Thirty Years of Treason

Also by Eric Bently

AUTHOR OF:

A Century of Hero-Worship
The Playwright as Thinker
Bernard Shaw
In Search of Theatre
The Dramatic Event
What Is Theatre
The Life of the Drama
The Theatre of Commitment
A Time to Die
The Red White and Black
Are You Now
The Great R.
Theatre of War

EDITOR OF:

The Importance of Scrutiny
From the Modern Repertoire
(three volumes)
The Play
The Modern Theatre *(six volumes)*
The Classic Theatre *(four volumes)*
Let's Get a Divorce!
The Genius of the Italian Theatre
The Theory of the Modern Stage
Shaw on Music
The Works of Bertolt Brecht
The Storm over The Deputy
The Brecht-Eisler SOng Book
The Great Playwrights

TRANSLATOR:

twelve plays of Brecht, five plays of Pirandello,
Filumena Marturano *by Eduardo de Filippo,*
The Wire Harp *by Wolf Biermann,* and other items

Eric Bentley is heard, as either reader or singer, on the following record albums:

Bentley on Brecht
Brecht before the Un-American
Activities Committee
Songs of Hanns Eisler
The Exception and the Rule
A Man's a man
The Elephant Calf
Bentley on Biermann
The Queen of 42nd Street

THIRTY YEARS OF TREASON

Excerpts from Hearings before the House Committee on Un-American Activities 1938-1968

Edited by Eric Bentley

Thunder's Mouth Press/Nation Books-New York

THIRTY YEARS OF TREASON

Published by
Thunder's Mouth Press/Nation Books
161 William St., 16th Floor
New York, NY 10038

First published in 1971 by The Viking Press, Inc.

Nation Books is a co-publishing venture of the Nation Institute and Avalon Publishing Group Incorporated.

Library of Congress Cataloging-in-Publication Data is available.

ISBN 1-56025-368-1

9 8 7 6 5 4 3 2 1

Printed in the United States of America

Distributed by Publishers Group West

Grateful acknowledgment is made to the following for permission to reprint:

THE AMERICAN LEGION MAGAZINE: *The Truth about the Blacklist* by Roy M. Brewer. Copyright 1962 by The American Legion Magazine.

ALVAH BESSIE: From *Inquisition in Eden* by Alvah Bessie. Copyright © 1965 by Alvah Bessie.

HERBERT BIBERMAN: From *Hollywood on Trial* by Gordon Kahn. Copyright 1948 by Herbert Biberman.

BENJAMIN BLOM, INC.: Hallie Flanagan, *Arena: The History of the Federal Theatre* (New York: Benjamin Blom, Inc., 1965).

BOOKMAILER, INC.: From *The Martin Dies Story* by Martin Dies. Copyright © 1963 by Martin Dies.

DODD, MEAD AND COMPANY, INC.: From *The Trojan Horse in America* by Martin Dies. Copyright 1940 by Dodd, Mead and Company, Inc. Copyright renewed 1968 by Martin Dies.

ESTATE OF ALBERT EINSTEIN: From *Einstein on Peace* (New York: Schocken Books, 1968).

HOLLYWOOD REPORTER: For excerpts from the issues dated September 8, 1950; June 6, 1951; and May 28, 1951.

ELIA KAZAN: For "A Statement."

ALFRED A. KNOPF, INC. AND LONGMANS GREEN AND CO. LTD.: From *Wanderer* by Sterling Hayden.

MILLARD LAMPELL AND THE NEW YORK TIMES: *I Think I Ought to Mention I Was Blacklisted* by Millard Lampell. © 1966 by The New York Times Company.

STEFAN BRECHT AND SUHRKAMP VERLAG, ROBERT LANTZ–CANDIDA DONADIO LITERARY AGENCY, INC., AND METHUEN AND CO. LTD. From Volume 19 of *The Collected Works of Bertolt Brecht*. Copyright © 1967 by Suhrkamp Verlag KG.

RING LARDNER, JR.: From *My Life on the Blacklist* by Ring Lardner, Jr. Copyright © 1961 by Ring Lardner, Jr. Originally appeared in *Saturday Evening Post.*

LITTLE, BROWN AND COMPANY AND ROBERT LANTZ–CANDIDA DONADIO LITERARY AGENCY, INC.: From *An Unfinished Woman* by Lillian Hellman. Copyright © 1969 by Lillian Hellman.

LOS ANGELES EVENING CITIZEN NEWS: From *Reds Beaten in Hollywood* by Ronald Reagan, July 30, 1951.

LOS ANGELES TIMES: From *The Case of Larry Parks,* editorial, March 23, 1951. Copyright 1951 by The Los Angeles Times.

NORTON MOCKRIDGE: For column from the August 16, 1955, issue of the *World-Telegram,* by Norton Mockridge and Frederick Woltman.

RAMPARTS: *Two, Three, Many Columbias* by Tom Hayden. Copyright Ramparts Magazine, Inc., 1968.

PAUL ROBESON: From *Here I Stand* by Paul Robeson.

RUSSELL AND VOLKENING, INC.: From *Where We Came Out* by Granville Hicks. Copyright 1954 by Granville Hicks.

SATURDAY REVIEW AND RICHARD M. NIXON: From *A Plea for an Anti-Communist Faith* by Richard M. Nixon, May 24, 1952. Copyright 1952 by Saturday Review Associates, Inc.

WILLARD UPHAUS: *My Witness* by Willard Uphaus.

VARIETY: From an article from the April 11, 1951, issue.

For P.P.

“All I love America for is contained in men and women like you.”

Contents

Acknowledgments xv
Introduction xxiii
Foreword xxv

1938

The Federal Theater Project 3

Hallie Flanagan 6

An Affidavit from Upton Sinclair 48

1947

The Eislers 55

Gerhart Eisler 57
Ruth Fischer 59
Hanns Eisler 73

"Communist Infiltration of the Motion-Picture Industry" 110

Ayn Rand 111
Adolphe Menjou 119
Robert Taylor 135
Ronald Reagan 143
Gary Cooper 147
John Howard Lawson 153
Edward Dmytryk 165
Emmet Lavery 169
Ring Lardner, Jr. 184
Bertolt Brecht 207
Louis J. Russell 225

1948

"Proposed Legislation to Curb or Control the Communist Party" 247

Arthur Garfield Hays 248
James Burnham 272

1951

"Communist Infiltration of Hollywood" 291

Larry Parks 308
Sterling Hayden 348
Edward Dmytryk 376
José Ferrer 407
Budd Schulberg 434

1952

Michael Blankfort 461
Elia Kazan 484
Edward G. Robinson 496
Clifford Odets 498
Lillian Hellman 533
Abe Burrows 544

A Voice from the Future 569

"Plea for an Anti-Communist Faith" by Richard M. Nixon 569

1953

The Infiltration of Harvard 575

Robert Gorham Davis 577
Daniel J. Boorstin 601
Granville Hicks 612

Hollywood and Broadway, Continued 625

Jerome Robbins 625
Lionel Stander 634
Lee J. Cobb 653

A Letter from Albert Einstein 667

Testimony of a Bishop 669

G. Bromley Oxnam 670

1955

Song and Dance 683

Pete Seeger 686
Zero Mostel 708

1956

"Unauthorized Use of United States Passports" 725

William Uphaus 728
Paul Robeson 770
Arthur Miller 791

1957

"Communism in the Metropolitan Music School" 829

Earl Robinson 831

1958

The New York Shakespeare Festival 847

Joseph Papp 847

1966

"Assistance to Enemies of the United States in Time of Undeclared War" 859

Richard Mark Rhoads 860
Steven Cherkoss 868

1968

"Subversive Involvement in Disruption of 1968 Democratic Party National Convention" 879

Tom Hayden 879
Rennie Davis 896
Dave Dellinger 910

Afterword 933

Appendix 1: House Un-American Activities Committee Membership 1938-1970 955

Appendix 2: *The Measures Taken,* By Bertolt Brecht and Hanns Eisler 959

Appendix 3: A Statement by Paul Robeson 977

Index, with a Note on How to Find Things 981

ACKNOWLEDGMENTS

Various colleagues, friends, and acquaintances supplied me with information and documents. Among these I should specially like to thank Donna Allen, Carey McWilliams, and Frank Wilkinson. One colleague who has himself written a book about HUAC let me inspect a large bundle of press clippings on the subject, and some items from his bundle then found their way into the present text. My benefactor was Frank J. Donner. For much secretarial help and research, not to slight the sheer muscular effort of carting Committee records around for me, I am grateful to two excellent research assistants: Kelley Snodgrass and Robert Silberman. Finally, I have to report that this book was not my idea, and credit the person whose idea it was: my friend and editor Ann Hancock.

E.B.

New York
March 1970

From *Martin Dies' Story* (New York, 1963)

On August 12, 1938, we began our public hearings. To the press, the committee members and the audience in the caucus room, I made a preliminary statement in which I said:

"The chair wishes to reiterate what he has stated many times—namely, that this committee is determined to conduct its investigation upon a dignified plane, and to adopt and maintain throughout the course of the hearings, a judicial attitude. The committee has no preconceived views of what the truth is respecting the subject matter of this inquiry. Its sole purpose is to discover the truth and report it as it is, . . . with such recommendations, if any, as to legislation on these subjects as the situation may require and as the duty of Congress to the American people may demand.

"We shall be fair and impartial at all times and treat every witness with fairness and courtesy. We shall expect every witness to treat us in the same way. This committee will not permit any character assassinations or any smearing of innocent people. We wish to caution witnesses that reckless charges must not be made against any individual or organization. The chair wishes to emphasize that the committee is more concerned with facts than with opinions, and with specific proof than with generalities. Opinions, conclusions and generalities have no probative force in any court of justice, and they cannot be made the basis of any findings on the part of this committee. . . . It is easy to smear someone's name or reputation by unsupported charges, and an unjustified attack, but it is difficult to repair the damage that has been done. . . . When any individual or organization is involved in any charge or attack made in the course of the hearings, that individual or organization will be accorded an opportunity to refute such a charge or attack. In investigating un-American activities, it must be borne in mind that because we do not agree with opinions or philosophies of others, does not make such opinions or philosophies un-American. The most common practice engaged in by some people is to brand their opponents with names when they are unable to refute their arguments with facts and logic. Therefore, we find a few people of conservative thought who are inclined to brand every Liberal's viewpoint as communistic. Likewise, we find some so-called Liberals who stigmatize every conservative idea Fascistic. The utmost care therefore must be observed to distinguish clearly between what is obviously un-American, and what is more or less an honest difference of opinion with respect to some economic, political or social question."

From *Inquisition in Eden* by Alvah Bessie (New York, 1965)

In addition to permanent exclusion from one's chosen field of employment, social ostracism, divorce, and voluntary exile (a list that numbers many hundreds if not thousands), there have been even greater tragedies that cannot be forgotten. For in the roll call of victims of the proliferating local, state, and national witch-hunting committees, there are many who cannot answer. Their premature deaths from "natural" causes and from suicide may be laid directly or indirectly at the doors of these inquisitorial outfits.

Number among them: John Garfield, heart attack preceding his second scheduled appearance before the un-Americans; Harry Dexter White, assistant to the Secretary of the Treasury, heart attack following appearance before the Committee, where he denied Whittaker Chambers' accusations that he had headed an espionage ring; Mady Christians, actress, died following blacklisting, which followed Committee testimony; John Brown, actor, died following blacklisting by all media after decades of performing on radio; Edwin Rolfe, poet, blacklisted, unemployable, heart attack.

Also, Frances Young, blacklisted actress-wife of blacklisted actor-writer, suicide; Madelyn Dmytryk, former wife of then-blacklisted director, suicide; Philip Loeb, blacklisted actor, suicide; E. Herbert Norman, Canadian ambassador to Egypt, accused by a Senate committee of having been a Communist, suicide; Lawrence Duggan, State Department official, suicide following charges before the un-Americans that he had been a courier for Whittaker Chambers; Abraham Feller, UN general counsel, suicide following appearance before the Senate Internal Security Committee; Raymond Kaplan, Voice of America engineer, suicide following attack by Senator McCarthy's committee.

Also, Francis O. Matthiessen, Harvard professor and renowned critic, suicide following accusation by J. B. Matthews before a Massachusetts legislative committee that he was a Communist-front member; Walter Marvin Smith, Justice Department attorney, suicide after being mentioned as a notary in a transaction involving Alger Hiss; Morton E. Kent, former State Department official, suicide following FBI hounding; John Winant,

U.S. ambassador to Britain under FDR, suicide following charges that he had failed to facilitate entry of U.S. troops into Berlin; William K. Sherwood, brilliant young Stanford University research scientist, suicide by poison two days before his scheduled appearance before the un-Americans in San Francisco.

Sherwood's widow, Barbara, attempted to read a statement before the Committee in June of 1957. She was thrown out of the hearing room. This is her statement:

"Members of the Un-American Activities Committee:

"You have helped kill my husband and make my four children fatherless.

"That is our personal tragedy.

"It is as nothing to the crime you have committed against the children of America and the children of the world.

"For when you drove my husband to his death, you destroyed a man of bright promise, a talented fighter in the army of devoted men who are warring against disease.

"My husband thought that he had found an important clue to the understanding of cancer and schizophrenia. Perhaps he was mistaken. Only time, and the opportunity to continue his researches, could have supplied the answer.

"This opportunity your committee has denied him, and the loss is not only mine.

"Throughout his lifetime, my husband had but one goal: to ease the suffering of mankind.

"It was this goal that drew him to support the Loyalists in the Spanish Civil War, that inspired his youthful identification with radical causes.

"It was this goal that led him, when greater maturity had mellowed and deepened his understanding, to abandon politics completely and devote himself single-mindedly to science.

"Is it a crime for a young man in his twenties to dream of a bright new world?

"Must the children of our country leave their idealism in the cradle so that their future careers will not be blighted by the Un-American Activities Committee?

"And is it fitting, now that he is dead, that you insinuate he was a traitor to his country?

"Is not his death enough for you?

"Must you also besmirch his honor, now that he is no longer able to answer you?

"Members of the Committee, what you have done and what you are doing is an evil thing. Do not persist in it. Go away, go home, bow your heads in prayer and ask forgiveness of your God."

From *Additional Dialogue: Letters of Dalton Trumbo, 1942–1962* (New York, 1970)

The blacklist was a time of evil and . . . no one on either side who survived it came through untouched by evil. Caught in a situation that had passed beyond the control of mere individuals, each person reacted as his nature, his needs, his convictions, and his particular circumstances compelled him to. There was bad faith and good, honesty and dishonesty, courage and cowardice, selflessness and opportunism, wisdom and stupidity, good and bad on both sides; and almost every individual involved, no matter where he stood, combined some or all of these antithetical qualities in his own person, in his own acts.

Introduction

When Eric Bentley published *Thirty Years of Treason* some thirty years ago, America was still in the throes of Vietnam—a war whose many casualties included memory. Though Vietnam was nothing if not in part a byproduct of Congressional witchhunts—no one in State or Defense would ever again risk being crucified for "losing" any part of Asia—the heyday of the House Committee on Un-American Activities already seemed like ancient history. In Hollywood, the blacklist was over, and one of those jailed for refusing to name names, Ring Lardner, Jr., was not only back from exile but was about to receive the 1971 Oscar for "M*A*S*H," a popular anti-war film. Yes, HUAC's successor, the House Internal Security Committee, had taken on the New Left rebels of the late Sixties—as is documented near the end of this volume—but this time history was being replayed as farce, or at least street theater. In 1970, it seemed an almost quixotic publishing venture to devote a fat book mainly to the ideological warfare of the era that took its name from a dead and discredited Senator from Wisconsin—faded black-and-white archival stuff next to the bloody ongoing warfare, in Asian jungles and American cities, of the apocalypse now.

As we begin the twenty-first century, the importance of this history is a given. An avalanche of red scare literature, movies, and plays (including Bentley's own invaluable *Are You Now or Have You Ever Been?*) followed in the wake of *Thirty Years of Treason* and even at this writing, well after the end of the Cold War, the hostilities of the time still glow like a pilot light just beneath the surface of our political culture, waiting to reignite at almost any provocation. Merely the presentation of an honorary Academy Award to Elia Kazan in 1999 was enough to spark a rancorous ideological melee and the reopening of supposedly healed wounds, as well as a certain modish revisionism. Perhaps HUAC went overboard in its methods, this argument goes, but might not an abridgment of American democratic principles be justified in the cause of smiting (however ineffectually) the greater evil of totalitarianism?

To wrestle with this question, you must look at the record—starting with what follows in these pages, the public trials of alleged subversives by politicians on an unchecked crusade. Were Washington's red hunters principled anti-communists with the sole goal of unmasking those who aided and abetted an evil empire? Or were they vigilantes using the pretext of national security to vanquish political foes advancing progressive domestic causes? Were their targets patriots or traitors, martyrs or dupes, or did interrogators and witnesses alike sometimes come in shades of gray? HUAC didn't expire completely until 1975, and only in 2001 have scholars started to gain complete access to the Committee's 444 linear feet of records. The answers will keep coming.

As Bentley knew, the voices of the actual confrontations in all their "human fullness" are essential evidence. Yet at the time he assembled his book, that basic part of the public record was all but inaccessible. He discovered that even the libraries at his own academic home, Columbia University, had not bothered to collect the complete record of HUAC transcripts as they emerged over the years from the Government Printing Office. As an antidote to this national amnesia, *Thirty Years of Treason* was a heroic act in its time, both by Bentley and his publisher, The Viking Press.

This book is not, however, merely a document of our political past, but also a shadow history of mid-twentieth century American culture, featuring an all-star cast of artists and intellectuals high and low, admirable and not, from academe to Broadway to Hollywood. As one of America's greatest drama critics, Bentley was perfectly suited to pick the scenes that would dramatize the HUAC story and to select the other documentary material that would provide the proscenium frame and illuminate the subtext. *Thirty Years of Treason* is the twentieth century theatrical epic—alternately absurd, tragic, fiery, pathetic, and nightmarish—that Shaw, Pirandello, and Brecht never got together to write.

FRANK RICH
August, 2001

Foreword

> Hundreds of hearings, a thousand publications, a library of expert testimony, qualify the work of the [Un-American Activities] Committee as a supremely valuable repository of expert knowledge on the scope and meaning and particularities of the Communist enterprise, a source more valuable by far than what the typical student, taking every course in the curriculum, is likely to come up against in a major university in his quest for a profound understanding of the most vital problem of our time.
>
> —WILLIAM F. BUCKLEY, JR.

> Department of Defense investigators check HUAC files approximately 120 times a week. During fiscal year 1967 the U.S. Civil Service Commission made approximately 288,000 searches against the HUAC files.
>
> —Official answers to letters of inquiry sent by Representative Don Edwards, August 1967

As its subtitle states, this book is made up of excerpts from hearings before the House Un-American Activities Committee, 1938–1968. Since to hold hearings is the Committee's function, transcripts of those hearings are the main record of the Committee's existence, its footprints in the sands of time. Given that the Committee is important (a thesis I subscribe to) the reprinting of its records would seem to require no pleading for, all the less so as they are hard to get at, and much too long for most people to read, in their original printed form. The Government Printing Office duly issues them one and all, but only in a small edition that is soon out of print and is never on sale through bookstores. To get at the complete transcript, unless you have a friend who is a specialist and has gone to the trouble of securing a copy, you would have to have recourse to a very large library. I myself, in preparing this volume, found even the Columbia University Libraries insufficient: they had not bothered to acquire the records of the early years (1938–1945) or to bind them up in book form after 1960. I had to repair to the New York Public Library, which has a complete file in one of its branches (Forty-second Street).

Had The Viking Press elected to reprint the whole record, it would have run to several dozen volumes as big as the one you now hold in your hand. You wouldn't have bought these, so a job of selection had to be done. On what principles? Different editors would proceed very differently. The wish that I started out from was *to present the encounter between Committee and witness in its human fullness.* I soon found that such a wish is quixotic. Neither Congressman nor witness went to the committee room to bare his breast. Some of the friendly witnesses did say they were doing this. It is another question whether even they actually did it. They were more apt to bare the breast of some creature of their fantasy. Many outright lies have been told in the hearings of HUAC. We shall probably never know *how* many, and the corollary of this is that it is hard to know what, in these records, is true. They are no open book. They need a lot of interpreting, and even scholars who have done a maximum amount of homework on the material will not be able to interpret everything correctly, because much of the necessary information is locked up either in FBI files or in the hearts of men who have swallowed the key. And by this time, in many cases, death has swallowed *them*. Scholar and layman, professional and amateur, we should all alike approach this material with an acknowledgment of our ignorance and its possible consequence of dire misunderstanding.

I would sympathize with the man who proposed to leave these records completely alone on the ground that a little learning would be a dangerous thing, but in the end I part company with him because all our learning is "little," it is all "out of context," it is all misleading, without that supplementation from omniscience which it is never going to get. History as we in our adolescent demand for the Whole Truth would have it can never be written, and the record of HUAC, though humanly fragmentary, is no more so than the record of most other institutions.

The encounters of this book between Committee and witness are not rendered in their human fullness, but I have always kept such fullness in mind as the desirable thing, the luminous Platonic Idea of my presentation, if not its shadowy actuality. Which will explain another feature of the book. Background material is added to the testimony, not to make the book a comprehensive history of HUAC, which it is not, but to flesh out human beings whom the record too often renders only as skeletons. Even this is not as easy as it may sound. We cannot go directly at our pound of flesh, like Shylock. Sometimes we find our man not in what is said, even if said by him, but in a seemingly accidental detail, or in what seems a detail but is not—like his tone of voice or, if we have only nonauditory materials to work with, the tone of his prose, the nature of his syntax and vocabulary.

How much the reader gets from this book will depend a good deal on his ability to take a hint, to pick up that evidence which is not offered as such.

The *problem* is that both Congressman and witness were busy concealing things from us, not least their own souls, if any, when our reader-spectator demand upon them is that they exhibit themselves to us. And it would be an insoluble problem but for an aspect of human nature that has been observed by Sigmund Freud: however much men seek to conceal themselves, there is a drive in them to undo the concealment and reveal all. Murder will out, because, in the end, the murderer insists on it. This "end" is sometimes too long in coming, and yet the astute observer can pick up small intimations of the message long before the final confession comes pouring out. If, on the one hand, language is a way of not communicating, it communicates willy-nilly: all manner of messages break through the barriers-to-messages. In some degree, truth may be found to break through the barriers even of mendacity. A liar says yes, but there may be something in his eye, or tone of voice, gesture, or stance, which says no: such signs are never mendacious, it is a matter of being able to read them. Offered half a chance—and appearance before a Committee is often three-quarters of a chance—men give themselves away. That is the *solution* to what I have posed as the problem.

Another quixotic wish of mine was to reprint the encounters with the Committee in unabridged form so that the reader would know he was getting the whole thing and not being manipulated by me. In the finished book now in your hand the encounters appear in cut form; and even so the book is long. Let me minimize the anxieties about manipulation thus engendered by stating forthwith what kind of cuts were made. Two kinds: redundancies, generally of several words at a time, were removed from many individual sentences and, secondly, whole passages, sometimes running to many consecutive pages, were left out. Where I thought it would be helpful to the reader to know that a cut had been made, I inserted three asterisks. I would have liked to indicate any and all cuts, however small, by some typographical device, but there is none that would not disfigure the page to the point of unreadability. Where suspicion is aroused that some of my editing may have been unfair—we are none of us incarnations of justice—the reader has the choice between offering me the benefit of the doubt and consulting the full text. He will realize, too, that the existence of such a text in public places would operate as a brake upon the editorial waywardness.

For all the cuts, I did not abandon my initial preference of a few ample encounters to snippets from many. The latter might well have looked more impressive on the title page, for I could have chosen some short passage from the testimony of every well-known person who ever came before HUAC. Undoubtedly my preference robbed the book of many amusing and otherwise striking quotes. But as to "big names," magnitude in the sense that phrase implies was not sought. Nor was I after those who wielded most political power, though the Committee offered me J. Edgar Hoover and Henry A. Wallace, Sumner Welles and Earl Browder, Harry Dexter White, Averell Harriman, Ramsey Clark. The Alger Hiss case began as a HUAC affair, and the Committee's testimony on it is crucial and dramatic. It is also so plentiful that it would need a book to itself. Better still, it should be incorporated in books that tell the Hiss-Chambers story from beginning to end; and, to a degree, it has been.

Another part of the record that is not done justice to in the present book is the testimony of "friendly" witnesses of, shall we say, the crudest type: leaders of right-wing organizations and the like. The reader will probably never conceive of the relentlessness of some of these unless he reads at least one piece of such testimony right through—for example, the testimony on July 21, 1947, of Walter S. Steele, Chairman, National Security Committee of the American Coalition of Patriotic, Civic, and Fraternal Societies: its 176 pages have doubtless contributed to my own education, yet I did not feel I could assign 176 pages of my book to it, and excerpts give no impression of Mr. Steele's approach, which is essentially torrential in style and all-inclusive in scope. His contribution in 1947 was not even his first: he had given the Government Printing Office a 100-page contribution already in August 1938, when HUAC started. Similar in type, if less exhaustive in treatment, is the testimony of Colonel John Thomas Taylor, Director, National Legislative Committee, American Legion, his colleague, James F. Green, chairman of the Legion's Americanism Commission, and his sister-under-the-skin, Mrs. Julius Y. Talmadge, President General, Daughters of the American Revolution. In chatting (on taxpayers' money) with the friendly Louis E. Starr, Commander in Chief, Veterans of Foreign Wars, Congressman John McDowell asked this question:

> Well, Commander, I wonder if you would not agree with me that it should be said in this year of 1947 for the record that Karl Marx was what in modern times, these days, would be known as a bum, a rather shiftless scoundrel, who would do anything but work, who lived all his life on somebody else, whose family also lived on somebody else, whose family was kept in near starvation most of their life, the ideals that he wrote about died, apparently, with Karl Marx; I think it should be written into the record that although this political crowd is running Russia and spreading this business throughout the world, the only connection they have with Karl Marx is merely to mention his name once in a while, that Marshal Stalin refers frequently to the sayings and the philosophy of Karl Marx, but practices none of them. Would you agree with that?

That Stalin's neglect of Marxism doesn't make Marxism all right is, however, more than hinted at in many parts of the HUAC record, as for instance when Averell Harriman, asked whether Marx's writings should be banned in the schools of the free old U.S.A., replied:

> Our high-school students should be taught by competent teachers who are opposed to Marxist philosophy.

More influential in HUAC than philosopher-kings like Harriman, or even than the listers of subversive organizations like Walter S. Steele, were no doubt the namers of personal names, particularly those who named them by the dozen, such as Martin Berkeley and Richard Collins of Hollywood or, higher on the informer echelons, Elizabeth Bentley, the Russian agent's widow who played a sizable role in the Hiss and Remington cases, and Louis Budenz, former editor of the *Daily Worker,* whose confessions of 1946 touched off that crisis in the Eisler family which is documented below.

It is hardly necessary to read Budenz' lists of names in order to follow the narrative. I was able, I think, to fill this book with matter both more interesting and more instructive than any of the types of testimony just mentioned by limiting myself to a single part of the Committee records: the part that concerns artists and intellectuals. Obviously the choice reflects my own interests: an anthology that does *not* reflect its editor's interests is likely to prove an arid affair. In any case, intellect is not confined to intellectuals (on the contrary, I am tempted to say), nor is art addressed to other artists. ("The artist is not a special kind of man. Every man is a special kind of artist."—Eric Gill.) I believe that, however unintelligent some of the intellectuals represented in this book may be and however minor some of the artists, their testimony has universal import. Though the artist and the intellectual are not necessarily brighter than other men, they are, in general, more vulnerable—and therefore more visible: if nothing else, they are open wounds. Far from exemplary, they do serve as examples, which indeed was one reason why HUAC sadistically enjoyed making "examples" of them. When that happens, we see, for instance, the actor Larry Parks acting out the anxieties and rationalizations of a generation, and, given a little of the Committee's cruelty, we might ask, what else is an actor for? Any contempt we feel for such a man must be qualified by a compassion that is not free of self-pity. (A fellow traveler of HUAC would see this differently. The nation was to be punished, forgiven, and purified vicariously: Larry Parks was a scapegoat.)

The reader may ask why so many of the witnesses quoted in this book are performing artists. Again, I would not duck the imputation of professional bias: my own background is theatrical. But HUAC itself betrayed theatrical bias. Its first substantial target in the thirties was the Federal Theater, and throughout its Great Decade (1946–1956) it recurred again and again to the performers, whether movie stars, Broadway actors, or folk singers. If one remarks that one of the Committee's star witnesses and stanch supporters became Governor of California, one should not forget that until this happened Ronald Reagan was known to the public exclusively as a movie actor. Things changed in the sixties, but in what way? Radical politics became street theater. For that decade the testimony included here is that of "agitators" pure and simple. But they were the star performers of their time.

There have always been other theaters besides the professional playhouse and the political arena, notably the law court, the church, and the schoolroom. Witnesses from each of these are also present below. In a degree, they may be thought of as bringing their theaters with them: we hear the characteristic style of each different setting. But then again, the theater environment imposed by HUAC soon takes over and asserts its own character. The transaction is called Investigation. The scene is the Old House Office Building in Washington, Room 1105 in the United States Court House, Foley Square, New York, or some high rectangular chamber in some other governmental building designed in the grand Greek post-office manner. In the early years, before television, HUAC hearings were often heard on the radio, which meant that the drama was played to a national audience. Later, Speaker Sam Rayburn forebade that, but, since hearings were nationally reported in the papers, the occasion was never contained within the room where it took place. As in a play, the actors were never really talking *to* each other but *for* an audience, and HUAC could always confidently feel that its audience was not limited to guests physically present. The Committee performed for the nation, present and future. If not the Judaeo-Christian God, then Clio, Muse of History, sat in the royal box.

It is important not to think of the hearings as the drama of the witnesses only, be they friendly or unfriendly, famous or obscure, honest or nefarious. It was the drama of the witness *and the other fellow,* who was either a Congressman or an investigator paid by the Congress. No one had the authority (or temerity?) to ask the other fellow *his* name, address, date of birth, party allegiance, religious affiliation, and so on. He really did enjoy the protection of the First Amendment; which the historian must regret, as the background of a Robert E. Stripling, a Frank S. Tavenner, or a Richard Arens could not fail to be fascinating, not to mention the background of a Martin Dies, a Parnell Thomas, or a Francis Walter. But, as Freud would have predicted, these chaps did give themselves away. The drama is there. All it needs is a reader.

1938

The Federal Theater Project

One of the first victims of the Un-American Activities Committee was the Federal Theater. In fact the victimization began before the Committee actually met—namely, in July 1938, when Congressman J. Parnell Thomas (1895–1970) announced that both the Theater and the Writers' Project were hotbeds of Communism and infested with radicals from top to bottom. "Practically every play presented under the auspices of the Project," said Thomas, "is sheer propaganda for Communism or the New Deal." And since the Chairman, Martin Dies, is rather soft-spoken in the dialogue with Hallie Flanagan (1890–1969) printed below, it would be well to be clear in advance that he fully agreed with Thomas. Here is the summing up from his book, *The Trojan Horse in America* (New York, 1940):

W.P.A. was the greatest financial boon which ever came to the Communists in the United States. Stalin could not have done better by his American friends and agents. . . .

All over the United States, the Federal Theater Project produced plays which were nothing but straight Communist propaganda. This is not at all surprising in view of the personnel chosen by the New Deal to supervise the Project. Let us take a look at one of these Communist plays.

At the Adelphi Theatre in New York in May, 1936, a capacity audience of theater goers saw W. H. Auden's poetic play, *The Dance of Death.* As the play opened, an announcer stepped in front of the curtain and recited the following lines:

> We present to you this evening a picture of the decline of a class. Of how its members dream of a new life, but secretly desire the old; for there is death inside them. We show you that death as a dancer.

Near the beginning of the Auden play, an imaginary audience, one McLaughlin, and a chorus spoke the following lines:

> AUDIENCE: One, two, three, four—the last war was a bosses' war. Five, six, seven, eight—rise and make a workers' state. Nine, ten, eleven, twelve—seize the factories and run them yourselves.
>
> MCLAUGHLIN: We will liquidate—
>
> CHORUS: The capitalist state!
>
> AUDIENCE: Overthrow!
>
> CHORUS: Overthrow!
>
> AUDIENCE: Attaboys!

The revolutionary seizure of our factories; the overthrow of the capitalist state: such was the theme of the play which an audience just off Broadway was witnessing on that opening night in May, 1936. How the play ended may best be told in the words of the *Daily Worker* a few days later. That official newspaper of the Communist Party hailed the production as a great achievement in the theater. It described the ending, as follows:

> With Death the Dancer dead, we witness the appearance of a huge shadow on the backdrop. It is Karl Marx, who announces: "The instruments of production have been too much for him. He is liquidated." Exeunt, to a Dead March, as capitalism is borne out on the shoulders of four pallbearers.

That and scores of other plays equally freighted with Moscow's propaganda were what the American people spent millions of dollars to have produced all over the country. A great deal of time would be required to find a parallel for such a betrayal of the American people by their own federal officials. Of course, it was all done in the name of humanitarianism and in the name of relief for the needy. The situation became so intolerable that the Congress of the United States stepped into the picture and made an end of the whole shameful use of the taxpayers' money to spread Communist propaganda. The Communists and their fellow travelers are, of course, clamoring for the restoration of the Federal Theater Project. Naturally, they want the feed-bag put back to the mouth of their Trojan Horse, but they also want the Government of the United States to pay for Stalin's propaganda.

And evidently Dies didn't change his mind, for the further summary which his Committee had issued in January 1939 is reprinted in his autobiography, *Martin Dies' Story* (New York, 1963):

We heard some of the employees and former employees in the Federal Theater Project in New York. These witnesses testified that Communistic activities have been carried on in the Federal Theater Project for a long time; that Communist meetings have been held on the project during work hours; that some of the employees had participated in these Communist meetings during their work hours; that Communist literature had been distributed on the project from time to time, and that Communist posters had been printed on the official bulletin board; that all of these activities had been carried on in the premises of the Federal Theater Project and during the very time that the employees were paid to work. It is also clear that certain employees felt under compulsion to join the Workers' Alliance in order to retain their jobs.

On the director of the Theater Project, the Committee's chief informant seems to have been one Hazel Huffman, who testified on August 19, 1938, "I cannot prove that Mrs. Flanagan has Communist membership as I have never seen a card bearing her name; but I can prove Mrs. Flanagan was an active participant in Communist activity, and that her Communist sympathies, tendencies, and methods of organization are being used in the Federal Theater Project."

The Committee at this date had the following members: Martin Dies, Texas; Arthur D. Healey, Massachusetts; John J. Dempsey, New Mexico; Joe Starnes, Alabama; Harold G. Mosier, Ohio; Noah M. Mason, Illinois; J. Parnell Thomas, New Jersey. Its Secretary, later to be called Chief Investigator, and as such to play a part in the Hiss case, published his reminiscences in 1949 (*The Red Plot Against America* [Drexel Hill, Pennsylvania, 1949] by Robert E. Stripling) and, in a section called "500 Things You Should Know About Communism" asks and answers the following questions about Federal Theater:

> How did the Communists use the Federal Theater, Writers' and other such projects?
>
> To present Communist propaganda plays, to feature Communist actors, to distribute Communist propaganda in Government books, pamphlets, and art work.
>
> Can you give a sample of Communism in the WPA theatre project?
>
> Here is the testimony of a confidential investigator . . . *Triple-A Plowed Under* . . . was one play which on the opening night required 30 New York policemen to guard the play and prevent a riot. . . . Such characters as George Washington and Andrew Jackson were removed from the play in order to give a prominent part to the secretary of the Communist Party, Earl Browder.

Mrs. Flanagan told her own story in *Arena* (New York, 1940). The job that the Un-American Committee began was completed during 1939 by the House Appropriations Committee: without funds, the Theater Project was dead. Among the notables in the House of Representatives who helped kill it was Everett Dirksen, who considered its plays "salacious tripe," citing as evidence such titles as *Up in Mabel's Room*. And pornography was not the only infallible sign of Marxism on the premises: "Also, *A New Kind of Love*. I wonder what that can be. It smacks somewhat of the Soviet."

DECEMBER 6, 1938:

Hallie Flanagan

THE CHAIRMAN: Will you please state what your position is, Mrs. Flanagan?

MRS. FLANAGAN: I am national director of the Federal Theater Project under the Works Progress Administration.

THE CHAIRMAN: How long have you held that position?

MRS. FLANAGAN: Since the inception of the Project, Congressman Dies, on August 29, 1935.

MR. THOMAS: Mrs. Flanagan, who appointed you as national director?

MRS. FLANAGAN: I was appointed by Mr. Harry Hopkins.

MR. THOMAS: Before you were appointed, did Mr. Hopkins approach you or did you approach Mr. Hopkins in relation to this appointment?

MRS. FLANAGAN: Mr. Hopkins approached me. I made no approach to Mr. Hopkins or to any Government official on this Project.

MR. THOMAS: Do you know who recommended your name to Mr. Hopkins?

MRS. FLANAGAN: I do not.

MR. THOMAS: You have no idea who recommended your name to Mr. Hopkins?

MRS. FLANAGAN: I do not.

MR. THOMAS: Mr. Hopkins didn't tell you who recommended your name to him?

MRS. FLANAGAN: He did not.

THE CHAIRMAN: Now, will you just tell us briefly the duties of your position?

MRS. FLANAGAN: Yes, Congressman Dies. Since August 29, 1935, I have been concerned with combating un-American inactivity.

THE CHAIRMAN: Inactivity?

MRS. FLANAGAN: I refer to the inactivity of professional people who, at that time when I took office, were on the relief rolls, and it was my job to expend the appropriation laid aside by Congressional vote for the relief of the unemployed as it related to the field of the theater, and to set up projects wherever in any city twenty-five or more such professionals were found on the relief rolls.

MR. THOMAS: Mr. Chairman, I think it is of great importance that we know something about her history—where she went to college, and so forth.

THE CHAIRMAN: We are going to get to that. I think that you said you are the director of all these activities?

MRS. FLANAGAN: Yes. May I add that the Project is national in scope, and that we have projects in Washington, Oregon, California, in Colorado and Michigan, in Ohio and Illinois, in Oklahoma and North Carolina, in Maine and New Hampshire, in New York State and Massachusetts, and New Jersey and Delaware, in other words, in any place where there were a sufficient number of qualified relief applicants.

MR. STARNES: When was the Federal Theater Project set up, Mrs. Flanagan?

MRS. FLANAGAN: It was set up on August 29, 1935.

MR. STARNES: What was the primary purpose of setting up this Federal Theater Project?

MRS. FLANAGAN: To put back to work the unemployed professional people, rehabilitate them, and conserve their skills. That was then and always has been the prime purpose of the Theater Project. Now, if I may say so, the fact that we have returned to private industry some two thousand people would seem to prove that we are considering that always as our major objective.

MR. STARNES: You say now yourself that the primary purpose of setting up the Federal Theater Project was for the purpose of giving relief to professional theatrical people?

MRS. FLANAGAN: Of putting back to work such people; yes.

MR. STARNES: You have made statements, however, to the contrary, have you not?

MRS. FLANAGAN: I have never made a statement to the contrary.

MR. STARNES: Haven't you made the statement repeatedly that the primary purpose to be considered in separating people from the relief rolls is the welfare of the Theater Project first, and that relief was secondary?

MRS. FLANAGAN: Never. I would like to turn to that point in the testimony with your permission.

MR. STARNES: In other words, it is said that in a letter you said—

MRS. FLANAGAN: Yes, I have it here. May I quote first from the allegation?

MR. STARNES: Yes.

MRS. FLANAGAN: Miss [Hazel] Huffman stated in the Hearing in volume 1, page 781: "Mrs. Hallie Flanagan, our national director, stated in 1936 that the Federal Project was set up for relief and our foremost consideration must be the Federal Theater Project." Mr. Thomas then said, "What did she mean by that?" And Miss Huffman said, "The matter of this being for relief or to provide work for relief was to be placed in a secondary consideration." Then she quotes a director's letter. The fact is that by reason of reductions in appropriated funds at the time, the Project was being cut from fifty-seven hundred to four thousand; and that of the four thousand only two hundred people not certified for relief were to be retained. Consequently, the letters sent out at that time referred to the relief persons being cut; that is, of two people, both from relief rolls, both therefore presumably equally in need, my orders to executives were to retain on the Project—of these two relief people, gentlemen—the one best suited to carry on the work of the Project.

MR. STARNES: Just a minute. In your language you have here: "In making the necessary separations from the payroll, supervisors were directed to give primary consideration to the needs of the Federal Theater Project rather than to the relief status or need situation of the individual." Just what did you mean by that statement if you didn't mean the primary consideration was to be the Federal Theater Project?

MRS. FLANAGAN: I did not make that statement.

MR. STARNES: Do you deny making that statement at all?

MRS. FLANAGAN: This is the letter, which I would like to read: "To all workers on the Federal Theater Project: Reduction of personnel. The following instructions were received from Washington June 9: This is to inform you that a new employment quota has been established for the Federal Theater Project. This quota will go into effect on July 15, 1937. Reductions to conform with the new quota should begin as soon as possible to be sure that this quota is reached by the effective date. However, workers should, whenever possible, be given two weeks' notice. The July 15 quota for maximum employment for the Federal Theater Project in New York City is 4016. The procedure of reaching the new quota will be as follows: First, the elimination of nonessentials on relief—"

MR. STARNES: Oh, you had nonrelief people in on these plays and on these projects, did you?

MRS. FLANAGAN: Yes.

MR. STARNES: As high as thirty-seven per cent at one time, didn't you?

MRS. FLANAGAN: We had at one time a national over-all exemption which allowed us to take on twenty-five per cent—distributing that per cent over the entire nation.

MR. STARNES: At one time you had thirty-seven per cent on one of your projects?

MRS. FLANAGAN: I think at one time, in New York, that was the figure.

MR. THOMAS: What is the percentage in New York at the present time?

MRS. FLANAGAN: The percentage is very low at the present time. It is, I believe, thirteen and a half. I would like to call on Mr. Paul Edwards, who is present, for that exact figure. But may I read that letter, because it is very important?

MR. DEMPSEY: Do you know of any of these projects that does not have nonrelief people on it, and things of that kind? They all have those people, don't they?

MRS. FLANAGAN: They do, Congressman, but may I read this letter because I wouldn't want to leave with this Committee a totally false impression: that is, that I have ever put the artistic record on this Project before the human record. Every word that I have written on this Project, every word that I have said for three years, has attested to the fact that the artistic job that we do can be no better than the human job that we are doing. Consequently, my orders were, first, the elimination of nonessential nonrelief; and, second, the elimination of all nonessential administrative and supervisory staffs on the whole Project and on individual projects. It was only after giving those two orders, my first two points, that I then said, "Coming to the consideration of cutting direct and other theatrical personnel"—that is the relief personnel—"we should be guided by, first, actual value to the Federal Theater Project; second, professional training and achievement in acting." Those are my words here in this letter, which is in my brief, which I trust can be written into your record. My prime job is dealing with relief people, and always has been.

MR. STARNES: You issued another order, didn't you? You issued director's letter No. 2, didn't you?

MRS. FLANAGAN: This *is* director's letter No. 2. I have just read it.

MR. STARNES: What about No. 1? You never did send out No. 1?

MRS. FLANAGAN: It has nothing to do with this. It is not in the record, is it?

MR. STARNES: There is nothing in No. 1 about separation from rolls?

MRS. FLANAGAN: Nothing. That was a misunderstanding of someone who read this, who did not read it carefully, did not understand that the crux—

MR. STARNES: Did you later, in December of 1937, appear before a Congressional Committee and advocate the establishment of the National Theater Project?

MRS. FLANAGAN: I never did. I appeared before the Congressional Committee called, I believe, by Congressman [William] Sirovich, at his request, and at the order of my superior officers, Mrs. [Ellen] Woodward and Mr. Hopkins. I presented a brief explaining the whole conception and development of the project, and that brief, gentlemen, is also appended in my record. At that time I never advocated the National Theater Project; nor have I—

MR. STARNES: You never advocated it?

MRS. FLANAGAN: I have never advocated it. I have never even referred to the Federal Theater as a national theater.

MR. STARNES: You never have? Now, let us get into your background, as bearing somewhat on this proposition, because the question has been raised of the artistic qualifications as a background. We are not questioning your background in the slightest, but at the same time, as a matter of record, we think such things should be made of record.

MRS. FLANAGAN: I think you are quite within your rights.

MR. STARNES: You are a graduate of Grinnell College?

MRS. FLANAGAN: I am.

MR. STARNES: And you have had some experience, I believe, according to the testimony of Mrs. Woodward, in Radcliffe or in Chicago.

MRS. FLANAGAN: Yes; I took my master's degree in Radcliffe.

MR. STARNES: That was in what year?

MRS. FLANAGAN: That was in 1923. I became production assistant to Professor [George Pierce] Baker, who was at that time in charge of The 47 Workshop, and assisted in the production of plays.

MR. STARNES: You did not take charge of a class in dramatic training?

MRS. FLANAGAN: No, I did not.

MR. STARNES: Your work at Vassar has been in the experimental field?

MRS. FLANAGAN: I was professor of English and in charge of the Experimental Theater.

MR. THOMAS: At the present time are you a professor of English there?

MRS. FLANAGAN: I am. On leave.

MR. THOMAS: And you spend how much time at that work?

MRS. FLANAGAN: I spend possibly a month in the summer when I take leave. I have spent no time at Vassar at which I have not taken leave from my Federal job.

MR. THOMAS: Don't you go there each month to lecture?

MRS. FLANAGAN: I do.

MR. THOMAS: That is outside of the one month that you spend there entirely?

MRS. FLANAGAN: Yes; I have a month's leave.

MR. THOMAS: You lecture how often at Vassar?

MRS. FLANAGAN: It is irregular. It depends entirely upon the planning that is done during the summer for the projects. I am not connected actively with them. I am a professor on leave, but I am helping to shape the policy of the dramatic department.

MR. THOMAS: Do you spend as much as a day a week at Vassar?

MRS. FLANAGAN: No.

MR. THOMAS: A day a month?

MRS. FLANAGAN: Yes; I should say possibly two days a month.

MR. STARNES: You are the first woman in America to receive the Guggenheim Foundation scholarship? Is that correct?

MRS. FLANAGAN: Yes; that is correct.

MR. STARNES: You went abroad for twelve or fourteen months to study the theater?

MRS. FLANAGAN: I did.

MR. STARNES: What date was that?

MRS. FLANAGAN: That was in 1926 and 1927.

MR. STARNES: You spent most of that time in what country?

MRS. FLANAGAN: In Russia.

MR. STARNES: In Russia. Was the statement true which was attributed to you in the *New York Daily Times* [*sic*] of September 22, 1935, on or about the time of your appointment, in which it was said that you said that the continental theater was a tiresome and boresome matter, but the Russian theater was a live and vital theater?

MRS. FLANAGAN: Congressman Starnes, that remark, if it is an exact quotation, is so casually given that I could not identify it. I have here in my brief a statement of the countries visited, of the records—

MR. STARNES: How much time did you spend in Russia, Mrs. Flanagan?

MRS. FLANAGAN: I spent two months and a half in Russia out of the fourteen months. But let me say, gentlemen, that—

MR. STARNES: Did you spend more time there studying the theater than you did in any other country?

MRS FLANAGAN: I did, because there are many more theaters in Russia than there are in any other country.

MR. STARNES: Did you or not make the statement that the theaters in Russia are more vital and important?

MRS. FLANAGAN: Yes; I did find that. And I think that opinion would be borne out by any dramatic critic that you cared to call to this chair.

MR. STARNES: What is it about the Russian theater that makes it more vital and important than the theaters of the continent and the theaters of the United States?

MRS. FLANAGAN: I have maintained consistently that we are starting an American theater, which must be founded on American principles, which has nothing to do with the Russian theater.

MR. STARNES: I know, but you are not answering the question, Mrs. Flanagan.

MRS. FLANAGAN: Well, I will go back and answer it. The Russians, if we are to go into this, are a very gifted people. They are temperamentally equipped for the stage. They have had a long and an exciting history of theatrical development. And I found a great variety of Russian productions extremely interesting. For instance, I went to their ballet a great deal. They gave a beautiful ballet based on fairy tales. . . .

MR. STARNES: All those fairy tales have a little moral to them, don't they? What we call a moral?

MRS. FLANAGAN: Not that I know of.

MR. STARNES: I don't know whether it would be a moral in Russia or not.

MRS. FLANAGAN: In the ballet that is not true.

MR. STARNES: We are talking about the theater. Let us stay with the theater.

MRS. FLANAGAN: In the theater I saw a great many classics, and I saw a great many plays that advocated the Soviet form of government. That is quite true. I had been sent by the Guggenheim Foundation to make a comparative study of the tendencies—

MR. STARNES: That is not answering the question.

MR. DEMPSEY: I think the witness ought to be allowed to finish her answer.

MR. STARNES: I think the witness's answer should be responsive to the question.

MR. THOMAS: You are interrupting her all the time. I should like to hear what the witness has to say.

MR. STARNES: Go ahead.

MRS. FLANAGAN: The Guggenheim Foundation had sent me to make a study of the comparative tendencies in some twelve European countries in the course of a single year. In the course of that year I went to England, Ireland, Norway, Sweden, and Denmark, to Latvia, Hungary, to Austria, to Germany, Italy, France, as well as to Russia. The record of that trip is embodied in a book called *Shifting Scenes,* and I have here the clippings from all over the world and from every leading paper in the United States on that book. And I can only say, gentlemen, and leave it to your own proof as you go over the testimony, that not one newspaper critic, when that book came out in 1927, not one critic picked out anything that was subversive or un-American. Would you like to have me read quotations from the press clippings?

MR. STARNES: No, because that is not responsive to my question.

MR. THOMAS: But she was answering several questions, and you interrupted the witness when you didn't like the answer. I would like to hear what the answer is.

MR. STARNES: I would like to also, if it is responsive.

THE CHAIRMAN: The correct procedure is that which is followed in court. The witness's testimony is supposed to be responsive, and then if the witness has any explanation to make, she may make it.

MR. STARNES: Part of the witness's statement was responsive and part was absolutely not.

MR. DEMPSEY: The witness makes her statement and you don't let her finish it. You interrupt her, and I object to that.

MRS. FLANAGAN: Do you want me to continue with a discussion of the Russian theater?

Mr. Starnes: No. I have some questions, Mrs. Flanagan. Did you make any later trips to Russia to study the theater?

Mrs. Flanagan: I went to Russia in 1931.

Mr. Starnes: Did you attend the Olympiad there?

Mrs. Flanagan: I did.

Mr. Starnes: Did you attend as a delegate?

Mrs. Flanagan: I did not.

Mr. Starnes: You went as an observer?

Mrs. Flanagan: I went as an observer.

Mr. Starnes: Did you accompany a delegate to the Olympiad?

Mrs. Flanagan: No. I went with a group of American women, and I later recorded a record of that trip in the Theater Guild magazine. And the magazine articles were reviewed very widely without one newspaper picking up anything subversive or un-American about their tone.

Mr. Starnes: Was this at the time of the Fifth Red International of Labor Unions that you attended?

Mrs. Flanagan: I wouldn't know that. I was going to see the theater. That was my one concern.

Mr. Starnes: Was that at the time of the Kharkov conference? *

Mrs. Flanagan: I don't know.

Mr. Starnes: Or at the time of the first Olympiad of the theaters of the Union National U.S.S.R.?

Mrs. Flanagan: Yes. It was.

Mr. Starnes: Was this Olympiad a section of the Fifth Red International?

Mrs. Flanagan: Not that I would know of.

Mr. Starnes: Have you made other trips to Russia besides that?

Mrs. Flanagan: I have been in Africa and Greece and Sicily and Italy in 1934. I did not go to Russia on that trip. I was again studying the theater, particularly the Greek chorus.

Mr. Starnes: How long did you stay in Russia in 1931?

Mrs. Flanagan: Three weeks.

Mr. Starnes: At the time of your trip—in 1931, I believe you said it

* The importance of this question to the HUAC is spelled out in Roy M. Brewer's article (page 203, below). The Second International Conference of Revolutionary Writers was held in Kharkov in November 1930. The proceedings were published in English in *Literature of the World Revolution,* Special Number, 1931. The masthead of the magazine included the following American names: John Dos Passos, Michael Gold, A.B. Magil, Upton Sinclair. The American delegation to the conference consisted of (or at any rate included) Michael Gold, Josephine Herbst, John Herman, Joshua Kunitz, A.B. Magil, and Harry A. Potamkin. (It is interesting, particularly in view of Sinclair's affidavit below, that he was declared unreliable at the conference by Potamkin. Incidentally Potamkin was one of the most brilliant movie critics America has had.) The editor-in-chief of *Literature of the World Revolution* was a young Pole, Bruno Jasienski: he was arrested in Stalin's terror, 1937, and died in one of the camps four years later (see Eugenia Semyonovna Ginzburg, *Journey into the Whirlwind,* pp. 237–38). —E.B.

was—did you meet, at any of those theater festivals, any of the Americans that you saw here or that you employed in the Federal Theater Project?

MRS. FLANAGAN: I did not.

MR. STARNES: Did you meet Elmer Rice there?

MRS. FLANAGAN: I did not.

MR. STARNES: Was he at that play?

MRS. FLANAGAN: I do not know.

MR. STARNES: You have not been there since 1931?

MRS. FLANAGAN: I have not.

MR. THOMAS: May I ask a question?

MR. STARNES: Yes.

MR. THOMAS: Are you a member of any Russian organization at the present time?

MRS. FLANAGAN: I am not.

MR. THOMAS: Have you been a member of any Russian organization?

MRS. FLANAGAN: I have not.

MR. THOMAS: Have you ever been trustee of a Russian university or Russian college?

MRS. FLANAGAN: I was at one time on the board of Dr. Stephen Dugan, who was at that time connected with the International Educational Board. Dr. Dugan, together with a number of other people whose names I have forgotten, had a theory that it would clear up a great many misapprehensions if there were a system of exchanging professors between such schools as Harvard and Yale and the University of Moscow.

MR. THOMAS: You mean that Harvard would take some professors from the University of Moscow, and the University of Moscow would take some professors from Harvard?

MRS. FLANAGAN: That was the general plan.

MR. THOMAS: What was the purpose of the plan?

MRS. FLANAGAN: To clarify the existing definitions. It was just after we had recognized the Soviet Union, and I believe that Mr. Dugan's idea was that we should know what it was that we had recognized. And I believe he thought it might be well for Russia to understand what the American system of government was. It was a plan which did not materialize, and I cannot give any more information on that.

MR. THOMAS: But you were on that board?

MRS. FLANAGAN: I was.

MR. THOMAS: Why did the plan fail?

MRS. FLANAGAN: I could not tell you, because Mr. Dugan called a meeting and said that the plan which had seemed feasible to him no longer seemed so, and consequently the whole thing was dropped.

MR. THOMAS: Was the meeting of the board held in the United States or held in Russia?

MRS. FLANAGAN: It was held in the United States. In the Hotel Astor.

MR. THOMAS: Did you consult with anyone in Russia about that plan?

MRS. FLANAGAN: I did not. I was not in the close councils of that body at all. They simply asked me to be on the board.

MR. STARNES: Now, Mrs. Flanagan, would you go back to this question again of un-American Communistic activities on the Federal Theater Project? The charge has been made that the *Daily Worker* and Red pins and other Communistic propaganda have been disseminated on the Project on Project time. Do you know whether or not that is true, of your own personal knowledge?

MRS. FLANAGAN: Congressman Starnes, I am submitting in this brief administrative orders which absolutely forbid the dissemination of any such literature on Project time or money. I have never seen such literature distributed. I have never seen such notices on bulletin boards. I know that in the testimony of some of your witnesses these allegations have been made, and I can only tell you that when such an allegation is made, any person who is found guilty of such improper use of Project time or property would be dismissed.

MR. STARNES: All right. In other words, if such has been done, it has been done without your knowledge and without your consent?

MRS. FLANAGAN: That is absolutely true.

MR. STARNES: Against express orders on your part?

MRS. FLANAGAN: Against such express orders, Congressman.

MR. STARNES: You don't say, though, it has not been done?

MRS. FLANAGAN: I could not, of my own knowledge.

MR. STARNES: All right. Now, you were speaking of the Russian theater a moment ago. Do you believe that the theater is a weapon?

MRS. FLANAGAN: Shall I discuss the American theater or talk about the Russian?

MR. STARNES: I refer to the theater generally. Do you believe that the theater is a weapon?

MRS. FLANAGAN: I believe that the theater is a great educational force. I think it is an entertainment. I think it is an excitement. I think it may be all things to all men.

MR. STARNES: The Russians use it as a means of teaching class consciousness, do they not?

MRS. FLANAGAN: I think they do.

MR. STARNES: Practically every play you saw was along those lines, was it not, Mrs. Flanagan?

MRS. FLANAGAN: Yes. I should say that that was the main theme of the Russian theater.

MR. STARNES: And they use the system of selling block groups of seats at reduced prices to the working classes. Is that right?

MRS. FLANAGAN: That has been done in Russia, in Germany, and in France.

MR. STARNES: In Germany in Rhineheart [Reinhardt] * theaters?

MRS. FLANAGAN: Yes.

MR. STARNES: He, of course, was accused at least of being a radical Communist?

MRS. FLANAGAN: Rhinehart* used them for years.

MR. STARNES: You make mention of the fact in your own book *Shifting Scenes*. You say, 'The task of these actors, drawn from many provinces and fields of labor, is to build a theater which shall draw a vast audience, unaccustomed to theatergoing, in the principles of Communism. The struggle that Russia is making for a universal culture is bigger than anything that you say about it. You must serve this thing bigger than itself." What "this thing" that you serve means I don't know, unless it is training those people in Communism who are not Communists.

MRS. FLANAGAN: I was reporting, Mr. Starnes, on the Russian theater.

MR. STARNES: That is right. "Forty to sixty per cent of all theater seats are sold at low rates to the trade unions and passed on for a nominal price to the workers. Hard that the intelligentsia and the bourgeoisie must pay more than the worker? Yes, but the greatest need must be met first. The state must accommodate first those who have in the past been denied theatergoing." That is a quotation from your *Shifting Scenes*.

MRS. FLANAGAN: Yes.

MR. STARNES: That is the purpose of course, of the Russian theater?

MRS. FLANAGAN: It has been ten years since I have read that book myself, but I would accept your word if you say that that is in there. I think it is a very good account of what happened in Russia.

MR. STARNES: This is on page 114, beginning with the second paragraph. Let me refer you to the article and you see if I read it correctly.

MRS. FLANAGAN: Oh, no, Congressman Starnes, I don't see any need of that. I won't question it. I was just being facetious. I am rather honored by having it read.

MR. STARNES: I am quoting an article in which you said that the theater was a weapon for teaching class consciousness, and that it should be used for the purpose of giving the public something that is vital and alive, that the theater should stress strikes and antilynching scenes and class consciousness.

MRS. FLANAGAN: I think you are referring now again to a piece of reporting, Congressman Starnes, and I would like to turn to the place in my own brief where I have mentioned that. May I do so?

MR. STARNES: Yes. You may do so.

MRS. FLANAGAN: This is on page 19 of my brief. "Mrs. Huffman al-

* Such errors, albeit only the stenographer's, seemed worth keeping as indicating the distance between certain procedures and reality. —E.B.

leged that, in being present at a meeting of the workers' theaters in November 1931, I assisted in setting up this workers' theater. She attributes to me the calling together of the various organizations present at the meeting." This is completely untrue. I was in no way connected with the setting up of these workers' theaters. I went, as did many professional theater people, to any opening meeting as an onlooker interested in theaters in general, and I reported my observations, at the request of Miss Edith Isaacs, to the *Theatre Arts Monthly*.

MR. STARNES: You wrote for the *Theatre Arts Monthly* of November 1931, did you not?

MRS. FLANAGAN: That is the article I have just been quoting.

MR. STARNES: I quote this from that same article, on page 908 of the *Theatre Arts Monthly*. "The theater being born in America today is a theater of workers. Its object is to create a national culture by and for the working class of America. Admittedly a weapon in the class struggle, this theater is being forged in the factories and the mines." Is that a correct statement?

MRS. FLANAGAN: That is a correct statement. Again, Congressman Starnes, I was reporting for the *Theatre Arts Monthly* on a very important theatrical movement of workers throughout America. It has nothing whatsoever to do with the Federal Theater. It is a piece of reporting. I have had nothing to do with setting up workers' theaters. I was teaching at Vassar College.

MR. STARNES: But this is a quotation from you. What I am quoting from is an article headed "A Theater Is Born" by Hallie Flanagan.

MRS. FLANAGAN: Exactly, but the theater was not born through me, Mr. Starnes.

MR. STARNES: That is true. The point I am making is this—

MRS. FLANAGAN: Mr. Starnes, let us not get into a controversy over this, because it is so simple. At that time, in 1931, the workers' theaters were being set up in mines and schools and all sorts of places in America. The *Theatre Arts Monthly* asked me if I would go to this meeting and report on it. If you will read on a little bit further, you will see that it describes a meeting of some of these workers' theaters. It even describes some of the plays that they were doing. Every word that you have read is there as it was quoted. That is a report of the setting up of this workers' theater.

MR. STARNES: This thing here purports to be an article written by you as a reporter. We will see, then, if we can make a distinction. You are the author of that article?

MRS. FLANAGAN: I am.

MR. STARNES: This is an expression of your thoughts right down here?

MRS. FLANAGAN: Quite true.

MR. STARNES: This is a statement made here by you with no quotations from anyone?

MRS. FLANAGAN: That is right.

MR. STARNES: That is your theory? That is an expression of your belief about the new theater of America?

MRS. FLANAGAN: More than a theory, Congressman Starnes, it was an actual fact.

MR. STARNES: That is right.

MRS. FLANAGAN: I had seen these projects. I was quoting factual material.

MR. STARNES: Now, there is another statement you have made here, that some of the plays that were put out by the Federal Theater Project are propagandistic or that they breed class consciousness—is that true or untrue?

MRS. FLANAGAN: When we remember—

MR. STARNES: Not all of them, because the testimony is that nine hundred twenty-four plays have been produced, and only twenty-six, as I recall, were in question. Let us confine ourselves to those that are in question.

MRS. FLANAGAN: I do want to go into the matter of the twenty-six plays as much as this Committee will allow me to do. But before I go into that I would like to say that I could not say that we never did a propaganda play. But I should like to go to the actual definition of "propaganda." Propaganda, after all, is education. It is education focused on certain things. For example, some of you gentlemen have doubtless seen *One Third of a Nation,* and I certainly would not sit here and say that that was not a propaganda play. I think in the discussion yesterday the word "propaganda" was used in this connotation only—that any play which was propaganda was necessarily propaganda for Communism. I should like to say very truthfully that to the best of my knowledge we have never done a play which was propaganda for Communism, but we have done plays, which were propaganda for democracy, propaganda for better housing—

MR. THOMAS: I think you ought to develop that point right there. You said that some plays were propaganda for democracy. What do you mean by that? Propaganda for what forms of democracy and what particular things? Like housing, as you just mentioned?

MRS. FLANAGAN: Yes.

MR. THOMAS: What others?

MRS. FLANAGAN: I would say—shall we go into a discussion of democracy?

MR. THOMAS: No. Just name some of the things that the Federal Theater Project has put out propaganda plays for.

MRS. FLANAGAN: Yes. Well, let us say first, *One Third of a Nation*. In that the definite propaganda was for better housing for American citizens.

MR. THOMAS: What others?

MRS. FLANAGAN: I would say that in general, Mr. Thomas, the Living Newspaper* would be propaganda for—

MR. THOMAS: But you are not answering the question. You mentioned housing?

MRS. FLANAGAN: Yes.

MR. THOMAS: How about *Power*?

MRS. FLANAGAN: Yes. I would say that *Power* was propaganda for a better understanding of the derivation and the scientific meaning of power and for its wide use—

MR. THOMAS: Was it for public ownership of power?

MRS. FLANAGAN: —that portrayed as effectively as possible both sides of that controversy, and quoted both sides.

MR. THOMAS: How about this new play, *Medicine*? What is that going to be like? What is that going to be for?

MRS. FLANAGAN: I wish I could answer that question. I am sorry to say that the play is not at the present time ready, and I could not possibly tell you, but I can tell you that it will not be a passionate brief, it will be rather in the nature of a scientific inquiry as to the whole history of medicine. You probably know that many people quarrel with the Living Newspaper because they say that we have gone into the matter too historically.

MR. THOMAS: Will it also be propaganda for the socialism [sic] of medicine?

MRS. FLANAGAN: Well, I couldn't tell you that, because the play is not complete, and I have not seen the scenario. I believe that *Prologue to Glory* could be called a propaganda play in its intense emphasis on the distinct value of sturdy American qualities and simple living.

MR. THOMAS: How about *Injunction Granted*?

MRS. FLANAGAN: *Injunction Granted* is propaganda for fair labor relations and for fairness to labor in the courts.

MR. STARNES: In other words, it does teach class consciousness, doesn't it?

MRS. FLANAGAN: I am trying to give you my definition of propaganda and just what it teaches.

MR. STARNES: Yes. Well, that is what this play teaches, isn't it?

MRS. FLANAGAN: I was trying to explain more clearly and more definitely what I mean by propaganda.

MR. STARNES: Yes. But the play *Injunction Granted* was an attack against our present system of courts, wasn't it?

MRS. FLANAGAN: No. I should say that that play was a historical study of the history of labor in the courts.

MR. STARNES: I know, but don't you believe that it does attack the present system of courts?

* A form of documentary theater invented by the Project. Arthur Arent wrote the most notable scripts. —E.B.

MRS. FLANAGAN: I do not believe that it fosters class hatred. No, I do not believe so.

MR. STARNES: All right. Now, I want to read from your article "A Theater Is Born," on page 908: "Strong he must be, however; for the theater, if it is to be of use to the worker, must be divorced from the nonessentials which have become synonymous with it—divorced from expensive buildings, stage equipment, painted sets, elaborate costumes and properties, made-up plays; above all, divorced from actors who want to show off or make money. If the theater can throw all these things into the discard it may perhaps become, as it has been at certain great moments of its history, a place where an idea is so ardently enacted that it becomes the belief of actors and audiences alike."

MRS. FLANAGAN: Well, that is a better article than I remember.

MR. STARNES: You subscribe to that? You agree with it?

MRS. FLANAGAN: Read it again. I would like to know whether the gentlemen around this table would not subscribe to it.

MR. STARNES: I can read that again if you would like to have me, but I want to read some other excerpts.

MRS. FLANAGAN: That is all right. Don't read it.

MR. STARNES: I continue to read: "Where are these theaters to exist? According to the pamphlet I am quoting, everywhere."

MRS. FLANAGAN: Notice, please, that I am quoting.

MR. STARNES: I am quoting from you: "If you are a worker in a shop, a factory, or a mine, where struggle for existence makes one day as dark as the next, if you are oppressed by capitalism and want to cry out in protest—organize a dramatic group."

MRS. FLANAGAN: May I interrupt one minute? Please notice that this is a quotation.

MR. STARNES: That is correct. I said so. "Start dramatic groups in unions, in fraternal organizations, in social clubs, in company unions, in YMCAs. Start dramatic groups in the North, South, East, and West. Let dramatic groups dot the land from coast to coast. Don't expect profit in money. These theaters exist to awaken the workers." Now, you wrote that in your article? I mean, you quoted that with approval in your article, did you not?

MRS. FLANAGAN: I did. I quoted it in my article—

MR. STARNES: With approval?

MRS. FLANAGAN: I quoted it because it was a piece of reporting in which I was showing how these theaters came into being, and I was quoting from their own magazine.

MR. STARNES: Yes. You are the protagonist for this new theater. Isn't that correct? Didn't they use some of your plays in this new theater that was being born in America at that time, Mrs. Flanagan?

MRS. FLANAGAN: I don't know.

MR. STARNES: Didn't they use some?

MRS. FLANAGAN: I did approve of the workers' theater.

MR. STARNES: *Can You Hear Their Voices?* * That was used, wasn't it?

MRS. FLANAGAN: That was done in Baptist churches and educational institutions and all sorts of—

MR. STARNES: Yes, but wasn't this new theater using your plays, Mrs. Flanagan?

MRS. FLANAGAN: Not that I know of.

MR. STARNES: I will quote directly from your article. This is from the same article. This is you speaking. Page 909: "More than a prophecy, however, these words, for theaters of workers exist in America today. On June 13, 1931, I attended in New York a conference of workers' cultural societies, the object of which was to organize these groups as a base for the federation in the near future of all the workers' theaters in the United States. At this meeting delegates from two hundred twenty-four workers' cultural groups in New York and vicinity were present and reports were read from scores of other theaters throughout the country. The John Reed Club, which, together with the *New Masses,* sponsored this initial meeting, states that there are in the United States today, some two thousand cultural organizations of workers." Now, John Reed, of course, is a Communist?

MRS. FLANAGAN: I was reporting on a meeting. I must go back and back to that point.

MR. STARNES: Please answer my question. John Reed was a Communist, wasn't he?

MRS. FLANAGAN: He was.

MR. STARNES: He was a Communist all through?

MRS. FLANAGAN: He was.

MR. STARNES: And the *New Masses* is alleged to be a Communist publication, isn't it?

MRS. FLANAGAN: Alleged to be.

MR. STARNES: Now, I again quote from your article: "The international aspect of the meeting was evident, not only from the many messages read from foreign theater groups—but from the nationality of the speakers and actors themselves—Germans, Finns, Hungarians, Russians, Negroes, and Chinese. The red banner, WORKERS OF THE WORLD UNITE, across the wall back of the platform, and the many messages from theaters in the Union of Soviet Socialist Republics, suggested that these workers' theaters were to be modeled entirely upon those of the Russian Soviets." Did you make that statement or didn't you?

MRS. FLANAGAN: I did make the statement, and it was a true statement. It was published by the *Theatre Arts Monthly,* and many people commented on it, and, so far as I know, no one picked up the point which you

* Mrs. Flanagan's and Margaret Ellen Clifford's play, based on a story by Whittaker Chambers, and published by Vassar College, 1931. —E.B.

are trying to allege. The only possible point of your reading it, of course, is to show that it has to do in some way with the Federal Theater Project; and I claim that it has nothing whatsoever to do with it.

MR. STARNES: It has nothing to do with the Federal Theater Project?

MRS. FLANAGAN: Read the next sentence there. Read article after article in which I have said that our theater was made in America.

MR. STARNES: But you also said in article after article that these theaters in America must stress class consciousness? Isn't that right?

MRS. FLANAGAN: Show me a quotation.

MR. STARNES: I am asking you if you haven't advocated that.

MRS. FLANAGAN: I do not.

MR. STARNES: Do you advocate it or do you not?

MRS. FLANAGAN: I do not.

MR. STARNES: You do not? You do not believe that plays in America should have the social significance that you say the plays of Russia have?

MRS. FLANAGAN: Now you are using another of those polite phrases that I thought you barred yesterday, but if you want to take up that phrase, I will tell you what I mean by it. I was guilty of using it myself once. When I say that a play is socially conscious I mean that it has something to do with the world today—

MR. STARNES: It is a changing world, isn't it?

MRS. FLANAGAN: It is a changing world, and the theater must change with it, Congressman, if it is to be any good.

MR. STARNES: That is right. People have got to change. That is true. I notice that you quote here, apparently with approval, some comment in reference to theaters in this country by Michael Gold. Who is he?

MRS. FLANAGAN: Michael Gold? I think he is a Communist.

MR. STARNES: I quote further from page 910.

MRS. FLANAGAN: Is this the same article?

MR. STARNES: Yes. I am quoting from Michael Gold as quoted by you. Michael Gold says, "We must have not only ideas, but fitting stage forms for those ideas," he said. "A worker will not come to a workers' theater where the production is poor when he can go to a bourgeois theater where the production is good. It is not enough that we are doing a new thing. We must do it in a new way and we must do it well." That is the end of Gold's quotation. Here comes your article: "How are they to be trained, these workers, unused to the simplest technique of the stage, men and women who work by day in shops, factories, or mines, and come together at night to make a theater? They will not be trained in the art of illusion, for their object is to remain themselves—workers—expressing workers' problems. Their object is to attack those evils from which they themselves are suffering; wage cuts, unemployment, deportation, lynching, race prejudice, legal discrimination, war, and all oppression and injustice. Being craftsmen, however, they are not oblivious to the fact that the dramatic medium is a new craft to them. They will learn this craft from the only theater at hand, the theater of the class they are attacking." Did you make that statement?

MRS. FLANAGAN: I wrote it in my article in which I was reporting on the situation in the workers' theaters in 1931.

MR. STARNES: You are the author of that article?

MRS. FLANAGAN: I am.

MR. STARNES: That is your thought and what you believe? You are giving your ideas on this new theater that is born in America or being born?

MRS. FLANAGAN: I am reporting.

THE CHAIRMAN: What is the difference? When you are making your opening statement here you don't say that this is the opinion of someone else, do you?

MRS. FLANAGAN: Yes. I quote from their own magazine and pamphlet and from Michael Gold and from various people who were aiding them at that time. I had nothing whatsoever to do with setting up the workers' theater, nor with their projects, nor was I ever associated with one.

THE CHAIRMAN: Do you have anything to do with this Workers' Laboratory Theater in New York?

MRS. FLANAGAN: Now?

THE CHAIRMAN: No.

MRS. FLANAGAN: I am not concerned with any theater except the Federal Theater, nor have I ever been connected with the Workers' Laboratory Theater in any way.

THE CHAIRMAN: Do you use any of the artists of the Workers' Laboratory Theater in New York? Do you use any of their plays? Do you collaborate with them in any way or do any of the members of the Workers' Laboratory Theater sit on your board up here?

MRS. FLANAGAN: I am under the impression, which may be wrong, that the Workers' Laboratory Theater is not now in existence.

THE CHAIRMAN: It is supplanted by what?

MRS. FLANAGAN: Well, I couldn't answer that, but we on the Federal Theater have no collaboration with any of those groups.

THE CHAIRMAN: How many people are engaged in these Federal Theater Projects in New York?

MRS. FLANAGAN: Over four thousand.

THE CHAIRMAN: Out of how many altogether?

MRS. FLANAGAN: Out of a total of some nine thousand throughout the United States.

THE CHAIRMAN: You recently made a report of your activities and you gave the number of people you estimated you have played to since the establishment of the Project. How many people do you figure you had as audiences in the United States for these plays?

MRS. FLANAGAN: The recorded figure, Congressman Dies, was something like twenty-five million people.

THE CHAIRMAN: In other words, you have reached approximately twenty-five per cent of our population with your plays?

MRS. FLANAGAN: Something like that. One of the great problems, if you will permit me to speak for just a minute—

THE CHAIRMAN: Yes, ma'am.

MRS. FLANAGAN: One of the great problems is that, while in the other art projects it is possible to establish them in every state in the Union, which we would also like to do here, it is not possible with us, because, while an artist can paint or a musician play or a writer write if there is no audience or only one or two people involved, we cannot set up theaters except in states where there are twenty-five or more people of satisfactory type on the relief rolls. So that one of our problems is this centralization of the theater industry.

THE CHAIRMAN: Where have your audiences been? What localities have you played mostly?

MRS. FLANAGAN: We have played, I think I am safe in saying, the widest variety of American audiences that any theater has ever played.

THE CHAIRMAN: In what localities, Mrs. Flanagan?

MRS. FLANAGAN: The chief localities are, first, New York City, and next Los Angeles and Chicago, because that is where the greatest unemployment exists. They are the three largest cities. But if you are speaking now of the audiences themselves—I want to pick up that point, if you don't mind—

THE CHAIRMAN: I merely want to know the places where you have played, but if you want to discuss audiences, it is all right.

MRS. FLANAGAN: I do want to discuss them, because that allegation was made here by one of your witnesses, which I would not like to remain in the minds of any of you around this table. My impression is that you are trying to get at all the facts.

THE CHAIRMAN: That is correct. And if this statement is untrue, we want you to refute it.

MRS. FLANAGAN: I want to quote from her allegation. Miss Huffman says, "They couldn't get any audiences for anything except Communistic plays." Now, gentlemen, I have here the proof that that is an absolutely false statement. We have, as sponsoring bodies for the Federal Theater, lists of organizations covering twenty pages of this brief, which I intend to write into the record; and I will summarize them for you. Two hundred and sixty-three social clubs and organizations, two hundred and sixty-four welfare and civic organizations, two hundred and seventy-one educational organizations, ninety-five religious organizations, ninety-one organizations from business industries, sixteen mass organizations, sixty-six trade-unions, sixty-two professional unions, seventeen consumers' unions, twenty-five fraternal unions, and fifteen political organizations. Note, gentlemen, that every religious shade is covered and every political affiliation and every type of educational and civic body in the support of our theater. It is the widest and most American base that any theater has ever built upon, and I request you not only to write that into the record but to read the list of public schools and universities and churches and the civic and social groups that are supporting this Federal Theater.

MR. STARNES: I want to quote finally from your article "A Theater Is Born," on page 915 of the *Theatre Arts Monthly,* edition of November 1931.

MRS. FLANAGAN: Is this the same article, Mr. Starnes?

MR. STARNES: Yes. "The power of these theaters springing up everywhere throughout the country lies in the fact that they know what they want. Their purpose—restricted, some will call it, though it is open to question whether any theater which attempts to create a class culture can be called restricted—is clear. This is important because there are only two theaters in the country today that are clear as to aim: one is the commercial theater which wants to make money; the other is the workers' theater which wants to make a new social order. The workers' theaters are neither infirm nor divided in purpose. Unlike any art form existing in America today, the workers' theaters intend to shape the life of this country, socially, politically, and industrially. They intend to remake a social structure without the help of money—and this ambition alone invests their undertaking with a certain Marlowesque madness." You are quoting from this Marlowe. Is he a Communist?

MRS. FLANAGAN: I am very sorry. I was quoting from Christopher Marlowe.

MR. STARNES: Tell us who Marlowe is, so we can get the proper reference, because that is all that we want to do.

MRS. FLANAGAN: Put in the record that he was the greatest dramatist in the period immediately preceding Shakespeare.

MR. STARNES: Put that in the record because the charge has been made that this article of yours is entirely Communistic, and we want to help you.

MRS. FLANAGAN: Thank you. That statement will go in the record.

MR. STARNES: Of course, we had what some people call Communists back in the days of the Greek theater.

MRS. FLANAGAN: Quite true.

MR. STARNES: And I believe Mr. Euripides was guilty of teaching class consciousness also, wasn't he?

MRS. FLANAGAN: I believe that was alleged against all of the Greek dramatists.

MR. STARNES: So we cannot say when it began.

MRS. FLANAGAN: Wasn't it alleged also of Gibson [Ibsen] and against practically every great dramatist?

MR. STARNES: I think so. Now, I am quoting again: "When we see, as we probably shall during the next year, their street plays and pageants, their performances on trucks and on street corners, we shall doubtless find them crude, violent, childish, and repetitious. Yet we must admit that here is a theater which can afford to be supremely unconcerned with what we think of it. It does not ask our advice, our interest, our advertising, or our money. We need not deplore the lack of art in the workers' theater for we shall not be invited to witness its performances. It is only in the event of the success of its herculean aim—the reorganization of our social order—that we shall become involuntary audience."

MRS. FLANAGAN: Well, you understand, Mr. Starnes, that that did not take place, did it? The great hope of the workers' theater—together with the commercial theater—failed, and some ten thousand theater professionals landed right in the lap of the United States Government, and I can again say that I am concerned today, and have been for three years, with the rehabilitation of those people.

MR. STARNES: That is all I have to ask, Mr. Chairman.

THE CHAIRMAN: Do you have any questions, Mr. Thomas?

MR. THOMAS: I have a few questions. You heard the testimony yesterday relative to *The Revolt of the Beavers*?

MRS. FLANAGAN: I did. I was very sorry that Mr. Brooks Atkinson, whose skill as a critic and whose learning are valued very greatly, was disturbed by this play, and that the police commissioner was disturbed, but we did not write this play for dramatic critics, nor did we write it for policemen. We wrote it for children, and I wish to write into the record what the children thought about the play.

MR STARNES: Of course, you know they were not criticizing it because they thought that it was not an amusing play for policemen?

MRS. FLANAGAN: They were criticizing it because they said that they thought that it was poisoning the minds of youth.

MR. STARNES: That is correct.

MRS. FLANAGAN: Now I wish to write into the record a survey on *The Revolt of the Beavers* which was conducted under the supervision of Dr. Francis Holder of the Department of Psychology of New York University, together with fourteen honor students of the college, on the reactions of the children. They made many tests covering a number of public schools, and I would like to read you the questions which they asked, not only about this play, but about every play which we do, because one function of the Committee, as you mentioned yesterday, is to be sure that the plays that we do are good for children.

MR. STARNES: They asked those questions of whom?

MRS. FLANAGAN: Of fifty children in the public schools. And I have the answers of each one of the fifty briefed for you. I don't propose to read the whole thing. I propose to read the questions and a number of the answers. It is very short and I think it will interest you. I know, and I want you to know, that I would not wish to poison the minds of children. These are the questions:

"1. Could the child see and hear everything in the play clearly?

You understand that these are not just on *The Revolt of the Beavers*. This has to do with every play that we do.

THE CHAIRMAN: But this questionnaire was sent out in connection with *The Revolt of the Beavers*?

MRS. FLANAGAN: Yes. But the answers that I will read have to do only with that.

"2. Was the story or idea of the play thoroughly understood by the child?

"3. Was any part of the play unclear to the child?

"4. If possible, get the child to express an opinion or preference on the acting and scenery, lighting, music, dancing, and the meaning of the play; what characters were liked or disliked by the child, and why; whether anything in the play has left the child upset or afraid. Would he like to see and hear more plays of this type, or would not the child like to see them?"

The first answer was: "The play teaches us never to be selfish, never to be selfish because you don't get anything out of it." "The acting—how to get around on the stage. That is what I like, the acting big people do as small children, and how good they acted as beavers on roller skates." "I thought that the grown people acted their parts as children very well, especially on roller skates." "That it is better to be good than bad. That beavers have manners just like children. To teach that if you are unkind any time in your life, you will always regret it. Never to be selfish." "To show you the ways of beavers in Beaverland. The way that big people act to make them look just like children and beavers, and the way they act, and the way they work." "How the children would want the whole world to be nine years old and happy." "To get the beavers to be like children nine years old, thinking it would be more fun if everyone was nine years old and a land of talking beavers on roller skates." "How the beavers live in Beaverland. How a boy and girl can make beavers be happy."

MR. THOMAS: I think their reaction is very interesting, but at the same time what was the reaction of Mr. Atkinson?

MRS. FLANAGAN: Oh, I thought you were barring critics.

MR. THOMAS: And the reaction of the police commissioner in New York City. What attention did you pay to their reaction?

MRS. FLANAGAN: Let us divide that into two parts. What attention did we pay to Mr. Brooks Atkinson? We value his critical opinion on the subject, as any play producer must.

MR. THOMAS: Did you, in regard to this particular play?

MRS. FLANAGAN: As to this particular play we found that the children, the audience for which it was planned, enjoyed it and found, as I have told you, nothing subversive in it, and we were went right on giving it. To the best of my knowledge, the police commissioner did not say in his letter that he had seen the play. He was alleged to have seen it.

MR. THOMAS: Now quite a bit has been said here today about the theater as a weapon. Have you read the script of *Injunction Granted*?

MRS. FLANAGAN: I have, and I saw the production also.

MR. THOMAS: I have here the script of *Injunction Granted*. The last part of the script is all devoted to a criticism of the legislature in the State of New Jersey. It has to do with the Workers' Alliance coming into the halls of the legislature in the State of New Jersey and sitting there and taking over the government. Do you think that that is the proper kind of propaganda to put out through the Federal Theater Project?

MRS. FLANAGAN: I think that that episode was necessary in the development of a study of labor in litigation.

MR. THOMAS: This latter part has nothing to do with labor in litigation. It has to do with the Workers' Alliance's criticism of the state legislature.

MRS. FLANAGAN: It was headline news of that period which had a direct relevance to the theater. You see, in the Living Newspaper, everything is factual. The records from which any Living Newspaper is taken are always open to all of you and to anyone. And I think it is rather a remarkable fact, gentlemen, that in the three years of the existence of the Living Newspaper, not one allegation has been made that the news were untrue. Nobody has ever proved that we have ever misquoted.

MR. THOMAS: I want to read a few lines from this play. The first man on the dais, who is a member of the Workers' Alliance, says this, (*Putting up his hand for silence*): " 'Brothers, we of the Workers' Alliance, a relief organization, have taken over this house to protest against the inaction of our elected legislators.' " I happened to be a member of that legislature at that time, and I happen to know that there was nothing in the way of inaction at that time.

MRS. FLANAGAN: I beg your pardon, but that was a quotation.

MR. THOMAS: A quotation, yes, from one of the members of the Workers' Alliance who were sitting in our seats in the legislature.

MRS. FLANAGAN: From a newspaper.

MR. THOMAS: Here is another line: "We consider the Workers' Alliance a responsible labor organization, and as such we have been reorganized by the American Federation of Labor. The cause of demonstrations such as these is not agitation, but rather the continuance of six years of mass unemployment." Now certain members of the state legislature at that time offered jobs to different members of the Workers' Alliance who were sitting in the house at Trenton, and those jobs were not accepted.

MRS. FLANAGAN: May I break in there to say that if you had written to us at that time and given us that material over your signature, we would have tried to get that into the play. We have done that many times, gentlemen, for members of Congress.

MR. THOMAS: Do you know about all the plays that are put out by the Federal Theater Project?

MRS. FLANAGAN: No. But we are doing, in the eyes of expert historians, a very good critical job.

MR. THOMAS: But how can I select anything out of any of these plays and make a suggestion to you unless it has been called to my attention by somebody?

MRS. FLANAGAN: You quoted something you would like to have seen in there, and I say that it might have been in there, if you had called it to our attention.

MR. THOMAS: Again I quote: "Mimics the compass of the legislature." "Sister Speaker, fellow representatives, and the great American public outside. Things have come to a hell of a pass. We have been dillydallying," and so on. Spain—this man Spain, as I understand it, was one of the heads of the Workers' Alliance, and is still one of the heads of the Workers' Alliance. He says in the last two or three pages, Spain says: "Motion carried. Well, this is only our first day, but we have done just as much as the legislature did in three months, which seems practically nothing. (*Laughter and applause as Powell committee returns.*) Hello, Powell. What does the Governor have to say?" Now, that is in this play *Injunction Granted*. Do you, as the Director of the Federal Theater Project, think that that is the right kind of propaganda to put out against the government of a particular state, against the legislators who were elected by the people of that particular state?

MRS. FLANAGAN: I think that the scene was taken from newspaper reports—

MR. THOMAS: I want an answer to my question.

MRS. FLANAGAN: I do. I think that plays dealing with real problems facing all of us as Americans today may be one phase of the work that the Federal Theater should do. Remember that on the children's plays, religious plays, and musical plays—

MR. THOMAS: I want an answer to my question specifically, and I want to say that representatives of the Federal Theater Project and the Art Project who have come before this Committee—and this is my personal opinion—have evaded question after question. Now I want to find out, Mrs. Flanagan, whether you, as National Director of the Federal Theater Project, think that it is proper for the Federal Theater Project, an agency of the Federal Government, to put out this kind of propaganda against the elected legislators of a particular state.

MRS. FLANAGAN: It is not propaganda against the elected legislators.

MR. THOMAS: You said it was propaganda, originally.

MRS. FLANAGAN: I said it was propaganda for fair labor relations, and I must insist that I think that that is one thing that the Federal Theater should do.

MR. THOMAS: What has that play to do with labor relations? It has to do with the question of the relations between the state legislature and the Workers' Alliance, who said at that time that they were working in behalf of unemployment.

MRS. FLANAGAN: It was all information from the daily papers. It was intended to prove that during the time when there was this mass need and this mass unemployment, their people were not getting sufficient help from their legislative bodies. It was taken from the daily papers bearing on that point.

MR. THOMAS: Then you will admit that we should use the Federal Theater Project, through their plays, to encourage mass movements? That is practically what you just said. Do you admit it or don't you?

MRS. FLANAGAN: I think that the Living Newspaper, which I have discussed fully and would like to discuss more, may be one phase of proper activity for any theater.

MR. THOMAS: But you don't answer the question.

MRS. FLANAGAN: Yes. I am answering it.

MR. THOMAS: Do you admit it or don't you admit it?

MRS. FLANAGAN: I do think it is a proper use of Government funds.

* * *

MR. MOSIER: Mrs. Flanagan, in these plays that you produced, have you produced any anti-Fascist plays?

MRS. FLANAGAN: A number of people have claimed that the play *On the Rocks* [by Bernard Shaw] was anti-Fascist, and some people have claimed it was anti-Communist. That is another one of those words that it is very difficult to define. We never do a play because it holds any political bias. We do a play because we believe it is a good play, a strong play, properly handled with native material. Could you be a little more specific about that?

MR. MOSIER: Have you done any that are definitely anti-Communist?

MRS. FLANAGAN: Members of the press—I do not know where else to turn for reports—have said that *On the Rocks* was definitely: some say anti-Fascist and some say anti-Communist.

MR. MOSIER: You did one play, I believe, in which Earl Browder appeared as a character?

MRS. FLANAGAN: In *Triple-A Plowed Under*.

MR. MOSIER: I have not read the play, but in that play did Earl Browder expound his theory of Communism?

MRS. FLANAGAN: No, he does not. I will have that reference read if you would like to have it. I would like to say, however, that it seems to me we would be on very dangerous ground if we denominated and denounced as subversive any play in which any character opposing our own political faith appeared. For instance, you might as well say that Marlowe that we discussed a while ago, because he introduced the devil into the play had sold his soul to the devil. You might as well say the March of Time because it quotes from Stalin, is Communistic, or because it quotes from Hitler is Fascist. I do not think that is a tenable position. Would you like to have the Browder speech read?

MR. MOSIER: I just asked whether Browder appeared as a character and expounded his views in the play. If he did not, then the answer is no.

MRS. FLANAGAN: Browder appears together with Al Smith, Senator Hastings, and Thomas Jefferson, not as an actual person, but as a shadow on a screen.

MR. STARNES: He is in pretty good company with one exception.

MR. MOSIER: Have you produced any plays, Mrs. Flanagan, that are antireligious in character?

MRS. FLANAGAN: We certainly have not. On the contrary, we have produced—I think I am safe in saying—more plays religious in character than any other theater or organization. For example, gentlemen, last Christmas time, in every city in which we had projects, we did old religious scenes on the steps of libraries, on street corners, in trailer camps, and churches.

THE CHAIRMAN: Are there any other questions?

MR. STARNES: The statement has been made in the testimony that you are in sympathy with Communistic doctrines.

MRS. FLANAGAN: Congressman Starnes, I am an American, and I believe in American democracy. I believe the Works Progress Administration is one great bulwark of that democracy. I believe the Federal Theater, which is one small part of that large pattern, is honestly trying in every possible way to interpret the best interests of the people of this democracy. I am not in sympathy with any other form of government in this country.

MR. STARNES: That is your statement. You are absolutely not in sympathy with Communism. Now, have you, as director of this National Art Project, produced productions for the purpose of promoting class hatred?

MRS. FLANAGAN: I have not.

MR. STARNES: We understand that no restrictions have been placed on your employing people who might believe in a Communistic form of government. And unquestionably you have Communists working on the job, but the thing the Committee is interested in is the question of Communistic activity on the Project. Do you know of your own knowledge, personal knowledge, of any Communistic activities that are being carried on there, in other words, the promulgation of Communistic doctrines and theory, the recruiting of soldiers for Loyalist Spain, the dissemination of Communistic literature, or the collection of funds for the Workers' Alliance and for the Communist Party on Project time?

MRS. FLANAGAN: Congressman Starnes, those are opposed to the administrative restrictions, copies of which are in this brief.

MR. STARNES: You are opposed to it, and you know nothing of it personally, but you can't deny, of course, of your own personal knowledge, such is the case, but if it is the case, it is without your knowledge and consent?

MRS. FLANAGAN: Right.

* * *

THE CHAIRMAN: Mrs. Flanagan, I want to ask you one or two questions. What, in your opinion, as the director of the Federal Theaters, is the primary purpose to be kept in mind in the production of plays? What principal objective do you keep in mind, amusement, or, on the other hand, the teaching of a particular idea, or the presentation of facts or material in a way to leave a definite impression?

MRS. FLANAGAN: The basis of the choice of plays is that any theater supported by Federal funds should do no plays of a subversive or cheap, or shoddy, or vulgar, or outworn, or imitative nature, but only such plays as the Government could stand behind in a program which is national in scope and regional in emphasis and democratic in American attitude.

MR. THOMAS: Democratic!

MRS. FLANAGAN: Not democratic in the narrow sense.

THE CHAIRMAN: Then, in a sense, primarily it is for amusement, isn't that true?

MRS. FLANAGAN: The second objective, if I may go on, is wide diversity. I think we should do plays of as great diversity as the geographic range and the varieties of our people. I can't say just entertainment or education, Congressman Dies.

THE CHAIRMAN: You are not in a position to say whether the primary purpose should be to entertain the audience or instruct the audience?

MRS. FLANAGAN: A good play must always entertain the audience.

THE CHAIRMAN: That is the primary purpose of it?

MRS. FLANAGAN: The primary purpose of a good play *is* to entertain, isn't it?

THE CHAIRMAN: Entertain?

MRS. FLANAGAN: It must also, can also, often teach. It can inculcate religious principles. It can entertain simply, if it is a musical comedy. Think of the varieties of things that it can do to train people in the great field of the classics.

THE CHAIRMAN: It can be used as a vehicle, in other words, to impart to an audience certain ideas, either along moral lines, or along social lines or economic lines, isn't that a fact?

MRS. FLANAGAN: Yes.

THE CHAIRMAN: And in the production of these plays, while you have kept in mind primarily the objective of entertainment, you have considered it your duty likewise to convey such, we will say, instruction or to impart ideas along social and economic lines, isn't that true?

MRS. FLANAGAN: The list of the plays that we have done is open to you, and the proof of the types of plays that we do can be found there. Over five hundred of the nine hundred twenty-four plays are plays by tested American authors who have had previous successes on Broadway.

* * *

THE CHAIRMAN: But one of the important functions of the theater, as you recognize it—I am just asking you to get your opinion—is to promote an idea either along social, economic, or, we will say, political lines; is that true? Is that a legitimate function of the theater as you understand it?

MRS. FLANAGAN: I defined propaganda very clearly, or tried to, in the early stages.

THE CHAIRMAN: I know, but is that a legitimate function of the stage?

MRS. FLANAGAN: It is one legitimate function.

THE CHAIRMAN: It is one legitimate function?

MRS. FLANAGAN: Yes.

THE CHAIRMAN: Mr. Starnes read some excerpts from this article of yours. Now, I think it is fair to ask you how much of this is your opinion and how much of it is the mere reporting of the opinions of others? For instance: "Strong he must be, however; for the theater, if it is to be of use to the worker, must be divorced from the nonessentials which have been synonymous with it—divorced from expensive buildings, stage equipment, painted sets, elaborate costumes and properties, made-up plays; above all, divorced from actors who want to show off or make money. If the theater can throw off all these things into the discard, it may perhaps become, as it has been at certain great moments of its history, a place where an idea is so ardently enacted that it becomes the belief of actors and audiences alike." Now is that your opinion?

MRS. FLANAGAN: That was my opinion in regard to the workers' theaters, yes.

THE CHAIRMAN: Your opinion is, if it can throw off these costumes, and so forth, properties, and so forth—

MRS. FLANAGAN: Well, it had to throw those off. It had no money for those—

THE CHAIRMAN: —it can become a place where the idea is ardently enacted? That is your opinion?

MRS. FLANAGAN: That was my opinion about the thing I was discussing.

THE CHAIRMAN: But that is not reporting the opinion of others. You believe that to be true, do you not?

MRS. FLANAGAN: Of the workers' theaters, yes.

THE CHAIRMAN: Do you think that theaters should be created for the purpose of conveying ideas such as you have described in this article?

MRS. FLANAGAN: That article has nothing to do, as I have repeatedly said, with the Federal Theater.

THE CHAIRMAN: I know, but I am asking you if it is your opinion that the theater should do that thing?

MRS. FLANAGAN: Let us not be too solemn. Do you mean do I think without the decoration, some of the painted scenery, and some of the employees and embellishment, it would be a good thing? Yes, I think a great deal could be gotten rid of.

THE CHAIRMAN: I did not ask that. I asked you if you think the theater should be used for the purpose of conveying ideas along social and economic lines.

MRS. FLANAGAN: I think that is one justifiable reason for the existence of the theater.

THE CHAIRMAN: Do you think that the Federal Theater should be used for the one purpose of conveying ideas along social, economic, or political lines?

MRS. FLANAGAN: I would hesitate on the political.

THE CHAIRMAN: Eliminate political. Upon social and economic lines.

MRS. FLANAGAN: I think it is one logical, reasonable, and I might say imperative thing for our theater to do.

THE CHAIRMAN: And for educational purposes, is that right?

MRS. FLANAGAN: Yes.

THE CHAIRMAN: In other words, you believe it is correct to use the Federal Theater to educate people, audiences, along social or economic lines, is that correct?

MRS. FLANAGAN: Among other things, yes. I have pointed out to the Committee that only ten per cent of the plays that we do—

THE CHAIRMAN: I understand.

MRS. FLANAGAN: But I am not sure all of these people do understand, and I want them to. The definite proof is we have only done ten per cent of plays in that category.

THE CHAIRMAN: I am not questioning that fact. You have plays and dances that have nothing to do with economics.

MRS. FLANAGAN: Right. Among others we have plays that have to do with ideas. * * *

THE CHAIRMAN: But you do believe that it is proper that some of the plays produced by the Federal Theaters should be used for that purpose?

MRS. FLANAGAN: I do, Congressman Dies.

THE CHAIRMAN: I am just getting your idea, and those plays have been used for that purpose, have they not?

MRS. FLANAGAN: Yes.

THE CHAIRMAN: When you take plays like, we will say, *Stevedore*—was that one of your productions, *Stevedore*?

MRS. FLANAGAN: I know it was at one time on a production schedule.*

THE CHAIRMAN: You did produce *Sing for Your Supper,* didn't you?

MRS. FLANAGAN: We are planning to produce it.

THE CHAIRMAN: That is your plan, unless you are interrupted by lack of funds, or some action by Congress?

MRS. FLANAGAN: Yes.

THE CHAIRMAN: Now, here are a number of excerpts from this play, I presume authentic excerpts from it.

MRS. FLANAGAN: What play?

THE CHAIRMAN: *Sing for Your Supper.* For instance, in there Frank Hague sits at a desk, picks up phone. "Hello, Operator, give me Washington. I want to speak to John L. Lewis."

MRS. FLANAGAN: I am sorry to interrupt you, but the Hague scenes have been cut out of the play.

THE CHAIRMAN: You think it is entirely proper that the Federal Theater produce plays for the purpose of bringing out some social idea that is a heated issue at a particular time?

MRS. FLANAGAN: It is one of the things that the theater can do.

THE CHAIRMAN: One of the important things. Now on this *Stevedore,* the reason I ask you about that play is because you said earlier you did not believe in producing any play that has any vulgarity in it, or profanity, or anything of that sort, didn't you say that?

MRS. FLANAGAN: I did not mention profanity. I did say a play which was vulgar.

THE CHAIRMAN: Do you think it is correct to produce a play that has a great deal of profanity in it?

MRS. FLANAGAN: Could you be specific?

THE CHAIRMAN: I will take *Stevedore,* according to the statement here on page 24: "Lonnie: God damn dem, anyhow. What dey think I am? Do I look like some kind of animal? Do I look like somebody who'd jump over a back fence and rape a woman?" I am not going to read all of the things in here, but there are numerous examples of absolutely vulgar statements and the frequent use of the Lord's name in a profane way. Now, what I am asking you is this: Do you think it is proper that the taxpayers' money of America should be used to produce a play to an American audience that contains such vulgarity and such profanity as that? I am not undertaking to indict you or anything you have done. I am just getting your idea as to whether you think that is a proper thing to do?

MRS. FLANAGAN: I have no defense for blasphemy.

THE CHAIRMAN: I know you have not. Do you think it is proper that

* And it was produced, in Seattle, 1936. —E.B.

the Federal Theater should produce a play in which vulgarity and profanity appears throughout, as it does in *Stevedore*?

MRS. FLANAGAN: No, I do not.

THE CHAIRMAN: Then you will agree with me that the play should not have been produced?

MRS. FLANAGAN: I think that we should look into the matter.

THE CHAIRMAN: Do you not also think that since the Federal Theater Project is an agency of the Government and that all of our people support it through their tax money, people of different classes, different races, different religions, some who are workers, some who are businessmen, don't you think that no play should ever be produced which undertakes to portray the interests of one class to the disadvantage of another class, even though that might be accurate, even though factually there may be justification normally for that, yet because of the very fact that we are using taxpayers' money to produce plays, do you not think it is questionable whether it is right to produce plays that are biased in favor of one class against another?

MRS. FLANAGAN: I think we strive for objectivity, but I think the whole history of the theater would indicate that any dramatist holds a passionate brief for the things he is saying.

THE CHAIRMAN: I am talking about plays that you are authorized, as a representative of the American people, to supervise, plays that all of us help to finance, people of different conditions and different opinions. Now, do you think it proper that a play be produced which represents the desires and the viewpoint of one class to the disadvantage of another class?

MRS. FLANAGAN: I think that if every play that you did expressed one class opinion, that it would be a loaded theater, and quite out of keeping with a theater subsidized by Government funds. However, I think you would have to take into consideration the many plays done, the many types of plays. I think that you gentlemen would have to go to some of these plays.

THE CHAIRMAN: I am not arguing with you. I am just asking you. You are the source of our information. We are not asking this in any sarcastic manner.

MRS. FLANAGAN: Yes.

THE CHAIRMAN: This is for the purpose of eliciting information from you, who are the servant of our Administration in this important matter.

MRS. FLANAGAN: Quite true.

THE CHAIRMAN: And to you we come for the information.

MRS. FLANAGAN: Yes.

THE CHAIRMAN: So, I am asking you if you do not think you are treading upon dangerous ground when you use an agency of the Government—no matter how laudable it may be in private life—but when you use that agency to portray the interests or the arguments of the Workers' Alliance, or the CIO, or any other class or group, so that by subtle portrayal you paint that group, or you paint the other class, in a disadvantageous role, don't you think that is more or less dangerous?

MRS. FLANAGAN: We are not doing plays to stir up class hatred.

THE CHAIRMAN: Is it not a fact that when you do produce a play that gives all the breaks to one class, such as the Workers' Alliance, or such as the CIO, or such as the workers of the country generally, gives them breaks over another class, over the employers or the business people, would you not join with me in condemning that as a dangerous policy?

MRS. FLANAGAN: Could you give me a specific example?

THE CHAIRMAN: I am asking you if that is done. I am not assuming it is done.

MRS. FLANAGAN: We do not do plays that stir up class hatred. If you can give me quotations I will be glad to answer.

THE CHAIRMAN: Can you give me a single play, not among the group now dealing with historical plays, or things of that sort, but among the ten per cent that you say deal with social and economic questions, can you submit to this Committee one play that does not convey a subtle impression throughout, so that when the audience is left with the play, the Workers' Alliance or the CIO or organized labor does not have the best of the other fellows?

MRS. FLANAGAN: Why, Congressman Dies, I could sit in this room until the end of the day and give you such plays—*Spirochete,* for example.

THE CHAIRMAN: What is that?

MRS. FLANAGAN: It is a Living Newspaper of the study of syphilis, which was backed by the Surgeon General of the United States.

THE CHAIRMAN: I am not talking about that.

MRS. FLANAGAN: And by all of the health departments. That is one of the plays that comes in the category you have just mentioned.

THE CHAIRMAN: All right.

MRS. FLANAGAN: It is one of the plays in the ten per cent—it is definite propaganda for education in regard to social diseases. . . .

THE CHAIRMAN: All right.

MRS. FLANAGAN: And, as I say, it is backed and sponsored by the medical associations of this country. That is a perfectly clear example, isn't it? Another one—

THE CHAIRMAN: What others?

MRS. FLANAGAN: Another one is a Living Newspaper on flood control. Another one is on Bonneville Dam, in which the whole thing is a history of the development of Bonneville Dam.

THE CHAIRMAN: Showing the necessity for it?

MRS. FLANAGAN: Yes, to some extent.

THE CHAIRMAN: And the great value of it?

MRS. FLANAGAN: To some extent. Showing also the great heroism of it and the scientific knowledge necessary to put it through.

THE CHAIRMAN: Now give us some more.

MRS. FLANAGAN: *The Spanish Grant,* which is the whole history of the trek of our forefathers across the plains and the founding of California.

THE CHAIRMAN: That is historical?

MRS. FLANAGAN: Yes, but it comes right down to present-day events. It is one of the big regional dramas that I spoke of that is being developed on the Project on the West Coast.

THE CHAIRMAN: Give us another one.

MRS. FLANAGAN: *Clown's Progress,* which is the history of vaudeville in the United States, showing its close applicability to everyday life, which is also written on the Project. *Two a Day,* which is in that same category on the development of the vaudeville trades throughout the country. Many of our plays deal with these pressing situations around us, some of them springing from unemployment, but without the slightest attempt to stir up class hatred.

THE CHAIRMAN: Do you agree, then, with the proposition that no play should be presented that will give advantage to one class over another class where there is a controversy involved?

MRS. FLANAGAN: I do not think you can possibly take that position. I think that, there again, I would have to go back to my original premise that I want a good play, a powerful play, preferably of native material, and that, in at least ten per cent of the cases, I would feel we should do a play that had something to do with modern life.

THE CHAIRMAN: Then this Federal Theater is a very powerful vehicle of expression, isn't it, and of propaganda, because, as you say, it reaches twenty-five million people. It therefore can be used or abused.

MRS. FLANAGAN: Yes.

THE CHAIRMAN: With serious consequences, can it not?

MRS. FLANAGAN: Yes, sir.

THE CHAIRMAN: And do you know of any way in which it could be more seriously abused than it would be to portray, as I said a few moments ago, one class, putting them at an advantage over another class?

MRS. FLANAGAN: I have been giving a long list of illustrations of the fact that we do not so do.

THE CHAIRMAN: I am not asking you that. I say, isn't that a fact?

MRS. FLANAGAN: I am asking you for illustrations where we have done that. I claim you are stating a hypothetical case, Congressman Dies.

THE CHAIRMAN: Then, will you say that you have not produced a play in which one class of workers is not portrayed in an advantageous role?

MRS. FLANAGAN: First you asked me if I could give you a single play in which we have not done that—

THE CHAIRMAN: You gave that.

MRS. FLANAGAN: I say I can show you a myriad, so I would not take the position you have said; that is too strong a position. For instance, in *Power,* the central character is the consumer, and the whole play shows that all of us, as consumers of power, have some question as to how it came into being, and what makes it, and what is the best possible use of it.

THE CHAIRMAN: What is the objective of the play, what impression is it designed to bring in the mind of the audience—the play *Power*—that public ownership is a good thing?

MRS. FLANAGAN: I think the first thing the play does is to make you understand more about power, where it comes from, and how it is evolved, about its whole historical use.

THE CHAIRMAN: All right.

MRS. FLANAGAN: I think it also does speak highly for the public ownership of power.

THE CHAIRMAN: Let us just take that one instance. We will assume, for the sake of argument, that maybe the public ownership of power is a desirable thing. Do you not think it improper that the Federal Theater, using the taxpayers' money, should present a play to the audience which champions one side of a controversy?

MRS. FLANAGAN: No, Congressman Dies, I do not consider it improper. I have just said that I felt that in a small percentage of our plays, and pointed out that it is ten per cent that do hold a brief for a certain cause in accord with general forward-looking tendencies, and I say—

THE CHAIRMAN: Who is to determine what is a forward-looking tendency?

MRS. FLANAGAN: Why, our play-policy board chooses these plays.

THE CHAIRMAN: They are to determine that question? As to what is a forward-looking tendency? They, therefore, would have the idea that public ownership of utilities was a forward-looking tendency?

MRS. FLANAGAN: Also with the idea, Congressman Dies, that, first, the play must be good, it must have the power to hold the audience.

THE CHAIRMAN: I am assuming that. But we are confining ourselves to the proposition—take *Power*—you say that your policy board must first pass on this, isn't that right?

MRS. FLANAGAN: Yes.

THE CHAIRMAN: Then your policy board approves the public ownership of utilities. Then you think that, because they approve the principle of public ownership of utilities, it is proper that the Federal Theater shall exhibit a play in which it champions the right of public ownership, do you not?

MRS. FLANAGAN: I do think so.

THE CHAIRMAN: All right. Now, would the same thing be true with reference to the public ownership of railroads, because the policy board—

MRS. FLANAGAN: I do not know. We never choose plays that way, Congressman Dies.

THE CHAIRMAN: I understand that. But assume that a play is submitted to you that champions the cause of public ownership of railroads, and the majority of the policy board say, "We are in favor of public ownership of railroads," then would you believe it right to exhibit that play to twenty-five million people?

MRS. FLANAGAN: That is the very grave responsibility, Congressman Dies, with which I am charged.

THE CHAIRMAN: Do you think it would be right to show that play under those circumstancse?

MRS. FLANAGAN: Yes. Absolutely.

THE CHAIRMAN: Do you think that type of play should be done?

MRS. FLANAGAN: I think that is entirely too hypothetical a question, Congressman Dies.

THE CHAIRMAN: Having accepted one principle, the principle that you have the right to exhibit a play championing the public ownership of utilities, how could you draw the line?

MRS. FLANAGAN: Each play draws its own line. Each play makes its own contribution and has its own question.

THE CHAIRMAN: But having established that precedent of public ownership of utilities, how could you stop where plays are presented to your policy board dealing with the ownership of railroads, dealing with the ownership of land and other matters? Would it not be the same principle involved?

MRS. FLANAGAN: I told you over and over again that the basic principle is: Is it a good play?

THE CHAIRMAN: You have established the precedent of exhibiting a play championing the cause of ownership of public utilities. You said that was proper, and you yourself thought you had a right to do that?

MRS. FLANAGAN: I think so.

THE CHAIRMAN: What would keep you or the policy board from continuing that same type of plays so as to cover other ranges of public ownership?

MRS. FLANAGAN: If someone came up with a very good play proving that the private ownership of railroads was the best possible thing, and the play was a good play, we would do it.

THE CHAIRMAN: Then, on the other hand, if the play proved that the public ownership of railroads was a good thing, you would do it too, would you not?

MRS. FLANAGAN: Absolutely. The test is: Is it a good play?—within the general range we have established.

THE CHAIRMAN: And if someone came with a play showing the public ownership of all the property in the United States, and it was a good play, you would also exhibit that, would you not?

MRS. FLANAGAN: Well, that is a very clever move on your part to maneuver me into a certain position.

THE CHAIRMAN: I do not pretend to any cleverness. I would not undertake to match my cleverness with you on this subject, because you are thoroughly acquainted with it.

MRS. FLANAGAN: No, I would not, we would stop with that, because that would be recommending the overthrow of the United States Government, and I do not want that, gentlemen, whatever some of the witnesses may have intimated.

THE CHAIRMAN: In other words, you would favor doing it by degrees, but not all at once, isn't that right?

MRS. FLANAGAN: Well, we probably would not agree—

THE CHAIRMAN: Well, but you have said under oath, of the exhibition of a play championing the ownership of public utilities or railroads, that, if it were an entertaining play, you would show it. You have said that yourself. Now, that is just the degree, is it not?

MRS. FLANAGAN: Well, it is a degree that the Congress of the United States has passed upon, isn't it?

THE CHAIRMAN: Not yet—the question of public ownership of utilities, it has not passed on that.

MRS. FLANAGAN: You did it one time.

THE CHAIRMAN: Not that I know of.

MRS. FLANAGAN: During the war.

THE CHAIRMAN: Oh, well, you are going back now to emergency legislation.

MRS. FLANAGAN: Of course, we have gone back into history and covered so much geographic range that perhaps I—

THE CHAIRMAN: So, as I understand from your testimony, when a play is presented to you championing the public ownership of power, of railroads, if it is a good play, you said you would exhibit it. Now, what I want to ask you is: Would you stop with those two forms of ownership? Or would you go further and exhibit a play that would champion the public ownership of other forms of private property?

MRS. FLANAGAN: I came up here under the distinct understanding that I was to refute testimony given by witnesses before your Committee. You are proposing a long series of hypothetical questions.

THE CHAIRMAN: You say you are here to refute testimony of other witnesses. You can't refute any of the testimony that appeared in this record dealing with Communistic activities on the projects, can you, because you admit you were not there?

MRS. FLANAGAN: I want to take it up charge by charge.

THE CHAIRMAN: I see. But you have already stated that you did not know of any of those Communistic activities, you did not see it.

MRS. FLANAGAN: I say, to my own knowledge, in the offices which I have frequented, it has not been true. I cannot have been in every office all the time.

THE CHAIRMAN: So you yourself are not in a position to deny under oath, to refute, any of the testimony that has appeared in this record dealing with Communistic activities on the projects, are you?

MRS. FLANAGAN: I can submit administrative orders proving that such—

THE CHAIRMAN: That does not prove it did not take place—the fact that you issued administrative orders.

MRS. FLANAGAN: I have many affidavits in this brief personally denying under oath testimony offered by some of your witnesses on this very point, Congressman.

THE CHAIRMAN: I am talking about what you are prepared to say yourself. Are you in a position to deny under oath any of the statements in the record dealing with Communistic activities?

MRS. FLANAGAN: Oh, yes!

THE CHAIRMAN: Give us the ones that you yourself, of your personal knowledge, can refute.

MRS. FLANAGAN: All right, will you turn to volume 1, pages 939–40, Mr. [Wallace] Stark's testimony on Miss [Madelyn] O'Shea. He calls her *Mrs.* O'Shea. I am reading now from the testimony:

> MR. STARK: Mrs. O'Shea at the present time is in charge of the Employment Division of actors on the Federal Theater and also handles the Little Theater groups and the amateur theater projects.
>
> MR. THOMAS: Have you ever had any conversation with Mrs. O'Shea?
>
> MR. STARK: To this extent, that she broke up a group that I had started at one time, because I would not advocate Communistic theories in plays I was putting on with a group that I had organized under the heading of the Little Theater Group.
>
> MR. THOMAS: Will you tell the Committee what Mrs. O'Shea said?
>
> MR. STARK: She said she had no position for me, because I did not carry out the theories of the Project. I suppose she meant the political theories of the Project.

"What were the political theories on the Project?" the Chairman asked.

> MR. STARK: From what I understand—
>
> THE CHAIRMAN: Not from what you understand, but from what you know. What do you know?
>
> MR. STARK: The propaganda plays, the putting on of propaganda plays.

"What kind of propaganda, to do what?" the Chairman asked.

> Mr. Stark: To advocate Communism—social-problem plays of a revolutionary nature.
>
> The Chairman: Did you ever try to put on any other kind?
>
> Mr. Stark: Yes, I did. And I had my scenery slashed, I had my lights cut out on me, and my actors taken out of cast.
>
> Mr. Starnes: Who did that, Mr. Stark?
>
> Mr. Stark: I would like to know. Those things were done to me.
>
> The Chairman: Name some of the plays that she [Miss O'Shea] produced or wrote or had anything to do with.
>
> Mr. Stark: *The Revolt of the Beavers* is one play.
>
> The Chairman: What was Communistic about that play?
>
> Mr. Stark: The story is about two children going up north with the North Wind. They were supposed to get to the North, and they found the beavers working there. There were two groups of beavers, the working beavers, and those who were the bosses. In the story, the beavers were supposed to advocate a revolutionary theory of smuggling, into the places where they worked, guns and arms, to overthrow the bosses and overthrow constituted authority. That play was banned by the New York Police Department after three weeks' production in New York.

That is a completely inaccurate statement. Miss O'Shea had absolutely nothing to do with that.

The Chairman: You are dealing with the production of plays?

Mrs. Flanagan: I am dealing with other allegations made by your witnesses which I can, of my personal knowledge, refute. Mr. [Leo A.] Dawson, in this same connection, goes on:

> Mr. Dawson: There is another thing I want to say, and that is it is common knowledge that Madelyn O'Shea is a cousin of Mrs. Hallie Flanagan. It is commonly known among the people on the Project that Mrs. Flanagan is a cousin of Madelyn O'Shea. Madelyn O'Shea has complete control over the actors and actresses cast in the Project. There is no actor or actress on the Project without her signature.

Congressman Dies, that statement is an absolute falsehood. Madelyn O'Shea is no relation of mine by blood or marriage, nor is there any person employed at any place throughout the United States on the Project that is related to me by blood or marriage.

The Chairman: But I said any statement made by any witness in the record dealing with Communistic activities on the project.

Mrs. Flanagan: Mr. Thomas says, "Do you know whether Miss O'Shea is a member of the Communist Party?

> Mr. Dawson: I do not think anyone knows as to that. There is no criterion—
>
> Mr. Thomas: Do you know whether Miss O'Shea has spent any time recently in Moscow?
>
> Mr. Dawson: I cannot say that; no, sir."

I can only say that Miss O'Shea—I have here her affidavit—has never been in Moscow and is not in any way related to me.

THE CHAIRMAN: Nobody said she was in Moscow there. The witness said he didn't know.

MRS. FLANAGAN: The chief point was to spread the idea that Miss O'Shea, in the occupation of hiring people, was not only a Communist but was a cousin of mine and was put in that position by me. I am stating from my personal knowledge it is not true.

THE CHAIRMAN: Give us any testimony of any witness in this record that Communist activity took place, that pamphlets were distributed, that speeches were made, and that meetings were held on the Project during pay time, give us a single part of that testimony that you yourself can refute under oath.

MRS. FLANAGAN: I cannot refute that under oath, because I have not been present.

THE CHAIRMAN: All right. So it boils down: the things that you can refute deal with whether or not plays were exhibited?

MRS. FLANAGAN: I feel there are certain other charges that I could refute.

* * *

THE CHAIRMAN: All right, give us some more that you yourself can personally refute.

MRS. FLANAGAN: I can refute all charges on three basic points: that the plays we have done were subversive—

THE CHAIRMAN: I agree to that, I am not asking—

MRS. FLANAGAN: —that the people either on my staff or on my policy board are unprincipled, that they are anything except the type of people that they should be.

THE CHAIRMAN: Was a charge made that any of them were unprincipled?

MRS. FLANAGAN: By inference. Throughout the whole record. It is said that the Workers' Alliance is in charge of the Project. That is untrue, and I can refute it.

THE CHAIRMAN: You would not undertake to disprove that six of your supervisors on one project were Communists, would you?

MRS. FLANAGAN: You mean the ones mentioned in the brief?

THE CHAIRMAN: The ones in the testimony.

MRS. FLANAGAN: We have every one of those cases listed here with accompanying affidavits.

THE CHAIRMAN: That they are not Communists?

MRS. FLANAGAN: No. On the charges.

THE CHAIRMAN: Did you ever secure from any of the supervisors affidavits as to whether they were not Communists?

MRS. FLANAGAN: No.

THE CHAIRMAN: So you are not able to produce any evidence on the question as to whether they are not Communists?

MRS. FLANAGAN: No.

THE CHAIRMAN: So that it comes down to this, does it not, that with reference to the plays you can say unequivocally that none of them were Communistic?

MRS. FLANAGAN: Right.

THE CHAIRMAN: But, outside of that, you are not in a position to refute any of the testimony by any of the witnesses?

MRS. FLANAGAN: Oh, yes, I am.

THE CHAIRMAN: Dealing with the Communistic activities charged on the Project?

MRS. FLANAGAN: Yes. For example, I quoted this morning Miss Huffman as saying we could not get any audiences except for Communistic plays.

THE CHAIRMAN: But that is not Communistic activities on the Project.

MRS. FLANAGAN: Let us narrow it down to the solicitation of funds, and the posting of notices on bulletin boards, and so forth.

THE CHAIRMAN: We heard considerable testimony that numerous people working on the Project were Communists. We got that from one or two who are members of the Communist Party themselves. We got it from their own signatures and statements that they were Communists, and received testimony that Communist literature was disseminated through the premises during Project time, that they were printed on the bulletin board until this investigation began and it stopped, that meetings of the Communist units were held on Project time in the premises. I am just citing you some of the highlights.

MRS. FLANAGAN: May I ask is that all in the record which I have studied or are you referring to other records?

THE CHAIRMAN: I do not know what record you have studied, but that is in all of the records.

MRS. FLANAGAN: I think you must be confusing some of our testimony, because I have read it very carefully, and I have not found a single witness brought up before us that said he was a Communist.

THE CHAIRMAN: Before us?

MRS. FLANAGAN: Before you.

THE CHAIRMAN: Well, Mr. [Ralph] DeSola said he was a Communist.

MRS. FLANAGAN: But he is not on the Federal Theater Project.

THE CHAIRMAN: He is on the Writers' Project.

MRS. FLANAGAN: Yes, but not our Project.

THE CHAIRMAN: You do remember the statements with reference to dissemination of Communistic literature on the premises?

MRS. FLANAGAN: I have never seen subversive literature or Communistic literature on the Project bulletin boards, nor have I ever known of Communist meetings being held on Project property. So that what I have to go on is that your principal witnesses alleged that such things took place.

* * *

MR. STARNES: In view of the fact that we have testimony that *Stevedore* has been produced, I think that we should set out in the record here these excerpts.

> (Page 24) LONNIE: God damn dem, anyhow. Whey dey think I am? Do I look like some kind of animal? Do I look like somebody who'd jump over a back fence and rape a woman?
>
> (Page 29) WALCOTT: You're too Goddamn uppity. . . . You black ——— of a ——— you can't talk to me that way.
>
> (Page 42) RAG WILLIAMS: Dat li'l skinny boy! Lawd, he couldn't rape nothing.
>
> JOE CRUMP: Why dey have to go and start dat rape stuff up again?
>
> (Page 43) RAG WILLIAMS: He just a big hunk of horse rump, dat's all.
>
> (Page 53) LONNIE: God damn you, let go.
>
> (Page 60) AL: Well, I'll be God damned if you can use my car to help rape a nigger.
>
> LEM: Christ Almight? Rape nigger.
>
> (Page 61) AL: Well, by God, some nigger raped her.
>
> MARTY: Rape, my eye.
>
> AL: Yeah, rape. You let 'em get away with it, and no white woman will be safe on the streets any more. Christ, if a nigger raped your woman in your back yard how would you feel if we helped him?
>
> (Page 62) LEM: Don't be such a Goddamned fool.
>
> LEM: Aw, for Christ's sake, Al.
>
> AL: Yeah. Like a Goddamned nigger-lover.
>
> (Page 86) AL: Yeah! That "red" bastard! Nigger-lover.
>
> MOB: Let's get that bastard. Nigger-lover! Throw him out of here! Goddamned nigger-lover.
>
> (Page 90) MITCH (*looking her over lecherously*): Um-m, I'll bet you're a hot mamma. Think I'm your size, brown sugar?
>
> BINNIE: No. You couldn't handle me. You ain't man enough.
>
> (Page 122) MITCH: We'll kill every black bastard behind dat woodpile.
>
> (Page 123) BINNIE: That red-headed ——— of a ———, I got him!"

THE CHAIRMAN: What time is it, please?

MR. STARNES: A quarter past one.

THE CHAIRMAN: We will adjourn for one hour.

MRS. FLANAGAN: Just a minute, gentlemen. Do I understand that this concludes my testimony?

THE CHAIRMAN: We will see about it after lunch.

MRS. FLANAGAN: I would like to make a final statement, if I may, Congressman Dies.

THE CHAIRMAN: We will see about it after lunch.

In her book *Arena* Mrs. Flanagan completed the story:

> We never saw about it after lunch. "We don't want you back," [Parnell Thomas] laughed. "You're a tough witness, and we're all worn out."

An Affidavit from Upton Sinclair

Upton Sinclair (1878–1968) was never a witness before the Committee, but he was one of many who felt they had been traduced by it, and he was among a certain number who protested to the Committee itself. He put his name to the following affidavit on December 28, 1938.

It has been widely reported in the press that at least two of the witnesses before the Dies Committee have said that I was a Communist; that I had held positions in the Communist Party, and had taken part in consultations for the determining of Communist policies.

The fact is that I have never been a member of the Communist Party and have never been a Communist. I have never advocated Communism, but on the contrary, in every book, pamphlet, and magazine article in which I have discussed the subject I have explained that I am not a Communist and why. I have been for more than thirty-five years a Socialist, and for the greater part of that time have been a member of the Socialist Party. In 1904, I founded the Intercollegiate Socialist Society, which is now the League for Industrial Democracy; in 1906, I was candidate of the Socialist Party for Congress from New Jersey; in 1917, I resigned from the Socialist Party in a public statement declaring my support of the United States Government in the World War. After the war I rejoined the Socialist Party and ran for Congress in California in 1920; for the United States in 1922; for Governor of California in 1926; and again in 1930. In 1933 I joined the Democratic Party and won its nomination for the governorship of California in 1934. Just recently I joined the National Progressive Party.

For more than thirty-five years past I have used the following definition of Socialism as the doctrine and procedure which I advocate: the social ownership and democratic control of the instruments and means of production. I believe and teach that the change from private competitive or monopoly ownership to public and cooperative ownership can be brought about peaceably and gradually under our present Constitution. I have written many books and pamphlets in the effort to prove this, and I have never, in my writings or in any other way, advocated the bringing about of the change by any other method.

Bolshevism, which is the doctrine now known as Communism, or Leninism, advocates the overthrow of capitalist governments by the workers and the establishment of a dictatorship of the proletariat. This was the method used in Russia, and from the time that it occurred I have defended the right of the Russian workers to settle their own affairs. I opposed the armed intervention of the United States Government to put down the Russian revolution. I have always and everywhere defended the right of the Russians, the Spanish, the Chinese, and all other peoples, to determine their own form of government, without military intervention such as we ourselves took part in against the Russian people. I have denounced the attacks of Germany and Italy upon the people of Spain, and the policy of our government in denying the duly elected people's government of Spain the right to purchase arms for its own defense. But in discussing the domestic affairs of the American people, I have invariably argued that, since they enjoy democratic institutions and have the ability to change their government and their business affairs at any time they please, they should make the necessary changes by democratic and orderly process, and under the Constitution.

In my book, *The Brass Check,* published in 1920, appears a chapter entitled "The Case of Russia." I wrote on page 385: "Let me make clear at the outset my point of view, oft repeated. I am not a Bolshevik, and have never been a Bolshevik." I then went on to define the word Bolshevik and explain my belief in the democratic method of procedure, adding: "I am well aware that this method will be slower, but I believe it will be quicker in the long run, because it will avoid the waste incidental to civil war, and the possibilities of failure and temporary reaction." On page 386 I added: "But such a program, of course, can be effective only in a country where political rights are recognized."

This is a perfectly obvious distinction which any honest person can understand at once. Where people have political rights they should use them to get such economic changes as they need and desire. Where they have no political rights they have to win them, by the same method that our forefathers won them in 1776, and as the British and French and other people won them through a long series of struggles.

In *The Book of Life,* published in 1922, I give a detailed study of all these problems, occupying more than one hundred pages. There is a chapter beginning on page 179, entitled "Confiscation or Compensation," in which I defend the method of compensation of the owners of industry. The following chapter demonstrates the futility of efforts to bring about a proletarian revolution in the United States. The entire work defends the cooperative method and advocates peaceable, orderly, cooperative change.

In the pamphlet, "Letters to Judd," first published in 1925 and reprinted in 1932 and 1933, are several chapters endeavoring to maintain this same thesis. I presented an edition of one hundred thousand copies of this book to the Socialist Party, and it was used in the Presidential campaign of 1932.

The pamphlet, "The Way Out," first published in 1933, presents long arguments to the same effect. Near the end of 1933, I launched the so-called Epic Plan to End Poverty In California. This plan proposed to put the unemployed at productive labor to produce the goods which they themselves were going to consume. In the first pamphlet, "I, Governor of California: And How I Ended Poverty," of which nearly a quarter of a million copies were circulated during the campaign in California, I took the utmost pains to make clear the democratic procedure proposed for this plan. The book was from beginning to end an account of an imaginary democratic procedure by which I, as elected governor of California, would bring about the end of poverty in California by peaceable and orderly methods.

I told what the opposition of the Communists to this plan would be, and the opposition of the Communists to the plan was in actual fact exactly as I had foretold in the pamphlet. The evidence of this is given in detail in the history of the Epic campaign which I published immediately after the campaign, under the title of, "I, Candidate for Governor: And How I Got Licked." The fact that I was called a Communist during the campaign meant nothing except that the opponents of the plan were afraid of its success, and in order to defeat it they told lies about Upton Sinclair and his ideas. They even went so far as to print a fake circular, attributed to the Communists, endorsing our Epic campaign. This trick was first tried during the primary campaign and was fully exposed, but nevertheless the same fraudulent circular was used during the general election campaign.

The Communists fought the Epic campaign as hard as they knew how. They printed circulars denouncing Epic and threw handfuls of these circulars from the balconies at mass meetings where I spoke. The Communist organ of San Francisco referred to the Epic Plan as "one more addled egg from the blue buzzard's nest." They printed cartoons ridiculing me and my idea.

Every Communist in the United States knows that I am not a Communist. So does every reactionary know it. The reactionaries desire to have no economic change in the United States, but to continue the present system of exploiting labor for the benefit of a small class. They find it a cheap and easy method to discredit all advocates of economic reform by calling them Communists. This saves the need of argument and is supposed to keep the people from finding out the truths which scientific Socialism has to offer to the world.

The hired agents of big business who traveled from California, provided with elaborate typewritten copies of fraudulent material to be laid before the Dies Committee, knew that Upton Sinclair is not and never has been a Communist, and does not advocate and never has advocated Communism.

One of these witnesses stated that I had taken part in a conference in Senator Olson's [office] in November 1935, in which plans had been made to advance Communism in California. I have not been in Senator Olson's office since the 1934 election, and in November 1935, I was on an automobile tour with my wife in which we covered some twelve thousand miles and I lectured about the Epic Plan in a score of cities in the Middle West and on the Atlantic Coast from Albany to Boston and on down to Florida. I have a mass of newspaper clippings and other evidence concerning this tour.

1947

The Eislers

The collision of the Committee with the Eisler family—Elfriede Eisler (Ruth Fischer) (1895–1961), Gerhart Eisler (1897–1968), and Hanns Eisler (1898–1962)—is best described by the Chief Investigator himself, Robert E. Stripling, in his book *The Red Plot Against America* (Drexel Hill, Pennsylvania, 1949):

> In October, 1946, Louis Budenz, who had quit Communism the year before and resigned as editor of *The Daily Worker*, said in a broadcast from Detroit that a shadowy figure, unknown even to himself, was the real head of Communism in America.
>
> Within a few days, those two great New York reporters on Communism, Frederick Woltman and Howard Rushmore, had brought out a connection between Budenz's shadowy figure and "Edwards," "Brown," "Berger," and Eisler.

Allegedly, Edwards, Brown, and Berger were not the only names Eisler sometimes used. On a passport application signed by one Samuel Liptzin the photograph was said to show the face of Gerhart Eisler: Stripling reports that he got Eisler's own sister Ruth to testify to this. Gerhart, he says, then made "two frantic attempts" to leave the United States.

> Through our request to the Department of Justice that he be kept under twenty-four-hour surveillance, and the alertness of immigration officers, he was stopped both times. He finally went before us on February 6, 1947. It was a sharp, flinty hearing, and my last remaining doubts that something big had been bagged disappeared when he appeared in the Caucus Room with Carol King as his attorney. Miss King had represented Harry Bridges and Earl Browder.

This "appearance" before HUAC is reported below. A little later, Stripling tells in his book, Eisler was sentenced to jail. "He remains at liberty on bail at this writing, moving about the clandestine domain he did so much to fashion."

In its obituary of March 22, 1968, *The New York Times* told the rest of the story:

> [Eisler] jumped bail of $23,500 by stowing away aboard the Polish liner Batory when she sailed from New York on May 7, 1949. . . . When the Batory arrived in Southampton, he was arrested, but a London court declined to extradite him to the United States and instead allowed him to proceed to East Germany. . . . Mr. Eisler died in the Armenian Soviet Republic after attending to a contract beween the East German and Russian radio networks.

Ruth's testimony against her brother, as printed below, will speak for itself. It led, naturally, to an intensive investigation of her other brother, the composer Hanns, and it was this investigation—not that of Hollywood writers—which led to the investigation of perhaps the greatest artist ever summoned before HUAC: Bertolt Brecht. Investigator Russell's testimony, also printed below, would also suggest that, through Gregory Kheifetz, an official of the Russian consulate in San Francisco, HUAC hoped to open up the Oppenheimer-Chevalier controversy and involve Brecht and Hanns Eisler in it. As for Hanns Eisler's fate after his encounter with the Committee, Stripling continues:

> It was not until late in 1948 that the Department of Justice, acting on evidence the Committee produced long before, issued orders to deport Hanns Eisler and his wife. They were permitted to leave the U.S. voluntarily on the promise that they would never return.

Hanns Eisler was received with open arms by the newly created German Democratic Republic. He composed their national anthem for them and had his songs published in ten large volumes, living out his last years as a highly successful man. Many of his thoughts were tape-recorded by Dr. Hans Bunge and published in a paperback volume, *Fragen Sie Mehr Ueber Brecht* (Munich, 1970).

One year after Oxford University Press published Hanns Eisler's *Composing for the Films* (1947), Harvard University Press published Ruth Fischer's history of Stalinism in Germany, *Stalin and German Communism*. In this book she reprinted an article on Brecht as "minstrel of the GPU" which had earlier appeared in Dwight MacDonald's magazine *Politics* (April 1944). This piece on Brecht would appear to explain the emphasis placed by HUAC on the Brecht-Eisler work, *Die Massnahme* (*The Measures Taken*). Arthur Koestler was to place a similar stress on this work in his autobiography (*The Invisible Writing*, Boston, 1954).

FEBRUARY 6, 1947:

Gerhart Eisler

The Committee met at 10 a.m., the Honorary J. Parnell Thomas (Chairman) presiding. All members present: Karl E. Mundt, South Dakota; John McDowell, Pennsylvania; Richard M. Nixon, California; Richard B. Vail, Illinois; John S. Wood, Georgia; John E. Rankin, Mississippi; J. Hardin Peterson, Florida; Herbert C. Bonner, North Carolina.

Staff members present: Robert E. Stripling, Chief Investigator; Louis J. Russell, Investigator.

MR. STRIPLING: Mr. Gerhart Eisler, take the stand.

MR. EISLER: I am not going to take the stand.

MR. STRIPLING: Do you have counsel with you?

MR. EISLER: Yes.

MR. STRIPLING: I suggest that the witness be permitted counsel.

THE CHAIRMAN: Mr. Eisler, will you raise your right hand?

MR. EISLER: No. Before I take the oath—

MR. STRIPLING: Mr. Chairman—

MR. EISLER: I have the floor now.

MR. STRIPLING: I think, Mr. Chairman, you should make your preliminary remarks at this time, before Mr. Eisler makes any statement.

THE CHAIRMAN: Sit down, Mr. Eisler. Mr. Eisler, you are here before the Committee on Un-American Activities in response to a subpoena served on you January 25, 1947, which summoned you to appear before this Committee this morning. This Committee's authority which is derived from Public Law 601, is authorized to investigate:

> (1) The extent, character, and objects of un-American propaganda activities in the United States;
>
> (2) The diffusion within the United States of subversive and un-American propaganda that is instigated from foreign countries or of a domestic origin and attacks the principle of the form of government as guaranteed by our Constitution; and
>
> (3) All other questions in relation thereto. . . .

The Committee considers the Communist Party of the United States to be a subversive organization, and the testimony or activities of any individual connected with the Communist Party of the United States is considered to be the purview of this Committee's authority. There has been considerable testimony before the Special Committee on Un-American Activities, and this Committee, its successor, which link you with the activities of the

Communist Party. The questions which will be asked you this morning will be aimed at determining the facts, and it is therefore requested that your answers be responsive and direct. It is not the policy of this Committee to permit witnesses to make a statement. After you have completed your testimony, if you desire to make a statement, the Committee will permit you to put it in the record. Now, Mr. Eisler, you will be sworn in. Raise your right hand.

MR. EISLER: No.

THE CHAIRMAN: Mr. Eisler, in the first place, you want to remember that you are a guest of this nation.

MR. EISLER: I am not treated as a guest.

THE CHAIRMAN: This Committee—

MR. EISLER: I am a political prisoner in the United States.

THE CHAIRMAN: Just a minute. Will you please be sworn in?

MR. EISLER: You will not swear me in before you hear a few remarks.

THE CHAIRMAN: No, there will be no remarks.

MR. EISLER: Then there will be no hearing with me.

THE CHAIRMAN: You refuse to be sworn in? Do you refuse to be sworn in, Mr. Eisler?

MR. EISLER: I am ready to answer all questions, to tell my side.

THE CHAIRMAN: You refuse to be sworn in? Do you refuse to be sworn in?

MR. EISLER: I am ready to answer all questions.

THE CHAIRMAN: Mr. Stripling, call the next witness. The Committee will come to order, please. We have strived to put on a witness, Mr. Gerhart Eisler. Mr. Eisler refused to be sworn in.

MR. EISLER: I did not refuse to be sworn.

THE CHAIRMAN: What is the pleasure of the Committee?

MR. STRIPLING: Mr. Chairman, I think that the witness should be silent, or take the stand or be removed from the room, one or the other, until this matter is determined.

MR. MUNDT: Mr. Chairman, suppose you ask him again whether he refuses to be sworn.

MR. RANKIN: Not "sworn in," but to be sworn.

THE CHAIRMAN: Mr. Eisler, do you refuse, again, to be sworn?

MR. EISLER: I have never refused to be sworn in. I came here as a political prisoner. I want to make a few remarks, only three minutes, before I be sworn in, and answer your questions, and make my statement. It is three minutes.

THE CHAIRMAN: I said that I would permit you to make your statement when the Committee was through asking questions. After the Committee is through asking questions, and your remarks are pertinent to the investigation, why, it will be agreeable to the Committee. But first you have to be sworn.

MR. EISLER: That is where you are mistaken. I have to do nothing. A political prisoner has to do nothing.

THE CHAIRMAN: Then you refuse to be sworn?

MR. EISLER: I do not refuse to be sworn. I want only three minutes. Three minutes to make a statement.

THE CHAIRMAN: We will give you those three minutes when you are sworn.

MR. EISLER: I want to speak before I am sworn.

MR. MUNDT: Mr. Chairman, I make the motion that the witness be cited for contempt.

MR. RANKIN: I second the motion.

THE CHAIRMAN: Any discussion? All in favor signify by saying, "Aye." Motion carried. The witness will be cited for contempt.

MR. STRIPLING: Mr. Chairman, before the witness leaves I would like to know in whose custody he leaves.

THE CHAIRMAN: Who brought the witness?

MR. STRIPLING: These gentlemen. Will you give your name?

MR. GRENNMAN: Steve Grennman.

MR. STRIPLING: And what is your position?

MR. GRENNMAN: Security Officer, Department of Justice, Immigration and Naturalization Service.

MR. STRIPLING: And your name?

MR. BROSMAN: R. J. Brosman.

MR. STRIPLING: Your position?

MR. BROSMAN: Security Officer, Department of Justice, Immigration and Naturalization Service.

MR. STRIPLING: Did you bring Gerhart Eisler to the Committee?

MR. GRENNMAN: Yes.

MR. STRIPLING: Is he now in your custody?

MR. GRENNMAN: Yes, sir.

MR. STRIPLING: Can you tell the Committee where he will be taken?

MR. GRENNMAN: To the county jail in Washington.

MR. STRIPLING: Do you know where he will go from the county jail?

MR. GRENNMAN: Back to Ellis Island, I believe.

FEBRUARY 6, 1947:

Ruth Fischer

MR. STRIPLING: The next witness will be Ruth Fischer.

MR. RANKIN: At this point I want to acknowledge the presence of the distinguished gentleman from Alabama, Mr. Starnes, who was one of the members of the Dies Committee on Un-American Activities, and who rendered valuable assistance to that committee.

THE CHAIRMAN: Mr. Starnes is always welcome.

MR. STARNES: Thank you very much.

MR. STRIPLING: Miss Fischer, you are appearing before the Committee in response to subpoena served on you Monday, February 3: is that correct?

MISS FISCHER: Yes.

MR. STRIPLING: Miss Fischer, I understand you are known as Ruth Fischer?

MISS FISCHER: Yes.

MR. STRIPLING: However, for the record, will you please state and spell your full name?

MISS FISCHER: My name is Elfriede Eisler. Fischer is my mother's name, which I use for writing.

MR. STRIPLING: When and in what country were you born?

MISS FISCHER: I was born in Leipzig, Germany, 1895.

MR. STRIPLING: Will you state the name of your father and mother?

MISS FISCHER: My father's name was Rudolph Eisler. My mother's name was Marie Edith Fischer.

MR. STRIPLING: Will you also state the names of your relatives presently living in the United States?

MISS FISCHER: My relatives in the United States are Gerhart Eisler, my second brother, and Hanns Eisler, my youngest brother, and an old uncle, Ernand Eisler and his wife.

MR. STRIPLING: You are the sister of Gerhart Eisler, is that right?

MISS FISCHER: Yes.

MR. STRIPLING: At this point, Mr. Chairman, I want to introduce into the record the sworn statement of Mr. Eisler before a Board of Special Inquiry, held at Ellis Island, New York, June 14, 1941. As Mr. J. Edgar Hoover pointed out, Mr. Eisler has consistently made false statements under oath to authorities in the United States, both in his applications to the State Department and also in this sworn testimony when he entered this country. He was asked these questions:

> Who is your nearest relative in the U.S.?
> I have a brother Hanns Eisler, 122 Waverly Place, New York City.
> How long has your brother resided in the U.S.?
> Either end of 1937 or the beginning of 1938.
> Have you other relatives besides this brother?
> No.

Now, you are a full sister of Gerhart Eisler?

MISS FISCHER: Yes.

MR. STRIPLING: You were residing in the United States at that time?

MISS FISCHER: Yes. I had just arrived.

MR. STRIPLING: Miss Fischer, will you state whether or not you have been a member of the Communist Party of Germany?

MISS FISCHER: I was a member of the Communist Party of Germany until 1926.

MR. STRIPLING: Did you hold any position in the Communist Party of Germany?

MISS FISCHER: For a time I was in charge of the Berlin organization; for another time I was in charge of the Politburo; and I was also a member of the Presidium in Moscow.

MR. STRIPLING: During the course of your association with the German Communists you, of course, became familiar with the activities of your brother?

MISS FISCHER: I was in the beginning responsible for the activities of Gerhart Eisler because he entered the Party at the same time I did. He lived in Vienna until 1920.

THE CHAIRMAN: We are having a hard time hearing.

MISS FISCHER: And he followed me to Berlin. My father lived in Vienna. We are all of Austrian origin. We were born in Leipzig, but my father was an Austrian citizen. I went to Berlin in September 1919, and my brother Gerhart followed me in 1920. He entered the Austrian Communist Party after his return from the front in November 1918.

MR. STRIPLING: I would like for you to give the Committee the association between you and your brother as to Communist activities.

MISS FISCHER: I was a charter member of the Austrian Communist Party, and when my brother returned from the war—we were both very young—he joined the organization at my request and at my initiative. In Berlin, where I was very active in the Communist organization, Gerhart became immediately an organizer and propagandizer in the German Communist Party. At that time, our relationship was friendly, not only from the point of view of family relations—we are very close in age and have grown up together—but we were also of the same political ideas. This personal and political friendship lasted until 1923, when we had a very deep conflict about the policy of the German Communist Party, the year of the occupation of the Ruhr region by the French Army. From that moment, our political relationships were broken, and I was expelled from the German Communist Party in 1926 because of my opposition to Stalin and to the Comintern and to the Politburo. My relationship with Gerhart became more and more hostile to the point where I am forced to testify against him today because I regard him as a most dangerous terrorist, both to the people of America and to the people of Germany, where he wants to go and whom he pretends to love so much. On this particular question, may I read this statement as to why, I, a sister by blood, and having been very near to my brother in our childhood, why I am forced to testify before a House

Committee of the United States against my own brother, if I may read a few lines here, Mr. Chairman—

THE CHAIRMAN: That is all right.

MISS FISCHER: Yes.* I consider Eisler the perfect terrorist type, most dangerous for the people of both America and Germany. The fact that this man is my brother has only given me a deeper insight in the technique of Stalin's NKVD and the terror system it imposes on the peoples of Europe. In a totalitarian party, all human relations are deteriorated; a man who serves Stalin is conditioned to hand over to the GPU his child, his sister, his closest friend. Since I learned that Eisler was in this country I have been exposing him. He has used the sympathy of the American people for the suffering and tortured victims of Nazism to mask his dirty work. I consider him particularly dangerous for the German workers, whom he now pretends to love so much. For years he relentlessly demanded the purge of the German people—that is, decided the slaughter and enslavement of millions on the arbitrary decision of the GPU. In the inner circles of the Comintern, it is well known that Eisler denounced to the GPU many [anti-?] Nazi refugees living in Moscow. He is particularly responsible for the death of the German Communist Hugo Eberlein, the leader of Eisler's own caucuses, and of Nikolai Bukharin, the great Russian theorist, his one-time friend and protector. Eisler's presence in Germany will help to build up another Nazi system which will differ from the old one only by the fact that the Fuehrer's name will be Stalin.

MR. STRIPLING: Mr. Chairman, one of the main reasons of the hearing is to show that Mr. Eisler has been active in the United States prior to June 13, 1941. Last year the Committee heard Mr. Louis F. Budenz, former managing editor of the *Daily Worker*. Mr. Budenz is here today and will testify this afternoon. He testified at that time that Gerhart Eisler, under the name of Hans Berger, and under the alias of Edwards, had directed Communist Party activities in the United States. We are, therefore, interested in placing Mr. Eisler in the United States.

THE CHAIRMAN: Prior to that date?

MR. STRIPLING: Yes, sir, prior to 1941, which he admits. Will you state for the record in what European countries you have seen your brother Gerhart other than Germany since the year 1929?

MISS FISCHER: I saw him in June 1933, in a French apartment, 4 Place de Vaugirard, Paris, where I met him in the house of my younger brother, Hanns Eisler.

MR. STRIPLING: Did he state to you at that time where he had been or where he was going?

MISS FISCHER: I had been estranged from Gerhart for years and I hadn't seen him since 1928, when he was summoned to Moscow, and where he entered the services of the Comintern. I was a refugee from Berlin, just

* Perhaps the whole of this speech was read, but the record does not show it. —E.B.

arrived in Paris, and meeting there my youngest brother, Hanns Eisler, renewing relationships after the shock of Hitler's victory. When I came home one evening, as a surprise, Gerhart was there, just arrived from Moscow, and wished to speak to me, something we hadn't done for at least six or seven years. He was on his first trip to the United States, directly dispatched from Moscow to take over Communist affairs in this country.

MR. STRIPLING: Pardon me. Could you give the Committee exactly what he said, to the best of your recollection?

MISS FISCHER: He said: "I am going for the Comintern to the United States, and I will change the policy of the Communist Party there completely and entirely."

MR. STRIPLING: How long did he remain in Paris?

MISS FISCHER: He remained in Paris one or two weeks. I cannot remember that precisely, but I was together with him not just once but at least eight or ten times during a week, during which time we tried to make up and couldn't do it because our opinions concerning Russia were too different.

MR. STRIPLING: Mr. Chairman, I would like to refer again to this passport application which was executed August 30, 1934, and which passport was issued in the name of Samuel Liptzin. In other words, this was one year later than Miss Fischer saw her brother. Miss Fischer, I show you the picture which is appended to this passport, with the seal of the Department of State, and ask you if you can identify the individual.

MISS FISCHER: That is unmistakably Gerhart Eisler.

MR. STRIPLING: Mr. Chairman, there is also the record subpoenaed from the files of World Tourists, Inc., in connection with this passport and passage. I ask you, Miss Fischer, if you can identify that picture?

MISS FISCHER: That is also Gerhart Eisler.

MR. STRIPLING: Also the records subpoenaed dealing with the passport and passage of April 22, 1936. I ask you if you can identify that picture?

MISS FISCHER: That is also Gerhart Eisler, but of a different year.

MR. STRIPLING: In other words, does he appear to be older to you there?

MISS FISCHER: Yes.

MR. STRIPLING: Now, you state that you saw Gerhart—by the way, what name was your brother known by in the Party?

MISS FISCHER: In the Party by his first name, Gerhart. He never used the name Eisler.

MR. STRIPLING: I should like to point out that is the name Mr. [William O'Dell] Nowell has testified Mr. Eisler was known by in Moscow, Mr. Chairman. You are certain that he was known as Gerhart throughout his Communist activities?

MISS FISCHER: He used other names, many other names, but I didn't follow these names because my informants in the Comintern circles always spoke about Gerhart.

MR. STRIPLING: Was Gerhart ever given a reprimand by Stalin?

MISS FISCHER: Gerhart pretends to be a German anti-Nazi refugee. I want to underscore that he has not lived in Germany since 1929. He had neither residence nor a family there. He married his wife in Vienna and took her to Moscow, where his only child was born in 1931. He was not permitted to return to Germany on political missions because he was under the surveillance of the GPU and of the Communist Party for a certain period because I conspired against Stalin in 1928. He has not touched German soil since 1929. He may have done that in transit, with a false passport, and just for the purpose of going through from Moscow to another mission. He has not lost one single book, manuscript, or any other belonging by the victory of the Nazis. He was never imprisoned one day in Germany for anti-Nazi activities, and he has not taken part against the Nazis since 1928, because he entered at that time the services of the Comintern apparatus, which he has not left until now.

MR. STRIPLING: Mr. Chairman, in connection with Mr. Eisler's marital status, I should like to put in the record at this point a document which is in the Government's file in which it is stated:

> Mrs. Ella Eisler, née Tune. Born November 15, 1908, at Vienna, Austria, called at the legation and reported that she had read article and said that Eisler is her husband and was born February 20, 1897, at Leipzig, Germany, that she married him on July 22, 1931, at Vienna; article stated that he is now in the United States with his wife who accompanied him to the United States from France in 1941, but Mrs. Ella Eisler states that she is not divorced from her husband, and that the woman he brought with him and with whom he is now living in the United States is not his legal wife. Mrs. Ella Eisler stated she last saw her husband in July 1936, at Prague, Czechoslovakia, when he left for Paris, France, and she departed for Moscow, where they were to meet and settle down. However, Eisler, she states, failed to come to Moscow, and in May 1938 she left Moscow for Stockholm, Sweden, with her daughter, Anna Eisler, born November 2, 1931, at Moscow, with intention of joining her husband in France. Since they could obtain no visa permitting them to enter France, Mrs. Ella Eisler and her daughter remained in Stockholm. Mrs. Ella Eisler states that she has endeavored to locate her husband through his brother, Hanns Eisler, Hollywood cinema composer, but he failed to reply to her letters.

Miss Fischer, could you give us information concerning Mr. Eisler's first marriage?

MISS FISCHER: He was first married to the sister of his second wife.

MR. STRIPLING: Who was the second wife?

MISS FISCHER: The second wife was Mrs. Ella Eisler.

MR. STRIPLING: He was first married to her sister?

MISS FISCHER: Yes.

MR. STRIPLING: Could you give us any dates?

MISS FISCHER: No, because, he married in Vienna and I was in Berlin. I have never seen or met the third Mrs. Eisler.

MR. STRIPLING: In that connection, Mr. Chairman, when Mr. Eisler entered this country he was accompanied by a woman by the name of Brunhilda Rothstein.*

THE CHAIRMAN: When was that date?

MR. STRIPLING: That was June 13, 1941—June 14, 1941. Under oath he was asked by the immigration authorities: "Have you ever been married at any time?" Answer: "No." Miss Fischer, will you state to the Committee the second time that you saw your brother?

MISS FISCHER: I saw him in 1936, by coincidence, in a small Parisian restaurant. We didn't speak to each other any longer, and he was more frightened to see me than I was disgusted to see him.

MR. STRIPLING: Would you care to go into the circumstances of that?

MISS FISCHER: In 1936 the first "show" trial in Moscow took place against the former chairman of the Comintern and others who were accused of conspiracy against Stalin and to have plotted to assassinate him. In this trial my name was mentioned by a defendant, that I had sent him to Moscow with the task of assassinating Mr. Stalin and several other dignitaries of the Politburo. The fact was well known to the Comintern circles, and Vishinsky, who was prosecutor, had several times asked Dr. Lurge [Moissei I. Lurye], who was executed with fifteen other defendants, about my initiative in this conspiracy against Stalin. Gerhart was trembling. He said he would be drawn in. He knew as well as everybody in the Comintern that I had not sent Dr. Lurge to Moscow and that the whole thing was a frame. But he wasn't sure that Vishinsky might not ask hadn't Gerhart conspired with Ruth Fischer in the assassination of Stalin. Therefore, he was under surveillance by his own comrades. He felt it could be used as evidence by Vishinsky that we had met in this Parisian restaurant to conspire.

MR. STRIPLING: Miss Fischer, can you give the circumstances of the meeting? Do you want to mention your son?

MISS FISCHER: My son, who studied in Cambridge, England, was coming to see me for the holidays. He has the same name as Gerhart. He was called after his uncle. He knew him very well. He was not informed about the turn of events in our family circle and in our political life. He was young and I didn't want to trouble his peace of mind. So when I was sitting with him at the window of the restaurant, and Gerhart came in, the boy said, "There is Uncle Gerhart." But Gerhart went on through, with his Bolshevik-trained eyes; he didn't see either his nephew or me; and I said to my son, "Please sit down, you don't understand. Don't approach your uncle."

MR. STRIPLING: Now, in that connection, Mr. Chairman, I should like

* Later, as Hilde Eisler, a prominent magazine editor in East Germany. Eisler's first wife, Hede Massing, had an important part in the Hiss case. —E.B.

to point out that the records here show that Mr. Eisler traveled under the name of Samuel Liptzin again a second time, at which time he sailed on the *Île de France,* and it was the same time that Miss Fischer saw him in Paris.

* * *

MR. CHAIRMAN: Mr. Russell has certain questions that he would like to ask the witness.

MR. RUSSELL: Miss Fischer, this morning you testified that the last time you saw your brother—that is, prior to the time you saw him in the United States—was during the year 1936 in Paris, France.

MISS FISCHER: Yes.

MR. RUSSELL: When did you next learn the whereabouts of your brother and what country was he in?

MISS FISCHER: I heard constantly about Gerhart Eisler when in Paris, about his activities in the United States, because his mission to the United States was regarded in the Comintern circles in Europe as a promotion for services of a special character. Eisler had been in disgrace during 1928, 1929, and 1930, and everybody of the Communist Party in Berlin expected his expulsion from the Communist Party of Germany, because of his rebellion against Stalin at that time. Then he was sent to a mission into China, with the GPU delegation, to purge rebellious Chinese Communists. At that time Eisler's mission was not a very high one, in China; he was one of a group of men sent there to carry out orders. In these Chinese purges he behaved so cruelly and carried out the orders so well that the report about him in Berlin said that he was really the hangman of the rebellious Chinese Communists, who were sentenced by the decisions of Moscow. After the Chinese trip he came back in 1930 or 1931 to Moscow, where he then married his wife,* and where his daughter was born, and where he remained until 1933. In 1933, when I met him in Paris, on his first mission to the United States, he was in the best of spirits, because his second Comintern assignment was a much higher one than his previous assignment to China, and he regarded it as a complete rearrangement of his relationship with the Politburo. In the Russian Communist organization there is a fight for survival, and only the fittest survive, and the fittest have always complete obedience and carry out every order of whatever character. So in Paris I heard constantly that Gerhart was carrying out his mission to the United States to the full satisfaction of his boss in Moscow, and said that he was just doing fine, and that the American Communist Party, which had attacked the late President Franklin Roosevelt as a Fascist, had changed its line, and had accepted a reasonable line of popular front, of a united front, with all the elements who wanted to fight together with the Communists and Russia.

*** Contradicts statement just read by Stripling. —E.B.**

***

MR. RUSSELL: Miss Fischer, when did you first learn that your brother was actually in the United States?

MISS FISCHER: I heard about it the first time in 1942, when I was a year in this country, but I didn't believe it. I thought it was a false rumor and said he must be in Mexico, because I had learned that he had been in Ellis Island in June 1941, and I was sure that the authorities here must have a complete file about him, and that it was impossible that he could go around freely and take up his old activities. I didn't believe it until 1943, when the evidence that he was really here—and didn't write his articles, by Hans Berger, and send them air mail from Mexico—the evidence was too overwhelming. I had to realize that he was in this country. Then a few months later, when I published material on contemporary Communism, in January 1944, I exposed him as head of the Comintern activities in this country; or, to put it better, as the head of a network of agents of the secret Russian state police.

MR. RUSSELL: Do you still have those writings in your possession?

MISS FISCHER: Yes.

MR. RUSSELL: Will you send them to the Committee or possibly produce them the next time you are subpoenaed?

MISS FISCHER: Yes.

MR. RUSSELL: In other words, we want to bring out that you made public the activities of your brother prior to the time there was any publicity in the newspapers concerning his actual connections in the United States, which first came to the attention of the press in 1946.

THE CHAIRMAN: Miss Fischer, why do you say that Gerhart Eisler was head of the Russian secret police in the United States?

MISS FISCHER: I don't say he was head of the secret police, because there are various ranges of activities, and I am sure that the Russian secret police has other agents than Mr. Eisler, but I regard all those who work for the Moscow headquarters, under whatever names they are working, as branches of said Russian secret state police. The Comintern is nothing else but a branch, a division, of the Russian secret state police, with international branches in all the countries. So whoever poses as a representative of the Communist Party in other countries, is, for me, nothing else than an agent of the Russian state police, a GPU agent, identical with a Gestapo agent at the time when the Nazis were in power.

THE CHAIRMAN: You would say that every American Communist was, in effect, a member of the Russian secret police?

MISS FISCHER: I wouldn't say that, Mr. Chairman, because I am sure that the American Communist Party is divided into various groups. Only those really considered as reliable—

THE CHAIRMAN: As what?

MISS FISCHER: —as reliable and tested for the secret police are taken in. There are many others who are regarded as innocent and incapable of doing this type of work and have to carry other kinds of missions—propaganda, trade-union work, or all kinds of organization work, and who are not informed about the activities of the secret branches, and are kept completely in the dark.

MR. STRIPLING: In that connection, Mr. Chairman, I would like to introduce at this time certain questions and answers from the sworn statements of Mr. Eisler. Mr. Eisler, as I have previously stated, came here June 13, 1941. He is still here. In other words, the United States has been a haven for him during the entire period of the war. Now, I have yet to find any statement which Mr. Eisler has made under oath to this Government which was correct. For example, when he was sworn before the Special Board of Inquiry at Ellis Island in New York Harbor on June 14, 1941, he was asked this question: "Are you now or have you ever been a member of any Communist organization?" The answer was: "No." The next question: "Were you ever sympathetic to the Communist cause?" The answer was: "No." Then, again, on January 6, 1942, his application to depart, which was a sworn statement, Question No. 23: "State the names of all organizations, groups, societies, clubs, or associations of which you are or have been a member, or with which you are or have been affiliated." And his answer was: "None." A good example of Mr. Eisler's veracity.

MR. RUSSELL: Miss Fischer, on September 5, 1945, Gerhart Eisler applied to the Secretary of State of the United States for permission to leave the United States. At that time he requested permission to proceed directly to Berlin, Germany. In August 1946 he filed another application with the Secretary of State requesting permission to return to Europe by way of Soviet Russia. In your opinion, what was the reason for his change in plans?

MISS FISCHER: He could have left the country immediately after Hitler's defeat. He could have gone to Russia much earlier and fought with the others in the Battle of Stalingrad, which is so much propagandized in the Communist press. In fact, his comrades in the German Communist Party had all missions to carry out at the Russian front and had to go with the Red Army for various propaganda affairs among the Nazi soldiers, and it was always absolutely clear that he had a special arrangement in this country, that he didn't go back to Russia to fight with the Red armies against the Nazis, and stayed here. When he first tried to go to Berlin it was considerably after the time when he could proceed to Germany. Then he must have had an order to stay here from his boss, and to carry out further work in other parts of the United States. When a year passed, and it was obvious he wouldn't get a permit to go to Germany, he must have got an order to try to get a visa to Russia, because his superiors may have thought that the State Department would not refuse a visa to Russia, in order not to hurt the feelings of an allied power.

MR. RUSSELL: The Committee has been told that all Communist Party members, or former Communist Party members, who desire to return to the Soviet zone in Germany must return by way of Vladivostok, Russia. Do you know whether or not that is true?

MISS FISCHER: That depends on where they are. I know that many Communists in Stockholm have returned from Stockholm to Berlin, and I don't know exactly at what Russian port or town they have been questioned. But every Communist who has been outside Russia cannot return to Germany before having a hearing before the GPU branch with which he is connected. He must give first a full report about his activities in the other countries and must be cleared of all charges that he hasn't performed his duties according to orders. I can give you a very striking example. Deputy Poulnerker [Paul Merker], who was with me in the Reichstag during 1924–28, was in Mexico City during 1941–45, and was the head of a substantial group of German Communists, about eight important Party members who lived during the war in Mexico City, and who, of course, checked with Eisler-Berger in New York City, as many other Communist groups in Latin America and also in Canada. Mercher [Merker], today in Berlin, he took over the job which was done by Albrecht [Walter Ulbricht], who was with the Army from Moscow. He had to proceed with the Russian boat from Mexico to Vladivostok and was delayed in Moscow for several months, so that many of his friends were asking if he had not fallen under the purge, because he was sometimes not in complete agreement with Mr. Eisler-Berger here, who asked relentlessly for the slaughtering of all Germans, but Mercher [Merker] has arrived, after some months' delay, during which he was undoubtedly questioned and scrutinized by the GPU headquarters before he got permission to go to Berlin. If Gerhart Eisler would have gone on a Russian boat, a much more strict investigation than the American investigation would have met him there. He would have had to give a full report about his activities in this country.

MR. RUSSELL: Do you know of any other countries besides China and the United States in which your brother has acted as an agent of the Communist International?

MISS FISCHER: I don't know where he had an official mission. I know for certain China, the United States, but he had missions in Spain, in France, in Czechoslovakia, and in Austria.

MR. MUNDT: Miss Fischer, what year did you leave the Communist Party, or are you still a member of the Party?

MISS FISCHER: I left the Communist Party in 1926.

MR. MUNDT: What was the reason for your break with the Party?

MISS FISCHER: The reason for my break with the Party was that Stalin was transforming the Comintern into a branch of the secret Russian police.

MR. MUNDT: The *New York Times,* about ten years ago, said editorially that the Communist Party is not a political party but a conspiracy which uses the defenses of the democracy to destroy the functioning of the democracy when it can, and resorts to bullets when ballots won't do the job. From your experience in Communist Party matters and as an observer, do you think that is a correct definition of Communism as it is practiced today?

MISS FISCHER: I think it is a more or less adequate description, but it is, even in this strong form, simplification. I don't want to go into too long an exposé about this, but the kernel of the question is that all the branches, tied to Moscow, have only one aim: to carry out the policy in accordance with orders of the Russian state. The Russian state may wish, in certain cases of policy, a softening down of Communist activity, and in other stages it may wish a speeding up of Communist activity. That makes the thing rather complicated for the outsider to see, but there is only one yardstick: namely, how to proceed in the interest of the Russian state, and all Communist organizations are completely under the control of the Communist state. So if the Politburo wants no disturbance in one country, for one reason or another, for a time, the activities are slowed down or stopped, and then taken up again later, but the entire organization is a conspiratory organization, as it is an organization connected with the secret-police system, which has the very definite orders.

MR. MUNDT: Mr. Stripling read from the application for exit permit that your brother filed that he had spent two years in a Nazi concentration camp. Do you know whether that is a fact or a falsehood?

MISS FISCHER: He was not in a Nazi concentration camp, but he was in a camp in France where all natives of Germany were put at the time of the Vichy government.

MR. MUNDT: In other words, he was put in prison by the French government on the suspicion that he might have been a Nazi rather than the fact that he was an anti-Fascist?

MISS FISCHER: He was put in the camp as a suspicious character of German origin.

MR. MUNDT: Not because of anti-Fascist activities?

MISS FISCHER: No. Because of his Communist activities in France, and I am sure that the French police knew exactly that he was a Comintern representative of high standing and wanted to put him out of circulation.

MR. MUNDT: They were afraid that he might be aiding in the aggressive campaign of the Germans at that time?

MISS FISCHER: Exactly.

MR. BONNER: How have you been able to keep up with all of these activities if your membership in the Communist Party stopped in 1926?

MISS FISCHER: I have continued to study Communist affairs and I have written a lot about it, and I have personal connections with friends and have been able to follow the thing from the inside much better than someone with no personal experience.

MR. BONNER: In what year did you come to the States?

MISS FISCHER: In 1941.

MR. BONNER: For what purpose did you come?

MISS FISCHER: I came here to live.

MR. BONNER: Where did you come from, exactly?

MISS FISCHER: From France, via Lisbon.

MR. BONNER: You came as a French citizen or German citizen?

MISS FISCHER: I came as a French citizen.

MR. BONNER: What has been your occupation?

MISS FISCHER: I was a social worker and writer.

MR. BONNER: Who employed you?

MISS FISCHER: A Parisian municipality.

MR. BONNER: I mean since you have been in the United States?

MISS FISCHER: Here in the United States I do only writing.

MR. BONNER: Who do you write for?

MISS FISCHER: I write for the Harvard University Press. I have another contact. I give out a newsletter.

MR. MUNDT: Do you have an article in the *Reader's Digest*?

MISS FISCHER: No, in the *American Mercury*.

MR. MUNDT: It was reprinted in the *Reader's Digest*.

MISS FISCHER: Yes.

THE CHAIRMAN: Mr. Nixon?

MR. NIXON: Have you applied for citizenship?

MISS FISCHER: Yes.

MR. NIXON: You have indicated, Miss Fischer, that you had a break with the Communist Party and with your brother in 1926, and from your testimony you seem to indicate that the reason for the break was that you did not like the methods which they use to accomplish their ends. Do I gather that you may still have some sympathy with the Marxist philosophy and the ends which Communism attempts to achieve but do not agree with the methods which Stalin and his group are using to achieve those ends?

MISS FISCHER: At this moment what we have to face is an empire of Stalin going into many countries. We have to fight his terrorist methods, and do everything in our power to hinder that movement.

MR. NIXON: Well, you have inferred that your brother was a terrorist, and you also gave inference that your brother may have been responsible for the death of some people who were on the other side. Do you have any specific information on that, or do you say that from hearsay, or what is your reason for saying that your brother is a terrorist and has been guilty of what might be considered the destruction of people who disagreed with him politically?

MR. MCDOWELL: Murdered.

MISS FISCHER: Well, I want to go back to this first promotion he got in his involvement in the Chinese Communist affairs. Until this time he was an ordinary Communist in the sense that he carried out political tasks and that he fought, in his way, for what he thought was the best policy in Germany. Then he was taken in the apparatus in Moscow in 1929. He was trained in the carrying out of terrorist orders. He became another man. He was transformed. He was conditioned by his participation in GPU activities in China. When he came from China he was another type of man from the man sent from Moscow in 1929. The second point I would like to make—why I am convinced that he is a terrorist—is his behavior. It is not a well-known fact, but a fact that will come out rather soon, that many anti-Nazi refugees have been killed in Moscow during the middle thirties in connection with the purge carried out against those groups in Russia who resisted the terrorist dictatorship of the Communist Party. One group after the other became involved in the purge, and hundreds of outstanding Russians have been killed, and thousands, tens of thousands, have been sent into labor camps, many into Siberia. Among these Russians who were executed was one special friend and protector of Gerhart Eisler, namely the great Russian terrorist and economist, Nikolai Bukharin. He had protected Eisler in the 1929 affair against his expulsion from the Party. It is my opinion that it was mainly due to Bukharin that Eisler got his grace from Stalin in 1929. In the same period, a German Communist of old reputation, Hugo Eberlein, had been together with Eisler in caucuses in this intrigue he made in 1928 in Berlin. Hugo Eberlein was called to Moscow and was killed. He was not killed after a public hearing, but after a secret hearing, where the evidence was gathered by the GPU. Eisler went in 1937 to Moscow, and he gave evidence against most of his friends—Eberlein and Bukharin. Not he alone; many others were taken there for the same purpose. And Bukharin was sentenced to death in 1938 and executed. But I regard Eisler as responsible not only for the death of these two outstanding men but for many unknown little people who have been caught in the purge. And I have got material that I am publishing that women from Germany, Communist women, were taken from a labor camp in Russia and transferred, in 1940, under the pact with Hitler, to the Gestapo, in the prison at Lublin, and were given over and have been for five years in the famous camp of Ravensbruck, which was a women's hell, and which is now under investigation and indictment in Germany. The GPU transferred these girls directly into the hands of the Gestapo. In all these terrorist activities Eisler had a leading hand.

THE CHAIRMAN: I want to say to the Committee that we will have to cut this short because there is an important vote in the House.

MR. MUNDT: In further substantiation of the terrorist activities of this man Eisler, it might be interesting to quote from Hans Berger in the *Daily Worker* for March 8, 1945, in an attack on Dr. [George] Shuster. He says this:

> I put it this way: If a German Nazi parades as a Communist, he should be unmasked and hanged. But when reactionaries of all kinds parade as Catho-

> lics to save their skins and propose to save "Catholic Germany" against Bolshevism, they should be unmasked and hanged, too. Sauce for the goose and the gander. And all of this is directly connected with Dr. George Shuster, a well-known Catholic, who also comes forward with the same ideas.

He would like to hang Dr. Shuster, if he could.

MR. VAIL: You mentioned you had another brother. Is he in this country?

MISS FISCHER: Yes.

MR. VAIL: In France the two brothers made contact, when you met Gerhart for the first time. Have they maintained contact in this country?

MISS FISCHER: Yes.

MR. VAIL: Where does your brother now reside, this other brother?

MISS FISCHER: My brother is in Hollywood.

MR. VAIL: Are your relations with that brother pleasant?

MISS FISCHER: As hostile as with Gerhart, for the last five years, because he is in contact with Gerhart I have broken off my contact with him.

MR. VAIL: You have broken off relationship for the same reason that it was broken off with Gerhart?

MISS FISCHER: Yes.

MR. MUNDT: Is your brother in Hollywood a Communist?

MISS FISCHER: He is a composer of films and he is a Communist in a philosophical sense.

MR. MCDOWELL: Did you say films?

MISS FISCHER: He composes music for films. He makes music, accompanying music for films.

MR. NIXON: You said he was close to Gerhart Eisler.

MISS FISCHER: Yes, he was close to Gerhart.

MR. BONNER: From your knowledge of all these activities you have spoken of, approximately how many Communist workers, directed from the International in Moscow, would you think there are in this country?

MISS FISCHER: Several thousand.

SEPTEMBER 24, 1947:

Hanns Eisler

The Committee met at 10:30 a.m., the Honorary J. Parnell Thomas (Chairman) presiding.

THE CHAIRMAN: The Committee will come to order. Will the record show that a Subcommittee is sitting, consisting of Mr. McDowell, Mr. Wood, Mr. Rankin, and Mr. Thomas. Staff members present are Mr. Robert E. Stripling, Chief Investigator, and Mr. Louis J. Russell and Mr. Donald T. Appell, Investigators.

MR. EISLER: I wish to repeat the requests made by my counsel yesterday. First, I ask that my hearing be adjourned until the same date as the hearing of the other witnesses of the motion-picture industry. The Committee has stated that it would adjourn the hearings for the industry because it was necessary to have a full Committee. There is no reason to separate me from the rest of the industry. I should be given the same treatment and privileges which you will give to other witnesses you call from Hollywood. Second, I request the right for my counsel to cross-examine any witnesses who may testify about me. For a long time now this Committee has smeared me and done everything possible to prevent me from earning a living. I think I am now entitled to the elementary protection of the cross-examination of witnesses. Should the Committee deny me this basic privilege I request permission to submit questions to the Chairman to put to the witnesses. This privilege was recently granted to Mr. Howard Hughes, and the late Mr. Wendell Willkie propounded questions to the Chairman of this Committee for interrogation of witnesses.

MR. STRIPLING: Mr. Chairman, on the first point which Mr. Eisler raises, I submit that this hearing is on an entirely different subject matter than the Hollywood hearing. This hearing has to do entirely with the activity of Mr. Eisler. As to the question of the cross-examination, it has never been the policy of this Committee, and in very few cases any committee in the history of the Congress, to permit cross-examination.

THE CHAIRMAN: It is the unanimous consent of the Committee that the answer is no on both one and two.

MR. STRIPLING: The third point, Mr. Chairman, was whether or not he can submit questions to the Committee to be asked other witnesses, questions which would serve as a cross-examination?

THE CHAIRMAN: The answer is no on number three.

MR. EISLER: Then, Mr. Chairman, may I ask the permission to read a statement?

THE CHAIRMAN: Let me see your statement, please.

MR. EISLER: Will you be so kind?

(*Statement handed to the Chairman.*)

THE CHAIRMAN: Mr. Eisler, we have read this statement. The Chair is going to rule exactly the same in your case as it did in the case of your brother. We are taking the statement under advisement. The statement will not be read at this time.

MR. EISLER: I object to not being allowed to read my statement after all that I went through in the last year—

THE CHAIRMAN: The objection is overruled. Go ahead and proceed with your questions, Mr. Stripling.

MR. STRIPLING: When and where were you born, Mr. Eisler?

MR. EISLER: 6 July 1898, Leipzig, Germany.

MR. STRIPLING: You are a citizen of what country at the present time?

MR. EISLER: I am in possession of first citizenship papers of the United States.

MR. STRIPLING: Mr. Eisler, of what country were you a citizen before you filed for citizenship papers of the United States?

MR. EISLER: Austria.

MR. STRIPLING: Do you have any relatives in the United States?

MR. EISLER: Yes.

MR. STRIPLING: Will you name them for the Committee?

MR. EISLER: Gerhart Eisler, Miss Ruth Fischer.

MR. STRIPLING: What is your occupation?

MR. EISLER: Musical composer—may I add, of international reputation.

MR. STRIPLING: Of international reputation?

MR. EISLER: Yes.

MR. STRIPLING: In what institutions did you receive your musical education?

MR. EISLER: In Vienna, at the academy. I am the pupil of the famous composer, Arnold Schoenberg, one of the greatest living masters of modern music.

MR. STRIPLING: Mr. Eisler, when did you leave Austria? And will you talk into the microphone, please, and address the Committee?

MR. EISLER: Yes. I left Austria, I think, in '24, and went to Berlin.

MR. STRIPLING: How long did you remain in Berlin?

MR. EISLER: Till 1933, February, when I have to flee Germany, after Hitler made Reichstag fire.

MR. STRIPLING: And where did you go?

MR. EISLER: I went to Paris.

MR. STRIPLING: How long did you remain in Paris?

MR. EISLER: I was there at least from March, I think, until July.

MR. STRIPLING: What other European countries have you resided in?

MR. EISLER: I lived for quite a time in London.

MR. STRIPLING: During what period?

MR. EISLER: I lived in London, February, I think—no, the fall of '34 until around February or March, so far as I remember—and went back to London—let me see—'36, February, and stayed the whole year in London.

MR. STRIPLING: Were you ever in Denmark?

MR. EISLER: Sure. I was quite often in Copenhagen. I spent my summer on a small island—Funen—in a little fishing village, to compose there.

MR. STRIPLING: Were you ever in the Soviet Union, Mr. Eisler?

MR. EISLER: Yes. I was also in the Soviet Union for short trips.

MR. STRIPLING: How many times have you been in the Soviet Union?

MR. EISLER: The last time I remember was '35. I must have been there at least in '32, '31.

MR. STRIPLING: '31, '32, and '35?

MR. EISLER: Possibly I was there once more, but I really cannot remember, you know.

MR. STRIPLING: You remember three times?

MR. EISLER: Three times, yes. It could have been '29 or so, I cannot recall that.

MR. STRIPLING: Why did you go to the Soviet Union, Mr. Eisler?

MR. EISLER: I made moving pictures there. *Youth Takes the Floor* is the title of the moving picture. That made two trips necessary.

MR. STRIPLING: What years?

MR. EISLER: That was '31 and '32, or '33; '35 they had some concerts there, some lectures there. The state publishing house prints a symphony of mine. I also had talks with this publishing house. I stayed five or six weeks, I would say.

MR. STRIPLING: Were you ever employed by the Soviet Union in any capacity?

MR. EISLER: No. I was, like many, many artists, a guest.

MR. STRIPLING: Did you ever receive any money from the Soviet government?

MR. EISLER: No. Naturally, I got my fee from the publishing house, as every author gets from every publishing house in the world.

MR. STRIPLING: Did you ever receive any money from any individuals other than the publishing house you referred to?

MR. EISLER: No.

MR. STRIPLING: Mr. Eisler, when did you first come to the United States?

MR. EISLER: I came first in the United States, to be exact, in '35, it must be April, the second of April, or the end of February, if I am not mistaken.

MR. STRIPLING: How long did you remain?

MR. EISLER: I made a lecture and concert trip. It must be two and a third or three months. I was traveling under the auspices of the Lord Morley committee. Lord Morley had a kind of committee to help the children of refugees which were living in great hardship, even in camps, in France.

* * *

MR. STRIPLING: Now, Mr. Eisler, with the exception of the brief period which you spent in Mexico, you have been residing in the United States since 1940?

MR. EISLER: Yes.

MR. STRIPLING: During this period have you been employed in various capacities?

MR. EISLER: Yes.

MR. STRIPLING: Will you outline those for the Committee—your employment?

MR. EISLER: I was employed as professor of music at the New School for Social Research. And I got a grant from the Rockefeller Foundation—

MR. STRIPLING: Just a moment. The New School for Social Research in New York City, is that right?

MR. EISLER: Yes. I was working under a grant from the Rockefeller Foundation. I taught and studied and composed.

MR. STRIPLING: You taught and what?

MR. EISLER: I composed my music. I was a teacher. I did my research work for the Rockefeller Foundation.

MR. STRIPLING: Now, besides the New School for Social Research, were you ever employed by the Federal Government?

MR. EISLER: Never.

MR. STRIPLING: Didn't you assist in the making of a film for the Department of Agriculture?

MR. EISLER: Yes, but wouldn't call it employment. It was a small picture. I wanted to do it free. I got, I guess, one hundred or two hundred dollars for it.

MR. STRIPLING: Were you ever employed by the Federal Theater Project?

MR. EISLER: Never.

MR. STRIPLING: Have you ever been employed in the motion-picture industry?

MR. EISLER: Absolutely. I am a free lancer. Whenever somebody likes something exceptional in modern music he hires me.

MR. STRIPLING: You write background music for motion pictures?

MR. EISLER: Yes. That is only one part of my profession. I am a composer. I have written many many symphonic—chamber music—songs. And once or twice a year I write a motion picture. It interests me and I need the money.

MR. STRIPLING: Would you outline for the Committee the various studios by which you have been employed?

MR. EISLER: I was one, two, three times hired by Independent Producers. I made *Hangmen Also Die,* for United Artists. Then I made the picture *Scandal in Paris,* that was made by the same independent outfit. Then a picture, *Jealousy,* which was done, I guess, by Gong Productions, a small independent outfit. Then I made five—let me see—*None But the Lonely Heart, Deadline at Dawn, Spanish Main, Woman on the Beach,* and *So Well Remembered*—five pictures for RKO Studio. But I was only there as a free lancer, I was hired from job to job.

MR. STRIPLING: Your latest employment was with RKO–Keith?

MR. EISLER: RKO. Correct, sir. I wrote a score to a picture which they did in England—*So Well Remembered.*

MR. STRIPLING: Now, Mr. Eisler, are you now, or have you ever been, a Communist?

MR. EISLER: I was, as I told you in my first hearing*—I am not now a

* In Hollywood, the previous spring. —E.B.

Communist. And I remember I made, when I was a young man, in 1926, an application for the German Communist [Party] but I found out very quick that I couldn't combine my artistic activities with the demand of any political party, so I dropped out.

MR. STRIPLING: You dropped out?

MR. EISLER: Dropped out.

MR. STRIPLING: I thought you said you made application.

MR. EISLER: Yes.

MR. STRIPLING: You wouldn't drop out if you made application.

MR. EISLER: Oh, yes, sir. Look! If I join a union and don't pay union dues, after a couple of months I will be suspended.

MR. STRIPLING: I understood you made application.

MR. EISLER: Yes.

MR. STRIPLING: Well, did you join?

MR. EISLER: You know that is the implication, but I didn't take any more care of it, I just let it run.

MR. STRIPLING: You did join the Communist Party?

MR. EISLER: I made application.

MR. STRIPLING: Did you join?

MR. EISLER: It is so: you make an application, you get an answer—

MR. STRIPLING: What I have asked is, "Are you now, or have you ever been, a member of the Communist Party?"

MR. EISLER: I say I am not now a member of the Communist Party. I tried to explain to you that I made, in 1926, an application for the Communist Party in Germany, but I didn't follow the activities, I dropped out, I got an answer, but I was not active in political groups—

THE CHAIRMAN: Mr. Eisler, let me ask that question a little differently. You did make application?

MR. EISLER: Yes, sir.

THE CHAIRMAN: And you did join, did you not?

MR. EISLER: I did not really join. I made an application, and I got an answer, but I neglected the whole affair.

THE CHAIRMAN: Then your answer is you were never a member of the Communist Party?

MR. EISLER: Not in the real sense.

THE CHAIRMAN: Never mind the real sense. Were you a member or were you not a member?

MR. EISLER: I told you, Mr. Chairman, and I repeat, I made an application but neglected—

THE CHAIRMAN: I know. But is your answer yes or no?

MR. EISLER: That is my answer, Mr. Chairman.

THE CHAIRMAN: No. You will have to be more specific. We want to know whether you were a member of the Communist Party.

MR. EISLER: In the Communist Party, I would say I never was a member. When a man who doesn't follow up—

THE CHAIRMAN: But you made application to be a member?

MR. EISLER: Yes.

THE CHAIRMAN: And was the application accepted?

MR. EISLER: Yes.

THE CHAIRMAN: That is all.

MR. STRIPLING: Mr. Eisler, have you ever participated in any Communist Party meetings?

MR. EISLER: Any Party meeting? No.

MR. STRIPLING: Mr. Eisler, as a matter of fact, you have been the foremost figure in the revolutionary movement of the Soviet Union in the musical field, have you not?

MR. EISLER: No, sir. The Soviet Union has wonderful composers, and I never was in the foreground movement of the Soviet Union at all.

MR. STRIPLING: Mr. Chairman, I have here a copy of the *Daily Worker,* an excerpt from a copy of the *Daily Worker* of January 15, 1935. I should like to introduce this into the record. It states:

> HANNS EISLER WILL ARRIVE HERE JANUARY 27. . . . This famous revolutionary composer, who has been living in exile in Paris and London since the advent of Hitler, is well known both in Europe and America for his brilliant compositions, which include

K-u-h-l-e W-a-m-p-e—

MR. EISLER: *Kuhle Wampe.* This is a motion picture which I did in 1932 in Berlin.

MR. STRIPLING (*continues reading*):

> *—Hell on Earth, Comintern,*

M-a-s-s-n-a-h-m-e—

MR. EISLER: What is that last one, please?

MR. STRIPLING: M-a-s-s-n-a-h-m-e.

MR. EISLER: M-a-s–Would you be so kind, please?

(*Mr. Stripling exhibits clipping.*)

MR. EISLER: *Massnahme,* which is a German word meaning "expedient."

MR. STRIPLING: And the next one.

MR. EISLER: *Tempo der Zeit,* which means "the tempo of our times."

MR. STRIPLING: And the next one.

MR. EISLER: *Rot Front,* which means "red front."

MR. STRIPLING: "Red front?

MR. EISLER: Yes.

MR. STRIPLING: Did you compose all of those?

MR. EISLER: Yes.

MR. STRIPLING: The article goes on to state, Mr. Chairman:

> His arrival in America marks the further extension of an international tour which has so far included lectures and concerts in Leningrad, Moscow, Copenhagen, Brussels, Paris, and London. The Hanns Eisler Tour Committee, composed of representatives of the Workers Music League, John Reed Club, League of Workers Theaters, Workers Dance League, Anti-Nazi Federation, German Workers Clubs, and other groups are preparing for an outstanding reception for this courageous revolutionary musician and composer for February 8.

MR. RANKIN: Well, Mr. Chairman, what is that from?

MR. STRIPLING: It is from the *Daily Worker,* official organ of the Communist Party.

MR. RANKIN: That is what I wanted to know.

MR. STRIPLING: Now, Mr. Eisler, it is stated here that the Workers Music League was a part of the Hanns Eisler Tour. Are you familiar with the Workers Music League?

MR. EISLER: I remember there was nice young men which were very friendly to me and interested in composing music for labor, for which I have a lot of sympathy.

MR. STRIPLING: Now, do you conceive the Workers Music League to be a Communist organization?

MR. EISLER: No. There must be some Communists in it, but it is a music organization which has social tendencies.

MR. STRIPLING: Social tendencies?

MR. EISLER: Absolutely.

MR. STRIPLING: I have here, Mr. Chairman, the issue of the *Workers Music League,* dated December 1932, volume 1, No. 1, official organ of the Workers Music League, 55 West Nineteenth Street, New York City. The emblem of the organization I will ask Mr. Eisler to explain and identify to the Committee because it has the hammer and sickle and some musical notes.

MR. EISLER: Would you be so kind and look at the date? It says "1932." I was not in this country—

THE CHAIRMAN: The question is, Mr. Eisler, will you describe the emblem on that.

MR. EISLER: The sickle and hammer is the Communistic sign.

THE CHAIRMAN: The hammer and sickle?

MR. EISLER: Yes. But it is with a violin clef, so it is not—

MR. STRIPLING: You don't consider the Workers Music League to be a Communist organization, Mr. Eisler?

MR. EISLER: No. A Communistic organization is one which declares itself a Communistic organization.

MR. STRIPLING: Wasn't it the United States affiliate of International Music Bureau?

MR. EISLER: I remember darkly some music bureau.

MR. STRIPLING: You are very familiar with the International Music Bureau with headquarters in Moscow?

MR. EISLER: Yes. It was one of my ideas.

MR. STRIPLING: It was your idea?

MR. EISLER: Yes.

MR. STRIPLING: You helped organize it, didn't you?

MR. EISLER: No. I would—

THE CHAIRMAN: Did you help organize it? That was the question.

MR. EISLER: No.

MR. STRIPLING: You didn't help organize the International Music Bureau?

MR. EISLER: No. It was a voluntary collaboration between artists and labor groups. I am not an organizer. I am a composer. I advised them.

MR. STRIPLING: That is all right, Mr. Eisler. We will get to the International Music Bureau in just a few minutes.

MR. EISLER: Yes.

MR. STRIPLING: I am sure you will admit that you were quite instrumental in its organization and in its reorganization?

MR. EISLER: I gave my best advice when somebody asked me, but I am not what you call an organizer.

MR. STRIPLING: Next, Mr. Chairman, I have the *Daily Worker* of February 18, 1935, which contains an article entitled "Noted Composer of Comintern Arrives for United States Concert Tour." "Hanns Eisler Exiled from Germany and Music Banned." This article is by Sergei Radamsky:

> Hanns Eisler, the famous revolutionary German refugee composer, arrived in this country a few days ago.

I won't read the article in its entirety, Mr. Chairman. But I would like to read certain excerpts:

> The spreading of revolutionary music among the German workers was not an accident, nor was it easily accomplished. The Communist Party in Germany had to fight the old beer-garden atmosphere and nationalist ditties of the middle class which had gone their way to the masses. In this cultural and musical development the German workers were led by Hanns Eisler. The class struggle in Germany, strikes, barricades, first of May celebrations, and other demonstrations are bound up with his name. . . .
>
> Eisler, however, was not happy in the surroundings of the musical bourgeoisie. To be one of a great number of decadent musicians meant a futility stagnating to his talents. Only when Eisler came into the struggle of the working class did he find his medium, and with it grew his power of composing music which expressed not only the life and battles of the German workers but of the working class of the entire world.

THE CHAIRMAN: What is it you are reading from now?

MR. STRIPLING: From the *Daily Worker,* Mr. Chairman, concerning Mr. Eisler's arrival in the United States in 1935.

MR. RANKIN: Is that the Communist *Daily Worker,* the organ of the Communist Party in the United States?

MR. STRIPLING: It is the official organ of the Communist Party.

MR. RANKIN: That is what I wanted the record to show.

MR. STRIPLING:

> Those who are acquainted with his "Solidarity Song" from the *Kuhle Wampe,* "The Ballad of Soldiers," "On Guard," "Roter Wedding," "Comintern," "Address to a New Born Child," know the stirring message he tells in his music. The workers and peasants of the Soviet Union were quick to appreciate this, and his "On Guard," "Comintern," and others are tremendously popular. One hears them wherever workers gather. . . .
>
> This Hanns Eisler has done with remarkable success. We, in the United States, are acquainted with some of his songs, but not, by far, to the degree deserved by him or needed by us. He is one of the leading spirits in music for the worker, an outstanding musician, a comrade, and always on the battle line with rank and file.

Do you take any disagreement with this article which Sergei Radamsky wrote in the *Daily Worker* of February 18, 1935?

* * *

MR. EISLER: I cannot identify all newspaper articles written about me, but I think it was well meant, and they want to show that in Germany I wrote a lot of music, especially in the last years before Hitler came to power, and that I did my best as an artist to help with my music in this very difficult struggle. If you like, I can show you clippings for the same time from the Hearst press which say I am a monarchist and wanted the return of Kaiser Wilhelm.

MR. STRIPLING: Mr. Eisler, I checked the entire New York press for the same period and I don't find such clippings.

MR. EISLER: I will give you such a clipping.

MR. STRIPLING: Now, five days later the New York *Daily Worker,* the official organ of the Communist Party, carried a picture under the heading "Eisler greeted in New York." It has here a picture of what appears to be several hundred persons, all giving the Communist salute, with the clenched fist. And it says:

> Part of soprano section of a chorus of 1,000 hails Hanns Eisler, . . . noted German revolutionary composer, as he arrives to conduct rehearsals for his concerts here.

Now, in the forefront of this picture, Mr. Eisler, is yourself, also giving the Communist salute.

MR. EISLER: This is a German salute, which is not—

MR. STRIPLING: Would you identify yourself from that picture?

MR. EISLER: Yes, absolutely. Here.

MR. STRIPLING: There is no question but that you are giving the salute?

MR. EISLER: Yes, but—

MR. STRIPLING: Would you demonstrate to the Committee the salute you gave?

(*Mr. Eisler demonstrates salute.*)

MR. EISLER: May I add this salute was invented in Germany and was not only used by Communists but by our anti-Fascists. It is not a Party salute.

MR. RANKIN: What paper was that in?

MR. STRIPLING: That is the *Daily Worker*.

MR. RANKIN: The Communist *Daily Worker*?

MR. STRIPLING: Yes. Now, on March 1, 1935, Mr. Eisler, there is an article here by Joe Foster in the *Daily Worker* from which I would like to read excerpts:

> In every city of the world, hundreds of thousands of workers pound along the pavements, voicing in mass protest, the outrages and exploitations of their ruling classes. They remember their tortured and imprisoned comrades, the untold sufferings and brutality that has been their lot. As they march, thousands of voices eagerly catch up in militant determined song their struggles and their fight for liberation. In the pulsating, stirring rhythms of these revolutionary songs they forge their common challenge, which hurls itself in a volume of sound against the very walls of their ruling-class enemies. Behind this music stands Hanns Eisler—foremost revolutionary composer.

* * *

Mr. Eisler, I have here the *Daily Worker* of October 7, 1935, an article by Charles Hatchard, under the headline "Music unifies workers—Eisler describing experiences in Europe." This article was written after you had returned from Moscow, is that right?

MR. EISLER: I don't remember the article.

MR. STRIPLING: This is October 1935.

MR. EISLER: I don't remember this article.

MR. STRIPLING: It starts out:

> Hanns Eisler, German exile and world's leading composer of music and songs for workers, returned to America Friday from a tour of France, Czechoslovakia, and the Soviet Union as world chairman of the International Music Bureau. A pink-cheeked man with sparkling gray eyes, the composer brought news of workers' musical achievements in Europe which he himself had no small part in developing.

Later it says:

> The International Music Bureau, which he has headed for three months, is having marked success in bringing together professional and amateur musicians and contemporary composers.

And it also states:

> A large edition of his compositions is being published this year by the State Publishing House of the Soviet Union. Eisler is also at work on the score for a Soviet movie directed by [Joris] Ivens—

MR. EISLER: Yes, directed by Ivens.

MR. STRIPLING: We will get to Mr. Ivens later. The article concludes:

> In the heat of the October revolution, Eisler reminds all musicians, proletarian love of music was powerfully promoted and developed by the Soviet. The fourth number of Pravda after the seizure of power featured a long article calling upon all workers and Red Army men to learn songs and music. "For music identifies and unifies the workers," Eisler remarks with a warm smile. "The songs of the workers will rise in this present conflict from the trenches on either side of every no man's land. In that unity of voices and of action lies our hope for the world's future."

Do you have any disagreement with what Mr. Hatchard has said?

MR. EISLER: This writer has the right to write what he likes. I can only speak for myself. I am not responsible for every article written about me.

* * *

MR. STRIPLING: Mr. Eisler, the Committee has quite a bit of evidence here—

MR. EISLER: I see.

MR. STRIPLING: Concerning the International Music Bureau.

MR. EISLER: Yes.

MR. STRIPLING: Which you organized and which you reorganized. Now, would you give the Committee a complete statement of your activities in that connection?

MR. EISLER: Yes, I would be delighted. It was my idea to group together anti-Fascist artists, composers, and try to make some kind of a music bureau. I spoke with several friends in France and in Berlin and we decided to do such a thing. Unfortunately, it never materialized. We were all too busy. There may have been some talk about it. Since I had written some songs for moving pictures and the theater which became quite popular in the labor movement, it was natural that my colleagues in London and Paris said that I should try to make this thing go. We would exchange cultural experiences. Don't forget this is music, and nothing else.

MR. STRIPLING: Mr. Eisler, you say it is music and nothing else. Haven't you on a number of occasions said, in effect, that music is one of the most powerful weapons for the bringing about of the revolution?

MR. EISLER: Sure. Napoleon the First said—

THE CHAIRMAN: Never mind Napoleon. You tell what you said.

MR. EISLER: I consider myself, in this matter, a pupil of Napoleon. I think in music I can enlighten and help people in distress in their fight for their rights. In Germany we didn't do so well. They are friendly words, from this man in the *Daily Worker,* but the truth is songs cannot destroy Fascism, but they are necessary. It is a matter of musical taste as to whether you like them. I am a composer, not a lyric writer. If you don't like them, I am sorry; you can listen to "Open the Door, Richard."

MR. STRIPLING: You have written a lot of songs, Mr. Eisler, have you not?

MR. EISLER: I have written not only songs, but I have written everything in my profession. Here is a book printed by a subversive organization, the Oxford University Press, but I couldn't say that I am a member of the Oxford University Press. This came out two weeks ago. I would ask you, Mr. Stripling, to study this book. I did work for the Rockefeller Foundation.

MR. STRIPLING: Mr. Eisler, when we get through with the International Music Bureau we will take up your work with the Rockefeller Foundation, for which you received twenty thousand dollars.

MR. EISLER: My salary was exactly sixty-five dollars a week.

MR. STRIPLING: We will go into the exact amount which you received.

MR. EISLER: Yes.

MR. STRIPLING: The International Music Bureau was organized in Moscow, was it not?

MR. EISLER: I spoke with some of the German refugees in Moscow.

THE CHAIRMAN: Was it organized in Moscow?

MR. EISLER: No. If it ever came to having an office, we wanted it in Paris, London, or Prague. I was not in Moscow. How could there be an office in Moscow, if I am the head? It was my idea to organize such a thing.

THE CHAIRMAN: Just a minute. The question was, "Was the International Music Bureau organized in Moscow?"

MR. EISLER: No.

THE CHAIRMAN: You can answer that in one word.

MR. EISLER: No.

MR. STRIPLING: Mr. Chairman, in connection with that, I should like to introduce a translation of an article which appeared in *Soviet Music,* No. 2, the March and April 1933 issue, pages 126 and 127, entitled "For a Solid Front of all Proletariat and Revolutionary Musicians," by P. Weis:

> In November of 1932 was held the First International Musical Conference in which participated representatives of the following countries: United States of America, Japan, France, Hungary, Austria, Holland, Belgium, Mexico, and Lithuania. The first International Music Bureau was elected, the object of

which was to prepare the ground for creating an international union of revolutionary musicians because the need for this was apparent—

MR. EISLER: I was not present—

THE CHAIRMAN: Just a minute.

MR. STRIPLING:

> Creating a revolutionary single front in the musical movement can be accomplished only by politicalization. We should not diverge one single iota from a program of progressive class struggle. We can be successful in our efforts only if we know how to transplant our political slogans to the sphere of music. It isn't sufficient just to expose the treachery of reform leaders; we should also be able to show how the socialist fascistic ideology displays itself in special forms of musical movements and musical creations. It is not sufficient only to point out to the crisis of capitalization in general; we should also show concretely the decadence of all bourgeois culture and particularly musical culture. We should prove that the only right road for artistic creations, which include also that of musicians, is in service to the objectives of proletarian revolution.

* * *

You said that you were the inspiration for the International Music Bureau. Then state the origin and genesis of it.

MR. EISLER: I was not in this country, Mr. Chairman. May I object to the reading of articles of this kind, old articles from a different time, because it can only create a kind of hysteria against me. If you want to do something for me, please ask me about these things.

THE CHAIRMAN: Mr. Stripling, what is the purpose of your reading these excerpts?

MR. STRIPLING: The purpose is to show that Mr. Eisler is the Karl Marx of Communism in the musical field and he is well aware of it.

MR. EISLER: I would be flattered.

MR. STRIPLING: In California he indicated that the only thing he ever did was to file an application to join the Communist Party—he had no knowledge of Communism. When he was asked by the Board of Special Inquiry, when he entered this country, if he was familiar with Communism, he said no. When he was asked if he had ever cooperated with the Soviet Union, his answer was no.

MR. EISLER: But did I deny I was in Moscow? Did I deny any of the works which I have written? Was not I questioned about every song which I wrote and I gave answers? What do you mean, Mr. Stripling?

MR. STRIPLING: Mr. Chairman, I intend to show that the International Music Bureau, as a section of the Communist International, was a major program of the Soviet Union in their effort to bring about a world revolution and establish a proletarian dictatorship. This International Music Bureau, which Mr. Eisler conceived and reorganized in 1935, after he had been in the United States, carried on extensive activities, which I shall be glad to introduce into the record. Now I would like to question Mr. Eisler about the origin of it. You have admitted that it was your idea?

MR. EISLER: It was my idea and the idea of my friends. I assure you, it was the idea of my friends.

THE CHAIRMAN: You have answered the question.

MR. EISLER: Yes. I take all responsibility for such a thing, but I assure you—

THE CHAIRMAN: You have already answered the question, Mr. Eisler. Ask another question.

MR. EISLER: Could I finish my sentence, Mr. Chairman?

THE CHAIRMAN: You have answered. Please go ahead and ask the next question.

MR. STRIPLING: The *Soviet Music* issue of January and February of 1933, No. 1, page 142, entitled "International Bureau of Revolutionary Music," has the following to say:

> In February of 1932 there was laid down a firm beginning for the International Union of Revolutionary Musicians. At the initiative of the secretariat of the International Union of Revolutionary Theatres, there has been established within this organization a musical section.
>
> During a comparatively short period the musical section of MORT has done considerable work in strengthening the international musical bonds.
>
> In November 1932, the first international music conference of great historical significance took place in Moscow, which was organized through the efforts of the musical section of the MORT and Union of Soviet Composers. . . .
>
> It was decided to create in place of the musical section of the MORT an International Music Bureau, which was to have the functions of organizing committees for establishment of an International Union of Revolutionary Music. The following members were elected to this bureau: Comrade Eisler (Germany), Shafer (London), Adomian, Keller (United States of America)—

I won't list the other members of the bureau, Mr. Chairman. I want to point out that Mr. Eisler was the first one selected as a member of the bureau. It continues:

> For directing the work of the bureau, a secretariat was formed, which included the following members—

It lists the members, and there is the name of Mr. Eisler.

> The principal tasks of the IMB are to unite all of the revolutionary musical forces in all countries, to exchange musical experience and musical material among different countries, to attract into the ranks of the revolutionary musical front the better representatives of the workers' intelligentsia, to create sections in the capitalistic countries, and to call a world congress for the

> organization of the International Union of Revolutionary Music. The American Workers' Musical League, the German Union for the Advancement of Revolutionary Music, and the Japanese Union of Proletariat Musicians have already become national sections of IMB.

Mr. Eisler, when I asked you to identify the emblem of the Workers Music League, you said that it was not affiliated with the international union.

MR. EISLER: I don't really know. This was a copy from 1932. I don't know how that affiliation was. I was here as a composer. If somebody asked me about music, I would talk about it. I would make speeches about Beethoven for amateur orchestras, and so on.

MR. STRIPLING: Mr. Eisler, who composed the "Internationale"?

MR. EISLER: A man called Pierre Degeyter. It was written around 1888.

MR. STRIPLING: Did you ever belong to an organization known as the Pierre Degeyter Music Club?

MR. EISLER: I had a lecture there once.

MR. STRIPLING: In the United States.

MR. EISLER: Yes. In the Pierre Degeyter Club.

MR. STRIPLING: Do you consider it to be a Communist organization?

MR. EISLER: Mr. Stripling, I don't ask anybody is he a Communist or not when I go to a club and speak. I was in many clubs and in many concerts. I don't check up on them.

MR. STRIPLING: Well, now do you know whether or not it is a Communist organization?

MR. EISLER: I don't know.

MR. STRIPLING: Mr. Eisler, did you ever lecture at the Communist Party headquarters?

MR. EISLER: No.

MR. STRIPLING: In November of 1935 didn't you appear at the Communist Party headquarters with your brother, Gerhart Eisler?

MR. EISLER: My best recollection is I do not remember.

MR. STRIPLING: You lectured on the cultural movement in the United States.

MR. EISLER: I was never elected to anything by the Communist Party.

MR. STRIPLING: Your answer is that you did not?

MR. EISLER: To my best memory and recollection, this is not true.

THE CHAIRMAN: Your memory is better today than it was in Los Angeles, isn't it?

MR. EISLER: Yes.

THE CHAIRMAN: So you can recall whether you attended such a meeting with your brother Gerhart.

MR. EISLER: I really cannot recall. I am not a coward. I really do not recall.

THE CHAIRMAN: Is your answer yes or no?

MR. EISLER: My answer is that I don't remember it.

MR. STRIPLING: Were you a member of the Pierre Degeyter Club?

MR. EISLER: Never.

MR. STRIPLING: You were not?

MR. EISLER: I was a guest. At this time I was exactly ten days in New York. When I came back it was already dissolved. How could I be a member? Maybe they made nice remarks about me, but I don't know.

MR. STRIPLING: Mr. Chairman, we have here the record of the Pierre Degeyter Club. Here is the membership roll of the Pierre Degeyter Club. Under the E's is listed as, I assume, member No. 12, as Eisler, 147 Abbey Road, London. I think it is in your handwriting.

MR. EISLER: It is very nice for this young man to elect me, but I lived in London, didn't know anything about it.

MR. STRIPLING: Is this your handwriting?

MR. EISLER: No.

MR. STRIPLING: Was that your address at that time?

MR. EISLER: In London, yes.

MR. STRIPLING: This states, Mr. Chairman, "Membership roll." Now, is this your handwriting?

MR. EISLER: Absolutely. It is.

MR. STRIPLING: It is written in German, and I wonder if you would translate it for the Committee.

MR. EISLER: "The heartiest greetings and wishes"—"revolutionary greetings and wishes to the Pierre Degeyter Club."

MR. STRIPLING: You wrote that?

MR. EISLER: Yes.

MR. STRIPLING: Now, Mr. Chairman, among the records which the Committee has on the Pierre Degeyter Club is one which states, "Pierre Degeyter Club, predecessor of the American Music League." Pierre Degeyter Club was changed to the American Music League. Here are the minutes of the American Music League for the meeting June 15, 1936:

> The minutes of meeting of June 8, 1936, were read and accepted. Communications were read:
>
> 1. Letter from district 2 of the Communist Party asking us to adopt a resolution of protest against the action of the Supreme Court in voiding the minimum-wage law and against the power of the Supreme Court. A motion was made to send telegrams to our Congressional representative and to President Roosevelt protesting recent Supreme Court decisions and requesting that action be taken to curb their power. The motion was amended to send letters instead of telegrams, and the amended motion was carried. . . .
>
> 4. Letter from the Soviet Union on the subject of the exuberance of musical culture of the peoples of the Union of Soviet Socialist Republics. A motion was made and carried that this rather lengthy letter be read at next Monday's open meeting and to be part of the program.

I offer these, Mr. Chairman, to indicate the complexion, so to speak, of the organization. The Pierre Degeyter Music Club published a number of songs, some of which were Mr. Eisler's, but its activities were not as extensive as those of the International Music Bureau, which I would like to return to. I have here, Mr. Chairman, what is entitled *International Collection of Revolutionary Songs*. On the front is the hammer and sickle. Inside, under the date of 1933, it has the hammer and sickle. It says "International Music Bureau of IURT, International Collection of Revolutionary Songs." On page 24 there appears a song entitled "The Comintern March," by Hanns Eisler. Now, Mr. Eisler, did you compose the music for "The Comintern March"?

MR. EISLER: I composed a march for a theater play in 1926 or 1927,* which was later popular and got a different title. I am the author of the song.

MR. STRIPLING: Of "The Comintern March"?

MR. EISLER: Yes.

MR. STRIPLING: Will you explain to the Committee what the Comintern is?

MR. EISLER: The Comintern was an international organization of labor.

THE CHAIRMAN: I didn't hear you.

MR. EISLER: An international organization of labor. There was the First, Second, and Third International. They come together to try to unify.

MR. STRIPLING: Mr. Chairman, this appeared in three different languages. In the foreword they have gone to great lengths to point out what a great weapon music is in the class struggle. It says:

> We know of some very important historical examples when the song served as a mighty weapon for revolutionary agitation, such as the period of the Russian Revolution in 1917.
>
> Its extreme importance was again demonstrated by the fact that about three-fourths of an editorial article in one of the first issues of *Pravda* in 1917 (issue No. 5) was devoted to the question of song.

The quote from *Pravda* goes on to say that the workers sang the "Internationale" while behind barricades, and it was an inspiration, and so forth. Here is another edition published in 1935 in the Soviet Union by the International Music Bureau, with the title in four languages, and it says "Workers of the World Unite." Isn't that the slogan of the Communist Party?

MR. EISLER: Yes. Also the slogan of many political groups. Not exclusively the Communist Party.

MR. STRIPLING: The slogan is well known, Mr. Chairman. In this particular edition, published in four languages, in Moscow, there appears another song by Hanns Eisler, entitled "Fifty Thousand Strong." Did you compose that, Mr. Eisler?

* It is from a program entitled "Ten Years of the Comintern" presented in Berlin in 1929. The tune was used in the Hollywood film *Hangmen Also Die*—one of the few instances of authentic "infiltration"! —E.B.

Mr. Eisler: Yes, I composed it in Berlin in 1930.

Mr. Stripling: Would you refer to it as revolutionary music?

Mr. Eisler: Absolutely. Revolutionary music is a little high-hat for it. I would call it a song for labor.

Mr. Stripling: Would it aid in the class struggle?

Mr. Eisler: Pardon me?

Mr. Stripling: Would your song aid in the class struggle?

Mr. Eisler: I hope it was.

Mr. Stripling: You hope that it was?

Mr. Eisler: I hope it was.

Mr. Stripling: You have also entertained that hope since you have been in the United States?

Mr. Eisler: My songs are completely forgotten. This is really, I would say, a past affair.

Mr. Stripling: Mr. Eisler, well, let's see whether it is forgotten. I have here a song book, entitled *Red Song Book*. This was published, prepared by the Workers Music League, with the hammer and sickle on the front, which you said was not a Communist organization, and they feature on the back your song, "Comintern," by Hanns Eisler. I will read to the Committee the words of the song.

Mr. Eisler: A pleasure.

Mr. Stripling: Would you like to read them?

Mr. Eisler: You have a better pronunciation than I.

Mr. Stripling:

Oh, you who are missing,
Oh, comrades in dungeons,
You're with us, you're with us,
This day of our vengeance.
No Fascists can daunt us,
No terror can halt;
All lands will take flame
With the fire of revolt.

The Comintern calls you,
Raise high Soviet banner,
In steeled ranks to battle
Raise sickle and hammer.
Our answer: Red Legions
We raise in our might
Our answer: Red Storm Troops
We lunge to the fight.

From Russia victorious
The workers' October
Comes storming reaction's
Regime the world over

We're coming with Lenin
For Bolshevik work
From London, Havana,
Berlin and New York.

Rise up fields and workshops
Come out workers, farmers;
To battle march onward,
March on, world stormers.
Eyes sharp on your guns,
Red banners unfurled,
Advance, Proletarians
To conquer the world.

Is this one of your little ditties that someone adopted [adapted]?

MR. EISLER: This song was written in 1926. This is a translation. When was the song printed here?

MR. STRIPLING: This was published in 1932 in New York.

MR. EISLER: In 1932 I was in Berlin. I am not responsible for literary translations. My song was written in Germany for a theater performance on the anniversary of the German revolution in 1918.

MR. MCDOWELL: Who wrote the words, Mr. Stripling?

MR. STRIPLING: By Victor Jerome. Other songs which appear in this issue are the "Internationale," "The Barricades," "The Builders," "Comrades, the Bugles Are Sounding," "Solidarity," "The Workers' Funeral March," and others.

MR. EISLER: Very beautiful melody there.

MR. STRIPLING: I have another one here, Mr. Eisler, entitled *America Sings*.

MR. EISLER: Yes.

MR. STRIPLING: That was published by the Workers' Bookshop, 50 East Thirteenth Street, New York, New York, which is the official publishing house of the Communist Party. It has a foreword by Earl Robinson. Among the songs which are contained in *America Sings* are the "Comintern," on page 11, "Comrades, the Bugles Are Sounding," "Internationale," "Red Air Fleet," "Red Flag," "Rounds," "Salute to Life," "Scottsboro Boys," "Solidarity Forever," and, for some unknown reason, "The Star-Spangled Banner," on page 5. I have here, Mr. Chairman, an article entitled "The Revolutionary Musical Front," by G. Schneerson, which appeared in the *Soviet Music,* No. 3 of May and June of 1933. It says, "The league"—referring to the Workers League—

> has published . . . songs by Eisler and by Soviet composers which have been translated into the English language. . . . The American comrades have succeeded in getting into the movement a number of outstanding musicians and theorists. . . .

> Great assistance in the matter of solving the greatest problem of theoretical courses is shown by a musical club called Pierre Degeyter in New York, organized by the league. The work in the club is being conducted by such great musicians as Prof. Henry Cowell, Charles Seeger, and others. The league has over 6,000 active members. A number of large choruses and orchestras make the league one of the strongest and outstanding factors in the International Musical Revolutionary front.

* * *

This is the organization which you autographed revolutionary greetings to?

MR. EISLER: Sure.

* * *

MR. STRIPLING: Mr. Eisler, when you were in Moscow in 1935 did you give out some interviews or write some articles?

MR. EISLER: I think I gave interviews, as usual. Mostly ideas about Germany.

MR. STRIPLING: I have an article here written by you, which appeared in *Sovetskoe Iskusstvo,* July 29, 1935, page 2, and it has your picture, and is printed in Russia. The title is "The Destruction of Art." I won't read it all. If you want it all read, I will be glad to do so. You state:

> Still, I am an optimist with regard to the future because I believe in the inexhaustible strength of organized masses. The dark epoch of fascism makes it clear to each honest artist that close cooperation with the working masses is the only way leading to creative art. Only in a revolutionary struggle will an artist find his own individuality. . . .
>
> Similar developments can be observed in America where the recognized composer, Aaron Copland, has composed a mass song, "The First of May." An active role is also played in the workers' musical movement by Henry Cowell of San Francisco.
>
> All these events, which only three years ago could hardly have been foreseen, show that for a real artist there is only one way in the field of art: the road toward revolution. It would not be long before there would not be left a single great artist on the other side of the barricades.
>
> Revolutionary music is now more powerful than ever. Its political and artistic importance is growing daily.

Mr. Eisler, what do you mean by "on the other side of the barricades"?

MR. EISLER: Will you repeat the title of this article?

MR. STRIPLING: The title of it was "The Destruction of Art."

MR. EISLER: By whom?

MR. STRIPLING: By Hanns Eisler.

MR. EISLER: No, I didn't destroy art. You can't criticize me there. I spoke on—I guess you can find it—how Fascism has destroyed art.

THE CHAIRMAN: I don't think that is responsive to the question. What was your question, Mr. Stripling?

MR. STRIPLING: I asked him what he meant when he referred to "on the other side of the barricades."

MR. EISLER: I mean in Germany to fight against Hitler. That was my real belief.

* * *

MR. STRIPLING: Mr. Eisler, did you write a song entitled "In Praise of Learning"?

MR. EISLER: Yes.

MR. STRIPLING: I will read the words to this one verse. It says:

> Learn now the simple truth,
> You, for whom the time has come at last;
> It is not too late.
> Learn now the A, B, C,
> It is not enough, but learn it still.
> Fear not, be not downhearted,
> Begin, you must learn the lesson
> You must be ready to take over.

What do you mean, "You must be ready to take over?"

MR. EISLER: This song appeared in a play which I wrote the music for.* It was written in 1929 in Berlin. The play was based on the famous novel by Maxim Gorky. This theater piece was sung by workers on the stage. Again, this song became popular to a certain extent. It was in this historical play about the struggle of the Russian people from 1905 to 1917.

THE CHAIRMAN: You didn't mean that you must be ready to take over now, did you?

MR. EISLER: I can't understand your question.

THE CHAIRMAN: You said that it applied to Germany.

MR. EISLER: Not only to Germany. It was a show, a musical song in a show. It applied to the situation on the stage.

THE CHAIRMAN: Would it also apply here to the United States?

MR. STRIPLING: It was shown in the United States. He wrote the music for it in the United States.

MR. EISLER: No, I wrote the music in 1929 or 1930 in Berlin. It was produced in Copenhagen, in New York—I guess in Paris. It was a theater play.

THE CHAIRMAN: It doesn't apply only to Germany but applies to France and Italy and the United States?

MR. EISLER: It is from a quotation by Maxim Gorky, the famous

* The play is *The Mother*. In a published interview given later in East Germany, Eisler states that he protected Brecht before HUAC by claiming authorship of Brecht's works. This he did not do; but he obviously did go to some pains to avoid the use of Brecht's name. See Hans Bunge, *Fragen Sie Mehr Ueber Brecht*, pp. 203–207. —E.B.

writer. The song is based on the idea of Maxim Gorky. This song applies to the historical structure of the Russian people from 1905 until 1917.

THE CHAIRMAN: Would you write the same song here now?

MR. EISLER: If I had to write a historical play about Russia, I would write it—and the poet would let me have the words.

THE CHAIRMAN: Would you write the same song here in the United States now about "you must take over" here in the United States?

MR. EISLER: No.

THE CHAIRMAN: You have changed your opinion, then?

MR. EISLER: No, but I am a guest, a stranger here, and the labor movement can handle their affairs themselves. That is what I mean.

MR. STRIPLING: Mr. Eisler, did you ever send greetings to the Soviet Union?

MR. EISLER: Sure. I don't remember but there must be some.

MR. STRIPLING: *Soviet Music* of October 1936, No. 10, page 6, has an article, "Musicians Abroad on the Subject of Stalin's Constitution." You don't hate Stalin, Mr. Eisler?

MR. EISLER: Pardon?

MR. STRIPLING: Do you hate Stalin?

MR. EISLER: No.

MR. STRIPLING: Why did you tell the immigration authorities that you hated Stalin?

MR. EISLER: I cannot remember the fact. If I really made such a stupid remark I was an idiot.

MR. STRIPLING: You said, "I hate Stalin just as I hate Hitler," when you were before the immigration authorities.

MR. EISLER: I am surprised. There must be a misunderstanding, or it is a completely idiotic, hysteric remark.

THE CHAIRMAN: Do you remember?

MR. EISLER: I don't remember the remark. I think that Stalin is one of the greatest historical personalities of our time.

MR. STRIPLING: This message, Mr. Chairman, refers to Stalin's constitution, by Hanns Eisler, and reads:

> Hearty greetings to the constitution of the great socialistic state, based on the great principle "From each one according to his abilities—and to each one according to his labor." It is almost impossible to encompass with thought all those huge results which your constitution will have for future instruction of the new socialistic culture. Each success for the Soviet Union is success for the international proletariat. It gives us courage in struggle and binds us to give all our strength in the defense of the Soviet Union.

That was written in 1936 after you had been in this country.

MR. EISLER: Did I write this?

MR. STRIPLING: It says, "By Hanns Eisler, hearty greetings."

MR. EISLER: I cannot remember. It is quite possible that I did it. But where was it written?

MR. STRIPLING: It appears in *Soviet Music.*

MR. EISLER: I see.

MR. STRIPLING: October 1936, number 10.

MR. EISLER: Then I wrote it, naturally.

MR. STRIPLING: *The Great Soviet Encyclopedia,* Mr. Eisler, of Moscow, published in Moscow, 1933, volume 63, columns 157–158, gives your picture and says:

> Hanns Eisler—born 1898, composer, Communist, is at the head of the proletarian movement in German music.

Is that an error on the part of this *Great Soviet Encyclopedia* to refer to you as a Communist?

MR. EISLER: It is an error. They call everybody Communist which was active like me. I admitted, gentlemen—I am not afraid about anything—I would admit it. I have no right, especially today, in which the German Communists in the last fifteen years have sacrificed so much, and fought, too—I would be a swindler if I called myself a Communist. I have no right. The Communist underground workers in every country have proven that they are heroes. I am not a hero. I am a composer.

THE CHAIRMAN: Mr. Eisler, on that point, you said that you made application—

MR. EISLER: Yes.

THE CHAIRMAN: —to become a member.

MR. EISLER: Yes.

THE CHAIRMAN: And that application was accepted.

MR. EISLER: Yes.

THE CHAIRMAN: How long were you a member?

MR. EISLER: I tell you, I remember I made this application around January or February in Berlin. I went—it must have been March or May, 1926—to Paris, and forgot about the thing, never attended a political meeting. I stick to my music. I don't know about politics.

THE CHAIRMAN: For how many years were you a member of the Communist Party?

MR. EISLER: I was not really a member. I didn't pay the membership dues. I was not active in the political organization of the Communist Party.

THE CHAIRMAN: You admitted you made an application to become a member of the Communist Party.

MR. EISLER: 1926, in Berlin.

THE CHAIRMAN: You admitted that you had been accepted.

MR. EISLER: Yes.

THE CHAIRMAN: I want to know how long you were a member.

MR. EISLER: Mr. Chairman, since I went immediately to Paris and came back in the fall, to Berlin—

THE CHAIRMAN: That is all right. How many years?

MR. EISLER: No years.

THE CHAIRMAN: How many months were you a member?

MR. EISLER: Technically, maybe for a couple of months.

THE CHAIRMAN: Two months?

MR. EISLER: Look, Mr. Chairman, if you join a union and don't pay union dues and don't participate in union activities—I am automatically suspended if I do that.

THE CHAIRMAN: You said before that you withdrew as a member.

MR. EISLER: I dropped out.

THE CHAIRMAN: You dropped out. How long a time was it between the time you made application and were accepted and the time you dropped out?

MR. EISLER: I made application—

THE CHAIRMAN: Wait a minute. Was it two months?

MR. EISLER: I cannot state. I would like to answer it.

THE CHAIRMAN: Do you think it was two months?

MR. EISLER: I cannot say so.

THE CHAIRMAN: What is your opinion?

MR. EISLER: My opinion is that when I came back to Berlin again—I don't really join up, you know—and I lived my life as an artist.

THE CHAIRMAN: Would you say two months was a fair assumption?

MR. EISLER: I wouldn't say so.

THE CHAIRMAN: How long, then? What would you say would be a fair time?

MR. EISLER: I couldn't say.

THE CHAIRMAN: What?

MR. EISLER: I couldn't answer the question. I explained.

THE CHAIRMAN: How did you withdraw, by the way?

MR. EISLER: The very simple thing that I didn't join, really, a political organization of the Communist Party in Germany. I didn't pay my membership dues, and I was automatically suspended.

THE CHAIRMAN: You were suspended?

MR. EISLER: Automatically.

THE CHAIRMAN: Automatically. When was that?

MR. EISLER: That must be end of 1926.

THE CHAIRMAN: You joined when?

MR. EISLER: January 1926.

THE CHAIRMAN: That is all.

MR. STRIPLING: Mr. Chairman, I don't think there is any question about whether Mr. Eisler is a Communist or not. The point of the Committee putting all of this material in the record is to show that Mr. Eisler was permitted to go in and out of this country time and time again when the immigration laws of this country say a Communist shall not be permitted in this country.

MR. EISLER: I told you before that my relations to the Communist Party was such a loose thing—

THE CHAIRMAN: You have already admitted that you were a Communist for almost a year. Go ahead, Mr. Stripling.

MR. STRIPLING: The Soviet government, the Comintern, wouldn't invite a person to come to Moscow to reorganize the International Music Bureau if that person wasn't a Communist, do you think, Mr. Eisler?

MR. EISLER: We were refugees. We all stick together, regardless of our political beliefs—details of our political beliefs. We stick together. It was not even possible in 1933 to join the Communist Party. This was a very fighting organization. They wouldn't accept a composer or a fool like me.

MR. STRIPLING: Mr. Chairman, I have next *International Literature,* published in Moscow in 1933. It is an issue issued in January and carries the title "1933–34." It has an article by S. Tretyakov, entitled "Hanns Eisler: Revolutionary Composer—a Soviet writer about a German musician." You are referred to, Mr. Eisler, throughout this article as a comrade, "Comrade Eisler."

MR. EISLER: Yes. That is usual in the Soviet Union. You don't call a man "mister."

MR. STRIPLING: He says:

> Eisler sits down to the piano. He pats it with the palms of his small hands like a child pats the water in its tub. He doesn't pedal; he stamps the pedal as if it were a vicious thing. He breathes loud in rhythm with the march. His voice is hoarse and passionate. . . .

Eh, hosts, we are your guests.
   Unasked we're here.
Into our bones you pressed
   Your crutches dear.
You said: False limbs are best—
   And hand and foot surpass.
You said: Blind folk in the dark
   Push better than the rest.
No matter. Let the other foot
   Be also torn away,
But to our bosses' necks
   Our hands will find the way.
An army of stumps we are
On wooden claws that ply,
And standing we bring news—
   The world October's night.

That is not like "Open the Door Richard," Mr. Eisler?

MR. EISLER: Pardon me. I didn't write this. This is a writer that writes about me.

MR. STRIPLING: Here is a direct quote—

MR. EISLER: What book is that?

MR. STRIPLING: *International Literature,* published in Moscow, in 1933–1934, a feature article about Hanns Eisler:

> "These choruses," says Eisler, "are not just music compositions performed for listeners. They are a particular kind of political seminar on problems of party strategy and tactics. The members of the chorus work these problems out, but they do so in the easily remembered and practiced form of a chorus singing. We build this play not for concerts. It is only a method of pedagogic work with students of Marxian schools and proletarian assemblies. . . .
>
> "Thus Communist music becomes the heavy artillery of the battle for Communism. . . ."

MR. EISLER: He has written his interview and he does it in his own way. It is not an article by myself.

* * *

MR. STRIPLING: Did you write the music for a play *Die Massnahme*?

MR. EISLER: Sure.

MR. STRIPLING: Would you describe it to the Committee? Describe the plot.

MR. EISLER: This play goes back to an old Japanese play and was written by a German writer.* I wrote the music to it. Three or four men are involved in organizational struggle. That is the general tone of the play. It is really a condensation of an old Japanese play. It was written in 1929 in Germany.

MR. RANKIN: May I ask what time you are going to recess?

THE CHAIRMAN: We will recess in just a few minutes, and will reconvene at two o'clock, at which time Mr. Sumner Welles will be the first witness.

MR. RANKIN: I have a conference with the Red Cross in regard to relief for the stricken areas along the Gulf Coast at one o'clock, and I may not get back by two.

MR. STRIPLING: Mr. Eisler, you—

MR. EISLER: The play was written after an old classic Japanese play. I have forgot the name. It was just brought up to date by the writer, and was a symbolic philosophical play and that is all.

MR. STRIPLING: It dealt with party strategy?

MR. EISLER: Yes.

MR. STRIPLING: It had to do with four young Communists, did it not?

* Again Brecht's name is avoided. —E.B.

Mr. Eisler: Yes, sir.

Mr. Stripling: And three of the Communists murdered the fourth one because they felt he would be a menace to the cause; is that correct?

Mr. Eisler: Yes.

Mr. Stripling: That is the theme of it?

Mr. Eisler: Yes.

Mr. Stripling: We won't go into it further. When the immigration authorities questioned you about this play do you remember what you told them?

Mr. Eisler: I think, that I wrote the music to the play.

The Chairman: You said it was just a play?

Mr. Stripling: When questioned about it, Eisler referred to the play as *An Expedient* and stated it was not Communistic in nature. The real title of the play is *Disciplinary Measures,* isn't that right?

Mr. Eisler: Yes, it is a poetical philosophical play.

Mr. Stripling: Mr. Chairman, I don't think we can finish with Mr. Eisler before lunch.

* * *

Mr. Stripling: Mr. Eisler, you stated that you have a sister in the United States.

Mr. Eisler: Yes.

Mr. Stripling: By the name of Ruth Fischer.

Mr. Eisler: Yes.

Mr. Stripling: Do you recall receiving a letter from her on April 24, 1944, addressed to you and your wife?

Mr. Eisler: I don't recall it. What kind of letter was it, please?

Mr. Stripling: In this letter she accused you and her brother Gerhart of being agents of the GPU. She stated as follows:

> If the local branches of the GPU can succeed in making clever arrangements for a natural death it will not succeed this time. Not for you nor for Gerhart Eisler, Chief of the German GPU division in the United States. . . . This time it will not be made so easy for you. You always play with terror and are always afraid to take your responsibility for your acts.
>
> I have made the following preparation: No. 1, three physicians have given me a thorough examination. I am now in good health. There is no cause for natural death. I am constantly under a physician's care and am taking care of myself in a sensible manner. The doctors are informed that in case of any trouble they will testify accordingly. 2, a number of reputable journalists and politicians have been informed and possess a copy of this letter. A number of German immigrants have also been apprised.

Do you recall receiving that letter?

Mr. Eisler: Really not. I don't recall getting such a letter. I think the letter is absolutely idiotic.

THE CHAIRMAN: Don't you think, Mr. Eisler, if you had received such a letter you would be able to recall whether you had gotten it or not?

MR. EISLER: Maybe it was sent to the wrong address?

THE CHAIRMAN: Beg your pardon?

MR. EISLER: But I read similar things.

THE CHAIRMAN: Would you say you never received that letter?

MR. EISLER: It could be possible.

THE CHAIRMAN: Would you say that you did receive the letter?

MR. EISLER: Oh, let's say I don't recall exactly.

THE CHAIRMAN: Now, now, you better jog that memory of yours a little bit, because it is getting right back to where it was in California.

MR. EISLER: Yes.

THE CHAIRMAN: If I had received a letter like that, or anyone else in this room had received a letter like that, they would know, particularly if it was from our sister. They would remember whether they received it or not.

MR. EISLER: Yes.

THE CHAIRMAN: So I want you to answer whether you received that letter or whether you didn't receive the letter.

MR. EISLER: It is quite a possibility that I received the letter.

THE CHAIRMAN: That is not an answer to the question.

MR. EISLER: I say, Mr. Chairman, it is quite a possibility that I received the letter. This must be a sufficient answer. I don't recall this letter. I have no reason to deny it, but I don't know exactly.

THE CHAIRMAN: Yes, but don't you think that if you had received it you would recall it?

MR. EISLER: No. It is so foolish and idiotic—

THE CHAIRMAN: That is why you would recall, if you say it was foolish.

MR. EISLER: Maybe my wife put it away. It is possible. But let's say, for the sake of the record, I received this letter.

THE CHAIRMAN: You received it. All right, for the sake of the record, he received it.

MR. STRIPLING: All right.

THE CHAIRMAN: I don't want to burden the Committee with putting in any more of this evidence. I would like, however, to put into the record as exhibits a number of books containing songs of Mr. Eisler. For example, I have one here published by the Rand School in New York, entitled *Rebel Song Book,* which contains "We're Marching, O Comrades," by Hanns Eisler.

MR. EISLER: It is the song "Comintern," with a different title in this book.

MR. STRIPLING: I also have another one, Mr. Chairman, entitled *Workers' Song Book,* published by the Workers Music League in 1935 "Forward, We've Not Forgotten," by Hanns Eisler.

THE CHAIRMAN: Are those the only ones you have, Mr. Stripling?

MR. STRIPLING: No. I have one or two others I would like to put in. I have here *Soviet Russia Today,* May issue, 1936. It says, on page 33:

> For May Day and every day, timely records of workers' songs. One is "Rise Up"; another is the "Internationale"; and another one is "In Praise of Learning," which was written by Hanns Eisler and Bertolt Brecht for *Mother,** a musical play based on Maxim Gorky's novel of the same name.
>
> The recorded version has been rearranged by the composer, who supervised the recording. The fresh note this song strikes, coupled with its splendid vigor, makes this a recording of particular interest.

MR. EISLER: That is just what I told you—

MR. STRIPLING: The other songs listed, as I say, are the "Internationale," "Forward, We've Not Forgotten," and also "The Soup Song" and "United Front," by Brecht and Eisler.

MR. EISLER: I offer as evidence my book, too.

MR. STRIPLING: Mr. Chairman, those are the only questions I have at this time of Mr. Eisler. I should like to point out, however, that it might be necessary to bring him back as a witness. He will have to be subpoenaed back in the Hollywood hearing.

MR. RANKIN: Mr. Chairman, under the law, it is not necessary to resubpoena a witness. Just direct him to stay within the call of the Chair.

THE CHAIRMAN: I am quite confident that you will stay within the call of the Chair.

MR. EISLER: Absolutely.

MR. GREENBERG: Are you putting any geographical limitation on him when you say, "Within the call of the Chair"?

THE CHAIRMAN: Anywhere within the United States, but not outside of the United States.

MR. EISLER: Oh, yes. Surely.

THE CHAIRMAN: Mr. McDowell, do you have any questions?

MR. MCDOWELL: Yes. Mr. Eisler, you were born in Austria?

MR. EISLER: I was born in Leipzig, but I always was an Austrian citizen.

MR. MCDOWELL: During the First World War were you a member of either army—the Austrian or the German Army?

MR. EISLER: The Austrian Army.

MR. MCDOWELL: Did you work before you became a soldier? Did you have a job?

MR. EISLER: No, I was in school.

MR. MCDOWELL: You were a student?

MR. EISLER: Yes.

MR. MCDOWELL: And after the war was over did you return to your school and continue your studies?

* In short, Stripling already had the "dope" on Brecht, and Eisler's avoidance of the name made no difference. —E.B.

MR. EISLER: Yes.

MR. MCDOWELL: Have you ever worked for anybody? Have you ever had what we call in America a job?

MR. EISLER: Yes. I was a professor of music in the Conservatory of the City of Vienna.

MR. MCDOWELL: You taught? You were a teacher?

MR. EISLER: I was a student, a postgraduate musical student. I taught there.

MR. MCDOWELL: In the song "Red Front," which I have before me—music by Hanns Eisler—in the publication the *Worker Musician,* among other things, it says this: "We carry the flag of the working class, in the face of our class enemy," and so forth. Now, from your testimony here I conclude that your opinion on matters of work, as we understand work in the United States, is purely academic.

MR. EISLER: I am a composer and composing is my whole life. That is working, too.

THE CHAIRMAN: Mr. Eisler, on this question of work, you are now employed with RKO?

MR. EISLER: No. I was only a free lancer. I didn't get any job the last—

THE CHAIRMAN: What is the total amount of pay that you have received from RKO?

MR. EISLER: I have to reckon this out. I cannot recall it.

THE CHAIRMAN: It would be in excess of twenty thousand dollars?

MR. EISLER: In the last four years, yes.

MR. MCDOWELL: Mr. Eisler, did you write "The Ballad to Paragraph 218"?

MR. EISLER: I write only music.

MR. MCDOWELL: You remember the words?

MR. EISLER: Sure I remember the words.

MR. MCDOWELL: Did you write the ballad "Address to the Crane 'Karl' "?

MR. EISLER: I wrote the music to it.

MR. MCDOWELL: Only the music?

MR. EISLER: I never write words.

MR. MCDOWELL: Have you read the words?

MR. EISLER: Sure.

MR. MCDOWELL: Did you write "The Ballad of the Maimed"?

MR. EISLER: Of what, please?

MR. MCDOWELL: Of the maimed—the hurt, the injured?

MR. EISLER: I wrote the music to it.

MR. MCDOWELL: Did you write the words?

MR. EISLER: No. I never write words.

MR. MCDOWELL: Have you read the words?

MR. EISLER: Yes.

MR. MCDOWELL: Did you write "Ballad of Nigger Jim"?

MR. EISLER: I wrote the music.

MR. MCDOWELL: You didn't write the words?

MR. EISLER: No.

MR. MCDOWELL: You read the words?

MR. EISLER: I read the words.

MR. MCDOWELL: Did you write "Song of the Dry Bread"?

MR. EISLER: Yes. It was in a play.

MR. MCDOWELL: Did you write the words?

MR. EISLER: No. I never write the words.

MR. MCDOWELL: Did you read the words?

MR. EISLER: Sure.

MR. MCDOWELL: Did you write "Song of Demand and Supply"?

MR. EISLER: It is one of the songs of the—

MR. MCDOWELL: Did you write the words?

MR. EISLER: No.

MR. MCDOWELL: Did you read the words?

MR. EISLER: Yes.

MR. MCDOWELL: As a composer of the music for the various pieces that I have named here, would you be consulted in the words that would go with this music?

MR. EISLER: No. I get the text and then I write the music to it.

MR. MCDOWELL: I would like to say, Mr. Chairman, that I think all members of the Committee should examine these exhibits that I have just named to Mr. Eisler, who maintains he is a composer of the music. This is matter that couldn't be sent through the mails in the United States. It deals with affairs that are entirely out of political matters, entirely out of anything except perhaps that of medicine. "Obscenity" is a poor word for it. I don't know what the custom is in Germany or in Austria, but such words as are in those sheets have no place in any sort of a civilization.

MR. EISLER: They are considered as great poetry.

MR. MCDOWELL: They are considered as what?

MR. EISLER: Great poetry.

MR. MCDOWELL: Great poetry?

MR. EISLER: Yes.

MR. MCDOWELL: Well, great poetry as we are taught in America has nothing to do with that kind of truck. Among other things, there is a song in there apparently dedicated or written because of the laws prohibiting abortion.

MR. EISLER: Yes.

MR. MCDOWELL: In Germany.

MR. EISLER: Yes.

MR. MCDOWELL: This song ridicules the law—

Mr. Eisler: Yes.

Mr. McDowell: Opposing the prohibition of abortions.

Mr. Eisler: Yes.

Mr. McDowell: In other words, this song would, I presume, in your Communist fashion of thinking, urge that the law opposing abortion be disregarded.

The Chairman: I would suggest that we don't get very deep into the question of abortion.

Mr. Rankin: I understand that you have complained that this Committee had smeared you.

Mr. Eisler: Yes, Mr. Rankin.

Mr. Rankin: When you make that charge you are making that charge against a Committee of the Congress of the United States. You realize that, do you?

Mr. Eisler: Yes.

Mr. McDowell: Nothing that this Committee has done is in violation of the rules of the House, or in conflict with the laws of common decency. Now, where do you get any authority for saying that this Committee has smeared you?

Mr. Eisler: I haven't any authority at all, but if you had made such a hearing without giving [out], every week the last twelve months, things about me which are not even sometimes the truth, it would be different. But when you have distortions or inventions of somebody which told it to one of the members of the Committee, when you go into this fantastic press campaign against an artist, I am sure every red-blooded artist will be, after one year, after you nearly ruined him, very angry about this.

Mr. Rankin: I am conscious, when I look at this filth here, to which Mr. McDowell has referred—

Mr. Eisler: Pardon me, Mr. Rankin. It is not filth.

Mr. Rankin: I am conscious that anybody that would write that stuff would certainly not have much respect for the Congress of the United States. But this Committee has given you more than a fair deal, more than a fair trial, more than you would have gotten in any other country in the world.

Mr. Eisler: I don't know, Mr. Rankin, how you are familiar with American poetry.

Mr. Rankin: American what?

Mr. Eisler: Poetry.

Mr. Rankin: Poetry.

Mr. Eisler: And American writing. This is not American poetry or American writing. This was written in German. It is not translated. It was written in Berlin in 1927 or 1928 or 1929. I say, again, it is great poetry. We can have different tastes in art, but I cannot permit, Mr. Rankin, that you call my work just in such names. I protest against that.

MR. RANKIN: I suppose that I am as familiar with American poetry and with English poetry generally as any Member of either House. And anybody that tries to tell me that this filth is poetry certainly reads himself out of the class of any American poet that has ever been recognized by the American people.

MR. MCDOWELL: Mr. Eisler, you wrote the poem about killing, "About Killing"?

MR. EISLER: It was a quotation from poetry.

MR. MCDOWELL: It was a quotation?

MR. EISLER: Quotation.

MR. MCDOWELL: But you were the author of the poem?

MR. EISLER: No, I just put it together from poetry. I cannot write words, you know.

MR. MCDOWELL: You merely put this together?

MR. EISLER: Yes, from the poetry. I am not a writer.

MR. MCDOWELL: Mr. Chairman, I would like permission to read these nine lines, which is the entire poem, that Mr. Eisler put together.

MR. RANKIN: I reserve the right to object. But we will hear him read it.

MR. MCDOWELL:

Terrible it is to shed blood
Hard it is to learn to kill
Bad it is to see people die before their time
But we must learn to kill
We must see people die before their time
We must shed blood
So that no more blood will be shed.

MR. EISLER: This is a correct anti-Fascist sentiment—

THE CHAIRMAN: Mr. Stripling, do you have any more?

MR. EISLER: —written in 1929 and 1930 in Germany. And when Heydrich was killed in Prague by the Czech people, I agreed with this. He is a gangster and he killed innumerable goodhearted people. This is poetry and not reality. The difference between art and real life has to be reconsidered. Take Hollywood: At every street corner you can see the most cruel pieces of art, and you can read stories in mystery magazines that you can buy in every drugstore which are horrible. I don't like such stuff. This is a little philosophical poem directed against gangsters.

MR. RANKIN: Mr. Chairman, the American people, of course, have just whipped Hitler, but the thing that shocks me is that, while our boys were dying by the thousands over there to get Hitler's heel off their necks, some of these people come here and attempt to foment revolution in the United States. It is about time the American people woke up and put a stop to it.

THE CHAIRMAN: Mr. Eisler, the Chair wishes to direct you to remain in the United States.

MR. EISLER: I will.

THE CHAIRMAN: Until you are released by us.

MR. EISLER: Yes.

MR. STRIPLING: And have him remain for the hearings, Mr. Chairman.

THE CHAIRMAN: And be subject to a call from us at the coming hearings, which will start on October 20.

MR. EISLER: Yes. Do I have to remain in Washington? Do you need me tomorrow or another day?

THE CHAIRMAN: Do you want him any more?

MR. STRIPLING: Mr. Chairman, I would like for him to remain this afternoon, please.

THE CHAIRMAN: Stay throughout the day in Washington.

MR. EISLER: I am to stay in this room?

MR. STRIPLING: In this room.

THE CHAIRMAN: In this room.

Hanns Eisler had been given a visa to enter the United States in 1940. Among those mentioned in the Committee's records as having helped him to get this visa—in most cases by writing a testimonial to the American Consul in Havana, Cuba—are: Dorothy Thompson, Freda Kirchwey, Malcolm Cowley, Raymond Gram Swing, George Cukor, Clifford Odets, William Dieterle, Joseph Losey, and Harold Clurman. But the big document was the following letter from Caesar's wife (so to speak) to Sumner Welles, Under Secretary of State, dated January 11, 1939.

Dear Sumner: All these papers were brought to me yesterday by a friend of Mr. Eisler. The man who brought them is a perfectly honest person and very much disturbed. He thinks the State Department has really told the Cuban Consul that they do not wish to admit the Eislers, and he is perfectly sure that the Eislers are not Communists and have no political affiliations of any kind. He is sure that they believe our form of government is "heaven" and would be entirely agreeable without reservation to take an oath of allegiance.

I believe it is said that the Labor Department did not examine the case carefully enough. Why not do it all over again and bring it out in the open and let the Eislers defend themselves?

Cordially, Eleanor Roosevelt

Yet in truth Eleanor Roosevelt was so far from being above suspicion that she was suspected above everyone else. Arguably she was the principal target of HUAC in its early years. How the Committee members took aim is well illustrated by a further page in the Hanns Eisler dossier, a page which also takes in, and takes on, the New School for Social Research.

MR. RANKIN: Mr. Appell, you say this [the New School for Social Research] was a Communist school of instruction?

MR. [Donald T.] APPELL [Investigator]: No, sir, I do not say that it is a Communist school. I don't think there is any evidence in our records that would designate that it was.

MR. RANKIN: It was spreading Communist propaganda?

MR. APPELL: I can't say that the school itself—I have no evidence that the school itself, Mr. Rankin—has put out any Communist propaganda, but I know that the members of the faculty of the New School of Social Research have been checked against our files, and that a considerable number of the members of the faculty are very prominently displayed in our files.

MR. RANKIN: Do you know whether or not Mrs. Roosevelt was familiar with that situation when she urged the admission of Hanns Eisler into the United States?

MR. APPELL: I do not, sir.

MR. RANKIN: You do not know?

MR. APPELL: No, sir. My investigation dealt with the New School, and there was nothing in their file to show any connection with Mrs. Roosevelt.

MR. RANKIN: Did you read her recent article in the *Ladies' Home Journal*? *

MR. APPELL: No, sir, I haven't.

MR. RANKIN: It is the most insulting, Communistic piece of propaganda that was ever thrown in the faces of the women in America. I am just wondering if she was familiar with all of this Communist infiltration when she was trying to get Hanns Eisler into the United States.

The statement Hanns Eisler was not allowed to read to HUAC was printed in *The New Masses,* October 14, 1947, under the title, "Fantasia in G-Men." In its November 27 issue *Les Lettres Françaises* published the news that Charles Chaplin, by Mackagy Radio, had requested Pablo Picasso to form a committee in Hanns Eisler's defense. This committee had sent a strongly worded protest to the American

* Eleanor Roosevelt answered questions in a regular one-page feature of the *Ladies' Home Journal* under the title "If You Ask Me." Rankin is presumably referring to the September 1947 issue, in which Mrs. Roosevelt suggested that Southern reactionaries in Congress should be replaced by liberals. —E.B.

Embassy in Paris. The signatories included Picasso, Matisse, Cocteau, Jean-Louis Barrault, Louis Aragon, Paul Eluard, and Louis Jouvet. It has also been stated in print (though the present editor has been unable to confirm) that Thomas Mann and Albert Einstein raised their voices in behalf of Hanns Eisler.

"Communist Infiltration of the Motion-Picture Industry"

The Committee's Chief Investigator, Robert E. Stripling, wrote in *The Red Plot Against America:*

> Chairman Thomas, Representative McDowell, Investigator Louis Russell and I went to Hollywood in the Spring of 1947. Our primary task was to uncover and subpoena Hanns Eisler. With Eisler served and heard in a short executive session, we began calling in key Hollywood figures . . . we obtained enough preliminary testimony to make a public hearing imperative.

Here is reprinted evidence from five witnesses friendly to the Committee: Ayn Rand, Adolphe Menjou (1890–1963), Robert Taylor (1911–1969), Ronald Reagan, and Gary Cooper (1901–1961). Nineteen unfriendly witnesses were scheduled to appear, though eight of them did not—at any rate not in 1947. The eight who did not then appear were: Richard Collins, Gordon Kahn, Howard Koch, Lewis Milestone, Irving Pichel, Larry Parks, Robert Rossen, and Waldo Salt, three of whom (Collins, Parks, and Rossen) would later be friendly witnesses. Of the other eleven, ten stood on the First Amendment and refused to testify: they were Alvah Bessie, Herbert Biberman, Lester Cole, Edward Dmytryk, Ring Lardner, Jr., John Howard Lawson, Albert Maltz, Samuel Ornitz, Adrian Scott, Dalton Trumbo. Of these, one (Dmytryk) later became a friendly witness, while two (Lardner, Trumbo) later publicly declared themselves ex-Communists. The eleventh man was Bertolt Brecht, whose position is defined below. Since the unfriendly witnesses are referred to below as "the witnesses of Mr. Kenny and Mr. Crum," it may be well to explain that Robert W. Kenny and Bartley Crum served as counsel to these men.

OCTOBER 20, 1947:

Ayn Rand

The Committee met at 10:30 a.m., the Honorable J. Parnell Thomas (Chairman) presiding.

THE CHAIRMAN: The meeting will come to order. The record will show that the following members are present: Representatives John McDowell, Richard B. Vail, Richard M. Nixon, Mr. John S. Wood, Mr. Thomas. A Subcommittee is sitting.

Staff members present: Robert E. Stripling, Chief Investigator; Louis J. Russell, Robert B. Gaston, H. A. Smith, and A. B. Leckie, Investigators; and Benjamin Mandel, Director of Research.

MR. STRIPLING: That is A-y-n?

MISS RAND: That is right.

MR. STRIPLING: R-a-n-d?

MISS RAND: Yes.

MR. STRIPLING: Is that your pen name?

MISS RAND: Yes.

MR. STRIPLING: And what is your married name?

MISS RAND: Mrs. Frank O'Conner.

MR. STRIPLING: Where were you born, Miss Rand?

MISS RAND: In St. Petersburg, Russia.

MR. STRIPLING: When did you leave Russia?

MISS RAND: In 1926.

MR. STRIPLING: How long have you been employed in Hollywood?

MISS RAND: I have been in pictures on and off since late in 1926, but, specifically as a writer this time, I have been in Hollywood since late 1943 and am now under contract as a writer.

MR. STRIPLING: Have you written various novels?

MISS RAND: Yes, I have written two novels. My first one was called *We, the Living,* which was a story about Soviet Russia and was published in 1936. The second one was *The Fountainhead,* published in 1943.

MR. STRIPLING: Was that a best seller—*The Fountainhead*?

MISS RAND: Yes, thanks to the American public.

MR. STRIPLING: Do you know how many copies were sold?

MISS RAND: The last I heard was three hundred sixty thousand copies. I think there have been some more since.

MR. STRIPLING: You have been employed as a writer in Hollywood?

MISS RAND: Yes, I am under contract at present.

MR. STRIPLING: Could you name some of the stories or scripts you have written for Hollywood?

MISS RAND: I have done the script of *The Fountainhead,* which has not been produced yet, for Warner Brothers, and two adaptations for Hal Wallis Productions, at Paramount, which were not my stories but of which I did the screenplays, which were *Love Letters* and *You Came Along.*

MR. STRIPLING: Now, Miss Rand, you have heard the testimony of Mr. [Louis B.] Mayer?

MISS RAND: Yes.

MR. STRIPLING: You have read the letter I read from Lowell Mellett?

MISS RAND: Yes.

MR. STRIPLING: Which says that the picture *Song of Russia* has no political implications?

MISS RAND: Yes.

MR. STRIPLING: Did you at the request of Mr. Smith, the Investigator for this Committee, view the picture *Song of Russia*?

MISS RAND: Yes.

MR. STRIPLING: Within the past two weeks?

MISS RAND: Yes, on October 13, to be exact.

MR. STRIPLING: In Hollywood?

MISS RAND: Yes.

MR. STRIPLING: Would you give the Committee a breakdown of your summary of the picture relating to either propaganda or an untruthful account or distorted account of conditions in Russia?

MISS RAND: Yes. First of all, I would like to define what we mean by propaganda. We have all been talking about it, but nobody has stated just what they mean by propaganda. Now, I use the term to mean that Communist propaganda is anything which gives a good impression of Communism as a way of life. Anything that sells people the idea that life in Russia is good and that people are free and happy would be Communist propaganda. Am I not correct? Now, here is what the picture *Song of Russia* contains. It starts with an American conductor, played by Robert Taylor, giving a concert in America for Russian war relief. He starts playing the American national anthem and the national anthem dissolves into a Russian mob, with the sickle and hammer on a red flag very prominent above their heads. I am sorry, but that made me sick. That is something which I do not see how native Americans permit, and I am only a naturalized American. That was a terrible touch of propaganda. As a writer, I can tell you just exactly what it suggests to the people. It suggests literally and technically that it is quite all right for the American national anthem to dissolve into the Soviet. The term here is more than just technical. It really was symbolically intended, and it worked out that way. The anthem continues, played by a Soviet band. That is the beginning of the picture. Now we go to the pleasant love story. Mr. Taylor is an American who came there apparently voluntarily to conduct concerts for the Soviet. He meets a little Russian girl from a village who comes to him and begs him to go to her village to direct concerts there. There are no GPU agents and nobody stops her. She just comes to Moscow and meets him. He falls for her and decides he will go, because he is falling in love. He asks her to show him Moscow. She says she has never seen it. He says, "I will show it to you." They see it together. The picture then goes into a scene of Moscow, supposedly. I don't know where the studio got its shots, but I have never seen anything like it in Russia. First you see Moscow buildings—big, prosperous-looking, clean buildings, with something like swans or sailboats in the foreground. Then you see a Moscow restaurant that just never existed there. In my time, when I was in Russia, there was only one such restaurant, which was nowhere as luxurious as that and no one could enter it except commissars and profiteers. Certainly a girl from a village, who in the first place would never have been allowed to come voluntarily, without permission, to Moscow, could not afford to enter it, even if she worked ten years. However, there is a Russian restaurant with a menu such as never existed in Russia at all and which I doubt even existed before the revolution. From this restaurant they go on to this tour of Moscow. The streets are clean and prosperous-looking. There are no food lines anywhere. You see shots of the marble subway—the famous Russian subway out of which they make such propaganda capital. There is a marble statue of Stalin thrown in. There is a park where you see happy little children in white blouses running around. I don't know whose children they are, but they are really happy kiddies. They are not homeless children in rags, such as I have seen in Russia. Then you see an excursion boat, on which the Russian people are smiling, sitting around very cheerfully, dressed in some sort of satin blouses such as they only wear in Russian restaurants here. Then they attend a luxurious dance. I don't know where they got the idea of the clothes and the settings that they used at the ball and—

MR. STRIPLING: Is that a ballroom scene?

MISS RAND: Yes, I have never seen anybody wearing such clothes and dancing to such exotic music when I was there. Now, after this tour of Moscow, the hero—the American conductor—goes to the Soviet village. The Russian villages are something—so miserable and so filthy. They were even before the revolution. What they have become now I am afraid to think. You have all read about the program for the collectivization of the farms in 1933, at which time the Soviet government admits that three million peasants died of starvation. Other people claim there were seven and a half million, but three million is the figure admitted by the Soviet government as the figure of people who died of starvation, planned by the government in order to drive people into collective farms. That is a recorded historical fact. Now, here is the life in the Soviet village as presented in *Song of Russia*: You see the happy peasants. You see they are meeting the hero at the station with bands, with beautiful blouses and shoes, such as they never wore anywhere. You see children with operetta costumes on them and with a brass band which they could never afford. You see the manicured starlets driving tractors and the happy women who come from work singing. You see a peasant at home, with a close-up of food for which anyone there would have been murdered. If anybody had such food in Russia in that time he couldn't remain alive, because he would have been torn apart by neighbors trying to get food. But here is a close-up of it and a line where Robert Taylor comments on the food and the peasant answers, "This is just a simple country table and the food we eat ourselves." Then the peasant proceeds to show Taylor how they live. He shows him his wonderful tractor. It is parked somewhere in his private garage. He shows him the grain in his bin, and Taylor says, "That is wonderful grain." Now, it is never said that the peasant does not own this tractor or this grain because it is a collective farm. He couldn't have it. It is not his. But the impression he gives to Americans, who wouldn't know any differently, is that certainly it is this peasant's private property, and that is how he lives, he has his own tractor and his own grain. Then it shows miles and miles of plowed fields.

MR. STRIPLING: Miss Rand, may I bring up one point there? At this peasant's village or home was there a priest or several priests in evidence?

MISS RAND: Oh, yes, I am coming to that, too. The priest was from the beginning in the village scenes, having a position as sort of a constant companion and friend of the peasants, as if religion was a natural accepted part of that life. Well, now, as a matter of fact, the situation about religion in Russia in my time was—and I understand it still is—that for a Communist Party member to have anything to do with religion means expulsion from the Party. To continue with the story, Robert Taylor proposes to the heroine. She accepts him. They have a wedding, which, of course, is a church wedding. It takes place with all the religious pomp which they show. They have a banquet. They have dancers, in something like satin skirts and performing ballets such as you never could possibly see in any village and certainly not in Russia. Later they show a peasants' meeting place, which is a kind of marble palace with crystal chandeliers. Where they got it or who built it for them I would like to be told. Then later you see that the peasants all have radios. When the heroine plays as a soloist with Robert Taylor's orchestra, after she marries him, you see a scene where all the peasants are listening on radios, and one of them says, "There are more than millions listening to the concert." I don't know whether there are a hundred people in Russia—private individuals—who own radios. And I remember reading in the newspaper at the beginning of the war that every radio was seized by the government and people were not allowed to own them. Such an idea that every farmer, a poor peasant, has a radio, is certainly preposterous.

You also see that they have long-distance telephones. Later in the picture Taylor has to call his wife in the village by long-distance telephone. Where they got this long-distance phone, I don't know.

Now, here comes the crucial point of the picture. In the midst of this concert, when the heroine is playing you see a scene on the border of the U.S.S.R. You have a very lovely modernistic sign saying U.S.S.R. I would just like to remind you that that is the border where probably thousands of people have died trying to escape out of this lovely paradise. It shows the U.S.S.R. sign, and there is a border guard standing. He is listening to the concert. Then there is a scene inside kind of a guardhouse where the guards are listening to the same concert, the beautiful Tchaikovsky music, and they are playing chess. Suddenly there is a Nazi attack on them. The poor, sweet Russians were unprepared. Now, realize—and that was a great shock to me—that the border that was being shown was the border of Poland. That was the border of an occupied, destroyed, enslaved country which Hitler and Stalin destroyed together. That was the border that was being shown to us—just a happy place with people listening to music. Also realize that when all this sweetness and light was going on in the first part of the picture, with all these happy, free people, there was not a GPU agent among them, with no food lines, no persecution—complete freedom and happiness, with everybody smiling. Incidentally, I have never seen so much smiling in my life, except on the murals of the World's Fair pavilion of the Soviet. If any one of you have seen it, you can appreciate it. It is one of the stock propaganda tricks of the Communists, to show these people smiling. That is all they can show. You have all this, plus the fact that an American conductor had accepted an invitation to come there and conduct a concert, and this took place in 1941, when Stalin was the ally of Hitler.

Now, then, the heroine decides that she wants to stay in Russia. Taylor would like to take her out of the country, but she says no, her place is here, she has to fight the war. Here is the line, as nearly exact as I could mark it while watching the picture: "I have a great responsibility to my family, to my village, and to the way I have lived." What way had she lived? This is just a polite way of saying the Communist way of life. She goes on to say that she wants to stay in the country because otherwise, "How can I help to build a better and better life for my country." What do you mean when you say "better and better"? That means she has already helped to build a good way. That is the Soviet Communist way. But now she wants to make it even better. All right. Now, then, Taylor's manager, who is played, I believe, by [Robert] Benchley, an American, tells her that she should leave the country, but when she refuses and wants to stay, here is the line he uses: He tells her in an admiring friendly way that "You are a fool, but a lot of fools like you died on the village green at Lexington." Now, I submit that that is blasphemy, because the men at Lexington were not fighting just a foreign invader. They were fighting for freedom, and what I mean—and I intend to be exact—is they were fighting for political freedom and individual freedom. They were fighting for the rights of man. To compare them to somebody, anybody, fighting for a slave state, I think is dreadful. Then, later, the girl also says—I believe this was she or one of the other characters—that "the culture we have been building here will never die." What culture? The culture of concentration camps.

At the end of the picture one of the Russians asks Taylor and the girl to go back to America, because they can help them there. How? Here is what he says: "You can go back to your country and tell them what you have seen and you will see the truth both in speech and in music." Now, that is plainly saying that what you have seen is the truth about Russia.

Now, here is what I cannot understand at all: If the excuse that has been given here is that we had to produce the picture in wartime, just how can it help the war effort? If it is to deceive the American people, if it were to present to the American people a better picture of Russia than it really is, then that sort of attitude is nothing but the theory of the Nazi elite, that a choice group of intellectual or other leaders will tell the people lies for their own good. That I don't think is the American way of giving people information. We do not have to deceive the people at any time, in war or peace. If it was to please the Russians, I don't see how you can please the Russians by telling them that we are fools. To what extent we have done it, you can see right now. You can see the results right now. If we present a picture like that as our version of what goes on in Russia, what will they think of it? We don't win anybody's friendship. We will only win their contempt, and as you know the Russians have been behaving like this. My whole point about the picture is this: I fully believe Mr. Mayer when he says that he did not make a Communist picture. To do him justice, I can tell you I noticed, by watching the picture, where there was an effort to cut propaganda out. I believe he tried to cut propaganda out of the picture, but the terrible thing is the carelessness with ideas, not realizing that the mere presentation of that kind of happy existence in a country of slavery and horror is terrible because it is propaganda.

* * *

MR. WOOD: Do you think that it was to our advantage or to our disadvantage to keep Russia in this war, at the time this picture was made?

MISS RAND: That has absolutely nothing to do with what we are discussing.

MR. WOOD: Well—

MISS RAND: But if you want me to answer, I can answer, but it will take me a long time to say what I think, as to whether we should or should not have had Russia on our side in the war. I can, but how much time will you give me?

MR. WOOD: Well, do you say that it would have prolonged the war, so far as we were concerned, if they had been knocked out of it at that time?

MISS RAND: I can't answer that yes or no, unless you give me time for a long speech on it.

MR. WOOD: Well, there is a pretty strong probability that we wouldn't have won it at all, isn't there?

MISS RAND: I don't know, I think we could have used the lend-lease supplies that we sent there to much better advantage ourselves.

MR. WOOD: We were furnishing Russia with all the lend-lease equipment that our industry would stand, weren't we?

MISS RAND: That is right.

MR. WOOD: And continued to do it?

MISS RAND: I am not sure it was at all wise. Now, if you want to discuss my military views—I am not an authority, but I will try.

MR. WOOD: What do you interpret, then, the picture as having been made for?

MISS RAND: I ask you: What relation could a lie about Russia have with the war effort? I would like to have somebody explain that to me, because I really don't understand it, why a lie would help anybody or why it would keep Russia in or out of the war. How?

MR. WOOD: You don't think it would have been of benefit to the American people to have kept them in?

MISS RAND: I don't believe the American people should ever be told any lies, publicly or privately. I don't believe that lies are practical. I think the international situation now rather supports me. I don't think it was necessary to deceive the American people about the nature of Russia. I could add this: If those who saw it say it was quite all right, and perhaps there are reasons why it was all right to be an ally of Russia, then why weren't the American people told the real reasons and told that Russia is a dictatorship but there are reasons why we should cooperate with them to destroy Hitler and other dictators? All right, there may be some argument to that. Let us hear it. But of what help can it be to the war effort to tell people that we should associate with Russia and that she is not a dictatorship?

MR. WOOD: Let me see if I understand your position. I understand, from what you say, that because they were a dictatorship we shouldn't have accepted their help in undertaking to win a war against another dictatorship.

MISS RAND: That is not what I said. I was not in a position to make that decision. If I were, I would tell you what I would do. That is not what we are discussing. We are discussing the fact that our country was an ally of Russia, and the question is, What should we tell the American people about it—the truth or a lie? If we had good reason, if that is what you believe, all right, then why not tell the truth? Say it is a dictatorship, but we want to be associated with it. Say it is worthwhile being associated with the devil, as Churchill said, in order to defeat another evil which is Hitler. There might be some good argument made for that. But why pretend that Russia was not what it was?

MR. WOOD: Do you think it would have had as good an effect upon the morale of the American people to preach a doctrine to them that Russia was on the verge of collapse?

MISS RAND: I don't believe that the morale of anybody can be built up by a lie. If there was nothing good that we could truthfully say about Russia, then it would have been better not to say anything at all.

MR. WOOD: Well—

MISS RAND: You don't have to come out and denounce Russia during the war, no. You can keep quiet. There is no moral guilt in not saying something if you can't say it, but there is in saying the opposite of what is true.

MR. MCDOWELL: You paint a very dismal picture of Russia. You made a great point about the number of children who were unhappy. Doesn't anybody smile in Russia any more?

MISS RAND: Well, if you ask me literally, pretty much no.

MR. MCDOWELL: They don't smile?

MISS RAND: Not quite that way, no. If they do, it is privately and accidentally. Certainly, it is not social. They don't smile in approval of their system.

MR. MCDOWELL: Well, all they do is talk about food.

MISS RAND: That is right.

MR. MCDOWELL: That is a great change from the Russians I have always known, and I have known a lot of them. Don't they do things at all like Americans? Don't they walk across town to visit their mother-in-law or somebody?

MISS RAND: It is almost impossible to convey to a free people what it is like to live in a totalitarian dictatorship. I can tell you a lot of details. I can never completely convince you, because you are free. It is in a way good that you can't even conceive of what it is like. Certainly they have friends and mothers-in-law. They try to live a human life, but, you understand, it is totally inhuman. Try to imagine what it is like if you are in constant terror from morning till night and at night you are waiting for the doorbell to ring, where you are afraid of anything and everybody, living in a country where human life is nothing, less than nothing, and you know it. You don't know who or when is going to do what to you because you may have friends who spy on you, where there is no law and any rights of any kind.

MR. MCDOWELL: You came here in 1926, I believe you said. Did you escape from Russia?

MISS RAND: No.

MR. MCDOWELL: Did you have a passport?

MISS RAND: No. Strangely enough, they gave me a passport to come out here as a visitor.

MR. MCDOWELL: As a visitor?

MISS RAND: It was at a time when they relaxed their orders a little bit. Quite a few people got out. I had some relatives here and I was permitted to come here for a year. I never went back.

MR. MCDOWELL: I see.

THE CHAIRMAN: Mr. Nixon?

MR. NIXON: No questions.

OCTOBER 21, 1947:

Adolphe Menjou

The Committee met at 10:30 a.m., the Honorable J. Parnell Thomas (Chairman) presiding.

THE CHAIRMAN: The record will show that a Subcommittee is present, consisting of Mr. McDowell, Mr. Vail, Mr. Nixon, Mr. Wood, and Mr. Thomas.

Staff members present: Mr. Robert E. Stripling, Chief Investigator; Messrs. Louis J. Russell, Robert B. Gaston, H. A. Smith, Investigators; and Mr. Benjamin Mandel, Director of Research.

MR. STRIPLING: Mr. Menjou, what is your occupation?

MR. MENJOU: I am a motion-picture actor, I hope.

MR. STRIPLING: When and where were you born, Mr. Menjou?

MR. MENJOU: I was born in Pittsburgh, Pennsylvania, February 18, 1890.

MR. STRIPLING: How long have you been in the motion-picture industry?

MR. MENJOU: Thirty-four years.

MR. STRIPLING: And how long have you been in Hollywood?

MR. MENJOU: Twenty-seven years.

MR. STRIPLING: Mr. Menjou, were you in the First World War?

MR. MENJOU: Yes, sir.

MR. STRIPLING: In the armed services?

MR. MENJOU: Yes, sir. I served abroad for two years. I was in the Army three years, one year in America. I served in Italy, with the Italian Army, being attached to the Italian Army; attached to the French Army; and with the Fifth Division until the surrender on November 11, 1918.

MR. STRIPLING: Were you in World War II?

MR. MENJOU: I served six months with the U.S. Camp Shows, Inc., entertaining troops—for four months in England, two months in North Africa, Sicily, Tunisia, Algeria, Morocco, Brazil, and the Caribbean.

MR. STRIPLING: Mr. Menjou, have you made a study of the subject of Communism, the activities of the Communists, in any particular field in the United States?

MR. MENJOU: I have. I have made a more particular study of Marxism, Fabian Socialism, Communism, Stalinism, and its probable effects on the American people if they ever gain power here.

MR. STRIPLING: Based upon your study, have you observed any Communist activity in the motion-picture industry or in Hollywood, as we commonly refer to it?

MR. MENJOU: I would like to get the terminologies completely straight. Communistic activities—I would rather phrase it un-American or subversive, anti-free enterprise, anticapitalistic.

MR. STRIPLING: Have you observed any Communist propaganda in pictures, or un-American propaganda in pictures which were produced in Hollywood?

MR. MENJOU: I have seen no Communistic propaganda in pictures—if you mean "Vote for Stalin," or that type of Communistic propaganda. I don't think that the Communists are stupid enough to try it that way. I have seen in certain pictures things I didn't think should have been in the pictures.

MR. STRIPLING: Could you tell the Committee whether or not there has been an effort on the part of any particular group in the motion-picture industry to inject Communist propaganda into pictures or to leave out scenes or parts of stories which would serve the Communist Party line?

MR. MENJOU: I don't like that term "Communist propaganda," because I have seen no such thing as Communist propaganda, such as waving the hammer and sickle in motion pictures. I have seen things that I thought were against what I considered good Americanism, in my feeling. I have seen pictures I thought shouldn't have been made.

MR. STRIPLING: Mr. Menjou, do you have any particular pictures in mind?

MR. MENJOU: Well, I wonder if I could preface it by a short statement?

MR. STRIPLING: Yes, if you please.

MR. MENJOU: I am not here to smear. I am here to defend the industry that I have spent the greater part of my life in. I am here to defend the producers and the motion-picture industry. Now, you wanted me to name a picture?

THE CHAIRMAN: I want to say that the Committee is, also, not here to smear the industry or to smear people working in the industry. The Committee wants to get the facts, and only the facts. We are going to hear both sides of all of these questions. We want to make it very clear that the Committee is not out to censor the screen. Proceed, Mr. Menjou.

MR. MENJOU: Will you repeat the question, please?

MR. STRIPLING: Yes. Well, we will approach it this way. We have had testimony here to the effect that writers who were members of the Screen Writers Guild have attempted to inject un-American propaganda into motion pictiures. Are you aware that that is the case, or has been the case, in Hollywood at any time?

MR. MENJOU: I don't think that I am competent to answer that question. If you want to ask me if I know of any un-American propaganda in any pictures that I appeared in, I will be glad to give you my thoughts.

MR. STRIPLING: Will you give an example?

MR. MENJOU: I don't think the picture *Mission to Moscow* should have been made. It was a perfectly completely dishonest picture. If it was to have been an adaptation of the book by Mr. [Joseph E.] Davies it should have included the entire story in Moscow, including the Moscow trials where Mr. Davies was a witness and over which Mr. Vishinsky presided. That was not in the picture. Therefore, I consider that a completely dishonest picture and distortion of the adaptation of the book. I also do not think that the picture *North Star* was a true picture, from what I have been able to learn after reading over a hundred and fifty books on the subject. This was a picture showing the German attack on the Russians, and certain parts of it were not true. I thought that picture would have been better unmade. Fortunately, those pictures were unsuccessful.

MR. STRIPLING: As a generality, would you say that the more entertaining the picture is, the better opportunity there might be to put across propaganda?

MR. MENJOU: Yes. The better the entertainment the more dangerous the propaganda becomes, once it is injected into the picture.

MR. STRIPLING: Do you know of any anti-Communist pictures that are being produced in Hollywood at the present time?

MR. MENJOU: No, sir, I do not. And I would like to see one. I think the producers of anti-Fascist pictures should turn around and make an anti-Communist picture. I believe it would be an enormous success, if it were made.

MR. STRIPLING: Mr. Menjou, if a picture is produced, as for example *Mission to Moscow,* which gives a false portrayal or which has propaganda in it, who do you hold responsible in your own mind as a veteran actor in the motion-picture industry?

MR. MENJOU: Well, I believe that the manufacturer of any product is responsible in the end for the quality of his product.

MR. STRIPLING: In other words, the producers would be held responsible?

MR. MENJOU: They should be.

MR. STRIPLING: What do you think could be done to correct that?

MR. MENJOU: I think a great deal already has been done. The eternal vigilance of the Motion Picture Alliance for the Preservation of American Ideals, by its vigilance, has prevented an enormous amount of sly, subtle, un-American class-struggle propaganda from going into pictures.

MR. STRIPLING: Do you consider that the Alliance is doing a good job —that is, has been doing a good job?

MR. MENJOU: I think they have done a magnificent job, and I am very proud to be a member of the board of directors.

MR. STRIPLING: Are you a member of the Screen Actors Guild?

MR. MENJOU: Yes, sir, I am.

MR. STRIPLING: Have you ever noticed any effort on the part of Communist individuals to gain influence in the Screen Actors Guild?

MR. MENJOU: I don't know any members of the Screen Actors Guild who are members of the Communist Party. I have never seen their cards. I am a firm believer that the Communist Party in the United States is a direct branch of the Comintern—which, in my opinion, has never been dissolved —direct from Moscow. It is an Oriental tyranny, a Kremlin-dominated conspiracy, and it is against the interests of the people to admit that they are Communists. Very few admit it.

MR. STRIPLING: Do you have your very definite suspicions about some members of the Screen Actors Guild?

MR. MENJOU: I know a great many people who act an awful lot like Communists.

MR. STRIPLING: As an actor, Mr. Menjou, could you tell the Committee whether or not an actor in a picture could portray a scene which would in effect serve as propaganda for Communism or any other un-American purpose?

MR. MENJOU: Oh, yes. I believe that under certain circumstances a Communistic director, a Communistic writer, or a Communistic actor, even if he were under orders from the head of the studio not to inject Communism or un-Americanism or subversion into pictures, could easily subvert that order, under the proper circumstances, by a look, by an inflection, by a change in the voice. I have never seen it done, but I think it could be done.

MR. STRIPLING: You don't know of any examples?

MR. MENJOU: I cannot think of one at the moment, no, sir.

MR. STRIPLING: Do you know Mr. John Cromwell?

MR. MENJOU: Yes, sir.

MR. STRIPLING: He was identified before the Committee yesterday by Mr. Sam Wood as being one who sought to put the Screen Directors Guild into the Red river. Do you consider Mr. Cromwell to be a Communist?

MR. MENJOU: I don't know whether he is a Communist or not.

MR. STRIPLING: Does he act like one?

Mr. Menjou: In my opinion, he acts an awful lot like one.

Mr. Stripling: Did he ever make any statement to you relative to his—

Mr. Menjou: Mr. Cromwell, in his own house, said to me that capitalism in America was through and I would see the day when it was ended in America. A very strange statement from a man who earns upwards of two hundred and fifty thousand dollars a year, who owns a great deal of Los Angeles and Hollywood real estate. It is rather difficult to reconcile that. He is profiting by the capitalistic system, and yet he is against it. He told me so with his own lips.

Mr. Stripling: Mr. Menjou, what have been your observations regarding Communist activity in Hollywood in the past ten years? We received testimony yesterday that their activity increased after 1936.

Mr. Menjou: Well, I became very much interested as to what socialism was during the last war, when I was stationed in the birthplace of Karl Marx with the Fifth Division. It interested me greatly. I did a considerable amount of reading. I tried to wade through *Das Kapital*. It was a very difficult job. I read the Max Eastman condensation of it. When I got to California later, we heard very, very little about it. Socialism at that time was spoken of. It had very few followers in this country. About 1932 or 1933, when the Russian question began to loom in the picture, with the mass starvations of the poor Russian peasants because they would not conform to the demands of Mr. Stalin—why, they shocked the world with the testimony of some of the witnesses. Then, later on, identified by various committees, groups began to be formed, which have been labeled, and I think documented, as being Communistic-front organizations. I particularly refer to the Independent Citizens Committee of the Arts, Sciences, and Professions. This was labeled a Communist-front organization. I understand that at a meeting of the board of directors it refused to make an anti-Communist statement, that they were anti-Communist, whereupon there were wholesale desertions. One of the first was the son of the president, Mr. James Roosevelt. He left the thing just prior to the elections. Then there were many, many other people who left. Those people who still remained in it, in my opinion, would be pro-Communist. I do not understand any other reason for a person belonging to an organization in which he knew Communists were in and were dominating. Then the PCA [Political Action Committee] was formed. It also refused to come out with an anti-Communist platform, whereupon the ADA, the Americans for Democratic Action, was formed, I believe by Mrs. Roosevelt, Leon Henderson, Melvyn Douglas, and some other people. They do not permit Communists in their organization, I understand.

Mr. Stripling: Yes. Now, these various front organizations which have sprung up in Hollywood—

Mr. Menjou: There is the American Youth for Democracy, which is the new name for the Young Communist League. I am not an expert on the organizations here in America, although I have a list of names here which I have gathered and will be glad to produce.

MR. STRIPLING: The Committee has evidence that innumerable Communist-front organizations mushroom in Hollywood. We received testimony yesterday from Mr. Wood to the effect that they set up an organization, and after they milk it dry they form another one. In the Screen Actors Guild, have there ever been any resolutions offered by any of the members which had as their purpose to aid these front organizations?

MR. MENJOU: I think a member of the board of directors would be far more capable of answering that question than myself.

MR. STRIPLING: Yes. Mr. Chairman, we will have officials of the Screen Actors Guild before the Committee later in the week. As a student of Communism, did you note an increased alliance with the Communists in Hollywood during the period of the war emergency, when we had a military allied relationship with the Soviet Union?

MR. MENJOU: Well, I spent practically seven months out of every year after Pearl Harbor away, and I was not in Hollywood most of that time. I find it rather difficult to answer that question.

MR. STRIPLING: Would you say that Communist activity increased?

MR. MENJOU: Oh, yes.

MR. STRIPLING: In Hollywood after Pearl Harbor, 1941? Was it intensified?

MR. MENJOU: It was intensified with the nonaggression pact between Mr. Molotov and Mr. Von Ribbentrop.

MR. STRIPLING: Do you recall some of the figures in Hollywood who were very active in the American Peace Mobilization during the period?

MR. MENJOU: I do not. I am not familiar with that part of the picture at all.

MR. STRIPLING: Would you say the Communists in Hollywood follow the party line, directions laid down by Moscow?

MR. MENJOU: Rigidly.

MR. STRIPLING: It is requested in all of their activities there?

MR. MENJOU: Yes, sir.

MR. STRIPLING: Could you elaborate on that point any, Mr. Menjou?

MR. MENJOU: I am trying to think how I can help you. We have had a very disastrous strike in Hollywood, and a very long one. It has been going on now for more than a year. Mr. [Herbert K.] Sorrell is the head of the organization whose members are out on strike. I believe that Mr. Sorrell is a member of the Communist Party under the name of Herbert K. Stewart. I have a photostatic copy of the purported Communist card and the sworn testimony of Mr. Sellers, admittedly the world's greatest handwriting expert. Based on the fact, I believe, that Mr. Sorrell is a Communist, I would be very suspicious of any of the people who either stood on a platform with him or supported any of his activities or statements. This strike was a particularly bloody strike.

MR. STRIPLING: Could the Committee have that photostat?

MR. MENJOU: Yes, sir.

MR. STRIPLING: Do you know of some of the actors or other people who are prominent in the motion-picture industry who did associate with Mr. Sorrell in his activities?

MR. MENJOU: I attended a meeting of the entire membership of the Screen Actors Guild. I am not too certain of this date, but it might have been a year ago. The meeting was called in order to try to settle the strike. Now, the board of directors of the Screen Actors Guild had exerted all of their efforts to settle this strike in every way possible. I think a magnificent job was done by the board of directors, particularly Mr. [Ronald] Reagan, the president. After long, long deliberations and trips to Chicago and everywhere else, they finally came to the conclusion that it was a jurisdictional strike and could have been settled, but Mr. Sorrell did not want to settle it. That was the conclusion made. This meeting was called by a group of three hundred fifty people. I think that is the necessary amount, according to our bylaws, to call such a meeting. Mr. Reagan spoke for, I think, more than an hour and a half, explaining the position and the work and the labors that he had gone through to try to determine who was right or who was wrong, because there was an effort to call all the actors out on strike, which would have thrown some thirty-odd thousand people out of work. Now, then, that particular evening the opposition wanted to be heard. Mr. Sorrell spoke. Following Mr. Sorrell appeared Mr. Edward G. Robinson, Mr. [Hume] Cronyn, Mr. Alexander Knox, and Mr. Paul Henreid. They all admitted what a wonderful job Mr. Reagan had done, but they wanted the strike settled on Mr. Sorrell's side, which, in my opinion, would have meant more trouble, more chaos, and no solution to the trouble, excepting that the unions would have been under the complete domination of the Communist Party. I think sanity prevailed. There was a motion presented by myself that the membership stand by its duly elected board of directors, which was majority voted, and the meeting was over. Now, I personally would never have been seen with Mr. Sorrell if I could help it. He is responsible for the most incredible brutality—beatings, the overturning of cars on private property in front of the Warner Brothers studio, shocking parades, where one man almost lost an eye in front of the M-G-M studio—a most outrageous performance and violation of the picketing laws in California. I think he did everything possible to embarrass the producers. I don't believe the Communist Party has any intention of ever having any peace of any kind, and I would regret the day that a man of Mr. Sorrell's characteristics should ever be in charge of the labor unions in California. God help us if he ever does!

MR. STRIPLING: Do you know Mr. John Howard Lawson?

MR. MENJOU: I do not.

MR. STRIPLING: Have you ever heard a charge that he was head of the Communist Party in Hollywood?

MR. MENJOU: Yes, sir.

MR. STRIPLING: He directed their affairs?

MR. MENJOU: I have heard that, but I cannot testify to it, because I do not know.

MR. STRIPLING: Do you know whether or not he participated in the picket line at Warner Brothers studio, when the cars were overturned?

MR. MENJOU: I do not know that; I am sorry.

MR. STRIPLING: Mr. Menjou, what do you think is the best way to go about combating Communism in Hollywood?

MR. MENJOU: Well, I think a great deal already has been done. The first meeting of this Committee has already alerted many apathetic people, many people who are not aware of the incredibly serious menace that faces America. They don't take the trouble to read. I am sure that some of my fellow actors who have attacked this Committee and myself, had they taken the time to read and study, would be of exactly the same opinion as I am. I believe that ninety-five per cent of the people in California are decent, honest American citizens. The Communist Party is a minority, but a dangerous minority. I believe that the entire nation should be alerted to its menace today. In my opinion, the Comintern has never been dissolved and the new Cominform which meets in Belgrade is simply an opening. No one seems to know why they have come out into the open. They have always been underground before. The proof that they are in existence is the letter Mr. DuBois [Jacques Duclos], the pastry cook, one of the heads of the Communist Party, wrote to the Communist Party in New York, which was published in the *Daily Worker*. It forced Mr. Browder, the former head of the Communist Party, out of the party. Presumably Mr. Browder had no trouble getting a passport to go to Moscow and returned to represent the Communist book trust in New York. I don't think anybody is being fooled by this. But the American people are not alert. If a Gallup poll in California shows that fifty per cent of the people have never heard of the Taft-Hartley bill, you can imagine how apathetic and how ignorant most of them are of this subject. I have a list of books here—I published a list of over thirty-five books—and if you will bear with me and if I have the time I would like to read a list of books which I would advise every man, woman, and child in America to read. They will then get a picture of this Oriental tyranny, this Communist-dominated conspiracy to take the world over by force. It will take the words out of Mr. Lenin's mouth, out of Mr. Stalin's mouth. Mr. Molotov is a member of the Politburo. Mr. Vishinsky I consider simply a puppet. First, I would like to ask them to read *Das Kapital,* by Karl Marx; then the Max Eastman condensation; then a magnificent book called *The Red Prussian* [by

Leopold Schwarzschild]; *The Dream We Lost,* by Fred A. [Freda] Utley; *Report on Russians,* by Paul Winiton, who spent fourteen years in Moscow as a correspondent; *Towards Soviet America,* by William Z. Foster, present head of the Communist Party in America, where on page 275 he advocates the liquidation of the American Legion, the Rotary clubs, all fraternal organizations, arming of the farmers and arming of the workers, with a dictatorship of the proletariat to take America over by force. That is page 275 of *Towards Soviet America.* You will have trouble getting the book. You will have to advertise for it. *Yogi and the Commissar,* by Arthur Koestler, one of the magnificent writers living today who was a Communist member of the Party. He spent a great deal of time in Russia. *Dark Side of the Moon.* I defy anyone to read that without being frightened to death. That is a documentary testimony, edited by T. S. Eliot, of the 1,750,000 estimated, innocent Polish people taken into concentration camps by the Russians in early 1939. The three books by Mr. [David J.] Dallin, particularly his book, which will be in *Look* magazine, *Slave Labor in Communist Russia.* Over at Uncle Joe's,* a magnificent book [by Oriana Atkinson]; *Russian Report,* by William White; *I Chose Freedom,* by Victor Kravchenko; *One Who Survived* [by Alexandre Barmine]; *Why They Behave Like Russians,* by [J.] Fischer; *In Search of Soviet Gold,* by [John D.] Littlepage; and one of the best books of all, *Pattern for World Revolution,* written anonymously. This is only a very, very small list of books, but I guarantee you that anyone that reads them will fear for the safety of America.

MR. STRIPLING: Mr. Menjou, yesterday Mr. Sam Wood testified that he considered members of the Communist Party in this country to be the agents of a foreign principal. Do you share that opinion with Mr. Wood?

MR. MENJOU: The members of the Communist Party in the United States unquestionably, in my mind, are agents of the Comintern in Moscow, or the Cominform in Belgrade, or wherever it is. The papers found, on—I think it was—Professor [Alan Nunn] May, who is now in jail, the Polish-born member of the Canadian Parliament, would prove to me conclusively that the Comintern has never stopped working.

MR. STRIPLING: Do you consider that the Communist Party members in this country are engaged in treasonable activities?

MR. MENJOU: Definitely.

MR. STRIPLING: Mr. Menjou, this Committee also has a legislative function as well as an investigative function. During this session there were two bills introduced which sought to outlaw the Communist Party. Do you think that the Communist Party should be outlawed by legislation?

MR. MENJOU: I believe that the Communist Party in the United States should be outlawed by the Congress of the United States. It is not a political

* Actually, *Forced Labor in Soviet Russia* by David J. Dallin and Boris I. Nicolaevsky. —E.B.

party. It is a conspiracy to take over our Government by force, which would enslave the American people, as the Soviet government—fourteen members of the Politburo—hold the Russian people in abject slavery.

MR. STRIPLING: Mr. Menjou, there has been quite a bit said and written in the Communist publications and certain left-wing organizations have circulated pamphlets to the effect that this Committee is trying to bring about thought control.

MR. MENJOU: Well, I also have heard many other words—"witch-hunting." I am a witch-hunter if the witches are Communists. I am a Red-baiter. I make no bones about it whatsoever. I would like to see them all back in Russia. I think a taste of Russia would cure many of them. Unfortunately, people in Europe who have not faced the Russians do not realize the method. That is one of the great troubles in France. They are faced with French Communists and not Russians. All of those nations—Rumania, Bulgaria, Hungary, Austria, the Russian zone in Germany—that have had to come in contact with the Russian Army realize what a menace this is. There would have been much more of an overwhelming vote for General de Gaulle if these people realized it. They don't realize it. They don't read. They don't study. The masses of Russian officers who have come to the American headquarters and asked how they can get into America! The escape of the Russian general who is now in Buenos Aires! The capture of the young senior lieutenant who tried to commit suicide rather than to return to his country! With the hundreds of suicides of those who faced return there, I think it is shocking that the United States should ever return anybody to the Soviet Union.

MR. STRIPLING: Mr. Menjou, yesterday there was placed in the record the salaries of three writers who were employed in the motion-picture industry, whose salaries exceeded seventy thousand dollars per year. They had been identified as Communists, and the Committee had records concerning these three men. How do you account for a person who would have such an income subscribing to the Communist philosophy?

MR. MENJOU: Well, Frederick Engels, who supported Karl Marx his entire life, was a millionaire. He had a very large textile factory in Germany and a very large one in England. We find crackpots everywhere. We have in California what I call the lunatic fringe, the political idiots, the morons, the dangerous Communists, and those who have yet to be convinced. I don't accuse anybody, because we are curing people every day. There has been an amazing change in Hollywood in the attitude of many people since this Committee has started to function and also due to the activities of the Motion Picture Alliance. These people only have to be told and have to see. The only dangerous one is the hard, disciplined core of the Communist Party themselves. These people I do not know. I have never seen one. The only Communist I ever met was Mr. Maisky, the [Russian] Ambassador to

London, and I fear he has either been liquidated or shunted off somewhere for some deviation. His name has disappeared completely from the newspapers.

MR. WOOD [now present]: Mr. Menjou, do I understand from your testimony that it is your opinion that the producers themselves and the responsible studio heads in Hollywood are not Communistic?

MR. MENJOU: They are as fine a group of men as I ever met. I have worked with them for thirty-four years, and I don't think any of them are Communists. I think the fact that the Communist Party in America is a legal party has prevented them from taking certain action against very excellent writers. There are some very excellent writers among those leftist writers. They don't have to always write Communistically, at all. Some of them have contributed much to some of our finest motion pictures, in which there was no Communism whatsoever. I think the producers in California are as patriotic a group of Americans as you will meet anywhere.

MR. WOOD: It was suggested yesterday that the producers themselves should get together and by concerted action eliminate these people who are affected with Communist tendencies from the industry. Do you agree with me that that would involve some very serious legal implications?

MR. MENJOU: I believe it would.

MR. WOOD: Under existing law?

MR. MENJOU: I spoke to Senator [Robert A.] Taft about that the other day, and he agreed also.

MR. WOOD: Would you then feel that a recommendation to the Congress by this Committee to so modify existing law as to permit just that to be done would have a wholesale effect?

MR. MENJOU: I am told by Mr. Edgar Hoover, who is a very close personal friend of mine, that he is against driving the Communist Party underground. They are now underground. I want to bring them out so we can see who they are. I feel, about pictures, that propaganda pictures should be labeled propaganda as such and propaganda should be not injected into entertainment. I feel that if an anti-Fascist picture is made, an anti-Communist picture should be made next, because I am anti-Fascist as well as I am anti-Communist. The German-American Bund was driven underground, if you want to call it such. I believe all their members are known. But they cannot go on the air. They cannot have meetings. They cannot get converts. Therefore, they are made impotent. I am not afraid of Communism in America if it is out in the open. The American people will reject it openly, if they know what it is. I would like to see it outlawed.

MR. MCDOWELL: Mr. Menjou, on this matter of outlawing the Communist Party, the party has been outlawed in Canada, Panama, and various other nations of the world. So far as I could study their situations, the results haven't been much different. There are many Communists now in

Canada. Canada now faces the business or arresting those that are known Communists and proven Communists. They go through trials. But it hasn't apparently slowed the number of Communists that are in Canada.

MR. MENJOU: You are not going to slow down the hard core of the disciplined Communist. He is going to be there all the time. He simply has to be watched. To take the producers in the picture business—if I may partially answer Mr. Wood again—a man, let us say, like Mr. Mayer or Mr. [Jack] Warner, who testified yesterday, it is practically impossible for them to see every foot of film made in their studios. They make too many. They haven't the time. Both of them are anti-Communist to the core; that I know. You will see, and have seen, very, very little of what I would call anything like subversion because, as I say, of the activities of the Alliance and due to the publicity that has been given out. This publicity is healthy. That is why I am proud to be before the Committee, because these things can be heard and brought out. Being so busy that they cannot do it, the underproducers in the studio do the engaging of the writers. Mr. Mayer doesn't hire any writers. That is done by other people. Now, if these people are watched constantly, they can do no harm. I wouldn't want to deprive anybody from making his bread and butter. I think these people can be taught. If the capitalistic system does as well in the next fifty years as it has done in the last fifty, there will be no trouble at all in this country, believe me.

MR. MCDOWELL: Mr. Menjou, I believe I told you last May, on the West Coast, that, of all the thousands of people I have discussed Communism with, you have the most profound knowledge of the background of Communism. With that knowledge, with your study of Karl Marx and modern Communism, I would like to ask another question. There has been a great deal of propaganda in the United States and other countries here in the last two years that the Soviet government has relaxed its opposition to religion. I have even heard speakers from the Soviet Union say that church attendance was encouraged. Do you think the ardent Soviet government has changed in any respect from the original Marxian Communism?

MR. MENJOU: It was somebody from the government some four or five years ago that requested they relax their attitude toward religion. The Communist Party itself will never relax it. They are anti-God. They are atheistic. The Party itself. The Russian people are deeply, deeply religious people, and their cry for religion is very great. They have been permitted to go to church, yes, but I think that everybody has been watched very carefully. Father Brown, who was the only Catholic priest permitted in Russia for many years, had a small group of people coming to his church. The government itself has never relaxed its attitude toward religion at all. It is still there in the Red Square that "religion is the opiate of the masses." And the Communist Party itself, they have relaxed nothing, nothing. They allow a few more people to go to church, but they watch everybody. The secret police watch the people so carefully that they have complete control. The

Russian people are completely enslaved. Mr. Vishinsky is enslaved. Mr. Molotov is enslaved. They are all frightened to death. Mr. Stalin would just as soon kill them as look at them. He killed all his close friends. There is excellent evidence that he poisoned Lenin, Gorky, and that he also executed the pharmacist, the head of the NKVD at the time, who was the witness. He acted very much like Mr. Capone. He committed the murders and then killed the witnesses.

MR. MCDOWELL: Mr. Chairman, in addition to being a great American, here is one of the greatest American patriots I have ever met.

MR. VAIL: Mr. Menjou, do you think there is justification for the action of this Committee in instituting an investigation of Communist activities in Hollywood?

MR. MENJOU: Do I think so? Certainly.

MR. VAIL: In the daily papers in the past few days I noticed a statement that was signed by a number of prominent Hollywood actors and actresses deploring the investigation and describing it as a smear. What is your impression of the people who were signatory to that statement?

MR. MENJOU: I am just as shocked and amazed—which I believe were their words—as they said they were shocked and amazed. I don't believe any of them has ever made a serious study of the subject. I believe they are innocent dupes. I guarantee not one of them could name four men on the Politiburo. If these people will only read and read and read and read, they will wake up. I have all the sympathy in the world for them. I am sorry for them.

MR. NIXON: Mr. Menjou, from what you have said, to charge a person with being a Communist is a very serious thing?

MR. MENJOU: Yes, sir.

MR. NIXON: You would not want that charge made?

MR. MENJOU: Without substantiation, that is right. That is playing right into the Communists' hands.

MR. NIXON: In answer to a question by Mr. Stripling, you indicated that, although you might not know whether a certain person was a Communist, I think you said he certainly acted like a Communist.

MR. MENJOU: If you belong to a Communist-front organization and you take no action against the Communists, if you do not resign from the organization when you know the organization is dominated by Communists, I consider that a very, very dangerous thing.

MR. NIXON: Have you any other tests which you would apply which would indicate to you that people acted like Communists?

MR. MENJOU: Well, I think attending any meetings at which Mr. Paul Robeson appeared, and applauding or listening to his Communist songs in America. I would be ashamed to be seen in an audience doing a thing of that kind.

MR. NIXON: You indicated you thought a person acted like a Communist when he stated, as one person did to you, that capitalism was through.

MR. MENJOU: That is not Communistic per se, but it is very dangerous leaning, it is very close. I see nothing wrong with the capitalistic system, the new dynamic capitalism in America today. Mr. Stalin was very worried when he talked to Mr. [Harold H.] Stassen. He asked him four times when the great crash was coming in America. That is what they are banking on, a great crash, and I do not think it is coming.

MR. NIXON: You indicated that belonging to a Communist-front organization—in other words, an association with Communists—attending these planned meetings, making statements in opposition to the capitalistic system are three of the tests you would apply.

MR. MENJOU: Yes, sir.

MR. NIXON: Do you have any other tests from your experience you would like to give this Committee?

MR. MENJOU: I don't know of any better ones.

MR. NIXON: Do you believe that the motion-picture industry at the present time is doing everything it can to rid itself of subversive un-American influences?

MR. MENJOU: Yes, I do. I believe it has been that way for almost a year, or maybe a little more than a year.

MR. NIXON: You see no further steps the industry can take at this time that it has not taken in the past?

MR. MENJOU: Except eternal vigilance that every American and every citizen of the United States should exercise toward Communism. I would rather label it as Stalinism; there is no such thing as Communism.

MR. NIXON: Do you feel Congressional action is necessary in order to assist the industry in going any further with this campaign?

MR. MENJOU: This is a secret organization. Very few people admit to being members of it, only a few, and of course their records are disgraceful. Mr. Mate [Henri Martin?] of the French Communist party was sentenced to twenty years for mutiny; Mr. Torres [Maurice Thorez] was sentenced to six years for desertion. Mr. Eugene Dennis, one of the members in New York, has a police record in California. I think I would keep away from those kinds of people; at least I have been taught that way.

MR. NIXON: Getting down to specific cases as to what the industry should do to rid itself of un-American activities in Hollywood. If, for example, a producer were to be given unequivocal proof that one of his star actors was a member of the Communist Party, do you believe that that producer has the responsibility as an American not to renew that person's contract?

MR. MENJOU: Well, I would not want to say that. I was one of the persons most deeply shocked when Mr. Cecil B. DeMille was deprived of his job on the radio. I thought that was perfectly shocking. I asked Mr. Cromwell about that and he said, "He is rich." I said, "What has wealth to do with the matter?" I think Mr. DeMille showed incredible moral courage, more than I have, in giving his job up. He cannot work any more on the radio because he refused to put up a dollar for political purposes. The Taft-Hartley Act has negated all that. I don't believe that an actor, if he is a member of a Communist Party and is careful to state that—I think the public will take care of him.

MR. NIXON: In other words, you believe the producer in that case would be justified in keeping him in his employment?

MR. MENJOU: He won't last long if he is labeled as a Communist.

MR. NIXON: What if a producer is informed that a writer he has in his employ is a member of the Communist Party, what should his action be?

MR. MENJOU: We have many Communist writers who are splendid writers. They do not have to write Communistically at all, but they have to be watched.

MR. NIXON: Your answer would be the same in case he learned that a director or one of the top employees in the particular industry was a member of a Communist Party?

MR. MENJOU: Yes, sir. I am firmly convinced of the evils of Stalinism or Marxism. It is so evil and it is such a menace to the American people that I think it should be watched and watched and watched.

MR. NIXON: Then so far as your program is concerned, what you advocate is publicity of the fact that certain people in the industry are Communists?

MR. MENJOU: If they are members of the Communist Party they should say so.

MR. NIXON: And once that publicity is given, by vigilance on the part of the producers they can see that no un-American propaganda gets into those films?

MR. MENJOU: Yes, sir. I have no objection, Mr. Nixon, to Communistic picture propaganda if it is so labeled. I would like to see pictures of the people at the place where Mr. [Henry A.] Wallace made his speech; I would like the American people to see that. That would be an honest picture of what is going on in Russia today.

MR. NIXON: If we refuse to allow a Communist picture to be made and advertised as such, we would probably be falling into the same error that we criticize the Communists for in Russia, is that right?

MR. MENJOU: I agree.

MR. NIXON: In other words, they will not allow a picture showing the democratic way of life in Russia?

MR. MENJOU: I also believe the Russians should be treated exactly as they treat us. I would treat them visa for visa. If there are 218 Americans in Moscow today, there shouldn't be 3046 Russians in America—because they are all spies, every one of them. There should be 218 Russians in America.

THE CHAIRMAN: Mr. Menjou, why have no anti-Communist films been made in the United States?

MR. MENJOU: There are a great many anti-Nazi films made; I do not know. Some have been announced as being in preparation. The title "The Iron Curtain" is, I think, copyrighted by a number of producers. I hope to see that made. I would like to see an honest anti-Communist picture and I would like to see it labeled as such, not as entertainment.

THE CHAIRMAN: We heard yesterday from witnesses that at least one, possibly two, anti-Communist films were being planned. What have you heard from Hollywood as to the feeling on the part of the producers about producing anti-Communist films?

MR. MENJOU: I believe they would be an incredible success. After the first picture was made, I think there would be many many more made. I would like to see a picture of the Bulgarian situation. I would like to see the execution of Mr. Patkoff [Nikolai Petkov] by Mr. Dimitrich [Georgi Dimitrov], who was former head of the Comintern.

THE CHAIRMAN: It has been said in the press, by certain individuals in the United States, that these hearings now being held by the Un-American Activities Committee are a censorship of the screen. What have you to say about that?

MR. MENJOU: It is perfectly infantile to say this Committee is trying to control the industry. How could they possibly control the industry? They wouldn't know anything about it. You wouldn't know how to make a picture or anything else. I don't see how that could be said by any man with the intelligence of a louse.

THE CHAIRMAN: When the actors testify and when the writers testify, when persons in labor testify, will their testimony and the fact that they have testified before this Committee injure their livelihood in any way?

MR. MENJOU: I shouldn't think it would injure it seriously. I believe there are many people in the picture industry that would not have me in a picture with them. I think this has gone too far in Hollywood. The line of cleavage is very straight. It isn't like a good Republican or a good Democrat. This is foul philosophy and it has embittered many, many people. I think Mr. Vishinsky and Mr. Molotov have done a most magnificent job of awakening the American people. The more information the American people get, the more they will turn against it. It is completely against the American philosophy. I would move to the State of Texas if it ever came here because I think the Texans would kill them on sight.

THE CHAIRMAN: Have you heard or do you know of any efforts made on the part of anyone to intimidate witnesses that might come before this Committee?

MR. MENJOU: No, I have not. When I went out to campaign for Mr. [Thomas E.] Dewey and Mr. [John W.] Bricker in 1944 I was told by various people it would injure my career. I don't think it has. There is no way of proving that. In Hollywood when your name comes up for a picture you are one of seven or eight actors. I believe a person who was friendly toward Communism, if I came up for a job, he would choose another man in preference, everything else being equal. I do not consider that a loss of a job, because we lose jobs in many other ways, and we get them in many other ways.

THE CHAIRMAN: You believe, then, it is the patriotic duty of a witness to speak very frankly and freely and he should be pleased to come before the Committee and testify?

MR. MENJOU: Definitely. I believe that any man who is a decent American, who believes in the Constitution of the United States and the free-enterprise system which has made this country what it is and which has given its people the highest standard of living of any country on the face of the earth, I believe he should be proud to stand up for it and not be afraid to speak.

MR. MCDOWELL: I would like to tell Mr. Menjou something to add to his already great knowledge of Communism. Recently I have been examining the borders of the United States. I would like to tell you, Mr. Menjou, that within weeks, not months but weeks, busloads of Communists have crossed the American border.

MR. MENJOU: That is right. We have no air border patrol, not a sufficient one, and we haven't enough guards. The frontier is very long which we are guarding, and it is very easy for people to infiltrate from Mexico over the border. There was a great, profitable industry in smuggling Chinese [?] over the border. One of my good friends made a great deal of money doing it. I believe America should arm to the teeth. I believe in universal military training. I attended Culver Military Academy during the last war and enlisted as a private. Due to my military training, I was soon made an officer and it taught me a great many things. I believe if I was told to swim the Mississippi River I would learn how to swim. Every young man should have military training. There is no better thing for a young man than military training for his discipline, for his manhood, for his courage, and for love of his country.

THE CHAIRMAN: Mr. Menjou, we thank you very much for coming. We appreciate your being here. (Loud applause.)

OCTOBER 22, 1947:

Robert Taylor

The Committee met at 10:30 a.m., the Honorable J. Parnell Thomas (Chairman) presiding.

THE CHAIRMAN: The meeting will come to order. The record will show that the following members are present: Mr. McDowell, Mr. Vail, Mr. Nixon, and Mr. Thomas. A Subcommittee is sitting.

Staff members present: Mr. Robert E. Stripling, Chief Investigator; Messrs. Louis J. Russell, Robert B. Gaston, H. A. Smith, Investigators; and Mr. Benjamin Mandel, Director of Research.

I would like to ask all these still photographers to stay there for a few more minutes, take a few shots, then come down here and take your positions. We do not want to have any confusion in the chambers. Moving around brings about some confusion.

MR. STRIPLING: Please state when and where you were born, Mr. Taylor.

MR. TAYLOR: I was born in Filley, Nebraska, August 5, 1911.

MR. STRIPLING: You are here before the Committee on Un-American Activities in response to a subpoena which was served upon you on October 3, 1947, are you not?

MR. TAYLOR: That is correct.

MR. STRIPLING: What is your present occupation, Mr. Taylor?

MR. TAYLOR: I am presently employed as an actor by Metro-Goldwyn-Mayer Studios in Culver City, California.

MR. STRIPLING: How long have you been an actor?

MR. TAYLOR: I have been employed as an actor since 1934.

MR. STRIPLING: How long have you been in Hollywood?

MR. TAYLOR: I have been in Hollywood since 1933.

MR. STRIPLING: Were you in the last world war?

MR. TAYLOR: Yes, sir.

MR. STRIPLING: In what branch of the service?

MR. TAYLOR: The United States Naval Air Service.

MR. STRIPLING: What was your rank?

MR. TAYLOR: I was discharged from the Navy as a full lieutenant.

MR. STRIPLING: During the time you have been in Hollywood has there been any period during which you considered that the Communist Party or the fellow travelers of the Communist Party were exerting any influence in the motion-picture industry?

MR. TAYLOR: Well, of course, I have been looking for Communism for a long time. I have been so strongly opposed to it for so many years; I think in the past four or five years, specifically, I have seen more indications which seemed to me to be signs of Communistic activity in Hollywood and the motion-picture industry.

MR. STRIPLING: In any particular field?

MR. TAYLOR: No, sir. I suppose the most readily determined field in which it could be cited would be in the writing of scripts. I have seen things from time to time which appeared to me to be slightly on the pink side, shall we say. At least, that was my personal opinion.

Mr. Stripling: Could we have a little better order?

The Chairman (*pounding gavel*): Please come to order.

Mr. Stripling: Mr. Taylor, in referring to the writers, do you mean writers who are members of the Screen Writers Guild?

Mr. Taylor: I assume that they are writers of the Screen Writers Guild. There seem to be many different factions in skills in Hollywood. I don't know just who belongs to what sometimes, but I assume they are members of the guild.

Mr. Stripling: Are you a member of any guild?

Mr. Taylor: I am a member of the Screen Actors Guild; yes, sir.

Mr. Stripling: Have you ever noticed any elements within the Screen Actors Guild that you would consider to be following the Communist Party line?

Mr. Taylor: Well, yes, sir, I must confess that I have. I am a member of the board of directors of the Screen Actors Guild. Quite recently I have been very active as a director of that board. It seems to me that at meetings, especially meetings of the general membership of the guild, there is always a certain group of actors and actresses whose every action would indicate to me that, if they are not Communists, they are working awfully hard to be Communists. I don't know. Their tactics and their philosophies seem to me to be pretty much Party-line stuff.

Mr. Stripling: Mr. Taylor, these people in the Screen Actors Guild who, in your opinion, follow the Communist Party line, are they a disrupting influence within the organization?

Mr. Taylor: It seems so to me. In the meetings which I have attended, at least on issues in which apparently there is considerable unanimity of opinion, it always occurs that someone is not quite able to understand what the issue is, and the meeting, instead of being over at ten o'clock or ten thirty, when it logically should be over, probably winds up running until one or two o'clock in the morning on such issues as points of order.

Mr. Stripling: Do you recall the names of any of the actors in the guild who participated in such activity?

Mr. Taylor: Well, yes, sir, I can name a few who seem to sort of disrupt things once in a while. Whether or not they are Communists I don't know.

Mr. Stripling: Would you name them for the Committee, please?

Mr. Taylor: One chap we have currently, I think, is Mr. Howard Da Silva. He always seems to have something to say at the wrong time. Miss Karen Morley also usually appears at the guild meetings.

Mr. Stripling: That is K-a-r-e-n M-o-r-l-e-y?

Mr. Taylor: I believe so, yes, sir. Those are two I can think of right at the moment.

Mr. Stripling: Mr. Taylor, have you ever participated in any picture as an actor which you considered contained Communist propaganda?

MR. TAYLOR: I assume we are now referring to *Song of Russia*. I must confess that I objected strenuously to doing *Song of Russia* at the time it was made. I felt that it, to my way of thinking, at least, did contain Communist propaganda. However, that was my personal opinion. A lot of my friends and people whose opinions I respect did not agree with me. When the script was first given me I felt it definitely contained Communist propaganda and objected to it upon that basis. I was assured by the studio that if there was Communist propaganda in that script it would be eliminated. I must admit that a great deal of the things to which I objected were eliminated. Another thing which determined my attitude toward *Song of Russia* was the fact that I had recently been commissioned in the Navy and was awaiting orders. I wanted to go ahead and get in the Navy. However, it seems at the time there were many pictures being made to more or less strengthen the feeling of the American people toward Russia. I did *Song of Russia*. I don't think it should have been made. I don't think it would be made today.

MR. STRIPLING: Mr. Taylor, in connection with the production of *Song of Russia,* do you know whether or not it was made at the suggestion of a representative of the Government?

MR. TAYLOR: I think the script was written and prepared long before any representative of the Government became involved in it in any way.

MR. STRIPLING: Were you ever present at any meeting at which a representative of the Government was present and this picture was discussed?

MR. TAYLOR: Yes, sir, in Mr. L. B. Mayer's office. One day I was called to meet Mr. Mellett, whom I met in the company of Mr. Mayer, and, as I recall, *Song of Russia* was discussed briefly. I don't think we were together more than five minutes. It was disclosed at that time that the Government was interested in the picture being made and also pictures of that nature being made by other studios as well. As I say, it was to strengthen the feeling of the American people toward the Russian people at that time.

MR. STRIPLING: The Mellett you referred to is Mr. Lowell Mellett?

MR. TAYLOR: Yes, sir.

MR. STRIPLING: He was the Chief of the Bureau of Motion Pictures of the Office of War Information?

MR. TAYLOR: That is right. However, may I clarify something?

MR. STRIPLING: Yes, go right ahead.

MR. TAYLOR: If I ever gave the impression in anything that appeared previously that I was forced into making *Song of Russia,* I would like to say, in my own defense, lest I look a little silly by saying I was ever forced to do the picture, I was not forced, because nobody can force you to make any picture. I objected to it, but, in deference to the situation as it then existed, I did the picture.

MR. STRIPLING: Did you have any special qualification, Mr. Taylor, for the particular part they wanted to fill? I understand you were selected, among other reasons, because of the fact that you were a musician.

MR. TAYLOR: Well, I assume that that might have been a qualification for doing a part in *Song of Russia*. Yes, I had studied music quite extensively in college and previous to college.

MR. STRIPLING: Could you tell the Committee whether or not in your experience in Hollywood any scripts have ever been submitted to you which contained any lines of material which you considered might be un-American or Communistic—any lines which you objected to?

MR. TAYLOR: Oh, yes, sir. I think from time to time you are bound to run into lines and situations and scenes which I would consider objectionable. One script was submitted to me quite some time ago, but not officially from the studio, which I objected to on the basis that it seemed to foster ideologies which I did not personally agree with. However, nothing more came out of it. The script has not been made and I have heard nothing more about it.

MR. STRIPLING: Mr. Taylor, there has been quite some testimony here regarding the presence within the motion-picture industry of a number of writers who are considered to be Communists. Are you personally acquainted with any writers whom you consider to be Communists or who follow the Communist Party line?

MR. TAYLOR: I know of several writers in the motion-picture business who are reputedly fellow travelers or possibly Communists.

MR. STRIPLING: You have no personal knowledge of it yourself?

MR. TAYLOR: I know one gentleman employed at the studio at which I am employed, Mr. Lester Cole, who is reputedly a Communist. I would not know personally.

MR. STRIPLING: Would you say that after Pearl Harbor the activities of the Communists in the motion-picture industry increased or decreased?

MR. TAYLOR: I think quite obviously it must have increased. The ground for their work in this country was obviously more fertile. I would say yes, it did definitely increase following Pearl Harbor.

MR. STRIPLING: Mr. Taylor, have you ever joined any Communist-front organization?

MR. TAYLOR: No, sir, believe me.

MR. STRIPLING: Have you ever played in any picture with people whom you had any doubts about as to their loyalty to the Government?

MR. TAYLOR: Not that I know of. I have never worked with anyone knowingly who is a Communist. Moreover, I shall never work with anyone who is a Communist.

MR. STRIPLING: You would refuse to act in a picture in which a person whom you considered to be a Communist was also cast, is that correct?

MR. TAYLOR: I most assuredly would, and I would not even have to know that he was a Communist. This may sound biased. However, if I were even suspicious of a person being a Communist with whom I was scheduled to work, I am afraid it would have to be him or me, because life is a little too short to be around people who annoy me as much as these fellow travelers and Communists do.

MR. STRIPLING: You definitely consider them to be a bad influence upon the industry?

MR. TAYLOR: I certainly do, yes, sir.

MR. STRIPLING: They are a rotten apple in the barrel?

MR. TAYLOR: To me they are, and I further believe that 99.9 per cent of the people in the motion-picture industry feel exactly as I do.

MR. STRIPLING: What do you think would be the best way to approach the problem of ridding the industry of the Communists who are now entrenched therein?

MR. TAYLOR: Well, sir, if I were given the responsibility of getting rid of them I would love nothing better than to fire every last one of them and never let them work in a studio or in Hollywood again. However, that is not my position. If I were producing a picture on my own—and I hope I never do—but if I were, I would not have one of them within a hundred miles of me or the studio or the script. I am sure the producers in Hollywood are faced with a slightly different problem. They are heads of an industry, and, as heads of an industry, they might be slightly more judicial than I, as an individual, would be. I believe firmly that the producers, the heads of the studios in Hollywood, would be and are more than willing to do everything they can to rid Hollywood of Communists and fellow travelers. I think if given the tools with which to work—specifically, some sort of national legislation or an attitude on the part of the Government as such which would provide them with the weapons for getting rid of these people—I have no doubt personally but what they would be gone in very short order.

MR. STRIPLING: Mr. Taylor, do you consider that the motion picture primarily is a vehicle of entertainment and not of propaganda?

MR. TAYLOR: I certainly do. I think it is the primary job of the motion-picture industry to entertain; nothing more, nothing less.

MR. STRIPLING: Do you think the industry would be in a better position if it stuck strictly to entertainment without permitting political films to be made?

MR. TAYLOR: I certainly do. Moreover, I feel that, largely, the picture business does stick to entertainment. I do not think they let themselves be sidetracked too much with propaganda films and things of that sort. Every once in a while things do sneak in that nobody catches. If the Communists are not working in the picture business there is no motive for their sneaking things in.

MR. STRIPLING: Mr. Taylor, returning to the picture *Song of Russia* for a moment, Miss Ayn Rand gave the Committee a review of the picture several days ago. In the picture there were several scenes, particularly a wedding scene at which a priest officiated; also several other scenes at which the clergy was present. When you were making this picture were you under the impression that freedom of religion was enjoyed in Russia?

MR. TAYLOR: No, sir, I never was under the impression that freedom of religion was enjoyed in Russia. However, I must confess, when it got down to that part of the picture, the picture was about two-thirds gone, and it didn't actually occur to me until you mentioned it just a minute ago.

MR. MCDOWELL: Mr. Taylor, you have been interested in this matter for quite a long time, and probably know as much about the situation in Hollywood as any person who lives there. There have been many statements made since Mr. Thomas and I went to Hollywood last May and began this investigation into the Communist activities on the West Coast, to the effect that the Committee on Un-American Activities was attempting to control thought or frighten the producers out there into producing some sort of picture. Has that been your impression of our activities?

MR. TAYLOR: No, sir, not at any time did I get that impression.

MR. MCDOWELL: I am very glad to hear you say that. I thought a great deal about things I have read in various columns of the papers as to our attempting to control the great American movie industry. It is silly. We are not concerned with liberals or conservatives or anything of that kind. We are hunting enemies of the nation. We know some are in Hollywood.

MR. NIXON: Mr. Taylor, as a result of your appearance before the Subcommittee on Un-American Activities in Hollywood a few months ago, you were subject to considerable criticism and ridicule from certain left-wing quarters, were you not?

MR. TAYLOR: I am afraid so, yes, sir. It didn't bother me, however.

MR. NIXON: And as the result of your testimony and your appearance before this Committee today and the stand you have taken on this issue, you will be the subject of additional ridicule and criticism from those quarters, will you not?

MR. TAYLOR: I suppose so. However, any time any of the left-wing press or individuals belonging to the left wing or their fellow-traveler groups ridicule me, I take it as a compliment, because I really enjoy their displeasure.

MR. NIXON: You realize, however, that your success as an actor, your livelihood as an actor, depends to a great extent upon the type of publicity you receive?

MR. TAYLOR: Yes, sir.

MR. NIXON: And that ridicule and abuse heaped upon you has a much more serious effect than it would have upon a person who does not depend upon public acceptance of what he does? Yet you feel that under the circumstances it is your duty as an American citizen to state your views on this matter?

MR. TAYLOR: I most assuredly do, sir.

MR. NIXON: As far as you are concerned, even though it might mean that you would suffer, possibly, at the box office, possibly in reputation or in other ways, for you to appear before this Committee, you feel you are justified in making the appearance and you would do so again if requested to do so?

MR. TAYLOR: I certainly would, sir. I happen to believe strongly enough in the American people and in what the American people believe in to think that they will go along with anybody who prefers America and the American form of government over any other subversive ideologies which might be presented and by whom [*sic*] I might be criticized.

(*Loud applause.*)

THE CHAIRMAN: Mr. Taylor, are you in favor of the motion-picture industry making anti-Communist pictures, giving the facts about Communism?

MR. TAYLOR: Congressman Thomas, when the time arrives—and it might not be long—when pictures of that type are indicated as necessary, I believe the motion-picture industry will and should make anti-Communist pictures. When that time is going to be I don't happen to know, but I believe they should and will be made.

MR. STRIPLING: I would like to ask Mr. Taylor if he thinks the Communist Party should be outlawed, for this reason: This Committee presently has before it two bills which seek to do that very thing, legislation which would in fact outlaw the Party. Do you think that would reach this Communist influence in the motion-picture industry?

MR. TAYLOR: Well, in order to answer that, I personally, with all due regard to Mr. [J. Edgar] Hoover, whose opinion I respect most highly, certainly do believe that the Communist Party should be outlawed. However, I am not an expert on politics or on what the reaction would be. If I had my way about it they would all be sent back to Russia or some other unpleasant place (*Loud applause*) and never allowed back in this country.

THE CHAIRMAN: I am going to ask the audience to please not applaud. We are trying to get the facts here. This is not a show, or anything like that. Do not applaud any of the witnesses who are on the stand or at any other time! Go ahead, Mr. Taylor.

MR. TAYLOR: If outlawing the Communist Party would solve the Communist threat in this country, then I am thoroughly in approval and accord with it being outlawed.

MR. CHAIRMAN: Mr. Taylor, we want to congratulate you for your very frank statement. We are going to ask all the audience and all the photographers to please keep your seats while the witness is leaving.

OCTOBER 23, 1947:

Ronald Reagan

The Committee met at 10:30 a.m., the Honorable J. Parnell Thomas (Chairman) presiding.

THE CHAIRMAN: The record will show that Mr. McDowell, Mr. Vail, Mr. Nixon, and Mr. Thomas are present. A Subcommittee is sitting.

Staff members present: Mr. Robert E. Stripling, Chief Investigator; Messrs. Louis J. Russell, H. A. Smith, and Robert B. Gaston, Investigators; and Mr. Benjamin Mandel, Director of Research.

MR. STRIPLING: When and where were you born, Mr. Reagan?

MR. REAGAN: Tampico, Illinois, February 6, 1911.

MR. STRIPLING: What is your present occupation?

MR. REAGAN: Motion-picture actor.

MR. STRIPLING: How long have you been engaged in that profession?

MR. REAGAN: Since June 1937, with a brief interlude of three and a half years—that at the time didn't seem very brief.

MR. STRIPLING: What period was that?

MR. REAGAN: That was during the late war.

MR. STRIPLING: What branch of the service were you in?

MR. REAGAN: Well, sir, I had been for several years in the Reserve as an officer in the United States Cavalry, but I was assigned to the Air Corps.

MR. STRIPLING: That is kind of typical of the Army, isn't it?

MR. REAGAN: Yes, sir. The first thing the Air Corps did was loan me to the Signal Corps.

MR. MCDOWELL: You didn't wear spurs?

MR. REAGAN: I did for a short while.

THE CHAIRMAN: I think this has little to do with the facts we are seeking. Proceed.

MR. STRIPLING: Mr. Reagan, are you a member of any guild?

MR. REAGAN: Yes, sir, the Screen Actors Guild.

MR. STRIPLING: How long have you been a member?

MR. REAGAN: Since June 1937.

MR. STRIPLING: Are you the president of the guild at the present time?

MR. REAGAN: Yes, sir.

MR. STRIPLING: When were you elected?

MR. REAGAN: That was several months ago. I was elected to replace Mr. [Robert] Montgomery when he resigned.

MR. STRIPLING: When does your term expire?

MR. REAGAN: The elections come up next month.

MR. STRIPLING: Have you ever held any other position in the Screen Actors Guild?

MR. REAGAN: Yes, sir. Just prior to the war I was a member of the board of directors, and just after the war, prior to my being elected president, I was a member of the board of directors.

MR. STRIPLING: As a member of the board of directors, as president of the Screen Actors Guild, and as an active member, have you at any time observed or noted within the organization a clique of either Communists or Fascists who were attempting to exert influence or pressure on the guild?

MR. REAGAN: Well, sir, my testimony must be very similar to that of Mr. [George] Murphy and Mr. [Robert] Montgomery. There has been a small group within the Screen Actors Guild which has consistently opposed the policy of the guild board and officers of the guild, as evidenced by the vote on various issues. That small clique referred to has been suspected of more or less following the tactics that we associate with the Communist Party.

MR. STRIPLING: Would you refer to them as a disruptive influence within the guild?

MR. REAGAN: I would say that at times they have attempted to be a disruptive influence.

MR. STRIPLING: You have no knowledge yourself as to whether or not any of them are members of the Communist Party?

MR. REAGAN: No, sir, I have no investigative force, or anything, and I do not know.

MR. STRIPLING: Has it ever been reported to you that certain members of the guild were Communists?

MR. REAGAN: Yes, sir, I have heard different discussions and some of them tagged as Communists.

MR. STRIPLING: Would you say that this clique has attempted to dominate the guild?

MR. REAGAN: Well, sir, by attempting to put over their own particular views on various issues, I guess you would have to say that our side was attempting to dominate, too, because we were fighting just as hard to put over our views, and I think we were proven correct by the figures—Mr. Murphy gave the figures—and those figures were always approximately the same, an average of ninety per cent or better of the Screen Actors Guild voted in favor of those matters now guild policy.

MR. STRIPLING: Mr. Reagan, there has been testimony to the effect here that numerous Communist-front organizations have been set up in Hollywood. Have you ever been solicited to join any of those organizations or any organization which you considered to be a Communist-front organization?

MR. REAGAN: Well, sir, I have received literature from an organization called the Committee for a Far-Eastern Democratic Policy. I don't know whether it is Communist or not. I only know that I didn't like their views and as a result I didn't want to have anything to do with them.

MR. STRIPLING: Were you ever solicited to sponsor the Joint Anti-Fascist Refugee Committee?

MR. REAGAN: No, sir, I was never solicited to do that, but I found myself misled into being a sponsor on another occasion for a function that was held under the auspices of the Joint Anti-Fascist Refugee Committee.

MR. STRIPLING: Did you knowingly give your name as a sponsor?

MR. REAGAN: Not knowingly. Could I explain what that occasion was?

MR. STRIPLING: Yes, sir.

MR. REAGAN: I was called several weeks ago. There happened to be a financial drive on to raise money to build a badly needed hospital called the All Nations Hospital. I think the purpose of the building is so obvious by the title that it has the support of most of the people of Los Angeles. Certainly of most of the doctors. Some time ago I was called to the telephone. A woman introduced herself by name. I didn't make any particular note of her name, and I couldn't give it now. She told me that there would be a recital held at which Paul Robeson would sing, and she said that all the money for the tickets would go to the hospital, and asked if she could use my name as one of the sponsors. I hesitated for a moment, because I don't think that Mr. Robeson's and my political views coincide at all, and then I thought I was being a little stupid because, I thought, Here is an occasion where Mr. Robeson is perhaps appearing as an artist, and certainly the object, raising money, is above any political consideration: it is a hospital supported by everyone. I have contributed money myself. So I felt a little bit as if I had been stuffy for a minute, and I said, "Certainly, you can use my name." I left town for a couple of weeks and, when I returned, I was handed a newspaper story that said that this recital was held at the Shrine Auditorium in Los Angeles under the auspices of the Joint Anti-Fascist Refugee Committee. The principal speaker was Emil Lustig [Ludwig?], Robert Burman took up a collection, and remnants of the Abraham Lincoln Brigade were paraded on the platform. I did not, in the newspaper story, see one word about the hospital. I called the newspaper and said I am not accustomed to writing to editors but would like to explain my position, and he laughed and said, "You needn't bother, you are about the fiftieth person that has called with the same idea, including most of the legitimate doctors who had also been listed as sponsors of that affair."

MR. STRIPLING: Would you say from your observation that that is typical of the tactics or strategy of the Communists, to solicit and use the names of prominent people to either raise money or gain support?

MR. REAGAN: I think it is in keeping with their tactics, yes, sir.

MR. STRIPLING: Do you think there is anything democratic about those tactics?

MR. REAGAN: I do not, sir.

MR. STRIPLING: As president of the Screen Actors Guild, you are familiar with the jurisdictional strike which has been going on in Hollywood for some time?

MR. REAGAN: Yes, sir.

MR. STRIPLING: Have you ever had any conferences with any of the labor officials regarding this strike?

MR. REAGAN: Yes, sir.

MR. STRIPLING: Do you know whether the Communists have participated in any way in this strike?

MR. REAGAN: Sir, the first time that this word "Communist" was ever injected into any of the meetings concerning the strike was at a meeting in Chicago with Mr. William Hutchinson, president of the carpenters' union, who were on strike at the time. He asked the Screen Actors Guild to submit terms to Mr. [Richard] Walsh, and he told us to tell Mr. Walsh that, if he would give in on these terms, he in turn would run this Sorrell and the other Commies out—I am quoting him—and break it up. I might add that Mr. Walsh and Mr. Sorrell were running the strike for Mr. Hutchinson in Hollywood.

MR. STRIPLING: Mr. Reagan, what is your feeling about what steps should be taken to rid the motion-picture industry of any Communist influences?

MR. REAGAN: Well, sir, ninety-nine per cent of us are pretty well aware of what is going on, and I think, within the bounds of our democratic rights and never once stepping over the rights given us by democracy, we have done a pretty good job in our business of keeping those people's activities curtailed. After all, we must recognize them at present as a political party. On that basis we have exposed their lies when we came across them, we have opposed their propaganda, and I can certainly testify that in the case of the Screen Actors Guild we have been eminently successful in preventing them from, with their usual tactics, trying to run a majority of an organization with a well-organized minority. In opposing those people, the best thing to do is make democracy work. In the Screen Actors Guild we make it work by insuring everyone a vote and by keeping everyone informed. I believe that, as Thomas Jefferson put it, if all the American people know all of the facts they will never make a mistake. Whether the Party should be outlawed, that is a matter for the Government to decide. As a citizen, I would hesitate to see any political party outlawed on the basis of its political ideology. We have spent a hundred and seventy years in this country on the basis that democracy is strong enough to stand up and fight against the inroads of any ideology. However, if it is proven that an organization is an agent of a foreign power, or in any way not a legitimate political party—and I think the Government is capable of proving that—then that is another matter. I happen to be very proud of the industry in which I work; I happen to be very proud of the way in which we conducted the fight. I do not believe the Communists have ever at any time been able to use the motion-picture screen as a sounding board for their philosophy or ideology.

* * *

MR. CHAIRMAN: There is one thing that you said that interested me very much. That was the quotation from Jefferson. That is just why this Committee was created by the House of Representatives: to acquaint the American people with the facts. Once the American people are acquainted with the facts there is no question but what the American people will do the kind of a job that they want done: that is, to make America just as pure as we can possibly make it. We want to thank you very much for coming here today.

MR. REAGAN: Sir, I detest, I abhor their philosophy, but I detest more than that their tactics, which are those of the fifth column, and are dishonest, but at the same time I never as a citizen want to see our country become urged, by either fear or resentment of this group, that we ever compromise with any of our democratic principles through that fear or resentment. I still think that democracy can do it.

OCTOBER 23, 1947:

Gary Cooper

MR. STRIPLING: When and where were you born, Mr. Cooper?

MR. COOPER: I was born in Helena, Montana, in 1901.

MR. STRIPLING: What is your present occupation?

MR. COOPER: An actor.

MR. STRIPLING: Mr. Cooper, you are here in response to a subpoena which was served upon you on September 26, are you not?

MR. COOPER: Yes, I am.

MR. STRIPLING: Mr. Chairman, the interrogation of Mr. Cooper will be done by Mr. Smith.

THE CHAIRMAN: We will have more order, please.

MR. SMITH: Mr. Cooper, how long have you been an actor?

MR. COOPER: I have been an actor since 1925.

MR. SMITH: And how long have you been in Hollywood?

MR. COOPER: Since 1924.

MR. SMITH: I believe you made many pictures, some of which pictures are *Unconquered, Pride of the Yankees, Saratoga Trunk, Mr. Deeds Goes to Town,* and you are presently making *Good Sam,* is that correct?

MR. COOPER: Yes.

MR. SMITH: Are you a member of the Screen Actors Guild?

MR. COOPER: Yes, I have been a member since the guild was organized.

MR. SMITH: During the time that you have been in Hollywood, have you ever observed any Communistic influence in Hollywood or in the motion-picture industry?

MR. COOPER: I believe I have noticed some.

MR. SMITH: What do you believe the principal medium is that they use [in] Hollywood or the industry to inject propaganda?

MR. COOPER: Well, I believe it is done through word of mouth—

THE CHAIRMAN: Will you speak louder, please, Mr. Cooper?

MR. COOPER: I believe it is done through word of mouth and through the medium of pamphleting—and writers, I suppose.

MR. SMITH: By "word of mouth," what do you mean, Mr. Cooper?

MR. COOPER: Well, I mean sort of social gatherings.

MR. SMITH: That has been your observation?

MR. COOPER: That has been my only observation, yes.

MR. SMITH: Can you tell us some of the statements that you may have heard at these gatherings that you believe are Communistic?

MR. COOPER: Well, I have heard quite a few, I think, from time to time over the years. Well, I have heard tossed around such statements as, "Don't you think the Constitution of the United States is about a hundred and fifty years out of date?" and—oh, I don't know—I have heard people mention that, well, "Perhaps this would be a more efficient Government without a Congress"—which statements I think are very un-American.

MR. SMITH: Have you ever observed any Communistic information in any scripts?

MR. COOPER: Well, I have turned down quite a few scripts because I thought they were tinged with Communistic ideas.

MR. SMITH: Can you name any of those scripts?

MR. COOPER: No, I can't recall any of those scripts to mind.

THE CHAIRMAN: Just a minute. Mr. Cooper, you haven't got that bad a memory.

MR. COOPER: I beg your pardon, sir?

THE CHAIRMAN: I say, you haven't got that bad a memory, have you? You must be able to remember some of those scripts you turned down because you thought they were Communist scripts.

MR. COOPER: Well, I can't actually give you a title to any of them, no.

THE CHAIRMAN: Will you think it over, then, and supply the Committee with a list of those scripts?

MR. COOPER: I don't think I could, because most of the scripts I read at night, and if they don't look good to me, I don't finish them, or if I do finish them I send them back as soon as possible to their author.

Mr. McDowell: That is the custom of most actors, most stars, Mr. Cooper?

Mr. Cooper: Yes, I believe so, yes, sir. As to the material, which is more important than the name of the script, I did turn back one script because the leading character in the play was a man whose life's ambition was to organize an army in the United States, an army of soldiers who would never fight to defend their country. I don't remember any more details of the play, but that was enough of a basic idea for me to send it back quickly to its author.

Mr. Smith: Mr. Cooper, have you ever had any personal experience where you feel the Communist Party may have attempted to use you?

Mr. Cooper: They haven't attempted to use me, I don't think, because, apparently, they know that I am not very sympathetic to Communism. Several years ago, when Communism was more of a social chit-chatter in parties for offices, and so on, when Communism didn't have the implications that it has now, discussion of Communism was more open and I remember hearing statements from some folks to the effect that the Communistic system had a great many features that were desirable. It offered the actors and artists—in other words, the creative people—a special place in Government where we would be somewhat immune from the ordinary leveling of income. And as I remember, some actor's name was mentioned to me who had a house in Moscow which was very large—he had three cars, and stuff, with his house being quite a bit larger than my house in Beverly Hills at the time—and it looked to me like a pretty phony come-on to us in the picture business. From that time on, I could never take any of this pinko mouthing very seriously, because I didn't feel it was on the level.

Mr. Smith: Mr. Chairman, we have several official documents that we have obtained through the State Department, which I believe clearly shows that the Communist Party attempts to use actors individually throughout the world to further their cause. With your permission, I would like to show one of those documents to Mr. Cooper and have him read it to the Committee. This document from which Mr. Cooper is going to read was distributed in pamphlets in Italy during May of 1947—

Mr. Cooper: Shall I read it?

Mr. Smith: —by the Communist Party. Yes, sir, go ahead.

Mr. Cooper:

> Gary Cooper, who took part in the fights for the independence of Spain, held a speech before a crowd of ninety thousand in Philadelphia on the occasion of the consecration of the banner of the Philadelphia Communist Federation. Between other things, he said: "In our days it is the greatest honor to be a Communist. I wish the whole world to understand what we Communists really are. There could be nobody then who might say that we are enemies of mankind and peace. Those who want to discuss Communist ideas should first get to know them. Americans learn this with great difficulty. Millions of

people from other continents regard America as a center of modern civilization, but only we Americans can see how false this opinion is. Let us be frank. Our country is a country of gold, silver, petrol, and great railways. But at the same time it is a country where Rockefeller, Ford, and Rothschild use tear gas against workers fighting for their legitimate rights. Our country is the fatherland of Lincoln and Roosevelt, but at the same time it is a country of men like Senator Bilbo and many of his type. It is a country where redskins were exterminated by arms and brandy."

MR. SMITH: Were you ever in Philadelphia, Mr. Cooper?

MR. COOPER: No, sir, I was never in Philadelphia.

MR. SMITH: Do you have any comment to make regarding this letter?

MR. COOPER: Well, a ninety-thousand audience is a little tough to disregard, but it is not true.

THE CHAIRMAN: I want to help you along, Mr. Cooper—

MR. COOPER: No part of it is true, sir.

THE CHAIRMAN: I happen to know it is just a plain, ordinary, ruthless lie. We know that for a fact. So you don't have to worry any more about that.

MR. MCDOWELL: And also, Mr. Cooper, in order to get it into the record, don't you think there wouldn't be ninety thousand people in Philadelphia who were Communists?

MR. COOPER: Well, I believe it was Mr. Smith here that said you would have a hard time getting ninety thousand people out in Philadelphia for anything. I don't know about that.

MR. SMITH: Mr. Chairman, I have in my possession another similar document. Some portions of it should be read into the record. It was distributed on Saturday, July 19, 1947, by the Communist Party in Yugoslavia, in various cities therein; and, with your permission, I would like to read a few paragraphs therefrom.

In the usual column on the sixth page entitled "Fascist Shooting on Broadway," appeared the following: In the middle of June, in Hollywood, Gary Cooper, Tyrone Power, and Alan Ladd, well-known film stars, were imprisoned because they were marked as leftists and denounced un-Americans, but before that happened, something else was going on, about which the American newspaper agencies did not speak, and that is very characteristic of conditions today in the United States. The film actor, Buster Crabbe, lost his life in a mysterious way. The background of this tragic and mysterious death of Buster Crabbe was set forth by the New York paper, *Red Star*. From the articles of Immy Stendaph, we can see that Buster Crabbe was very popular in the United States. He organized a movement in the Army to protest against the investigation of un-American activities against Cooper, Chaplin, and other film stars. The beginning of Buster Crabbe's tragedy was when he found valuable documents, through which documents he could give light and prove the criminal and aggressive plans of reactionary circles in America. . . . On May 31, Buster Crabbe came to the apartment of the well-known film actor,

> Spencer Tracy, also well-known as a leftist, and they had a long talk in the presence of Tyrone Power. . . . On June 3, on Broadway, on the corner of Seventh Avenue, Crabbe was riddled with bullets from a machine gun from a closed car. This tragic death of Crabbe provoked terrific unrest in Hollywood. At the funeral of Buster Crabbe, 150,000 men were present, and the coffin was carried by Comrades Gary Cooper, Tyrone Power—

THE CHAIRMAN: I don't think we will have to have any more of that letter. But what I would like to have you do, Mr. Smith, is to identify the source.

MR. SMITH: Yes, sir, there is just one more paragraph.

THE CHAIRMAN: All right, read on, if you want to.

MR. SMITH:

> This case is very characteristic of the conditions which are now prevailing in the United States. This is the method of Fascist liquidation [with] which this country of freedom and democracy is dealing with a political opponent. It is quite possible that this crime was committed by the KKK and inspired by the elements who were interested in Crabbe's disappearance—that he stop talking.

My point, Mr. Chairman, is to show not only in Hollywood, but throughout the world, the extent to which the Communist Party can go to use an actor to further their cause. This particular document we have from the State Department.

THE CHAIRMAN: Well, you see from that, Mr. Cooper, to what extent they will go.

MR. COOPER: Yes, sir.

THE CHAIRMAN: So when they used your name in that regard you can almost consider it a compliment.

MR. COOPER: Thank you.

MR. MCDOWELL: May I ask, Mr. Chairman, if Crabbe is living? Is Mr. Crabbe living?

MR. SMITH: So far as I know, he is living.

MR. COOPER: Mr. Crabbe is a very healthy specimen of American manhood.

MR. STRIPLING: Mr. Cooper, witnesses who have preceded you from Hollywood have said that they consider members of the Communist Party to be agents of a foreign government. Do you consider the members of the Communist Party to be that?

MR. COOPER: I am not in nearly as good a position to know as some of the witnesses that have been ahead of me, because I am not a very active member in our guild. They, therefore, know much more about the politics and the workings of what Communists there are in the guild than I. From the general, over-all things that you hear in Hollywood, I would assume that there is such a close parallel, and I think this document which Mr. Smith gave me is a pretty good indication that there is a direct connection in the material that comes from abroad and the material that is given to them here.

MR. STRIPLING: Do you think that the Communist group or clique in Hollywood, whether it is in the Screen Actors Guild or the Screen Writers Guild, is a good influence or bad influence for the motion pictures generally?

MR. COOPER: Well, to go back to one or two examples that I quoted before, I think it is a very bad influence because it is very un-American. I mean, it is very shocking to hear someone with a lot of money say such a thing as, "The Constitution of the United States is a hundred and fifty years out of date."

MR. STRIPLING: Have you ever been solicited to join the Communist Party or any of its fronts, Mr. Cooper?

MR. COOPER: No, I have not.

THE CHAIRMAN: Mr. Cooper, during the wartime, the moving-picture industry made anti-Nazi films. Don't you think it would be a good idea if now the moving-picture industry produced anti-Communist films showing the dangers from Communism in the United States?

MR. COOPER: I think some very sound and real fine pictures, more of them, should be made on selling what is really Americanism. A great many good pictures have been made, and I have tried to do some of them, but I think there is great room for reselling people the idea of what we have got in this country, which is the finest thing there is in the world. I know that the great majority of people in this country would not exchange our country or government for any other.

THE CHAIRMAN: Do you think that Communism is on the increase or on the decrease out in Hollywood?

MR. COOPER: It is very difficult to say right now, within these last few months, because it has become unpopular and a little risky to say too much. You notice the difference. People who were quite easy to express their thoughts before begin to clam up more than they used to.

THE CHAIRMAN: In other words, some of them are "getting religion"?

MR. COOPER: Well, I don't know, but they do their discussions in corners, I guess, in huddles of their own where they are surrounded with their own.

THE CHAIRMAN: Now, you heard about these bills that are before the Un-American Activities Committee, bills to outlaw the Communist Party in the United States, just as the Communist Party is outlawed in Canada and the Communist Party is outlawed in some South American countries?

MR. COOPER: Yes.

THE CHAIRMAN: Do you believe, as a prominent person in your field, that it would be wise for us, the Congress, to pass legislation to outlaw the Communist Party in the United States?

MR. COOPER: I think it would be a good idea, although I have never read Karl Marx and I don't know the basis of Communism, beyond what I have picked up from hearsay. From what I hear, I don't like it because it isn't on the level. So I couldn't possibly answer that question.

OCTOBER 27, 1947:

John Howard Lawson

The Committee met at 10:30 a.m., the Honorable J. Parnell Thomas (Chairman) presiding.

Staff members present: Mr. Robert E. Stripling, Chief Investigator; Messrs. Louis J. Russell, H. A. Smith, and Robert B. Gaston, Investigators; and Mr. Benjamin Mandel, Director of Research.

THE CHAIRMAN: The record will show that a Subcommittee is present, consisting of Mr. Vail, Mr. McDowell, and Mr. Thomas.

MR. LAWSON: Mr. Chairman, I have a statement here which I wish to make—

THE CHAIRMAN: Well, all right, let me see your statement.

(*Statement* handed to the Chairman.*)

THE CHAIRMAN: I don't care to read any more of the statement. The statement will not be read. I read the first line.

MR. LAWSON: You have spent one week vilifying me before the American public—

THE CHAIRMAN: Just a minute—

MR. LAWSON: —and you refuse to allow me to make a statement on my rights as an American citizen.

THE CHAIRMAN: I refuse to let you make the statement because of the first sentence. That statement is not pertinent to the inquiry. Now, this is a Congressional Committee set up by law. We must have orderly procedure, and we are going to have orderly procedure. Mr. Stripling, identify the witness.

MR. LAWSON: The rights of American citizens are important in this room here, and I intend to stand up for those rights, Congressman Thomas.

MR. STRIPLING: Mr. Lawson, will you state your full name, please?

MR. LAWSON: I wish to protest against the unwillingness of this Committee to read a statement, when you permitted Mr. Warner, Mr. Mayer, and others to read statements in this room. My name is John Howard Lawson.

MR. STRIPLING: When and where were you born?

MR. LAWSON: New York City.

MR. STRIPLING: What year?

* The statement is printed below, right after the testimony. —E.B.

MR. LAWSON: 1894.

MR. STRIPLING: Give us the exact date.

MR. LAWSON: September 25.

MR. STRIPLING: Mr. Lawson, you are here in response to a subpoena which was served upon you on September 19, 1947; is that true?

MR. LAWSON: That is correct.

MR. STRIPLING: What is your occupation, Mr. Lawson?

MR. LAWSON: I am a writer.

MR. STRIPLING: How long have you been a writer?

MR. LAWSON: All my life—at least thirty-five years—my adult life.

MR. STRIPLING: Are you a member of the Screen Writers Guild?

MR. LAWSON: The raising of any question here in regard to membership, political beliefs, or affiliation—

MR. STRIPLING: Mr. Chairman—

MR. LAWSON: —is absolutely beyond the powers of this Committee.

MR. STRIPLING: Mr. Chairman—

MR. LAWSON: But—

(*The Chairman pounding gavel.*)

MR. LAWSON: It is a matter of public record that I am a member of the Screen Writers Guild.

MR. STRIPLING: I ask—

(*Applause.*)

THE CHAIRMAN: I want to caution the people in the audience: You are the guests of this Committee and you will have to maintain order at all times. I do not care for any applause or any demonstrations of one kind or another.

MR. STRIPLING: Now, Mr. Chairman, I am also going to request that you instruct the witness to be responsive to the questions.

THE CHAIRMAN: I think the witness will be more responsive to the questions.

MR. LAWSON: Mr. Chairman, you permitted—

THE CHAIRMAN (*pounding gavel*): Never mind—

MR. LAWSON: —witnesses in this room to make answers of three or four or five hundred words to questions here.

THE CHAIRMAN: Mr. Lawson, you will please be responsive to these questions and not continue to try to disrupt these hearings.

MR. LAWSON: I am not on trial here, Mr. Chairman. This Committee is on trial here before the American people. Let us get that straight.

THE CHAIRMAN: We don't want you to be on trial.

MR. STRIPLING: Mr. Lawson, how long have you been a member of the Screen Writers Guild?

MR. LAWSON: Since it was founded in its present form, in 1933.

MR. STRIPLING: Have you ever held any office in the guild?

MR. LAWSON: The question of whether I have held office is also a question which is beyond the purview of this Committee.

(*The Chairman pounding gavel.*)

MR. LAWSON: It is an invasion of the right of association under the Bill of Rights of this country.

THE CHAIRMAN: Please be responsive to the question.

MR. LAWSON: It is also a matter—

(*The Chairman pounding gavel.*)

MR. LAWSON: —of public record—

THE CHAIRMAN: You asked to be heard. Through your attorney, you asked to be heard, and we want you to be heard. And if you don't care to be heard, then we will excuse you, and we will put the record in without your answers.

MR. LAWSON: I wish to frame my own answers to your questions, Mr. Chairman, and I intend to do so.

THE CHAIRMAN: And you will be responsive to the questions or you will be excused from the witness stand.

MR. LAWSON: I will frame my own answers, Mr. Chairman.

THE CHAIRMAN: Go ahead, Mr. Stripling.

MR. STRIPLING: I repeat the question, Mr. Lawson: Have you ever held any position in the Screen Writers Guild?

MR. LAWSON: I stated that it is outside the purview of the rights of this Committee to inquire into any form of association—

THE CHAIRMAN: The Chair will determine what is in the purview of this Committee.

MR. LAWSON: My rights as an American citizen are no less than the responsibilities of this Committee of Congress.

THE CHAIRMAN: Now, you are just making a big scene for yourself and getting all "het up." (*Laughter.*) Be responsive to the questioning, just the same as all the witnesses have. You are no different from the rest. Go ahead, Mr. Stripling.

MR. LAWSON: I am being treated differently from the rest.

THE CHAIRMAN: You are not being treated differently.

MR. LAWSON: Other witnesses have made statements, which included quotations from books, references to material which had no connection whatsoever with the interest of this Committee.

THE CHAIRMAN: We will determine whether it has connection. Now, you go ahead—

MR. LAWSON: It is absolutely beyond the power of this Committee to inquire into my association in any organization.

THE CHAIRMAN: Mr. Lawson, you will have to stop or you will leave the witness stand. And you will leave the witness stand because you are in contempt. That is why you will leave the witness stand. And if you are just trying to force me to put you in contempt, you won't have to try much harder. You know what has happened to a lot of people that have been in contempt of this Committee this year, don't you?

MR. LAWSON: I am glad you have made it perfectly clear that you are going to threaten and intimidate the witnesses, Mr. Chairman.

(*The Chairman pounding gavel.*)

MR. LAWSON: I am an American and I am not at all easy to intimidate, and don't think I am.

(*The Chairman pounding gavel.*)

MR. STRIPLING: Mr. Lawson, I repeat the question. Have you ever held any position in the Screen Writers Guild?

MR. LAWSON: I have stated that the question is illegal. But it is a matter of public record that I have held many offices in the Screen Writers Guild. I was its first president in 1933, and I have held office on the board of directors of the Screen Writers Guild at other times.

MR. STRIPLING: You have been employed in the motion-picture industry, have you not?

MR. LAWSON: I have.

MR. STRIPLING: Would you state some of the studios where you have been employed?

MR. LAWSON: Practically all of the studios, all the major studios.

MR. STRIPLING: As a screen writer?

MR. LAWSON: That is correct.

MR. STRIPLING: Would you list some of the pictures which you have written the script for?

MR. LAWSON: I must state again that you are now inquiring into the freedom of press and communications, over which you have no control whatsoever. You don't have to bring me here three thousand miles to find out what pictures I have written. The pictures that I have written are very well known. They are such pictures as *Action in the North Atlantic, Sahara*—

MR. STRIPLING: Mr. Lawson—

MR. LAWSON: —such pictures as *Blockade,* of which I am very proud. and in which I introduced the danger that this democracy faced from the attempt to destroy democracy in Spain in 1937. These matters are all matters of public record.

MR. STRIPLING: Mr. Lawson, would you object if I read a list of the pictures, and then you can either state whether or not you did write the scripts?

MR. LAWSON: I have no objection at all.

MR. STRIPLING: Did you write *Dynamite,* by M-G-M?

MR. LAWSON: I preface my answer, again, by saying that it is outside of the province of this Committee, but it is well known that I did.

Mr. Stripling: *The Sea Bat,* by M-G-M?

Mr. Lawson: It is well known that I did.

Mr. Stripling: *Success at Any Price,* RKO?

Mr. Lawson: Yes, that is from a play of mine, *Success Story.*

Mr. Stripling: *Party Wire,* Columbia?

Mr. Lawson: Yes, I did.

Mr. Stripling: *Blockade,* United Artists, Wanger?

Mr. Lawson: That is correct.

Mr. Stripling: *Algiers,* United Artists, Wanger?

Mr. Lawson: Correct.

Mr. Stripling: *Earth Bound,* Twentieth Century–Fox.

Mr. Lawson: Correct.

Mr. Stripling: *Counterattack,* Columbia.

Mr. Lawson: Correct.

Mr. Stripling: You have probably written others, have you not, Mr. Lawson?

Mr. Lawson: Many others. You have missed a lot of them.

Mr. Stripling: You don't care to furnish them to the Committee, do you?

Mr. Lawson: Not in the least interested.

Mr. Stripling: Mr. Lawson, are you now or have you ever been a member of the Communist Party of the United States?

Mr. Lawson: In framing my answer to that question I must emphasize the points that I have raised before. The question of Communism is in no way related to this inquiry, which is an attempt to get control of the screen and to invade the basic rights of American citizens in all fields.

Mr. McDowell: Now, I must object—

Mr. Stripling: Mr. Chairman—

(*The Chairman pounding gavel.*)

Mr. Lawson: The question here relates not only to the question of my membership in any political organization, but this Committee is attempting to establish the right—

(*The Chairman pounding gavel.*)

Mr. Lawson: —which has been historically denied to any committee of this sort, to invade the rights and privileges and immunity of American citizens, whether they be Protestant, Methodist, Jewish, or Catholic, whether they be Republicans or Democrats or anything else.

The Chairman (*pounding gavel*): Mr. Lawson, just quiet down again. Mr. Lawson, the most pertinent question that we can ask is whether or not you have ever been a member of the Communist Party. Now, do you care to answer that question?

Mr. Lawson: You are using the old technique, which was used in Hitler Germany in order to create a scare here—

THE CHAIRMAN (*pounding gavel*): Oh—

MR. LAWSON: —in order to create an entirely false atmosphere in which this hearing is conducted—

(*The Chairman pounding gavel.*)

MR. LAWSON: —in order that you can then smear the motion-picture industry, and you can proceed to the press, to any form of communication in this country.

THE CHAIRMAN: You have learned—

MR. LAWSON: The Bill of Rights was established precisely to prevent the operation of any committee which could invade the basic rights of Americans. Now, if you want to know—

MR. STRIPLING: Mr. Chairman, the witness is not answering the question.

MR. LAWSON: If you want to know—

(*The Chairman pounding gavel.*)

MR. LAWSON: —about the perjury that has been committed here and the perjury that is planned—

THE CHAIRMAN: Mr. Lawson—

MR. LAWSON: —permit me and my attorneys to bring in here the witnesses that testified last week and permit us to cross-examine these witnesses, and we will show up the whole tissue of lies—

THE CHAIRMAN (*pounding gavel*): We are going to get the answer to that question if we have to stay here for a week. Are you a member of the Communist Party, or have you ever been a member of the Communist Party?

MR. LAWSON: It is unfortunate and tragic that I have to teach this Committee the basic principles of American—

THE CHAIRMAN (*pounding gavel*): That is not the question. That is not the question. The question is: Have you ever been a member of the Communist Party?

MR. LAWSON: I am framing my answer in the only way in which any American citizen can frame his answer to a question which absolutely invades his rights.

THE CHAIRMAN: Then you refuse to answer that question; is that correct?

MR. LAWSON: I have told you that I will offer my beliefs, affiliations, and everything else to the American public, and they will know where I stand.

THE CHAIRMAN (*pounding gavel*): Excuse the witness—

MR. LAWSON: As they do from what I have written.

THE CHAIRMAN (*pounding gavel*): Stand away from the stand—

MR. LAWSON: I have written Americanism for many years, and I shall continue to fight for the Bill of Rights, which you are trying to destroy.

THE CHAIRMAN: Officers, take this man away from the stand—

(*Applause and boos.*)*

THE CHAIRMAN (*pounding gavel*): There will be no demonstrations. No demonstrations, for or against. Everyone will please be seated. All right, go ahead, Mr. Stripling. Proceed.

MR. STRIPLING: Mr. Chairman, the Committee has made exhaustive investigation and research into the Communist affiliations of Mr. John Howard Lawson. Numerous witnesses under oath have identified Mr. Lawson as a member of the Communist Party. I have here a nine-page memorandum which details at length his affiliations with the Communist Party and its various front organizations. I now ask that Mr. Louis J. Russell, an Investigator for the Committee, take the stand.

In order to give the Committee the type of affiliations that Mr. Lawson has had with the Communist Party, I should like to refer, Mr. Chairman, to an article which appeared in the *Daily Worker,* the official organ of the Communist Party. This article is dated September 6, 1935, and appears on page 5 of the *Daily Worker*. Under the headline "Artists, writers," it says: "We cannot let the *Daily* go under—" referring to the *Daily Worker*. It says: "Need for *Daily Worker* has grown a thousand times since 1934." By John Howard Lawson. The article bears a picture of Mr. Lawson, and it appears on the front page of the *Daily Worker*. Under the *Daily Worker* heading, the following language appears: *"The Daily Worker*—central organ of the Communist Party of the United States, section of the Communist International." I have here, Mr. Chairman, another article from the *Daily Worker* by John Howard Lawson, dated February 26, 1935, page 5: "The Story of William Z. Foster, a tribute on the occasion of his fifty-fourth birthday, by John Howard Lawson." I have here, Mr. Chairman, over one hundred exhibits showing Mr. Lawson's affiliations with the party.

Your name is Louis J. Russell?

MR. RUSSELL: That is right.

MR. STRIPLING: You are a member of the investigative staff of the Committee on Un-American Activities?

MR. RUSSELL: I am.

MR. STRIPLING: You were formerly with the FBI for ten years?

MR. RUSSELL: I was.

MR. STRIPLING: Were you detailed to make an investigation as to the Communist Party affiliations of John Howard Lawson?

MR. RUSSELL: I was.

MR. STRIPLING: What did your investigation disclose?

MR. RUSSELL: We were furnished—or I was—with copies of Communist Party registration cards pertaining to certain individuals for the year 1944.

THE CHAIRMAN: Speak louder, please.

MR. RUSSELL: One of those cards bears the number 47275 and is made

*** As Lawson is taken away by officers. —E.B.**

out in the name of John Howard Lawson, 4542 Coldwater Canyon; City, Los Angeles; County, Los Angeles; State, California. There is a notation contained on this registration card: "New card issued on December 10, 1944." Other information contained on this card, which referred to the personal description of the John Howard Lawson mentioned, on Communist Party registration No. 47275—the description is as follows: "Male, white. Occupation, writer. Industry, motion pictures. Member of CIO–A. F. of L." "Independent union or no union," "Independent union" is checked. There is a question asked on this registration card: "Is member club subscriber for *Daily Worker*?" The answer, "Yes," is checked.

MR. STRIPLING: That is all, Mr. Russell. Now, Mr. Chairman, what is the Committee's pleasure with regard to the nine-page memorandum? Do you want it read into the record or do you want it made a part of the record?

THE CHAIRMAN: The Committee wants you to read it.

MR. STRIPLING:

INFORMATION FROM THE FILES OF THE COMMITTEE ON UN-AMERICAN ACTIVITIES, UNITED STATES HOUSE OF REPRESENTATIVES, ON THE COMMUNIST AFFILIATIONS OF JOHN HOWARD LAWSON

John Howard Lawson is a screen writer and one of the most active Communists in the Hollywood movie industry. . . .

The files of the House Committee on Un-American Activities show that—

1. Rena M. Vale, a former member of the Communist Party and a screen writer, testified before the Special Committee on Un-American Activities on July 22, 1940, that Mr. Lawson had been identified to her as a Communist Party member when she met him at a Communist Party fraction meeting. She further testified that Mr. Lawson during the meeting gave advice on inserting the Communist Party line into drama. The State legislative committee investigating un-American activities in California has cited Mr. Lawson as "one of the most important Marxist strategists in southern California," in its 1945 report, page 118. The California report notes on the same page that Rena M. Vale also testified before the State legislative committee and that the witness identified Lawson as a member of the Communist Party fraction of the Screen Writers Guild who had given advice on the Communist Party program in the writing of the play *Sun Rises in the West*. The State legislative committee states further, in its 1947 report, page 260, that Mr. Lawson directed a Communist bloc of about sixty-five members in local 47, the Hollywood local of the American Federation of Musicians, AFL, between the years 1937 and 1940.

2. The Communist Party has been publicly defended by John Howard Lawson. The *Daily Worker,* in an article on April 16, 1947, page 2, and reprinted in the Sunday edition of April 20, 1947, page 8, announced that Mr. Lawson was one of the signers of a statement opposing any legislative attempts to restrict the activities of the Communist Party. The organization sponsoring the statement was the Civil Rights Congress, which the House Committee on Un-American Activities, in a report published September 2,

1947, declared to be "dedicated not to the broader issues of civil liberties, but specifically to the defense of individual Communists and the Communist Party." The Civil Rights Congress is now defending such persons as Gerhart Eisler, an agent of the Communist International convicted of passport fraud, and Eugene Dennis, Communist Party general secretary, convicted of contempt of Congress. The Civil Rights Congress is the successor to the International Labor Defense, former legal arm of the Communist Party, according to former Attorney General Francis Biddle. John Howard Lawson also came to the support of the Communist Party on another occasion, according to the *Daily Worker* for March 18, 1945, page 2. Mr. Lawson was listed in this issue as one of the signers of a statement hailing a War Department order allowing military commissions for Communists. Sponsor of the statement was the National Federation for Constitutional Liberties, which was cited as a Communist front organization by former Attorney General Biddle. Biddle pointed out the organization's defense of such prominent Communist leaders as Sam Darcy and Robert Wood, party secretaries for Pennsylvania and Oklahoma, respectively. The organization was also cited as a Communist front by the Special Committee on Un-American Activities on June 25, 1942, and March 29, 1944.

3. John Howard Lawson has given his support to a number of individual Communists. The *People's World,* official west coast Communist organ, reported on October 22, 1942, page 2, that Mr. Lawson was backing Mrs. LaRue McCormick, a candidate for the California State Senate on the Communist Party ticket. Mr. Lawson was one of the signers of a statement in defense of the Comintern agent Gerhart Eisler, according to the *Daily Worker* for February 28, 1947, page 2. The organization sponsoring this statement in behalf of Eisler was the Civil Rights Congress.

The "statement" which Lawson was not allowed to read into the record was published in *Hollywood on Trial* by Gordon Kahn (New York, 1948), and is here reprinted uncut:

A Statement by John Howard Lawson

For a week, this Committee has conducted an illegal and indecent trial of American citizens, whom the Committee has selected to be publicly pilloried and smeared. I am not here to defend myself, or to answer the agglomeration of falsehoods that has been heaped upon me, I believe lawyers describe this material, rather mildly, as "hearsay evidence." To the American public, it has a shorter name: dirt. Rational people don't argue with dirt. I feel like a man who has had truckloads of filth heaped upon him; I am now asked to struggle to my feet and talk while more truckloads pour more filth around my head.

No, you don't argue with dirt. But you try to find out where it comes from. And to stop the evil deluge before it buries you—and others. The immediate source is obvious. The so-called "evidence" comes from a parade of stool-pigeons, neurotics, publicity-seeking clowns, Gestapo agents, paid informers, and a few ignorant and frightened Hollywood artists. I am not going to discuss this perjured testimony. Let these people live with their consciences, with the knowledge that they have violated their country's most sacred principles.

These individuals are not important. As an individual, I am not important. The obvious fact that the Committee is trying to destroy me personally and professionally, to deprive me of my livelihood and what is far dearer to me—my honor as an American—gains significance only because it opens the way to similar destruction of any citizen whom the Committee selects for annihilation.

I am not going to touch on the gross violation of the Constitution of the United States, and especially of its First and Fifth Amendments, that is taking place here. The proof is so overwhelming that it needs no elaboration. The Un-American Activities Committee stands convicted in the court of public opinion.

I want to speak here as a writer and a citizen.

It is not surprising that writers and artists are selected for this indecent smear. Writers, artists, scientists, educators, are always the first victims of attack by those who hate democracy. The writer has a special responsibility to serve democracy, to further the free exchange of ideas. I am proud to be singled out for attack by men who are obviously—by their own admission on the record—out to stifle ideas and censor communication.

I want to speak of a writer's integrity—the integrity and professional ethics that have been so irresponsibly impugned at these hearings. In its illegal attempt to establish a political dictatorship over the motion picture industry, the Committee has tried to justify its probing into the thought and conscience of individuals on the ground that these individuals insert allegedly "subversive" lines or scenes in motion pictures. From the viewpoint of the motion picture producer, this charge is a fantasy out of the Arabian Nights. But it is also a sweeping indictment of the writer's integrity and professional conduct. When I am employed to write a motion picture, my whole purpose is to make it a vital, entertaining creative portrayal of the segment of life with which it deals. Many problems arise in writing a picture. Like all honest writers, I never write a line or develop a situation, without fully discussing its implications, its meaning, its tendency, with the men in charge of production. Where a line or a situation might relate to controversial issues, I am particularly insistent on full discussion, because such issues affect studio policy, critical response and popularity of the picture.

My political and social views are well known. My deep faith in the motion picture as a popular art is also well known. I don't "sneak ideas" into pictures. I never make a contract to write a picture unless I am convinced that it serves democracy and the interests of the American people. I will never permit what I write and think to be subject to the orders of self-appointed dictators, ambitious politicians, thought-control gestapos, or any other form of censorship this Un-American Committee may attempt to devise. My freedom to speak and write is not for sale in return for a card signed by J. Parnell Thomas saying "O.K. for employment until further notice."

Pictures written by me have been seen and approved by millions of Americans. A subpoena for me is a subpoena for all those who have enjoyed these pictures and recognized them as an honest portrayal of our American life.

Thus, my integrity as a writer is obviously an integral part of my integrity as a citizen. As a citizen I am not alone here. I am not only one of nineteen men who have been subpoenaed. I am forced to appear here as a representative of one hundred and thirty million Americans because the illegal conduct of this Committee has linked me with every citizen. If I can be destroyed no American is safe. You can subpoena a farmer in a field, a lumberjack in the woods, a worker at a machine, a doctor in his office—you can deprive them of a livelihood, deprive them of their honor as Americans.

Let no one think that this is an idle or thoughtless statement. This is the course that the Un-American Activities Committee has charted. Millions of Americans who may as yet be unconscious of what may be in store for them will find that the warning I speak today is literally fulfilled. No American will be safe if the Committee is not stopped in its illegal enterprise.

I am like most Americans in resenting interference with my conscience and belief. I am like most Americans in insisting on my right to serve my country in the way that seems to me most helpful and effective. I am like most Americans in feeling that loyalty to the United States and pride in its traditions is the guiding principle of my life. I am like most Americans in believing that divided loyalty—which is another word for treason—is the most despicable crime of which any man or woman can be accused.

It is my profound conviction that it is precisely because I hold these beliefs that I have been hailed before this illegal court. These are the beliefs that the so-called Un-American Activities Committee is seeking to root out in order to subvert orderly government and establish an autocratic dictatorship.

I am not suggesting that J. Parnell Thomas aspires to be the man on horseback. He is a petty politician, serving more powerful forces. Those forces are trying to introduce fascism in this country. They know that the only way to trick the American people into abandoning their rights and liberties is to manufacture an imaginary danger, to frighten the people into accepting repressive laws which are supposedly for their protection.

To anyone familiar with history the pattern for the seizure of dictatorial power is well known. Manufactured charges against "reds," "communists," "enemies of law and order" have been made repeatedly over the centuries. In every case, from the Star Chamber in Stuart England to the burning of the Reichstag in Nazi Germany, the charges have included everyone with democratic sympathies; in every case the charges have been proven false; in every case, the charges have been used to cover an arbitrary seizure of power.

In the terrible wave of repression that swept England at the end of the eighteenth century, Charles James Fox asked a simple question: "We have seen and heard of revolutions in other states. Were they owing to the freedom of popular opinions? Were they owing to the facility of popular meetings? No, sir, they were owing to the reverse of these." The writers and thinkers who were jailed and silenced at that time were all cleared a few years later. The great scientist, Priestley, whose home was burned, was forced to flee to America where he was honored as an apostle of liberty. The persecutions under the Alien and Sedition Acts in our own country in 1798 were all proved to be the irresponsible means by which a reactionary political party sought to maintain itself in power. Congress officially repaid all the fines collected under the Sedition Act. The cry of sedition was again raised through the land in 1919 in order to build up the illusion of a nonexistent national emergency and thus justify wholesale violations of the Bill of Rights, designed solely to crush labor, prevent American participation in the League of Nations, and keep reaction in power.

Today, we face a serious crisis in the determination of national policy. The only way to solve that crisis is by free discussion. Americans must know the facts. The only plot against American safety is the plot to conceal facts. I am plastered with mud because I happen to be an American who expresses opinions that the House Un-American Activities Committee does not like. But my opinions are not an issue in this case. The issue is my right to have opinions. The Committee's logic is obviously: Lawson's opinions are properly subject to censorship; he writes for the motion picture industry, so the industry is properly subject to censorship; the industry makes pictures for the American people, so the minds of the people must be censored and controlled.

Why? What are J. Parnell Thomas and the Un-American interests he serves, afraid of? They're afraid of the American people. They don't want to muzzle me. They want to muzzle public opinion. They want to muzzle the great Voice of democracy. Because they're conspiring against the American way of life. They want to cut living standards, introduce an economy of poverty, wipe out labor's rights, attack Negroes, Jews, and other minorities, drive us into a disastrous and unnecessary war.

The struggle between thought-control and freedom of expression is the struggle between the people and a greedy unpatriotic minority which hates and fears the people. I wish to present as an integral part of this statement, a paper which I read at a Conference on Thought Control in the United States held in Hollywood on July 9th to 13th. The paper presents the historical background of the threatening situation that we face today, and shows that the attack on freedom of communication is, and has always been, an attack on the American people.

The American people will know how to answer that attack. They will rally, as they have always rallied, to protect their birthright.

OCTOBER 29, 1947:

Edward Dmytryk

The committee met at 10:30 a.m., the Honorable J. Parnell Thomas (Chairman) presiding.

THE CHAIRMAN: The record will show that a Subcommittee is sitting, with Mr. McDowell, Mr. Vail, and Mr. Thomas present.

Staff members present: Mr. Robert E. Stripling, Chief Investigator; Messrs. Louis J. Russell, H. A. Smith, Robert B. Gaston, Investigators; and Mr. Benjamin Mandel, Director of Research.

Now, the Chair at this point would like to make a brief recapitulation with reference to the Committee's investigation of Communist influences in the motion-picture industry. Responding to the demand of the people, the present Committee on Un-American Activities made a preliminary investigation which produced ample evidence that a full-scale investigation was in order of the extent of Communist infiltration in Hollywood. This Committee has utilized the services of trained investigators, all former FBI agents, to assemble this evidence in this manner. The Committee's authority to conduct such an investigation, under authority of Public Law 601, is crystal-clear. We have not violated and we are not violating the rights of any American citizen, not even the rights of the Communists whose first allegiance is to a foreign government. The Committee is well aware that powerful influences have sought in every manner to divert this Committee from its main course of inquiry. I am proud to say that this Committee has not been swayed, intimidated, or influenced by either Hollywood glamor, pressure groups, threats, ridicule, or high-pressure tactics on the part of high-paid puppets and apologists for certain elements of the motion-picture industry. The people are going to get the facts, just as I announced on the opening day.

MR. STRIPLING: Mr. Dmytryk, when and where were you born?

MR. DMYTRYK: I was born on September 4, 1908, in Grand Forks, British Columbia, Canada.

MR. STRIPLING: When and how did you become a citizen of the United States?

MR. DMYTRYK: I was nationalized [naturalized?] in 1939 in Los Angeles.

MR. STRIPLING: What is your occupation?

MR. DMYTRYK: I am a motion-picture director.

MR. STRIPLING: How long have you been acting in that occupation?

MR. DMYTRYK: Well, I have been a director since 1939. However, I first entered motion pictures early in 1923.

MR. STRIPLING: With what studios are you now associated?

MR. DMYTRYK: I am with RKO.

MR. STRIPLING: What studios were you associated with in the past?

MR. DMYTRYK: I have worked at Universal. Most of my years were spent at Paramount.

MR. STRIPLING: Would you give the Committee the names of some of the pictures you have directed?

MR. DMYTRYK: Mr. Chairman, I have a statement here that I would like to make. The names of some of the pictures I have directed are included in here. May I please make this statement?

MR. CRUM: Show it to the Chairman.

THE CHAIRMAN: Let me see the statement. (*After a pause.*) This statement is typical of the other statements that we have inspected. It is not at all pertinent to this inquiry. Therefore, the Chair rules it cannot be read.

MR. DMYTRYK: Mr. Chairman, I feel that since this statement concerns the questions which have been brought up here as to the effect of this investigation—

THE CHAIRMAN: The Chair has ruled that the statement was not pertinent at all. The Chief Investigator will ask questions, and you will please answer them.

MR. DMYTRYK: All right.

MR. STRIPLING: Mr. Dmytryk, are you a member of the Screen Directors Guild?

MR. DMYTRYK: Mr. Stripling, I feel that these kinds of questions are designed to—

THE CHAIRMAN: Just a minute. It is not up to you to "feel" what the design is. It is up to you to answer the questions and be responsive to the questions. Go ahead.

MR. DMYTRYK: Mr. Chairman, if you will let me I will answer the question. However, most other witnesses, certainly the witnesses the first week, were given the right to answer as they pleased. Some went on at great length—

MR. STRIPLING: Pardon me, Mr. Dmytryk. About how long a time would you require to answer whether or not you were a member of the Screen Directors Guild? Would five minutes be long enough?

Mr. Dmytryk: It would take me a lot less than five minutes.

The Chairman: It would take you five minutes to answer whether you are a member of the Screen Directors Guild?

Mr. Dmytryk: I said it would take me a lot less than five minutes, Mr. Chairman.

The Chairman: A lot less than five minutes. Can't you answer yes or no, are you a member of the Screen Directors Guild?

Mr. Dmytryk: There aren't many questions that can be answered yes or no—

The Chairman: I am referring to this one question. Can you answer it yes or no?

Mr. Dmytryk: I would like to answer the question. I would like to answer it in my own way.

The Chairman: We want you to answer the question, but we want a specific answer. That question can be answered yes or no.

Mr. Dmytryk: I don't feel you should tell me how to answer the question. I have told you that I would like to answer the question in my own way.

The Chairman: Well, you try to answer the question to the best of your ability, but you must make it very plain whether you are a member or not a member of the Screen Directors Guild.

Mr. Dmytryk: I will be glad to answer.

The Chairman: If it takes a long time to answer it, why, something is wrong.

Mr. Dmytryk: I don't think it will take long enough to bore you, Mr. Chairman.

The Chairman: Go ahead.

Mr. Dmytryk: I think that this kind of questioning is designed to bring about a split in many of the guilds, among the members of the guilds, at a time when we have just succeeded in getting unity between the guilds. I do want to say, however, that it is a matter of public record, since a fight some of us had against Mr. Wood—Sam Wood—in which Mr. Wood wound up on the losing end, with the entire guild against Sam Wood, that I was an officer of the Screen Directors Guild.

Mr. Stripling: Are you now or have you ever been a member of the Communist Party, Mr. Dmytryk?

Mr. Dmytryk: Well, Mr. Stripling, I think that there is a question of constitutional rights involved here. I don't believe that you have—

The Chairman: When did you learn about the Constitution? Tell me when you learned about the Constitution?

Mr. Dmytryk: I will be glad to answer that question, Mr. Chairman. I first learned about the Constitution in high school and again—

Mr. McDowell: Let's have the answer to the other question.

Mr. Dmytryk: I was asked when I learned about the Constitution.

MR. STRIPLING: I believe the first question, Mr. Dmytryk, was: Are you now, or have you ever been, a member of the Communist Party?

MR. DMYTRYK: All right, gentlemen, if you will keep your questions simple, and one at a time, I will be glad to answer.

MR. STRIPLING: That is very simple.

MR. DMYTRYK: The Chairman asked me another question.

THE CHAIRMAN: Never mind my question. I will withdraw the question.

MR. DMYTRYK: I have been advised that there is a question of constitutional rights involved. The Constitution does not ask that such a question be answered in the way that Mr. Stripling wants it answered. I think that what organizations I belong to, what I think, and what I say cannot be questioned by this Committee.

MR. STRIPLING: Then you refuse to answer the question?

MR. DMYTRYK: I do not refuse to answer it. I answered it in my own way.

MR. STRIPLING: You haven't answered whether or not you are a member of the Communist Party.

MR. DMYTRYK: I answered by saying I do not think you have the right to ask—

MR. STRIPLING: Mr. Chairman, it is apparent that the witness is pursuing the same line as the other witnesses.

THE CHAIRMAN: The witness is excused.

Like the "statements" of all of the Hollywood Ten, Edward Dmytryk's statement was published in *Hollywood on Trial*. Since, however, it was emended, if not canceled out, by a subsequent appearance of Dmytryk before the Committee, it has been thought more important to reprint the transcript of the reappearance (under date April 25, 1951, below).

Emmet Lavery had helped prepare the "brief" which Hallie Flanagan hoped to present to HUAC on behalf of the Federal Theater in 1938. He mystified the vigilantes because he was not only a Catholic but a liberal. Translated into their terms, it meant that he was a Communist masquerading as a Catholic. His views, to be sure, were closer to John XXIII than to Cardinal Spellman; and he merits a place in this book precisely as representing such views. Incidentally, Lavery won one of the few victories for anti-anti-Communists in those years. The lawsuit which he mentions (below) having brought against Ginger Rogers' mother was later settled in his favor.

OCTOBER 29, 1947:

Emmet Lavery

MR. STRIPLING: When and where were you born, Mr. Lavery?

MR. LAVERY: I was born at Poughkeepsie, New York, Dutchess County, November 8, 1902.

MR. STRIPLING: What is your occupation?

MR. LAVERY: I am a playwright, screen writer, and member of the Bar of the State of New York.

MR. STRIPLING: How long have you been a writer?

MR. LAVERY: I have written, alternately, for the stage and screen, since the year 1934. At the present time I am about to rehearse, in New York, a play which has been variously described and was described before this Committee. In Hollywood, I am currently preparing for an independent film production, an adaptation of a play about the Jesuits, *The First Legion.*

MR. STRIPLING: Would you give us the names of some of your plays, Mr. Lavery?

MR. LAVERY: Gladly. I think the play with which the Committee is probably most familiar is *The Magnificent Yankee,* a dramatization of the life of Mr. Justice Holmes from the biography by Francis Biddle, former Attorney General of the United States. My screen plays best known are two that dealt with war topics: *Hitler's Children,* and an adaptation from *Education for Death,* by Gregor Ziemer, and *Behind the Rising Sun*—both produced by RKO. My writings for the theater have included *The First Legion,* which has been produced in twelve languages since it was first done in the United States in 1914; *Monsignor's Hour; Second Spring,* a play about Cardinal Newman and Cardinal Manning; *Brother Petroc's Return,* an adaptation of the English novel by an English nun; *Brief Music; Kamiano,* a play about Damien; *Murder in a Nunnery,* an adaptation of the English novel by Eric Shepherd.

MR. STRIPLING: Mr. Lavery, now long have you been in Hollywood?

MR. LAVERY: I first went to Hollywood in 1934. I remained there until approximately 1937. I was in the East from 1937 to 1941. I returned to Hollywood in 1941. I remained in 1942. I came back East. I returned in 1943. And I have been there since. And let me volunteer, if permitted, that I am now serving my third term—

MR. STRIPLING: Just a moment, Mr. Lavery.

MR. LAVERY: All right, Mr. Stripling.

MR. STRIPLING: Will you answer this question—

MR. LAVERY: Surely.

MR. STRIPLING: —without an outburst: Are you a member of the Screen Writers Guild?

MR. LAVERY: Well, I wanted to volunteer the information that I am both a member and serving my third term as president.

MR. STRIPLING: Do you see anything incriminating in any way to a person answering whether or not he is a member of the Screen Writers Guild?

MR. LAVERY: For myself, I am delighted and proud to answer that I am president of the guild, to which I have been greatly devoted.

MR. STRIPLING: Well, isn't it true that the Screen Writers Guild is the one big writers' organization or union within the motion-picture industry?

MR. LAVERY: We are the only one. We are the recognized bargaining agency for screen writers in Hollywood, and our position there corresponds, roughly, to that of the Dramatists Guild in New York or the Radio Writers Guild or the Authors League. As a matter of fact, we are affiliated with the Authors League of America.

MR. STRIPLING: Can you explain to the Committee why there is so much reluctance on the part of the previous witnesses to answer the simple question as to whether or not they belong to a recognized guild in the motion-picture industry?

MR. LAVERY: Mr. Stripling, I can't go into their minds. I would like to remind the Chair at this time that in order to expedite the discussion, I would appreciate the opportunity to make several very brief motions—

MR. STRIPLING: This is not a discussion, Mr. Lavery. It is for the purpose of obtaining facts.

MR. LAVERY: Well, I stand corrected.

THE CHAIRMAN: May I ask if these are motions to be made by you as a witness, or motions to be made by you as an attorney, or motions made by your organization?

MR. LAVERY: Well, I guess it is all three, Mr. Chairman. I am here as myself, as counsel for myself, and as the only authorized spokesman for the Screen Writers Guild of Hollywood, which has been mentioned considerably by witnesses before this Committee. So, on my own behalf, in various capacities, I simply wanted to make one or two requests of the Chair, to straighten out the record. If the rule is no, why, we can simply go on with the examination.

MR. STRIPLING: Mr. Chairman, I should like to state Mr. Lavery is here in response to a subpoena—

MR. LAVERY: I do want to say that I would be here, whether you gave me a subpoena or not.

THE CHAIRMAN: I just want to find out whether these motions are pertinent to the inquiry of alleged Communism in Hollywood.

MR. LAVERY: I think so, Mr. Chairman. I wouldn't offer them if they weren't.

MR. STRIPLING: Do you have them in writing?

MR. LAVERY: Well, the motions are oral, but a statement that I would like to offer I have here in writing.

THE CHAIRMAN: Which do you want to offer first, the motion or the statement?

MR. LAVERY: I would like to offer the motions first, if I might.

THE CHAIRMAN: All right; without objection, so ordered.

MR. LAVERY: Thank you, Mr. Chairman. My first request for the record will be: Would the Committee recall to the stand Mr. Jack L. Warner, of Warner Brothers Studios, and subpoena all pertinent records of Warner Brother Studios, in order to establish by Mr. Warner's own records that it was at my request, and not Mr. Warner's, that our association was dissolved early in 1946.

MR. MCDOWELL: Mr. Chairman, I move the Committee take the motion under consideration.

THE CHAIRMAN: Without objection, so ordered.

MR. LAVERY: Mr. Chairman, I would like to ask whether, in the course of the examination by Mr. Stripling, I may have the opportunity to reply specifically to serious misstatements of fact made by three witnesses last week. I refer to Mr. Jack Moffitt, who made serious misinterpretations about a play on Congress which I have written. I refer to Mr. Morrie Ryskind, who said that the Screen Writers Guild, under my leadership, was under Communist domination. And I refer to Mr. Rupert Hughes, who made the serious implication, if not direct charge, that I was a Communist masquerading as a Catholic. And as a Catholic, I ask the opportunity to establish in this record how far from the truth Mr. Hughes is. Will I have the opportunity to reply specifically to those three witnesses?

THE CHAIRMAN: Without objection, the Chair will give you permission to reply to those. That is just why you are here. Charges have been made against you and against your organization.

MR. LAVERY: Thank you, Mr. Chairman.

THE CHAIRMAN: We subpoenaed the other side, and you are the only one to date, however, willing to come here and be very frank. And it is very refreshing, I will tell you that.

MR. LAVERY: Thank you, Mr. Chairman. I would like to offer in evidence at this time, if I may, an official transcript of the testimony which I gave to Senator Jack Tenney and the California Joint Fact Finding Committee on Un-American Activities on October 7, 1946, drawing particular attention to the remarks of Chairman Tenney, who wrote into the record that in his opinion I am not a Communist and the guild is not Communist-controlled. I want to have a notation made for the record that in October 1946, a few weeks after I appeared before the Tenney committee, I appeared voluntarily before the office of the FBI in Los Angeles—the office of Mr. Richard B. Hood—and I asked him to make a notation that, as president of the guild, I had appeared before the FBI voluntarily and had offered to put myself and any records of our guild completely at his disposal at any time. I have not heard from him.

THE CHAIRMAN: When was that?

MR. LAVERY: That was in October 1946. I think the records of Mr. Hood in the Los Angeles office of the FBI will bear me out on that. I would also ask the Chairman to permit me to have a notation made for the record that when the Committee held its hearings in Los Angeles, in the spring of last year, I was not subpoenaed then, nor were any records of my guild subpoenaed. Now, Mr. Chairman—and this will dispense with my preliminary motions—I have a piece of information that I would like to put in the record on my own motion and on my volunteering, because I am not sure, as a student of constitutional law, whether the Committee does have the authority to demand it of me, but let me break the suspense immediately and tell you that I am not a Communist. I never have been. I don't intend to be. I will make open confession and admit that I am a Democrat, who in my youth was a Republican. And if the Committee wants to know why I changed from Republican to Democrat—

THE CHAIRMAN: No, we are not interested in why you changed. (*Laughter.*)

MR. STRIPLING: You are now the president of the Screen Writers Guild, is that true?

MR. LAVERY: That is correct.

MR. STRIPLING: How many times have you been president?

MR. LAVERY: I am serving my third and last term.

MR. STRIPLING: And when were you last elected?

MR. LAVERY: A year ago this November.

MR. STRIPLING: How many members are there of the Screen Writers Guild?

MR. LAVERY: I think our active voting members number approximately 937. Our nonvoting associate members number approximately 531.

MR. STRIPLING: And what is the purpose of the guild?

MR. LAVERY: We are the official bargaining agency for screen writers in Hollywood. We correspond roughly to the position of the Dramatists Guild in the theater and are unaffiliated with either the A.F. of L. or the CIO. Our only affiliation is with the Authors League of America.

MR. STRIPLING: Now, the Authors League of America, was that established by the guild?

MR. LAVERY: No. The Authors League of America is a much older organization. It is a, you might call it, federation which unifies the Radio Writers Guild, the Authors League, the Dramatists Guild, and ourselves, although we are not full members of the league. We are merely an affiliate.

* * *

Mr. Stripling: Now, Mr. Lavery, as president of the guild, have you ever noticed or observed or are you aware of any Communist infiltration within the Screen Writers Guild?

Mr. Lavery: Mr. Stripling, I am willing to make the assumption that there are Communists in the Screen Writers Guild.

Mr. Stripling: What influence do you think they exert within the guild?

Mr. Lavery: Well, Mr. Stripling, our Screen Writers Guild has what this Committee would probably consider an extreme left, and it has an extreme right, but the great rank and file of the membership is what I call liberal center. And, like any guild, we have our discussions. We try to keep them in the family. I think we keep our guild on a good, even keel. My only concern with respect to this whole proceeding, Mr. Chariman, is merely that people might go back home and think that they have been political martyrs. An election in November which is coming up in our Screen Writers Guild might be seriously affected, and not for the better, if people thought that Government had interfered more than was necessary in the normal operations of the guild.

Mr. Stripling: Are you familiar with Mr. John Howard Lawson?

Mr. Lavery: Yes. I have known John Howard Lawson for some years.

Mr. Stripling: Is it true that he was the first president of the guild?

Mr. Lavery: I think way back in the early days, prior to reorganization of the guild in 1937, John Howard Lawson was president, yes.

Mr. Stripling: Is he now a member of the guild?

Mr. Lavery: Yes.

Mr. Stripling: Do you think that John Howard Lawson is a member of the Communist Party?

Mr. Lavery: Mr. Stripling, I don't know whether he is or not. I have never seen his card. But I have heard the testimony that has been offered here this week.

Mr. Stripling: Does Mr. Lawson conduct himself in guild affairs along the Communist Party line?

Mr. Lavery: Well, the truth of the matter is, Mr. Stripling, that Mr. Lawson hasn't been as active in the affairs of the guild, at least on the floor of meetings that I have chaired, as he was in years gone by.

Mr. Stripling: What about Mr. Dalton Trumbo? Do you know Mr. Dalton Trumbo?

Mr. Lavery: Yes, I know Mr. Trumbo.

Mr. Stripling: And Mr. Trumbo was editor of the *Screen Writer,* the official publication of the guild, was he not?

Mr. Lavery: At one time Mr. Dalton Trumbo was editor of the *Screen Writer,* the monthly publication of the Screen Writers Guild.

Mr. Stripling: Do you know if he holds any other position in the Screen Writers Guild at this time?

MR. LAVERY: I don't think so.

MR. STRIPLING: Do you think Mr. Dalton Trumbo is a Communist?

MR. LAVERY: Mr. Stripling, I have no information beyond what I have heard here this week. I heard the charge made that there was a membership card in his name.

MR. STRIPLING: Are you familiar with the statement which the *Hollywood Reporter* carried, asking Mr. Trumbo and others who are members of the Screen Writers Guild to deny that they held party card so-and-so?

MR. LAVERY: Yes. But the reason that perhaps I don't attribute too much weight to what the *Hollywood Reporter* says, Mr. Stripling, is that one time they said the same things about me until I threatened to sue Mr. Wilkerson for libel: he published a two-page retraction at his own expense.

THE CHAIRMAN: Isn't it quite strange, then, that they don't threaten to sue?

MR. LAVERY: Well, maybe I like to sue more than other people, Mr. Chairman.

THE CHAIRMAN: These days everybody likes to sue, I can tell you that.

MR. LAVERY: I have a libel suit pending in the State of California against one of the star witnesses of this Committee. I have sued Mrs. Lela Rogers in the Superior Court of California for one million dollars in libel and slander for remarks made about a play of mine, *The Gentleman from Athens,* in a Town Hall broadcast on September second.

THE CHAIRMAN: Wasn't that all in the newspapers?

MR. LAVERY: It was also in the records of this Committee, Mr. Chairman.

THE CHAIRMAN: Well—

MR. LAVERY: Everything except the fact that I sued her for libel.

THE CHAIRMAN: Well, is it pertinent to this inquiry?

MR. LAVERY: I think it is pertinent as to the credibility of whatever Mrs. Rogers said.

MR. STRIPLING: I don't think Mrs. Rogers made any mention of it during her testimony, Mr. Lavery.

MR. LAVERY: No, but she talked about Communism in Hollywood.

MR. STRIPLING: But we are now asking you about Communism in the Screen Writers Guild.

MR. LAVERY: All right, let us discuss Communism in the Screen Writers Guild.

MR. STRIPLING: What influence do the six people* who have been here in the last three days exercise in the guild?

MR. LAVERY: Mr. Stripling, they do not have control of the guild, and, if they did have control of the guild, I would have stayed home long ago.

* John Howard Lawson, Dalton Trumbo, Albert Maltz, Alvah Bessie, Samuel Ornitz, and Herbert Biberman. —E.B.

MR. STRIPLING: Did they ever have control of the guild?

MR. LAVERY: Not while I have been president.

MR. STRIPLING: Did Mr. Trumbo? He was the editor of the *Screen Writer*.

MR. LAVERY: Yes, that is true, but—

MR. STRIPLING: I think some of these others have held prominent positions in the guild.

MR. LAVERY: Yes, but we are a guild of many, many members, Mr. Stripling—937 or 931 active members. You have mentioned the names of perhaps a half dozen.

MR. STRIPLING: There will be others.

MR. LAVERY: I will be glad to discuss them, if I can.

MR. STRIPLING: Would you think it is possible for a few Communists to exert tremendous influence within unions and organizations?

MR. LAVERY: I think it is possible for them to try. I don't think in a group of writers it is possible for them to get away with it. Have you ever tried to organize a group of writers to do anything?

(*Laughter. The Chairman pounds gavel.*)

MR. STRIPLING: Mr. Lavery, are you familiar with an organization known as the Hollywood Writers Mobilization?

MR. LAVERY: Yes. I was its wartime chairman. And may I point out that there was an error the other day in one of the dossiers describing the Hollywood Writers Mobilization. I don't know where your investigators got their information, but I am sure the FBI in Los Angeles can tell you that the Hollywood Writers Mobilization was not the successor of the League of American Writers. Nobody who knows the Hollywood scene would ever make that observation. The Hollywood Writers Mobilization was roughly what you might call a writers' war board, formed on the West Coast during the war, to service the agencies of the Government in their need for various scripts in various parts of the war effort. And I have brought with me here today, if the Committee is interested, a medal—not an important medal, but a medal anyway—which the Treasury Department of the United States sent to me, as chairman of the Writers Mobilization in return for the work that I did in the war years.

THE CHAIRMAN: Mr. Lavery, the Committee has gone over your statement. In view of the fact that you have indicated your attitude very fully up to now—and you will probably have more to add—plus the additional fact that there is much in your statement that is not pertinent to the inquiry, we decline to have you read the statement in these hearings.

MR. LAVERY: May I have a notation made for the record, Mr. Chairman, that I respectfully dissent?

THE CHAIRMAN: That is your right.

MR. LAVERY: And may I carry the further notation that I am always available and at the service of the Committee for any questions. I don't want to leave this stand, Mr. Chairman, without going exhaustively into any questions—

THE CHAIRMAN: Oh, we are not asking you to leave the stand.

MR. STRIPLING: Mr. Lavery, can you tell me what position, if any, you ever held in the Hollywood Writers Mobilization?

MR. LAVERY: I was its wartime chairman.

MR. STRIPLING: Do you know whether the Writers Mobilization ever attempted any censorship?

MR. LAVERY: I don't see how they would be in a position to, Mr. Stripling. They wrote literally on assignment to Government agencies.

MR. STRIPLING: Would you describe for the Committee just what the Writers Mobilization did do?

MR. LAVERY: Briefly, it was a clearing house set up by six or seven guilds in Hollywood, to pool their common functions as writers, actors, directors, and producers, in the preparation of scripts for war-bond drives; documentaries for use of the Army or Navy or Treasury Departments; and similar activity—the preparation of speeches during the war drive. This was definitely a cooperative research agency placed at the disposal of the Government. The speeches or films or scripts were never produced by us. They were written by us and then turned over to the people who had ordered them.

MR. STRIPLING: Mr. Lavery, in connection with the Hollywood Writers Mobilization, did they ever take a position regarding the production of *Abie's Irish Rose*?

MR. LAVERY: I can't recall, Mr. Stripling.

MR. STRIPLING: Mr. Chairman, I would like to introduce into the record a letter from Bing Crosby dated March 11, 1947, addressed to Mr. Howard Koch, chairman of the Hollywood Writers Mobilization.

MR. LAVERY: May I point out that by that time I had resigned from the Mobilization?

MR. STRIPLING: Why did you resign, Mr. Lavery?

MR. LAVERY: Increase of other work.

THE CHAIRMAN: Well, even though it hasn't anything to do with this witness, is the letter pertinent to the inquiry?

MR. STRIPLING: Yes. I think it deals with the objections on the part of the Hollywood Writers Mobilization to the production of *Abie's Irish Rose*. Mr. Bing Crosby wrote a letter concerning it.

THE CHAIRMAN: All right, go ahead and read it.

MR. STRIPLING: It is addressed to Mr. Koch, chairman of the Hollywood Writers Mobilization.

DEAR MR. KOCH:

I feel the production *Abie's Irish Rose* is a victim of a very unfortunate turn of events. When I was approached to lend my name to a group concerned with the production of this picture—and that is all I ever did—lend my name—I consented on the representation, entirely credible, that such a film would prove an effective means of advancing interracial amity. The film was made with complete script and dialogue approval of all sects and with proper representatives of such groups in attendance on the set. It is inconceivable to me now that any group can, in conscience, object to the film or any part thereof. But a concerted campaign is being waged against the booking of the picture, in the motion-picture business, and against its exhibition to the public. In the most liberal interpretation possible, such action can only be construed as unfair, unjust, and restraint of trade.

Sincerely yours,
BING CROSBY.

MR. LAVERY: There are matters of taste in the theater. There are many people, both Catholic and Jew, who work in the theater who don't like the oversimplification of those types. I can conceive of lots of people protesting the production of *Abie's Irish Rose* as merely perpetuating stage types that have gone out of fashion and that don't do justice to the racial groups concerned. I don't think one has to be a Communist to take exception to *Abie's Irish Rose*.

MR. MCDOWELL: On the other hand, Mr. Lavery, one wouldn't be some sort of Fascist to have enjoyed *Abie's Irish Rose*.

MR. LAVERY: I agree absolutely, Mr. McDowell.

MR. MCDOWELL: If I recall, I saw it four or five times, and millions of Americans did and thought it was a delightful story and well played.

MR. LAVERY: I agree with you. I think that one could have a difference of opinion over the merits of *Abie's Irish Rose* without either being a Fascist on the one side or a Communist on the other.

THE CHAIRMAN: If you people don't stop pretty soon, I'll be reading the book.

MR. STRIPLING: Mr. Lavery, in regard to the presence, within the Screen Writers Guild, of Communists, do you think that any action should be taken to remove these people from the guild?

MR. LAVERY: Mr. Stripling, I stand with Mr. Edgar Hoover, of the FBI. Mr. Hoover says he thinks it would be bad policy to outlaw the Communist Party and to drive it underground. I think so, too. I think that under our existing contract with the producers and our existing constitution, it would be next to impossible for us to remove anybody from our guild for political belief, private political belief or action. In our guild, I have said many times that, if any individual members are guilty of indictable offenses, let a proper complaint be brought to the FBI, and an indictment sought by a Federal grand jury and action taken accordingly. But short of that, particularly in time of peace, it would be disastrous for a guild to attempt to project a standard of conduct not yet embodied in the law by the Congress of the United States.

MR. STRIPLING: What is your opinion as to the Communist Party of the United States? Do you think they are a political party, or do you consider them to be the agent of a foreign principal?

MR. LAVERY: Mr. Stripling, like many Americans, I am confused. I don't know. I like my country. I don't think I would like a party that was devoted to a foreign power or that was an agent of a foreign power. I think the basic difficulty is that it is [not?] a demonstrable point in each individual case. If a man is an unregistered agent of a foreign power, then I think he ought to be indicted and tried for any offense that is appropriate under the Federal law. But to make the general observation, I don't know. I haven't the access to the information.

MR. STRIPLING: Have you ever heard that J. Edgar Hoover testified before this Committee that Communists were agents of a foreign power?

MR. LAVERY: Yes, I think I have heard something to that effect, Mr. Chairman.

THE CHAIRMAN: Well, then, won't you, too, agree with J. Edgar Hoover that Communists were agents of a foreign power?

MR. LAVERY: I would still say, Mr. Chairman, that it was a case of proof and fact in each individual case. We toss the word "Communism" around. I have heard nobody on this stand, or in the Committee either, define the kind of Communism we are talking about. I assume it is Marxian Communism. But there are shades and shades of people in this country who consider themselves Communists, and there are shades and shades of people who are called Communists without being it. So when counsel asks me to generalize, do I think the Communists are agents of a foreign power, I will say, "Well, how can anybody under oath answer with any assurance." I don't know. I don't have the facts.

MR. STRIPLING: We will limit it to Stalinists. Do you think the Stalinist Communists are the agents of a foreign power?

MR. LAVERY: Mr. Stripling, I have no way of knowing who is or who is not a Stalinist. If I was a member of the FBI, or if I were a member of the research staff of this Committee, perhaps I would have such information. I don't. And as a matter of fact, under the constitution of the guild of which I am president, I am discouraged from inquiring into the political or religious belief of our members—and, I think, wisely. We would have no guild if the president could begin to examine each member on his political or religious beliefs.

THE CHAIRMAN: Nothing has been brought up about religion, Mr. Lavery, except by yourself.

MR. LAVERY: No. Mr. Rupert Hughes brought up religion. He said that I was a Communist masquerading as a Catholic.

THE CHAIRMAN: Well, I want to tell you something. I didn't hear Rupert Hughes say that, but I want to tell you that this Committee is never interested in one's religion.

Mr. Lavery: Thank you, Mr. Chairman.

Mr. Stripling: Mr. Lavery, what is your opinion about outlawing the Communist Party?

Mr. Lavery: I think the best answer to Communism is to live a better life, run a better guild. I think if we make political martyrs out of them we make it easy for the Communists. I think Mr. Hoover is absolutely right. Certainly, in time of peace, if we are not on the verge of war, I think it would be fatal to outlaw any one political party.

Mr. Stripling: Mr. Lavery, for example, we take Mr. Albert Maltz. Are you familiar with Mr. Maltz?

Mr. Lavery: Yes, I know Mr. Maltz.

Mr. Stripling: Do you remember that Mr. Maltz wrote an article which appeared in the *New Masses,* official organ of the Communist Party?

Mr. Lavery: I heard reference made to it.

Mr. Stripling: Yes. Are you familiar with the letter which he wrote and the article which he subsequently wrote in which he did a complete somersault?

Mr. Lavery: No, I am not.

Mr. Stripling: Well, would you say that a person in the Screen Writers Guild who consistently followed the exact line as laid down by the Soviet Union is following the Communist Party line of Stalinism or do you think that he is exercising his freedom of political belief?

Mr. Lavery: Mr. Stripling, I just don't know. I mean, this is a—

Mr. Stripling: There are a number of these people, Mr. Lavery, in your guild, a number of them, very prominent.

Mr. Lavery: Yes.

Mr. Stripling: Now, you have been president three times. You certainly must have observed their activities, and I think you are a little more aware than you have told the Committee of just how they operate.

Mr. Lavery: Mr. Stripling, if you want me to make myself counsel for the prosecution, that is rather difficult. That is your job. I am not here either as prosecutor or as defendant. I'll admit I have had arguments with a lot of these people in the guild, but I am not here as an alarmist. I say we have a good guild. I say that some of the people who have appeared before you with tales about our guild are sincere, but they are mistaken. I don't know why you rate so highly the influence of Mr. Maltz, Mr. Lawson, Mr. Trumbo. They are able men. They are articulate men. And they are competent screen writers. But they are only a few of a membership of nine hundred some. We have often had our arguments within the family. I think so far I have had the upper hand. I have nothing to complain about. And when Mr. Stripling says, "Aren't you worried about Mr. Maltz," I say, "Not particularly."

Mr. Stripling: Mr. Lavery, during this year, in the spring of this year, did Mr. Eric Johnston come to Hollywood and appear before a meeting of the Screen Writers Guild?

MR. LAVERY: Yes, indeed. I had been urging Mr. Johnston to come over and speak to our guild for a year.

MR. STRIPLING: How long did that meeting last?

MR. LAVERY: Oh, perhaps an hour and a half, maybe two hours.

MR. STRIPLING: Did Mr. Johnston urge the guild to oust the Communists within it?

MR. LAVERY: I can't honestly say that I recall Mr. Johnston telling the guild to get rid of any group of members. As a matter of fact, it was a very peaceful meeting. If Mr. Johnston made that kind of a speech, we probably would have been there until two o'clock that morning.

THE CHAIRMAN: Why would that be?

MR. LAVERY: Why, Mr. Chairman, because writers will argue at the drop of a hat. And if somebody tells them they can't do something, particularly if he be a producer or a representative of a producer, we will stay there all night with him, just perhaps to be negative.

MR. STRIPLING: It wasn't a very heated meeting, in other words?

MR. LAVERY: I don't think so.

MR. STRIPLING: Was his appearance there regarding the problem of picture making, or was it regarding the issue of Communism within the guild?

MR. LAVERY: Ever since Mr. Johnston had become president of the Motion Picture Association I had been urging him to come and speak to the writers, and I think Mr. Johnston was anxious to come and speak to us. As you can imagine, in an industry as diversified as ours, relations between producers, employers, and writers, particularly at the creative level, are often, shall we say, competitive. There is not always understanding and sympathy between the man who is paying for the script and the man who is writing it. Both Mr. Johnston and myself thought it was a good opportunity for closer understanding between production management, on the one hand, and writers on the other.

MR. VAIL: Mr. Witness, aren't you aware of the development of Communism all over the world?

MR. LAVERY: Yes. I read the headlines every day, Mr. Congressman.

MR. VAIL: And isn't it your feeling, too, that Communism has gained a foothold in this country, and its influence is spreading rapidly?

MR. LAVERY: I don't think it is spreading as rapidly in this country as it is elsewhere in the world.

MR. VAIL: But it is spreading rapidly today?

MR. LAVERY: Elsewhere.

MR. VAIL: That is the general consensus. In the Gallup poll not long ago the American people indicated, by their ballot, that only one per cent felt that Communism was a serious threat to this country. Now, don't you believe that the American people should be alerted to the danger that exists in the form of Communism today?

MR. LAVERY: Mr. Congressman, I think that they are alert to the general danger abroad of Communism, but I think that the alerting at home requires a different approach, if we are really to meet the menace and be equal to it. I think, in our own domestic American life, the way to meet the challenge of Communism is not repressive legislation or scareheads, but to show that we have a better way of life, to dramatize that life. Now, this Committee has asked previous witnesses as to whether they think anti-Communist pictures should be made. Mr. Chairman, I think that there is nothing that sends an audience out of a theater quicker than an anti picture about anything, special propaganda in any form. But I do believe, with all my heart and soul, that this is a great time for all of us to dramatize the American way of life, in any medium, at any level of life that is available for us. The more attractive we make our American scheme of life, I think the more secure we are.

MR. VAIL: Don't you think that the gentlemen who appeared before this Committee have dramatized Communism to some degree by the exhibition they put on? Don't you think today that it is vital that the American citizen be as militant and American as these Communists are militant throughout the world?

MR. LAVERY: Mr. Congressman, if we are to keep harping on the note of fear, it is like the old-fashioned revival or the old-fashioned mission, where you scare the devil out of the parishioners for a week, and after that they are rather accustomed to the notion of fear. I don't think it is enough to make people afraid. It is very easy to make them afraid. I think the problem is how to make people aware of the active love that they have. I think that the negative force of fear is distinctly noncreative. The challenge of the theater and the screen is to project an American way of life, particularly an historical drama, that vitalizes the whole tradition of which we are a part. Believe me, I am much more interested, as a playwright and a screen writer, in trying to show, for instance, what Mr. Justice Holmes would be like than showing how bad Mr. Stalin is. It would be very easy to show how bad Mr. Stalin is, but the positive virtues of our great American leaders are the thing that the screen should be showing at this time.

MR. VAIL: Well, I think that it is the general opinion today that anyone who seeks to temper the public acceptance of the menace of Communism is doing a distinct disservice to their country.

MR. LAVERY: Well, Mr. Congressman, there were three editorials in the *Osservatore Romano* last spring, front page, on the international situation. The Pope himself, speaking through the editorial in the *Osservatore Romano,* reminded people that perhaps the time had come to slow down the push toward war. Now, I don't think anybody calls the Holy Father a warmonger for trying to slow down the feeling of national pride and security. I think he is a man that is trying to put out fires. And I think that if sincere people come before this Committee and say that they think the positive picture of the American life is the better way to do it, that doesn't mean they are less loyal Americans. I think it means they are more vital Americans, and they are trying to do it on a deeper and more stable basis than merely a lot of attacks on a potential enemy.

THE CHAIRMAN: Mr. McDowell, do you have any questions?

MR. MCDOWELL: Yes. Mr. Lavery, it is a great relief to have you testify.

MR. LAVERY: Thank you, Mr. Congressman.

MR. MCDOWELL: Without waving your arms and screaming and insisting that something was being done to you—about the Bill of Rights. It is good to hear somebody from the Screen Writers Guild talk as freely as you have. I think you are a good example of, shall I say, a liberal coming before this Committee. We have been many times accused of trying to do something to liberals. We are not. Liberals are a part of America, just the same as I am, and I am not a liberal. You sort of pooh-poohed the idea that a small minority of Communists can have much influence. Well now, the facts don't bear out that thought. There is a very tiny minority of Communists that run two hundred million people in Russia, which has become a slave state.

MR. LAVERY: I merely say we have beaten them. They have not run away with the opera house.

* * *

MR. STRIPLING: Go ahead, Mr. Lavery.

MR. LAVERY: Just replying specifically, Mr. Chairman, to a point made last week by a previous witness—I think it was Mr. Jack Moffitt—who said that I had written a play which attempted to slur the Congress of the United States. I have the greatest respect for the Congress of the United States. I tried to run for Congress last spring. The voters of my district, perhaps wisely, decided in the primary election that I wasn't the man to come to Congress, but one doesn't run for a thing that he doesn't value, and I assure you that this play that we are working on, *The Gentleman from Athens,* will be a tribute to the democratic process.

MR. MCDOWELL: What is the name of it?

MR. LAVERY: *The Gentleman from Athens.* And when we open, Mr. Chairman, I would be delighted to have this Committee come and see it. I thought, If I can't go to Congress, at least I will try to write about it in terms that will be acceptable to people who hold this thing dear.

MR. MCDOWELL: Well, not that the Committee will have anything to do with the play, but *The Gentleman from Athens* is a play about the United States Congress?

MR. LAVERY: Yes. It is a mythical town called Athens, California.

MR. MCDOWELL: Oh.

MR. LAVERY: I would also like to point out that, in the nature of picture making, Mr. Chairman, it so happens that our guild does not qualify the writers who are members of it. I think people might get the idea that perhaps we just go out any week that we are short of members and recruit a few more and that, if the membership committee were not extraordinarily alert, we might get a lot of Stalinists in. Oddly enough, our guild accepts members only after they are qualified in the industry. If a man works twenty-six weeks in pictures, or comes to us on transfer from the Authors League, he is an active member of our guild, but he cannot be a voting or an active member of our guild unless he works twenty-six weeks in the picture industry or comes to us on transfer from the Authors League. Another point: I feel that very few people here have had the opportunity to discuss the making of pictures. When people talk about the content of what gets on the screen, I wonder if any witness has told this Committee that it is not like the writing of a novel or the making of a play, which is often a rather individual and solitary effort. It has often been said in Hollywood that the making of pictures is a kind of collaborative compromise: the world and his brothers are in it. Fifty or more departments are involved in the preparation of the script, from the time that it is bought to the time it goes on the screen. Everybody and his brother has a hand in that script—"Put it in for Harry," "Take it out for Joe"—the advertising department, the location department—

THE CHAIRMAN: I think we understand that.

MR. LAVERY: One more point: I feel at this time the Congress of the United States and this Committee could do a great thing, to raise the sights of picture making. If somebody would go to Congress and ask for enough money to permit the Library of Congress to organize an international film festival in which the best films—

THE CHAIRMAN: Organize a what?

MR. LAVERY: An international film festival in which the best work in the films of each country is presented at a festival, better than any that have been held. Now, there are many international film festivals, but not one that we give. And sometimes the rivalries are international and rather bitter. It seems to me that the Congress of the United States and the Library of Congress could do a great thing for picture making the world over, for better understanding between nations, if they would say, "Let us hold in Washington a great international film festival, with the best work of each country brought here and shown in the Library of Congress."

THE CHAIRMAN: Do you have in mind inviting all of the nations of the world to that festival?

MR. LAVERY: Mr. Chairman, I will leave that to Congress and the Library of Congress.

THE CHAIRMAN: Well, I was wondering if we invited Russia whether they would attend.

MR. LAVERY: Your guess is as good as mine. Perhaps they would. But I was not thinking only of the Russians, Mr. Chairman. I was thinking that pictures, after all, are one of the great mediums of international communication. It is probably the only way the French people know what Americans as a whole are like—we know what the French people are like. Most of our people never meet—the French, the British, and even the Germans, the Austrians, and the Hungarians. Here is this great medium of communication which could do so much for better understanding between nations. I think it would be a graceful thing if the Library of Congress and the Congress of the United States would say, "Why don't we have a festival, without prizes, where the best work of each nation is presented, so that we can understand what the creative force of pictures in the world is today."

OCTOBER 30, 1947:

Ring Lardner, Jr.

The Committee met at 10:30 a.m., the Honorable J. Parnell Thomas (Chairman) presiding.

THE CHAIRMAN: The record will show that a Subcommittee is sitting, consisting of Mr. McDowell, Mr. Vail, and Mr. Thomas.

Staff members present: Mr. Robert E. Stripling, Chief Investigator; Messrs. Louis J. Russell and Robert B. Gaston, Investigators; and Mr. Benjamin Mandel, Director of Research.

MR. STRIPLING: When and where were you born, Mr. Lardner?

MR. LARDNER: On August 19, 1915, in Chicago, Illinois.

MR. STRIPLING: What is your occupation?

MR. LARDNER: A writer.

MR. STRIPLING: How long have you been a writer?

MR. LARDNER: I have been a writer about ten years. Mr. Chairman, I have a short statement I would like to make.

(*The witness hands statement to the Chairman. The witness hands statement to Mr. Stripling.*)

THE CHAIRMAN: Mr. Lardner, the Committee is unanimous in the fact that after you testify you may read your statement.

MR. LARDNER: Thank you.

MR. STRIPLING: Mr. Lardner, are you a member of the Screen Writers Guild?

Mr. Lardner: Mr. Stripling, I want to be cooperative about this but there are certain limits to my cooperation. I don't want to help you divide or smash this particular guild, or to infiltrate the motion-picture business in any way for the purpose which seems to me to be to try to control that business, to control what the American people can see and hear in their motion-picture theaters.

The Chairman: Now, Mr. Lardner, don't do like the others, if I were you, or you will never read your statement. I would suggest—

Mr. Lardner: Mr. Chairman, let me—

The Chairman: —you be responsive to the question.

Mr. Lardner: I am—

The Chairman: The question is: Are you a member of the Screen Writers Guild?

Mr. Lardner: But I understood you to say that I would be permitted to read the statement, Mr. Chairman.

The Chairman: Yes, after you are finished with the questions and answers.

Mr. Lardner: Yes.

The Chairman: But you certainly haven't answered the questions.

Mr. Lardner: Well, I am going to answer the questions, but I don't think you qualified in any way your statement that I would be allowed to read this statement.

The Chairman: Then I will qualify it now. If you refuse to answer the questions, then you will not read your statement.

Mr. Lardner: Well, I know that is an indirect way of saying you don't want me to read the statement.

The Chairman: Then you know right now you are not going to answer the question. Is that correct?

Mr. Lardner: No, I am going to answer the question.

The Chairman: All right, then, answer that question.

Mr. Lardner: All right, sir. I think these points I am bringing out are relevant to the question, because I have to consider why the question is asked—

The Chairman: We will determine why the question was asked. We want to know whether you are a member of the Screen Writers Guild.

Mr. Lardner: Yes—

The Chairman: That is a very simple question. You can answer that yes or no. You don't have to go into a long harangue or speech. If you want to make a speech, you know where you can go out there.

Mr. Lardner: Well, I am not very good in haranguing, and I won't try it, but it seems to me that, if you can make me answer this question, tomorrow you could ask somebody whether he believed in spiritualism.

The Chairman: Oh, no, there is no chance of our asking anyone whether they believe in spiritualism, and you know it. That is just plain silly.

MR. LARDNER: You might—

THE CHAIRMAN: Now, you haven't learned your lines very well.

MR. LARDNER: Well—

THE CHAIRMAN: I want to know whether you can answer the question yes or no.

MR. LARDNER: If you did, for instance, ask somebody about that you might ask him—

THE CHAIRMAN: Well, now, never mind what we might ask him. We are asking you now, Are you a member of the Screen Writers Guild?

MR. LARDNER: But—

THE CHAIRMAN: You are an American—

MR. LARDNER: But that is a question—

THE CHAIRMAN: —and Americans should not be afraid to answer that.

MR. LARDNER: Yes, but I am also concerned as an American with the question of whether this Committee has the right to ask me—

THE CHAIRMAN: Well, we *have* got the right, and until you prove that we haven't got the right, then you have to answer that question.

MR. LARDNER: As I said, if you ask somebody, say, about spiritualism—

THE CHAIRMAN: You are a witness, aren't you? Aren't you a witness?

MR. LARDNER: Mr. Chairman—

THE CHAIRMAN: Aren't you a witness here?

MR. LARDNER: Yes, I am.

THE CHAIRMAN: All right, then, a Congressional Committee is asking you: Are you a member of the Screen Writers Guild? Now you answer it yes or no.

MR. LARDNER: Well, I am saying that in order to answer that—

THE CHAIRMAN: All right, put the next question. Go to the sixty-four-dollar question.

THE WITNESS: I haven't—

THE CHAIRMAN: Go to the next question.

MR. STRIPLING: Mr. Lardner, are you now or have you ever been a member of the Communist Party?

MR. LARDNER: Well, I would like to answer that question, too.

MR. STRIPLING: Mr. Lardner, the charge has been made before this Committee that the Screen Writers Guild which, according to the record, you are a member of, whether you admit it or not, has a number of individuals in it who are members of the Communist Party. This Committee is seeking to determine the extent of Communist infiltration in the Screen Writers Guild and in other guilds within the motion-picture industry.

MR. LARDNER: Yes.

MR. STRIPLING: And certainly the question of whether or not you are a member of the Communist Party is very pertinent. Now, are you a member or have you ever been a member of the Communist Party?

MR. LARDNER: It seems to me you are trying to discredit the Screen Writers Guild through me, and the motion-picture industry through the Screen Writers Guild, and our whole practice of freedom of expression.

MR. STRIPLING: If you and others are members of the Communist Party you are the ones who are discrediting the Screen Writers Guild.

MR. LARDNER: I am trying to answer the question by stating, first, what I feel about the purpose of the question which, as I say, is to discredit the whole motion-picture industry.

THE CHAIRMAN: You won't say anything first. You are refusing to answer this question.

MR. LARDNER: I am saying my understanding is, as an American resident—

THE CHAIRMAN: Never mind your understanding. There is a question: Are you or have you ever been a member of the Communist Party?

MR. LARDNER: I could answer exactly the way you want, Mr. Chairman—

THE CHAIRMAN: No—

MR. LARDNER: —but I think that is a—

THE CHAIRMAN: It is not a question of our wanting you to answer that. It is a very simple question. Anybody would be proud to answer it—any real American would be proud to answer the question, "Are you or have you ever been a member of the Communist Party?"—any real American.

MR. LARDNER: It depends on the circumstances. I could answer it, but if I did, I would hate myself in the morning.

THE CHAIRMAN: Leave the witness chair.

MR. LARDNER: It was a question that would—

THE CHAIRMAN: Leave the witness chair.

MR. LARDNER: Because it is a question—

THE CHAIRMAN (*pounding gavel*): Leave the witness chair.

MR. LARDNER: I think I am leaving by force.

THE CHAIRMAN: Sergeant, take the witness away.

(*Applause.*)*

THE CHAIRMAN: Mr. Stripling, next witness.

MR. STRIPLING: Mr. Russell, you were detailed to make an investigation to determine whether or not Ring Lardner, Jr., was ever a member of the Communist Party?

MR. RUSSELL: I was.

MR. STRIPLING: Will you give the Committee the benefit of your investigation?

* As the sergeant obeys the order. —E.B.

MR. RUSSELL: During the course of my investigation I obtained information regarding the Communist Party registration card of Ring Lardner, Jr. This card bears the number 47180. It is made out in the name of Ring L., which, during the course of the investigation, developed to be the name of Ring Lardner, Jr., as contained on his Communist Party registration card. This card contains a notation: "1944 Card No. 46806." The address of Ring Lardner is given as 447 Loring; City, Los Angeles; County, Los Angeles; State, California. The card contains a notation, "New card issued on November 30, 1944." The description of Ring Lardner as contained on the card is as follows: "Male; occupation, writer; industry, m. picture." The question is then asked: "Member of CIO, A.F. of L., independent union, no union"? "Independent union" is checked. Another question asked is: "Is member club subscriber for *Daily Worker*?" The answer, "Yes" is checked.

MR. STRIPLING: That is all, Mr. Russell. Mr. Chairman, the Committee has prepared a memorandum concerning the Communist affiliations of Ring Lardner, Jr.

1. Under date of August 22, 1946, the *Hollywood Reporter,* a publication in Los Angeles, Calif., carried an editorial headed "More Red Commissars." This editorial is quoted, in part, as follows:

"Now let us take a look at another member of the Screen Writers Guild's executive board—Ring Lardner, Jr. As chairman of the Guild's powerful original materials committee Lardner incubated and sponsored the James M. Cain plan for literary dictatorship through the so-called American Authors Authority.

"The *Reporter* has this to ask Ring Lardner, Jr.: 'Are you a member of the Communist Party? Are you at present assigned to the Party's Northwest (propaganda) section? Do you hold Party Book No. 25109?' " The article continues: "Lardner has a long record of activity in Communist front organizations. The March 1937 issue of the *Western Worker* listed him as one of the signers of an open letter which denounced the demands of the American Committee for the Defense of Trotsky for an investigation of the Russian 'purge' trials. . . ."

One of the Hollywood Ten wrote a book about, or largely about, his experience with the Committee: *Inquisition in Eden* by Alvah Bessie (New York, 1965). Of the others, the one who did the most talking about it in public was Ring Lardner, Jr.* The *New York Herald Tribune* ran a long interview with him on January 7, 1948. The "statement" he was not allowed to read before the Committee was published in *Hollywood on Trial.* Finally, in the *Saturday Evening Post,* October 14, 1961, came a retrospective account, part of which is reprinted here. This drew a rejoinder from Roy M. Brewer, which appeared in

* That is, until recently. In 1970 Dalton Trumbo's letters appeared under the title *Additional Dialogue.*

the *American Legion Magazine,* March 1962, and is reprinted in full here.

"My Life on the Black List" by Ring Lardner, Jr.

A famous writer reveals that he was once a Communist, and tells about his career since he "declined to testify"

This extraordinary personal statement is revealing not only of the author's character but of the climate of thought that prevailed in many segments of American society in the 1930's and 1940's. The Post *in no way is pleading justification for Mr. Lardner. We believe merely that any thoughtful reader will find his story a contribution to the history of our times.*

—The Editors [of the *Saturday Evening Post*]

The blue prison fatigues hung loosely on the weary, perspiring man whose path across the quadrangle was about to meet mine. I felt I looked comparatively dapper in the same costume after a day of mild stenographic labor in the Office of Classification and Parole, but his job, while not exactly strenuous, kept him in the August sun all day. He was custodian of the chicken yard at the Federal Correctional Institution, Danbury, Connecticut, and his name was J. Parnell Thomas, formerly chairman of the Committee on Un-American Activities of the House of Representatives.

He had lost a good deal of weight, and his face, round and scarlet at our last encounter, was deeply lined and sallow. I recognized him, however, and he recognized me, but we did not speak. It would have been hard for either of us to pick up the thread after our sole previous exchange which, according to the official record, had ended:

MR. LARDNER: I could answer the question exactly the way you want, Mr. Chairman—

THE CHAIRMAN: No—

MR. LARDNER: —but I think that is a—

THE CHAIRMAN: It is not a question of our wanting you to answer that. It is a very simple question. Anybody would be proud to answer it—any real American would be proud to answer the question, "Are you or have you ever been a member of the Communist Party?"—any real American.

MR. LARDNER: It depends on the circumstances. I could answer it, but if I did, I would hate myself in the morning.

THE CHAIRMAN: Leave the witness chair.

MR. LARDNER: It was a question that would—

THE CHAIRMAN: Leave the witness chair.

MR. LARDNER: Because it is a question—

THE CHAIRMAN (*pounding gavel*): Leave the witness chair.

MR. LARDNER: I think I am leaving by force.
THE CHAIRMAN: Sergeant, take the witness away.

Nearly three years had elapsed between that bit of repartee before a battery of microphones and newsreel cameras, and our meeting in the jailyard in the summer of 1950. Along with nine other Hollywood writers and directors, I had lost an appeal of my conviction for contempt of Congress, and the Supreme Court had denied our request for a review of the constitutional issues in the case.

During the same period Mr. Thomas had been brought to trial for putting nonworkers on the Government payroll and appropriating their salaries to himself. Offering no defense and throwing himself on the mercy of the court, he had received an eighteen-months prison sentence, later reduced by parole to an actual term of about nine months.

My own stint was one year, reduced by "statutory good-time" to ten months and by "meritorious good-time" to nine and a half. This last concession of fifteen days was a tribute to my spelling and punctuation, which, I was told by a grateful official at the Connecticut spa, were markedly superior to the institutional norm.

Though far from happy at being where I was, I was sharply aware of the difference between my situation and that of this pathetically aging man. Even if the torch of super-Americanism he had brandished so fiercely during his two years of glory had not already been picked up by Sen. Joseph McCarthy, there was no conceivable political future for Thomas. Perhaps he could return to the obscurity of the insurance business in New Jersey, but no business or social contacts would ever again be easy for a man whose downfall had been so pitilessly publicized.

My own future was at least speculative. I had taken the position that, while public servants are answerable to the people, citizens cannot be summoned, in the absence of even an allegation of an illegal act, to account to government for their beliefs and associations—matters that have traditionally been an American's own business. It was a position that had commanded a good deal of support, some of it quite respectable. In fact, I had based it on what seemed to be unequivocal language in a 1943 Supreme Court decision: "If there is any fixed star in our constitutional constellation, it is that no official, high or petty, can prescribe what shall be orthodox in politics, nationalism, religion or other matters, of opinion, or force citizens to confess by word or act their faith therein."

Forced confessions, or disavowals, were what the committee was clearly demanding, and I felt it was an abuse of the legislative function that needed challenging. Unfortunately the only legal way to challenge it involved the risk of losing the argument.

The impulse to resist such assaults on freedom of thought has motivated witnesses who could have answered "no" to the Communist question as well as many, like myself, whose factual response would have been "yes." I was at that time a member of the Communist Party, in whose ranks I had found some of the most thoughtful, witty and generally stimulating men and women of Hollywood. I also encountered a number of bores and unstable characters, which seemed to bear out Bernard Shaw's observation that revolutionary movements tend to attract the best and worst elements in a given society.

With both these extremes the relationship had been a confidential one, and an added reason for taking the chance of a contempt citation was the fact that I had no legal defense at all if I first admitted my own membership and then declined to implicate other people.

For reasons of no particular pertinence to this story, my political activity had already begun to dwindle at the time Mr. Thomas popped the question, and his only effect on my affiliation was to prolong it until the case was finally lost. At that point I could and did terminate my membership without confusing the act, in my own or anyone else's head, with the quite distinct struggle for the right to embrace any belief or set of beliefs to which my mind and my conscience directed me.

It was clear, in any event, that my uncooperative attitude had not improved my status. Long before going to jail I had lost my job. A scant month after my 1947 appearance there was a top-level meeting of the industry that had previously awarded me one of its Academy Oscars—for the picture *Woman of the Year* with Katharine Hepburn and Spencer Tracy—and a salary of $2000 a week at the age of thirty-one. It ended with a joint public statement declaring my colleagues and me unemployable.

This blacklisted status, expanded to cover more than 400 people from various crafts in movies, television and radio, has persisted ever since. A few of the writers among these outcasts have been able to operate under other names in the "black market." Others have had to find new occupations entirely, among them carpentry, selling women's clothing, bartending, driving a school bus, and waiting on tables in a restaurant.

For actors, of course, pseudonyms were out of the question, and the only branch of the entertainment world remaining more or less open to them has been the ailing Broadway theater.

While I didn't anticipate, during my Danbury sojourn, how long and how zealously my former employers would maintain their decree of exile, I could see, in the ample time for reflection provided by my Government, that the prospects were tougher than anything I had faced in a rather sheltered life.

I could assume that the newspaper and publicity businesses, in which I had been briefly employed before becoming a screen writer at the age of twenty-one, were not likely to welcome me back. I had no experience whatsoever as a novelist or playwright, and even these relatively open fields were somewhat restricted by the knowledge that my work could not be sold to the movies.

Writing for any of the major magazines was a highly dubious proposition and remained so up to the time of my present assignment. The only two blacklisted writers I know of who have sold their work profitably to magazines in recent years have had to do so under assumed names, despite the fact that both had previously been in considerable demand under their real ones.

The situation clearly demanded a readjustment for which my background had done nothing to equip me. When you are descended from a Lardner who sat on the Governor's Council in colonial Pennsylvania, and an Abbott who fought with the minutemen at Lexington and Bunker Hill, you find it hard to accept the "un-American" designation. And the fact that I bore, through no fault or merit of my own, a well-known name in American letters simply made it the most easily remembered among the "Hollywood Ten" by people who read about the case in the newspapers.

As a complicating detail, in the summer of 1947 my wife and I had bought a large house with a tennis court in Santa Monica, on the strength of a new contract with Twentieth Century–Fox. We had just begun the process of moving in when my subpoena from Mr. Thomas was delivered in September by the local United States marshal.

My employer's reaction to my Washington debut the following month was provocatively erratic. A week after I returned to work, I was asked to waive a contractual provision limiting the studio's use of my services to two pictures annually and to undertake a third screenplay for the current year. Then, after the industry heads had convened at the Waldorf Astoria in New York in November, I was directed to quit the premises on approximately two hours' notice.

I held out in the new house while the case against us progressed slowly from citation by the House of Representatives to indictment, arraignment, trial, conviction and appeal. My tennis game improved; my wife conceived and bore another child, making five for whose rearing and education I was financially responsible; what insecurity I felt was tempered by the general sentiment in Hollywood that the whole thing would blow over like other periodic tempests in the movie business. Among liberals at least, including those who considered my conduct unwise or quixotic, it was widely conceded that I had a clear legal right to take the stand I had.

Reflecting this attitude, the blacklist was not as rigid during this interim as its formal announcement had seemed to indicate. True, the doors of all the major studios were closed to me. But independent and semi-independent producers and the stars and directors who were beginning the now-prevalent practice of forming their own corporations were not nearly so timid as they later became about making furtive arrangements with the proscribed ten.

On completing one piece of work for a prominent star, I met him at his bank, where he drew and paid over my compensation in cash. The amount, while considerably more than I was accustomed to carry about, was much less formidable than it would have been before the blacklist, since even the most friendly of such secret employers were motivated in part by the opportunity to hire our services at cut rates.

There was also for some of us the chance to work abroad, where we encountered the almost unanimous opinion that what had happened to us was a piece of temporary American insanity. A European producer who came to Hollywood to employ me and to borrow one of Twentieth Century–Fox's leading stars found himself in negotiation with the same executive who had signed my dismissal notice. Before he was permitted to sublet the actor, for a fee of $200,000, he was asked who was doing the script. Given my name, the studio executive said, "Good man," and O.K.'d the deal.

These and other clandestine movie jobs enabled me to keep the food supply moving into hungry young mouths until April 10, 1950, when the Supreme Court announced its refusal to consider the issues in the two pilot cases on which the other eight of us had agreed to stand. This meant the imminent end of my precarious liberty and a distinctly reduced standard of living for my family. The first step was to finance their upkeep during my absence by selling the house, into which all my savings had gone, and moving them to rented quarters.

Quick sales of property were common amid the sudden changes of fortune in Hollywood, and the local trade papers often carried advertisements with such eye-catching captions as OWNER GOING ABROAD or OWNER RETURNING TO BROADWAY. I composed a notice featuring the line OWNER GOING TO JAIL and inserted it in one of these publications. A national news magazine, whose space rates I could scarcely have afforded, picked it up as a news story, reprinting the entire ad, and a Beverly Hills physician who was doing research in emotional stress at the gaming tables of Las Vegas, read it there, mounted his Cadillac before dawn and concluded by midday a deal that left me with a net loss of $9000.

The Danbury prison featured hygienic austerity and a clientele that specialized in nonviolent offenses such as mail theft, traffic in narcotics, driving stolen automobiles across state lines, embezzlement, tax evasion and using the mails to defraud. We also had a smattering of murderers, armed robbers and rapists, mostly transfers from Army disciplinary barracks who were permitted to pass their final months before release in our less stern surroundings.

The atmosphere in Hollywood had changed considerably when I returned in the spring of 1951. The blacklist up till then had covered only the ten of us and a few others who were bracketed with us by reason of marriage or an overly ardent support of our position. Now the Un-American Activities Committee had resumed the offensive; and what had been one of the main issues all along was clearly exposed for the first time in the case of an actor, Larry Parks.

Summoned before the committee, he admitted a nominal association with the Communist Party that had ended five years previously. "I would prefer," he added, "if you will allow me, not to mention other people's names." He was told sharply that in testifying about himself he had forfeited the protection against self-incrimination in the Fifth Amendment, a right none of the ten of us had invoked because, among other reasons, almost no one at the time considered Communist Party membership a crime. Between our appearance and his, however, had occurred the first prosecution and conviction of Communists under the Smith Act.

Parks pleaded with his inquisitors: "Don't present me with the choice of either being in contempt of this committee and going to jail or forcing me to really crawl through the mud to be an informer. . . . I beg of you not to force me to this."

The Congressmen remained unmoved, and Parks proceeded to provide them with what they wanted, setting a pattern that reached its high point later in the year when Martin Berkeley, a writer who specialized in movies whose main characters were horses, listed 162 men and women he alleged had been party members with him.

The industry blacklist policy was extended to cover every person subpoenaed by the committee who failed to answer all the questions put to him, or who having been named by a witness, did not appear voluntarily to clear or purge himself. It didn't matter whether, as in the case of writers and directors, they might conceivably exert a subversive influence on the content of movies, although all the studio heads had sworn to the committee that even this was impossible under their vigilant control. Actors, musicians, technicians and stenographers were chopped from the payrolls with equal dispatch.

It also didn't matter whether the grounds for not answering was the First Amendment, which the appellate-court decision in our case had rated as invalid protection, or the Fifth, which the Supreme Court had meanwhile upheld as a fully applicable use of a precious freedom that no man might legally construe as evidence of guilt.

Nor did it matter that some witnesses took a position that came to be known as the "diminished Fifth," declaring that they were not now Communists but declining to say whether they ever had been. They, too, were promptly added to the blacklist.

"The Truth About the 'Blacklist'" by Roy M. Brewer

An answer to communist propaganda
which tries to prove that red is black

This is an article that was offered to the Saturday Evening Post *as an answer to a piece written by Ring Lardner, Jr., that appeared in the October 14, 1961 issue of that publication. Mr. Brewer, who fought the communist infiltration of Hollywood, and who knew at first hand what such people as Lardner were doing, felt that the* Post *had done a disservice in setting forth the Lardner premise, actually the Party line, on "blacklists." He requested the opportunity of answering the article but permission was refused. Brewer made another appeal, pointing out: "There is a general misunderstanding of the so-called blacklisting problem in Hollywood, and this article has compounded the misunderstanding . . ." The* Post's *answer was another refusal.*

So, for the record and since The American Legion has long opposed the employment of communists in a communications media as important as motion pictures, we have opened our pages to Mr. Brewer's remarks.

My Life on the Blacklist
By Ring Lardner, Jr.

A famous writer reveals that he was once a Communist, and tells about his career since he "declined to testify."

Ring Lardner, Jr., who was a member of the Communist Party, got the opportunity to do another service for communism in this *Saturday Evening Post* article on Blacklists.

—From *The American Legion* magazine

A few months ago a friend, who happens to be a bank official, expressed his strong opposition to "the Hollywood blacklist." Such "persecution of people for political beliefs," he insisted, was unthinkable in this enlightened age.

"Would you employ a member of the Mafia as a cashier in your bank?" I asked him.

"Certainly not," he replied, "but that is different. I'm talking about respectable people—writers, actors, directors. You're talking about hoodlums who couldn't be trusted with bank funds and whose very presence in a bank would destroy public confidence in it."

Actually my friend the banker was citing the very reasons why communists have no business in motion pictures. What he had failed to recognize is that communism is not a political belief, but is, in fact, a world-wide organization of gangsters which is irrevocably dedicated to destroy every government in the world which it does not control. Many of the persons in it are deceived as to its real nature but as long as they are subject to its discipline they can never be trusted and their very presence in the industry destroys public confidence in it. Like the Black Hander in a bank, the communist has no allegiance to his employer but to an outside gang intent on plunder. And it has been demonstrated that the public has little liking for films in which communists have a part. Indeed, it was Hollywood's belated realization of this fact which brought into being the so-called "blacklist."

During World War II the communists had extended their influence in Hollywood but at the close of the war, as the true nature of communism became apparent, Americans decided that they wanted no part of those who served the criminal conspiracy then headed by Stalin. They therefore stopped patronizing films in which known communists and sympathizers were featured. Worried by this boycott, the industry decided it was bad business to try to jam red writers, actors and directors down the throats of a reluctant public. In a gesture that, in retrospect, seems to have been inspired more by a sense of public relations than sincerity, the industry assured the public that henceforth it would not knowingly employ communists or those who refused to answer questions asked by the House Un-American Activities Committee about communist affiliations. This it did in the famous Waldorf Declaration of 1947.

Reaction from the communist element was not long in coming. With their amazing talent for distortion, and with their fantastic ability at enlisting support from influential muddleheads, the communists set about selling the American public the idea that they were the pitiable victims of a diabolical "blacklist."

No right-thinking person believes in "blacklists." The term has evil overtones, echoes of a time when powerful employers created secret lists of employees they considered troublesome. By circulating these "blacklists" among themselves they were able to punish the unfortunate workers cruelly by depriving them of a chance to make a living. The practice has long since been outlawed and is recognized as unethical, immoral and illegal. Hollywood's communists cynically donned martyrs' robes as "victims of a blacklist," no doubt assuming that many Americans would overlook the fact that they were part of an international conspiracy aimed against the U.S.A.

The motion picture industry was not anxious to face up to the problem that communist infiltration presented. Most of its leaders found it much more convenient to accept the denials of the leftists and join them in their denials. Indeed, when the hearings of the House Committee on Un-American Activities of 1947 were being prepared, industry leaders joined with the fronts and the leftists in proclaiming such hearings "a witch hunt." The Motion Picture Producers Association took full-page ads charging that the industry was being persecuted for politically supporting the New Deal. Much of America accepts this analysis, assisted by the press which portrayed Hollywood's anti-communists as crackpots.

But when the hearings began and guards were required to drag the communist witnesses from the stand while they screamed invective at the Committee and called the chairman a Hitler, the American people suddenly realized that these people, reacting with the viciousness of a pack of cornered rats, were not the persecuted idealists they had pretended to be. Americans decided they wanted no part of such characters, and stayed away from films in which they had a part.

Their lush livelihood threatened, the communist element received powerful support in their efforts to prove that *they* were the ones who deserved sympathy—not the American people they were trying to sell out. As they cried "blacklist" their howls of anguish were echoed in some of the most influential publications in the country. But the American people were not impressed. As the cry began to die down the matter was revived in a widely distributed "study" made by the Fund for the Republic. This amateurish contribution to confusion did not make much of a case but it was enough for the same people who had previously been crying alligator tears over Hollywood's "persecuted" commies. These people seized upon the Fund's "study" as further proof that a lot of fine people were being victimized by a sinister crowd of superpatriots.

Now, after a lapse of several years, the same cry has been raised once again, and this time it has resounded from a strange quarter indeed—the once highly conservative *Saturday Evening Post*. In an article in the October 14, 1961 issue entitled "My Life on the Blacklist," Ring Lardner, Jr., acknowledged his Communist Party membership at the time of the 1947 hearings but then proceeded to use the pages of the *Post* to generate sympathy for himself and others who allegedly suffered as a result of the Waldorf Declaration.

There is no doubt that Lardner suffered economically when hearings of the HCUA exposed him as a communist. However, it would appear that, "blacklist" notwithstanding, he continued to live substantially, if not luxuriously, after his exposure. Nor does it follow that the industry was wrong in firing Lardner and his ideological soul-mates. It was Lardner's own action and his own decision that forced the industry's hand. He had the alternative of renouncing his communist obligations but he chose not to do so.

Lardner is a persuasive writer, and in his article he did an effective job of making it appear that the evil in Hollywood was the "blacklist" when, in reality, the problem was the communist penetration of the movie industry. Regrettably, the *Saturday Evening Post* did not see fit to present this side of the picture.

Communist attempts to penetrate Hollywood started about 30 years ago, when the commies embarked on a long-range plan to take over the industry and use it as an instrument of its program for world revolution. The ultimate objective, of course, was to overthrow the government of the United States and destroy our Judeo-Christian civilization. There is substantial evidence to establish that this effort was Moscow-directed and, to a large degree, Moscow-financed. Mr. Lardner was a part of this effort.

When the members of the industry finally became aware of what was going on they fought back, and some of the communists got hurt. But then so did many anti-communists, and the suffering of the reds who had started the trouble was nothing compared to injuries sustained by thousands of innocent persons who were thrown out of jobs by the strikes fomented by the communists—or whose legs or ribs were broken in the violence, or whose homes were bombed by red-inspired goon squads, or who were threatened with disfigurement because they refused to take the communist side.

Those who were there will not soon forget the sight of the mass picket lines around the Warner Brothers Studio in Burbank in October of 1945. Of Mr. John Howard Lawson and his so-called "intellectual" leaders, marching in the picket lines while Hollywood workers beat their fellow workers with stones, chains, bricks and broken bottles. Of their "peaceful" demonstrations, with strike leaders carrying rolled-up newspapers which concealed lead pipes or steel rods to strike down those who dared to resist them. Of the squad of "pros" who with a short piece of "two by four" could hit a locked car door so it would pop open and they could drag out and beat the occupants whose unions were not on strike and whose only crime was their desire to go to their jobs.

These "demonstrations" paralyzed the law enforcement agencies in the area of the Warner Brothers Studio for a period of ten days. Mr. Jack Warner could not get into his own studio. After one such demonstration seven tons of "instruments of persuasion" were cleaned up in the form of broken bottles, chains, rocks, bricks, etc. And to add insult to injury, the so-called "intellectuals" who were supporting the strike, headed by John Howard Lawson, sent a telegram to Mr. Warner blaming him for the violence because he would not submit to their blackmail.

It is little wonder that the industry fought back. If any criticism is justified it is because it didn't fight back hard enough or soon enough. Or because some of the members didn't really fight back at all as is indicated by Mr. Lardner's description of the manner in which some producers dealt with him surreptitiously and passed money "under the table."

Lardner's *Saturday Evening Post* article is unfair to the thousands of members of the industry who fought the fight to keep this important industry from falling into the hands of the communists, but it is more than that. It presents a completely distorted view of what the Communist Party is and how it works. It is the image which the Party wants us to have, but one which we had better not swallow if we want to survive.

To understand the true picture let us start with Mr. Lardner's effort to explain his motives. His effort to justify his action as a dedication to constitutional principles leaves us a little cold. Can anyone be so naive, at this late date, as to give credence to this explanation from a man who acknowledged his membership in a movement which denies all of the basic protection of personal rights which our Constitution guarantees? There is no evidence of his concern for the fact that the communist world denies its citizens *all* the rights which he says the Committee is denying to him and others. This is typical of the double standard by which communists judge the free world. Or, as Mrs. Khrushchev so dramatically put it . . . "But you don't understand—our bombs are for peace." Mr. Lardner's attitude towards American institutions then and now is still the same as that prescribed by the Communist Party position.

Let us next take his statement that the reason he chose the course of defiance was because he, personally, thought the Committee was invading *his* rights. What Mr. Lardner, obviously, hopes we will forget, is that his conduct before the Committee was identical in pattern, to that of the other nine recalcitrant reds. His conduct was in keeping with a decision of the Communist Party. The orders came from the Party, through the three communist lawyers who made up the group of five which represented the ten witnesses.

The manner in which this was put over is a typical example of communist treachery. One of the ten witnesses was Edward Dmytryk. He had actually left the Party at the time of the hearings, and he later broke completely and joined the anti-communist forces in Hollywood. The communists then tried to destroy him but they were unsuccessful. He is now high on their "hate list."

Although he had left the Party at the time of the hearings he was still in the periphery but not subject to strict Party discipline. He therefore hired a non-communist lawyer, the late Bartley Crum, who represented him. Crum had a national reputation as a lawyer but he was not wise to the ways of the red fraternity. At a "pre-trial" conference he agreed that his client, along with the other nine witnesses, would take a position which was to be formulated by a majority vote of the five lawyers. What Crum didn't know was that three of these five were disciplined Party members. Through them the Party directed the witnesses to defy the Committee on the grounds that the hearing was an illegal and unethical invasion of their individual rights to personal beliefs and associations. Dmytryk went along and wound up serving a term in the Federal penitentiary for contempt of Congress.

Mr. Lardner states that after the case was lost he terminated his membership, "without confusing the act, in my own or anyone else's head, with the quite distinct struggle for the right to embrace my belief or set of beliefs to which my mind and my conscience directed me." The language is ambiguous but what Mr. Lardner seems to be saying, in a quiet sort of way, is that after he was convinced he had lost his legal fight he terminated his membership in the Communist Party. He states it, however, in such a way as to imply that he has to say it but he hopes no one will notice. Somewhat like the double talk artist when he makes a statement but wipes his hand across his lips as he says it so the words are indistinct.

If this incident changed his basic relationship to the Party, more convincing evidence of it is needed. Indeed, he was challenged on this point by Rep. Francis E. Walter, Chairman of the House Committee on Un-American Activities, in a letter published in the *Saturday Evening Post,* January 13, 1962. Said Congressman Walter: "Actually, Lardner has avowed his concern for the success of both the local and Soviet Communist movements many years after his alleged termination of Party membership in 1950, and he has continued to play a starring role in the Party's front organization up to the very date of this communication."

The Congressman then cited some of Lardner's activities in this area. To this charge Lardner replied that he had not been a communist in "more than a decade," but he went on to say: "I did not say that I had ceased all political activity or that I had taken the path of contrition prescribed by the committee. . . ." He concluded his letter saying that Congressman Walter's charge was "utter and easily disprovable nonsense," without attempting to disprove it.

As late as December 6, 1961 Lardner played a prominent part at a meeting of the New York Committee to Abolish the House Un-American Activities Committee held at Manhattan Center. Present were such stalwarts as Pete Seeger, Willard Uphaus and Mrs. Frank Wilkinson, and the chairman was Otto Nathan, who has been denied a passport and who has been cited for contempt. Lardner spoke and introduced all the people who had had difficulties with the HCUA.

The technical formalities of Party membership have in the past proven quite flexible. For example, there was a time when Party law prescribed that if you, as a member of the Party, were asked about your Party membership by a member of an investigating committee, your membership was automatically terminated as of that moment. Thus you could swear that you were not a member without committing perjury. It would appear, though, that this tactic has gone out of style since the Party has discovered the manifold blessings of the Fifth Amendment.

There is also flexibility in the Party regulations as it applies to a person who holds public office or whom the Party is grooming for public office. In order to avoid the possibility of defection and thus exposure of a political figure such persons are sworn into membership in secret by a high official of the Party, without any other formal recognition of Party membership in terms of written records. This is probably the reason that the membership of Alger Hiss was so well concealed.

When appraising the completeness of a person's break with the Party, it is not so important to determine whether the person has left the Party as it is to determine whether the Party has left him. It is quite a common practice among persons who find Party discipline a burden to withdraw from formal Party membership by agreement with Party officials but to continue to serve the Party in some area where strict discipline is not required. Such persons may then take a moderate anti-communist position. They may even mildly criticize the foreign policy of the Soviet Union without coming in for Party criticism. However, if they offend the Party on some major point, then the Party will leave THEM and they will be denounced in Party organs and ostracized in every phase of communist activity. It is usually at this point that such a person learns for the first time the real nature of the apparatus to which he was attached.

The experience of Edward Dmytryk, the only one of the original ten who has completely broken with the Party, points up this flexible arrangement. He joined the Party in 1944. Shortly thereafter he was approached by John Howard Lawson, who requested him to direct the picture he was working on in accordance with communist concepts. Dmytryk rebelled at such instructions. Lawson then advised him that as a member of the Party he had no right to refuse such instructions—that if Dmytryk didn't expect to accept Party discipline he should resign and confine his communist activity to work in fronts. It was all very friendly. Dmytryk agreed and did, in fact, resign. It is significant to note, however, that the Party's hold on him was sufficiently strong to cause him to accept the Party's position when he appeared before the HCUA in 1947.

It is clear now that Dmytryk was under Party influence until he returned from serving the sentence imposed on him for contempt of Congress. At this point he determined to throw it off and solicited the help of the anti-communists to do so. On April 25, 1951 he appeared as a cooperative witness before the HCUA. The Party then attacked him and for the first time he learned the true nature of the Communist apparatus with which he had been associated. It also seems clear that Lardner has not yet reached this point in his relationship with the Party. He may have formally left the Party as he says but the Party has not yet left him.

The communists have tried very hard to destroy those persons who have testified before the Committee as friendly witnesses. Unfortunately, many Americans have rendered support to this effort by their failure to understand the deceptive nature of the communist appeal. The communists have sold the idea that such witnesses are informing on their associates rather than helping a government agency uncover a diabolical conspiracy aimed at the freedom of all of us, including those who were duped. The public must understand that the vast majority of Americans who found themselves involved in the communist conspiracy were well-intentioned persons who never had any thought of harming America. They were deceived into believing they were serving a good, humanitarian purpose. Thus, when they discover the deception they want to make a clean breast of it.

Those who do so can expect the full measure of communist wrath. At this point they need the support and understanding of all anti-communists, and failure to give it only serves the communist end. It is, however, important that such persons be sincere and their break with the Party complete. Their good intentions do not lessen the harm done by their actions but it does make it possible to bring them over to the American side. This is why it is so important that they name names for this is the only way by which one can determine with certainty that the Party has actually left *them*. The communists attempt to maintain the delusion that to testify is to betray their former associates. Such betrayal is the unpardonable sin. Mr. Lardner's effort to smear such witnesses as Martin Berkeley, Robert Rossen, etc., follows the pattern by which the Party hopes to destroy such persons. It is remarkable how successful such attacks have been.

It is not the dupes who are real enemies. They are important only if the communists have a line of communication with them. It is the hard core that we are after, those persons who are in reality an extension of the worldwide military machine which is threatening our very survival. The American communist is as much a part of the effort to destroy us as the general who commands the Red Army. As the strength of these armies grows the American communist becomes potentially a greater threat to our survival. The dupes are not blameless but those who fail to distinguish between the dupe and those in the hard core not only do an injustice to well intentioned Americans but they also help to hide the extremely dangerous hard core. Mr. Lardner's article is a masterpiece for the creation of such confusion.

The last issue which is raised by Mr. Lardner is the question of motion picture content. He does not dwell on this but he implies that any such allegation is ridiculous and not really worthy of comment. Actually this is the most important issue of all, for if Hollywood was *really* important to the program of world revolution it was important in this area.

Hollywood officialdom has always vigorously denied that there has been any influence of film content by communist writers of screen plays. However, such denials usually come from persons who have otherwise demonstrated their inability to recognize communism and how it works.

Recently a prominent Hollywood producer, who specializes in "message" pictures, publicly stated, in answer to criticism leveled at him for hiring known communist writers, that he would assume full responsibility for seeing to it that no communist propaganda reached the screen. This same producer, during the 1940's, was a teacher in a communist school in Hollywood. When asked why he agreed to teach there he stated that he did not know it was a communist school. It is difficult to understand how he could be so sure he would recognize communist propaganda in screen plays when he could actually teach in a communist school and not know that it was communist. The truth is that his "message" pictures, some of them written by communist writers, have been a source of great satisfaction, down through the years, to those who have been directing the communist program in America.

I am sure most of the people who "defended" Hollywood against the charge of communist influence sincerely believed they had frustrated the efforts of the communist movement to "doctor" our films. But if they didn't understand what the communists were trying to achieve, it is not logical that they could determine whether or not they had achieved it.

It is clear that they did not understand. But in this they were not alone. During the same period, communist influence within the areas of our national life has helped to create many of the problems plaguing the free world. Hollywood was no better or no worse than the rest of the nation in this regard. But its industry was more important. More important, because the communists were using it to help prepare the world for the confusion that has made it possible for them to conquer half the world without firing a shot.

Hollywood movies during the 1930's and 1940's occupied 75 percent of all the screen time in the free world. And if our American producers didn't understand the propaganda value of their pictures, the communists did. They had discovered that movies were the most effective force ever created for playing on the emotions, frustrations and fears of peoples of the world—peoples, who in many cases were being prepared to throw off the structure of our western civilization without having a stable structure to take its place. The movies were only a part of communism's program of confusion, but they were important. The new line was not to sell communism as such but to subtly undermine western institutions.

In Hollywood the center of communist influence was the Screen Writers Guild. The communist program to seduce the creative writers of America first took form at the second meeting of the International League of Revolutionary Writers held in Kharkov, Russia in 1930. The original program was an open revolutionary movement—its revolutionary purpose was not disguised. Its first effort in America was the formation of John Reed Clubs named after the young Harvard student who wrote "The Ten Days That Shook the World."

While these early efforts attracted some important writers, they were not successful in making serious inroads into American thought. Then the communists discovered the "Yenan Way." This was the name given to the tactic of the popular front—the "boring from within" technique. It was called this because it was first developed by the Chinese Communists of Yenan Province.

It was presented to Stalin, who, realist that he was, had it tried out in Chile by a young communist named Euducio Ravines. Ravines later broke with the Party and became a militant anti-communist. Recently he appeared in Chile at a Moral Rearmament Rally and apologized for the work he had done there in perfecting the popular front.

This new tactic was so successful that in the middle thirties it became the official communist program in America and in most of the world. Its success in America was no less phenomenal than in South America. The New Deal was dominating the political life of America so the reds moved in on it. In a short time they had not only infiltrated our political life but our government as well. New Deal legislation had released a pent-up demand for union organization so the communists infiltrated the unions. For quite some time they dominated the CIO. They moved into the field of literature and education, into the theatre and the arts—and Hollywood.

In Hollywood their key man was John Howard Lawson. He first appeared on the scene in 1932 as an organizer of the first John Reed Club formed in New York. He next appeared as the organizer of the Screen Writers Guild in Hollywood in 1934. He became its first vice-president and its mentor until after the hearings in 1947. Recognized as the Cultural Commissar of Hollywood, he was the Party authority on all matters affecting the creative arts in Hollywood.

With the advent of the popular Front technique, Lawson came into his own. "Revolutionary Writers" became "Progressive Writers" and instead of writing about World Revolution they began to write about poverty, corruption, injustice, bigotry and discrimination. They downgraded patriotism and religion in American life.

Heretofore movies had been considered an entertainment medium. Controversial subjects had been avoided because they cut the entertainment potential and usually made less money. The first real victory of communist influence in Hollywood was the discarding of this practice. The reds won acceptance of the idea that the movies should carry a social message. The next step was to sell the idea that movies should deal with the "realities of life," and to write about realities it was necessary to experience them. Thus writers were urged to march on picket lines and otherwise taste the sordid side of life. Out of this came a tendency toward stories dealing with violence, sex, divorce, prostitution and miscegenation. Pictures began to make heroes and sympathetic characters out of persons who were outside the pale of social acceptability. The underlying theme of all these motion pictures was that America was a nation of "decadent bourgeoisie."

This, of course, was not communist propaganda in the fullest sense but it developed naturally from Hollywood's communist influence on creative artists. Those who failed to fall in line were scorned as having sold their literary soul. Better to write a flop that had social significance than a successful screenplay that only entertained!

Communist influence was not confined to Party members. Generally the reds were successful in getting most of what they wanted by convincing those who fell for the "progressive" line, that they were rendering a great humanitarian service.

They were able to set the fashion for what was accepted as "good" writing. Most writers followed their lead. How was this possible, you might ask? It wasn't too difficult. First they were a disciplined, secret group who had a definite program. They were lavish with their praise for those who went along and they were ruthless in their attacks on those who fought them. They were uninhibited by any scruples. They had good connections with the press. Hollywood personalities soon learned that it was *much* more comfortable to be on their side.

During the same period that the Screen Writers Guild was developing in Hollywood, the American Newspaper Guild was being formed in the East. While the Newspaper Guild ultimately threw off its pro-communist leadership, the influence of the Party at that time was clearly discernible. This influence extended to the press agents who were a bridge between the newspapermen and the screen writers. At one point both of the Screen Publicists Guilds, one in Hollywood and the other in New York, were under communist domination. Thus the reds not only sold the idea to the writers that "progressive" writing was good but they were in a strategic position to sell it to the public as well.

Obviously they had to handle themselves very carefully. During this period the industry was under tight control of the major producing companies, whose officials had no sympathy with communism even though they were not knowledgeable on the subject. However, the heads of the producing companies didn't want to be considered reactionary, so many went along with much of the "progressive" program. The communists utilized all the issues of the day to gain positions of leadership. They made a bold bid to get control of the labor unions but they were frustrated in this by the solidarity and the determination of the American Federation of Labor. Had they achieved this control, they would certainly have become more aggressive, but fortunately they never achieved the strength of this position. It was as a result of their failure to win the labor fight that the anti-communist forces finally solidified and the hearings which ultimately deposed the reds were made possible.

And where was Mr. Lardner during this? He was at the right hand of Mr. Lawson along with about 40 or 50 others who constituted the "hard core" of the Hollywood communist apparatus, manipulating many others who were actually their victims, whose well-intentioned efforts to serve humanity and human injustice were exploited to help build the most inhuman institution in the history of man.

While the communists were frustrated in gaining the control they had hoped for during this period—the effort is by no means dead. The fight is still going on and the deterioration of the American film industry in relation to foreign industry is traceable in part to this continuing fight. Most of the goals of the "progressive writers" in terms of picture content have been achieved.

The communist issue will never be a black and white issue in America. It will always be disguised and confused as it was in Hollywood. But we must learn to understand, expose and isolate the communist influence if we are to combat it successfully. To do this we must learn a few fundamentals and the first is to remember that you can never judge a communist by what he *says*—only by what he *does*.

He does not accept our standards of truth—for truth to him is what the Party says it is—it has no relation to fact.

He cannot be depended upon to do what is right in terms of our moral and ethical standards for right is to him that which serves the interest of the Party.

Thus when a writer says he is not using his position to inject propaganda into films such assurances mean nothing when they come from a disciplined member of the Party.

When the American people come to know the conspiracy as we in Hollywood saw it, I am sure they will conclude that there is no place for communists in Hollywood, or, for that matter, in any other place in American life.

Only the eleventh of the Hollywood Ten was a writer of the first rank, but the Committee was far from aware of finer points of this kind. Rather, as some wit put it, they were apes who had taken to studying the biologist. The testimony of Bertolt Brecht (1898–1956) seems to be unique in one other respect that it has survived in aural form. Although for its official record, the Committee has always used stenographers, not tape recorders, the Hollywood hearings were broadcast, live, all over the United States. The Brecht testimony was recorded as it came over the radio, and is preserved in a Folkways album (FD 5531). Brecht's unread "statement" is read in the album by the present Editor, Eric Bentley, and is reprinted below. The collected works of Brecht in German (1967) contain an additional piece by Brecht called "We Nineteen," written in 1950 and also printed here, in which he gives it as his opinion that as a foreigner he was not entitled to protection by the Constitution and so could not cite any of its amendments. Who told him this, if anyone, is not stated. It is, of course, not true, and just adds another snarl to a very snarled record. (A second highly dubious assertion is that Hollywood people had been "told" to make anti-Soviet movies. A third is that "most" of the Ten were not Communists.) Incidentally, while the subject is inaccuracies, the case of Brecht permits scholars to compare the actual spoken record with the stenographer's transcript and to note that the latter deviates in many small ways from the former: which would be something to bear in mind when reading any textual record of HUAC proceedings.

OCTOBER 30, 1947:

Bertolt Brecht

MR. STRIPLING: Mr. Brecht, will you please state your full name and present address for the record, please? Speak into the microphone.

MR. BRECHT: My name is Bertolt Brecht. I am living at 34 West Seventy-third Street, New York. I was born in Augsburg, Germany, February 10, 1898.

MR. STRIPLING: Mr. Brecht, the Committee has a—

THE CHAIRMAN: What was that date again?

MR. STRIPLING: Would you give the date again?

THE CHAIRMAN: Tenth of February 1898.

MR. McDOWELL: 1898?

MR. BRECHT: 1898.

MR. STRIPLING: Mr. Chairman, the Committee has here an interpreter, if you desire the use of an interpreter.

MR. CRUM: Would you like an interpreter?

THE CHAIRMAN: Do you desire an interpreter?

MR. BRECHT: Yes.

MR. STRIPLING: Where are you employed, Mr. Baumgardt?

MR. [DAVID] BAUMGARDT [interpreter]: In the Library of Congress.

MR. BRECHT: Mr. Chairman, may I read a statement in English?

THE CHAIRMAN: Yes, but has the Chief Investigator completed his investigation of both the interpreter and the witness?

MR. STRIPLING: No, sir, I have not. What is your position in the Congressional Library, Mr. Baumgardt?

MR. BAUMGARDT: Consultant of philosophy of the Library of Congress.

MR. STRIPLING: Now, Mr. Brecht, will you state to the Committee whether or not you are a citizen of the United States?

MR. BRECHT: I am not a citizen of the United States. I have only my first papers.

MR. STRIPLING: When did you acquire your first papers?

MR. BRECHT: In 1941, when I came to the country.

MR. STRIPLING: When did you arrive in the United States?

MR. BRECHT: May I find out exactly? I arrived July 21 at San Pedro, California.

MR. STRIPLING: July 21, 1941?

MR. BRECHT: That is right.

MR. STRIPLING: You were born in Augsburg, Bavaria, Germany, on February 10, 1888, is that correct?

MR. BRECHT: Yes.

MR. STRIPLING: I am reading from the immigration records—

MR. CRUM: I think, Mr. Stripling, it was 1898.

MR. BRECHT: 1898.

MR. STRIPLING: I beg your pardon.

MR. CRUM: I think the witness tried to say 1898.

MR. STRIPLING: I want to know whether the immigration records are correct on that. Is it '88 or '98?

MR. BRECHT: '98.

MR. STRIPLING: Were you issued a quota immigration visa by the American vice-consul on May 3, 1941, at Helsinki, Finland?

MR. BRECHT: That is correct.

MR. STRIPLING: And you entered this country on that visa?

MR. BRECHT: Yes.

MR. STRIPLING: Where had you resided prior to going to Helsinki, Finland?

MR. BRECHT: May I read my statement? In that statement—

THE CHAIRMAN: First, Mr. Brecht, we are trying to identify you. The identification won't be very long.

MR. BRECHT: I had to leave Germany in 1933, in February, when Hitler took power. Then I went to Denmark, but when war seemed imminent in '39 I had to leave for Sweden, Stockholm. I remained there for one year and then Hitler invaded Norway and Denmark. I had to leave Sweden and I went to Finland, there to wait for my visa for the United States.

MR. STRIPLING: Now, Mr. Brecht, what is your occupation?

MR. BRECHT: I am a playwright and a poet.

MR. STRIPLING: Where are you presently employed?

MR. BRECHT: I am not employed.

MR. STRIPLING: Were you ever employed in the motion-picture industry?

MR. BRECHT: Yes. I sold a story to a Hollywood firm, *Hangmen Also Die,* but I did not write the screenplay myself. I am not a professional screenplay writer. I wrote another story for a Hollywood firm but that story was not produced.

MR. STRIPLING: *Hangmen Also Die*—whom did you sell to, what studio?

MR. BRECHT: That was to, I think, an independent firm, Pressburger at United Artists.

MR. STRIPLING: When did you sell the play to United Artists?

MR. BRECHT: The story—I don't remember exactly, maybe around '43 or '44—I don't remember, quite.

MR. STRIPLING: And what other studios have you sold material to?

MR. BRECHT: No other studio. Besides the last story I spoke of, I wrote for Enterprise Studios.

Mr. Stripling: Are you familiar with Hanns Eisler? Do you know Johannes Eisler?

Mr. Brecht: Yes.

Mr. Stripling: How long have you known Johannes Eisler?

Mr. Brecht: I think since the middle of the twenties, twenty years or so.

Mr. Stripling: Have you collaborated with him on a number of works?

Mr. Brecht: Yes.

Mr. Stripling: Mr. Brecht, are you a member of the Communist Party or have you ever been a member of the Communist Party?

Mr. Brecht: May I read my statement? I will answer this question, but may I read my statement?

Mr. Stripling: Would you submit your statement to the Chairman?

Mr. Brecht: Yes.

The Chairman: All right, let's see the statement.

(Mr. Brecht hands the statement to the Chairman.)

The Chairman: Mr. Brecht, the Committee has carefully gone over the statement. It is a very interesting story of German life, but it is not at all pertinent to this inquiry. Therefore, we do not care to have you read the statement.*

Mr. Stripling: Mr. Brecht, before we go on with the questions, I would like to put into the record the subpoena which was served upon you on September 19, calling for your appearance before the Committee. You are here in response to a subpoena, are you not?

Mr. Brecht: Yes.

Mr. Stripling: Now, I will repeat the original question. Are you now or have you ever been a member of the Communist Party of any country?

Mr. Brecht: Mr. Chairman, I have heard my colleagues when they considered this question not as proper, but I am a guest in this country and do not want to enter into any legal arguments, so I will answer your question fully as well I can. I was not a member, or am not a member, of any Communist Party.

The Chairman: Your answer is, then, that you have never been a member of the Communist Party?

Mr. Brecht: That is correct.

Mr. Stripling: You were not a member of the Communist Party in Germany?

Mr. Brecht: No, I was not.

Mr. Stripling: Mr. Brecht, is it true that you have written a number of very revolutionary poems, plays, and other writings?

Mr. Brecht: I have written a number of poems and songs and plays in the fight against Hitler and, of course, they can be considered, therefore, as

* It is printed below, right after the testimony. —E.B.

revolutionary because I, of course, was for the overthrow of that government.

THE CHAIRMAN: Mr. Stripling, we are not interested in any works that he might have written advocating the overthrow of Germany or the government there.

MR. STRIPLING: Yes, I understand. Well, from an examination of the works which Mr. Brecht has written, particularly in collaboration with Mr. Hanns Eisler, he seems to be a person of international importance to the Communist revolutionary movement. Now, Mr. Brecht, is it true you have written articles which have appeared in publications in the Soviet zone of Germany within the past few months?

MR. BRECHT: I do not remember to have written such articles. I have not seen any of them printed. I have not written any such articles just now. I write very few articles, if any.

MR. STRIPLING: I have here, Mr. Chairman, a document which I will hand to the translator and ask him to identify it.

MR. BRECHT: May I explain this publication?

MR. STRIPLING: Yes. Will you identify the publication?

MR. BRECHT: Oh, yes. That is not an article, that is a scene out of a play I wrote in, I think, 1937 or 1938 in Denmark. The play is called *Private Life of the Master Race,* and this scene is one of the scenes out of this play about a Jewish woman in Berlin in the year of '36 or '37. It was, I see, printed in this magazine *Ost und West,* July 1946.

MR. STRIPLING: Mr. Translator, would you translate the frontispiece of the magazine, please?

MR. BAUMGARDT: *"East and West,* Contributions to Cultural and Political Questions of the Time, edited by Alfred Kantorowicz, Berlin, July 1947, first year of publication enterprise."

MR. STRIPLING: Mr. Brecht, do you know the gentleman who is the editor of the publication whose name was just read?

MR. BRECHT: Yes, I know him from Berlin and I met him in New York again.

MR. STRIPLING: Do you know him to be a member of the Communist Party of Germany?

MR. BRECHT: When I met him in Germany I think he was a journalist on the Ullstein Press. That is not a Communist—was not a Communist—there were no Communist Party papers, so I do not know exactly whether he was a member of the Communist Party of Germany.

MR. STRIPLING: You don't know whether he was a member of the Communist Party or not?

MR. BRECHT: I don't know, no; I don't know.

MR. STRIPLING: In 1930 did you, with Hanns Eisler, write a play entitled, *Die Massnahme*?

MR. BRECHT: Yes, yes.

MR. STRIPLING: Would you explain to the Committee the theme of that play—what it dealt with?

MR. BRECHT: Yes, I will try to.

MR. STRIPLING: First, explain what the title means.

MR. BRECHT: *Die Massnahme* means (*speaking in German*).

MR. BAUMGARDT: Measures to be taken, or steps to be taken—measures.

MR. STRIPLING: Could it mean disciplinary measures?

MR. BAUMGARDT: No, not disciplinary measures, no. It means measures to be taken.

MR. STRIPLING: All right. You tell the Committee now, Mr. Brecht, what this play dealt with.

MR. BRECHT: Yes. This play is the adaptation of an old religious Japanese play, called [a] Noh play, and follows quite closely this old story which shows the devotion for an ideal until death.

MR. STRIPLING: What was that ideal, Mr. Brecht?

MR. BRECHT: The idea in the old play was a religious idea. This young people—

MR. STRIPLING: Didn't it have to do with the Communist Party?

MR. BRECHT: Yes.

MR. STRIPLING: And discipline within the Communist Party?

MR. BRECHT: Yes, yes, it is a new play, an adaptation. It had as a background the Russia-China of the years 1918 or 1919, or so. There some Communist agitators went to a sort of no man's land between the Russia which then was not a state and had no real—

MR. STRIPLING: Mr. Brecht, may I interrupt you? Would you consider the play to be pro-Communist or anti-Communist, or would it take a neutral position regarding Communists?

MR. BRECHT: No, I would say—you see, literature has the right and the duty to give to the public the ideas of the time. Now, in this play—of course, I wrote about twenty plays—but in this play I tried to express the feelings and the ideas of the German workers who then fought against Hitler. I also formulated in an artistic—

MR. STRIPLING: Fighting against Hitler, did you say?

MR. BRECHT: Yes.

MR. STRIPLING: Written in 1930?

MR. BRECHT: Yes, yes. Oh, yes, that fight started in 1923.

MR. STRIPLING: You say it is about China, though. It has nothing to do with Germany?

MR. BRECHT: No, it had nothing to do about it.

MR. STRIPLING: Let me read this to you.

MR. BRECHT: Yes.

MR. STRIPLING: Throughout the play reference is made to the theories and teachings of Lenin, the ABC of Communism, and other Communist classics, and the activities of the Chinese Communist Party in general. The following are excerpts from the play.*

Now, Mr. Brecht, will you tell the Committee whether or not one of the characters in this play was murdered by his comrade because it was in the best interest of the Communist Party, is that true?

MR. BRECHT: No, it is not quite according to the story.

MR. STRIPLING: Because he would not bow to discipline he was murdered by his comrades, isn't that true?

MR. BRECHT: No, it is not really in it. You will find, when you read it carefully, like in the old Japanese play where other ideas were at stake, this young man who died was convinced that he had done damage to the mission he believed in and he agreed to that and he was about ready to die, in order not to make greater such damage. So he asks his comrades to help him, and all of them together help him to die. He jumps into an abyss and they lead him tenderly to that abyss. And that is the story.

THE CHAIRMAN: I gather from your remarks, from your answer, that he was just killed, he was not murdered?

MR. BRECHT: He wanted to die.

THE CHAIRMAN: So they kill him?

MR. BRECHT: No, they did not kill him—not in this story. He killed himself. They supported him, but of course they had told him it were better when he disappeared, for him and them and the cause he also believed in.

MR. STRIPLING: Mr. Brecht, could you tell the Committee how many times you have been to Moscow?

MR. BRECHT: Yes. I was invited to Moscow two times.

MR. STRIPLING: Who invited you?

MR. BRECHT: The first time I was invited by the Voks Organization for Cultural Exchange [Society for Cultural Relations with Foreign Countries]. I was invited to show a picture, a documentary picture I had helped to make in Berlin.

MR. STRIPLING: What was the name of that picture?

MR. BRECHT: The name—it is the name of a suburb of Berlin, Kuhle Wampe.

MR. STRIPLING: While you were in Moscow, did you meet Sergei Tretyakov?

MR. BRECHT: Tretyakov, yes. That is a Russian playwright.†

MR. STRIPLING: A writer?

MR. BRECHT: Yes. He translated some of my poems and, I think, one play.

MR. STRIPLING: Mr. Chairman, *International Literature* No. 5, 1937,

* The Committee's translation appears in full below as Appendix 2. Stripling read from sections 1, 2a, 3b, and 10. —E.B.

† Shot by a people's court in 1939, on which subject Brecht had written an as yet unpublished poem. —E.B.

published by the State Literary Art Publishing House in Moscow had an article by Sergei Tretyakov, leading Soviet writer, on an interview he had with Mr. Brecht. On page 60, it states:

> "I was a member of the Augsburg Revolutionary Committee," Brecht continued. "Nearby, in Munich, Leviné raised the banner of Soviet power. Augsburg lived in the reflected glow of Munich. The hospital was the only military unit in the town. It elected me to the revolutionary committee. I still remember Georg Brem and the Polish Bolshevik Olshevsky. We did not boast a single Red guardsman. We didn't have time to issue a single decree or nationalize a single bank or close a church. In two days General Epp's troops came to town on their way to Munich. One of the members of the revolutionary committee hid at my house until he managed to escape."
>
> He wrote *Drums at Night*. This work contained echoes of the revolution. The drums of revolt persistently summon the man who has gone home. But the man prefers quiet peace of his hearthside.
>
> The work was a scathing satire on those who had deserted the revolution and toasted themselves at their fireplaces. One should recall that Kapp launched his drive on Christmas Eve, calculating that many Red guardsmen would have left their detachments for the family Christmas trees.
>
> His play, *Die Massnahme,* the first of Brecht's plays on a Communist theme, is arranged like a court where the characters try to justify themselves for having killed a comrade, and judges, who at the same time represent the audience, summarize the events and reach a verdict.
>
> When he visited in Moscow in 1932, Brecht told me his plan to organize a theater in Berlin which would re-enact the most interesting court trials in the history of mankind.
>
> Brecht conceived the idea of writing a play about the terrorist tricks resorted to by the landowners in order to peg the price of grain. But this requires a knowledge of economics. The study of economics brought Brecht to Marx and Lenin, whose works became an invaluable part of his library.
>
> Brecht studies and quotes Lenin as a great thinker and as a great master of prose.
>
> The traditional drama portrays the struggle of class instincts. Brecht demands that the struggle of class instincts be replaced by the struggle of social consciousness, of social convictions. He maintains that the situation must not only be felt, but explained—crystallized into the idea which will overturn the world.

Do you recall that interview, Mr. Brecht?

MR. BRECHT: No. (*Laughter.*) It must have been written twenty years ago or so.

MR. STRIPLING: I will show you the magazine, Mr. Brecht.

MR. BRECHT: Yes. I do not recall there was an interview. (*Book handed to the witness.*) I do not recall—Mr. Stripling, I do not recall the interview in exact. . . . I think it is a more or less journalistic summary of talks or discussions about many things.

MR. STRIPLING: Yes. Have many of your writings been based upon the philosophy of Lenin and Marx?

MR. BRECHT: No, I don't think that is quite correct, but, of course, I studied, had to study as a playwright who wrote historical plays, I, of course, had to study Marx's ideas about history. I do not think intelligent plays today can be written without such study. Also, history written now is vitally influenced by the studies of Marx about history.

MR. STRIPLING: Mr. Brecht, since you have been in the United States, have you attended any Communist Party meetings?

MR. BRECHT: No, I don't think so.

MR. STRIPLING: You don't think so?

MR. BRECHT: No.

THE CHAIRMAN: Well, aren't you certain?

MR. BRECHT: No—I am certain, yes.

THE CHAIRMAN: You are certain you have never been to Communist Party meetings?

MR. BRECHT: Yes, I think so. I am here six years—I am here those—I do not think so. I do not think that I attended political meetings.

THE CHAIRMAN: No, never mind the political meetings, but have you attended any Communist meetings in the United States?

MR. BRECHT: I do not think so, no.

THE CHAIRMAN: You are certain?

MR. BRECHT: I think I am certain.

THE CHAIRMAN: You think you are certain?

MR. BRECHT: Yes, I have not attended such meetings, in my opinion.

MR. STRIPLING: Mr. Brecht, have you, since you have been in the United States, have you met with any officials of the Soviet government?

MR. BRECHT: Yes, yes. In Hollywood I was invited, sometimes, three or four times, to the Soviet consulate with, of course, many other writers.

MR. STRIPLING: What others?

MR. BRECHT: With other writers and artists and actors who . . . they gave some receptions at special Soviet (*speaking in German*)—

MR. BAUMGARDT: Festivities.

MR. BRECHT: Festivities.

MR. STRIPLING: Did any of the officials of the Soviet government ever come and visit you?

MR. BRECHT: I don't think so.

MR. STRIPLING: Didn't Gregory Kheifets visit you on April 14, 1943, vice-consul of the Soviet government? You know Gregory Kheifets, don't you?

MR. BRECHT: Gregory Kheifets?

THE CHAIRMAN: Watch out on this one.

MR. BRECHT: I don't remember that name, but I might know him, yes. I don't remember—

Mr. Stripling: Did he come and visit you on April 14, 1943?

Mr. Brecht: It is quite possible.

Mr. Stripling: And again on April 27, and again on June 16, 1944?

Mr. Brecht: That is quite possible, yes, that somebody—I don't know. I don't remember the name, but that somebody, some of the cultural attachés—

Mr. Stripling: Cultural attachés.

Mr. Brecht: Yes.

The Chairman: Spell the name.

Mr. Stripling: Gregory, G-r-e-g-o-r-y. Kheifets, K-h-e-i-f-e-t-s.

Mr. Brecht: Kheifets?

Mr. Stripling: Yes. Do you remember Mr. Kheifets?

Mr. Brecht: I don't remember the name, but it is quite possible. But I remember that from the—I think from the—yes, from the consulate, from the Russian consulate some people visited me, but not only this man, but also I think the consul once, but I don't remember his name either.

Mr. Stripling: What was the nature of his business?

Mr. Brecht: He—it must have been about my literary connections with German writers. Some of them are friends of mine.

Mr. Stripling: German writers?

Mr. Brecht: Yes, in Moscow.

Mr. Stripling: In Moscow?

Mr. Brecht: Yes. And there appeared in the Staats Verlag [State publishing house] the Sergei Tretyakov translations of my plays, for instance, *Private Life of the Master Race, A Penny for the Poor,* and poems, and so on.

Mr. Stripling: Did Gerhart Eisler ever visit you, not Hanns, but Gerhart?

Mr. Brecht: Yes, I met Gerhart Eisler, too. He is a brother of Hanns and he visited me with Hanns and then three or four times without Hanns.

Mr. Stripling: Could you tell us in what year he visited you? Wasn't it the same year that Mr. Kheifets visited you?

Mr. Brecht: I do not know, but there is no connection I can see.

Mr. Stripling: Do you recall him visiting you on January 17, 1944?

Mr. Brecht: No, I do not recall such date, but he might have visited me on such date.

Mr. Stripling: Where did he visit you?

Mr. Brecht: He used to ask for his brother who, as I told you, is an old friend of mine, and we played some games of chess, too, and we spoke about politics.

Mr. Stripling: About politics?

Mr. Brecht: Yes.

The Chairman: What was the last answer? I didn't get the last answer?

MR. STRIPLING: They spoke about politics. In any of your conversations with Gerhart Eisler did you discuss the German Communist movement?

MR. BRECHT: Yes.

MR. STRIPLING: In Germany?

MR. BRECHT: Yes, we spoke about, of course, German politics. He is a specialist in that, he is a politician.

MR. STRIPLING: He is a politician?

MR. BRECHT: Yes, he, of course, knew very much more than I knew about the situation in Germany.

MR. STRIPLING: Mr. Brecht, can you tell the Committee, when you entered this country did you make a statement to the Immigration Service concerning your past affiliations?

MR. BRECHT: I don't remember to have made such a statement, but I think I made the usual statements that I did not want to, or did not intend to, overthrow the American Government. I might have been asked whether I belonged to the Communist Party, I don't remember to have been asked, but I would have answered what I have told you, that I was not.

MR. STRIPLING: Did they ask you whether or not you had ever been a member of the Communist Party?

MR. BRECHT: I don't remember.

MR. STRIPLING: Did they ask you whether or not you had ever been to the Soviet?

MR. BRECHT: I think they asked me, yes, and I told them.

MR. STRIPLING: Did they question you about your writings?

MR. BRECHT: No, not as I remember; no, they did not. I don't remember any discussion about literature.

MR. STRIPLING: Now, you stated you sold the book, the story, *Hangmen Also Die,* to United Artists. Is that correct?

MR. BRECHT: Yes, to an independent firm, yes.

MR. STRIPLING: Did Hanns Eisler do the background music for *Hangmen Also Die*?

MR. BRECHT: Yes, he did.

MR. STRIPLING: Do you recall who starred in that picture?

MR. BRECHT: No, I do not.

MR. STRIPLING: You don't even remember who played the leading role in the picture?

MR. BRECHT: I think Brian Donlevy played it.

MR. STRIPLING: Do you remember any of the other actors or actresses who were in it?

MR. BRECHT: No, I do not. You see, I had not very much to do with the filmization itself. I wrote the story and then [gave] to the script writers some advice about the background of Nazis, Nazism in Czechoslovakia, so I had nothing to do with the actors.

THE CHAIRMAN: Mr. Stripling, can we hurry this along? We have a very heavy schedule this afternoon.

MR. STRIPLING: Yes. Now, Mr. Brecht, since you have been in the United States have you contributed articles to any Communist publications in the United States?

MR. BRECHT: I don't think so, no.

MR. STRIPLING: Are you familiar with the magazine *New Masses*?

MR. BRECHT: No.

MR. STRIPLING: You never heard of it?

MR. BRECHT: Yes, of course.

MR. STRIPLING: Did you ever contribute anything to it?

MR. BRECHT: No.

MR. STRIPLING: Did they ever publish any of your work?

MR. BRECHT: That I do not know. They might have published some translation of a poem, but I had no direct connection with it, nor did I send them anything.

MR. STRIPLING: Did you collaborate with Hanns Eisler on the song "In Praise of Learning"?

MR. BRECHT: Yes, I collaborated. I wrote that song, and he only wrote the music.

MR. STRIPLING: Would you recite to the Committee the words of that song?

MR. BRECHT: Yes, I would. May I point out, that song comes from another adaptation I made, of Gorky's play, *Mother*. In this song a Russian worker woman addresses all the poor people.

MR. STRIPLING: It was produced in this country, wasn't it?

MR. BRECHT: Yes, '35, New York.

MR. STRIPLING: Now, I will read the words and ask you if this is the one.

MR. BRECHT: Please.

MR. STRIPLING: [reads the eight lines of verse printed on page 94.]

MR. BRECHT: No, excuse me, that is the wrong translation. That is not right. (*Laughter.*) Just one second, and I will give you the correct text.

MR. STRIPLING: That is not a correct translation?

MR. BRECHT: That is not correct, no. That is not the meaning. It is not very beautiful, but I am not speaking about that.

MR. STRIPLING: What does it mean? I have here a portion of *The People,* which was issued by the Communist Party of the United States, published by the Workers' Library Publishers. Page 24 says: "In praise of learning, by Bert Brecht; music by Hanns Eisler." It says here:

> You must be ready to take over; men on the dole, learn it; men in the prisons, learn it; women in the kitchen, learn it; men of sixty-five, learn it. You must be ready to take over—

MR. BAUMGARDT: The correct translation would be, "You must take the lead."

THE CHAIRMAN: "You must take the lead"?

MR. BAUMGARDT: "The lead." It definitely says, "the lead." It is not, "You must take over." The translation is not a literal translation of the German.

MR. STRIPLING: Well, Mr. Brecht, as it has been published in these publications of the Communist Party, then, if that is incorrect, what did you mean?

MR. BRECHT: I don't remember, never—I never got that book myself. I must not have been in the country when it was published. I think it was published as a song, one of the songs Eisler had written the music to. I did not give any permission to publish it. I don't see—I think I have never saw the translation.

MR. STRIPLING: Do you have the words there before you?

MR. BRECHT: In German, yes.

MR. STRIPLING: It goes on:

> You must be ready to take over; you must be ready to take over.
> Don't hesitate to ask questions, comrade—

MR. BRECHT: Why not let him translate from the German, word for word?

MR. BAUMGARDT: I think you are mainly interested in this translation, which comes from—

THE CHAIRMAN: I cannot understand the interpreter any more than I can the witness.

MR. BAUMGARDT: Mr. Chairman, I apologize. I shall make use of this [the microphone].

THE CHAIRMAN: Just speak in that microphone and maybe we can make out.

MR. BAUMGARDT: The last line of all three verses is correctly to be translated: "You must take over the lead," and not, "You must take over." "You must take the lead," would be the best, most correct, most accurate translation.

MR. STRIPLING: Mr. Brecht, did you ever make application to join the Communist Party?

MR. BRECHT: I do not understand the question. Did I make—

MR. STRIPLING: Have you ever made application to join the Communist Party?

MR. BRECHT: No, no, no, no, no, never.

MR. STRIPLING: Mr. Chairman, we have here—

MR. BRECHT: I was an independent writer and wanted to be an independent writer and I point that out, and also theoretically, I think, it was the best for me not to join any party whatever. And all these things you read here were not only written for the German Communists, but they were also written for workers of any other kind. Social Democrat workers were in these performances; so were Catholic workers from Catholic unions; so were workers which never had been in a party or didn't want to go into a party.

THE CHAIRMAN: Mr. Brecht, did Gerhart Eisler ever ask you to join the Communist Party?

MR. BRECHT: No, no.

THE CHAIRMAN: Did Hanns Eisler ever ask you to join the Communist Party?

MR. BRECHT: No, he did not. I think they considered me just as a writer who wanted to write and do as he saw it but not as a political figure.

THE CHAIRMAN: Do you recall anyone ever having asked you to join the Communist Party?

MR. BRECHT: Some people might have suggested it to me, but then I found out that it was not my business.

THE CHAIRMAN: Who were those people who asked you to join the Communist Party?

MR. BRECHT: Oh, readers.

THE CHAIRMAN: Who?

MR. BRECHT: Readers of my poems or people from the audiences. You mean—there was never an official approach to me to publish—

THE CHAIRMAN: Some people did ask you to join the Communist Party.

MR. KENNY: In Germany. (*Aside to witness.*)

MR. BRECHT: In Germany, you mean in Germany?

THE CHAIRMAN: No, I mean in the United States.

MR. BRECHT: No, no, no.

THE CHAIRMAN (*to Mr. Kenny*): He is doing all right. He is doing much better than many other witnesses you have brought here. Do you recall whether anyone in the United States ever asked you to join the Communist Party?

MR. BRECHT: No, I don't.

MR. STRIPLING: I would like to ask Mr. Brecht whether or not he wrote a poem—a song, rather—entitled, "Forward, We've Not Forgotten."

MR. MCDOWELL: "Forward" what?

MR. STRIPLING: "Forward, We've Not Forgotten."

MR. BRECHT: I can't think of that. The English title may be the reason.

MR. STRIPLING: Would you translate it for him into German?

(*Mr. Baumgardt translates into German.*)

MR. BRECHT: Oh, now I know, yes.

MR. STRIPLING: You are familiar with the words to that?

MR. BRECHT: Yes.

MR. STRIPLING:

> Forward, we've not forgotten our strength in the fights we've won.
> No matter what may threaten, forward, not forgotten, how strong we are as one.
> Only these our hands now acting, built the road, the walls, the towers. All the world is of our making.
> What of it can we call ours?

The refrain:

> Forward. March on to the tower, through the city, by land the world;
> Forward. Advance it on. Just whose city is the city? Just whose world is the world?*
> Forward, we've not forgotten our union in hunger and pain, no matter what may threaten, forward, we've not forgotten
> We have a world to gain. We shall free the world of shadow; every shop and every room, every road and every meadow,
> All the world will be our own.

Did you write that, Mr. Brecht?

MR. BRECHT: No. I wrote a German poem, but that is very different from this. (*Laughter.*)

MR. STRIPLING: That is all the questions I have, Mr. Chairman.

THE CHAIRMAN: Thank you very much, Mr. Brecht. You are a good example to the witnesses of Mr. Kenny and Mr. Crum.

The Unread Statement

For the record, this is reprinted here exactly as given in *Hollywood on Trial* by Gordon Kahn. In the album *Brecht Before the Un-Amer-*

---

* This translation actually reads:

> Forward, march on to power
> Through the city, the land, the world,
> Forward, advance the hour
> Just whose city is the city?
> Just whose world is the world?

But these particular errors are the stenographer's, not Stripling's, as the audio-record proves. Stripling's own liberties with text are better illustrated from his use of *Die Massnahme* and the Tretyakov piece above. For details, consult *Brecht Before the Un-American Activities Committee.* —E.B.

ican Activities Committee (Folkways, FD 5531), a lightly edited version of the same text is used. The original German was not published until the collected works came out in German in 1967. From which it would seem that the original (anonymous) translator had made some mistakes. For example, the last sentence should read: "Art can make such ideas clearer and even nobler." But it would also seem that the editors of the German edition have made at least one deletion—of the sentence: "We applied for American citizenship (first papers) on the day after Pearl Harbor."

I was born in Augsburg, Germany, the son of an industrialist, and studied natural sciences and philosophy at the universities of Munich and Berlin. At the age of twenty, when participating in the war as a member of the medical corps, I wrote a ballad which the Hitler government used fifteen years later as the reason for my expatriation. The poem *Der tote Soldat* (*The Dead Soldier*) attacked the war and those wanting to prolong it.

I became a playwright. For a time, Germany seemed to be on the path of democracy. There was freedom of speech and of artistic expression.

In the second half of the 1920's, however, the old reactionary militarist forces began to regain strength.

I was then at the height of my career as a playwright, my play *Dreigroschenoper* being produced all over Europe. There were productions of plays of mine at Berlin, Munich, Paris, Vienna, Tokyo, Prague, Milan, Copenhagen, Stockholm, Budapest, Warsaw, Helsinki, Moscow, Oslo, Amsterdam, Zurich, Bucharest, Sofia, Brussels, London, New York, Rio de Janeiro, etc. But in Germany voices could already be heard demanding that free artistic expression and free speech should be silenced. Humanist, socialist, even Christian ideas were called "undeutsch" (un-German), a word which I hardly can think of without Hitler's wolfish intonation. At the same time, the cultural and political institutions of the people were violently attacked.

The Weimar Republic, whatever its faults had been, had a powerful slogan, accepted by the best writers and all kinds of artists: *Die Kunst dem Volke* (*Art Belongs to the People*). The German workers, their interest in art and literature being very great indeed, formed a highly important part of the general public of readers and theatre-goers. Their sufferings in a devastating depression which more and more threatened their cultural standards, the impudence and growing power of the old militarist, feudal, imperialist gang alarmed us. I started writing some poems, songs and plays reflecting the feelings of the people and attacking their enemies who now openly marched under the swastika of Adolf Hitler.

The persecutions in the field of culture increased gradually. Famous painters, publishers and distinguished magazine editors were persecuted. At the universities, political witch hunts were staged, and campaigns were waged against motion pictures such as *All Quiet on the Western Front.*

These, of course, were only preparations for more drastic measures still to come. When Hitler seized power, painters were forbidden to paint, publishing houses and film studios were taken over by the Nazi party. But even these strokes against the cultural life of the German people were only the beginning. They were designed and executed as a spiritual preparation for total war which is the total enemy of culture. The war finished it all up. The German people now have to live without roofs over their heads, without sufficient nourishment, without soap, without the very foundations of culture.

At the beginning, only a very few people were capable of seeing the connection between the reactionary restrictions in the field of culture and the ultimate assaults upon the physical life of a people itself. The efforts of the democratic, anti-militarist forces, of which those in the cultural field were, of course, only a modest part, then proved to be weak altogether; Hitler took over. I had to leave Germany in February, 1933, the day after the Reichstag fire. A veritable exodus of writers and artists began of a kind such as the world had never seen before. . . . I settled down in Denmark and dedicated my total literary production from that time on to the fight against Nazism, writing plays and poetry.

Some poems were smuggled into the Third Reich, and Danish Nazism, supported by Hitler's embassy, soon began to demand my deportation. Of course, the Danish government refused. But in 1939 when war seemed imminent, I left with my family for Sweden, invited by Swedish senators and the Lord Mayor of Stockholm. I could remain only one year. Hitler invaded Denmark and Norway.

We continued our flight northward, to Finland, there to wait for immigration visas to the U.S.A. Hitler's troops followed. Finland was full of Nazi divisions when we left for the United States in 1941. We crossed the U.S.S.R. by the Siberian Express which carried German, Austrian, Czechoslovakian refugees. Ten days after our leaving Vladivostok aboard a Swedish ship, Hitler invaded the U.S.S.R. During the voyage, the ship loaded copra in Manila. Some months later, Hitler's allies invaded that island. We applied for American citizenship (first papers) on the day after Pearl Harbor.

I suppose that some poems and plays of mine, written during this period of the fight against Hitler, have moved the Un-American Activities Committee to subpoena me.

My activities, even those against Hitler, have always been purely literary activities of a strictly independent nature. As a guest of the United States, I refrained from political activities concerning this country even in a literary form. By the way, I am not a screen writer. Hollywood used only one story of mine, for a picture showing the Nazi savageries in Prague. I am not aware of any influence which I could have exercised in the movie industry whether political or artistic.

Being called before the Un-American Activities Committee, however, I feel free for the first time to say a few words about American matters: looking back at my experiences as a playwright and a poet in the Europe of the last two decades, I wish to say that the great American people would lose much and risk much if they allowed anybody to restrict free competition of ideas in cultural fields, or to interfere with art which must be free in order to be art. We are living in a dangerous world. Our state of civilization is such that mankind already is capable of becoming enormously wealthy but, as a whole, is still poverty-ridden. Great wars have been suffered, greater ones are imminent, we are told. One of them might well wipe out mankind, as a whole. We might be the last generation of the specimen [species?] man on this earth.

The ideas about how to make use of the new capabilities of production have not been developed much since the days when the horse had to do what man could not do. Do you not think that, in such a predicament, every new idea should be examined carefully and freely? Art can present clearly and even make nobler such ideas.

(1947)

"We Nineteen"

From the United States we receive the almost incredible news that some of their best writers will now be sent to jail. Since I sat next to them on the defendants' bench in Washington two and a half years ago, I can report it—I'm told that some of the people who have seen my plays do not consider me a liar. What saved me then was not that no un-American activities could be proved in my case—they could not be proved against those who are now going to prison either—but rather that I was not an American. They had called us nineteen, writers, film directors, actors, to Washington before a Congressional Committee to ask us if we were members of the Communist Party. At the time, two years after the war, the artists in the big film studios of Hollywood had been told to make movies that were against America's wartime ally, the Soviet Union. The industry had set aside large sums for this purpose, and several scripts had been commissioned. Strangely, they did not materialize. The good script writers would not; the poor ones could not. Not all good script writers were progressive, but the population was not yet ready to see the heroes of Stalingrad abused: they had saved America from making so many sacrifices. It [the population] had to be worked on first. An example had to be set, and every refusal to obey orders from on high had to be publicly punished. This was the reason why a number of artists were to be publicly queried as to whether they were members of the Communist Party.

For such membership no prison term or fine had been fixed; the Party was not illegal at the time. However, there were punishments in that country which appear much more harmless but aren't. The State does not put in an appearance but the execution does take place. One could call it Cold Execution—a certain form of peace is called Cold War there. This Cold Execution is carried out by the industry: the delinquent is not deprived of his life, only of the means of life. He does not appear in the obituary column, only on the blacklists. Whoever has witnessed the horrors of poverty and humiliation which, in the land of the dollar, fall upon the man without a dollar, will not prefer the punishment of unemployment to any punishment that the State could inflict. In our case, incidentally, the State collaborated with the industry: it played the role of the snooper. It asked the suspects under oath about their party membership. Now the Constitution of the United States of America was written at a time when the goddess of freedom had oil in her lamp, not in her face. Thus the Constitution forbade the newly founded State to be the snooper for the powerful and rich: no one could be asked about his religion, opinions, and party membership. The writers, directors, and actors had recourse to this clause* when the Congressional Committee examined them under oath. They refused to answer. And one has to know that by no means all of them were members of the Communist Party. Most of them were not, and, had they answered, could have made replies that would not have harmed them; they refused to answer only because they wanted to see the Constitution respected. What thereupon happened was bad for them, but even worse for their country. Signifying their respect for the Constitution, they were sentenced to jail terms for contempt of Congress. I myself escaped being sentenced because, as a non-American, I had to answer the question; I was not protected by the Constitution. My American colleagues were protected by the Constitution; it was the Constitution that was not protected. In fact, they realized that they were exposing themselves to danger by relying on their Constitution. But they did not heed that danger; they were trying to tell the country that *it* was in danger. These fearless people called out to the judges of their country, "Show everyone who you are! Take up a club and smash the innocent, before the eyes of all! So that you can deceive no one any longer." Well, the judges took up the club and smashed the innocent, before the eyes of all. And what have we learned? We have learned what that "justice" is. We have also learned that there are people ready to sacrifice themselves so that their countrymen as well as the rest of the world may learn the truth. Salud, my friends!

(1950)

(*Translated by Hugo Schmidt, 1970*)

* The First Amendment. Note that the Fourteenth Amendment, Section 1, states: "No State shall . . . deny to any person within its jurisdiction the equal protection of its laws." —E.B.

The day before Bertolt Brecht testified word had gone around that Chairman Thomas was about to produce a surprise witness. Then, on the day, some people thought Brecht was it. But no, it was the Committee's own Investigator, Louis J. Russell, some of whose testimony is given here as an exception to the pattern of artists and intellectuals only. The Russell testimony provides a fair sample of what witnesses both "friendly" and "expert" had to offer and includes the surprise that Thomas had in mind: here is first released to the American public the story of Eltenton's alleged attempt to extract atom secrets from J. Robert Oppenheimer through the mediation of Haakon Chevalier. It is fair also, for our purposes here, to let Russell cite all of a long report by V. J. Jerome since, in the view of the Committee, Jerome was a key figure in the cultural history of these United States.

OCTOBER 30, 1947:

Louis J. Russell

MR. STRIPLING: Will you state your full name?

MR. RUSSELL: Louis J. Russell.

MR. STRIPLING: Will you give the Committee again your past employment background, particularly with the Federal Bureau of Investigation?

MR. RUSSELL: I was employed by the Federal Bureau of Investigation for a period of ten years. I have also been employed by the Thomas A. Edison Company Incorporated, of West Orange, New Jersey, as director of plant protection. I have been associated with the Committee on Un-American Activities since May 1945.

MR. STRIPLING: Mr. Russell, during your investigation of the Hollywood movie industry did you conduct any research work which would reflect the interest of the Soviet Union in the Hollywood motion-picture industry?

MR. RUSSELL: Yes. In the publication called *International Theater,* which was published in Moscow, Russia, as the official publication of the International Union of the Revolutionary Theater, there is contained a great deal of information concerning the interests of the Communist International in the motion pictures as a means of furthering the class struggle.

MR. STRIPLING: I also ask unanimous consent of the Committee to put into the record a speech which was delivered by V. J. Jerome in the summer of 1938 to the National Convention of the Communist Party on the Cultural Commission within the United States.

REPORT ON THE NATIONAL CONVENTION IN RELATION TO CULTURAL MOVEMENT

INTRODUCTORY REMARKS

First report in the National Convention on Culture, an achievement. Hope that writers in the field will make demands on the editors of the *Communist*.

SURVEY OF ACTIVITIES

Necessary to supplement leaflets and papers with cultural media which should be used by us. There is also the subjective factor—the winning over of professionals to our party increases forces and modes of expression for our agitation and education through the medium of culture. Result: Beginnings of people's culture fusing with the life of our movement in the form of films, plays, recitations, chalk talks, and the like. Our party should remember the use of these things in the campaign of 1937—the use of schools, settlement houses, organized camera clubs, presenting actual scenes of the living conditions of the people in the communities. The East Side Players of New York wrote and produced a play on housing, presented the play to indoor and outdoor audiences, helping to build the Tenant's League. These experiences should be assembled. The section could regularly carry on such work.

In the trade-unions this work is important. Plays such as *Plant in the Sun,* representing through the medium of drama the idea of solidarity, Negro rights, etc. Dramatic presentations facilitate political campaigns in the trade unions by emotional appeal, making it easier for us to come with our programatic campaigns.

Detroit Automobile Theater has presented a play on Spain to 50,000 auto workers.

In Chicago a play was presented on industrial unionism to A.F. of L. audience using the theme of sit-down strike.

Theater groups developing forms of workers' education. Our comrades must utilize—get firmer grasp of cultural activity. . . .

Think of the fund of cultural tradition that can be exploited among the Negro groups in line with the emphasis that Comrade Browder has given in his report for the general need for vitalizing our activity among national groups. Think of the tasks among the Negro people. In the Negro People's Theater of Richmond, Va., a start was made through some assistance of certain comrades in New York. Harlem Suitcase Theater. Actual demand for cultural equality of Negroes must become part of our struggle for Negro culture. Remove discrimination against Negroes. And remove the condition of making Negroes menials in the hall of culture.

American youth: A special duty on our party, our resolve to give increased guidance and assistance to YCL [Young Communist League] centering on cultural work.

Work among women: Leadership shown must be emphasized and developed in terms of their special problems.

Consider the children and their cultural demands—winning through them their families.

Basis for these developments in organizations such as Artists Congress,

American Artists Union, League of American Writers. Similar work in this field has been done by Theater Arts Committee for Peace and Democracy with its splendid radio division. Note with special appreciation the work done by Comrade Reid in helping establish this organization.

New Theatre League doing educational work in trade unions and mass organizations and which has brought forward a series of excellent playlets before audiences in many towns and cities.

Frontier Films: *Heart of Spain* and *China Strikes Back.*

Associated Film Audiences stopped the showing of *Siege of Alcazar.*

Choruses, musicians, dancers, entertainment unions, WPA projects; campaign for the enactment of Federal art bill is now in full swing and should have the full support of the party.

Publications: *New Masses, Daily Worker,* column of Mike Gold.

PROBLEMS

How can we coordinate cultural activities with the movement as a whole. We need a far more positive approach to cultural work; to realize the opportunities of cultural movements that mass agitation offer to our party. This approach of necessity will lead to the solution of the second problem, that of developing cultural personnel in our party.

We have made advances; yet in regard to the opportunities and in general needs we have scarcely made a turn. We have still in our party a certain evil remaining from the past—the evil of pulling up stakes. We should recognize that there is still a tendency in the committees, units, etc., to divert the comrades doing cultural work to assign them to new work. It is an indication of development when a comrade shows himself fit to be transferred to varied activities. We should not discourage such transfers. But we should bear in mind—concern must always be given to condition of the work that the comrade has been doing so there will not be pulling up of stakes, which we have got rid of successfully in many fields of our endeavor.

In dealing further with the question of coordinating the work, we can only speak experimentally. We have done so little because actually we are groping for particulars, methods in building up coordinating activity.

We have had in certain districts, and in certain sections, certain enterprising districts and sections, cultural committees that have undertaken to do work set up by districts and committees. In the course of recent months we have made a survey of certain of these committees. We found in many instances that these committees, while doing certain valuable work, did not always yield the fruits that the planters had looked for; and in examining causes we found that committees were left to drift for themselves. They were invested with too much autonomy. Experience would show us that where such cultural committees are established by sections it is best to regard them as subcommittees, let us say, of the education and organization committees, or if a separate committee apart from the educational committee, then responsible to the lending committee of the section to which it gives regular reports and accounts of its activities, having its activities placed on the agenda for review, discussion, and planning. Without this they will really be drifting. They need integrated cultural committees. If we examine the way a committee has been set up, we would find that the organization tie-up is that of integration; but the emphasis cannot be overstated, the work of such committees must be considered a work of importance, of cultural importance, along the central activity of the party as a whole.

Another difficulty in regard to these committees, or to cultural work carried on without committees by some of our party bodies, is the tendency to limit cultural activity to festive occasions, to Lenin Memorial, May Day, and other red-letter days, etc. It is very good to feel that we have forces who come to the assistance of the party and beautify and intensify the party's agitational work, but the time has come when we must register our dissatisfaction with any policy which limits cultural activities to simply occasional entertainment, to gala entertainment, even though it be Bolshevist-gala entertainment. We have to have day-to-day cultural activity as part of the class struggle, as part of the general struggle for building the front of the American people for democracy, for culture, and in doing this the party everywhere will, in the course of time, realize that [if] there is anything to be regretted it is the late start in integrating this cultural work with our general campaign—the minutest day-to-day activities.

The problem that I want particularly to stress tonight is the problem which has caused us real concern in the course of our experience—that of our responsibility to the cultural workers. And we are dealing with human factors. We are dealing with heterogeneous human factors—much more heterogeneous than any other social components of the Communist Party. The Communist Party is a monolithic party. The working class is a homogeneous class but it becomes monolithic to the extent that we bolshevize the membership of our Party, make them thoroughbred Communists.

A realistic view of the situation shows us that in the cultural forces much work has to be done by our party, and when we speak of our party I do not mean just the leadership of the party, but every party comrade, both in regard to himself and everyone with whom he comes in contact.

We have won many cultural people to our fold as members and friends and sympathizers, but recruiting, unless it is followed by the next step, the step of solidifying, helping, rendering permanent this recruiting, we have not really done the recruiting; in other words, solidifying our gains in the course of winning these people.

If this is a problem for the party as a whole, how much more is it a problem in regard to the workers in the cultural field, for with their valuable equipment they bring in varying forms draw-backs which reflect themselves in their work, unless we help them to overcome it. Draw-backs that are hang-overs of past environments, past miseducation, past outlook on life and society. Such traits are liberalism, which has nothing in common with progressivism. Speaking of liberalism, or to round out the word, rotten liberalism, such traits as academicism, viewing a topic, an issue, almost with a Hamletic waver, between yea and nay. What has this in common with the Communist theory and practice? But we find it still in our midst—pure and simple professionalism. It is merely a carry-over of an organized notion of our function in which one has not yet learned to make the synthesis between his political program and his professional contribution to the carrying out of that program.

And, of course, hyperindividualism, that direct curse of them all—all of which institutes susceptibilities to Trotskyism and other alien classes.

Certain examples which will illustrate at the present moment the danger of permitting such notions to remain in our midst. How often do we come across certain individuals mingling with us who advance the following idea about the people's front; for example, that Dimitrov's report* finally recognized that they were right all the time. In other words, that Dimitrov's report is a concession to the petty bourgeoisie. What does this mean? Can we allow such notions to manifest themselves politically? Comrade Browder's people's front illustrated for us to see that the adoption of a new line does not constitute a repudiation but, on the contrary, it constitutes a necessary historic transition to a new tactic rendered requisite by a developing situation. Now, he who is opposed to the adoption on the part of the working-class party of the correct tactic stands on the side lines sneering that "They have changed their line." This sneering reflects itself in shadows of grimaces on the part of some of our weaker comrades. We must overcome such notions in our midst, and welcome them (the comrades) but we do not welcome their interest on the basis of their understanding that that which they are joining is not a party of communism. It is our duty to clarify these comrades.

We have a task to perform; we are educators; we are transformers of consciousness; and that transformation of consciousness does not end with the registration of a given candidate to the party but begins with that moment, for then we have the administrator—the channel through which to do it.

Another manifestation of this—the tendency to abuse and distort the criticism contained in the word "sectarianism." How often do we not find that when a certain liberalism begins to insinuate itself and when it is criticized correctly that very often we find countercharges that criticism is sectarianism. Yes, we have—we hope for good—thrown sectarianism out the window. We have established ourselves as being on the highroad to becoming a mass party. We hope before very long to count our numbers in terms of hundreds of thousands. That is a prospective with a program.

We build qualitatively as well as quantitatively, and we cannot, and should not, permit the charge contained in the word "sectarianism" to cover the employment of opportunism, conscious or unconscious.

To illustrate this with an instance: The book *Red Star Over China* [by Edgar Snow] which has created confusion in the party and around the party. The action of the party in adopting a critical attitude to the book, in keeping the book from circulation in our party bookshops, has not been completely understood by many comrades. I think it should be stated in all due fairness to those comrades that the party did not come out quickly enough with an authentic opinion on the book; and, of course, there were many speculations. It was necessary and imperative to have prompt reviews of the book, to make the matter clear before our members. Of course, the party has an attitude to the book; there were reviews in several periodicals. Here is a book written by a man who undoubtedly is disposed as a friend and well-wisher of the Chinese people. A man who is, you might say, profoundly sympathetic, and attached to the Chinese Soviets, and who wrote a book that is in many pages inspiring.

* To the Congress of the Comintern, 1935. —E.B.

Yet those who have read the book carefully, those who have followed the review in the *Communist,* will come to the conclusion that the book brings forward Trotskyite conclusions that actually damage an otherwise valuable documentary account. In fact, the philosophy of the book is that communism is adorable if it arises as a Chinese phenomenon. A sort of new exceptionalism cut off from international communism—not only cut off, but Snow's thesis seems to be that wherever the Communist International enters as a factor it brings about tragedy and ruin in the wake of the Chinese revolution. And as for the Soviet Union, that is the villain of the piece. Snow maintains that the Communist International is, or is used as, a sort of vest-pocket bureau of the Soviet Foreign Office. This is purveying Trotskyism. We do not say that Snow is a Trotskyite, but we do say that by his unclarity and by his failure, his professional failure, to check on data, a responsibility which he owes to himself as a foreign correspondent, he has made himself a vehicle for carrying Trotskyite poison into his book; and, therefore, notwithstanding the great value of his book in many other ways, we have to register this deep-going criticism in the hope that thereby he will perhaps put forth a new edition in which he will make the corrections that we have indicated.

There is an antitoxin to drive out this remaining poison in the system of certain of the people that come toward us. This antitoxin is the valuable flow of education—of study of Marxism, Leninism, which we owe as educators, as members of the party, to those who come toward us. We have to devise the necessary methods to help overcome this. Of course, we don't mean in the book learning; we mean practice.

Far too many of these people somehow or other are members at large, not because they have been assigned due to the strategic posts that they may occupy in the camp of the enemy, in Wall Street or other places. They have sort of placed themselves at large.

I cite an instance where a representative of the central committee set out to visit a certain group at large to conduct an instructive talk on a vital political subject and he was told that they couldn't reveal themselves. In other words, they don't know us and we don't know them. They missed the study, the work, the activity, the helpful guidance, and the contact with the life of the basic party organizations.

There are two ways for intellectuals to come into the party. One is the way of perennially skirting the fringe. The other is the way to come—weave himself right into the cloth of the banner of Leninism. Every one of us knows what the results of two such ways of coming are.

For instance, I think that in certain places and in certain professions it is advisable to have special units of workers in a given profession established in WPA units, or perhaps units of a given establishment. But, to say, as we have observed in certain cities not farther than a stone's throw from here, that everyone who wields a pen shall therefore belong to our writers unit—and there are such demands I notice, in Chicago, in Philadelphia and here—I think this means isolating themselves from the party. It means a life of inbreeding, failure to live the life of the party. There is no blanket judgment on this. In every district or section the leadership exercises its due discretion to see where in special places professional units can be and should be set up.

They have their place and should function where they have their place; but where they have no reason for being, there is absolutely nothing but loss in such an arrangement.

I was in Los Angeles last year and came upon a unit consisting of one or two lawyers, one or two medicos, publicity agents, a couple of storekeepers and teachers. I visited that unit, and I was told that this is an industrial unit. That was not the opinion of the county leadership. Actually it seemed that it was some sort of mushroom growth; and in investigating the basis upon which they had built themselves—they had not a single profession, let alone an industrial profession—the common denominator upon which they existed, I found, was the desire to keep from being open party members. In other words, the negative policy of concealment was the basis for joint work.

Certainly, we have to safeguard professionals. We cannot adopt the same methods of work, nor can we always nor should we always have the general policy of open work, dependent upon who the professionals are. But to say that there can be such a thing as a basis of work which hasn't a positive program, but rather a negative program of withdrawal, is the opposite. Well, as to that unit, they disbanded, and some of them became attached to factory groups and units, helped put out factory papers, and began to find themselves in the party, making themselves useful. They gave their equipment to basic party units, began to register their party attitude to things. Before leaving I spoke to some of those comrades. There was a different light in their eye in speaking of the party.

Promote the party press among our professionals. I don't like to embarrass gatherings of professionals by asking how many have really read the *Daily Worker,* and I don't mean page 7 * only. How many read the *Party Organizer*? How many read the *Communist*? Very few, comrades. And where will this transformation come about? Where shall we equip ourselves for further education? . . . It is a very important question. Ask yourselves; probe your consciences tonight. I think if we can all answer in the affirmative there would be a much wider circulation of the *Daily Worker* and of the entire press.

We must begin to educate through the medium of study groups. The question of study groups is a fundamental problem, of course, not only educational work in the units, but actual study groups where groups of party comrades build around themselves nonparty people, and begin bringing in the policies of our party through a program of education related to the current topics of the hour.

I would say that if the comrades of the section could see their way to instituting such study groups around the professional units it would really be a basic achievement—it would be a preparation for the bolshevizing of the comrades—for making genuine Communists of the entire circle of party comrades and their familiars. The leading committees should actually do the building of these study groups.

And further, we must more than ever impress the professionals—our friends and sympathizers, that we have a positive approach also to their work. It isn't just a question—they shouldn't imagine that they are just brought into

* At the time the seventh page of the *Daily Worker* was devoted to feature articles, such as the regular "Change the World" by Mike Gold. —E.B.

the party as though to be turned into instruments apart from their work, but on the contrary, that their coming into the party was their being friends of the party and sympathizers as in terms of their actual work. We do not always make this clear. The party increasingly cherishes and values specific qualities that the professionals bring into our midst. Gone is the day when we just took a professional comrade and assigned him to do nondescript party work. We say, on the contrary, "Comrades, you have something specific to give. You have the general contributions to make, in your loyalty, in your dues payments, your attendance, and your various duties and tasks to perform. But you have also a different contribution to make, whether you are a writer, a film artist, a radio performer. We need this no matter how valuable you are to the party on the picket line, and if in your turn you do not contribute, you would not really be valuable to us." This is important to register. And we must also register the fact that the party is not satisfied with anything save the best in terms of quality and caliber and talent that the comrades can produce. Our motto is: Nothing is too good for the working class—and not, as some say, and possibly by their inferior work, not because they are unable to do better, but a sort of sloppy arrangement, that anything is good enough for the working class. We want quality. We want good leaflets, splendid posters, such as the Communist Party of Germany used to put out when artists such as Käthe Kollwitz gave of their best to poster production. And, of course, murals, and everything that is good. We want our basic agitational work to reflect that we have talented professionals in our midst—good sketches, good plays. In fact unless the form is there the content is not there.

I came across something recently—a translation of a poem—Rossetti's translation of François Villon—"Where are the snows of yesteryear?" An American paper carried in translation of that same line: "What's become of last year's snow?" Is it really the same? The form is not there. And as Marxists, as dialecticians, we believe in the daily unity and interpenetration of form and content.

I was present last night at a cabaret—TAC [Theater Arts Committee]. I want to say that I think the comrades of TAC deserve a cheer for this innovation that they have brought into our movement; it opens an avenue for very fine achievements. Speaking in terms of medium as to its possibilities, its possibilities are great. There was some fine singing, good schnitzelbank, and yet at the end we had something tacked on the end of the program about Mayor Hague in the form of a round. The form, the words particularly, and music, were nothing to write home about. And I feel that, although the content was intended with the form, especially I was a little ashamed of the thing, because these comrades can do so much better. The content wasn't there because there wasn't that medium of presenting the thing effectively. I say that as party comrades we must be the first to demonstrate that it is not true what the [Max] Eastmans say, "Artists in uniform, crushing art out of creation." On the contrary, we have to demonstrate by our creations that we are the ones that are the guardians of art. Quality. Stimulate; criticize. And we demand the best that the comrades can offer.

We have had another tendency, comrades. A tendency—part of the same thing—of utilizing certain names of notables for public statements. Very good, and we need more of such names. But I think, comrades, that if we get these signatures and let it go at that we are not really doing the right thing by these people; for who will deny the fact that if they are prepared to give their signatures for a progressive cause, even for a direct Communist cause, they are also prepared in one way or another to vitalize those signatures into action? Don't we shy off? Just leave them and then call upon them again? We don't want to use these people for window trimming. These are people who demonstrate by that that they want to do something. We are the stimulators. We should draw them. Do we? You will find that very often we neglect these people. To draw them means to draw them to do something. Why can't we draw some of these people and ask them to become pamphleteers for our cause?

We can ask them to become poster artists, mural makers. They can embellish our shop papers and do various performances in our day-to-day work and struggle. They are waiting for their invitations. Let's give them a ring. I think we have neglected some very important and useful people in America. We need and we can get cultural workers to temper the press with protests, with letters, to write to Congressmen in behalf of various causes that we promulgate. These are important activities, and these are the beginnings to bring these people closer, and this has to become a systematic activity. Units should put this on the agenda—how to draw these people and for what occasion. This will help to Americanize our work. It will help to bring our message to greater numbers; and not only will the party gain but we will thereby make use of the special talents which are remaining idle in our midst, and we shall be making happier and more devoted party comrades of these professionals. Let us remember that the enemy class bludgeons the masses with every form of clubbing—the radio, press, and so forth. Let us bear in mind the demagogic use to which they are put. Let us not abandon a single cultural field to reaction. The Communist Party is by its valiant leadership administering its role as vanguard of progressive humanity. Let our party demonstrate its role of vanguard of modern culture.

MR. STRIPLING: Mr. Russell, will you name the bulletins of the *International Theater* which you have referred to?

MR. RUSSELL: Yes. Bulletin No. 2 of *International Theater* published in 1934, pages 1, 3, 4, 5, and 7. The October 1934 issue of *International Theater,* on page 3, contains an article describing the growth of the revolutionary theater in the United States. This particular article states that such dramatists as Alfred Kreymborg, John Wexley, Albert Maltz, George Sklar, Lee Simonson, and others are coming over to the revolutionary theater. John Wexley and Albert Maltz have been employed by the Hollywood motion-picture industry. Page 56 of issue 3 and 4 of *International Theater* for the year 1934 contains information concerning the training of cadres in the United States. We might also discuss an article, "Straight From the Shoulder," in the November 1934 issue of the *New Theater,* on page 11, by John Howard Lawson, the movie writer. The comment of the editors of the *New Theater* is as follows:

However, John Howard Lawson's argument that a united-front theater cannot produce specifically Communist plays is certainly true, and he has brought up real but not insurmountable difficulties facing playwrights, whether Socialists, Communists, or just sympathetic, who write for such united-front organization and audience. His article indicates the immediate need for a Communist professional theater that will produce plays as Lawson and others will write, plays with a clear Communist line and straightforward political statements and references.

MR. STRIPLING: Mr. Russell, can you tell the Committee whether or not the Soviet government has ever sent an official representative to the motion-picture industry?

MR. RUSSELL: During the summer of 1943, one Mikhail Kalatozov made his appearance in Hollywood. According to the Soviet Embassy in Washington, D.C., the purpose of Kalatozov's being in Hollywood was to strengthen the artistic and commercial ties with the cinema people of the United States. Just prior to Kalatozov's arrival, announcement of the fact was made by Miss Pauline Swanson of the National Council of American-Soviet Friendship, 814–816 Broadway, Arcade Building, Los Angeles, California. According to this announcement, Mr. Kalatozov was to be presented to the Hollywood film colony at a reception and cocktail party given at the Mocambo Restaurant on the afternoon of August 12, 1943. An article in the West Coast organ of the Communist Party, the *People's World,* carried the following item concerning Kalatozov in its issue of September 10, 1943.

Moscow Liaison

Mikhail Kalatozov, Soviet film director, is in Hollywood to give first-hand advice on pictures dealing with Russia and to study Hollywood methods. They are starting him off with a reception at the Mocambo.

MR. STRIPLING: Mr. Russell, can you tell the Committee where Mr. Kalatozov resided while he was in Los Angeles?

MR. RUSSELL: While in Hollywood, Kalatozov resided at 4744 Los Feliz Boulevard, which is located close to the Soviet consulate and near the homes of some of Hollywood's best-known stars.

MR. STRIPLING: Mr. Russell, to what extent did Mr. Kalatozov contact people in the motion-picture industry?

MR. RUSSELL: During the course of my investigation I became familiar with the content of several cablegrams which indicated that Kalatozov had contacted various motion-picture studios in Hollywood.

MR. STRIPLING: Would you read the content of those telegrams to the Committee?

MR. RUSSELL: Yes. One of these cablegrams was dated December 7, 1943, wherein it is indicated that Kalatozov cabled his superior, Alexander Andreivsky, in Moscow, as follows:

> Lawrence agrees to distribute our films in Africa, Italy, France. Agreement advantageous to us. Imperative that we receive immediate reply.

As you know, Mr. Chairman, we are presently investigating this matter and there will be an identification made of Lawrence at the time a report is submitted.

MR. STRIPLING: Do you have other cablegrams, Mr. Russell?

MR. RUSSELL: Yes. A copy of a cablegram which was received by Mikhail Kalatozov on January 20, 1944, from his superior in Moscow, Alexander Andreivsky, reads as follows:

> Agreement RKO not received. Will cable after receipt. Regarding radio concert you should receive detailed cable.

This cablegram indicates an agreement with the RKO studio in Hollywood had been reached between Kalatozov and that studio.

MR. STRIPLING: Do you have cablegrams indicating connection with other studios in Hollywood?

MR. RUSSELL: Yes. In a cablegram dated January 23, 1944, addressed to Alexander Andreivsky, of the cinema committee in Moscow, is stated:

> Immediately inform if Warner Brothers films brought to Moscow were seen by you.

MR. STRIPLING: Mr. Russell, do you recall that several weeks ago the Committee held a hearing on Hanns Eisler?

MR. RUSSELL: Yes.

MR. STRIPLING: Did you assist in the investigation of Hanns Eisler?

MR. RUSSELL: Yes, sir.

MR. STRIPLING: Did you go to California early this year to assist in that investigation?

MR. RUSSELL: I did.

MR. STRIPLING: Could you furnish the committee with some information regarding the association of Hanns Eisler with certain individuals in Hollywood?

MR. RUSSELL: Yes. On October 13, 1943, Hanns Eisler and his wife, Louise, attended a gathering in the home of Paul Jarrico, 727 Linda Flora Drive, Los Angeles, California, which was addressed by Joseph North, former editor of the *New Masses*.

MR. STRIPLING: I believe it has been placed in the testimony here, Mr. Chairman, that Paul Jarrico was one of the original script writers of the picture *Song of Russia*.

MR. RUSSELL: On November 9, 1943, the Hanns Eislers were invited to an affair given by V. V. Pastoev, who at that time was the Soviet vice-consul in Los Angeles. On November 16, 1943, the Eislers entertained the Pastoevs at a party in their home. On January 10, 1944, Gregory Kheifets, a Soviet vice-consul from San Francisco, California, visited Hanns Eisler.

MR. STRIPLING: Mr. Chairman, for the purpose of the record, Hanns Eisler is now subject to deportation, and the Immigration and Naturalization Service has arrested him, and he is out on bond awaiting a hearing on a deportation order.* At the time of the hearing he was shown to be the head of the International Music Bureau with headquarters in Moscow. Mr. Russell, did you receive any information during your investigation regarding the brother of Hanns Eisler, Gerhart Eisler, who has been convicted in the court in the District of Columbia for being in contempt of Congress and also for violation of the passport regulations?

MR. RUSSELL: Yes. During the year 1940 certain people in the United States were engaged in a campaign to purchase Gerhart Eisler's way out of a concentration camp in France. This campaign started when Hanns Eisler, the brother of Gerhart Eisler, received a cablegram from Gerhart asking him for money which he needed for an operation. This money was actually to be used for the purpose of buying Gerhart Eisler's way out of the concentration camp in France.

MR. STRIPLING: Could you give the Committee the details regarding this matter?

MR. RUSSELL: Yes. One person active in this matter was Charles A. Page, who was in 1940 a free-lance writer in Hollywood. Also active, Louise Bransten. It is a known fact that Page requested Louise Bransten's advice as to how the situation could be handled and it was resolved that the best way of securing information concerning the method of handling the situation would be to contact an individual known as Otto Katz, who was then in Connecticut. It might be recalled at this point that Gerhart Eisler, when he first entered the United States, stated before the immigration officials who examined him that he was en route to see Otto Katz, who was at that time residing in Mexico.

MR. STRIPLING: Could you further identify Otto Katz, Mr. Russell?

MR. RUSSELL: Yes. Otto Katz, whose real name is André Simone, and who has numerous other names and aliases, is a known agent of the Soviet government who was very active in Mexico City during the period of the late war. At present he is in Czechoslovakia.† He was also very active in Hollywood at one time, particularly during the year 1935. During the testimony of Joseph Savoretti in the hearing regarding Hanns Eisler, Mr. Savoretti made several statements regarding a warrant which had been issued for the arrest of Hanns Eisler. I quote from the record of the hearing:

> The warrants were thereupon sent to our district office in Philadelphia by the New York office under date of August 15 for service. The investigator of the Philadelphia office learned that the aliens had proceeded to 2738 Outpost Drive, care of Page, Hollywood, California.

* Subsequently Hanns Eisler was permitted to make a "voluntary" departure from the United States. —E.B.

† He was liquidated in the Czech purges around 1950. —E.B.

Yesterday the Committee dispatched a telegram to the chief of police to determine whether Charles A. Page was identical with the person mentioned in the testimony of Savoretti regarding the warrant which had been issued for the arrest of Hanns Eisler. The reply of V. B. Horrall, chief of police, Los Angeles, California, states:

> Re tel Charles A. Page and Mary Page. Page registered at 2736 Outpost Drive, Hollywood, from 1938 to 1941.

I believe this establishes the residence of the Pages at 2736 Outpost Drive when this address we requested was 2738 Outpost Drive, Hollywood, California.

MR. STRIPLING: Mr. Russell, will you identify Louise Bransten?

MR. RUSSELL: Yes. She was born on October 10, 1908, at Berkeley, California, the daughter of Abraham Rosenberg and Alice Greenbaum. She is the former wife of Richard Bransten, also known as Bruce Minton, former owner of *New Masses,* and at present the husband of Ruth McKenney, the writer. Both of them were recently expelled from the Communist Party of the United States on a charge of revisionism. McKenney and Bransten have both been employed in the movie industry. Louise Bransten's father died in 1929 and left an estate valued at over two million dollars. Louise was the beneficiary of a five-hundred-thousand-dollar trust fund which provided that two hundred fifty thousand dollars be given to her on her twenty-fifth birthday and the other half upon reaching the age of forty-five. At the age of twenty-five, she made an agreement with the executors of her father's estate to accept shares of stock in a particular company in lieu of two hundred fifty thousand dollars in cash. In view of the fact that I have made no investigation regarding the company mentioned, I would rather furnish its name in executive session because if the name of the firm is mentioned there might be an unjust reflection on its character. In 1943, after her mother's death, Louise Bransten inherited a large sum of money, some of which is held in trust. In June 1933 Louise Bransten, accompanied by her husband Richard, made a six weeks' tour of the Soviet Union. During the waterfront strike in San Francisco Louise and Richard Bransten carried out assignments for the Communist Party, working with Earl Browder and Gerhart Eisler. In 1944 Louise Bransten made a loan of fifty thousand dollars to the *People's World,* which is the West Coast organ of the Communist Party. She has also contributed through the Rosenberg Foundation, of which she is a member of the board of directors, six thousand dollars to the American-Russian Institute, and ten thousand dollars to the California Labor School. She has also contributed to the Joint Anti-Fascist Refugee Committee. At present she is living in New York City and is married to Lionel Berman, who is interested in documentary films. Bransten is now employed by the New York Committee To Win the Peace.

MR. STRIPLING: Now, would you identify Charles A. Page?

MR. RUSSELL: Yes. The last-known address of this person, insofar as I know, is the Jefferson Apartments, Sixteenth and M Streets NW., Washington, D.C. He was employed by the State Department from about the year 1928 through the year 1933. During the years 1934 through 1941 he was a free-lance writer in Hollywood, California. When he discontinued this type of work he returned to the State Department. He has been in contact with Louise Bransten, Haakon Chevalier, Vassili Zublin, a Soviet diplomatic official, Herbert Biberman, John Howard Lawson, Gerhart Eisler, Otto Katz, and Hanns Eisler. He at one time attempted to obtain a position for Haakon Chevalier.

MR. STRIPLING: Do you know where he attempted to obtain such position?

MR. RUSSELL: Yes, with the Office of War Information.

MR. STRIPLING: Do you know through whom he tried to get the job?

MR. RUSSELL: Through Robert E. Sherwood.

THE CHAIRMAN: Through Robert E. who?

MR. RUSSELL: Sherwood, S-h-e-r-w-o-o-d.

MR. STRIPLING: Do you know whether or not he obtained a position?

MR. RUSSELL: No, he did not obtain a position.

MR. STRIPLING: Do you know whether or not he was ever contacted in Washington by Louise Bransten while he was in the State Department?

MR. RUSSELL: Yes. On January 3, 1944.

MR. STRIPLING: Can you tell the Committee the nature of work or the place of employment of Page while he was in the State Department?

MR. RUSSELL: Yes. At one time he was assigned to the American Embassy in Montevideo, Uruguay. During this employment he corresponded frequently with Herbert Biberman and John Howard Lawson of the Hollywood movie colony. This person was referred to upon one occasion by a leading Communist in Mexico as being "one of our men." This Communist said of Page; "We have one of our men right inside the American Embassy and we get the real inside dope from there." I could name the person who said this, if the Committee considers it necessary.

MR. STRIPLING: Mr. Chairman, Page was also the cultural attaché at the Embassy in Paris for a while.

MR. RUSSELL: He was also in New York with the cultural section of the State Department.

MR. STRIPLING: Mr. Russell, during your investigation of Louise Bransten did you determine whether or not she was in communication with various officials of the Soviet government?

MR. RUSSELL: On April 25, 1945, Louise Bransten was contacted by Stepan Apresian of the Soviet consulate. Apresian was attached to the Soviet consulate in San Francisco. She, Louise Bransten, was contacted by this individual in San Francisco at the Hotel Canterbury on April 25, 1945.

The purpose of this meeting, which was arranged by a Mr. Khrameev, of the Soviet consulate, was to arrange for the distribution of forty thousand copies of a speech to be made by Molotov before the United Nations Conference at San Francisco. On the 24th of April 1945, Bransten was requested to work on the translation of this speech at the Soviet consulate in San Francisco, California. Ten thousand copies of Molotov's speech were purchased by the International Workers Order, as a matter of information. The forty thousand copies of Molotov's speech were to be distributed after they had been printed by a particular lithographing and printing company in San Francisco.

MR. STRIPLING: Mr. Chairman, we prefer to give the name of the company in executive session.

THE CHAIRMAN: Without objection, so ordered.

MR. STRIPLING: Can you tell the Committee whether or not your investigation disclosed whether or not Louise Bransten entertained any of the officials of the Soviet government?

MR. RUSSELL: On May 19, 1945, Dmitri Manuilsky, the Ukraine Communist leader, was the guest of honor at a dinner given by Louise Bransten in her home. Dimitri Manuilsky was a member of the three-man board which functioned as the Communist International during the late war. This was during the time that the Communist International had supposedly been dissolved. Other persons who attended the dinner given by Bransten for Manuilsky were Frederick Thompson, Holland Roberts, president of the California Labor School, and Max Yergan.

MR. STRIPLING: Mr. Russell, will you tell the Committee the various connections between Louise Bransten and persons in the motion-picture industry?

MR. RUSSELL: Yes. First, we have the direct connection between Louise Bransten and Charles A. Page, who operated as a free-lance writer in Hollywood for a period of seven years. Then there is the association of Gregory Kheifets, the Soviet consul, with Hanns Eisler and Louise Bransten.

MR. STRIPLING: Mr. Chairman, I would like to point out that Mr. Bertolt Brecht, the witness this morning, admitted having met with Kheifets on several occasions and of Kheifets coming to his home.

MR. RUSSELL: Hanns Eisler, of course, was employed by the Hollywood moving-picture industry. Then there is a tie-up between Page, the associate of Bransten, and Herbert Biberman and John Howard Lawson of the movie colony. Also it might be stated at this point that when Louise Bransten went to New York City in November 1945 she was contacted by an individual known as George George, a member of the Communist Party, and a contact of Hanns Eisler in Los Angeles, California. George at one time worked for one of the studios in Hollywood as a free-lance writer.

MR. STRIPLING: Did he work for Metro-Goldwyn-Mayer, Mr. Russell?

MR. RUSSELL: Yes.

MR. STRIPLING: Can you at this point furnish the Committee with any information concerning contacts in Hollywood, California, which have been made by outstanding or notorious leaders of the Communist Party?

MR. RUSSELL: On May 3, 1942, Alexander Stevens, also known as J. Peters, and whose real name is Goldberger, visited Los Angeles, California. When he arrived in Los Angeles he was met by Herbert Biberman at the Union Station. During that day a meeting was held by Alexander Stevens, Waldo Salt, and Herbert Biberman. Also on that same date another meeting was held at Herbert Biberman's home, which was attended by Paul Jarrico, Morton Grant, Robert Rossen, and Hyman Kraft. Rossen, Biberman, Salt, and Jarrico are also associated with the motion-picture industry. Also on that same date a third meeting was held by Alexander Stevens, J. Peters, R. Goldberger, as he is known, Morton Grant, John Howard Lawson, and Vera Harris, the wife of Lou Harris, a screen writer. During the evening of May 3, 1942, another meeting was held in Herbert Biberman's home between Stevens or Peters, John Howard Lawson, Lester Cole, Madeline Ruthven, and Herta Uerkvitz. Lester Cole is a screen writer, while Ruthven and Uerkvitz are Communist Party functionaries in Los Angeles, California. Ruthven, Lawson, Stevens, and Salt also held a meeting on the same date, late at night, in the home of Waldo Salt. During this visit, among other things, Stevens was working on the Communist-inspired movement to secure the release of Earl Browder, Communist Party president [*sic*] at that time, from a Federal penitentiary, where he had been incarcerated on a charge of using a false passport to travel to the Soviet Union. Stevens also had a very successful financial trip, since he collected fifteen hundred dollars, or furnished this sum to Communist Party functionaries in California, which he had received from Louise Bransten. He also received the sum of twenty-two hundred dollars from a Ruth Wilson, whom I can identify in executive session, the reason being that she at the present may have a connection with a leading department store in the United States and I am certain that any mention of her name in connection with that department store would cast an unjust reflection upon the particular store, because I know its reputation.

THE CHAIRMAN: Without objection.

MR. STRIPLING: Mr. Chairman, with reference to J. Peters, or Stevens, I should like to state that the Committee issued a subpoena calling for his appearance before the committee yesterday. However, we have been unable to serve the subpoena. It was issued several months ago. He was arrested by the immigration authorities about three weeks ago in Poughkeepsie, New York. The Committee has evidence to show that J. Peters, or Alexander Stevens, or Isadore Boorstein, as he is also known, has for years been the leader of the underground section of the Communist Party in the United

States. The Committee has the passport, a fraudulent passport, by the way, which he traveled to the Soviet Union on, on October 7, 1931, under the name of Isadore Boorstein. When and if we can obtain Mr. Peters and have him before the Committee we will go into great detail concerning his activities.

THE CHAIRMAN: Well, the Government agencies that we have asked to aid us in getting Mr. Peters haven't been either very alert or cooperative. They have known that we have wanted Peters for a long time. But I do want to point out that the Government agencies that I have in mind do not include the Federal Bureau of Investigation.

MR. STRIPLING: Mr. Russell, did your investigation disclose whether or not Louise Bransten was ever contacted by Gerhart Eisler?

MR. RUSSELL: Yes. On December 29, 1943, she was a guest at a dinner given by Lement U. Harris, of Chappaqua, New York, at his home. Gerhart Eisler was present at this dinner.

MR. STRIPLING: Could you identify Lement Harris further for the Committee.

MR. RUSSELL: Yes, Lement Harris is high in the Communist Party circles of the United States. He has charge of the Party's work among the agricultural workers in the United States as well as the Western Hemisphere. He also has something to do with Communist Party financing in the United States, since it is known that he attempted to persuade Louise Bransten to invest ten thousand dollars in the *Salute* magazine.

MR. STRIPLING: S-a-l-u-t-e?

MR. RUSSELL: S-a-l-u-t-e.

MR. STRIPLING: Can you tell the Committee whether your investigation disclosed whether or not Peters was, or Alexander Stevens was, very successful in raising funds in the motion-picture industry in behalf of Earl Browder?

MR. RUSSELL: Well, the donations that I know about are those received from Louise Bransten and Ruth Wilson. However, it is known that Bransten—or, that Stevens, or Peters, as he is known, visited a bank with Herbert Biberman and that Biberman entered a safety-deposit box in the bank. However, I can't state whether or not he got money from the box.

MR. STRIPLING: He did enter the bank with Peters?

MR. RUSSELL: That is right.

MR. STRIPLING: Mr. Russell, do you have any information regarding further contacts on the part of Louise Bransten with other persons associated with the Soviet government?

MR. RUSSELL: Yes, she has been associated with Vassili Zublin, of the Soviet Embassy in Washington, D.C. She has also been associated with Gregory Kheifets, of the Soviet consulate in San Francisco, and Mr. V. V. Pastoev, of the Soviet consulate in Los Angeles, California. For instance, on May 12, 1944, Gregory Kheifets, Aubrey Whitney Grossman, and John Tripp McTernan, were in attendance at a party in San Francisco which was given by Louise Bransten.

MR. STRIPLING: Did your investigation disclose whether or not Bransten is an important figure in the Communist setup in the United States?

MR. RUSSELL: Bransten is what would be termed in a confidence-game racket as the sharper or the loader. That is, in Communist Party circles, she directs the manner in which contacts with certain people are to be made, whether or not these persons are connected with the Communist Party of the United States or other countries, or whether they are connected with the Communist Party at all. She has contacts, did have them, in numerous Government agencies.

MR. STRIPLING: Could you tell the Committee whether or not Louise Bransten was in communication with certain individuals who were approached by an agent of the Soviet government regarding certain espionage activities?

MR. RUSSELL: Yes. Louise Bransten was closely associated with Peter Ivanov, the Russian vice-consul in San Francisco, California. He was also a secretary in that consulate. I understand Mr. Ivanov has returned to Soviet Russia.

MR. STRIPLING: Can you tell the Committee whether or not Louise Bransten was associated with a man by the name of George Charles Eltenton?

MR. RUSSELL: Yes, she was very closely associated with George Charles Eltenton, and his wife, Dolly.

MR. STRIPLING: Could you identify George Charles Eltenton?

MR. RUSSELL: Yes, Charles Eltenton was an employee of the Shell Development Corporation in Emoryville, California, from 1938. He possibly is still employed there.

MR. STRIPLING: Do you know whether or not George Charles Eltenton ever made any trips to the Soviet Union?

MR. RUSSELL: Yes, he lived in the vicinity of Leningrad. While there, was requested to translate a book written by a Victor Konratiev entitled *The Free Hydroylem.** Konratiev is a friend of [Abraham] Joffe, who developed the first atom-smashing machine in the Soviet. Mr. Eltenton, along with his wife, Dolly, attended a party given by Louise Bransten on November 10, 1944, and at the time Eltenton was trying to educate a scientist along Soviet lines since he had loaned this particular scientist a copy of the Soviet constitution which he asked him to read. I can identify that scientist if necessary.

MR. STRIPLING: Was this scientist employed at the radiation laboratory in California?

* Given as *Free Hydroxyl* by Victor Kondratyev in *World's Who's Who in Science.* But no English translation is traceable. —E.B.

MR. RUSSELL: He was employed at the radiation laboratory at the University of California.

MR. STRIPLING: At Berkeley?

MR. RUSSELL: At Berkeley.

MR. STRIPLING: Do you know whether or not Eltenton attended a reception in the honor of Molotov in the St. Francis Hotel in San Francisco on May 7, 1945?

MR. RUSSELL: Yes, he did attend the reception for Molotov in the St. Francis Hotel on May 7, 1945, during which he held quite a conversation with Mr. Molotov.

MR. STRIPLING: Do you have any information regarding further association between Louise Bransten and Eltenton?

MR. RUSSELL: Yes, it is known that Louise Bransten at one time attempted to secure employment for Dolly Eltenton with the American-Russian Institute through Gregory Kheifets. Also Louise Bransten requested Eltenton to send a telegram of congratulations to a Russian scientific society in the Soviet Union, and during the month of July 1940 it was sent. The person in charge of this scientific gathering in Soviet Russia was an individual known as Peter Kapitza.

MR. STRIPLING: Mr. Russell, tell the Committee whether or not Eltenton was ever contacted by an official of the Soviet government regarding espionage activity.

MR. RUSSELL: Yes, during the year 1942, the latter part, Eltenton was contacted by Peter Ivanov, whom I have identified as a vice-consul of the Soviet government and a secretary in its consulate in San Francisco. Ivanov offered Eltenton money in return for his cooperation in securing information regarding the secret work which was being conducted at the University of California, Berkeley, in its radiation laboratory.

MR. STRIPLING: Do you know whether or not Eltenton, in furtherance of this offer, contacted anyone else?

MR. RUSSELL: Yes. In order to cooperate with Ivanov he approached Haakon Chevalier, who was a professor at the University of California, and requested him to find out what was being done at the radiation laboratory, particularly information regarding the highly destructive weapon which was being developed through research. Eltenton told Chevalier that he had a line of communication with an official of the Soviet government who had advised him that, since Russia and the United States were allies, Soviet Russia should be entitled to any technical data which might be of assistance to that nation. At the time of this particular conversation Chevalier advised Eltenton that he would contact a third person who was working in the radiation laboratory and attempt to secure information regarding the type of work conducted there or any information which he could regarding technical developments which might be of assistance to the Soviet government.

MR. STRIPLING: Mr. Russell, can you tell the Committee whether or not Mr. Chevalier did contact a scientist employed in the radiation laboratory?

MR. RUSSELL: Yes, Chevalier approached this third person.

MR. STRIPLING: Was that third person J. Robert Oppenheimer?

MR. RUSSELL: That is right. Chevalier approached this third person, J. Robert Oppenheimer, and told him that George Charles Eltenton was interested in obtaining information regarding technical developments under consideration by the United States and also that Eltenton was interested in obtaining information regarding the work being performed at the radiation laboratory at the University of California.

MR. STRIPLING: Did Chevalier tell J. Robert Oppenheimer that he had the means of communication whereby he could transmit such information to the Soviet Union?

MR. RUSSELL: Yes, he did. He told J. Robert Oppenheimer that Eltenton had a source through which he could relay the information to the Soviet government.

MR. STRIPLING: What did Mr. Oppenheimer reply to this approach on the part of Mr. Chevalier?

MR. RUSSELL: He said that he considered such attempts as this to secure information a treasonable act and that he certainly would not have anything to do with such a thing.

MR. STRIPLING: Can you tell the Committee whether or not J. Robert Oppenheimer subsequently worked on the atomic project at Los Alamos, New Mexico, in the development of the atomic bomb?

MR. RUSSELL: Yes, he did. He was in charge of it.

THE CHAIRMAN: The Chair would like to make this statement. The hearings today conclude the first phase of the Committee's investigation of Communism in the motion-picture industry. While we have heard thirty-nine witnesses, there are many more to be heard. The Chair stated earlier in the hearing he would present the records of seventy-nine prominent people associated with the motion-picture industry who were members of the Communist Party or who had records of Communist affiliations. We have had before us eleven of these individuals. There are sixty-eight to go.

I want to emphasize that the Committee is not adjourning sine die, but will resume hearings as soon as possible. The Committee hearings for the past two weeks have clearly shown the need for this investigation. Ten prominent figures in Hollywood whom the Committee had evidence were members of the Communist Party were brought before us and refused to deny that they were Communists. It is not necessary for the Chair to emphasize the harm which the motion-picture industry suffers from the presence within its ranks of known Communists who do not have the best interests of the United States at heart. The industry should set about immediately to clean its own house and not wait for public opinion to force it to do so.

1948

"Proposed Legislation to Curb or Control the Communist Party"

The American Civil Liberties Union has always, naturally enough, been a target of HUAC. On one page of *The Trojan Horse in America* the position of Roger Baldwin, "who has run the ACLU ever since its beginning," is completely identified with Marxism, and on another page of the same book the following sentence appears: "Only such persons as Robert Morse Lovett, secretary of the Virgin Islands, Roger Baldwin, director of the ACLU, Malcolm Cowley, editor of the *New Republic,* Donald Ogden Stewart, Hollywood writer, Vito Marcantonio, member of Congress, and Leane Zugsmith, writer, have records that compare in volume with that of Rockwell Kent."

In which a man is judged by the fatness of his file in the Committee's office.

All this being so, it is the more important to let a voice from the ACLU itself be heard because such a voice would not characteristically be that of a Communist sympathizer, and in what follows we hear Arthur Garfield Hays (1881–1954), describing the Communists as "crackbrained." Some people, Sidney Hook, for example, have taken the position that, if you're not pro-Communist, you've got to be anti. Hays agrees to the extent of considering the Communists eccentric but he cannot raise the wind of hatred that Hook was to demand. Which would be important for anyone asking what really was going on in America at mid-century and what the different schools of opinion actually were. The characteristic locus of intense hatred, as far as intellectuals are concerned, was with the ex-Communists, and one of them—the ex-Trotskyist James Burnham—is heard from right after Arthur Garfield Hays.

As for this whole campaign by Richard Nixon and others to outlaw ("curb," "control") the Communist Party, its success can be measured less by the legislation that ensued than by the state of mind to which it reduced liberals such as the movie star John Garfield who said to HUAC in 1951, "How do you protect people like me? That is what I want to know. That is why I feel we should outlaw the Party."

FEBRUARY 10, 1948:

Arthur Garfield Hays

The Subcommittee met at 10 a.m. in room 225, Old House Office Building, the Honorable Richard M. Nixon (Chairman of the Subcommittee) presiding.

Subcommittee members present: Representatives Nixon, F. Edward Hébert, and John McDowell.

Also present: Representative Rankin.

Staff members present: Robert E. Stripling, Chief Investigator, and Robert B. Gaston, Investigator.

MR. NIXON: The hearing will come to order.

MR. HAYS: My name is Arthur Garfield Hays, 24 East Tenth Street, New York City.

MR. STRIPLING: For the purpose of identification will you please give the Committee a resume of your professional background?

MR. HAYS: I was graduated from Columbia College in 1902, from Columbia Law School in 1905 with L.B., LL.B., and M.M.A. degrees. I started practicing law in New York with Bowers & Sands. I established my own firm in 1907. I was very active in 1912 in politics in the Bull Moose Party. I went to England during the last war and practiced in the prize courts in England for about two years. When I came back home, and after we got into the war, I became interested in the work of the American Civil Liberties Union and have been general counsel for the American Civil Liberties Union ever since the early 1920s. Politically I was a Republican for Hughes in 1916. I joined the Farmer-Labor Party in 1920. I was state chairman of the Progressive Party in New York City for LaFollette and Williams. Since 1928 I have been a good Democrat. My practice today is largely constitutional law and commercial law, and I have an office at 120 Broadway, New York City.

MR. STRIPLING: Mr. Hays, do you have a prepared statement?

MR. HAYS: Yes, sir.

MR. STRIPLING: In line with the Committee's procedure, if you will read your statement at this time, when you reach its conclusion the members will direct questions to you.

MR. HAYS: This is a statement on laws banning the Communist Party from the ballot and others affecting that party. Neither democratic principles nor practical expediency can justify these proposals.

OUTLAWRY OF THE COMMUNIST PARTY*

In principle this is wrong, and in my judgment is unconstitutional. In practice it would be futile and defeat the very purpose intended.

So long as people have the right freely to persuade and secretly to vote we have a method by which changes in government, no matter how revolutionary, can be brought about without force or violence.

The Bill of Rights guarantees the freedom to advocate changes in the American form of government, to belong to a political party for that purpose, and to run for office. Any denial of these freedoms for Communists inevitably challenges the rights of all political minorities.

To outlaw the Communist Party or to bar its members from public office would be to substitute totalitarian practices for democratic principles.

The kind of law proposed is one in which Congress would find as a fact that the Communist Party is not a political party, but an international conspiracy which advocates revolution and the overthrow of our Government by force. For Congress to become a fact-finding body would seem to me to be putting itself in the place of the judiciary. It is the business not of Congress but of the judiciary to find facts. The Communists deny the facts, and the alleged facts and conclusions are difficult, if not impossible to prove.

The limitations on the power of Congress were recently reaffirmed in *United States* v. *Lovett* (328 U.S. 303 (1946)).

There, Mr. Justice [Hugo] Black said:

> . . . legislative acts, no matter what their form, that apply either to named individuals or to easily ascertainable members of a group in such a way as to inflict punishment on them without a judicial trial are bills of attainder prohibited by the Constitution . . . (p. 315).
>
> Those who wrote our Constitution well knew the danger inherent in special legislative acts which take away the life, liberty, or property of particular named persons because the legislature thinks them guilty of conduct which deserves punishment. They intended to safeguard the people of this country from punishment without trial by duly constituted courts. . . . (p. 317).

We believe, moreover, that, like attempts to bar the Communist Party by name from the ballot, any restrictions on the freedom of expression of individuals merely because they belong to a particular organization is a denial of due process. This has been decided in two cases arising under state laws which sought to bar the Communist Party: *Communist Party* v. *Peek* (20 Cal. 2d 536, 127 P. 2d 889 (1942)), and *Feinglass* v. *Reinecke* (48 F.

* Printed here uncut. —E.B.

Supp. 438 (N.D. Ill. 1942)), in which, incidentally, I represented the Communist Party.

In the Peek case, there was a statute prohibiting the use of the ballot by the Communist Party or any organization which used the name "Communist." The law also prohibited the ballot to organizations which advocated the forceful overthrow of the Government. There was no proof that the Communist Party came within the latter category. The court held that the statute was invalid insofar as it sought to ban the party by name on the ground that there was no reasonable basis for this. The court also held that judicial notice could not be taken of the contention that the Communist Party in fact advocated the overthrow of the Government by force.

In the Feinglass case, an Illinois statute was before the court. This prohibited the use of the ballot by an organization connected with Communist "or other un-American principles" or which taught "subservience to the political principles and ideals of foreign nations" or which sought to overthrow the Government by force. Again there was no showing that the party advocated the overthrow of the Government by force. Judge Holly held that the party had the right to be on the ballot, that the mere use of the name was no ground for barring it, and that the other terms of the statute were too vague to justify exclusion. He said:

> Such terms as "un-American" and "the political principles of foreign nations" lack the precision required in a statute which affects the rights of a political group to appeal to the electorate. Any political idea that happens to conflict with the economic or political notions of an individual is apt by him to be deemed un-American.

In the matter of *Schneiderman* v. *United States* (320 U.S. 118 (1942)), there was presented to the court the usual material showing the basis of the Communist Party's principles and ends. The court held that on analysis none of this material proved that the party necessarily advocated the overthrow of the Government by force. Justice Murphy referred to the 1938 constitution of the Communist Party as one which "ostensibly eschews resort to force and violence as an element of party tactics" and, said Justice Murphy (p. 157):

> A tenable conclusion from the foregoing is that the party in 1927 desired to achieve its purpose by peaceful and democratic means, and as a theoretic matter justified the use of force and violence only as a method of preventing an attempted forcible counteroverthrow once the party had obtained control in a peaceful manner, or as a method of last resort to enforce the majority will if at some indefinite future time because of peculiar circumstances constitutions or peaceful channels were no longer open.

No bill would be constitutional, in my judgment, except a general bill which might make it a crime for a party to advocate the overthrow of the Government by force. However, we have plenty of that kind of legislation on the books. There already is the Federal act (the Smith Act), and there are criminal anarchy laws in all the states to that effect. The difficulty is one of proof. We have plenty of legislation today to stop all Communist activity if we could prove that the party and the members thereof advocate force and violence.

In practice, any such legislation would be futile, as has happened incidentally, in Canada.

If the law applied to the Communist Party, the law could be evaded by the Communist Party changing its name. Experience shows that laws of this kind would merely drive the movement underground, give it the advantage of the emotionalism that arises from secrecy, and lend to its members the halo of martyrdom. Suppression would promote its growth, not halt it. Measures like this might be used as a threatening gag to all those who favor any change in the *status quo*. This kind of legislation seems to me to be wholly un-American, indicates lack of faith in our institutions, would arouse fear and timidity, and invite attacks upon sincere liberal thought.

The bill H.R. 4422 introduced by Mr. Mundt, of Illinois [South Dakota], and now before the Committee on Un-American Activities, would require certain persons to register as agents of foreign principals and mark all propaganda sent out by them. The bill covers all members of the Communist Party or of any group "dominated, directed, or controlled by the Communist Party."

Any matter circulated in interstate or foreign commerce or by use of the mails, which might reach two or more persons, must contain a statement that it has been published in compliance with the laws governing agents of foreign principals. All such matter must also contain an elaborate statement that the transmitter has registered, giving the name and address of the agent and his foreign principal, that the registration statement is open for inspection and that the Government has not, by accepting the registration statement, indicated its approval of the material sent out. The bill provides that the Attorney General may prescribe the language in which these statements shall be printed, and that he may require that additional information from the registration statement be included.

This bill is likewise subject to attack on constitutional grounds as a bill of attainder and a denial of due process and infringement of free speech. It imposes penalties on individuals merely by reason of their association and without any hearing. In effect the bill constitutes a Congressional determination that all members of the Communist Party or of groups controlled by it actually are agents of a foreign principal. *United States* v. *Lovett, supra,* is particularly in point here.

We also have the objection that this is not general but specific legislation and that it is indefinite.

The bill is clearly a restriction on the freedom of expression of the persons covered. Whatever may be the right of Congress to require agents of foreign principals to register and, in connection with their activities on behalf of such foreign principals, to indicate that they are so acting, it is quite another matter to require persons to indicate that they have registered as agents of foreign principals in all of their activities. Unless an individual when he expresses his opinion is acting on behalf of his foreign principal, it would seem wholly inappropriate to require him to state that he is in fact an agent of a foreign principal. Congress, moreover, has not adopted any such general rule with regard to agents of foreign principals, and no proper basis seems to exist for imposing this restriction on freedom of expression of all individual members of the Communist Party.

If the Communist Party and the members thereof are foreign agents, they are subject to the requirement of registration today and they could be prosecuted for violating the law. The difficulty again is one of proof.

Now, I have a bill to propose in order to eliminate the Communist nuisance, and this is my proposed bill:

(*Mr. Hays proposed the following bill which was referred to the Committee on Un-American Activities:*)

A BILL to provide means to eliminate the Communist nuisance

Whereas this was a happy land with no troubles until hordes of Communists overran us, causing high prices, strikes, conspiracies—and treason; and

Whereas Communists have, since the beginning of our history, caused all the hell raising in the United States; and

Whereas experience during the late war proved conclusively that the FBI, the police, the military, and all of our courts and laws are incapable of doing their jobs of apprehending traitors; and

Whereas treason is hard to prove under the Constitution of the United States; and

Whereas Communists advocate deceit, confusion, and are traitors; and

Whereas one of our chief difficulties is that we cannot distinguish a Communist from anyone else; and

Whereas there is a pressing need for some means of easy distinction; and

Whereas we have all sorts of investigations, committees, and commissions but no machines to read a man's mind: Therefore be it

Enacted by the Senate and House of Representatives of the United States of America in Congress assembled:

1. That all suspected Communists or people we don't like be submitted to a mental test.
2. That we appropriate $10,000,000,000 to set up a commission to invent a mental reading machine which when applied will say "Communist" when the individual is not a loyal citizen.
3. Until such machine is fully developed, all Communists must wear boots, red shirts, fur caps (both male and female) and grow beards (both male and female).
4. This law shall be self-enacting and shall take effect immediately.

I propose that bill as a test of the kind of bills proposed in Congress today.

In my judgment no laws should be passed. It is about time our legislators realized that the American people are to be trusted and need no laws to save them from bad propaganda or bad thinking. After one hundred fifty years of history, our people have shown that they are entitled to be trusted.

Justice Holmes once said that democracy is an experiment, as all life is an experiment. So long as we are trying this experiment and feel it works, as I imagine any good American does, we should let people alone to think, talk, and develop propaganda as they choose. We should encourage those of radical thought to come out into the open and to act along political lines. If their views are obnoxious, it is the American belief that they will not get very far.

I know of no better evidence of this than the Communist Party itself. After twenty-five years, the Communists cannot get enough votes even in the State of New York, where a large proportion of them are centered, to keep their name on the ballot. They have been unable to elect a representative to Congress although some people claim there is one exception. They have none in the New York State Legislature.

In New York City, through proportional representation, two Communists managed to get elected to the city council, and we timidly changed the voting system to prevent this in the future. The situation with the Communists today is quite parallel with that of the Socialists in the 1920s.

As a matter of fact, if we had a more radical party than the Communists today, that party would make the Communists respectable, just like the Communists made the Socialists respectable.

It was claimed that the Socialists were not a real political party but engaged in a conspiracy to overthrow the Government by force, acting as agents of foreign countries. There is hardly a crackbrained movement in the United States that cannot get a million followers within a comparatively short time. These movements rise and fall. Sometimes people are afraid of them.

Referring to history, I have in mind the Jacobin Republicans around 1800, the Catholics in the middle of the century, the Anarchists and Knights of Labor in the 1880s, the A.F. of L., at first quite radical, the IWW, the Socialists, the Communists, the CIO and, again, the Communists.

The method of the Fascists, of Hitler and Mussolini, was to stir up a Red scare and then repress the liberties of the people in order to save them from the Reds. It is about time we realized that this technique of passing laws to save us from imagined dangers is inimical to freedom. What we need are men in this country who not only believe in, but who are not afraid of freedom.

MR. NIXON: Does that conclude your statement, Mr. Hays?

MR. HAYS: Yes, it does, sir.

MR. NIXON: Do you have a statement to make, Mr. McDowell?

MR. MCDOWELL: Mr. Chairman, in view of the fact that the entire world around the United States is in flames, a great part of that world has disappeared under this thing called Communism. People have died, nations have been destroyed, customs and laws have been broken. Hence I would have no question to ask of the witness after listening to this startling statement.

MR. NIXON: Mr. Hébert?

MR. HÉBERT: I want to concur with what Mr. McDowell has said. It is an amazing statement to have come from an acceptedly intelligent individual who has a string of degrees behind his name. I did not hear "Red" behind any of these letters.

MR. HAYS: That has been said before, if you please, and if your idea about me is that I am a Communist, you can call me that if you would, but those are my views and those views are quite in accord with our Constitution and our Bill of Rights. I cannot understand you men. You say you are Americans. You are so little American, you have so little faith in our institutions. The idea of being afraid of Communists is ridiculous. You are doing what they have done in every Fascist country. You are building up a Red scare and then you will pass laws as though we are contaminated and not allow us to do our own thinking. I don't know of anybody who is afraid of taking a look. I don't know of anybody who is corrupt. Freedom is the right to hear an opinion, and the idea of passing laws to keep people's names off the ballot—those are views of the totalitarians, and if those views are contrary to Americanism, if that is Communistic, then I am a Communist.

MR. HÉBERT: I am sure that the gentleman will agree that the people of the overthrown countries of Europe had no reason to feel fear of the spread of Communism there. It was just merely a Red scare set up by the Fascists and the Nazis, and so forth.

MR. HAYS: I don't agree that they had no right to fear.

MR. HÉBERT: Just a moment, I will let you make a speech.

MR. HAYS: I beg your pardon.

MR. HÉBERT: I am sure the gentleman will agree with me that Communism as we recognize Communism—the influence of the Kremlin in Moscow, the influence of the Communist government of Russia—has encompassed more of Europe today under a totalitarian government in which all civil liberties have been destroyed, in which the dignity of the individual has been flaunted, than Hitler controlled at the height of his power with the same totalitarian government. Do you agree with me there?

MR. HAYS: No, I don't.

MR. HÉBERT: What do you call these countries of the Balkan states—Greece, Rumania, Yugoslavia, Czechoslovakia, and all these places that are overrun by totalitarian government under the direction of Moscow and the Kremlin—what form of government have they got if it is not Communist?

MR. HAYS: If you tell me Russians are a danger to Europe and a danger to the United States, I agree. I don't know how to meet that danger. As far as this country is concerned, we can meet all dangers as a free country a whole lot better than if we pass oppressive laws. I agree that Russia is a totalitarian state, and I hate totalitarianism. But what does impress me is the fear you have of the present Communist Party members and what they may do to the laws of the United States. Is it just a matter of chance that the most progressive countries in the world have always been the freest countries? Countries like Sweden, New Zealand, Australia, Canada, and the United States—they are all free countries. If you pass laws of oppression because you are fearful of the present Constitution, because you feel it don't [won't?] work, you will destroy freedom in the United States. If you bring people out in the open and face them in the open, you can get much farther than if you drive them underground, and I cannot see anything in these bills except an attempt to drive the Communist movement underground. I think they are very dangerous.

MR. HÉBERT: Of course, we disagree. I think it would be very helpful to bring them out [in the open], and I am the last person in the world to stop any man from having an expression of what he wants to say: I am letting you make a speech.

MR. HAYS: People who are willing to allow a man to talk but want to bring about a situation whereby he must pay for it! His kids will be slighted at school, he will lose his job, and he will get social discrimination. When you impose penalties on free speech you are corrupting free speech. How far have the Communists gotten in the United States in the last twenty-five years? They have gotten nowhere. What is all the excitement and danger about, Congressman?

MR. HÉBERT: Your expression, "They got nowhere," and my opinion are two different opinions. When I see what happened in different countries, and in this one, with Communist-influenced strikes that kept planes on the ground when they were instantly needed in other parts of the world, I think they have gotten somewhere.

MR. HAYS: If they have been responsible for them [the strikes]. Nothing outrages us more than the general idea that the Communists deserve all the credit in the United States. They don't deserve that credit. It is that kind of credit that builds up the Communist Party. They think they are important, and then a lot of people think they are important. After all, it is a large movement. We in the American Civil Liberties Union see that every time a meeting of Communist Party was broken up in New York they would get hundreds of new adherents. After all, it is exciting to be in a movement where you are up against the authorities. I think all this publicity builds up the Communist Party more than the Communists themselves can do in ten years. They have gotten millions of dollars worth of publicity. I think we ought to regard them as the ridiculous, insignificant, futile crowd that they are. Whenever there is any difficulty in the labor unions the Communists are blamed. You would think that a couple of Communists could lead millions of Americans around by the nose. That is an insult to Americans. Every time there is a disorder in the United States the Communists must be blamed for it. I don't think they deserve the credit.

MR. HÉBERT: In your general statement, "Every time there is a disorder we blame the Communist," you are merely expressing an individual opinion.

MR. HAYS: You have told me that all the strikes and troubles are stirred up by the Communists.

MR. HÉBERT: I did not say all of them; I said many of them. I am trying to protect the American form of government and American free speech. I believe everybody should have a right to speak. It is probably a rather hackneyed phrase, it is Voltaire's expression, "I may not agree with what you say, but I certainly will fight to defend your right to say it." And I agree with that, of course. However, when a disease is spreading either on the body politic or on the body human, it behooves us as intelligent human beings to do something to retard it. We ought to treasure our way of life. You must know that freedom can destroy freedom.

MR. HAYS: Congressman, you mean to say that under our form of government we should protect people from ideas that may contaminate them? Isn't it the very fundamental of our Government that people are entitled to protection from everything but ideas, and do you think by law you can protect people from ideas we don't like?

MR. HÉBERT: I propose to do something about them. That same argument, the spread of disease—all these signs around—particularly the drive against venereal disease—the more you say about it, the more you make it popular?

MR. HAYS: If you cancel the spread of books or literature that will contaminate you, the Congress interrupts us in spreading ideas. Either it is free speech or nothing.

MR. HÉBERT: I believe in a Communist being able to come up and say anything he wants to say.

MR. HAYS: But aren't you going to put a curb on him?

MR. HÉBERT: No, just what they stand for and where they are getting it. I want the Communist Party to be out in the open where we can see them, and I want them to have a chance to call me whatever they want to call me and the opportunity to prove I am what they call me.

MR. HAYS: Tell me what laws you want, then.

MR. HÉBERT: I cannot speak for the Committee. I am quite impressed by the Mundt bill and its exposition procedure where we know where we stand. In the same token we don't want thieves and criminals running around rampant.

MR. HAYS: They are not protected by the courts.

MR. HÉBERT: We won't let them run rampant. They pursue that kind of life and the majority of the people are not going to have it.

MR. HAYS: But you yourself told me you were not going to prevent the spread of ideas.

MR. HÉBERT: Yes, that is right.

MR. HAYS: Why make it a parallel with criminals running loose?

MR. HÉBERT: I am taking your own statements to show how fallacious they are.

MR. HAYS: My theory on this is: The best way to prevent an evil is to meet the evil by truth and meet the evil in the open market. You mentioned the statement made by Louis Waldman* the other day. As I understand it, either a man must repudiate the stand of the Communists politically or say he is a Communist. Suppose he is not a Communist. Suppose he believes what Roosevelt said: "I will let anybody vote for me who believes in my ideas." Does he say he is a Communist? How did Waldman act when LaFollette was running for Congress? Was LaFollette obliged to say we were Socialists when we were not, and, if you're not supporting the Socialists, you won't have to vote for us? I am amazed that anybody could give credit to that idea. That, to me, is the most crackedbrain one in the world.

MR. HÉBERT: We probably did not read the same statement. What impressed me most about Waldman's statement was he did not want to call any party by name.

MR. HAYS: I thought his purpose was if [Henry A.] Wallace accomplished getting the support of the Communists, Wallace should be obliged to state he believes in Communist principles.

MR. HÉBERT: That he had to accept the support of the individual party, whether Communist, Republican, or Democrat.

MR. HAYS: That he accepted the support of Communist principles and believed in them. That was the report in the *New York Times*. Was Roosevelt asked to do that? Was LaFollette asked to do that? Why should Wallace be asked if he believes in something that is voting for him? He [Waldman] would have all Communists register as foreign agents, whether they were foreign agents or not. That is a disputable point. Congress has not proved they are foreign agents. Today you can lock up every Communist in the United States under your foreign-agents registration law. As they are not foreign agents, Congress has no right to pass a bill saying that they are.

MR. HÉBERT: Congress has a right to pass any law it wants to pass.

MR. HAYS: Congress has no right to find the facts. Congress under that bill would find that all Communists are foreign agents. Just like the Mundt

* Louis Waldman was general counsel to United Hatters, A.F. of L. In this period he was supporting the Mundt-Nixon Communist Control Bill. He also wanted Eleanor Roosevelt to run for President with Walter Reuther as running mate.

bill, they would find the Communist Party advocated the overthrow of the United States Government by force. The only difficulties you would have in a bill like that would be constitutional, if it referred to the Communist Party, but if you made it a crime to overthrow the Government by force—you have that bill—it is the Smith Act.

MR. HÉBERT: The Attorney General has testified the present laws are inadequate to prosecute.

MR. HAYS: Surely they are inadequate. That way the jurisdiction—let us do away with the three-branch system—the legislative, the judicial—

MR. HÉBERT: And executive.

MR. HAYS: —and executive. Let us do away with that system in order to get a crowd like the Communist Party. I can understand, Congressman, why people say freedom is no longer adequate, our institutions are no longer adequate. It won't do to let anybody vote. It won't do to let anybody spread propaganda. So we want to change our institutions. But for men to say we believe in the American system but we are afraid of it—

MR. HÉBERT: I am not afraid of it.

MR. HAYS: —I cannot understand that.

MR. HÉBERT: I have great faith in it and that is why I want to drive these subversive people above ground. I want to hear all the crackpot ideas, because I have great faith in the American people and that is the reason we are trying to bring it into the open and I am for everybody expressing themselves.

MR. HAYS: Where do you and I differ? You want to put them in a certain class because they believe in certain things. You want them to register or you want them to engage in political action openly and they are afraid. You want to make it clear whether or not a fellow belongs to a certain group. Those things put curbs on free speech, that men won't express themselves freely, if they are to be put in a special class, or condemned by society. I don't like Communism, but I would not put a curb on their expression of opinion of any kind. You say they can express their opinion but they must do certain things.

MR. HÉBERT: Certainly, that is the requirement of expressing the opinion. We don't prevent them from expressing it.

MR. HAYS: They will be afraid to do it. For instance, in a fight we had with Mayor Hague, one of our chief supporters, who was a high-school principal, would not contribute, and neither would a small businessman for fear of retaliation. People in this day and age will express an opinion only if they don't have to pay a penalty for it. If we are going to put people in such a class and have them pay penalties to express their opinions, that is the end for free speech. It is like Hitler saying you can have free speech but we will send you to a concentration camp if we don't like what you say.

MR. HÉBERT: If we let that freedom be destroyed it can happen here, and I am going to do everything I can in preventing our freedom from being destroyed.

MR. HAYS: Am I not right that Hitler and Mussolini got into power by whipping up a Red scare?

MR. HÉBERT: They did not get into power merely by building up a Red scare.

MR. HAYS: I was in Germany in 1933 when it came under Hitler in the days of the Reichstag fire. He had two scapegoats—the Communists and the Jews. The Communists were most important. He was saving the people from the Reds and they passed a law barring all Communists from the Reichstag and as a result the anti-Communists had the authority and they repealed the German constitution. He did exactly what you are doing here. He barred the Communists from the Reichstag, and if Congress adopts this principle, Congress must bar a minority party or their delegates of voters. Suppose you turn your mind to the situation in the early 1800s where all the early Jeffersonians were called Jacobins and they were Republicans. They were charged with getting money from France. They were charged with being foreign agents. They were charged with loyalty not to the United States but to France, and the people in power, the Federalists, put all the important Jacobins in jail, and some of those stories are vicious reading today. And what happened? Jefferson got in office and pardoned all the people in jail and we passed the earliest sedition law. That was passed, just as you are passing these laws today, to protect the people from dangerous thoughts. That was early in our history. Don't you realize that in the early part of our history the Catholics were a dangerous force to our people? They were supposed to be run through foreign influence. Their churchmen were jeered, their altars were desecrated, they were supposed to be a dangerous group, but nobody thought of barring them from the ballot, and today the situation is different. It was that way with the Anarchists in the year 1880, and so with the Knights of Labor, the American Federation of Labor, the IWW workers and laborers. In those days they did a lot more hell raising than the Communists. A lot of them were jailed. They were jailed under the antisedition laws. And then came the Socialists in the twenties. And if you read the proceedings you found exactly the same arguments and actions at law to force the Socialists out of the New York Assembly as with the Communists today.

MR. NIXON: In other words, there is an honest difference of opinion.

MR. HÉBERT: An honest difference with this gentleman's opinion. And he has a right to express himself. One of us is a little wrong. I don't think it is I.

MR. HAYS: You see, I do. My regret is so many people in the United States are following you men, and I think what you are doing is very dangerous to what America stands for and to American rights.

MR. HÉBERT: If you want the American form of government, the majority rules. We have the majority on our side, according to your own statement.

* * *

MR. NIXON: Mr. McDowell?

MR. MCDOWELL: I said I would not ask Mr. Hays any questions and I don't intend to ask him any. Mr. Hays has come to Washington presupposing that we are for all of these bills. As a matter of fact, I have discarded in my mind all but one of these bills and I am by no means sure I am willing for that to become a law. I don't think the witness should come here with the idea, "You were doing this, you were doing that, you were giving this law." That is not the case at all, Mr. Hays.

MR. HAYS: I know that, Congressman, and I recognize the difference between this Subcommittee and the way the Dies Committee and the Thomas Committee acted before this branch of the investigation was started. This, of course, is what a Congressional Committee, in my judgment, is supposed to do: hold hearings in connection with legislation, and when I used the word "you," I gathered from the Congressman that all of you thought I was wrong and I was a minority of one.

MR. MCDOWELL: I think you are dead wrong in belittling the danger of Communists. You are dead right in expressing your opinions. Certainly I will agree to that. But you are dead wrong in assuming that these matters are going to become law, when we are now trying to find out what we should do with them. We have asked the best minds of America, and that includes yours. Some of whom we knew we opposed before they came here too, and that includes you.

MR. HAYS: You say I don't recognize the danger of Communists. I do. I don't realize the danger of the Communists *in the United States* and I think Communism is so foreign to American ideas that they never can get to first base, just like the Socialists were never able to get to first base. According to J. Edgar Hoover's statement, there are approximately one hundred thousand Communists in this country and an equal number of fellow travelers. Suppose we had a million who think wildly? I think, in the first place, the Communists do one thing valuable in this country: that is they are gadflies. Whatever their purpose may be, they have been fighting the cause of all mean injustices in the United States, starting with the Sacco-Vanzetti case, then the Scottsboro case, then cases of workingmen all over the country, fighting against Negro oppression in the South—and all the way through they have done a job that the rest of us ought to do and, so long as we ignored it, we give the Communists arguments. I think it is very fortunate that we have some people in this country who do wake up the public mind to these injustices. I wish these people did not go to the Communists. I wish the American Civil Liberties Union was the only group that acted in that behalf and all cases came to us. A lot go to the Communist Party, like the case of interracial difficulty.

I remember the Scottsboro case. I remember going down to Scottsboro with Clarence Darrow to defend the Negroes there. We were in Birmingham and were told these boys wanted to be defended by Interracial Defense, which was a Communist organization. They said, "Mr. Hays, we would be glad to have you in the case and Mr. Darrow, but under certain conditions." Mr. Darrow replied that it was unusual for people to let me in a criminal case on conditions, particularly when I am not getting paid for it. Then Mr. Darrow asked, "What are the conditions?" They replied that "First, we must run the defense so that if you want to insult the Governor or the people who pass on this case, I have to let you insult them. And secondly, you will have to act for the Interracial Defense." Mr. Darrow and I refused to do it. We were then pilloried in the Communist papers as pulling the rope that would hang these Negroes. Then they stirred up public opinion all over the United States. They would write these insulting letters. They developed what is called a mass movement. I don't know if Darrow and I could have saved those Negroes or not. They stirred up public opinion by getting money for propaganda. But none of those Negroes were hung. You have to credit the Communists with being gadflies, with stirring up things. Their purpose is different from my purpose, because I hate the injustice of it, but after all they do fulfill a function.

* * *

MR. McDOWELL: You have made a statement about the Communist Party, that they are gadflies. You wished the rest of us had done that.

MR. HAYS: Instead of the Communists.

MR. McDOWELL: Don't you think there is anything doing good or that has done good in the United States in your day but the Communist Party? Don't you credit the great Democratic Party with bringing about some very much needed labor reforms and hasn't the Republican Party at some time or another come up with something decent and proper and good?

MR. HAYS: Why certainly. As a matter of fact, in 1924 when I was state chairman of the Progressive or LaFollette Party in New York, we were regarded as radical or Reds because we supported the Socialists. At the time Roosevelt had been President for two years, the Government was so far ahead of what we stood for that our movement of 1924, when we were designated as Reds, we would have been regarded as conservatives. We have made tremendous gains. I know the Communist and his role. I hate totalitarianism of any kind. I think they have a divided loyalty. I wouldn't trust a Communist. Some may be idealists and I don't think they have any mental integrity whatever. These people who changed their position overnight, when they signed that treaty with Germany. I don't see how anybody could have any faith in the mental integrity of people of that sort.

We don't trust them at all. When I say they are gadflies, all I say is the people of the Left take advantage of everything wrong in the present system and awaken our conscience.

MR. MCDOWELL: Mr. Hays, the Committee on Un-American Activities is not concerned with what the people on the Right or the people on the Left are saying. We are concerned with the enemies to the Constitution.

MR. HAYS: Who are the enemies of the Constitution? They must be people charged as enemies by the courts or traitors under our system. They cannot be people who have ideas we think dangerous. They must be people who are convicted.

MR. MCDOWELL: I say those people who blame the United States for causing the Second World War, who charge that we financed the war, and so on. You said Mr. Hoover stated there are only one hundred thousand Communists in the United States. In my home community there is a great labor union of some nineteen thousand members, largely intelligent people, all of whom can read and write and everything of that kind. To date I have been able to card exactly seventeen Communists in those nineteen thousand people. Those seventeen Communists run everything that happens in that nineteen-thousand-man union. Every expression of opinion, every political policy, everything that goes on, those seventeen people run. I am deadly afraid of these one hundred thousand Communists in the United States. When Russia was overthrown, when the old Czarist system was overthrown, there were less than thirty thousand Communists in Russia and one hundred fifty million Russians who never had heard of the Bolsheviks, but the Commies took over.

* * *

MR. MCDOWELL: Do you think it is all right for the Ku Klux Klan and the German-American Bund to march with swastikas on?

MR. HAYS: I happened to defend a Fascist crowd in Jersey City where the police refused to allow them to hold meetings. My argument was that I had known Fascists. I was in Germany. Some belonged because they were Germans, some belonged because they don't like the Treaty of Versailles, some belonged because they thought Hitler would lead Europe, some belonged because they were sadists. Let them alone. But as long as you are denying their rights, you are building up that organization that had backing of a foreign power. Individuals are the same way. The police enjoined the crowd not to interfere with the movements, and within six months the whole movement had gone to pieces in north Jersey. I believe that is the way freedom works. It works out more practically than in any other system. Fellows who call us idealists, people who believe in force and oppression, they are the idealists, they have had force and oppression for years, and it is a very much more practical method in letting these fellows alone and not showing this terrible fear of small groups of people. It is the most effective weapon against the Communists.

MR. MCDOWELL: Mr. Hays, you have defended the Fascists, you have defended the Communists, you have defended various others, those accused of murder.

MR. HAYS: Always when their civil rights are involved. I have never defended any other case.

MR. MCDOWELL: Someday you will defend the Committee on Un-American Activities.

MR. HAYS: I will defend the Subcommittee. I won't defend the Commitdetee. (*Laughter.*) Years ago the Communists in New York were being defended by the Civil Liberties Union in their right of free speech and it is only in that respect I have ever defended Communists or Fascists. The right to free speech, the right to a fair trial and not on un-American activities. We wrote a letter to the Communist Party saying we thought it was impertinent for them to ask us to defend their right to free speech when they were breaking up the meetings of other people. They wrote to us and said, "You defend our right to free speech because you believe in free speech. We break up these meetings because we don't believe in free speech." I defended these people because I believe in freedom of speech and the Constitution. I want to ask you a question. What bill is it you are thinking of supporting?

MR. MCDOWELL: Very frankly, it is the Mundt bill I think I will support.

MR. HAYS: When you take this Mundt bill, where these fellows must register as foreign agents, isn't it a judicial question to determine whether they are foreign agents? I also thought the Communists were supported by Russia and they followed Soviet orders. Then, on the other hand, it has occurred to me that a lot of people believe in things the same way the Communists do. They don't get orders, but they are doing the same thing automatically, and I don't believe for a moment they are necessarily Russian agents. I think they may do the same things, but to ask Congress to call men Communists merely by saying so, it is beyond my comprehension how it can be done constitutionally. The courts have to determine if they are foreign agents or not. You can't make a man white by calling him white, and Congress can't make a man a foreign agent by calling him a foreign agent. And if they *are* foreign agents, all you have to do is pass a foreign-agent registration law.

MR. MCDOWELL: Of course, Mr. Hays, your knowledge of Communists has been gained from life's experience. Mine has been gained as a member of this Committee. Many thousands of dollars have been allocated by Congress to hire skilled men to go where they ought to go to examine and analyze and everything of the kind. As the evidence pours in here I get in and analyze it, and so do these other gentlemen on both sides of me, and we are, of course, cognizant that the Communists of the United States are directed by the Communist Party head, whether it be Stalin or the Politburo or whatever it may be. We have reached that conclusion. Now, whether the House of Representatives and the Senate and the President will reach that conclusion I don't know.

MR. HAYS: If you have investigated the facts, that conclusion may be right, but Congress is not a fact-finding body and, if they are agents of Russia, I don't see why they are not prosecuted under the Foreign Agents Acts in failing to register and, if you can't prove that, you have no right to say these men are agents. *We* find that the Communist Party has as its objective the overthrow of the Government by force. The Communists deny it. The courts say, "We can't take findings of disputed fact."

MR. NIXON: In order that the position of the American Civil Liberties Union can be made doubly clear, I have noted in my study of the matter before the hearing today that the American Civil Liberties Union in 1940, on February 6, barred from office all Communists and Fascists in the Civil Liberties Union. After your discussion, how can you reconcile the American Civil Liberties Union action when you say at present your policy is to bring them out in the open.

MR. HAYS: I am glad you asked that question.

MR. NIXON: If you can, answer it very quickly.

MR. HAYS: We had one very well-known Communist, Elizabeth Gurley Flynn, and several fellow travelers on our board. We just couldn't do any business. We would get together on our directors meetings and these people would talk and talk and talk. We would hold evening meetings and at twelve o'clock we would all go home, and we found ourselves going over the same things time and time and time again and our whole work was simply ruined by these Communists. The Communists regarded civil liberties as a means to an end, where the rest of us regard civil liberties as an end in itself. In other words, they were influenced whenever it hit a workingman, but they objected very much to, say, that Henry Ford had a right to go into court and defend his particular view on labor unions. We would defend industrialists just as well as labor unions. Then the question came up: what to do about it. There were four obstructionists in a board of twenty-five. Some of them wanted to get these people off the board on the ground that they did not belong there. Some thought we are an organization that stood to the right of everybody. When Elizabeth Gurley Flynn came out with an article in the *Daily Worker* that attacked us all as insincere, that said we did not believe in what we were doing, that we are defending big interests, and that we are a bunch of hypocrites, then we discharged Miss Flynn from the board and the rest resigned.

MR. NIXON: The only people who resigned from the board of directors were either Communists or fellow travelers, as a result of that action?

MR. HAYS: Yes.

MR. NIXON: In other words, this change in the board that was made was directed against Communists. In other words, you did not feel that the American Civil Liberties Union could do a proper job with the Communists, so you passed a rule against them, but you wouldn't want us to do that on a national level? (*Laughter.*)

* * *

MR. HAYS: No, because the United States is prohibited from doing that by a Constitution adopted one hundred fifty years ago.

MR. NIXON: You mean the American Civil Liberties Union guarantees liberties to a lesser degree than the Constitution of the United States?

MR. HAYS: We guarantee the civil liberties of Communists.

MR. NIXON: But not to your own members.

MR. HAYS: We have members who belong to the Communist Party. We did not want directors who were Communists because we adopted the principle we wanted people running the union who believe in free speech as an end in itself, not as a means to an end. These people believe in ideology as in Russia and we thought people who were on the board should have the same ideas we had.

MR. NIXON: That is the way *we* feel.

MR. HAYS: But you have no right to do it. In 1940 we passed a resolution to the effect that only those could serve as directors who believe in free speech as an end in itself and who did not believe in totalitarian doctrines, and every member had to state that he was not a Communist or Fascist and did not believe in those things.

MR. NIXON: I think that makes the position of the Civil Liberties Union quite clear to the Committee. The matter has already arisen after hearing the very interesting discussion between Mr. McDowell, Mr. Hébert, and you. Do I understand you to say that in your opinion, looking at the record of the Communist Party in the United States since its inception, that it has been an influence for good in our country?

MR. HAYS: I would not say that.

MR. NIXON: But you are pointing out that it was the Communist Party that defended labor, it was the Communist Party that defended the Negroes, the minority groups, when other parties would not do it. You said that was a good thing. Do you think it is an over-all good influence in the United States?

MR. HAYS: I am not sure. I would not judge these Communists—I would not say the Communists are the only ones who supported these minorities. For instance, there are thousands of us.

MR. NIXON: Do you consider the Communist Party was or was not an influence for good? If you don't know the answer, you won't say yes or no, of course.

MR. HAYS: I hate to make a judgment, but I would say in general, any leftist party, any man who promotes an ideal, helps, because I think progress is made from ideals.

MR. NIXON: And the term "leftist" would include the Communist Party?

MR. HAYS: Yes.

MR. NIXON: And so, by implication, you would like to leave with the membership of the Committee the thought that the Communist Party in your opinion has been an influence for good in the United States?

MR. HAYS: I would like to leave the impression that the Communist Party has done some good, and we would lose a good deal if we could not have a Communist Party.

MR. NIXON: In other words, you cannot answer the question directly?

MR. HAYS: I cannot answer that they have done more harm than good. I don't know.

MR. NIXON: You feel they have done harm? In what instances?

MR. HAYS: I think they did us a great deal of harm for all our people when they made that tremendous flop when the Germans went into Russia, and I think altogether they are an untrustworthy crowd.

MR. NIXON: Do you think, Mr. Hays, when the Communists did attach themselves to a worthwhile cause, such as, for example, the Scottsboro case, that they were doing the cause of the Negro a service?

MR. HAYS: I think they are doing the cause of nine Negroes a service.

MR. NIXON: Are they helping the group that they pretend to help in that case, or would that group be helped more, if, say, the Civil Liberties Union did it by itself?

MR. HAYS: I am sure we could do more for them.

MR. NIXON: In other words, taking the specific example of the Scottsboro case, had the Communists not entered that case, it would have been better for the boys involved and for the Negroes generally.

MR. HAYS: I would not say that.

MR. NIXON: You again would prefer not to answer the question directly?

MR. HAYS: Darrow and I are respectable lawyers who do not do these shocking things. We do not raise a lot of money and spend it to arouse public opinion and try to influence the courts indirectly. The Communists do. I have grave doubt that anybody could have tried that case any more effectively than Lebowitz,* and I have grave doubt that those boys would have been saved by respectable lawyers like ourselves, although they were saved by that mass movement. I just know what the result is. What it would have been otherwise, I do not know.

MR. NIXON: In other words, on both of these series of questions you are in doubt as to whether or not the Communists have been a harmful or a good influence.

* A stenographic error for Leibowitz—who did not "try" the case but was defense counsel. —E.B.

MR. HAYS: Oh, yes, except I do not know if I am in doubt on the Negro movement. I think when the Communists go to the South and try to introduce Negro equality with whites, and try to do these things in order to stir up incitement, that probably they are doing the Negroes more harm than good. I was chairman or one of the members of LaGuardia's committee investigating the Harlem riots a few years ago, when they used a lot of incidents to stir up incitement. I think they did an infinite amount of harm to the Negroes. So it works differently under different circumstances. I would not say that they are helping the Negroes at all. I should say the most effective influence on the Negroes is the National Association for the Advancement of Colored People, men like Walter White and Wendell Johnson.

MR. NIXON: Neither of whom is a Communist.

MR. HAYS: No.

MR. NIXON: I was making that as an observation, not a question.

MR. HAYS: There is an old saying that anyone who is not a radical before he is twenty-five has no heart; but if he is a radical after twenty-five he has no brains. The assumption is that men are the same all the time. I think we change our minds as life goes on.

MR. NIXON: I might say, Mr. Hays, that that quotation has been already inserted in the record by a member of the Committee at a previous hearing. It certainly is quite apropos. But like all rather general statements, and particularly like the statement on page 9 of your statement, I would like to pin it down to know exactly what you mean. On page 9 you refer—and again I am just clarifying the record to see that you do not say something you do not intend to say—to this:

> The situation with the Communists today is quite parallel to that of the Socialists in the 1920s. . . . It was claimed that the Socialists were not a real political party but engaged in a conspiracy to overthrow the Government by force, acting as agents of foreign countries.

Do I understand you correctly to mean that the Communists today are like the Socialists of the twenties, and that there is no basic difference?

MR. HAYS: No, I did not mean that. I mean in public opinion the same charges are made against Communists today that were made against Socialists in 1920.

MR. NIXON: But there is a great difference between the Socialists and the Communists, is there not?

MR. HAYS: Oh, not the slightest doubt of it.

MR. NIXON: The Socialists, as far as persons like Mr. [Norman] Thomas are concerned, are not working for a totalitarian government and certainly owe their allegiance only to our own Government.

MR. HAYS: Oh, yes.

MR. NIXON: Whereas you could not say that about a Communist like Mr. [William Z.] Foster.

MR. HAYS: Certainly not.

MR. NIXON: You would not like to leave the implication in the record, then, that when you referred to Communists and Socialists, as you have in answer to several questions, they are just two peas in a pod.

MR. HAYS: Altogether different. I know Foster. I know Bob Minor. I knew Earl Browder. I knew all these men. To me they are confused, futile men with wild ideas, who have been able to get nowhere in all these years. Why we treat them as important people developing a big political movement is beyond my comprehension. If we just ignore them and laugh at them, as I often do, and kid them along, and treat them as they deserve to be treated, we would get rid of Communists a lot sooner in this country.

MR. NIXON: You say public opinion was the same then toward the Socialists as it is toward the Communists today?

MR. HAYS: Yes, sir.

MR. NIXON: But you admit that the Communists are very different from the Socialists.

MR. HAYS: Certainly.

MR. NIXON: In other words, the fact that public opinion was the same toward the Socialists in the twenties as it is toward the Communists today does not necessarily prove the point that you are trying to make, that public opinion should be different today toward Communists than toward Socialists. In other words, they are different people, and should be treated differently.

MR. HAYS: Certainly, but my point was that we are guided by our emotions at the time. The American people are, and so is the Congress. We were ashamed of what we did to the Socialists ten years afterward. I think if you pass these laws today, some time a more radical party may come up and then we would be ashamed of what we had done in the Congress.

MR. NIXON: Do you feel that the Socialists of the twenties were as dangerous, to use the word which the Committee has used and some of the witnesses have used before the Committee, to our form of government as the Communists are today?

MR. HAYS: I do, because I do not think either of them are at all dangerous.

* * *

MR. NIXON: You have used the term on page 9: "There is hardly a crackbrained movement in the United States that cannot get a million followers within a comparatively short space of time." You refer in connection with that statement to the Communists, and to the Socialists, and then to the Jacobin Republicans, the Catholics, the Anarchists, Knights of Labor, the A.F. of L., the IWW, and the CIO. I assume you did not mean to refer to all of those movements as being crackbrained.

MR. HAYS: Not at all. I think most of these movements are very sound, particularly the labor movements.

MR. NIXON: Do you consider the Communist movement to be crackbrained?

MR. HAYS: Yes.

MR. NIXON: Do you consider the Socialist movement to be crackbrained?

MR. HAYS: Yes.

MR. NIXON: The Jacobin Republicans?

MR. HAYS: No.

MR. NIXON: The Catholics?

MR. HAYS: No.

MR. NIXON: The Anarchists?

MR. HAYS: Of course, the Catholics were charged with things they were not responsible for. The Anarchists, crackbrained, yes.

MR. NIXON: The Knights of Labor?

MR. HAYS: Somewhat. It is a little doubtful.

MR. NIXON: The CIO?

MR. HAYS: No.

MR. NIXON: I think that clears the record up.

MR. HAYS: I had in mind movements like Huey Long, the Townsend plan, the "ham-and-egg" plan, Upton Sinclair's movement, the Coughlin movement, and Lemke movement.

MR. NIXON: Mr. Hays, do I understand that you feel that the Communist movement in the United States is no more dangerous than the "ham-and-eggs" movement in California to the security of the country?

MR. HAYS: I hate to compare them. I do not think the "ham-and-eggs" movement was dangerous to the Government security at all.

MR. NIXON: You do not consider the Communist movement to be dangerous at all, either.

MR. HAYS: Not in the United Sattes.

MR. NIXON: Then as far as you are concerned, Communism and "ham-and-eggs" are at the same level as far as danger is concerned.

MR. HAYS: I would say not dangerous at all.

MR. MCDOWELL: How about Henry Wallace?

MR. HAYS: I never got over the impression that I got when I was told that Henry Wallace was a soothsayer. I do not think he has feet on the ground. I asked my friends who belong to the PCA to point out some instance in which their policy differs from the Communist Party line. I was asked that question and I did not know. The answer I got was that, "The fact that we believe certain things that the Communists believe does not make us Communists." I said, "No, but I would like to know some points on which you differ." I have not had the answer yet. But I have very high respect for Wallace. I think he is a great idealist. I think his criticism of the Marshall plan, to the effect that it should have been done by the United Nations, is sound, but I think the whole idea is foolish today, because we have gotten beyond that. It will not be done by the United Nations; it has to be done by the United States alone.

MR. NIXON: You still think he is pretty hot?

MR. HAYS: I think he is pretty hot. I would not vote for him.

* * *

MR. NIXON: I think the final point which should be made, and I think your discussion has brought it out quite clearly, is that what we are talking about here today is not a question of procedures—that is, how we can constitutionally control a group. There has been no argument about that point because we have never gotten by the original premise which is necessary before any legislation can be passed. It is on that original premise that we disagree. You feel, as you have indicated, that the Communists in the United States are not a danger to our form of government.

MR. HAYS: Yes.

MR. NIXON: And that no steps should be taken.

MR. HAYS: No. If any steps are needed, they should be taken, if they are steps against *acts* of Communists that are dangerous to this Government, but not against their preaching doctrines.

MR. NIXON: But you recommend no specific steps, see no need to recommend specific steps, because they are no danger.

MR. HAYS: I see no need to recommend any laws whatever.

MR. NIXON: You see no more reason to recommend steps against the Communists than against the "ham-and-eggers" in California?

MR. HAYS: So far as their ideas are concerned, none whatever.

MR. NIXON: Now ask your question, if you like.

MR. HAYS: I was going to ask: If you did not have the Communists as a political party, how would you ever know in the State of New York that they did not have fifty thousand voters? One of the ways we check up on the influence of movements is by how many voters they can get.

MR. NIXON: I think, Mr. Hays, that you apparently did not get the impression that both Mr. Hébert and Mr. McDowell tried to make, and that is that the majority sentiment on this Committee is against definitely outlawing the Communist Party as a party. At the present time the majority sentiment of the Committee is toward exposure more than suppression. On that you disagreed with us. I might say, too, that the Committee appreciates, and I say this in all sincerity, the very stimulating discussion that you have given us of these issues; that although we are in disagreement, I think you can see from the attitude of the Committee today that we are attempting to find the proper laws in the American tradition to control what may to us appear to be somewhat more of a danger than appears to you. I assure you, in recommending those laws, that we shall bear in mind what I would call the very healthy criticism against any legislation which you have made today.

MR. HAYS: Mr. Chairman, that confirms my faith in the American system of government, and I hope it will not be changed.

MR. NIXON: Thank you.

MR. HAYS: Let me make this comment: When Mr. Dies was running the Un-American Committee—

MR. MCDOWELL: Un-American Activities Committee.

MR. HAYS: I called it the Un-American Committee. One time when I met Mr. Dies he said, "Why do you attack me all the time?" I said, "Because you are a dangerous man. I think you are doing a great deal to stir up a Red scare in the United States." I said, "The attitude that your Committee takes is very clear. Like all human beings, your work is more interesting if it is important. There can't be anything more important than saving the country, and how can you save the country without first finding something to save it from?" So we find the Fish Committee, the Dixon Committee, the Dies Committee, the Thomas Committee, the Lusk Committee in New York, which was finally thrown out by Al Smith: all of these committees must find and always do find something to save the country from. Where there is a will to believe, it is very hard to answer people of that type. I know they are sincere men, and that is what troubles me. Throughout our history we have had these dangers. We have always found that letting people alone and not repressing them works the thing out according to American traditions. And I hope we continue along that line.

MR. MCDOWELL: Of course, the Ferguson Committee had a similar object when they discovered General Meyers, and the Walsh Committee had a similar object when they discovered Teapot Dome.

MR. HAYS: No, I do not think so. Those committees went after specific things.

MR. MCDOWELL: So are we.

MR. HAYS: You are going after ideas. I say Congress has no right to go after the ideas of the American people, or to do anything that makes people timid in expressing their ideas. Those people were after things. One more word, please. Morris Ernst is coming here tomorrow. He is a colleague of mine in the Civil Liberties Union. His position is that there ought to be some law by which all people engaged in political propaganda should disclose their activities. I am against that, because that is a curb on free speech. I want you men to consider how far the abolitionist movement would have gotten in this country if at the beginning everybody who favored abolition had to come out in the open. You have good as well as bad movements in a free country so far as expression is concerned. I do not think we can distinguish between bad propaganda and good propaganda. All propaganda is allowable under the Constitution.

MR. NIXON: Will you call the next witness, Mr. Stripling?

James Burnham's claim to a place in the present book can best be suggested by a despatch to the *New York Times* of April 26, 1970, under the byline of Tad Szulc, which reads, in part, as follows:

> The United States Information Agency has instructed its overseas libraries to order conservative-oriented books from a special list that included works by Governor Ronald Reagan of California, Senator Barry M. Goldwater of Arizona, and the late Whittaker Chambers to assure balance between "the liberal and conservative viewpoints."
>
> The list has a blue cover. . . .
>
> According to agency officials, the blue list was prepared on the basis of recommendations in a report submitted late last year by James Burnham, an editor of the conservative magazine, *National Review*. Mr. Burnham wrote the report on the suggestion of William F. Buckley, Jr., the *National Review*'s editor and since last July a member of the United States Advisory Commission on Information, which is the agency's public overseer. . . .
>
> Mr. Burnham observed in his report that conservative writers tended to support United States foreign policy while those whose books were in the libraries included "the most vicious opponents" of official policy.

FEBRUARY 19, 1948:

James Burnham

The Subcommittee met at 10 a.m., in room 225, Old House Office Building, the Honorable Richard M. Nixon (Chairman of the Subcommittee) presiding.

Subcommittee members present: Representatives Nixon, Vail, Peterson, and McDowell.

Also present: Representative Gordon L. McDonough.

Staff members present: Robert E. Stripling, Chief Investigator, and Robert B. Gaston, Investigator, of the Committee on Un-American Activities.

MR. NIXON: The Committee will come to order.

The record will show that the following members are present: Mr. Vail, Mr. McDowell, Mr. Peterson, and Mr. Nixon.

MR. STRIPLING: When and where were you born, Mr. Burnham?

Mr. Burnham: In Chicago in 1905.

Mr. Stripling: What is your profession?

Mr. Burnham: I am a teacher. I have been on the faculty of New York University since 1929.

Mr. Stripling: Would you give the Committee a brief resume of your professional background?

Mr. Burnham: Let me see, I have been on the faculty of New York University since 1929. Most of the time in the department of philosophy, with a few years in other departments. I have also, during the past twenty years been an active student of modern political movements, in particular totalitarian movements, and I have written a great variety of articles and essays and books on the general subject of these modern movements. The chief books have been *The Managerial Revolution* which was published in 1940, *The Machiavellians* published in 1942, and last year a book called *The Struggle for the World*.

Mr. Stripling: Mr. Burnham, you are here at the request of the Committee and at the invitation of the Committee?

Mr. Burnham: Yes, sir.

Mr. Stripling: You are here at the invitation of the Committee to give your opinion on certain legislative provisions now before the Committee which seek to outlaw the Communist Party. Do you have a prepared statement?

Mr. Burnham: Yes, I have.

Mr. Stripling: In line with the procedure of the Committee, if you will read that statement* at this time, the Committee will direct questions to you afterward.

Mr. Burnham: Revolutionary totalitarianism, of both the Communist and the Fascist varieties, is a development of the twentieth century. In the late eighteenth century, when the basic ideas and institutions of modern democratic government took form, totalitarianism did not exist, and had not even been thought of. It is not surprising, therefore, that we find unprecedented difficulties today when we try to solve the problem of totalitarianism.

Two facts are of decisive significance:

First, totalitarianism has never won a free democratic majority within any nation; it has always taken power by force and subversion, counter to the majority will.

Second, totalitarianism has nevertheless, since its first major eruption in 1917, conquered a steadily expanding percentage of the nations and peoples of the earth. The defeat of the major Fascist totalitarianisms in the Second World War has already been more than counterbalanced by the further spread of Communist totalitarianism.

* Reprinted here without cuts. —E.B.

These two facts seem to prove that the methods so far used for the defense of democracy are not adequate. If the process of the past thirty years continues unchecked, we must anticipate the world defeat of democracy.

Within the United States there is at the present time no strong and organized Fascist movement. Whatever may be the case in the future, the specific totalitarian threat today is from Communism.

Communism is in no sense an ordinary political party comparable to the political parties that have functioned in the United States or in other nations with parliamentary institutions. Communism is a world-wide, conspiratorial movement, politically based upon terror and mass deception, which has for its objective the conquest of a monopoly of world power. In spite of frequent shifts in tactics and propaganda, the fundamental Communist program has never varied. The Communists do not aim at any "reforms" of existing institutions, or at any changes that can be achieved by peaceful or constitutional means. Their object, as stated in their own words and proved by their own actions, is to smash and destroy the institutions of non-Communist society, and to substitute new revolutionary social arrangements that will guarantee their own monopoly of power.

Communism is a world movement, which operates within all nations, and already holds full power over a vast area comprising the former Russian Empire together with the territories and peoples conquered since 1939. So long as Communism remains a major world force, it is impossible for any given nation to solve fully its own internal Communist problem by purely internal measures. The full solution requires an adequate world policy. However, a partial solution for the internal problem can be provided by correct internal measures; and these in turn can contribute to a world solution.

The proper and necessary internal measures for the defense of democracy against Communism should be planned with three principal purposes in mind:

1. Education. The people should be informed, accurately and fully and continuously, about the nature and activities and strategy and tactics of Communism. This educational task can be in part accomplished by qualified and concerned private citizens. Its scope and importance are such, however, that supplementary activities by the Government are also needed.

2. Exposure. Communism is peculiarly characterized by the systematic use of deception. Communists perform in a perpetual masquerade. As individuals and in groups they appear before the public today as "progressives," tomorrow as "patriots," last week as "liberals," next month as "simple humanitarians," tonight as "defenders of free speech," yesterday as "honest trade-unionists," at breakfast as "Twentieth-Century Americans," and at dinner as "the voice of the people." It is impossible for an ordinary citizen to keep track of all the disguises. The defense against Communism requires, therefore, a continuous campaign of exposure. The masks should

be stripped from Communist individuals and from Communist-front organizations. They must be labeled for what they are, so that every citizen may know, and may be guided by his knowledge. This continuous exposure also needs the aid of Government resources and agencies. I understand the bill introduced by Representative Mundt (H.R. 4422) to be designed to implement this work of exposure.

If the exposure of the Communists is to function in fact as a defense of democracy, it must be carried out with the most scrupulous care and accuracy. The reactionary tendency to lump genuine Communists together with Socialists, liberals, honest progressives, and others who may in one or another legitimate way be critical of certain abuses in our society or who may advocate some project reform is one of the greatest services that can be rendered to Communism. The precise purpose of exposure must be to separate and isolate the Communists from all the rest.

3. Illegalization. The experience of the past thirty years proves that in the end education and exposure will not be a sufficient defense against Communism. The Communist movement will have to be outlawed. The only real question is one of timing. Whether the action will be taken while its object can be accomplished by ordinary methods of legal enforcement, or whether it will wait until a future when the issue will have to be decided by a civil war. If we permit a murderer the free run of our house, we can expect that in the end someone is going to get killed. If we are willing to accept in a football league a team that makes up its own rules and stabs opponents instead of tackling them, then we shouldn't be surprised if that team wins.

No serious student of modern politics questions the facts. The objective of the Communist movement in the United States, as in every other non-Communist nation, is to destroy the existing government by illegal means, by violence and terror. The Communist movement is the agent of a sovereignty other than that of the United States Government. Even under existing laws, its illegalization is called for. Nevertheless, the contemporary Communist movement is unique. It seems to me to be the duty of Congress to establish the facts, and by specific statute to define unambiguously the intention and policy of the Government.

The objections that have been brought against the policy of illegalizing the Communist movement do not stand against the weight of the facts.

It is argued, for example, that illegalization would merely "drive the Communist underground." The fact is that the most serious part of the Communist movement is already underground. Illegalization would deprive the underground apparatus of the cover and protection and funds that they now enjoy from the legal organizations.

It is argued that illegalization would violate the constitutional guarantees of free speech and assembly. But these guarantees have never been and could never be interpreted in an absolute sense. Democracy does not give its citizens the right, for example, to advocate and organize for mass murder, rape, and arson. In general, the principles of democratic government cannot be interpreted in practice in such a way as to make democratic government itself impossible. The rights and freedoms of democracy are properly extended only to those who accept the fundamental rules of democracy. If this is not the interpretation, the democratic government is necessarily self-defeating. It cannot defend itself. It welcomes and fosters, in effect, its own murderer.

The specific goal of Communism (as of Fascism also) is to destroy democratic government, and to replace democratic government by totalitarianism. The rules of democracy cannot be intelligibly interpreted as providing for the free operation of a force specifically designed for their own destruction. On the contrary, if democratic government is historically workable, its rules must not only permit but enjoin it to combat and eliminate any such force.

The most important objection to illegalization, however, is of another kind. It is said that the suppression of the Communist movement would start a political chain reaction. Next would come the suppression of Socialists; then of liberals and progressives; and finally of all opposition. Totalitarianism would have entered by a rear door.

There is no doubt that this objection points to a real danger. The danger is, indeed, so real, that in spite of theoretical considerations it would argue against any statute of suppression unless the counterbalancing danger to democracy were still greater. It would never be correct, from a democratic point of view, to suppress a relatively small and weak group, no matter how far outside the boundaries of democracy that group's program and activities might be. But when the antidemocratic group becomes, like the present Communist movement, a clear, present, and powerful threat, democracy must defend itself, in spite of the risk.

The danger to democracy from any act of suppression will remain. It can be guarded against, in part, by the careful definition of the terms used in any statute that may be proposed or enacted. In particular, it is necessary to designate with the utmost clarity just whom the statute is directed against. It will do little good merely to refer to "the Communist Party," since the day after enactment the Communist Party could change its name, as it has often been changed in the past. It would be even worse to use such vague and loose language as is found in Representative McDonough's bill (H.R. 4581), the exact application of which could not be objectively determined.

An adequate statute will, I think, have to define the official Communist movement historically, in order to show that what is at issue is the United States section of the world-wide political movement that was initiated through the Communist International, that has had a continuous historical, programmatic, and organizational development since then, and that happens for the moment to be called "the Communist Party of the United

States." The definition must at the same time be so drawn as to exclude any group other than the official Communists. It is the Communists, and they alone, that constitute a clear, present, and powerful threat.

A well-drawn statute, and even its scrupulous execution, would not, however, end the problem or the risk. The final result would depend, as it always must depend in a democratic nation, upon the value that all of us, as citizens, place upon our rights and freedom.

MR. NIXON: Mr. McDowell, do you have any questions you would like to ask?

MR. MCDOWELL: I doubt if I have any questions after that great statement. You phrase it in a fashion I have never heard before. It is very interesting. I think, however, that you said something I have heard so many times, both here in this chamber and very many places where Communism is discussed. When the point is made of outlawing Communism, some person always brings in the argument you just referred to a minute ago: next would be the Socialists, then the liberals, then the progressives, and there would be no stopping. The Communists have succeeded apparently all over the world in associating themselves with liberals and progressives and things that are advanced, and so forth. It seems to me that the smart people of America should begin to connect Communism with what it really is. There is nothing progressive about it. Absolutely nothing. It is the most reactionary thing there is. In other words, Communists are the most reactionary group in the world.

MR. BURNHAM: I think it is unfortunate that Communism is referred to as the "left wing." It is actually the most "right wing."

MR. MCDOWELL: It is, unfortunately, the most right-wing method of operation. I certainly appreciate your statement.

MR. PETERSON: I think you made a fine statement, and I was following the things you said. Have you worked out a definition? Would you attempt to rough one out yourself?

MR. BURNHAM: I am not legally trained, so I don't think I can be the one to put it in proper form in terms of legally acceptable language. I approached it from the point of view of political science.

MR. PETERSON: Could you put it in your own language and let us polish it up in proper form? We wouldn't expect you to do it today. I was very much impressed. If we outlaw the Communist Party and the next day it pops out with another name— We have got to outlaw the conspiracy, the plans they are making, and, as you say, "the long historical basis of what they have been doing." We take those historical facts and put that in the definition of the thing we want to outlaw.

MR. BURNHAM: There has been a good deal of work done in content analysis. I believe that an effort has been made on the part, I understand, of some of the people who have worked in the Department of Justice—how to show, by following from day to day the activities, propaganda, behavior of a given group, it can obviously be established just what that group is, and what its policy is, in a way that the older rules of evidence did not provide for.

MR. McDONOUGH: You referred to my bill as being vague; and in my bill I attempted to put, in very brief language, what I thought Communism stood for. Do you disagree with any of the things I referred to in my bill? Do you have a copy of it?

MR. BURNHAM: I think I do.

MR. McDONOUGH: I would like to know what sections you disagree with or what you consider vague about it.

MR. BURNHAM: One point that puzzled me in your bill was the conception of treason from a legal point of view. As I understand it, or as it has been explained to me, that has a restricted meaning under our Constitution and legal history. I am not convinced that under that legal meaning, strictly speaking, one can call the activities of the Communist Party treasonable, since I think treason has to apply against those with whom we are making war—our enemies. Now, it is true that Communism is making continuous war against us, and they are not making a distinction against war. It is a war fought by various techniques. We are legally not at war with them. No statute has been passed. It also seems to me to speak of such concepts as confusion and atheism and antireligious ideology—while it is true in a lot of instances, it is true of other movements than the Communist movement. In other words, if we made it criminal to create confusion, I would not be sure how many of us would be left in any organization. (*Laughter.*)

MR. McDONOUGH: My idea is that the confusion in the ideology of Communism is created to overthrow the Government—it is not the confusion that might exist in this room between two people—such as the confusion on the part of the political party in France, to confuse the whole nation by sudden strikes, that is certainly treasonable: it is against the government, and it is not to the best interest of the people over there. So it is not the interpretation you give the word "confusion," in that confusion of any kind could be prosecuted. That is not the point.

MR. BURNHAM: Incidentally, I just returned from France, and while there I had discussions with the leaders of France on the same problem we are facing today and the difficulty they are facing with the French Communist Party. It seems to me from a positive point of view that any definition of "Communism" must refer to the historical relation of the Communist International. Of course, in words, they deny this today, and we must refer not so much to the theoretical ideology but to their political doctrine as it is connected with our political practice.

MR. McDONOUGH: Do you believe that the Communist Party, having as its directing energies and force from foreign countries, could exist as a legal party in the United States—or should exist in the United States?

MR. BURNHAM: Should exist? No, I think it should not.

Mr. McDonough: You take it the American Communist Party is that kind of a party?

Mr. Burnham: There is no question about it. The Communist Party here and in all countries, whatever name it calls itself, is part of the international movement and is at present directed from the Soviet Union.

Mr. McDonough: Therefore, the Communist Party should not exist in the United States if it is directed by the Soviet Union.

Mr. Burnham: As long as this movement exists its operatives will be active here. Of course, the Communist Party is only one part of the Communist set of activities in this country. I assume you gentlemen have all read the report of the Canadian Royal Commission, which seems a marvelous analysis of the several networks which were simultaneously operating—the Military Intelligence, the Intelligence of the Russian party itself, and the NKVD, or, as it is now called, the MVD.

Mr. Kersten*: I want to congratulate you on your very fine statement. A frequent objection to any law pertaining to Communism is that we already have laws, criminal laws, espionage laws, which, if put into practice, will take care of whatever the Communists do. What would you say as to that? Would you say that perhaps our present criminal laws could take care of the situation, or do you think we need specific further laws?

Mr. Burnham: Well, as I explained, I do not have legal training myself, so I have to speak as an amateur about the law itself.

Mr. Kersten: Yes.

Mr. Burnham: I would believe that under the present laws the prosecution and illegalization of the Communist Party could be justified. However, the Communist Party is a very special organization. Nothing like it has ever existed in history, and certainly the existing laws did not have such an organization in mind. It raises problems not only in the eyes of the courts from the legal points of view, but also in the minds of the citizens in the country, including some very excellent citizens who are deceived by the Communist Party, who, not realizing what it is and not seeing that it fits under the older laws, will join its various fronts, and even work openly with Communists for what they consider to be a specific good goal. That is why it has seemed to me that whatever action—apart from such matters as treatment of aliens and specific individuals who are engaged in court and criminal activities—whatever general action about the Communist movement is taken should be motivated in a way that would be intelligible to the courts and to the public, so that they will see that it is a particular and special problem.

Mr. Kersten: You have pointed out that the particular vice of Communism is its international aspect in its present-day ambitions, and so forth. Do you think, Mr. Burnham, that there is presently available evidence to

* At this point Congressman Charles J. Kersten of Wisconsin, though not a member of HUAC, took part in the proceedings. —E.B.

prove on this international hookup, available here in the United States, apart from the examples that we read of in Europe, so that if a person was suspected of Communism he could be proved linked with the international setup?

MR. BURNHAM: Do you mean in terms of one particular person or the organization's activities?

MR. KERSTEN: The terms of definitions.

MR. BURNHAM: Yes.

MR. KERSTEN: Or statements, authoritative statements, of the Communist Party here in the United States.

MR. BURNHAM: If you mean in terms of one individual Communist who happens to be investigated, I would say no, because he may himself be perfectly innocent. There are many members of the Communist Party who do not understand what the Communist Party is, who are simply used by the inner circles of the Party. But, for the organization as a whole, for its direction, for the decision on its policies, for its press and its general activities, I think one can establish objectively that it is part of the international movement and establish that it is such on the basis of evidence in this country. There are several varieties of evidence. There is the evidence from those who have prominently participated in the Communist movement. In this country there are now a dozen or so who have been quite prominent and who you could give direct evidence of; there is evidence from the international figures, at least a number of whom are in this country, who can give evidence about the relations between the international organizations and the United States organization. Content analysis can establish by what is the equivalent of circumstantial evidence that over a period of twenty-five years there is a complete pattern of political action that coincides exactly with the demands of the Communist Party of the Soviet Union and the Soviet interests. Now, although this might be a coincidence over a period of a month or two, it becomes unquestionable when it goes longer than that period. A careful investigation would unquestionably show, and doubtlessly has shown to our own investigators, the direct channels whereby often policies are transmitted from the international center to the United States in terms of Soviet operatives, in terms of the use of the employees of the Soviet Embassy, and the other Soviet organizations in this country, who give the directives through the operations of men like Gerhart Eisler, through the men who are taken on and off Soviet ships, and so on, to give the directives. The French link resulted in the dismissal of Browder. After the publication of the condemnation of Browder in France.

MR. KERSTEN: Would you think that a person capable of being proved to be a Communist could be prevented from taking an elective office, say, in the United States here which required the oath to support the Constitution of the United States?

MR. BURNHAM: Well, he certainly is necessarily committing perjury when he takes such an oath.

MR. MCDOWELL: Mr. Chairman, I am a little loath to let Mr. Burnham go. His various writings indicate that he has devoted a great deal of time and work to the business of subversive activities. I wish you were a member of this Committee. And if you were a member of this Committee, I am wondering what you would consider the most dangerous. We found Communists in labor, of course; we have discovered Communists connected with radio and the publishing business; and, of course, many times we have found they were connected with the seafaring affairs of ships that go to sea. We have found Communists in plants and at various places, Communists on the farms sometimes. Where would you think the dangers to be most acute if we were to have trouble in this country?

MR. BURNHAM: Well, the immediate tactics of the Communist Party are devoted to the preparation for what they consider to be the inevitable third world war—that is, in terms of the immediate. They do not believe they can take power in this country. Ultimately, they hope to take power in the world, but they do not expect this in the coming decade, let us say. They do, however, expect or consider very probable a war, so that their objective is to entrench themselves in key places in the country, throughout the country, to be ready to act for the war. Everything else is really secondary for them: to take as many people into their apparatus, to have them situated in every sensitive spot of the country, of the Government, and so on. I am not sure that in that light one can say that any one place is any more dangerous than another. But their concentration indicates pretty clearly what they have in mind. For instance, in the maritime industry they have devoted a tremendous amount of energy and money, to try to get in there to hold up, in the case of war, transport. In land transport they have not done so well in this country, though they have made a great effort, and in the New York local transit situation they have got a good deal. Then, in international communications, it is very interesting that their primary concentration is the union that handled the international cables and radios. They have not been able to do very much in the internal telegraph lines, but in the international local they have a good many people. Then, in the public-opinion industry, they believe that many people who are in no way Communists will pick up their ideas and confuse the country, which will make it possible to divide opinion. Of course, in politics, their supreme concentration is on the Wallace movement. They, of course, constitute the one serious organized force that is furthering the Wallace candidacy, and I must say they did quite a job in the Bronx two days ago.*

* On February 17, 1948, in the 24th Congressional District the ALP candidate, endorsed by Wallace, won the special election by almost two-to-one in a four-way race. —E.B.

MR. MCDOWELL: It must be obvious to most Americans, whether they are Communists or Republicans or Democrats, that Mr. Wallace cannot be elected President. Mr. Wallace himself has committed the cardinal sin against Communism many times by saying that he does not like Communism, even though he accepts these people and works along with fellow travelers and will accept their votes and even urges the election of men who are deep in Communism. Would you think that the Communist Party's chief objective is to establish a third party, any third party that they may have a finger in so that some day it may be necessary to the election of one or the other parties, that they may some day become part of a coalition government such as has occurred in practically all of the countries which have disappeared behind the Iron Curtain? In not one of those countries was there a majority of Communists.

MR. BURNHAM: No.

MR. MCDOWELL: Would you not think that that was the chief reason for this third-party movement now? They are not particularly anxious about Mr. Wallace. I do not think they care any more about him than they care about me.

MR. BURNHAM: They are more contemptuous of Mr. Wallace than of you, sir. Of course, he is not a Communist, but he is an unconscious front for them—unconscious in the sense that he does not know what he is doing, and they do. I think that their primary purpose, this year, in connection with this movement, though I agree with you about their long-term purpose, is in connection with the Soviet plans in world politics, especially in European politics, for 1948. There is every reason to believe that the Communists look upon the present year as comparable to the year 1936—I think it was 1936, perhaps 1935—when Hitler went into the Ruhr. There he consolidated the position which enabled him to make his further expansions, and he chose the moment of the French election, when the French government had been dissolved. He counted on paralysis in France because of the elections, that would prevent them from taking the comparatively small action that would have kept the Reichwehr, which had no real arms, out of the Ruhr. This year, as indicated in the speech of Zhdanov to the Communists last autumn, the Communists want to consolidate their European position in a way that will prevent them from ever being thrown back, and they are stretching out as fast as they can before the year is over, and they will make new moves, I am sure, in France and Italy. They count upon the difficulties of an election situation in this country. They count on the fact that that will tend to make the Government unable to act decisively, and putting Wallace in makes the situation a hundred times more confused, because he tends to get a balance-of-power position. He tends to weaken the hand of the existing Administration; he tends to make the existing Administration attempt to try to appease him, which, from an international point of view, is in a sense appeasing Soviet policies. I was in France when

Wallace's nomination was announced, and it was astounding the effect it made on French opinion, because the first day a large editorial by the chief editorial writer appeared in the official Communist paper welcoming this as the greatest step forward that Americans have made in the past fifteen years.

MR. MCDOWELL: Thank you, Dr. Burnham. I just wanted to make one correction as a loyal Republican, Mr. Chairman. Mr. Wallace has not been nominated for anything. He just announced he was going to run.

MR. MCDONOUGH: In further reference to some of the other points of my bill, let me ask you this: Do you believe the Communists practice deceit?

MR. BURNHAM: They certainly do.

MR. MCDONOUGH: Do you believe they are subversive?

MR. BURNHAM: They are.

MR. MCDONOUGH: Do you believe they are antireligious?

MR. BURNHAM: As a movement, yes. As a movement they are atheistic. Individual Communists in some cases are not, and they are prepared to sacrifice that tactic. For instance, in Italy, in order to get along well in the periods following the war they suddenly became friendly toward the church, and Togliatti, the Italian leader, was conspicuously photographed going to mass on Sunday.

MR. MCDONOUGH: Do you believe they subordinate their subjects to the will of the state?

MR. BURNHAM: There one has to distinguish the question of fact from the question of theory. In fact, they do perhaps more strictly adhere to the Communist Party leadership. In theory they say that they do this only because through it ultimately they will bring a new flower into the human individual.

MR. NIXON: Mr. Burnham, you distinguished between what you term the inner circle of the Party, and the people who might be Party members but who did not perhaps subscribe to the degree of loyalty to the Party that the inner-circle people did. I understand you to mean by that that there may be American Communists, members of the Party in this country, whose loyalty would be to the United States rather than to a Communist-dominated country.

MR. BURNHAM: In their own minds.

MR. NIXON: I see.

MR. BURNHAM: Yes, because they do not understand what they have done by joining the Party.

MR. NIXON: I see. In other words, even within the Communist Party itself there are some—and certainly this would include all of the leaders—the policy makers of the Party, who owe their loyalty, their primary loyalty to the Communist-dominated countries as such.

MR. BURNHAM: Yes, and they have said so publicly on occasion. For instance, the leader of the movement in Brazil has quite openly said that he would fight for the Soviet Union instead of Brazil in case of a war.

MR. NIXON: But, on the other hand, there are members of the Communist Party in this country, and in other countries which have not yet been dominated by Communist government, who might not necessarily owe their loyalty to other governments?

MR. BURNHAM: That is my opinion, yes, sir.

MR. NIXON: For that reason then, the problem that this Committee faces in legislation is made particularly difficult, in that, in order to draft a bill which will be effective, we would have to start on the premise that legislation was necessary because members of the American Communist Party are potentially disloyal to the country. Now, as a practical matter, in enforcing any piece of legislation, as you probably recognize, a law is enforced not against an organization as such, generally speaking, because such enforcement is not particularly effective, but it is enforced against individuals, for doing certain acts. But, as you have pointed out, the difficulty we would be facing in this case would be that, depending upon the individual that we attempted to prosecute, we might in some cases run into a Communist—in fact, on several occasions we have—who was, shall we say, a theoretical Communist in the old Marxian sense, and not an active practicing Communist in the modern Stalin sense. You might find Communists of that type who would not be covered by laws that we have passed, isn't that the case?

MR. BURNHAM: Well, of course, I suppose in general, if there is any question of prosecution, the effective prosecution, of course, always applies to the leaders of such an organization in such a case. In terms of their activities, unfortunately, even these Communists who are misled and who do not realize what they are doing are nevertheless aiding the Communists. Those Canadian hearings bring that out very interestingly: for instance, there were several of the university professors who were involved in it. In their own minds it is plain from their testimony that they were perfectly honest and humanitarian men, but still they found out that they were led into a situation where they were getting the atomic secrets for the Soviet Union, and where ultimately they turned over the blueprints and samples of uranium 235 and so forth.

MR. NIXON: In other words, it was the so-called theoretical Communists who did the really most effective work against the Canadian government and for the Soviet government.

MR. BURNHAM: Because they were manipulated by the members of the inner apparatus; but they were indispensable to it.

MR. NIXON: As far as you can see, though, insofar as the policy makers are concerned, the inner circle, the so-called hardened Communists, we would not have any difficulty, in your opinion, proving that such people in ordinary cases owed their primary loyalty to a Communist-dominated country, rather than the United States, assuming that a conflict existed between the two.

MR. BURNHAM: Well, I think you would have no difficulty in proving that the organization is of that sort that operates in that way. In the case of any particular individual, I suppose, you always have a question of direct evidence that bears on that individual.

MR. NIXON: I know you have read some of the other legislative proposals which have been made for controlling the Communists of the United States. One thesis which is generally followed in most of those proposals is that the Communist Party advocates the overthrow of this Government by force and violence. That is point number two. First is the problem of disloyalty. Here again, we have a practical difficulty, have we not? For example, is it not true that at the present time the constitution of the American Communist Party, for obvious reasons, specifically departs from the usual Communist line, which was rather typical of the Party, say, in 1930, at the time William Foster appeared before this Committee [HUAC did not exist in 1930. Foster testified in 1945. E.B.], and does not include force and violence as one of the methods that would be used in overthrowing the so-called capitalist Government of the United States?

MR. BURNHAM: Yes, that is right. The official charter—whatever it is called—and the pledge that the member signs when he joins the Party no longer contains a sentence that could be clearly interpreted as advocating overthrow by force and violence. However, on that point, there seems to me to be another approach, or other approaches. For instance, the literature and the courses that are taught in the Party training schools, as well as the testimony that ex-members of the Party can give directly, and thirdly, the necessary inferences that can be drawn are other approaches. If a Communist will testify at all, he will lie about many things, but certain things he feels a little worried about lying in connection with. He will say that the only kind of a government that can possibly work is a Soviet government, and then he will say the United States has a parliamentary government, but a parliamentary government will never give up peacefully, and so, by putting four or five statements together you get the combination of them yielding an inevitable conclusion of what they believe in. Or you can ask them, "Do you believe in such and such a statement by *Pravda,* by the Communist International, certain resolutions that have been passed, and so forth?

MR. NIXON: Then, as a matter of fact, the present charter of the Communist Party, and the membership application which the person signs, do not represent, in fact, what the Communist Party member is agreeing to, and what he stands for insofar as membership in the Party is concerned.

MR. BURNHAM: No, that is another element in the Communist deception, and it is adopted, as you say, primarily in this case for legal purposes.

Mr. Nixon: And force and violence then is a necessary part of the code which the American Communists generally subscribe to when they become active members of the Party?

Mr. Burnham: Force and violence, and specifically always the overthrow of what they call bourgeois parliamentary institutions.

Mr. Nixon: By any means whatever, legal, or illegal.

Mr. Burnham: They further add, and their theory adds, and they teach their members that this can be done only by violent means, as they put it, because a ruling class never yields power willingly.

Mr. Nixon: This morning the witness before the Committee was Dr. George Dimitrov, former head of the Bulgarian Agrarian Party, and he testified, from his experience in Bulgaria, that the only effective way of meeting the Communists in any country which had not already been dominated by them was to use the same means that they use. Would you subscribe to going that far in, say, the United States?

Mr. Burnham: No, by no means. In fact, if I had reached that conclusion I would have no longer any interest in the question. It is not just Communism as a name that I am opposed to, but I am precisely opposed to the means that they try to use to solve social questions, and unless we can preserve at least a reasonable amount of decency and democracy, it is not worth fighting against Communism. I do think, however, that we have to use, and use more dynamically, means that we have neglected or have not developed up to the present time in combating the Communists. Some of them go right down to grass roots. You take that situation in the Bronx on Tuesday. It is partly because the Communists worked so hard, so energetically, and they get out and do so much, and they are willing to sacrifice for their ideas, that they can bring about a result of that sort for the candidate that they favor.

Mr. Nixon: Is it not also true that the Communists there seized upon issues which were not true Communist issues in attempting very cleverly to build up their candidate and defeat the other candidate?

Mr. Burnham: They picked, as they usually do, the issue that will get by best with the group they are dealing with. In the Midwest later on in the year they will probably use just the opposite issues to get votes in the rural districts.

Mr. Nixon: Is it your opinion that the American people today are not sufficiently aware of the Communist danger? I note that you advocate education of the people, constant vigilance, as one of the steps which you think should be taken.

Mr. Burnham: Well, if you ask the people, "Are you against Communism?" the great majority says, "Yes." In that sense you might say they are aware, at least, of the word; they are aware enough that they do not want it. But they do not really understand what it is. The very people who will say, "I am certainly not a Communist," will turn up the next night at some

Communist-front organization or will applaud a speaker who is defending a policy which is merely a thinly disguised version of the Soviet foreign policy. In instances like that, I feel that the American people are by no means sufficiently aware of the real meaning of Communism.

MR. NIXON: Do you believe that the American Communist Party and the American Communists constitute a potential danger to the country which would justify the legislative steps which you have suggested in your statement?

MR. BURNHAM: If the Communist Party were a purely national party, if it had no international support, and, in particular, if it did not have the enormous Soviet empire which, in a sense, is back of it, I would say no. In terms of actual numbers, as merely a native movement, being able to rely upon native resources, I think it could be handled without any new or extreme or serious steps. But, in the light of the real world situation, where it is the extension of this great Communist empire, where it is linked with the Communists of all other nations, and in particular because of the extremely acute international situation that now exists, I think it is a very serious danger. I think one has to be very experimental. I would not say, for instance, that tomorrow it should be outlawed without further discussion and the exploring of further possibilities. I have talked to many people, seriously concerned with the Communist question, who think that a bill, something like Representative Mundt's bill, would be a good experimental approach.

MR. NIXON: An interim approach.

MR. BURNHAM: Yes, to see how that works; and then check up in six months or a year and consider whether further legislation is necessary. I have heard very well-argued cases made for that approach.

MR. NIXON: Although you made out a theoretical case for illegalization, as you put it, you do not advocate that that step should be taken at the present time. There is still the element of timing involved?

MR. BURNHAM: Timing, and in a way psychological and public preparation for it. I think that it would be very unfortunate if illegalization should come before everyone understood exactly why it had to be done, and what was involved in it. It should be done in such a way that separates a Communist from everyone else; it does not make those who are genuine liberals and genuine Democrats sorry for them. I tend to believe, basing my beliefs on historical evidence, that in the end the Party will have to be illegalized. When we look at one country after another, and we see that they are able to take power in spite of the fact that they are often a very small minority, in some of these Eastern European countries sixteen, seventeen per cent, and when we look at the situation such as that which exists in France now, where under the ideas of traditional Socialists and Radical Socialists and under people like Blum and Herriot, the Communists have had an almost free hand, and see where France is virtually on the verge of a civil war and of insoluble internal crisis, I am inclined to believe that democracy will have to face directly this problem.

MR. NIXON: The Committee is very appreciative of your statement, Mr. Burnham, and we know it was a considerable personal sacrifice for you to come down here. I assure you that your reasoning will be very helpful to us in considering the problems before us.

1951

"Communist Infiltration of Hollywood"

The Korean War started in 1950 and, among its many other effects, reopened the war on Hollywood Communists and those suspected of Communism. This page from the *Hollywood Reporter*, September 8, 1950, gives the information as well as re-creating the atmosphere:

CLOSING RANKS

Closing ranks in the motion picture industry in fervent support of the CRUSADE FOR FREEDOM, the Motion Picture Alliance for the Preservation of American Ideals and Walter Wanger, Los Angeles Chairman of the Crusade, have pledged utmost cooperation in the campaign headed by Generals Eisenhower, Clay and Eaker, and are jointly publishing the following letters:

September 5, 1950

DEAR MR. WANGER:

Announcement of your acceptance of the Chairmanship for Los Angeles division of CRUSADE FOR FREEDOM is to us happy evidence of the heightening realization in motion picture circles of the need for tightening our ranks to defend liberty. At this time of relentless threat to our national existence and to free men everywhere, we must forget old disagreements and heal old wounds in the interests of a cause more important than any of us and certainly more important than any memories we may have of ancient dispute.

Consequently, we of the Motion Piction Alliance for the Preservation of American Ideals pledge ourselves to do our best to further the purposes expressed by Generals Eisenhower, Clay and Eaker and to help you rouse Southern California and the film colony to the grim and present danger of our times.

Not, then, out of pique, or resentment, but merely to keep the record clear, we recall to you that the Motion Picture Alliance for nearly seven years has recognized this danger and has tried to wake our fellow workers to awareness of the threat. We take no particular credit for being first; somebody had to be.

We must, however, ask you at this time to correct the misunderstanding you had in the past as to our purpose.

On May 26, 1944, you wrote us a letter which included this passage:

> Your organization has made unsupported charges of Communism in the motion picture industry—it has linked throughout the nation the word "Hollywood" and "Red" and without proof.

We wish you had been right and we had been wrong. It is no satisfaction to us that there are now and were then a tight group of Communist conspirators in our midst, treasonably obeying the dictates of a foreign tyranny. Time and history have furnished the proof. Two American juries and four American judges have supported the charges and the U.S. Supreme Court has upheld them.

We didn't make "Hollywood" and "Red" synonymous—the Communists, their fellow travellers and their dupes did that damaging job. We foresaw this result and tried to persuade our fellow workers of the need for cleaning our own house. We intend to continue doing so, since, even yet, too few people recognize that need.

Now that the issue is clear between freedom and slavery, we feel confident that you will want to correct our former disagreement.

Again, with a pledge of all cooperation in the Crusade for Freedom, we are,

Sincerely,
Motion Picture Alliance for the
Preservation of American Ideals
By JOHN WAYNE, President.

September 6, 1950

Motion Picture Alliance for the
Preservation of American Ideals,
159 South Beverly Drive,
Beverly Hills, Calif.
GENTLEMEN:

My thanks for your pledge of help in the Crusade for Freedom. It is most welcome.

I am glad to accept your suggestion that we bury old disagreements and unite to face the common enemy.

Having known so many of the leading figures of the Motion Picture Alliance intimately and for many years, I must assert that I never questioned their integrity or the honesty of their purpose, and if any words of mine hurt your group, or any member of it, I can only express my regret.

If I, along with others in the motion picture industry, disagreed, it was not that we had any sympathy for Communism, but rather that we were reluctant to believe that any American would knowingly and secretly engage in an insidious conspiracy against his country and against the industry which had done so much for him.

Wendell Willkie once told me that the world needed more men who were willing to admit mistakes when they made them and ready to take action to correct them.

In that spirit, I recognize that time and history have proven the correctness of the judgment of the Motion Picture Alliance and its foresight in recognizing the Communist menace.

Gladly, I accept your assurance of support in the great task of our lives: that of tightening ranks here and everywhere in defense of freedom and against our proven enemies—Communism and all those who espouse or support it.

Sincerely yours,
(*signed*) WALTER WANGER.

Motion Picture Alliance for the Preservation of American Ideals

Officers

John Wayne, President; Charles Coburn, 1st Vice-President; Hedda Hopper, 2nd Vice-President; Morrie Ryskind, 3rd Vice-President; Robert Arthur, Secretary; Clarence Brown, Treasurer; John Klorer, Assistant Treasurer.

Executive Committee

Roy M. Brewer, Chairman; Ralph Clare, Vice-Chairman; Ward Bond, Charles Cane, Carl Cooper, Gary Cooper, Steve Fisher, John Ford, Clark Gable, Cedric Gibbons, Richard H. Gordon, Alex Kempner, Gunther R. Lessing, Louis Lighton, Cliff Lyons, John Lee Mahin, Ben A. Martinez, Leo McCarey, Howard A. McDonnell, James K. McGuinness, Adolphe Menjou, Alan Mowbray, Fred Niblo, Jr., Pat O'Brien, LeRoy Prinz, Kane Richmond, Robert Taylor, Joseph Tuohy, Herbert J. Yates.

By July 30, 1951, Ronald Reagan was ready to write an article for the *Citizen News* under the title, "Reds Beaten in Hollywood":

(Victor Riesel is on vacation. Ronald Reagan, president, Screen Actors Guild [AFL], is substituting for him today as special guest columnist.)

HOLLYWOOD, July 30. — Communism failed in Hollywood because the overwhelming majority of the members of the Screen Actors Guild, the Screen Extras Guild, the writers' and directors' guilds and the workers in the Hollywood studio craft unions are and always have been opposed to communism.

Day after day in this year's hearings by the House Committee on Un-American Activities, the same story has been unfolded—a story of communist frustration and failure in the party's bold plot to seize control of the talent guilds and craft unions, through which the subversive brethren hoped eventually to control contents of films and thus influence the minds of 80,000,000 movie goers.

The extent of Hollywood's victory over the Communist Party is all the more remarkable because Hollywood for many years was a prime target of the Red propagandists and conspirators in this country.

They were trying to carry out orders from Joseph Stalin, who had said: "The cinema is not only a vital agitprop (active propaganda) device for the education and political indoctrination of the workers, but is also a fluent channel through which to reach the minds and shape the desires of people everywhere. The Kinofikatsiya (turning propaganda into films) is inevitable. The task is to take this affair into your hands, and vigorously execute it in every field."

So the Red enemies of our country concentrated their big guns on Hollywood. And they failed completely. But not before they had succeeded in bringing about two years of disastrous strikes and bloody fighting in which American workmen battled other American workmen at the studio gates. And, unfortunately, not before the communists had fooled some otherwise loyal Americans into believing that the Communist Party sought to make a better world. Those dupes know today that the real aim of the Communist Party is to try to prepare the way for Russian conquest of the world.

The Screen Actors Guild members are justifiably proud of the key role they played in bringing about the final defeat of the communist conspirators in Hollywood.

Actually, there were very few actors in Hollywood who became Party members. But there were quite a number who were tricked many years ago into lending their names or giving money to organizations or causes that later proved to be influenced or dominated by communists.

Today, even the fellow traveller has disappeared from the Hollywood scene.

But it was not so in 1945 and 1946 when the communist-backed Conference of Studio Unions battled with the anti-communist International Alliance of Theatrical Stage Employes, led by Richard Walsh and Roy Brewer.

To win, the Reds had to get the actors to join in the jurisdictional strike on the side of the strikers. If the actors didn't go to work, the studios would shut and the Reds would have won a great victory.

They tried every trick in the bag but the actors, led by the Board of Directors of Screen Actors Guild, out-thought them and out-fought them. We fought them on the record and off the record.

We fought them in meetings and behind the scenes.

Our Red foes even went so far as to threaten to throw acid in the faces of myself and some other stars, so that we "never would appear on the screen again." I packed a gun for some time and policemen lived at my home to guard my kids.

But that was more than five years ago and those days are gone forever, along with the deluded Red sympathizer and fellow traveller.

Never again can the communists hope to get anywhere in the movie capital. And it looks to me as if the die-hard Reds in this country are now concentrating their plotting in other industries such as defense plants. I hope that all such industries will take a leaf out of Hollywood's book and actively combat the communist conspirators wherever they may be found.

And any American who has been a member of the Communist Party at any time but who has now changed his mind and is loyal to our country should be willing to stand up and be counted; admit, "I was wrong," and give all the information he has to the government agencies who are combatting the Red plotters.

We've gotten rid of the communist conspirators in Hollywood. Let's do it now in other industries!

Testimony below from Larry Parks (March 21), Sterling Hayden (April 10), Edward Dmytryk (April 25), José Ferrer (May 22), and Budd Schulberg (May 23) makes clear just what Reagan's victory was like. The Ferrer testimony needs supplementing from the press. Ferrer was up for an Academy Award. Ward Bond of the Motion Picture Alliance for the Preservation of American Ideals chose this moment to publish an accusation of Communist associations. Ferrer got the Award, and threatened a libel suit. The background is filled in by this news story in the weekly *Variety,* April 11, 1951:

GARFIELD, FERRER 'INVESTIGATE' SELVES AS PRELUDE TO APRIL 20 RED HEARINGS

Hearings slated for April 20 to wind up the present series of sessions by the House Un-American Activities Committee on alleged Red leanings in Hollywood promise to be the most unusual the House group has held to date in any field.

In place of the general denials or refusals to answer, which have been normal procedure, the committee's two principal witnesses, John Garfield and José Ferrer, will come into the hearing room with painstakingly detailed cases. Both are preparing to explain and defend every action of their professional and personal lives.

Both have employed top counsel and spent a large amount of time and money in recent weeks going over their own actions and motives. Both have strongly denied any tie with Communism now or in the past, and they are preparing to prove their denials.

They are understood to have gone so far as to hire investigators of their own to dig up anything derogatory to themselves, so that they'll be thoroughly prepared with answers whether the point is false rumor or based on some shred of fact. It is understood that attorneys for the two actors have insisted upon such procedure as a prelude to taking on the cases. They've questioned the actors exhaustively themselves and sought outside evidence in order to be assured that they are not putting themselves on the spot by defending clients of dubious political backgrounds.

Garfield's attorney is Louis Nizer, of Phillips, Nizer, Benjamin & Krim, New York law firm which reps Paramount, J. Arthur Rank and many other major outfits in and out of the film industry.

Ferrer is repped by a whole battery of lawyers. In New York he has his regular counsel, Edwin M. Reiskind, and in California Greg Bautzer. His principal defender, however, will be Abe Fortas, of the Washington firm of (Thurman) Arnold, Fortas & (Paul) Porter.

Fortas is the attorney who last year defended Owen Lattimore when he was accused of leading the State Dept. along Communist lines when he was principal adviser on China. Lattimore is generally conceded in Washington to have come off better than any other witness. He is in top demand now as a lecturer, and thousands of copies of his book on his testimony have been sold, both in a $3.50 and 25¢ edition.

Both Ferrer and Garfield have heavy commercial incentives in demanding their names be cleared. Garfield is the star of a new picture, *He Ran All the Way,* of which he is part owner and which is just about to go into release. Ferrer is star of *Cyrano de Bergerac,* Stanley Kramer production, which is now winding up roadshow dates and will go into general release in July. He is also under contract to Paramount to appear in *Anything Can Happen,* film version of the George and Helen Papashvily book.

Paramount is extremely concerned and watching results of the hearings very carefully. Ferrer is felt by producers George Seaton and William Perlberg to be the only actor who could really satisfactorily play the part in *Anything,* and an adverse decision in Washington might require ditching of the whole project.

It is only fair to add that Ferrer got it coming and going. Here is how his former admirers on the Left now saw him (David Platt in the *People's Daily World,* March 27, 1951):

New York

In October, 1947, screen actor John Garfield put his signature to the following statement issued by the Hollywood Branch of the Committee for the First Amendment. (This committee was set up to aid John Howard Lawson and 18 other Hollywood artists subpoenaed by the un-American committee.)

"We, the undersigned, as American citizens who believe in constitutional democratic government, are disgusted and outraged by the continuing attempts of the House un-American Activities committee to smear the motion picture industry. We hold that these hearings are morally wrong because any investigation into the political beliefs of the individual is contrary to the basic principles of our democracy. Any attempt to curb freedom of expression and to set arbitrary standards of Americanism is in itself disloyal to both the spirit and the letter of our Constitution."

Recently, however, when Garfield was himself subpoenaed by the un-American committee, he hastened to "clear" himself in advance with the same committee which disgusted and outraged him three years ago.

"I have always hated communism. It is a tyranny which threatens our country and the peace of the world. Of course, then, I have never been a member of the Communist party, or a sympathizer with any of its doctrines. I will be pleased to cooperate with the committee."

Somehow the title of John Garfield's next film which United Artists will release in April, fits his about-face. His new film is called *He Ran All the Way.*

Broadway actor José Ferrer, who was subpoenaed by the un-American committee took a full page ad in the *Hollywood Reporter* to deliver himself of the following knee-bending oath:

"I attest, and will so swear under oath, that I am not, have never been, could not be, a member of the Communist party; nor, specifically, am I a sympathizer with any Communist aim, a fellow traveler, or in any way an encourager of any Communist party concept or objective."

Do these two gentlemen of the theater and screen realize what they are saying?

"I attest that I am not a sympathizer with any Communist aim," says Ferrer.

"I have never been a sympathizer with any Communist doctrine," says Garfield.

But the aims and doctrines of American Communists are directed toward making our country a better place to live in, a place where the Negro people will have full equality, where there will be no exploitation of man by man, no unemployment, no periodic economic crises or depressions, where everyone will have the opportunity to work in the field of his or her choosing, where the finest of world culture will be accessible to all, where warmongering and anti-Semitism will be capital offenses on a par with premeditated murder and treason, where science and art will serve constructive rather than destructive ends, where there will be government of, by and for the people instead of misgovernment by, of and for Morgan and duPont. These are some of the aims and doctrines of the American Communists.

But Garfield and Ferrer say they are "not sympathetic with any Communist aim."

Are we to assume then, that they are opposed to first-class citizenship for Negroes; that they want big business to continue amassing fabulous profits out c^ the hides of the workers; that they see nothing wrong in the jailing of men and women for fighting for peace while the warmonger and the anti-Semite are free to spout their poisonous hates; that they are content to see the brutalization of the youth of America by gangster films and gangster culture; that they are fully satisfied with things as they are—that is, fully satisfied and convinced that Truman is serving the best interests of the nation and not the best interests of U.S. Steel, General Motors, General Electric?

That they are fully satisfied that the FBI and its army of stoolpigeons are serving democracy and not fascism; fully satisfied and convinced that the rearming of Nazi Germany by Wall Street will lead to world peace and not world war?

Garfield says: "Communism threatens our country."

How? Where? Is it the Communists who are lynching Negroes? Rattling the atom bomb? Stirring up anti-Semitism? Burning books? Depriving a great artist like Paul Robeson of his passport?

Is it the Communists who are building war bases in every part of the world? Burning huts of Koreans to keep warm without looking first to see if women and children are inside? Strafing everything that moves? The Communists want peace—does peace now threaten America?

Ferrer says: "I swear that I am not in any way an encourager of any Communist party concept or objective."

Some of the objectives of the Communist party include the freeing of Willie McGee and other Negroes framed on phony "rape" charges; the outlawing of the Ku Klux Klan, the adoption of laws banning war propaganda; the curbing of monopolies; independent political action on the part of organized labor; low cost housing; opening of the Metropolitan Opera to Negro voices; halting of the Catholic hierarchy's drive to dictate the thought content of all film and plays shown in America; stopping the witchhunt against Hollywood and Broadway actors such as Garfield and Ferrer; stopping the drive toward world war and atomic ruin.

Are we to assume that Garfield and Ferrer are opposed to these objectives?

If they are, then they are betraying America—betraying the tens of millions of Americans who have the same objectives, including the cessation of hostilities in Korea—and every mother who does not want to see her son mangled in an unjust, unpatriotic war should hate Garfield and Ferrer for their betrayal—should hate them for lending their talents, their names, their influence to such a murderous cause.

For make no mistake about it, Garfield and Ferrer are betraying everything that's decent and honorable in our land to the fat pigs of Wall Street who are wallowing in their blood-soaked profits.

They are just as guilty, just as dishonorable, as the German actors Werner Krauss and Emil Jannings who joined Hitler's fight against communism in the early '30's. Krauss and Jannings also said "Communism is a tyranny which threatens our country and the peace of the world."

Today the entire world knows that the tyranny which threatened Germany and the peace of the world was fascism, not communism. The entire world now knows that behind the "red" scares, behind the witchhunts and the "loyalty" oaths and the book burnings and the midnight raids, behind the attacks on the Communists, the extermination of six million Jews was being planned by Hitler as part of his program to enslave humanity.

Actors like Werner Krauss and Emil Jannings were guilty of cooperating in this horrible slaughter. They betrayed their talents to Hitler's murder machine.

Now the Garfields and the Ferrers are doing the heiling, allying themselves with all that's degrading in our country, cooperating to bring about a third world war so destructive of human life and property it defies the wildest reaches of the imagination. Their guilt is immensely greater than that of Krauss and Jannings. They are contributing to the incitement of a holocaust alongside of which World War II was child's play.

As for Larry Parks, his testimony is perhaps the most pathetic in all the annals of the Committee, particularly as there was no joy in Heaven over this particular sinner's repentance. Here are the *Los Angeles Evening Herald & Express* and the *Los Angeles Times,* both of March 23, 1951:

LOYAL ACTORS CALL FOR FILM INDUSTRY PURGE OF ALL SUBVERSIVES

Hollywood has treated the Communist menace in its midst "too lightly" and the time has come for the film industry to purge itself of subversive elements, according to Actor John Wayne, who today started his third term as president of the Anti-Red Motion Picture Alliance for the Preservation of American Ideals.

Speaking last night at the Alliance's eighth annual meeting, Wayne took Actor Larry Parks to task for waiting 10 years before making public confession that he was once a Communist Party member. Wayne said that his earlier statement that Parks' admission was "commendable" was a "snap comment" and that the long interval of silence on Parks' part was "not to his credit."

"Let no one say that a Communist can be tolerated in American society and particularly in our industry," Wayne declared. "We do not want to associate with traitors.

"We want patriotism and justice. We hate no one. We hope those who have changed their view will cooperate to the fullest extent. By that I mean names and places, so that they can come back to the fellowship of loyal Americans.

"The bankers and stockholders must recognize that their investments (in the movie industry) are imperiled as long as we have these elements in our midst," Wayne told the 1000 film workers, actors and writers jammed into the Hollywood American Legion auditorium.

A box office boycott of Red actors was urged by another speaker, Victor Riesel of New York, syndicated labor columnist.

"It was the Communists themselves who started the boycott system," he said. "The Commies called it a 'blacklist.' The time has come to turn the tables with a 'Red' list.

"To hell with Parks and all the late confessors," Riesel shouted. He lambasted Actors John Garfield and Charlie Chaplin and Singer Paul Robeson, all of leftist persuasion, and attacked Actress Gale Sondergaard and Actor Howard Da Silva, who earlier this week balked at testifying before the House Un-American Activities Committee.

Wayne presented a $1000 check to William B. Keene, 26, of Manhattan Beach, a law student at the University of California at Los Angeles, as the first annual James K. McGuinness Award for Outstanding Americanism shown by a student on an American college campus.

Keene told of his battle to keep Communists from establishing a foothold on the Westwood campus through appointments to the staff of the *Daily Bruin* while he was president of the university's student body in 1949.

Another speaker was Hollywood Columnist Hedda Hopper, who hit at Parks, saying:

"The life of one American soldier is worth all the careers in Hollywood. We must be careful lest we give sympathy to those who do not deserve it—and Parks certainly does not."

THE CASE OF LARRY PARKS

The first Hollywood character to admit publicly past membership in the Communist Party is the actor Larry Parks. Parks says he joined the party in 1941 because he thought it was "liberal" and that he dropped out about four years later because it had ceased to interest him. He seeks to pass the whole matter off as a youthful indiscretion.

Parks may deserve credit for frankness and courage; but on the other hand he admitted what was practically common knowledge, and what the committee probably would have been able to prove if necessary, since it had in its possession Communist Party membership cards bearing his name.

He said his testimony may cost him his career. But if his career is hurt it will not be through truthtelling but because he once chose to associate with a subversive organization.

Behind closed doors he gave the committee some names of people he said were Hollywood Communists. The committee says it already had most of the names. So his testimony in this regard does not seem to be particularly valuable.

Before Parks is praised too much, therefore, his attitude may be contrasted with that of Whittaker Chambers, who under somewhat parallel circumstances did sacrifice his career on the altar of patriotism and who did give valuable information, which resulted in the conviction of Alger Hiss and the unmasking of others.

By coincidence Alger Hiss surrendered to serve his five-year sentence shortly after Parks concluded his testimony.

A close parallel to what Parks has actually done is the case of Lee Pressman, who similarly admitted past membership in the Communist Party and named Nathan Witt, John Abt and Charles Kramer as other Communists.

Since Pressman and all three of the men he named had been in government offices and on the public payroll his information was rather more useful than that given by Parks. But no one has voted Pressman any medals.

The public will consider that Parks would have been deserving of more credit had he made a public confession without being under any compulsion. He says he dropped out of the Communist cell about 1945, which is five or six years ago; and Parks has been all that time under suspicion, which he took no steps to dispel.

The Un-American Activities Committee also heard from Actor Howard Da Silva and Actress Gale Sondergaard, but not much from either. Both declined to testify on the ground that their evidence might serve to incriminate them—a legitimate ground for refusal, according to a recent Supreme Court decision.

Their declination may, of course, be taken note of by the public, which may draw conclusions from it if it wishes. Miss Sondergaard is the wife of

Herbert Biberman, who was one of the "Hollywood 10" who served terms in jail after refusing to tell the committee whether they were Communists. Their refusal was not based on the possibility of self-incrimination; they denied the right of the committee to ask the question. That is what Miss Sondergaard meant by saying her husband had been in prison "for defending the First Amendment."

The committee should pursue the inquiry, as it no doubt will. The crowd which flew to Washington in December, 1947, to protest the imprisonment of the "Hollywood 10" should furnish some interesting testimony. Of these only Humphrey Bogart disclaimed Communism and the purpose of the trip; he said it was "ill advised, foolish and impetuous."

A whole galaxy of Hollywood names has been drawn under suspicion by the various inquiries and the committee owes it to the public and to the great majority of decent, self-respecting and patriotic Americans who work in Hollywood to clear up the matter. The committee, when it resumes after Easter, should particularly insist on knowing who has bank-rolled the Communist conspiracy; that the party has obtained large sums from Hollywood is notorious.

Some indication of how these matters were handled in popular magazines is provided by the following pages of *Hollywood Life* (July 13 and March 30, 1951):

JIMMIE TARANTINO

DORE SCHARY AND DASHIELL HAMMETT COMMUNIST CONNECTIONS

The active participation of top-flight Hollywood stars and personalities in the Communist Party cause, is reaching the sickening stage. The rats, who have helped the commie cause, in an attempt to sell America down the river, are slowly (but surely), being revealed and exposed. Commie revelations of the past few months, such as **Jose Ferrer, Judy Holliday, Johnny Garfield** and dozens of others, is just the beginning. The next six months will witness sensational findings of scores of big and small names. Men and women will be deported, and jailed and others handed long overdue shame. The present Washington House Committee on Un-American Activities accomplishments extends further than is commonly known. But, come September, **Senator Pat McCarran** and a powerful 19 Senators' committee will heave-ho with rocking blows that will shock the nation. McCarran, as fearless as they come in Washington, is dead set on cleaning out communism in its entirety.

SCHARY, THE SCHEMER

As I indicated several weeks ago, **Dore Schary,** executive producer and a production boss at MGM, is a Red Fellow Traveler and has been a serious Red Sympathizer for many years. Schary can scream and yell all he wishes; still the facts and records are clearly recorded.

Actually, Schary is one of the smartest schemers in the Hollywood Red Influence. He is brilliant, studious and highly educated. For these reasons it is pathetic that, with his eyes wide open, he became a victim of the **commie hokum.**

Nevertheless, Schary has associated himself with numerous dangerous communists and red fellow travelers. It is said, often, that Schary from time to time favored his **"Red Boy Friends"** with many studio writing and acting jobs. A few years ago, I'm told, Schary was set and scheduled to be one of the **"Hollywood Un-Friendly Ten,"** who have since cooled their heels in Federal prisons for contempt of Congress. How Schary ever escaped that punishment is another story.

Schary has written many articles for the benefit and interest of the communist cause.He has advised and discussed commie matters with many commies such as **Dalton Trumbo** and **John Howard Lawson.** His entire secret red affiliation would out-do most of his screen scenes.

Schary has been connected with a minimum of three red front organizations, in a membership capacity of some sort. They included, The American Youth for Democracy, Hollywood Writers Mobilization Committee, and, as an Executive, of the **Hollywood Independent Citizens Committee of the Arts, Sciences and Professions Committee. The latter three are important and have been dangerous commie outlets. This is practically an original expose on Schary, but it won't be the last.**

DASHIELL HAMMETT
A BIG TIME RED

Dashiell Hammett, noted author and creator of the **"Thin Man"** stories and "Sam Spade," deserves an American Tragedy title. **Hammett** is one of the most dangerous (if not **THE**) influential communists in America. **Communism has been his first love for many years,** and he has aided the Moscow methods with thousands of dollars, and most of his spare time. **Hammett** is said to be responsible for selling the red banner to dozens of men and women including actor **Howard Duff,** alias **Sam Spade.** Duff is also a member of one or more red fronts, and a **definite red sympathizer.**

Truthfully, **Dashiell Hammett should be indicted for participating in subversive activities and aiding in matters which seek and conspire to overthrow the United States Government.** Earlier this week, he was jailed for refusing to reveal the secret communist bankroll usd to free commies and red fellow travelers whenever jailed. Proving over again that **Hammett is without any question one of the red masterminds of the nation, with main headquarters in Hollywood and a sub-office in New York.**

The actual record of the numerous red fronts of which Hammett is a member, executive or organizer, runs far past 35 organizations. I doubt if there is any notorious communist front organization that doesn't bear the phony Dashiell Hammett name.

When you're a commie and a member of more than 35 red organizations, you're in the high, top brackets of the caviar-vodka set.

CRUMMIE DASHIELL HAMMETT has been a member and has helped organize more than 35 organizations and, for the sake of the record, here are a few important ones: **Citizens Committee for Harry Bridges, Hollywood Writers' Congress, Civil Rights Congress, Abraham Lincoln Brigade, Motion Picture Artists' Committee, American Committee for the Protection of the Foreign Born, Jefferson School of Social Science, and he once signed a letter, sent to President Roosevelt,** protesting the alleged persecution of communist leaders. The above amounts to approximately 10% of **Dashiell Hammett's** efforts to help further the cause of communism.

JIMMIE TARANTINO

JOHN GARFIELD — LENA HORNE — JUDY HOLLIDAY — JOSE FERRER — DUFF — WELLES — SUPPORT COMMUNIST PARTY

The Communist Party and its leaders **have been slowly but surely placing a RED NOOSE around the neck of many Hollywood personalities.** The inside story of how the Reds and the commie party wormed their way into the movie and radio industry ranks with the most traitorous movements in history. **It's shocking! Shameful! Deceitful!**

If anyone in the world, short of HIS HOLINESS, POPE PIUS, had told me a few short years ago that this could happen in America, I would have shooed them away. It is almost unbelievable that so many so-called intelligent and prominent people would turn their affections and sympathies to butcher **Joe Stalin** and the Communist Party.

How in the world so many men and women can pretend to love America,

while supporting and aiding our number one enemy, **Communism,** is beyond normal thinking. And most of them, born in this country. It was common knowledge for years that the Communist Party's chief aim was to control our nation. And in recent years it became obvious that the Reds have been in an all out fight to overthrow our Government. Stalin has it mapped out on blueprint plans. The Korean war is on his timetable. **It followed his cold war conquest of RED CHINA.** The present Korean war finally taught us a lesson we have shunned. To prepare. To be ready to fight on a twenty-four hour notice, with sufficient manpower and arms.

Still, it is difficult to understand how a person can rise from practical poverty, or from an average earning family, to great fame and wealth, and then give aid, comfort and money to a known enemy nation. A person must be temporarily nutty to support or defend the commie party, or any of their many RED FRONT ORGANIZATIONS. (A Red Front is a commie alibi.) Well, here is the most shocking list of Communist members, Red Fellow Travelers and Red Sympathizers ever revealed at one time. Three persons on the following list have confessed in my presence. This list is factual. **I have the proof.** So has the U. S. Government and many federal agencies, and the Washington Committee Investigating UN-American Activities.

JOHN GARFIELD, ACTOR . . . Garfield is a Communist from way back. He is said to have once signed a commie card. On 8/6/45 he was a sponsor for the American Committee for Yugoslav Relief. A Red Front outfit . . . 4/27/46 he sponsored a Civil Rights Congress affair in Detroit, Mich. . . . In 1941 he issued a statement in the publication, "SOVIET RUSSIA TODAY" in support of Russia and what it stands for . . . In 1944 he became an executive member of the Hollywood Democratic Committee. A RED FRONT . . . He is a member of the Theater Arts Committee, also a RED FRONT . . . In 1948, Garfield was a sponsor on the committee of the NATIONAL COUNCIL of the ARTS, SCIENCES AND PROFESSIONS organization, which **attempted to abolish** the present Washington House Committee on Un-American Activities . . . Garfield has supported the commie cause by lending his name and has given money to more that 20 commie or commie front outfits.

LENA HORNE, SINGER-ACTRESS . . . Horne is a supporter of the commie party in many ways. Her name has been used in countless cases bringing in support and money . . . The Daily Worker has had her help . . . In 1945, Lena received an award from the **NEW MASSES,** a commie publication . . . She was a fund raiser for the PEOPLE'S DAILY WORKER . . . She once acted as a speaker for the Civil Rights Congress, a red front . . . Lena gave free entertainment to the Communist Party State Committee of N.Y. in the Golden Gate Ballroom, N.Y.C. in an affair honoring the commie election of Ben J. Davis, a noted Communist . . . La

Horne was a performer who aided in a radio program, "FIGHTERS FOR FREEDOM," a known commie red front . . . Lena Horne, has aided red front affiliations other than those listed.

JUDY HOLLIDAY, SINGER-ACTRESS . . . Holliday is up for an Academy Award "Oscar," for her work in the Columbia film, "Born Yesterday" . . . Judy only acts dumb. She's a smart cookie . . . The Commies got her a long time ago . . . She was a singer with the National Council of Arts and Sciences and Professions, a commie red front, who supported the UN-Friendly Ten Hollywood Writers who went to jail . . . Judy, in 1948, was a guest speaker during a rally in the N.Y. Hotel Astor, for the STOP CENSORSHIP COMMITTEE, a communist front . . . She was a sponsor for the WORLD FEDERATION of DEMOCRATIC YOUTH, a known communist front . . . In 1948, Holliday wired **greetings** of good luck and best wishes to the MOSCOW ART THEATER . . . She is a supporter of the CIVIL RIGHTS CONGRESS, a red outfit . . . A few years ago, Judy performed free of charge at a dance and affair in the Hotel Capitol, N.Y.C., that was sponsored by the Commie Daily Worker . . . Judy Holliday always knew what she was doing.

JOSE FERRER, STAGE-SCREEN ACTOR . . . Ferrer has made wild statements denying he has commie affiliations. He has threatened to sue various people. Well, **he can sue me,** and have the following, plus other data read off in court . . . In the first place he has lent his name, given time and money to more than 15 red front commie outfits . . . Here are a few. Artists Front to Win the War, Scientific and Cultural Conference for World Peace and Win the Peace Conference . . . He once spoke on behalf of the **Abraham Lincoln Brigade** during a N.Y.C. rally in 1945 . . . On 6/26/44 he entertained at a commie front rally for the Negro Labor Victory Committee . . . In 1945 he acted as a sponsor and aided the election of Ben J. Davis, noted Communist . . . Ferrer was a member of the National Henry Wallace for President Committee . . . He was Chairman of the Commie front Theater Division of the Independent Citizen Committee of the Arts and Sciences and Professions in 1945 . . . Ferrer was a sponsor on a committee of the National Council of the Arts, Sciences and Professions organization, who attempted to abolish the present Washington House Committee on Un-American Activities . . . Jose Ferrer has acted in many official capacities for commie causes. It may yet be proven he is a card carrying member of the Commie party.

HOWARD DUFF, RADIO AND SCREEN ACTOR . . . Sam Spade Duff is a red fellow traveler and red sympathizer. He has also given comfort and his well-advertised name to many commie fronts . . . He was an un-friendly witness before the Washington House on Un-American Activities . . . A member of the Committee for the First Amendment, a commie setup . . . Duff on 10/3/47 was a member of the Actors Division of the Progressive Citizens of America, a red front deal . . . He signed a petition to the U. S. Supreme Court to review the conviction of Lawson and Trumbo, two of the Un-Friendly Hollywood writers who were sent to jail.

ORSON WELLES, RADIO AND SCREEN STAR . . . Welles has been affiliated with several commie fronts . . . He is a definite red fellow traveler and has aided the Communist Cause . . . He has lent his name to commie setups.

HOWARD DaSILVA, SCREEN AND RADIO ACTOR . . . DaSilva recently refused to testify before the Washington House on Un-American Activities. He had a good reason. DaSilva is a member of the Communist Party . . . He was a participant during a rally in 1946 to abolish the Wood-Rankin Committee . . . He was a sponsor of the WIN THE PEACE CONFERENCE, a red setup . . . He was a sponsor on a committee for the re-election of Ben J. Davis, noted Communist Party member . . . He also signed a petition to the U. S. Supreme Court to review the conviction of Lawson and Trumbo, who were sent to jail. On 6/6/46 he took part in a handbill rally for the benefit of the Council on American Affairs, a red front . . . In 1949 DaSilva was an Executive member of the Actors Laboratory Theater, a red outfit . . . Howard DaSilva is a commie member, and an active one.

SAM WANAMAKER, ACTOR, DIRECTOR ON RADIO AND SCREEN . . . Wanamaker has acted as a speaker at **affairs praising** the Communist ideology . . . He belongs to red fronts . . . Wanamaker acted as a sponsor and entertainer at a rally for the benefit of the Abraham Lincoln Brigade, a noted red front.

ARTIE SHAW, ACTOR AND BAND LEADER . . . This Shaw fellow became involved in Communist Party affairs early in 1941 . . **Kathleen Winsor,** his ex-wife, testified under oath that he was a member of the Communist Party . . . He has affiliated himself many times with known commies and is a member of many red fronts. Also as a red front sponsor.

CHARLIE CHAPLIN, ACTOR . . . Chaplin has been a card-carrying member of the Communist Party for many years . . . He has lent his name and given money to commie organizations.

LIONEL STANDER, RADIO AND SCREEN ACTOR . . . Stander is a definite red fellow traveler and red sympathizer for many years . . . He has spoken for the commie cause and aided the reds in many ways.

BEN GRAUER, NOTED RADIO ANNOUNCER . . . Grauer has been affiliated with the Communist cause for many years.

MARCH 21, 1951:

Larry Parks

The Committee on Un-American Activities met at 10:35 a.m. in room 226, Old House Office Building, the Honorable John S. Wood (Chairman) presiding.

Committee members present: Representatives John S. Wood (Chairman), Francis E. Walter, Clyde Doyle, James B. Frazier, Jr. (appearance as noted in transcript), Harold H. Velde, Bernard W. Kearney, Donald L. Jackson, and Charles E. Potter.

Staff members present: Frank S. Tavenner, Jr., Counsel; Thomas W. Beale, Sr., Assistant Counsel; Louis J. Russell, Senior Investigator; William A. Wheeler, Investigator; John W. Carrington, Clerk; and A. S. Poore, Editor.

MR. TAVENNER: The Committee on Un-American Activities has succeeded to a marked degree in exposing Communists' infiltration into labor organizations, with the result in many instances that the organizations have rid themselves of Communist domination and influences, and that the Congress has been informed of many important facts as the basis for legislative action. I need only remind you that the testimony of Matthew Cvetic virtually destroyed, for the time being at least, the power and influence of the Communist Party in western Pennsylvania. Then there have been many witnesses who have told this Committee of the circumstances under which they were duped into joining the Communist Party, the Communist Party activities observed by them while they were members, and the reasons for their breaking with the party. This has required courage, but, in so testifying, they have performed a service of inestimable value to their country and should receive the plaudits of their fellow citizens.

The hearing today is the first of a series designed by the Committee to accomplish the same results in the entertainment field as have been accomplished in labor and other fields. It is hoped that any witness appearing during the course of these hearings, who made the mistake of associating himself or herself with the Communist Party, will have sufficient courage and loyalty to make an honest disclosure of all they know about Communist Party activities. Now, Mr. Chairman, I would like to call, as the first witness, Mr. Larry Parks.

MR. TAVENNER: Are you represented by counsel, Mr. Parks?

MR. PARKS: Yes, I am. My counsel is Mr. Mandel.

MR. TAVENNER: Will counsel identify himself?

MR. MANDEL: Louis Mandel, 1501 Broadway, New York City. In the light of the testimony that Mr. Parks will give here, he has prepared a statement that he would like to read at this point. I think it is a proper background to the testimony he will give and be very enlightening to the Committee as his testimony unfolds. May he read that statement?

MR. WOOD: At the conclusion of his testimony, if he desires to read the statement that has been presented to the members here, he will be given that privilege, or he can put it in the record, as he desires.

MR. MANDEL: I would, in fairness to the witness, urge very strongly that he be permitted [to read the statement], because there is a connecting link to what he will testify, here in this statement. And I think, in proper consideration of the witness and what he will do, this opportunity ought to be given to him. I urge it very strongly.

MR. WOOD: Proceed, Mr. Tavenner.

MR. TAVENNER: Mr. Parks, when and where were you born?

MR. PARKS: I was born on a farm in Kansas. I suppose the legal town would be Olathe. That was the closest town.

MR. TAVENNER: Will you relate briefly to the Committee the details regarding your educational background?

MR. PARKS: I moved when I was quite small to Illinois. I attended the high school in Joliet, Illinois, and I also attended and graduated from the University of Illinois, where I majored in chemistry and minored in physics. I sometimes wonder how I got in my present line of work.

MR. TAVENNER: What was the date of the completion of your work at the university?

MR. PARKS: 1936.

MR. TAVENNER: Now, what is your present occupation?

MR. PARKS: Actor.

MR. TAVENNER: Mr. Parks, I believe you were present when I made a statement as to the purpose of this series of hearings.

MR. PARKS: Yes, I was present, and I heard you.

MR. TAVENNER: There has been considerable testimony taken before this Committee regarding a number of organizations in Hollywood, such as the Actors' Laboratory Theater. Have you been connected in any way with any of those organizations?

MR. PARKS: I have.

MR. TAVENNER: Will you state the names of those organizations which you have been affiliated with? To aid you, I will hand you the list.

MR. PARKS: (*looking at sheet of paper containing list*): Well, most of them I'm not familiar with. I'm familiar with the Actors' Laboratory.

MR. TAVENNER: Well, did you hold any official position in that organization?

MR. PARKS: For a time I was sort of honorary treasurer of this organization.

MR. TAVENNER: Was that in 1949 and 1950 or when was that?

MR. PARKS: Well, I can't recall the exact date.

MR. TAVENNER: Will you proceed?

MR. PARKS: I believe that I for a time was a member of the Hollywood Independent Citizens Committee of the Arts, Sciences, and Professions.

MR. WOOD: We will have to ask the photographers to not block the view.

MR. TAVENNER: Do you recall whether or not the Progressive Citizens of America was the outgrowth or successor to what was known as the Hollywood Democratic Committee?

MR. PARKS: I believe that's true.

MR. TAVENNER: Were you a member of it?

MR. PARKS: Yes, I was.

MR. TAVENNER: Did you hold any official position in the organization?

MR. PARKS: No, I don't believe so. Not that I recall.

MR. TAVENNER: What other organizations listed there were you affiliated with?

MR. PARKS: What do you mean "affiliated with"?

MR. TAVENNER: Well, either by way of membership or by way of aid and support.

MR. PARKS: Well, I don't—

MR. TAVENNER: And if you aided in any way by entertainment.

MR. PARKS: Those two are the only ones that I can think of at the moment. Perhaps if you could refresh my memory I would appreciate it.

MR. TAVENNER: Well, were you affiliated with the Civil Rights Congress in any manner?

MR. PARKS: No, I don't believe so.

MR. TAVENNER: Well, did you appear at any meeting of that organization to your knowledge?

MR. PARKS: It's quite possible that I did.

MR. TAVENNER: According to the *Evening Star,* of Washington, D.C., November 3, 1947, you are reported to have been one of the speakers—

MR. PARKS: As I say, it's quite possible at that particular time—

MR. TAVENNER: —at a reception given Gerhart Eisler. Do you recall that?

MR. PARKS: No, I don't recall ever being at a reception for Gerhart Eisler. To the best of my knowledge, I have never seen him. When I was in Washington last time I attended many meetings and many receptions. I'm not familiar with the names of these. If you ask me if I was at this reception, it's quite possible that I was. What the name of it is I can't recall at this time, and I probably didn't know at that time.

MR. TAVENNER: Now, referring back to the Actors' Laboratory, of which you were an officer—you were the treasurer, I believe?

MR. PARKS: In name I was treasurer, yes.

MR. TAVENNER: What do you mean by stating that you were treasurer "in name"?

MR. PARKS: Well, this was more of an honorary position than an active one. My job as the treasurer was to sign a batch of checks, and that's the extent of my knowledge of the money matters of the Lab.

MR. TAVENNER: Will you tell the Committee whether or not there were, to your knowledge, Communists in these various organizations, particularly those that you were a member of?

MR. PARKS: I think that I can say yes to that.

MR. TAVENNER: Well, who were these Communists?

MR. PARKS: There were people in the Actors' Lab, for instance. This, in my opinion, was not a Communist organization in any sense of the word. As in any organization, it has all colors of political philosophy. I know nothing about who belonged, other than myself, to the Independent Citizens Committee of the Arts, Sciences, and Professions. This I won't say because I don't know. There were Communists attached to the Lab.

MR. TAVENNER: Well, were there Communists attached to these other organizations which you say you were a member of?

MR. PARKS: This I'm not familiar with. I don't know. I don't know who else was a member of them besides myself.

MR. TAVENNER: You do not recall who were members of those other organizations?

MR. PARKS: I think that that is the gist of my answer, yes.

MR. TAVENNER: But you do recall that at the Actors' Laboratory there were members of the Communist Party?

MR. PARKS: That's true.

MR. TAVENNER: Did those Communist Party members endeavor to obtain control of the activities of the organization and of its various offices?

MR. PARKS: No, the Lab was a school for acting and sort of a showcase for actors. I left the Lab because I was in favor of forming a permanent repertory theater. It was felt by the majority of the Lab that they wanted it the way it was, as a school.

MR. TAVENNER: Well, what was your opportunity to know and to observe the fact that there were Communists in that organization?

MR. PARKS: I knew them as Communists.

MR. TAVENNER: Well, what had been your opportunity to know them as Communists?

MR. PARKS: May I answer this fully and in my own way?

MR. TAVENNER: I would like for you to.

MR. PARKS: I am not a Communist. I would like to point out that, in my opinion, there is a great difference between being a Communist, say in 1941, ten years ago, and being a Communist in 1951. To my mind this is a great difference and not a subtle one. It is also, I feel, not a subtle difference to be a member of the Communist Party and being a Communist. I do not believe in my own mind that this is a subtle difference either. I would furnish you with—I guess you would call it an allegory [analogy?] as to what I mean, so that you will see why I say it is not a subtle difference. The President of this country is the head of the Democratic Party. There are many people who call themselves Democrats. There are certain Southern Democrats, for instance, that do not follow the aims and platform of the Democratic Party, yet they are called Democrats. They, in my opinion, are Republicans really.

MR. TAVENNER: Well, now, that could be said and a similar analysis could be given of the Progressive Party or any other party, but let us—

MR. PARKS: Yes.

MR. TAVENNER: —confine ourselves to the question of Communism—

MR. PARKS: Yes. Well, I'm drawing an [analogy?] allegory.

MR. TAVENNER: —rather than speaking in terms of [analogy?] allegory.

MR. PARKS: Well, I felt that it was necessary, so that you could see that this is not a subtle difference, you see.

MR. TAVENNER: No, I think the Committee can understand by speaking plainly—

MR. PARKS: Yes.

MR. TAVENNER: —and to the point—

MR. PARKS: I'm trying to.

MR. TAVENNER: —on Communism.

MR. PARKS: As I say, I am not a Communist. I was a member of the Communist Party when I was a much younger man, ten years ago.

MR. TAVENNER: I wish you would tell the Committee the circumstances under which you became a member of the Communist Party, if you left the Communist Party, when you did it and why you did it.

MR. PARKS: Being a member of the Communist Party fulfilled certain needs of a young man that was liberal in thought, idealistic, who was for the underprivileged, the underdog. I felt that it fulfilled these particular needs. I think that being a Communist in 1951 in this particular situation is an entirely different kettle of fish, when this is a great power that is trying to take over the world. This is the difference. I became a Communist—

MR. TAVENNER: In other words, you didn't realize that the purpose and object of the Communist Party was to take over other segments of the world in 1941? But you do realize that that is true in 1951?

MR. PARKS: This is in no way an apology for anything that I have done, you see, because I feel I have done nothing wrong ever. Question of judgment? This is debatable. In 1941 the purposes, as I knew them, fulfilled simply—at least I thought they would fulfill as I said before—a certain idealism, a certain being for the underdog, which I am today, this very minute. This did not work out. I wasn't particularly interested, after I did become a member, I attended very few meetings, and I petered out the same way I drifted into it. I petered out about the latter part of 1944 or 1945.

* * *

MR. TAVENNER: Let me see if this information in the Committee files would be of any value in refreshing your recollections: That your Communist registration card for the year 1944 bore the number 46954 and for the year 1945 the number 47344. Does that happen to refresh your recollection?

MR. PARKS: No, sir, it doesn't, because to the best of my recollection I never had a Communist Party card.

MR. TAVENNER: Now, do I infer that shortly after 1945 or, say, in 1946 you became disillusioned about the Communist Party and withdrew as a member?

MR. PARKS: As I said before, to the best of my recollection it was in 1944 or 1945.

MR. TAVENNER: But by 1946, at least, you had definitely broken with the Party?

MR. PARKS: That is correct.

MR. TAVENNER: Have you participated in any Communist Party activities since that date, 1946?

MR. PARKS: I don't recall ever having participated in a Communist Party activity since that time.

MR. TAVENNER: Now, will you state to the Committee where you first became a member of the Party?

MR. PARKS: In Hollywood, California.

MR. TAVENNER: Who recruited you into the Party?

MR. PARKS: Well, a man by the name of Davidson, I believe.

MR. TAVENNER: What was Davidson's first name and what was his position?

MR. PARKS: I don't remember his first name. I haven't seen him for ten years, and I do not know what his position was.

MR. TAVENNER: Where did he live? Do you know?

MR. PARKS: This I have no idea.

MR. TAVENNER: What was his occupation?

MR. PARKS: This I do not know either.

MR. TAVENNER: Can you give us some descriptive data of the individual?

MR. PARKS: Average-looking man, young, dark hair.

MR. TAVENNER: Well, what were the circumstances under which you met?

MR. PARKS: Well, this is hard for me to recall, too.

MR. TAVENNER: Was it at a meeting in your home or where?

MR. PARKS: Well, as I say, I really don't remember. I'm being as honest as I know how.

MR. TAVENNER: I just wanted you to give the Committee what information you recall about how you got into the Communist Party.

MR. PARKS: As I told you, I was a good deal younger than I am now, about twenty-five, with certain liberal tendencies, idealism.

MR. TAVENNER: Well, did you seek this individual out, or did he seek you out?

MR. PARKS: Well, I certainly didn't seek him out. It's hard for me to say whether he sought me out.

MR. TAVENNER: Did others counsel you in regard to your uniting with the Communist Party before you were recruited by this individual by the name of Davidson?

MR. PARKS: No, I did it of my own volition.

MR. TAVENNER: Were you assigned to a Communist Party cell?

MR. PARKS: I was.

MR. TAVENNER: What was the name of that cell, and where was it located?

MR. PARKS: Well, it had no name that I know of. It was a group of people who were Communists, and I attended some meetings with them.

MR. TAVENNER: Well now, you were a member of that particular group from 1941 up to possibly as late as 1945?

MR. PARKS: That's correct.

MR. TAVENNER: Will you tell us what you know about the organization of the Communist Party from your own observations during that period of time in Hollywood?

MR. PARKS: Well, I'm afraid that I was a pretty bad member by their lights. I didn't attend too many meetings—maybe ten, twelve, fifteen meetings. And what I really know about the Communist Party is very little. If you will ask me some questions, I would be happy to answer them to the best of my ability.

MR. TAVENNER: Do you know whether or not the writers and actors in Hollywood were members of any particular branch or group of the Communist Party?

MR. PARKS: I know that certain actors were a group that met. This I do know. The other things I do not know.

(*Representative James B. Frazier, Jr., enters hearing room.*)

MR. TAVENNER: What was the name of the group to which the actors were assigned?

MR. PARKS: Well, no name that I know of. The majority of the members of this particular group were actors.

MR. TAVENNER: Well, were there several groups to which the actors belonged, depending upon the geographical location of the actor?

MR. PARKS: I wouldn't say for certain. I'm not under that impression.

MR. TAVENNER: Well, who was the chairman of the group to which you were assigned?

MR. PARKS: Well, it had no chairman that I know of.

MR. TAVENNER: Well, who was the secretary of the group?

MR. PARKS: This I do not recall either. I don't know if there were any actual officers of this particular group.

MR. TAVENNER: Well, to whom did you pay your dues?

MR. PARKS: To various members. No one in particular that I can recall was the treasurer.

MR. TAVENNER: Well, a person who was responsible for the collection of dues would certainly be performing the duty of a treasurer, even if he did not go by that name, isn't that true?

MR. PARKS: That's very true.

MR. TAVENNER: Well, who were those persons to whom you paid your dues?

MR. PARKS: Well, this is hard for me to answer, too, because the few times that I paid dues, as I recall, were to different people.

MR. TAVENNER: You cannot recall the name of any one individual to whom you paid?

MR. PARKS: No one individual can I recall that I paid the dues to.

MR. TAVENNER: Well, was Communist Party literature distributed to the members at any of the meetings or through any medium?

MR. PARKS: Certain pamphlets were available if you wished to buy them.

MR. TAVENNER: Who was the individual who had charge of the distribution or sale of those pamphlets?

MR. PARKS: This I don't know either, because the pamphlets were there and you could buy them if you wished.

MR. TAVENNER: Well, was there any secret about who was handling the literature of the Party?

MR. PARKS: No secret at all.

MR. TAVENNER: What was the total membership of this cell in which you were a member?

MR. PARKS: I would say that it ranged from as little as five, and I think it went up to maybe, oh, possibly ten or twelve.

MR. TAVENNER: And did the personnel change considerably between 1941 and 1945, or did it consist of the same members during all that period of time?

MR. PARKS: Well, I do know that, as I say, I attended rather irregularly, and at some of the meetings I would see someone that I didn't know, I didn't recognize, and I would never see them again.

MR. TAVENNER: Did speakers or organizers, Communist Party organizers, appear before your group from time to time—people from the East, let us say?

Mr. Parks: No, I don't recall ever seeing anyone from the East, as you say, or any "big shot," if you will allow me to put it that way.

Mr. Tavenner: Well, are you acquainted with V. J. Jerome?

Mr. Parks: To the best of my knowledge, I have never met the man.

Mr. Tavenner: Have you ever seen him in Hollywood?

Mr. Parks: I don't believe I have even seen him. I would not recognize the man if he walked into the room.

Mr. Tavenner: Are you acquainted with Lionel Stander?

Mr. Parks: I have met him.

Mr. Tavenner: Have you ever attended a Communist Party meeting with him?

Mr. Parks: I don't recall ever attending a Communist Party meeting with this Lionel Stander.

Mr. Tavenner: Do you know whether or not he is a Communist Party member?

Mr. Parks: No.

Mr. Tavenner: Are you acquainted with Karen Morley?

Mr. Parks: I am.

Mr. Tavenner: Is she a member of the Communist Party?

Mr. Parks: Well, counsel, these— I would prefer not to mention names, if it is at all possible. I don't think it is fair to people to do this. I have come to you at your request. I will tell you everything that I know about myself, because I feel I have done nothing wrong, and I will answer any question that you would like to put to me about myself. I would prefer, if you will allow me, not to mention other people's names.

Mr. Walter: Do you take the same position with respect to the obvious leaders of the Communist movement?

Mr. Parks: I do, because I don't know any of the leaders of the Communist movement.

Mr. Walter: Of course, you do know who was active in the movement in California?

Mr. Parks: No, I only know the names of people who attended certain meetings that I attended, and these were not active, big leaders of the Communist Party.

Mr. Walter: Who directed the meetings that you attended?

Mr. Parks: The meetings consisted mainly of—we were in a war then —discussions of how the war was going, current events, problems of actors in their work. It was more of a social occasion than a stereotyped kind of meeting. Does that answer your question, Congressman?

Mr. Walter: It's an answer.

Mr. Parks: Hmm?

Mr. Walter: It's an answer.

Mr. Parks: Well, I would like to answer your question, if you're not satisfied with that answer.

MR. WALTER: What I am interested in knowing is who directed the activities that this group were engaged in.

MR. PARKS: And I repeat again that no one to my knowledge directed any kind of activities.

MR. POTTER: Who would call the meetings together?

MR. PARKS: Well, I don't really know.

MR. POTTER: Did you have a set, scheduled meeting once every month or once every week, or was it upon the call of some individual?

MR. PARKS: Well, as I recall, various individuals would call. I don't believe that there was any set—

MR. POTTER: Certainly it wasn't run by mental telepathy.

MR. PARKS: No. I didn't say that. I say certain individuals would call, and, to the best of my knowledge, there was no set schedule of meetings.

MR. POTTER: Somebody had to issue a call?

MR. PARKS: That's correct.

MR. POTTER: Did you ever issue a call for your cell to get together?

MR. PARKS: No, I didn't.

MR. POTTER: Then, somebody would have to tell you when the meetings would take place and where they would take place, is that not true?

MR. PARKS: I would get a call from a member of the group and they would say, "Well, let's have a meeting tonight, tomorrow night."

MR. KEARNEY: Were the meetings always held at the same place?

MR. PARKS: No, they were not.

MR. KEARNEY: Were they held in halls or in your own homes?

MR. PARKS: These were held at homes.

MR. KEARNEY: Did you ever have any meetings at your own home?

MR. PARKS: Never.

MR. KEARNEY: Where were some of the meetings held?

MR. PARKS: These were people like myself, small-type people, no different than myself in any respect at all, and no different than you or I.

MR. KEARNEY: Where were some of these meetings held?

MR. PARKS: As I say, these were held in various homes in Hollywood.

MR. KEARNEY: Can you name some of them?

MR. PARKS: Well, as I asked the counsel and as I asked the Committee, if you will allow this, I would prefer not to mention names under these circumstances: That these were people like myself who—and I feel that I—have done nothing wrong ever. I mean along this line. I am sure none of us is perfect. Again, the question of judgment certainly is there, and even that is debatable, but these are people—

MR. WOOD: Just a moment. Do you entertain the feeling that these parties that you were associated with are likewise guiltless of any wrong?

MR. PARKS: This is my honest opinion: that these are people who did nothing wrong, people like myself.

MR. WOOD: Mr. Parks, in what way do you feel it would be injurious to them, to divulge their identities, when you expressed the opinion that at no time did they do wrong?

MR. PARKS: If you think it's easy for a man who has—I think I have worked hard in my profession, climbed up the ladder a bit. If you think it's easy for me to appear before this Committee and testify, you're mistaken, because it's not easy. This is a very difficult and arduous job for me for many reasons. One of the reasons is that as an actor my activity is dependent a great deal on the public. To be called before this Committee at your request has a certain inference, a certain innuendo that you are not loyal to this country. This is not true. I am speaking for myself. This is not true. But the inference and the innuendo is there as far as the public is concerned. Also as a representative of a great industry—not as an official representative—but as an actor of the motion-picture industry that is fairly well known, in that respect I am a representative of the industry. This is a great industry. At this particular time it is being investigated for Communist influence.

MR. WOOD: Don't you think the public is entitled to know about it?

MR. PARKS: Hmm?

MR. WOOD: Don't you feel the public is entitled to know about it?

MR. PARKS: I certainly do, and I am opening myself wide open to any question that you can ask me. I will answer as honestly as I know how. And at this particular time, as I say, the industry is—it's like taking a pot shot at a wounded animal, because the industry is not in as good a shape today as it has been—economically, I'm speaking. It has been pretty tough on it. And, as I say, this is a great industry, and I don't say this only because it has been kind to me. It has a very important job to do to entertain people, in certain respects to call attention to certain evils, but mainly to entertain, and in this I feel that they have done a great job. Always when our country has needed certain help, the industry has been in the forefront of that help.

MR. TAVENNER: You are placing your reluctance to testify upon the great job that the moving-picture industry is doing or can do?

MR. PARKS: On the question of naming names, it is my honest opinion that the few people that I could name, these names would not be of service to the Committee at all. I am sure that you know who they are. These people I feel honestly are like myself, and I feel that I have done nothing wrong. Question of judgment? Yes, perhaps. And I also feel that this is not—to be asked to name names like this is not—in the way of American justice as we know it, that we as Americans have all been brought up, that it is a bad thing to force a man to do this. I have been brought up that way. I am sure all of you have. And it seems to me that this is not the American way of doing things—to force a man who is under oath and who has opened himself as wide as possible to this Committee—and it hasn't been easy to do this—to force a man to do this is not American justice.

MR. WOOD: Well, I am glad, of course, to give considerable leeway to the range of your statement, because I for one am rather curious to understand just what the reasons are in your mind for declining to answer the question.

MR. PARKS: I'm not declining. I'm asking you if you would not press me on this.

MR. WOOD: I'm not going to press the point, unless other members of the Committee wish to.

MR. POTTER: Are any of the members in the particular Communist cell that you were in, to your knowledge, still active members in the Communist Party?

MR. PARKS: I can't say this, Congressman, because I have divorced myself completely. I have no way of knowing this at all. I know what I think inside: My opinion is that ninety-nine per cent of them are not.

MR. POTTER: If you knew people in Hollywood that were identified with the Party then, would you be reluctant to cite their names if they were active members at the present time?

MR. PARKS: I would be reluctant on only one score: that I do not think that it is good for an American to be forced to do this. Only on this score. But I feel that a man—the people that I knew—it is my opinion that they are not members of the Communist Party at this time. This is my opinion only. If they are, they shouldn't be.

MR. POTTER: If you had knowledge of a man who committed murder, certainly you wouldn't be hesitant to give that information to the proper authorities?

MR. PARKS: That is correct.

MR. POTTER: Now, I assume that you share the belief that we share, that an active member of the Communist Party believes in principles that we don't believe in, in overthrowing our Government by force and violence. Now, you say you would readily give information concerning a man you have knowledge has committed murder. Wouldn't you also give information to the proper authorities of a man you knew or a woman you knew or believed to be working to overthrow our Government by force and violence?

MR. PARKS: I will say this to you: If I knew a man that committed murder, this is against the law of our land, and I'm not drawing a fine line for my own protection when I say this, I'm not doing this at all. This is a reprehensible thing to do, to commit murder, and I certainly would name him immediately. The other question is—even now it is not against the law of our land. Do you understand the difference that I mean?

MR. POTTER: So when we are drafting men to fight Communist aggression, you feel that it is not your duty as an American citizen to give the

Committee the benefit of what knowledge you might have?

MR. PARKS: I think that there is a difference, Congressman, between people who would harm our country and people who in my opinion are like myself, who, as I feel, did nothing wrong at the time—

MR. POTTER: I'm not questioning that point, when you say that people like yourself may be misguided, or because of faulty judgment were members of the Party. But you don't believe today that anyone can be naïve enough to be an active member of the Communist Party and not know what he's doing?

MR. PARKS: That is correct. That is what I believe.

MR. POTTER: For that reason I can't see your consistency in saying you won't name someone who you know today is an active member of the Party.

MR. PARKS: But I do not know anyone today that is an active member of the Party.

MR. POTTER: If you did know, you would tell?

MR. PARKS: Yes, I think I would.

MR. TAVENNER: Mr. Parks, it seems to me that your argument in substance is this: that this Committee should investigate Communism but not find out who is a Communist.

MR. PARKS: No, counsel, that is not my—

MR. TAVENNER: In the final analysis, isn't that your argument?

MR. PARKS: No, this is not my argument at all.

MR. TAVENNER: You are taking the position that it is not important to find out who may be in Communism in Hollywood—

MR. PARKS: No.

MR. TAVENNER: —rather than for this Committee to determine what its obligations are under the statute which created it to investigate Communism?

MR. PARKS: No, counsel, I didn't say this at all.

MR. TAVENNER: But isn't that the result of your argument?

MR. PARKS: No, counsel, what I say is that the few people that I knew at that time are people like myself who are as loyal to this country as you.

MR. TAVENNER: And if every witness who came before this Committee were permitted to take that position, then the extent of the investigation that this Committee could conduct would be limited entirely by the attitude of the witness, wouldn't it?

MR. PARKS: But I told you the circumstances surrounding my small activity with the Communist Party, you see, and this makes quite a difference.

MR. TAVENNER: In your judgment?

MR. PARKS: Not only in my judgment. I know—at least inside of myself—that these people were like myself, and the most that you can accuse them of is a lack of judgment. I say none of this in apology for what I did, because a young man at twenty-five, if he's not a liberal, if he is not full of idealism, is not worth his salt. And if you make a mistake in judgment like this, I don't particularly, myself, believe that it is serious.

MR. TAVENNER: Yes, but if every witness who took the stand before this Committee would be the final judge of when a thing was serious and when it was not, and the Committee would be limited accordingly, how could this Committee carry out its statutory duty?

MR. PARKS: But I'm asking you as a man, having told you and opened myself to you, that—

MR. TAVENNER: And I'm only asking that you see the other side of it.

MR. PARKS: I do see the other side.

MR. TAVENNER: Now you have placed Hollywood on a very high pedestal here.

MR. PARKS: I have.

MR. TAVENNER: But there has been testimony here involving the scientific professions, persons in Government, persons in numerous industries, and I take it that there is no preference of any kind that should be allowed to your profession over that of the scientific professions or any other calling in life.

MR. PARKS: That is true. But I have told you and, as I say, opened myself as wide as I know how. What little I know, as you can judge for yourself, as I told you, and it's the truth, I was probably the poorest member of the Communist Party that has existed, and the few people that I knew, you probably know their names. I can see no way that this would be of additional help to this Committee. And, counsel, I am sure that you realize that if this was really consequential, I would do it, but you must realize the position.

MR. TAVENNER: Pardon me?

MR. PARKS: I say you must realize that, as inconsequential as I was in it, the few people that I knew, that it is very distasteful to me to be forced into that position.

MR. TAVENNER: I recognize that. There certainly can be no difference in opinion about that. It is a distasteful position to be in.

MR. PARKS: And I—

MR. TAVENNER: And you have avowed here that because of the difference in the situation with regard to the Party now from what it was in 1941 you have withdrawn, because you now understand the purposes of this organization which you joined years ago. Now, if you would be equally frank with regard to other people who are connected with this organization, then this Committee would be permitted to function in line with the statutory duty that rests upon it. And, therefore, I am going to ask you who it was who acted as secretary of this group.

MR. PARKS: And I can honestly say to you that I do not know, to the best of my remembrance.

MR. TAVENNER: Do you know Elizabeth Leech?

MR. PARKS: I don't recall ever meeting an Elizabeth Leech.

MR. TAVENNER: Do you know a person by the name of Elizabeth Glenn?

MR. PARKS: No, to the best of my knowledge, I do not know any person by that name.

MR. TAVENNER: Do you know a person by the name of Marjorie Potts?

MR. PARKS: To the best of my knowledge, I do not know anyone by the name of Marjorie Potts. I don't recall ever meeting these people.

MR. TAVENNER: Now, do you know Karen Morley?

MR. PARKS: I do.

MR. TAVENNER: Was Karen Morley a member of this group with you?

MR. PARKS: And I ask you again, counsel, to reconsider forcing me to name names. I told you that I was a member only for a short time and at that particular time, in my opinion, the people I knew were like myself. I don't think that this is really American justice, to force me to do this, when I have come to you three thousand miles and opened myself as I have.

MR. WALTER: Mr. Chairman, may I ask counsel a question? How can it be material to the purpose of this inquiry to have the names of people when we already know them? Aren't we actually, by insisting that this man testify as to names, overlooking the fact that we want to know what the organization did, what it hoped to accomplish, how it attempted to influence the thinking of the American people through the arts? So why is it so essential that we know the names of all of the people?

MR. PARKS: May I answer your question?

MR. WALTER: No, I am directing my question to counsel.

MR. TAVENNER: Although there is information relating to some of these individuals, some of them have evaded service of process, so that we cannot bring them here. That is one point. Another is that this Committee ought to be entitled to receive proof of information which it has in its files. There would be no way to really investigate Communist infiltration into labor without asking who are Communists in labor. And the same thing is true here in Hollywood.

MR. WALTER: But isn't it far more important to learn the extent of the activity, and what the purpose of the organization actually was, than to get a long list of names of bleeding hearts and fools, suckers, hard-boiled Communist politicians? I don't know as it makes too much difference. As long as we have a witness anxious to cooperate in carrying out what I conceive to be our purpose, I think the rest is all immaterial.

MR. TAVENNER: As to the various organizations, that was the subject of the testimony of about twenty witnesses or more here.

MR. WALTER: May I ask this witness a question, Mr. Chairman?

MR. WOOD: Yes, Mr. Walter.

MR. WALTER: Were you instructed to attempt to influence the thinking of the American people through various exhibitions on the stage or on the screen? Was that the purpose of your organization?

MR. PARKS: I was never instructed at any time to do this, and I think that if you are a follower of the motion-picture industry—if you go to the movies is what I mean—it is almost evident that this was not done in pictures.

MR. WALTER: Well, was it talked about? Was it the purpose of the Communist organization to attempt to set up a hard core in Hollywood that would slant pictures and performances so as to influence the thinking of the American people?

MR. PARKS: Not to my knowledge, Mr. Congressman. As I say, I was with a small group of actors, but, as a person who is close to the industry, I think that this is almost an impossibility. If you are familiar—you probably aren't—with the making of pictures, first of all it's impossible to do this as an actor. I was never asked to do it. It was never discussed. A script that is written is the important thing about making a picture. You can only make a stinker if you have a poor script.

MR. WOOD: On that point, wouldn't it be true that the writer of that script is in a position to very decidedly slant—

MR. PARKS: I really don't believe that this is true. There are, I think, on the average about four hundred pictures [per annum?] made in Hollywood, approximately. I don't know the exact number. This is divided up among a number of studios. A script passes through usually—and unfortunately—through too many hands. My opinion is that a script should be written by one man and directed by the same man. But this happens hardly ever. It passes through several writers, usually. They think if one man is good for jokes, they put him in for jokes, and another man, if they want a tear-jerker, they will assign him to that particular portion of it. It goes to an associate producer, a producer, the heads of the studios. I think you are familiar with the men that are the heads of the studios in Hollywood, and it is my studied opinion that this is an impossibility.

MR. WOOD: And didn't happen?

MR. PARKS: I do not believe that this has ever happened.

MR. WOOD: Now, you're leaving a very decided impression on my mind that there was no attempt to influence the character of the pictures that emanated from the studios that your group was connected with, that there was nothing off-color about the conduct of any of the people that belonged to it. Then, how could it possibly reflect against the members of this group for the names to be known, any more than it would if they belonged to the Young Men's Christian Association?

MR. PARKS: You cannot find one picture that has been slanted adversely, deliberately. Again, a man can make a mistake in judgment, Congressman. Now, to answer your last question, I feel as I do about it because myself I am a good example. As I said before, it's not easy, personally, for me to be here. Anybody who thinks it is is out of their mind. Over and above that, it is doubtful whether, after appearing before this Committee, my career will continue. It is extremely doubtful. For coming here and telling you the truth. You see, there were other things open to me that I could have done. But, feeling that I have not done anything wrong, I will tell you the truth. There were other things that were open to me that I could have done, and I chose not to do them.

MR. WALTER: Actually, the producers, particularly in recent years, have been very careful to examine scripts so that they would not be slanted. Is that not the fact?

MR. PARKS: I think that this is correct.

MR. DOYLE: Mr. Parks, have you any knowledge of the extent to which the movie industry, if it has, has made a conscientious effort to clean out any subversive influence in the industry either on the part of the actors or otherwise? Are you conscious of any fixed determination since 1946?

MR. PARKS: Yes, this is common knowledge.

MR. DOYLE: Well, is it part of your knowledge?

MR. PARKS: When I say "common knowledge" I mean mine, yours, everybody's. Everyone knows there has been a conscious effort to be absolutely free of any kind of Communism.

MR. DOYLE: May I ask this? A few minutes ago you said you were for a time honorary treasurer of one of these two groups that you stated you believed you were a member of. I think you said the extent of your duty as honorary treasurer was to sign a batch of checks.

MR. PARKS: That's right.

MR. DOYLE: To whom were those checks written or for what purpose?

MR. PARKS: Well, these were written to pay the office help, the secretaries, the clean-up man, the teachers, electric company, the utility bills, bills for lumber and paint for scenery, et cetera.

MR. DOYLE: What secretaries? How many secretaries and what office help for what organization?

MR. PARKS: For the Actors' Lab.

MR. DOYLE: How many secretaries did you have?

MR. PARKS: Well, it varied from none to one to, at certain times, when a show was being given and tickets were being mailed out to—I don't really recall—possibly three, four.

MR. DOYLE: Now, with reference to the cell which you said you attended some twelve or fifteen times, to the best of your recollection—

MR. PARKS: Yes.

MR. DOYLE: Was that attendance spread over from 1941 to 1945?

MR. PARKS: That's correct.

MR. DOYLE: Inclusive?

MR. PARKS: That's—

MR. DOYLE: I think you said your attendance averaged from five to twelve or fifteen.

MR. PARKS: Well, as I recall, it averaged from five, ten, twelve, in that—

MR. DOYLE: Were the majority of those in attendance men or women?

MR. PARKS: I had never thought about it. I suppose equally divided.

MR. DOYLE: Did you recognize at each meeting at which you were in attendance some actors and some actresses?

MR. PARKS: That's correct.

MR. DOYLE: About what proportion of the attendance, when twelve or fifteen were in attendance, were members of the actors' or actresses' group?

MR. PARKS: Well, when I say twelve, this as I recall—I'm using this number. I don't recall the exact number. I think that probably was the largest meeting. And these were all in the acting profession.

MR. DOYLE: Then, am I to understand that the entire attendance was, as far as you knew, members of the actors' profession?

MR. PARKS: I believe that this is true.

MR. DOYLE: Was this one cell limited to members of the actors' profession?

MR. PARKS: I believe it was limited to that.

MR. DOYLE: And I think you said you more or less had a social affair. Did you have refreshments?

MR. PARKS: Yes, we did. Coffee. Well, I'm serious when I say that. Coffee, doughnuts.

MR. DOYLE: Did the cell have dues?

MR. PARKS: It did.

MR. DOYLE: How much were the dues?

MR. PARKS: Well, I'm not, I don't think, a stingy man, but I'm known as a close man with a dollar. And, to the best of my knowledge, during the short time I was connected with this organization I could not have contributed more than fifty, sixty dollars.

MR. DOYLE: You mean you were connected with this one cell from 1941 to 1945, inclusive, yet you only paid a total of fifty or sixty dollars in those four years?

MR. PARKS: Well, the dues, as I recall, when you weren't working were about seventy-five cents a month, as I recall, and if you were working I think you paid some percentage. I didn't.

MR. DOYLE: To what organization did you pay the dues as a member of the cell?

MR. PARKS: I gave them to—right at the meeting.

MR. DOYLE: In check?

MR. PARKS: No, I believe I gave them in cash.

MR. DOYLE: Did you get a receipt for it?

MR. PARKS: No.

MR. DOYLE: Didn't ask for one?

MR. PARKS: Didn't ask for it.

MR. DOYLE: You mentioned that the cell members during the war discussed how the war was going. What did you mean by that?

MR. PARKS: Well, at that particular time, this was the major topic of conversation for most people in the country, and this was certainly true of myself and the actors that were at these particular meetings.

MR. DOYLE: Were there ever any resolutions submitted to the cell for consideration and action? I mean, were ever any communications read to you in the meeting from any other segment of the Communist Party? Did you ever listen to any communications read to you in any cell meeting those four years? If so, what?

MR. PARKS: I honestly cannot say that I ever heard any such communication. I don't believe so.

MR. DOYLE: Well, did anyone ever give you a report of any kind on Communist Party activities in those four years at any of these cell meetings? If so, what report? Weren't you interested in the progress of the Communist Party? Didn't anyone send you reports or give you an oral report?

MR. PARKS: Well, I think that certain things were mentioned at some of these meetings, that a certain number of people had been approached as far as our particular group was concerned, and this was about the extent of it.

MR. DOYLE: Basing this question on the fact that you deliberately laid the groundwork that you were idealistic, liberal, and progressive at the age of twenty-five, and so forth, and that is perhaps one reason you joined the Communist Party, or at least you gave it as one reason for your joining it—

MR. PARKS: No, that *is* the reason.

MR. DOYLE: Now, you made an effort—didn't you?—as a member of the cell—didn't that cell make efforts to increase its own membership in Hollywood?

MR. PARKS: I personally, to the best of my knowledge, never made such an effort.

MR. DOYLE: No, but you heard reports of what was being done by the cell?

MR. PARKS: That's correct.

MR. DOYLE: Well, what reports were given as to the activities of the cell?

MR. PARKS: Well, I don't remember. It's been a long time, as I told you.

MR. DOYLE: Well, now, you notice, Parks, I'm deliberately avoiding at this time asking you names of any other person.

MR. PARKS: Yes.

MR. DOYLE: I am assuming you want to be helpful to the Committee and tell the activities of the cell that you were in.

MR. PARKS: That's correct, and I am doing this.

MR. DOYLE: Now, manifestly, the cell was trying to increase its membership, wasn't it?

MR. PARKS: That's correct.

MR. DOYLE: And you were a member of the cell?

MR. PARKS: That's correct.

MR. DOYLE: You testified that you heard reports—

MR. PARKS: Well, as I say—

MR. DOYLE: —of what the cell was doing to increase its membership.

MR. PARKS: Well, you're really going a bit further than I said, Congressman.

MR. DOYLE: Well, you go as far as you honestly can and tell us what activities the cell participated in to increase its membership.

MR. PARKS: Well, I think that certain members of the group approached people about becoming a member of the Communist Party. I myself never did this.

MR. DOYLE: Well, names were submitted of other prospective members in your presence, were they not? Names of prospective members were read off, or possibilities were read off, weren't they?

MR. PARKS: It's possible that this was done.

MR. DOYLE: Well, was it done?

MR. PARKS: As I say, it's been a long time.

MR. DOYLE: Well, was any difference in philosophy between Communism and our form of government ever discussed in the cell? What did you discuss, besides drinking coffee?

MR. PARKS: Well, we didn't discuss drinking coffee, we just drank it. As I told you, at that particular time, the war was going on, and this was of major importance to every American, and was the major topic of conversation. Then, the discussions also had to do with conditions of actors—how we could get more money and better conditions.

MR. DOYLE: Well, was it discussed among you that you could get more money as a member of the Communist Party than you could just being a plain Democrat or Republican?

MR. PARKS: No, this was never discussed, to my knowledge.

MR. DOYLE: What was the Communist Party membership in this cell going to do for you in Hollywood? What were the benefits of it? Why did you join the cell? What did you get out of it or hope to get out of it?

MR. PARKS: As I told you, as a young man of twenty-five, with ideals and a feeling for the underdog, I felt that this was a legitimate political party, like you would join the Democrats or Republicans. I felt that this was the most liberal of the political parties of the time. All of this time I was a registered Democrat. I still am. And I have voted, from that time and before it, the straight Democratic ticket, because this was the practical thing to do. The other was an idealistic thing.

MR. DOYLE: About how many years were you in that cell before you began to be disillusioned?

MR. PARKS: Well, "disillusion" is not the exact word that I would choose.

MR. WOOD: Do I understand from that answer, sir, that you are not yet disillusioned about it?

MR. PARKS: No, no. Don't bend it. It was a question of lack of interest, of not finding—you may call it disillusionment if you want—not finding the things that, as a young man with those particular feelings, I thought I would find.

MR. DOYLE: Were most of the twelve or fifteen occasions on which you attended in 1941, 1942, and 1943? Or were most of them in 1944 and 1945?

MR. PARKS: I began to work more, and when I worked I didn't go. It would be hard for me to say. I do know that it just petered out like a spent rocket.

MR. DOYLE: Of course, you were well acquainted with some of the members of the cell?

MR. PARKS: Could I just explain one other thing when I say "when I worked I didn't go"? If you know anything about an actor's work, it goes from six in the morning till seven-thirty, eight at night, and when you do work you really don't have much time for anything else. And I have finished my forty-first picture in ten years. And this means I have been working pretty hard.

MR. DOYLE: I greatly respect the dedication of you artists to your profession and the diligence with which you work at it. Now, let me ask this further question: You, of course, in these four or five years, became acquainted with some of the members of the cell?

MR. PARKS: That's correct.

MR. DOYLE: Now, did you ever discuss the fact that you were becoming less satisfied? That you didn't find in the Communist Party membership that which you had hoped?

MR. PARKS: I believe that I did.

MR. DOYLE: With men or women?

MR. PARKS: I don't recall.

MR. DOYLE: Did they agree with you or did they disagree with you?

MR. PARKS: Well, as I recall, many times people agreed with what I felt. This is one of the reasons that I feel as I do about the people that I knew. I don't recall anyone giving me a really serious argument about the way I felt.

MR. DOYLE: While you were a member of that cell from 1941 to 1945, did it come at all clearly to you that the Communist Party was part of an international conspiracy against our form of government?

MR. PARKS: No, not while I was a member of that particular group.

MR. DOYLE: Did you, while a member of that cell, come to the conclusion that the Communist Party program was aimed at world domination?

MR. PARKS: Not at that particular time, I did not.

MR. DOYLE: When did you come to that conclusion, if at all?

MR. PARKS: Well, I think the way most everybody has come to that conclusion, with the recent and not so recent events in the history of the world, in the history of our country.

MR. WOOD: General Kearney.

MR. KEARNEY: Mr. Parks, I cannot understand your lack of interest in the Communist Party, when, from your own testimony, no member of the Communist Party ever appeared at any of the meetings attended by yourself and spoke.

MR. PARKS: I don't understand the question. Would you repeat it?

MR. KEARNEY: Well, you testified some few minutes ago that no member of the Communist Party ever spoke before any of the meetings that you attended.

MR. PARKS: No, I don't believe I said this.

MR. KEARNEY: That is my strong recollection of your testimony.

MR. PARKS: What I said, that to my recollection no—I think I used the words "big shot."

MR. KEARNEY: Well, were there members of the Communist Party who appeared at your meetings and spoke to your group?

MR. PARKS: We were all at that particular time members of the Communist Party.

MR. KEARNEY: I mean from other cells outside of your own.

MR. PARKS: There was one instance that I do recall when this did happen.

MR. KEARNEY: Can you give his name?

MR. PARKS: Again I wish you would not press me.

MR. WOOD: I will state for the benefit of the members: We are going to take a recess for lunch, at which time I ask the Committee to assemble back in the room for the purpose of determining this matter of policy. After we resume, the witness will be advised what the disposition of this Committee is with reference to his apparent disinclination to answer questions.

MR. VELDE: You stated that you now believe that the Communist Party of the United States is a subversive organization. Is that true?

MR. PARKS: Yes, I do.

MR. VELDE: But at that time that you went into the Communist Party, you felt that it was not a subversive organization?

MR. PARKS: That is quite correct.

MR. VELDE: Well, do you now know that at the time you belonged to the Communist Party it actually was a subversive organization—at that time?

* * *

MR. PARKS: I think a great change has occurred in this particular organization. That is my opinion.

MR. WALTER: In other words, you feel that the "do-gooders" have gotten out of it and there is nothing remaining now except the hard-boiled politicians?

MR. PARKS: I would say that in substance I agree with this.

MR. VELDE: Mr. Parks, how could you possibly know how other members of your particular cell felt about the purposes of the Communist Party organization?

MR. PARKS: Well, during the war a common purpose united all of the people of this country—practically all of the people of this country.

MR. VELDE: I don't think you are answering my question, Mr. Parks. I realize your reluctance in telling the membership of your organization.

MR. PARKS: Would you repeat the question then?

MR. VELDE: We had a witness down here last year, Lee Pressman, who was likewise reluctant to answer questions concerning his association with members of his own Communist Party cell, but eventually he did, and the Committee received his testimony, and it did the Committee a lot of good to realize that he would give the testimony. We realize that is true, and I understand your reluctance, but I think you will agree that the Committee is a legally organized committee and has a function.

MR. PARKS: I agree with this perfectly.

MR. VELDE: And as such it has the right to inquire as to the names of members of the Communist Party during the past.

MR. PARKS: This is your right.

MR. TAVENNER: I would like to ask just one or two questions. Mr. Parks, you are no doubt acquainted with Mr. Samuel G. Wood, a motion-picture producer and director?

MR. PARKS: Well, I'm quite— If this is the man that died a year or two ago, I'm an admirer of his work as a director. I don't believe I have ever met him.

MR. TAVENNER: But you know of whom I am speaking?

MR. PARKS: Yes, I do. Sam Wood? Right?

MR. TAVENNER: Yes. Now he testified as follows: "The Laboratory Theater, I think, is definitely under the control of the Communist Party. Any kid that goes in there with American ideals hasn't a chance in the world." Do you agree with his statement?

MR. PARKS: I disagree with it emphatically.

MR. TAVENNER: But do you agree that Mr. Wood is a man of honor and integrity?

MR. PARKS: But I disagree with this emphatically.

MR. TAVENNER: But do you still feel that, in light of that testimony, you should be the judge as to whether or not you testify as to who were connected with the theater—

MR. PARKS: At no time did I say that I was to be the judge. I was explaining my position to you. I have opened myself to you. And I am asking you gentlemen to be the judge, because this is not my duty here. I am a witness.

MR. TAVENNER: But you see there is a vast difference, apparently, between your opinion of the activities of that organization and the opinion of others.

MR. PARKS: Well, let me tell you then about the activities of this organization, and then you form your own opinion. This I think would be the only fair thing to do.

MR. TAVENNER: Proceed.

MR. PARKS: The activities of the Lab I think were admirable. I didn't happen to agree with certain of the objectives from a professional point of view. This was my disagreement. The work of the Lab I think has been very fine. I feel that the Actors' Lab as a training ground for actors was probably the finest of its kind, with the finest courses and the finest directors. It had the cream of the talent appearing on its stages and for the Army. I personally, for instance, appeared in three shows that we toured all over the Army camps, like *Three Men on a Horse, Arsenic and Old Lace, Kiss and Tell.* They had the greatest casts. You couldn't possibly have afforded these kinds of casts on Broadway. No producer could be this rich. Because these people from the bits to the starring parts were giving of their time. These are the reasons. I think the record of the Lab speaks for itself. I can't prove to you that it was a good acting school—this is impossible—but, in my opinion as an actor, this was a fine acting school.

MR. TAVENNER: I am not questioning the skill of the group.

MR. PARKS: Now, if you go down the list of the plays and the classics and the modern plays that the Lab has done, everything from Shakespeare and before, playwrights of all countries, this is the only way I think that you can judge the worth of an organization like this.

MR. TAVENNER: Well, do you agree that it was the purpose of the Communist Party to exert an influence through the professionals in Hollywood in the advancement of the cause of Communism?

MR. PARKS: No, I cannot agree with this at all.

MR. TAVENNER: Are you acquainted with the "Report on the National Convention in Relation to Cultural Movement" by V. J. Jerome, delivered in 1938?

MR. PARKS: No, I am not.

MR. TAVENNER: Well, let me read this paragraph to you:

> . . . The party increasingly cherishes and values specific qualities that the professionals bring into our midst. Gone is the day when we just took a professional comrade and assigned him to do nondescript party work. We say, on the contrary, "Comrades, you have something specific to give. You have the general contributions to make, in your loyalty, in your dues payment, your attendance, and your various duties and tasks to perform. But you have also a different contribution to make, whether you are a writer, a film artist, a radio performer. We need this no matter how valuable you are to the party on the picket line, and if in your turn you do not contribute, you would not really be valuable to us." . . .*

Doesn't that indicate to you a very definite plan on the part of the Communist Party to use its cells in the advancement of its program in Hollywood as well as elsewhere?

MR. PARKS: That would be my impression from listening to you read that.

MR. JACKSON: Mr. Parks, why in your opinion were you solicited for membership in the Communist Party?

MR. PARKS: Well, I imagine I wasn't working at the time, so it was not from a standpoint of getting any kind of working actor. I imagine that it was because I was young and probably, as I said, idealistic, and my views on the underprivileged and the underdog were probably known at the time, and I imagine that this was the reason.

MR. JACKSON: You think it had nothing to do with your potentialities as an actor? That you were solicited just as someone down on Skid Row might have been taken into the Party?

MR. PARKS: Well, I hope it wasn't quite to that extreme, but at the time—I started to say, "I hate to admit it," but I really don't—I was not considered to have much talent as an actor by many people.

MR. JACKSON: You say that today you are entirely out of sympathy with the Communist philosophy and with its outward manifestations in recent years.

MR. PARKS: I certainly am. I think that any power that is trying to, in my opinion, take over the world in this manner is wrong.

MR. JACKSON: I think a concomitant of that would be, then, that in case of armed conflict between the United States and the Soviet Union you would bear arms in defense of the United States?

MR. PARKS: Without question.

MR. WOOD: We will take a recess at this time until two thirty.

* Full text in Louis J. Russell's testimony above, pp. 226–233. —E.B.

Afternoon Session

MR. WOOD: The Committee will be in order. Let the record show that the members present are: Messrs. Walter, Doyle, Frazier, Velde, Kearney, Jackson, Potter, and Wood.

MR. MANDEL [counsel for the witness]: Mr. Chairman, Mr. Parks would like to talk to the Committee about the question of naming names. He would appreciate it if the Committee would hear what he has to say on the subject.

MR. WOOD: I thought he expressed himself pretty fully this morning. We are taking a good deal of time on this hearing. I think counsel has a few more questions. Maybe they will bring out what he wants to say.

MR. MANDEL: What he has to say, I think, is very pertinent at this point. I don't think we can judge it until he says it. It will only take him three minutes or so to say it. In view of the fact he has cooperated so completely with the Committee, I think he should be granted three minutes to say what he has to say. Then he is willing to be guided by the Committee.

MR. WOOD: I see no objection to it. Make it as brief as you can, Mr. Parks.

MR. PARKS: I will, Mr. Chairman. To be an actor, a good actor, you must really feel and experience, from the top of your head to the tip of your toes, what you are doing. As I told you, this is probably the most difficult morning and afternoon I have spent, and I wish that if it was at all possible —you see, it is a little different to sit there and to sit here, and for a moment if you could transfer places with me, mentally, and put yourself in my place . . . My people have a long heritage in this country. They fought in the Revolutionary War to make this country, to create this Government, of which this Committee is a part. I have two boys, one thirteen months, one two weeks. Is this the kind of heritage that I must hand down to them? Is this the kind of heritage that you would like to hand down to your children? And for what purpose? Children as innocent as I am or you are, people you already know . . . I don't think I would be here today if I weren't a star, because you know as well as I, even better, that I know nothing that would be of great service to this country. I think my career has been ruined because of this, and I would appreciate not having to— Don't present me with the choice of either being in contempt of this Committee and going to jail or forcing me to really crawl through the mud to be an informer. For what purpose? I don't think this is a choice at all. I don't think this is really sportsmanlike. I don't think this is American. I don't think this is American justice. I think to do something like that is more akin to what happened under Hitler, and what is happening in Russia today. I don't think this is American justice for an innocent mistake in judgment, if it was that, with the intention behind it only of making this country a better place in which to live. I think it is not befitting for this Committee to force me to make this kind of a choice. I don't think it is befitting to the purpose of the Committee to do this. As I told you, I think this is probably the most difficult thing I have done, and it seems to me it would impair the usefulness of this Committee to do this, because God knows it is difficult enough to come before this Committee and tell the truth. There was another choice open to me. I did not choose to use it. I chose to come and tell the truth. If you do this to me, I think it will impair the usefulness of this Committee to a great extent, because it will make it almost impossible for a person to come to you, as I have done, and open himself to you and tell you the truth. So I beg of you not to force me to do this.

MR. TAVENNER: Mr. Parks, there was a statement you made this morning which interested me a great deal. This is what you said: "This is a great industry"—speaking of the moving-picture industry—"and I don't say this only because it has been kind to me. It has a very important job to do, to entertain people, in certain respects to call attention to certain evils, but mainly to entertain." Now, do you believe that the persons who are in a position to call attention to certain evils ought to be persons who are dedicated to the principles of democracy as we understand them in this country?

MR. PARKS: I certainly agree.

MR. TAVENNER: Do you believe, on the other hand, that the persons who are in those responsible positions should be people who are antagonistic to the principles of democracy and our form of government, and who are members of a conspiracy to overthrow our Government?

MR. PARKS: Most assuredly I don't.

MR. TAVENNER: Then what is your opinion as to whether or not members of the Communist Party should be in positions of power and influence in the various unions which control the writing of scripts, the actors, and various other things which we have mentioned during the course of this hearing relating to the great industry of the moving pictures?

MR. PARKS: I thought I had made myself clear. I certainly do not believe that those people should be in any position of power to be able to direct this.

MR. TAVENNER: Then we will ask your cooperation, before this hearing is over, in helping us to ascertain those who are or have been members of the Communist Party. Mr. Parks, it is generally recognized that the Communist Party must raise money by various methods. Will you tell us what you know of the methods by which money was raised to promote the purposes of the Communist Party while you were a member?

MR. PARKS: I don't believe I can help you on this because I really don't know.

MR. TAVENNER: Did you take any part in fund-raising campaigns which were engineered by the Communist Party or by organizations known to you to be Communist-front organizations?

MR. PARKS: I don't recall at the moment. This is like asking a man what he did in 1941, and he says, "I don't remember." If you say to him, "Did you go fishing up on the Oregon River?" he will say, "Yes, yes, I did." If you would accommodate me in this way perhaps I can answer your question.

* * *

MR. TAVENNER: I am merely asking what you know about the raising of Communist Party funds.

MR. PARKS: At the moment I don't recall knowing anything about it. As I just told you, I have appeared in many benefits over the past few years for many organizations, and if you could be more specific perhaps I could be more specific. I am not trying to avoid the question.

MR. TAVENNER: I have no trick question here through which I am attempting to lead you into denial of something we know about.

MR. PARKS: I have come here and have been as open and aboveboard as I can. I think the testimony will bear me out. I am willing to help you all I can if you could be more specific. As I told you, I have appeared at many benefits over many years.

MR. TAVENNER: As far as you know, were any of these fund-raising benefits conducted for the benefit of the Communist Party?

MR. PARKS: I don't recall any at the moment. But again I say, I have been to many benefits over many years.

MR. TAVENNER: At the beginning of the afternoon session, you made a statement which I cannot let go by without challenging it. You said you were subpoenaed here because you were a star. Mr. Parks, you were subpoenaed here because the Committee had information that you had knowledge about Communist Party activities and that you had been a member.

MR. PARKS: All I meant was that I know nothing of any conspiracy that is trying to overthrow this Government. You know this even better than I. And my point was that if I was working in a drugstore I doubt whether I would be here.

MR. TAVENNER: We have had many people before this Committee who have been engaged in very menial forms of making a livelihood, and that will be so in the future.

MR. PARKS: Please don't take that in the wrong spirit, because it was not meant in the wrong spirit.

MR. TAVENNER: I did not fully understand your reference to the possible destruction of your career by being subpoenaed here. You did not mean to infer by that that this Committee was bringing you here because of any effect it might have on your career?

MR. PARKS: No, I didn't infer that at all. What I meant, and what I said, was that because of this, in my opinion, I have no career left.

MR. TAVENNER: Don't you think that that question might be influenced to some extent by the fullness of the cooperation that you give the Committee in a situation of this kind?

MR. PARKS: I have tried to cooperate with the Committee in every way that I feel that I can, but I think the damage has been done. This is my personal opinion.

MR. JACKSON: Don't you think that more than the damage that possibly has been done you by this Committee—which, after all, is an expression of the will of the American people and operates under the mandate of the people—don't you think the great damage occurred when you became a member of an organization which has been found to advocate the overthrow of every constitutional form of government in the world? Is this Committee more to blame than your own act in affiliating with that organization?

MR. PARKS: As I told you, Congressman, when I was a good deal younger than I am now, ten years ago, I felt a certain way about certain things. I was an idealist, I felt strongly and I still do about the underdog, and it was for these reasons that this organization appealed to me. I later found that this would not fulfill my needs. At that time, this I don't even believe was a mistake. It may have been a mistake in judgment. This is debatable. But my two boys, for instance—I would rather have them make the same mistake I did under those circumstances than not feel like making any mistake at all and be a cow in the pasture. If a man doesn't feel that way about certain things, then he is not a man. I do not believe that I did anything wrong.

MR. JACKSON: You say, Mr. Parks, that your association at best was haphazard, and, in your own words, you are afraid you were not a very good Communist.

MR. PARKS: That is correct.

MR. JACKSON: Upon what do you base the opinion that the people whose names you have in your possession probably have severed their relations with the Communist Party?

MR. PARKS: In my opinion, the few people that I knew are people like myself and feel the way that I do.

MR. JACKSON: Well, of course, that is merely your judgment of the matter. Have you discussed their Party affiliations with those with whom you were affiliated in the Party?

MR. PARKS: I have not. But these people I knew, and this is my honest opinion. You know these people. You know them as well as I do.

MR. JACKSON: I will point out to you that in a recent case [Presumably that of Hiss. —E.B.] here in Washington some of the highest officials in Government testified to their honest belief that a man with whom they had been associated had never been a member of the Communist Party and in no way constituted any threat to our institutions, but every man who reads the newspapers knows how fallacious that opinion was. I merely point out that after all, in all good faith, you might be wrong as to the present status of membership in the Communist Party of some people whose names you evidence hesitancy about disclosing.

MR. PARKS: These men you speak of did not act as informers in any sense of the word. I told you about these people. You know who the people are. And I have told you my opinion of them. And I have told you that I think to force me to do something like this is not befitting this Committee. I don't think the Committee would benefit from it, and I don't think this is American justice to make me choose one or the other or be in contempt of this Committee, which is a Committee of my Government, or crawl through the mud for no purpose. Because you know who these people are. This is what I beg you not to do.

MR. JACKSON: That is also problematic, Mr. Parks. I know who they are, maybe you are entirely right, but I still think it is within the province of the Committee to determine how far they will go.

MR. PARKS: I am asking the Committee not to do it. I am not setting myself up as a judge. I am asking you to judge.

MR. VELDE: I think you are wrong in assuming we know all of the activities in which you were engaged and all the people you were engaged in those activities with. I am satisfied you are wrong in that, and possibly you could furnish us with a lot of information we do not have, and I feel sure you would be willing to do that to serve the best interests of the United States, of which you are a citizen.

MR. PARKS: I have told you, to the best of my ability, of my activities.

MR. WOOD: We will ask at this time to [make a] break in the testimony of this witness. I request that he not leave the jurisdiction of the Committee until later this afternoon.

* * *

The Committee on Un-American Activities met in executive session at 4 p.m. in room 226, Old House Office Building, the Honorable John S. Wood (Chairman) presiding.

Committee members present: Representatives John S. Wood (Chairman), Francis E. Walter, Clyde Doyle, James B. Frazier, Jr., Harold H. Velde, Bernard W. Kearney, Donald L. Jackson, and Charles E. Potter.

Staff members present: Frank S. Tavenner, Jr., Counsel; Louis J. Russell, Senior Investigator; William A. Wheeler, Investigator; Thomas W. Beale, Sr., Assistant Counsel; and A. S. Poore, Editor.

MR. WOOD: Mr. Parks, at the conclusion of the morning session, the Committee had a meeting, and it was the unanimous expression of the members of the Committee that we were going to seek your further cooperation in an executive session for further testimony that will not be publicized until such time, if at all, as the Committee itself may deem expedient.

It may never happen, but it is only fair to say to you that it is in the discretion of the Committee at any time to make public any information that you may see fit to give in this executive session. Until such time, if it does happen, it will be kept in the confidential files of the Committee. With that statement, counsel will now propound additional questions.

MR. MANDEL: Is it the intention of the Committee that unless he answers these questions in private—that is, in executive session—they intend to cite him for contempt of this Committee?

MR. WOOD: The Committee makes no threats.

MR. MANDEL: We haven't approached it as a matter of threat. Just to clear his thinking so that he is fully informed in his own mind of the consequences of following that path.

MR. WOOD: Counselor, the Committee did not discuss that phase of it. It is entirely possible, if Mr. Parks placed himself in the position here of being in contempt of Congress, that the Committee may request a citation for that purpose. On the other hand, it may not. I cannot speak for the Committee. Does that answer your question?

MR. MANDEL: No, not quite. I would like to spend another minute on it. In view of Mr. Parks's general attitude of being cooperative—and everyone easily understands here what is motivating him—he feels so bad about what he has to do, and if he thought there was any chance that you would elicit from him information that was important to you, he would very gladly give it to you. It is only saving that little bit of something that you live with. You have to see and walk in Hollywood with that. You have to meet your children and your wife with it, and your friends. It is that little bit that you want to save. Although I don't want to ask the Committee to commit itself, in fairness to Mr. Parks, he may have to sacrifice the arm with gangrene in order to save the body. Even though he doesn't like it, he will walk around the rest of his life without an arm. I realize the purposes of this Committee, and our attitude has been one of cooperation. We want to go right through with that. Now, if that is going to be the penalty that he eventually will have to pay, then I have to help him think a different way. I have to urge him a different way. His honest and sincere opinion is that what he is going to give you will only eat up his insides and you will get nothing, no more than you have today. This is a conviction of this man.

MR. WOOD: Mr. Attorney, the Committee has to be the judge of what information has pertinency and relevancy. It can't take the opinions of other people. I have tried to be frank about it, and the Committee is very anxious—I think you will agree—to be considerate of this man. The Committee is in no sense responsible for the position he finds himself in, but we are responsible for the position we find ourselves in.

* * *

MR. TAVENNER: Mr. Parks, are you acquainted with an effort made to raise funds for the *New Masses* magazine, which was in the form of a party held at the home of Frank Tuttle on June 8, 1945?

MR. PARKS: No, sir, I don't recall any such party at Frank Tuttle's house. I was at his house, I believe, only once, and as I remember it there were maybe two or three people, and it was purely a social evening. This is the best of my recollection.

MR. TAVENNER: I have just learned there are two Frank Tuttles in Hollywood. Are you acquainted with that fact?

MR. PARKS: No. I only know one Frank Tuttle, who is a director in Hollywood.

MR. TAVENNER: He is the one that I had reference to.

MR. PARKS: That is the one that I was acquainted with. I don't know whether he is out there now.

MR. TAVENNER: Did you attend a meeting of a cultural group of the Communist Party at the home of Hugo Butler?

MR. PARKS: I have been to Hugo Butler's house twice, I think. One was on a matter of—I believe I read a script of his. The other time, to the best of my recollection, was a party given for—as I recall, it was given for the people who had come before your Committee in 1947. This is the best of my recollection. I don't recall ever going to a party for—what was it? *New Masses?*

MR. TAVENNER: No. This party that I am speaking of now did not necessarily have anything to do with *New Masses*. This is a different meeting that I am referring to now at the home of Hugo Butler. It is alleged to have taken place on January 3, 1945.

MR. PARKS: No, I don't recall going there for a party at that time at all. I am being very honest when I say that. As I say, I know where he lives, and I think I have been there twice.

MR. TAVENNER: Was Hugo Butler a member of the Communist Party, to your knowledge?

MR. PARKS: No, sir, I have no knowledge of Hugo Butler at all being a member.

MR. TAVENNER: Did you ever attend a Communist Party meeting at which he was present?

MR. PARKS: Not to my recollection.

MR. TAVENNER: Was Frank Tuttle a member of the Communist Party, to your knowledge?

MR. PARKS: This, counsel, I do not know. I don't believe I have ever heard that. I don't believe that I have ever, to the very best of my knowledge, ever attended any meeting of such a nature with Frank Tuttle.

MR. TAVENNER: Who were the members of the cell of the Communist Party to which you were assigned during the period from 1941 on up to the time you disassociated yourself from the Party about 1945?

MR. PARKS: This is what I have been talking about. This is the thing that I am no longer fighting for myself, because I tell you frankly that I am probably the most completely ruined man that you have ever seen. I am fighting for a principle, I think, if Americanism is involved in this particular case. This is what I have been talking about. I do not believe that it befits this Committee to force me to do this. I do not believe it befits this Committee or its purposes to force me to do this. This is my honest feeling about it. I don't think that this is fair play. I don't think it is in the spirit of real Americanism. These are not people that are a danger to this country, gentlemen, the people that I knew. These are people like myself.

MR. TAVENNER: Mr. Chairman, if the witness refuses to answer the question, I see very little use in my asking him about other individuals.

MR. WOOD: The witness, of course, has got to make up his own mind as to whether he will or will not do it. It isn't sufficient, as far as this Committee is concerned, to say that in your opinion it is unfair or un-American. The question is: Do you refuse to answer or will you answer it?

MR. MANDEL: At this point I would like to ask the Chairman whether he is directing the witness to answer.

MR. WOOD: The witness has been asked. He must answer or decline to answer.

MR. MANDEL: I think a little more is needed. He must be directed to answer, and if he refuses to answer, just merely asking him and not going beyond I don't believe under law is sufficient. I think he has to be directed and told, "You have got to answer."

MR. WOOD: I don't understand any such rule, but, in order to avoid any controversy, I direct the witness to answer the question.

MR. PARKS: I do not refuse to answer the question, but I do feel that this Committee is doing a really dreadful thing that I don't believe the American people will look kindly on. This is my opinion. I don't think that they will consider this as honest, just, and in the spirit of fair play.

MR. JACKSON: Mr. Chairman, might I interpose at this point? Mr. Parks, we are, each one of us, individually responsible to the American people. I think that our concept of our responsibility is a thing which we ourselves are fully conscious of. That determination must rest with the individual members of the Committee and the Committee as a whole. I, for one, resent having my duties pointed out to me.

MR. PARKS: I am not pointing the duty out.

MR. JACKSON: The inference is that we are doing something which is un-American in nature. That is a personal opinion of yours, and I merely think that it should be in the record. We have accountability for which we must account and for which we must answer.

MR. WOOD: The witness has said he doesn't refuse to answer, so I assume he is ready to answer.

MR. MANDEL: I think the Committee and the individual members of the Committee are all seeking within themselves to do the right thing. There is no question about that. I think, in the same spirit, no one can, with the heritage that Mr. Parks has to uphold, think that he isn't as loyal as any member of this Committee, and that he has to do the right thing as we Americans in our elections do and choose. Of course, when the final gong goes down, he intends, as he indicated, to respect the will of this Committee, but, I think justly, he reserves the right to talk to you gentlemen and possibly persuade you to think differently.

MR. WOOD: The Committee took the view, sir, that perhaps there might be some merit in your contention if we were still in an open hearing, but we are not. It is an executive session.

MR. MANDEL: I realize that, and I want to thank the Committee for this consideration. I think it should have been done first before we started here, but this session is a very private session or executive session, which is very considerate of the Committee, and the record should so state. May I have a minute to talk to Mr. Parks?

MR. WOOD: Yes. You may retire if you like.

MR. MANDEL: I make this request of the Committee: I want no promise from you, but just as a matter of finding what is the sportsmanlike attitude, that what he gives you will not be used in that way if it can be helped, without embarrassing these people in the same position he finds himself in today.

MR. WOOD: Nobody on this Committee has any desire to smear the name of anybody. That isn't of benefit to this Committee in the discharge of its duties. I think all of the American people who have viewed the work of the Committee dispassionately and impartially will agree with that.

MR. MANDEL: The reason I asked is because, in the struggle that Mr. Parks is going through, I think the internal struggle would go a little lighter having that statement from you.

MR. TAVENNER: If you will just answer the question, please. The question was: Who were the members of the Communist Party cell to which you were assigned during the period from 1941 until 1945?

MR. PARKS: Well, Morris Carnovsky, Joe—

MR. TAVENNER: Will you spell that name?

MR. PARKS: I couldn't possibly spell it. Carnovsky, Joe Bromberg, Sam Rossen, Anne Revere, Lee Cobb.

MR. TAVENNER: What was the name?

MR. PARKS: Cobb. Gale Sondergaard, Dorothy Tree. Those are the principal names that I recall.

MR. TAVENNER: What was the name of Dorothy Tree's husband? Was it not Michael Uris?

MR. PARKS: Yes.

MR. TAVENNER: Was he a member?

MR. PARKS: Not to my knowledge.

MR. TAVENNER: Do you know whether Michael Uris was a member of any other cell of the Communist Party?

MR. PARKS: No, I don't know this at all.

MR. TAVENNER: I believe he was a writer, was he not, as distinguished from an actor?

MR. PARKS: I think he was a writer, yes.

MR. TAVENNER: The persons whose names you have mentioned were all actors?

MR. PARKS: Yes, that's correct.

MR. TAVENNER: Can you recall the names of others who were at one time members of that cell?

MR. PARKS: That's about all I recall right now.

MR. TAVENNER: Was Howard Da Silva a member?

MR. PARKS: No, I don't believe that I ever attended a meeting with Howard Da Silva.

MR. TAVENNER: Was Howard Da Silva a member of the Communist Party, to your knowledge?

MR. PARKS: Not to my knowledge.

MR. TAVENNER: Was Roman Bohman [Bohnen?] a member?

MR. PARKS: Yes.

MR. TAVENNER: He is now deceased, I believe.

MR. PARKS: He is dead.

MR. TAVENNER: Was James Cagney a member at any time?

MR. PARKS: Not to my knowledge. I don't recall ever attending a meeting with him.

MR. TAVENNER: Was he a member of the Communist Party, to your knowledge?

MR. PARKS: I don't recall ever hearing that he was.

MR. TAVENNER: Sam Jaffe?

MR. PARKS: I don't recall ever attending a meeting with Sam Jaffe.

MR. TAVENNER: Was he a member of the Communist Party, to your knowledge?

MR. PARKS: I don't recall any knowledge that Sam Jaffe was ever a member of the Communist Party.

MR. TAVENNER: John Garfield?

MR. PARKS: I don't recall ever being at a meeting with John Garfield.

MR. TAVENNER: Do you recall whether John Garfield ever addressed a Communist Party meeting when you were present?

MR. PARKS: I don't recall any such occasion.

MR. TAVENNER: Marc Lawrence, was he a member of that cell?

MR. PARKS: I believe he was. I wouldn't say with certainty. I believe so.

MR. TAVENNER: What is there in your memory that leads you to believe that he was a member of the Communist Party?

MR. PARKS: Well, as I told you, I didn't attend very many meetings, and I believe I recall that he was there. I don't swear to it.

MR. TAVENNER: Was it during the early part or the latter part of your membership that you have that recollection of him?

MR. PARKS: Well, this I couldn't say. I really don't remember.

MR. MANDEL: May I suggest to counsel, in view of the general feeling of the witness—I don't mean to rush you, but this whole thing being so distasteful—I wonder if we can proceed a little faster so he doesn't suffer so much while this is going on.

MR. TAVENNER: I want him to be accurate on it. I purposely do not want to rush him into answering about matters as important as these.

MR. MANDEL: I didn't mean that. I am just trying to be considerate of the man's feelings, doing something that—

MR. TAVENNER: I asked you this morning about Karen Morley. Was she a member of the Communist Party?

MR. PARKS: Yes, she was.

MR. TAVENNER: Was she in this particular cell that you have described?

MR. PARKS: Yes, she was.

MR. TAVENNER: Richard Collins, were you acquainted with him?

MR. PARKS: I know Richard Collins. He was not to my knowledge a member of the Communist Party.

(*At this point Representative Clyde Doyle left the hearing room.*)

MR. TAVENNER: Did Communist Party organizers from the State of California appear before your committee from time to time?

MR. PARKS: Not to the best of my recollection. I don't believe I ever met any of them or ever saw any of them.

MR. TAVENNER: Were lectures given at any time or study courses given in your cell in which persons outside of your cell took part?

MR. PARKS: The only one that I recall at this time was a talk by John Howard Lawson.

MR. TAVENNER: What was John Howard Lawson's connection with the Communist Party?

MR. PARKS: I don't really know.

MR. TAVENNER: Fred Graff, was he a member of this group?

MR. PARKS: The name doesn't ring a bell at all.

MR. TAVENNER: Georgia Backus?

MR. PARKS: No, I don't recall ever being at a meeting with Georgia Backus.

MR. TAVENNER: Meta Reis Rosenberg?

MR. PARKS: I don't believe I know the lady.

MR. TAVENNER: Robert Rossen?

MR. PARKS: No, I don't recall ever being at a meeting with him.

MR. TAVENNER: Do you know whether he was a member of your cell, even if you were not in a meeting with him?

MR. PARKS: No. To the best of my knowledge, I have no information at all.

MR. TAVENNER: Philip Loeb?

MR. PARKS: No, I don't recall I know the gentleman at all.

MR. TAVENNER: Lloyd Gough?

MR. PARKS: Yes, I believe he was a— I saw him at a couple of meetings.

MR. TAVENNER: Sterling Hayden?

MR. PARKS: No, I don't recall ever being at a meeting with Sterling Hayden.

MR. TAVENNER: Will Geer?

MR. PARKS: No, I don't recall ever being in a meeting with Will Geer.

MR. TAVENNER: Victor Killian, Sr.?

MR. PARKS: Yes, I recall that he attended at least one meeting.

MR. TAVENNER: Victor Killian, Jr.?

MR. PARKS: I don't believe I am acquainted with the gentleman at all.

MR. TAVENNER: Lionel Stander?

MR. PARKS: I have met him. I don't recall ever attending a meeting with him.

MR. TAVENNER: Andy Devine?

MR. PARKS: I don't recall ever attending a meeting with Andy Devine.

MR. TAVENNER: Edward G. Robinson?

MR. PARKS: No, I don't recall ever attending a meeting with Edward G. Robinson.

MR. TAVENNER: Mr. Chairman, I think nearly all of these people have either been subpoenaed or we have tried to find them. Some of them unquestionably are attempting to avoid service. Do you know Hester Sondergaard?

MR. PARKS: No, I don't recall ever meeting her. I believe that is Gale Sondergaard's sister.

MR. TAVENNER: Do you know whether she is married?

MR. PARKS: No, I don't.

MR. TAVENNER: Francis Edwards Faragoh?

MR. PARKS: No.

MR. TAVENNER: Vera Caspary?

MR. PARKS: No, I don't believe that I know the woman.

MR. TAVENNER: Madeleine Carroll?

MR. PARKS: No, I don't recall ever attending a meeting with Madeleine Carroll.

MR. TAVENNER: Was she a member of this group, to your knowledge?

MR. PARKS: I have no knowledge of that.

MR. TAVENNER: Gregory Peck?

MR. PARKS: I have no remembrance of ever attending a meeting with Gregory Peck.

MR. TAVENNER: Humphrey Bogart?

MR. PARKS: I don't recall ever attending a meeting with Humphrey Bogart.

(*At this point Representative Donald L. Jackson left the hearing room.*)

MR. WALTER: I think you could get some comfort out of the fact that the people whose names have been mentioned have been subpoenaed, so that if they ever do appear here it won't be as a result of anything that you have testified to.

(*At this point Representative Bernard W. Kearney left the hearing room.*)

MR. PARKS: It is no comfort whatsoever.

MR. TAVENNER: Do you know of any other person now whose name comes to your recollection?

MR. PARKS: No, I don't recall anyone else.

MR. TAVENNER: I think that is all, Mr. Chairman.

MR. POTTER: I would like to say, Mr. Chairman, that Mr. Parks's testimony has certainly been refreshing in comparison with the other witnesses that we have had today.

MR. WOOD: I am sure you reflect the sentiments of the entire Committee. We appreciate your cooperation. You are excused.

* * *

(By order of the Committee the following letters are being included in the record at this point:*)

July 23, 1953

HON. HAROLD VELDE,
Chairman, House Committee on Un-American Activities,
Washington, D.C.

DEAR CHAIRMAN VELDE:

I have your letter of July 17, and it was so good to hear from you.

Pursuant to your suggestion, I'm enclosing a sworn copy of the letter I sent you and also authorize you and your Committee to release the testimony I gave you in executive session.

Again let me take this opportunity to thank you for your consideration, I remain

Respectfully,
LARRY PARKS

* "This point" is 1953, because the testimony given in executive session was not released till then. —E.B.

(Sworn letter mentioned by Larry Parks in his letter dated July 23, 1953:)

July 15, 1953

HON. HAROLD VELDE,
Chairman, House Committee on Un-American Activities,
Washington, D.C.

DEAR CHAIRMAN VELDE:

After careful consideration, I wish to file a clarifying statement of my point of view on the Communist problem with your Committee. In rereading my public testimony before the House Committee on Un-American Activities, I am now convinced that it improperly reflects my true attitude toward the malignancy of the Communist Party.

If there is any way in which I can further aid in exposing the methods of entrapment and deceit through which Communist conspirators have gained the adherence of American idealists and liberals, I hope the Committee will so advise me. Perhaps some of the confusion now apparent to me in my testimony before your Committee can best be explained by the fact that I was the first cooperative witness from Hollywood to appear before your Committee and at the time I was under really great strain and tension. Upon reflection, I see that I did not adequately express my true beliefs—beliefs which have even deepened and strengthened since my appearance.

Above all, I wish to make it clear that I support completely the objectives of the House Committee on Un-American Activities. I believe fully that Communists and Communist intrigues should be thoroughly exposed and isolated and thus rendered impotent.

In the light of events which have transpired since I appeared as a witness before your Committee, it is crystal clear that no one who really believes in a progressive program for humanity can support any part of the Communist program. No true liberal can doubt that Soviet Communism constitutes as grave a threat to the rights of man today as once did Hitler Fascism. The most recent attack by the Soviet Army on unarmed German workers makes it crystal-clear that their interest in labor is only to increase their power.

Liberals must now embrace the cause of anti-Communism with the same dedication and zeal as we once did that of anti-Nazism. The enemy is the same though the labels have changed.

It is my conviction that to assist your Committee in obtaining full information about the Communist Party and its activities is the duty of all who possess such evidence. Certainly, if I were to testify today I would not testify as I did in 1951—that to give such testimony is to "wallow in the mud"—but on the contrary I would recognize that such cooperation would help further the cause in which many of us were sincerely interested when we were duped into joining and taking part in the Communist Party.

My statement about not wanting my sons to become "cows in the pasture" obviously needs clarification. The thought I really meant to convey was that my sons should not become indifferent to the plight of the people less fortunate than themselves. It is my conviction that through sympathetic understanding and aid to the repressed peoples, we Americans cannot only best represent American traditions but also effectively aid in combating the false power of Communism. I want my sons to participate fully in the search for democratic answers to the continuing threat of totalitarianism—Communist or Fascist. To that end, I will do all within my power as one who once was duped but has since learned the hard way about the guileful traps which Communism can set for an unwary idealist or liberal.

I sincerely hope the Committee will publish the statement of my militant anti-Communist beliefs at the earliest possible date.

Sincerely,
LARRY PARKS

The early 1950s—the McCarthy era—had different effects upon different people: character is fate. Propelled against his will into bearing witness against Communists, Larry Parks came to believe one should willingly bear witness against Communists. This shift was called "repentance" in that period, and quite without irony: we shall find certain people, below, complaining that Arthur Miller was not "repentant." Sterling Hayden, for his part, repented his *anti*-Communism. Readers of the testimony here will have a shock when they open his autobiography—*Wanderer* (New York, 1963)—and find that two of the three people to whom it is dedicated are Rockwell Kent and Warwick M. Tompkins, "Sailormen, Artists, Radicals." On page 371, we find:

> You know, I don't know why I got out of the Party any more than I know why I joined. I could say a lot of things about those people I knew in the Party—and you know something? It would all be good.
>
> I'd like to take a two-page spread in the *Hollywood Reporter* and in *Variety* and I'd let go the goddamnedest blast, let people know who the real subversives are. I wrote this out last night: "You loud-mouthed self-styled patriots in this business had better wake up. . . . You think those people are trying to subvert your precious Hollywood? They're not. They happen to believe in planned social order. They look up to Russia as the leader of the world socialist movement. . . . Now you people allegedly believe in free competition. You want the world to follow in our footsteps, so you invest million of bucks all over hell and go on trying to influence people. Yet when the socialist world does this you scream Foul."

And on page 378, again remarks addressed by the narrator to his psychoanalyst:

I'll say this too, that if it hadn't been for you I wouldn't have turned into a stoolie for J. Edgar Hoover. I don't think you have the foggiest notion of the contempt I have had for myself since the day I did that thing. . . . Fuck it! And fuck you too.

APRIL 10, 1951:

Sterling Hayden

The Committee on Un-American Activities met at 10 a.m. in room 226, Old House Office Building, the Honorable John S. Wood (Chairman) presiding.

Committee members present: Representatives John S. Wood, Francis E. Walter, Morgan M. Moulder, Clyde Doyle, Harold H. Velde, Bernard W. Kearney (appearance as noted in transcript), Donald L. Jackson, and Charles E. Potter.

Staff members present: Frank S. Tavenner, Jr., Counsel; Thomas W. Beale, Sr., Assistant Counsel; Louis J. Russell, Senior Investigator; William A. Wheeler, Courtney E. Owens, and James A. Andrews, Investigators; John W. Carrington, Clerk, and A. S. Poore, Editor.

MR. WOOD: I will ask the members of the press and photographers taking pictures here to try to disturb the proceedings as little as possible. Mr. Counsel, are you ready to proceed?

MR. TAVENNER: Yes, Mr. Chairman. We are ready to proceed this morning with the continuance of the Hollywood hearings.

MR. WOOD: Is Mr. Hayden in the hearing room?

MR. HAYDEN: Yes.

MR. TAVENNER: When and where were you born, Mr. Hayden?

MR. HAYDEN: March 26, 1916, Montclair, New Jersey.

MR. TAVENNER: What is your present occupation?

MR. HAYDEN: Actor.

MR. TAVENNER: Will you please state for the Committee your educational background, just briefly?

MR. HAYDEN: Well, I went to public schools in Montclair, New Jersey, up until the time I was ten years old. After that we started moving around, and I finished about half of my second year high school at various places in New England, and then quit and went to sea.

MR. TAVENNER: How old were you when you went to sea?

MR. HAYDEN: Fifteen.

MR. TAVENNER: What do you mean, you "went to sea"?

MR. HAYDEN: Well, I simply left home and started working on ships, and worked seven years sailing vessels, fishing boats, and so forth.

MR. TAVENNER: You followed that occupation for seven years?

MR. HAYDEN: Yes. That was my trade.

MR. TAVENNER: During that period of time did you become master of a ship?

MR. HAYDEN: When I was twenty-one I finally got a master's license and took command of a ship and started making long voyages.

MR. TAVENNER: During that period of time did you become acquainted with a Captain Warwick Tompkins?

MR. HAYDEN: Yes. I met him when I was fourteen, in Boston, Massachusetts. He had a schooner and I wanted to go to work on it, but he said I was too young. I never got to know him too well personally at that time.

MR. TAVENNER: After the completion of your experiences at sea, when you became shipmaster, what calling did you follow?

MR. HAYDEN: Another fellow and I tried to operate a schooner. We didn't have much success. We lost the ship, finally. I was broke and in New York, and through accident I met a producer with Paramount and made a test and got a contract May 1, 1940, as an actor.

MR. TAVENNER: And how long did you follow that occupation?

MR. HAYDEN: Well, ever since, except for the war years. I left Hollywood in the fall of 1941 and returned to Hollywood under contract in the spring of 1946, so I was away for five years.

MR. TAVENNER: Then you were in Hollywood under your first contract between 1940 and 1941?

MR. HAYDEN: Yes, sir.

MR. TAVENNER: Will you tell the Committee how you obtained your first contract with Paramount?

MR. HAYDEN: Well, I was pretty much of a fluke. I had never given a thought to going into the acting profession, but the seafaring thing was washed up, and I simply met a correspondent in Boston who knew a producer, and he told the producer about me, and he contacted me in New York and made a test, a very bad test, but it got me a contract with Paramount and I went to work as an actor.

MR. TAVENNER: While you were on the West Coast serving under this first contract, was Captain Warwick Tompkins on the West Coast also?

MR. HAYDEN: Yes. He had at that time—I believe in 1938 or 1937—he had shifted his base of operations from Boston to San Francisco, therefore he was in San Francisco in 1940 when I first got there. I felt kind of lost in Hollywood, not really being an actor by inclination, and one time when I was feeling particularly low I decided to pay him a visit. I went to San Francisco and saw him. He at that time, or previously, had become, I believe, an open and avowed Communist. He made no bones about it. He talked about very little else, and he started to deluge me with propaganda.

MR. TAVENNER: Were you a Communist at that time?

MR. HAYDEN: No. It had never entered my head.

MR. TAVENNER: Do you recall meeting any other persons at that time who you either knew then or have found out since were members of the Communist Party, through your connections with Captain Tompkins?

MR. HAYDEN: On one of those visits, I believe probably that it was in 1941, while he was in San Francisco living on his ship, he said he wanted to introduce me to what he called "an old warrior in the class struggle," "Pop" Folkoff. I met him at a luncheon. I thought he was a retired tailor at that time. What he was I don't know to this day. Who else I may have met that year I don't remember too clearly.

MR. TAVENNER: What was the way in which Captain Tompkins went about consulting with you regarding Communism?

MR. HAYDEN: I wouldn't say he consulted with me. I think he recognized I was at a peculiar stage in my life. I was sort of betwixt and between. The sea had always been my calling. This was now denied me, or I had denied myself it. I was feeling restless and dissatisfied in Hollywood. He used the device of talking and talking and asking why I didn't read more. I had never thought in political terms at all. That was another world, which I am not particularly proud of today.

MR. TAVENNER: Had you been engaged in the production of any particular movies prior to your leaving Hollywood?

MR. HAYDEN: I had only been in Hollywood two weeks when I was cast in second lead in *Virginia,* and a short while later in *Bahama Passage*. All during the summer of 1941 I was churning inside, thinking about the war. I would like to claim, but I can't claim, I knew this country was in danger, but I knew something was going on, and I wanted to get in it. September 15, 1941, I went to the heads of Paramount and said I would like to break my contract and leave for an indefinite length of time. They wanted to know why. I didn't know what to tell them. I said I didn't want to act, I didn't know what I wanted to do, I just wanted to leave. So I did leave. I went East. I contacted Colonel Donovan, who was then Coordinator of Information. I knew him through his son, who had sailed around the world with me in a schooner. He said he was setting up an organization in which men would be needed to train American troops—because this was prior to Pearl Harbor—in guerrilla warfare, and one of the men thought it a good idea to go to England or Scotland. I went to Scotland and trained with the Argyle and Sutherland Highlanders three months, went to England, went to a parachute school, broke my ankle on the sixth jump, and came back to the United States. I was unable to continue with the training because of my broken ankle, and I did not want to be placed in some administrative capacity, so I went to the Elco Boat Works in Bayonne, New Jersey, and worked with test crews. Then I was offered a commission as ensign in the Navy, which I declined because I thought I should have a higher rank, since I had been master of ships. I thought I could operate a schooner to the West Indies, because of the shortage of cargo vessels.

MR. TAVENNER: Was that during the period when the waters in that area were infested with German submarines?

MR. HAYDEN: I think there were quite a few down there, yes. So I went to the West Coast, bought a half interest in a schooner, and hauled freight for the War Shipping Administration through the late summer and fall of 1942. This was rather a lucrative thing, really.

MR. TAVENNER: How lucrative was it?

MR. HAYDEN: If things went smoothly, we stood to gross between eight and eleven thousand dollars per voyage. We were taking detonators and explosives, the theory being it was better to put them on a small vessel, so if it was lost it wouldn't make much difference, rather than put them with the cargo on a large ship. In October of that year I met with a bunch of Marines in the West Indies, and it entered my head to enlist. I sold the schooner, went to New York, enlisted, and went to Parris Island. That started another phase. I went through boot camp at Parris Island. At that time two men were selected out of each company for OSS [Office of Strategic Services] at Quantico. I changed my name to John Hamilton because I wanted to get away from Hollywood as much as possible. I was commissioned as second lieutenant. I went back to OSS. I don't know the exact date that the Coordinator of Information became OSS. The OSS shipped us first to Cairo. We were supposed to go to Greece, but we were shipped to Bari, Italy. Then began a long term of duty with the Yugoslav partisans there.

MR. TAVENNER: What was the general character of your work with the Partisans of Yugoslavia?

MR. HAYDEN: They claimed they wanted supplies. The first assignment I had was to coordinate the handling of a fleet of twenty-eight or thirty schooners. Two weeks later I was placed in charge of the port at Monopoli, Italy. We built up the staff and operated these schooners across the Adriatic. I don't remember the exact dates, but we would frequently go off on reconnaissance expeditions along the coast, along the mainland, trying to get new routes. We got up to Trieste on one trip.

MR. TAVENNER: Will you try to fix the date when you began your assignment at Bari and took over control of the port of Monopoli?

MR. HAYDEN: I would say that was the first week in December 1942.

MR. TAVENNER: And then try to coordinate the narrative with dates.

MR. HAYDEN: All right, sir. I would say we were in Monopoli six weeks to two months, and during that period of time I made two or three reconnaissance expeditions over into Yugoslavia.

MR. TAVENNER: What was the purpose of those?

MR. HAYDEN: To find a more efficient route of supplies to the partisan forces in the interior, to get the supplies through the German blockade to the forces fighting in the mountains.

MR. TAVENNER: That means you had to pass a German sea blockade as well as a land blockade?

MR. HAYDEN: Yes, it did.

MR. TAVENNER: And your work was behind the German lines?

MR. HAYDEN: Yes, it was, particularly later on when we were working in the interior. At that time we were operating along the periphery of the coast. Before I got in the work on the interior, I was put in command, told to take a small fishing boat, and operate it across the Adriatic. We could carry five to six tons of medical and other supplies into Albania, islands off the Greek coast, and Yugoslavia. I think we made eighteen or twenty trips before the E boats patrolling the coast really got wise to what was going on, and it became unhealthy. That operation was abandoned probably early in the summer of 1944. The next step seemed to be to supply them by air, so we were flown in to various places in Bosnia, in Slovenia—I beg your pardon: we never could get into Slovenia by air, so we were ordered to march into Slovenia. We had guides and they would take us through swamps where there was no liaison, and we tried to lay out an airfield to bring supplies through.

MR. TAVENNER: How long did you continue in your work with the underground in Yugoslavia?

MR. HAYDEN: Until late in November of that year, when I was sent home for a thirty-day leave in the States.

MR. TAVENNER: When you operated with the underground in Yugoslavia, just how close was your relationship with the leaders and the rank and file of that movement?

MR. HAYDEN: Well, of course, being a very junior officer myself—I was a second lieutenant at that time, most of us were lieutenants—we didn't actually come in contact on an operative level with the so-called brass. We established a tremendously close personal feeling with these people. We had unlimited respect for the way they were fighting. I think that respect was reciprocated. We tried to do the best we could. We got quite steamed up by it. I had never experienced anything quite like that, and it made a tremendous impression on me. We knew they were Communist-led, we knew they had commissars, but there was very little discussion of that. We couldn't discuss those things very much because we didn't know the language.

MR. TAVENNER: And you were fighting a common foe at that time?

MR. HAYDEN: That we were, and I think we conducted ourselves fairly well.

MR. TAVENNER: You say your relationship with the partisan movement had a deep effect upon you. What do you mean by that?

MR. HAYDEN: In 1940, when I was still an actor, and in 1941 I had had conversations with this man Tompkins. I wish I could describe my first reaction, because I think it would be typical of the experience so many people have had. I was appalled at the idea of what he was telling me about, but I did listen. He would give me literature, propaganda, and I would scan it briefly and burn it up. When this Yugoslavia thing came up, I wrote to him, "Maybe you were not so wrong. These people are doing a magnificent job." I thought I had better figure this thing out. He, in turn, reciprocated by bombarding me with Communist literature—*People's World, Daily Worker, New Masses,* and others I can't remember. I was impressed by the fact that the reports printed in the United States in this literature were accurate as regards the partisans in Yugoslavia. Apparently the people in the States knew this. This had an effect on me because it made me conscious of what these people knew that apparently the rest of us didn't know. I engaged in quite a lot of correspondence with Tompkins at that time. I can remember, in the interior of Yugoslavia, the crews of planes would leave their shoes, anything they could spare, with the partisans, they were that impressed, and I don't think a GI impresses too easily as a rule. This had a strong emotional impact on all of us.

MR. TAVENNER: Did you have political discussions with the partisans or any groups of them?

MR. HAYDEN: No. Once in a while, when we were back in Italy, we would sit around, and a few at Bari headquarters would talk a little bit about what was going on, but we never got very much involved in it. I remember a couple of times, when I would have a story in some of this literature Tompkins sent me, I would show it to them, and they were very pleased.

MR. TAVENNER: What was the final result upon you of the correspondence you were having with Captain Tompkins and the experience that you were undergoing in Yugoslavia?

MR. HAYDEN: There was a sort of thing churning inside me that I didn't know how to handle, but it seemed there was something in this world that I ought to find out about. When I got home on leave in December 1944, one of the first things I wanted to do, on a purely emotional basis, was go back and see Tompkins and talk to him about this thing, which I did. I flew out to the Coast and basked in the reflected glory of the partisan movement. Tompkins sort of showed me off as an exhibit.

MR. TAVENNER: Before leaving the Yugoslavian section of your testimony, were you recognized in any way by the government of Yugoslavia or by the partisans for your services in working with the underground?

MR. HAYDEN: I was given a decoration called the Order of Merit.

MR. TAVENNER: Was that the second highest decoration that could be awarded to a person foreign to Yugoslavia?

MR. HAYDEN: I have heard that it was, but I am not sure.

MR. TAVENNER: You received a Silver Star as a decoration?

MR. HAYDEN: Yes, sir.

MR. TAVENNER: On your return to the United States for your thirty-day leave, did you again see Captain Warwick Tompkins?

MR. HAYDEN: That was the first thing I did. I didn't know where I was going to be sent. The Yugoslav situation seemed to be more or less under control at that time. They had gotten the partisans a great deal more equipment and built them into some semblance of strength, so some of us were sent back to the States, and I was anxious to get in the same kind of work somewhere else. I didn't know where, but I hoped it would be possible to get into guerrilla outfits, because it is very stimulating. So I contacted Tompkins. Subsequently, through him, I contacted people in New York who I thought would know about guerrilla outfits elsewhere, as they had had accurate dope about Yugoslavia. I flew out to San Francisco, met Tompkins, and for five or six days I was on a merry-go-round. He took me around and I talked *ad nauseam* about Yugoslavia, but they were apparently interested. I met a great many people, some of whom may or may not have been Communists. Some I know now were. At that time I wasn't paying too much attention to that.

MR. TAVENNER: You were the guest of Captain Tompkins on your trip to the West Coast at that time?

MR. HAYDEN: Yes, I was.

MR. TAVENNER: Do you recall whether, on the day after your arrival there, you had dinner with three individuals, including Captain Tompkins, one of whom was Isaac Folkoff?

MR. HAYDEN: I remember having dinner or lunch with this fellow called "Pop" Folkoff, yes.

MR. TAVENNER: Do you remember where that lunch was held?

MR. HAYDEN: I do not.

MR. TAVENNER: Was there some other person present at that luncheon with the three of you?

MR. HAYDEN: I vaguely recall that there was, but I am not sure.

MR. TAVENNER: Do you recall his name?

MR. HAYDEN: No, sir, I do not.

MR. TAVENNER: Do you know a person by the name of Leo Baroway?

MR. HAYDEN: I have heard the name. You mean at that time, was this the man in question?

MR. TAVENNER: Yes.

MR. HAYDEN: I could not say.

MR. TAVENNER: Do you know whether or not Isaac Folkoff was a functionary in the Communist Party at that time?

MR. HAYDEN: I do not. I had the idea that he was in some way retired from the "struggle" at that time, as they put it, but from what I have heard since, this is open to question.

MR. TAVENNER: Will you describe what else occurred on that trip, where you went and what you did while you were a guest of Tompkins?

MR. HAYDEN: We went from place to place. Either at that time or on a subsequent visit he took me to the offices of the daily *People's World.* I remember meeting Bill Schneiderman and Harrison George. I don't remember anyone else. We went to San Francisco and went aboard a Russian vessel and had a drink.

MR. TAVENNER: Did you on that occasion meet a person by the name of Steve Nelson?

MR. HAYDEN: I met Steve Nelson. I don't remember if I met him then or after the war. I know I met him either in December of that year, 1944, or after the war when I saw Tompkins again.

MR. TAVENNER: Regardless of the correct date, will you tell the Committee the circumstances under which you met Nelson?

MR. HAYDEN: It was at a party, or rather a group get-together in someone's home in Oakland or in San Francisco one evening. There were ten or fifteen people sitting around. Nelson was one of them. I remember being introduced to him because he was supposed to be an outstanding figure.

MR. TAVENNER: An outstanding figure in what capacity?

MR. HAYDEN: In their world. I don't remember exactly what I was told he had done that made him outstanding, but I remember Tompkins' saying to me in the car, "Steve Nelson will be there. He is quite a guy," or something like that.

MR. TAVENNER: Do you know whether he was the organizer for the Communist Party for Alameda County at that particular time?

MR. HAYDEN: I didn't know that.

MR. TAVENNER: Can you recall in whose home you met Nelson?

MR. HAYDEN: Usually it was at the home of Tompkins' brother-in-law, a doctor whose last name slips me this minute.

MR. TAVENNER: Is it Dr. Lyman?

MR. HAYDEN: Dr. Lyman is right. Frequently when I was in San Francisco visiting Tompkins we would go see Tompkins' sister and brother-in-law.

MR. TAVENNER: Is that Dr. Ellwood W. Lyman?

MR. HAYDEN: I know it is Ellwood.

MR. TAVENNER: Do you remember anything that took place at that meeting attended by Steve Nelson?

MR HAYDEN: I vaguely recall that they asked if I would say a few words about Yugoslavia, and I did. What I said was in the same vein as what I have said here today, except at that time I was fresh from the place.

MR. TAVENNER: How long did you remain as the guest of Captain Tompkins?

MR. HAYDEN: I think five or six days.

MR. TAVENNER: When you returned to Washington did you bring any Communist Party literature or documents with you?

MR. HAYDEN: I may have. I think every time I ever saw Tompkins I would end up with, if not an armful, at least a handful of pamphlets, so I probably had some with me that I was going to read in the plane or carry with me.

MR. TAVENNER: Will you give the Committee your best opinion as to the effect of this trip upon you?

MR. HAYDEN: Well, I was trying to look ahead, figure out what I wanted to do after the war. I didn't know if I wanted to go back to Hollywood or not. I felt a sort of reluctance to accept what seemed to me to be the very lucrative and easy life Hollywood had offered me. The main thing was it planted a seed in me that said, if I could do something about the condition of the world, I could probably justify my position as an actor with a good salary and good working conditions. This was something boiling inside of me.

MR. TAVENNER: What did you do when you went back to New York?

MR. HAYDEN: I remember I went back to OSS headquarters, and my future assignment had not been determined, and it seemed to me that inasmuch as the Communist press had analyzed Tito accurately, they might know of other guerrilla outfits such as the partisans. I wrote or wired Tompkins asking who I could contact in New York, and he wired me to contact V. J. Jerome in New York. I picked up the phone and called the *Daily Worker* office and I said, "This is Lieutenant John Hamilton, United States Marine Corps. I would like to talk to V. J. Jerome." There was some consternation at the other end of the line, and I was told, if I was in New York later to call again, which I did. Jerome said we could meet at the Golden Eagle Café on West Twelfth Street just off Fifth Avenue. I went in and sat at the bar. About half an hour later a man scuttled through the back room and I thought, "This must be Jerome." I looked at him. He looked at me. I walked up, introduced myself, and sat down. My purpose was to find out if he had any idea where there were other guerrilla movements going on. He wouldn't talk to me. I think he was suspicious. I got nowhere that day. I called and talked to a man named Joe North, whom he had mentioned to me. I went up and talked to him in this building that I guess was headquarters for the whole caboodle. There was general conversation.

MR. TAVENNER: Did you also go see a person by the name of Allan Chase, who is an avowed Communist, having been a candidate for Congress on the Communist ticket?

MR. HAYDEN: I met him. I think even prior to my trip to see Tompkins I had met him. I didn't know until you told me that he was a Communist. I thought possibly he was. He was particularly interested in the situation in Spain. He talked about that angle of it, the fact there was a movement there, the remnants of a movement, and I met friends of his at his apartment near Central Park, and so forth. I went back to Washington and talked to someone in OSS about the possibility of going to Spain. They said there were already men in Spain. They said I would be sent to Paris. I went to Paris and was attached directly to the First Army Headquarters.

MR. TAVENNER: You referred to having met a number of Allan Chase's friends. Was Communism discussed with his friends?

MR. HAYDEN: No. Communism was never discussed. There was a discussion of the war going on and the role in it of the guerrillas.

MR. TAVENNER: Did you meet any other Communists while you were in New York?

MR. HAYDEN: The only two I met that I considered Communists were V. J. Jerome and Joe North. I thought possibly Chase was connected, but I didn't know.

MR. TAVENNER: Did you attempt to make any connection with the underground in Spain after you arrived in Paris?

MR. HAYDEN: No. When I went overseas I had two or three letters of introduction from friends of Chase to be used in case I got into Spain. I don't remember what I did with these letters. As soon as I got to Paris I was told to get into a jeep and go to Belgium, which I did, and I guess I threw the letters away or burned them; I don't know.

MR. TAVENNER: What was the nature of your work in Belgium?

MR. HAYDEN: OSS detachment, G-2 headquarters. The work at the detachment was in two levels: First, on an operational level, to infiltrate German civilians or German prisoners who had indicated a desire to work with the Allies back through the lines. Colonel B. A. Dickson was anxious to find out if there were any guerrilla anti-Nazi elements that were liberated as we went along that we could contact. I had a team of six or eight men, American Army personnel, who spoke German. We worked together quite closely and went to Marburg, Germany, which is where we were on V-E Day. We didn't meet many anti-Nazis that I remember. After V-E Day I returned to Paris and was told to take a photographic team and make a photographic study of all the ports of northern Europe, including Germany, Denmark, and Norway, which we did. We covered almost all of Norway, all of Denmark, all of Germany, and I was sent back to the States and discharged.

MR. TAVENNER: During the time of your second assignment on the German front, what was your connection with Captain Warwick Tompkins? Did you continue to obtain Communist literature and propaganda from him?

MR. HAYDEN: I kept up a desultory correspondence with him, and I presume he continued to send me Communist newspapers and literature. I don't remember, actually.

MR. TAVENNER: When was your assignment terminated?

MR. HAYDEN: I was discharged the 24th of December 1945. I think I returned to the States the end of November.

MR. TAVENNER: What did you do upon arriving in the United States?

MR. HAYDEN: There were two forces working inside me. One was to go back to sea; and the other was this political thing. At that time, it had never occurred to me to join the Communist Party. It seemed this whole thing had introduced me to a new world that I had never known. I tried to raise money to get a schooner. I couldn't raise the money. Then someone in Paramount contacted me to sign a new contract. I said, "O.K. Here we go."

MR. TAVENNER: Who was that?

MR. HAYDEN: Russell Holman, of Paramount's New York Office.

MR. TAVENNER: Was that prior to your leaving the East Coast for the West Coast?

MR. HAYDEN: We made the deal in New York. I then went out to Nevada, where I got a divorce from my then wife, Madeleine Carroll, and then went to San Francisco and spent six weeks with Tompkins, and then reported to Paramount in Hollywood.

MR. TAVENNER: Did Holman know of your past associations and connection with Captain Warwick Tompkins?

MR. HAYDEN: I don't know.

MR. TAVENNER: At the time of your second employment by the moving-picture industry, did your employer have any knowledge, as far as you know, of your associations with other Communist functionaries in California, such as William Schneiderman and Isaac Folkoff?

MR. HAYDEN: No. I think that was more or less lost in the shuffle of the war. There was so much going on, and I was fortunate enough to come out of the war better—publicitywise or otherwise—and they felt I had done pretty well in the war, and let it go at that.

MR. TAVENNER: As a result of your signing the contract in New York, you went to the West Coast. At that time, did you see Captain Warwick Tompkins again?

MR. HAYDEN: I saw him as soon as I left Nevada. I returned to Hollywood by way of San Francisco and spent some time with him on his schooner there. I don't remember how long.

MR. TAVENNER: What was the date?

MR. HAYDEN: I would say it was approximately the last week in March 1946.

MR. TAVENNER: What occurred on the occasion of this visit to Captain Tompkins?

MR. HAYDEN: He said he wanted to write a book about me. He was a very good writer. He had written for yachting magazines and had written several books with no political content whatever, and he thought it would be a good idea to write a biography of my life, and the slant he wanted to give it was "the development of a typical nonpolitical American youth into a militant participant in the class struggle," something like that. I said O.K.

So I went down to Hollywood and purchased a boat which I made my home on. Shortly thereafter, I would say in April, for three weeks he came on the schooner with me and took notes copiously. He followed me wherever I went on the boat, and eventually he got seventy-five thousand words written on the story, before I "came to" sufficiently to call on him one day and call the whole thing off.

MR. TAVENNER: When was it you called it off?

MR. HAYDEN: A long time later.

MR. TAVENNER: Before we go into that, I would like to know what occurred in the meantime. After your arrival in Hollywood, did you become associated with any particular organizations there?

MR. HAYDEN: I joined the Communist Party.

MR. TAVENNER: You joined the Communist Party?

MR. HAYDEN: Yes.

MR. TAVENNER: Will you tell the Committee the circumstances leading up to your actually becoming a member of the Communist Party?

MR. HAYDEN: As I began to operate around Hollywood, I continued to talk, almost incessantly, about this thing built up in me in Yugoslavia and the feeling I wanted to do something for a better world. Through Tompkins, I was put in contact with a woman, Bea Winters. One day she said to me, "Why don't you stop talking and join the Communist Party?" I remember my first reaction, which was, "This is ridiculous." However, I went ahead. She had a paper which I signed. I don't know whether I signed Sterling Hayden or John Hamilton. John Hamilton was my legal name. I signed one of the two names and was almost immediately accepted into the party.

MR. TAVENNER: How do you spell Bea?

MR. HAYDEN: B-e-a.

MR. TAVENNER: How was she employed?

MR. HAYDEN: She was a secretary in the office of my agent.

MR. TAVENNER: What was the name of your agent?

MR. HAYDEN: Berg—Allen Berg, Inc.

MR. TAVENNER: Is that agency in existence today?

MR. HAYDEN: It has since become amalgamated with the William Morris office.

MR. TAVENNER: Do you know whether Bea Winters' membership in the Communist Party was known to the agency?

MR. HAYDEN: I think it is safe to say it was not, or she wouldn't have been employed there.

MR. TAVENNER: How is she employed now, do you know?

MR. HAYDEN: I have heard she was secretary to a producer. I can't think of his name.

MR. TAVENNER: Can you fix the date when you joined the Communist Party?

MR. HAYDEN: It was approximately between the 5th and 15th of June 1946.

MR. TAVENNER: Over how long a period of time were you acquainted with Bea Winters?

MR. HAYDEN: I had known her before the war when she was with the Berg—Allen Berg Agency. Nothing political was ever discussed. I saw her again after the war, and I believe it was Tompkins who told me she was very active politically.

MR. TAVENNER: How long were you acquainted with her after you became a member of the Communist Party?

MR. HAYDEN: She was a member of the cell or group that I was assigned to up until the time that I broke with them, which was in December of that same year, 1946.

MR. TAVENNER: To what group of the Communist Party were you assigned?

MR. HAYDEN: I was told that for security reasons I should not be with any prominent people in the motion-picture industry but should be with people known as back-lot workers, carpenters, electricians, and so forth.

MR. TAVENNER: Will you explain that a little further? Security for whom?

MR. HAYDEN: Security for me, I presume. It was never discussed very much. I believe this cell was composed primarily of people from Universal, RKO, Columbia, and Paramount, but these people were never known to me by their last names. It was only first names. Everybody called everybody else comrade.

MR. TAVENNER: How many composed that cell?

MR. HAYDEN: I don't know what the official membership was, but an average meeting would have from ten to twenty-two or twenty-three people. I think they were happy if they had more than eight.

MR. TAVENNER: Who were the officers?

MR. HAYDEN: When I first joined there was a man who functioned as secretary, whose last name I do not know, whose first name was Hjalmar.

MR. TAVENNER: How was he employed?

MR. HAYDEN: I don't know.

MR. TAVENNER: Do you know where he lived?

MR. HAYDEN: I have no idea, although I may have gone to his house. I went to different houses by address. I don't know if I ever went to his house. He functioned as secretary. He kept records, collected dues, and so forth.

MR. TAVENNER: To whom did you pay your dues?

MR. HAYDEN: To him.

MR. TAVENNER: What were your dues?

MR. HAYDEN: The same as everybody else. They were computed at a percentage of salary, but I was not included in the percentage deal. I paid what everybody else paid. It seems to me it was a dollar-seventy-five, two dollars, or two-fifty a month.

MR. TAVENNER: Can you recall the names of anybody else who were members of that group?

MR. HAYDEN: I remember the names Bernie and Frank. I never knew their last names. I knew Bea Winters, of course.

MR. TAVENNER: Was she a member of that same group?

MR. HAYDEN: She was.

MR. TAVENNER: Do you know how Bernie was employed?

MR. HAYDEN: I do not.

MR. TAVENNER: Do you know where he lived?

MR. HAYDEN: I do not know that.

MR. TAVENNER: Did you say a person named Frank?

MR. HAYDEN: Somebody named Frank.

MR. TAVENNER: Are you able to identify any of these people to the Committee, as to how they were employed and where, or where they lived, that might lead to a discovery of who they actually are?

MR. HAYDEN: Only the man named Bernie. I would say he was employed in a white-collar capacity. He was more of an intellectual type than the others. He frequently would hold a discussion on the dialectical phases of Communism, and so forth and so on.

(*Representatives Doyle, Velde, and Jackson left the hearing room.*)

MR. TAVENNER: Can you recall the names of any of the persons in whose homes the meetings were held?

MR. HAYDEN: No, because when a meeting broke up somebody would say, "We will meet next Friday night at such and such a time at such an address." I would write down the address. I wasn't sure whose house it was.

MR. TAVENNER: Do you know an individual by the name of Abe Polonsky?

MR. HAYDEN: Yes. The meetings were frequently held at Abe's house.

MR. TAVENNER: Was he a member of this group?

MR. HAYDEN: He was later. About the time I terminated he began to show up at meetings.

MR. TAVENNER: Was he known to you as a member of the Communist Party?

MR. HAYDEN: Yes.

MR. TAVENNER: Is he currently a writer for Twentieth Century–Fox?

MR. HAYDEN: I don't know anything about him.

MR. TAVENNER: Will you give any further information you have as regards Abe Polonsky and his activities in the Communist Party?

MR. HAYDEN: In all honesty, I know little on that score. Initially, I had the feeling he was involved elsewhere. While the meetings were held at his house, he was seldom present until two or three months had elapsed, after which he began to appear fairly regularly, and after that functioned as sort of head of the group.

MR. TAVENNER: Were you acquainted with Robert Lees?

MR. HAYDEN: Robert Lees was a member of this group.

MR. TAVENNER: How often do you think he was there while you were there?

MR. HAYDEN: I could only guess, and I don't like to guess on things like this. I would say ten or twelve times.

MR. TAVENNER: Do you recall whether you met at his home on any occasion?

MR. HAYDEN: I think we did on one occasion.

MR. TAVENNER: What was the purpose of the holding of these meetings?

MR. HAYDEN: Simply that these people were Communists and they met to discuss what was going on. In a meeting the discussion would usually be split up into what was going on in the industry that concerned them, and then part of the meeting would be devoted to the world situation, theoretical diagnoses, and so forth.

MR. TAVENNER: Part of the time was devoted to the study of the principles of the Communist Party?

MR. HAYDEN: Yes.

MR. TAVENNER: How long did you continue in that cell?

MR. HAYDEN: That was the only cell I ever belonged to.

MR. TAVENNER: Did you have any particular assignment while you were a member of that cell?

MR. HAYDEN: I was told that it would be very helpful and important if the Screen Actors Guild could be swung into line in support of this strike.

MR. TAVENNER: You were told that by whom?

MR. HAYDEN: I don't know; somebody in this group.

MR. TAVENNER: It was a Communist order or suggestion?

MR. HAYDEN: That is the way it came to me.

MR. TAVENNER: It came to you in a Communist meeting by members of the Communist Party?

MR. HAYDEN: Yes. So I went first—and I don't remember who told me to go to it—to a large cocktail party where sixty or seventy people interested in this phase of endeavor were present, and through this meeting I began to meet a group of actors and actresses who all felt the same way. This was a very loose category of people, however.

MR. TAVENNER: Was that the group with whom you were directed to work?

MR. HAYDEN: No. I still attended meetings with this same group, but they told me I should be concerned primarily with actors, and they thought I should contact the Screen Actors Guild for support of the position of the

Conference of Studio Unions, which is a sort of amalgamation of locals in the industry, and I was told to associate with these people.

MR. TAVENNER: Who were working for the same purpose?

MR. HAYDEN: There were a great, great many people involved here. I don't know what percentage of the actors and actresses involved were a long, long, long way from being Communists in any sense of the word.

MR. TAVENNER: You have given a list of the persons connected with that movement to the investigators of this Committee, have you not?

MR. HAYDEN: Yes, I have.

MR. TAVENNER: Are there any of that group whom you can identify as members of the Communist Party? I am not asking you for names of people who were with you in this project unless they were known to you to be members of the Communist Party.

MR. HAYDEN: I wouldn't hesitate to say Karen Morley, inasmuch as in 1947, a long time after I had completely severed connections with any form of Communist activities, she came and asked me to come back, so it is safe to assume that she was a member. Over and above that, it would have to get into the realm of conjecture.

(Representative Doyle returns to hearing room.)

MR. TAVENNER: I want to ask you about this meeting which you were directed to attend in carrying out your Communist Party obligations. You said there were fifty or more people present, as I understood you?

MR. HAYDEN: There were sixty or seventy people there.

MR. TAVENNER: Did that group narrow down to a comparatively few who actually functioned?

MR. HAYDEN: I would say there was a nucleus that would attend meetings more regularly. When there were gatherings to see what could be done, there were certain people who would appear more regularly. There were people on the periphery, on the edge, who would be there sometimes; and other people were there more regularly.

MR. TAVENNER: How frequently did you meet to work on that enterprise?

MR. HAYDEN: I would say once or twice a week.

MR. TAVENNER: Did Karen Morley meet with you?

MR. HAYDEN: Yes.

MR. TAVENNER: Where were these meetings held?

MR. HAYDEN: Some were held at Karen Morley's house. Some were held at a house owned by a man named Morris Carnovsky, who, I might say, was never present. And others were held at homes which I only knew at that time by address.

(Representative Jackson returns to hearing room.)

MR. TAVENNER: Are you acquainted with a person by the name of Lloyd Gough?

MR. HAYDEN: Yes.

MR. TAVENNER: Did he attend those meetings?

MR. HAYDEN: Yes, he did.

MR. TAVENNER: Do you have any knowledge as to whether he was a member of the Communist Party?

MR. HAYDEN: Well, it would probably be safe to assume that he was.

MR. TAVENNER: I don't want to assume it.

MR. HAYDEN: I have absolutely, categorically, no knowledge that he was.

MR. TAVENNER: Are you acquainted with Howard Da Silva?

MR. HAYDEN: Yes.

MR. TAVENNER: Did he attend those meetings?

MR. HAYDEN: Yes.

MR. TAVENNER: Have you any personal knowledge as to whether he was a member of the Communist Party?

MR. HAYDEN: Only in his behavior before this Committee.

MR. TAVENNER: I understand that you terminated your connection with the Communist Party the same year in which you joined it?

MR. HAYDEN: That is right.

MR. TAVENNER: Will you tell the Committee what led up to the termination of your relationship with the Communist Party, and whether your break was a final break with the Communist Party?

MR. HAYDEN: I do not mean to imply that I was dragged into the thing in any way, shape, or manner. I went into the thing voluntarily. Certainly I think it was the stupidest, most ignorant thing I have ever done, and I have done a good many such things, but I did go into it with a very emotional and very unsound approach. I hadn't been in very long—I would say it took me three or four months to realize the true nature of what I had done. One thing that decided me against the whole business was the manner in which everything is predetermined. I had become susceptible to and, in a sense, perhaps, a victim of the idea that they had a form of democracy in mind. That was in my mind during the Yugoslav days and the time I joined. The belief is that they have the key, by some occult power, to know what is best for people, and that is the way it is going to be. I think any Communist or pseudo-Communist who pretends it is other than this is falsifying the fact. When I learned about this and began to digest it a bit, I decided to get out, and I got out. That is all there is to it, and anybody who insinuates it is not is mistaken.

MR. TAVENNER: Have you become a member of any other organizations, since you terminated your relationship with the Communist Party, which has been cited as a Communist front, or has had Communist Party leanings, so far as you know?

MR. HAYDEN: I know of one instance, and I would like to set that straight. There was an outfit in Hollywood, the Committee for the First

Amendment, formed in October 1947. I broke once and for all with the Communist thing in December 1946. The break coincided with the fact I was living on my boat in Santa Barbara. That summer my wife and I went East, on the coast of Maine, and when we came back I had a call from Alexander Knox saying this Committee for the First Amendment was being formed, and would I join. I was told who was sponsoring it, spearheading it. I thought it over very carefully, and I assured myself that this was in no way a Communist front at that time. So I joined, and I came to Washington in the fall, I think, October of that year, 1947. I think you are probably familiar with the membership list of that organization, and if it has since been determined that this thing was spearheaded by Communists, believe me, these people didn't know it. The people who lent their names and gave money to this Committee for the First Amendment had no idea that it was a Communist front any more than I had.

MR. TAVENNER: Who were those who spearheaded the Committee for the First Amendment, to your knowledge?

MR. HAYDEN: The first name that comes to mind is Humphrey Bogart. And his wife [Lauren Bacall]. It would be hard for me to remember. I wish I had a list. I know it runs into hundreds of so-called Hollywood names. I know there was a gathering at Ira Gershwin's house at which a couple of hundred people were present. The spokesmen were John Huston and Phil Dunne.

MR. TAVENNER: When you joined the Communist Party, were you advised by anyone that to do so would improve your chance of promotion in Hollywood?

MR. HAYDEN: On the contrary, I kept completely quiet about my association with the Communist Party. I didn't think it would help me in any way, shape, or manner. On the contrary.

MR. TAVENNER: In the course of your experience in Hollywood, did you at any time become acquainted with any Communist activity on the part of any high official of the motion-picture industry?

MR. HAYDEN: Yes, there was one instance. Shortly after I joined—I would say in July—Bea Winters said there was an important man who would like to come and talk with me. We met at the restaurant Victor's on Sunset Boulevard. He came in. I don't know the name by which he was introduced to me. After reading certain newspaper stories subsequent to this event I figured his name was John Stapp. I know he was introduced as John.

MR. TAVENNER: S-t-a-p-p?

MR. HAYDEN: Yes. I think he has other names. He asked what made me think I wanted to be a Communist.

MR. TAVENNER: Was he a member of the Hollywood motion-picture industry?

MR. HAYDEN: I have no idea.

MR. TAVENNER: He was a high functionary in the Communist Party?

MR. HAYDEN: I was told he was an important man.

MR. TAVENNER: But not in the Hollywood motion-picture industry?

MR. HAYDEN: I don't think he was in any way employed in the industry; not in any way.

MR. TAVENNER: Go ahead with your experience.

MR. HAYDEN: He asked why I had joined, and I went into the Yugoslavia thing. He asked if I had any militant trade-union background, and I said I did not. The conversation was more or less parallel with the conversation I had with Jerome, where I figured he was doing some calculating. He didn't say anything to me at all. I think he said he doubted that I would make a good Communist, but I am not sure.

MR. TAVENNER: Going back to my original question, did any knowledge come to you at any time of activities on the part of any high-ranking official in the Hollywood motion-picture industry that would indicate Communist Party membership on the part of any such individual?

MR. HAYDEN: No.

MR. TAVENNER: Were you acquainted with Edward G. Robinson?

MR. HAYDEN: I met Mr. Robinson backstage at a rally for Israel one evening and chatted with him a couple of minutes before he made a speech.

MR. TAVENNER: Did he attend any Communist Party meetings which you attended?

MR. HAYDEN: No.

MR. TAVENNER: Please proceed to sum up what you had in mind saying.

MR. HAYDEN: As soon as I got back in Hollywood I joined the Hollywood Independent Citizens Committee of the Arts, Sciences, and Professions, HICCASP. I paid dues through December. I never participated in a single thing in their behalf. I joined the American Veterans Committee at the same time. I made two speeches for them on Yugoslavia, one in Pomona and one in Santa Barbara. Then there is the Committee for the First Amendment, which I suppose could be construed as such since it has since been cited as a front organization. And, as I indicated earlier, this is the total, without reservation or limitation.

MR. TAVENNER: What were the organizations to which you contributed?

MR. HAYDEN: I contributed a hundred dollars to HICCASP. Three hundred dollars, one check, to Abe Polonsky. As I remember, this was for the families of the strikers in the CSU [Conference of Studio Unions]. That may be wrong. It may have been for the Communist Party. I paid my Communist Party dues. I paid my AVC dues, two dollars and seventy-five cents per month. I paid my HICCASP dues. I once gave Tompkins seventy-five dollars for the *People's World* when they were trying to keep on printing. That was the total.

MR. TAVENNER: Were all these contributions made prior to your leaving the party?

MR. HAYDEN: Except for one hundred dollars to the Committee for the First Amendment.

MR. TAVENNER: You have indicated that, after your relationship with the Communist Party was severed, Karen Morley came to you and asked you to come back into the Party.

MR. HAYDEN: Yes.

MR. TAVENNER: Will you give the Committee the entire transaction as it occurred?

MR. HAYDEN: I had remarried in June of that year. She came to our house, I believe, right after or before the Committee for the First Amendment was formed. She said she wanted me to consider coming back in, and I said, "There is nothing to be considered. This is it. There is nothing to discuss," and so forth. As she left, I took her out to the front hall, and she said, "I hope you realize that, having made that decision, it will be extremely hard for you to ever get back in." And I said, "Nothing will please me more." That ended it.

MR. TAVENNER: During the course of the conversation, was anything said about your becoming a passive member?

MR. HAYDEN: Yes. I forgot that. She said, "Since you don't want to be an active member, will you contribute money?" I said, "No."

(*Representative Velde returns to the hearing room.*)

MR. TAVENNER: In other words, in Hollywood there is such a thing as a passive membership, or a contributing membership, without attending meetings and so forth?

MR. HAYDEN: That is the way I understood it.

MR. TAVENNER: Do you know of any instance in which that type of membership is being maintained?

MR. HAYDEN: I do not.

MR. TAVENNER: You have cooperated with the Committee by telling the investigators, in advance of this hearing today, what you have known of Communism in your own life and in Hollywood. Have you taken any other action, besides that, which would indicate good faith on your part in the break which you claim you have made with the Communist Party?

MR. HAYDEN: I believe I have. One month after South Korea was invaded, through my attorney, a letter was sent to Mr. J. Edgar Hoover, Federal Bureau of Investigation, in which was set forth the fact that for a period of five to six months I had been a member of the Communist Party, and with the world going the way it was, it seemed entirely probable that a conflagration would develop, and I hope, if that was the case, my services would not be denied—if the Marine Corps could use me—on the basis of this mistake I had made. I have a photostatic copy of that letter I would like to produce or read for the record.

MR. TAVENNER: Suppose you produce it *and* read it into the record.
MR. HAYDEN:

July 31, 1950.

Federal Bureau of Investigation
Washington, D.C.
(Attention Mr. J. Edgar Hoover)
DEAR SIR:

This office has a client who has discussed with us a problem which I believe can only be answered through your organization.

In June of 1946 this young man, in a moment of emotional disturbance, became a bona fide member of the Communist Party in the State of California. In November of 1946 he decided that he had made a mistake and terminated his membership and his association with the Communist Party. Ever since November of 1946 this client has had no connection whatsoever with the Communist Party or with an organization affiliated with it.

The gentleman in question is an American-born citizen with a distinguished war record. He enlisted in the Marine Corps as a private and received his termination as a captain. Because of his distinguished services he received the Silver Star medal with citation from the commanding general, Mediterranean Theater of Operations, United States Army. The citation recognized his gallantry in action in the Mediterranean Theater of Operations with the United States Marine Corps Reserve.

Our client is not engaged in any activity where security is involved. However, since the commencement of the operation in Korea, he has felt that the time may come, in the near future, when his services might be of aid to the United States. He is concerned with the fact that his brief membership in the Communist Party, as aforesaid, may operate to prevent the use of his services.

In addition to the foregoing, he is married and has young children. If his services are not needed by the United States, conditions may develop so as to require an answer in connection with ordinary employment to the query: "Are you now or have you ever been a Communist?"

Our client can, of course, answer honestly and frankly that he is not now a member of the Communist Party. He could not answer the rest of the compound question without (a) either lying, or (b) if he told the truth he would probably find himself unable to earn a living.

While it must be admitted that a mistake was made in 1946, it does appear that justice requires some method by which one mistake does not operate (a) to prevent the United States from making use of the services of our client, (b) to prevent our client from earning a living.

He is perfectly willing to submit to any interrogation or examination by the Federal Bureau of Investigation so that that organization may be convinced of his sincerity and of the truth of all the statements related herein.

The purpose of this, of course, is to permit our client, if the compound question is asked him, to say in answer to the question, "Please inquire of the Federal Bureau of Investigation." The Federal Bureau of Investigation could then notify the prospective employer that there was no reason for not employing our client.

We would appreciate hearing from you at your earliest convenience.

Sincerely yours,
GANG, KOPP & TYRE
By MARTIN GANG.

MR. TAVENNER: Was a reply received from the Director of the Federal Bureau of Investigation?

MR. HAYDEN: Yes.

MR. TAVENNER: Will you read it into the record?

MR. HAYDEN:

August 15, 1950.

Mr. Martin Gang
401 Taft Building
Los Angeles 28, California
DEAR SIR:

Your letter of July 31, 1950, has been received and I want to thank you for making these facts available to me. I have given your letter careful consideration and I am fully cognizant of the problem which confronts you and your client.

I regret to inform you, however, that it has been a long-standing policy of this Bureau not to grant a clearance to any person and I am, therefore, unable to assist you in the manner which you suggest.

May I suggest, however, that inasmuch as this Bureau has primary investigative jurisdiction of matters concerning the internal security of our country, it is considered advisable that your client furnish our Los Angeles office with details concerning his membership in the Communist Party together with the nature of the party activities during that period.

In order to comply with this request may I suggest that you contact Mr. R. B. Hood, special agent in charge of our Los Angeles office, 900 Security Building, Los Angeles 13, Calif., in order to arrange for an interview of your client.

Very truly yours,
(*S*) J. E. HOOVER
John Edgar Hoover, Director.

MR. TAVENNER: Did you report as requested in that letter?

MR. HAYDEN: Yes, I did. I don't remember just how soon after we received this letter from Mr. Hoover. I believe it was early in August. And subsequently I met with them on two other occasions and discussed the thing in complete detail, as I have today.

MR. TAVENNER: Have you anything further you desire to add?

MR. HAYDEN: I would like to say that I appreciate very much, very, very much, the opportunity to appear here today. I think that there is a tremendous service to be rendered, not only to the country at large but to the motion-picture industry and also to those individuals who find themselves in a similar position to mine. I have heard that there are hundreds of thousands of ex-Communists who don't know what to do about it. I would like, if it is not presumptuous, to suggest, in all humility, that perhaps some provision could be made by law to permit people who had had a similar experience to make their position known and clear, so that they could get this thing off their chest, because, believe me, it is a load to carry around with you.

MR. TAVENNER: I might say, in that connection, that the Chairman of this Committee, in a broadcast not long ago, invited those who were in this category to make that fact known to this Committee—and they would keep it in confidence if that was desired—but to make known their participation so that it would be a matter of record now as to just what their participation had been, and there has been a very fine response to that.

MR. HAYDEN: I didn't realize that.

MR. DOYLE: Mr. Hayden, you said you are very, very grateful to the Committee for the opportunity to get this thing off your chest. Then you added, "Believe me, it is a load." What did you mean by that?

MR. HAYDEN: Well, conditions, of course, it seems to me, from my personal experience, were a great deal different in 1946 than today. As I have indicated, I went into the thing of my own free will, impulsively, stupidly, but I did get into it. When I realized I was wrong, I got out.

MR. DOYLE: What happened to cause you to come to the conclusion you had committed error?

MR. HAYDEN: One of the prime things was taking refuge in certain amendments to the Constitution. At that time I was pretty much of a greenhorn, but as soon as I realized the Communists were taking refuge under the amendments to our Constitution that they under no circumstances would permit others to take—

MR. DOYLE: Taking refuge from what?

MR. HAYDEN: Taking refuge in the Fifth Amendment or the First Amendment and considering that their political connections could not be questioned.

MR. DOYLE: What led you to believe they were taking refuge in the First and Fifth Amendments?

MR. HAYDEN: I believe in this investigation certain people have stood on the Fifth Amendment.

MR. DOYLE: That is only in the last year or so, and you resigned from the Communist Party in 1946. That is four [five?] years ago. What did you discover prior to the time you resigned which caused you, if anything did cause you, to come to the conclusion that you could not consistently continue longer as a member of the Communist Party?

MR. HAYDEN: One thing was when I became aware of the totalitarian idea of Communism, which had been obscured by the fog in the war years.

MR. DOYLE: I believe you testified when you accepted Bea Winters' invitation to join the Communist Party, the meetings of the cell indicated, did they not, the totalitarian nature of the Communist Party?

MR. HAYDEN: Yes, they did, but unfortunately, it took some time for my awareness of this to overcome the initial headway I had built up.

MR. DOYLE: What does "totalitarian nature of the Communist Party" mean to you?

MR. HAYDEN: That a very few people, or a certain group of people, know what is best for the majority, and the will of the majority has no bearing on what is done for the majority.

MR. DOYLE: Did you discover at any time that the Communist Party was encouraging devious ways to overthrow, by force if necessary, the republican form of government that we have under our Constitution in the United States?

MR. HAYDEN: I certainly believe that to be the case.

MR. DOYLE: When did you come to that conclusion?

MR. HAYDEN: Approximately at the time I severed my connection.

* * *

MR. DOYLE: Did you ever receive any literature from Tompkins or anyone else that caused you to conclude that the Communist Party was interested in revolution against the American form of government?

MR. HAYDEN: As I recall, it was always couched in other terms. I think a more perceptive person would have seen it. I did not at the time.

MR. DOYLE: You believe the literature you received from Tompkins did advocate the overthrow of the American form of government?

MR. HAYDEN: I think that was the ultimate objective, yes.

MR. DOYLE: Do you have any of that literature now?

MR. HAYDEN: No.

MR. DOYLE: Do you know where any of it could be had?

MR. HAYDEN: No. I know it used to be out in plain sight in some of the bookstores.

MR. DOYLE: Can you identify any of those bookstores by name or location?

MR. HAYDEN: I cannot offhand.

MR. DOYLE: Do you think your memory could be refreshed?

MR. HAYDEN: I remember a bookstore—I don't know if it is in existence any more: the Lincoln Bookstore, I think it was. I don't know where it was.

MR. DOYLE: When was that?

MR. HAYDEN: 1946.

MR. DOYLE: Did you ever receive literature from that bookstore?

MR. HAYDEN: I went in there once or twice.

MR. DOYLE: Did they ever hand you some literature for free distribution?

MR. HAYDEN: There was a lot of throwaway stuff on the table, as I remember it.

MR. DOYLE: You stated you came to think there was a great service to do the country and the industry. Does the moving-picture industry, in your judgment, need any service in connection with who are and who are not Communists, and if so, what service?

MR. HAYDEN: My thought on that was simply that if ex-Communists, or people who had been affiliated with Communist fronts, felt they could stand up and be counted and be judged on the facts, it would clarify the situation.

MR. DOYLE: Has the moving-picture industry been endeavoring to clean up its own house?

MR. HAYDEN: I certainly think it has.

MR. DOYLE: Do you think it is doing a pretty good job of it?

MR. HAYDEN: I think it is, so far as I know.

MR. DOYLE: I quickly made notes of this part of your testimony: "I was boiling inside. If I could do something about conditions, it might justify my being an actor with high income and pleasant working conditions." What were the conditions that you were boiling up inside about, that you wanted to help correct?

MR. HAYDEN: I came into the industry with no background in the conventional way of earning a living, having always been at sea. I suddenly found myself making a lot of money and not doing a great deal of work for it, and I felt a responsibility I should have had earlier as an American citizen. I had never thought politically before. All of this came to focus at one time, and unfortunately perhaps, the increment that set it off was my experience in Yugoslavia.

(*Representative Kearney enters hearing room.*)

MR. DOYLE: At that time you were not interested in any economic conditions facing our country. It only involved your personal boiling up inside?

MR. HAYDEN: That is very close to being correct.

MR. DOYLE: When Bea Winters in June 1946 handed you an application and asked you why you didn't join the Party— I believe that was your testimony?

MR. HAYDEN: Yes.

MR. DOYLE: And then told you you could not be a member of a cell where all members were actors, for security reasons, didn't it then occur to you there was something phony or dangerous about the Communist Party, when, for security reasons, you could not belong to a cell where actors belonged?

MR. HAYDEN: Yes, it did.

MR. DOYLE: What occurred to you?

MR. HAYDEN: As I said before, it was a rash move, an impulsive move, but I was under such a head of steam at the time I simply did not think the thing out very carefully. I went ahead anyway.

MR. DOYLE: In other words, you were so enraptured with the partisans of Yugoslavia, their bravery and heroism, and you had so tied yourself up with Tompkins and others, that you could not immediately withdraw from the Communist Party?

MR. HAYDEN: I could have withdrawn, but I couldn't see clearly at that time.

MR. DOYLE: Did it ever occur to you, between June and December 1946, what the security reasons were?

MR. HAYDEN: I felt that, had it been known to Paramount that I was a member of the Communist Party, I would no longer be employed by Paramount.

MR. DOYLE: You stated Captain Tompkins got some seventy-five thousand words written on your biography before you "came to" sufficiently to go to him and call the whole thing off.

MR. HAYDEN: That is right.

MR. DOYLE: What was it that caused you to "come to" sufficiently to go to this long-time friend of yours? He had been an adviser, I take it?

MR. HAYDEN: Yes.

MR. DOYLE: What gave you the backbone to go to him? What did you discover about the seventy-five thousand words?

MR. HAYDEN: The first draft he had knocked out actually fell by the wayside when I realized what I had done. It was not the book, I never read the book.

MR. DOYLE: Was the book published?

MR. HAYDEN: Heaven forbid. No.

MR. DOYLE: Was it ever reduced to typewritten form?

MR. HAYDEN: Only the first draft. My wife has frequently suggested I get it back. I don't know what happened to it.

MR. DOYLE: Do you feel, if you made a demand on Tompkins for it, you would get it back?

MR. HAYDEN: I have no idea.

MR. DOYLE: Did you accept money or anything of value for the script?

MR. HAYDEN: Nothing whatever. I have heard since he has been expelled from the Party. I don't know anything about that.

MR. VELDE: I wish you would go back and review your associations in Yugoslavia and name the persons you were associated with there who were in the partisan movement at that time.

MR. HAYDEN: The first names that come to my mind are Colonel Manola, who at one time functioned in some executive capacity in Bari headquarters in Bari, Italy, and Colonel Sergei Mackiedo, who was the man who notified me I had received this decoration from the Yugoslav government.

MR. VELDE: Were they American citizens?

MR. HAYDEN: No. These are partisans. Do you want American citizens?

MR. VELDE: I want both.

MR. HAYDEN: These two are partisans. I can remember a man named Ivosevich, who was first mate.

MR. VELDE: Did you meet Tito?

MR. HAYDEN: I never met Tito.

MR. VELDE: Proceed.

MR. HAYDEN: I don't think of any other names.

MR. VELDE: What about Americans?

MR. HAYDEN: American OSS officers in Bari: Captain Haus Tofte; Lieutenant Bob Thompson; Lieutenant Ward Ellen; Lieutenant Benson; Sergeant John Harnicker, Marine Corps; Major Koch; Major Linn Farish, who was killed in Greece. I guess there are a lot of others. Their names don't come to mind.

MR. VELDE: If any of those you have listed are known to you to be or to have been members of the Communist Party, so state.

MR. HAYDEN: To my knowledge, none of them had any connection whatever.

MR. VELDE: Was there an OSS officer from Pittsburgh?

MR. HAYDEN: There were a number from around the Pittsburgh district.

MR. VELDE: Can you identify any of them as members of the Communist Party?

MR. HAYDEN: No. I have heard subsequently that one of them, George Wuchinich, was in some way connected with the Communist Party. The others were strictly anti-Communist.

MR. VELDE: Will you tell the Committee how you felt, or know, that George Wuchinich was associated with the Communist Party?

MR. HAYDEN: I don't know when or how I heard it, but at some time since the war I have heard that mentioned.

MR. VELDE: Scuttle butt?

MR. HAYDEN: Let's say scuttle butt.

* * *

MR. MOULDER: During the period of your membership in the Party, you decided that the philosophy they were discussing was not in accord with your philosophy of government?

MR. HAYDEN: Yes. In the first place, if I may say so—and I say it because probably a good many people have been in a similar position—I never understood it. I was constantly told, if I would read forty pages of

Dialectical and Historical Materialism [by Stalin], I would understand Communism. I never got beyond page 8, and I tried several times.

MR. DOYLE: I am asking for your honest-to-God truthful opinion. I have never asked [this] question before, but I think in view of the manner in which you have come before this Committee, and the apparent frankness with which you have answered questions, if you have any criticism of the manner in which this Committee functions, I would like to know what that criticism is. You have now been before us three hours.

MR. HAYDEN: I think of no criticism whatever.

MR. DOYLE: Have you any suggestions to make of ways and means in which we might be more helpful in meeting this problem of the determination of the Communist Party of the United States to overthrow, if necessary by force, our Government?

MR. HAYDEN: I think that the suggestion that was made by the Chairman of the Committee, that people come up and speak up, is the thing I came here today thinking it was an extremely fine thing, a constructive thing. I don't mean to attach any importance to myself as an individual who is out of balance, but I have had the feeling that my appearance before the Committee could serve a very useful purpose. I hope it does.

* * *

MR. VELDE: Did you attend a Progressive Party rally at Madison Square Garden in 1947?

MR. HAYDEN: At which Mr. Wallace spoke? Yes.

MR. VELDE: Whom did you go there with?

MR. HAYDEN: My wife, who is here today.

MR. VELDE: Was there anyone else in your group?

MR. HAYDEN: I am strongly of the impression we went alone.

MR. VELDE: Did you meet any persons at that rally you can identify as being members of the Communist Party?

MR. HAYDEN: To the best of my recollection we went in, sat down, got out of the meeting, and left.

* * *

MR. TAVENNER: I asked you to name those whom you know to be members of the Communist Party who were connected with the Screen Actors Guild with which you worked, and you named those that you knew?

MR. HAYDEN: I did.

MR. TAVENNER: And you named several others, members of the Communist Party, with which you had come in contact. Then, in the course of your testimony, you indicated that you could name others, but it would be a matter of conjecture, and I stated to you that I did not want you to testify from conjecture. Have you given to the invesigators of this Committee a list of names of those to whom you have referred?

MR. HAYDEN: Yes, I have.

MR. WOOD: By that I understand that the list of names you have given the investigators are in addition to those you have named before this Committee.

MR. HAYDEN: Yes, they are.

MR. WOOD: And do I understand those names have been furnished the investigators by you only upon some conjecture you have that they may have been members of the Party?

MR. HAYDEN: My feeling is that the only ones I know to have been members are those active in the cell and Karen Morley. Any others would have to be conjecture.

MR. WOOD: Do I understand that the list of names you have furnished the investigators, that you have no knowledge as to whether they have ever been members of the Communist Party or not?

MR. HAYDEN: That is true. I do not know.

MR. WOOD: But your purpose in furnishing the list of names to the investigators was that, by proper investigation on the part of the investigators of the Committee and the Committee itself, their connection with the Communist Party might be revealed with reference to some of them?

MR. HAYDEN: I think, if they were asked, it would be developed.

MR. WOOD: Was that your purpose in furnishing to the staff of this Committee that list of names?

MR. HAYDEN: It was.

MR. WOOD: And no other reason?

MR. HAYDEN: No, sir.

APRIL 25, 1951:

Edward Dmytryk

The Committee on Un-American Activities met at 10:20 a.m., in room 226, Old House Office Building, the Honorable John S. Wood (Chairman) presiding.

Committee members present: Representatives John S. Wood (Chairman), Francis E. Walter, James B. Frazier, Jr., Harold H. Velde (appearance as noted in transcript), Bernard W. Kearney (appearance as noted in transcript), Donald L. Jackson, and Charles E. Potter.

Staff members present: Frank S. Tavenner, Jr., Counsel; Thomas W. Beale, Sr., Assistant Counsel; Louis J. Russell, Senior Investigator; William A. Wheeler, Investigator; and A. S. Poore, Editor.

MR. WOOD: Let the record show that there are present members of the

Committee as follows: Mr. Walter, Mr. Frazier, Mr. Jackson, Mr. Potter, and Mr. Wood, a quorum of the full Committee.

MR. TAVENNER: What is your name, please?

MR. DMYTRYK: Edward Dmytryk.

MR. TAVENNER: And the spelling is D-m-y-t-r-y-k?

MR. DMYTRYK: That is right.

MR. TRAVENNER: When and where were you born, Mr. Dmytryk?

MR. DMYTRYK: I was born in Canada—Grand Forks, British Columbia, September 4, 1908.

MR. TAVENNER: Are you a naturalized American citizen?

MR. DMYTRYK: I am.

MR. TAVENNER: When were you naturalized?

MR. DMYTRYK: I was naturalized in 1939.

MR. TAVENNER: What is your profession?

MR. DMYTRYK: I am a screen director.

MR. TAVENNER: I wish you would give the Committee a brief statement of your educational training.

MR. DMYTRYK: Well, I went through grammar school, went through Hollywood High School, and I attended a year the California Institute of Technology before I went back to pictures, where I had worked previously.

MR. TAVENNER: You say you had worked prior to that time in pictures?

MR. DMYTRYK: Yes. I left home when I was fourteen, just when I entered high school, and I worked after school and during vacations at Paramount in order to work my way through school.

MR. TAVENNER: Where did you work?

MR. DMYTRYK: At Paramount Studios. I worked in the laboratory as a messenger boy first, and then as a projectionist.

MR. TAVENNER: What salary did you receive?

MR. DMYTRYK: I started at six dollars a week.

MR. TAVENNER: Will you outline to the Committee what your professional career has been since that time?

MR. DMYTRYK: After I quit college and went back to Hollywood, I went to work as a projectionist, which I had been doing for some time before, after school. About that time sound came in, in the late twenties, and there was great expansion, and I became assistant cutter, then cutter for Paramount, until 1939, at which time I got a break directing pictures. I directed B pictures, three or four at Paramount, at Columbia, one at Universal, and one at RKO. At RKO I made a picture, *Hitler's Children,* which was a quickie, but it made many millions of dollars, and from then on I directed A pictures, from 1943 until 1947.

MR. TAVENNER: What were some of the principal productions directed by you?

MR. DMYTRYK: *Behind the Rising Sun; Tender Comrade; Till the End of Time; Back to Bataan; Murder, My Sweet; Cornered; So Well Remembered,* which was made in England; and the last picture, *Crossfire*.

MR. TAVENNER: At the time you directed this picture, *Crossfire,* how did your weekly salary compare with the time you started?

MR. DMYTRYK: I was making twenty-five hundred dollars a week, fifty-two weeks a year.

MR. TAVENNER: Mr. Dmytryk, you were subpoenaed as a witness before this Committee in 1947?

MR. DMYTRYK: I was.

MR. TAVENNER: And you are one of those commonly referred to as the Hollywood Ten?

MR. DMYTRYK: I was.

MR. TAVENNER: I notice you say you "were," rather than "are."

MR. DMYTRYK: I don't think I will be considered so much longer.

MR. TAVENNER: Your testimony today will throw considerable light on that subject?

MR. DMYTRYK: I imagine so, yes.

MR. TAVENNER: I believe you were one of the group who were prosecuted for contempt of Congress, and that you received a sentence, and that you have served that sentence?

MR. DMYTRYK: I have, yes.

MR. TAVENNER: Were you a member of the Communist Party at the time you were subpoenaed before this Committee in 1947?

MR. DMYTRYK: No, I was not.

MR. TAVENNER: Had you ever been a member of the Communist Party?

MR. DMYTRYK: Yes, I had been a member from sometime around the spring or early summer 1944 until about the fall of 1945. Most of this was during the period when the Communist Party as such was dissolved and the Communist Political Association had taken its place.

MR. TAVENNER: While you were a member of the so-called Hollywood Ten, did you have opportunity to further observe the workings of the Communist Party?

MR. DMYTRYK: I think I can truthfully say that I had much more opportunity to observe the workings of the Communist Party while I was a member of the Hollywood Ten than I did while I was a member of the Communist Party.

MR. TAVENNER: This Committee is endeavoring very strenuously to investigate the extent of Communist Party infiltration into the entertainment field. Are you willing to cooperate with the Committee in giving it the benefit of what knowledge you have, from your own experiences, both while a member of the Communist Party and later?

MR. DMYTRYK: I certainly am.

MR. TAVENNER: And that is true notwithstanding you refused to testify before this Committee in 1947?

MR. DMYTRYK: Yes, it is true. The situation has somewhat changed.

MR. TAVENNER: What do you mean by that?

MR. DMYTRYK: There is a great deal of difference between 1947 and 1951, as far as the Communist Party is concerned, or at least as far as my awareness of what is going on is concerned. In 1947 the Cold War had not yet gone beyond the freezing point. I wanted to believe that Russia was very sincere in wanting peace, and I didn't feel the Communist Party in this country was any particular menace, and I felt the Committee before which I appeared was invading a field they could not properly invade—that is, freedom of speech and freedom of thought. And I also sincerely believed the procedures used by the Committee were not completely in keeping with an honest investigation. On those grounds, I refused to testify at the time. Since that time a number of very important developments have taken place. In the first place, I had never heard, before 1947, anybody say they would refuse to fight for this country in a war against Soviet Russia. I think I was in England when I first saw an article about an Australian Party member who said he would not fight against Soviet Russia. Then I saw articles about American Party members taking the same position; I believe Paul Robeson was one.* Since then other Party members in this country have stated they would not fight for their country. I think in a democracy each person takes upon himself the duty to defend his country in time of war. Along with other people, I signed the Stockholm Peace Petition. I believe in peace, as everybody does. I hoped they were sincere. However, the Korean War made me realize that they were not. I think any intelligent person must realize that the North Koreans would not have attacked the South Koreans unless they had the backing of very strong forces. I can't prove it, but I believe those forces are Communist China and Communist Russia. This, too, disturbed me tremendously, and made me realize there is a Communist menace and that the Communist Party in this country is a part of that menace. The third thing was the spy trials, the development of the Hiss, Coplon, and Greenglass cases, and the Fuchs case in England. To me, there is a significant thing about the spy trials. The thing that impressed me was that these people did not get any money, or not much. There are spies who work for their country, and we have respect for them. There are other spies who receive money for their work, and there may be a certain admiration for them, because they risk their necks. These people are doing it for love of the Party. This is treason. I think the party that has used them is treasonable also. I don't say all members of the Communist Party are guilty of treason, but I think a party that encourages them to act in this capacity is treasonable. For this reason I am willing to talk today.

MR. TAVENNER: I would like to have you state to this Committee what

* But Robeson denied Party membership. See p. 769. —E.B.

the real object of the Communist Party is, in its efforts to organize and infiltrate the moving-picture industry in Hollywood.

MR. DMYTRYK: Well, I had no access to inner-Party circles, so I can't tell you officially, but my opinion is they had probably three chief purposes. The first one was to get money. Hollywood is a very wealthy community, and it is a great source of capital. The next one was to get prestige. And the third and most important one was, through the infiltration and eventual taking over of Hollywood guilds and unions, to control the content of pictures. The only way they could control the content of pictures was to control studios, and the only way they could do that was to completely take over the guilds and the unions.

MR. TAVENNER: Let us go back to the first of those purposes that you mentioned, the matter of money. What information do you have regarding the effort of the Communist Party to obtain sizable sums of money out of its membership in Hollywood?

MR. DMYTRYK: I know that at least some of the members were making sizable salaries. This was not true in all cases, but there was in some cases a tithing system under which members gave a percentage of their salaries. Sometimes it amounted to quite a bit of money. There was also the opportunity to hold a great many affairs—parties, dinners, meetings of various sorts—not so much directly for the Communist Party as for Communist-front organizations, for which they were always able to get very sizable donations, and I think over a period of years, particularly when the love feast was on between Russia and America during the war, and for some years afterward, a great deal of money was taken from Hollywood.

MR. TAVENNER: Did you make any sizable contribution to the Communist Party?

MR. DMYTRYK: No. I wasn't making much at that time. I also had a business manager. A Hollywood business manager is a very unique institution. In order to try to save your money, he gives you a very, very small allowance. I had an allowance of twenty-five dollars a week. I sometimes gave five or ten dollars, but I couldn't give a tithing because I would have had to go to my business agent. Business agents are capitalists, and I couldn't ask for money for the Communist Party. Then, too, I was never indoctrinated enough to know if I would become a serious member of the Communist Party. As it turned out, I didn't.

MR. TAVENNER: You referred to another purpose of the Communist Party in its work in Hollywood as being the purpose of obtaining prestige. What did you mean by that?

MR. DMYTRYK: I don't know that the Party itself ever recruited any large number of prestige people. However, through what are now called Communist-front organizations, they were able to approach a large percentage—I would say majority—of the name people in Hollywood and get their names on resolutions or as members of boards of the Communist fronts. This is a complicated thing. When you say "Communist front," you get the impression it is run by Communists. This isn't always true. I have seen Communist fronts where there are as few as one or two Communists. Also, there are two kinds of fronts. One kind is organized by the Communist Party itself, or by certain Communists; and another is an organization that starts out as an ordinary liberal organization and is infiltrated by Communists. The Communists are tireless workers. One tireless worker in an organization can usually take over that organization. A Communist doesn't want to be president. He wants to be secretary. As secretary, he very soon takes control and will run the organizaiton as a Communist organization. Another important point is that the Communist-front organizations were never engaged, at least overtly, in any activities that seemed undemocratic or unpatriotic, and that is why they were able to attract so many people. Actually, the work they did during the war was really good work. That is the way they were able to trap so many people. I would say that for every Communist in a Communist-front organization in Hollywood, there were a hundred non-Communists, and very few of them had any idea they were dominated by a Communist group. This was not because they were fools, but the Communists are clever enough to cover up that fact, and the work they do overtly appeals to many public-minded citizens.

MR. TAVENNER: You spoke of a third and most important aim and object of the Communist Party as being the purpose of eventually obtaining control of the guilds and unions, as I understood you to say?

MR. DMYTRYK: Yes.

MR. TAVENNER: What guilds were they that you referred to?

MR. DMYTRYK: In the first two points I mentioned I think the Communists had considerable success in Hollywood. In this last point they had only limited success. Hollywood is split up into probably two sections. First the talent guilds: Screen Writers Guild, unaffiliated; Screen Directors Guild, unaffiliated; and Screen Actors Guild, which is affiliated with the American Federation of Labor but is largely autonomous. Then there are the craft unions: mostly IATSE—International Association of Theatrical and Stage Employees. I know that the Communists were successful for a time in taking over or largely controlling—they didn't take over but controlled for a long time—the Screen Writers Guild. They got a number of men on the board to pass their resolutions and that sort of thing. They were not successful at all in the Screen Directors Guild. There were only a very few Communists in the Screen Directors Guild at any time.

MR. TAVENNER: Were you in the Screen Directors Guild?

MR. DMYTRYK: Yes, from 1939 on.

MR. TAVENNER: How many were there in the Screen Directors Guild?

MR. DMYTRYK: The total membership, full directors, was 225 or 230.

MR. TAVENNER: And of that number there were a few known to you to be members of the Communist Party?

MR. DMYTRYK: As far as I know there were seven.

MR. TAVENNER: Will you give us the names of the seven?

MR. DMYTRYK: Yes. Frank Tuttle.

MR. TAVENNER: He was a director?

MR. DMYTRYK: Yes. Herbert Biberman. Jack Berry.

MR. TAVENNER: Can you identify him further?

MR. DMYTRYK: I heard the Chairman this morning give the address. He is the Berry who lives on King's Road. The meeting was at his house. That is why I know. Bernard Vorhaus.

MR. TAVENNER: I believe you have named four.

MR. DMYTRYK: Then Jules Dassin. And myself.*

MR. TAVENNER: Do you have any definite knowledge of any of the others' having left the Communist Party?

MR. DMYTRYK: No, I don't. I think it is quite possible that some of them have.

MR. TAVENNER: I understood you to say the meeting you described was held at the home of Jack Berry?

MR. DMYTRYK: That is right.

MR. TAVENNER: What was the purpose of the meeting?

MR. DMYTRYK: As far as I can remember, I think it had to do with trying to elect one of us to the board of directors of the Directors Guild.

MR. TAVENNER: Why was the Communist Party interested at that particular time in placing one of its members on the board of directors of the guild?

MR. DMYTRYK: Well, that was part of a very long-term plan. They wanted to get as many people as they could on the board of directors of the guilds so that they could eventually control the policy of those guilds, particularly in relation to an eventual coalition for the backing of the various unions.

MR. TAVENNER: In other words, this is one instance in which the Communist Party was endeavoring to obtain control of the guilds?

MR. DMYTRYK: Yes.

MR. TAVENNER: Continuing with your discussion of what you referred to as the third and most important aim of the Communist Party, what other efforts do you know of that the Communist Party resorted to to control either pictures, or the guilds, or the executives of the industry?

MR. DMYTRYK: The chief effort was in the craft unions. In my opinion, the Communist Party never had any control over any major executive in any major studio, nor did they at any time have any effective control over the content of pictures. It is true that somebody may have slipped in a line or something that made them happy, but that is not the kind of thing that would be effective in the least degree, and certainly they never had any control over any major executive that I know of. But in the craft unions

* No seventh was named. —E.B.

they were successful in organizing a group called the Conference of Studio Unions that did have a great deal to do with the policies. They eventually got so strong that they risked a strike against the IATSE. However, they lost the strike after a very, very long and serious battle, and that attempt came to nothing.

MR. TAVENNER: During that period, did the Communist Party attempt to influence the guilds in the matter of the strike?

MR. DMYTRYK: I know the three guilds got together and appointed committees to investigate the strike. In almost every case they came out in favor of the Conference of Studio Unions.

MR. TAVENNER: You were speaking of the craft unions. What do you know about the existence of Communism in the craft unions?

MR. DMYTRYK: Well, I know very little except that within the Conference of Studio Unions, in particular, they were quite well organized. I also believe that they were actually very few. I don't believe there were over fifty or so in that group.

* * *

MR. TAVENNER: Will you state what you know about the activity of the Communist Party within the Screen Writers Guild, if you know?

MR. DMYTRYK: Well, I don't know a great deal about that, except many of my friends were in the Screen Writers Guild. The Communists elected enough members to the board of directors to control that guild for a large number of years, actually until 1947, I believe. As a result of that, they largely led the fight in Hollywood on various Communist-front activities. They usually led the fight to get the other talent guilds—what we call prestige guilds—they tried to get them to take the side of the CSU against the IATSE.

MR. TAVENNER: Do you know the names of individuals within that group who were members of the Communist Party at that time?

MR. DMYTRYK: Yes. I know several. John Howard Lawson was one of them. Lester Cole was a leader in that group. Those are the only two whom I can positively identify as Communists. Gordon Kahn, by the way, was also rather important in the group.

MR. TAVENNER: Just how did the Communist Party plan to function, or did it function, in its effort to control or to obtain control or influence in these various guilds?

MR. DMYTRYK: They didn't get to the point, in my opinion, of ever controlling any kind of content in pictures, which is actually what they were aiming for in the long run. The Communists for years have realized the importance of any public mediums of propaganda and education. Lenin said way back that the cinema would probably be the most important medium of propaganda and education, and they were trying to take over that medium. They could not walk in and start controlling the content from the beginning. The only way they could control content was through control of the unions and guilds. They could get a stranglehold of the executives. It is very difficult to obtain control, because you have to go through the line, and you would have to have a chain of Communists from beginning to end, five or more, and they never did.

MR. TAVENNER: Do you know of any instance in which an effort was made to control the content of a picture?

MR. DMYTRYK: Well, in a vague way, yes. That is, the attempt to control was vague. I know the instance very well because it happened to me. This is the thing that actually got me out of the party. In 1945 Adrian Scott and I made a picture called *Cornered*. The picture was the story of a Canadian pilot immediately after the war who had been married to a French girl who had been in the underground and been killed, and, with very little to go on, this pilot started looking for the person who had killed her. Many Germans were reported to have escaped to Argentina, and he followed him there, trying to pin him down. In that picture we had an opportunity to say many things about Fascism, which we did. While the first script was being written by John Wexley, I found the script had long speeches, propaganda—they were all anti-Nazi and anti-Fascist, but went to extremes in following the Party line. I objected—not because of this, but because the picture was undramatic, too many speeches, and I suggested to Adrian that we get another writer, which we did. We got John Paxton, a very fine writer, who had worked for us previously. And since I have mentioned him, he is not a Communist, by the way. He rewrote the script, we shot it, and made a fairly good melodrama out of it. After they were making prints to go out to the theaters, so that I knew no changes could be made in it, Adrian Scott received a note from Wexley saying he wanted to have a conference with us. Wexley had had an arbitration on credits and had lost.

MR. TAVENNER: What do you mean by "credits"?

MR. DMYTRYK: He wanted a larger share of credit, and there are means of arbitration on writers' disputes about that. They gave Wexley adaptation credit. The meeting was at my house. I was surprised to see the meeting was of Communists, and the whole meeting was along Communist lines. Adrian Scott and I were attacked by Wexley and by two people he brought with him at the time, Richard Collins and Paul Trivers.

MR. TAVENNER: What was Paul Trivers' occupation?

MR. DMYTRYK: He was a writer. I think he is now with the Bob Robert–John Garfield Company as a writer. The whole attack on us was along this line: by removing Wexley's line, we were making a pro-Nazi picture instead of an anti-Nazi picture. To say the least, we were startled.

MR. TAVENNER: Was Adrian Scott a member of the Communist Party?

MR. DMYTRYK: Yes, he was. His experience with the Party was about the same as mine.

MR. POTTER: Where did this meeting take place?

Mr. Dmytryk: At my apartment.

Mr. Potter: When?

Mr. Dmytryk: Late summer of 1945 or fall of 1945.

Mr. Tavenner: Was John Wexley also a member of the Communist Party?

Mr. Dmytryk: I would say he was a member of the Communist Party because this was unquestionably a Communist Party affair. This was the only time I ever saw him at anything that I considered Communistic.

Mr. Tavenner: Other than John Wexley, how did you know the other persons you mentioned to be members of the Communist Party? Take first Adrian Scott.

Mr. Dmytryk: I had attended meetings with Scott.

Mr. Tavenner: Another you mentioned was John Howard Lawson.

Mr. Dmytryk: No. I mentioned him earlier. I mentioned Collins and Trivers.

Mr. Tavenner: How did you know Trivers to be a member of the Communist Party?

Mr. Dmytryk: Only by reputation and by the conduct of this committee hearing. This was a little committee. There was no question then, and there is no question now, but that this was a Communist meeting, as I will develop later on. Of course, we refused to admit any of the charges made by Wexley and the other two. Nevertheless, they asked for a further meeting. At the further meeting, they brought John Howard Lawson, who was the "high lama" [Dalai Lama?] of the Communist Party at that time.

Mr. Tavenner: Why do you say that?

Mr. Dmytryk: He settled all questions. If there was a switch in the Party line, he explained it. If there were any decisions to be made, they went to John Howard Lawson. If there was any conflict within the Communist Party, he was the one who settled it. We had a third meeting at which Adrian Scott brought in Albert Maltz, who was a more liberal Communist, to defend us. These meetings ended in a stalemate. There were several by-products of these meetings. I think Albert Maltz had been concerned with the lack of freedom of thought in the Communist Party for some time, and this was the trigger for the article he wrote for the *New Masses* on freedom of thought which was so widely discussed.

Mr. Tavenner: It is your view that this incident you have described had a very strong effect upon Albert Maltz?

Mr. Dmytryk: I know it did, because I talked to him about it, and he was very much concerned with this effort to control the thought of members. So he wrote the article which he later had to repudiate or get out of the Party, and he chose to repudiate it. Adrian Scott was also concerned, and he thought we should have a meeting with John Howard Lawson and discuss the broad subject with him. We had luncheon with John Howard Lawson at the Gotham Café in Hollywood. It was a very unsatisfactory meeting. John Howard Lawson was very uncommunicative. He would not explain his actions, would give no reason for them. He said we obviously showed we could not accept Party discipline, and if we felt that way it would probably be better that we get out of the Party. We made no official decision at that time. Adrian Scott was loath to make any decision. I never attended any meeting after that. So, although that was not an official getting out of the Party—very few write letters of resignation or anything of that kind—I never attended any other meeting of the Communist Party as such.

MR. TAVENNER: Have you anything further to say regarding point three that you mentioned, as to the most important of the aims of the Communist Party in Hollywood?

MR. DMYTRYK: I feel sure that the Communist Party is now a completely ineffective element in Hollywood.

MR. TAVENNER: I have been rather struck with some of the testimony here as to the station in life and the measure of success that various people apparently had when they became members of the Communist Party. What appeal was there in the Communist Party which aided them in recruiting members? How was it that individuals—for instance, such as [Paul] Jarrico, as to whom there has been testimony that he was a member of the Communist Party—how was it they would become members?

MR. DMYTRYK: Writers are, of course, traditionally concerned with people. These are the bones of their work. To understand people properly they have to understand the society in which they live and the economic conditions under which they live. So any writer worthy of the name studies these problems. Probably he becomes a writer because he is a humanitarian. There is at least a streak of altruism and idealism in him. So they usually come in contact with Communists more than the average person. Most of these people do not come from poor backgrounds of poverty and deprivation. Most of them come from good backgrounds. They become troubled about poverty, especially where there is such a discrepancy, where a man making twenty-five hundred dollars a week is working next to a man making twenty-five dollars a week. They consider this unfair. It is a characteristic purely of Hollywood. You hear in Hollywood more than anywhere else the word "break" used. If you ask a successful person in Hollywood how he got there, he will never say, "I got here by hard work and personality." He will say, "I got the breaks." Of course, hard work and personality count a great deal, but "breaks" count too. When I was a projectionist, the head of the cutting department came to me and an older man who was also a projectionist and gave both of us an opportunity to become a cutter. The older man wouldn't take it. He wanted security and preferred to remain as a projectionist. I took it. He is still a projectionist, and I am a high-salaried director. I took the chance. We think, There but for the grace of God go I, when we see somebody not so successful. As a result, a person in Hollywood is really interested in bringing up the general level of people around him. He knows he can't do it individually. He knows it wouldn't do any good to give five bucks here or there. He looks around for some organization in which he can work that does these things. He finds Marxism because it is waiting for him. Of course, it is not that simple. He doesn't just open his eyes and see Marxism and say, "That is for me." The Communist Party has laid very clever flytraps for him. These organizations are all around him. And most of the work they do is very good. Their overt purpose is certainly good. They may eventually be used for other purposes. These organizations are not for the long-term work of the Communist Party. They are used to attract many people. They not only attract those who become Communists, but they attract many who never become Communists but who give the Communists the advantage of their time, their work, and their money. I think Koestler said seven out of every ten who joined the Party got out. The phrase has been used that the same ideals that took them in the Party took them out again. The average person who goes in finds there is no freedom of thought; that the discipline is a very harsh one. If it had not been for my experience in connection with *Cornered,* I might have gone on for some time. The Party has a very good explanation for everything that troubles a man. If he says he doesn't have freedom, the great explainer, whoever he is in that locality, will point out that he has freedom to tell the truth; that the Communist Party has discovered the ultimate truth; and within that limit he can speak. Anything outside of the Party line is a lie. Of course, anything capitalistic is basically a lie because it comes from a system they consider dishonest to begin with. So when a man accepts this thing, he believes he is following the truth. When a man leaves, like Albert Maltz, he is brought back in line or thrown out. Many go out. Something else takes place. You are isolated. You are surrounded by people who believe as you do. The people talk a lot, but they all agree with each other. You go to a party or to a friend's house, and you simply make statements and agree with each other, and, of course, damn the capitalists. You become isolated so much that after a while you don't know what the truth is, and it takes some shocking event to get you out of it. I would say the majority of members are not used in subversive activities. They are concerned with the organization and running of the Communist fronts, and many of them can go to their deaths believing they were working in a decent organization, if they don't look on the outside to see what is happening in Russia. It is the "end" policy of the Communist Party which explains everything. Whatever is done, they say, "This had to be done to achieve a good end." The end overtly [ostensibly?] is Utopia. For instance, many people questioned the Communist purges. The answer was, "These people are [counter?] revolutionists. We must hold them back." The same thing is true of the Hitler-Stalin Pact and the Finnish War. The Hitler-Stalin Pact was to achieve a good end. My wife had an interesting experience while I was in jail. My wife is not political at all, but she wanted me to get home very badly and was doing what she could, together with other wives of the Ten, to get me home. She was called and asked to go with one of the wives of the Ten to Sacramento, where all three parties—Democratic, Republican, and Progressive—were holding conventions. My wife noticed that the woman she was with, and others she had made contact with up there, were doing things that she didn't think were quite proper. For instance, they were getting information. In one particular instance they asked a small clerk, getting a small salary, to give them a secret list. My wife said, "You are asking him to risk his livelihood. He might lose his job and his reputation." The answer was, "It doesn't matter if one person gets hurt if thousands will eventually benefit." That answer is a very corrupt thing. You cannot get a perfect end by using a corrupt means, because the corrupt means corrupts you so that you don't know what a perfect end is.

MR. WALTER: How do the Communists explain the eighteen million slave laborers in Russia?

MR. DMYTRYK: In this country they deny it. They say the capitalist press does not print the truth. I have had arguments on that. They will admit some people are liquidated, but they say it is for the good of humanity.

MR. TAVENNER: Tell us now the circumstances of your own joining of the Communist Party, when it was and how it occurred.

MR. DMYTRYK: I joined, as I said before, in 1944.

MR. TAVENNER: Prior to that time, were you a member of various Communist-front organizations?

MR. DMYTRYK: Probably as early as 1942 I had begun to be interested in what later became Communist fronts. There was a school started that eventually became the People's Educational Center. Before that it was a small school, and there was one class for readers, and they wanted me to come and give them a talk on the editing of pictures, which I did. In preparing a lecture I had to try to arrive at certain theories of cutting, and in doing this I found I was finding out things about my profession—which I still did on my own pictures—which I had never learned before. I was very excited about that. I was asked to repeat the lecture, which I did, and improved on it. About this time, in 1943, the People's Educational Center was organized, and one of the classes was a class in screen direction. We had twelve lectures by directors—how a screenplay is directed, Technicolor, cutting, and so forth. I became one of the lecturers. Some of the lecturers were Communists, but most of them were not, and most of the students were not Communists. Then I learned the Communists were running this organization. It was during the war, and I didn't say, "How horrible." I said, "The Communists are doing something I think is good." The Writers' Congress was held about 1943. This was a meeting of writers from all over the country and from foreign countries. A message from President Roosevelt was read at the Congress. Gordon Sproul was honorary chairman. I think

Darryl Zanuck was in it. I later found that some of the people connected with the Congress were Communists. This was a good thing. I thought one of the things we needed was a meeting of cultural minds. When I found out this, too, had been organized by Communists, I thought it showed the Communist Party was engaged in good things. The Writers Mobilization was formed about this time. The Writers Mobilization, Emmet Lavery testified in 1947, got a medal for work they did for the war effort. They were writing speeches for patriotic organizations, writing scripts for USO, and that sort of thing. This, too, I found out had been very largely organized by a few Communists. During this time I was approached by people—I can't say by whom—to join the Communist Party. I was curious. I had tried to read Marx, but never got beyond the first chapter [of *Das Kapital*?]. So I agreed to go to a recruiting meeting, and eventually I went to a Communist Party meeting. Immediately after that the Communist Party was dissolved as such and became the Communist Political Association. At this time the line was that Communism can work with capitalism because capitalism is now enlightened; there is no need for revolution, and no need for conflict.

MR. TAVENNER: That doctrine was very short-lived?

MR. DMYTRYK: About a year, I think. Browder got kicked out for it. Also, during this time there was a good deal of disorganization in Hollywood. I attended only about six or seven regular group meetings and perhaps three special group meetings in all the time I was in the Party.

MR. POTTER: Who asked you to attend the first recruiting meeting?

MR. DMYTRYK: The man who spoke at this meeting was Alvah Bessie, later one of the Hollywood Ten.

MR. TAVENNER: Who were some of the others in that group with you?

MR. DMYTRYK: At that recruiting meeting, which was held at Frank Tuttle's house, although he was not there, the only one I knew was Alvah Bessie, because he spoke. That was not a regular Communist meeting. Later I went with a friend of mine—I won't mention his name because he has since died—I went to a meeting in San Fernando Valley at which I signed a Communist Party card.

MR. TAVENNER: Was that a cell?

MR. DMYTRYK: We didn't call them cells. This was a neighborhood group.

MR. TAVENNER: Can you give the names of people with you in that group?

MR. DMYTRYK: One was Lester Cole. Another was a man named Sackin. I had known him in the picture business. I think his first name was Lou or Moe. I think there are two of them. I cannot positively identify him.

MR. TAVENNER: You mean there are two separate people?

MR. DMYTRYK: Yes. The others I didn't know. There is a reason for that. When you first come to a Communist Party meeting you are not introduced by your last name, nor are the others introduced to you by their last names, so, unless you happen to know them, you don't know who they are for a long time. I went to only a couple of these meetings. Later I moved to Beverly Hills and went to a couple of meetings there, and then moved to another group, so I never got to know any of these people.

MR. TAVENNER: Describe each of these groups to which you were assigned.

MR. DMYTRYK: The second group I was assigned to met in Hollywood. In this group I saw Herbert Biberman, Arnold Manoff, Mickey Uris, and Leonardo Bercovici.

MR. TAVENNER: Then you were transferred to another group?

MR. DMYTRYK: I was transferred to a special group. This was toward the end of the Communist Political Association. I don't know exactly why this special group was organized. I was told later they were called the Davis group. They started naming the groups after famous dead Communists. They wouldn't use live ones because they didn't know how they would wind up. That group met in San Fernando Valley. They were people either considered supersecret or superprestige. I have no idea what the ultimate purpose of the group was, but I know it was a secret thing. I attended two meetings of this group. One meeting was at Sidney Buchman's house, although Sidney Buchman was not present. In this group were John Howard Lawson; Adrian Scott and myself; a writer named Francis—this is the masculine Francis—Faragoh and his wife, Elizabeth Faragoh; and a couple I had never met before: the man's name, I believe, is George Corey, a writer.

* * *

MR. TAVENNER: Did you at any time attend a fraction meeting of the Communist Party?

MR. DMYTRYK: Yes, I attended at least three special meetings. One I have already taken up, the directors' group. Now, there was another group at Paul Trivers' house. I can't remember who was present there. I haven't even the faintest recollection of what it was all about, and the only one I can identify at that particular meeting is Paul Trivers. Then there was another group, which met for the purpose, I think, of some sort of affair that had to do with the fight against anti-Negro prejudice. That was composed of small committees, as it were, from several neighborhood groups throughout the town. Most of them I didn't know. I knew just a few from Hollywood. The meeting was held at Ben Margolis's house, and Mr. Margolis was present, and Henry Blankfort was present. And a man named George Pepper. Now, also at one or another of these groups—it may have been at this one and may not—there were a couple of men. Sam Moore from Radio was present, and Maurice Clark, about whom I know nothing except he was concerned with the People's Educational Center.

MR. TAVENNER: This first meeting that you described was at the home of Ben Margolis?

MR. DMYTRYK: Yes.

MR. TAVENNER: Was he known to you to be a member of the Communist Party?

MR. DMYTRYK: Well, this was definitely a Communist Party meeting.

MR. WALTER: What is Mr. Margolis's occupation?

MR. DMYTRYK: He is an attorney.

MR. WALTER: Is he the man who has appeared here on several occasions with witnesses?

MR. DMYTRYK: I believe so. He appeared with us back in 1947.

MR. WALTER: Perhaps that accounts for the reluctance on the part of some of the witnesses to testify.

MR. TAVENNER: I understood you to say that you had learned a good deal about Communism through your associations with the group known as the Hollywood Ten. What did you have reference to?

MR. DMYTRYK: After the hearings here in 1947, when we went back to Hollywood, we organized. We had—it couldn't be called an organization, but a group who shared lawyers, called the Nineteen. Of these, ten appeared before the Committee and were cited for contempt, and so we organized the Hollywood Ten in Hollywood for the sharing of expenses, because we were all pretty broke by that time. We had to pay our attorneys. We conducted certain public-relations campaigns—not very successfully, but we did—that took a good deal of money. We had to hold affairs to collect money from private people, functions, dinners, and that sort of thing. And we held meetings quite frequently in order to discuss the various problems that came up. Right after the hearings in 1947 a number of speeches were made at various places. We were hot copy then, and, as a matter of fact, I think I made a couple of speeches myself. I left the country shortly after that. I couldn't work in Hollywood. We were all fired, those of us who were under contract by the studios, five out of the Ten. I went to England to make a couple of pictures. I went there early in 1948, and I came back in 1949, at the time when it was assumed that our case would get up in the Supreme Court, and we would either go to jail or not. One thing happened in England, however, that might be of interest. That is, Kravchenko, who had written a book—

MR. TAVENNER: Victor Kravchenko?

MR. DMYTRYK: Yes. Had written a book [*I Chose Freedom*] exposing Russian Communism, I believe. I never read the book. Anyway, a Communist newspaper in Paris printed the story about it, said that it was composed of lies. He sued the paper for libel. While I was in England a subpoena was sent over to England from France for me to appear at the trial. I was called and asked to accept a subpoena. They wanted me to come and testify.

MR. TAVENNER: Who wanted you?

MR. DMYTRYK: The newspaper side. In other words, the Communist side in this case wanted me to come over and testify, in the light of my experiences in the United States, that there was a great deal of repression and persecution in the United States. This didn't seem to me to have any bearing on whether or not Kravchenko had been libeled, and, besides, I think no man, even if he feels a grievance, should wash his dirty linen in public in a foreign country. Anyway, I was asked three different times to accept the subpoena, and I refused, and they finally stopped calling me. Now, when I came back to this country, we had a great many meetings then of the Hollywood Ten. We used to meet at least every week. There were several committees. And during this time I, too, I attended all the meetings. I got into arguments. I noticed that a change had taken place in the time while I was gone, and that the group was, without question, following the Party line all the way down the line. I know the basis of my argument was primarily that I thought that, since we were conducting a fight on civil liberties, that we ought to include as many people in our fight as we could, liberals, middle-of-the-roaders, progressives, everybody, and that the only way we could do this was make an honest fight on an honest issue. However, the group usually voted to support every cause they could. That is, they put stuff out in defense of the New York Eleven, the Communists in New York, the Harry Bridges case, every case of this sort that came up. Sometimes others would agree with me on my point of view, but I noticed that, when the argument got hot, somebody would call on John Howard Lawson, and then eventually on Ben Margolis, and the dialectical reasoning would come, and in effect, the Party-line dictate would come. A small group of these people probably used to meet before the meetings and lay out the agenda. In the long run it would wind up always, of course, in favor of the broad Communist Party line of action.

MR. TAVENNER: The time you were subpoenaed to appear before this Committee, was there any indication to you that the Communist Party was endeavoring in any way to influence the course of action that you as a group should take?

MR. DMYTRYK: Well, I certainly had no idea of it at the time. In looking back, of course, and remembering how the Nineteen were organized, I would say the answer to that would probably be yes.

MR. TAVENNER: Well, describe that to the Committee.

MR. DMYTRYK: When we first got the subpoenas, Adrian Scott and I accepted subpoenas from the marshal at RKO studios. We had been in touch with nobody else; nor did we get in touch with anybody else at that time. We decided we wanted to get a lawyer. I think that Adrian Scott had had some contact with Bartley Crum, whom we knew as a liberal Republican from San Francisco, a man who had been very active in Willkie's campaign. So we decided to contact Bartley Crum and ask him to serve as our counsel. He agreed. We told him our experience, that we had been members of the Party. We had both gotten out. Now we came back to Hollywood, and we were asked to attend a very loose meeting of a group of other people who had gotten subpoenas and who were not friendly to the Committee. This meeting was held at Edward G. Robinson's house. He was not there. The only reason it was held there is that Senator Pepper was visiting in Hollywood at the time, and whether he was a house guest with the Robinsons— I know he was quite friendly. They thought it would be wise if we could get together with Senator Pepper and just find out from him what the situation was in Washington. He spoke, extemporaneously, of course, compeletely harmlessly. At the end of the meeting, however, we were approached by people like Herbert Biberman, Adrian Scott, and asked to attend a further meeting, at which we would discuss procedure for our mutual benefit. We had another meeting. We had several after that, and found out that these other people had obtained other attorneys. So we finally decided that, since the expenses would be heavy and since there were quite a few members of that group who hadn't worked for a long time and had no money and that we would, in effect, have to carry them, we should pool our attorneys, as it were. I would assume that the thing was carefully planned by a certain number, but we went into it not realizing. We came back to Washington and worked as a unit, not in discussing what our testimony would or wouldn't be so much as on financial questions, on broad political questions. We were at the Shoreham Hotel part of the time; we had a large suite there, used to hold meetings regularly every day and discuss the various problems that came up.

MR. TAVENNER: Did any persons appear before your meeting to discuss matters?

MR. DMYTRYK: Two I can remember. One was Lee Pressman, who delivered a little informal speech.

MR. TAVENNER: What was the subject of his speech?

MR. DMYTRYK: We were in the forefront of a battle for freedom, and we were on the barricades. The other person was Harry Bridges.

MR. TAVENNER: Did you gain the impression that your group was being encouraged by Lee Pressman and Harry Bridges in the stand that it was taking?

MR. DMYTRYK: There was no question about that.

MR. TAVENNER: Well, the result of your concerted agreement was you would refuse to testify?

MR. DMYTRYK: Yes. It was generally agreed. We were fighting it purely on the standpoint of civil liberties and the First Amendment. The principle was that since we believed the procedures of the Committee at that time were not proper, the only way to test it was to take them into court, or have them take us into court—which is literally what happened—on a constitutional issue. We were sure that we would be cited for contempt, and we hoped and sincerely believed at the time that, on the question of the First Amendment, we could get at least a Supreme Court decision in our favor.

MR. TAVENNER: Was there an agreement by all to resort to that general procedure of refusing to testify, or was there difference of opinion?

MR. DMYTRYK: We were very careful not to discuss this in the group. We felt there was some danger that this might constitute conspiracy, and most of the decisions were made by individual consultation with the attorneys. The attorneys gave the same advice to everybody. There was disagreement at first to some extent among the attorneys. Bob Kenny and Bartley Crum were on the more conservative side, but they were outvoted, and I frankly don't know how strong they were in their private conversations. I am sure Bartley Crum disapproved of the tactics pretty much, but he went along. There were other elements that led us to believe that the tactics might be successful. For a while the motion-picture industry as such —that is, their spokesmen—fought the Committee, too. We were led to believe they would support us.

MR. TAVENNER: What do you mean?

MR. DMYTRYK: There had been several hearings into the industry by this Committee at that time, and before that, and I think by a Senatorial Committee. Wendell Willkie defended Hollywood at that time. And there was fear in Hollywood that the Committee was really out to try to intimidate Hollywood. So many of the executives in Hollywood were not in favor of the Committee and were anxious to get subpoenas and testify before the Committee to defend Hollywood.

MR. TAVENNER: You mentioned the fact that a meeting was held at the home of Edward G. Robinson. Do you have any knowledge of Communist Party membership or activity by Edward G. Robinson?

MR. DMYTRYK: To the best of my knowledge, he was never a Communist. It is true that he gave some money to Communist-front organizations, but many people did this without knowing what they were doing. I don't think, however, that he ever gave any money to the Hollywood Ten.

MR. TAVENNER: We have a list here of about twenty-four individuals whom you have named as being known to you to be members of the Communist Party and whose names you have given in the course of your testimony. I want to ask you about one of those to make certain what your testimony was: Alvah Bessie.

MR. DMYTRYK: I mentioned a meeting at which Alvah Bessie spoke about the Party. He had fought in the International Brigade in Spain and was a bit of a heroic figure at that time. He spoke at that party to recruit me and anybody else who was recruitable.

MR. TAVENNER: Recruit you into what?

MR. DMYTRYK: In the Communist Party.

* * *

MR. TAVENNER: Did you sit in a Communist Party meeting at any time with Richard Collins?

MR. DMYTRYK: Only in this particular affair. A person can be in the Communist Party for a long time and still not know that many people are Communists, because these groups are kept fairly separate. There is no secret handshake or password, and I have never heard anybody come up to me and say, "I am a Communist." It just doesn't happen. And you can suspect fifty people or a hundred people, but you cannot be sure unless you have worked with them in a meeting.

MR. TAVENNER: Now, for instance, Richard Collins, to give an example of what you are speaking of, testified that he had been a member of the Communist Party in Hollywood for around nine years, that he attended meetings about twice a week during all that period. And yet you never sat in a meeting with him?

MR. DMYTRYK: Never sat in a meeting with him outside of the incident I mentioned.

MR. TAVENNER: Sterling Hayden was one who testified that he had attended a number of meetings. Did you ever sit in a meeting with him?

MR. DMYTRYK: I was very surprised when he admitted being a member of the Communist Party. I had no idea he was even close.

MR. TAVENNER: Larry Parks has testified he was a member of the Communist Party and attended meetings. Did you ever attend a meeting at which he was present?

MR. DMYTRYK: No. At the time of the original hearings I was convinced Larry Parks was one of those—and there were several in the Nineteen—who was not a Communist.

MR. TAVENNER: Mrs. Meta Rosenberg testified to attendance at a number of meetings. Did you ever attend a meeting with her?

MR. DMYTRYK: I never did.

MR. TAVENNER: The twenty-four persons you have named are persons known to you to be members of the Communist Party?

MR. DMYTRYK: Yes.

MR. TAVENNER: You were a member, I believe, of the Council of the Hollywood Arts, Sciences, and Professions.

MR. DMYTRYK: Yes. . . . The reason for my being on the board was, about that time—that is, around, I should say, the middle of 1949, at the latest—the Council of Arts, Sciences, and Professions took the case of the Hollywood Ten as their leading cause, . . . and in general I think it can be said to have been run by Communists.

MR. TAVENNER: Was it affiliated with the Progressive Citizens of America?

MR. DMYTRYK: I believe so.

MR. TAVENNER: When the Progressive Citizens of America dissolved into the Wallace Progressive Party movement in 1948, do you know what effect that had upon the Council of Arts, Sciences, and Professions?

MR. DMYTRYK: I would say that the Council of Arts, Sciences, and Professions was one of the Progressive Party's chief supporters, because I know they ran affairs to collect money for the Wallace movement. That was their chief job.

MR. TAVENNER: Now, you have described to us in great detail the experience you have had in connection with the picture *Cornered,* when you were told at the conclusion of that incident by [John] Howard Lawson that, if you could not accept the discipline of the Communist Party, probably the best thing for you and Scott to do was to get out.

MR. DMYTRYK: Yes.

MR. TAVENNER: I understood you to say that that incident had a lot to do with your determining that you would get out of the Party.

MR. DMYTRYK: Yes, it did.

MR. TAVENNER: Now, explain that more in detail.

MR. DMYTRYK: I had always believed in the right of every individual to think as he wished, and particularly for every artist to be perfectly free in what he had to say. I had never gone along with any kind of thought control, and before that actually I had never myself experienced any such instances. The fact that they tried to tell us what to do, that others got together and tried to tell us what to do, shocked me very deeply. I knew myself that I could never submit to that kind of discipline.

MR. TAVENNER: There has come to our attention an incident of a similar circumstance that came over the radio today, and a few moments ago we were able to locate it in the newspaper. I am going to read it to you:

(Washington *Daily News,* April 25, 1951, p. 7)

SOVIET OPERA FAILS AT COLLECTIVE FARMING

> The Russian Government has fired the director of its state-owned Bolshoi Theater for staging an opera which failed to show the best qualities of Soviet farmers. A brief radio Moscow announcement yesterday said A. V. Solodovnikov had been replaced as theater director by A. I. Anisimov for unsatisfactory direction. But *Pravda* provided some details a week ago. It said Herman Zhukovsky's opera, *From All Our Hearts,* failed to reflect the riches and joyfulness of life on a collective farm. Authors, composers, and stage designers were jolted by the *Pravda* blast, because the opera had received a Stalin prize only last month. Furthermore, Stalin had attended the opera shortly after. *Pravda* even assailed the All-Union Committee of Fine Arts, final authority on new artistic works, for permitting the production of an unhealthy, inartistic opera.

That was based upon the failure of this play to properly describe the best qualities of collective farming. Now, is that the type of discipline to which you refer as being objectionable and as being accepted in the Communist Party?

MR. DMTYRYK: It certainly is. For instance, the famous case of the

Communist musicians who were reprimanded by the Party—and I remember asking, "How can anybody, any commissar or committee say what is people's music? It doesn't make sense to me, because a note doesn't propagandize, as far as I am concerned." But they said, "No. If you really study it very carefully there is a great deal to this. There is a certain kind of music people understand. If they understand it, it is people's music, and it should be done. On the other hand, if the music isn't understood by the people, then it is counterrevolutionary and as such should be forbidden." I have had these arguments with Communists in Hollywood.

MR. TAVENNER: And was that argument equally valid with regard to the Duclos letter, which has been mentioned here in the testimony a number of times?

MR. DMYTRYK: The Duclos letter was a little bit different. I'd say this was what happened. Browder recently, and his associates, decided they could cooperate with the capitalistic government, that revolution or war was not necessary, that the capitalist form itself would eventually evolve into a socialist form of government. Now, after the war was over and there was no longer need on the part of Russia to cooperate with the United States, Duclos, who was a French Communist, a powerful worker in the French underground, went to Russia. When he came back to Paris he wrote his famous letter in which he criticized severely the American Party line as it had been followed under the Communist Political Association. This even had some repercussions in Hollywood, because John Howard Lawson, who had been a Browder supporter, and who had been a strong preacher of the cooperative policy, had to do a lot of very fast tightrope walking to save himself. A lot of the Communists in Hollywood were a little bit happy about this, because even they had resented the Lawson touch. And so they hoped he would get thrown out, too, but he made his peace with the new group.

MR. TAVENNER: Well, do you recall any instance in which a leader in the Party may have argued in behalf of one thing at one time and then very shortly afterward been compelled to change entirely?

MR. DMYTRYK: There was a well-known incident that everybody got a good laugh out of in Hollywood, even the Communists. They were the only ones who actually knew about it. It was where Herbert Biberman had made a very powerful speech, impassioned speech, in favor of—I don't know if it was a personality or Party line, one day. The official Party line changed the following afternoon. The following day he made an equally impassioned speech in direct contrast to the speech he had made two days before.

MR. TAVENNER: When do you consider you withdrew from the Communist Party?

MR. DMTYRYK: In the fall of 1945. However, I was active in what are now called Communist Party fronts. I was still teaching at the People's Education Center until 1947. I was on the board of the Arts, Sciences, and

Professions Council. I was a member of the Hollywood Ten. So actually I didn't break, I want to explain that, too. As a man who had taken a gamble, who had made his choice in my appearance before the 1947 Committee, I felt that I should follow this choice to its logical conclusion—that is, until such a time as the Supreme Court either decided we were right, or we were wrong and went to jail. I felt if I suddenly started crying uncle, I was doing it simply to avoid the consequences of the decision, which was going to jail, although, before I went to jail, I had already made up my mind, as soon as my jail sentence was over, I would issue an affidavit and disclose whether I had been a member of the Party. Actually, I issued such an affidavit, a partial disclosure, because a complete disclosure would have taken far too much time and space to explain while I was in prison. I did this, because the Korean War—the way the Korean War was going so bothered me that I felt I had better make my position clear on that.

MR. TAVENNER: To whom did you give this affidavit?

MR. DMYTRYK: Well, Bartley Crum and Milton Diamond, two attorneys. We took the deposition in the presence of Mr. Thieman, who was the superintendent of the Mill Point Prison. I have heard rumors, two different kinds: One that I made the affidavit because I had been offered a job at M-G-M at five thousand dollars a week if I would make such an affidavit. This obviously had been proven untrue. The other is Bartley Crum said somebody, not a Communist, had approached him in New York and said, "I understand that they really put the works to Dmytryk in jail, they put the pressure on him, and that is why he made his affidavit." This is not true. There was no pressure, nor has there been of any kind, nor have I ever been offered a bribe or job of any kind—I wish I had—to make either the affidavit or to come here.

MR. TAVENNER: This was a statement dictated by your own conscience?

MR. DMYTRYK: Dictated by my own conscience, absolutely.

MR. TAVENNER: Has there been any effort made since that time to recruit you again into the Communist Party?

MR. DMYTRYK: Well, there was when I came back from England. Herbert Biberman asked me to go back in the Party. I told him I couldn't.

MR. TAVENNER: Do you recall an occasion when Mrs. Faragoh approached you about your uniting again in the Communist Party back, I think, in 1945?

MR. DMYTRYK: As a matter of fact, I was out on the street washing my car when Elizabeth Faragoh asked me to re-sign. She said she wanted to issue a new Communist Party card for me. I described to her what had gone on between Scott and Lawson and myself and said that I was very doubtful about the Party. She said, "Well, it won't hurt just to put your name in. You can do as you please about it, because actually things are in a great state of flux. We ourselves don't know what is going to happen." I must say I said

O.K. I did not want to continue the discussion. I had already made up my mind I wasn't going back, but I didn't object to her putting my name back in again.

MR. WALTER: Mr. Dmytryk, it is refreshing to find that there are people who are willing to assist in our feeble efforts to make a contribution in this world-wide struggle against Communism. I think that you have made a very great contribution.

MR. DMYTRYK: Thank you.

* * *

MR. JACKSON: Mr. Dmytryk, much has been said with respect to legislation directed to the outlawing of the Party. Objections have been made to such proposal on the grounds that it might tend to drive the Communist Party underground. Would you care to make any comment, so far as the operations of the Party are concerned?

MR. DMYTRYK: I would like to read a wire I got. The important part of this wire is simply that it relates an interview on last Sunday night between Louella Parsons and a man named Matt Cvetic. I believe he is the man who wrote a book called *I Was a Communist for the FBI*. Louella Parsons asked him, "What about the argument that these trials drive the Reds further underground?" He replied, "Don't fall for that. The Reds try to put that idea across to discourage these trials, but the truth is the Commies *always* work underground. Anything that brings them in the open hurts them." Then he says, "That is why Hollywood must support Parks and Hayden, to encourage more people to speak out." Parsons then asked how smart personalities like Parks and Hayden could be gotten in the Party. He replied, "The really frightening cleverness of the Communists is how they understand appealing to people's best emotions—their tolerance—their broad-mindedness, and then use those good emotions for their own end."* * * I think the Communist Party is conspiratorial, subversive, and even in certain cases treasonable. There is no question in my mind—and there is certainly no question in these days of present danger—that the Communist Party should be outlawed.

MR. JACKSON: One more question, if I may, Mr. Chairman. What would you call the final test of credibility of a witness purporting to be a former Communist? Would you say the test of credibility would have to be primarily the willingness to name names, places, and circumstances surrounding such membership?

MR. DMYTRYK: I personally believe so. That is why I am doing it. I think if a man says that he is convinced that the Communist Party is a subversive or criminal organization, that he certainly shouldn't mind giving names. I know that there have been comments—I don't mean by the Communists but even among certain progressives and liberals—that people who talk are, in effect, informers. I heard that so much that I went to the dictionary and looked up the word. An informer, roughly speaking, is a man who informs against colleagues or former colleagues, who are engaged in criminal activity. I think the Communists, by using this word against people, are in effect admitting they are engaged in criminal activity. I never heard of anybody informing on the Boy Scouts.

MR. JACKSON: What is your opinion of the sincerity or devotion to American ideals of those witnesses who refuse to answer any questions posed by the Committee which touch upon membership in the Communist Party or Communist-front organizations?

MR. DMYTRYK: I knew the minute I refused to testify everybody in the United States who heard about it assumed I was a Communist.

MR. JACKSON: Do you think that is an unreasonable assumption?

MR. DMYTRYK: I make the same assumption myself.

MR. JACKSON: So do I.

* * *

MR. WOOD: Permit me, Mr. Dmytryk, to add my feeble expression of appreciation for your coming here, and for the information that you have given to the American people, millions of whom haven't the vaguest conception of what the Communist movement in America stands for.

Storm Over Dmytryk

Dmytryk repeated his story in a *Saturday Evening Post* article, "What Makes a Hollywood Communist," signed by Richard English (May 10, 1951). This brought forth the following letter from Albert Maltz, reprinted from the *Hollywood Reporter*, May 29, 1951, which in turn brought forth the statement signed by Ronald Reagan and others, reprinted from the *Hollywood Reporter*, June 6, 1951.

May 28, 1951.

Editors, *Saturday Evening Post*.

DEAR SIRS:

The *Post* has been made a victim of a fraud. Richard English, author of your recent article, "What Makes a Hollywood Communist," is presumably an equal victim. Edward Dmytryk, the subject of the article, is a deliberate faker and liar. I will prove it.

In your pages Dmytryk represents himself as a man of principle and idealism who was misled into joining the Communist Party in the spring of 1944, but who left it in disillusionment and resentment in the fall of 1945. Very good! Now let us ask some questions.

Why did Dmytryk oppose the 1947 investigation into Communism in Hollywood? Why didn't he support it as others did? Dmytryk swears now that he left the Communist Party in 1945 because Party members tried to dictate to him the manner in which one of his films should be written and produced. Is this true? If it is true, why did he not testify to it in 1947? The entire thesis of the House Committee was precisely this: That the Communist Party was involved in a conspiracy to influence and dominate the content and production of Hollywood films. Dmytryk swears to this thesis in 1951. Why did he not do so in 1947? It was crucial testimony. If it is true now, it was true then. Why was he silent about it?

Only one conclusion is possible. Either his present testimony about the Communist Party is false, and therefore he is a perjurer; or else, in 1947, he self-confessedly was a citizen without principle, honor or sense of public duty.

I do not know when Dmytryk joined the Communist Party or when he left it. I was not witness upon either occasion. Furthermore I would not speak of it if I knew. I did not go to prison myself, or accept blacklisting in the film industry, to give over the principles upon which I stood—that no American should be compelled to disclose matters involving his freedom of thought and the secrecy of the ballot. And therefore I will not comment upon those sections of Dmytryk's biography which touch upon such matters. But I will prove by public record that Dmytryk's story of himself is a falsehood.

The truth about Dmytryk is simple and ugly: He believed in certain principles, no doubt very sincerely, until the consequences of those beliefs became painful. He has not now made a peace with his conscience, he has made it with his pocket book and his career. Here is the evidence:

In September, 1947, some thirty individuals in Hollywood received subpoenas to testify before the House Committee on Un-American Activities. Nineteen of these witnesses were opposed to the investigation and to the Committee. They voluntarily joined together to combat both by means of a public campaign. Dmytryk was one of them. Why? Some of these individuals, he now testifies, were members of the Communist Party. Why did he ally himself with them? Several were among those very Communists, he also testified, who participated in the effort in 1945 to make him an artist in uniform. Over this he quit the Communist Party. Why then did he join hands two years later with these same men?

When the nineteen men contributed money to the expenses of their common effort, why did Dmytryk contribute also—some $2500? Why did he appear in a public meeting at the Shrine Auditorium in Los Angeles on the eve of the investigation, joining with those others in a wholesale condemnation of the House Committee?

Why did he travel from Los Angeles to Washington in the same plane with the other witnesses unfriendly to the Committee? Why did he join with them in speaking to a public meeting in Chicago? Why also did he join them in a public meeting in Washington during the crucial first week of the testimony in which the Committee declared, and took testimony, concerning the evil influence of Communism in the film industry? Why did he not at that time withdraw from this group of nineteen men since, as he now asserts, the Committee thesis was true?

Dmytryk says he believed then that the Committee was trying to acquire censor power over the films. For this reason he opposed it. Very admirable! But why did he not state in public, or on the witness stand, what he now testifies he knew about the Communist Party? Unless it was false, both then and now.

Dmytryk maintains that he was merely a fellow-traveler of the Hollywood Ten in the period that followed the citation for contempt. His interest was in civil liberties, he asserts, and for this very reason his two and a half year association with the other men taught him to detest Communism even more deeply. For we others were not truly interested in civil liberties or the constitution. Indeed! If this is true, then it may be asked at what point Dmytryk saw the light of this truth?

Was it in 1945 when, as he now testifies, he left the Communist Party? No—because two years later he participated intimately, fully and voluntarily in the private and public efforts of the nineteen witnesses opposed to the House Committee.

Was it a little later, after he had been cited for contempt? No, because he joined the group known as the Hollywood Ten—retained the same attorneys—appeared on public platforms—voluntarily signed joint public statements—voluntarily raised funds in the Hollywood Community—and joined with the other nine men in two legal suits against the film companies, one of them early in 1948, the other in the summer of 1949.

Did he see the light after his first trip to England in 1948, where he remained for some months arranging for film work? No, because he returned to speak on platforms as a member of the Hollywood Ten. What truth is there to his statement that the other members of the Ten were becoming abhorrent to him, since I myself was witness and best man at his marriage to Jean Porter in Elicott City, Md., on May 12, 1948, the only one of his friends present? And since I traveled with the bride and groom from Washington to Philadelphia by auto, and appeared on a public platform with Dmytryk on the evening of his marriage, he scarcely can assert that I was repugnant to him, or he to me, at that time.

Was it after Dmytryk's second trip to England, which ended in August, 1949, that he saw the great light? He maintains so. I quote him from your article: "After you've been away, your eyes are really clear. . . . The second thing that got me was the way the Ten were being turned into martyrs. . . . When I left, it had basically been a good civil liberties case. Now it was being used as a spearhead against all attacks on Communism.

. . . The hardest thing I had to live with was the realization that they were trying to protect communism in this country by invoking the Constitution and civil liberties. . . . This was on my conscience constantly."

Was it? If this is true, then Dmytryk has a most flexible conscience. Five months after his clear-eyed return from England, he was one of the three member Steering Committee of the Hollywood Ten, the group responsible for day to day conduct of our private and public affairs. Two months later, in April, 1950, he joined with the other members of the Hollywood Ten in a public statement, before press and television, condemning the refusal of the Supreme Court to hear our case. A month later, in May, he joined with all other members of the Hollywood Ten in appearing and speaking in a two reel film on our case, a film designed for distribution all over the world. This film was not made in 1947, early in the case, as Dmytryk deliberately implies in your article, but in May, 1950, after the Supreme Court had rejected us.

Two weeks or so later, on a June night, he appeared at the Los Angeles Airport with other members of the Ten for a farewell public meeting. A night later he appeared with us at Town Hall, in N.Y., at a meeting under the auspices of the Arts, Sciences, and Professions Council, a meeting at which Paul Robeson spoke and sang. And in N.Y. that day at LaGuardia Airport, and in Washington the next day at the Shoreham Hotel, he spoke with us to the press and mentioned nothing about his troubled conscience. And where finally was his conscience, and what motivated him or compelled him, when he signed the Stockholm Peace Petition, before a photographer, on the steps of the District Court in Washington on the day he went for formal trial and sentence?

So, it was not then either that he saw the light! Not in 1945, when he says he left the Communist Party, and not in 1947 when the Committee asserted, and he denied, what he now eagerly testifies to, and not in 1949 when he returned from England with clear eyes.

Dmytryk lies further when he says that he finally broke with the Hollywood Ten over the issue of the Korean War. Neither he nor I can have direct evidence on those conversations in the jail yard, to which he refers. I grant him now, as I granted him then, the right to his own opinion. But his statement that the nine men had one interpretation of those new and terrible events, and were opposed to him in a solid phalanx, is a flat lie, and he knows it.

And if what I say is not true—if Dmytryk at last, and finally, learned that he had been associated with a group of malevolent scoundrels whom he now repudiated—then let me ask further: Why did his wife continue to function publicly as a member of the Committee of the Wives of the Hollywood Ten? Why also did his wife join mine in August, 1950, in appearing in Sacramento, Calif., before the Platform Committees of the Democratic and Republican Parties and before the convention of the Progressive Party, to ask all three parties to include a statement on the case of the Hollywood Ten in their platform on civil liberties? And why, at the end of August, did Mrs. Dmytryk join my wife in a common visit to prison? Why did they sleep in the same hotel room, hire a car together, travel 120 miles from Charleston to Mill Point, W.Va., visit, remain over night and travel back together? The prison records show they were together and twenty officers and inmates will testify to it.

Yet there is still more to this fraud. Dmytryk decided in September to issue a statement from prison asserting his loyalty to the U.S. And I, he says, pleaded with him not to issue it. He even presumes to invent words that he puts in my mouth. What a scoundrel! The truth is that his attorney, Bartley Crum, one of the several attorneys in our case, was requested by Mrs. Dmytryk to visit her husband. I knew nothing of this until the Saturday morning he appeared. The prison records will show that the interview between them was in the presence of the Superintendent of the camp—and that I was not present. Dmytryk had neither told me beforehand that he intended to issue a statement nor consulted me about it. After the interview he had no text to show me. The statement came over the radio on Sunday night but I did not hear it, other inmates told me. I first read it on Tuesday, when the Monday *New York Times* came to the camp. Indeed I did disapprove of it because the statement implied that there had been an element of disloyalty in the constitutional position taken by the Hollywood Ten and that only he, Dmytryk, was truly loyal to the U.S. and therefore was obliged to make a statement.

The truth is much simpler. The truth was revealed a few weeks before he issued the statement when he said to me one day, very suddenly, "I'm NEVER going to prison again." The truth was equally naked when he replied to my criticism of his public statement by saying that I analyzed it too closely, that most people would not do that, that all he wanted was to try to get work in Hollywood again. I'm still opposed to the Committee, he told me, I'm still heart and soul against the Motion Picture Alliance, I'm still the same man I always was—but it is necessary for Progressives to go underground for a while.

This to me in prison in mid-September, 1950. The night before he left prison, Nov. 14, this man shook my hand warmly, doing so in the presence of several inmates and an officer, offering me his deep sympathy, because I had received double his sentence. At the Christmas season he received Herbert Biberman, another of the Hollywood Ten, in his home, listened to Biberman's invitation to join families for a holiday in the snows, watched, smiling, as Biberman played with his infant son.

This is the man of conscience who now tells his story in your pages. What conscience? A conscience that was quickly and cheaply refurnished by four and a half months in prison and is now a commodity for hire. This is the man who swears that he speaks the truth. What truth? He has lied and befouled others with his lies; he has traduced the good principles for which he once stood; and now he buys his way back into the film industry by trampling the careers of thirty others. Who but the blind, the stupid and the prejudiced will believe anything he says?

Very truly yours,
ALBERT MALTZ

YOU CAN BE FREE MEN AGAIN!

When the Communist Party traps an American into its unholy conspiracy, it is almost unbearably hard to break away. The Party sees to that, for the Party must enforce its discipline or die.

The Communist Party is now trying to destroy Edward Dmytryk for breaking with the party and exposing its secrets to the proper government agencies. Dmytryk is not the first ex-communist to be called "faker" and "liar" and "scoundrel" and "perjurer." These same accusations have been levelled by the Communist Party against such militant ex-communists as Arthur Koestler, Louis Budenz, Elizabeth Bentley and Whittaker Chambers.

In each case, the records of these persons show that their disillusionment with Communism came slowly, but with it came determination to help destroy the menace which once had trapped them. The attack upon Dmytryk merely confirms what veteran fighters against communism already know, namely, that the party has been hit where it hurts.

Any American who associates with the Communist Party is befouled. He is befouled, not by the person who exposes him, but by his own act in joining a traitorous conspiracy against his own country. This has been confirmed by the U.S. Supreme Court decision upholding the Smith Act. Read then a story which should interest you, a story of a person who finally realized that he had been besmirched by his association with the Communist Party and who sought our help in rising from Communist slime to cleaner ground:

We are just a few of the many loyal Americans in Hollywood who have helped bring about the complete frustration and failure of the Communist Party in the motion picture capital. On February 2, 1951, we met with Edward Dmytryk at his request. Dmytryk told us he wished to rehabilitate himself and he asked our advice and help. We questioned him at length and searchingly. We told him that we were not interested in him personally or whether he ever got a job again. We made sure in our own minds that it was not principally economic pressure which had led Dmytryk to want to come clean, although, of course, that had something to do with it. We made sure that Dmytryk was really trying to escape the Communist trap.

The advice we gave Dmytryk was tough and drastic. No one without courage and sincerity could have followed that advice. An appointment was made for Dmytryk with the F.B.I. Another meeting was arranged with investigators for the House Committee on Un-American Activities. We suggested his voluntary appearance before the committee. We suggested a magazine article. In meeting after meeting with Dmytryk, we watched the man change and gradually lose his fear that for the ex-Communist there is no road back to decent society. We watched as, with his intellectual blinders removed, he slowly realized with growing anger the truth and the enormity of the Communist conspiracy against our land. We warned him to expect vicious attacks by the Communist Party.

Not one item of fact in the Communist Party line attack on Edward Dmytryk was unknown to us nor to the Federal Bureau of Investigation nor to the House Committee on Un-American Activities. Dmytryk himself told us the facts, in proper sequence and perspective and not pervertedly twisted to serve the Communist Party line. The one thing we could not know in advance, of course, was the one BIG LIE in the attack on Dmytryk, namely the unsupported claim that Dmytryk had said Progressives must go underground. We are certain Dmytryk never said anything like that. This BIG LIE was fashioned as the supposed "clincher" for a collection of half-truths and distortions in time and fact. The BIG LIE is an official technique of the Communist Party.

The attack on Eddie Dmytryk was not unexpected and it came as no surprise to those who know how the Communist Party operates. But the Communist Party has failed in its effort to destroy Edward Dmytryk. Were it otherwise, it would be a victory for the Communist Party and a defeat for Americanism.

We will be surprised if there are not other attacks by the Communist Party on other former Communists who have the guts to stand up and be counted and to tell the truth to the proper government agencies. It takes courage and desire and time for an American to work free of the tentacles of the Communist Party. And it takes help. But there is a way out. To any Communist Party members who may be seeking that way, we say: "You too can be free men again!"

ROY BREWER — RONALD REAGAN
I. E. CHADWICK — JACK DALES
ART ARTHUR — ALEXANDER KEMPNER

The Motion Picture Industry Council, composed of Hollywood's key guild, union and management groups, endorses the above statement in accordance with the MPIC policy announced March 21, 1951, of urging all persons subpoenaed by the House Committee on Un-American Activities to tell the whole truth, and of offering "commendation and encouragement" to those former members of the Communist Party who have repudiated party ties and who join their fellow Americans in the fight for freedom.

MAY 22, 1951:

José Ferrer

The Committee on Un-American Activities met at 10:30 a.m. in room 226, Old House Office Building, the Honorable John S. Wood (Chairman) presiding.

Committee members present: Representatives John S. Wood (Chairman), Francis E. Walter (appearance as noted in transcript), Morgan M. Moulder (appearance as noted in transcript), Clyde Doyle, Harold H. Velde, Bernard W. Kearney, and Donald L. Jackson.

Staff members present: Frank S. Tavenner, Jr., Counsel; Thomas W. Beale, Sr., Assistant Counsel; Louis J. Russell, Senior Investigator; John W. Carrington, Clerk; Raphael I. Nixon, Director of Research; and A. S. Poore, Editor.

MR. TAVENNER: Will you state your name, please?

MR. FERRER: José Ferrer.

MR. TAVENNER: Are you represented here by counsel?

MR. FERRER: I am, sir.

MR. TAVENNER: Will counsel please identify themselves for the record?

MR. FORTAS: I am Abe Fortas.

MR. REISKIND: I am Edwin Reiskind.

MR. TAVENNER: Mr. Ferrer, after the service of a subpoena on you, the Committee received a letter from you, through counsel, in which you stated, "I attest and will so swear under oath that I am not, have never been, could not be, a member of the Communist Party, nor, specifically, am I a sympathizer with any Communist aim, a fellow traveler, or in any way an encourager of any Communist Party concept or objective." Is that substantially your statement?

MR. FERRER: Yes.

MR. TAVENNER: Are you now or have you ever been a member of the Communist Party?

MR. FERRER: No, sir, I am not now nor have I ever been.

MR. TAVENNER: Are you now or have you ever been a sympathizer?

MR. FERRER: No, sir.

MR. TAVENNER: Paraphrasing the language of your statement, have you been a sympathizer with any Communist aim, or have you been a fellow traveler or in any way an encourager of any Communist Party concept or objective?

MR. FERRER: The only time I could even remotely be said to have been in sympathy with any Communist aim was when it coincided with the aim of our Government. For instance, when they wanted us to win the last war, I certainly was in sympathy with that.

MR. TAVENNER: The Committee is in possession of information indicating your affiliation or connection with quite a number of organizations which have from time to time been cited by various governmental agencies as Communist-front organizations. You, of course, are aware that affiliations with or activities in Communist-front organizations, if true and unexplained, leave the implication that one is in fact a member of the Communist Party or has been, or that he is in fact a sympathizer of the Communist Party or an encourager of Communist Party concepts and objectives. You agree with that, do you not?

MR. FERRER: Yes. This has been made dramatically clear to me recently, Mr. Tavenner.

MR. TAVENNER: The Committee is quite concerned about the use of Communist fronts in exploiting the objectives of the Communist Party, and that is particularly true with regard to Hollywood.

MR. FERRER: Yes, sir.

MR. TAVENNER: A witness who appeared here before this Committee last week, Mr. Roy M. Brewer, whose position with a labor union in Hollywood over a long period of time has put him in a position of having special knowledge on this subject, states that the real power that they (the Communists) had in Hollywood was through their front organizations. He also testified at some length regarding the Communist fronts in Hollywood. This may in one way or another be true as to all the entertainment fields. At least, it applies to Hollywood. Mr. Brewer testified as follows, on page 131 of the transcript:

> . . . The Communist fronts played a very important part in publicizing the class struggle and publicizing their efforts to infiltrate and take control of all trade-union activities which they felt would promote the philosophy of their party.
>
> But in this Hollywood situation the fronts played an even more important part in this control of the thought of the community, which certainly followed over into the unions and made it very difficult for those of us who were trying to expose the Communist nature of this thing to get that idea across.
>
> During this period the fronts played a very important part in controlling the thought of the community, which I testified to yesterday. This was really the instrument by which they got all these people, most of whom were honest, sincere people who wanted to do the right thing, who wanted to serve humanity in a practical way, and wound up finding themselves in an organization that had been manipulated by the Communist Party day after day, week after week, and month after month.

That illustrates what has been testified to here as to the importance of Communist-front activities in the entertainment field. Now, the Committee desires to ask you a number of questions relating to your own special knowledge of Communist fronts in Hollywood, not only for the purpose of finding what your own connection with those organizations was but to ascertain the manner in which your assistance was secured, if that be true, and the method by which these organizations function. So, I will start off asking you about various Communist-front organizations with which we have information that you have at one time or another been connected. First of all, do you have any comment to make upon the testimony of Mr. Brewer that I have just read to you?

MR. FERRER: Undoubtedly what Mr. Brewer says probably is very perceptive and very accurate, not only as regards Communist-front activities but also, very importantly, from my personal point of view, the way innocent and well-intentioned people have been deceived and lured into participation in causes which at one time seemed worthy and later on appeared unworthy.

MR. TAVENNER: I have before me a pamphlet entitled "Artists' Front to Win the War," published by that organization October 16, 1942. It reflects that you are one of the sponsors of the theater section of that organization. Were you affiliated with it in any way?

MR. FERRER (*after examining document*): It is entirely possible, and even probable.

MR. TAVENNER: This pamphlet, under date October 16, 1942, has a heading, as you noticed, in the center of the pamphlet, "For a Second Front This Year." You do recall, do you not, that that was the Communist Party line during that period in 1942, to urge the establishment of a second front?

MR. FERRER: I recall that in the light of later knowledge. I did not know at the time that it was the Communist Party line.

MR. MOULDER: A second front in what?

MR. TAVENNER: In World War II. That is correct, isn't it?

MR. FERRER: I think so.

MR. TAVENNER: In fact, that is the only purpose shown for the establishment of this organization, Artists' Front to Win the War?

MR. FERRER: Would you like me to explain why I probably allowed my name to be used?

MR. TAVENNER: Yes.

MR. FERRER: The general technique is to come to someone, by letter or otherwise, and say, "You realize that a second front must be established." And to make yourself appear to be a person of some sagacity, you say yes. Then they say, "Important people are ready to move in that direction," and they show you a list of distinguished names, leaders in cultural and various fields, names you associate with integrity and authority, and if it seems a worthwhile cause—and I am speaking only for myself—you say, "Certainly, use my name."

MR. TAVENNER: And you were one of the distinguished persons in the field of actors?

MR. FERRER: I don't think I was very distinguished in 1942, Mr. Tavenner. There is a question whether I am distinguished now.

MR. TAVENNER: Do you recall who solicited your affiliation with this organization?

MR. FERRER: No, I don't.

MR. TAVENNER: You do recall that sometime later this organization was cited as a Communist front by the Committee on Un-American Activities and the California committee, do you not?

MR. FERRER: I recall it in the light of the work and the research that I have done recently, yes, sir.

MR. TAVENNER: There was a committee known as the American Committee for Protection of Foreign Born. The Committee possesses information indicating that your name was listed as the sponsor of a dinner given by the American Committee for Protection of Foreign Born held April 17, 1943, at the Hotel Biltmore in New York City. Do you recall sponsoring that dinner and attending it?

MR. FERRER: I am pretty sure I did not attend it, Mr. Tavenner, and I will say I think I remember sponsoring it simply because it has been proven to me time and again, especially in the last few weeks, that one's memory can be treacherous.

MR. TAVENNER: What association did you have with the American Committee for Protection of Foreign Born, if any?

MR. FERRER: I don't remember any connection whatever. What probably happened, again, is that I received a letter saying, "We are having this dinner; will you lend us your name?" Then they cited some distinguished names. I don't remember who they were, but wasn't Mrs. Roosevelt's name used in soliciting sponsors?

MR. TAVENNER: I do not see the name you mentioned. I am handing you the list of sponsors.

MR. FERRER (*examining list*): Dorothy Thompson, William Allen White, and Edward G. Robinson were among the people who spoke at that dinner. In connection with the foreign-born, Mr. Tavenner, I would say that I would probably be predisposed emotionally to help the foreign-born in any legitimate cause in this country, because of the fact that I am a Puerto Rican.

MR. TAVENNER: But are you familiar with the extent to which the Communist Party has endeavored to infiltrate organizations that may be interested in that cause?

MR. FERRER: Unfortunately, I have become aware only in recent months.

MR. TAVENNER: Did you know that this organization has been cited as subversive?

MR. FERRER: I know that now.

MR. TAVENNER: By this Committee and also by the California committee. I want to ask you questions now concerning the Joint Anti-Fascist Refugee Committee. The December 21, 1943, issue of *New Masses,* at page 31, contains an advertisement indicating that José Ferrer, among others, was to be an entertainer at an all-star show to be held on January 26, 1944, at the Imperial Theater in New York under the auspices of the Joint Anti-Fascist Refugee Committee. Did you appear as an entertainer on that occasion?

MR. FERRER: No, sir, I did not.

MR. TAVENNER: Will you explain to the Committee how your name happened to appear in the advertisement?

MR. FERRER: I did agree to appear, and just didn't.

MR. TAVENNER: You were more or less active, were you not, with the Joint Anti-Fascist Refugee Committee?

MR. FERRER: I was from time to time, yes, sir.

MR. TAVENNER: Did you make contributions to it?

MR. FERRER: I don't believe so. If I may ask counsel, they would be able to tell you better than I can.

(*The witness conferred with his counsel.*)

MR. FERRER: They are of the opinion I did not.

MR. FORTAS: We have a list, Mr. Tavenner, of all contributions Mr. Ferrer made to any cause so far as they can be ascertained from his own records, and will be glad to supply that if you want it.

MR. TAVENNER: Will you take a hurried glance at the list and see if you have made contributions to this organization?

MR. FERRER: I suspect they will take careful glances.

MR. FORTAS: Would you like to have a copy, Mr. Tavenner?

(*Copy of document was handed to Mr. Tavenner.*)

MR. WOOD: May I inquire if there are extra copies of the list available for the members of the Committee?

MR. FORTAS: Yes, sir (*handing copies to members of Committee*).

MR. TAVENNER: I have looked at the list, and I do not see any contributions to this organization. Does that mean that you did not make any contributions as far as you know?

MR. FERRER: As far as I know, Mr. Tavenner. Any contribution I would have made I would have made by check, and this list is made from a thorough search of my checkbooks.

MR. TAVENNER: Did you engage in other activities with regard to the raising of money or benefits for what was known as the Spanish Refugee Appeal?

MR. FERRER: I probably did, Mr. Tavenner.

MR. TAVENNER: You were acquainted with the fact that the Spanish Refugee Appeal was one of the projects of the organization with which you say you were connected, the Joint Anti-Fascist Refugee Committee?

MR. FERRER: I am aware now. Whether I was then I am not sure. I certainly linked them together in my mind. I am not trying to evade your question.

MR. TAVENNER: The Committee is in possession of information indicating you were the guest of honor at a meeting sponsored by the Joint Anti-Fascist Refugee Committee in San Francisco on March 10, 1945. Do you recall that?

MR. FERRER: If it is the one at which Walter Huston spoke, then I do recall it, yes, sir.

MR. TAVENNER: Tell us about that meeting.

MR. FERRER: I suspect the purpose was, so far as I knew, and so far as Mr. Huston's speech indicated—which is what I remember about the meeting—action against Franco. We who called ourselves liberal Democrats considered Franco a dictator, a man who was against the democratic processes, as Hitler had been and as Stalin is today, and anytime there was an occasion to oppose him I, for one, rather unquestioningly did so.

MR. TAVENNER: The Committee is in possession of information that you spoke at a Spanish Refugee Appeal benefit held for the purpose of raising funds on May 5, 1945, at the University of Wisconsin, Madison, Wisconsin, which was sponsored by the Joint Anti-Fascist Refugee Committee. Do you recall that?

MR. FERRER: I know I spoke.

MR. TAVENNER: Tell us what the arrangements were by which you were to appear at these various meetings.

MR. FERRER: During the season 1944 to 1945 I was on tour with *Othello,* and what would happen would be that I was asked would I appear and speak, and I agreed to, my sole thought being anti-Franco activity.

MR. TAVENNER: Was any arrangement made prior to your leaving on this tour with *Othello* for you to appear in behalf of the Joint Anti-Fascist Refugee Committee at various places?

MR. FERRER: I seem to recall having been told that, if the schedule coincided, they might contact me and that I would be asked to speak, and I said I would.

MR. TAVENNER: Who guided and directed that course of procedure?

MR. FERRER: Gosh, I wish I could remember, Mr. Tavenner. I would get a letter or phone call and be asked to appear, and I would say yes, and I would appear and that would be the end of it.

MR. TAVENNER: You were rather active, I take it, in connection with the Joint Anti-Fascist Committee, over a considerable period of time?

MR. FERRER: Active only in appearing at public functions. I never appeared at private meetings or anything of that sort.

MR. TAVENNER: We find, for instance, in the issue of the *Daily Worker* of September 25, 1945, an article listing you as a speaker before a group of seventeen thousand persons at Madison Square Garden on September 24,

1945, at a function held under the auspices of the Spanish Refugee Appeal. Were you a speaker on that occasion?

MR. FERRER: I think I introduced Paula Laurence, Josh White, and the CIO chorus. That was my function during the evening. I acted as master of ceremonies, if that is the occasion.

MR. TAVENNER: The article mentions that, so I guess that is the meeting.

MR. FERRER: I think that is the night Mr. [Harold J.] Laski spoke from England—

MR. TAVENNER: Yes. He is chairman of the English Labour Party.

MR. FERRER: —and made remarks supposed to be derogatory to the Catholic Church, and Frank Fay—

MR. TAVENNER: This is another meeting?

MR. FERRER: This is the meeting which provoked Frank Fay.

MR. TAVENNER: And at that same meeting Dr. Edward K. Barsky, chairman of the Joint Anti-Fascist Refugee Committee, spoke and made a special appeal for funds for the Spanish cause?

MR. FERRER: I don't remember that.

MR. TAVENNER: And at the same meeting Mr. Nikolai Novikov, acting head of the Russian Embassy, was a speaker and called for the prosecution of Franco as a war criminal. Do you recall that?

MR. FERRER: No. I don't know if you have ever attended any of the meetings at the Garden, but I can give you my view of what happened.

MR. TAVENNER: Any explanation you wish to make.

MR. FERRER: Say a meeting is scheduled for seven-thirty. They would say, "We want you to introduce some of the speakers." I would say, "I am engaged in a production on Broadway"—which I was at that time: I was working on *Strange Fruit*—and I would say, "If you will submit the material you want me to use, and write the introductions, I will be there at that time, and as soon as I am through I will leave." If they say, "We want you at nine-thirty," I arrive at nine-thirty. The activity is taking place on an elevated platform, something like a prize-fighting ring. Around the bottom of this arena is a tremendous hustle and bustle of newspaper people, photographers, people coming and going, and one very seldom listens to what is happening on the stage, because one is busy preparing one's own material, and when he is through, he leaves.

MR. TAVENNER: It was charged, was it not, that this meeting sponsored by the Joint Anti-Fascist Refugee Committee was a Communist-inspired program that was being conducted there, you recall that?

MR. FERRER: Yes, I do, sir.

MR. TAVENNER: Did you make any investigation to determine for yourself whether there was any substance to that charge?

MR. FERRER: I regret to say that I didn't, and one reason I may not have was that the charges of Communism were made by Frank Fay, who, although he turns out to have been factually right in regard to this meeting, behaved in such a scandalous and ill-advised manner throughout that charges were brought against him by his own union.

MR. TAVENNER: Wouldn't it have been a warning? Wasn't it a flag in your face?

MR. FERRER: I admit I was wrong, but listening to Mr. Frank Fay is something that doesn't come easily to me.

MR. TAVENNER: How did you become connected with the Joint Anti-Fascist Refugee Committee?

MR. FERRER: Mr. Tavenner, my connection with the organization was that they would call me up and say, "Will you appear?" and I would say yes.

MR. VELDE: Do you remember any of the names of persons who called you?

MR. FERRER: I do not, Mr. Velde.

MR. TAVENNER: This meeting to which we referred was September 24, 1945, as to which we spoke of the flag which should have notified you of the Communist Party purposes of this organization. The Special Committee on Un-American Activities cited this organization on March 29, 1944, more than a year prior to that. Weren't you aware of the fact at that time, in September 1945, that the Communist Party infiltration into the organization was a publicly known charge?

MR. FERRER: I don't believe I was, Mr. Tavenner. I should like to explain something else about appearing at this sort of meeting. Before any member of an actors' or entertainment union is allowed to appear at any function and lend his services, he has to check with an organization known as Theater Authority, the chairman of which was Alan Corelli. If they say, "Do not appear," you do not appear, because if you do appear against their instructions, Equity, my union, takes a very, very serious view of it. Theater Authority was established by Equity, Screen Actors Guild, and other unions. I can only say, to explain my answer, that there were people in the organization whom I considered not subversive, including the CIO chorus, and because of that fact, plus the fact Theater Authority gave me permission to go ahead, I did appear.

MR. TAVENNER: You did secure authority on that occasion?

MR. FERRER: I would have to.

MR. TAVENNER: Who was in charge of Theater Authority in September 1945?

MR. FERRER: Alan Corelli has been in charge for many, many years until just recently.

MR. TAVENNER: Was it brought to your attention through any source that this Committee had cited that organization?

MR. FERRER: I don't know if it was or not, sir.

MR. TAVENNER: When did you first learn it?

MR. FERRER: I suspect that I first learned it recently, when I had to do a lot of studying that I probably should have done long ago.

* * *

MR. WOOD: Are the organizations or meetings at which you do appear selected for you, or do you exercise some choice about it yourself?

MR. FERRER: This body, Theater Authority, when you are asked to appear at a function, if you decide that you want to appear—

MR. WOOD: Then you have to clear it with them?

MR. FERRER: That is right.

MR. WOOD: And if they turn thumbs down, you can't appear?

MR. FERRER: You cannot appear.

MR. WOOD: Can they require you to appear?

MR. FERRER: No.

MR. WOOD: So your appearance is voluntary?

MR. FERRER: Yes, sir.

MR. WOOD: And it was in this instance?

MR. FERRER: Yes, sir.

Mr. WOOD: It was not compulsory?

MR. FERRER: It was not compulsory. I take full blame.

* * *

MR. TAVENNER: The American Committee for Spanish Freedom was an organization formed after the civil war in Spain. According to a letterhead of the American Committee for Spanish Freedom bearing date January 21, 1946, you are named as one of the sponsors of this organization. Will you please explain to the Committee what motivated you in becoming a sponsor of that organization, if you did, and how your sponsorship was obtained?

(*Representative Donald L. Jackson left hearing room.*)

MR. FERRER: I do not remember this specific organization, Mr. Tavenner. However, once more I must plead guilty to the charge of carelessness. If I was approached on an anti-Franco question, the chance is I would agree to sponsor it. Without knowing, I suspect that probably the same people sponsored it, the same set of people, as sponsored the Joint-Anti-Fascist Refugee Committee, and that there was a community of activity which I accepted without question.

MR. TAVENNER: In other words, an interlocking membership or these organizations?

MR. FERRER: Certainly in my mind. In January 1946 *Strange Fruit* was on its last legs, a financial crisis for me, and I was preparing for *Cyrano,* and my feeling is that I would be very cursory in my examination, and if I was asked to appear and it was something at which I wanted to appear, I would say yes and forget about it.

MR. TAVENNER: When was that?

MR. FERRER: January 1946, when I was preparing *Cyrano*.

MR. TAVENNER: At an earlier date, in May 1945, you were listed as a member of the Arts and Sciences Division of the American Committee for Spanish Freedom. In other words, it is a more formal sponsorship in that it is of a special division.

MR. FERRER: In May 1945 we were completing our tour of *Othello*, which had taken us out of New York for ten months. I probably allowed them to use my name.

MR. TAVENNER: This organization was cited also by this Committee, but at a later date, 1948, and by the Attorney General in 1949. The Committee is in possession of information indicating that on June 22, 1944, you were introduced as a guest speaker at a Negro Freedom Rally sponsored by the Negro Labor Victory Committee at Madison Square Garden, New York City, and that you were one of the entertainers at this function. Did you take part in that meeting?

MR. FERRER: The chances are I did. I worked with a great number of Negro artists in the theater. I have seen them suffer injustices, and I am extremely sympathetic to their situation. I have here a note to the effect that this June 26, 1944, rally of the Negro Labor Victory Committee which you mentioned—one of the speakers at that rally was Mayor LaGuardia.

MR. TAVENNER: Do you recall that you took part in it?

MR. FERRER: No. Even the name of Mayor LaGuardia does not make me remember being there.

MR. TAVENNER: You do know that the Negro Labor Victory Committee had been cited as a Communist-front organization?

MR. FERRER: I know that now, yes.

MR. TAVENNER: Both by this Committee and twice by the Attorney General.

MR. FERRER: To the best of my knowledge, I think that is my only connection with the Negro Labor Victory Committee. Isn't it?

MR. TAVENNER: Can you recall anything about that meeting at all? You made mention of the fact that Mayor LaGuardia was there. Do you recall whether Benjamin J. Davis spoke there?

MR. FERRER: I don't remember anything about the meeting. In fact, I do remember that in some of the research I made in connection with this appearance I read that Mayor LaGuardia did not appear because of illness. I don't remember this occasion. I remember meeting Mr. Davis on another occasion.

MR. TAVENNER: What was the other occasion?

(*Representative Morgan M. Moulder left hearing room.*)

MR. FERRER: The other occasion was, I believe, in April 1944. It was a birthday celebration in honor of Paul Robeson at one of the armories, I believe the armory on Park Avenue in the thirties.

MR. KEARNEY: Thirty-fourth Street?

MR. FERRER: That would be the one. I do remember meeting Mr. Davis then because he was a speaker that night.

MR. TAVENNER: What official position did he hold at that time in the City of New York?

MR. FERRER: I don't remember whether he already was councilman of the City of New York or running for councilman, but it was one or the other.

MR. TAVENNER: That was in April 1944?

MR. FERRER: Yes, sir.

MR. KEARNEY: When he did run for re-election you lent your name in support of his candidacy, did you not?

MR. FERRER: I am not sure that I did, Mr. Kearney, but if I did it was because, in my mind, he was being presented to me as being endorsed by the Democratic Party.

MR. KEARNEY: Was that endorsement subsequently withdrawn?

MR. FERRER: At the time he ran? I don't know.

MR. KEARNEY: Did you contribute anything toward Mr. Davis's re-election?

MR. FERRER: I don't know. I don't think so.

MR. TAVENNER: According to the September 25, 1945, issue of the *Daily Worker,* you became one of the group of sponsors for the election of Mr. Davis. The heading is THOUSAND ARTISTS, WRITERS BACK DAVIS. "Formation of an artists', writers', and professionals' group for re-election of Benjamin J. Davis was announced yesterday by Paul Robeson, chairman of the new group." Then the article gives the names of sponsors, among whom your name, José Ferrer, appears. Does that refresh your recollection?

MR. FERRER: My name does appear there, yes; and I probably authorized it, but I don't remember.

MR. WOOD: You say you *probably* authorized it. Have you any recollection?

MR. FERRER: I have no recollection, but there are so many names of people I know and whom I have associated with that I would accept this as evidence against myself if it should be submitted.

MR. WOOD: Mr. Davis was serving at that time as a member of the council?

MR. FERRER: I don't remember.

MR. WOOD: You had met him?

MR. FERRER: I had met him a few months before.

MR. WOOD: Didn't you know that at that time he was serving as councilman, and that he had been elected on the Communist ticket?

MR. FERRER: I did not.

MR. WOOD: You didn't know that?

* * *

MR. FERRER: I did not know it at the time, because if I had known that Davis was to all intents and purposes a candidate of the Communist Party, that he was affiliated with the Communist Party, and that he was serving allegiance to the Communist Party, I would never have lent my name to support him.

* * *

MR. TAVENNER: I believe you stated that you first became acquainted with Benjamin Davis at the birthday party that was given in April 1944 for Paul Robeson. Did I understand you to say that?

MR. FERRER: Yes.

MR. TAVENNER: How long had you known Paul Robeson?

MR. FERRER: I met Paul Robeson, I believe, in the spring of 1942—it was either the spring or the early summer—at a brief interview, which lasted a few minutes, the purpose of which interview was for him to meet me and either approve or disapprove of me as the actor to play the role of Iago in *Othello*. Apparently, I met with his approval. I did not see him again until we began rehearsing in the late summer of 1942. We rehearsed for two weeks and we played for two weeks; one week in Cambridge, Massachusetts, and one week in Princeton, New Jersey. Then I don't believe I saw him again for a year, until we began rehearsals in the late summer of 1943 for the Broadway engagement of *Othello*. The Broadway engagement, after a number of weeks out of town, in September and October, opened in New York on, I believe, October 19, 1943—I think it was around that time—and ran into June, I think, of 1944. We had a few weeks off that summer, during which time we recorded an album of records of almost the entire play of *Othello* for Columbia Records. And then in the fall of 1944 we started this ten-month tour, visiting, I believe, forty-odd cities that I mentioned earlier in my testimony.

MR. TAVENNER: When you say "we," to whom do you refer?

MR. FERRER: I am referring to the theatrical company involved in rehearsal.

MR. TAVENNER: Was Paul Robeson associated in all those trips?

MR. FERRER: Oh, yes. He was the star of the play. He played Othello.

MR. TAVENNER: And that was through the year 1945?

MR. FERRER: Until June of '45. Then we disbanded in June.

MR. TAVENNER: He is the person named as the chairman in the press release of this artists' group to promote the election of Ben Davis.

MR. FERRER: Yes, sir.

MR. TAVENNER: Did he talk to you about your support of Ben Davis?

MR. FERRER: Mr. Tavenner, I don't remember whether he did, or not, but it is entirely possible that he did, yes.

MR. TAVENNER: Did he ever discuss with you the Communist Party?

MR. FERRER: No, sir.

MR. TAVENNER: Did he ever make any statement to you with reference to the Communist Party?

MR. FERRER: No, sir.

MR. VELDE: You are sure about that, but you are not sure about the support of Ben Davis?

MR. FERRER: Because, strange as it seems, I don't believe I recognized Mr. Davis as a Communist candidate. Had Mr. Robeson ever spoken to me about the Communist Party or Communist matters at all, I would have been very aware of the conversation.

MR. KEARNEY: Would that be true of all Communist-front organizations?

MR. FERRER: If they had Communist conversations with me?

MR. KEARNEY: Yes.

MR. FERRER: Oh, it certainly would be true, yes, sir.

MR. KEARNEY: And that would be also true as far as your attitude, of course, toward Communist organizations?

MR. FERRER: Definitely. Definitely.

MR. KEARNEY: I would like to show the witness, Mr. Counsel, a picture appearing in the *Daily Mirror* and ask him to inform the Committee under what circumstances that picture was taken.

MR. FERRER: I know the picture, Mr. Tavenner, if you want me to answer the question without looking. I saw enough from what Mr. Kearney had in his hand. The picture appeared in the *Daily Mirror,* I believe, and under a column by Victor Riesel.

MR. TAVENNER: That is right.

MR. FERRER: And the name of the man in the photograph with me is Charles Collins.

MR. TAVENNER: That is correct.

MR. FERRER: I had completely forgotten this incident, and I don't to this day remember it, but my press agent in *Cyrano* does remember it. He is the man who is working for me now as press agent for Twentieth Century and for my more recent production, *Stalag 17*. When this appeared in the paper, I showed it to him and I said, "This man Riesel says that I left the theater in make-up and costume to be photographed with Mr. Collins." And I said to him, "I remember very distinctly that the only time I ever left the theater in make-up or in costume in *Cyrano* was on three occasions." I then named the three occasions. I am very definite about everything that happens to me in the theater. My memory is extremely accurate about my theatrical activity and I do not go out in the street wearing a long nose, a wig, a beard, a mustache, and a flowery two-hundred-year-old costume casually. I did not leave the theater for that photograph despite what Mr. Riesel says. Mr. Lipsky remembers that we were taking press photographs in the theater at this occasion and that a phone call came in, and somebody whom I know—whom I knew—whose name I don't remember—I don't even remember whether it was a man or a woman—said, "There is a Negro called Charles Collins running for office in New York. Would you endorse him?" And very stupidly again, I said, "Sure. Send him over and we will take a picture." So they took a picture of a man I have never seen before or since. I have completely forgotten the incident.

MR. KEARNEY: You did not even know what party ticket the gentleman in question was running on?

MR. FERRER: Only to this extent, sir, that I was probably told what the party ticket was, and it was not the Communist Party.

MR. KEARNEY: Is it your custom to endorse candidates that are running on any political ticket?

MR. FERRER: Generally speaking, no, sir.

MR. KEARNEY: In this particular instance, did you endorse the candidacy of Charles A. Collins?

MR. FERRER: I was asked to be photographed with him shaking hands, and I did. I never endorsed Mr. Collins, that I know of.

MR. KEARNEY: At that time, did you know what political party Mr. Collins was running on and for what office?

MR. FERRER: I was probably told at the time, yes, sir.

MR. KEARNEY: You do not remember now?

MR. FERRER: I only remember what I have read since.

MR. KEARNEY: If I refreshed your memory by saying that I read from this article that he was a candidate for senator in the State of New York, on the American Labor Party ticket, would that refresh your recollection?

MR. FERRER: I have read the article, Mr. Kearney, and I don't remember the incident.

* * *

MR. WOOD: A list has been furnished here to counsel and to the members of the Committee, which is headed "Contributions of José Ferrer, 1943 through 1950, based on information derived from check stubs and the records of the Subcommittee, including all identifiable contributions." Does this list contain an itemized statement of all the contributions that you made either to charitable, eleemosynary institutions, or individuals about which you now have any knowledge?

MR. FORTAS: May I answer that, Mr. Chairman?

MR. WOOD: I do not see how you could possibly answer what was within the witness's knowledge.

MR. FORTAS: I can tell you how this list was prepared, if you would like to know. Counsel went through all of Mr. Ferrer's check stubs.

Mr. Wood: Then, as I understand it, these items that are here listed are reflected in stubs of checks.

Mr. Fortas: Yes, sir, and they are all available.

Mr. Wood: Then do I understand that contributions made in cash are not now within your recollection?

Mr. Ferrer: Mr. Wood, the only item of that nature would be the sort of thing when you are stopped on the street and asked to buy a poppy or to help the orphans. I never, never make contributions except by check, because that is one thing that I like to keep a record of.

* * *

Mr. Tavenner: I want to ask you now regarding various May Day celebrations which you participated in in one form or another, either as a sponsor or otherwise. I have before me the April 22, 1946, issue of the *Daily Worker,* which shows a headline: NOTED ARTISTS, PROFESSIONALS, BACK MAY DAY. The article proceeds to state:

> Some of the outstanding names in the cultural and other professional fields today lent their support to the forthcoming May Day parade and urged a unity of professionals and trade-unionists in the battle for peace and security. Famous names of stage, among writers, artists, and radio topnotchers were included in the list, who urged a gigantic turnout on May Day as a fitting answer to the war makers by the American people.

And your name, "José Ferrer, actor," appears as one of those enunciating that position.

Mr. Ferrer: Sponsoring the May Day parade?

Mr. Tavenner: Yes. Will you tell the Committee the circumstances upon which you sponsored that parade and urged the turnout that it referred to here?

Mr. Ferrer: Well, Mr. Tavenner, I don't remember sponsoring the parade. However, it is possible that I did, because I did not know at the time, and I only found out a few weeks or a couple of months ago, that May Day was the annual celebration of the American Communist Party. Yes, I knew that May Day had a connection with Soviet Russia. If I sponsored this parade it was with the thought that, since Russia had been our ally in the recent war, this was, along with a great many other people, a casual tribute to Russia. I never urged any turnout for the May Day parade. I never spoke in behalf of the May Day parade. And if I endorsed it at all, somebody came up to me and said, "Can we use your name?" and I said yes, and forgot about it.

Mr. Tavenner: Well, this language is also included in the endorsement; it says: ". . . topnotchers were included in the list, who urged a gigantic turnout on May Day as a fitting answer to the war makers by the American people." Now, this was in 1946.

MR. FERRER: Yes, sir.

MR. TAVENNER: Who were the war makers?

MR. FERRER: I have never seen the *Daily Worker* and I don't want to have their words put into my mouth.

MR. KEARNEY: Mr. Ferrer, do you want this Committee to believe that during all the years you lived in New York City, that you never knew that May Day was the Communist Party day in the City of New York and all over the nation?

MR. FERRER: I would like them to believe, but even if they don't, it is the truth.

MR. TAVENNER: Now, you supported the May Day on more than one annual occurrence, did you not?

MR. FERRER: I am supposed to have; I don't think I did. I am supposed to have supported it in 1949 also.

MR. WOOD: You said you are supposed to?

MR. FERRER: Yes, sir.

MR. WOOD: On what do you base that statement, Mr. Ferrer?

MR. FERRER: On the fact that in *Red Channels,* I believe, and in other lists that have appeared in newspapers against me, my name is listed as a supporter of the May Day parade of 1949.

MR. WOOD: Is that the only evidence of your alleged support that you know of?

MR. FERRER: There may be other photostatic evidence, Mr. Wood.

MR. WOOD: Do you have any independent recollection?

MR. FERRER: No, sir, I do not.

MR. WOOD: In 1949?

MR. FERRER: By 1949 I was beginning to understand some of these issues, and I would have been very, very chary of lending my support to the May Day parade of 1949.

MR. KEARNEY: When you acted as a sponsor for this one May Day celebration, did you take the trouble to find out whether it was sponsored by the Communist Party, or not?

MR. FERRER: Mr. Kearney, subsequent research has shown that this May Day parade in 1946 was endorsed, among other people, by the American Federation of Labor and the CIO. I have relied on the names of other people, the names of organizations in whom I had faith, to guide me in letting my name be used. If I may make an analogy: if any of you gentlemen were to come to New York and, say, you wanted to see a show, you would pick up a newspaper, and if you saw the name of Helen Hayes, the name of Alfred Lunt and Lynn Fontanne, or the name of Katharine Cornell, you would assume that it is worth seeing because these people have built up a reputation through the years. When I see something endorsed by the American Federation of Labor, of which I am a member, and the CIO, when I see Mrs. Eleanor Roosevelt's name, or Fiorello LaGuardia's name, or Mayor [William] O'Dwyer's name, I drop my guard and say, "Yes, I think it is safe to go along with these people." I have been wrong time and time again.

MR. KEARNEY: So have some of the individuals you mentioned.

MR. TAVENNER: How did your support of all those organizations come about? You just do not go out looking for those things.

MR. FERRER: No, sir, I certainly don't. I know that one of the purposes of this investigation is to find that out, and if I were able to think of a name or remember a person who said, "Come here, will you sign this paper?" I would hasten to give it to you, Mr. Tavenner.

MR. TAVENNER: According to the letterhead of the American Relief for Greek Democracy, bearing date of November 15, 1946, you were one of the sponsors of that organization. Will you tell us how you became a sponsor of that organization?

MR. FERRER: Could I see a document on the subject, sir, please?

MR. TAVENNER: Yes, sir (*handing document to witness*).

MR. FERRER: Thank you.

(*After examining document*): I do not remember, Mr. Tavenner, how I became associated with this organization.

MR. TAVENNER: Were you affiliated with the Civil Rights Congress?

MR. FERRER: I don't know, sir.

MR. TAVENNER: According to the January 19, 1946, issue of the *Daily Worker,* page 12, there is an article entitled ANTI-BIAS VETS WIN HUNTER COLLEGE FOR RALLY, at which you were listed as a speaker for the Veterans Against Discrimination, of the Civil Rights Congress of New York.

MR. FERRER: I would like to make a positive statement at this time. I generally have a very, very clear recollection of the auditoriums, theaters, and halls at which I speak, and that is why so often I ask to see the document, because if the document tells me where this took place, it refreshes my memory. I have appeared at Hunter College on one or two occasions, and I don't remember any of them being political. I do not remember appearing at Hunter College on this occasion. I very clearly do not. If I did, it will surprise me greatly, because I do not remember.

MR. TAVENNER: I should call to your attention and make it plain, if I have not already done so, that this stated that the meeting would be held. It does not state that you had spoken.

MR. FERRER: I see. Well, I have no recollection.

* * *

MR. TAVENNER: Do you recall having become a sponsor of the Veterans Against Discrimination, of Civil Rights Congress [as of May 11, 1946]?

MR. FERRER: No, sir, I do not. May 11, 1946, I was busy playing in Boston in *Cyrano*. We had received very bad notices, and I was killing myself trying to make a hit out of a flop.

MR. TAVENNER: This letter on the stationery of the Veterans Against Discrimination, of Civil Rights Congress advertises a mass rally to abolish the Wood-Rankin Committee. Does that refresh your recollection?

MR. FERRER: What date is this, Mr. Tavenner?

MR. TAVENNER: The date the meeting was to be held was May 23, 1946, at the Manhattan Center.

MR. FERRER: Yes. No, by then I was in Philadelphia, still worrying.

MR. TAVENNER: In fact, the letter, on its face, states: "The Un-American Committee can and must be abolished." Maybe you had better look at the document and see if that refreshes your recollection.

MR. FERRER (*after examining document*): No, it does not refresh my recollection. What is it you would like me to recollect?

MR. TAVENNER: As to whether or not you sponsored a meeting, a mass meeting, to be held to abolish the Wood-Rankin Committee.

MR. FERRER: I do not remember sponsoring that.

MR. TAVENNER: If you noted, the letter refers to the fact that Dr. Edward K. Barsky, chairman of the Joint Anti-Fascist Committee of which we have shown your activity—

MR. FERRER: Definitely.

MR. TAVENNER: —was to be one of the speakers. . . . Well, does that mean that at that time you held to the view that Dr. Barsky should not have been required by this Committee to produce evidence from its records as to what it was doing with the money which was being collected on the public assertion that it was going for relief in Spain?

MR. FERRER: No, sir, it does not mean that at all. It means that, along with a lot of other people, I did not always approve of the method of action of Mr. Dies, as later on I did not always approve of the method of action of Mr. Parnell Thomas.

MR. TAVENNER: Another speaker was the Reverend Richard Morford, executive secretary of the National Council of American-Soviet Friendship, who had also been subpoenaed before this Committee, and who had refused to give information about a subject of inquiry over which this Committee had jurisdiction.

MR. FERRER: To the best of my knowledge, I never heard of the Reverend Morford until this instant.

MR. TAVENNER: Another person who was to speak, according to this letter, the letter of the organization of which you were a public sponsor, was George Marshall, who was chairman of the national board, Civil Rights Congress. That was the board of the congress of which this very organization was a branch. And he likewise had appeared before this Committee and had refused to give it information relating to source of funds which they were inquiring about. Does that not bring to your mind that there was a definite connection?

MR. FERRER: No, sir. If you want, I can go through the list of sponsors and point out some very, very notorious anti-Communists, such as Mr. John Golden, whose name is very prominent there right below mine; a man who by no description could be called a sympathizer or interested in the least way in Communism, except to destroy it, a very important member of my profession, sir, a man whom I have known and admired for many years, and a man whose name I would hold impeccable.

MR. TAVENNER: Would you say, then, that as far as you are concerned, the Communist Party angle to this organization was not being endorsed by you?

MR. FERRER: No Communist Party angle has ever been endorsed by me knowingly, Mr. Tavenner.

MR. TAVENNER: Did you learn of this mass meeting after it was held?

MR. FERRER: I don't remember the meeting now, Mr. Tavenner, I don't know whether I did learn of it, or not, since I have no recollection of it. I was out of town at the time. I was in Philadelphia.

MR. TAVENNER: It would rather seem, then, if you disapproved of any of these movements, that you would have taken some action to see that it did not recur.

MR. FERRER: I am perfectly willing to assume the responsibility of ignorance, but I cannot assume the responsibility of knowledgeable guilt.

MR. TAVENNER: It is more than just a question of assuming responsibility. We want to know the circumstances under which it occurred and under which it was done.

MR. FERRER: In my particular case, I don't know how my name was gotten, who approached me, or in what manner. During this period I was working as hard as it seems possible for a human being to work.

* * *

MR. TAVENNER: It appears from the December 29, 1948, issue of the *Daily Worker* that José Ferrer was among the signers of a statement issued by the National Council of the Arts, Sciences, and Professions demanding the abolition of the Committee on Un-American Activities. Do you recall that—that you were a signer of such a letter?

MR. FERRER: I do not recall it, sir, but I—

MR. WOOD: Was the subject ever mentioned to you?

MR. FERRER: When you say "ever," do you mean—

MR. WOOD: The subject of the abolition of the Committee on Un-American Activities.

MR. FERRER: I cannot recall.

MR. WOOD: Well, for approximately three years, from early 1946 until the latter part of 1948—let us put it between those two dates—was the subject of the abolition of this Committee ever mentioned to you by any person?

MR. FERRER: I don't remember who I discussed it with, or how, but I remember discussing it. But I remember, for instance—if this is the sort of thing you want to know, Mr. Wood—that when I was in California shooting *Joan of Arc* with Ingrid Bergman, which was when the business of the Hollywood Ten began, along with most of the motion-picture colony, I felt a certain amount of disapproval of the way Mr. Thomas conducted the hearings.

MR. JACKSON: Mr. Chairman, I believe the record should stand corrected there. I do not believe that "most" of the motion-picture colony took that position.

MR. FERRER: All right, sir, then let us correct it.

MR. JACKSON: Let us say a small "minority" of the colony and the industry.

MR. WOOD: What activity did you exercise on behalf of such a move?

MR. FERRER: None whatever, sir. At the time I was in California there were two broadcasts given on subsequent Sundays—which is why I said a large part, Mr. Jackson—in which a great many stars and writers participated.

MR. WOOD: What support did you give it?

MR. FERRER: I didn't give any, sir. I didn't participate in any way whatsoever.

MR. KEARNEY: Were some of those writers later convicted?

MR. FERRER: I don't know, sir, because the only writer that was convicted that I ever met in my life was Ring Lardner, who was in college with me. I didn't know any of the other boys.

MR. TAVENNER: I did not ask that question with the idea of indicating that you did not have the right to oppose this Committee.

MR. FERRER: I know you didn't, Mr. Tavenner. I know you didn't.

MR. TAVENNER: On March 23, 1948, about a thousand writers and actors had a meeting at the Hotel Astor, at which was formed, so we understand, an anticensorship committee, which was instructed to carry out a strong campaign on a national scale against the House Committee on Un-American Activities, against the Tenney committee of California, and to fight against what was known as the Dewey plan of establishing a similar committee in New York State. You were alleged to be one of the speakers at this gathering.

MR. FERRER: I introduced several people, sir.

MR. TAVENNER: Tell us how that organization was formed.

MR. FERRER: To the best of my recollection, I was either phoned—I think I was probably phoned and told that this meeting was going to be held, and the names of some of the people who were going to be present—

MR. TAVENNER: Who phoned you?

MR. FERRER: I don't know. Among these names was Moss Hart. And because I like and admire Mr. Hart, and because all of us in the theater are against censorship, I agreed to appear.

MR. KEARNEY: Not because you were in favor of the abolishment of this Committee?

MR. FERRER: I didn't know enough about the Committee to be in favor of the abolishment of the Committee as a whole, Mr. Kearney. Censorship was the issue at this particular point.

MR. TAVENNER: Well, you were also concerned with the raising of funds for the defense of the Nineteen who had been subpoenaed before this Committee, at that meeting?

MR. FERRER: I don't believe I was concerned with that.

MR. TAVENNER: Well, that was the business of the meeting, was it not, in part?

MR. FERRER: I remember that I introduced a painter, and I introduced a writer, and I also said that I could not exist as an actor or as an artist if my art were controlled and if I were told how to do things and what to do. I said that the very essence of being an artist is liberty, and that, therefore, like a great many people in the arts, I was opposed to censorship.

MR. TAVENNER: We have information to the effect that you were one of a number of people who sent greetings to the Moscow Art Theater, on November 1, 1948.

MR. FERRER: Yes, sir.

MR. TAVENNER: Did you do that because of the same love that you expressed and the same necessity for freedom in the practice of your art and your profession?

MR. FERRER: No, sir. The reason was that this was the birthday of the Moscow Art Theater, and the Moscow Art Theater is the cradle of some of the most important developments of our modern theater. The Moscow Art Theater was the home of one of the greatest directorial geniuses the theater has ever known, Stanislavski. And on a cultural plane only, and completely divorced from any political implication, when I was asked, "Would you send a telegram to the Moscow Art Theater, saying, 'Congratulations on your fiftieth' "—or whatever it was—" 'birthday,' " I said yes. I would like to submit here a telegram from a gentleman you may have heard of, Mr. Lawrence Langner. Mr. Langner is one of the directors of the Theater Guild, and an extremely prominent patent attorney all over this country and in Europe. Mr. Langner is a very serious, very thoughtful businessman, a man who is not nearly as trifling as I am—

MR. TAVENNER: Before you submit that, let me finish my point.

MR. FERRER: Yes, sir.

MR. TAVENNER: All of the great things which you attribute to the Russian theater were things that were done earlier than 1934 and 1935, is not that true?

MR. FERRER: Yes, sir.

MR. TAVENNER: Had you taken the pains to study what had happened to the people of your profession in Russia since that date?

MR. FERRER: May I submit this in answer?

MR. TAVENNER: All right, if it has a bearing on it.

MR. FERRER: In answer to a request from my counsel, Mr. Reiskind, for an affidavit regarding Mr. Lawrence Langner's impression of my character and my Americanism, he wired back:

> Flying to Europe; hence unable to prepare affidavit. To the best of my knowledge, José Ferrer is loyal to this country and has expressed himself to me as being opposed to Communism. This came up in discussion regarding Soviet interference with creative artists in the theater. Regards.
>
> LAWRENCE LANGNER.

MR. TAVENNER: But yet you were congratulating the Moscow Theater.

MR. FERRER: I would congratulate the Moscow Theater in the same way, Mr. Tavenner, that I would disapprove of the discontinuance of, say, playing the music of Wagner while we were at war with Germany. The Moscow Art Theater is a symbol of something, and this is a congratulation divorced from political implications. I repeat that I have never had any sympathy for anything Communistic, and this conversation that Mr. Langner refers to I had completely forgotten until he mentioned it.

MR. JACKSON: That is in the nature of being a character reference, is it not?

MR. FERRER: Maybe so, Mr. Jackson. But the fact remains that he said I am opposed to Communism and "this came up in discussion regarding Soviet interference with creative artists in the theater."

MR. TAVENNER: When did that discussion take place?

MR. FERRER: It must have been when I was working for him in *The Silver Whistle,* which was the season of 1948 to 1949, sometime in that period.

MR. VELDE: You mentioned a moment ago that someone asked you to send this congratulatory telegram. Who was the person?

MR. FERRER: I believe it was Margaret Webster.

MR. VELDE: Who is she?

MR. FERRER: She was the director of *Othello* for the Theater Guild. She is an extremely prominent director in the theater.

MR. TAVENNER: The January 10, 1949, issue of the *Daily Worker* contains an article from which it appears that you were one of several who signed an invitation to a peace conference to be held March 25 through 27, 1949, at the Waldorf-Astoria Hotel, sponsored by the National Council of the Arts, Sciences, and Professions. Did you sign the invitation?

MR. FERRER: I am not sure, but I do know that the opening day of the conference I was in the Waldorf-Astoria—I broke through—which was picketed. The conference took place in the Waldorf-Astoria and I was in the Waldorf-Astoria. And although I was invited to the conference the opening day, I was at a party given for Ed Sullivan that night by the Circus Saints and Sinners, and I was a guest of Mr. Rutgers Nielsen of RKO pictures.

MR. KEARNEY: Did you ever repudiate the use of your name by any of these organizations?

MR. FERRER: No, I did not, sir. And I wish I had now. . . . I have learned a rather bitter lesson, Mr. Kearney.

MR KEARNEY: In other words, if you had to do it over again you would not allow your name to be connected with any of these organizations?

MR. FERRER: That is right, sir. I would not allow my name to be used by any organization that was a Communist organization, that I knew to be a Communist front, a Communist affiliate, Communist anything. And I have learned the hard way that there are agencies that inform you on these things, and I intend to avail myself of them in the future.

MR. KEARNEY: Do you still believe in the abolishment of the House Un-American Activities Committee?

MR. FERRER: No, I do not. I do think the House Un-American Activities Committee today is not only fulfilling an extremely important function, which I know that the FBI has been doing all along, but I know they are doing it in a way which I consider much more fair, much more decent.

MR. KEARNEY: When did you change your mind on that score?

MR. FERRER: Well, today, among other things.

MR. KEARNEY: In other words, since the subpoena was issued?

MR. FERRER: Yes, because I was not very much aware of the activity of the House Un-American Activities Committee personally until the subpoena was issued.

MR. KEARNEY: Did you make a study of it since that time?

MR. FERRER: To a certain extent, yes, sir. Superficial, as usual, but a study.

MR. TAVENNER: Mr. Ferrer, in a report by this Committee, of April 19, 1949, a rather lengthy report relating to the Scientific and Cultural Conference for World Peace, that organization was described as a "supermobilization of the inveterate wheel horses and supporters of the Communist Party and its auxiliary organizations." The report described the purposes of this conference, which the record shows you to have endorsed or sponsored, to be:

1. To provide propagandist forum against the Marshall plan, the North Atlantic Pact, the American foreign policy in general;
2. To promote support for the foreign policy of the Soviet Union;

3. To mobilize American intellectuals in the field of arts, sciences, and letters behind this program, even to the point of civil disobedience against the American Government;

4. To prepare the way for the coming world peace conference to be held in Paris on April 20 to 23, 1949, with similar aims in view on a world scale under similar Communist auspices;

5. To discredit American culture and to extol the virtues of the Soviet culture.

Is your knowledge of the work of that conference such that you recognized that the conference had those purposes?

MR. FERRER: If I had ever heard that the purpose of this conference was to discredit American culture or to advocate disregard for the American Government, I would have been extremely loud and unpleasant in opposition.

MR. TAVENNER: Did you take any steps to at that time ascertain what its true purposes were?

MR. FERRER: No, sir. And one reason I didn't take any steps was that I don't believe I ever authorized the use of my name, sir.

MR. TAVENNER: Have you taken any steps to repudiate your written sponsorship of—

MR. FERRER: No, I did not, sir.

MR. JACKSON: Did you know that your name was being used in that connection?

MR. FERRER: I probably did, Mr. Jackson.

MR. JACKSON: The newspaper accounts contained rather extensive coverage of the conference.

MR. FERRER: Yes, I think I did know. I would like to say, Mr. Jackson, that it presents a problem, as I say, to an actor who hasn't got the machinery set up around him how to repudiate it. If you write a letter to the people involved with your name on the letterhead, your name has been used. The damage has been done; they will probably disregard it. In those days I had not made very many motion pictures. I was not anywhere as near prominent as I am today, and if I had made some kind of a public statement to the effect, it probably would have been thrown in the wastebasket. That was my feeling.

MR. JACKSON: Of course, Mr. Ferrer, the thing that is perplexing many people is the fact that your situation at that particular time was not in the slightest degree unusual. The situation in which an artist was importuned to permit the use of his name was one which was shared by hundreds of artists in all fields of the cultural arts, hundreds of men and women upon whose names and characters no taint of suspicion has ever been cast. Your case was not at all unusual when considered in the same light and the same period during which the Cary Grants, Randolph Scotts, and John Waynes were climbing the success ladder. There were literally scores of others who avoided these pitfalls.

MR. FERRER: I know John Wayne and I know Cary Grant, and believe me, these men, when you get to be that successful and that prominent, you have either, through the studio or through your staff of secretaries—because when you are that successful and that well known, you have to have all kinds of machinery to dispose of, which a stage actor just never, never needs or can afford for that matter—

MR. JACKSON: Of course, there are, on the legitimate stage in New York, a number of actors and actresses who, during that same period were in very like situations. I mean that they were "top names." They were not people who were drawing down large salaries. They were people who, like yourself, were coming up the ladder and who were subject to the same pressures and the same unauthorized use of their names as you were.

MR. FERRER: I agree that I should have, Mr. Jackson. I am not arguing that point. I was just offering one more weak excuse.

* * *

MR. TAVENNER: Do you have any suggestion that you would like to make about the use of Communist-front organizations in your profession?

MR. FERRER: It is extremely important that in theatrical circles and in the entertainment profession it be highly publicized the availability of this Committee and the Attorney General's office rapidly to inform any member of the profession who wants instruction. I think that this service exists. But I don't think the people know about it. I think that if they knew we can go in and find out, if they had a place that they knew is set up just to help us out, to keep us out of this trouble, next to making it illegal, the Communist Party and all Communist activity—which would be the thing that I think would be the biggest help of all—I think some kind of a center where people who want information and want help can get it and can receive a welcome when they come asking questions and can get it rapidly so they can answer quickly when they ask a question. There is nothing like dragging something out into the open and exposing it to air.

MR. KEARNEY: That is what this Committee has been doing for years, and even on your admission you did not believe it until only a few days ago.

MR. JACKSON: Mr. Ferrer, what possible course of action could this Committee, or any other agency, take in advertising the fact that May Day is an international Communist celebration?

MR. FERRER: I think that is no longer necessary.

MR. JACKSON: What possible course can we take, as far as artists are concerned, in instances where they support, knowingly or unknowingly, Communist candidates for public office?

MR. FERRER: I think we have all learned a lot in the last few months, sir. I certainly have, Mr. Jackson. If the question ever comes up before me, I am going to very strongly advise people to find out and to tell them that this Committee exists and they should—

MR. KEARNEY: Why wait until the question comes before you? Why not start now?

MR. FERRER: Mr. Kearney, I will ask you for a few suggestions. If you tell me how, I will be glad to. I will. I am talking about other people—if it comes up in conversation, I mean. I mean younger members in the theater, young newcomers in the theater, that I come in contact with. They say, "Joe, how did you make out today? What are you going to do in the future?" and so on. I will tell them. Obviously, those are my juniors. Others will know better, those who didn't before. I think the youth, the people who are becoming the tomorrow of the theater, I think there is where we can all be very useful, because I think it is important that the motives that prompted this should not die, and I think it is important that the method that we employ be better.

MR. JACKSON: Do I understand, Mr. Ferrer, that you advocate and endorse the outlawing of the Communist Party?

MR. FERRER: Yes, sir, I do. Definitely. Emphatically.

MR. JACKSON: Would you assign a reason for your belief in that connection? Why do you think it should be outlawed?

MR. FERRER: Because, through conversations, investigation, and research that I have done because of the subpoena and my appearance here, I have been convinced and it has been pointed out to me irrefutably that the Communist Party of America is the instrument, definitely, of a foreign government, that its aims are those of a foreign government, and have nothing to do with our own life or our own welfare. And the mere fact that it is un-American seems to me to make it *ipso facto* illegal.

José Ferrer was recalled to the stand on May 25. Mr. Jackson introduced into the record an article from the *Daily Worker* of April 18, 1944, entitled "Happy Birthday Paul Robeson," with a photograph captioned: "Ben Davis, city councilman, being introduced by José Ferrer, the Iago in *Othello* and one of Robeson's dearest friends." Here are two brief excerpts from the further testimony:

MR. JACKSON: I don't believe you are a member, but I do believe that you have given aid and comfort to the Communist Party.

MR. FERRER: That may be so. The only platform I was on with Benjamin Davis was in April 1944 at a birthday party, at which point, to my mind, he was linked with the Democratic Party. As to my link with [Howard] Da Silva, in testimony at this hearing and before, my position has been diametrically opposed to him. I wrote a letter to this Committee offering all my records and checks. I had an informal hearing before appearing formally, at my request. I have done my very best to help you. I believe in what you want to do. I am against the Communist Party. I don't want it. And however negligent I may have been, my actions have never been other than anti-Communist and pro-American.

MR. JACKSON: I think that is a splendid statement.

MR. FERRER: It is also true, Mr. Jackson.

MR. JACKSON: Splendid and probably true. It would have carried twice as much conviction a year ago as it carries today, when your presence before this Committee follows service of a subpoena. I very frankly cannot place credence in some of the statements that you have made.

MR. FERRER: That I have just made?

MR. JACKSON: No, in your testimony.

MR. FERRER: In other words, I perjured myself?

MR. JACKSON: That I do not say. I say I can't place much credence in some of the things you have said. That is as much my constitutional right as the constitutional privilege claimed by some of the witnesses in refusing to testify.

* * *

MR. MOULDER: Do you care to elaborate on what action you could take to repudiate your activities along that [the Communist] line?

MR. FERRER: At this point I have publicly repudiated any and all Communist links and sympathies. I never had any, and I would like to say my statement was issued in the spirit of a complete repudiation and to clarify all positions along that line.

MR. MOULDER: When it was brought to your attention you did take action to repudiate it, is that so?

MR. FERRER: When the subpoena was served on me, yes.

MR. JACKSON: Will the gentleman yield?

MR. MOULDER: Yes.

MR. JACKSON: The repudiation followed acceptance of the subpoena?

MR. FERRER: Yes.

MR. MOULDER: Was that the first occasion you had to repudiate it?

MR. FERRER: This is the first time I have taken a public stand that I never was a Communist or Communist sympathizer.

MR. MOULDER: After you were informed of Davis's Communist affiliation, did you repudiate your action in favor of his candidacy? What action did you take on that?

MR. FERRER: I did not find out Mr. Davis was a Communist, to the best of my knowledge, until he was indicted. That was many years after 1945, and I took no action.

MR. MOULDER: Did you actively campaign for his re-election?

MR. FERRER: I did not.

MR. MOULDER: Did you vote for him?

MR. FERRER: No, sir.

MR. MOULDER: Are you a member of any church?

MR. FERRER: No, sir.

MAY 23, 1951:

Budd Schulberg

The Committee on Un-American Activities met at 10:45 a.m. in room 226, Old House Office Building, the Honorable John S. Wood (Chairman) presiding.

Committee members present: Representatives John S. Wood (Chairman), Francis E. Walter (appearance as noted in transcript), Morgan M. Moulder (appearance as noted in transcript), James B. Frazier, Jr., Harold H. Velde, Bernard W. Kearney, and Donald L. Jackson.

Staff members present: Frank S. Tavenner, Jr., Counsel; Thomas W. Beale, Sr., Assistant Counsel; Louis J. Russell, Senior Investigator; William A. Wheeler, Investigator; John W. Carrington, Clerk; Raphael I. Nixon, Director of Research; and A. S. Poore, Editor.

MR. WOOD: Let the record show that there are present of the full Committee Messrs. Frazier, Velde, Kearney, Jackson, and Wood, constituting a quorum of the full Committee.

MR. TAVENNER: When and where were you born, Mr. Schulberg?

MR. SCHULBERG: I was born March 27, 1914, in the city of New York.

MR. TAVENNER: Where do you live?

MR. SCHULBERG: I now live in New Hope, Pennsylvania.

MR. TAVENNER: What is your occupation?

MR. SCHULBERG: I am a writer.

MR. TAVENNER: Will you state for the Committee briefly your educational training?

MR. SCHULBERG: I went through the public-school system of the city of Los Angeles, graduated from Los Angeles High School, went to Deerfield Academy, and to Dartmouth College.

MR. TAVENNER: When were you at Dartmouth College?

MR. SCHULBERG: I was graduated in June of 1936.

MR. TAVENNER: Did you take additional educational training after that, or not?

MR. SCHULBERG: No, sir, I didn't. I received no other degrees except my B.A.

Mr. Wheeler: Mr. Schulberg, have you ever served in the Armed Forces of the United States?

Mr. Schulberg: Yes, I have.

Mr. Tavenner: What branch of the military service?

Mr. Schulberg: Naval Reserve.

Mr. Tavenner: When did you become active in the United States Navy?

Mr. Schulberg: March 10, 1943.

Mr. Tavenner: Did you enlist?

Mr. Schulberg: Yes, I enlisted.

Mr. Tavenner: Were you an officer?

Mr. Schulberg: I became a lieutenant in the Navy.

Mr. Tavenner: How long did you serve in the United States Navy?

Mr. Schulberg: Until March 17, 1946.

Mr. Tavenner: Did you have any foreign service?

Mr. Schulberg: Yes, I did. I received one battle star in the European Theater of Operations. I received commendation from the War Department for directing a security Nazi film to be used as evidence in the Nuremberg trial of major war criminals. I also received a commendation from Secretary [James] Forrestal.

Mr. Tavenner: When were you discharged from the United States Navy?

Mr. Schulberg: I was released to inactive status on March 17, 1946.

Mr. Tavenner: You still retain your commission in the United States Naval Reserve?

Mr. Schulberg: Yes.

Mr. Tavenner: When did you enter upon your profession?

Mr. Schulberg: It is a difficult question to answer, sir. I have been writing since about the age of eleven or twelve, I would say.

Mr. Tavenner: Will you outline to the Committee what your professional experience has been since you graduated from Dartmouth in 1936?

Mr. Schulberg: I will try to do it, sir, as briefly as I can. In the summer of 1936 I returned to Hollywood, California. During that summer I wrote short stories. In the fall I went to work at a film studio called the Selznick International, as a reader, and from that time to, I would say, 1939, on and off, I was what is known as a junior writer for the screen, although my main interest was in short-story writing and fiction. And from 1936 until the present I have been publishing almost constantly in international magazines, as well as writing some novels.

Mr. Tavenner: What novels have you written?

Mr. Schulberg: I have written three, sir. The titles of them are: *What Makes Sammy Run?*, *The Harder They Fall,* and *The Disenchanted.*

Mr. Tavenner: Mr. Schulberg, there has been testimony before the Committee by Mr. Richard Collins, who appeared here on April 12, 1951, that you had been a member of the Communist Party in Hollywood in the late thirties and that he had understood that you had withdrawn from the Communist Party as the result of a difficulty over the book *What Makes Sammy Run?*

MR. SCHULBERG: I guess some others run too, sir.

MR. TAVENNER: And shortly after that testimony—in fact, on April 14—this telegram was received by the Chairman of this Committee:

> I have noted the public statement of your Committee inviting those named in recent testimony to appear before your Committee. My recollection of my Communist affiliation is that it was approximately from 1937 to 1940. My opposition to Communists and Soviet dictatorship is a matter of record. I will cooperate with you in any way I can.
>
> BUDD SCHULBERG,
> NEW HOPE, PA.

Now, as a result of the receipt of that telegram, you were asked to appear at a time that the Committee could hear you.

MR. SCHULBERG: Yes, sir.

MR. TAVENNER: Had you at any time voluntarily made known to an investigative agency of the Federal Government, prior to the testimony of Richard Collins, that you had been a member of the Communist Party?

MR. SCHULBERG: Yes, sir, I had.

MR. TAVENNER: I would like to refer back for a moment to your educational training. You state that you completed your college course at Dartmouth in 1936. While at Dartmouth, did you become acquainted with William Remington?

MR. SCHULBERG: I believe when I was a senior at Dartmouth College that he was a freshman, and that when I was the editor of the college newspaper that he was one of the heelers, freshman heelers, for the paper. A heeler is someone bucking for a job on a newspaper. I did meet him at that time, yes, sir.

MR. TAVENNER: You had left Dartmouth College prior to his return to that institution after having been with the TVA in Tennessee?

MR. SCHULBERG: I left Dartmouth College in June 1936.

MR. TAVENNER: The testimony of Mr. Remington before this Committee was that he returned to Dartmouth in September 1937. That would have been after you had left the institution?

MR. SCHULBERG: Yes, sir.

MR. TAVENNER: Were you a member of the Communist Party at the time you attended Dartmouth College?

MR. SCHULBERG: No, sir.

MR. TAVENNER: Mr. Schulberg, there has been testimony before this Committee of efforts made by the Communist Party in Hollywood to influence the work of writers in Hollywood, such as the Albert Maltz incident, with which I am certain you are familiar.

MR. SCHULBERG: Yes, sir.

MR. TAVENNER: The screenplay written by Richard Collins, which you may recall from the testimony of Mr. Collins, and the adaptation of a book to the screen, I believe the title of which was *Cornered,* or possibly the title of which was *Crossfire*—do you recall which of the two it was with which Mr. Dmytryk was concerned in his testimony?

MR. SCHULBERG: I think he made them both.

MR. TAVENNER: The point is that Mr. Dmytryk testified at length regarding efforts made to influence the production of that picture, that is, efforts by the Communist Party.

MR. SCHULBERG: Yes, sir, I am aware of that, and that did strike a bell with me. I remember a somewhat similar incident in my life at a much earlier date.

MR. TAVENNER: I would like for you to tell the Committee in detail what your experience was while a member of the Communist Party.

(*Representative Morgan M. Moulder entered hearing room.*)

MR. SCHULBERG: From about 1937, I was first in a Marxist study group, which, without any formality that I remember, became a Young Communist League group and then, I believe, became a youth group, still more or less the same group, some changes here or there, a youth group of the Communist Party. I joined because at the time I felt that the political issues that they seemed to be in favor of—mostly I recall the opposition to the Nazis and to Mussolini and a feeling that something should be done about it—those things attracted me, and there were some others, too. At the same time I was very much interested in my own writing. In 1937, while a member of the group, and in 1938 also, I began to write short stories. These stories were published in many, many different magazines. I believe the feeling of the group was that these stories were not exactly what would be expected of someone writing as a Communist. Long before any difficulty that I got into for writing *What Makes Sammy Run?* I was told these stories were too realistic, they were too depressing, decadent, and there were many other words. Having some soft sides in my nature, and on some sides a little stronger, I decided that as a writer I had to go ahead and write as well as I could what I felt like writing. During these years, I would say through 1938, while there was a growing tension about this dispute, I must say I was, on the political side, still in favor of the immediate issues as the Communists seemed to be following them. I don't remember having any arguments then about trying to arouse people against the Nazis, and so forth, but I do remember many arguments about my writings. Though I had been somewhat of a zealot in 1936, I think I was much more of a zealot before I was in any organization. It is much easier before you are subjected to any discipline. By early 1939 I was definitely backsliding. I was trying to avoid as many meetings as I could and as many responsibilities as I could. I wasn't seeing the right people. Most of the people I was seeing were writers.

Some of these writers might have been strongly opposed to the Party. Some perhaps had not even heard of the Party. The subject of men writing was brought up at the meetings that I was attending, and my attitude toward my work was discussed, and it was suggested that I correct my errors, I suppose you would say. At that time I told them I had decided to write a book. The feeling of the group was: "That is fine. Writing is very important, books are very important, provided that they are useful weapons. What kind of a book do you intend to write?"—since I had used my book as an excuse for dropping out and not going to meetings. I said I had written a short story published in *Liberty* magazine in 1937 which was entitled "What Makes Sammy Run?", and that I had been thinking seriously of developing that into a novel. In fact, I had begun to write a series of short stories about a central character which were published in *Liberty* and other magazines and which later became a part of the book. The reaction to my idea for this book was not favorable, I would say. The feeling was that this was a destructive idea; that, again, it was much too individualistic; that it didn't begin to show what were called the progressive forces in Hollywood; and that it was something they thought should either be abandoned or discussed with some higher authority than the youth group before I began to work on it.

(*Representative Francis E. Walter entered hearing room.*)

MR. TAVENNER: Who in the Communist Party group made suggestions of that type to you?

MR. SCHULBERG: I believe the one who either felt most strongly or was most responsible at that time was Richard Collins. He disapproved strongly of my attitude toward writing and toward the Communists. When no agreement could be reached, and when both sides were adamant about this, it was suggested by Collins, as I recall, that I speak to John Howard Lawson and that possibly he could advise me on the changes of the approach or in some way direct my work so that it would not have the destructive and individualistic approach that the group felt I was taking, one which was in opposition to the program of the Party, I believe.

MR. TAVENNER: Well, as a result of that advice, did you confer with John Howard Lawson?

MR. SCHULBERG: Yes, sir, I did. I went to see Lawson. Either in the group or through Lawson it was suggested that I submit an outline and discuss the whole matter further, and [discover?] if it was considered a project that was useful—there was a lot of talk at that time about proletarian novels. That is a museum piece now, but at that time there was a great deal of talk about the proletarian novel and how writers could be useful.

MR. TAVENNER: Describe to the Committee the proletarian novel to which you refer.

MR. SCHULBERG: The writers were trying to write books about factories, about strikes, about opposition to capitalists, and so forth. Now that I look back, after having studied it more fully, I think it was very similar to what the writers in the Soviet Union were being told at the same time. They were being told that anything that helped the five-year plan, that made the workers happier in their role, was a good book; if it did not, it was not a good book. Looking back now, it seems that most of the best writers in the Soviet Union were silenced because they were not willing to take that command. But I don't pretend to have known that at the time I was having my squabbles and arguments with Richard Collins, John Howard Lawson, and other people in the Party.

MR. TAVENNER: All right. I interrupted you.

MR. SCHULBERG: I believe it was decided that this was not a worthy project unless I submitted to much more discipline. It is always called self-discipline, though I didn't find much self-discipline in it. Many people have submitted to this self-discipline, which, from what I can see, is imposed from without and does not have much to do with self. I decided I would have to get away from this if I was ever to be a writer. I decided to leave the group, cut myself off, pay no more dues, listen to no more advice, indulge in no more political literary discussions, and to go away from the Party, from Hollywood, and try to write a book, which is what I did. I went to Vermont in May of 1939. I settled there and I began to write.

MR. TAVENNER: When did you return to Hollywood?

MR. SCHULBERG: I believe in February or March 1940.

MR. TAVENNER: Well, had your book been published by that time?

MR. SCHULBERG: There is a long period of work, doing the manuscript cutting, going over the galleys, and so forth, before a book is published. The book finally was published on March 27, 1941.

MR. TAVENNER: Did you have any further difficulty, or did you receive any further advice from the Communist Party, before the publication of the book?

MR. SCHULBERG: Yes, sir, I did. When I returned, Richard Collins came to me. I think he had been treasurer of the group when I left. He seemed now to be in some position of greater authority. He came to me and said that they felt that my whole attitude had been sharply in opposition to the Party. I had gone away without announcement. You were not supposed to go away without saying where you were going and getting what was called a transfer. You were supposed to transfer, so that they could pick up your dues, and so forth, at the next place you went. I had simply broken off and gone away. They didn't think this was a very good idea. They didn't think finishing my book and turning it in to my publisher without further consultation was a very good idea.

MR. TAVENNER: You were requested to furnish to Lawson an outline of your book?

MR. SCHULBERG: Yes, I was.

MR. TAVENNER: Did you do that?

MR. SCHULBERG: No, sir, I did not. I think it was also suggested that I show him the book itself, which, also, I did not do. I feel very, very strongly that every writer has to choose his own guidance in these matters.

MR. TAVENNER: You were describing to us what had occurred prior to the publication and release of your book.

MR. SCHULBERG: Collins came to me and told me all the criticisms that had been made against me. By this time there was another problem. I didn't seem to be too much in favor of the Nazi-Soviet pact.

MR. TAVENNER: Let us confine ourselves for the moment to this pressure and influence brought to bear upon you as a writer.

MR. SCHULBERG: He said he thought I should come back to the group and not just go away and talk against them, as he had heard I had talked; not to be undisciplined, as he felt I had been for many years; and if I had these objections which he had heard I had told to others that I should come and at least present them and do it clean. I believe he said, "Are you in or out of this thing?" and that I said, "As far as I am concerned, since I left in May I am out." I had these discussions with the group, which were lengthy, both sides presenting their views, which continued to clash, and it was then suggested that I talk to John Howard Lawson, and that since they couldn't settle it, that maybe he could. And I did have a talk again with John Howard Lawson about the book. He felt that they should see it and felt that it was not the sort of thing I should do, and in a sense indicated that I was not functioning as a Communist writer. Finally it was suggested that I talk with a man by the name of V. J. Jerome, who was in Hollywood at that time. I went to see him. Looking back, it may be hard to understand why, after all these wrangles and arguments, I should go ahead and see V. J. Jerome. Anyway, I went. It was on Hollywood Boulevard in an apartment. I didn't do much talking. I listened to V. J. Jerome. I am not sure what his position was, but I remember being told that my entire attitude was wrong; that I was wrong about writing; wrong about this book; wrong about the Party; wrong about the so-called peace movement at that particular time. I don't remember saying much. I remember it more as a kind of harangue. When I came away I felt maybe, almost for the first time, that this was to me the real face of the Party. I didn't feel I had talked to just a comrade. I felt I had talked to someone rigid and dictatorial who was trying to tell me how to live my life, and as far as I remember, I didn't want to have anything more to do with them.

MR. TAVENNER: You have spoken several times of your conferences with a group. Will you identify that group more fully?

MR. SCHULBERG: This would be the tone of the group in general. Some would feel more strongly about it and others less so. We think of the Communists as a monolithic block. The individuals varied. There were some stronger and some weaker. But I believe it was also the view of Paul Jarrico, and not to the same extent that of Ring Lardner, Jr.

MR. TAVENNER: Who?

MR. SCHULBERG: Ring Lardner, Jr., who I felt always to be more tolerant in these matters than the others. Those are the principal members in the group itself that I remember discussing this with.

MR. TAVENNER: You were telling us what occurred after you returned to Hollywood in 1940 and prior to the release of your book in 1941.

MR. SCHULBERG: In the fall of 1940 I returned to New York to correct my galleys, and stayed there doing that and making last-minute changes until sometime early in 1941. It seems to me I returned to Hollywood again shortly before my book was actually supposed to appear. I was only there a short time then, but I gathered that the feeling of the Communist Party against the book had been mounting. I think advance copies had been read before it was out, and the feeling was that all the storm warnings that had been raised against me had been disregarded, and that the work that was about to come out was even worse than anyone could imagine. I was a little bit excited because it was my first novel and I was very curious as to what people would think of it, and I felt some people were not going to like it very well, and I decided to go down to a quiet spot and sit around on the beach. I went to Ensenada, and I thought I was waiting for it to blow over. I guess it hasn't quite blown over yet. I had been told that there was going to be a meeting against the book. When I returned to Hollywood after the book had been published, I ran into various people. It turned out to be rather a controversial book inside the Communist Party, apparently, and outside. People took rather violent sides on this. Some people disliked it intensely, and others were more favorable to it. There was a review in the *Daily Worker* about that time. I think it was early April sometime before I returned from Ensenada. The book review was a very favorable book review.

(*Representative Morgan M. Moulder left hearing room.*)

MR. TAVENNER: From the *Daily Worker*?

MR. SCHULBERG: Yes, sir. It said that this was "the Hollywood novel." It said that most of the novels before that treated with Hollywood had resorted to filth, and that this book was hearteningly free from all of this, that it dealt realistically with the Hollywood scene. I think I was called a realist; I think I was called an important comer; and, in general, it was a pretty good review. Apparently, the review was a mistake. I heard there was consternation about the review and that somehow the reviewer had missed a signal. I was told there was going to be a public meeting engineered by, but I don't believe confined to, Communists, at which the reviewer would be called to account and the real Party line on the book would be laid down. I was asked if I wanted to come to this meeting, and I said that I didn't believe any writer should defend his book in public. * * * It was pointed out at the meeting that this review was entirely opposite to what it should have been; that the book was not an honest book; that it was a dishonest book. The feeling was that I had slandered the progressive forces. I believe they said it was not a Hollywood novel at all. All the things brought out in the meeting which I am reporting, I neglected to say, appeared in a new review shortly after the meeting. A new review, by the same reviewer. It is the only time I have been reviewed good and bad by the same reviewer. It is the only time I ever remember one book reviewer reviewing the same book twice, ten days apart, and in almost every instance one review was completely at variance with the other, point by point. The book which was "not filthy" was "filthy"; the book which was "realistic" was "reactionary"; the book which was "healthy" was "diseased."

MR. VELDE: Was it reviewed by the same man in both instances?

MR. SCHULBERG: Yes. I remember his name. It was Charles Glenn.

MR. TAVENNER: Where was Charles Glenn then employed?

MR. SCHULBERG: I imagine both by the *Daily Worker* and the *People's World*. I believe those reviews appeared simultaneously in both newspapers.

MR. TAVENNER: Had you known Charles Glenn prior to that time?

MR. SCHULBERG: I may have met him once in Hollywood browsing around in a bookshop one day.

MR. WALTER: What was there in the book *What Makes Sammy Run?* that would cause the Communists to attack the book?

MR. SCHULBERG: The objection was to what I believe they called the whole approach to literature. I think they feel that you have to have a propagandistic point of view. They felt that I simply had not shown the things that they thought ought to be shown; that I had just written an individual story about one person. I never intended it to be typical of Hollywood. I didn't intend it to be typical of all the Hollywood producers. It was the story of one person as I saw him, that I thought could happen, but didn't happen in Hollywood all the time. It was at variance with what they thought a book about Hollywood should be.

MR. WALTER: In other words, they objected to the fact you had overlooked a chance to slant a story?

MR. SCHULBERG: I would say so, yes, sir.

MR. TAVENNER: In fact, one of the criticisms was that you had not dealt strongly enough with the work that had been done in the reorganization of the Screen Writers Guild?

MR. SCHULBERG: That was one of their many objections. They felt I had almost—I am not sure if the word "slandered" was used—but they felt I had completely overlooked the real work that had been done to build up the guild, and had not placed enough emphasis on the little people of Hollywood, and so on.

MR. TAVENNER: Mr. Chairman, I desire to introduce in evidence the book reviews referred to. The first is taken from *People's World* of April 2, 1941, page 5, the heading of which is "Novel—the story of a Hollywood heel," by Charles Glenn. I desire to offer it in evidence as Schulberg exhibit No. 1. The second is the issue of the *Daily Worker* of April 7, 1941 (p. 7), the heading of which is "What Makes Sammy Run?—story of a Hollywood heel," by Charles Glenn. I offer it in evidence as Schulberg exhibit No. 2. The third is the issue of the *Daily Worker* of April 8, 1941 (p. 7), and appears under the heading "News in the world of stage and screen," by Charles Glenn. I desire to offer it in evidence as Schulberg exhibit No. 3. The next is the April 24, 1941, issue of the *People's World* (p. 5), under the heading "Hollywood Vine," by Charles Glenn. I offer it in evidence as Schulberg exhibit No. 4. And finally, the issue of April 23, 1941 (p. 7), of the *Daily Worker,* an article entitled "Hollywood Can Be Won to the Side of the American People—Actors and Directors Respond to Criticism of Film Audiences," by Charles Glenn. I desire to offer it in evidence as Schulberg exhibit No. 5.

MR. WOOD: Let them be received.

(*Representative Bernard W. Kearney left hearing room.*)

MR. TAVENNER: Mr. Schulberg, I referred a moment ago to the review by Charles Glenn in which he made a favorable review, and the only criticism was that which I mentioned, that the battle to organize the Screen Writers Guild was sketched too lightly in the novel. And you have described in a general way the favorable comment that was made by the representative of the *Daily Worker.*

MR. SCHULBERG: Yes, sir, I tried to.

MR. TAVENNER: There was also an additional review by Charles Glenn on April 8, 1941, page 7, which has been introduced in evidence as Schulberg exhibit No. 3. Were you familiar with that second review which was also a favorable review?

MR. SCHULBERG: No, sir, that I don't know about. I was aware of two reviews, one favorable and another that was not.

MR. TAVENNER: In the course of this second review, exhibit 3, this statement is made:

> Originally, we passed on secondhand word about Budd Schulberg's new book, *What Makes Sammy Run?* Having finished it now, may we pass on word that while it doesn't qualify as the great American novel, it's still the best work done on Hollywood?

Showing that there had been a rather deliberate and painstaking review of your book by the reviewer of the *Daily Worker* which extended over a period of days. I would like to read into the record that portion of exhibits 4 and 5 in which Glenn explains the reasons for his change. In the *Daily People's World* of April 24, 1941, Mr. Glenn explained his about-face by this statement, and I quote:

> Since writing the review, I have received several criticisms on it. On the basis of these criticisms, I've done a re-evaluation of my work. It's rather important

that this re-evaluation be done, not in the light of breast beating, but in the light of constructive self-criticism, by which anyone who writes for this paper must work. Understanding your own mistakes is the first requirement of criticism. If you don't understand your own, how can you be expected to consistently understand the weaknesses and mistakes of those on the other side of the fence?

I also want to read into the record the explanation which appeared in the *Daily Worker* of April 23, 1941, which is exhibit 5. It is in this language, and I quote:

> On the basis of quite lengthy discussion on the book, I've done a little re-evaluating, and this helps me emphasize the points I've tried to make here. . . . To say I felt more than a trifle silly when these weaknesses (in the Schulberg novel) were called to my attention is putting it a bit mildly. It is precisely the superficial subjective attitude shown in this review which reflects the dangers of an "anti-Hollywood" approach, conscious or unconscious. This isn't breast beating. It's necessary criticism, because until the attitude reflected is cleaned up, Hollywood will not and cannot be considered the force for peace and progress it is and can be.

Those were the explanations given after the meeting which you have referred to, in which your book had been criticized and Glenn had been called on the carpet about his first favorable report on your novel.

MR. SCHULBERG: I had not realized there were two different reviews, but that does check with my memory of the one review I recall.

MR. TAVENNER: To emphasize clearly the way in which the Communist Party changed and followed the dictates of some directing authority, I want to read into the record some of those outstanding points which you mentioned in the course of your testimony. What I am going to read now is from the *Daily Worker* of April 7, 1941, and also from the *People's World* of April 2, 1941, being the favorable review of Charles Glenn. This is his language:

> For slightly fewer years than they have awaited the great American novel, whatever that may be, American bibliophiles and critics have been awaiting the Hollywood novel. While they may argue its merits and demerits I've a feeling that all critics, no matter their carping standards, will have to admit they've found the Hollywood novel in Budd Schulberg's *What Makes Sammy Run?*

Now, in the retractive statement of Charles Glenn published in the *People's World* of April 24, 1941, this is what he says, and I quote:

> The first error I made was in calling the book the Hollywood novel.

And I quote again, from the *Daily Worker* of April 23, 1941:

> Recently I wrote a review on Budd Schulberg's book, *What Makes Sammy Run?* I said it was the story of a Hollywood heel and could be regarded as the

> Hollywood novel. On the basis of quite lengthy discussion on the book, I've done a little re-evaluating, and this helps me emphasize the points I've tried to make here.

He then makes various criticisms, and adds:

> Can it then be termed "the Hollywood novel"?

I want the record to also show one or two other points, so that it may be plain. I quote from the *Daily Worker* of April 7, 1941, and the *People's World* of April 2, 1941, which was the favorable review:

> Former works on the film city have been filthy with four-letter words, spoken and implied. . . . None of these things hold true for Schulberg's novel.
>
> There is nothing vulgar in what he says, nothing superficially vulgar, that is. . . .
>
> Writing in the first person, Schulberg tells of the good as well as the bad.

Then, after the meeting, from the *Daily Worker* of April 23, 1941, appears this statement:

> We do not intend to go into all the aspects of the conscience of a writer, a conscience which allows him (with full knowledge of the facts) to show only the dirt and the filth.

And from the *People's World* again, of April 24, 1941, after the meeting, I quote:

> In a full-drawn portraiture of either Sammy Glick or Hollywood, the people must be seen in action, living the lives they lead. Even more effective would the filth of Sammy Glick become when counterposed to the cleanliness of the people.

MR. VELDE: Mr. Counsel, may I make a comment at this point?

MR. TAVENNER: Yes, sir.

MR. VELDE: I feel very definitely that this illustrates the degree of control the Communist Party had over the *People's World* and the New York *Daily Worker* and all writers in their jurisdiction.

MR. TAVENNER: I call attention to one other point which I desire to be shown in the record. In the *Daily Worker* of April 7, 1941, and the *People's World* of April 2, 1941, which are the favorable reviews, this language appears:

> Characters [referring to former books on Hollywood] have been drawn black and white, most Hollywood denizens turning out to be unadulterated heels. . . . None of these things hold true for Schulberg's novel.

Then, after the meeting, from the *People's World* of April 24, 1941, appears this language:

> Some day that story of the Guild will be thoroughly told, well dramatized, and done in all the shades of gray which entered the picture, not on the plain black and whites drawn in the Schulberg book.

* * *

Mr. Tavenner: Mr. Schulberg, is this effort within the Communist Party of the United States to control the work of writers, which you have so graphically described in your own case, consistent with what is occurring in Russia?

Mr. Schulberg: I believe it is, yes, sir.

Mr. Tavenner: Have you been in the Soviet Union?

Mr. Schulberg: Yes, I was.

Mr. Tavenner: When was that?

Mr. Schulberg: In 1934, during the summer. Two or three months ago I did begin to write an article on the subject of what has happened to writing in the Soviet Union between my first visit in 1934, when I must say I was very impressed, and 1951. I have done a great deal of research on the subject.

Mr. Tavenner: Will you give the Committee the benefit of your research?

Mr. Schulberg: In the late twenties and early thirties writing was controlled by a proletarian group—I have forgotten the name of the organization. Those writers who didn't conform to that were silenced. I think the very best writers, Isaac Babel and many others, felt they could not write under those circumstances. They had slogans for writing. One slogan was: "All novels must make workers feel happier under the five-year plan." If the book suggested it was not altogether true, or only 99.9 per cent true, there was a good chance it would not be published. If it suggested it was only 50 per cent true, there was a good chance the writer would not be around any more. One day, according to my research, Stalin looked around and said, "Our writing is pretty dull." They said, "Let's find the man who is making it dull." They got the man, who was the head of this group, and sent him to Siberia and shot him. For two years there was a lessening up. When I went there in 1934 there was a writers' congress, which was more or less a welcoming back of all the people who had been silenced and under cover. The reason for that was that Gorky, head of the writing organization, believed there should be a more lenient attitude. I was on the platform at that writers' congress, and that is what did impress me. I remember Gorky speaking, and a man named Bukharin spoke, and Isaac Babel spoke, and many of the great poets, Pasternak, and so forth. I think it is a striking fact that every man who appeared on the platform and called for greater leniency—I think it was called a new silver age of literature—every one of these men by 1938 had either been shot or been silenced, and after that none of these writers, who were trying to follow their individual line, were able to function any more. Some were silenced. Some committed suicide. Some disappeared. Some decided to conform and wrote in the approved style and made a lot of money and did very well. I believe that is much the situation today. I really believe that you have to conform or in some way you get out or they put you out. I don't know if I should say it in connection with this, but there is an organization called Friends for Intellectual Freedom.

MR. TAVENNER: I was just going to ask you about that.

MR. SCHULBERG: The organization is interested in helping those writers who have suffered under those conditions and who are able to get out and to try to rehabilitate them and to help them write as they please. For that reason, a number of writers, novelists—Arthur Koestler, Aldous Huxley, Graham Greene, John Dos Passos, James T. Farrell, Richard Rovere, Stephen Spender, and myself, among others—have decided to try to raise funds if they can, to help these people. * * * I believe through these people we will have an opportunity to get firsthand information on what has actually been happening. For instance, I have heard a number of stories. One is that a very distinguished Soviet critic, Corvely Zelinsky, decided he would try to write the history of the Soviet literature. He began with high hopes after the writers' congress I have described, but so many changes had to be made—for instance, one chapter would have to be thrown out because it was written about a writer who was just arrested, and so forth, that he decided after three years that it was impossible to write a history of literature in the Soviet Union that would be honest.

MR. TAVENNER: In other words, the changes were probably for the same reason that John Howard Lawson was required to change his history that he was writing, if you are familiar with that testimony?

MR. SCHULBERG: I believe it does have exactly the same effect, yes, sir. I was very interested in finding out that meetings are held and writers are denounced and, from that time on, their works are no longer in publication.

MR. TAVENNER: Have there been any instances where you have obtained direct information from a person who has been subjected to that type of treatment in Russia?

MR. SCHULBERG: Yes, sir. In the preparation of this article—which I began, as I said, three months ago—I wrote to someone who was somewhat of an authority in this field, who had come out of Russia only in the last two or three years, and I told him of my experience in 1934, when I had been impressed. I told him I had met Gorky and a playwright by the name of Afinogenov, and many others, and it had begun to strike me that all the people who told me how hopeful they were in 1934 weren't around any more. I said I didn't know any more about it than that writers' congress I had attended. I asked if he could fill me in on what happened after that time, and he did write me a letter which I found extremely enlightening, and I will read some parts of it.

> You were very fortunate to be in Moscow in 1934. The period from April 1932 (decree abolishing the special proletarian groups in literature and art) to 1935 was a time of good and new hopes. During that period the Soviet litera-

ture was under the strong and friendly leadership and protection of Maxim Gorky. The apogee of that short "silver age" was the first convention of the Soviet writers in September 1934. The principal speakers at the first convention were Gorky ("Soviet Literature and Socialistic Realism") and Nicholai Bukharin ("The Problems of Soviet Poetry"). The last name certainly shows what a tolerant atmosphere was present at the convention. Among the many speakers was Isaac Babel. This gifted novelist was silenced since 1927 (or 1928) and I still remember how surprised and pleased I was to see him on the podium speaking a brilliant speech in his usual sharp-witted manner.

"All the materials of the first convention seemed to be unorthodox, doubtful, and unreliable for Stalin. This is very important for clear understanding what had happened in 1936 and 1937. It is easy to remark that all repressions and liquidations in the literature and in the literary circles which took place during the Yernov era—

I don't know what that is—

were tightly connected with the first convention, its most important speakers and organizers. Gorky was poisoned (1936), Bukharin was dismissed from his office as editor in chief of *Izvestia,* arrested (1937) and shot (1938). . . .

Then there were a bunch of Russian names

and many other novelists were arrested—the same as poets Pavel Vassiliyev, Boris Kornilov, Zaholotsky, Smelyakoff, and others. Some of their colleagues —prominent Soviet writers and poets—completely stopped their creative activity—among them, Selvinsky, Pasternak, Sholokhov, Fedin, and Leonov.

After 1937 Soviet literature was like a big army retreating after unsuccessful decisive battle. Some generals were missing, some retreated in silence, trying not to show their fear and doubts. Others tried to make a gay look and impression that nothing of importance was happening. This group did not stop their activity during the Yernov era and produced some bad plays and novels. . . .

Some of the writers who belonged to the silent group later (in 1939 or 1940) broke the silence and started to write in the new orthodox way. It was a great creative degradation for them. So did Tolstoy, Sholokhov, Fedin, poet Antokolsky. Some of the writers never tried again—like Boris Pasternak—the finest poet of contemporary Russian and an extremely noble and honest person. So far as I know he only translates from English and French. During the war he translated *Hamlet*. But I have never heard that any of them did something active "anti" like Meyerhold.

I might say when I went to the Soviet Union in 1934 one of the things that had impressed me most was that I had an opportunity to meet Meyerhold, who was the foremost stage director in the Soviet Union and probably one of the outstanding ones in the world, and he showed me through his theater.

The case of Meyerhold was a unique one. It certainly was a very rare combination of the big mistakes of the Government. . . .

I think I should explain he is writing something that is known to me. Meyerhold had been a director until 1937. At that time his technique fell into disrepute and he was under a very strong cloud. I don't think he was allowed to produce anything at all in 1937. In 1939 there was a meeting of the stage directors in Russia, and Meyerhold, who had been silenced for a long time, asked for an opportunity to speak. He got up and spoke on June 14, 1939, and I honestly believe that his speech will go down as one of the great speeches in defense of individual conscience in the field of art.* He told them he had always done the best that he could in his own way; that he couldn't follow anybody else's line or point of view; but that if he was a formalist, and if all the plays he saw on the stage at that time were Socialist realism, he was glad to be a formalist, and so forth. The day after that speech Meyerhold disappeared, and when the yearbook came out at the end of the year, giving all the speeches of the directors at this convention, Meyerhold's speech was conspicuous by its absence. I think in another twenty or thirty years probably nobody in that country will have ever heard of Meyerhold. I think he will be completely removed and will be what is called a nonperson.

* * *

MR. TAVENNER: I wish you would now tell the Committee the circumstances under which you became a member of the Communist Party, fixing the date as nearly as you can.

MR. SCHULBERG: In the summer of 1936 I returned to Hollywood and in the fall of that year I went to work as a reader in a studio, as what they call a junior writer. I was disturbed by the unemployment problem and what seemed to me the rising tide of aggression in Europe. It was during that period that somebody came to me by the name of Stanley Lawrence.

MR. TAVENNER: Stanley Lawrence?

MR. SCHULBERG: Yes, sir. I have been trying to fix the place where we met, and I can't. I have the impression of his just coming up to me somewhere, either at home—I am just not sure any more—and saying that he heard that I was interested in this problem, that I was concerned about the growth of Nazism and so forth, and that I might be interested in joining a Marxist study group. I said that I thought I would be interested in joining it.

MR. TAVENNER: Do you know or did you know at that time whether or not Lawrence held a high position within the Communist Party in Hollywood?

MR. SCHULBERG: No, sir, at the time I had no idea who he was. He said that he had done a good deal of teaching of Marxism and had a job during the day and was interested in teaching this class at night. As far as I know, at that time that was the only way I could identify him.

* Presumably the text as given in Jelagin's *Taming of the Arts,* on which doubt has subsequently been cast. —E.B.

MR. TAVENNER: Did you subsequently discover how high his position was in the Communist Party?

MR. SCHULBERG: I would say in the next year and a half I definitely did, sir, yes. By degrees, I would say.

MR. TAVENNER: Will you describe what his function was in the Communist Party as far as you are able to do so?

MR. SCHULBERG: We began this study group—it seems to me it was somewhere early in 1937. I think that the teaching of Marx was fairly elementary, and I honestly don't think I ever mastered it. After the study group was going for some time, Lawrence dropped out of it and only would come once in a while. It was only later on that I did find out that he had started, I suppose, many groups like this one group that I was in and that he had become the head of the Communist movement in Hollywood at that time. I believe that would be around 1938.

MR. TAVENNER: Did other individuals confer with you either before Stanley Lawrence spoke to you or soon thereafter about your joining the Communist Party?

MR. SCHULBERG: There were two people about the same time late in 1936 or early in 1937 who talked to me about the Communist Party in general and told me that they felt that it was sort of leading the way in trying to work up as much feeling as possible against the Nazis and against aggression in Europe and so on. They talked to me in pretty general terms, but they did talk to me about the Communist Party. They didn't ask me to join it directly, no. I should say that this first study group was not part of the party. When Stanley Lawrence came to me he simply said, "Do you want to join this study group," and I said yes, not conscious that this was actually a part of the Community [Communist] Party. In fact, I suppose in some ways it wasn't.

MR. TAVENNER: Who were the individuals who approached you?

MR. SCHULBERG: Their names were Robert Tasker and John Bright.

MR. TAVENNER: Tasker is now deceased, I believe.

MR. SCHULBERG: Yes, I think he is.

MR. TAVENNER: Can you give us any information as to the present occupation of John Bright?

MR. SCHULBERG: He was a screen writer at the time. I haven't seen him in many years, and I don't know where he is.

MR. TAVENNER: Now will you proceed to tell us further about your recruitment into the Party?

MR. SCHULBERG: The group was studying Marx, and Lawrence at that early time would relate these things to current events. At some point which I can't identify exactly there was a change—I think one reason I can't is that it wasn't a formal change and was pretty much the same group, as I remember, and I remember them mostly because these were the people who went on with me as being the ones I mentioned this morning, Richard Collins and Paul Jarrico, and Ring Lardner. At some point it was suggested by Lawrence that these things that we were talking about and all believed in, which at that time were very, very general issues because the feeling in those days seemed to be extremely broad, they said that any man of good will, anybody opposed to Fascism, really could join the Party. I believe it was even said that you didn't have to believe in all of the points of the program. You could even disagree with some. I am pretty sure that was said to me at that time. It was also said that this was not a revolutionary organization and that it supported the Constitution and so forth.

MR. WALTER: Then what actually happened was that Stanley Lawrence set up this organization and after giving the members some fundamental instructions he moved on to continue the same sort of work elsewhere?

MR. SCHULBERG: That is exactly the way it seemed to me, sir.

* * *

MR. TAVENNER: He joined the Abraham Lincoln Brigade and was killed in overseas fighting, was he not?

MR. SCHULBERG: I heard that he did, yes, sir. I don't remember exactly. It seems to me it was in 1938 sometime.

* * *

MR. TAVENNER: Will you give us the names of other persons who from time to time became affiliated with that group—that is, the group in the Communist Party to which you belonged?

MR. SCHULBERG: Besides the ones I remember definitely in 1937, there was Waldo Salt.

MR. TAVENNER: Waldo Salt?

MR. SCHULBERG: Yes. I don't believe he was in the original group, but came in at some later time. I couldn't place the time. It seems to me early in 1938, but I am not too clear on these dates.

MR. TAVENNER: In whose homes were meetings held?

MR. SCHULBERG: They would be held at the various homes of the people in the group. As far as I recall, it would rotate. Once in a while, mine, sometimes at Jarrico's or Collins' apartment, at the house of Ring Lardner.

MR. TAVENNER: Did you meet at the home of Waldo Salt?

MR. SCHULBERG: I believe so. I can't say for sure, but I believe so.

MR. TAVENNER: Now, are there others?

MR. SCHULBERG: Meta Reis Rosenberg. At that time her name was Meta Reis. She was in it. It seemed to me that at some point, as I remember, she was there for not very long and then went to some other group.

MR. TAVENNER: Are there others?

MR. SCHULBERG: The others that I remember are Mrs. Tuttle, Tania Tuttle, who was also in this group. She may have replaced Meta Reis in it.

MR. TAVENNER: Go ahead.

MR. SCHULBERG: When I came back in 1940 and talked to Collins and told him I didn't want to come back at all and he urged me at least to present my point of view, at that time I also had written out my reasons for being against the Nazi-Soviet pact. I had felt all through the thirties that this was a good thing and that this was really a leading force against Fascism and that it should be supported. After that pact I didn't feel the same way about it and I told him. * * * When I came back [to Hollywood] the nature of the group had changed. There were still a few of the people I had seen before, but now two or three or four older persons as well.

MR. TAVENNER: Who were they?

MR. SCHULBERG: I believe Herbert Biberman was in that group. I say "believe" because he had come to meetings before, of the Young Communist League group, and he might have come to this group especially because of me. Lester Cole was in that group and somebody by the name of Kelly. Incidentally—no, sir, it was not Gene Kelly.

MR. TAVENNER: Are you acquainted with Albert Maltz?

MR. SCHULBERG: Yes, sir, I knew Albert Maltz, and my one distinct memory of him is during the time of the attack on my book by the Party. I couldn't definitely identify him in the Party, as he was never in a meeting with me, but he called me one day at a time when I was telling everybody how I felt about what was happening. He asked me to drop over and see him if I was ever going by. Mr. Maltz said that he heard that I felt very strongly about the attack that had been made on my book by Lawson and by all these people, and that he felt rather sympathetic, that he felt there was too tight a control of writing by the Communists and that I was somewhat on the right track but much too impulsive and wanting to solve the whole thing overnight. He gave me the impression that he agreed with me, but felt that it could be done possibly in a more gradual way. That is why, very frankly, I was extremely interested when I heard about the testimony of Mr. Dmytryk, because when Mr. Dmytryk was under the same sort of attack six or seven years later and strangely enough by much the same people, I believe, I forget now, but I think John Lawson and Richard Collins were also involved in that. I believe he said it was Albert Maltz who was more or less the voice of reason there who tried to get them to ease off. That did interest me very much because that was much the same kind of conversation that I remembered having with him that day.

MR. TAVENNER: Were there outside speakers who attended your group meetings?

MR. SCHULBERG: In the Young Communist League days the two that I definitely remembered were Herbert Biberman and Lester Cole. Local issues seemed to be more Lester Cole's province; the over-all approach seemed to fall to John Howard Lawson.

MR. TAVENNER: Was there any individual within the Communist Party whom you can identify with reference to the so-called great proletarian novel?

MR. SCHULBERG: Even for a short story as early as 1937 I was criticized very severely along the lines that I stated this morning. About this time a writer known to me as a Communist by the name of Harry Carlisle just called on me at my home and talked to me about the Communist approach and told me that there was a young Communist writer living in Santa Monica who had just written some very effective labor stories for one of the Communist periodicals. He said he thought if I talked more with her and got a better understanding of what a Communist writer's responsibilities were I might be able to strengthen my own work. I had several meetings with her.

MR. TAVENNER: With whom?

MR. SCHULBERG: With a young writer by the name of Tillie Lerner. She was then writing a proletarian novel.

MR. TAVENNER: Can you further identify Harry Carlisle—that is, as to his position?

MR. SCHULBERG: No, sir, I can't.

MR. TAVENNER: Can you give us the names of any other persons who became associated with your group from time to time, particularly after your return in 1940?

MR. SCHULBERG: Besides those I have tried to tell you, there was Kelly, Biberman, Cole, I believe—I am almost sure that Gordon Kahn was there.

* * *

MR. TAVENNER: Notwithstanding the break with the Party which you have described, you did continue from time to time, did you not, to make contributions of writings to the Communist press, such as *New Masses*?

MR. SCHULBERG: On two specific occasions I was asked specifically by the *New Masses* to make some comment on a particular event. I believe the first time was when Germany invaded Russia. I did send them a statement. The other one was about a year later, some sort of controversy between a Republican Congressman, I think it was, and Mrs. Roosevelt over the appointment of Melvyn Douglas. I believe the particular objection had been that Melvyn Douglas had changed his name. This was used as a reason for feeling he shouldn't have some sort of civilian office. I was queried directly by them, and I answered them, saying that I felt, especially in the film business, that many people changed their names. I didn't feel in either case that I was endorsing the *New Masses* as a magazine.

MR. TAVENNER: The Committee is in possession of information indicating that you either joined or continued your affiliation with several organizations which have been referred to generally as Communist-front organizations. Is that correct?

MR. SCHULBERG: I remember lending my name to a kind of circular letter put out by the Council of Arts, Sciences, and Professions in favor of the candidacy of Henry Wallace. I was in favor of Henry Wallace.

MR. VELDE: Do you remember the approximate date of that, Mr. Schulberg?

MR. SCHULBERG: It must have been sometime early in the campaign.

MR. VELDE: 1948?

MR. SCHULBERG: 1948. I wasn't unaware of the ways that the Communists had used Mr. Wallace. As the campaign went on, I became increasingly sure that this was being done. I spoke about it to people, not that I didn't feel that Mr. Wallace was an honorable and also an independent man, and a pretty good American. Finally after the campaign, however, I did write to Mr. Wallace and tell him I thought that he might have had some chance to win some support from the American people if he hadn't lent himself completely to the line of the Communist Party, which seemed to increase as the campaign went on.

MR. TAVENNER: I believe you were associated with certain activities of the Council of Arts, Sciences, and Professions, such as the signing of a letter requesting the abolition of the Committee on Un-American Activities. I am not asking you about your views as to this Committee, but I would like to know the manner in which your endorsement of the letter was secured and what you know about the formation of the plan to abolish this Committee.

MR. SCHULBERG: Letters like this do pour in every day, and I suppose you sign one for ten that you either say no or toss in the wastebasket. This one I did sign, and I remember doing so. I think it was late in 1948, although the date might have been 1949. As far as I recall, it simply came to my desk in the general mail and I signed it. If you are interested in knowing why I should sign it, I will be glad to tell you.

MR. WALTER: Please state your reason.

MR. SCHULBERG: I felt a definite concern that had nothing to do with love for the Communist Party at the fact that people should be called in and their political views inquired into. I felt that there was a great danger in that. I felt there was also information about the Communist Party and the Communist operation that could be of no value [of value?] to the American people. I tried to decide which is the greater danger. I also had a kind of personal reason which I have never told anybody to this moment anywhere, but if you are curious I will also tell you that.

MR. WALTER: Please do.

MR. SCHULBERG: In 1940 this Committee under a different leadership came to Hollywood at just about the time I believe I had broken with the

Communist Party. I believe it was under the chairmanship then of Martin Dies. On the day he arrived an announcement was made in the paper that there were six leading Communists in Hollywood, I think it was, and I was named as one of the six. The statement also said that anybody who didn't feel that he was being treated quite fairly was invited to come down to the committee room, which was at the Hotel Biltmore, and present himself. I just hopped in the car and drove down to the Hotel Biltmore. I telephoned upstairs to the investigator. I told him, "My name is Budd Schulberg. I am downstairs. I saw the note in the paper. I feel that there is something that isn't quite just about making an announcement in the paper about people before they have had a chance to come down and at least talk with you." I said, "I can't prove it, but I just have a strong hunch that that list is a faulty list."

MR. WALTER: At that time you were no longer a member of the Communist Party, is that the fact?

MR SCHULBERG: That is right, sir. I was told, "Well, we are very busy now, but call back in half an hour or so and we will see." I did. I called back in half an hour. I remember the date very well. I don't know why these things end up with my going to a bar, but I went to a bar in the Hotel Biltmore and listened to a speech by Wendell Willkie. In about thirty-five or forty minutes I called back again, and I was told, "We can't see you again, but call back in another half hour." At five o'clock, at the end of the day, I called again and I was told, "We are going to San Francisco on the next train. We have to leave and we are sorry we can't see you." Frankly, that didn't give me the most favorable impression. Maybe I should have been more reasonable later. But, as I say, it was on one side a matter of principle and on the other side a sense of personal pique that induced me to sign that letter in 1949.

MR. WALTER: If your views at that time had been followed, there wouldn't be in existence today a vehicle to give to the American people and to the world the valuable information you have given.

MR. SCHULBERG: Thank you, sir.

* * *

MR. TAVENNER: Mr. Schulberg, your name appears as one of the signers of a brief *amicus curiae* which was filed in the Supreme Court of the United States in the case against John Howard Lawson and also in the case against Dalton Trumbo. You recall that, I suppose?

MR. SCHULBERG: I do, sir.

MR. TAVENNER: What were the circumstances under which your signature was obtained to that brief?

MR. SCHULBERG: It was sent to me in the mail at my farm; I believe from the office of the principal signer. I think it was Max Radin. I wouldn't want to say whose office, but it came there. I read it, I suppose, not too carefully. I have been told by some lawyers that this was not very good legally, but I did sign it. I believe I signed it for somewhat the same reasons as I signed the others, although in this case I had an additional feeling at the time that possibly this was something that should be tested in the courts.

* * *

MR. DOYLE: You mentioned the word "fear." Do I understand that there is anything done directly or indirectly in these young Communist groups to instill in the members a fear of something happening to them if they withdraw?

MR. SCHULBERG: Before the step is taken, you don't know quite how to make it. You sit there for a long time wanting to get out, and you can't find the words to say it. You go on maybe for a year in which you think about how to get out and not really agreeing with it, but still in it. One day you say, What am I doing here, I am not a Communist, and finally you go. I happened to read an interesting book the other day by the editor of the British *Daily Worker*. It is called *I Believed* [by Douglas Hyde]. He said for two years he edited the *Daily Worker* of England, was one of the top men in the Communist Party of England, and at the same time he was taking instructions, planning to join the Catholic Church. Every day, in a sense, he was doing both. This might seem the behavior of a very dishonest man, of a hypocrite, but I don't think it really was in that case.

* * *

MR. DOYLE: I am sure that I, as a member of the Committee, would not want to lose the opportunity to give you every opportunity to give us any suggestion you might have, if you have any, any processes or any action, any attitude that we should take with reference to any possible remedial legislation to meet the present subversive misconduct of people.

MR. SCHULBERG: On the subject of outlawing the Communist Party, my mind itself is not made up.

* * *

MR. JACKSON: Do you believe that a member of the Communist Party can at the same time be dedicated to a free America as we understand it and to the dignity of the individual?

MR. SCHULBERG: Not if he knows the whole story of what Communism and the Communist Party is. I think there are innocents in there that might fit that category, yes.

MR. JACKSON: You mean at the present time there are Communists who could be Communists and at the same time loyal Americans?

MR. SCHULBERG: I think there might be some who are not presently in the process of getting out who might become loyal Americans. I do, yes, although I wouldn't make a strong point of that. It is something I haven't really thought through.

MR. JACKSON: Mr. Chairman, may I ask one more question just in conclusion? Knowing the Communist Party line, what would your reaction be to a set of principles which I will enumerate here? "Washington is a very unhealthy place." These are from minutes. "The Un-American Committee is a modern inquisition. The Committee members are self-centered tyrants. Parks, Hayden, and Collins are mentally ill—"

MR. VELDE: I think there is something added to that one line which modesty forbids your reading.

MR. JACKSON: It says,

> The Committee members are self-centered tyrants, especially a man named Jackson. Pressure of people for peace is greatly retarding the war. . . . We demand immediate peace negotiations with People's China. . . . We must demand immediate withdrawal of troops from all nations. . . . We must demand immediate recognition of People's China in the United Nations. . . . Our goal is to work for peace. . . . We have never deviated from the aim of working forces. . . . The role of the Dance Division is to entertain labor and minority groups. . . . The present task is to cooperate with the Marine Cooks and Stewards in the fund-raising campaigns. . . . Our duty is to enlighten people who read the Washington investigations and liken the investigations to the inquisition. . . . The newspapers all slant to testimony of the witnesses, and people are losing their sense of direction. . . . We must assume the leadership.

Does that strike a familiar chord?

MR. SCHULBERG: That does, yes.

(*Representative James B. Frazier, Jr., left hearing room.*)

MR. JACKSON: What is the song? What is the music?

MR. SCHULBERG: That sounds like a very familiar line.

MR. JACKSON: The Communist Party line.

MR. SCHULBERG: It sounds like the Communist line.

MR. JACKSON: This is a report of the membership committee of the Council of Arts, Sciences, and Professions in Los Angeles, April 12, 1951, and I insert it in the record so people may know the words and the music.

MR. WALTER: Mr. Schulberg, this Committee is indebted to you for making one of the most constructive statements that I have heard since I have been a member of this Committee. It can only come through the lips of people who have had the experiences that you have had, the information that the American people should have, so as to bring home to everybody in every community of America an awareness of the menace of this world-wide conspiracy, and in our efforts to enlighten our people you have made a very fine contribution. We thank you.

MR. SCHULBERG: Thank you, sir.

1952

JANUARY 28, 1952:

Michael Blankfort

The Committee on Un-American Activities met at 10:10 a.m., in room 226, Old House Office Building, the Honorable Francis E. Walter, presiding.

Committee members present: Representatives Francis E. Walter, Morgan M. Moulder, Clyde Doyle, James B. Frazier, Jr. (appearance as noted in record), Harold H. Velde (appearance as noted in record), Bernard W. Kearney, Donald L. Jackson, and Charles E. Potter.

Staff members present: Frank S. Tavenner, Jr., Counsel; Thomas W. Beale, Sr., Assistant Counsel; John W. Carrington, Clerk; Raphael I. Nixon, Director of Research; William A. Wheeler and Courtney E. Owens, Investigators; and A. S. Poore, Editor.

MR. TAVENNER: When and where were you born, Mr. Blankfort?

MR. BLANKFORT: December 10, 1907, in New York.

MR. TAVENNER: Will you state for the Committee, please, what your educational training and background has been?

MR. BLANKFORT: I was educated in the public schools of New York City. I was an undergraduate at the University of Pennsylvania. I graduated with the degree of bachelor of arts in 1929. I was an instructor of psychology at Bowdoin College, Brunswick, Maine. I was an instructor in psychology at Princeton University.

MR. TAVENNER: During what years?

MR. BLANKFORT: At Princeton it was from 1930 to 1932, where I took graduate work as well as teaching, and received my master's degree. My educational record includes teaching at New York University in the adult education, in playwriting; a session at the University of Heidelberg in Germany, as a student of the language.

MR. TAVENNER: What is your profession?

MR. BLANKFORT: I am a writer.

MR. TAVENNER: How long have you been actively engaged in the writing profession?

MR. BLANKFORT: Since the early 1930s.

MR. TAVENNER: Will you tell the Committee briefly what some of the more outstanding productions have been?

MR. BLANKFORT: I am both a novelist and a screen writer. I have particular pride in my novels, since they are the sole product of whatever ability I have, and they are not collaboration efforts, as moving pictures sometimes are. My first novel was called *I Met a Man,* published in 1936 or

1937. I published a novel in 1938 called *The Brave and the Blind;* one in 1942 called *A Time to Live;* another in 1946 called *The Widow Makers*. I published a biography of Brigadier General Evans Carlson in 1946. They are my books, generally speaking. I may have left out one or two that I wrote under a pseudonym, but they are just mystery stories, and I wrote them to earn a living. My screen productions have been—I believe the first one was *Blind Alley*. Perhaps the best known of my screen work is *Broken Arrow* . . . ; *Halls of Montezuma*.

MR. TAVENNER: Did you at any time serve with the Marine Corps?

MR. BLANKFORT: Yes, sir. Immediately after Pearl Harbor, though I was married and had two children, and was above draft age—and also had a contract at Columbia Pictures as a writer—I volunteered. I received my commission in the summer of 1942 as a first lieutenant, and I served for a little over two and one half years, and was honorably discharged as a captain.

MR. TAVENNER: Mr. Blankfort, during the course of the hearings conducted here in Washington on January 15, 1952, Mr. Louis Francis Budenz was a witness. I will read to you [from the testimony]:

> MR. JACKSON: During the course of the hearings in the Senate Subcommittee on Internal Security dealing with the Institute of Pacific Relations, I believe you were a witness?
>
> MR. BUDENZ: Yes, sir.
>
> MR. JACKSON: I would like to direct your attention to the testimony in those hearings when the matter of Evans P. Carlson's book *The Big Yankee* was under discussion. There was one quotation given from that book, and you were asked as to whether or not, in your opinion, this quotation represented Communist propaganda, and your answer to that, as quoted in the record, was "Yes, I also would recognize the author of General Carlson's biography as a Communist, Michael Blankfort. He is well known to myself as a Communist. He had many consultations with me as such." Inasmuch as his name has occurred a number of times during the course of the Committee hearings in the Hollywood matter, I should like to ask several questions on that particular individual. When did you first meet Mr. Michael Blankfort?
>
> MR. BUDENZ: In 1935, at the *Daily Worker*.
>
> MR. JACKSON: Do you recall the occasion of the meeting, or what brought it about, or in what connection you met him?
>
> MR. BUDENZ: Yes, he was then writing for the *Daily Worker*, that is, I wouldn't say he was a regular member of the staff, although in a way he was. He wrote reviews and other articles for the *Daily Worker*.
>
> MR. JACKSON: Over how long a period of time did your association with Mr. Michael Blankfort continue?
>
> MR. BUDENZ: Well, it continued—I cannot tell you the exact year at the moment, but until he went out to Hollywood. In the first place, when he came to me and had a three-hour conference with me in regard to how to penetrate the ranks of the Catholics of the West Coast, he told me he had received instructions from the Politburo to endeavor to look into that while he was on

the West Coast. He was driving through, by the way, and came to see me before he left.

Mr. Jackson: You say "effort to penetrate the Catholics"? Do you mean on behalf of and for the Communist Party?

Mr. Budenz: That is correct.

Mr. Jackson: Did you know Mr. Michael Blankfort to be a member of the Communist Party?

Mr. Budenz: Yes, sir, he came to me as such.

Mr. Jackson: These consultations that you had with Mr. Blankfort took place in the offices of the *Daily Worker*?

Mr. Budenz: Yes, sir.

Mr. Jackson: Did you ever see Mr. Michael Blankfort in the Communist Party meeting or Communist Party function where those present would have to be presumed to be Communists?

Mr. Budenz: Oh, yes, I have seen him, not in a branch meeting, or anything of that sort, but I have seen him in the *Daily Worker*.

Mr. Jackson: Was Mr. Michael Blankfort an open member of the Party, or was he a concealed member?

Mr. Budenz: I should say he was a concealed member, although he did not conceal it very much while he was around the Party.

Mr. Jackson: He did not conceal it to you?

Mr. Budenz: No, he did not.

* * *

Mr. Tavenner: Were you acquainted with Mr. Louis Budenz in 1935?

Mr. Blankfort: Yes, sir. May I comment generally on the point?

Mr. Tavenner: Yes.

Mr. Blankfort: * * * This alleged discussion with [which?] Mr. Budenz said that I had with him took place between fifteen and seventeen years ago, although he couldn't remember the exact year. Right now and here, and first of all, I want to categorically deny that any such discussion ever took place between me and Mr. Budenz. * * * I am going into detail as to what discussion I may have had with Mr. Budenz, not at that time. Now, since Mr. Budenz, in his testimony, stated that he met me for the first time in 1935, as I said, I have tried to remember when I did meet Mr. Budenz. I associate him with a group of people around a man named V. F. Calverton, a member of the magazine called the *Modern Quarterly,* when I first met him in about 1933 or 1934. It later became the *Modern Monthly*. I had just left Princeton. Mr. Calverton was the first man I met who was a major writer, and I was a disciple of his. It is here, through Mr. Calverton, where I met such men as John Chamberlain, Henry Hazlitt, Thomas Wolfe, the great novelist. There was a Professor Dewey, a Professor Hook, Max Eastman, and others of that kind. There, to the best of my recollection, was the first time I met Mr. Budenz. Of all the people of that group that I can recall now, he is the only one who became a member of the Communist Party.

MR. TAVENNER: He was not a member of the Communist Party at that time?

MR. BLANKFORT: No, sir, he wasn't, because the distinguishing characteristic of this group was that it was anti-Communist, it was attacked frequently as a group and as individuals as anti-Communists during that period and, to the best of my recollection, I never saw Mr. Budenz after the time he left this group and became a member of the Communist Party.

MR. WALTER: You say this group was under attack. By whom?

MR. BLANKFORT: By the *New Masses* and the *Daily Worker*. It was well known as an anti-Communist group.

MR. TAVENNER: You spoke of Dewey. Was that John Dewey?

MR. BLANKFORT: Yes, sir.

MR. TAVENNER: And Hook?

MR. BLANKFORT: Yes, sir.

MR. TAVENNER: Was that Sidney Hook?

MR. BLANKFORT: Yes, sir.

* * *

MR. MOULDER: Are you now or have you ever been a member of the Communist Party?

MR. BLANKFORT: No, sir, I have not, and I am not. I was brought up in an orthodox Jewish family. Anyone who knows me can confirm that I have always been a deeply religious person. It is incredible to me that I should be charged with antireligious opinion or activity. The first thing I did when I settled in Los Angeles was to join and become active in the B'nai B'rith. I helped edit the newsletter which was fighting totalitarianism and hate groups at the time. Why would I do anything like that if I had the slightest interest in penetrating the ranks of the Catholics and making them Communists? Mr. Budenz states that the conversation he had with me was right before I left for Hollywood. That was in the fall of 1937. The last time, to the best of my recollection—I am pretty certain of this—that I ever wrote for the *Daily Worker* was around the end of 1935. I would like to tell you about my writing for the *Daily Worker*. I wrote play reviews. I am not ashamed to say that there was a certain amount of opportunism involved in this, because to be a play reviewer meant that I could get free tickets to all the plays. Well, it turned out that I didn't get tickets to all the plays, because not all the managers and producers would give tickets to the *Daily Worker*. After 1935 I stopped writing for the *Daily Worker*, and I had no occasion ever to go up to the offices of the *Daily Worker*.

MR. TAVENNER: Did you call upon Mr. Budenz at or about the time that you left for Hollywood?

MR. BLANKFORT: I did not see Mr. Budenz before I left for Hollywood. I had no reason to see him. During the very same years during which Mr. Budenz calls me a Communist Party member, I was dropped as a writer by both the *New Masses* and the *Daily Worker*. I was dropped as a writer because I refused to fit my play reviews into the political theory of the moment.

MR. TAVENNER: What was the time when you state you were dropped by the *New Masses*?

MR. BLANKFORT: I would say probably in 1934.

MR. TAVENNER: And when were you dropped as a writer of the *Daily Worker*?

MR. BLANKFORT: 1935.

MR. TAVENNER: Can you explain why the *Daily Worker* would accept you as a writer if the *New Masses* had dropped you?

MR. BLANKFORT: At that time there were many, many people who wrote for the *New Masses* and the *Daily Worker* who were not even Communist sympathizers. I have always expressed an independent view, and I expressed it to the *New Masses,* when I was dropped because of a play review. The *Daily Worker,* I am sure, anxious to increase its circulation—perhaps I impressed people with my ability—hoped that, by my reviewing plays, I might increase the interest in the *Daily Worker*. I got no money for it. I never was "hired." Perhaps it was Mike Gold, whom I knew, who said, "How would you like to write reviews for the *Daily Worker*?" And I grabbed at it. Now, whether the *New Masses* people told the *Daily Worker* people that I had "geed" at slanting a play review, I don't know.

MR. TAVENNER: Well, what was this review which you said you "geed" at?

MR. BLANKFORT: Interestingly enough, both plays were written by the same playwright. His name is Clifford Odets. The first play was *Awake and Sing,* I believe. It was produced, I think, in January 1935. I felt that there were many weaknesses in the play. Apparently—now, this is assumption on my part—the Communist Party did like the play. Now, I had no personal knowledge that Mr. Odets was a Communist or wasn't a Communist. But they liked *Awake and Sing* and I didn't. So after presenting my review, I found, in both cases, that the review was being held up, it wasn't being published, and I may have called a man named Joe North who, I think, was editor of the *New Masses* at the time, or it may have been Joe Freeman—I don't recall—and said, "What about this?" And they said, "Well, we are going to publish it sometime, but are you sure that you are right about the play?" I said yes. He said, as far as I can recall now, "We think it is a fine play." I said, "Well, I don't think it is such a fine play." The next thing I knew there were no more tickets for me, and someone else began writing play reviews, one of the editors. The same thing happened in the *Daily Worker*. The play was also by Mr. Odets. It was called *Paradise Lost*. This time I loved the play, and this time the play was not loved by the Communist Party. The same thing happened. "Well, we will get another reviewer. We will try someone else out." In this case, I can't tell you who it was, because it happened after the opening-night performance. I was shocked by this. Of course, there was no deadline, I didn't have to go out and write the review, and maybe six of us went for coffee, and I heard this thing, "Do you like it or don't you?" And I said, "I loved it." They said, "Oh, you are wrong. It can't be so good." As a result, I didn't get any more tickets.

MR. TAVENNER: Was this first play which you mentioned, and which you were reviewing for the *New Masses,* of political implications?

MR. BLANKFORT: General political implications, yes. It didn't say anything about the Communist Party in the play. There was no reference to revolution or Marxism or Communism or Russia. Both plays were analyses of middle-class attitudes. Now, for the life of me, I can't tell the difference between Mr. Odets's attitude toward his material in the first play or the second play. The material was pretty much the same. It was the craftsmanship and the way he did it that concerned me. I had been primarily concerned with craft.

MR. TAVENNER: Well, did you know Joe North at that time to be a member of the Communist Party?

MR. BLANKFORT: I assumed that he was.

MR. TAVENNER: What was the reason you can assign as to why you were dropped as a reviewer by the *New Masses* and the *Daily Worker*?

MR. BLANKFORT: That I didn't fit into the current Party line at the moment on the plays. I had, during these years that Mr. Budenz says I was a member of the Communist Party, this experience with the *Daily Worker* and *New Masses.* There was a club in New York called the John Reed Club, which consisted of artists and writers. I applied for membership in the John Reed Club, and the Communist influence in the John Reed Club was so powerful that I was not accepted.

MR. TAVENNER: Was that before your experience with the *New Masses* and the *Daily Worker*?

MR. BLANKFORT: I can't honestly say. I want further to add that during this very period I maintained a close and constant friendship with people who were well known in vocal anti-Communist groups, something no Party member would be permitted to do. If I could have accepted every political tenet of the Communist Party, one of the reasons which would have prevented me from becoming a Communist Party member was that it transcended personal friendship. If you were a Communist you just were not friends with people who were anti-Communist. I maintained relationships throughout this whole period of time with well-known anti-Communists.

* * *

MR. BLANKFORT: Mr. [Martin] Berkeley, who is present, reminded me this morning that he had been instructed to recruit me into the Communist Party, and he tried for two years. This would have been 1937 or 1938, when I first met Mr. Berkeley. During those years, Mr. Budenz saw and talked to thousands of people, Communists and non-Communists and anti-Communists, and I think we would all agree that events and incidents over a twenty-year period tend to become confused and jumbled in one's mind. No human memory is so infallible. Mr. Budenz is clearly in error. I had no such conversation with him, to the best of my recollection, I never saw him after he became a Communist Party member. I am not nor have I been a member of the Communist Party.

MR. TAVENNER: You were interviewed, I believe, by a member of the Committee staff in April 1951, were you not?

MR. BLANKFORT: Yes, sir.

MR. TAVENNER: You denied at that time having ever been a member of the Communist Party?

MR. BLANKFORT: Yes, sir.

MR. TAVENNER: You were asked if you had at any time come under the influence of the Communist Party and replied, as I am informed, "Yes, I think that, while critical of much of it or part of it, in the early 1930s I was influenced by what I felt was not so much the Communist Party as the Communist view of Marxism." Will you explain further what you meant by that?

MR. BLANKFORT: I don't think that I have ever been thoroughly conversant with Marxism, but in the early thirties I tried to understand what Marxism was. I never did finish *Das Kapital,* but I read a lot of popularizations. The Socialist Party considered themselves Marxists. The Stalinist group of Communists considered themselves Marxists. The Trotskyite group considered themselves Marxists. When I speak of the Communist view of Marxism, I am talking specifically about the Stalinist view. During those years I looked for opportunities to partake in the alleviation of human distress. Of all these groups, only the Communist Party group seemed to be active. They were the ones who, at least to my knowledge, the ones who were big, important, and did things like fight for unemployment insurance, for example. Unemployment insurance was a very serious thing in those days. I don't think there had ever been unemployment insurance in this country. I am not giving the Communist Party credit for *getting* unemployment insurance, but they did *call* for unemployment insurance. So that when I say that I came under the influence of the Communist view of Marxism, I meant that I joined organizations which subsequently, I have now become convinced, were Communist-front organizations. If you, Mr. Tavenner, had told me, in 1935 or 1934, that the Committee to Get Unemployment Insurance for the Unemployed was a Communist front, I would have joined it anyway. I believed, at that time, that the Communist movement represented a progressive force in the American life.

* * *

MR. TAVENNER: I would like to show you a photostatic copy of a clipping taken from the *Daily Worker* of April 27, 1934. This article does not appear to be a review, but it appears to be an article on the problems connected with producing a play called *The Stevedore*. According to the *Daily Worker,* the article was written by Michael Blankfort, director of *The Stevedore*. Do you recall the article?

MR. BLANKFORT: I didn't recall it until I saw it.

MR. TAVENNER: In the first line of the last paragraph, there appears the words, "a familiar canard of the white chauvinism." Would you tell the Committee what meaning you intended to convey by the use of those words?

MR. BLANKFORT: Yes, sir. This took place in 1934, but I think I can say that it was difficult for Negro actors to get work. I said, "A familiar canard of the white chauvinism is that Negro casts are unreliable," which was a stereotyped reaction that producers and directors gave about Negro actors.

MR. TAVENNER: Was not the language the stereotyped language of the Communist Party?

MR. BLANKFORT: It may well be. I was reading Communist literature.

MR. TAVENNER: Were you reading it under the supervision of some leader of the Communist Party?

MR. BLANKFORT: No, sir. I was reading it because I was interested in everything that was going on around me.

MR. TAVENNER: In the second column appears these words: "There are no stock Mammies or night-club jazz babies or comic butlers, or any other of the false characters which colored actors or actresses are called on to play in the bourgeois theater." Will you tell the Committee what you meant by "bourgeois theater"?

MR. BLANKFORT: The whole French theater of the nineteenth century has been called, in many histories, not necessarily left wing, the theater of the bourgeoisie.

MR. TAVENNER: Was that not the stereotyped language of the Communist Party in referring to anything which was not Communist?

MR. BLANKFORT: The word "bourgeois" goes back long before the Communists took it as a stereotype.

MR. VELDE: Do you still use the term "bourgeoisie"?

MR. BLANKFORT: I don't, no, sir.

MR. VELDE: Do you recall when you stopped using it, or any of the other well-known Communist terms?

MR. BLANKFORT: No, sir, I don't recall.

MR. TAVENNER: Of course, it is a term that has been used back in French history, but was it not adopted in the Communist Manifesto itself? Did you learn of it there?

Mr. Blankfort: No. I read the word "bourgeois" long before I read the Communist Manifesto.

Mr. Tavenner: I understand, but you do know it was recognized as a Communist Party term in the Communist Manifesto?

Mr. Blankfort: Well, the Communist Manifesto preceded the Communist Party by a long number of years, and the writings of the American Socialists, Jack London, and [Eugene V.] Debs used the word "bourgeois" often.

Mr. Tavenner: You mean to tell the Committee that at the time you were using language of that type, while working for the Communist Party organs, you were not a member of the Communist Party?

Mr. Blankfort: Yes, sir.

Mr. Tavenner: I show you a photostatic copy of the clipping from the *Daily Worker* of December 21, 1935. This article is entitled "Introducing the Staff." The name of Michael Blankfort appears as the theater editor. Does that refer to you?

Mr. Blankfort: That is me.

Mr. Tavenner: Does it not show that you had a definite position with the *Daily Worker*?

Mr. Blankfort: I did no more for the *Daily Worker* than I described. I cannot be responsible for the way the *Daily Worker* advertised my appearance as a play reviewer in it.

Mr. Tavenner: Well, were you not the theater editor of the paper?

Mr. Blankfort: As far as I know, I never was responsible for anything but my play reviews.

Mr. Tavenner: According to this same article, the editors of the *Daily Worker* are C. A. Hathaway, Joseph North, James Allen, and Edwin Seaver. Were you personally acquainted with each of those individuals?

Mr. Blankfort: The only two that I was personally acquainted with were Edwin Seaver and Joseph North.

Mr. Tavenner: You have already testified regarding Joseph North. Was Edwin Seaver known to you to be a member of the Communist Party?

Mr. Blankfort: No, sir.

Mr. Tavenner: Do you recall a meeting held in Philadelphia in April 1936 and referred to as the National Conference of the New Theater League?

Mr. Blankfort: I don't recall it at all.

Mr. Tavenner: Well, I show you a photostatic copy of a clipping from the *Daily Worker* of April 23, 1936. It is an article by Ben Irwin regarding the conference. In the last column appear these words: "Greetings from John Howard Lawson, Michael Blankfort, and from a number of exiled German playwrights now in the Soviet Union received prolonged applause from the delegates."

MR. BLANKFORT: I am pretty certain I wasn't there.

MR. TAVENNER: Did you and John Howard Lawson send greetings to that meeting of the National Conference of the Theater League?

MR. BLANKFORT: I don't know about Mr. Lawson. I may have sent greetings.

MR. TAVENNER: Well, do you recall having collaborated with John Howard Lawson in regard to it?

MR. BLANKFORT: No, sir. I have never collaborated with John Howard Lawson.

MR. TAVENNER: Did you know John Howard Lawson at that time, in 1936?

MR. BLANKFORT: I think I met him in two ways: one was in the League of American Writers and the other was in the Theater Union, which produced his play.

MR. TAVENNER: Was he known to you to be a member of the Communist Party prior to your going to Hollywood?

MR. BLANKFORT: No, sir.

MR. TAVENNER: Referring again to the greetings alleged to have been sent by you to the National Conference of the New Theater League, it would indicate that you were a member of the New Theater League, is that true?

MR. BLANKFORT: I wrote for a magazine called the *New Theater Magazine,* which may have been the organ of the New Theater League.

MR. TAVENNER: Will you tell the Committee what the New Theater League was?

MR. BLANKFORT: It was an organization of theaters. There was a theater in Los Angeles. There were Little Theaters throughout the country doing plays like *Bury the Dead, Waiting for Lefty*.

* * *

MR. TAVENNER: I show you a photostatic copy of another article appearing in the *Daily Worker,* June 6, 1936. This article is by Michael Gold and Michael Blankfort, and begins with these words: "We have been asked by the editor of the *Daily Worker*'s feature page to comment on the matters that impelled us to write *Battle Hymn,* the drama about John Brown, the abolitionist, which is now playing at Daley's Experimental Theater of the WPA." Do you see that?

MR. BLANKFORT: Yes, sir.

MR. TAVENNER: Further along in the article you said: "There is a great and epic pathos in the fact that an abolitionist like John Brown, who was hounded by spies, cursed as a madman, beaten, and finally hung, just as our Tom Mooneys and Vanzettis are today, and for almost the same reasons, and by the same exploiters." Will you explain to the Committee what you meant?

MR. BLANKFORT: I can't, because I didn't write this. I wrote a play called *Battle Hymn* with Michael Gold. He had written a play called *John Brown,* which was not right. He brought it to me and I rewrote the play and it subsequently was produced by the Federal Theater in San Francisco. Michael Gold at this time, I suspect, was writing for the *Daily Worker* and wrote this article. He credited me with co-authorship of the article.

MR. TAVENNER: You were employed by the *Daily Worker* at that time, were you not?

MR. BLANKFORT: Not to my recollection did I work for the *Daily Worker* as late as June 6, 1936. I use the word "work." I don't feel like I worked for the *Daily Worker.*

MR. TAVENNER: You were making contributions during this period of time to the *Daily Worker,* were you not?

MR. BLANKFORT: I don't recall any. I have no files, Mr. Tavenner.

MR. TAVENNER: Well, you saw the article at the time that it appeared, or shortly thereafter, did you not?

MR. BLANKFORT: I have no recollection of seeing this article before this.

MR. TAVENNER: Later in the article appears another statement: "The proletarian writer who will help revivify this great tradition will find himself well rewarded." Will you tell the Committee what a proletarian writer is?

(*Representative Francis E. Walter left the hearing room at this point.*)

MR. BLANKFORT: Well, that phrase kind of tips it off to me that I didn't write it. I may have used the phrase "proletarian writer," but I sometimes tried to qualify it because at that time there was a great discussion as to what is a proletarian writer. Is he a man who works as a member of the proletariat—that is, the working class—or is he a man who writes about the working class? The feeling was that a writer should participate in the deep currents of his time. I don't believe that a man can be a good writer without loving people. Now, I don't mean to say that people are limited to just a working-class people. I think we are all workers. But you had to go out and you had to love these people if you were going to be a good writer. You had to feel them. I came from a closed corporation. I didn't know much of the world. I certainly had never known a union man.

MR. TAVENNER: This was another of those stereotyped expressions of the Communist Party?

MR. BLANKFORT: These were current words of the time.

(*Representative Francis E. Walter returned to the hearing room at this point.*)

MR. TAVENNER: I show you a photostat copy of an article that appeared in the *Daily Work*er on December 9, 1936. It is an announcement of the twenty-fifth celebration of *New Masses.* At this celebration it appears that they played *Anniversary Cavalcade* by Michael Blankfort. Would you tell the Committee the circumstances?

MR. BLANKFORT: The *New Masses* was an outgrowth of a magazine called the *Masses,* which, in turn, was an outgrowth of the magazine called, I think, the *Liberator,* which, in turn, I believe, was an outgrowth of a magazine published by the Intercollegiate Socialist Society. I believe Max Eastman was the editor of the old *Masses,* as was perhaps John Reed or Jack London, and so on. Obviously, someone asked me whether I would write a history of the *New Masses.* I wrote one. It was called *Anniversary Cavalcade.*

MR. TAVENNER: This was some years after you say they had dropped you because of your attitude toward your work on reviewing plays?

MR. BLANKFORT: That is true. They dropped me as a contributor.

MR. TAVENNER: And then came to you again to perform this particular work?

MR. BLANKFORT: Yes, sir.

MR. TAVENNER: I show you another photostatic copy of a page from the March 9, 1936, issue of *New Masses.* It contains a review by Michael Blankfort of *An Actor Prepares,* by Constantin Stanislavski. Do you recall that occasion?

MR. BLANKFORT: Yes. I still have the book.

MR. TAVENNER: Was that a contribution made by you to *New Masses*?

MR. BLANKFORT: Well now, there is confusion here. I said that I had stopped contributing as a regular contributor to *New Masses* and *Daily Worker* at a certain time.

MR. TAVENNER: I understood you to say you had been dropped by them.

MR. BLANKFORT: Yes, they stopped asking me to contribute play reviews. I don't know how long it was before they stopped sending me books. In this case, I may have begged for the book. I may have run into Joe Freeman or Joe North and said, "Will you send me a book to review?" There are no two ways about this. To review books—for which, by the way I was paid nothing—means that you got the book. That means you owned it. This book cost $2.50; it was a book I wanted. I begged to review for the *New York Times.* I begged to review for the *Nation* and *New Republic.* I wanted those books.

MR. TAVENNER: Yes, but the fact that you were continuing to make reviews for the *New Masses,* regardless of what purpose you had in mind, is inconsistent with your prior statement that they dropped you because of your attitude.

MR. BLANKFORT: Well, they knew that I would not write play reviews to fit their design. Now, if I had said in this review that I thought that Stanislavski was something that they didn't like, they wouldn't have published this review.

MR. TAVENNER: I show you a photostatic copy of a pamphlet published by the National Committee Against Censorship of the Theater Arts.

According to this pamphlet, you were a member of that committee. Will you tell us when that committee was created, the purpose of its creation, and who solicited your support, if you were a member?

MR. BLANKFORT: I can't even remember the committee. This was 1935. As I look over the names, I am impressed by the number of people that I knew and didn't know, people like Brooks Atkinson and Bennett Cerf and Clifton Fadiman.

MR. TAVENNER: Do you know whether [any] of those persons were members of the Communist Party?

MR. BLANKFORT: I think this list characterizes the spirit of the times. There were people whom we now know as Communists there, and there are people quite unlike the others, Charles Angoff and others. I think an examination of this list would show people who were Communist Party members, as we now know, people who were generally sympathetic, people who were liberals, people who were interested only in the theater. These were the people interested in the fight against censorship.

MR. WALTER: What attempt was being made at that time to impose any sort of censorship?

MR. BLANKFORT: I don't remember the details.

MR. TAVENNER: I show you a photostatic copy of the letter head of the American Society for Technical Aid for Spanish Democracy. According to information in the files of this Committee, some of this technical aid was the recruiting of Americans to fight in the Loyalist Army during the Spanish Civil War. The name of Michael Blankfort appears as a member of the board. Will you tell the Committee how this organization was formed, its purposes, and how your support of it was solicited?

MR. BLANKFORT: I never attended as a member of the board, I never attended as a member of the committee, I have no recollection of anybody asking for my name, or giving it. The other thing that I want to say is that if I had been asked I would have given it. I was for the Loyalists. This is something I believe in. I believed in the Loyalists, and I wanted them to win. I was opposed to Franco and the Spanish Fascists.

MR. TAVENNER: Mr. Blankfort, I show you a photostatic copy of the program of the banquet given Mother Bloor on the forty-fifth anniversary of—and I quote—"your [Mother Bloor's] never-ceasing fight in the ranks of the revolutionary movement for the liberation of the American toilers." The name of Michael Blankfort not only appears as a sponsor but personal greetings by Michael Blankfort appear in the form of "All power to Mother Bloor." At the time when you were interviewed by Mr. Wheeler in April 1951 you stated that you were not a sponsor of that banquet. Does this photostatic copy of the program refresh your recollection?

MR. BLANKFORT: No, it doesn't, Mr. Tavenner.

MR. TAVENNER: Did you ever permit anyone to use your name in sending greetings to Mother Bloor?

MR. BLANKFORT: No, sir. But someone may have said to me, "They are having a birthday party for Mother Bloor," and I might have said "That is fine, all power to her."

MR. TAVENNER: The date on the program is January 24, 1936, so this was prior to your going to Hollywood.

MR. BLANKFORT: Yes, sir. Mother Bloor is an old lady.

MR. TAVENNER: Would you say an old Communist lady?

MR. BLANKFORT: I certainly would.

MR. TAVENNER: I show you a printed record of the First Congress of American Writers published by the International Publishers in 1935.

MR. BLANKFORT: Yes, sir.

MR. TAVENNER: Among the articles submitted to this conference was one entitled "Social Trends in the Modern Drama," by Michael Blankfort and Nathaniel Buchwald.

MR. BLANKFORT: Yes, sir.

MR. TAVENNER: You are aware of the fact, are you not, that the publishing company, International Publishers, which published this book, has been cited as a Communist Party publishing house headed by Alexander Trachtenberg?

MR. BLANKFORT: When was that cited?

MR. TAVENNER: The date is September 24, 1942, that it was cited by Attorney General Francis Biddle.

MR. BLANKFORT: Yes, sir. This is published in 1935.

MR. TAVENNER: Did you know at the time that the International Publishing House was a part of the Communist Party?

MR. BLANKFORT: I suspected strongly that it was a Communist Party publishing house, although sometimes it published non-Communist stuff.

MR. TAVENNER: I show you a photostatic copy of a clipping from the *People's World,* of May 2, 1942. According to this article, you were a master of ceremonies of the feature presented by the school for writers of the League of American Writers. Do you recall that occasion?

MR. BLANKFORT: Yes, I recall it now.

MR. TAVENNER: Were you affiliated with the school of writers?

MR. BLANKFORT: Yes, sir, I was.

MR. TAVENNER: I show you a photostatic copy of a circular concerning the American people's meeting held at Randall's Island, New York, on April 5, 1941. This was a meeting of the American Peace Mobilization. According to the circular you were a sponsor of the American Peace Mobilization. Is that correct?

MR. BLANKFORT: If at any time I have ever been connected with the American Peace Mobilization, it is the one thing of which I am deeply ashamed. I did not sponsor it.

* * *

Mr. Tavenner: Did you write the book *The Big Yankee*?

Mr. Blankfort: Yes, sir.

Mr. Tavenner: Was this book based on the life of Evans F. Carlson?

Mr. Blankfort: Yes, sir.

Mr. Tavenner: Were you personally acquainted with Evans F. Carlson?

Mr. Blankfort: The first time I met the then Colonel Evans F. Carlson was at Camp Pendleton, when I served in the Marine Corps. This is a man whose reputation, as it came to me, was as a Marine Corps leader who had won the adoration of every marine who ever heard of him. My friendship with General Carlson is one of the dearest things of my memory. I cannot tell you with what outrage I responded to the allegation that General Carlson was a member of the Communist Party. I knew him well; but more than that, his public record as a God-fearing man, whose eulogy after his death at Guadalcanal, in which his own words were used, stated, "This experience reaffirms our belief in the Supreme Being." This is a man who fought at Guadalcanal, at Tarawa, at Makin, was wounded twice, and at Saipan. I would like to point out that his father is a Congregationalist minister. When I was at General Carlson's home, grace was said before meals. His total attitude toward life is that of a very deep-feeling religious man. If one calls General Carlson a Communist, this is good for the Communists, it is not good for the country.

Mr. Tavenner: The book which you wrote was distributed by the Liberty Book Club, a new book club organized in New York to distribute Communist books.

Mr. Blankfort: I was very happy that they did. It meant an additional royalty.

Mr. Tavenner: Well, aside from the question of royalties, what special purpose would the Communist Party have in circulating your book?

Mr. Blankfort: Has the Liberty Book Club been cited as a Communist Party organization?

Mr. Walter: Who ever charged General Carlson with being a Communist?

Mr. Blankfort: Mr. Budenz, sir.

Mr. Walter: Are you sure that Mr. Budenz described General Carlson as being a Communist, or did he say that the author of the biography was?

Mr. Tavenner: According to the testimony which I read, there was no identification of Carlson.

Mr. Blankfort: I have it here on page 581, the date is August 1951, part II, Mr. Budenz, in answer to a question [before the Senate Internal Security Committee] said, "Yes, sir, General Carlson was a member of the Communist Party."

Mr. Tavenner: You have been listed in an advertisement of the Civil

Rights Congress as a sponsor of the Los Angeles chapter of the Civil Rights Congress. In this advertisement it is said that "The Civil Rights Congress is defending Gerhart Eisler, world-renowned anti-Fascist fighter." Do you recall that?

MR. BLANKFORT: Yes. I joined the Civil Rights Congress. I got out pretty quick, and I joined the American Civil Liberties Union. The American Civil Liberties Union, of which I became a member afterward, will defend Communists and anti-Communists and Fascists. That is what I believe civil rights should be.

MR. TAVENNER: I desire to introduce in evidence a photostatic copy of the daily *People's World* of May 2, 1947. This advertisement of the Civil Rights Congress, which lists you as a sponsor, also says that Gerhart Eisler was framed by this Committee, and it calls for the abolishment of this Committee. Upon what evidence do you base the statement that Eisler was framed by this Committee, if you had any part in the sponsorship of the movement which the article says you were a sponsor of?

MR. BLANKFORT: I say this, and it is no credit to me, I repeat again I never saw that ad. I am not in a position to say or to have said that Mr. Eisler was ever framed by anybody.

MR. WALTER: Why did these Communists feel that they could use your name without consulting you?

MR. BLANKFORT: In this connection, I am reasonably certain they asked me.

MR. WALTER: Why is it that your name is always used?

MR. BLANKFORT: I was intellectually lazy. Someone would ask me would I join the Civil Rights Congress, and I just didn't go and say, "Well, let me see who is connected with it? What does it stand for?"

MR. WALTER: You want us to believe, then, that you were asked to join the Civil Rights Congress because of your anti-Communist expressions?

MR. BLANKFORT: No, sir, I didn't mean to say that.

MR. WALTER: I think that is what it adds up to.

MR. BLANKFORT: I am not sure but what General Carlson was a member of the Civil Rights Congress, and I am not certain but what I joined just on his say-so. You have the record of the national sponsorship there; I don't. But, if it were General Carlson, I guess I would have followed him without question at all.

MR. TAVENNER: Well, were you not also a member of the Committee for the First Amendment? Or were you not a sponsor of it?

MR. BLANKFORT: Whether I was a sponsor or not, I would have been a sponsor, and I certainly would have been a member. I believe that the Committee for the First Amendment had a good point.

MR. TAVENNER: Who solicited your support?

MR. BLANKFORT: Maybe Phil Dunne asked me. I think I was at his studio at the time.

MR. TAVENNER: Who asked you to become a sponsor?

MR. BLANKFORT: Well, on this list, any one of these people could have asked me. It depended on what studio I was working at at the time. It may have been Bob Ardrey. It may have been Dunne. It may have been a man named Gomberg. I don't know who asked me.

MR. TAVENNER: Then, after looking at the exhibit, you are convinced that you did become a sponsor of it, are you not?

MR. BLANKFORT: Yes, sir, I am.

MR. TAVENNER: Let me read to you the opening statement: "We, the undersigned, as American citizens who believe in constitutional democratic government, are disgusted and outraged by the continuing attempt of the House Committee on Un-American Activities to smear the motion-picture industry." Do you believe that the efforts of this Committee to expose the Communist infiltration into the moving-picture industry constituted a smear of that industry?

MR. BLANKFORT: Was it this Committee that this refers to, this present Committee?

MR. TAVENNER: Of course, that is dated, as you will see, 1947.

MR. BLANKFORT: Then it wasn't the Committee which is presently constituted.

MR. TAVENNER: The Committee is the same regardless of the membership of it. A corporation doesn't go out of existence because the board of directors are changed.

MR. BLANKFORT: I don't have to tell you, Mr. Tavenner, what the opinion of Hollywood was about the earlier 1947 Committee.

MR. TAVENNER: I am not asking you to make any comparisons. I do want to know whether you think it was smeared.

MR. BLANKFORT: Whether I think Hollywood was smeared?

MR. TAVENNER: Yes, in light of the evidence as you now know it.

MR. BLANKFORT: Well, "smear" is a word which is a color word. Certainly it has not helped Hollywood. I don't mean that the Committee has had anything to do with it, but the fact that it has come out that people in the moving-picture industry have been Communist Party members certainly is not helpful.

MR. WALTER: Do you not think that this Committee would have been derelict in its duty if it did not expose the machinations of these Communists?

MR. BLANKFORT: I think it would have been. I think this is the function of your Committee, sir.

MR. TAVENNER: Why did you permit the use of your name as a sponsor of a committee which was organized to try to destroy the work of this Committee?

MR. BLANKFORT: Well, again, you force me to make the perhaps invidious comparison. There are committees and there are committees. There is a way of handling interrogation, and a different way. That was our impression. Hollywood, as perhaps one man, was under the same impression of that earlier Committee. And that is why, if we look at the list, it contains the names of the foremost people in Hollywood. I was not an active member of this committee, but I did speak to some of the active members of this committee much later. And I found out, to my amazement, which I had not known before, that the active members of the committee had tried to persuade those ten men from pleading as they did. They tried to get them to cooperate with the Committee.

MR. JACKSON: The activity of the previous Committee, after all, was the opening gun in an investigation which was to disclose the presence of a highly organized, well-integrated group of Communists in Hollywood. I think that that is historically on the record today to the satisfaction of everyone, even those who at the time said, "There is no organized Communist movement in Hollywood. There may be a few individuals running around who are doing no damage; but, as far as organized Communism is concerned, there isn't any." The activities of this Committee through the years has proven quite the contrary: that there was a very effective organization. I agree with the gentleman from Pennsylvania, Mr. Walter, when he says that much of the furor created by the Committee for the First Amendment was furor created in self-defense by others who had not been subpoenaed before the Committee but who had every reason to believe that they would be subpoenaed.

MR. TAVENNER: The Committee has information that you also joined in an *amicus curiae* brief to the Supreme Court on behalf of Dalton Trumbo and John Howard Lawson. Is that true?

MR. BLANKFORT: Yes, it is true.

MR. TAVENNER: What were the circumstances under which your assistance in that matter was obtained?

MR. BLANKFORT: As I remember it, I got a letter asking for my support. It was signed, I believe, by a professor at the University of California, or Stanford. His name was Max Radin.

MR. WALTER: Do you suppose that the eminent professor wrote that letter because he knew of your anti-Communist utterances?

MR. BLANKFORT: Sir, I was under the impression that he wrote to everybody. I think he wrote to everyone.

MR. WALTER: By "everybody" you mean whom?

MR. BLANKFORT: I mean that he probably got a list of the subscribers to the *Nation* and the *New Republic*. He probably got a list of the members of the Screen Actors Guild or Screen Directors Guild.

MR. TAVENNER: I believe you have informed the Committee prior to this that you supported a resolution to deprive members of the Communist Party from membership in the American Veterans Committee.

Mr. Blankfort: Yes, sir, that is true. I was an active member of the Beverly Hills Chapter of the American Veterans Committee.

Mr. Tavenner: Let me show you a photostatic copy of a letter of the National Council of the Arts, Sciences, and Professions. I believe your name appears there as one of the signers?

Mr. Blankfort: I have no recollection of this letter.

Mr. Tavenner: You will notice that it is directed to the Members of the Eighty-first Congress.

Mr. Blankfort: Yes, sir.

Mr. Tavenner: And it uses this language: "The Eighty-first Congress can and must abolish the Committee on Un-American Activities." Will you tell the Committee who solicited your signature to that letter?

Mr. Blankfort: To the best of my recollection, I never saw this letter before now.

Mr. Tavenner: Aside from the fact that you may never have seen it, did you authorize the use of your name?

Mr. Blankfort: Not to my recollection.

Mr. Walter: Did you advocate the abolition of this Committee at that time?

Mr. Blankfort: I advocated a change in procedure. That was my chief criticism.

Mr. Walter: Was that because you were fearful that the Committee would continue its investigation of Hollywood?

Mr. Blankfort: I was fearful that the investigation would not be fair, let us say, or reasonable.

Mr. Tavenner: Attached to the letter which I handed you is a photostatic copy of an article appearing in the *Daily Worker* of December 29, 1948, which says,

> A group of distinguished writers, clergymen, actors, and other notables, called upon the Eighty-first Congress to abolish the Un-American Activities Committee. The request was made in a statement released by the National Council of the Arts, Sciences, and Professions. Signers of the statement included . . .

Michael Blankfort.

Mr. Blankfort: Doesn't that come from the same list?

Mr. Tavenner: Yes. But I want you to look at the article from the *Daily Worker* and state whether or not you saw that article.

Mr. Blankfort: I can answer that without looking at it. I never saw the article. I have never seen the *Daily Worker*.

Mr. Tavenner: Then, as far as the use of your name in that particular article is concerned, it was done without your permission?

Mr. Blankfort: To the best of my knowledge, yes.

Mr. Walter: What do you propose to do now that your name has been used without authority to find out why people had the temerity to use your name without permission?

MR. BLANKFORT: I don't think these organizations are still in existence. If they were I would write them a letter and express my view on this.

MR. JACKSON: You can write the Hollywood Chapter of the Arts, Sciences, and Professions. It is still in existence.

MR. BLANKFORT: I have. I cannot tell you the date, but I perhaps could find out when I did and resigned from my membership. Has that committee ever been classed subversive?

MR. TAVENNER: Yes, it has been. The National Council of the Arts, Sciences, and Professions was cited as a Communist front by the Committee on Un-American Activities on April 26, 1950.

MR. BLANKFORT: When you are a member of an organization, I never understood that they would have to have special permission to use your name for any function of that organization.

MR. TAVENNER: I am very much surprised to hear you state that, because I don't see how anyone could be assumed to have agreed to the use of his name in any project in which an organization may be interested without permission. I have never heard that advanced before.

MR. BLANKFORT: I didn't think I was advancing original theory.

MR. TAVENNER: I think a great many of the names of people were used without permission, but this is the first time I have ever heard it suggested that the mere joining of the organization was tantamount to a consent to use the individual's name without specific permission. I show you a photostatic copy of a program of the Cultural and Scientific Conference for World Peace held in New York City in March 1949. Your name appears as one of the sponsors. Will you tell the Committee who received your sponsorship of that group, if you actually sponsored it?

MR. BLANKFORT: This took place in March 1949. I was in Israel. I wasn't present. I received a letter asking for my permission, and I did not give it. As I remember the letter, a card was enclosed, I am not certain, "Will you sponsor or give permission"—or whatever the thing is for—"this conference."

MR. TAVENNER: Now, Mr. Blankfort, you stated that the pattern of your conduct had been such as to show that you could not have been a member of the Communist Party at the time that Mr. Budenz testified you were, and that you could not have, or did not, go to Hollywood for the purpose of looking into Communist activities out there. You have testified here about your membership in many Communist-front organizations in Hollywood.

MR. BLANKFORT: Parallel with these activities were other activities. I was a member of organizations which had taken decided stands against Communists: the American Jewish Congress, the B'nai B'rith, the American Veterans Committee. My whole life has been one of independent radicalism. I suppose "radicalism" is the word for it. It is apparent that I am an organization joiner.

MR. TAVENNER: Then, in the final analysis, you are saying that you are not now and never have been a member of the Communist Party?

MR. BLANKFORT: Exactly.

MR. JACKSON: Mr. Blankfort, can you assign any possible reason for the testimony given by Mr. Budenz before this Committee on January 15?

MR. BLANKFORT: You mean do I have a theory as to why he testified this way?

MR. JACKSON: Yes. Why would Mr. Budenz, in your opinion, say that? Could it have grown, perhaps, out of a personal disagreement? Have you ever had a personal disagreement with Mr. Budenz?

MR. BLANKFORT: No. If the sense of your question is that this could have been a personal matter, no.

MR. JACKSON: Because the situation with which the Committee is confronted is that of a positive identification on the one hand and a positive denial on the other, up to this moment. Did you know Michael Gold to be a member of the Communist Party?

MR. BLANKFORT: I sure assumed that he was. I may add at this point that Michael Gold told me never to join the Communist Party.

MR. JACKSON: That is recruitment in reverse. Did you know Gerhart Eisler?

MR. BLANKFORT: No, sir.

MR. JACKSON: Do you feel, Mr. Blankfort, that in light of the identification made before the Committee by Mr. Budenz, and in the light of the many suspect groups with which you have been associated, that the Committee was doing the proper thing in asking you to appear before it to explain the situation?

MR. BLANKFORT: I certainly do. I appreciate the opportunity.

MR. JACKSON: You used the word "smeared" in connection with the previous Committees that antedated this one. Do you know anyone who has been smeared by this Committee either now or in times past?

MR. BLANKFORT: This present Committee, no, sir.

MR. JACKSON: I am speaking of the Committee generally. I would like to know who has been unjustly accused.

MR. BLANKFORT: I don't think anybody who was brought before the Committee has been unjustly accused.

MR. WALTER: We have not accused anybody of anything. When these witnesses have been subpoenaed it is because we have every reason to believe they possess information that will aid us in letting the American people see to what extent this Communist conspiracy has gone in our society.

MR. BLANKFORT: Yes, sir, I realize that.

MR. WALTER: We do not accuse anybody of anything.

MR. BLANKFORT: I agree with you.

* * *

MR. TAVENNER: You stated that Michael Gold advised you not to become a member of the Communist Party. What were the circumstances of his giving you that advice?

MR. BLANKFORT: The first time I met Michael Gold was probably when I got the manuscript of that play, and he just complained about the fact that he was a writer, and any writer who is a member of the Communist Party was just insane.

MR. TAVENNER: You know Michael Gold was a member, wasn't he?

MR. BLANKFORT: He certainly was.

MR. WALTER: We appreciate your cooperation, and it is only because of the willingness of people like you to come here and give us a full statement of the facts as you know them that we are able to point up to the American people the danger of this conspiracy.

The Committee handled Elia Kazan with kid gloves. He was heard in executive session on January 14, 1952, and that testimony has never been made public. Even the testimony given here was originally presented in executive session, no doubt to preserve Kazan from hecklers in the audience, and it was released to the press a day later, April 11, 1952. One day after that, the *New York Times* carried a paid advertisement, as follows:

A STATEMENT
by Elia Kazan

In the past weeks intolerable rumors about my political position have been circulating in New York and Hollywood. I want to make my stand clear:

I believe that Communist activities confront the people of this country with an unprecedented and exceptionally tough problem. That is, how to protect ourselves from a dangerous and alien conspiracy and still keep the free, open, healthy way of life that gives us self-respect.

I believe that the American people can solve this problem wisely only if they have the facts about communism. All the facts.

Now, I believe that any American who is in possession of such facts has the obligation to make them known, either to the public or to the appropriate Government agency.

Whatever hysteria exists—and there is some, particularly in Hollywood—is inflamed by mystery, suspicion and secrecy. Hard and exact facts will cool it.

The facts I have are sixteen years out of date, but they supply a small piece of background to the graver picture of communism today.

I have placed these facts before the House Committee on Un-American Activities without reserve and I now place them before the public and before my co-workers in motion pictures and in the theatre.

Seventeen and a half years ago I was a twenty-four-year-old stage manager and bit actor, making $40 a week, when I worked.

At that time nearly all of us felt menaced by two things: the depression and the ever growing power of Hitler. The streets were full of unemployed and shaken men. I was taken in by the Hard Times version of what might be called the Communists' advertising or recruiting technique. They claimed to have a cure for depressions and a cure for Naziism and Fascism.

I joined the Communist Party late in the summer of 1934. I got out a year and a half later.

I have no spy stories to tell, because I saw no spies. Nor did I understand, at that time, any opposition between American and Russian national interest. It was not even clear to me in 1936 that the American Communist Party was abjectly taking its orders from the Kremlin.

What I learned was the minimum that anyone must learn who puts his head into the noose of party "discipline." The Communists automatically violated the daily practices of democracy to which I was accustomed. They attempted to control thought and to suppress personal opinion. They tried to dictate personal conduct. They habitually distorted and disregarded and violated the truth. All this was crudely opposite to their claims of "democracy" and "the scientific approach."

To be a member of the Communist Party is to have a taste of the police state. It is a diluted taste but it is bitter and unforgettable. It is diluted because you can walk out.

I got out in the spring of 1936.

The question will be asked why I did not tell this story sooner. I was held back, primarily, by concern for the reputations and employment of people who may, like myself, have left the party many years ago.

I was also held back by a piece of specious reasoning which has silenced many liberals. It goes like this: "You may hate the Communists, but you must not attack them or expose them, because if you do you are attacking the right to hold unpopular opinions and you are joining the people who attack civil liberties."

I have thought soberly about this. It is, simply, a lie.

Secrecy serves the Communists. At the other pole, it serves those who are interested in silencing liberal voices. The employment of a lot of good liberals is threatened because they have allowed themselves to become associated with or silenced by the Communists.

Liberals must speak out.

I think it is useful that certain of us had this kind of experience with the Communists, for if we had not we should not know them so well. Today, when all the world fears war and they scream peace, we know how much their professions are worth. We know tomorrow they will have a new slogan.

Firsthand experience of dictatorship and thought control left me with an abiding hatred of these. It left me with an abiding hatred of Communist philosophy and methods and the conviction that these must be resisted always.

It also left me with the passionate conviction that we must never let the Communists get away with the pretense that they stand for the very things which they kill in their own countries.

I am talking about free speech, a free press, the rights of property, the rights of labor, racial equality and, above all, individual rights. I value these things. I take them seriously. I value peace, too, when it is not bought at the price of fundamental decencies.

I believe these things must be fought for wherever they are not fully honored and protected whenever they are threatend.

The motion pictures I have made and the plays I have chosen to direct represent my convictions.

I expect to continue to make the same kinds of pictures and to direct the same kinds of plays.

ELIA KAZAN

APRIL 10, 1952:

Elia Kazan

Executive Hearing (released April 11)

A Subcommittee of the Committee on Un-American Activities met at 4:25 p.m., in room 330, Old House Office Building, the Honorable Francis E. Walter, presiding.

Committee member present: Representative Francis E. Walter.

Staff members present: Frank S. Tavenner, Jr., Counsel; and Raphael I. Nixon, Director of Research.

MR. TAVENNER: Mr. Kazan, you testified before this Committee on January 14, 1952, in an executive session, did you not?

MR. KAZAN: That's correct.

MR. TAVENNER: In that hearing, you testified fully regarding your own membership in the Communist Party approximately seventeen years ago and your activity in the Party, did you not?

MR. KAZAN: That is correct.

MR. TAVENNER: However, you declined at that time to give the Committee any information relating to the activities of others or to identify others associated with you in your activities in the Communist Party?

MR. KAZAN: Most of the others, yes, sir. Some I did name.

MR. TAVENNER: But you declined at that time to name all of them?

MR. KAZAN: That is correct.

MR. TAVENNER: Now I understand that you have voluntarily requested the Committee to reopen your hearing, and to give you an opportunity to explain fully the participation of others known to you at the time to have been members of the Communist Party.

MR. KAZAN: That is correct. I want to make a full and complete statement. I want to tell you everything I know about it.

MR. TAVENNER: Now, in preparation for your testimony here, have you spent considerable time and effort in recalling and in reducing to writing the information which you have?

MR. KAZAN: I spent a great deal of time, yes, sir.

MR. TAVENNER: Do you have prepared, in written form, the full and complete statement which you say you would like to make to the Committee?

MR. KAZAN: Yes, sir, I have such a statement prepared.

* * *

(*Statement of Elia Kazan:*)

New York City, N.Y., April 9, 1952.

The House Committee on Un-American Activities,
Washington, D.C.

GENTLEMEN:

I wish to amend the testimony which I gave before you on January 14 of this year, by adding to it this letter and the accompanying sworn affidavit.

In the affidavit I answer the only question which I failed to answer at the hearing, namely, what people I knew to be members of the Communist Party between the summer of 1934, when I joined it, and the late winter or early spring of 1936, when I severed all connection with it.

I have come to the conclusion that I did wrong to withhold these names before, because secrecy serves the Communists, and is exactly what they want. The American people need the facts and all the facts about all aspects of Communism in order to deal with it wisely and effectively. It is my obligation as a citizen to tell everything that I know.

Although I answered all other questions which were put to me before, the naming of these people makes it possible for me to volunteer a detailed description of my own activities and of the general activity which I witnessed. I have attempted to set these down as carefully and fully as my memory allows. In doing so, I have necessarily repeated portions of my former testimony, but I believe that by so doing I have made a more complete picture than if I omitted it.

In the second section of the affidavit, I have tried to review comprehensively my very slight political activity in the 16 years since I left the party. Here again, I have of necessity repeated former testimony, but I wanted to make as complete an over-all picture as my fallible memory allows.

In the third section is a list of the motion pictures I have made and the plays I have chosen to direct. I call your attention to these for they constitute the entire history of my professional activity as a director.

Respectfully,
ELIA KAZAN.

State of New York,
County of New York, ss:

I, Elia Kazan, being duly sworn, depose and say:

I repeat my testimony of January 14, 1952, before the House Committee on Un-American Activities, to the effect that I was a member of the Communist Party from sometime in the summer of 1934 until the late winter or early spring of 1936, when I severed all connection with it permanently.

I want to reiterate that in those years, to my eyes, there was no clear opposition of national interests between the United States and Russia. It was not even clear to me that the American Communist Party was taking its orders from the Kremlin and acting as a Russian agency in this country. On the contrary, it seemed to me at that time that the Party had at heart the cause of the poor and unemployed people whom I saw on the streets about me. I felt that by joining, I was going to help them, I was going to fight Hitler, and, strange as it seems today, I felt that I was acting for the good of the American people.

For the approximately 19 months of my membership, I was assigned to a "unit" composed of those party members who were, like myself, members of the Group Theater acting company. These were—

Lewis Leverett, co-leader of the unit.

J. Edward Bromberg, co-leader of the unit, deceased.

Phoebe Brand (later Mrs. Morris Carnovsky). I was instrumental in bringing her into the Party.

Morris Carnovsky.

Tony Kraber; along with Wellman (see below), he recruited me into the Party.*

Paula Miller (later Mrs. Lee Strasberg): We are friends today. I be-

* When Kazan's testimony was cited to Kraber before HUAC, August 18, 1955, the latter asked, "Is this the Kazan that signed the contract for $500,000 the day after he gave names to this Committee? Would you sell your brothers for $500,000?" —E.B.

lieve that, as she has told me, she quit the Communists long ago. She is far too sensible and balanced a woman, and she is married to too fine and intelligent a man, to have remained among them.

Clifford Odets: He has assured me that he got out about the same time I did.

Art Smith.

These are the only members of the unit whom I recall and I believe this to be a complete list. Even at this date I do not believe it would be possible for me to forget anyone.

I believe that in my previous testimony I mentioned that there were nine members in the unit. I was including Michael Gordon, but in searching my recollection I find that I do not recall his having attended any meeting with me.

As I testified previously, two Party functionaries were assigned to "hand the party line" to us new recruits. They were—

V. J. Jerome, who had some sort of official "cultural" commissar position at Party headquarters; and

Andrew Overgaard, a Scandinavian, who was head, as I recall, of the Trade Union Unity League.

There was a third party official who concerned himself with us, although whether he was officially assigned or merely hung about the theater when he was in New York, I never knew. He told us that he was state organizer for the Party in Tennessee. He was obviously stagestruck and he undertook to advise me. He was—

Ted Wellman, also known as Sid Benson.

Our financial contributions and dues were on a puny scale. We were small-salaried actors, frequently out of work, and it was depression time.

What we were asked to do was fourfold:

(1) To "educate" ourselves in Marxist and Party doctrine;

(2) To help the party get a foothold in the Actors Equity Association;

(3) To support various "front" organizations of the Party;

(4) To try to capture the Group Theater and make it a Communist mouthpiece.

The history of these efforts in my time, were as follows:

(1) In the "education" program we were sold pamphlets and books and told to read them. There were also "discussions" of these. The "discussions" were my first taste of totalitarian methods, for there was no honest discussion at all, but only an attempt to make sure that we swallowed every sentence without challenge.

(2) The attempt to gain a foothold in Actors Equity was guided by an actor, Robert or Bob Caille (I think that was the spelling). He was also known as Bob Reed. I have been told that he died some years ago.

The tactic—and the sincere effort of many individuals—was to "raise a demand" that actors receive pay during the weeks when they rehearsed for shows. The long-range plan was, by leading a fight for a reasonable gain for the actors, to gain prestige for individual Communists and sympathizers who, the party hoped, would then run the union.

Pay for the rehearsal period was obtained, but at no time that I saw, either then or after I left, did the Party come within sight of controlling the actors' union.

(3) Most of our time, however, went directly or indirectly into providing "entertainment" for the meetings and rallies of front organizations and unions. The "entertainment" was strictly propaganda.

There were two front organizations in the theater field, but off Broadway, whose purpose was to provide such propaganda entertainment and with whom I had dealings. They were the League of Workers Theaters (later the New Theater League) and the Theater of Action. It was into these that my time went. I acted, I trained and directed other actors and, with Art Smith, I co-authored a play called *Dimitroff,* which had to do with the imprisonment of the Bulgarian Communist leader by the Nazis following the Reichstag fire. It is my memory that the play enjoyed either two or three Sunday-night performances before benefit audiences and was then retired.

I taught at the school for actors and directors run by the League of Workers Theaters. This was unquestionably a Communist-controlled outfit. Its officials were never bona fide theater people and it was my impression that they had been imported by the Party from other fields to regiment the political novices in the theater. To the best of my knowledge, when he league came to an end, they retired from the theater again. I do not recall any Communist meeting which I attended with them, but my impression that they were all Communists is very strong. The ones I remember were—

Harry Elion, president;

John Bonn, a German refugee;

Alice Evans (I am told she later married V. J. Jerome);

Anne Howe.

In the Theater of Action, there was a Communist thought and behavior and control, but I did not attend their political meetings so I cannot tell which of the actors were Party members and which were not. I did some acting training here and I co-directed with Al Saxe a play called *The Young Go First,* and I directed another called (I think) *The Crisis.*

About 1936, I began a connection with an outfit called Frontier Films, but the Party had nothing to do with my making this connection. The organization consisted of four or five men, of whom I remember Paul Strand, Leo Hurwitz, and Ralph Steiner. From long friendship with Steiner, I believe him to be a strong anti-Communist. I do not know the Party affiliations of the others. They were trying to raise money to make documentary films. They put me on their board, but I attended few meetings. I wanted to make a picture. This I did, with Ralph Steiner, in 1937. It was a two-reel documentary called *The People of the Cumberlands.*

That was my last active connection with any organization which has since been listed as subversive.

(4) I want to repeat emphatically that the Communists' attempt to take over the Group Theater failed. There was some influence and a great deal of talk, the members of the Communist unit consumed a great deal of time at group meetings, they raised some money from the non-Communist members for Communists' causes and they sold them some Communist pamphlets; they brought the prestige of the group name to meetings where they entertained as individuals, but they never succeeded in controlling the Group Theater.

This was because the control of the group stayed firmly in the hands of the three non-Communist directors, Harold Clurman, Lee Strasberg, and Cheryl Crawford. (In 1937 Clurman became sole director and remained so until the theater broke up in 1940.)

In a small way, I played a part in blocking the Communist unit's maneuvers to get control. In the winter of 1935–36 I was a member of the actors' committee of the group. This was an advisory committee, but it was the nearest the actors ever came to having any voice in the running of the theater. I was instructed by the Communist unit to demand that the group be run "democratically." This was a characteristic Communist tactic; they were not interested in democracy; they wanted control. They had no chance of controlling the directors, but they thought that if authority went to the actors, they would have a chance to dominate through the usual tricks of behind-the-scenes caucuses, block voting, and confusion of issues.

This was the specific issue on which I quit the party. I had enough regimentation, enough of being told what to think and say and do, enough of their habitual violation of the daily practices of democracy to which I was accustomed. The last straw came when I was invited to go through a typical Communist scene of crawling and apologizing and admitting the error of my ways. The invitation came from a Communist functionary brought in for the occasion. He was introduced as an organizer of the Auto Workers Union from Detroit. I regret that I cannot remember his name. In any case, he probably did not use his own name. I had never seen him before, nor he me.

He made a vituperative analysis of my conduct in refusing to fall in with the Party line and plan for the Group Theater, and he invited my repentance. My fellow members looked at him as if he were an oracle. I have not seen him since, either.

That was the night I quit them. I had had enough anyway. I had had a taste of police-state living and I did not like it. Instead of working honestly for the good of the American people, I had found that I was being used to put power in the hands of people for whom, individually and as a group, I felt nothing but contempt, and for whose standard of conduct I felt a genuine horror.

Since that night, I have never had the least thing to do with the Party.

II

After I left the Party in 1936, except for the making of the two-reel documentary film mentioned above, in 1937, I was never active in any organization since listed as subversive.

My policy in the years after 1936 was an instinctive rather than a planned one. I could usually detect a front organization when I first heard about it and I stayed away from it. I never became a member of such an organization, although I was pressed to join dozens of them.

Contradictorily, on a few of the many occasions when I was asked to sign a statement or a telegram for a specific cause, I may have allowed my name to be used, even though I suspected the sponsoring organization. They insidiously picked causes which appealed to decent, liberal, humanitarian people; against racial discrimination, against Japanese aggression, against specific miscarriages of justice. There was a piece of spurious reasoning which influenced me to let them use my name in rare instances. It went like this, "I hate the Communists but I go along with this cause because I believe the cause is right."

Today I repudiate that reasoning, but it accounts for those of the instances listed below in which I may have done what is alleged. I repudiate the reasoning because I believe that all their fights are deceitful maneuvers to gain influence.

My connections with these front organizations were so slight and so transitory that I am forced to rely on a listing of these prepared for me after research by my employer, Twentieth Century–Fox. I state with full awareness that I am under oath, that in most of the cases I do not remember any connection at all. It is possible that my name was used without my consent. It is possible that in a few instances I gave consent.

I am told that the *New Masses* of November 4, and the *Daily Worker* of November 8, 1941, list me as an entertainer at a meeting sponsored by the American Friends of the Chinese People. I remember no connection whatsoever with this organization and especially since I ceased all "entertaining" in 1936 when I left the Party, I can only suppose that my name was used without my permission in this instance.

I am told that I signed an appeal put out by the Committee for a Boycott Against Japanese Aggression. I do not remember this either, but it is possible that I signed such an appeal. No date is given, but it must have been before Pearl Harbor.

I am told that the official program of the Artists Front To Win the War listed me as a sponsor in October 1942. I have no memory of this either, but it is possible that I gave my consent to the use of my name.

I am told that on July 19, 1942, I signed an open letter sponsored by the National Federation for Constitutional Liberties, which denounced Attorney General [Francis] Biddle's charges against Harry Bridges. I have no recollection of this either, but again it is possible that I did so, for I remember that, in contrast to what I had heard about the New York water front, what I had heard about San Francisco suggested that Bridges had done a good job for his union. And I remember that I believed the story, current at that time, that he was being hounded for this. At that time I did not believe him to be a Communist.

I have been reminded that my name was used as a sponsor of the publication, *People's Songs*. I have no doubt that I gave permission for this. The date could be found by referring to the first issues of the publication. Beyond allowing my name to be used initially, I had no contact with it.

The only money contribution which I remember between 1936 and 1947 or 1948—and I remember it with regret—was one of $200 which I gave to Arnaud d'Usseau when he asked for help in founding what he said was to be a new "liberal literary magazine." This magazine turned out to be *Mainstream* and from its first issue was a patently Communist publication altogether detestable and neither liberal nor literary.

Now I come to the only case or cause in which I got involved, even to a limited extent, in those sixteen years between 1936 and 1952. It was what became known as the case of the Hollywood Ten.

I would recall to this Committee the opening of the first investigation into Communism in Hollywood by the previous committee under the chairmanship of J. Parnell Thomas. I would recall that a large number of representative people in the creative branch of the picture industry, regardless of their politics, were alarmed by the first sessions. They signed protests and they banded in organizations which certainly did not look to me like front organizations at their inception, although later the Communists plainly got control of them.

I am listed as sponsoring a committee to raise funds for the defense of the Ten and as having sent a telegram to John Huston on March 5, 1948, when he was chairman of the dinner for them. I do not remember these specific actions, but I certainly felt impelled to action of that sort at that time and did this or something like it. I also made a contribution of $500 to a woman representative of the committee for the Hollywood Ten. This was in New York. If I am able to recall her name, I will advise you of it, but I cannot recall it at the moment. I am also listed as supporting a radio program for the Ten as late as August 1950. I am surprised at the date. It is possible that I was approached and gave permission to use my name as late as this, but it seems to me more likely that my name was reused without asking me, since I had allowed its use earlier.

For by that time I was disgusted by the silence of the Ten and by their contemptuous attitude. However, I must say now that what I did earlier represented my convictions at the beginning of the case.

That is the end of the list of my front associations after 1936, insofar as I can remember them, with the assistance of the memorandum prepared for me.

I should like to point out some of the typical Communist-front and Communist-sympathizer activities which I stayed away from:

From the day I went to Hollywood to direct my first picture, in 1944, I had nothing to do with any front organization there. Neither had I anything to do with them on three earlier trips as an actor. I had nothing to do with the Actors' Lab. I never gave a penny to any front organization on the West Coast.

I did not sign the Stockholm peace pledge. I saw what that was. I resented the Communist attempt to capture the word "peace."

I did not sponsor or attend the Waldorf Peace Conference. My wife's name was used as a sponsor without her permission. She protested and asked for its withdrawal in a letter to Prof. Harlow Shapley of Harvard University, who had some official post. She received no answer from him, but she did get an apology from James Proctor, who had given her name without her permission.

I had nothing to do with the Arts, Sciences, and Professions or any of its predecessors or successors.

I did not support Henry Wallace for President.

I do not want to imply that anyone who did these things was one of the Communists; I do submit that anyone who did none of them was a long way away from them.

III

There follows a list of my entire professional career as a director, all the plays I have done and the films I have made.

Casey Jones, by Robert Ardrey, 1938: The story of a railroad engineer who comes to the end of his working days. It is thoroughly and wonderfully American in its tone, characters, and outlook.

Thunder Rock, by Robert Ardrey, 1939: This is a deeply democratic and deeply optimistic play, written at a time when there was a good deal of pessimism about democracy. It told of a group of European immigrants headed for the West about 1848, and showed how they despaired of reforms which this country has long since achieved and now takes for granted. A failure in New York, this play was a huge hit in wartime London.

Café Crown, by Hy Kraft, 1942: A comedy about Jewish actors on New York's East Side. No politics, but a warm and friendly feeling toward a minority of a minority.

The Strings, My Lord, Are False, by Paul Vincent Carroll, 1942: An Irishman's play about England under the bombings. Not political. It shows human courage and endurance in many kinds of people, including, prominently, a priest.

The Skin of Our Teeth, by Thornton Wilder, 1942: One of the plays I am proudest to have done. It celebrates the endurance of the human race and does so with wit and wisdom and compassion.

Harriet, by Florence Ryerson and Colin Clements, 1943: The story of Harriet Beecher Stowe, who wrote *Uncle Tom's Cabin.*

One Touch of Venus, by S. J. Perelman, Ogden Nash, and Kurt Weill, 1943: Musical comedy. The goddess Venus falls in love with a barber.

Jacobowsky and the Colonel, by S. N. Behrman, 1942: Humorous-sad tale of the flight of a Jewish jack-of-all-trades and a Polish count before the oncoming Nazis. Not political, but very human.

A Tree Grows in Brooklyn (my first picture), 1944: A little girl grows up in the slum section of Brooklyn. There is pain in the story, but there is health. It is a typically American story and could only happen here, and a glorification of America not in material terms, but in spiritual ones.

Sing Out Sweet Land, by Jean and Walter Kerr, 1944: A musical built around old American songs. Nonpolitical but full of American tradition and spirit.

Deep Are the Roots, by Arnaud d'Usseau and James Gow, 1945: This was a very frank and somewhat melodramatic exploration of relations between Negroes and whites. It was shocking to some people but on the whole both audiences and critics took it with enthusiasm.

Dunnigan's Daughter, by S. N. Behrman, 1945: A comedy drama about a young wife whose husband was too absorbed in his business to love her.

Sea of Grass (picture), 1946: The conflict between cattle ranchers and farmers on the prairie.

Boomerang (picture), 1946: Based on an incident in the life of Homer Cummings, later Attorney General of the United States. It tells how an initial miscarriage of justice was righted by the persistence and integrity of a young district attorney, who risked his career to save an innocent man. This shows the exact opposite of the Communist libels on America.

All My Sons, by Arthur Miller, 1947: The story of a war veteran who came home to discover that his father, a small manufacturer, had shipped defective plane parts to the Armed Forces during the war. Some people have searched for hidden propaganda in this one, but I believe it to be a deeply moral investigation of problems of conscience and responsibility.

Gentlemen's Agreement (picture): Picture version of the best-selling novel about anti-Semitism. It won an academy award and I think it is in a healthy American tradition, for it shows Americans exploring a problem and tackling a solution. Again it is opposite to the picture which Communists present of Americans.

A Streetcar Named Desire, by Tennessee Williams, 1947: A famous play. Not political, but deeply human.

Sundown Beach, by Bessie Breuer, 1948: A group of young Army fliers and their girls at a hospital in Florida. Not political, but a warm and compassionate treatment.

Lovelife, by Alan Jay Lerner and Kurt Weill, 1948: Musical comedy. Story of a married couple, covering 100 years of changing American standards and customs.

Death of a Salesman, by Arthur Miller, 1949: It shows the frustrations of the life of a salesman and contains implicit criticism of his materialistic standards.

Pinky (picture), 1949: The story of a Negro girl who passed for white in the North and returns to the South to encounter freshly the impact of prejudice. Almost everybody liked this except the Communists, who attacked it virulently. It was extremely successful throughout the country, as much so in the South as elsewhere.

Panic in the Streets (picture), 1950: A melodrama built around the subject of an incipient plague. The hero is a doctor in the United States Health Service.

A Streetcar Named Desire (picture), 1950: Picture version of the play.

Viva Zapata (picture, my most recent one), 1951: This is an anti-Communist picture. Please see my article on political aspects of this picture in the *Saturday Review* of April 5, which I forwarded to your investigator, Mr. Nixon.

Flight into Egypt, by George Tabori, 1952: Story of refugees stranded in Cairo and trying to get into the United States.

I think it is useful that certain of us had this kind of experience with the Communists, for if we had not, we should not know them so well. Anyone who has had it is not to be fooled by them again. Today, when all the world fears war and they scream peace, we know how much their professions are worth. We know tomorrow they will have a new slogan.

Firsthand experience of dictatorship and thought control left me with an abiding hatred of these. It left me with an abiding hatred of Communist philosophy and methods.

It also left me with the passionate conviction that we must never let the Communists get away with the pretense that they stand for the very things which they kill in their own countries.

I am talking about free speech, a free press, the rights of labor, racial equality and, above all, individual rights. I value these things. I take them seriously. I value peace, too, when it is not bought at the price of fundamental decencies.

I believe these things must be fought for wherever they are not fully honored and protected whenever they are threatened.

The motion pictures I have made and the plays I have chosen to direct represent those convictions.

I have placed a copy of this affidavit with Mr. Spyros P. Skouras, president of Twentieth Century–Fox.

ELIA KAZAN.

Sworn to before me this 10th day of April, 1952.

MR. TAVENNER: Mr. Kazan, the staff or members of the Committee may desire to recall you at some future time for the purpose of asking you to make further explanations of some of the matters contained in your sworn statement.

MR. KAZAN: I will be glad to do anything to help—anything you consider necessary or valuable.

MR. WALTER: Mr. Kazan, we appreciate your cooperation with our Committee. It is only through the assistance of people such as you that we have been able to make the progress that has been made in bringing the attention of the American people to the machinations of this Communist conspiracy for world domination.

One of the characteristic types which should certainly be set forth is the Hollywood celebrity who had Communist friends without knowing it. One example was Charles Laughton, who was close to Bertolt Brecht and Hanns Eisler. When he found out the FBI considered Eisler had Communist sympathies, Laughton said, "But that's ridiculous: his music is just like Mozart." That was in December 1947. By 1956, when Brecht died and Laughton received a wire from East Berlin inviting him to a memorial meeting, the now informed and "co-ordinated" actor at once phoned the FBI to ask if it was all right that he had received a wire from such a source, after all he couldn't help it, etc., etc.

In the brave days of 1948, Edward G. Robinson could be cited by the Hollywood Ten in their book *Hollywood on Trial* as a witness most friendly to them, alongside Frank Sinatra, Fredric March, Lucille Ball, Myrna Loy, Burt Lancaster, Judy Garland, and Bennett Cerf. But by 1952 another epoch had opened. In Robinson's testimony this exchange occurs:

> MR. WALTER: Mr. Robinson, you stated that you were duped and used. By whom?
>
> MR. ROBINSON: By the sinister forces who were members, and probably in important positions, in those organizations.
>
> MR. WALTER: Well, tell us what individuals you have reference to.
>
> MR. ROBINSON: Well, you had Albert Maltz, and you have Dalton

Trumbo, and you have—what is the other fellow, the top fellow who they say is the commissar out there?

MR. WALTER: John Howard Lawson?

MR. ROBINSON: Yes, John Howard Lawson. I knew Frank Tuttle. I didn't know Dmytryk at all. There are the Buchmans, that I know, Sidney Buchman and all that sort of thing. It never entered my head that any of these people were Communists.

Students of the loyalty tests which the Committee encouraged will note how Robinson cites the fact that the play he is in is Koestler's *Darkness at Noon*. Kazan (as quoted on page 493) had even cited such details as a good priest in one of his productions.

APRIL 30, 1952:

Edward G. Robinson

A Subcommittee of the Committee on Un-American Activities met, at 2 p.m., in room 226 Old House Building, Washington, D.C., the Honorable Francis E. Walter, presiding.

Committee members present: Representatives Francis E. Walter, Morgan M. Moulder, Bernard W. Kearney, and Donald L. Jackson.

Staff members present: Frank S. Tavenner, Jr., Counsel; Thomas W. Beale, Sr., Assistant Counsel; Raphael I. Nixon, Director of Research; Donald T. Appell and James A. Andrews, Investigators; John W. Carrington, Clerk; and A. S. Poore, Editor.

MR. TAVENNER: I understand, Mr. Robinson, that this morning you requested of the Committee that you be permitted to appear before it?

MR. ROBINSON: That is quite right, sir.

MR. TAVENNER: And that privilege was granted you?

MR. ROBINSON: Yes, sir.

MR. TAVENNER: Will you state for the Committee your purpose in desiring to appear before the Committee at this time?

MR. ROBINSON: I have just finished my season with *Darkness at Noon,* Monday night in West Virginia, and I had come to Washington on a personal matter. I hoped that I would have the opportunity of appearing before your Committee, so that I could give you an idea of just what my feelings and my thoughts are in this matter since the revelations that have been made during 1951 and 1952 by your Committee. I have prepared a written statement, and I should like to read it to you. My voice is a little hoarse—I have had a very arduous part for a long time. If you will permit me to read this statement—

MR. WALTER: You may proceed, sir.

Mr. Robinson: Thank you, sir. Mr. Chairman and members of the Committee, as on previous occasions, I have asked for this opportunity to appear before you so as to make unmistakably clear my feeling about Communism and Communists. As on previous occasions when I have appeared, I desire to repeat under oath a denial that I am or ever have been a Communist or knowingly a fellow traveler. I have always been a liberal Democrat. The revelations that persons whom I thought were sincere liberals were, in fact, Communists, has shocked me more than I can tell you. That they persuaded me by lies and concealment of their real purposes to allow them to use my name for what I believed to be a worthy cause is now obvious. I was sincere. They were not. I bitterly resent their false assertions of liberalism and honesty through which they imposed upon me and exploited my sincere desire to help my fellow men. Not one of the Communists who sought my help or requested permission to use my name ever told me that he or she was a member of the Communist Party. My suspicions, which should have been aroused, were allayed by the fact that I had been falsely accused of Communist sympathies, and I was, therefore, willing to believe that other accused persons were also being unfairly smeared.

My conscience is clear. My loyalty to this nation I know to be absolute. No one has ever been willing to confront me under oath, free from immunity, and unequivocably charge me with membership in the Communist Party or any other subversive organization. No one can honestly do so. I now realize that some organizations which I permitted to use my name were, in fact, Communist fronts. But their ostensible purposes were good, and it was for such purposes that I allowed use of my name and even made numerous financial contributions. The hidden purpose of the Communists, in such groups, was not known to me. Had I known the truth, I would not have associated with such persons, although I would have and intend to continue to help to the extent of my ability in worthwhile causes, honestly calculated to help underprivileged or oppressed people, including those oppressed by Communist tyranny.

The Committee will, I am sure, appreciate the fact that I have been active in groups opposed to the Communists. For instance, my memory was recently refreshed concerning the support I gave the William Allen White Committee to aid the Allies at a time when Hitler and Stalin sympathizers were using the slogan "The Yanks are not coming." I was at that time urging aid for Great Britain, which was fighting the Communist-Nazi alliance. My stand was definitely contrary to the stand of the Communists. I have helped other anti-Communist causes, but this has somehow been lost sight of by those who seem intent upon trying to make me out a Communist, in spite of my repeated denials under oath of Communist sympathies.

May I add that of the very many civic, cultural, philanthropic, and political organizations of which I have been a member and a contributor, but a small percentage I later discovered were tinged with the taint of Communism. It is a serious matter to have one's loyalty questioned. Life is less dear to me than my loyalty to democracy and the United States. I ask favors of no one. All I ask is that the record be kept straight and that I be permitted to live free of false charges. I readily concede that I have been used, and that I have been mistaken regarding certain associations which I regret, but I have not been disloyal or dishonest.

I would like to find some way to put at rest the ever-recurring innuendoes concerning my loyalty. Surely there must be some way for a person falsely accused of disloyalty to clear his name once and for all. It is for this purpose that I come again voluntarily before this Committee to testify under oath. What more can I do? Anyone who understands the history of the political activity in Hollywood will appreciate the fact that innocent, sincere persons were used by the Communists to whom honesty and sincerity are as foreign as the Soviet Union is to America. I was duped and used. I was lied to. But, I repeat, I acted from good motives, and I have never knowingly aided Communists or any Communist cause.

I wish to thank the Committee for this opportunity to appear and clarify my position. I have been slow to realize that persons I thought sincere were Communists. I am glad, for the sake of myself and the nation, that they have been exposed by your Committee.

While you have been exposing Communists, I have been fighting them and their ideology in my own way. I just finished appearing in close to two hundred and fifty performances of *Darkness at Noon* all over the country. It is, perhaps, the strongest indictment of Communism ever presented. I am sure it had a profound and lasting effect on all who saw it.

MAY 19–20, 1952:

Clifford Odets

A Subcommittee of the Committee on Un-American Activities met at 11 a.m., in room 226, Old House Office Building, the Honorable John S. Wood presiding.

Committee members present: Representative John S. Wood (Chairman), James B. Frazier, Jr., Harold H. Velde (appearance noted in transcript), and Bernard W. Kearney.

Staff members present: Frank S. Tavenner, Jr., Counsel; Thomas W. Beale, Sr., Assistant Counsel; John W. Carrington, Clerk; Raphael I. Nixon, Director of Research; and A. S. Poore, Editor.

MR. TAVENNER: Mr. Odets, you appeared before the Committee in executive session on April 24, 1952. The purpose of your appearance here today is to obtain your testimony in open hearings and to question you further on matters discussed at the earlier hearings. Will you please state the time and place of your birth?

MR. ODETS: I was born in Philadelphia, Pennsylvania, July 18, 1906.

MR. TAVENNER: What was your formal education?

MR. ODETS: Two years of high school, and elementary school, in the Bronx, New York City.

MR. TAVENNER: What is your occupation?

MR. ODETS: I am a playwright and a theater director.

MR. TAVENNER: Have you also engaged in the acting profession?

MR. ODETS: I have in the past been an actor. I have written and directed for movies.

(*Representative Harold H. Velde entered the room at this point.*)

MR. TAVENNER: Where do you now reside?

MR. ODETS: In New York City.

MR. TAVENNER: Where have you lived during your professional career? That is, as an actor and as a playwright and director.

MR. ODETS: I have lived in Philadelphia, I have worked and lived in Camden, New Jersey, Chester, Pennsylvania, Hollywood, California.

MR. TAVENNER: Well, would you tell us as nearly as you can the periods when you were in Hollywood?

MR. ODETS: 1935. After that I will guess two or three excursions to Hollywood between the years of 1936 and perhaps 1941. I went one time to make a picture for Paramount called *Gettysburg*. I went one time for United Artists to make a picture called *The River Is Blue,* which I did not finally write. I went at another time to write *The Life of George Gershwin.* Finally in 1943 I went to Hollywood for a period of slightly over four years.

MR. TAVENNER: When did you leave Hollywood and return to New York?

MR. ODETS: I will guess in 1947 and a half or 1948.

MR. TAVENNER: And since that time how have you been employed or in what work have you been engaged?

MR. ODETS: I have since then, in New York City, written and produced two plays, one of which I directed, my last one.

MR. TAVENNER: What are their names?

MR. ODETS: The first one was called *The Big Knife,* and the second one was called *The Country Girl.*

MR. TAVENNER: *The Big Knife* was in 1948 and *The Country Girl* in 1951, I believe.

MR. ODETS: I think so.

MR. TAVENNER: When did you cease being an actor and become a playwright?

MR. ODETS: I think this happened at the end of 1934 or the beginning of 1935, in there.

MR. TAVENNER: What are the principal plays that were written by you after you became a playwright in 1934 or 1935?

MR. ODETS: The first play I wrote was called *Awake and Sing*. The second two plays after that were called *Waiting for Lefty* and *Till the Day I Die*.

* * *

MR. TAVENNER: What was your next play?

MR. CDETS: The next play was called *Paradise Lost*.

MR. TAVENNER: And it was produced in 1936, was it not?

MR. ODETS: About, I guess so.

MR. TAVENNER: Was the *Golden Boy* the next in order?

MR. ODETS: I think so, yes.

MR. TAVENNER: Produced in 1937?

MR. ODETS: I think so, yes, sir. Then after that would come *Rocket to the Moon*.

MR. TAVENNER: In 1939?

MR. ODETS: I think so. Or maybe a little earlier, 1938 or 1938 and a half.

MR. TAVENNER: Prior to the production of *Rocket to the Moon,* did you write a play entitled *Silent Partner*?

MR. ODETS: Yes, except that was not produced. It was imperfectly written, therefore it was not produced.

MR. TAVENNER: Then, after your play *Rocket to the Moon,* did you write and produce *Night Music*?

MR. ODETS: Correct.

MR. TAVENNER And the date of that was in 1940, was it not?

MR. ODETS: Yes, sir.

MR. TAVENNER: And what was the next after that?

MR. ODETS: After that Billy Rose produced a play of mine called *Clash by Night*.

MR. TAVENNER: That was in 1942?

MR. ODETS: I think so.

MR. TAVENNER: Did that compose the entire list, with the addition of the three pictures you produced in Hollywood?

MR. ODETS: I have written more movies. Not many of them saw production, and frequently I was employed as a play doctor in Hollywood to improve other writers' scripts.

MR. TAVENNER: Mr. Odets, there has been testimony before the Committee that you were at one time a member of the Communist Party. Was that testimony correct?

MR. ODETS: Yes, sir, it was.

MR. TAVENNER: When were you a member of the Communist Party?

MR. ODETS: My best guess would be from toward the end of 1934 to the middle of 1935, covering maybe anywhere from six to eight months.*

MR. TAVENNER: How were you recruited into the Communist Party and by whom?

MR. ODETS: Of a total Group Theater membership of perhaps thirty-five, there were four or five people who were connected with the Communist Party. Literature was passed around, and, in a time of great social unrest, many people found themselves reaching out for new ideas, new ways of solving depressions or making a better living, fighting for one's rights.

MR. KEARNEY: What were those rights?

MR. ODETS: The right to be steadily employed, for instance. There were perhaps fifteen or sixteen million unemployed people in the United States, and I myself was living on ten cents a day. Therefore, I was interested in any idea which might suggest how I could function as a working actor who could make a living at a craft he had chosen for his life's work. These were the early days of the New Deal, and I don't think that one has to describe them. They were horrendous days that none of us would like to go through again. On this basis, there was a great deal of talk about amelioration of conditions, about how should one live, what values should one work for, and in line with this there was a great deal of talk about Marxist values. One read literature. There were a lot of penny and two-cent and five-cent pamphlets. I read them, along with a lot of other people, and finally joined the Communist Party, in the honest and real belief that this was some way out of the dilemma in which we found ourselves.

MR. TAVENNER: You have not told us the exact circumstances under which you were recruited into the Party.

MR. ODETS: Well, you read some pamphlets, you listened to someone talk, and finally a person would ask you if you didn't want to join the Communist Party. In my case it happened: "No, I don't. When I am ready, I will." I was not ready that month, I was ready a month or two later.

MR. TAVENNER: Who was the individual who made that suggestion to you?

MR. ODETS: This would be an actor friend of mine named J. Edward Bromberg.

MR. TAVENNER: Was he a member of the Group Theater?

MR. ODETS: Yes, he was.

MR. KEARNEY: Was he the actor who died a few months ago?

* Kazan (above) had stated: "He [Odets] has assured me that he got out about the same time I did," this time being late winter or early spring 1936. The discrepancy between the two accounts is hardly a vast one, but it is of interest that Odets' reports on autobiographical matters *are* apt to be inaccurate, if not even a little fanciful. Evidence on this point has been rather abundantly provided by an Odets biographer, Gerald Weales, in his *Clifford Odets, Playwright*: New York, 1971. See especially pp. 101–104. —E.B.

MR. ODETS: Yes, sir, he is.

MR. TAVENNER: Who actually recruited you into the Party?

MR. ODETS: My best memory would be that Mr. Bromberg did.

MR. TAVENNER: When you were recruited into the Party, were you assigned to a particular cell or group?

MR. ODETS: Yes, it would be connected with those few people who were in the Group Theater.

MR. TAVENNER: Who were the other persons who were members of the cell?

MR. ODETS: Well, they have been mentioned here as Lewis Leverett, a young actress named Phoebe Brand, and an actor about whom you refreshed my memory the last time I was here named Art Smith. And then, from my reading of the *New York Times,* a couple of other members were mentioned that I have no memory of, as I told you.

MR. TAVENNER: Elia Kazan? Was he a member of that group?

MR. ODETS: Yes, Mr. Kazan.

MR. TAVENNER: Did you meet with all of those persons as members of the Communist Party—that is, those you have named up to the present time?

MR. ODETS: Yes, sir.

MR. TAVENNER: Tony Kraber?

MR. ODETS: He, too.

MR. TAVENNER: He is included in the group. Also, do you recall a person by the name of Sid Benson, also known as Ted Wellman?

MR. ODETS: Yes, sir, I knew him.

MR. TAVENNER: Was he an attendant at your Communist Party meetings in this Group Theater?

MR. ODETS: He came in as an occasional visitor.

MR. TAVENNER: Was he known to you as a functionary in the Communist Party?

MR. ODETS: Well, I actually did not know what he did. I thought for a while he was a man who wrote newspaper articles. Then my impression became that he was some kind of Party functionary.

MR. TAVENNER: But he was not a member of the Group Theater as such?

MR. ODETS: No, sir, he was not an actor.

MR. TAVENNER: Did this person, Wellman or Sid Benson, ever visit in your home?

MR. ODETS: Yes, sir, he did. He was a friend of mine.

MR. TAVENNER: What was the purpose of his visits at your home in New York?

MR. ODETS: They were always social visits. We both were interested in music, fine classical music, records. We might go out to dinner.

MR. TAVENNER: Did any of those visits have anything to do with his interest or his work in the Communist Party?

MR. ODETS: No, sir, in no way.

MR. TAVENNER: Were you acquainted with a person by the name of Andrew Overgaard?

MR. ODETS: Yes, I met him.

MR. TAVENNER: Under what circumstances did you meet him?

MR. ODETS: In some way that I wouldn't remember. He came backstage in one of our plays. And perhaps we went out to get a bit to eat or something to drink, some coffee.

MR. TAVENNER: Did he attend the Communist Party cell meetings to which you referred?

MR. ODETS: I would guess that he was introduced to people who were connected with this group within the group, so to speak.

MR. TAVENNER: Did you recognize him as a functionary of the Communist Party?

MR. ODETS: This would be my good guess.

MR. TAVENNER: On what do you base that statement?

MR. ODETS: Well, the Communist Party functionaries, when they are such, are always secretive. They never announce themselves as Communist Party functionaries. But they have a quality of authority, a quality of talking with knowledge, and one makes the surmise that this is some kind of functionary.

MR. TAVENNER: And it was on the basis of that conduct on his part that your judgment was that he was a functionary of the Communist Party?

MR. ODETS: Yes, sir.

MR. TAVENNER: Do you recall any occasions when his advice was sought on Communist Party problems?

MR. ODETS: I remember one such occasion. The occasion, as I think I have stated before, was we thought that actors should get rehearsal pay, which was an unheard of thing and rather a lunatic idea in those days. We wanted or perhaps we did first go to an Actors Equity Association meeting and made no headway at all. My best memory is that we then in some way consulted with Mr. Overgaard, who suggested certain tactical moves to make to get our proposal on the floor, and I have no memory of details, but I do know that this small group within the Group Theater did get, for every actor in the United States, rehearsal pay. That is, we were the beginning of such a movement.

MR. TAVENNER: Do you know whether Overgaard was connected with any Communist trade-union organization at that time?

MR. ODETS: There was some such talk. It was obvious that he was a trade-union man. It was on that basis that we would have consulted with him. But what exactly it was I am not sure.

MR. TAVENNER: During the course of your membership in the Party, were you required to make a study of Marxist literature?

MR. ODETS: Yes, sir, it was a great day for literature. One read and one was supposed to read constantly.

MR. TAVENNER: Did you take up those studies in meetings of your group?

MR. ODETS: I personally did not do too much because it was a little beyond me, and my interest was going toward writing plays. These matters required really months of very serious study, which I did not give them.

MR. TAVENNER: Did you attend meetings where the principles of Marxism were discussed and studied?

MR. ODETS: I never studied in such groups. It would be a matter of taking home a newspaper or pamphlet and reading it.

MR. TAVENNER: Where did you obtain the material?

MR. ODETS: The material was bought at the Workers' Bookshop. Or it was given to you or bought for you by some other member.

MR. TAVENNER: How many meetings did you attend in the group?

MR. ODETS: I am quite certain they were very few.

MR. TAVENNER: Were meetings held regularly?

MR. ODETS: I think that meetings are held regularly—let us say, for instance, once a week—and that special meetings would be called on the basis of some complaint or something that had to be fixed. I gave you what seemed to be a rather silly example of saying, "Well, we don't get clean drinking glasses around here." They would call a meeting at ten or eleven o'clock that night to discuss that subject. I thought it was a little silly, and I refused to attend such meetings.

MR. TAVENNER: Were any of the meetings held in your home?

MR. ODETS: No, I don't think I had a home then. I was a very poor man.

MR. TAVENNER: When was the period of time that Wellman was visiting you in your home?

MR. ODETS: I might think in the next six months or a year.

MR. TAVENNER: Will you fix the time as nearly as you can by giving us the months of the year that it may have occurred?

MR. ODETS: Well, if I said he visited me once or twice in 1935 and then perhaps later in 1936, this would be my best judgment.

MR. TAVENNER: Did he visit you at any time after 1936?

MR. ODETS: Yes, a number of times.

MR. TAVENNER: Will you give us the occasion of those visits and the time, approximate time?

MR. ODETS: I sleep very late, sometimes until two or three o'clock in the afternoon, because I work very late. I work frequently until five or six in the morning. So, I might get up in the afternoon and he might telephone me and say, "What are you doing for dinner?" I would say, "Nothing. Come on over and we will go for a walk and go to such-and-such a restaurant." The visits would be of that sort.

MR. TAVENNER: When, over what period of time did that take place?

MR. ODETS: I would guess up until 1938, perhaps 1939, I don't know.

MR. TAVENNER: In the course of the hearing conducted by this Committee regarding [William Walter] Remington, there was testimony by Mr. [Howard Allen] Bridgman that Ted Wellman was the organizer of the Communist Party for the State of Tennessee. That was at the time that Remington was employed at the Tennessee Valley Authority. And the period of time that Wellman was the state organizer of Tennessee was during this period that you say he visited you in New York, 1938 and 1939, and earlier. Do you know what Ted Wellman's business was in New York on those occasions when he visited you?

MR. ODETS: I have no way of knowing. My best memory would be that around 1939, perhaps even 1940, that he lived in New York. My memory is not that good on dates.

MR. TAVENNER: Mr. Remington testified before this Committee that he knew Ted Wellman and that he met him in Tennessee in the spring of 1937 and again in June of that year. Now, did he visit you during the period of 1937?

MR. ODETS: I am sorry, I have no way of remembering that.

* * *

MR. TAVENNER: How long did you remain a member of the Party?

MR. ODETS: I would say between six and eight or nine months.

MR. TAVENNER: What were the circumstances under which you terminated your Party membership?

MR. ODETS: I was connected with the "cultural front," and it came to the point where I thought, If I can't respect these people on a so-called cultural basis—that is, as literary or theater critics, I don't know what I am doing here. I remember telling you that, when my plays came out, they received fantastically bad notices, although a play like *Waiting for Lefty* was widely used, not only by the Communists but by all liberal organizations and trade-union movements. I not only disagreed with their critical statements of my work, but I disagreed with their critical estimates of anybody's work, writers that I didn't know, like Steinbeck and Hemingway. I had a great number of fights about that. And I simply thought, This is not for me, there is no reason for me to be mixed up in there. I am a playwright. I have established myself as a playwright. I have a great deal of work to do. I have enough to say out of my own mind and heart, and I had better leave. This would be the general attitude under which I left.

MR. TAVENNER: Can you be specific as to the month of the year in which you left the Party?

Mr. Odets: I am sorry, I can't. Well, I would guess it was somewhere in the latter half of 1935.

Mr. Tavenner: During the time of your affiliation with the Communist Party, did you engage in any special activity for the Party?

Mr. Odets: None that I remember, no.

Mr. Tavenner: Do you recall having been made chairman of the American Commission to Investigate Labor and Social Conditions in Cuba?

Mr. Cdets: Yes, sir, I distinctly remember that.

Mr. Tavenner: Well, did you make a trip to Cuba as a member of that commission?

Mr. Odets: Yes, that was in June of 1935.

Mr. Tavenner: According to the information in the files of the Committee, this commission was composed of yourself as chairman, representing the League of American Writers. That is correct, is it not?

Mr. Odets: I did not have that memory of it until you mentioned it the last time. It is correct, I know that now.

Mr. Tavenner: And the other members of the commission of which you were the chairman were Fred L. Gordo, secretary, representing the League of American Writers; also, Manning Johnson* of the Food Workers Industrial Union; Herman Reissig, of the American League Against War and Fascism; Mary Gruber, also of the American League Against War and Fascism; Celeste Strack of the National Students League; Elsa Waldman of the National Students League; Paul Crosbie, of the American League of Ex-Servicemen; Lucille Perry, of the Provisional Committee for Cuba; Dora Zucker of International Ladies' Garment Workers Union; Conrad Komorowski, of the All American Anti-Imperialist League; Paul Irving of the Unemployed Teachers Association; José Santag, representing thirteen Latin-American organizations in New York; Mason Shaffer, of the International Workers' Order; and Frank Griffin of the International Labor Defense. Did you know any of these people before you made the trip to Cuba with them?

Mr. Odets: No, sir, not one of them.

Mr. Tavenner: Did you know any of them to be members of the Communist Party or did you discover their membership in the Communist Party while on your trip to Cuba or in a subsequent period?

Mr. Odets: I would say on the boat I discovered that some of them were members of the Communist Party. Some of the names, I just wrote

* Before the Subversive Activities Control Board, Manning Johnson answered the following question in the affirmative: "In other words you will tell a lie under oath in a court of law rather than run counter to your instructions from the FBI. Is that right?" For further details on Mr. Johnson see the Paul Robeson testimony below and all the literature on the informers of this period down through Melvin Rader's *False Witness*: Seattle, 1969, especially p. 192. —E.B.

them down, and you did mention them the last time. I actually, right now, do not remember but about half of these people.

MR. TAVENNER: Can you tell us which of them were members of the Communist Party?

MR. ODETS Well, I am going to guess that Komorowski was. I am going to guess that Manning Johnson was. I am going to guess that Celeste Strack was. And that is where I shall have to stop.

MR. TAVENNER: How was this commission chosen?

MR. WOOD: Mr. Counsel, I do not think we should leave the record in that condition, unless the witness has some knowledge about it. The fact that he said he would guess at it, the record ought to be clarified on the three names that were mentioned. See if you can clarify that. If not, there is the mere fact that he is guessing.

MR. KEARNEY: Do you know, as a matter of fact, that any of the three names that you mentioned were members of the Communist Party and, if so, you can name them.

MR. ODETS: I should think that Komorowski was a member of the Communist Party, definitely.

MR. KEARNEY: When you say you "should think" that Komorowski was a member of the Communist Party, upon what do you base that assumption?

MR. ODETS: I was only nominally the chairman of this committee. When I got on the boat and the committee started for Cuba, I discovered—should I say, to my disgust—that this man actually was the expert and I was the idealist, so to speak. I was the idealist who had some kind of publicity value and he was the expert on Latin-American affairs. He spoke with such authority and such knowledge that I simply supposed, if there were other Communist Party delegates on this commission, that he was the top one.

MR. KEARNEY: Did he ever tell you that he was a member of the Communist Party?

MR. ODETS: No, they never do.

MR. KEARNEY: What else transpired on the voyage from New York to Cuba that would lead you to believe that this individual was a member of the Communist Party? Did you discuss with him Communist Party affairs?

MR. ODETS: No, but there were tactical discussions, what do you do when you get there, what happens, what kind of statements shall one give the press. And since this man led the discussion, since this man planned the tactics, I would say that he was a Communist Party member and was really the head of the delegation.

MR. KEARNEY: What do you mean by planning tactics? Do you mean Communist Party tactics?

MR. ODETS: No, I mean in relation to this particular junket. I was, for instance, astonished to learn on the boat that, when we got to Cuba, we were going to be arrested. So there would be a meeting on what do we do when we get arrested. And this was the man who seemed to know what we do.

MR. KEARNEY: Did they tell you what you were to be arrested for?

MR. ODETS: Well, the grounds were that we were *persona non grata* in Cuba at that time.

MR. KEARNEY: Were you accused directly of being members of the Communist Party?

MR. ODETS: The delegation was being accused of being a Communist delegation. Actually, there were a lot of people on this delegation who, in my opinion, had nothing to do with Communists or Communism.

MR. KEARNEY: Were you arrested, or were the members of the delegation arrested, by the Cuban authorities?

MR. ODETS: We were promptly arrested and promptly lined up and marched to jail.

MR. KEARNEY: Were you asked whether you were members of the Communist Party or not by the police of Cuba?

MR. ODETS: No, sir, we were not asked anything. We were just arrested.

MR. KEARNEY: Arrested and put in jail. Were there any charges placed against you?

MR. ODETS: No. We were held incommunicado, except for a phone call or two, for about twenty-four hours. And I asked with a great deal of honest indignation why we were arrested.

MR. KEARNEY: Was this the time that you yourself were a member of the Communist Party?

MR. ODETS: I might have been. Yes, I was.

MR. KEARNEY: That was the time that you asked with honest indignation what it was all about?

MR. ODETS: I believe the indignation was honest, sir. I went there as a citizen of the United States. I didn't go there as a Communist Party member.

MR. KEARNEY: I inferred from your answers that the group was arrested because they were members of the Communist Party.

MR. ODETS: We weren't told why we were arrested. As a matter of fact, after reading the newspaper when I got back to New York City—because I couldn't read the Spanish newspapers—I learned that that is why we had been arrested. I, of course, suspected—I am not going to be naïve—I suspected that that is why we were arrested.

MR. KEARNEY: Did you see the American consul or talk with him?

MR. ODETS: I saw him one time, and he said very coyly, "You know, you know." A very coy gentleman.

MR. KEARNEY: And you were held there for twenty-four hours?

MR. ODETS: Twenty-four or thirty-six, something like that.

MR. KEARNEY: What happened after that?

Mr. Odets: Then we were very carefully marched back to another boat going back to New York.

Mr. Tavenner: You later found out that the person originally selected to act as chairman of this commission was Mother Bloor, did you not?

Mr. Odets: That is correct.

Mr. Tavenner: And why was it that Mother Bloor did not go through with the proposed assignment?

Mr. Odets: I went back to New York with a great deal of indignation, and later spoke to someone in New York, and was rather aroused by this idea that we had been manhandled, because we were. I was indignant because no one semed to make a fight about that. During this time I also said it was very dangerous, which it was, because there were dozens of secret police there with machine guns, some of them dressed as dock workers in overalls. I said it was a very dangerous matter and they said, "Yes, it was so dangerous that we had originally intended to send Mother Bloor down as head of the delegation, but it was so dangerous we didn't send her." She was an old lady.

Mr. Kearney: They sent you down as chairman instead of Mother Bloor?

Mr. Odets: So I said he might have at least told me this, and given me the chance to decide whether I wanted to face machine guns.

Mr. Tavenner: Well, actually, this was nothing more than a Communist Party idea to send this commission to Cuba for its own propaganda purposes?

Mr. Odets: Well, today, with a little more sophistication, I would say so.

Mr. Tavenner: Well, Manning Johnson, to whom you referred as a person that you guessed was a member of the Communist Party, testified before this Committee and admitted his former Communist Party membership, and in the course of his testimony he stated:

> I was secretary of the American Commission to Cuba and I was sent to Cuba to help the revolutionary forces there. I might say from the point of view of background that Cuba at that time was in a state of revolution. They had overthrown the government of Machado and the Mendieta-Batista revolutionary junta had come into power. We were assigned to tour the islands and assist the Communist forces to overthrow this Mendieta-Batista junta and put in power Grau San Martin and his group. They considered the Grau San Martin government would be a government that would permit Communists to operate openly. That is all I can recall at the present time. But I do know we were thrown in jail down there and I never will forget the experience.

Mr. Velde: Referring to your guess that Celeste Strack, I believe it was, was a member of the Communist Party, on what do you base it?

Mr. Odets: As a matter of fact, quick, smart girl. Knew how to move tactically.

MR. VELDE: Are all smart, quick people Communist Party members?

MR. ODETS: Well, there is a certain kind of professionalism. My guess about her comes from simply her tactical smartness.

MR. VELDE: And you had a conversation or several conversations with her, I suppose, on the trip?

MR. ODETS: Yes.

MR. VELDE: Did she ever mention that she was a member?

MR. ODETS: They do not.

MR. TAVENNER: Mr. Odets, will you tell the Committee just how this commission was created, and the circumstances under which you were designated as chairman?

MR. ODETS: I listened very carefully to what you read there, the statement of Manning Johnson. He is talking awfully big. He is talking awfully big, in a sense, that eight or ten, or whatever the number is, left and liberal people from New York City could go down to Cuba and change the course of this horrible Cuban revolution. If we were going to do what Mr. Johnson said, we certainly should not have announced in a public press that we were all getting on a boat and going down there to make a fuss. The point of the mission could not have been what he said. If you would contact anybody in Cuba, you would go down there silently and slip in.

MR. VELDE: What was *your* purpose in going to Cuba on this mission?

MR. ODETS: The purpose that attracted me was that there were oppressive measures taken against thousands of intellectuals and college students. They were thrown into jail, under the previous Machado regime, which was a horrible regime. I was glad to go down. If nothing else did happen, we would dramatize what the issues were down there. Of course, the stories that were coming out were very garbled. No one knew what was happening. I frankly think that, later, the American Embassy straightened out the whole thing and was a salutary and moderating influence.

MR. WOOD: What did you propose to do about it when you went down there?

MR. ODETS: I would guess, sir, that our arrival would encourage and hearten certain sections of the Cuban people, in the sense of saying, "You see, here are people from the United States who are interested in you and your problems and your employment."

MR. WOOD: Did you have a plan as to the course of conduct when you got there?

MR. ODETS: Well, the plan was that we were going to get arrested, which I did not know about. I was politically extremely naïve, and I remember distinctly the night before the boat docked, which was a festive occasion on an excursion boat, we were called together and told, I believe by Komorowski, that this is what was going to happen.

MR. TAVENNER: You found that you were not in command of your own commission but that Komorowski was?

MR. ODETS: Yes, sir.

MR. TAVENNER: And it was known that you were to be arrested, before you reached Cuba?

MR. ODETS: Evidently a lot of these people had far more background than I did in political scuffling, and they knew that that was going to happen. I didn't.

MR. TAVENNER: Then if it was planned that your group should be arrested, this was nothing more than a propaganda stunt?

MR. ODETS: It finally turned out that way.

MR. KEARNEY: In the parlance of everyday language, you were known as the fall guy, is that it?

MR. ODETS: A little bit.

MR. VELDE: Do you know whether Komorowski had definite knowledge that you were going to be arrested?

MR. ODETS: He had that much grace to say, the night before the boat lands, to be prepared for this.

MR. TAVENNER: Now, you have spoken of being rather naïve in political matters yourself, and others such as Komorowski being experienced. You are referring there to experience in Communist Party tactics, aren't you? You are not speaking of experience in the broad field of politics?

MR. ODETS: I am actually speaking of both. There are Communist Party tactics which are exclusively their own, and there are Communist Party tactics which are shared typically by many politicians.

* * *

MR. WOOD: Who paid your expenses?

MR. ODETS: I paid my own expenses.

MR. WOOD: Did you get it back?

MR. ODETS: No. On this idealistic swing I wouldn't think of taking any expenses, I would pay my own.

MR. WOOD: You don't recall now who procured you to go?

MR. ODETS: No. I know I was approached by someone and asked about it. I was anxious to get out of the country, I was anxious to take a trip. It was a beautiful trip on the water. My mother had just died three or four weeks before and I went.

MR. FRAZIER: Who were you supposed to contact when you reached Cuba?

MR. ODETS: We had some letters to various college professors and students. There was a packet of letters, and when the police boarded the ship these letters were scuttled, they were torn up and thrown overboard.

MR. FRAZIER: Who were these letters from?

MR. ODETS: They would be from people in the United States, I don't know.

MR. FRAZIER: Who gave you the letters?

MR. ODETS: I didn't have them, Komorowski had them. But they were passed like a hot plate from one to the other. The police were in earnest boarding that ship with machine guns, and it got to be like a scene from a Charlie Chaplin movie. They were torn up and thrown overboard. I just remembered that for the first time!

MR. FRAZIER: You didn't know who you were going down there to see?

MR. ODETS: No, I didn't know.

MR. FRAZIER: Yet you were chairman of the committee?

MR. ODETS: I was the nominal chairman. I wouldn't let that happen today.

MR. TAVENNER: Did you write any articles for publication about the trip to Cuba?

MR. ODETS: Yes, I wrote an article for the New York *Evening Post*. I was an accredited correspondent for the *Evening Post* on that trip.

MR. TAVENNER: Do you recall any other articles written by you?

MR. ODETS: It is possible there was a pamphlet written by two or three persons, of which I was one.

MR. TAVENNER: Who were the other persons who assisted in the writing?

MR. ODETS: I am going to guess a very interesting man named Carleton Beals. He was not a Communist, but he was a fighting liberal and a very interesting man.

MR. TAVENNER: I hand you a pamphlet entitled "Rifle Rule in Cuba," by Carleton Beals and Clifford Odets.

MR. ODETS: That is more than I had in my files.

MR. TAVENNER: At the end of the pamphlet is a report entitled "Report of the American Commission to Investigate Labor and Social Conditions in Cuba." At the end of which appears the name "American Commission to Investigate Labor and Social Conditions in Cuba, Clifford Odets, chairman, Manning Johnson, secretary," and giving the names of the other members of it. On the last page is this statement:

> The provisional committee for Cuba was organized precisely for the task of unifying the efforts of the American people for assistance in the struggle of the Cuban people for freedom. It is especially vital that the American people help, for the way to freedom is barred primarily by American imperialist domination of Cuba.

Did you write that?

MR. ODETS: No.

* * *

MR. TAVENNER: You recognize fully at this time, do you not, that this was all a part of the Communist Party propaganda, that it was embarking upon at that time?

MR. ODETS: Except that I still don't know this was exclusively a Communist affair. I am almost certain that Carleton Beals is not and was not a Communist.

MR. TAVENNER: But the Communist Party is well known for the manner in which it uses other people.

MR. WOOD: Was Carleton Beals on the mission with you?

MR. ODETS: No, sir, he was not.

MR. WOOD: Mr. Odets, who got you out of jail? Did they open the doors and turn you out?

MR. ODETS: No, they carefully waited until another ship was ready and carefully, under guard, marched us on the ship, and said, "Don't come back again." I said, "We will come back, and I will bring people you can't touch, I will bring famous liberals in New York." And that is what I wanted to do. But that never happened.

MR. WOOD: Was there ever any formal charge made against you while you were in jail?

MR. ODETS: None.

MR. TAVENNER: Do you recall having written any other articles relating to a commission to Cuba?

MR. ODETS: I may have, but I don't remember them.

MR. TAVENNER: I show you a photostatic copy of an issue of *New Masses* for July 16, 1935, where there appears an article entitled "What Happened to Us in Cuba," by Clifford Odets. Will you examine it, please, and state whether or not you wrote it?

MR. ODETS: This one I know I wrote: when I read it, I recognize my style.

MR. TAVENNER: What were the circumstances under which you wrote that article for *New Masses*?

MR. ODETS: I must have been asked to.

MR. TAVENNER: Who was the person that asked you to write that article for *New Masses*?

MR. ODETS: I don't know, but it might have been Joe North.

MR. TAVENNER: In the article you summed up your adventure in Cuba in part as follows:

> This impartial commission of investigation has shown its uncertainty of purpose by being honored by deportation by the present Cuban military dictatorship in collusion with the American Embassy officials. Their collusion is clearly marked out by their negative response to our call for help.

I am interested in the term used in referring to your commission as an "impartial" commission of investigation. Are you now of the opinion that this commission, which was in fact headed by Komorowski, though you were used as a cover for it, was actually an impartial commission?

MR. ODETS: Although it had all sorts of left and liberal elements in it, the commission was definitely Communist Party slanted.

MR. TAVENNER: Well, it was Communist Party controlled under the *de facto* leadership of Komorowski, wasn't it?

MR. ODETS: They don't quite do it that way, sir. There is always a certain, what I call a democratic, procedure. Things are put to a vote. The only thing is, it doesn't help to put things to a vote, they have the know-how, and you don't have the know-how.

MR. KEARNEY: Mr. Odets, I just hastily scanned your article in the pamphlet entitled "Rifle Rule in Cuba," by Carleton Beals and Clifford Odets, your article headed "Machine-Gun Reception." I can see the indignant manner in which you write concerning your treatment by the Cuban police, but I fail to see any indignant protest of yours over the manner in which the Communist Party used you.

MR. ODETS: I simply didn't know about this all until later.

MR. KEARNEY: After you found out about it, did you make an effort to change your statement?

MR. ODETS: No, I made no effort to change my statement. It would have been much too late.

MR. TAVENNER: When you discovered the real facts relating to the mission to Cuba you withdrew from the Communist Party?

MR. ODETS: A short time after.

MR. TAVENNER: Well, did this experience have any motivating effect upon your decision to either stay in or get out of the Communist Party?

MR. ODETS: I would say it had considerable effect on my decision. I resented the professionalism, the cut-and-dried way in which this was done. I said, This is not for me, I am not a professional businessman, my business is writing plays and I better get out of this, I don't want to be used. The expedition was largely responsible for me leaving the Communist Party.

* * *

MR. TAVENNER: Mr. Odets, in your earlier testimony before the Committee, you referred to the manner in which your plays had been received by the Communist Party. I recall that you stated that your play *Waiting for Lefty* was referred to as a Trotskyite production, and that that was one of the reasons that impelled you to fall out with the Communist Party. In our examination of the Communist press, we have been unable to find any statement that your play *Waiting for Lefty* was ever referred to as a Trotskyite play. You stated that you thought you had a clipping that would so indicate.

MR. ODETS: Yes, Mr. Tavenner. When I left Washington the last time I was here I went through my press-clipping books and found for every play that I produced very bad critical reception from the Left. So, as of two or three nights ago, I copied some of these out in my own handwriting, on a pad, and brought them along. I found that the phrase "Trotskyite tendencies" had been marked down as left tendencies: I had better be careful of left tendencies. Which in those days meant that one had better be careful not to be a Trotskyite.

MR. TAVENNER: In other words, it was your interpretation that the criticism meant Trotskyite, although there was no actual reference to Trotskyite?

MR. ODETS: There was a rather amusing detail. One of the papers was Yiddish, from a paper called the daily *Freiheit,* which was or is—I don't know whether the paper is still in existence—which is the Yiddish *Daily Worker*. My memory would be in that, in the translation of that, the actual phrase "Trotskyite" was used.

MR. TAVENNER: You spoke of the severity of the criticisms. The criticisms that you referred to were criticisms of a technical character regarding your plays, were they not, as distinguished from the criticism of your ability and your skill in portraying the characters?

MR. ODETS: I would like to put a few of them in the record by reading them, and then let you make your own judgment of those. I think that they are generally very bad notices.

MR. TAVENNER: You say "generally" bad. Was there a period of time in which the Communist press seemed to change its attitude regarding your plays?

MR. ODETS: Well, I can only say that, from the very first play, *Waiting for Lefty,* on until my plays of a year ago, the criticisms were sometimes good and sometimes bad, shockingly bad. I dislike being called a hack writer, but [for] my last play I was called a hack writer in the *Daily Worker*. I don't know how you would categorize this sort of criticism, but I call it very severe and very shocking.

MR. TAVENNER: What was the purpose of the criticism, do you know?

MR. ODETS: The purpose, I would think, would be to say, "This man has gone off the track, and while he has talent we mourn his loss," so to speak, "We wish we could get him back."

MR. TAVENNER: Did it also take on the character of a challenge to you to produce more plays depicting the strike as in your play *Waiting for Lefty*.

MR. ODETS: That was in the beginning. It was suggested that I produce or write another strike play.

MR. TAVENNER: Who suggested that?

MR. ODETS: Well, the suggestion was general among Communist friends.

MR. TAVENNER: Did that go beyond the cell of the Communist Party of which you were a member?

MR. ODETS: I might meet people in the theater and they would say, "When are you going to write another play like *Waiting for Lefty*? We need more strike plays." However, in the reviews, what they were griping about might become more evident if I were permitted to read you a few of them.

MR. TAVENNER: Before coming to that, did you gain the impression that the type of criticism which your plays received constituted an effort on the part of the Communist Party to direct you in your course of writing?

MR. ODETS: I would say that some of the criticisms were open to that interpretation, but most of them took me to task for what they called my defections. I would be expressed that way: "It is a pity that this man is wasting his time about this trifling subject matter when he could be writing, let us say, about the American workers, when he could be writing about the war in Spain. Why is he writing about a dentist in an office?"

MR. TAVENNER: When you speak of a dentist in an office, you are speaking of *A Rocket to the Moon*. That was in 1939. Now, coming back to the time when you were in the Party—because you were in the Party when you wrote *Waiting for Lefty,* were you not?

MR. ODETS: Yes, sir, I was.

MR. TAVENNER: Were you in the Party at the time you wrote the earlier production, *Awake and Sing*?

MR. ODETS: No, I was not, even though it was produced at the time I was in the Party. It was written maybe a year and a half before.

MR. TAVENNER: Which was produced first?

MR. ODETS: *Awake and Sing* was written and no one wanted to do it. Then I wrote *Waiting for Lefty,* which was very successful. And then other people wanted to do *Awake and Sing*. So *Awake and Sing* was produced second.

MR. TAVENNER: During the period of your membership did you meet and associate with functionaries of the Communist Party who were interested particularly in cultural activities?

MR. ODETS: Well, the few people that I did meet were people on the cultural front, like V. J. Jerome. I might meet occasionally a drama critic of the *Daily Worker*.

MR. TAVENNER: Who was that?

MR. ODETS: A man named Nathaniel Buchwald. He wrote, I must say, really scurrilous reviews of my plays. I don't know why.

MR. TAVENNER: Any others?

MR. ODETS: I undoubtedly met at that time an editor or two of the *New Masses,* Joe North.

MR. TAVENNER: Were you acquainted with Michael Blankfort?

MR. ODETS: I knew him vaguely. But I didn't like him. That is because he was a budding playwright, too, I think. He wrote scurrilously of my plays.

MR. TAVENNER: Well, he placed you highly too, didn't he?

MR. ODETS: Well, when he had to he did, but when he could get away from it, he didn't. As I said before, there was not always unanimity of opinion, so that a play of mine might be reviewed very badly, and then someone else on the Left would say, "Just a minute, this play is much better than you put in *New Masses*, so you must let me write a second article."

MR. TAVENNER: Can you assign any reason for that change of attitude?

MR. ODETS: They would have liked to have had me write what they would call "progressive plays." They would like me to write plays on themes they would think burning issues of the day. I am sure, for instance, the Communist Party thought that the war in Spain was a burning issue of the day. I think a great number of liberals did, too.

MR. TAVENNER: And they attempted to direct you in that course of writing?

MR. ODETS: In the sense, sir, of saying, "This man is wasting his time writing about ordinary, middle-class life when he could be writing a glorious play about the war in Spain."

MR. TAVENNER: Well, did you follow the suggestion?

MR. ODETS: I am afraid I never did.

MR. TAVENNER: Why?

MR. ODETS: I didn't respect any person or any party or any group of people who would say to a young creative writer, "Go outside of your experience and write a play." I knew that, as fumbling as my beginnings were, I could only write out of my own experience. I couldn't be given a theme and handle it. It was not my business. It meant to me, if I may say it this way, a loss of integrity. And so I persisted in going along on my own line and writing what did come out of my true center. And whenever this happened, I got this violent opposition in the press, and I became further disgusted and estranged.

MR. TAVENNER: Then that was an effort on the part of the Communist Party to dictate to you what you should write?

MR. ODETS: I would say so.

MR. TAVENNER: And you rebelled against that type of Communist Party discipline?

MR. ODETS: By then I had, so to speak, loosened these ties, and I had no connection with them. So one read what they said as one read other criticisms. I was much more apt to be interested in what a critic like Stark Young would say in the *New Republic* or Brooks Atkinson in the *New York Times*.

MR. TAVENNER: If I understand you correctly, the Communist Party had its own methods of thought control in dealing with the writers who were members of the Communist Party.

MR. ODETS: They tried that, but they drove all of the good writers away. So far as I know offhand, they don't have a first-grade writer, and they haven't for years, because of these tactics.

MR. TAVENNER: Now let us return to the criticisms of your plays. Let us have the instances in which there was a criticism of a severe type.

MR. ODETS: Here is one from the *Daily Worker* review of the *Waiting for Lefty* production in February of 1935, by Nathaniel Buchwald:

> The very gush of his dramatic say [?] has resulted in a woeful looseness of play structure and its strident overtones all but vitiate his message . . . exhortations which now and then deteriorate into mere sloganism or rhetoric . . . though each episode is eloquent in itself, all of them put together fail to make a play.

MR. TAVENNER: Well, now, the same reviewer, in the issue of January 12, 1935, which is earlier than the one you referred to, had this to say:

> Propelled by his burning revolutionary fervor, and by an essentially clear guiding idea, this young playwright swept the audience off its feet by the sheer power and sincerity of dramatic utterance which was amplified and given vibrant resonance by the magnificent performance of the Group Theater players.

In the issue of January 5, 1935, Nathaniel Buchwald does criticize certain technical matters, but he also concedes that Odets will learn and that he is splendidly equipped for a young revolutionary dramatist, and that the play is "a high watermark of revolutionary drama and probably the most effective agitprop play written in this country thus far." Now, that is a very high commendation, is it not?

MR. ODETS: I think so, yes, sir.

MR. TAVENNER: Particularly from the Communist standpoint. Now, what is meant by "agitprop play," when he says it is a "most effective agitprop play"?

MR. ODETS: "Agitprop" is short for the phrase "agitational propaganda."

(*Representative John S. Wood left the room at this point.*)

MR. TAVENNER: Though he criticized certain technical aspects of your plays, would you not say that at that time the Communist Party was very enthusiastic about *Waiting for Lefty*?

MR. ODETS: Yes, I remember telling you distinctly in our last meeting that they were delighted with the play.

MR. TAVENNER: I find the *New Masses* review in its issue of January 29, 1935. [Stanley] Burnshaw had this to say: "On January 5, when the curtain ran down on the first performance of Clifford Odets' *Waiting for Lefty* the audience cheered, whistled, and screamed with applause." In the course of his review, he stated that "some persons referred to the play as a disjointed, structurally arbitrary piece of playwright." In fact, that is about what John Howard Lawson had said about it, is that correct?

MR. ODETS: I remember Jack Lawson. I don't remember what he said.

MR. TAVENNER: It says:

> Yet a second seeing by the *New Masses* reviewer provides sufficient perspective for discerning in the juxtaposition of scenes a clear logic, binding them

> into a solid dramatic role. The *New Masses* reviewer said there were some weak scenes in the play, but that the terrific emotional drive of the play as a unit is more than the toal effectiveness of the eight scenes.

So that was a commendation by the *New Masses*. Now, John Howard Lawson, according to our study, was concerned in his criticism with the technique, as he referred to it, but he does not question your talent, about which he says it is of "outstanding significance, his skill, vitality, and honesty rarely found in the current theater." Lawson states that while *Lefty* represents a tremendous advance over *Awake and Sing,* nevertheless there are structural flaws, which he referred to. And he predicts for you a great future. Well, that certainly is not a severe criticism of your work from the standpoint of the Communist Party. If, up to this point, there had been criticism, it has been with regard to what the reviewers referred to as structural flaws.

MR. ODETS: Well, may I say a few words about that?

MR. TAVENNER: Yes.

MR. ODETS: A Marxist believes that if you would straighten out your ideology in terms of Marxist orientation, that when you do that, you will no longer have structural flaws. So to say that something has structural flaws means that this young writer must attend more Marxian ideology and Marxian study. I happen to know, from reading a book or two, that John Howard Lawson very thoroughly believes that. I do not. I do not think that if you spoil your inner life by Marxian ideology you will then have no structural difficulties in writing a play. The essence of John Howard Lawson's meaning would be that: in fact, he has written two whole books about it. I have respect in many areas for Jack Lawson. As, for instance, a once very, very gifted playwright. But the part that I am discussing is, I think, arrant nonsense. What was happening here was that they had a hot potato in their hands, and one fellow would say, "This has great value," another fellow would say, "No, he is not very good." They would keep contradicting each other, and I suppose somewhere they made a rule and said, "Now, look, let's don't drive these people away. Now let's send a more important man to review the play." So frequently the same play would be reviewed two or three times, and—I am guessing—on the basis of trying to tie the writer closer. "Don't chase him away, don't say harsh things. Ameliorate these statements by a second review."

MR. TAVENNER: Now, I think I should read part of the review made by Michael Blankfort, which appeared in *New Masses* on March 5, 1935, when he reviewed *Awake and Sing*. Now, he took the position that *Awake and Sing* was not as great a work as *Waiting for Lefty*. But he said this: "*Awake and Sing* is worth seeing because Odets is one of the new revolutionary voices, because he has something invigorating to say, because he says it in a fresh way." He also criticizes one of the play's characters for realizing his mission out of mysticism, rather than out of an understanding of social forces, as it should be in a revolutionary play. Blankfort concedes that Mr. Odets was growing in a revolutionary understanding of those matters. Now, what was your interpretation of that criticism?

MR. ODETS: You are taking out of his review of March 5, 1935, certain praise. Well, what I have taken out is certain *dis*praise:

> The types . . . are no more than characters in a play, well-documented puppets . . . nothing advances through them and they do not grow. . . . Reminds me of etchings you can catch with the first superficial glance. . . . If the characters in *Awake and Sing* aren't burlesqued, the credit must go to the director. . . . Too often for the health of a play, a situation is created out of nothing just to get across a wisecrack or a laugh. . . .*

This was the most serious play I had written. This had been received by the leading newspapers of New York as a minor masterpiece. Here were my friends on the Left publishing these sort of things.

MR. TAVENNER: And he followed it by stating that if the audience was staying for a laugh it would miss the real revolutionary message in the play, didn't he?

MR. ODETS: Something like that.

MR. TAVENNER: So your position is that these various items of criticism and praise were designed to pressure you, as a member of the Party, into writing more in line with the Party dictates and the Party policy?

MR. ODETS: Yes, they would want me to write more from their world point of view.

MR. TAVENNER: Well, didn't you write later on Communist themes?

MR. ODETS: I have always tried to write, not out of any themes to one side of myself, but to themes that were central and germane to my own life. I do remember stating at our last meeting that if I were moved by certain situations of poverty, this would be because my mother worked in a stocking factory in Philadelphia at the age of eleven and died a broken woman—and an old woman—at the age of forty-eight. When I wrote, sir, it was out of central, personal things. I did not learn my hatred of poverty, sir, out of Communism.

MR. TAVENNER: Did you ever write a play which was based on your experience in the Communist Party?

MR. ODETS: No, I never did. I have never written a Communist play, because I want always to write plays for the largest American audiences that I can reach. I want to write American plays. I want to talk to average Americans. I don't want to talk to a special minority group. I believe that the Communists have a very special and narrow view of American life. There is another reason that I broke with them.

MR. TAVENNER: You spoke a moment ago of the Communist Party

* Some of this is paraphrase. Tavenner's summaries may be honest, but they are inexact. —E.B.

taking one view of your works on one occasion and then a different view later. I am referring particularly in that respect to your play *Paradise Lost.* You find in the *Daily Worker* of December 13, 1935, that Michael Blankfort praised *Paradise Lost* as being a better play than *Awake and Sing* in many respects. And Robert Forsythe, in *New Masses,* issue of December 24, 1935, praised *Paradise Lost* as much better than both *Awake and Sing* and *Waiting for Lefty*. Then we find the *Daily Worker* of February 7, 1936, just several months later, the reviewer, Jay Gerlando, took the contrary position and criticized your play. And I think it is important to bring it to your attention here and ask for your comment. This reviewer took the position that the characters in *Paradise Lost* grow out of the theater more than out of real life, and he says, "And the Marxists have an advantage in making real characters because they understand the forces that shape human beings."

MR. ODETS: One reviewer would go to see a play. He might write a favorable review and then someone else in the Communist Party would say, "That isn't true, that play is not so good. This play demonstrates dangerous tendencies and we must send somebody to review the play and point out the dangerous tendencies to our readers." Or it might go the other way around. The first review was bad and they said, "Wait a minute. Don't drive this young playwright away. Let us send a second reviewer." You mentioned *Paradise Lost,* you read a favorable review or two, and then, before, you read a favorable review of Burnshaw correcting some other reviewer of *Awake and Sing*. I happen to have here a *New Masses* review by Burnshaw of *Paradise Lost* which is quite bad.

MR. TAVENNER: Now, in addition to that criticism on February 7, we find that four days later in *New Masses* the reviewer Stanley Burnshaw—which is probably the thing that you are referring to—in commenting on *Paradise Lost,* said, "It is the lack of Marxism which has deprived the play of its fundamental social truth." And then he also stated, "It is regrettable to see a left writer proceeding on an utterly false premise, portray as doomed objects of decay that very middle class which will be enlisted as a vigorous ally in the growing people's front against Fascism and war." Now, how do you explain the difference in the reviews from December of 1935, from both the *Daily Worker* and the *New Masses,* and the reviewers from both *Daily Worker* and the *New Masses* in February of 1936?

MR. ODETS: When a playwright presents a new work, there would be a review and then there would seem to be conferences about the review and then they would send out another reviewer to make a re-evaluation if they thought that was necessary. This, of course, was with the obvious intention of binding the writer to the Communist Party and the Marxist world point of view. So here again is Burnshaw recommending that if I were a better Marxist I would be a better playwright and a better constructor of plays. There is also a horrifying review by James Farrell, in a Communist publication, of *Paradise Lost*. He says it is a burlesque of my previous work. "The lines are gags. I don't understand how he could have written a play so consistently, so ferociously bad. It is mistitled. It should be known as *Lay Down and Die*." This is from *Partisan Review and Anvil,* which was another magazine like the *New Masses* in those days.

MR. TAVENNER: What was the date?

MR. ODETS: The date was February 1936.

MR. TAVENNER: The Communist Party seemed to have changed its approach to your work between December 1935 and February 1936.

MR. ODETS: I vaguely remember Mike Gold answering James Farrell and saying he was much too harsh, that it was a beautiful play. Now we have five reviews of the play. It was a very hectic and tumultuous time. However, I believe that the intention is clear through all of these. "Let us not chase this young writer away. If he is not Marxist enough, let us try to teach him." Some of these people are rascals, but on the other hand some of them were people of high seriousness and integrity in their feelings.

MR. TAVENNER: Were you acquainted with Herbert Kline?

MR. ODETS: Yes. I met him as an editor of a magazine called *New Theater*.

MR. TAVENNER: He was a witness before the Committee in separate [?] hearings of last year, but refused to testify. Did you know him to be a member of the Communist Party?

MR. ODETS: No, I did not.

MR. TAVENNER: The *New Theater* magazine, of which you say he was the editor, was the official publication of the New Theater League, was it not?

MR. ODETS: I don't know about that. I am willing to say it is, if you have notes about it.

MR. TAVENNER: Well, I show you the issue of February 1935. Will you examine it, please, and state what appears from pages 13 to 20?

MR. ODETS: It does say that it is an organ of the New Theater League, National Film and Photo Workers League, and this edition prints *Waiting for Lefty* in its entirety.

MR. TAVENNER: From pages 13 to 20. This play was based on a taxicab strike in New York City in February 1934, was it not?

MR. ODETS: That is what they say. But it is just something I kind of made up.

MR. TAVENNER: Wasn't it based on that strike?

MR. ODETS: I didn't know anything about a taxicab strike. I had a few boyhood friends who were cab drivers. I knew their lingo. I have never been near a strike in my life.

MR. TAVENNER: There was a taxicab strike in February 1934 which you were familiar with, wasn't there?

MR. ODETS: No. I learned later there was such a strike.

MR. TAVENNER: Were the pictures appearing in that article on pages 14, 17, 18, and 20 from the first production of the play?

MR. ODETS: Yes, sir, they were.

MR. TAVENNER: Did John Garfield appear in the play?

MR. ODETS: Yes, sir, he did.

MR. TAVENNER: Were you acquainted with John Garfield at that time?

MR. ODETS: Oh, yes.

MR. TAVENNER: Did you ever know John Garfield to be a member of the Communist Party?

MR. ODETS: No, sir.

MR. TAVENNER: I believe you received an award from the New Theater League for the production of *Waiting for Lefty*, did you not?

MR. ODETS: They came to me and said, "We have had a one-act play contest and no good material has shown up. Do you mind if we give you the prize?" I said, "No, I don't mind."

MR. TAVENNER: In the February 2, 1939, issue of the *Daily Worker,* it is stated: "In 1935 the New Theater League first attracted wide attention when *Waiting for Lefty* by Clifford Odets, who had been known as a playwright before, was chosen as the best among hundreds of scripts submitted."

MR. ODETS: That made a good story.

MR. TAVENNER: Returning to the magazine *New Theater,* according to a note by the author appearing at the end of the script of *Waiting for Lefty,* no production of the play could be presented without your permission. Is that correct?

MR. ODETS: I didn't know about copyrights when the play was written. But I would doubt that in my entire life I earned one thousand dollars out of that play. People just did it. It was kind of public property. As a matter of fact, one of the few times permission was asked for that play was from the United States Army. They did it in Japan just after the war.

MR. TAVENNER: According to the *Daily Worker* of January 23, 1948, *Waiting for Lefty* was produced under the auspices of the Communist Party of New Jersey, at a mass demonstration on January 25, 1948. Did you grant permission to the Communist Party of New Jersey to produce your play?

MR. ODETS: I haven't granted permission for that play, to my knowledge, I would guess, for eight or ten years. The play is now handled by my agent, Brandt and Brandt, in New York City, and is rather infrequently done by colleges.

* * *

MR. TAVENNER: The Communist Party has made use of the play, regardless of the amount of criticism that it may have received by technical reviewing writers.

MR. ODETS: They have used the play a great deal. I would not like you to misconstrue anything I have said as saying that the Communist Party didn't think the play was not a very fine play, particularly to produce. It was at one time a kind of light machine gun that you wheeled in to use whenever there was any kind of strike trouble.

MR. TAVENNER: According to the March 16, 1937, issue of the *Daily Worker,* the Chicago Repertory Group produced *Waiting for Lefty* for the reason assigned that it hits the nail on the head so perfectly. It deals with the problem of taxicab drivers to form their own union and to strike for better living conditions, as stated. With the taxicab strike on Chicago's own doorstep, the Chicago Repertory Group, it was said, was able to respond perfectly at the psychological moment. So again, the play was used in special instances, apparently, by the Communist Party. Do you know of any other instances?

MR. ODETS: I know that the play has been translated into almost every language in the world, and I know that that play must have played in over two hundred different American cities in its fifteen or seventeen years of existence.

MR. TAVENNER: This would all seem to confirm your statement that the criticism made of your play was done for the purpose of influencing you in your future writings.

MR. ODETS: That is about the only one of my plays that they have done that with.

MR. TAVENNER: Mr. Odets, there is considerable information in the files of the Committee that reflects your interest in, your support of, or your affiliation with a number of organizations of a Communistic nature, usually referred to as Communist-front organizations. Inasmuch as all of this so-called activity occurred after you say you left the Communist Party, the Committee would like to know how you were approached for support of these different groups, what induced you to lend your name, if you did do so, and any other explanation that you care to offer. * * * I show you a photostatic copy of an article that appeared in the January 18, 1935, issue of the *Daily Worker*. This article is a call for a Congress of American Revolutionary Writers, on May 1. I want to read several paragraphs from the article.

> The capitalist system crumbles so rapidly before our eyes that whereas ten years ago scarcely more than a handful of writers were sufficiently farsighted and courageous to take a stand for proletarian revolution, today hundreds of poets, novelists, dramatists, critics, short-story writers, and journalists recognize the necessity of personally helping to accelerate the destruction of capitalism and the establishment of a workers' government.
>
> We propose, therefore, that a Congress of American Revolutionary Writers be held in New York City on May 1, 1935, that to this congress shall be invited all writers who have achieved some standing in their respective fields,

> who have clearly indicated their sympathy to the revolutionary cause, who do not need to be convinced of the decay of capitalism, of the inevitability of the revolution.
>
> We believe such a congress should create the League of American Writers, affiliated with the International Union of Revolutionary Writers. The program of the League of American Writers would be evolved at the congress, basing itself on the following: Fight against imperialist war and fascism, defend the Soviet Union against capitalist aggression, for the development and strengthening of the revolutionary labor movement, and so forth.
>
> The call was signed by such well-known and outstanding Communists as Earl Browder, Theodore Dreiser, Michael Gold, Clarence Hathaway, Herb Kline, John Howard Lawson, Lewis Lozowick, Joseph North, M. J. Olgin, Isidor Schneider, Alexander Trachtenberg, Ella Winter, and Richard White. The congress was held in New York City on April 27, 1935, and the League of American Writers was formed.

Did you participate in this congress?

MR. ODETS: I have no memory of that, but I would have been glad to have been there in 1935.

MR. TAVENNER: In other words, the purpose met with your approval?

MR. ODETS: Well, what is there is very highfalutin, very high-flown. I think when I hear it, and follow it with my eye as you are reading, it is silly, foolish, but at that time one believed that perhaps all of our problems could be worked out by some kind of socialism.

MR. TAVENNER: I show you the official proceedings of that meeting as published by the International Publishers. Will you look at page 188 and state whether your name appears as one of those selected to the National Council of the League of American Writers?

MR. ODETS: Yes, I see my name there.

MR. TAVENNER: Were you at that time a member of the Communist Party?

MR. ODETS: I don't know. I should say so.

MR. TAVENNER: Will you turn now to the last page of the book. Do you not find that the official report closes with this language: "When the applause died down, James Farrell arose and suggested that the congress conclude its final session by singing the 'Internationale.' This was done." Do you recall that?

MR. ODETS: No, I don't remember being at such a meeting, but, in those days, these kind of things could happen very easily.

MR. TAVENNER: How long were you affiliated with the League of American Writers?

MR. ODETS: It might have been a year. I began to have quarrels with them in public on their platforms at their meetings. I attended a number of meetings of the League of American Writers.

MR. TAVENNER: What do you mean you had quarrels?

MR. ODETS: John Howard Lawson got up and made a critical evaluation of the Broadway Theater season, and I disagreed with him. I would ask for the floor and get up on the platform and have a fight with him about it. This kind of made me *persona non grata* and resulted, finally, in a real cooling off between myself and most of these people. Many of these people have become since violent anti-Communist.

* * *

MR. TAVENNER: I show you a circular reproduced and circulated by the Communist Party. It is a statement labeled "In Defense of the Bill of Rights." A most casual reading reveals it is a statement in defense of the Communist Party and known Communists. This statement was released on December 14, 1939. The name of Clifford Odets appears as one of the signers.

MR. ODETS: Again I regret to say that I have no memory of this.

MR. TAVENNER: That article shows it is directly a Communist Party matter, doesn't it?

MR. ODETS: Well, it is headlined "In Defense of the Bill of Rights," and I don't see that as strictly a Communist matter.

MR. TAVENNER: Then it follows with one paragraph regarding the Bill of Rights, and the rest of it is defense of the Communist Party.

MR. ODETS: My eye falls on a statement here that "we are not Communists and we are not concerned at this moment with the merits or demerits of the doctrines advocated by the Communists."

MR. VELDE: Mr. Odets, do you believe now that the Communist Party has been interested in preserving our Bill of Rights and the Constitution?

MR. ODETS: I would think that the Communist Party was interested in preserving its existence.

MR. VELDE: And what do you deem as the program of the Communist Party in this country?

MR. ODETS: My relationship with the Communist Party over the years was a very distant one. Anything I tell you would be my guess or my speculation.

MR. VELDE: You still have an opinion, don't you?

MR. ODETS: Well, my opinion is that the Communist Party is interested in preserving itself as a minority political party. I believe, sir, that that is their right under the United States Constitution. I do not think that their essential purpose is the preservation of the Constitution. I think they want to bring about some kind of social disorder. I find some of their practices reprehensible. I am against secrecy in any political party. I would not advocate the Communist Party for anyone to join because of their secrecy. One of the elements that made me leave the Communist Party was secrecy. I saw no reason to be conspiratorial in the United States. I see no reason now for any political party to be conspiratorial in the United States. I believe in free speech. I believe in open political practice. I advocate these things.

Frequently I have gotten in trouble because I have stood up for free speech at moments when it seemed to be even taking the Communist Party point of view. I have fought for civil rights and civil liberties, again when it seemed to be taking the Communist Party point of view. This is why I find myself on some of these documents, because, as I said a few weeks ago, the lines of liberalism and the lines of left thought frequently cross each other. However, if one winnows out and deals only with the Communist Party position in the United States, I am frankly against it.

MR. VELDE: Then, do you believe that the avowed purpose of the Communist Party in the United States is not to overthrow our form of government, our Constitution, by force and violence?

MR. ODETS: I don't think that is their purpose.

MR. VELDE: Even in view of the fact that it was proven to be true in the case of the trial of the eleven Communists?

MR. ODETS: Well, sir, if I may say so, you have a split of opinion about that, even in the Supreme Court of the United States. I frankly agree with the minority opinion of Justice Douglas and Justice Frankfurter.

* * *

MR. TAVENNER: Are you acquainted with the *Manual of Organization of the Communist Party* which was written by J. Peters?

MR. ODETS: I am sorry, sir, I never heard of that document.

MR. TAVENNER: Let me read you a paragraph from the book:

> As the leader and organizer of the proletariat, the Communist Party of the United States of America leads the working class in a fight for the revolutionary overthrow of capitalism, for the establishment of the dictatorship of the proletariat, for the establishment of a Socialistic Soviet republic in the United States, for the complete abolition of classes, for the establishment of Socialism, as the first stage of classless, Communist society.

So I again ask you: Do you maintain that Communism is just a political party, as distinguished from a conspiracy to overthrow the Government of the United States, directed from a foreign country?

MR. ODETS: If I may say so, Mr. Tavenner and Mr. Velde, you have me here in a rather singular position. You have me here defending Communism. I am not here for that purpose.

MR. TAVENNER: I only asked you the question to explain your very loose use of the term "political party."

MR. ODETS: I understand that the Communist Party is a legally recognized minority political party in the United States. Am I correct about that, sir?

MR. TAVENNER: No, this Committee has never considered it a political party. It considers that it is a conspiratorial group.

MR. ODETS: Well, then, I think that recommendation should be made, if I may be so bold as to say so, to have this party declared illegal, because at the moment my best knowledge is that this is a legal political party in the United States.

* * *

MR. VELDE: What was your recommendation with reference to outlawing the Communist Party?

MR. ODETS: My recommendation was that any party or any group of people that wanted to stand as a political party in the United States had to stand up and move in the open and had to be willing to be counted in public.

MR. VELDE: But by making that statement you don't mean to infer that the Communist Party should be such a recognized—

MR. ODETS: I think we need a liberal party in this country. I don't think the Communist Party is it, by the widest stretch of imagination. But when I talk this way, I am talking about the possibility of some kind of liberal-labor party that I would like to see come into existence. If I may say so, the foolish position of a man like myself is that he has no party to belong to. And I think that I share this foolish, empty position with thousands of sincere and earnest-thinking liberals in the United States. We have no party to join because we cannot give our allegiance to the Communist Party.

* * *

MR. TAVENNER: Were you acquainted with Hanns Eisler?

MR. ODETS: Yes, I knew him.

MR. TAVENNER: I show you the *Daily Worker* for September 26, 1947. On page 12 there is an article regarding Hanns Eisler, and lists a number of persons who expressed strong interest in the case. Your name appears on the list. What was your interest in Hanns Eisler's case?

MR. ODETS: I met Hanns Eisler first in New York City in 1939 or 1940, as a very gifted composer, and later had the pleasure of employing him to write music for a play of mine, *Night Music,* for which he wrote a very gifted score. We developed a friendship. Then, when I later went out to California and began to not only write but to direct movies, I was interested, naturally, in getting the best musical score that I could, and I asked the studio, RKO, to hire Hanns Eisler for a picture I directed called *None But the Lonely Heart,* and we remained friends. When he was in trouble, as a friend, I tried to help him. I knew him as a totally nonpolitical figure. I saw him a number of times in Hollywood. I knew he had indulged in no political activity of any sort, that he lived very quietly, that he was essentially an artist, and I saw him and recognized him as a friend.*

* Hanns Eisler has given his own account of his relationship with Odets in Hans Bunge, *Fragen Sie Mehr Ueber Brecht* (Munich, 1970), pp. 234–35. The following

MR. TAVENNER: Then it was purely on a personal basis that you were interested in that case?

MR. ODETS: Absolutely, sir.

* * *

MR. TAVENNER: According to the *Daily Worker* of June 22, 1950, page 10, the National Council of Arts, Sciences, and Professions conducted a town rally to free Hollywood writers convicted of contempt of Congress. You are listed as having wired the organization as follows:

> I believe that yours is truly the American way and salute you all in the name of your convictions and courage.

Do you remember sending that telegram?

MR. ODETS: My best guess would be that I did send this telegram.

MR. TAVENNER: Did you send the telegram because you believed that the Hollywood Ten were not in contempt of Congress?

MR. ODETS: I, by the way, did not agree with their stand. But I felt that it was very American to fight for what you conceived to be your constitutional rights, and I felt impelled to send this wire.

MR. TAVENNER: Then why did you send this telegram praising them so highly for the stand they were taking?

MR. ODETS: I thought they were making a good fight. And, by the way, I must tell you frankly that at that [time] I did not believe that a number of them were Communists. I, for instance, must tell you that in Hollywood I was very frequently with one of the finest human beings I had ever met. That is Adrian Scott. I thought some of these people were being prosecuted for what they were not, and I later was surprised to learn that apparently all of them were Communists. I did not have many who were friends of Hollywood, but Adrian certainly astounded me.

MR. TAVENNER: I show you a photostatic copy of page 7 of the *Daily Worker* of August 23, 1937. Apparently, this was on the occasion of your return to New York from Hollywood, and considerable space was given to you and your plays in that article. The article evidently represents an interview by a reporter for the *Daily Worker*. In this article you are identified as "Clifford Odets, well-known, left-wing playwright." According to the article, you were questioned as to whether you had made an effort to turn out scenarios with social content while in Hollywood. You will observe that you were quoted as saying:

---

sentences, literally translated from this book, are of special interest: "Meanwhile Clifford Odets—I think in 1951—behaved badly. He was called before the House Committee for Investigation of Un-American Activities. . . . He behaved deplorably there. I thereupon broke off relations with him. He was very outraged about this. There's nothing I can do for him, and I've no idea what has become of him. I think he's writing films in Hollywood. . . ." —E.B.

> Well, I got away with some stuff in *The General Dies at Dawn* and in the other two scripts that I did, *The River Is Blue* and *Gettysburg,* but they have been careful with me. They go over my stuff with a fine-tooth comb. It is difficult to do anything with social significance.

Do you recall the interview?

MR. ODETS: I remember reading this from your hands a few weeks ago and saying that I thought the whole matter was nonsense because *The General Dies at Dawn* is a picture that starred Gary Cooper and [was] done by Paramount. There was nothing of any subversive or propaganda nature in it. *Gettysburg* is a picture in which Abraham Lincoln is the hero. And *The River Is Blue* I did not write. Therefore, I couldn't have made this statement. I go to Hollywood to make an honest living, writing entertaining scripts. I have never gone to Hollywood as a propagandist. I think nothing gets by anybody in Hollywood. I don't think Hollywood has ever made a movie with left propaganda in it. And I think the whole matter of social messages from Hollywood [is] something that really cannot happen. All scripts are carefully written and rewritten and gone over with fine combs in Hollywood, and I never in my life had any intention of going to Hollywood and making a two-million-dollar picture which was a propaganda picture.

MR. WOOD: Then you were misquoted?

MR. ODETS: I am misquoted all the way through there. I suppose if the interview took place it could not have been a friendly interview, because when I look at the top of it, it very sneeringly refers to me as a man who gave up his career and went to Hollywood to make his gold. The opening of the interview is extremely unfriendly. So I could not have been very friendly with the interviewer.

MR. TAVENNER: Do you recall that an interview took place with the person whose name is mentioned as the interviewer?

MR. ODETS: I think it says Burns. I have no idea who that is, and I have no memory of the interview—1937 is fourteen years ago. I was quoted as saying, "Social drama isn't dying, it never really lived." That is what he quotes me as saying.

MR. WALTER: Isn't the screening so thorough it would be an utter impossibility to slant a picture? There are so many people that examine it for that particular purpose?

MR. ODETS: You are right. There is nothing less possible in Hollywood.

* * *

MR. TAVENNER: I show you another pamphlet entitled "Guide to Readings on Communism," issued by the Workers' Bookshop. On the inside of the front cover you will find this statement:

> This guide has been compiled to help those workers, students, and intellectuals who are finding their way to Communism. The titles of books and

> pamphlets included in this pamphlet are by no means complete. What we have attempted to do here is to list the minimum required readings for an understanding of the fundamental, theoretical, and practical questions facing the international as well as the American revolutionary movement.

Then on page 19 you will find listed the two plays of yours, *Waiting for Lefty* and *Till the Day I Die,* and they are described as two of the important revolutionary plays. Do you have any comment to make on that?

MR. ODETS: As early as 1937 they, of course, were on the Wilson Library Index and were required reading in most of the colleges and universities of the United States. One of the reasons I left the Communist Party was that I did not want my work or my meaning to be narrowed down to their meaning. Here in this pamphlet they narrowed down the meaning of what I write to their meaning. I would much rather be taught and have my plays as required reading in American universities than in this pamphlet.

MR. TAVENNER: You say you joined the Communist Party in 1935 and remained a party member only a few months—I think probably nine months. You also say that your break with the Communist Party was complete and final. How do you reconcile your statement that your break with the Communist Party was complete and final with this record of affiliation with Communist-front organizations?

MR. ODETS: Well, Mr. Tavenner, the lines of leftism, liberalism, in all of their shades and degrees, are constantly crossing like a jangled chord on a piano. It is almost impossible to pick out which note is which note. I have spoken out on what I thought were certain moral issues of the day, and I found myself frequently on platforms with Communists that I did not know about then but evidently are now known Communists. Many of these people have some very good tunes. They have picked up some of our most solemn and sacred American tunes and they sing them. If I as an American liberal must sometimes speak out the same tune, I must sometimes find myself on platforms, so to speak, with strange bedfellows. I have never wittingly, since these early days, joined or spoken on an exclusively Communist program or platform. I see that one must do one of two things: One must pick one's way very carefully through the mazes of liberalism and leftism today or one must remain silent. Of the two, I must tell you frankly I would try to pick the first way, because the little that I have to say, the little that I have to contribute to the betterment or welfare of the American people could not permit me to remain silent.

The first witnesses before HUAC to be characterized as "unfriendly"—the Hollywood Nineteen of 1947—had taken their stand on the First Amendment: you were free to believe what you chose, and the Government had no right to pry into this choice. Beginning with the actor Howard Da Silva in 1951, more and more Hollywood witnesses stood, instead, on the Fifth Amendment: the privilege of declining to testify against oneself. By a misunderstanding which has been professionally explicated by Telford Taylor in his *Grand Inquest* (New York, 1953), the Fifth Amendment came in this era to be regarded among liberals as a device for protecting one's friends and associates. As Taylor explains, it was really meant to protect *you,* even if you were guilty: for even the guilty have rights.

For lawyers then, there was an irony about the twist which Lillian Hellman gave to things in 1952, when she agreed, as it were, to testify "against" herself, provided that she was not forced to testify against others. By another irony, just one year before Miss Hellman felt called upon to take this stand, the Supreme Court had ruled that "disclosure of a fact waives the privilege as to details." If, for example—and it was *the* example—you disclosed that you had been a member of the Communist Party, you had thereby waived the privilege of withholding any further facts about the Party, including the names of other members. Miss Hellman, as we now know from her autobiography *An Unfinished Woman* (New York, 1969), never had been a Communist, but has related in private conversation with the editor of this book that her attorney became very nervous about her losing the "privilege as to details" by disclosure of whatever she might disclose.

> MR. WOOD: Can you fix a period during which you have not been a member of the Communist Party? Were you yesterday?
>
> MISS HELLMAN: No, sir.
>
> MR. WOOD: Were you last year at this time?
>
> MISS HELLMAN: No, sir.
>
> MR. WOOD: Were you five years ago at this time?

At this point, Miss Hellman relates, her attorney was kicking her so vigorously under the table that she answered, "I must refuse to answer." But Wood continued: "Were you two years ago from this time?" And perhaps the kicking had subsided a little, for Miss Hellman answered, "No, sir." "Three years ago from this time?" "I must refuse to answer." And thus it was, Miss Hellman says, that the report could circulate that she had left the Communist Party between two and three years earlier.

This anecdote, if believed—and the present editor believes it—is interesting evidence of the way in which others than Party members did stand on the Fifth. It is also evidence of the terrible confusions of those years. What were the laws, and how was the nonlawyer to understand them? What did the Constitution mean, and when was a given amendment applicable and why? But most important—a landmark, actually—was the position taken by Miss Hellman in her letter.

She tells that her best memory of this melancholy occasion was a voice from the audience: "At last someone's done it." The final irony was that, at a time when people, including some of her closest friends, were going to jail for far less, she got away with it. History isn't all bad.

MAY 21, 1952:

Lillian Hellman

A Subcommittee of the Committee of Un-American Activities met, at 11 a.m., in room 226, Old House Office Building. The Honorable John S. Wood (Chairman) presiding.

Committee members present: Representatives John S. Wood and Francis E. Walter.

Staff members present: Frank S. Tavenner, Jr., Counsel; Thomas W. Beale, Sr., Assistant Counsel; John W. Carrington, Clerk; Raphael I. Nixon, Director of Research; and A. S. Poore, Editor.

MR. WOOD: Are you represented by counsel? Counsel will please identify himself for the record.

MR. RAUH: My name is Joseph L. Rauh, Jr.

MR. TAVENNER: You are Miss Lillian Hellman?

MISS HELLMAN: Yes, I am.

MR. TAVENNER: Where were you born?

MISS HELLMAN: I was born in New Orleans, Louisiana, in June 1905.

MR. TAVENNER: Will you give to the Committee, please, in a general way, what your educational training has been?

MISS HELLMAN: Yes. I went to public schools in New Orleans, Louisiana, and in New York City. I went to New York University and Columbia University.

MR. TAVENNER: What is your occupation?

MISS HELLMAN: I am a writer, a playwright.

MR. TAVENNER: How long have you been a playwright?

MISS HELLMAN: Since about 1933.

MR. TAVENNER: Will you tell the Committee, please, what some of the principal productions have been—that is, your productions as a playwright?

MISS HELLMAN: Not a full list, just some?

MR. TAVENNER: Some of the most prominent.

MISS HELLMAN: *The Children's Hour, The Little Foxes, Watch on the Rhine, Another Part of the Forest, The Autumn Garden, The Searching Wind.*

MR. TAVENNER: Where have you engaged in the practice of your profession?

MISS HELLMAN: In the practice of playwriting, in New York City, principally.

MR. TAVENNER: Well, were you not located in Hollywood for a while?

MISS HELLMAN: Yes, sir. I have done screen writing, a great deal of it.

MR. TAVENNER: Over what period of time?

MISS HELLMAN: From about the beginning of 1935 through about 1945, and one short job since then.

MR. TAVENNER: When was the work that you say was a short job since then?

MISS HELLMAN: I think in about 1948 or 1949.

MR. TAVENNER: What was the title?

MISS HELLMAN: It wasn't a title. I went out to California to work for two weeks to do a so-called ten-page treatment on *Streetcar Named Desire,* which the producer, the owner at that point, wished to submit to the Breen office. In other words, I did not do a script, I simply did a suggestion for Mr. Breen.

MR. TAVENNER: For what studios have you worked?

MISS HELLMAN: I have worked mostly for Samuel Goldwyn, for whom I worked off and on for ten years. I also did a picture for Warner Brothers, and *The Searching Wind* was produced by Mr. Hal Wallace [Wallis] of Paramount Pictures.

MR. TAVENNER: What do you consider the major screen credits which you have received for your work in Hollywood?

MISS HELLMAN: An adaptation of my own play *The Children's Hour,* which was called *These Three,* a picture called *The Dark Angel.* I did the screenplay of my own play *The Little Foxes.* I edited the screenplay of my own play *Watch on the Rhine.* I did the screenplay of my own play *The Searching Wind.* I worked for short periods on other pictures. But those are the major ones.

MR. TAVENNER: When did you go to Hollywood?

MISS HELLMAN: I went first in 1930 and worked at Metro-Goldwyn-Mayer as a reader and translator, reader chiefly. I went back in 1935, I think, to the first screen-writing job. I also did a picture called *Dead End,* which I had forgotten.

MR. TAVENNER: How long did you remain in Hollywood when you were there in 1935?

MISS HELLMAN: I couldn't say, Mr. Tavenner. I would think it was a period of four or five months.

MR. TAVENNER: And what was the occasion of your next trip to Hollywood?

MISS HELLMAN: I think my own play *The Children's Hour,* which would have been 1936. I am not certain of these dates.

MR. TAVENNER: How long did you remain in 1936 in Hollywood?

Miss Hellman: I think about the same period off and on. I never really lived in Hollywood. I would live two or three months and then come back for a month or two. I think the longest period I ever lived was about six or seven months, which was 1937 or 1938.

* * *

Mr. Tavenner: In the course of your visits to Hollywood, did you become acquainted with Martin Berkeley?

Miss Hellman: I must refuse to answer, Mr. Tavenner, on the ground it might incriminate me.

* * *

Mr. Tavenner: Miss Hellman, during the course of the hearings in California in September 1951, Mr. Martin Berkeley testified regarding the holding of a meeting of members of the Community Party in June of 1937 at his home. This appeared, according to his testimony, to have been one of the early organizational meetings of the Communist Party in Hollywood. I want to read you his testimony regarding that meeting:

> Mr. Tavenner: I would like you now to tell the Committee when and where the Hollywood section of the Communist Party was first organized.
>
> Mr. Berkeley: Well, sir, by a very strange coincidence the section was organized in my house. From the time I got out here in January, the Party grew pretty rapidly. Jerome was working hard, Mike Pell was working hard, Lou Harris was working hard, and all of us were working pretty hard to recruit members. And we felt—you see, at that time there was no real organization, you were a Party member but you had no place to go and meet. There were no real groups, there were a few study groups, but that is about all. It was felt that numerically we were strong enough to have our own organization, which was called the Hollywood section. In June of 1937, the middle of June, the meeting was held in my house. My house was picked because I had a large living room and ample parking facilities, it was out on Beverly Glen, which was out in the country, at least in those days, and my lease was up in two days. So we had the meeting at my house. And it was a pretty good meeting. We were honored by the presence of many functionaries from downtown, and the spirit was swell.
>
> Mr. Tavenner: Will you give us the names of those who were in attendance at that meeting, who were members of the Communist Party?
>
> Mr. Berkeley: Well, in addition to Jerome and the others I have mentioned before—and there is no sense in me going over the list again and again—I would like to get to the newer people, if I may. Eva Shafran, who was then, I believe, the educational director of the county, downtown, and who is now dead. Also present was Harry Carlisle, who is now in the process of being deported, for which I am very grateful. He was an English subject. After Stanley Lawrence had stolen what funds there were from the Party out here and to make amends had gone to Spain and gotten himself killed, they sent Harry Carlisle here to conduct Marxist classes. He was at the meeting.

> Also at the meeting was Donald Ogden Stewart. Dorothy Parker, also a writer. Her husband, Allen Campbell. My old friend Dashiell Hammett, who is now in jail in New York for his activities. That very excellent playwright, Lillian Hellman . . .

Miss Hellman, in the light of that testimony, I want to ask you whether or not you agree that that is a correct statement, and if it is not, wherein it is in error; and, if you did attend this meeting as represented and as sworn to by Mr. Berkeley, I would then want to ask you regarding the activities of any other persons who were there. First of all, I will ask you the question, is that statement true?

MISS HELLMAN: I would very much like to discuss this with you, Mr. Tavenner, and I would like at this point to refer you to my letter. I have every desire to discuss this with you. To be fair to myself, I think I have worked very hard over this letter, and most seriously. I would like to ask you once again to reconsider what I have said in the letter.

MR. TAVENNER: In other words, you are asking the Committee not to ask you any questions regarding the participation of other persons in the Communist Party activities?

MISS HELLMAN: I don't think I said that, Mr. Tavenner.

MR. WOOD: In order to clarify the record, Mr. Counsel, at this point would it be wise to put into the record the correspondence that has been had between the witness and me, as Chairman of the Committee.

MR. TAVENNER: I have here the letter of Miss Hellman, addressed to the Chairman, May 19, 1952, and a copy of the reply by the Chairman of May 20, 1952. I notice the press is passing around copies. Are those copies being disseminated by you?

MR. RAUH: By me, Mr. Tavenner. I thought you had accepted them in the record and that was proper. I am sorry if I had done anything that was not proper.

MR. TAVENNER: Not at all. I was just interested to know whether you were prepared to do that before you came here.

MR. RAUH: We had to have the copies, Mr. Tavenner. If you had not put them in the record, I would not have done it. I thought it was proper once you made it a part of the record.

MR. TAVENNER: There is no objection to that.

MR. WOOD: It is my view that, in the function of this Committee, we cannot be placed in the attitude of trading with the witnesses as to what they will testify to. And that is the substance of my reply, which is in the record and which I think should be read publicly now, in view of the fact that the witness has been circulating them among the press.

MR. TAVENNER: The letter by Miss Hellman reads as follows:

> DEAR MR. WOOD:
>
> As you know, I am under subpoena to appear before your Committee on May 21, 1952.

I am most willing to answer all questions about myself. I have nothing to hide from your Committee and there is nothing in my life of which I am ashamed. I have been advised by counsel that under the Fifth Amendment I have a constitutional privilege to decline to answer any questions about my political opinions, activities, and associations, on the grounds of self-incrimination. I do not wish to claim this privilege. I am ready and willing to testify before the representatives of our Government as to my own opinions and my own actions, regardless of any risks or consequences to myself.

But I am advised by counsel that if I answer the Committee's questions about myself, I must also answer questions about other people and that if I refuse to do so, I can be cited for contempt. My counsel tells me that if I answer questions about myself, I will have waived my rights under the Fifth Amendment and could be forced legally to answer questions about others. This is very difficult for a layman to understand. But there is one principle that I do understand: I am not willing, now or in the future, to bring bad trouble to people who, in my past association with them, were completely innocent of any talk or any action that was disloyal or subversive. I do not like subversion or disloyalty in any form, and if I had ever seen any, I would have considered it my duty to have reported it to the proper authorities. But to hurt innocent people whom I knew many years ago in order to save myself is, to me, inhuman and indecent and dishonorable. I cannot and will not cut my conscience to fit this year's fashions, even though I long ago came to the conclusion that I was not a political person and could have no comfortable place in any political group.

I was raised in an old-fashioned American tradition and there were certain homely things that were taught to me: to try to tell the truth, not to bear false witness, not to harm my neighbor, to be loyal to my country, and so on. In general, I respected these ideals of Christian honor and did as well with them as I knew how. It is my belief that you will agree with these simple rules of human decency and will not expect me to violate the good American tradition from which they spring. I would, therefore, like to come before you and speak of myself.

I am prepared to waive the privilege against self-incrimination and to tell you everything you wish to know about my views or actions if your Committee will agree to refrain from asking me to name other people. If the Committee is unwilling to give me this assurance, I will be forced to plead the privilege of the Fifth Amendment at the hearing.

A reply to this letter would be appreciated.

Sincerely yours,
LILLIAN HELLMAN.

The answer to the letter is as follows:

DEAR MISS HELLMAN:

Reference is made to your letter dated May 19, 1952, wherein you indicate that in the event the Committee asks you questions regarding your association with other individuals you will be compelled to rely upon the Fifth Amendment in giving your answers to the Committee questions.

In this connection, please be advised that the Committee cannot permit witnesses to set forth the terms under which they will testify.

We have in the past secured a great deal of information from persons in the entertainment profession who cooperated wholeheartedly with the Committee. The Committee appreciates any information furnished it by persons who have been members of the Communist Party. The Committee, of course, realizes that a great number of persons who were members of the Communist Party at one time honestly felt that it was not a subversive organization. However, on the other hand, it should be pointed out that the contributions made to the Communist Party as a whole by persons who were not themselves subversive made it possible for those members of the Communist Party who were and still are subversives to carry on their work.

The Committee has endeavored to furnish a hearing to each person identified as a Communist engaged in work in the entertainment field in order that the record could be made clear as to whether they were still members of the Communist Party. Any persons identified by you during the course of Committee hearings will be afforded the opportunity of appearing before the Committee in accordance with the policy of the Committee.

Sincerely yours,
JOHN S. WOOD, *Chairman*.

Now, the question was asked you of whether or not you attended this organizational meeting of the Communist Party that was described by Mr. Martin Berkeley.

MISS HELLMAN: I must refuse to answer, on the ground that it might incriminate me.

MR. WOOD: You might refuse to answer it. The question is asked, do you refuse?

MISS HELLMAN: I am sorry, I refuse to answer on the ground that it might incriminate me.

MR. TAVENNER: I desire to continue to read additional testimony as given by Mr. Berkeley.

MR. TAVENNER: Did you later obtain information that some of these individuals were made members of the Communist Party at large?

MR. BERKELEY: I did, sir.

MR. TAVENNER: Which of these persons whom you have named became members at large of the Communist Party?

MR. BERKELEY: Well, I have to put it this way, sir. After this meeting I never saw Stewart or Parker or Campbell or Hammett or Hellman at a Party meeting. They were at that meeting at my house and I spoke to Jerome and Lawson at a subsequent date and I asked them where Stewart and Dash were —I was very fond of Dash Hammett—and he said that they had been assigned to a group known as Party members at large. They were no longer assigned to any particular group in the Hollywood section and that I had seen the last of them as far as organizational matters were concerned. I imagine right now they wish they hadn't come in the first place. There are throughout the country those who are members at large of the Communist Party.

> Mr. Tavenner: Will you tell the Committee what you mean by member at large, or what the Communist Party meant by the designation "member at large"?
>
> Mr. Berkeley: Well, if you are pretty important and you don't want to be exposed— Well, suppose Congressman Jackson here decided to become a Communist, God forbid—
>
> Mr. Jackson: Would you pick somebody else, please?
>
> Mr. Berkeley: —it would be pretty important that no one knew that such was the case, and the Party would probably not issue a formal book. You would take your oath to the Communist Party, you would pay your dues to the Communist Party, you would take your directives from the Communist Party, and you would function as you were told to function, but you would not go to meetings with other Congressmen or other writers, or other members of the top echelon in the trade-unions or the arts. From time to time you might meet with a man like—I am sure these five writers I have mentioned as members at large, they undoubtedly met out here in secret with John Howard Lawson or in New York with V. J. Jerome or a gentleman called Brown, a member of the Politburo. You would meet with these people and get your instructions from the Party, but you would have no contact with anybody else in the Party.

Were you at any time a member at large of the Communist Party?

Miss Hellman: I refuse to answer, Mr. Tavenner, on the same grounds.

Mr. Tavenner: Were you acquainted with V. J. Jerome?

Miss Hellman: I refuse to answer on the same grounds.

Mr. Tavenner: John Howard Lawson?

Miss Hellman: I refuse to answer on the same grounds.

Mr. Tavenner: Are you now a member of the Communist Party?

Miss Hellman: No, sir.

Mr. Tavenner: Were you ever a member of the Communist Party?

Miss Hellman: I refuse to answer, Mr. Tavenner, on the same grounds.

Mr. Wood: See if we can be of mutual assistance to each other. You testified that you are not now a member of the Community Party. On the grounds of possible self-incrimination, you have declined to answer whether you were ever a member.

Miss Hellman: Yes, sir.

Mr. Wood: What I would like to know is can you fix a date, a period of time in the immediate past, during which you are willing to testify that you have not been a member of the Communist Party?

Miss Hellman: I refuse to answer, Mr. Wood, on the same grounds.

Mr. Wood: Were you yesterday?

Miss Hellman: No, sir.

Mr. Wood: Were you last year at this time?

Miss Hellman: No, sir.

MR. WOOD: Were you five years ago at this time?

MISS HELLMAN: I must refuse to answer.

MR. WOOD: Were you two years ago from this time?

MISS HELLMAN: No, sir.

MR. WOOD: Three years ago from this time?

MISS HELLMAN: I must refuse to answer on the same grounds.

MR. WOOD: You say you must refuse. Do you refuse to answer whether you were three years ago?

MISS HELLMAN: I am so sorry, I forget. I certainly don't mean to forget.

MR. WALTER: Were you a member of the Communist Party in the middle of June 1937?

MISS HELLMAN: I refuse to answer, Mr. Walter, on the same ground.

MR. WALTER: As I remember your letter to the Chairman, you didn't want to testify because you were afraid that you might bring "bad trouble" to people whose names might be mentioned in connection with your testimony. In view of the fact that Martin Berkeley has already admitted that he was a member of the Communist Party, what bad trouble do you think you would bring to him if you were to admit that you attended the meeting at his home?

MISS HELLMAN: I must stand by the letter, Mr. Walter. I have worked very hard on it, and I tried very hard to explain exactly what I meant by it. I must refer back to it at this point.

MR. WALTER: But the principal reason why you do not want to testify is because you do not want to bring, to quote you, "bad trouble" to other people. Martin Berkeley has already admitted that he was a member of the Communist Party. You decline to answer the question of whether or not you attended a meeting at his home. What "bad trouble" could you bring to him if you would mention his name?

MISS HELLMAN: Since I don't quite understand, may I speak with my counsel?

MR. WALTER: Yes.

(*Witness conferred with her counsel.*)

MISS HELLMAN: Because I didn't understand that that was the principal reason and because I don't understand the legalities, may I refer you to Mr. Rauh. I didn't really understand the question. I would prefer Mr. Rauh answer it, if it is possible.

MR. WALTER: No, I am not interested in that. I know about what he would say.

MR. TAVENNER: On February 12, 1948, the National Institute of Arts and Letters addressed a letter to the Speaker of the House of Representatives protesting the investigation of the Communist infiltration of the motion-picture industry as a subversion of the traditional American sense of fair play and human decency. Your name appears as having been signed to this letter. That is February 12, 1948. Were you a member of the Communist Party at that time?

MISS HELLMAN: I refuse to answer, Mr. Tavenner, on the same ground.

MR. TAVENNER: You have stated in answer to a question from one of the members of the Committee that three years ago you were not a member of the Communist Party, if I understood you correctly.

MR. RAUH: I am sorry, Mr. Tavenner.

MR. TAVENNER: Two years ago. But you refused to answer as to whether you were a member of the Communist Party three years ago. There is one great advantage [sic] between those two periods which is uppermost in my mind, and I want to ask you whether it has any bearing or significance with respect to your answer. The Korean episode began in 1950. Does that have any bearing upon your answer as to the time in which you were willing to testify you were not a member of the Communist Party?

MISS HELLMAN: No, sir, I don't think so.

MR. TAVENNER: Well, what event, if any, occurred which makes you willing to testify that you were not a member of the Communist Party two years ago?

MISS HELLMAN: I must refuse to answer that, Mr. Tavenner, on the same ground.

MR. WOOD: You are still not under any compulsion.

MISS HELLMAN: I am very sorry, Mr. Wood. It is a way of talking, I suppose. It is rather hard to cure myself.

MR. WOOD: But I cannot let it stay in the record that you are under any compulsion.

MISS HELLMAN: I am sorry. I will try very hard not to do it.

MR. TAVENNER: Your answer, then, is that you decline to answer on a constitutional ground, the Fifth Amendment in particular.

MISS HELLMAN: Yes, sir.

From *An Unfinished Woman*
by Lillian Hellman (1969)

Nothing, of course, begins at the time you think it did, but for many years I have thought of those days in the lonely London hotel room as the root-time of my turn toward the radical movements of the late thirties. (I was late: by that period many intellectuals had made the turn. So many, in fact, that some were even turning another way.) It saddens me now to admit that my political convictions were never very radical, in the true, best, serious sense. Rebels seldom make good revolutionaries, perhaps because organized action, even union with other people, is not possible for them. But I did not know that then and so I sat down to confirm my feelings with the kind of reading I had never seriously done before. In the next few years, I put aside most other books for Marx and Engels, Lenin, Saint-Simon, Hegel, Feuerbach. Certainly I did not study with the dedication of a scholar, but I did read with the attention of a good student, and Marx as a man, and Engels and his Mary became, for a while, more real to me than my friends.

In 1939, soon after *The Little Foxes,* I bought a Westchester estate, so called—large properties were cheaper in those days than small ones—and turned it into a farm. [Dashiell] Hammett, who disliked cities even more than I did, came to spend most of his time there, and maybe the best of our life together were the years on the farm. At night, good-tired from writing, or spring planting, or cleaning chicken houses, or autumn hunting, I would test my reading on Dash, who had years before, in his usual thorough fashion, read all the books I was reading, and a great many more. They must have been dull and often irritating questions I threw at him—my father had once said that I lived within a question mark—but Hammett used to say he didn't mind the ragging tone I always fall into when I am trying to learn, because it was the first time in our life together I had been willing to stay awake past ten o'clock.

But this time the ragging, argumentative tone came for a reason I was not to know about for another ten years: a woman who was never to be committed was facing a man who already was. For Hammett, as he was to prove years later, Socialist belief had become a way of life and, although he was highly critical of many Marxist doctrines and their past and present practitioners, he shrugged them off. I was trying, without knowing it, to crack his faith, sensed I couldn't do it, and was, all at one time, respectful, envious, and angry. He was patient, evidently in the hope I would come his way, amused as he always was by my pseudo-rages, cold to any influence. I do not mean there were unpleasant words between us. None, that is, except once, in 1953, after he had been in jail and gone back to teaching at the Jefferson School. I was frightened that his official connection with the school would send him back to jail and was saying that as we walked down 52nd Street. When we were a few steps from Sixth Avenue, he stopped and said, "Lilly, when we reach the corner you are going to have to make up your mind that I must go my way. You've been more than, more than, well, more than something-or-other good to me, but now I'm trouble and a nuisance to you. I won't ever blame you if you say goodbye to me now. But if you don't, then we must never have this conversation again." When we got to the corner, I began to cry and he looked as if he might. I was not able to speak, so he touched my shoulder and turned downtown. I stood on the corner until I couldn't see him anymore and then I began to run. When I caught up with him, he said, "I haven't thought about a drink in years. But I'd like one. Anyway, let's go buy one for you."

* * *

He had made up honor early in his life and stuck with his rules, fierce in the protection of them. In 1951 he went to jail because he and two other trustees of the bail bond fund of the Civil Rights Congress refused to reveal the names of contributors to the fund. The truth was that Hammett had never been in the office of the Congress, did not know the name of a single contributor.

The night before he was to appear in court, I said, "Why don't you say that you don't know the names?"

"No," he said, "I can't say that."

"Why?"

"I don't know why. I guess it has something to do with keeping my word, but I don't want to talk about that. Nothing much will happen, although I think we'll go to jail for a while, but you're not to worry because"—and then suddenly I couldn't understand him because the voice had dropped and the words were coming in a most untypical nervous rush. I said I couldn't hear him, and he raised his voice and dropped his head. "I hate this damn kind of talk, but maybe I better tell you that if it were more than jail, if it were my life, I would give it for what I think democracy is, and I don't let cops or judges tell me what I think democracy is." Then he went home to bed, and the next day he went to jail.

* * *

But Goldwyn and I—and Washington, behind the scene—went on talking about a Russian picture and finally came to what seemed like, and could have been, a sensible solution: we would do a simple, carefully researched, semi-documentary movie to be shot in Hollywood. I have, during the last year, read again my script for *North Star*. It could have been a good picture instead of the big-time, sentimental, badly directed, badly acted mess it turned out to be. Halfway through the shooting, Mr. Goldwyn and I parted company. (The picture, now called *Armored Train* when it is shown on television, has printed titles explaining the Russians were once our allies but haven't turned out so nice. If apologies were needed, and they were needed for the silliness of the movie, then the picture should have been scrapped. But the convictions of Hollywood and television are made of boiled money.)

But I think the picture was one of the reasons why the Russians invited me on a cultural mission in 1944 and why Washington—acting with faceless discretion—wanted me to go. (True, that when I got to Moscow I found they thought *North Star* a great joke, but I guess outside Moscow there were some simple peasant folk glad to find themselves so noble on the screen.)

NOVEMBER 12, 1952:

Abe Burrows

A Subcommittee of the Committee on Un-American Activities met at 11:20 a.m., in room 226, Old House Office Building, the Honorable John S. Wood (Chairman) presiding.

Committee members present: Representatives John S. Wood, Morgan M. Moulder, James B. Frazier, Jr., and Harold H. Velde.

Staff members present: Frank S. Tavenner, Jr., Counsel; Thomas W. Beale, Sr., Assistant Counsel; John W. Carrington, Clerk; and A. S. Poore, Editor.

MR. TAVENNER: Are you represented by counsel?

MR. BURROWS: I am. Mr. Martin Gang.

MR. TAVENNER: When and where were you born, Mr. Burrows?

MR. BURROWS: I was born in New York City, December 18, 1910.

MR. TAVENNER: Will you tell the Committee briefly what your educational training has been?

MR. BURROWS: I went to elementary school, high school, in New York City and in Manhattan and in Brooklyn; went to College of the City of New York and New York University School of Finance, Pace Institute of Accounting.

MR. TAVENNER: What is your present occupation?

MR. BURROWS: I am a writer and director of the theater, and I also appear periodically as a performer on television.

MR. TAVENNER: Will you tell the Committee what the record of your employment has been since, say, 1936?

MR. BURROWS: Well, in 1936 I gave up accounting and was in a business called the woven-label business, in which I didn't do very well. Then I worked as a salesman in this woven-label company for a while, and finally in 1938 I went into show business. I wrote gags for a great many comedians around town, and then finally started on a regular radio program for the Columbia Broadcasting System. Then in 1939 I was hired to do a program called the "Texaco Star Theater" in California. I went to California and wrote this "Texaco Star Theater" for Ken Murray and Frances Langford and Kenny Baker, and then in 1940 I was employed to write the Rudy Vallee–John Barrymore radio program. I started that in New York, went back to California with it. While in California, we got an idea for a program called "Duffy's Tavern." The idea was picked up and sponsored and I went back to New York. I was head writer of "Duffy's Tavern" for about five years, after which I left the field of radio and went to Paramount Pictures as a writer and producer. I didn't write or produce anything there. I wrote a program of my own—that is, one I owned myself and wrote—called "Holiday and Company." I did that in New York from about the end of 1945 until about June of 1946. I came back to California and didn't do anything for a couple of months. Then I wrote the Dinah Shore program and the Joan Davis program. Then I took on my own program called the "Abe Burrows Show" at the beginning of 1947. Then I went out in night clubs for about a year and a half and went back into television. Then I wrote a Broadway show. I was coauthor of *Guys and Dolls*. Since then I have done several other things in the theater. I did a play called *Three Wishes for Jamie,* which I was coauthor of and I directed, and it is a play that won the Christopher award. I am presently engaged in writing a new play for the spring, a musical, and I am employed on a weekly television show called "The Name Is the Same."

* * *

MR. TAVENNER: Mr. Burrows, you appeared in executive session of this Committee on March 20, 1951, at which time you were interrogated about your activities in California and New York, and at that time your testimony was very vague with regard to your knowledge of individuals who have been shown to be members of the Communist Party in Hollywood and your contacts with those individuals. The investigation by the Committee has continued, and during the course of our hearings in California there was a witness who appeared on October 2, 1952, before the Committee while sitting in California. His name was Mr. Owen Vinson. Now, Mr. Vinson testified as to his own Communist Party membership. He fixed the time at which he was a member of that group in Hollywood—that is, the Communist Party group within radio writers—as being from October 1945 or the middle of 1946—his recollection was not clear as to the exact date—for a period of approximately two years. During the course of his testimony he identified a number of persons as having been members of that group. And among them was yourself. The following questions were asked and answers given:

QUESTION: Were you acquainted with Abe Burrows?
ANSWER: Yes, sir.
QUESTION: Was Abe Burrows a member of the Communist Party to your knowledge?
ANSWER: Abe Burrows attended meetings of the Communist Party which I attended, yes, sir.
QUESTION: Have you collected dues from him?
ANSWER: I believe I have.

* * *

MR. TAVENNER: Now, the Chairman of the Committee has invited any person whose name had been adversely mentioned in the course of the testimony to appear before the Committee, to make denial or explanation, as the witness may think proper. Promptly upon taking of this testimony, we heard from you that you desired to appear before the Committee. And I assume it is in pursuance to that request that you are here now?

MR. BURROWS: I am, sir. First of all, I would like to say that I was very anxious to come back, outside of the fact that I wanted to clear up everything. The first time I was subpoenaed by this Committee I got in touch with my lawyer instantly and we asked to come down as quickly as possible. That was last year, in March. I would just like to say that I was very frightened when I got that first subpoena. I had been around in an atmosphere of people for a while who disliked this Committee very much, and I knew nothing about it except some of the stuff I had heard, and there had been a lot of—well, I might use the word "propaganda." So I was pretty scared. But I came down here and spoke to the people here and the investigators and everybody was very fair to me. There were no monsters here, no Fascists, nobody trying to kill me. The minute I heard Vinson had said something about me, I said I wanted to come back and talk to you people because I really want to get this whole thing cleared up, this whole point of my Americanism being under suspicion is very painful to me, not just painful economically but painful as it is to a guy who loves his country, loves his home, and loves his people. In answer to what Mr. Vinson said: I have no recollection at all of ever applying for Party membership. I have no recollection of ever having possession of a Communist Party card, although I have been told by a private source that somebody had seen a card with my name on it. I have never seen such a card and I don't believe it. I have no recollection of paying dues or anything that could be called dues. I have no recollection of any formal participation in anything that could be called this organization. However, I did associate with Communists. I went to various meetings, I belonged to a lot of their fronts, I attended lectures, what was called study groups or something like that. I entertained for their causes. I gave them money for these causes over a short time. And so, if someone testifies that he thought I was a Communist, I guess he is telling the truth as he sees it. I was around with those fellows, and he saw me. However, kind of a stubborn pride on my part makes me happy in the belief that maybe I didn't take the final step.

MR. TAVENNER: By "final step," what do you mean?

MR. BURROWS: I mean the actual applying or going through any of the ritualistic stuff which I always understood you had to go through before you became a member of the Communist Party.

MR. TAVENNER: Well, how did you learn where the ritualistic steps—

MR. BURROWS: I have read it in testimony from this Committee. I have read a lot of articles about Communism. You know, there was a period when I was around with these fellows, when the Communists weren't Communists as we know them or knew them before. Their role during the war was completely one of unity. They attacked anyone who talked about strikes, they talked about the war effort and unity and everything, and that was their whole approach. So they sounded like superpatriots. It wasn't until later that they began to show themselves. That iron fist in that intellectual glove, you know, began to show itself, and people began to recognize what they were. But in those days it wasn't like that, and a lot of them said they were Communists, a lot of them were on the masthead of the *New Masses,* other people spoke for Communist causes, and there was no hiding of it or anything like that. But since I have read about the conspiratorial nature of it, my role in this whole thing certainly doesn't jibe with the conspiratorial nature of it.

MR. MOULDER: When you referred to your association, was that at Communist cell meetings?

MR. BURROWS: Not anything that was called a Communist meeting. I have since read in testimony of other people, where they use the words "open Communist meetings," I don't know if it was anything like that. I don't recall ever being at anything that I could say was formally set up. You know, I have read a lot of stuff about it since.

MR. MOULDER: Was it an organization meeting of the Communist Party itself?

MR. BURROWS: Not to my recollection. Now, for instance, Owen Vinson: I only recall his name because I ran into him in front of the Beverly Hills Hotel about a year ago.

MR. MOULDER: I just want to be specific about what you testified to.

MR. BURROWS: I was in a great many of those front organizations. I was around with people. For instance, back in 1943, I met a fellow named Samuel Sillen, who was one of the editors of *New Masses*. And he introduced himself to me and we met somewhere in the country or somewhere and started to talk books. Then he introduced me to Joe North, who was editor of the *New Masses,* and another fellow named John Stewart, I think it was, and they would sit around and talk to me, and at one time they said to me, "You ought to be much closer to us." I associated with these fellows. When I came to California, about a week after I arrived, I was called by Albert Maltz, and Albert Maltz said, "Samuel Sillen said for me to get in touch with you." He came with his wife and visited me at my home.

MR. VELDE: Mr. Burrows, to your knowledge was Samuel Sillen a member of the Communist Party?

MR. BURROWS: Well, sir, he never said to me in those words, "I am a member." I don't ever remember anybody actually saying that to me. But I know he was literary editor of the *New Masses*. He wrote a column or something which was called "A Marxist Approach to the Theater." So I would assume, sir, he was a member of the Communist Party.

MR. VELDE: And Joe North, did you know him to be a member of the Communist Party?

MR. BURROWS: I would think the managing editor of the *New Masses* would have to be a member of the Communist Party. And when he spoke, he would say, "The Communists, we Communists." As a matter of fact, they once invited me to a lecture that was given under the auspices of the Communist Party in which Earl Browder had a debate with George Sokolsky. That is how everybody got along in those days. It was in 1943, I believe, in New York. And it was a big crowd and stuff like that.

MR. VELDE: How about John Stewart? Did you know him to be a member of the Communist Party?

MR. BURROWS: Well, he wrote a book with a fellow who used to give lectures in Hollywood, which I attended, a fellow named Bruce Minton. Bruce Minton gave lectures on what he called "A Marxist Approach to History," or something like that. Everything was called things like that, you know.

MR. VELDE: Do you know whether Bruce Minton used any other name?

MR. BURROWS: His real name was Richard Bransten, I believe.

MR. VELDE: How well did you know him?

MR. BURROWS: I knew him at his lectures and I was at his home a couple of times. His wife was Ruth McKenney, a writer, and they invited me there. In Hollywood, in those days, I was invited everywhere. I attended more parties, I guess, than anyone. The *Saturday Evening Post,* in 1945 or the end of 1945 [1944?], did an article about me and the fact that I played at parties all over Hollywood. As a matter of fact, it got a little out of hand. I used to go to too many, and I began to quit going when I started to get asked by people I didn't know. You know, people would say, "Come to the party," and you would sit, and then you would sit down to the party and go to work. So I attended parties, with all kinds of people, the right wing and the left wing, and the middle, and all down the line. I guess I never turned down an invitation to go to the piano. It was in a period before I became a performer, and I guess maybe I was hammy about it. I liked to sing. I played up these songs.

MR. VELDE: Now, with reference to Mr. Vinson, do you recall any time he attempted to collect dues from you for the Communist Party?

MR. BURROWS: Not in the terms of dues. The way I remember Mr. Vinson is that his wife was named Pauline Hopkins, and she was a Radio Writers Guild member. She came out from Chicago. She got very active in the Hollywood Radio Writers Guild. We used to have meetings at their house. I know one specific kind of meeting we did have at their house was a committee of the Radio Writers Guild. There was a ways and means committee meeting which would be held over there. I know she had meetings over there of the radio writers' division of HICCASP, which was the Hollywood Independent Citizens Committee of the Arts, Sciences, and Professions. I remember seeing Vinson there then, somewhere in 1945. I remember giving him, I don't know for what, really . . . there was an anti-Fascist fund some of those guys used to collect for . . . but I don't remember paying Vinson anything that you would call dues. He says he had trouble collecting dues from me, and that I used an excuse that I didn't have the money with me. Well, anyone who knows me knows I am not that sort of a fellow. If I had an obligation to pay dues, I would pay them.

MR. VELDE: Now, as to these study groups that you mentioned, you studied Communism in groups?

MR. BURROWS: I guess it was kind of to orientate people on what they called a Marxist approach to show business. You know, they used to have continual squabbles as to the role of a writer, and one group would hold the writer was a citizen, another group would hold that a writer was purely a writer. If you recall, it was a tremendous controversy that Albert Maltz had, I think it was, where he said art is a weapon and they said art isn't a weapon, or rather he said art isn't a weapon and they said it is a weapon. I used to find myself, periodically, engaged in arguments. I am a satirist, and one of my best-known satires is a satire of a kind of documentary radio program that was very common among the liberal and left-wing writers of the day. There was a big tendency in those days to do these very pontifical radio programs wth everybody talking very loud and introducing Thomas Jefferson and Abraham Lincoln at every opportunity. So I did a satirical thing on that at the piano. I remember the first time I did it was for some kind of a cause: I don't know what the cause was exactly, but I did it, and there was a pretty large left-wing crowd, I guess, and there was kind of a quiet in the room—it didn't go as well as it did with others of my friends. And then one of the fellows came over, I think it was Henry Blankfort. He came over and he said, "I think that is a very bad thing for you to do, Abe, you know." I said, "Why," and he said, "Because I think it is wrong." These guys had no sense of humor about themselves at all, I think that is one of the reasons that I wasn't too trusted.

MR. VELDE: Did you know Henry Blankfort as a member of the Communist Party?

MR. BURROWS: I know that he testified and took the Fifth Amendment, and I know that he has been around, he was around all of the time. In some of the cases, I don't know whether I know a fellow was a Communist from reading about it in this Committee's testimony or whether I knew it before. It kind of overlaps in your mind, you know.

MR. VELDE: Do you recall any of the instructors at these study groups? And the approximate date that they were held?

MR. BURROWS: Oh, somewhere in the 1945 period, I think. But some of them were the study groups that Bruce Minton ran. It was a lecture, a regularly organized lecture. They were called a study [group], but he just talked. He, at the moment, was engaged in a terrific controversy with John Howard Lawson over how history was to be interpreted. I frankly didn't know what either of them meant. Now, that was one group. Then there was a book put out called *Literature and Arts,* by Marx and Engels, or something. It was a collection. And a group gathered to discuss this and I think it was a group of people from—well, who I largely knew to be radio members of HICCASP, as I recall. I don't remember names. In my earlier testimony I said that a lot of the people were kind of faceless to me, and when I saw the list of people that Owen Vinson named as being part of the group that I was supposed to have been part of, I knew, maybe, two of them.

MR. VELDE: Do you remember them talking, in these groups, about the Duclos letter?

MR. BURROWS: I remember a great deal of conversation, socially and such, when the Duclos letter hit. And all over Hollywood there was a good deal of whispering and hushing and stuff like that. But I remember on one evening, one fellow, as I remember, was trying to make sense out of this thing. That seemed to be always the role of these guys, to try to make sense out of it. They spoke of how this would be a force for good. I remember, way back in 1936–37, that I had belonged to the American League for Peace and Democracy. When the Nazi-Soviet pact hit, I resigned with a letter to the league. But at that time they said, "This is going to be a force for peace, a great thing." And the talk after the Duclos letter hit was about the same. They said, "This is going to do a great thing." I didn't know what anybody meant.

MR. VELDE: Mr. Burrows, you are a fairly intelligent man; I think your testimony has shown that. Couldn't you tell from the way their Party line shifted that you were studying about Marxist Communism?

MR. BURROWS: Oh, yes, I knew that—

MR. VELDE: And if you were interested in Marxist Communism, don't you think it is reasonable to assume that you were a member of the Communist Party?

MR. BURROWS: But the study groups I mentioned, Mr. Velde, were in 1945, when there was absolutely no word mentioned of Marxist Communism as we know it. It was a case of the writers' aid in the war, the writers' role in the war, the writers' role in establishing unity, how the writers should treat minorities, how he should treat the war effort, he shouldn't make jokes about gas rationing—stuff like that, you know. I attended no such study groups, when it [the Party?] switched back to a revolutionary role.

MR. VELDE: But you know now, do you not, that in order to get into those study groups in the first place, you had to be considered for membership in the Communist Party?

MR. BURROWS: Well, I don't deny that I may have been considered for membership. I actually think that because of my work, my humor and my satire, I wasn't very well trusted, I was called chi-chi, phony, I will use any word I can think of, because I mingled with people who weren't of the Left.

I did satires, for instance, on folk songs in a period when the Communist Party had taken the folk song very dearly to its bosom, because the folk song and the square dance seemed to be a way to establish American roots.

MR. WOOD: May I ask a question at this point? During the period from 1943 to 1945 what was your annual income?

MR. BURROWS: In 1943 I guess I made about forty thousand dollars, and then in 1944 about fifty thousand, and in 1945 a little over fifty thousand.

MR. WOOD: When you made contributions to any organization, did you keep a list of them?

MR. BURROWS: No, sir. I did when they were charity contributions.

MR. WOOD: But you did make some that you knew were not for charity?

MR. BURROWS: Yes.

MR. WOOD: Can you name some of them?

MR. BURROWS: I made contributions to the Hollywood Independent Citizens Committee.

MR. WOOD: You knew what you were doing then.

MR. BURROWS: Yes, sir. The Hollywood Independent Citizens Committee at that time, when I joined it, was a very broad organization.

MR. WOOD: I understood that; I want to know if you knew.

MR. BURROWS: Yes, sir.

MR. WOOD: What other organizations?

MR. BURROWS: I said the Hollywood Independent Citizens Committee. I gave money once to a People's World fund.

MR. WOOD: You knew what you were doing then?

MR. BURROWS: Yes, sir.

MR. WOOD: You knew where the money was going to.

MR. BURROWS: To the People's World fund, yes, sir.

MR. TAVENNER: And the *New Masses*.

MR. BURROWS: Yes, sir.

MR. WOOD: You knew where that was going.

MR. BURROWS: Yes, sir.

MR. WOOD: All right, then, categorically, did you pay dues to the Communist Party?

MR. BURROWS: Not to my knowledge, sir, I never paid anything I thought could be called dues.

MR. WOOD: Categorically, were you ever requested to pay dues to the Communist Party as such?

MR. BURROWS: Not to my knowledge, sir.

MR. WOOD: Categorically, did you ever decline to pay dues because you didn't have the money with you?

MR. BURROWS: Well, categorically, no, sir. Because it just doesn't sound like me.

MR. WOOD: I am not asking you what it sounds like. Did you or did you not?

MR. BURROWS: No, sir.

MR. WOOD: Did you ever give Owen Vinson any money for any purpose?

MR. BURROWS: I may have, sir.

MR. WOOD: Do you know whether you did or not?

MR. BURROWS: I couldn't answer that for sure, sir.

MR. WOOD: Now, categorically, when he said that you paid to him money for Communist Party dues, was he telling the truth or not?

MR. BURROWS: He may have thought he was telling the truth.

MR. WOOD: I didn't ask you that.

MR. BURROWS: It is very difficult for me to say this, because I think when Owen Vinson said he thought I was a member of the Party—

MR. WOOD: The question I am asking you is: Did you pay him money as Communist Party dues, as he swore before this Committee?

MR. BURROWS: No, sir, not to my knowledge.

* * *

MR. TAVENNER: Mr. Vinson further testified as follows about the dues schedule. He said:

> As I recall, there was a certain set dues based on income up to—I do not recall exactly—I think it was fifty dollars a week, which was probably two dollars a month. And above that there was an assessment or dues of four per cent of the gross salary.

Did you know of the requirement to pay a certain percentage?

MR. BURROWS: Well, I had heard vague talk about people paying part of their money. I never knew it as something presented to me.

MR. TAVENNER: Does that mean that, at the time that you were associating with these people, you heard discussed the payment of part of their salaries?

MR. BURROWS: No, I don't mean that, sir. I mean I had heard talk around. It is one of those things that kind of comes through, like a process of osmosis. I knew that big-wheel Communists paid money. I had heard accusations about that in the paper. I heard that people gave portions of their income, et cetera.

MR. TAVENNER: Did anyone on any occasion ask you to contribute a percentage of your salary to any cause?

MR. BURROWS: No, sir.

MR. WOOD: By that you mean that there was never any demand made upon you to make a contribution of a specific percentage of income to the Communist Party?

Mr. Burrows: Never, sir.

Mr. Tavenner: Mr. Vinson told us that he was a member of that group of radio writers, and he named other persons. You stated that you knew two of them. Who were the two?

Mr. Burrows: I knew Sam Moore. From the list I remember Sam Moore, and I remember Georgia Backus. I remember her. She was very active in the American Federation of Radio Artists, and she was an actress. I knew her both socially and at a lot of HICCASP meetings, and stuff like that. The others, I knew of some of them, and some I didn't know at all.

Mr. Tavenner: Did you know Sam Moore to be a member of the Communist Party?

Mr. Burrows: Not to be a member of the Communist Party, in the sense that he never said to me, "I am a member of the Communist Party," or showed me a Communist Party card. He was active in a lot of these Communist things, and he seemed to be—he was around, you know. He seemed to be always around. And Sam was the first one who ever took me to the Hollywood Writers Mobilization.

Mr. Tavenner: Have you had any conversation with Sam Moore with regard to testifying before this Committee?

Mr. Burrows: Yes, sir. The last time I saw Sam Moore was right after I had made up my plans to come down to Washington and testify before this Committee. I got the subpoena, got in touch with my lawyer, and we agreed that we were going to ask for immediate hearing in Washington. We came down well in advance of the date we were called. And Sam called me up—I hadn't seen him for a number of years—and he said he would like to see me. I said, "I have a rehearsal today, at the Forty-eighth Street Theater." He said could I see him a few minutes, and I said I would meet him. We met at Moore's restaurant right next to the theater. Sam said, "I hear you got a subpoena." I said, "Yep," and he said, "I got one, too." I hadn't known that, it wasn't in the paper. He said, "What are you going to do with it?" I said, "Well, I think I have to keep that to myself." He said, "Well, I think the only thing to do is to stick with the Fifth Amendment." I said, "Sam, it is something I don't agree with you on, but I can't argue with you." It got very cold in the restaurant and I got up, and, as a matter of fact, we ordered coffee and I didn't finish the coffee. I paid the bill and went to my rehearsal, and he left, and I haven't seen him since.

Mr. Tavenner: Did he take the initiative of getting in touch with you at that time?

Mr. Burrows: Yes, sir. He called me. I hadn't seen him in a long time.

Mr. Wood: Why would he ask you to avail yourself of the protection of the Fifth Amendment in appearing before this Committee?

Mr. Burrows: His theory was that everybody ought to stick together.

Mr. Wood: Everybody?

MR. BURROWS: Everybody.

MR. WOOD: You mean the pastor of the First Presbyterian Church in Los Angeles ought to hide behind the Fifth Amendment?

MR. BURROWS: Well, Mr. Wood, back in the days when the first group of people from Hollywood were called, I remember reading a thing about them, in which one of them said that everybody, regardless of whether they had been members of the Communist Party, were to stick together in bucking the Committee.

MR. WOOD: Did you know twelve of them came from Hollywood before this Committee and claimed the protection of the Fifth Amendment? *

MR. BURROWS: I didn't know how many had done it, sir.

MR. WOOD: Did you know that every one of them have been identified, in sworn testimony before this Committee, that they were members? And a lot of them have come before the Committee voluntarily since they served their sentence in jail and admitted their membership?

MR. BURROWS: Yes, sir, I know that.

MR. WOOD: Why would this party be asking you or suggesting to you that you also avail yourself of the protection of the Fifth Amendment?

MR. BURROWS: I don't know if everybody who was subpoenaed back in, for instance 1948, whenever that was, was a Communist or not, but I know the Communists said they thought everybody should refuse to talk to the Committee.

MR. WOOD: Every Communist?

MR. BURROWS: No, everyone, regardless.

MR. WOOD: Do you know a single human being in the State of California who has been subpoenaed before this Committee that wasn't a Communist who availed himself of the protection of the Constitution?

MR. BURROWS: No, sir. I don't know of any of the background. All I know is that I have never asked to avail myself of it since the beginning. I said to my lawyer, you know—Sometimes it seems it might be easier for me if I just said, "Well, yes, I give up."

MR. WOOD: Now, Mr. Burrows, let's get down to cases. What this man suggested was that you refuse to answer the question as to whether or not you were a member of the Communist Party, or had been, on the ground that to do so would incriminate you.

MR. BURROWS: What he was referring to, I believe, was that a Communist Party member, in the Fifth Amendment, discovered a way to refuse to answer the questions of the Committee without being cited for contempt, and I believe they would like everyone who is called, and that includes non-Communists, to refuse to answer this Committee.

MR. WOOD: If I am called for any investigation that is empowered by law to administer an oath, and I take that oath that I will swear to the truth, the whole truth, and nothing but the truth, and then I am asked whether I

* The *Ten* who invoked the *First* Amendment are meant. —E.B.

am a Communist or not, and I say I won't answer that because to do so might have a tendency to subject me to criminal prosecution, is there any alternative in your thinking as to whether or not I am telling the truth, if I am a member of the Party? If I am not a member of the Party, I am swearing to a lie?

MR. BURROWS: No alternative, no, sir, none at all.

* * *

MR. TAVENNER: Was Georgia Backus known to you to be a member of the Communist Party?

MR. BURROWS: Not known. However, I kind of assumed it. She was very intense about everything, you know, the kind of thing you associate with that. She was very intense and terribly active.

MR. TAVENNER: Well, she was one of those named by Mr. Vinson as a member of this radio group of which he claimed you were a member. Do you recall attending meetings at which she was present?

MR. BURROWS: I recall meetings of the radio writers' group of HICCASP at Pauline Hopkins' house where Georgia Backus was present. I don't recall what kind of meetings other than that. I saw Georgia at meetings. You know, she was at everything. I saw her at meetings a couple of times a week.

MR. TAVENNER: With what regularity did these meetings occur that you attended?

MR. BURROWS: Well, no regularity, sir. Mr. Vinson himself says it. He says I was commuting, but actually I never attended any of these meetings with any regularity. I wasn't commuting.

MR. TAVENNER: Who acted as a chairman at those meetings?

MR. BURROWS: I don't recall any definite chairman.

MR. TAVENNER: Were you acquainted with Hy Alexander?

MR. BURROWS: I knew him as a radio writer, slightly, not well.

MR. TAVENNER: Did you attend meetings at which he was present?

MR. BURROWS: Various meetings. He was an active member of the Radio Writers Guild.

MR. TAVENNER: Was he chairman of any of the meetings that you attended?

MR. BURROWS: Not to my knowledge. He wasn't the type of fellow that was a chairman. I don't know him well, but I recall him being a very quiet fellow. I think he was married to Georgia Backus, was he not? I think so. He was married to somebody.

MR. VELDE: Mr. Burrows, do I understand you to say that you have never signed an application for the Communist Party?

MR. BURROWS: Not to my knowledge, sir. I think I would remember signing such an application.

MR. VELDE: And, furthermore, are you equally sure that you never signed your name on a Communist Party card?

MR. BURROWS: Yes, sir. As I said, somebody told me they saw a card with my name on it. First of all, I don't know how anybody would have a card that I signed, and I think to sign a Communist Party card would have seemed like the height of insanity to me. Even though I was around and listening and involved in the fronts and entertaining with them, I wasn't really one of the fellows.

MR. WOOD: Do you sign documents that you don't know what they are?

MR. BURROWS: What, sir?

MR. WOOD: Do you sign instruments without knowing what they are?

MR. BURROWS: No, sir.

MR. WOOD: Not ever, do you?

MR. BURROWS: No.

MR. WOOD: You read what you sign.

MR. BURROWS: Yes, sir.

MR. WOOD: Then why are you indefinite about whether you signed it?

MR. BURROWS: I am not indefinite about it.

MR. WOOD: You say now, categorically, you did not do it?

MR. BURROWS: To my recollection, I never signed any such thing.

MR. WOOD: That is still indefinite. You just testified that you do not sign documents without knowing what is in them, and what they are. On that basis, will you tell us whether or not you signed an application for membership in the Communist Party or signed a Communist membership card?

MR. BURROWS: No, sir.

MR. WOOD: You did not do it?

MR. BURROWS: I have no recollection of doing such thing.

MR. WOOD: I asked you did you do it or not.

MR. BURROWS: Well, I say, sir—

MR. WOOD: Do you want to leave the Committee in doubt?

MR. BURROWS: No, sir, I don't.

MR. WOOD: Then did you or not?

MR. BURROWS: I didn't.

MR. WOOD: Proceed, Mr. Tavenner.

MR. TAVENNER: Were you acquainted with Reuben Ship?

MR. BURROWS: No, not acquainted. I knew Reuben to be a radio writer. I have never attended any meetings with him that I knew of. I don't think I would know what he looked like, if I saw him.

MR. TAVENNER: Were you acquainted with Charles Glenn?

MR. BURROWS: I knew of him slightly. I remember him around some of these literature discussions.

MR. TAVENNER: When did these discussions regarding literature take place?

MR. BURROWS: What do you mean by "when"?

MR. TAVENNER: Under what circumstances.

MR. BURROWS: Somebody, either at the guild or HICCASP or something, would say, "A group of us are getting together for a talkfest Monday night," or something like that.

MR. TAVENNER: Who would notify you about those meetings to discuss literature and other things?

MR. BURROWS: Well, I sometimes would get a card, which would say, at so forth and so forth, literature and art is going to be discussed, or a new book or something.

MR. TAVENNER: Where were these meetings held?

MR. BURROWS: In various homes. From Owen Vinson's name coming up, I remember that some of them were held in his house.

MR. TAVENNER: Can you recall the names of other houses, the names of the owners of the homes?

MR. BURROWS: No, sir. As a matter of fact, a lot of them were held in places that didn't seem to be homes. They seemed to be houses but not homes. They were sparsely furnished. I remember one on the Crescent Heights Boulevard or something. Nobody seemed to live there. The reason I remember Vinson's house was he was the one who put up the chairs, you know. So you figure it is the host who is doing that.

MR. TAVENNER: Were any meetings of that character held at your home?

MR. BURROWS: There were HICCASP meetings held at my house, but none of these literature meetings that I know of. HICCASP meetings, Radio Writers Guild meetings.

MR. TAVENNER: Were you acquainted with Elizabeth Glenn?

MR. BURROWS: I wasn't acquainted with her. She was in my house once, I think, and I met her. She was never at any of the meetings that we were talking about. But she used to kind of wheel around at benefits and big functions. She seemed to be a person of some authority.

MR. TAVENNER: She was. She has been shown to have been a functionary of the Communist Party.

MR. BURROWS: I can remember her, because she was an exceptionally large lady.

MR. TAVENNER: What was her reason for being at your house?

MR. BURROWS: She came to my house one night with some other people. You see, a lot of these people on the Left would show up at my place socially, periodically, and she was brought by somebody. I think she was brought by Richard Bransten, by Bruce Minton.

MR. TAVENNER: What was the purpose of her visit?

MR. BURROWS: They dropped by. It was after some kind of thing, where everybody dropped by at somebody's house for a drink, and I knew him, and I guess I told him to drop by for a drink and I know her. It was after a rally or something, and he brought her. The only thing I remember is that she was engaged at the time. She introduced herself to me, and said, "Did you read Albert Maltz's new book?" Albert Maltz had just written *The Cross and the Arrow,* I think it was, a book about war in Germany, and I said "No," and she said it was terrible. She was very critical of it, and I guess I gave her a book, and that was all.

MR. TAVENNER: Did you know at that time that she was a functionary of the Communist Party?

MR. BURROWS: It was one of the things you felt. I don't know about the word "functionary," but I assumed she was a wheel.

MR. TAVENNER: Mr. Burrows, about the other persons whose membership in the radio group of the Communist Party has been testified to by Mr. Vinson. Were you acquainted with Billy Wolff?

MR. BURROWS: I knew him as a guy trying to get a job in radio, and he also belonged to the guild. I didn't know him in any political capacity.

MR. TAVENNER: You stated in the earlier part of your testimony that most of those whose names were mentioned by Mr. Vinson were faceless people, as far as you were concerned.

MR. BURROWS: Sort of, sir, yes.

MR. TAVENNER: Well, could Mr. Wolff have attended any of the meetings which you attended and you not have recognized him as Mr. Wolff?

(*Representative Harold H. Velde left the hearing room.*)

MR. BURROWS: He could have, sir. He could have.

MR. TAVENNER: Were you acquainted with Stanley Waxman?

MR. BURROWS: No, sir.

MR. TAVENNER: Were you acquainted with Dave Ellis?

MR. BURROWS: No, sir.

MR. TAVENNER: A radio actor and writer?

MR. BURROWS: No, sir, never heard the name.

MR. TAVENNER: Were you acquainted with Lee Barrie?

MR. BURROWS: I vaguely remember a radio actress by that name or a singer or something by that name, but I coud not really place her, sir, not in any real knowledge.

MR. TAVENNER: Were you acquainted with Lynn Whitney?

MR. BURROWS: She was a quite well-known radio actress. She worked, I believe, on some shows that I did, and also, I believe, she was a member of the Hollywood Independent Citizens Committee, I think.

* * *

MR. TAVENNER: Were you acquainted with Elaine Gonda?

MR. BURROWS: I remembered her when I read Charles Glenn's name because I think that they were having a kind of romance or something, it struck me, because I remember seeing them sitting—

MR. TAVENNER: Well, they became married, didn't they?

MR. BURROWS: Really? Well, that is the end of the romance.

MR. TAVENNER: That was Elaine Gonda.

MR. BURROWS: Well, I remember her in connection with— I don't quite remember what she looked like, but I remember they used to sit and hold hands, I think.

MR. TAVENNER: What type of meetings were these at which this occurred?

MR. BURROWS: Well, I think that they were present together at this one study group that I told you about which was based on this literature-and-art book.

* * *

MR. TAVENNER: You stated while in New York City you met Samuel Sillen, and also Joe North. Now, when was that?

MR. BURROWS: 1943. I met Sam Sillen somewhere in the country. I got a feeling it was somewhere up in the suburbs. I am not sure now. He was a very intelligent fellow. He was literary critic for the *New Masses* at the time. I didn't know it the night I met him. I knew that this was a very bright fellow who was saying good words about good books, when we talked, and I found him good company. He and his wife called me a week later and asked me over, and then I found out who he was. We talked, and he introduced me, as I say, to these other people from the *New Masses,* and they asked me to their houses, and we had—I don't know—seven or eight sessions of talk. They talked about the *New Masses.* As a matter of fact, if I recall, Joe North wanted me to do a column for the *New Masses,* which I wouldn't do. They said they hadn't had a humor column for a long time. You know, there wasn't anything very humorous in the publication. So, he asked me would I consider doing a humor column. And I said no.

MR. TAVENNER: Is that the first time that you met Mr. Sillen?

MR. BURROWS: Yes, sir.

MR. TAVENNER: And can you state the circumstances under which you were invited to this first meeting?

MR. BURROWS: Well, it wasn't a meeting. It was at his house. And he said, "Come for dinner." I came over with my former wife. We had dinner, and there were a few people there. Then Joe North, John Stewart— I don't remember who else, a couple of people. We all sat around and talked. Then, the next time, he called me about three days later, and I think I went up to the *New Masses* office. I think, when Joe North asked me would I be interested in maybe doing a humor column, he said, "A bright guy like you," and I think I recall then that they used the words, "A bright guy like you who is widely accepted." I believe that was the kind of phrase he used. You know how tough it is dredging up things from this far back, but, as you talk to me about it, I follow through.

(*Representative Harold H. Velde returned to the hearing room.*)

MR. TAVENNER: Why did you refuse to write the column for *New Masses*?

MR. BURROWS: I didn't want to do a column for *New Masses*. I never wrote for a Communist publication.

MR. TAVENNER: But, if you would associate with all of these persons who were known to you to be members of the Communist Party, if you would contribute to the support of the *People's World* and the *New Masses,* it isn't much of a distinction between those things and writing a column, is there?

MR. BURROWS: I never went all the way. I didn't go all the way.

MR. TAVENNER: You do not admit having been a member of the Communist Party, but you do admit that you were, in many respects, either similar to a member—

MR. BURROWS: I was considered a member, too. I will admit that. I don't deny that these fellows assumed that I was a member when Judge Wood questioned me today. I got a sharp insight. It hit me like a flash when he said to me, "Why did Sam Moore come to you?" It struck me I had never asked myself, Why did he come to me? And I realize Sam Moore thought I was a member, or he *wouldn't* have come to me. I think the judge was right.

MR. TAVENNER: What you are saying is that you believe Sam Moore had a right to think you were a member?

MR. BURROWS: The people I was around with could have thought I was a member; they really could have. I don't deny that they could have thought so, and I don't deny that my own sloppiness of action, my own thoughtlessness, or whatever it was, gave them the right to think I was.

MR. TAVENNER: Let's go back for a moment to these seven or eight meetings with Samuel Sillen and Joe North. Did they have reason to believe that you were a member of the Communist Party?

MR. BURROWS: I don't think so, and I will tell you why. They said "Why aren't you closer to us?" And I know that that follows, because, when I got to California, Albert Maltz called me at the request of Sillen.

MR. TAVENNER: And you knew Albert Maltz was a member of the Communist Party when he called you in California?

MR. BURROWS: Yes, sir, I assumed so.

MR. TAVENNER: Did anything else occur in California that would lead you to believe that word had been sent from New York?

MR. BURROWS: Some girl called, and said, "Wouldn't you like to get in touch with some progressive people?" She was the one who told me about Bruce Minton's lectures, I think. I got a call from a fellow named Abe Polonsky, who has been named, and who has testified here, or has refused to—I don't know what. But I got a call from him. When he came back from the war he was a pretty interesting guy. He had been with the Office of Psychological Warfare in London. I met him in some people's homes and he had a similar background to mine. He had been to City College and had written in radio. I knew that he was a—the word was a "progressive." I knew he was around these things. He became part of the Mobilization and things like that. He said, "I would like to have a drink with you. Where are you going to be this afternoon?" I said, "I am going up to Schwab's Drugstore." That is up on Sunset Boulevard. He said, "Will you drop by for a drink?" and I said, "All right." When I came to his house, beside him was a fellow named John Stapp, who, I was told by this Committee about a year and a half ago, was an organizer or something. I never knew him; he never spoke two words to me. He was a kind of violent, thin man. I remember seeing him once at some kind of benefit. Polonsky said to me, "Abe, why don't we ever see you around?" I said, "Well, I am busy." He said, "You are not. You are not working in any of the organizations." I said I was working very hard—the kind of evasive answers you give a guy in his house, you know. And he said, "Tell me frankly, Abe, don't you think there should be a left wing in the Communist Party?" I said, "Physically, I think that in every government there should be a left and a right. That balances each other. But I don't think the Communist Party is that." Incidentally, I made a note that I never got a drink. I was invited for a drink, you see. And so, all of a sudden, it got very chilly. He turned to Stapp and he said, "Well, at least he thinks there ought to be a left wing." And Stapp got up, and it was very funny, kind of like in a gangster movie. Stapp hadn't said a word to me. He just kind of sat there like—I don't know. And he turned and he walked out, just nodding to me. He hadn't said one word. And I said, "Well, I got to get to my errand," and he said, "O.K., so long." That is the last time I ever saw him. But he was there questioning me—this was about 1946—on my lack of activity.

MR. TAVENNER: Don't you think that you were considered a member of the Communist Party at that time?

MR. BURROWS: Well, nobody said that to me. There was a kind of reservation and caution, feeling me out how I felt about things.

MR. TAVENNER: Am I correct in assuming your connection with the people that you had been connected with before was terminated at this time, is that what you are saying?

MR. BURROWS: In all ways, you see, it was terminated even before this Polonsky visit. It was terminated socially, and then I had no— Well, you know, sometimes, when you cease being active in organizations like HICCASP, you may still go on seeing the people socially, but even that aspect of it in my life was terminated.

MR. TAVENNER: Were you acquainted with Carl Winter?

MR. BURROWS: Yes. When I first came out to Hollywood, right after I had spoken to Maltz and seen him and stuff like that, somebody called me and said that the Communist Party was putting on a series of radio programs which Carl Winter was going to speak at. He wanted somebody like me—you know, I was even then known as a kind of radio doctor. So I said, "What can I do?" They said, "Can you spare a few minutes to give us your professional opinion on the speech, and maybe give Mr. Winter a few pointers?" So, I said yes, as I always did, and I went over. They gave me the address, and I went to a house. I guess it was Winter's house, because he was sitting in his shirt sleeves. His wife was there, and I vaguely remember the house. It is kind of fuzzy. I remember him showing me the sketch. I remember him being very surly. I use "surly" because he wasn't friendly. If a fellow asks me to do him a favor and look at his speech, I figure he would be friendly, but he wasn't. Again, nobody even gave me a drink of water. I sat there, and it was very odd. It was right after I came to Hollywood, and I don't think I had even joined the Mobilization yet. However, there I was. I sat there with him, and he said, "What do you think of this?" So I looked at the speech, and right away it is one of those things that is hard to read, and it has everything in it. It has the poll tax in it, you know, he is talking about the war, and it has everything in it, all kinds of things, you know. It even had a thing, I remember, about rents in Harlem. He is talking on California, about the war, and he is trying to get it all into fifteen minutes. I start to doze after reading the first paragraph. So he said, "Now, look," and I said, "Well, it looks—" He said, "I don't want your opinion on the content," and he talked to me as if I was some kind of an idiot, as if to say, "Look, I want your radio technique and you are a good director, but you don't know a darn thing about what I am going to talk about, so don't stick your nose in." I said, "Well, sir, it looks a little long to me," and then he started to read. He said, "I am going to work slowly, because I have a very bad speaking voice." So I said what was probably an unfortunate thing: I said, "Why are you delivering it?" Well, immediately I stepped on somebody's toes, because it seemed he selected himself. I thought they would get the best one, but that isn't the way it would work. These guys are hams, too. So I left, and I never had a chance to do anything with his speech. I heard it subsequently on the air, and it was as dull as I thought it would be.

MR. TAVENNER: Do you know how they obtained your name?

MR. BURROWS: My guess is that I was referred by Sam Sillen to Albert Maltz as a very likely prospect.

MR. TAVENNER: Were you an instructor at the People's Education Center in Hollywood?

MR. BURROWS: I was.

MR. TAVENNER: Who solicited you for that work?

MR. BURROWS: I don't remember the man's name. It was somebody who was executive director. Kenneth, I think, but I don't know the whole name. He said to me, "We want to have a class in radio comedy writing, how would you like to do it?" I was always a kind of frustrated teacher, so I said, "I will take a whack at it." I taught it for a semester and a half.

MR. TAVENNER: Do you know what qualifications a person was required to have to teach in that People's Education Center?

MR. BURROWS: No, sir. I think that the basic thing was, actually, to get people who would do it and not ask for their money. For instance, I was told I was to be paid. I never did get paid. And I think there was that trouble in getting teachers. At the time, however, the school was a new experiment in adult education, so-called, and I understood, they told me, they had a veteran's license and things like that, and I was to teach shipyard workers, and I kind of liked the idea. But there was no question with me about qualifications in relations to that. I taught it, I kind of enjoyed it for a little while, and then I got tired of it. In my second semester, as I recall it, it took on a stronger coloration. I think they began to give a course in Marxist history, as I recall, and I remember I left it right in the middle. I left my class my second semester right in the middle.

MR. TAVENNER: Who was your superior?

MR. BURROWS: Nobody was my superior. There was an executive director of the school. I never could remember his name. Is there a name Kenneth something?

MR. TAVENNER: Yes, there is a person whose first name is Kenneth, but there may be a number of people by that name, so I wouldn't want to guess at it.

MR. BURROWS: Well, I don't know. I taught there for a while. I kind of enjoyed it for a little while, I was the kind of guy who loved to pop off.

MR. TAVENNER: Did you state that you were at one time affiliated with the Hollywood Writers Mobilization?

MR. BURROWS: Yes, sir—1943, I believe.

MR. TAVENNER: I believe you were treasurer of the organization.

MR. BURROWS: For a little while. Emmet Lavery was president and I was treasurer of it at that time.

MR. TAVENNER: Were you a member of the Hollywood Writers Mobilization after the war?

MR. BURROWS: No, sir.

MR. TAVENNER: Mr. Richard Collins testified at some length regarding the way in which that organization was used by the Communist Party. Are you familiar with any of the details?

MR. BURROWS: No. * * * I wrote some scripts for them and I made a speech for the Writers' Congress under the auspices of the Hollywood Writers Mobilization. There was a big congress of writers at UCLA. I made a speech on humor in wartime, in which I discussed the use of humor in wartime, and how writers by being irresponsible could cause a good deal of harm, by attacking rationing and stuff like that in wartime. And that is all. That was my only connection with the Mobilization.

MR. TAVENNER: You have referred to your activity with Hollywood Independent Citizens Committee of the Arts, Sciences, and Professions. Were you on the executive council of that organization?

MR. BURROWS: I think I might have been.

MR. TAVENNER: Do you recall who solicited your participation in that?

MR. BURROWS: I don't know. A bunch of people in the guild. When that thing was formed, almost everybody belonged to it. It was almost a social thing, sir. They had big functions and people came and said yes and gave money and entertained. I entertained for them a lot.

MR. TAVENNER: According to the January 25, 1945, issue of the *Daily Worker*, you were among a number of people from Hollywood who signed a telegram to the President of the United States to terminate the proceedings that were then being undertaken to deport Harry Bridges. Do you recall authorizing the use of your name on that telegram?

MR. BURROWS: No, sir. No, sir.

MR. TAVENNER: You mean you do not recall? Or that it did not occur?

MR. BURROWS: I think it did not occur.

MR. TAVENNER: I hand you a photostatic copy of the issue I referred to; and if you will look at the last paragraph, you will see the following language: "Among those signing the wire were Abe Burrows, writer of 'Duffy's Tavern' radio show," and the names of other people. Will you examine it?

MR. BURROWS: No, sir, I have seen this before: I didn't sign any such wire.

MR. TAVENNER: If your name was used in connection with it, it was without your authorization?

MR. BURROWS: Without my knowledge or permission.

MR. TAVENNER: Did you have any connection with the American-Russian Institute of Southern California? Were you affiliated in any way with the Joint Anti-Fascist Refugee Committee in Los Angeles?

MR. BURROWS: I don't know. Somebody called me and said, "Abe, would you do a benefit for Saturday night?"—some social friend. To this day, I do thousands of things, but I now watch them.

MR. TAVENNER: When did you begin watching them?

MR. BURROWS: Well, as soon as I realized what this whole thing was about, right after the end of the war. Right after the war, I immediately, when the Communist Party was completely opposed to building up American defenses, did a whole series of radio shows for the United States Army for Army recruiting. I recruited soldiers and Marines, wrote the shows, prepared them, and put them on for the Army. I got a citation from the United States Army for it. I did many recruiting shows. I have [this letter], for instance. It is from the Poor Richard Club of Philadelphia, which is a very famous club, and it says, "The officers and directors of the Poor Richard Club are gratified to learn that you have consented to join the club in honoring General Eisenhower at the Bellevue-Stratford Hotel, January 17."

MR. TAVENNER: What year?

MR. BURROWS: The letter is dated December 26, 1947, and I was invited to appear January 17, 1948, and with General Eisenhower at this thing, I was very, very thrilled about it, and I went to the dinner. If you recall, that was the first time they started the big Republican move for General Eisenhower.

* * *

MR. VELDE: You recall the days when the White House was being picketed here by the Communist Party members, don't you?

MR. BURROWS: Oh, that was during the period of the Nazi-Soviet pact and what they used to call the American Peace Mobilization. I was not any part of any organization at all like that. I got involved with these people in the 1943 period, sir. I belonged to the American League for Peace and Democracy in 1947 [1937?], and I resigned from it over the Soviet pact [1939?], and I wrote a letter in which I thought it was a dreadful thing and I hated the whole idea of it. When I got involved with these fellows, they were all sweetness and light, back in 1943, because my stand, however, on Communism itself, and on dictatorship, never changed. I am a man who has been kind of antiauthoritarian in my thinking, and their whole approach —I hate their whole approach, that says any means to an end is O.K.

MR. VELDE: Were you conscious of the fact that the American Communist Party line was being directed from Russia?

MR. BURROWS: I was during the pact, sir.

MR. VELDE: During the pact.

MR. BURROWS: During the Nazi-Soviet pact.

MR. VELDE: Up to June 21, 1941, you were conscious that the American Communist Party policy was being directed by Soviet Russia?

MR. BURROWS: I was.

MR. VELDE: And then after that you say you weren't conscious of the fact.

MR. BURROWS: Well, to my eternal regret, I was sucked back in. I knew that all of a sudden the Communist Party, on June 22, 1941, when the Soviet Union was attacked, all of a sudden said, "Let's go to war," and everything changed overnight. Somehow or other two years went by, it became 1943, and I must say I was sucked—

MR. VELDE: Did you think, then, in 1943, that the American Communist Party line was not being directed by Soviet Russia, is that the reason?

MR. BURROWS: Well, I guess I got sucked in by all of the statements that were made about unity. And, if you remember, Earl Browder was writing books—

MR. VELDE: Well, now, just tell me about your feeling at the time you got back in with them, so to speak.

MR. BURROWS: My feeling was that they were sincere when they said that they were an American-directed party who were acting on their own.

MR. VELDE: I must say, Mr. Burrows, you were pretty naïve.

MR. BURROWS: Well, I would go stronger than that. I would say I was stupid. But I will say, sir, that the Duclos letter, the letter—Mr. Duclos evidently said of all of the Communists, "They are all stupid and silly, and you guys," he said, "don't know what you are doing," and he accused them of the very thing you are saying, that I got sucked in by. He accused them of breaking away from the Soviet line, you see.

MR. VELDE: Well, I do not think he accused them of breaking away from the Soviet line, Mr. Burrows. All he wanted them to do was to return to the former militancy here in the United States.

MR. BURROWS: Yes. But as I recall, his letter was pretty strong. He accused them of a great many things. As far as Communism is concerned, I am the kind of fellow who could never go along with the kind of things that are called Marxist Communists [Communism?]: revolution, violence. I hate the whole idea of the dictatorship. They tell you that the means are justified by the end. I don't believe that. I don't believe you kill people for their own good. They say they kill people to make a better world. Well, the world is made up of human beings, and all you do by killing people is make the world nonexistent. I want to try, really, to fight it. I think I can fight it best with my own weapons, which are what talent I have. I have a couple of ideas for a play next year I would like to do, an anti-Communist comedy. I have a couple of magazine articles I want to write, and I do hope I can prove how much I hate this whole thing.

MR. WOOD: I will ask you the question now. Are you now a Communist?

MR. BURROWS: No, sir.

MR. WOOD: Have you ever been a member of the Communist Party?

MR. BURROWS: Well, as far as I have ever been, as I said, I have never applied for Party membership. If there is a Party card with my name, I know nothing about it. But, as I said, I did associate with these fellows.

MR. WOOD: I know, but you can answer that question as to whether or not you have ever been, or considered yourself as, a member of the Communist Party.

MR. BURROWS: I was considered a Communist.

MR. WOOD: You so considered yourself, too?

MR. BURROWS: I was considered a Communist. In my own heart, I didn't believe it, but I think I was considered a Communist, and that was the whole thing of my coming here to talk about Mr. Vinson's testimony.

MR. WOOD: You say you were considered by others to be. You know yourself whether or not you were, don't you?

MR. BURROWS: Well, you see, sir, by all of the actions I did, all of the material things, all of the facts, I guess I committed enough acts to be called a Communist. I am testifying here under oath.

MR. WOOD: Well, what would you call yourself? Would you have called yourself a Communist at that time?

MR. BURROWS: Not in my own heart, sir. But I am here under oath, and I am here to tell the truth, the whole truth, and nothing but the truth, and there is an element of truth in the statement that I was a Communist. But there is also an element of untruth.

MR. WOOD: We understand your position in that respect, but now can't you answer on your own as to whether or not you were ever a member of the Communist Party?

MR. BURROWS: Well, sir, let's put it this way: I don't deny the truth of the accusations of the witness.

MR. WOOD: Any other questions?

MR. TAVENNER: I might make one comment. You stated that you desired to use your weapons against Communism.

MR. BURROWS: Yes, sir.

MR. TAVENNER: Our observations have been that ridicule is about one of the most effective weapons against members of the Communist Party.

MR. BURROWS: They can't take it. I know in Russia, I read daily about what happens with writers there, and about Stalin likes an opera or doesn't like an opera, and he likes it to be serious. I read one item somewhere where they don't like jokes, they don't like funny stuff.

MR. WOOD: May I resume? I cannot understand how at this time you can emphatically say you are not now a member of the Communist Party, and why you cannot so clearly express yourself in the same manner as to whether or not you have ever been.

MR. BURROWS: Because of my associations, sir, and the fact that I was around with those fellows, and I did go to meetings with them, and attended things with them. I have to go by the objective facts of what other people thought and what it looked like. I was, by association—by association, sir, I can't under oath deny that.

MR. WOOD: Well, that is the point. You are not necessarily a Communist by association. I mean you weren't.

MR. BURROWS: I didn't say I was by association. But I say they thought me one, and I was assumed to be one, and I am not denying they had a right to.

MR. WOOD: You mean to say that, to a full extent, you conducted yourself and participated in all of the Communist activities at that time, with a reservation in your own heart?

MR. BURROWS: Yes, sir. That is very well put.

MR. VELDE: And you did attend Communist Party meetings, knowing them to be such?

MR. BURROWS: Well, I attended meetings at which Communists were present. Those were very bad years for me in the terms of personal trouble, and my mother and father both died, and I, as a matter of fact, had to seek help from a psychiatrist, and that whole period is kind of a painful, very painful period to me.

MR. WOOD: And they were Communist Party meetings?

MR. BURROWS: I imagine they could be called Communist Party meetings. I imagine so. I really am very vague on that. I am sorry if I sound overvague.

MR. WOOD: The witness will be excused.

MR. BURROWS: I would like to thank the Committee, if I may. Thank you very much, gentlemen.

In its issue of May 24, 1952, the *Saturday Review of Literature* ran several short reviews of *Witness* by Whittaker Chambers. One is reprinted here, not only because it is by the present President of the United States, but also because it is by a former member of HUAC. He was a Saul of Tarsus who never trod the road to Damascus, and there would have been no prosecution of Hiss but for his zeal, just as there might well have been no President Nixon but for the prosecution, and condemnation, of Hiss.

Readers of *Witness* will recall that Richard Nixon, if not the hero of the book (that role being pre-empted by his good friend the author), is that hero's hero. ". . . Nixon and his family, and sometimes his parents, were at our farm, encouraging me and comforting my family. My children have caught him lovingly in a nickname. To them, he is always 'Nixie,' the kind and the good. . . . I have a vivid picture of him, in the blackest hour of the Hiss Case, standing by the barn and saying in his quietly savage way (he is the kindest of men): 'If the American people understood the real character of Alger Hiss, they would boil him in oil.' "(*Witness,* pp. 792–793, footnote.)

"*Plea for an Anti-Communist Faith*"

BY RICHARD M. NIXON

United States Senator from California, formerly member of the House Un-American Activities Committee, which first probed the Hiss case.

It is regrettable that appraisal of *Witness* will in too many cases be determined not on the basis of its literary merit but according to the bias each reader may have on the Hiss-Chambers controversy. I can hear now the epithets which will be directed against it in the drawing rooms, around the dinner tables, and during the cocktail hours among the "better people"—"too emotional," "long and repetitious," "one of those anti-Communist things." After all, "how could anything good come from that fat, repulsive little creature who said those terrible things about a 100 per cent certified gentleman, Alger Hiss?"

But recognizing that mine will probably be a minority view and one that will be subject to the charge of prejudice, I say that *Witness* is a great book, and that the verdict of history will find it so.

Witness does a number of things well.

It is an amazingly accurate account of what happened during the Congressional "red herring" investigation of the Hiss Case.

It is a moving and stirring story of a dramatic conflict between two powerful and determined personalities—Hiss and Chambers.

It sheds a withering light on the netherworld of deceit, subversion, and espionage which is the Communist conspiracy.

It is a detective thriller of the first order.

If it did only these things *Witness* would be a significant book. But its greatness is derived from the fact that it answers the great question presented by the Hiss Case—Why? For five years I have been bombarded by that question all over the country. Why did Hiss do it? Why do people with good backgrounds and excellent educations become Communists in the first place?

How often have I heard my friends in the business and professional world give their own superficial answers to these questions: he must have done it for money; he did it for power; he lied to protect someone else; anyone who becomes a Communist must have been queer and unstable to begin with.

Never can they bring themselves to admit the truth—that Hiss did what he did because he was a Communist, and that despite his background he became convinced that the Communist ideology offered a better solution to the problems which face our civilization than our own system. Once he became convinced that this was the case he was willing to do anything, engage in espionage, run the risk of disgrace for himself and his family, in order to impose the Communist tyranny upon us and all the free peoples of the world.

It is here that Chambers renders his greatest service. *Witness* is the first book of its kind which acknowledges the great hold of Communism on the human mind—which does not dismiss it as a cellar conspiracy which can be abolished by police methods. Communism is evil because it denies God and defies man. "Man without God is a beast," says Chambers. "Never more beastly than when he is most intelligent about his beastliness." But evil though it is, Communism has a tremendously malignant and potent appeal all over the world and right here in the United States.

This, then, is the lesson for us—that men become Communists out of the best of motives and some of them cease to be Communists for the same motives once they learn that those who accept the pernicious doctrine of the end justifying the means will inevitably find that the means become the end.

And *Witness* goes further: it pleads eloquently and effectively for a counter-faith to combat the Communist idea—a faith based not on materialism but on a recognition of God. "Political freedom as the Western world knows it," Chambers says, "is only a political reading of the Bible.

Without freedom the soul dies. Without the soul, there is no justification for freedom."

There is much more that I would like to say about the book, but I would not want to end this comment without saying a word about the author. I know Whittaker Chambers well. During the early months of the investigation I had the same doubts about his story that many have even today. I felt it was essential to resolve those doubts before going forward with the investigation because to allow a fraud to be perpetrated upon the Committee would not only be a great wrong to Hiss and the others named by Chambers but it would be a death blow to effective and necessary investigation of the Communist conspiracy in the United States.

What kind of man is Chambers? How can one have any respect for a man who admits that he didn't tell the whole story the first time he appeared before the Committee? My answer is not one in justification but in extenuation. Is it not better to tell the whole truth in the end than to refuse as Hiss did to tell the truth at all? Is it not better to be one who has been a Communist than one who may still be one? After all, Chambers could have kept silent like the rest. He would still have his job with *Time* and the conspiracy of which he was a member would have remained unexposed.

Before I read *Witness* I had formed some opinions of its author based upon my personal acquaintanceship with him. He was a brilliant man. He was a shy man. He was a deeply religious man. In his treatment of his wife, Esther, and his two fine children, John and Ellen, I observed that he, himself, exhibited those traits which he said Alger Hiss possessed, "a man of great simplicity and a great gentleness and sweetness of character." But above all, I was convinced that here was a man who showed the greatness that was in him by his willingness to risk his job, his reputation, even his liberty to right the wrong which he had done to his country, by exposing the conspiracy he helped to create.

My reading of *Witness* confirmed that judgment.

1953

The Infiltration of Harvard

The three following pieces of testimony belong to a section of the HUAC record headed "Communist Methods of Infiltration (Education)," and all three are about the "infiltration" of Harvard University, no less, in the late 1930s by a group of faculty members. Since all three of our witnesses are "friendly," it may be as well to mention that a fourth, Wendell Furry, was unfriendly. (Mr. Furry subsequently informed Harvard that he had been in the Party until 1947. His encounter with Senator McCarthy can be heard, in part, on a Broadside disc, BR 450, "Senator Joseph R. McCarthy.") Although in some ways the three pieces of testimony duplicate each other, the personalities of the three men are so very different that it was thought worthwhile to let each do his own job of self-presentation here. Granville Hicks is of interest to us, as he was to HUAC, as a Star: the Star Communist become Anti-Communist Star Witness. It is interesting that his most popular book had been *I Like America:* one only had to extract the dialectics from it and what remained was a fine piece of "Americanism" and could apply for the imprimatur of HUAC. For the watered-down "Communism" of the CPUSA in Hicks's day was indeed "Twentieth-Century Americanism," and, by the same token, any revolt against Marxism, on Hick's part, was unnecessary, if not impossible, since, though the chief theoretician of the Left in his day, he had been so little a Marxist in the first place. Daniel Boorstin also "likes America," insisting that it is no sick society we have here but a healthy one, founded on the rock of ages—God. It is important to see that the popular mythology spread by HUAC could with so little trouble be given "dignified" forms in the universities. Increasingly, during the fifties and sixties, that has been what the universities were for. And since the clientele of the universities is nonacademic, one can also point to the receptiveness of nonacademic people to these academic formulations. The relatively highbrow Hollywood director, Robert Rossen, had come before HUAC in 1951 as an only partially repentant Communist. According to his own account, he then spent two years "thinking," only to return in 1953 with these conclusions:

> I wouldn't like to see young people today believe what I believed in. I wouldn't like to have them feel there is no growth left in this country . . . that it's a dead society. . . . It's a young society, it's a growing society, it's a healthy society. It . . . can . . . realize its hope only in terms of the system of government that's been devised.

And:

> I don't think, after two years of thinking, that any one individual can indulge himself in the luxury of individual morality or pit it against what I feel today very strongly is the security and safety of this nation.

The second point had to do with any accusation that might be made against him as an informer. "I don't feel that I'm being a stool pigeon," he said a little later in the day, "or an informer . . . that is rather romantic—that is like children playing at cops and robbers." For the Committee had got him to name names, as they had Hicks, Boorstin, and Davis. Of these three, it was Davis, probably, who was most concerned with this particular matter. Reviewing James Burnham's *Web of Subversion* in 1954, he wrote: ". . . those most opposed to 'informers' are often intellectuals whose profession it is to inform and be informed, and who fight for freedom of inquiry in every direction but this."

Now those, through the centuries, who have indeed fought for freedom of inquiry would be quite surprised to learn that, under that heading, could come inquiry into the beliefs and associations of former comrades. That is a kind of inquiry we associate with J. Edgar Hoover rather than Socrates, Galileo, or Voltaire. It is true that the Communists were equally disingenuous on the subject, since they would not allow anyone the right to turn against them in good conscience: it must always be a betrayal and have venal or other base motives. Two wrongs, however, don't make a right. The Communists and the anti-Communists, high- or low-browed, in vying with each other in disingenuousness, combined to evade the truth of every subject they touched.

"I believe," said the once-Communist Hollywood director Frank Tuttle, "there is a traditional dislike among Americans for informers, and I am an informer. . . . The aggressors are ruthless, and I feel it is absolutely necessary for Americans to be equally ruthless."

Neither side wanted to go into what actually underlies this traditional dislike, not merely American, of informers. The Communists were saying, "You know we are right, so any informing you do is in bad faith." The anti-Communists were saying, "You'd inform the police about arsonists, so you should inform Hoover about these political arsonists." Whereas someone who felt the traditional dislike without feeling that the Communist Party could command his loyalty might well have reasoned: "Tuttle exaggerates the threat in order to avoid complexity. In fact, there is not a clear and present danger of the kind he envisages, and it is quite dubious whether such utter ruthlessness is simply imposed upon us without any question. Since I owe the CP no loyalty, it is obvious that I don't think the Communists are right on all this. It is not obvious, though, that I should therefore give any information I may have about Communists to their enemies. I do not wish to protect the CP, but I may properly wish to protect past and even present members of it. And I dislike informers because they are phony avenging angels, 'phony' because their motives are seldom free of personal malice and perhaps suprapersonal vindictiveness. Tuttle says he is willing to be ruthless because it is absolutely necessary. That is phony: the testimony of these Hollywood people was in fact extremely unnecessary. The FBI had the information, such as it was, already. No, not an urgent political necessity, but fear and/or the American overconcern for public relations, was what made people like Frank Tuttle tick. In these circumstances, is not the traditional dislike of informing a better guide than the various 'rational' arguments? We feel there is something slimy about informing. Because there is."

FEBRUARY 25, 1953:

Robert Gorham Davis

The Committee on Un-American Activities met at 10:35 a.m., in the caucus room, Old House Office Building, the Honorable Harold H. Velde (Chairman) presiding.

Committee members present: Representatives Harold H. Velde (Chairman), Bernard W. Kearney, Donald L. Jackson, Kit Clardy, Gordon H. Scherer, Francis E. Walter, Morgan M. Moulder, Clyde Doyle, and James B. Frazier, Jr.

Staff members present: Frank S. Tavenner, Jr., Committee Counsel; Thomas W. Beale, Sr., Chief Clerk; Louis J. Russell, Chief Investigator; Raphael I. Nixon, Director of Research; Donald T. Appell and Earl L. Fuoss, Investigators.

MR. VELDE: Mr. Davis, it is our understanding that you are a member of the teaching profession. In opening this hearing, it is well to make clear to you and others just what the nature of this investigation is. From time to time, the Committee has investigated Communists and Communist activities within the entertainment, newspaper, and labor fields, and also within the professions and the Government. In no instance has the work of the Committee taken on the character of an investigation of entertainment organizations, newspapers, labor unions, the professions, or the Government, as such, and it is not now the purpose of this Committee to investigate education or educational institutions, as such. The Committee will follow its long-established policy of investigating Communists and Communist activities wherever it has substantial evidence of its existence.

When investigating Communists and Communist activities within certain labor unions, the Committee was met with the charge by alarmists and partisans within that field that the Committee was a group of Fascists and the enemy of labor, and that the real purpose of the investigation was to destroy labor unions. Similar and equally unfounded charges have been made with regard to this hearing. In pursuing its work within the field of labor, the Committee carefully refrained from taking any part in any internal disputes within labor or any disputes between employers and employees and confined its activities to the ascertainment and identification of leaders in the labor unions who were members of the Communist Party and were using their influence to promote the objectives of the Communist Party within the field of labor, and to the character, extent, and objects of their Communist Party activities. The work of the Committee in this respect has met with such growing success that many labor unions are now actively engaged in eliminating from positions of influence union officials known to be members of the Communist Party and engaged in Communist activities.

The purpose of the Committee in investigating Communists and Communist activities within the field of education is no greater and no less than its purpose in investigating Communists and Communist activities within the field of labor or any other field.

The Committee is charged by the Congress with the responsibility of investigating the extent, character, and objects of un-American propaganda activities in the United States, the diffusion within the United States of subversive and un-American propaganda that is instigated from foreign countries or of a domestic origin and attacks the principle of the form of government as guaranteed by our Constitution and all other questions in relation thereto that would aid Congress in any necessary remedial legislation.

It has been fully established in testimony before Congressional Committees and before the courts of our land that the Communist Party of the United States is part of an international conspiracy which is being used as a tool or weapon by a foreign power to promote its own foreign policy and which has for its object the overthrow of the governments of all non-Communist countries, resorting to the use of force and violence, if necessary. This organization cannot live except by the promulgation and diffusion of subversive and un-American propaganda and in the view of this Committee every person who remains a member of it is contributing to the ultimate accomplishment of its objectives. Communism and Communist activities cannot be investigated in a vacuum. The investigation must, of necessity, relate to individuals and, therefore, this morning the Committee is calling you as a person known by this Committee to have been at one time a member of the Communist Party.

The question is sometimes asked whether it is necessary to call as witnesses those who are no longer members of the Communist Party. It is quite obvious for a number of reasons that the answer should be yes. Such witnesses add immeasurably to the sum total of the knowledge of the character, extent, and objects of Communist activities. The testimony of former Communist Party members resulted virtually in immobilizing the Communist Party in Hollywood. These witnesses considered it their patriotic duty to answer under oath questions relating to their knowledge of Communist infiltration into the organizations of which they had been members, and to their knowledge of other Communist Party activities. Witnesses from the Screen Writers Guild, the directors' guilds, labor unions, the legal profession, the medical profession, and other groups have made a great contribution to the defense of their country by disclosing to this Committee facts within their knowledge.

Former Communist Party membership, in the view of the Committee, should not be held against an individual whose testimony admitting former Communist Party membership has that character of trustworthiness which convinces one that he has completely and finally terminated his Communist Party membership and has been given in all good faith. It is of great aid in determining who remain in the Communist Party to ascertain who have left it.

The Committee was greatly concerned with the evidence developed in the Hollywood hearings with respect to the type of "thought control" practiced by the Communist Party upon its members. Screen writers were told how and what they should write. The testimony of Budd Schulberg and Edward Dmytryk demonstrate the point as clearly as laboratory experiments would prove a chemical reaction. The same influence was found to exist in the field of art and music. An objective study of this testimony will lead to the inescapable conclusion that it is the Communist Party which is the enemy of academic freedom.

The Committee is equally concerned with the opportunities that the Communist Party has to wield its influence upon members of the teaching profession and students through Communists who are members of the teaching profession. Therefore, the objective of this investigation is to ascertain the character, extent and objects of Communist Party activities when such activities are carried on by members of the teaching profession who are subject to the directives and discipline of the Communist Party.

MR. TAVENNER: Now, when and where were you born, Mr. Davis?

MR. DAVIS: In Cambridge, Massachusetts, June 8, 1908.

MR. TAVENNER: How are you now employed?

MR. DAVIS: I teach at Smith College.

MR. TAVENNER: Will you state to the Committee, please, what your educational training has been?

MR. DAVIS: I was educated in the public schools of Cambridge, went to Harvard as a scholarship student in the class of '29, received my master's degree in 1930, returned to Harvard for further graduate work in 1933.

MR. TAVENNER: How long did you remain at Harvard when you went there in 1933?

MR. DAVIS: I taught ten years, until 1943.

MR. TAVENNER: I want to ask you at this stage whether you object to the cameras, the photographs that are being taken, and I believe the movies which are being taken?

MR. DAVIS: No, I do not.

MR. TAVENNER: Will you state, please, what your employment has been since the completion of your education?

MR. DAVIS: I taught at Rensselaer Polytechnic Institute from 1930 to 1933, was an assistant at Harvard from 1933 to 1934, an instructor from 1934 to 1940, a faculty instructor from 1940 to 1943. I went to Smith as a visiting lecturer and was made an associate professor in 1945 and full professor in 1952.

MR. TAVENNER: Professor Davis, are you now a member of the Communist Party?

MR. DAVIS: I am not.

MR. TAVENNER: Have you ever been a member?

MR. DAVIS: Yes.

MR. TAVENNER: Will you tell the Committee, please, the circumstances under which you became a member, how long you remained a member, and the circumstances under which you left the Party?

MR. DAVIS: I joined the Communist Party in January of 1937. I left the Communist Party in the fall of 1939, after the pact between the Germans and the Russians.

MR. TAVENNER: Since 1939, have you consistently been an opponent of the Communist Party?

MR. DAVIS: I have.

MR. TAVENNER: Now will you state more in detail the circumstances under which you became a member of the Party?

MR. DAVIS: Well, I should say that, ideologically, there were three elements: First, the fact of the depression. To my generation it seemed intolerable that men should be unemployed, that food and cotton should be destroyed while people were hungry in a country as advanced technologically as the United States, and with such tremendous natural resources. We sought to understand the reason for the depression, for the waste of human and natural resources, and were led, because of the spirit of the thirties, to concern ourselves with the Marxist explanation. One reason why Marxism appealed to my generation is because we were products of the twenties, educationally—a period of uncertainty and skepticism. Marxism seemed to offer a positive solution, an affirmative philosophy. We also had been taught that the First World War accomplished nothing despite the four years of suffering and slaughter. We were determined that another fruitless war of that kind should not occur. Finally, we were very much aware of the growing menace of Hitlerism, and it seemed that Hitlerism could be stopped internationally, and what might turn into a Fascist movement in this country could be stopped only by organizing a very broad, united front—and this the Communist Party purported to do. This was the period of the movement for collective security in the League of Nations. This was also the period of the Spanish Civil War, when the democracies seemed to be fighting against the armed forces of Hitler and Mussolini in Spain. All these influences converging made me feel, before I went into the Party, that it was my idea to align myself with this leadership. I discovered, in the two years which followed, that I had made a mistake, but my break did not come finally until after the Hitler-Molotov pact which initiated the Second World War. I left then not only because the shift of the line led me into a position which was politically and morally intolerable, but also because I had had such experience of the intrigues and duplicity that are inseparable from Communist Party membership, that as a person of morality and sincerity I could remain in that position no longer. I not only broke with the Party, but, increasingly in the years that have followed, have felt it necessary to fight the influence of the Communist Party in those areas where I could be most effective.

MR. CLARDY: And you regard your appearance here today as falling in that category, I take it?

MR. DAVIS: Yes. It is an unpleasant duty, but one I feel I must accept.

MR. TAVENNER: Did you have the feeling during the period of your membership that the Communist Party was being used as a tool by a foreign power for the advancement of its own foreign policy?

MR. DAVIS: That was less clear at the time, because the Russian policy then—the policy of collective security to which I refer—seemed an effective policy against Fascism, and, therefore, not only did I accept it, but, as you know, many liberals and progressives were ready at that time to unite with the Communist Party because it did seem to be working for peace and against Fascism.

MR. TAVENNER: Did your view change as a result of subsequent events?

MR. DAVIS: Yes. The shift of policy after 1939 and the rapidity with which the Communist Party in this country fell in line with the Russian policy, even though they didn't understand it, made it quite clear that they were acting for the Soviet Union, that they were in a certain sense Soviet nationalists and not working for the broader interests of the American people.

MR. TAVENNER: What type of a group of Communists were you assigned to upon joining the Party?

MR. DAVIS: It was a very small group. I think the active members were no more than six or seven at that time and they comprised two or three persons connected with Harvard and some townspeople.

MR. TAVENNER: Was it the type of an organization which has been frequently referred to as a neighborhood group?

MR. DAVIS: No. I think it had a rather more special connection than that. I think most of the people in it were professionals.

MR. TAVENNER: How long did you remain a member of that particular group?

MR. DAVIS: That is the only group I ever belonged to, but it changed its character after a few months.

MR. TAVENNER: Will you explain that, please?

MR. DAVIS: Because of the temper of the time, more teachers were coming into the Communist Party and, therefore, the group was made exclusively a Harvard teachers' or graduate students' group.

MR. KEARNEY: How many members were in that group when you first joined?

MR. DAVIS: I remember at the first meeting I went to—it is a very dim image now, but as I say, I don't think there were more than seven or eight.

MR. KEARNEY: Did the membership increase as time went on?

MR. DAVIS: It increased, but I don't believe that it ever comprised more than fifteen.

MR. MOULDER: Did you join somewhere else or did you just join that group?

MR. DAVIS: What I did was talk to a person whom I assumed to be a Communist Party member, and he invited me to the meeting.

MR. TAVENNER: What was his name?

MR. DAVIS: I am not certain, at this distance, which of two persons it was.

MR. TAVENNER: Then I will ask you to give the names of both of them.

MR. DAVIS: Louis Harap.

MR. TAVENNER: If you know what his subsequent connection was with the Communist Party, I think you should tell us.

MR. DAVIS: I have no firsthand knowledge. I have read writing by him in recent years which would suggest that his tendency had remained the same.

MR. KEARNEY: Is he a professor at Harvard?

Mr. Davis: No, he was not. He was employed in a very minor capacity as librarian, I believe, of the philosophy library.

Mr. Kearney: Is he still connected in that position?

Mr. Davis: No. He left Harvard many years ago.

Mr. Kearney: Do you know what he is doing now?

Mr. Davis: I believe he is editor of a magazine.

Mr. Kearney: Do you know the name of the magazine?

Mr. Davis: It is the *Jewish Affairs,* I believe.

Mr. Tavenner: Now will you give us the name of the second person who may have been the person whom you first interviewed with regard to joining the Communist Party?

Mr. Davis: William Parry.

Mr. Tavenner: Do you know whether he remained in the Communist Party?

Mr. Davis: I have known nothing of him since, I believe, 1938.

Mr. Tavenner: Were you required to sign a card?

Mr. Davis: For the purpose of collecting dues, the treasurer of the unit had a group of booklets in which stamps were pasted to show that the dues had been paid.

Mr. Tavenner: Did that card have your name on it?

Mr. Davis: No. It had either initials or a pseudonym, and the initials were not actually the initials of the person.

Mr. Tavenner: Will you tell the Committee the reason for that?

Mr. Davis: Professional units were always protected so that there would be no publicity which would be harmful to the careers of the individual members.

Mr. Tavenner: By that you mean that your Communist Party membership was kept secret from the rank-and-file members of the Communist Party?

Mr. Davis: Yes. To a very large extent.

Mr. Tavenner: What was your pseudonym?

Mr. Davis: I don't remember, because we simply made up one as the books were issued and didn't use it in any other connection. It was purely an aid to memory, so to speak, when the dues were paid. The treasurer called out the names and the persons identified themselves.

Mr. Tavenner: Was the decision to have the names kept secret one of national policy of the Communist Party in such organizations as yours, or was it the result of a decision of your own group?

Mr. Davis: This was regular practice, I believe.

Mr. Tavenner: Do you recall the names of any Communist Party functionaries who relayed the directives from the Communist Party to your group?

Mr. Davis: Yes. There was a paid functionary named Hy Gordon. There also was a girl named Margot Clark.

MR. CLARDY: Was she a paid functionary also?

MR. DAVIS: No, I don't believe she was a paid functionary, but she went back and forth between this unit and the officials.

MR. TAVENNER: Do you recall how Margot Clark was employed at that time?

MR. DAVIS: Then or later she ran a bookshop near Harvard Square called something like the Progressive Bookshop.

MR. KEARNEY: Was your group ever addressed by high functionaries of the Communist Party?

MR. DAVIS: Yes. A man named Phil Frankfeld.

MR. WALTER: Where is he now, Mr. Tavenner?

MR. TAVENNER: He was recently convicted at Baltimore along with others for violation of the Smith Act.

MR. KEARNEY: I think he is serving sentence now.

MR. TAVENNER: Will you state how frequently the group met?

MR. DAVIS: During the academic year I think it was once a week.

MR. TAVENNER: Where were these meetings held?

MR. DAVIS: In the apartments of the members.

MR. TAVENNER: What was the nature of the business that was conducted at the meetings?

MR. DAVIS: It consisted of three activities: First, discussing the policies of organizations to which we belonged, like the Teachers' Union or the front organizations, and determining upon the role that the individual member should play in those organizations. Secondly, the question of Marxist education—organizing study groups to which teachers would be invited. And thirdly, various fund-raising activities for united-front organizations or for the Party itself.

MR. TAVENNER: Let us consider each of those functions. What was the policy of the Communist Party with reference to your activities in outside organizations?

MR. DAVIS: We were to assume positions of leadership so that their policies would be as close to the policies desired by the Communist Party as possible.

MR. TAVENNER: How was that information transmitted to you as to what organizations you were to infiltrate?

MR. DAVIS: I think it hardly needed to be transmitted, because our immediate concern was with the Teachers' Union and with organizations like the [American] League for Peace and Democracy.

MR. TAVENNER: It may be well at this point for you to give us the names of all the organizations which your cell or group of the Communist Party infiltrated or endeavored to infiltrate.

MR. DAVIS: The so-called front organizations change so rapidly that it is hard for me to remember them. But during the period in which I was active we were concerned predominantly with the Teachers' Union.

MR. TAVENNER: Was that merely a local union at Harvard, or was that a national union?

MR. DAVIS: It was the national union affiliated with the American Federation of Teachers, which belonged to the A.F. of L.

MR. TAVENNER: Do you recall what instructions were given you by the Communist Party with regard to that particular organization?

MR. DAVIS: I think we were left pretty much to ourselves, as far as the local organization is concerned, because we all read the Party press and were aware of what the general line was. We got the various publications of the Teachers' Union—

MR. KEARNEY: But isn't it also true that from time to time you received instructions from national headquarters on your procedure?

MR. DAVIS: Oh, yes. As I say, persons like Frankfeld sat in with us, but that was to educate us, because the Party felt we were liberals and progressives, and we were not thoroughly grounded enough—not thoroughly disciplined enough—so that, as I recall these conversations, they were of a fairly general nature, since the persons who came to visit us were not very well informed about the Teachers' Union itself.

MR. TAVENNER: You were familiar with the teachings of Lenin on the subject of the activity of teachers and what they should endeavor to do, I assume?

MR. DAVIS: I have seen a passage quoted often since. I don't recall it from those days.

MR. TAVENNER: I have before me volume 23 of Lenin and I find at page 499 this statement:

> But today the chief task of those members of the teaching profession who have taken their stand with the International and the Soviet Government is to work for the creation of a wider and, as nearly as possible, an all-embracing teachers' union.

MR. DAVIS: Yes. That is correct.

MR. TAVENNER: And again on page 500 there is this statement:

> Your union should now become a broad teachers' trade-union embracing vast numbers of teachers, a union which will resolutely take up its stand on the Soviet platform and the struggle for Socialism by means of a dictatorship of the proletariat.

What activity did your group engage in which might be said to have carried out the policy, as expressed by Lenin, of assisting in the organization of teachers' trade-union movement which would be adaptable to the purposes of the Soviet Union?

MR. DAVIS: We worked very hard to build up the Teachers' Union, and we did this with a comparatively clear conscience because our immediate objectives were to improve teaching conditions, raise salaries, and so on, but also obviously we wished teachers to take the same position that we took on public questions.

MR. TAVENNER: Was there a local of that organization at Harvard?

MR. DAVIS: Yes.

MR. TAVENNER: Did it have a name?

MR. DAVIS: It was called the Cambridge Union of University Teachers, as I recall.

MR. TAVENNER: Will you explain the manner in which the Communist members of your group functioned within your local Teachers' Union?

MR. DAVIS: We usually discussed, before a meeting, what policies we would urge at the meeting, and, whenever there were elections, we would decide in advance what candidates we would propose or support.

MR. TAVENNER: And the purpose of that was to make certain that the plans of your group were carried out because the vast majority of members of your local were non-Communist?

MR. DAVIS: Yes.

MR. TAVENNER: Did the group of Communists who were working within the Teachers' Union also sponsor the passage of resolutions which the Communist Party as a whole was interested in having endorsed or adopted by various groups?

MR. DAVIS: Yes.

MR. TAVENNER: Can you recall any specific instance?

MR. DAVIS: No, but they would have to do again with the national political situation at that time. The Communists supported the Roosevelt Administration until the Russian pact of 1939, and many of the measures which they supported were, I think, good measures—against anti-Semitism, against Fascism, for minority rights.

MR. TAVENNER: Did your group of Communist Party members endeavor to control the selection of delegates from the local Teachers' Union to national conventions?

MR. DAVIS: Yes.

MR. TAVENNER: And also to district conventions?

MR. DAVIS: Yes.

MR. TAVENNER: Of what district was the local at Harvard a member?

MR. DAVIS: The Massachusetts Teachers' Union—whatever its title was.

MR. CLARDY: Can I interject there? Were you successful in your efforts to obtain that control in the selection of delegates?

MR. DAVIS: During that period, yes.

MR. CLARDY: Was that because you had been a cohesive body, knew where you were going, and worked hard at it?

MR. DAVIS: And also because, as I say, the policies we supported were policies supported by many liberals and progressives at that time.

MR. CLARDY: And you had the support of many other people who would probably have rebelled at Communism as a word or party?

MR. DAVIS: I am not even sure the last is true, because many were willing to work with Communists in the united front at that time.

MR. SCHERER: I believe you said, Professor, that the party at that time opposed anti-Semitism?

MR. DAVIS: Yes.

MR. SCHERER: Today, of course, you know it is as anti-Semitic as the Nazi Party?

MR. DAVIS: Yes. That's why I was particularly interested in the position of Louis Harap.

MR. CLARDY: I don't follow you there.

MR. DAVIS: Because, as editor of *Jewish Affairs,* I believe, he is now defending the Prague trials, contending that they are not anti-Semitic.

MR. TAVENNER: Now, will you proceed, please, to describe the method by which you endeavored to control the selection of delegates to the district and national convention of the Teachers' Union?

MR. DAVIS: One reason why Communists were successful was because in these organizations all service was voluntary. The teachers were very busy. Trips were expensive, and if a member of the Communist Party offered to go his offer was usually accepted.

MR. CLARDY: Witness, are you sufficiently acquainted with the facts as of today to tell us whether or not the same techniques are being followed today?

MR. DAVIS: Yes, except that the situation probably requires much more secrecy. These activities were comparatively open at that time.

MR. CLARDY: You think there is more of an underground now than there was at that time?

MR. DAVIS: Yes, and a much smaller one. And I should like to interject at this point the fact that, at the present time among teachers, the influence of Communists is very slight because the times have changed and because the teachers have been so shocked by the events in the Soviet Union in the last eight years. And among students at colleges like Smith any evidence of radical activity has disappeared entirely.

MR. CLARDY: Would you say the things you and others like you have been doing to combat the Communist influence may have had something to do with making it more difficult for the Communists to get along?

MR. DAVIS: A little, I hope, but mostly it is a matter of world events—the Korean War, the purge trials in the Soviet Union, and the inhumanities practiced by Communist regimes. It's very hard for anyone to defend those today.

MR. TAVENNER: Would you also say that knowledge of the manner in which the Communist Party endeavors to exert influence, and particularly their views as to academic freedom, have awakened the teachers and students to the dangers of Communism?

MR. DAVIS: Yes. I think those who entered the Communist Party for democratic and progressive reasons discovered that the activities of the Party were inconsistent with democracy and progressivism and left, and I think those who left have had a much greater insight into the dangers of Communism, both intellectually and politically, than they otherwise would have had. They've salvaged that at least from the experience.

MR. CLARDY: You wouldn't say the job of cleansing the temple has been finished, though, would you?

MR. DAVIS: No, but I am speaking now of general influence among teachers and students. The open influence is very slight now.

MR. VELDE: You mentioned something a while ago about the control the Communist Party has over the thinking of teachers.

MR. DAVIS: So far as my own experience goes, there was no direct attempt to influence teaching. There was never, in the unit to which I belonged, any discussion of what we did in class. It was always an indirect influence through Marxist-Communist political education.

MR. VELDE: Do you think a Communist Party member can have a free and open mind, especially in teaching in a classroom, even though he was given no instruction by the Communist Party as to what he should teach?

MR. DAVIS: It depends on his subject. I should think a teacher of music or mathematics might teach in a way that was quite unaffected by his political theories. In the political sciences, and even in the humanities, I doubt if this can be so, and I myself now feel that no one who is genuinely humane could be a defender of what goes on now in the Soviet Union and the Communist countries.

MR. VELDE: Then, within the classroom, it is possible, in your opinion, that a Communist can teach without instilling Communist philosophies in students, providing he taught the proper subjects. Now, how about his influences outside the classroom on our thinking?

MR. DAVIS: There he's likely to have more influence. This often, too, will be indirect, because of his influence on other faculty members, because of the talks he gives at public meetings. It's not been my experience that Communists, partly for reasons of security, try to indoctrinate students.

MR. VELDE: I would like to state, for the benefit of the public press that the fact that the testimony involves a Communist cell at Harvard is no reason that inferences should be drawn that we are investigating Communist activities only at Harvard University or that these activities are any more serious at Harvard than at any other of our great universities.

MR. KEARNEY: Professor Davis, a few days ago, in the newspapers, there was a hue and cry raised by certain educators throughout the country protesting against the investigation of Communists in the colleges. Do you believe that this Committee should proceed in exposing Communists in the colleges?

MR. DAVIS: I think that the Government should explore and expose the ramifications of the Communist Party, but I think this has to be done with great caution, by persons who are politically informed. I think that the testimony should be cautious testimony that would stand up in court. I think any loose charges, particularly a loose use of the word "Communist" or "Red" applied to teachers who are speaking their honest convictions, can be extremely harmful. I think it's entirely a question, therefore, of the manner in which this is done, the scrupulousness.

MR. KEARNEY: With that I heartily agree with you. But at the same time do you see any objection to the investigation of Communists and Communism in labor unions, in other phases of our national life?

MR. DAVIS: No. I do feel it necessary to have all possible information about the activities of the Communist Party itself for security reasons.

MR. CLARDY: If we treat the other witnesses as you have been treated thus far, would you not say we are conducting it fairly and as you would like it?

MR. DAVIS: So far, yes.

MR. SCHERER: Do you feel that your experience today here has interfered in any way with your academic freedom or the academic freedom of any professor at Smith College?

MR. DAVIS: That I will learn in the weeks to come.

MR. DOYLE: You came [here] as a result of being subpoenaed?

MR. DAVIS: Yes.

MR. DOYLE: Would you have felt it your duty to contact this Committee or any other governmental agency and reveal anything which you have today revealed if you hadn't been subpoenaed?

MR. DAVIS: I did not do so because I had reason to suppose that the facts were available to the Government agencies.

MR. TAVENNER: An investigator of this Committee came to see you before any subpoena had been issued?

MR. DAVIS: At the time of the issuing of the subpoena. It was not presented until after he talked to me.

MR. TAVENNER: So that the information you have given the Committee was given actually before any subpoena was served on you?

MR. DAVIS: Yes.

MR. TAVENNER: You indicated that the members of your group did not make an effort to recruit students into the Communist Party?

MR. DAVIS: The effort was to recruit faculty members.

MR. TAVENNER: Why?

MR. DAVIS: I think there were a variety of reasons, but the first one is that it would have been much too risky, as students join something and leave it, and they talk freely, and it would have led to the exposure of the individual members. But I also think, as I say, that the group at Harvard were at heart democrats, liberals, progressives. I think they disliked using any pressure they might have on individual students, even though this seems inconsistent with their policy and position as Communists.

MR. TAVENNER: Was it common knowledge at Harvard that a Communist Party cell existed among the faculty members?

MR. DAVIS: Yes, among liberals close to those who were Party members.

MR. TAVENNER: Well, that fact in itself would have been an inducement to members of the student body to unite in some group of their own, such as the Young Communist League, would it not?

MR. DAVIS: It might be an influencing factor, but there were so many other factors in that time. The students were even more politically conscious than the instructors, and there were all sorts of organizations for them which were directed from above, quite independently of this group. Even if the group hadn't existed, I think student organizations would have taken very much the same character.

MR. TAVENNER: I would like to turn now to the national conventions of the Teachers' Union.

MR. WALTER: Where were they held? You testified one was held in Buffalo. Where was the other convention?

MR. DAVIS: In a place in Ohio, on a lake.

MR. TAVENNER: How many of your associates from Harvard attended that convention with you?

MR. DAVIS: I remember only one other person.

MR. TAVENNER: What was his name?

MR. DAVIS: Let me preface the naming of names by expressing my extreme concern over the necessity of naming names—not because I don't agree with what I said earlier about the necessity of studying the ramifications of the Communist Party but because these events occurred from twelve to fifteen years ago. I knew many teachers in many different connections, professional and personal, and I have moments of doubt even among —about—those whom I assumed I knew best in these connections. But do you still wish me—

MR. TAVENNER: I do not want you to state in open session the name of any person as to whom you are in doubt as to membership. As to who it was that attended this Teachers' Union convention with you who was a member of the Communist Party with you at Harvard—

MR. DAVIS: Yes. That is why I hesitated.

MR. JACKSON: Is the doubt in your mind, Professor, as to whether or not this individual was a member of the Communist Party?

MR. DAVIS: One of the persons I have in mind was a member of the

Communist Party, yes, but I am not certain he is the one who went to the convention.

MR. VELDE: Well, will you state the name of that person and how you know he was a member of the Communist Party without reference to the convention?

MR. DOYLE: I want to compliment the witness on being extremely careful. I want to compliment our counsel on the statement he made. If there is any reasonable doubt in your mind as to whether or not this person, or any person about whom you are testifying, is a Communist, I don't want you to give the name.

MR. VELDE: I would like to concur, Mr. Doyle, and should any person be mentioned in public hearing, and that person feels that he would like to come forward and talk to the Committee counsel, he is certainly welcome to do so.

MR. TAVENNER: Mr. Chairman, I had planned, before the testimony is completed, to give him an opportunity to state who were associated with him in this work. I don't know whether it can be done very well by just asking him one particular name at a time.

MR. VELDE: All right, I will withdraw the question.

MR. TAVENNER: Now, will you describe the action that was taken in the caucus that you referred to?

MR. DAVIS: I remember more clearly a caucus which I attended in New York during the academic year and not at a time of convention. This was a caucus of representatives from different parts of the country. It was addressed by Jack Stachel.

MR. TAVENNER: What was Jack Stachel's position in the Communist Party?

MR. DAVIS: He was a high official of some kind.

MR. TAVENNER: He is one of those who was convicted in the first trial of the Communists in New York—

MR. DAVIS: Yes, under—

MR. TAVENNER: Under the Smith Act, was it not?

MR. DAVIS: Yes.

MR. TAVENNER: Was Samuel Sillen at that meeting?

MR. DAVIS: Not at the caucus in New York, but I met him at the Communist caucus at one of the two meetings of the American Federation of Teachers I attended.

MR. TAVENNER: Do you know whether he held any position within the Communist Party at that time?

MR. DAVIS: No, I know only he was a delegate to the convention, that he also was a Communist.

MR. VELDE: Is he an editor of *Masses and Mainstream* at present time, Mr. Davis?

MR. DAVIS: I think so, yes.

MR. TAVENNER: Now, can you recall the names of any other functionaries of the Communist Party who were present at that caucus which was addressed by Jack Stachel—

MR. DAVIS: Charles Hendley was present. He was at that time head of the New York local of the American Federation of Teachers.

MR. TAVENNER: Will you give us the names of others?

MR. DAVIS: I think Bella Dodd was present on that occasion.

MR. TAVENNER: Did she later become a member of the National Committee of the Communist Party?

MR. DAVIS: I believe so.

MR. TAVENNER: And she has now withdrawn from the Communist Party?

MR. DAVIS: Yes, she has testified in New York.

* * *

MR. TAVENNER: Well, let us turn now, then, to the second division of the activities of your group, that is, the conduct of Marxist study groups.

MR. DAVIS: It was fairly easy to form them because there was lively interest in Marxism, and though I think persons joining these groups had some idea that the instructors were close to the Communist Party they, nevertheless, were ready to discuss Marxism with them, and in some cases the persons whom the Party secured were not Party members but were intellectual social scientists who knew a good deal about Marxism and were willing to discuss it.

MR. TAVENNER: And what was the Communist Party purpose in establishing these Marxist groups?

MR. DAVIS: They had a double purpose: First, to disseminate Marxism, which is one of their important principles always and everywhere. And it was a very good way of recruiting members into the Communist Party.

MR. TAVENNER: Do you recall any instances in which members of the faculty at Harvard were recruited to the Communist Party through the Marxist group studies?

MR. DAVIS: I can't recall the names, because I don't remember now by what process the various parties came into the Party, but I am sure it was effective in two or three cases at least.

MR. TAVENNER: Would you describe it as an effective means of recruiting persons into the Communist Party?

MR. DAVIS: Extremely effective, yes, because intellectuals ordinarily joined for theoretic or intellectual reasons.

MR. TAVENNER: Were those study groups provided in any manner by functionaries of the Communist Party on a higher level?

MR. DAVIS: Not directly, no. They encouraged the formation of them, but they left this to the members of the teachers' group, who were better able to present it to other teachers.

MR. TAVENNER: Did these study groups include the issuance of Communist Party literature to the individuals and the requirements of study of particular documents and books in which the Communist Party was interested at the time?

MR. DAVIS: Yes, but primarily these were the classics—Marx's *Das Kapital,* the works of Engels, and so on.

MR. TAVENNER: The Communist Manifesto—

MR. DAVIS: Yes.

MR. TAVENNER: —I assume was one. *State and Revolution*?

MR. DAVIS: Yes.

MR. TAVENNER: *Left-Wing Communism*?

MR. DAVIS: I don't know that they were—that they would deal with quite so sectarian a work with a broad group.

MR. TAVENNER: *History of the Communist Party of the Soviet Union*?

MR. DAVIS: No, that again was a little too immediately a Party document and might alienate intellectuals. We were, however, instructed to distribute that book as widely as possible.

MR. TAVENNER: But the group thought it was a little dangerous to do so until the person invited in had become well indoctrinated in Marxian theory?

MR. DAVIS: Yes, that is right.

MR. TAVENNER: Did you read and study any of the works of Foster?

MR. DAVIS: Foster?

MR. TAVENNER: Yes, the head of the Communist Party of the United States.

MR. DAVIS: Not systematically.

MR. TAVENNER: I want to read you a paragraph from *Towards Soviet America* by William Z. Foster, printed in 1932, relating to the subject of education. I quote as follows:

> Among the elementary measures the American Soviet government will adopt to further the culture revolution are the following:
>
> The schools, colleges, and universities will be coordinated and grouped under the National Department of Education and its state and local branches.
>
> The studies will be revolutionized, being cleansed of religious, patriotic, and other features of the bourgeois ideology.
>
> The students will be taught on the basis of Marxian dialectical materialism, internationalism, and the general ethics of the new Socialist society.
>
> Present obsolete methods of teaching will be superseded by a scientific pedagogy.
>
> Religious schools will be abolished.

Do you recall?

MR. DAVIS: No. This is the pattern, however, that had been followed in Communist countries, and one could assume it would be followed if a Communist government came into power in the United States, but the Communist line had shifted somewhat in the later 1930s—that was the period when Browder's slogan "Communism Is Twentieth-Century Americanism" was being used—and again the Communists were reluctant to offend those they might bring into the broad united front, and they used a somewhat subtler approach.

MR. TAVENNER: And let me read you an excerpt from the *Communist* of May 1937, entitled "The Schools and the People's Front," by Richard Frank. Richard Frank was a member of the Education Commission of the Young Communist League. He had this to say:

> The task of the Communist Party must be, first and foremost, to arouse the teachers to class consciousness and to organize them into the American Federation of Teachers, which is the main current of the American labor movement.
>
> In the effort to organize the teachers, every care must be taken to bring together in united front actions all existing teacher organizations. Especial attention must be paid to secure such action with the American Association of University Professors, the National Educational Association, and the Guild. Our party members in these organizations must work actively toward this end.

Well, did your experience indicate that the Communist Party members in those organizations were working—

MR. DAVIS: What you just read was consistent with my experience of what occurred in the Teachers' Union.

MR. TAVENNER: * * * Now, it appears from that the Communist Party had for its objective the influencing of students without the student realizing or knowing that the teacher was, in fact, a Communist Party member. Did you recognize that that was the purpose and the objective of the Communist Party?

MR. DAVIS: That was quite clear from the publications of the American Federation of Teachers intended for the teachers in the public schools.

MR. TAVENNER: Did any of your students at any time suggest to you that they had concluded that you were a member of the Communist Party?

MR. DAVIS: No. As I told the investigator, quite the contrary happened. The year when I was most active as a member of the Communist Party—and it was also a year in which the students were also conscious politically—a politically conscious student came up to me at the end of the year and said he had been trying to figure all year just what my position was. And I think all of us who were at Harvard who were liberals had a somewhat ambiguous attitude toward this. We did want to influence our equals intellectually, but we had a lurking feeling that it wasn't quite good sportsmanship to try to influence young people—at least to make use of our position in the classroom to do this. It seems inconsistent. But I think the evidence of others in that same group will be of the same character.

MR. TAVENNER: Well, I am very glad to know you had that feeling about it, but how can you be certain that all had that feeling?

MR. DAVIS: Oh, I can't. I am speaking now only of the group of people in the unit at Harvard, most of whom broke with the Communist Party shortly afterward, because they were not indoctrinated Communists.

MR. TAVENNER: It is true, however, the opportunity for such influencing existed?

MR. DAVIS: It had.

MR. TAVENNER: And it is merely a matter as to whether the Communist Party took advantage of it?

MR. DAVIS: And I am quite sure, in many places, teachers did take advantage of it.

MR. TAVENNER: Continuing to read from the article mentioned: "To enable the teachers in the party to do the latter—" And by "latter" is meant the teaching of the working class—

> the party must take careful steps to see that all teacher comrades are given thorough education in the teachings of Marxism and Leninism.
>
> Only when teachers have really mastered Marxism and Leninism will they be able skillfully to inject it into their teaching at the least risk of exposure and at the same time to conduct struggles around the schools in a truly Bolshevik manner.
>
> Such teachers can also be used to advantage to conduct classes in Marxism-Leninism, for workers generally, and many such teachers should be assigned, not to school units, but to factory or industrial units where they can have great aid in party education in helping with leaflets, shock papers, and so forth. Others can play an important role in the educational activities of the Young Communist League.

Now, do you know, from your experience, whether any members of your group taught Marxist-Lenin classes in industry or in any group outside of the faculty at Harvard?

MR. DAVIS: Yes, I think they certainly did go to lecture to groups in various outlying suburbs.

MR. TAVENNER: Now, can you be more definite as to the places at which some classes were conducted?

MR. DAVIS: No, I can name only the towns.

* * *

MR. TAVENNER: Now, do you recall that your group engaged in the preparation of any pamphlets for use by the Communist Party?

MR. DAVIS: Yes, Granville Hicks and I collaborated on a pamphlet against anti-Semitism.

MR. TAVENNER: Was Granville Hicks a member of your group?

MR. DAVIS: For one year, yes.

MR. TAVENNER: I should state, Mr. Chairman, that Mr. Granville Hicks has cooperated with the investigators of the Committee and we are expecting his full cooperation. According to our investigation, he withdrew from the Communist Party at approximately the same time that the witness did and he's been active in his opposition to the Communist Party ever since.

MR. VELDE: I take it, Mr. Davis, that you also have been active against Communism since your withdrawal?

MR. DAVIS: Yes, I have some quotations from my published writings here, if anyone wishes to see them.

MR. TAVENNER: I am going to ask you about that in a few minutes. Now, did you submit the material which you were proposing to use in the pamphlet—that is, you and Mr. Granville Hicks—to any functionary of the Communist Party for review?

MR. DAVIS: Yes, Phil Frankfeld went over it with great care and attention.

MR. TAVENNER: Do you know whether Phil Frankfeld was capable of giving it the criticism that was given it or whether he, in turn, transmitted the material to some higher functionary such as V. J. Jerome, who was the cultural head of the Communist Party?

MR. DAVIS: He may have but I don't think this was important enough.

MR. TAVENNER: Did you have a memorandum in relation to that matter?

MR. DAVIS: Yes, I submitted—

MR. TAVENNER: I hand you a document, which I will ask be marked "Davis Exhibit 1" for identification only, and ask you whether or not that is the document to which you refer.

MR. DAVIS: It is.

MR. TAVENNER: Now, I desire, Mr. Chairman, to read this comment in evidence because it points out the approach of the Communist functionary not only to the particular subject under consideration but to writings generally.

Comment

Excellent material; the historical material and quotations are well selected and introduced.

The conclusions are not sharply drawn. The argumentation remains somewhat suspended in the air.

There is completely defensive argumentation on the question of the Jews and communism. There must be a straightforward presentation of the right of Jews to be revolutionists. The argument of the pamphlet follows almost exactly that of the American Jewish Congress.

The point should be introduced about the support given by the rich Jews to Hitler in his first stages of development. The poor Jews supported the Communist Party. There is no sufficiently sharp line drawn between the rich Jews and the poor Jews. A good illustration of this point would be the Boston garment workers' strike of 1936 when the Jewish bosses called out the Irish cops to club Jewish and Italian workers indiscriminately.

More facts should be introduced about numbers of Jews on relief, and so forth.

There is very little appeal made to the Protestants; also, the section on the Catholics should be strengthened.

At the close, introduce the relationship of anti-Semitism and the American reaction today. Illustrate the use of anti-Semitism against even Roosevelt, against [Herbert H.] Lehman in the recent election campaign. Point out that the only answer of Jews to [Father Charles E.] Coughlin must be to identify themselves more and more with the progressive camp, against reaction and Red-baiting, for the building of a strong peace movement, which is, itself, the struggle against fascism and anti-Semitism. Raise the question of the unity of the labor movement and building it, the support for social and labor legislation as the truest basis for democracy and the elimination of the basis for anti-Semitism.

MR. JACKSON: Is this the critique by Frankfeld on the work you had done, Mr. Davis?

MR. DAVIS: Yes, the rough draft of the pamphlet.

MR. JACKSON: Were those suggested changes incorporated in final draft?

MR. DAVIS: I believe so.

* * *

MR. TAVENNER: Now, let us go to the third and last division of the activities of your group—fund-raising.

MR. DAVIS: The Party was extremely greedy for money. Not only did we pay quite large dues, but extra donations or assessments were constantly being made. All sorts of means were being used to raise money, by having parties, dances, lectures, and so on. This was a very large part of our activity.

MR. TAVENNER: What were the dues that you paid?

MR. DAVIS: As I recall correctly, they were five per cent of one's salary.

MR. TAVENNER: Why, they charged you more than they did the directors in Hollywood! It was only four per cent there.

MR. CLARDY: The directors' salaries were slightly larger than yours, weren't they?

MR. DAVIS: Yes.

MR. TAVENNER: Then, were special assessments made for particular projects of the Communist Party?

MR. DAVIS: Constantly. It was always represented that the *Daily Worker* or some other magazine was in a state of emergency and that extra efforts must be made to obtain money.

MR. TAVENNER: Well, who was the contact with your committee on matters of that kind?

MR. DAVIS: Whoever was moving between us and the central office of the Party—people like the ones I mentioned this morning, such as Hy Gordon or Margot Clark. Then, also, we raised money for Spain, but a good deal of that, I suspect, went actually to the Party, not to Spain. I didn't know at that time. It was just as a result of subsequent revelations.

* * *

MR. TAVENNER: And I should ask you at this time, if you know of your own knowledge that any of these persons have since terminated their affiliations with the Communist Party, that you should state so. Daniel J. Boorstin?

MR. DAVIS: He was a member, but I know he has broken long since.

MR. TAVENNER: And, Mr. Chairman, Dr. Boorstin, according to our investigation, did withdraw many years ago from the Communist Party and has cooperated, and is cooperating, with this Committee in giving it the benefit of information he has and, like this witness, has been an outstanding opponent of Communism since taking that action. Richard Schlatter?

MR. DAVIS: Yes, he was also a member.

MR. TAVENNER: And what I had to say about Mr. Boorstin stands equally for Richard Schlatter. Were you acquainted with Richard Goodwin?

MR. DAVIS: Yes, he also was a member of the group of the Communist Party.

MR. TAVENNER: Do you have any information as to whether or not he has withdrawn from the Communist Party?

MR. DAVIS: I don't know directly, but all impressions I've gathered would lead me to suppose so.

MR. TAVENNER: Were you acquainted with a person by the name of George Mayberry?

MR. DAVIS: Yes, he was a member of the group.

MR. TAVENNER: Are you acquainted with Israel Halperin?

MR. DAVIS: I am. Yes, I was. He was a member of the group.

MR. TAVENNER: Was there anything outstanding or unusual about his contribution to the work of the Communist Party in your group, while you were a member?

MR. DAVIS: No, I don't recall any. I remember him very well. I know he was interested in the foundation of the magazine *Science and Society* but was also very critical of the editors of it.

MR. TAVENNER: Do you know where he is now?

MR. DAVIS: I know of his subsequent history from the accounts of the Canadian spy investigations. I know he was involved in that case but not convicted.

MR. TAVENNER: Herbert Robbins?

MR. DAVIS: He was a member the first year I belonged. He left Harvard the second year. I have every reason to believe, on the basis of a long conversation with him three years ago, that he broke perhaps before I did.

MR. TAVENNER: Were you acquainted with Rubby Sherr?

MR. DAVIS: Yes, he was a member of the group for a comparatively short time, but I think he was still a member when I left.

MR. TAVENNER: Or Wendell Furry?

MR. DAVIS: I knew him very well. He was a member of the group.

* * *

MR. TAVENNER: What has been the nature of your work against the Communist Party?

MR. DAVIS: It's been partly organizational, but mostly literary. I resigned in protest from the League of American Writers early in 1940 because of their attitude toward Hitler and the war. When I went to Smith I joined the Teachers' Union and struggled against the group there, led by Dorothy Douglas and Katherine Lumpkin, but the union took an increasingly Wallaceite position in the later forties, and I resigned from the union in protest in 1948. I was one of the eighty-eight intellectuals who signed the statement published in the *New York Times* on March 24, 1949, calling attention to the true nature of the Waldorf Scientific and Cultural Conference. I have been from the beginning a member of the Committee for Cultural Freedom, headed by Sidney Hook, and have contributed to *Partisan Review, Commentary,* and the *New Leader,* all magazines which have for years fought Stalinism. I have written for the *New York Times* regularly. I wrote, for *Commentary* in May 1951, an article showing the relationship between Soviet psychiatry and the destruction of the individual. May I read three sentences from that?

MR. TAVENNER: Yes, sir.

MR. DAVIS: There is a book by Dr. Wortis called *Soviet Psychiatry,* and I say:

> But what Dr. Wortis' book emphatically demonstrates—if it needed demonstrating—is the iron logic behind Communism's utter extinction of the individual self. This logic is orthodox in theory—it is explicit in Marx, Engels, and Lenin—and it has been appallingly proved and demonstrated in practice. The confessions of opponents of the regime at Communist trials show that by "immediate pressure of the environment," by torture, narcosis, hypnosis, and indoctrination in various combinations, the self's organic past can actually be negated, and that it can be made to "reflect" completely the party-partisan view of reality. Since those who do not come to reflect this reality are considered ultimate enemies of the people, there is no moral limit to the use which may be made of these psychological, physical, and medical means of extinguishing the self.

And then I say at the end of the article:

> A genuine struggle against Russian antihumanism should require our putting as much effort as we possibly can into discovering what social and political grounds still exist—or can be made to exist—in our contemporary society for the survival of what David Riesman calls the autonomous individual.

MR. TAVENNER: Mr. Chairman, I think that is all I desire to ask, unless the witness has something else to add?

MR. DAVIS: I think such investigations are necessary if they are carried out fairly and scrupulously. All I am afraid of is that so much political energy may be directed toward a preoccupation with the past that we may not have enough left to find creative solutions for problems that face us in the future. I think, for instance, that it's right to go back into the history of China and find out why that disaster occurred, and whether it occurred as the result of espionage, of improper influence by Communists within the Government, but we want to be sure that this will help us to solve the problems of India and Africa, for instance. It's not enough to discover what went wrong in China. We've got to keep the same thing from happening in other parts of the world, and it is this danger with which I, myself, am preoccupied at the present time.

MR. CLARDY: You mean we should profit from our past mistakes?

MR. DAVIS: We've got to profit from our experience and not let India, Africa, and Europe go as China went.

* * *

MR. CLARDY: You gave me an interim answer which got a little laughter earlier when I suggested you tell us whether our conduct was such that you approved. You said it had been, up to that time. Do I understand that you now are willing to say that you do think the manner in which we have conducted this is wholesome and good?

MR. DAVIS: Yes, I am entirely willing to say that.

* * *

MR. DOYLE: Professor Davis, I wrote down here that you used this language: "I feel that being here today is an unpleasant duty, but one I must accept." Why did you feel you must accept it? What compelled you to come in and cooperate with this Committee instead of pleading the First or Fifth Amendment or something?

MR. DAVIS: I broke with the Communist Party thirteen years ago because I could not stand the dishonesty and equivocation that were inseparable from being a member of the Party, expressing one's doubts, pretending to other people a certainty which one really did not feel. I felt I would have spoken out at any time in these fifteen years, but since I was summoned now, I was glad to use this opportunity to clear the record and say what I believed.

MR. DOYLE: Well, why don't more men of your mental capacity feel the same way and come forward and testify as you have?

MR. DAVIS: Prejudice has been built up over the years, partly by the Communists themselves, but also for reasons that are quite understandable to anyone who has to see the operations of an honor system in colleges, a prejudice against informing. I think the American people generally dislike informers.

FEBRUARY 26, 1953:

Daniel J. Boorstin

The Committee on Un-American Activities met at 9:35 a.m., in the caucus room, Old House Office Building, The Honorable Harold H. Velde, Chairman, presiding.

Committee members present: Representatives Harold H. Velde (Chairman), Bernard W. Kearney, Kit Clardy, Gordon H. Scherer, Francis E. Walter (appearance noted in hearing), Morgan M. Moulder, Clyde Doyle, and James B. Frazier, Jr. (appearance noted in hearing).

Staff members present: Frank S. Tavenner, Jr., Committee Counsel; Thomas W. Beale, Sr., Chief Clerk, Louis J. Russell, Chief Investigator; Raphael I. Nixon, Director of Research; Donald T. Appell and Earl L. Fuoss, Investigators.

MR. VELDE: The Committee will come to order. Let the record show that present are Messrs. Kearney, Clardy, Scherer, Foyle, Moulder, and the Chairman.

MR. TAVENNER: What is your name, please, sir?

MR. BOORSTIN: Daniel J. Boorstin.

MR. TAVENNER: When and where were you born?

MR. BOORSTIN: Atlanta, Georgia, October 1, 1914.

MR. TAVENNER: What is your present occupation?

MR. BOORSTIN: University professor.

MR. TAVENNER: At what institution?

MR. BOORSTIN: University of Chicago.

MR. TAVENNER: Will you give the Committee, please, a brief summary of your educational preparation?

MR. BOORSTIN: I was graduated from Harvard College with a B.A. degree in 1934; received the A.B. degree from Oxford University, England, in 1936; and a B.C.L. degree from Oxford University in 1937; the J.S.D. degree from Yale University in 1941.

MR. TAVENNER: Will you outline for the Committee, please, what your record of employment has been since the completion of your education?

MR. BOORSTIN: I was first employed by Harvard College as an instructor and tutor in history and literature in 1938. I was employed by Harvard College in 1942, during which time I taught briefly at Radcliffe College and the Harvard Law School. For several months during 1942—during the summer of 1942—I was employed on the legal staff of the Lend-Lease Administration. From 1942—from the fall of 1942—until the summer of 1944 I was employed as assistant professor of history at Swarthmore College, Swarthmore, Pennsylvania. Since the fall of 1944 I have been employed by the University of Chicago—first as visiting assistant professor of legal history, later as assistant professor of American civilization, and now as associate professor of American history.

MR. TAVENNER: Doctor, are you now a member of the Communist Party?

MR. BOORSTIN: No, sir.

MR. TAVENNER: Have you at any time been a member of the Communist Party?

MR. BOORSTIN: Yes, sir.

MR. TAVENNER: When and over what period of time were you a member of the Party?

MR. VELDE: Just a minute. Do you have any objection to being photographed by the newsreels?

MR. BOORSTIN: No, sir.

MR. TAVENNER: My question was, When and over what period of time were you a member of the Communist Party?

MR. BOORSTIN: For a period of something less than a year, terminating approximately in September 1939. That is about fourteen years ago that my association ceased.

MR. TAVENNER: Are you speaking now of the Communist Party of the United States?

MR. BOORSTIN: Yes, sir. Previous to that time I had been a member of a Marxist study group at Oxford University for about a year.

MR. KEARNEY: Were you a member of the Party at that time?

MR. BOORSTIN: It was about between fourteen and sixteen years ago, and it was not an important episode in my life in the sense that I had any position of leadership, or anything of that kind. It is very difficult for me to recall the precise nature of that group at Oxford. It may have been an affiliate of the Young Communist organization of England. It may not have been so. I don't recall clearly.

MR. TAVENNER: Have you been in opposition to the Communist Party since the time you withdrew in 1939?

MR. BOORSTIN: Yes, sir.

MR. TAVENNER: I would like for you to go back to the first connection that you had with the Communist Party, or a Communist Party group, and advise the Committee just the circumstances under which you were recruited into the group. I think you should begin with your experience at Oxford as a Rhodes scholar.

MR. BOORSTIN: I don't remember whether anyone ever tried to recruit me into that group. As best as I can remember, I was a member of the group and the precise details of how I ever got into the study group are difficult to recall in detail.

MR. TAVENNER: Did you pay dues in this group?

MR. BOORSTIN: I don't even remember that. I think I may have.

MR. TAVENNER: Were you issued a membership card of any description?

MR. BOORSTIN: I have a vague recollection of having signed a card of some kind.

MR. TAVENNER: Did you sign it with your own name or were pseudonyms used?

MR. BOORSTIN: As best as I can recall, it was with my proper name.

MR. TAVENNER: How many people were in the group?

MR. BOORSTIN: I don't remember exactly. In fact, it is hard for me to recall what the nature of its activities were. I would guess there might have been a hundred or so students—Oxford students—in the group together.

* * *

MR. CLARDY: Why don't we just ask him to tell us how they went about studying Marxism?

MR. BOORSTIN: I will give you the best of my recollection, Mr. Clardy. All I can recall is that students were reading Marxist literature at that time. There was a thing called a Left Book Club which existed in England and which had many, many members.

MR. VELDE: How do you spell that, Doctor?

MR. BOORSTIN: Left—L-e-f-t Book Club.

MR. TAVENNER: Did you study the Communist Manifesto?

MR. BOORSTIN: I don't recall specifically, sir.

MR. TAVENNER: Do you recall the book *State and Revolution*?

MR. BOORSTIN: I recall the name, but I don't recall specifically having studied it at Oxford.

MR. TAVENNER: Is there any other information that you can give the Committee regarding the activity of that group which you joined at Oxford?

MR. BOORSTIN: I have a vague recollection of a large meeting in a hall somewhere in Oxford during which there were about a hundred or a hundred and fifty people present. And I have a recollection that some of the students in the group may have rung doorbells for the Labour Party in some of the elections during the period that I was in England.

MR. CLARDY: I have a recollection of his having told the Committee at some time or other that pretty nearly all of the Rhodes scholars from this nation belonged to that group. Is that correct?

MR. BOORSTIN: I think I said that in executive session, Mr. Clardy. But since having made that statement—that was last summer—I have been thinking it over and trying to figure out exactly how many of the Rhodes scholars of my year I could remember as having been in that group—or of the Rhodes scholars who were there at the time. And I think as best I can recall it was about six. So I am afraid that was an exaggeration.

MR. CLARDY: Six out of how many?

MR. BOORSTIN: About seventy. There were about seventy-five American Rhodes scholars there during my period, but from any one year there were about thirty-two.

MR. CLARDY: So, comparing this with what you said earlier, it would be about six out of thirty-two instead of nearly all?

MR. BOORSTIN: No. My acquaintance included some Rhodes scholars from all the three classes, but I would not have known all of them.

MR. CLARDY: I see.

MR. BOORSTIN: So I would say it would be hard to say, sir.

(*Representatives Francis E. Walter and James B. Frazier, Jr., entered the hearing room at this point.*)

MR. MOULDER: I understand six actively participated in the meetings?

MR. BOORSTIN: There would be six whom I would remember. About six whom I would remember as having been interested in the materialist interpretation of history, and having been probably members of this group.

MR. MOULDER: Can you give us some statement as to how you expressed your opposition since that time?

MR. BOORSTIN: Yes, sir. My opposition has taken two forms: First, the form of an affirmative participation in religious activities, because I think religion is a bulwark against Communism. This has been expressed in my artivities in the Hillel Foundation at the University of Chicago, which is the local Jewish student group, and which is concerned in trying to develop in students an awareness of the importance of religion in their lives and in relation to the American tradition. I wrote a book on Jefferson some years ago, of which the motto was—it is a quotation from Jefferson—"Can the liberties of a people be thought secure if they have lost their only firm basis—the belief that those liberties are the gift of God?" I believe that, sir. The second form of my opposition has been an attempt to discover and explain to students, in my teaching and in my writing, the unique virtues of American democracy. I have done this partly in my Jefferson book, which, by the way, was bitterly attacked in the *Daily Worker* as something defending the ruling classes in America, and in a forthcoming book called *The Genius of American Politics*.* I have written articles and book reviews for *Commentary* magazine, which is a strongly anti-Communist journal.

* * *

MR. TAVENNER: After you entered Harvard in the fall of 1938 you then joined the Communist Party of the United States, as I understand it?

MR. BOORSTIN: Yes, sir.

MR. TAVENNER: Will you tell the Committee the circumstances under which you became a member of the Communist Party at that time?

MR. BOORSTIN: There were a number of circumstances that, as I can recall now, led me into the group. One was that those were the days of the so-called united front, during which the Communist Party was taking the position of supporting all liberal and progressive groups. Their motto was "Communism Is Twentieth-Century Americanism," at that time. They had somewhat succeeded in blurring the line between themselves and other groups. Also they were at that time taking a position against anti-Semitism and against the Nazis, and, as a Jew, that had a certain appeal to me, naturally. Also, during that year, Granville Hicks was a counselor in American studies, and he was a well-known person who had written a book about American literature. His presence lent a certain amount of glamor to the group. In addition, there were some old friends of mine who had been interested in Marxism at Oxford who were at Harvard at that time. As friends of mine, they added to the interest of the group.

MR. TAVENNER: Were these former associates of yours at Oxford members of the Communist Party group at Harvard?

MR. BOORSTIN: Yes, sir.

MR. TAVENNER: What were their names?

MR. BOORSTIN: Richard B. Schlatter and Richard M. Goodwin.

MR. TAVENNER: How closely were you associated with those two persons at Oxford?

MR. BOORSTIN: They were my roommates during my last year at Oxford.

MR. TAVENNER: Were both of them members of the group at Oxford?

MR. BOORSTIN: They were both in this study group. Yes, sir.

MR. TAVENNER: Was that the year in which Harvard began the counselor system in advising students in history?

MR. BOORSTIN: I think it was the first year. I wouldn't be sure if it was either the first or the second year.

MR. TAVENNER: Was it connected with that particular project that Mr. Granville Hicks had been engaged?

* And nearly twenty years later another Boorstin title could be added: *The Decline of Radicalism*: New York, 1970. —E.B.

MR. BOORSTIN: Yes, sir.

MR. TAVENNER: Was he a person known at that time openly as a member of the Communist Party?

MR. BOORSTIN: Yes, sir.

MR. WALTER: By "openly" what do you mean?

MR. BOORSTIN: He wrote for the newspapers and wrote frequently for Communist newspapers and journals, and admitted publicly that he was a member of the Communist Party.

MR. WALTER: So that, at the time he was selected as a counselor at Harvard, it was a well-known fact that he was an active member of the Communist Party?

MR. BOORSTIN: Yes, sir.

* * *

MR. TAVENNER: What was the general nature of your experience as a member of the Party at Harvard? What were the activities in which the members of the group engaged?

MR. BOORSTIN: From my point of view, sir, it was primarily a study group in which people talked about Marxism and the materialist interpretation of history. The activities of the group included an attempt to affect the policies and the leadership of the Harvard Teachers' Union.

MR. TAVENNER: Did you become a member of the local Teachers' Union?

MR. BOORSTIN: Yes, sir.

MR. TAVENNER: What part did the Communist Party play in your becoming a member of the union?

MR. BOORSTIN: I can't remember, sir. I may have become a member before I joined the group.

MR. TAVENNER: Was there any effort made by members of the Communist Party to require all of its members to be members of that particular union?

MR. BOORSTIN: I don't recall any requirement, but it is my impression that most of the members of the group were members of the Teachers' Union.

MR. TAVENNER: Did you at any time take part in a caucus of Communist Party members of the local union to decide ahead of meetings what action should be taken in the meetings?

MR. BOORSTIN: I was unaware of a special caucus, if there was one, but the meetings of the local Communist group would discuss this.

* * *

MR. WALTER: How many counselors were members of the Communist Party?

Mr. Boorstin: Granville Hicks is the only one I can recall in the group.

Mr. Kearney: How many counselors were there altogether?

Mr. Boorstin: I think there may have been ten or a dozen.

Mr. Kearney: Was the Party affiliation of Granville Hicks known to the university authorities?

Mr. Boorstin. To the best of my knowledge it was. Yes, sir.

Mr. Kearney: In other words, if he were writing articles for certain newspapers, it certainly should have been general knowledge.

Mr. Boorstin: Yes, sir.

Mr. Tavenner: Do you know whether the two persons that I first asked you about, Mr. Richard Schlatter and Mr. Goodwin, were members of the Party at the time you left the Party in September 1939?

Mr. Boorstin: As I can recall, they were members at the time I was a member. I do not know what they did thereafter, and I have not discussed political matters with them.

Mr. Kearney: Mr. Counsel, how would the witness know if they remained members of the Communist Party after he had left the Party?

Mr. Tavenner: We had the testimony here yesterday of the witness, Mr. Davis, that he knew that some of the persons he had named had withdrawn from the Party, and he gave various reasons for knowing some of them withdrew after he did and some before he did. I thought this witness might know the circumstances, if he was well acquainted with one or more of these individuals, and I think I should say that the Committee has information that Mr. Richard Schlatter has withdrawn from the Party and that he did withdraw back about very close to the same time this witness states that he did.

Mr. Kearney: That might be true, but what I am confused about is, if I belonged to an organization and I left, why should I know of my own knowledge that other members, that I knew to be members at the time I was a member, remained in the organization?

Mr. Tavenner: That would depend entirely on the type of information you have. You might have information that would warrant you in concluding that the man was no longer a member of the Party.

Mr. Kearney: Which would be practically hearsay evidence.

Mr. Tavenner: It would be the only type of evidence I think a person could act upon.

Mr. Clardy: He could know much better whether he was a member than whether he was not. It is like trying to prove everybody in this room didn't commit a murder.

Mr. Moulder: When you became a member of the Communist Party, was it then generally recognized as a political party and was it then known or not known as a world movement, or a plan or conspiracy inspired by the Kremlin to dominate the world?

MR. BOORSTIN: At that time my understanding, which I have since discovered to be erroneous, was that they were the most progressive and forward-looking of liberal groups.

MR. MOULDER: Then it is your explanation that your membership in the Communist Party was because of your interest, or your study, in the principles, or philosophy, of a government as then being proposed by the Communist Party?

MR. BOORSTIN: It was primarily an interest in a theory of history—the materialist interpretation of history—together with the feeling that these people were at that time standing up for humanitarian causes and fighting anti-Semitism in Nazi Germany, for example.

MR. SCHERER: Professor, I believe you said that was one of the primary reasons why you joined the Party, that you believed at that time that it was opposed to anti-Semitism. Now, today you know as a matter of fact that, instead of being opposed to anti-Semitism, the Communist Party of Russia is violently anti-Semitic.

MR. BOORSTIN: Yes, sir.

MR. SCHERER: Almost as much as the Nazi Party was, or perhaps more so?

MR. BOORSTIN: Yes, sir.

MR. CLARDY: The best reason in the world why that sort of folks should not go under the Communist Party, is it not?

MR. BOORSTIN: Yes, sir. One of many reasons.

MR. TAVENNER: Will you state, Doctor, just what, if any, influence this group of Communist Party members exerted over the students who were members of the classes of various professors, if you know?

MR. BOORSTIN: As a matter of fact, it was a curious sort of thing, as I think Mr. Davis said yesterday, that there was, as best as I can recall, never an effort made to affect what one said in the classroom, or to the student. Nevertheless, the fact that members of the faculty were interested politically and lent their names to political groups may have affected the attitudes of students.

MR. TAVENNER: Was it openly known in the university that there was a Communist Party cell within the faculty?

MR. BOORSTIN: I think it was generally known. There was a great deal of hocus-pocus connected with the group, but I—

MR. MOULDER: Your becoming a member of that cell was as much for the purpose of promoting the influence of the Communist Party, or was it for your own discussion as a student and in the study of it?

MR. BOORSTIN: I think it was primarily the latter, sir.

MR. WALTER: If it was the latter, then why was there all this hocus-pocus, and why did everybody conceal the fact that they were members of this Party? You know that isn't the fact. You know the reason why there was all this hocus-pocus is because you all had a feeling you were participating in some sort of a movement that was perhaps slightly un-American. Isn't that the fact?

MR. BOORSTIN: I think, Mr. Walter, the secrecy was part of the appeal of it also, especially to young people. That it had a kind of lodgelike appeal. I certainly had the impression what I was doing was not illegal, and I saw no illegal acts committed, but the notion that there was a cozy little group of people who had this certain rigmarole was part of the appeal.

MR. KEARNEY: While you were a member of the Party were you ever addressed at any of your meetings by any high functionaries of the party?

MR. BOORSTIN: My only recollection of that kind was that there was a representative. Frankfeld, I think, was his name. And he came to these meetings and attempted to discuss the books and talk about the policies of the group.

MR. WALTER: Did he discuss revolution?

MR. BOORSTIN: Not to the best of my recollection. The level of that discussion and his general approach to these problems was one of the many things that disgusted me with the group.

MR. WALTER: I have been curious to know whether or not the teachings of Frankfeld recently would have been any different than those that you knew about? I say that because he was recently sentenced to the penitentiary for those teachings.

MR. BOORSTIN: I am sorry, sir. I haven't seen him since 1939, and I had very slight contact with him then—only in these meetings.

MR. CLARDY: Witness, do I understand from your statement made a while ago that you are no longer a member of the Party, that you have not only done so because of the anti-Semitic angle, but also because you now reject the theory of Marxism and all those things that you were studying at the time?

MR. BOORSTIN: Yes, sir.

MR. CLARDY: In other words, you have come to realize at last that they were fallacious and that they were not good for America, and you quit the Party?

MR. BOORSTIN: Yes, sir. I consider that a part of the process of growing up.

MR. CLARDY: And your thought of the influence of groups of that kind you did belong to was that they were bad for America and should be disbanded?

MR. BOORSTIN: Yes, sir.

MR. KEARNEY: Do you know whether Frankfeld was ever a student in any university?

MR. BOORSTIN: No, sir. I do not.

MR. KEARNEY: Do you know, as a matter of fact, whether he ever attended any of the common schools or not?

MR. BOORSTIN: No, sir. I do not.

MR. KEARNEY: And still he addressed university professors at Harvard?

MR. CLARDY: Of course, Mr. [Owen] Lattimore never received a degree anywhere either, but he parades as a doctor.

MR. TAVENNER: What were the circumstances which induced you to leave the Communist Party? What occurred to make you change your mind?

MR. BOORSTIN: Well, Mr. Tavenner, it was a growing disgust with the way of thinking and the attitudes of people in the group. The most dramatic event which brought it out into the open was the Nazi-Soviet pact, which revealed both the willingness of the Soviet Union to collaborate with Nazism and the intellectual bankruptcy of the American Communists, who switched their line around according to what the *Daily Worker* said. As I recall, the day after the Nazi-Soviet pact, or just about then, the Communists denied everything they had been saying for years.

MR. SCHERER: Professor, do you feel today that an active member of the Communist Party should be a teacher in our public schools?

MR. BOORSTIN: No, sir.

MR. SCHERER: Do you feel that he should be a teacher in our colleges?

MR. BOORSTIN: In any area where I have any expert competence—that is, in the area of the humanities and social sciences—my answer would be no.

MR. WALTER: But, Doctor, don't you recognize the fact that students have such a high regard, even awe, for professors—and take a professor of trigonometry, for example—that it would create such an impression on a young man that if he were to indicate something or other that was not proper—something political—wouldn't that young man be apt to accept the suggestions made by that professor? And suppose that that professor engaged in any extracurricular activities? The fact that he had created an impression on his students, I should think, would make him a very strong force in the community in which he did lecture.

MR. BOORSTIN: Mr. Walter, my feeling is that no one should be employed to teach in a university who was not free intellectually, and, in my opinion, membership in the Communist Party would be virtually conclusive evidence that a person was not intellectually free.

MR. SCHERER: He would also believe in the overthrow of the American Government by force and violence if he was an active Communist Party member, as I asked, wouldn't he?

MR. BOORSTIN: It is my impression that the Supreme Court has held that leadership in the Communist Party is participation in a conspiracy.

MR. CLARDY: It was Hitler's theory to seize the minds of the youth by the method we have been talking about, was it not?

MR. BOORSTIN: Yes, sir.

* * *

MR. TAVENNER: While at Chicago, you have written the books and have taken the action that you have described as being in opposition to the Communist Party?

MR. BOORSTIN: Yes, sir.

MR. TAVENNER: Are there any other activities that you have engaged in since being at Chicago which would be in opposition to the Communist Party?

MR. BOORSTIN: Not that I can recall, sir. I am not basically a political person and I am not active politically. I do feel that the most effective way to fight Communism is—the one effective way in which I may have some competence is by helping people to understand the virtues of our institutions and their special values as those emerged from our history, and I have tried to do that.

MR. TAVENNER: Do I correctly understand that you are definitely of the opinion that no person should be employed as a teacher in our educational system who is subject to the discipline and the directives of the Communist Party, because they are not free to act? Is that in substance your view?

MR. BOORSTIN: I think a member of the Communist Party should not be employed by a university. I would not hire such a person if I were a university president.

MR. CLARDY: Witness, as I understand it, it is obviously your conclusion now that the work this Committee is undertaking is serving a good purpose, but I would like to have you tell us whether you do actually agree.

MR. BOORSTIN: Well, I think this is the second day of the public hearings, and I think that the Committee should be judged by the record which it makes.

MR. CLARDY: If we continue on the line we have followed, would you agree with us and the witness yesterday that it does serve a useful purpose?

MR. BOORSTIN: It is not for me to judge, sir. I have had little experience with legislation. I can't myself think of any legislation that would serve these purposes at the moment, but I am not expert in this field and I am afraid I just wouldn't be able to help you.

MR. CLARDY: Has there been anything that you have heard thus far, either in your own examination or that of Mr. Davis of yesterday, that in any way impinged upon this vague thing we call academic freedom, in your judgment?

MR. BOORSTIN: The Committee has been extremely courteous to me, sir.

MR. CLARDY: Well, answer my question directly, if you can.

MR. BOORSTIN: This Committee has not in any way impinged on my academic freedom. No, sir.

MR. VELDE: Dr. Boorstin, you also have contributed greatly to the fund of knowledge that this Committee has, in turning to the activities of the Communist Party in England and the Communist Party of the United States and the activities of the Soviet government generally to overthrow our form of government. I would like to thank you for coming before the Committee and, if you return to the University of Chicago, which happens to be in my home state, I am sure you will be able to give your students some of the same information which you have given to this Committee so ably, and that you will be able to convince the students who are in your classes and with whom you come in contact that the Soviet government is out to destroy our form of government.

FEBRUARY 26, 1953:

Granville Hicks

MR. TAVENNER: When and where were you born, Mr. Hicks?

MR. HICKS: I was born in Exeter, New Hampshire, on the 9th of September, 1901.

MR. TAVENNER: What is your present occupation?

MR. HICKS: I am a free-lance writer.

MR. TAVENNER: Will you state for the Committee, please, what your formal educational training has been?

MR. HICKS: I was educated in the public schools of New Hampshire and Massachusetts. I did undergraduate work at Harvard and was graduated in 1923 with my A.B. degree. From 1923 to 1925 I was at Harvard Theological School. In 1928–29 I was back at Harvard and took my master's degree in English.

MR. TAVENNER: Will you tell the Committee, please, what your work record has been since the completion of your formal education?

MR. HICKS: Well, from 1925 to 1928 I was an instructor at Smith College. Then I went back to Harvard in 1928–29, as I have already said. And from 1929 to 1935 I was assistant professor of English at Rensselaer Polytechnic Institute in Troy. Since then I have had— Well, except for one year in that period, I have been a free-lance writer. In the year 1938–39 I was a counselor in American civilization at Harvard College.

MR. TAVENNER: Mr. Hicks, you have appeared at a prior time before a Subcommittee of this Committee in executive session, have you not?

MR. HICKS: Yes, sir.

Mr. Tavenner: You have advised the Committee of most of the facts, I suppose, that you have within your recollection.

Mr. Hicks: Yes, sir.

Mr. Tavenner: When did you become a member of the Communist Party?

Mr. Hicks: In the winter of 1934–35.

Mr. Tavenner: And how long did you remain a member?

Mr. Hicks: Until September 1939.

Mr. Tavenner: What has been your attitude and your record since 1939 with reference to the Communist Party?

Mr. Hicks: I have been, I think, consistently anti-Communist.

Mr. Tavenner: Will you tell the Committee, please, the circumstances under which you first became a member of the Party?

Mr. Hicks: Well, I had been a rather close fellow traveler for a period of three or four years, so close that I was actually an editor of the *New Masses*. I was an editor at a time when I was not a member of the Party. It was very natural that I should be at some point or other recruited into the Party. And when I was asked, in the winter of 1934–35, I immediately agreed to join the Party, and I did so.

Mr. Tavenner: Were you then employed as an editor of *New Masses*?

Mr. Hicks: Well, "employed" is not the right word, since the *New Masses* never paid anything. I was an editor. I was employed at that time at Rensselaer Polytechnic Institute.

Mr. Tavenner: How long had you been on the editorial staff of the *New Masses* before you were invited into the Party?

Mr. Hicks: Approximately a year. I became the literary editor of the *New Masses* when it was made a weekly in January 1934.

Mr. Tavenner: Who asked you to become a member of the Party?

Mr. Hicks: Bernhard Stern.

Mr. Tavenner: How was he employed?

Mr. Hicks: He was employed in some capacity at Columbia University.

Mr. Tavenner: Tell the Committee the circumstances.

Mr. Hicks: We had dinner together and he simply asked me if I didn't feel I was now ready to join the Party, and after we discussed it a little while, I said that I did feel so.

Mr. Tavenner: Then you became a member of the same group or unit of which he was a member?

Mr. Hicks: That is true; which was a group of professional people, writers mostly, in New York City.

Mr. Tavenner: Were any other members of the teaching profession members of that group, other than Professor Bernhard Stern?

Mr. Hicks: Not to the best of my recollection.

MR. TAVENNER: What was the activity in which that group engaged?

MR. HICKS: I remember that at one meeting I attended there was a good deal of talk about preparations for the first Congress of American Writers.

MR. TAVENNER: Did you become a member of the first Congress of American Writers?

MR. HICKS: Yes. I presided, I think, at the opening meeting of that congress.

MR. TAVENNER: Was that an open meeting—open to the public generally?

MR. HICKS: Yes.

MR. TAVENNER: It was a matter that was public knowledge in the City of New York and carried in the newspapers?

MR. HICKS: Oh, very, very much so.

MR. TAVENNER: Were the other members of that Communist Party group to which you were assigned also members of that writers' conference?

MR. HICKS: I think so. The first Congress of American Writers led, as I recall it, to the formation of the League of American Writers, an organization that went on for a number of years. My guess would be that all of the members of the group I belonged to were also members of the League of American Writers. I know that some of them were.

MR. TAVENNER: What was the approximate date of the first Congress of American Writers over which you presided?

MR. HICKS: April or May 1935.

MR. TAVENNER: How long did you continue active in that organization?

MR. HICKS: I belonged to that until the winter of 1939–40, when I became convinced that the Communist domination was hopeless, and I got out. There were a good many of us who hoped during the fall and winter of 1939–40 that the league could be taken away from the Communists, but it proved to be impossible, and so most of us simply quit.

MR. TAVENNER: Were you of the opinion that it was under the control of the Communist Party from its inception?

MR. HICKS: The Communists were controlling it from the very beginning.

MR. TAVENNER: How long did you remain a member of the group?

MR. HICKS: Only until the following summer—the summer of 1935—when I asked to be transferred to the Street branch in Troy, where I was then living. This was partly because I thought it was foolish to belong to a branch in whose activities I could not really take any effective part. It was also because, having been fired from Rensselaer Polytechnic Institute, I felt I could afford to be a public and open member of the Communist Party, and I very much preferred to be in the open. So that I was transferred to the Troy branch, and from that time on went under my own name in the Party, made no effort whatever to conceal my affiliation with the Party, and spoke many times under direct Party auspices.

MR. TAVENNER: When you first became a member in the City of New York, your membership was kept secret?

MR. HICKS: Yes.

MR. TAVENNER: Did you use your own name?

MR. HICKS: No. I certainly had a Party name. I have no idea what it was, but I was given a Party name, I am sure.

MR. TAVENNER: Did you pay dues?

MR. HICKS: Yes.

MR. TAVENNER: What were the dues?

MR. HICKS: I don't know. The dues system changed several times during the period that I was in the Party, and sometimes it was on a sliding-scale basis, and sometimes it was on a direct-percentage basis. I think that dues ran somewhere around five per cent and up. Perhaps higher than five per cent of one's income.

MR. TAVENNER: Now you stated that you were teaching at Rensselaer College at the time you were editor of the *New Masses*. How long were you or did you occupy that dual relationship?

MR. HICKS: A year and a half.

MR. TAVENNER: How long was it after you became a member of the Communist Party that your services were dispensed with at Rensselaer College?

MR. HICKS: Five or six months.

MR. TAVENNER: Had you become openly known as a member of the Communist Party at that time?

MR. HICKS: No, I had not. I was certainly known as a very close sympathizer, as my being on the *New Masses* and presiding on the writers' congress, and so on, would indicate, but I concealed the fact that I was actually a member of the Communist Party.

MR. TAVENNER: Was there any connection between your release as a teacher at Rensselaer College and your Communist Party affiliations?

MR. HICKS: In his commencement address the acting president said that he did not fire me because I was a Communist but that if he had fired me because I was a Communist it would have been all right.

MR. TAVENNER: Did you at the time make any assertion as to the cause of your release?

MR. HICKS: Oh, I said as loudly as I could that I was being fired because I was a Communist sympathizer.

MR. TAVENNER: Did you at that time admit publicly that you were actually a member of the Party?

MR. HICKS: I did not.

MR. TAVENNER: Was it immediately after your release from Rensselaer College that you asked to be transferred to Troy?

MR. HICKS: It was.

MR. TAVENNER: Was that suggestion made to you by Communist sources?

MR. HICKS: It was a matter of my own decision, which was to some extent resisted by the Communists in New York.

MR. TAVENNER: At the time your connections were severed from Rensselaer College, did the Communists of your group take any position with regard to your making it known that you were a member of the Communist Party?

MR. HICKS: Bernhard Stern suggested that he thought it was very unwise. I remember that. Whether any of the others made similar suggestions I don't know, but in any case, whatever was said, I did what I wanted to do and became a public member.

MR. TAVENNER: Why was it you did not announce publicly that you were a member of the Communist Party while still a member of the group in New York, instead of waiting until you got to Troy and until you were assigned to the Troy group?

MR. HICKS: Because there would have been a danger then of exposing members of the unit in New York.

MR. TAVENNER: Wouldn't there have been an equivalent danger of exposing people in Troy?

MR. HICKS: Not really an equivalent danger. It was known a Troy branch did exist. The group in New York, on the other hand, was a highly secret group.

MR. TAVENNER: Was John Howard Lawson a member of that group?

MR. HICKS: That question I could only answer in terms of hearsay.

MR. TAVENNER: Do you know?

MR. HICKS: I do not ever remember seeing him at a meeting of that group.

MR. TAVENNER: Were any other members of the staff of *New Masses* members of that group?

MR. HICKS: No.

MR. TAVENNER: Can you recall the name at this time of any other persons who were members of that particular group?

MR. HICKS: I can. Do you think it is relevant to the interests of the Committee at the present time?

MR. TAVENNER: It isn't relevant to the issue we are immediately concerned with.

MR. HICKS: I have already given those names in private hearing and I would be glad to let that matter rest there for the time being.

MR. TAVENNER: When you were assigned to the unit in Troy did you immediately make known your membership in the Communist Party?

MR. HICKS: Not, at any rate, in the sense of sending a statement to the local papers saying I have joined the Communist Party, but almost immediately I began speaking at open Party meetings and broadcasting for the Party on the radio.

MR. TAVENNER: How long did you continue as an open Party member?

MR. HICKS: I was an open Party member as long as I was in the Party.

MR. TAVENNER: Your next employment, I believe, was at Harvard University?

MR. HICKS: Yes.

MR. TAVENNER: Will you tell the Committee the circumstances under which you were employed? Who initiated the movement or the suggestion of your employment?

MR. HICKS: As I recall it, the first suggestion came from a friend of mine at Harvard, F. O. Matthiessen the literary critic, who wrote to ask whether I would be interested in such an appointment if it were offered me. He had reason to ask that, since it was only a part-time job with part-time pay, and I would in any case have to go on with free-lance writing to support my family. He therefore approached the subject rather tentatively, telling what the plan involved. After thinking it over, I wrote back that I thought I would be very much interested.

MR. TAVENNER: Do you have any records showing how the official appointment was made?

MR. HICKS: I may have. I usually keep such things. But I think it would have come in the form of an impersonal letter from whatever official of the university handled that kind of thing.

(Representative Donald L. Jackson left the hearing room at this point.)

MR. TAVENNER: Do you know whether or not your activity in the Communist Party, or even the fact of the Communist Party membership at that time, was known to the appointive powers at Harvard?

MR. HICKS: It seems as if it must have been, but I don't know absolutely that it was.

MR. TAVENNER: I have seen an article in *The New York Times* stating that there was a considerable question raised at that time, was there not, about the appointment by Harvard of a person who was a known member of the Communist Party?

MR. HICKS: Particularly in the Boston newspapers.

MR. TAVENNER: Did your Communist Party membership have anything to do with your not being retained for an additional year?

MR. HICKS: That is a matter that was very much under dispute. I maintained at the time that it did.

MR. WALTER: Who passed on the question? The president of the university?

MR. HICKS: On the question of appointing me in the first place, or letting me go? I suppose that I could have been appointed without the president's having any immediate knowledge of it. This was a very unimportant position. I think he was very well aware of what went on when I left.

MR. TAVENNER: Well, during the period of your work at Harvard, did you continue in your Communist Party associations?

MR. HICKS: Oh, yes.

MR. TAVENNER: And membership?

MR. HICKS: Yes, indeed.

MR. TAVENNER: Were you very serious at that time about the subject of Communism?

MR. HICKS: I should say so, yes, very serious, indeed.

MR. TAVENNER: Did you have your membership transferred from Troy to Harvard University?

MR. HICKS: I suppose I must have.

* * *

MR. TAVENNER: We just had on the witness stand a professor from Harvard University, Dr. Wendell Furry.* Did you become acquainted with him while at Harvard?

MR. HICKS: Yes I did.

MR. TAVENNER: Was he a member of the Communist Party cell or group of which you were a member?

MR. HICKS: Yes, he was.

MR. TAVENNER: Was he a member when you came there?

MR. HICKS: Yes.

MR. TAVENNER: Was he a member when you left?

MR. HICKS: Yes.

MR. TAVENNER: Do you know anything about his continued membership in the Communist Party after you left?

MR. HICKS: No, I have no knowledge of that kind.

MR. TAVENNER: Did you become acquainted with a person by the name of Israel Halperin?

MR. HICKS: I did.

MR. TAVENNER: Was he a member of that cell of the Communist Party?

MR. HICKS: He was.

MR. TAVENNER: Do you recall Dr. Daniel J. Boorstin?

MR. HICKS: Yes.

MR. TAVENNER: Was he a member of the group or cell of the Party of which you were a member?

MR. HICKS: He was.

MR. TAVENNER: Do you recall a person by the name of Richard Schlatter?

MR. HICKS: Yes, I do.

MR. TAVENNER: Was he a member of your group?

MR. HICKS: Yes.

* See page 575. —E.B.

* * *

Mr. Tavenner: Now, what was the general purpose of the Communist Party in endeavoring to organize a cell or unit among the teaching profession at Harvard, or at any other university?

Mr. Hicks: What I thought then was that the Communist Party, having had a genuine change of heart in 1934 and 1935, when the new line was adopted, was interested in carrying on the fight against Fascism and in protecting democracy against Fascism and had postponed into some rather indefinite future the whole idea of world revolution. I believed that the Communist Party was interested in reaching all people who can mold public opinion, and among these, of course, would be the teachers. * * * Yes, certainly. Of course, I feel now that the popular front was simply a dodge that happened in those particular years to serve the foreign policy of the Soviet Union. So it seems to me that the Party, in organizing branches in the colleges, had two purposes. One was to carry out the existing line which they wanted to make a show of advancing, and then, of course, the other was to try to have a corps of disciplined revolutionaries whom they could use for other purposes when the time came.

Mr. Walter: Did you ever come in contact with the corps of trained revolutionaries?

Mr. Hicks: In the sense that the Party organizers, like Phil Frankfeld, for example, are?

Mr. Walter: I think he would faint if anybody showed him a gun, and I am sure that is true of a great many of the revolutionaries that testified before this Committee. I am just wondering, in view of these rather jacketed, hard-boiled revolutionaries, who they were.

Mr. Hicks: They were the Party functionaries as a rule, the professional Party members, the members who give the whole of their lives to it.

Mr. Kearney: In that category would you designate the group of Communists who were convicted in New York City?

Mr. Hicks: Certainly.

Mr. Tavenner: Now, will you elaborate further upon those two methods or purposes, rather, of the Communist Party?

Mr. Hicks: Most, and perhaps all, of the men who belonged to the unit at Harvard were people who felt as I did, who were thinking of Party activity in terms of the situation that then existed in the late thirties, a situation in which, to many people in this country, the great enemy was certainly Fascist Germany, and our potential ally was Soviet Russia.

Mr. Tavenner: Now, that was the situation as you have described it prior to, I assume you mean, the pact between Soviet Russia and Germany, which was August 23, 1939?

Mr. Hicks: Exactly.

Mr. Tavenner: What change occurred at that time?

MR. HICKS: Well, after a very brief period of confusion, the Party, of course, adopted its position. The fight against Fascism was a secondary matter, a matter of taste, as Molotov said, the war was an imperialist war and the chief aim of all Communists should be to prevent the United States from aiding England and France in their fight against Nazi Germany.

MR. TAVENNER: Did you have any difficulty in accepting that sudden change in Communist Party line?

MR. HICKS: I found it perfectly impossible to accept it and got out of the Party within a very short time after the pact was signed.

MR. TAVENNER: Were you concerned about it to the extent that you sought further information or advice from functionaries on a higher level?

MR. HICKS: Yes, I went to New York, had a talk with Earl Browder. I had given four years of my life to it. I didn't want to break. It was a very hard step to take. I went to talk with Browder, to see if he had anything to say that I hadn't already read in the *Daily Worker*. He simply paralleled the *Daily Worker* line, and I came home and wrote a public letter of resignation.

MR. TAVENNER: What he had said confirmed your opinions and judgment about the change in the Party policy?

MR. HICKS: It made clear to me what should have been clear to me earlier, and that is that the Communist Party in the United States was wholly under the domination of the Soviet Union. In my own case, it was very fortunate that I had been an open member of the Party because I had to make my decision openly. I had been saying all this about Fascism being the real enemy, and now I would have had to turn right around and say the exact opposite, and of course I couldn't bring myself to do that, and there was nothing to do but break with the Party. If I had been a secret member, I could have temporized for some months, worried and fretted, and then eventually come around and reconciled myself to the new Party line.

MR. TAVENNER: Well, I would like for you to give the Committee the benefit of such opinion as you have, based upon your knowledge of the Communist Party and its principles.

MR. HICKS: I think that every member of the Communist Party is an actual or a potential agent of the Soviet Union.

MR. TAVENNER: Now, knowing students at college, and understanding the motives of the Communist Party, what is your judgment about the advisability of maintaining a teacher who is under the discipline of the Communist Party?

MR. HICKS: Well, in most situations that is probably a very undesirable thing. I must say I would go along with Senator Taft in feeling that I would not want to make an absolute rule about that. I think there are situations in which it would be better to let a Communist keep his job than to disrupt the whole fabric of academic freedom.

* * *

MR. TAVENNER: Do you not agree that it is potentially dangerous to permit a member of the Communist Party, who is subject to its discipline, to be in a situation in a college where he is in a position to influence students or other faculty members, for that matter, and likewise to become potential agents of the Soviet Union by becoming Communist Party members?

MR. HICKS: You cannot protect all college students a hundred per cent. Some of them take to drink, and some of them take to Communism, and lots of other things happen to them, and there's nothing that anybody on God's earth can do that will look out for all college students. I think you have to just say that is a risk you run.

MR. TAVENNER: During the period of your membership were any efforts made to direct you in the character of writing you performed?

MR. HICKS: There were efforts made, but when I resisted them, I had no trouble.

MR. TAVENNER: Can you give us an illustration?

MR. HICKS: The one that comes to mind, because I have often quoted it as a joke, came when I did a review of the book *Selections from Marxism* for the *Communist,* the official theoretical magazine of the Party. In the course of the review I remarked on the fact that Marx and Lenin were very vivid writers as well as being great theoreticians. I received a telegram from V. J. Jerome asking, "What about Uncle Joe?"—meaning I had left out Stalin, and praise of Stalin was becoming obligatory in the *Communist,* as well as the papers in Russia. Since I happened to think one of the real evils that Stalin has brought is the corruption of the style of the Communist word, I wired back, "Nothing doing," and the review went as I had written it.

MR. TAVENNER: What has been the general nature of your opposition to the Communist Party since severing your connections with it?

MR. HICKS: I have written in the *Nation,* in the *New Republic, Harper's, Commentary,* and *Partisan Review*. I am on the editorial board of the *New Leader,* which is a leading anti-Communist paper. I've introduced the theme of anti-Communism in several of the books I have written in this period. I have taken part in the work of the Americans for Democratic Action and the American Committee for Intellectual Freedom.

MR. CLARDY: He mentioned the Americans for Democratic Action, which arouses my interest. Where did you slash that from the line of fronts? It followed a party line, almost identical in many particulars with the Communist Party line, did it not?

MR. HICKS: I think you will find ADA had disagreed with the Communist Party line again and again and again.

MR. KEARNEY: Well, as a matter of fact, the Communist is not eligible for membership in the ADA?

MR. HICKS: Exactly.

MR. WALTER: Now, you said a moment ago we perhaps were too worried about the menace of Communism and exaggerated the situation. If that is true, don't you feel that an atmosphere of fear is created throughout the United States which is not healthy?

MR. HICKS: I think that's absolutely true. The question is: How was it created?

MR. WALTER: Now, I don't think there is any question about how it was created, but how can we make the American people understand that the might and majesty of this great republic will not be abused, so that innocent, frustrated idealists, if you please, are not destroyed at a time when Congressional Committees are conducting a legitimate duty?

MR. HICKS: The fear in this country is in part a very real and understandable fear of the Soviet Union and its agents. It is a fear that we should all share. Over and above that, I think there is a mood of rather vague apprehension that is not rational and that is dangerous, and I do feel that that mood of irrational apprehension has been encouraged in part by legislative investigating committees. The emphasis in all these investigating committees always falls on the fact of how much Communism there is and never on how little there is.

MR. WALTER: That's right.

MR. HICKS: It seems to me I have been sitting around here for two days in which it has been demonstrated that there were ten or twelve Communists at Harvard fourteen years ago and that perhaps there is one still there. Now, I would honestly think, if you could just say to the public, "Look, that's all," instead of saying, "Look how much that is, isn't that terrible?" you might do a good deal to allay the fear that is sweeping over this country.

* * *

MR. DOYLE: When you say "revolutionaries," was it your experience that the Communist Party in America was advocating the use of force and violence?

MR. HICKS: The Communist Party at that time certainly was not advocating the use of force and violence. I think that [is] always in the background as part of the whole Marxist concept. It was being soft-pedaled, however, in the period 1935 to 1939. When we speak of trained revolutionaries, we're thinking of the sort of thing that Lenin recommended when he was building up the Bolshevik Party in Russia. What we have today is not even trained revolutionaries, but dependable agents.

MR. CLARDY: Agents of what?

Mr. Hicks: Agents. They are looking for dependable agents of the Soviet Union.

Mr. Walter: Well, then, can't this whole thing be dealt with adequately by making it a crime to be a Communist Party member and just arrest people, prosecute them for membership in the Communist Party, instead of searching all over the lot?

Mr. Hicks: I have sometimes felt that that was certainly the answer and would be much simpler. How much damage that would do I don't know—whether that would again give the impression that this big country is too much worried over a little party. It would be a simpler and, in many ways, I think, a more satisfactory way of handling the problem than what we've had in the last two or three years.

Mr. Kearney: No matter which way it was done, somebody would be bound to be hurt?

Mr. Hicks: Somebody will be hurt. There's no getting around it. I mean innocent people will be hurt.

Mr. Doyle: You are suggesting possibly outlawing the Communist Party?

Mr. Hicks: I am saying I have had times when I felt that was the only possible solution.

In his book *Where We Came Out* (1954) Granville Hicks takes issue with Whittaker Chambers' insistence that "anybody who was ever connected with the Communist Party in any way deserves to suffer," and adds the following information:

> What happened as a result of my testimony before the Velde committee? Of the men I named as having been members of the Communist branch at Harvard in 1938–39, eight were subpoenaed by the committee. Four testified, and four claimed immunity. Two of the latter had left academic life. One of the others lost his job, and one didn't—Wendell Furry, who satisfied an investigating committee at Harvard that he had quit the party in 1947. Of the three who testified publicly that they had been party members, none, so far as I know, has been subject to disciplinary action, though all of them have doubtless suffered the kind of inconvenience I have mentioned.
>
> In short, it appears that little damage was done, and I am happy that this is so. On the other hand, as I have already said, I cannot see that Communism was appreciably weakened by this particular inquiry. No conspiracy was exposed; no spies or saboteurs were apprehended. No record of current Communist activity of any sort was brought to light. Even as a piece of historical research, a study of Communism at Harvard fifteen years ago, the investigation produced no impressive results.
>
> And I know of one innocent person, or at any rate a person of whose

innocence I have no doubt, who was hurt by me, and might have been badly hurt. In naming men as Communists, I was careful to name only those whom I had actually seen at party meetings, but, in a different connection, when I was off my guard, I alluded to a certain individual as if I knew that he had been a Communist. I did think he had been, but I should have pointed out that that was not knowledge but inference, and, as it turned out, a not very logical inference. Subsequently subpoenaed by the committee, this man hired counsel, had photostats made of articles he had written, and went to Washington for a private hearing. His evidence apparently convinced the committee's investigators, but my slip—my inexcusable failure to distinguish between a fact and an assumption—had cost him time, money, and worry. If he had lost his head, as he might have done, or if he had not been able to produce rather impressive evidence, or if the investigators had been less reasonable, his career might have been blasted.

Hollywood and Broadway, Continued

MAY 5, 1953:

Jerome Robbins

The Committee on Un-American Activities convened in room 1105 of the United States Court House, Foley Square, New York, New York, at 3:20 p.m., the following Committee members being present: Representative Harold H. Velde, Chairman, Bernard W. Kearney, Kit Clardy, Gordon H. Scherer, and Clyde Doyle. Staff member: Frank S. Tavenner, Jr., Counsel.

MR. VELDE: I understand you desire the lights be turned off.

MR. ROBBINS: Yes.

MR. TAVENNER: Now, when and where were you born, Mr. Robbins?

MR. ROBBINS: I was born here at New York, 1918.

MR. TAVENNER: What is your profession?

MR. ROBBINS: I am a choreographer and a dancer.

MR. TAVENNER: How long have you been engaged in the profession of a choreographer?

MR. ROBBINS: As a choreographer since 1944.

MR. TAVENNER: Will you tell the Committee, please, what your formal educational training has been?

MR. ROBBINS: I attended grammar school and high school in Weehawken, New Jersey, graduated there. I attended NYU, Washington Square College, one year, in preparation for my profession. I was a dancer since 1937, studying all different kinds of dancing. I studied music.

MR. TAVENNER: Will you give the Committee, please, a better understanding of the nature of your profession?

MR. ROBBINS: Well, "choreography" is the technical word for creating dances, the same way as one would create a play or create music for a show. I conceive the ideas for the dances, create the steps, and instruct the dancers how to perform them, and then direct the performers.

MR. TAVENNER: Will you illustrate it a little more definitely?

MR. ROBBINS: Well, I work in two fields—both on Broadway, as far as musical comedy is concerned, and in the ballet field. I am represented on Broadway now by *The King and I.* In that show I had the problem of creating a ballet which was *Uncle Tom's Cabin,* but done in terms of the Siamese dancing, the way a Siamese court would do it, and I had to do some research on it, study the movements, make the point of the book, within the ballet itself, the story of the ballet. As far as the ballet field is concerned, I will have an idea for a ballet, select the music or have someone write it, conceive it, choreograph it, produce it finally.

MR. TAVENNER: Then, that type of work requires a highly creative art, doesn't it?

MR. ROBBINS: I think it is a highly creative art, yes.

MR. TAVENNER: Will you tell the Committee, please, the names of some of your principal productions?

MR. ROBBINS: On Broadway I have done the dances for *On the Town, Million-Dollar Baby, High Button Shoes, Call Me Madam, Miss Liberty, The King and I, Two's Company.* In the ballet I have done the ballets *Fancy Free, Interplay, Facsimile, Age of Anxiety, The Pied Piper, The Cage.*

MR. TAVENNER: Have you done this work in any countries besides the United States?

MR. ROBBINS: Yes. My ballets have been toured in Europe—most all the countries in Europe. I don't believe they've been performed in Mexico or Canada. That's about it.

MR. TAVENNER: What was your first ballet?

MR. ROBBINS: My first ballet was *Fancy Free.* It was created in 1944.

MR. TAVENNER: Was that the ballet which brought you prominence in your field?

MR. ROBBINS: Yes, it did. It was an immediate success, and I received a lot of attention because of it.

MR. TAVENNER: When did that go on the stage?

MR. ROBBINS: It was performed here in New York at the Metropolitan Opera House on April 18, 1944.

MR. TAVENNER: The investigation that the Committee has undertaken has disclosed information indicating that you were at one time a member of the Communist Party. Is that information correct?

MR. ROBBINS: Yes, it is.

MR. TAVENNER: For how long a period were you a member of the Communist Party?

MR. ROBBINS: I made application to the Communist Party—the Communist Association—

Mr. Tavenner: Communist Political Association?

Mr. Robbins: —Association—yes—around Christmas 1943. I attended my first meeting in the spring of 1944. The last meeting I attended, too, which was the only one I did, was in 1947, which was in the spring of that year.

Mr. Tavenner: Now, the Committee is very anxious to know from your experience in the Communist Party from 1944 to 1947 just how the Communist Party functioned in your field—that is, what the purpose of the Communist Party was in securing you as a member, what use it made of you, if it made any use of you, and what influence, if any, it attempted to bring to bear on you as a member of your profession.

Mr. Robbins: Well—

Mr. Tavenner: Let us first begin by your telling the Committee just, in your own way, what your experiences were in the Communist Party.

Mr. Robbins: I belonged to a group which was known as the theatrical transient group.

Mr. Tavenner: A theatrical transient group?

Mr. Robbins: Yes, well named because the group shifted around a lot. There was a shift of people within it, a shift of meeting places. It was divided and subdivided many times. It was part of the cultural division. As far as the way they tried to influence me or use me, at one of the earliest meetings I attended I was asked in what way did dialectical materialism help me do *Fancy Free*.

Mr. Tavenner: In what connection were you asked that question?

Mr. Robbins: Someone came up to me and just asked me this after a meeting. Someone asked me whether I would give a lecture on this to the club.

Mr. Tavenner: Now, that was as to how dialectical materialism influenced you in the production of *Fancy Free*—

Mr. Robbins: That's right.

Mr. Tavenner: —which had been a huge success?

Mr. Robbins: That's right. I had prepared *Fancy Free* before attending any meetings of the Association, and I found the question a little ridiculous and a little outrageous.

Mr. Tavenner: You had not been a member of the Communist Party when you created that ballet?

Mr. Robbins: No, sir.

Mr. Tavenner: But the assumption was, by at least some members of your group, that if you were a good Communist you would have permitted dialectical materialism to influence you in the production—

Mr. Robbins: Yes. I was asked to describe how dialectical materialism had helped me make *Fancy Free*.

Mr. Tavenner: Well, will you tell the Committee, briefly, about that ballet, of which you spoke, so that we may know what the Communist Party had in mind when you were asked that question.

MR. ROBBINS: It is about three sailors on shore leave in New York for the first time. This ballet was ultimately made into *On the Town*. The idea was mine. The purpose of it was to show how an American material and American spirit and American warmth and our dancing, our folk dancing, which is part of jitterbugging, part of jazz, could be used in an art form. The story concerns these three boys in New York for the first time, having a good time, trying to pick up some girls. It's always been identified everywhere, it's played as a particularly American piece, indigenous to America, and its theme has great heart and warmth, as far as representing our culture is concerned.

MR. TAVENNER: Then you, as I understand, had a feeling of resentment when you were asked to lecture upon the effect of Communism upon the production of that ballet?

MR. ROBBINS: Yes, sir. I had to laugh. I don't think I answered. I laughed back at this person and said that, in my opinion, there was no connection. I couldn't possibly do this, as I didn't see what one had to do with the other.

MR. TAVENNER: Then you did not attempt to make the lecture?

MR. ROBBINS: Not in the least, no, sir.

MR. TAVENNER: Well, did you acquire the feeling that the Communist Party was endeavoring to influence you in your product?

MR. ROBBINS: I believe this was part of the Communist attempt. I feel that constantly you are subjugated to propaganda and influence to make your art carry a political message. There was the Albert Maltz letter. He had written an article why the artist should be free to write what he wants to write about and how he wants to write it. This was severely criticized in the *New Masses* and the *Daily Worker,* and finally Maltz retracted. This became the subject of many meetings and much discussion back and forth.

MR. TAVENNER: Among your own group?

MR. ROBBINS: Yes. I could not understand how the Soviet musicians could be accused of writing—I think the word was—formalistic music and bourgeois music, having to repent publicly, and then get a benediction to move on and continue composing. I found this intolerable to an artist. I feel that they must be allowed to say what they want to say as they feel it, and that the minute they become subject to any dictums they're being false.

MR. [R. Lawrence] SIEGEL [Robbins' attorney]: May I refresh his memory as to one more incident?

MR. VELDE: Yes, certainly you may confer.

(*At this point Mr. Robbins conferred with Mr. Siegel.*)

MR. ROBBINS: Oh, yes. I attended one meeting in which someone reported to me that, the meeting before, a very great American dancer, not in the least Communist, had been called the Face of Fascism. I have the highest respect for this woman who was accused of portraying the Face of Fascism. This again floored me. I didn't understand what it was about, and it again brought forth this procedure to label things which did not conform Fascistic, bourgeois, decadent, degenerate. Other things which did conform, whether they were artistic or not, were seemingly praised.

MR. TAVENNER: Now, did you discover, during the course of your experience in the Party, any purposes that the Communist Party had in mind with respect to yourself?

MR. ROBBINS: No, sir. I was just always at meetings where this issue was kind of constantly brought forth, but outside of this one time, when I was asked to lecture, I did not receive any orders to make my work conform to their plans.

MR. DOYLE: May I ask one question there? Do I understand that, even though *Fancy Free* had been written—conceived and written—by you prior to the time you were a member of the Communist Party, after you became a member of the Communist Party you received orders, as you have just said, to give a lecture on how dialectical materialism or Communism had influenced you to write *Fancy Free*?

MR. ROBBINS: Yes, that's right.

MR. DOYLE: In other words, even though it had no influence on you, you received orders to give a lecture before other Communists that this—

MR. ROBBINS: This was not an order, sir. This was a request. It did not happen at the meeting. I want to put it straight. But someone did ask me to make a lecture to this effect after I had composed the ballet.

MR. TAVENNER: Were you requested at any other time to take part in any other meeting as a speaker?

MR. ROBBINS: No, not by the Party.

MR. TAVENNER: During the period of your membership did you come to the belief or the opinion that, as a Communist Party member, you should join front organizations?

MR. ROBBINS: At the time I was a member there was a lot of talk at the meetings about these organizations and that we should all attend them. I did join a large number of front organizations. I did not realize that they were front organizations to the effect that these were instigated by Communists and attempted to be controlled by them. I did realize Communists participated in them, but I was very much in favor of the things that they apparently stood for.

MR. TAVENNER: How active were you in the front organizations?

MR. ROBBINS: Not very.

MR. CLARDY: Too busy with your workaday life, I take it?

MR. ROBBINS: I think so, yes, sir.

MR. TAVENNER: Well, will you tell the Committee, please, what were the circumstances under which you first joined the Communist Party? What was the inducement that led you into the Communist Party?

MR. ROBBINS: The Communist Political Association had been presented to me as an organization which was very much for minorities and for advancing their causes. This interested me very much. I had had, prior to my joining, several instances of very painful moments because of minority prejudice. This was naturally an appeal for me.

MR. SCHERER: In other words, it was represented to you that the Communist Party at that time was opposed to anti-Semitism?

MR. ROBBINS: Yes.

MR. SCHERER: That was one of your reasons for joining?

MR. ROBBINS: Yes.

MR. TAVENNER: And if you had not had those experiences which you mentioned, you may not have gone to the Communist Party?

MR. ROBBINS: Perhaps not. It also was fighting Fascism, and Fascism and anti-Semitism were synonymous to me. It also gave one the feeling that the artist under Communism was a very free and secure person economically.

MR. SCHERER: Do you believe still today that the Communist Party is opposed to anti-Semitism?

MR. ROBBINS: In the past two summers I have traveled to Israel to teach there and to give what aid I can to that country, as far as my talent is concerned. In the light of the recent purges and waves of anti-Semitism, no, I do not believe—

MR. SCHERER: You would say today, as other witnesses have said to this Committee in the last four months, that the Communist Party is as anti-Semitic as the Nazi Party ever was?

MR. ROBBINS: It appears to be that way.

MR. TAVENNER: Now, you were telling us of the reasons why you went into the Communist Party.

MR. ROBBINS: And the other reason was that it was now frankly called the Communist Political Association, and I was given to believe that the Association was striving to make out of Communism an American form of Communism, and that it would coordinate with other political parties rather than be as secretive a thing as the Communist Party became when it changed back again.

MR. CLARDY: That is one thing I meant to suggest to you earlier. The change from a Communist Party to the Association and back again, I think, ought to be laid out pretty clear here.

MR. TAVENNER: Now, was there a time when you found that those representations that had been made to you at the time you entered the Party were not true?

MR. ROBBINS: If you're asking if I can put my finger specifically on those moments, no, sir, I can't. I did not like the shift from the Association back to the Party.

MR. TAVENNER: Why?

MR. ROBBINS: Because it seemed to be becoming more secretive. I did not understand the secrecy. My own feelings were that I wanted to put everything aboveboard, to be able to say, "Yes, I am a Communist," and when it shifted back, I did not understand the shift. As a matter of fact, I did not understand why Earl Browder was no longer the head and somebody else was. This was never explained clearly to me, and the shifts of policy were very disturbing to me.

MR. TAVENNER: Well, you have told the Committee that in 1947 you attended your last meeting.

MR. ROBBINS: Yes, sir.

MR. TAVENNER: Have you been connected in any way with the Communist Party since that meeting?

MR. ROBBINS: No, sir.

MR. TAVENNER: Will you tell the Committee, please, what brought about the termination of your relationship with the Communist Party?

MR. ROBBINS: Well, I suppose that the final straw was this last meeting. All these other reasons had been building up.

MR. TAVENNER: What other reasons?

MR. ROBBINS: One: There was no longer the Association, but now it had become the Party and had become smaller in its scope. Two: That the artist was not free, that he became a puppet to the Communist line, Communist propaganda. There was the attempt to move everything that way. Three: I did not feel it was working for minorities but had used it as a propaganda to get people into the Party. At this last meeting which I attended a fight broke out—not a fist fight—and this fight had to do with parliamentary procedure, and everyone began arguing and yelling, and I suddenly realized I was in the midst of chaos, of an unorganized, frantic group. The personalities there became involved with each other. I just thought it was too much. I didn't know what I was doing here, or what I was accomplishing by being present, and I had no more interest in continuing to participate.

MR. TAVENNER: Who recruited you into the Party?

MR. ROBBINS: Miss Lettie Stever.

MR. TAVENNER: How many persons were members of this group at the time you joined?

MR. ROBBINS: The personnel shifted constantly, sir. It would vary anywhere between ten to twenty.

MR. TAVENNER: How many meetings in all do you think you attended?

MR. ROBBINS: I think I attended twenty meetings over that period. I was busy with my work, going in and out of town.

MR. TAVENNER: Did you make any attempt to study Communism?

MR. ROBBINS: No. I was supposed to read Marx and Lenin, but I never did.

MR. TAVENNER: Will you give us the names of other persons who were in this group whom you can identify?

MR. ROBBINS: Lloyd Gough. Lionel Berman.

MR. VELDE: Do you know where Mr. Berman is?

MR. ROBBINS: No, sir.

MR. TAVENNER: Do you know whether or not he was a functionary in the Party?

MR. ROBBINS: He was identified as an organizer.

MR. TAVENNER: Can you give us the names of others? Or let me ask you the question this way: You said a Party member asked you to what extent dialectical materialism influenced you in the production of *Fancy Free*.

MR. ROBBINS: Yes.

MR. TAVENNER: Who was that person?

MR. ROBBINS: Madeline Lee.

MR. TAVENNER: Can you recall the names of other persons?

MR. ROBBINS: Elliott Sullivan.

MR. TAVENNER: Elliott Sullivan. Do you know how Elliott Sullivan was employed?

MR. ROBBINS: I believe he was an actor.

MR. TAVENNER: All right, now will you give us—

MR. ROBBINS: Edna Ocko.

MR. TAVENNER: How was she employed?

MR. ROBBINS: I don't know.

MR. TAVENNER: How can you identify her as a member? Is there any particular incident?

MR. ROBBINS: Yes. She was in the middle of this last argument at the last meeting.

MR. TAVENNER: In 1947?

MR. ROBBINS: Yes.

MR. TAVENNER: All right.

MR. ROBBINS: Jerome Chodorov.

MR. TAVENNER: Jerome Chodorov.

MR. ROBBINS: And Edward Chodorov.*

MR. TAVENNER: Edward Chodorov.

MR. ROBBINS: They both were at this last meeting.

MR. TAVENNER: Did you become acquainted with the names of all the persons who were members of your group?

MR. ROBBINS: No, I did not. Last names were not used usually, and, as I say, I attended meetings sporadically and the people at the meetings

* Edward Chodorov has informed the present editor that he was never in the C.P. at all. —E.B.

changed about, so that a first name might be all I would know of someone's identity.

MR. TAVENNER: Were you ever requested to rejoin the Communist Party after you left?

MR. ROBBINS: Mr. Chodorov asked me whether I was coming back. I said no.

MR. CLARDY: Which Mr. Chodorov?

MR. ROBBINS: Jerome.

MR. KEARNEY: I would like to express my own thanks to the witness for his very frank and honest testimony before the Committee this afternoon. I will say it was a bit unusual.

MR. CLARDY: I want to join with that, but also say I appreciate some of the work that I now know you are responsible for.

MR. ROBBINS: Thank you, sir.

MR. SCHERER: Just this, Mr. Robbins: You said the Communist Party pretended to be interested in the grievances of minority groups for the purpose of gaining converts?

MR. ROBBINS: Yes.

MR. SCHERER: Now, could it also have been for the purpose of gaining funds or money from some sources?

MR. ROBBINS: Might have been, sir. I am not cognizant of it.

MR. SCHERER: Thank you. I am going to see *The King and I* tonight, and I will appreciate it much more.

MR. ROBBINS: Thank you.

MR. DOYLE: I want to join in heartily complimenting you on doing what you have done. May I ask you this one question: We have had men and women before us, today and yesterday, who have referred to people who have come and testified before us and have not claimed the constitutional provisions and who have named other people as stool pigeons and informers. You realize, no doubt, that when you volunteered the names of other Communists whom you knew to be Communists that you would, by those people at least, be put in that class.

MR. ROBBINS: Yes, sir.

MR. DOYLE: In other words, you did it with your eyes open?

MR. ROBBINS: I did it according to my conscience.

MR. DOYLE: Now, I have a very personal question—and I have never met you, I have never talked with you before, have I?

MR. ROBBINS: No, sir.

MR. DOYLE: What is it in your conscience, or what was it in your experience, that makes you certainly one of the top men in your profession, one who has reached the pinnacle in your art, willing to come here, in spite of the fact that you knew some other people, who claim to be artists or authors or musicians, would put you down as a stool pigeon, and voluntarily testify as you have today?

MR. ROBBINS: I've examined myself. I think I made a great mistake before in entering the Communist Party, and I feel that I am doing the right thing as an American.

MR. DOYLE: Well, so do I. Again, I want to compliment you. You are in a wonderful place, through your art, your music, your talent, which God blessed you with, to perhaps be very vigorous and positive in promoting Americanism in contrast to Communism. Let me suggest to you that you use that great talent which God has blessed you with to put into ballets in some way, to put into music in some way, that interpretation.

MR. ROBBINS: Sir, all my works have been acclaimed for its [sic] American quality particularly.

MR. DOYLE: I realize that, but let me urge you to even put more of that in it, where you can appropriately.

MR. VELDE: Mr. Robbins, I do want to reiterate, you have performed a patriotic service to the Committee, and I am sure all Congress and the American people are very thankful to you for it.

MAY 6, 1953:

Lionel Stander

In 1971 Lionel Stander was interviewed by Guy Flatley, who reported in *The New York Times* (May 23) as follows:

> Hollywood's persecution of Lionel Stander began even before his celebrated jousts with the Committee (1940, 1953). "I've always been lefter than the Left, and I worked very closely with the Communist Party during the Thirties. But I never joined." Guilt by association, however, was sufficient guilt to hang Stander. "I remember very clearly that day in August, 1939, when my agent, Abe Lastfogel, came to me and said, 'Harry Cohn [head of Columbia Pictures] got up at a meeting of the MPAA [Motion Picture Association of America] last night and said that your contract was up for renewal but that he didn't want to renew it because you're a red sonofabitch and that anyone who hires you will have to pay $1000 to the MPAA. But don't worry, Lionel, it'll blow over.' Abe was right; it did blow over. But it took 24 years. Between 1939 and 1963 . . . I didn't work for a major studio except when somebody with courage, like Preston Sturges, decided to use me. . . . There were blacklisted actors who committed suicide. . . . But me, I have always lived on the champagne level. I figured that I needed $1,250 a week to break even, so I went to work on Wall Street, where

there is no blacklist. I became a customer's man, and I managed to live in the style to which Hollywood had accustomed me."

The Committee on Un-American Activities met at 10:10 a.m., in room 1105 of the United States Court House, Foley Square, New York, New York, the Honorable Harold H. Velde (Chairman) presiding.

Committee members present: Representatives Harold H. Velde (Chairman), Bernard W. Kearney, Kit Clardy, Gordon H. Scherer, Morgan M. Moulder, Clyde Doyle (appearance noted in transcript), and James B. Frazier, Jr. (appearance noted in transcript).

Staff members present: Robert L. Kunzig, Counsel; Frank S. Tavenner, Jr., Counsel; Raphael I. Nixon, Director of Research; Leslie C. Scott, Research Analyst; W. Jackson Jones, Earl L. Fuoss, and George C. Williams, Investigators; Dolores Anderson and Thelma Scearce, Staff Representatives; and Thomas W. Beale, Sr., Chief Clerk.

MR. STANDER: Before you ask me any questions, Mr. Velde, I would like it very much if you turned off the lights and discontinued the television cameras, as I am a professional performer and I only appear on TV for entertainment or for philanthropic organizations, and I consider this a very serious matter that doesn't fall into either category—

MR. VELDE: Well, now—

MR. STANDER: And it is certainly not right that a witness should have to have the lights and the television cameras on him.

MR. VELDE: Mr. Stander, do you feel the lights will affect your testimony?

MR. STANDER: Yes, I do. Furthermore, if this were a live television show in which my entire testimony would be seen by the American people just the way I make it, I don't think I would have as strenuous objections, but I still might object.

MR. VELDE: You mean a man who has been before the cameras and before the lights such as you have would have difficulty in testifying?

MR. STANDER: Yes, I do, because when I am before a camera I am before the camera as an actor and an entertainer, not as a witness.

MR. VELDE: You are before the United States Government now, a Committee of the Congress of the United States Government.

MR. STANDER: Which is a very serious thing, sir.

MR. VELDE: It is a very serious thing.

MR. STANDER: And I am not here just as an actor or an entertainer.

MR. VELDE: Let me tell you, Mr. Stander—

MR. STANDER: If I were here as an actor and entertainer, I wouldn't have any objection whatsoever, but—

MR. VELDE: Let me tell you, Mr. Stander, the Committee on Un-

American Activities desires to give the public the information that comes before it in all shapes and forms, and the excuse that you have that you are a professional entertainer—

MR. STANDER: That isn't an excuse, it is a fact.

MR. VELDE: —has no bearing whatsoever.

MR. STANDER: I resent the fact that you say it is an excuse. I am a professional entertainer, and it is quite different, as any actor will tell you, to come before the camera in a carefully rehearsed script and, on the other hand, to come before the camera as a witness before a Congressional Committee, which is a very serious thing, which isn't entertainment, and which certainly isn't a benefit for a charitable institution.

MR. VELDE: Now, Mr. Stander—

MR. STANDER: And that is my position, and I feel very strongly about this, and I would appreciate it very much if you would turn the lights off and turn the cameras off.

MR. BOUDIN [Leonard B. Boudin, counsel for Mr. Stander]: It's been done for other witnesses.

MR. VELDE: Certainly it has been done for other witnesses, but for other reasons, Mr. Stander. And the reasons were it would make them nervous and/or in some way interfere with the testimony they had to give.

MR. STANDER: I am not exactly calm this morning. I haven't had any sleep. As you know, I am playing in another city, and I haven't had any sleep at all tonight. I've traveled here, and I don't want to bore you with the details, but I was unable to get a room in a hotel and I stayed up. I can't give a good performance now that I haven't rehearsed, and inasmuch as I haven't had an opportunity to go over this matter and had time to consult with counsel—

MR. VELDE: Well, Mr. Stander, let me ask you—

MR. STANDER: I have been in Washington, and I have been in Philadelphia, and I was unable to secure counsel until I was in Washington—

MR. VELDE: If we do turn off the cameras, will you answer the questions that are put to you by counsel?

MR. STANDER: I intend to cooperate with this Committee and answer any questions to the best of my ability. I took an oath, and I believe in my oaths.

MR. VELDE: In that case, will the television and newsreel cameras please desist at the present time, and will the still photographers take their pictures and kindly retire during the witness's testimony?

MR. TAVENNER: What is your name, please, sir?

MR. STANDER: Lionel Stander.

MR. TAVENNER: Mr. Chairman, I think I should make a statement to the Committee of the purposes for the calling of this witness at this time.

MR. VELDE: Proceed, Mr. Counsel.

MR. TAVENNER: The witness previously appeared before this Committee in 1940, and at that time denied having been a member of the Communist Party and stated that he never intended to be.

(*Representative Clyde Doyle entered the hearing room at this point.*)
In 1951 information came to the Committee which resulted in the issuance of a subpoena on March 29, 1951. The Committee received a request from the then counsel for the witness that he would like a continuance. However, a witness by the name of Marc Lawrence testified before the Committee and alluded to this witness by name. On the following day a telegram was received from the witness in which he denied the statements made by Mr. Lawrence and requested that the Committee give him an immediate opportunity to appear before the Committee in regard to it. Then there was considerable correspondence backward and forward. During this correspondence the witness requested that he be given an opportunity to appear immediately. That was particularly in his letter of May 10.

MR. CLARDY: May 10 of what year?

MR. TAVENNER: 1951.

MR. VELDE: This matter has been before the Committee for approximately two years?

MR. TAVENNER: Yes. It was not our purpose in calling the witness now to go into any matter which was involved in his appearance before the Committee in 1940. It is only as the result of information received during the investigation which began in 1951 that we have called this witness.

MR. STANDER: I have voluminous correspondence here which shows I tried to get an immediate hearing. I sent a letter to each and every member of the Committee. I went in person to Washington and saw Congressman Kearney, who assured me—

MR. KEARNEY: Mr. Stander—

MR. STANDER: —that I would have an immediate hearing, because it was very important to me, because merely receiving the subpoena, with the press's announcement that I was subpoenaed, caused me to be blacklisted in radio, television, and motion pictures. So, I had an immediate economic motive for an immediate appearance. Congressman Kearney told me I would be heard within a day or two. I went back to New York and I received the telegram which said he assured me I would be heard immediately. At the same time I sued the witness who perjured himself before this Committee, Mr. Marc Lawrence, in the State Supreme Court of New York, who ruled that he enjoyed Congressional immunity. However, if he—

MR. VELDE: Now, Mr. Stander, we are not interested in those extraneous matters.

MR. STANDER: I don't think they are extraneous, when a man comes directly from the psychopathic ward under the care of two psychiatrists, Dr. Hannel and Dr. Orloff, and I wrote this letter and informed every one of the

Committeemen that this man, a psychopathic, was used as a witness against me and, under advice of counsel, fled to Europe and is still a refugee from this court case.

* * *

MR. VELDE: Mr. Stander, will you—

MR. STANDER: I asked for an appearance two years ago, and two years later I'm called, and—

MR. CLARDY: Do I understand, Mr. Stander, you are here to answer the sixty-four-dollar question when we ask it?

MR. STANDER: I will answer every question truthfully, to the best of my ability, and I am perfectly aware of the fact I have made an oath, and I am not in the habit of violating my word, even when I don't swear under oath.

MR. TAVENNER: Now, Mr. Stander, will you tell the Committee, please, when and where were you born?

MR. STANDER: New York City, January 11, 1908.

MR. TAVENNER: What is your occupation?

MR. STANDER: Well, I'm basically an actor. I have been a newspaper reporter. I have been a director of various stage entertainments for the Red Cross, the Air Force, the Kiwanis, junior and senior chambers of commerce, Elks, Moose, and other organizations with animal names. I've been an entertainer, director. I've produced two Broadway plays. I've been a theatrical person for the last twenty-six years, with an occasional venture into the field of journalism.

MR. TAVENNER: Have you also done screen writing or acting?

MR. STANDER: I have done screen acting. I have written a script or two for the screen.

MR. TAVENNER: How long were you engaged as a screen actor, and where?

MR. STANDER: Well, my very first jobs were in the old silent days as a kid actor, and then I made pictures for Warner Brothers. I worked with Marian Davies at the old Hearst Cosmopolitan, and went out under a Hollywood contract in January 1935.

MR. TAVENNER: How long did you remain in Hollywood as a screen actor?

MR. STANDER: Until I was the first person who exposed the criminal records of Browne and Bioff, the IATSE racketeer-gangster officials who later went to jail, and, because I exposed them one week before Mr. [Westbrook] Pegler exposed them in the paper I was blacklisted by the Motion Picture Producers Association—the major studios. So, in other words, that was from 1935 until the meeting in which I exposed these two racketeering gangsters who the Federal Government later put in the can.

MR. TAVENNER: My question to you was: How long did you continue to work as an actor?

Mr. Stander: I don't remember the exact date, but I have worked as an actor continually since then. After the major studios blacklisted me, I worked for independent producers—

Mr. Tavenner: Approximately—

Mr. Stander: —up until the time Mr. Marc Lawrence mentioned my name, or rather, up until the time Larry Parks said he didn't know me as a Communist.

Mr. Tavenner: Let me—

Mr. Stander: And that appeared in the paper, and just to have my name appear in association with this Committee—it seems like something, it shouldn't, I agree—I know it isn't the Committee's fault. It is like the Spanish Inquisition.

Mr. Tavenner: Let me remind you—

Mr. Stander: You may not be burned, but you can't help coming away a little singed.

Mr. Tavenner: Let me remind you of my question: How long did you continue to engage in the profession of screen acting?

Mr. Stander: In California, up until—outside of a period in which I enlisted in the Royal Canadian Air Force, United States Air Force, about two and one-half years, three years, it was from 1935 until 1948 or 1949. I'm not sure of the exact date. Then I made a few pictures, independent, New York.

Mr. Tavenner: And during that period of time you served in the armed forces, either of this or some other country, did I understand?

Mr. Stander: Well, not some other country. I enlisted in the RCAF, but I was in a show and had to give notice, and in the meantime the United States went to war and President Roosevelt issued an edict that nobody between the ages of eighteen and forty-five with any sort of pilot training cross the border. So I was unable to fulfill my enlistment in the Royal Canadian Air Force, and I enlisted subsequently, a few months later, for pilot training in the United States Air Force. Every one of the Committee received my war record, and I don't like to talk about it because it is there, and I do not like to match my patriotism with anybody.

Mr. Tavenner: I am just trying to ascertain dates. What is the approximate date you went into the armed forces?

Mr. Stander: I enlisted in the Royal Canadian Air Force in 1941.

Mr. Tavenner: From 1942 until what date were you in the armed services?

Mr. Stander: May 5, 1944. And, incidentally, while I'm looking at it here, I notice that the Chief of Staff, who was then Colonel Morgan, signed my character as excellent, and then Glenn O. Bacus, who I worked directly under—he was then commanding general of the headquarters' staff— He later got some very good publicity in the papers because of his heroic exploits—he is the man who made thirteen strikes with saber jets. I worked directly under him. Glenn Bacus and Colonel Morgan and every other officer of the headquarters' staff, upon my discharge, gave me letters and autographed pictures attesting to my excellent service record and character. In fact, the Chief of Staff initialed it himself.

MR. TAVENNER: Is it correct to say—

MR. STANDER: I see a citation from the Red Cross, the war bond drive, the Treasury Department, and here is a tribute to me from the Armed Forces Radio Service, November 12, 1947:

> DEAR MR. STANDER:
>
> May I extend my appreciation for your splendid cooperation—

MR. VELDE: Mr. Stander—

MR. STANDER:

> —Cooperation such as yours makes it possible here for the staff to carry on the work which means so much to our troops overseas—

MR. VELDE: Mr. Stander, let me—

MR. STANDER:

> —and the many combat casualties here at home.

MR. VELDE: You may elaborate later if there is some part of your career you are proud of.

MR. STANDER: I am proud of everything I said publicly or privately, and—

MR. VELDE: You have made some self-serving statements, and the Committee—

MR. STANDER: Does this Committee charge me with being a Communist?

MR. VELDE: Mr. Stander, will you let me tell you whether you are charged with being a Communist? Will you be quiet just for a minute while I will tell you what you are here for?

MR. STANDER: Yes, I would like to hear.

MR. VELDE: You are here to give us information which will enable us to do the work that was assigned to us by the House of Representatives, which is a duty imposed upon us to investigate reports regarding subversive activities in the United States.

MR. STANDER: Well, I am more than willing to cooperate—

MR. VELDE: Now, just a minute.

MR. STANDER: Because I have—I know of some subversive activities in the entertainment industry and, elsewhere in the country.

MR. VELDE: Mr. Stander, the Committee is interested—

MR. STANDER: If you are interested, I can tell you some right now.

MR. VELDE: —primarily in any subversive knowledge you have—

MR. STANDER: And I have knowledge of some subversive action.

MR. VELDE: —in the overthrow of the Government.

MR. STANDER: I don't know about the overthrow of the Government. This Committee has been investigating fifteen years so far, and hasn't even found one act of violence.

MR. VELDE: That is entirely—

MR. STANDER: I know of some subversion, and I can help the Committee if it is really interested.

MR. VELDE: Mr. Stander—

MR. STANDER: I know of a group of fanatics who are desperately trying to undermine the Constitution of the United States by depriving artists and others of life, liberty, and pursuit of happiness without due process of law. If you are interested in that, I would like to tell you about it. I can tell names, and I can cite instances, and I am one of the first victims of it, and if you are interested in that—and also a group of ex-Bundists, America Firsters, and anti-Semites, people who hate everybody, including Negroes, minority groups, and most likely themselves—

MR. VELDE: Now, Mr. Stander, let me—

MR. STANDER: And these people are engaged in the conspiracy, outside all the legal processes, to undermine our very fundamental American concepts upon which our entire system of jurisprudence exists—

MR. VELDE: Now, Mr. Stander—

MR. STANDER: —and who also—

MR. VELDE: Let me tell you this: You are a witness before this Committee—

MR. STANDER: Well, if you are interested—

MR. VELDE: —a Committee of the Congress of the United States—

MR. STANDER: —I am willing to tell you—

MR. VELDE: —and you are in the same position as any other witness before this Committee—

MR. STANDER: —I am willing to tell you about these activities—

MR. VELDE: —regardless of your standing in the motion-picture world—

MR. STANDER: —which I think are subversive.

MR. VELDE: —or for any other reason. No witness can come before this Committee and insult the Committee—

MR. STANDER: Is this an insult to the Committee?

MR. VELDE: —and continue to—

MR. STANDER: —when I inform the Committee I know of subversive activities which are contrary to the Constitution?

MR. VELDE: Now, Mr. Stander, unless you begin to answer these questions and act like a witness in a reasonable, dignified manner, under the rules of the Committee, I will be forced to have you removed from this room.

MR. STANDER: I am deeply shocked, Mr. Chairman.

MR. CLARDY: Mr. Stander, let me—

MR. STANDER: Let me explain myself. I don't mean to be contemptuous of this Committee at all.

MR. VELDE: Will you—

MR. STANDER: I want to cooperate with it. You said you would like me to cooperate with you in your attempt to unearth subversive activities. I know of such subversive activities. I began to tell you about them, and I am shocked by your cutting me off. You don't seem to be interested in the sort of subversive activities I know about.

MR. VELDE: You will be asked questions relative to subversive activities by counsel.

MR. STANDER: Let him ask me, and I will be glad to answer. And I am not a dupe, or a dope, or a moe, or a schmoe, and everything I did—I was absolutely conscious of what I was doing, and I am not ashamed of everything [anything?] I said in public or private, and I am very proud of my war record, my private record as a citizen, and my public record as an entertainer.

MR. DOYLE: Mr. Stander, won't you be courteous enough to let our general counsel ask you the questions?

MR. STANDER: But there was an inference of the Chairman that deeply irritated me.

MR. DOYLE: Well—

MR. STANDER: And that is I was out of order. I thought—

MR. DOYLE: You have made your record, and it is very glorious and very fine.

MR. STANDER: I am glad the Committee—

MR. DOYLE: Now, won't you go ahead and cooperate—

MR. STANDER: —thinks that is a very fine record.

MR. DOYLE: —and let somebody else do some talking?

MR. STANDER: I would like that put in the record.

MR. TAVENNER: Mr. Stander, is it correct to say, then, you were engaged as an actor in Hollywood between 1935 and 1948, with the exception of the period when you were in the armed services from 1942 to 1944?

MR. STANDER: Yes, sir.

MR. TAVENNER: What were some of the major screen credits as an actor?

MR. STANDER: I made about a hundred screenplays, and luckily I have forgotten most of them.

MR. TAVENNER: Will you just give us a few of the major ones?

MR. STANDER: Well, *Deeds Goes to Town, Specter of the Rose, A Star Is Born, The Milky Way, The Kid from Brooklyn*—a number of other titles that are completely unimportant to me—

MR. TAVENNER: Well, do you recall whether you left Hollywood in 1948 or in 1949?

MR. STANDER: I'm not sure. I went to make a personal appearance tour of the night-club circuit, which was the only thing left to me after being blacklisted by the major studios—

MR. TAVENNER: Will you tell—

MR. STANDER: —by merely newspaper accusation, without anybody charging me with anything. In fact, the last time I appeared here the Chairman very specifically said that this Committee didn't charge me with anything, and I swore under oath—I would like, if you want, to introduce the record of my testimony here in August 27, 1940.

MR. VELDE: Well, you are not—

MR. TAVENNER: I stated in the beginning—

MR. VELDE: —charged with anything.

MR. STANDER: I am not charged—

MR. VELDE: You are not charged with anything this time.

MR. STANDER: I am not charged with anything?

MR. VELDE: You are not charged with anything, Mr. Stander. You are here—

MR. STANDER: I would like the record to show I am not charged with being a member of the Communist Party; I am not charged with lying under oath, because I have made continuous oaths to various govermental agencies. You are not charging me with being a Communist, right?

MR. CLARDY: Will you subside until the Chairman finishes?

MR. VELDE: You are brought here as a witness.

MR. STANDER: I am a witness—

MR. VELDE: Please don't—

MR. STANDER: —not a defendant. I haven't been accused of anything. I want that very straight, because through newspaper headlines people get peculiar attitudes. Mere appearance here is tantamount—not just appearance, the mere fact, in my case, I was subpoenaed, is tantamount—to being blacklisted, because people say, "What is an actor doing in front of the Un-American Activities Committee?"

MR. CLARDY: Why did you want to appear before the Committee so badly, then, if that is the case?

MR. STANDER: Because I was told by my agent if I appeared before the Committee, and the Committee was a fair Committee, and allowed me to refute Lawrence's testimony, that I would be able to get back in television and motion pictures. I had made eleven television shows in a row, and one of the biggest TV agencies and producers had told my agent that if I went before the Committee and could again swear under oath that I wasn't [a Communist], I would have my own TV program, which meant one hundred fifty thousand dollars a year to me.

MR. CLARDY: Mr. Stander—

MR. STANDER: So, I had a hundred-and-fifty-thousand-buck motive—

MR. CLARDY: Mr. Stander, will you subside?

MR. STANDER: —for coming before the Committee.

MR. CLARDY: If you will just subside and answer the questions, I am sure you will accomplish your purpose.

MR. STANDER: Are you inferring—

MR. CLARDY: Now, just a minute, Mr. Stander.

MR. STANDER: —anything I said wasn't the truth?

MR. CLARDY: Unless you do that, your performance is not going to be regarded as funny.

MR. STANDER: I want to state right now I was not—

MR. CLARDY: Will you please subside?

MR. STANDER: —trying to be funny.

MR. CLARDY: If you continue with what you are doing, I am going to suggest to the Chairman that you are putting on a show, and I am going to ask him to turn on the lights and cameras so that your performance may be recorded for posterity. Now, if you will subside and go along, I am not going to make that request.

MR. STANDER: Mr. Chairman, may I state that, first, to clear up this misunderstanding, I have never been more deadly serious in my life.

MR. CLARDY: All right, then—

MR. STANDER: If anything I said seemed humorous or funny, I assure you it was purely coincidental and doesn't mirror what I deeply feel, because my entire career and the respect of my fellow artists and the American people is at stake, and I don't think that is very funny.

MR. CLARDY: I am a new member of this Committee, and I want to give you all possible opportunity to say what you have to say, but I want you to do it in the proper way.

MR. TAVENNER: Mr. Stander, will you tell the Committee, please, what your formal educational training has consisted of?

MR. STANDER: Well, I went to public schools in New York City, Mount Vernon. I went to various prep schools, a few colleges. I didn't complete my college education. The last university I went to was the University of North Carolina at Chapel Hill.

MR. TAVENNER: When did you attend the University of North Carolina?

MR. STANDER: I think it was 1927 or 1928. I think it was the class of 1930. It was so long ago I can't remember.

MR. TAVENNER: Now, Mr. Stander, I want to present to you some of the results of the investigation that the Committee has made in California relating to activities of the Communist Party and which, if true, would indicate that you have a special knowledge of things that the Committee is inquiring about; and, as a basis for further questioning, I want to read you certain portions of the testimony. Mr. Marc Lawrence, as mentioned before, was a witness before this Committee on April 24, the day you were expected to be, in 1951. In the course of his testimony he admitted having been a member of the Communist Party, and he was asked to describe the circumstances under which he became a Party member. This is part of his testimony:

> About 1938 I attended a number of cause parties. There was a girl who played the piano very well, and she introduced me to these parties. I went to these parties with her, and then I met an actor named Lionel Stander, who said to me, "You want to get to know how to talk to these people. The thing for you to do is to go to classes."

Then he testified he attended twelve meetings of the Communist Party as a member of a cell, and being asked the specific question as to where these meetings were held, Mr. Lawrence stated:

> They were held in different homes in Hollywood. Some I remember, some I don't.
>
> I remember a guy named Lester Cole. Lester Cole was there and the guy who introduced me to the Party, Lionel Stander—he was there.

Now, at our hearings which began in Hollywood on September 17, 1951, Mr. Harold J. Ashe told of his own connections with the Communist Party as a functionary, and he advised the Committee that it was at his instance that professional cells of the Communist Party were first established in Hollywood. Now, Mr. Ashe was asked this question:

> I wish you would give to the Committee the names of the members of these professional units whose membership was to be kept secret.

Mr. Ashe then proceeded to give information relating to various persons who were members of it, and in the course of that this is his testimony:

> Lucy Stander, who was the wife of J. Stander, also known as Lionel Stander—

MR. STANDER: I am not married.
MR. TAVENNER: Or your former wife.
MR. STANDER: Which one?
MR. TAVENNER: Well, the name mentioned here was Lucy.
MR. KEARNEY: Do you remember that name?
MR. STANDER: Yeah, I remember her, vaguely.
MR. TAVENNER: Let me read that again:

> Lucy Stander, who was at that time the wife of J. Stander, also known as Lionel Stander—

MR. STANDER: What time was that? What year?
MR. TAVENNER: I think it was along about 1936.
MR. STANDER: I wasn't married to Lucy in 1936.
MR. SCHERER: It was evidently the time you were married to Lucy. You would know when you were married to Lucy, wouldn't you?

MR. STANDER: Yes. We were separated in 1935.

MR. TAVENNER: I will attempt to read it again:

> Lucy Stander, who was the wife of J. Stander, also known as Lionel Stander—he was a character actor, I believe, in Hollywood. He, however, was not in the unit for any great length of time. I recall distinctly that he was brought in and a very short time later was transferred out. I don't know the reason for the transfer. I think it was arranged directly between Stander and the county office of the Party. However, his wife remained in one of these professional units.
>
> QUESTION: You are definite in your statement, however, that Lionel Stander was a member of this group?
>
> MR. ASHE: Lionel Stander was definitely a member of this group. He was transferred in and I handled the transfer. Of that I am positive.

MR. CLARDY: Who is speaking when you are saying that?

MR. TAVENNER: This is Mr. Ashe, a former functionary of the Communist Party. A further question was asked: "Do you recall from what place he was transferred?" Mr. Ashe said: "I believe New York City."

* * *

MR. TAVENNER: Then, there appeared the testimony of Mr. Martin Berkeley, who testified on September 19, 1951. Mr. Martin Berkeley described a meeting at the home of Mr. Frank Tuttle at which persons other than Communist Party members were present and at which V. J. Jerome spoke. And Mr. Berkeley, in naming the persons, had this to say:

> I also met for the first time Lionel Stander, who later became chairman of the actors' fraction. With him was his wife—his then wife—Alice Twitchell.
>
> It is interesting to know some time later during the strike at the *Hollywood Citizens' News,* for which I gave a benefit at my home for the striking newspapermen, at which we raised approximately a thousand dollars, I believe, to help the Newspaper Guild—and I am very proud that we did—Stander was at this meeting and called me over into a corner and introduced me to Comrade Harry Bridges.
>
> QUESTION: You refer to Stander as the chairman of the actors' fraction, if I understood you correctly.

Then he describes what is meant by "fraction."

(*At this point Mr. Stander conferred with Mr. Boudin.*)

MR. TAVENNER: He was then asked the question: "Did you ever attend a Communist Party meeting in the home of Lionel Stander?"

(*At this point Mr. Stander conferred with Mr. Boudin.*)

MR. TAVENNER: Mr. Berkeley replied: "I did, sir. There was a meeting called at the home of Stander, at which V. J. Jerome was present, that dealt with the matter of the struggle then going on in the Screen Actors Guild." Mr. Martin Berkeley testified before the Committee in executive session on

January 29, 1952, at which time he stated, with reference to Mr. [Cedric] Belfrage, who was a witness here yesterday: "My first official Party contact with Belfrage was at his home at a meeting attended by Herbert Biberman, Gale Sondergaard, Lionel Stander, and his wife, Alice."

(*At this point Mr. Stander conferred with Mr. Boudin.*)

MR. TAVENNER: "Nobody was there except Party members."

* * *

MR. TAVENNER: So, I want to ask you the question whether or not you were a member of the Communist Party at any time during the period when you were in California between 1935 and 1948?

MR. STANDER: This is a continuing Committee. I made a statement under oath in 1940. I would like you to read that into the record. You asked me a question that took about twenty minutes. This will take exactly three minutes. Would you mind reading this?

MR. TAVENNER: Will you answer my question?

MR. STANDER: I swore under oath before this Committee, in 1940, that I was not a member of the Communist Party. I also—

MR. TAVENNER: What do you say now?

MR. STANDER: I also swore in 1940 before the Los Angeles grand jury, its district attorney, and I forced my way in there. I was a voluntary witness, and one of the witnesses used here, and John Leech, who was later characterized by Judge Landis as a psychopathic liar, made similar statements to the statements made by Marc Lawrence and others. I swore under oath before the Los Angeles grand jury and the district attorney, and the district attorney's bureau saw fit to clear me and released a statement to the press absolving me of any participation whatsoever, and the grand jury also cleared me of the charges made before them. So, I have already been cleared by the district attorney, and the grand jury said I was a fine, patriotic, American citizen. I am reading from my 1940 testimony—

MR. VELDE: Now, Mr. Stander—

MR. STANDER: —which is the first time it ever has been released to the press—

MR. VELDE: —you promised me you would answer the question.

MR. STANDER: —and the story on that appeared on the front pages of all the Los Angeles newspapers.

MR. VELDE: Mr. Stander—

MR. STANDER: I have sworn under oath in 1940 twice. I swore under oath in an affidavit for the Royal Canadian Air Force and for the United States Air Force. I worked in a very sensitive spot, in the headquarters' staff, and, from my understanding, it is standard operating procedure to be cleared by the FBI. I cannot see it would serve the purposes of this Committee to ask me about periods during 1934, 1935, and 1936—

MR. VELDE: Mr. Stander—

MR. STANDER: And, incidentally, while you are mentioning that, there's obvious contradictions.

MR. VELDE: Mr. Stander, will you—

MR. STANDER: Miss [Mrs. Mildred] Ashe said in 1934 she collected dues from me—

MR. VELDE: Mr. Stander—

MR. STANDER: —and some people. I wasn't in Hollywood then. Her husband said it was in 1936.

MR. VELDE: Mr. Stander—

MR. STANDER: And my wife left me in 1935.

MR. VELDE: Mr. Stander, may I remind you that you have promised to answer the questions—

MR. STANDER: I have answered.

MR. VELDE: —and now will you—

MR. STANDER: I have sworn under oath, and if there is any—

MR. TAVENNER: I haven't asked you what you have done in the past.

MR. STANDER: If any of these charges be true, why haven't I been indicted?

MR. VELDE: Will you now answer the question—

MR. STANDER: I was asked a twenty-five-minute question and I can't even give a two-minute answer. I don't think that is fair.

MR. CLARDY: Mr. Stander, now, I suggested something to you a moment ago. You have been asked a straightforward question as to whether or not you were a Communist during a certain period. Now, answer that—

MR. STANDER: I swore under oath—

MR. CLARDY: —yes or no—

MR. STANDER: I swore—

MR. CLARDY: —or refuse to answer it on constitutional grounds.

MR. STANDER: I swore under oath in 1940, and that was covered by this same Committee.

MR. SCHERER: Why don't you swear under oath now whether you were?

MR. STANDER: You want me to give you the reason?

MR. SCHERER: Yes.

MR. STANDER: Because by using psychopaths—and I have the letter here giving the mental history of Marc Lawrence, who came from a mental sanitorium—he suffered a mental breakdown, and I gave you the names of the doctors—and you used that psychopath and used previously this man Leech, who the district attorney and the grand jury of Los Angeles didn't believe, throughout his charges, and they cleared me—so, I don't want to be responsible for a whole stable of informers, stool pigeons, and psychopaths and ex-political heretics, who come in here beating their breast and say, "I am awfully sorry, I didn't know what I was doing. Please, I want absolution, get me back into pictures," and they will do anything—they will name anybody—they will go to any extent necessary to get back into pictures, they will mention names and name anybody.

MR. VELDE: Now, will you answer the question?

MR. STANDER: Therefore, I decline to answer that question. It clearly is not relevant to the purpose of this Committee, and it violates my rights under the First and Fifth Amendments of the Constitution of the United States. And, incidentally, don't give me the routine about hiding, because the only people, witnesses, who hide here are witnesses like—

MR. VELDE: Mr. Stander—

MR. STANDER: —these people named here, who hide behind the cloak of legal responsibility, and I know, because I tried to get somewhere in the courts of New York, and I find the only people who hide behind immunity are the witnesses, the stool pigeons, used here, and that you are using, arrogating—

MR. TAVENNER: Have you finished?

MR. STANDER: No, this Committee arrogates judicial and punitive powers which it does not possess.

MR. CLARDY: Are you a Communist today?

MR. STANDER: No, I am not a Communist today. If you ask me was I a Communist yesterday, no, I wasn't, and I swore under oath, and it's a matter of public record—

MR. CLARDY: Were you at any time ever a member of the Communist Party?

MR. STANDER: You know that is a trick question to trap me to answer the same question. I would be an absolute idiot—

MR. CLARDY: No, I don't think you are.

MR. STANDER: Then, if you don't, you must think I am a political moron.

MR. CLARDY: Were you ever at any time a member of the Communist Party?

MR. STANDER: My record is absolutely clear. How many times do I have to swear under oath before governmental agencies?

MR. CLARDY: Just this once.

MR. STANDER: And how many times do you have to use my name to get headlines?

MR. CLARDY: Just this once.

MR. STANDER: And how many—

MR. CLARDY: Just this once.

MR. STANDER: I have already sworn under oath I am not now a member of the Communist Party.

MR. CLARDY: And never have been?

MR. STANDER: And I swore in 1940 I was never a member of the Communist Party, and never will be, and I would have to be pretty stupid if I swore that in 1940 and know the FBI automatically gets copies of every complaint that I joined the Communist Party later, I would have to be a complete idiot.

MR. TAVENNER: Will you read my question?

MR. STANDER: You want to repeat that twenty-five-minute question?

MR. TAVENNER: No, I only asked you a question which did not contain over fifteen or twenty words.

MR. STANDER: It seems to me this is a disgraceful experience for me to have to go through, when I answered and swore under oath in peacetime, and in wartime, when I was of draft age and enlisted in the RCAF, and then for the United States Air Force. This is a terribly disgraceful experience to go through, to be brought here because of these insinuations and accusations, and something which you don't dare charge me with. You said, and Congressman Dies stated specifically, I was not charged with anything, and this Committee says I am not charged with anything—

MR. MOULDER: Mr. Chairman, may I—

MR. STANDER: —yet, you are trying to trick me, depriving me of my constitutional rights. And it's two years since I requested an appearance—during which this fanatic group of subversives have blacklisted artists and are attempting to impose censorship on the free theater that we all believe in and love, and you people are in a way—I don't say consciously—instrumental in aiding them.

MR. DOYLE: Mr. Chairman—

MR. CLARDY: Mr. Stander—

MR. VELDE: The Committee is about to go into recess for ten minutes.

(*Whereupon, at 11:10 a.m., the hearing was recessed, to reconvene at 11:25 a.m., the following Committee members being present: Representatives Harold H. Velde* (*Chairman*), *Kit Clardy, Gordon H. Scherer, Morgan M. Moulder, Clyde Doyle.*)

MR. VELDE: Proceed, Mr. Counsel.

MR. STANDER: Will you turn out the lights?

MR. VELDE: Will the television cameras and newsreel cameras please desist? Will you please turn off the lights and desist from taking further film?

MR. TAVENNER: Mr. Reporter, I would like for you to read back the question to the witness which I asked—the last question.

(*The reporter read the question as follows:*)

> So, I want to ask you the question whether or not you were a member of the Communist Party at any time during the period when you were in California between 1935 and 1948?

MR. STANDER: I decline to answer this under constitutional rights which were just recently reaffirmed by Judge Youngdahl in the Lattimore case. I have a freedom of belief. You, as Congressmen, uphold the Constitution and you know that Federal judges have said it is not only your right, but your duty, whenever a Congressional Committee trespasses upon areas from which it's forbidden to, that it is the duty and right of the citizen to avail themselves of this privilege.

MR. VELDE: You are declining—

MR. BOUDIN: He hasn't completed his answer.

MR. STANDER: I decline under the First Amendment, which entitles me to freedom of belief; under the Fifth Amendment—

MR. SCHERER: Fifth Amendment?

MR. STANDER: Which states that I shall not be forced to testify against myself, and also in which there is no inference of guilt—it is designed to protect the innocent—and under the Ninth Amendment, which gives me other rights—for instance, the right to get up in the union hall, which I did, and introduce a resolution condemning this Congressional Committee for its abuse of powers in attempting to impose censorship upon the American theater.

MR. TAVENNER: Now, Mr. Stander—

MR. STANDER: And, finally, in my estimation, this entire question is not relative to the purposes of this Committee, because I can't understand why a question dating back to 1948, 1936, or 1935 concerning statements made by a bunch of stool pigeons and informers can aid this Committee in recommending any legislation to Congress, which I understand is the purpose of this Committee.

MR. TAVENNER: Mr. Stander, in the course of the testimony which I read you from Mr. Martin Berkeley—

MR. STANDER: I can save the time of the Committee. Anything else you will ask me, I will decline to answer on the aforementioned grounds and my constitutional privileges under the First, Fifth, and Ninth Amendments—

MR. TAVENNER: Mr. Stander, you have insisted you made a very earnest request to appear before this Committee to answer—

MR. STANDER: Answer what?

MR. TAVENNER: Answer testimony.

MR. STANDER: Answer charges?

MR. TAVENNER: No, not charges.

MR. STANDER: I attempted to do it in the courts, where I am protected by the Anglo-Saxon procedures—

MR. TAVENNER: Well, you were—

MR. STANDER: And under our Constitution, where I can cross-examine, and where a witness has complete legal responsibility.

MR. TAVENNER: Then, I understand—

MR. STANDER: Therefore, I don't choose to pit my word against a psychopathic liar, who was characterized as such by Judge Landis, or a man out of a mental institution, Marc Lawrence, who is a refugee from that case.

MR. TAVENNER: Are you acquainted with Martin Berkeley?

MR. STANDER: I told you any question along those lines by stool pigeons, informers, psychopathic liars, or anybody—for instance, Mr. Berkeley. I read in the minutes that, first, he said he was not a member of the Communist Party, then, when he realized you had the goods on him, he came here and rattled off one hundred fifty names. This is, in my idea, an incredible witness.

MR. VELDE: Do you decline to answer that question?

MR. STANDER: And I decline to answer under my constitutional rights, which I am proud of, and I resent the inference here that anyone who uses it, which our forefathers fought for, is guilty of anything.

(*Representative James B. Frazier, Jr., entered the hearing room at this point.*)

MR. STANDER: You know this is an ancient right of the American people.

MR. CLARDY: Mr. Counsel—

MR. STANDER: My name is Stander. It was adopted in 1943* because, unfortunately, in feudal Spain my ancestors didn't have the protection of the United States Constitution and were religious refugees. And you know that the Puritans used it, the people that established this country used this right, and I have done a little research on this since you called me, and the first experience of it was—

MR. TAVENNER: Will you answer the question I asked you?

MR. STANDER: —and I am not being sacrilegious—was when Jesus Christ was asked by Pontius Pilate, "These judges have a lot of witnesses against you?" and He said nothing.

MR. TAVENNER: I asked you a question—

MR. STANDER: Yes, and I answered the question, and I am a deeply religious man.

MR. TAVENNER: —which had nothing to do with religion.

MR. STANDER: Yes, it does, because that question is designed to trap me. You know, as I stated the first time I swore under oath—

MR. TAVENNER: You haven't sworn under oath in answer to these questions.

MR. STANDER: I swore under oath in 1950, I swore under oath before the Los Angeles grand jury, and I don't want to take up the time of the Committee—you get me excited—and any questions along that line I will decline to answer on the grounds of constitutional privileges.

* * *

MR. TAVENNER: Was Martin Berkeley—

MR. VELDE: Just a minute, counsel. It is very apparent that the witness is excited and nervous, as he stated.

* Possibly an earlier date is meant? —E.B.

MR. STANDER: Not as nervous as Marc Lawrence, who came out of a mental institution.

MR. VELDE: You said you would cooperate with the Committee and give it the benefit of your knowledge.

MR. STANDER: Against the blacklisting. Pardon me, I am sorry.

MR. VELDE: It is the order of the Chair and this Committee that you be continued under subpoena, and the investigation and hearing be continued in your case until a future date, at which time you will be notified by our counsel.

MR. STANDER: May I make one statement now?

MR. CLARDY: No.

JUNE 2, 1953:

Lee J. Cobb

An executive statement * given at 4:30 p.m., June 2, 1953, at room 1117, Hollywood Roosevelt Hotel, Hollywood, California.

Present: William A. Wheeler, Investigator.

MR. WHEELER: State your name, please.

MR. COBB: Lee J. Cobb.

MR. WHEELER: When and where were you born, Mr. Cobb?

MR. COBB: New York City, December 9, 1911.

MR. WHEELER: Your educational background, just briefly.

MR. COBB: Public schools and high school in New York City and CCNY at night.

MR. WHEELER: Did you obtain any degrees from New York City College?

MR. COBB: No.

MR. WHEELER: Your profession is that of an actor?

MR. COBB: That is correct.

MR. WHEELER: And how long have you been so employed?

MR. COBB: Twenty-two years or so.

MR. WHEELER: You have appeared both on the New York stage as well as in motion pictures?

MR. COBB: Yes, and radio and television.

MR. WHEELER: Mr. Cobb, are you presently under subpoena?

MR. COBB: No, sir.

MR. WHEELER: Are you represented by an attorney?

* HUAC reserved the right to make public any testimony given in private. Other examples in the present book are the Kazan testimony and the final part of the Parks testimony, though the release of this last was stated to be at Mr. Parks' behest. —E.B.

MR. COBB: No, sir.

MR. WHEELER: Do you desire counsel?

MR. COBB: No, sir.

MR. WHEELER: You realize by giving me this statement that it does not eliminate the possibility that in the future you may be called as a witness before the Committee?

MR. COBB: I do, and I shall be happy to appear wherever and whenever the Committee directs.

MR. WHEELER: Mr. Cobb, are you acquainted with Larry Parks?

MR. COBB: Yes, I am.

MR. WHEELER: I would like to refer to his testimony in executive session on March 21, 1951. Mr. Parks testified that he was a member of the Communist Party in Hollywood and was being questioned by Mr. Tavenner, Counsel for the Committee on Un-American Activities, and was asked to identify individuals whom he had known to be members of the Communist Party. Mr. Parks stated that he knew Lee Cobb to be a Communist. Is that a correct statement?

MR. COBB: Yes, that is correct.

MR. WHEELER: When did you join the Communist Party, Mr. Cobb?

MR. COBB: I joined in 1941, I believe, 1940 or 1941.

MR. WHEELER: In what city did you join?

MR. COBB: In New York City.

MR. WHEELER: Do you recall the circumstances that led up to your becoming a member of the Communist Party?

MR. COBB: I do.

MR. WHEELER: Would you relate them, please?

MR. COBB: In the pursuit of my professional endeavors I became a member of the Group Theater in New York. As a member, I made several friends, among them Phoebe Brand and Morris Carnovsky. It was at their invitation, after an association professionally and in friendship of a few years, that I attended a couple of meetings as a visitor and subsequently accepted the fact that I was a member. I put it that way because there didn't seem to be any formality involved, such as the signing of a card or indoctrination of any other kind.

MR. WHEELER: Well, Morris Carnovsky and Phoebe Brand, in all probability, did some kind of sales talk to promote the Communist Party so that you would become interested in it. What sold you on the Communist Party?

MR. COBB: As I recall, the atmosphere in the country as a whole at that time lent itself to rather a loose liberal, if not leftist, interpretation of events, local and international, and at that time we took each other for granted as subscribing generally to a similar interpretation of history. I was influenced greatly by their seniority within the group. I respected their opinions and, as I say, socially as friends we had known each other sufficiently long for me to accept an invitation of that kind.

MR. WHEELER: How long were you a member of the Communist Party in New York City?

MR. COBB: In New York City it was until the middle of or the beginning of 1942, at which time I went to a small town called Tyrone, Pennsylvania, where I undertook a Government course in flight training to improve my qualifications to become a flight instructor.

MR. WHEELER: How many months would you say you were a member of the Communist Party in New York, approximately?

MR. COBB: To the best of my recollection, it lacked a year. I imagine it was in the vicinity of eight or ten months.

MR. WHEELER: How many meetings did you attend over that period of time?

MR. COBB: I would say half a dozen.

MR. WHEELER: Do you recall who notified you of the meetings? The attendance was infrequent; therefore, I assume you would have to be notified.

MR. COBB: I would say that invariably it was either Phoebe Brand or Morris Carnovsky, since they were the ones I knew most intimately.

MR. WHEELER: Where were the meetings held?

MR. COBB: In a private house. At the Carnovskys'. I can't recall the names of several of the other people, although I have succeeded over the last week in isolating some of them visually, but I don't remember what their names were.

MR. WHEELER: Do you recall who was chairman of the group?

MR. COBB: No, sir. I am much more dependable with respect to recalling the names of the people in Hollywood than I seem to be with respect to the New York period, which is quite confused, because I had been attending meetings in connection with Actors Equity, as well as a caucus within Equity called the Forum, in addition to these party meetings. The Forum was a caucus within Equity, purportedly dedicated to liberal union issues, in which a Communist fraction played an important part.

MR. WHEELER: Well, how did you become aware of this fraction?

MR. COBB: I heard references among Communists to the fact that there were fraction meetings on Forum questions. Also, as a Communist, I was instructed to support certain issues or vote in certain ways on the floor of Equity meetings whenever these issues arose.

MR. WHEELER: Did you ever attend a meeting of this fraction?

MR. COBB: No, sir.

MR. WHEELER: Do you recall any specific issues that you were instructed to vote in a certain way on?

MR. COBB: No.

MR. WHEELER: Who controlled the Forum? Who was the actual leader of the caucus?

MR. COBB: Prominent in the Forum activities were, among others, Phil Loeb and Sam Jaffe, though I never knew them to be Communists. And I don't mean by mentioning their names to suggest that they were. But in answer to your question, they were very active in the Forum, as well as Bob Reed.

MR. WHEELER: Did you pay dues in New York, do you recall?

MR. COBB: In New York I don't remember paying any dues in the Communist Party. Possibly I paid the nominal twenty-five-cent minimum which was required. That, incidentally, goes for my dues-paying on the West Coast, too. I never paid any appreciable sum.

MR. WHEELER: Now, do you recall any of the members of this group, other than Phoebe Brand and her husband, Morris Carnovsky?

MR. COBB: On the occasion of my meeting with the Federal Bureau of Investigation I tried to recall the names for that purpose as well and was successful. Since then I have recalled one more name, and that is the name of Pete Lyon, or Pete Lyons.

MR. WHEELER: What was his occupation?

MR. COBB: I believe he was a radio writer. Also Bob Reed. I mentioned Bob Reed to the FBI.

MR. WHEELER: What was Mr. Reed's occupation?

MR. COBB: He was an actor.

MR. WHEELER: Would you please give your estimate of the number of people in this group in New York City of which you were a member?

MR. COBB: I would estimate about ten.

MR. WHEELER: I believe you testified that in 1942 you went to Pennsylvania to become a flight instructor, is that correct?

MR. COBB: Yes. I took this course and completed it and got my instructor's rating and commercial license.

MR. WHEELER: How long were you in Pennsylvania?

MR. COBB: About three months.

MR. WHEELER: Did you have any contact or association with the Communist Party or members of the Communist Party while receiving this instruction?

MR. COBB: No, sir, not at that time.

MR. WHEELER: After you received your certificate for instructor, where did you move to then?

MR. COBB: I went directly to Hollywood.

MR. WHEELER: And approximately what date would this be?

MR. COBB: Middle of August 1942.

MR. WHEELER: When you arrived in Hollywood, did you reaffiliate with the Communist Party?

MR. COBB: It was after a number of months, quite a few months.

Mr. Wheeler: Would you say as long as a year?

Mr. Cobb: Well, certainly six months.

Mr. Wheeler: That would bring it up to January or February of 1943.

Mr. Cobb: That's right. I was contacted here by the Party and advised that I was assigned to a local group and told to come to a meeting.

Mr. Wheeler: Do you recall who contacted you?

Mr. Cobb: I believe it was Gerry Schlein.

Mr. Wheeler: What was Mrs. Schlein's occupation?

Mr. Cobb: I don't think she had any professional occupation. She was a housewife, the wife of an artist by the name of Charles Schlein.

Mr. Wheeler: Did you know Charles Schlein as a member of the Communist Party?

Mr. Cobb: No, sir.

Mr. Wheeler: I assume that his wife, contacting you, was a member?

Mr. Cobb: Oh, yes, she was. We met at her home several times.

Mr. Wheeler: Were you assigned to a group in Hollywood?

Mr. Cobb: Yes. I don't know that the group was identified by any name or number, but virtually all of the people in it were.

Mr. Wheeler: How long did you remain a member of the Communist Party in Hollywood?

Mr. Cobb: With the exception of two years, during which I was in the Army, in the Air Force, I was with this group from the last date mentioned to sometime in 1946.

Mr. Wheeler: We established that you probably reaffiliated with the party in January or February of 1943. Now, can you tell us what date you entered the United States Army?

Mr. Cobb: I entered the Armed Forces of the United States on September 7, 1943.

Mr. Wheeler: Well, then, in 1943 you were a member of the Communist Party for approximately eight months. Do you recall how many individuals comprised this group you were assigned to?

Mr. Cobb: Oh, a dozen, roughly.

Mr. Wheeler: How many meetings did you attend?

Mr. Cobb: For the period before I went into the Army, must have been possibly ten or twelve.

Mr. Wheeler: How often did they meet?

Mr. Cobb: They met every three weeks, two or three weeks. It is evident that I was not regular in attendance. That accounts for the discrepancy in the number of times.

Mr. Wheeler: Do you recall who the members of this group were?

Mr. Cobb: Yes, I do. To the best of my recollection, the members were Ann Revere, Gale Sondergaard, Dorothy Tree, Larry Parks, Marc Lawrence, Gerry Schlein, Lloyd Bridges, Shimen Ruskin, Rose Hobart, Jeff

Corey, George Tyne, and Ludwig Donath. Several of these I had completely forgotten about until I was asked.

MR. WHEELER: On how many occasions would you say you met Ludwig Donath as a member of the Communist Party?

MR. COBB: His name is last on the list because he was the last one I recall, and I don't think I saw him more often than three or four times. It could have been because he was a member of the other group and I didn't see him until there was this unification. Elliott Sullivan is another one. Victor Killian, Sr., George Tyne, also known as Buddy Yarus.

MR. WHEELER: During this eight-month period, the first time you were in the Party here in Hollywood, did you pay dues?

MR. COBB: From time to time, yes, I would pay the minimum. I frankly explained that when I was working I was making a sizable salary and I didn't think it was fair the weeks that I worked to pay such a large fee.

MR. WHEELER: They had requested that you pay a percentage?

MR. COBB: A percentage of salary.

MR. WHEELER: Do you recall what the percentage was?

MR. COBB: No. I think there was a sliding scale, if I am not mistaken, but I never did it, so I didn't know.

MR. WHEELER: What would you estimate your dues amounted to over this eight-month period?

MR. COBB: Certainly no more than five or ten dollars.

MR. WHEELER: Do you recall who the chairman of this group was or any other officers of this particular club?

MR. COBB: I recall that Gerry Schlein was pretty much the driving force in the group.

MR. WHEELER: Do you recall whom you paid the dues to?

MR. COBB: No. I believe that varied from time to time. The treasurer would be a different one.

MR. WHEELER: What was the purpose of this group? What was the purpose of having a group of Communists comprised of actors?

MR. COBB: Well, I don't know what their affirmed purpose was. I do know in effect it seemed to serve no practical purpose, except the indoctrination and general orientation of actors.

MR. WHEELER: Was it possible that an actor can portray in any way the Communist Party line through the method of acting? Can he get over a political line or thought?

MR. COBB: No. I don't think that was at all possible. However, a project was undertaken, led by John Howard Lawson, to rewrite the precepts of Stanislavski's method on acting, to try as far as possible to color it by the prevailing Communist ideologies. The project failed miserably because the moment we departed from the text as published by Stanislavski we destroyed the most important aspect of it, and consequently I resigned from the project.

Mr. Wheeler: Who was Stanislavski and what was his method of acting?

Mr. Cobb: Stanislavski was an actor and director in Russia, before and since the revolution, who kept himself above all political questions of the time and dedicated his life to formulating an approach, a scientific approach, for the actor in his work, and for the first time broke down into scientific terms the elements involved in the creation of a role and thereby made possible a cogent practical attack for the actor.

Mr. Wheeler: Have you reached any conclusion in your own mind why John Howard Lawson wanted to change the writing of Stanislavski?

Mr. Cobb: The excuse was that however good Stanislavski was, he would be so much better if he were a Communist, and so the purpose was to add the Communist portion to Stanislavski, which he was not endowed with by God.

Mr. Wheeler: Stanislavski's method of acting has been widely adopted in the United States by members of the acting profession?

Mr. Cobb: All over the world. It had a profound effect upon acting in general.

Mr. Wheeler: How long did you state you were in the United States Army?

Mr. Cobb: Almost two years. I was discharged, honorably discharged, on August 24, 1945.

Mr. Wheeler: What was your rank at that time?

Mr. Cobb: Pfc.

Mr. Wheeler: Where did you serve in the United States Army?

Mr. Cobb: Mainly at Santa Ana with a radio-production unit.

Mr. Wheeler: While at Santa Ana, or, rather, while you were in the armed services, did you participate in any Communist meetings?

Mr. Cobb: No, sir. There was a strict directive in the Party prohibiting that.

Mr. Wheeler: Do you know for what reason?

Mr. Cobb: I can only suspect that, since that was a period of relative harmony as between the Allies, it was thought best not to do anything that might upset that.

Mr. Wheeler: Well, after you were discharged, did you resume your membership in the Communist Party?

Mr. Cobb: I waited until I was invited again, and attended some few additional meetings during which it became increasingly clear that I and Mrs. Cobb, who, incidentally, has the same attendance record as my own in the Party, were thorns in their sides and more and more didn't subscribe to the requirements and the general pattern of acquiescence.

Mr. Wheeler: What pattern of acquiescence did you object to?

Mr. Cobb: Well, a big point was made of adhering to a spirit of democratic centralism, and it was so obvious that the centralism obtained, and the democracy was only given lip service to. True, we were invited to discuss things and to raise questions, but if after that we still were unconvinced, invariably you were to be pitied and perhaps given some extra talking to and lecturing, and prevailing opinion as handed down was not to be questioned.

MR. WHEELER: Were you a member of the Communist Party at the time the Duclos letter was written?

MR. COBB: I know of its existence. I never read the letter. I know generally what its purpose was.

MR. WHEELER: Well, did it affect you in any way in your leaving the Communist Party?

MR. COBB: It was shocking to me and it coincided with my general disenchantment with the Party methods.

MR. WHEELER: After you reaffiliated in 1945, were there any additional new members of this group? I am going on the assumption that you were reassigned back to the actors' group.

MR. COBB: If there were, they were included in the [my?] general list of people.

MR. WHEELER: You have identified all the individuals you met as Communists in Hollywood?

MR. COBB: That's right.

MR. WHEELER: Did any outside instructors come in to give lectures?

MR. COBB: Yes, lectures and classes of a sort were held by Arnold Manoff.

MR. WHEELER: He is a screen writer?

MR. COBB: He is a screen writer, and, on one occasion, a functionary, whose name I never got, had a private talk with me in an attempt to congenially pull me back into line. I can only describe him. He was a man of more than average height. He had dark hair that was straight. He spoke with a German accent.

MR. WHEELER: When do you date the time you completely left the Party, or, rather, you quit attending meetings?

MR. COBB: In an endeavor to be completely certain, I was going to say 1947, but in discussing it with Mrs. Cobb, she was convinced that it must have been sometime in 1946.

MR. WHEELER: Well, would you say the first quarter or the second quarter or the third quarter? What would your estimate be?

MR. COBB: Well, to avoid error, I would rather be on the long side than the short side, so I would say perhaps even as late as the third or fourth quarter.

MR. WHEELER: We could estimate your membership after you returned from the Army [as] a period of about a year. That could vary one way or the other?

MR. COBB: That's right, a month or two.

MR. WHEELER: How many meetings would you say you attended?

MR. COBB: Very few. My ability to attend was circumscribed because I was sent on location on one or two occasions to Mexico.

MR. WHEELER: At that time you were under contract with Twentieth Century–Fox?

MR. COBB: Yes.

MR. WHEELER: Their records would show the period of time you were on location?

MR. COBB: Yes. That is true. I have some of the dates.

MR. WHEELER: Could you estimate the months that you were away?

MR. COBB: Yes, I could. I was about three months in Mexico, about five weeks in Connecticut and New York.

MR. WHEELER: Anyplace else?

MR. COBB: I was on location in Chicago in 1946 or 1947. I can estimate that the time I was away from Hollywood during my latter membership was about five months.

MR. WHEELER: I have no further questions to ask you about the period of time you were a Communist. I would like to ask you if you think we have covered most of the information you possess.

MR. COBB: I think so, and I want to make myself clear as being available should any further questions be necessary. If I should recall anything further that would be pertinent, may I amend?

MR. WHEELER: Certainly. Upon receipt of a letter, we can amend the testimony, with the permission of the Chairman. Were you a member of the Progressive Citizens of America?

MR. COBB: Is that the same organization that became ASP?

MR. WHEELER: Yes, it is.

MR. COBB: At one time I paid a dollar and got on the mailing list of ASP. If that makes me a member, I was.

MR. WHEELER: It is noted here that a conference on thought control, sponsored by the Hollywood Arts and Sciences and Professions Council, Progressive Citizens of America, was held in the Beverly Hills Hotel. This information indicates that you were a sponsor of the thought-control conference, is that correct?

MR. COBB: I was a speaker.

MR. WHEELER: You were a speaker?

MR. COBB: I was invited to speak at this panel, and when I demurred on the grounds that I was a poor speaker and hardly an authority, it was suggested that ASP would have the speech written for me, and when I examined the roster of what seemed to be respectable speakers from the university et cetera, I agreed to give this talk if the speech satisfied me.

MR. WHEELER: Do you remember the topic of the speech?

MR. COBB: It had to do with the historical role of the actor.

MR. WHEELER: Do you know who wrote it?

MR. COBB: No, I don't. It came unsigned.

MR. WHEELER: Was there any political content in it to your knowledge? Or Communistic content?

MR. COBB: It was not Communistic. It was liberal in tone and had no special pertinence to the present. It was mildly erudite and contained a lot of anecdotal information.

MR. WHEELER: Do you believe that the United States Government and Committees of Congress have the right—I am not speaking of the rights as set up by the laws of the United States—but the right to investigate Communists within any environment in the United States?

MR. COBB: Yes, sir, I do. I believe a reasonable interpretation of the laws and the Constitution would disclose not only a right but a duty on the part of the various agencies of the Government so to do.

MR. WHEELER: Do you believe that the Committee on Un-American Activities so-called set up a censorship of scripts in the motion-picture industry or of the products to be released by the motion-picture industry?

MR. COBB: No, sir, I have seen no instance of it.

MR. WHEELER: Now, the program of the American Peace Mobilization discloses that you signed a call to the American People's meeting to be held in New York City on April 5 and 6, 1941. I assume this was about the period of time you joined the Communist Party.

MR. COBB: That's right. It must have been around that time.

MR. WHEELER: Do you remember signing such a thing?

MR. COBB: No. I wouldn't deny it, but I don't specifically recall.

MR. WHEELER: Are you familiar with an organization known as the International Labor Defense?

MR. COBB: I have heard of it.

MR. WHEELER: Well, the *Daily Worker* of March 5, 1942, page 8, reports that Lee J. Cobb is going to be an auctioneer in the selling of books for this organization.

MR. COBB: I don't recall anything in that connection. I am strongly inclined to say that I don't remember ever being an auctioneer for anything.

MR. WHEELER: That would be a unique experience if you had been an auctioneer, and if so, you would recall it, wouldn't you?

MR. COBB: I would recall it. There is no doubt that at that time I permitted myself to be identified with organizations, that is, with themes of that kind.

MR. WHEELER: I notice from activities concerning the League of American Writers that they also had an auction and you were reported as the auctioneer and the reference is given as the *Daily Worker,* March 5, 1942, page 8. There must be a mistake made by whoever compiled it?

MR. COBB: That would be the same thing, wouldn't it?

Mr. Wheeler: Yes. So it would either be the International Labor Defense or the League of American Writers, I would assume.

Mr. Cobb: In either case, I must say that it is possible that I was tapped on the shoulder to do something like that. But, in all honesty, I don't recall the specific instance.

Mr. Wheeler: The *Daily Worker* of October 19, 1948, page 7, in an article, reports that you signed a statement in support of Henry Wallace, to which I certainly don't take exception. However, this was sponsored by the National Council of Arts, Sciences, and Professions.

Mr. Cobb: I probably did sign it.

Mr. Wheeler: You don't recall the background of who asked you?

Mr. Cobb: I think there was a banquet which I attended.

Mr. Wheeler: For Henry Wallace?

Mr. Cobb: I think it was for Henry Wallace. As I recall, it was quite an extensive affair. I think it was at Ciro's. A good representation of Hollywood society was there.

Mr. Wheeler: The *Daily Worker* of March 8, 1949, page 13, shows you as a sponsor of a Cultural and Scientific Conference for World Peace to be held on March 25 to 27, 1949. The article reports that you were also on the conference program. Do you recall anything about this particular item?

Mr. Cobb: I recall specifically signing the petition. I was never asked nor did I appear on any program in that connection. The occasion was a young high-school boy and girl coming backstage to the dressing room of the theater where I was then playing in New York City with the petition, acquainting me with the fact that it was a plea for peace, and I could see that quite a few prominent world figures had already signed, and I must say that I am most receptive where any efforts for the cause of world peace are concerned, and so I signed. I didn't look any further for any hidden political implications in this.

Mr. Wheeler: Were you a member of Actors' Lab?

Mr. Cobb: No, I was not a member of the Lab. I worked with the Lab and I taught one term.

Mr. Wheeler: Did you receive compensation?

Mr. Cobb: No, sir.

Mr. Wheeler: I just wondered, because the school was approved by the United States Government for GI—

Mr. Cobb: That was much later. When I taught at the Lab it was, I believe, before I went into the service.

Mr. Wheeler: To what degree did the Communist Party control the Actors' Lab?

Mr. Cobb: To the degree that there were several Communists on the board of the Lab. Incidentally, I declined, when I was invited to become a board member, because of my ideas about the theater which were in variance with theirs. Their intention was to make the Lab a mass people's organization, which obviously would have made impossible any real theater activity, and since I was interested in the theater, I did not lend myself to the attempt.

MR. WHEELER: Did the Communist fraction in the Lab in any way control the product of Actors' Lab?

MR. COBB: They influenced it insofar as they could influence other members on the board. I don't know whether, numerically, they were in the majority on the board, and, of course, I have no way of knowing to what extent they could have been an influence through personal association with the students and other people in the Lab.

MR. WHEELER: I note here by the *Daily Worker* of February 23, 1948, page 16, the Actors' Lab evidently formulated some type of protest against censorship. I note from this article or from the dossier that you were a supporter of this program. Do you recall any of the background of how you became a supporter?

MR. COBB: That was directed at the committee investigation, was it?

MR. WHEELER: I would go on that assumption, Mr. Cobb. Unfortunately, I don't have the article here.

MR. COBB: Did you say I signed something?

MR. WHEELER: It says you supported the Actors' Lab and protested against censorship.

MR. COBB: That may have been in connection with attacks on the Lab by the Tenney committee in California, which, in all honesty, I had considered as unfair. I think it must have been that.

MR. WHEELER: Are you familiar with the People's Drama?

MR. COBB: No, sir.

MR. WHEELER: The *Daily Worker* of August 22, 1949, page 11, reflects that you signed a call for a meeting. This was sponsored by the People's Drama.

MR. COBB: I perhaps did, but I still know nothing of the People's Drama.

MR. WHEELER: Well, the *Daily Worker* of September 2, 1949, page 4, discloses that you signed a statement on behalf of Robeson. I imagine, the Paul Robeson meeting.

MR. COBB: That was in 1949. I recall the time, and I recall that I deplored very deeply the physical violence that flared up then. What did it say I signed?

MR. WHEELER: On behalf of the Robeson meeting.

MR. COBB: It is my firm belief that any individual, whether I subscribe to his beliefs or not, does have the right to express himself publicly so long as he does not by so doing endanger the safety and rights of others.

MR. WHEELER: Are you familiar with an organization called China Welfare Appeals, Inc.?

Mr. Cobb: I am once again familiar with it. I say "once again," because recently I took the trouble to trace my past connection with it, which I had completely forgotten about. An organization which I believe was called the China Relief Ship in 1949, I think, asked for names for sponsorship in the theater. Richard Watts, Jr., the New York drama critic, approached me in this connection and I said he might use my name. I had completely forgotten about it. When it was called to my attention a couple of years later that another organization called China Relief, I believe, occupying the same address as the former, was then using my name on its letterhead in connection with its political activity—

Mr. Wheeler: The latter was undoubtedly the successor organization. I mean they changed names, so frequently they changed names.

Mr. Cobb: Yes.

Mr. Wheeler: However, this was prior to the Korean police action, and what would your attitude be now in regard to—

Mr. Cobb: Well, in line with my attitude now as well as last year, I last year sent them a registered letter insisting that they cease using my name in any way for their efforts, and that would still be my attitude today, of course. You did mention the Korean conflict. May I say now, in that connection, that in 1951 I offered my services to the Korean Consulate General in New York. I offered my services in behalf of South Korea to their Consulate General in New York in 1951 to be made use of in whatever way they might, in answer to which I received a very kind letter from David Y. Namkoom, the Consul General. The letter is dated November 16, 1951. Also may I say for the record that I have letters and commendations from the Treasury Department dated October 31, 1949, for my participation in transcribed radio programs. I also was happy to make several Navy recruiting programs in 1950 or 1951, and two big United Nations radio programs in 1949 and 1950. I have participated prominently in several other programs on radio and film in connection with our Government's efforts at home and abroad in the furtherance of the cause of democracy as expressed by our current foreign policy.

Mr. Wheeler: Mr. Cobb, do you have anything further you would like to add for the record?

Mr. Cobb: I would like to thank you for the privilege of setting the record straight, not only for whatever subjective relief it affords me, but if belatedly this information can be of any value in the further strengthening of our Government and its efforts at home as well as abroad, it will serve in some small way to mitigate whatever feeling of guilt I might have for having waited this long. I did hope that, in my delay to speak earlier, others of the people I had mentioned might have availed themselves of this opportunity for themselves to do likewise. I think by this time I can reasonably assume that those who have desired to do so have taken the opportunity to make their position clear, and I can only say that I am sorry for those who haven't and that more haven't done so.

MR. WHEELER: Thank you very much, Mr. Cobb, for giving the Committee the benefit of your knowledge of the Communist conspiracy.

(*Whereupon the interrogation of Lee J. Cobb was concluded.*)

A Letter from Albert Einstein

"That same year [1945, HUAC Member John] Rankin denounced Einstein on the floor of the House as a 'foreign-born agitator' and warned, 'It's about time the American people got wise to Einstein.' Also in 1945, Rankin told the House, 'These alien-minded Communistic enemies of Christianity and their stooges are trying to get control of the press. . . .' "

—From *A Quarter Century of Un-Americana,*
edited by Charlotte Pomerantz (New York, 1963)

On June 12, 1953, the *New York Times* published a letter from Albert Einstein to a New York schoolteacher named William Frauenglass, who had consulted him on the problem of how to confront Congressional investigations. "He was encouraged to do so," write the editors of *Einstein on Peace* (New York, 1968),

> by a recent statement of Einstein in which he had called himself "an incorrigible nonconformist whose nonconformism in a remote field of endeavor no Senatorial committee has as yet felt impelled to tackle." Frauenglass suggested that a statement from Einstein "at this juncture would be most helpful in rallying educators and the public to meet this new obscurantist attack." . . . The version of the Einstein letter which the *Times* published omitted the reference to the Fifth Amendment at the beginning of the fourth paragraph. The *Times* carried a statement of Frauenglass to the effect that the revision . . . had taken place at his request. While Einstein probably consented to the revision . . . his position as stated in the original never changed.

Thank you for your communication. By "remote field" I referred to the theoretical foundations of physics.

The problem with which the intellectuals of this country are confronted is very serious. Reactionary politicians have managed to instill suspicion of all intellectual efforts into the public by dangling before their eyes a danger from without. Having succeeded so far, they are now proceeding to suppress the freedom of teaching and to deprive of their positions all those who do not prove submissive, i.e., to starve them out.

What ought the minority of intellectuals to do against this evil? Frankly, I can only see the revolutionary way of noncooperation in the sense of Gandhi's. Every intellectual who is called before one of the committees ought to refuse to testify, i.e., he must be prepared for jail and economic ruin, in short, for the sacrifice of his personal welfare in the interest of the cultural welfare of his country.

However, this refusal to testify must not be based on the well-known subterfuge of invoking the Fifth Amendment against possible self-incrimination, but on the assertion that it is shameful for a blameless citizen to submit to such an inquisition and that this kind of inquisition violates the spirit of the Constitution.

If enough people are ready to take this grave step they will be successful. If not, then the intellectuals of this country deserve nothing better than the slavery which is intended for them.

P.S. This letter need not be considered "confidential."

It is hard to figure how wide the response was to Einstein's challenge. I. F. Stone supported Einstein in his *Weekly,* June 20, 1953, and contrasted his position with that taken by Bishop G. Bromley Oxnam. Stone was himself a voice crying in the wilderness, yet by that very token it remains of interest what his voice was saying, namely:

> Einstein has lent the world prestige of his name to such an effort. I propose an association of American intellectuals to take the "Einstein pledge" and throw down a fundamental challenge to the establishment of an inquisition in America.

Einstein died less than two years later. In a touching obituary, Stone wrote:

> The man who sought a new harmony in the heavens and in the atom also sought for order and justice in the relations of men. As the greatest intellectual in the world of our time, he fought fascism everywhere and feared the signs of it in our own country. This was the spirit in which he advised American intellectuals to defy the Congressional inquisition and refuse to submit themselves to ideological interrogation. In that position he was interpreting the First Amendment as Jefferson would have done.

Testimony of a Bishop

Bishop Oxnam was one of those who claimed to be more effective in their anti-Communism than HUAC, more royalist, as it were, than the king. Hence there is rivalry rather than true enmity in their confrontation. Which is sufficient reason in itself for including Oxnam's testimony in the present book: he represented a whole class of persons. To the same period belongs the J. Robert Oppenheimer crisis, and it is to be noted that when, in 1954, Oppenheimer was adjudged a bad security risk by the Atomic Energy Commission, even those who took his part did so on the ground that he was, too, a great anti-Communist. "He hates Russia," wrote Ward Evans, in a minority report asking that Oppenheimer be deemed a reliable citizen. Here again, one notes the quite precise tests which the ethos of those days, and particularly of HUAC, imposed as the proof of "Americanism." Before Oxnam came before the Committee there had been some sassy exchanges between him and Congressman Donald L. Jackson in the press and on radio. (See "Bishop Oxnam and the Un-American Activities Committee," Beacon Press, June 1953.) Ostensibly, he came before HUAC to be just as sassy, if not more so. Actually, HUAC proved the victor, and one sees how mistaken it is to write off the Committee as merely gauche, let alone stupid: they were masters of a certain kind of showmanship and public relations. At the close of the Oxnam hearing, the press photographed the Chairman beaming and taking Oxnam's hand; Oxnam beamed back. The testimony itself culminates, not in dramatic denunciation, à la Zola, as Oxnam seems to have intended, but in civilities such as this:

BISHOP OXNAM: I am leaving for Europe.

MR. VELDE: I am sure that the Committee will wish you Godspeed upon your journey.

MR. CLARDY: It may interest you to know some of us are going over to see what they are doing with Uncle Sam's dollars too, and don't forget the little private session you and I will have when we get back.

BISHOP OXNAM: We will have a good time, and you told me you were Irish, and we will have a wonderful time.

Which goes to show that, if only a witness is really anti-Communist, a good time can be had by all. Yet in a book called *I Protest* (1954), Oxnam seemed to admit he hadn't had as good a time as the Committee had: "I . . . am a little fearful that I went too far in courtesy . . . the procedure . . . is one that could destroy the reputation of any individual."

JULY 21, 1953:

G. Bromley Oxnam

The Committee on Un-American Activities met at 2:30 p.m., in the caucus room, 362 Old House Office Building, the Honorable Harold H. Velde (Chairman) presiding.

Committee members present: Representatives Harold H. Velde (Chairman), Bernard W. Kearney, Donald L. Jackson, Kit Clardy, Gordon H. Scherer, Francis E. Walter, Morgan M. Moulder, Clyde Doyle, and James B. Frazier, Jr.

Staff members present: Robert L. Kunzig, Counsel; Frank S. Tavenner, Jr., Counsel; Louis J. Russell, Chief Investigator; Raphael I. Nixon, Director of Research; George C. Williams, Investigator; and Mrs. Juliette Joray, Acting Clerk.

MR. VELDE: The Committee has as a witness today Bishop G. Bromley Oxnam of Washington, D.C. Bishop Oxnam is here at his own request and in keeping with an established policy of this Committee to grant a hearing to any citizen who asserts that he has been in any way adversely affected by virtue of any action taken by the Committee. Bishop Oxnam has informed the Committee that information in its files relating to him is in error and that he has been harmed as a result of public disclosure of such information. To the end that the facts of the allegations may be determined, the Committee extended an invitation to Bishop Oxnam to appear.

The hearing should not be interpreted as an investigation initiated by the Congress into the field of religion. It is incidental to this hearing that the witness is a man of the cloth. No inference should be drawn from this hearing as to the loyalty or disloyalty of any member of the clergy. The Committee has never instituted a hearing into any specific establishment of American life, whether the institution be labor, education, government, or entertainment, but has quite properly restricted its investigations and hearings to the area of individual representatives of those activities.

* * *

BISHOP OXNAM: Mr. Chairman and members of the Committee, I have requested opportunity to appear voluntarily before this Committee, in public session, to secure redress for the damage done to me by the release of information in the files of this Committee. I deeply appreciate the grant of this privilege. Such releases, made at various times for a period of nearly seven years, have contained material, much of which is irrelevant and immaterial, some of which is false and some of which is true, but all prepared in a way capable of creating the impression that I have been and am sympathetic to Communism, and therefore subversive. These files, so released, have been used by private agencies as evidence of Communist sympathies. A member of this Committee* apparently drew that conclusion. Speaking on the work of this Committee, upon the floor of the House of Representatives itself, he said:

> Bishop Bromley Oxnam has been to the Communist front what Man o' War was to thoroughbred horseracing, and no one except the good Bishop pays much attention to his fulminations these days. Having served God on Sunday and the Communist front for the balance of the week over such a long period of time, it is no great wonder that the Bishop sees an investigating committee in every vestry. If reprinting Bishop Oxnam's record of aid and comfort to the Communist front would serve any useful purpose, I would ask permission to insert it here, but suffice it to say that the record is available to any Member who cares to request it from the Committee.

If a member of the Committee can be so misled by this material, it is no wonder that uninformed citizens are similarly misled. When I declare, "I believe in God, the Father, Almighty," I affirm the theistic faith and strike at the fundamental fallacy of Communism, which is atheism. I thereby reaffirm the basic conviction upon which this republic rests—namely, that all men are created by the Eternal and in His image, beings of infinite worth, members of one family, brothers. We are endowed by the Creator with certain inalienable rights. The State does not confer them; it merely confirms them. They belong to man because he is a son of God. When I say, "I believe in God," I am also saying that moral law is written into the nature of things. There are moral absolutes. Marxism, by definition, rules out moral absolutes. Because I believe the will of God is revealed in the Gospel of Christ, I hold that all historically conditioned political, economic, social, and ecclesiastical systems must be judged by the Gospel, not identified with it. I reject Communism, first, because of its atheism. When I declare, "I

* Jackson. —E.B.

believe in Jesus Christ, His only Son, our Lord," I am affirming faith in a spiritual view of life. By so doing, I repudiate the philosophy of materialism upon which Communism is based and thereby undermine it. I reject the theory of social development that assumes social institutions and even morality are determined by the prevailing mode of production. When I accept the law of love taught by Christ and revealed in His person, I must, of necessity, oppose to the death a theory that justifies dictatorship with its annihilation of freedom. I am not an economist, but have studied sufficiently to be convinced that there are basic fallacies in Marxian economics. Believing as I do that personality is a supreme good and that personality flowers in freedom, I stand for the free man in the free society, seeking the truth that frees. I hold that the free man must discover concrete measures through which the ideals of religion may be translated into the realities of world law and order, economic justice, and racial brotherhood. As a result of long study and of prayer, I am by conviction pledged to the free way of life and opposed to all forms of totalitarianism, left or right, and to all tendencies toward such practices at home or abroad. Consequently, I have been actively opposed to Communism all my life. I have never been a member of the Communist Party. My opposition to Communism is a matter of public record in books, numerous articles, addresses, and sermons, and in resolutions I have drafted or sponsored in which powerful religious agencies have been put on record as opposed to Communism. It is evidenced likewise in a life of service and the sponsorship of measures designed to make the free society impregnable to Communist attack.

Loyalty to my family, my church, and my country are fundamental to me; and when any man or any committee questions that loyalty, I doubt that I would be worthy of the name "American" if I took it lying down. There are three considerations I desire to lay before this Committee: First, this Committee has followed a practice of releasing unverified and unevaluated material designated as "information" to citizens, organizations, and Members of Congress. It accepts no responsibility for the accuracy of the newspaper clippings recorded and so released and insists that the material does not represent an opinion or a conclusion of the Committee. This material, officially released on official letterheads and signed by an official clerk, carried no disclaimer, in my case, and the recipient understandably assumed it did represent a conclusion. I am here formally to request that this file be cleaned up, that the Committee frankly admit its inaccuracies and misrepresentations, and that this matter be brought to a close. It is alleged that the Committee has files on a million individuals, many of whom are among the most respected, patriotic, and devoted citizens of this nation. This is not the proper place to raise questions as to the propriety of maintaining such vast files at public expense, but it is the proper place, in my case, to request that the practice of releasing unverified and unevaluated material, for which the Committee accepts no responsibility, cease. It can be shown that these reports are the result of inexcusable incompetence or of slanted selection—the result being the same in either case—namely, to question loyalty, to pillory or to intimidate the individual, to damage reputation, and to turn attention from the Communist conspirator who pursues his nefarious work in the shadows while a patriotic citizen is disgraced in public. The preparation and publication of these files puts into the hands of irresponsible individuals and agencies a wicked tool. It gives rise to a new and vicious expression of Ku-Kluxism, in which an innocent person may be beaten by unknown assailants, who are cloaked in anonymity and at times immunity, and whose whips are cleverly constructed lists of so-called subversive organizations and whose floggings appear all too often to be sadistic in spirit rather than patriotic in purpose. I had planned at this point to set forth specifications of what I believe is false. The rules of this Committee give me but fifteen minutes for this statement. The specifications cannot be listed in fifteen minutes. Therefore, I must respectfully request the Committee members, or its counsel, to question me concerning some of the material released by the Committee, namely: First, a release dated July 3, 1946, in which it is alleged I sponsored the [American] League Against War and Fascism, and in which it is suggested by implication that I would substitute dialectical materialism for religious freedom. Second, a release dated September 4, 1946, in which it is alleged that I am "referred to as a collectivist bishop," that I presided at a meeting addressed "by one B. Gebert, president of the Polish section of the International Workers' Order," that I have been "associated with several groups in which Langston Hughes has also held membership." Third, a release dated September 13, 1950, in which, quoting the *Daily Worker* as authority, I am alleged to have been invited by the government of Yugoslavia to tour that country, in which I am alleged to have written an article for Stalin for a magazine called *Classmate*. Fourth, releases of different dates alleging I have delivered an address to the prisoners of the Indiana State Reformatory, February 10, 1930. Fifth, a letter from Mr. Frank S. Tavenner, Jr., dated March 21, 1953, relative to covering letters alleged to accompany releases. Sixth, a release sent out by the Chairman of this Committee dated March 31,1953. Seventh, letters from two members of this Committee, one dated March 19, 1953, and the other alleging the Committee did not release this material, dated March 13, 1953. If I may be asked questions concerning these items, I will leave it to any fair-minded man whether I have been misrepresented. In this connection I would like to file with the Committee a bibliography covering my personal position relative to Communism.

* * *

When I had the honor of debating this issue with the Honorable Donald L. Jackson, a member of this Committee, he said, "The Committee, in its work, accumulates all pertinent information relative to any given individual whose name is listed in the files. That is the only way by which one can determine the philosophical bent of any given individual." Can the philosophy of an individual be determined by a scissors-and-paste process of cutting out clippings that damn? Why did the individual who clipped derogatory statements concerning me fail to clip such announcements as the following: My appointment by the Joint Chiefs of Staff to visit the Mediterranean Theater and the European Theater of Operations during the war; or my appointment by Secretary Forrestal as a member of the Secretary of the Navy's Civilian Advisory Committee; or the announcement that the Navy had awarded me the highly prized Certificate of Appreciation for services during the war; or that I had been invited to be the guest of Archbishop Damaskinos, then Regent of Greece, and that the King of Greece had awarded me the Order of the Phoenix; or that I had represented the American churches at the enthronement of the Archbishop of Canterbury; or that I had been appointed by the President as a member of the President's Commission on Higher Education; or that I was chairman of the Commission approved by the President to study postwar religious conditions in Germany? This might be called pertinent information. I have held the highest offices it is in the power of fellow churchmen to confer upon me, such as the presidency of the Federal Council of the Churches of Christ in America. I am one of the presidents of the World Council of Churches, perhaps the highest honor that can come to a clergyman. We cannot beat down the Communist menace by bearing false witness against fellow Americans. The Communist wants a divided America, an America whose citizens are suspicious of each other, an America without trust, an America open to infiltration. I believe this Committee will wish to end a practice that plays into Communist hands. Third, Congress is considering proposals for the reform of investigating-committee procedures. It may, at first, seem drastic to propose that the so-called public files be closed out, but is there any need of any file other than the investigative files as they have been recently described? Could not all the material that is of value in the public files be included in the investigative files? If, for purposes of education or exposure, the Committee decides that public statements must be made, is there any reason why a careful statement that will stand scrutiny cannot be made by studying the material in the investigative files? The Committee informs us that it does not vouch for the accuracy of the public files, that everything in those files is available to the public elsewhere. Why, then, should public money be spent in maintaining such public files? Would it not be well for the Committee to appoint a subcommittee to investigate its own files and those who compiled them, and to secure answers to questions such as the following: How much duplication is there in the public and investigative files of this Committee and the files of the FBI? Is the FBI better equipped to get the facts on real subversives? If there is real misunderstanding, would it not be well to ascertain who is misinforming whom and why? I respectfully ask the Committee to order that my file be corrected so as to tell the truth, if that is all that can be done; that it publicly announce its mistakes in my case; but better, that the public files be closed out, and the releases of unverified material described herein be discontinued. When Mr. Jackson discovered that he had misunderstood the Chairman of this Committee with reference to an announcement concerning possible investigation of churchmen, he in the manly, the American, the Christian way apologized on the floor of the House. It takes a big man to admit a fault. I respectfully request Mr. Jackson to apologize on the floor of the House for his unprecedented and untrue statements made there concerning me. I will be the first to shake hands with him and to call the incident closed. I believe the churches have done and are doing far more to destroy the Communist threat to faith and to freedom than all investigating committees put together. I think the Chairman of this Committee, after a friendly interview, concurred publicly in that statement when I made it in his presence. This Committee might well have the cooperation of millions of citizens who belong to the churches if it would cease practices that many of us believe to be un-American and would turn itself to the real task and the real threat. But those citizens will never cooperate in practices that jeopardize the rights of free men won after a thousand years' struggle for political and religious freedom. They will cooperate effectively with agencies everywhere that honestly seek to build the free society, where free men may worship God according to the dictates of conscience, and serve their fellow men in accordance with Christ's law of love.

* * *

[Two hundred pages later in the printed record of this witness's testimony.]

MR. KUNZIG: Mr. Chairman, I have a document called "An American Churchman in the Soviet Union," by the Reverend Louie D. Newton, president of the Southern Baptist Convention. This is a publication of the American-Russian Institute, which is cited by Attorney General [Tom C.] Clark in 1949 as Communist. There is in this pamphlet an introduction by Bishop G. Bromley Oxnam. The question is: Do you recognize this book marked as "Oxnam exhibit No. 42," and did you write that introduction, sir?

BISHOP OXNAM: I do recognize it, and I did write it, and having answered the question, may I explain it?

MR. VELDE: Yes.

BISHOP OXNAM: Dr. Louie D. Newton is one of the most distinguished ministers of the Baptist Church. He was the president of the Southern Convention. Dr. Newton went to Russia. I have been related to the National Council. We have always hoped that someday our Southern Baptist brethren might be in the National Council. Dr. Newton is a dear, personal friend.

When he returned from Russia, he asked me if I would write an introduction to a booklet he was bringing out describing his visit. I would suggest the Committee read it. When it came out, I noticed it was put out by this agency. I have no relation to that. I wrote an introduction to a booklet written by a friend, a distinguished clergyman.

MR. KUNZIG: You did not know that this introduction would be put out by the American-Russian Institute?

BISHOP OXNAM: I did not know who was to publish that document.

MR. CLARDY: Incidentally, I find it a considerable apology for the Soviet Russian system.

BISHOP OXNAM: If you do, let me say I do not. This man is fundamentally opposed to Communism. He was trained as a journalist and was writing this as he saw it.

MR. KUNZIG: Was it within the last five or ten years?

BISHOP OXNAM: I will be glad to check and give you the date so it will be accurate. I should judge it was within the last five years, but I wouldn't want to say without checking the record.

MR. KUNZIG: I should like to offer this pamphlet, "An American Churchman in the Soviet Union," and ask that it be marked as "Oxnam exhibit No. 42."

MR. VELDE: Without objection, it will be admitted in the record.

(*Pamphlet referred to was received in evidence as "Oxnam exhibit No. 42."*)

MR. KUNZIG: I have a photostatic copy marked "Oxnam exhibit No. 43"—

BISHOP OXNAM: I have been a lot of trouble to this Committee. I am sorry. Forty-three exhibits is amazing!

MR. KUNZIG: Let me first ask: Did you know Dr. W. E. B. Du Bois, a Negro leader?

BISHOP OXNAM: I am afraid I don't know. I have heard his name.

MR. KUNZIG: Did Dr. Du Bois ever speak at your church?

BISHOP OXNAM: I think not.

MR. KUNZIG: Can you explain this exhibit marked "Oxnam exhibit No. 43"?

BISHOP OXNAM: What year are you talking about?

MR. KUNZIG: Let me show it to you. It states that he was listed to speak. The question I asked you was: Did he ever speak at your church?

BISHOP OXNAM: I have no recollection of it, but when somebody brings up a document that is twenty-six years back, that is a little difficult for anybody, even from this Committee, to answer.

MR. VELDE: I think the Chair would defer receipt of that until the Bishop has had an opportunity to check it.

MR. KUNZIG: I think it should be withdrawn.

Bishop Oxnam: Mr. Chairman, I am leaving for Europe. I hope it will not be a discourtesy if I have to get this information after I get back. I do not think I could do it in a day or two before I go.

Mr. Velde: I am sure that the Committee will wish you Godspeed upon your journey.

Mr. Clardy: It may interest you to know some of us are going over to see what they they are doing with Uncle Sam's dollars too, and don't forget the little private session you and I will have when we get back.

Bishop Oxnam: We will have a good time, and you told me you were Irish, and we will have a wonderful time.

Mr. Kunzig: I have no further questions to ask this witness, Mr. Chairman.

Mr. Jackson: I have no further questions, but I would like to ask that we interpose the citations in each instance of the various organizations, and I request that in cases of organizations where there are citations that those citations be included at the appropriate point in the record.

Mr. Velde: Without objection, that will be done.

Bishop Oxnam: Does that include organizations to which I do not belong?

Mr. Jackson: My motion deals with the organizations upon which you have been questioned and in which there are exhibits.

Mr. Velde: Does the gentleman reserve the right to object?

Mr. Doyle: Yes, unless our printed record also shows the date on which it was found to be subversive, if it was. In other words, the finding of the Attorney General will show the date upon which he arrived at the conclusion that it was subversive, if it was.

Mr. Velde: The gentleman knows that the files include those facts.

Mr. Doyle: I have seen some files that do not include that fact.

Mr. Jackson: I have no objection to that.

Mr. Doyle: Mr. Chairman, may I ask this question?

Mr. Velde: Let us get this matter straightened out first. Does the gentleman have objection to the listing of the citation if the date of the citation is mentioned?

Mr. Kunzig: The date is mentioned in every instance.

Mr. Clardy: I think there is cross-examination that identifies that, but I think it is customary to have it in and I would like to see it there.

Mr. Doyle: I think I will not object to that. I think it has been very unfortunate that a lot of organizations have been referred to which, only by inference, could this witness be entitled to have any connection with, even indirectly. I was hoping that it would not be printed and go out in the United States. It will be taken inferentially, and we all know it will. Those people will not read the fact that he was never a member of it, and the fact that his name was identified with it will be enough for them and the fact that he has testified he was not a member of it, and we have no evidence that he was a member, and I think that is the damnable part of it. I use that language because I feel just that way about it.

MR. VELDE: I understand the gentleman has no objection, so, without objection, the citations as asked by the gentleman from California, Mr. Jackson, will be inserted after each organization, and may the Chair say this: I believe that if the Bishop would not object to having this material in the record along with your denial, and it may be true, as the gentleman from California says, that some people may not read the Bishop's statement regarding this but unfortunately the Chairman cannot do anything about that.

MR. DOYLE: I was going to add to Mr. Jackson's request that it be plainly stated in our print that he has testified that he was not a member of this [or that] organization, and then if that page is torn out and used by some sneak thief we cannot help it, but I believe the Bishop is entitled to that protection. This witness has said two or three times that he was never a member of the Communist Party. I did not hear any member ask him plainly whether or not he ever had been. I want to ask him whether or not he has ever been.

MR. CLARDY: I want to object to it and I think that being in the record leaves a bad inference. I object.

MR. DOYLE: We have tied him up with a lot of organizations that we know have been identified as Communist fronts, and, so that there will be no question about what this Committee has in the way of evidence whether or not this witness was ever a Communist, I am asking that if we have any such evidence we now produce it. That will be helpful in clearing this man's record without any mistakes in this hearing.

MR. CLARDY: May I ask the Bishop a question?

MR. VELDE: Yes.

MR. CLARDY: You have been here all day, and haven't you heard us make it abundantly clear what we think about that, and aren't you satisfied with what we have said?

BISHOP OXNAM: I appreciate what Mr. Doyle has said. I do recall what Mr. Clardy has said, but it seems to me that the record that included what Mr. Doyle has said might be helpful. I don't know if this Committee learned how its documents are misused by organizations that deliberately seek to destroy one's character, but it seems to me that protection of that kind should be given, and I am not speaking for myself but for others.

MR. VELDE: What was the gentleman from California desiring in the listing of these citations? Will you ask unanimous consent or move?

MR. DOYLE: I move that the record show that this Committee has no record of any Communist Party affiliation or membership by Bishop Oxnam.

MR. JACKSON: I second the motion.

MR. VELDE: Is there objection to the motion of the gentleman from California? If not, the motion is carried.

MR. DOYLE: I make the further motion that, after every listing of the Bishop's name in any group which we have discussed today, it be clearly printed wherever the Bishop has denied membership that he did deny membership, and let the record stand on that, so that any person reading the list of names in our Committee publication, will see it right before him that the Bishop said he was never a member of that organization. We cannot do less. That is what the Bishop testified to. Why not let the people know what he testified to?

MR. JACKSON: We have been here for many, many hours taking testimony of denial or affirmation in the instances where it was pertinent. The record is voluminous, and it will speak for itself, as I believe it should speak for itself. Therefore, I am constrained to object to the motion.

MR. DOYLE: May I say that my distinguished colleague from California well knows that some pages of what we print will be read and some pages not, and many times, in the testimony of this witness, that he [said he] was not a member of this organization or that one, it will never be read by the people. They will read portions and they will never read his testimony that he was not a member. Consequently, the Bishop will again be done a rank injustice. It will not cost us any more money to say that Bishop Oxnam was not a member of that organization.

MR. VELDE: After the citation?

MR. DOYLE: Yes. It is only one line to print.

MR. VELDE: Does the gentleman from California object?

MR. JACKSON: Yes, on the ground that the positive denial is a matter of testimony. It is set forth not only once in most instances but several times, due to duplicating questions from Committee members or counsel. It is affirmatively set forth in all instances where the Bishop was not a member of the organization, and I believe it will be perfectly clear to anyone who reads the record that such a denial was in there. I am constrained to object to the motion largely due to the fact that it might establish precedent for further hearings where we would be forced into the position of having to annotate or make substantial additions to the actual physical testimony which is taken. Therefore, I object.

MR. CLARDY: It is doing the very thing that everybody objects to, of making this Committee draw conclusions they should not be drawing. What are you going to do in the case of the organizations to which the Bishop freely and frankly admitted he belonged? Are we going to put in yes, he belonged to that organization? You are doing him a disservice.

MR. DOYLE: Of course, the gentleman from Michigan is again wrong. I am not asking any such thing as he has indicated. The gentleman from

Michigan and my distinguished colleague from California want our printed record to be as clear as crystal that this witness has testified that he is not a member of this [or that] organization. Can that hurt anybody?

MR. JACKSON: On [the] ground that the printed words will *be* as clear as crystal, I object.

MR. VELDE: The question is on the motion of the gentleman from California, Mr. Doyle. All those in favor of the motion signify by raising their right hand; all those opposed to the motion signify by raising their right hand. Those in opposition are greater in number. The motion is defeated.

1955

Song and Dance

The *New York Herald Tribune* for August 19, 1955, reported:

> The House Committee on Un-American Activities yesterday ended a four-day hearing here at which only one of twenty-three show business witnesses cooperated in spotlighting Communist infiltration of the entertainment world. . . . During the hearings eighteen witnesses invoked the protection of the Fifth Amendment when asked about Communist activities in the theater, radio and television and in unions of entertainers. Four others defied the committee on other grounds and face contempt of Congress charges.

A representative report from the press of the time gives some indication of how the Committee followed through when names had been named. For example, the testimony of Jerome Robbins in 1952, cited above, is still a ferment here three years later. This report is from the *New York World-Telegram and Sun,* August 16, 1955. Incidentally, its co-author, Frederick Woltman, was one of the principal anti-Communist journalists of the forties and fifties, and claimed credit for the exposure of Gerhart Eisler, on whom he wrote in 1946.

Probe Head Says He Thought Some Would Talk Frankly

Bulletin

The 10th and 11th witnesses called before the House Un-American Activities Committee today refused, as have all the others, to answer any questions about their alleged Communist affiliations. They were Irma Jurist, composer, and Mrs. Susan d'Usseau, artist, wife of Arnaud d'Usseau, playwright.

By Frederick Woltman and Norton Mockridge, Staff Writers

Defied by every witness to appear before him, Rep. Francis E. Walter (D., Pa.), chairman of the House Un-American Activities Committee, said today he believes that pressure had been put on the witnesses to seal their lips.

Seven persons yesterday and two today, all charged with Communist associations—balked violently on the stand and refused to answer questions. Some ducked under the Fifth Amendment; some belligerently said the committee has no right to question them.

As the committee's hearings went into their second day in the U.S. Court House, Foley Square, Mr. Walter told reporters: "I am fairly convinced some pressure has been brought to bear. I was under the impression that some of our witnesses would testify openly and frankly."

Mr. Walter, admitting that the government so far has hit a blank wall in questioning theater people who are alleged to be Reds, said that some "surprise" witnesses would be called. These witnesses, he said, "will be cooperative."

Mr. Walter would not discuss how or when the pressure was brought to bear on the witnesses but he showed that he was considerably displeased.

Among the audience today in the crowded courtroom was Bernard Baruch who walked in unexpectedly this afternoon and was ushered to a leather chair at the front of the room.

When a break came in the questioning, Mr. Baruch shook hands with committee members and posed for pictures. In an impromptu speech he praised the work of the committee and criticized the close-mouthed witnesses.

"At a time like this," he said, "it isn't a case of giving associations. It's a case of giving comfort (to the Communists). Anyone who has nothing to fear can speak freely. They'll get a fair hearing."

Then he chuckled and added: "Why, I've been investigated more than they have."

The first witness today to fling defiance at the government was Elliott Sullivan, veteran stage, screen and TV actor. He refused to answer questions about his political beliefs or associations.

Mr. Sullivan, an important featured player for 26 years, did not take refuge in the Fifth Amendment. Instead, he told the committee that it had no right to question him.

The American Federation of Television and Radio Artists has the right to expel any actor who uses the Fifth Amendment to avoid answering questions put by a legislative committee.

The tall, gaunt, Texas-born actor who is noted for his gangster roles has been identified by four admitted Communists as a member of the Red cells to which they belonged. Mr. Sullivan, suave in manner but vitriolic in speech, admitted he knew the four but said they were "on the shameful list . . . people who sold their honor for a mess of pottage."

The four are Lee J. Cobb, Martin Berkeley and Nicholas Bela,* actors, and Jerome Robbins, choreographer.

Mr. Sullivan, 48, talked calmly most of the time to Frank S. Tavenner,

*** Actually, Bela was a writer. —E.B.**

committee counsel, but he shouted once when he got into conflict with Rep. Gordon H. Scherer (R., Ohio), a committee member.

Mr. Scherer, irked by the actor's balkiness, said he would be cited for contempt. Angry words were exchanged.

Rep. Francis E. Walter (D., Pa.), committee chairman, then told Mr. Scherer that he felt it wouldn't make any difference to the actor if he were cited for contempt.

"Of course it makes a difference," boomed the strong-voiced Mr. Sullivan. "I have a wife and two children. I want to work and earn a living and I resent your remark that it doesn't make any difference to me."

Mr. Sullivan admitted that one of the chores he performed to make a living had to do with the staging of shows at Wingdale Lodge, Wingdale, N.Y. Formerly known as Camp Unity, the lodge is the Communist party's summer resort at which party leaders are indoctrinated.

One of the skits he produced there recently, he agreed, featured a couple of actors who sold each other the Bill of Rights for a dollar and then, as FBI agents, arrested each other. Mr. Sullivan explained the dramatic value of this sketch by saying:

"We were entertaining an audience by satirizing a condition which exists in this country today. . . . It's as good a piece of American theater as you could possibly get, and it shows that people were trying to sell the Bill of Rights—members of the FBI or some other agency, and it's not terribly exaggerated."

Another witness today, Lee Hays, a folk singer, invoked the Fifth Amendment as soon as he got on the stand. A man who weighs close to 300 pounds, he said he sang bass in the now defunct quartet, "The Weavers," from 1949 to 1952.

Asked about his source of income, the singer from Little Rock, Ark., said he did "some folk singing, or folk research, or worked in factories, or as a laborer, farmhand or in greasy spoon restaurants."

He said he felt the committee had no right to "inquire into my personal associations."

He was on the stand only a brief period, unlike Mr. Sullivan who occupied the committee for the entire morning.

Time and again Mr. Sullivan was asked to say whether any of the four actors lied when they identified him as a Communist. Each time Mr. Sullivan refused to say yes or no. He merely insisted that the committee had no right to ask.

Many actors have complained that because of accusations, true or false, they have been blacklisted in entertainment fields and have not been able to get jobs.

This, most assuredly, is not true of Mr. Sullivan. Although he has been accused of being a Red a number of times since 1951, he has worked steadily. He said today he has appeared in some 80 movies, on 75 radio programs, in a number of Broadway shows including *Green Grow the Lilacs* and *Brigadoon* and on almost every major TV show—Goodyear, Philco, Robert Montgomery, "Big Story," Robert Q. Lewis, and many more.

"I got these jobs because of talent and ability, and not for any political reasons," he said. Then he charged that the committee has been helping blacklist actors for political reasons.

He then blasted the magazine *Red Channels* which lists persons in the entertainment field who are believed to have pinkish tinges.

"There are a great many names in there of people who are not members of the Communist party, but they are denied employment," he said.

Asked to give the names of persons who are not Communists, he refused to answer. Asked to tell which persons were Communists, he also refused.

Several times he referred scornfully to the four actors who accused him.

Mr. Walter declared that the four, admitting they were Communists and naming other Reds, had made a great contribution toward protecting this country. "They are now receiving recognition from the people of the country," he said.

"Not from the papers I read," said Mr. Sullivan.

"Well," replied Mr. Walter, "if you'd quit reading the *Daily Worker* you'd find out."

AUGUST 18, 1955:

Pete Seeger

A Subcommittee of the Committee on Un-American Activities met at 10 a.m., in room 1703 of the Federal Building, Foley Square, New York, New York, the Honorable Francis E. Walter (Chairman) presiding.

Committee members present: Representatives Walter, Edwin E. Willis, and Gordon H. Scherer.

Staff members present: Frank S. Tavenner, Jr., Counsel; Donald T. Appell and Frank Bonora, Investigators; and Thomas W. Beale, Sr., Chief Clerk.

MR. TAVENNER: When and where were you born, Mr. Seeger?

MR. SEEGER: I was born in New York in 1919.

MR. TAVENNER: What is your profession or occupation?

MR. SEEGER: Well, I have worked at many things, and my main profession is a student of American folklore, and I make my living as a banjo picker—sort of damning, in some people's opinion.

MR. TAVENNER: Has New York been your headquarters for a considerable period of time?

MR. SEEGER: No, I lived here only rarely until I left school, and after a year or two or a few years living here after World War II I got back to the country, where I always felt more at home.

MR. TAVENNER: You say that you were in the Armed Forces of the United States?

MR. SEEGER: About three and a half years.

MR. TAVENNER: Will you tell us please the period of your service?

MR. SEEGER: I went in in July 1942 and I was mustered out in December 1945.

MR. TAVENNER: Did you attain the rank of an officer?

MR. SEEGER: No. After about a year I made Pfc, and just before I got out I got to be T-5, which is in the equivalent of a corporal's rating, a long hard pull.

MR. TAVENNER: Mr. Seeger, prior to your entry into the service in 1942, were you engaged in the practice of your profession in the area of New York?

MR. SEEGER: It is hard to call it a profession. I kind of drifted into it and I never intended to be a musician, and I am glad I am one now, and it is a very honorable profession, but when I started out actually I wanted to be a newspaperman, and when I left school—

CHAIRMAN WALTER: Will you answer the question, please?

MR. SEEGER: I have to explain that it really wasn't my profession, I picked up a little change in it.

CHAIRMAN WALTER: Did you practice your profession?

MR. SEEGER: I sang for people, yes, before World War II, and I also did as early as 1925.

MR. TAVENNER: And upon your return from the service in December of 1945, you continued in your profession?

MR. SEEGER: I continued singing, and I expect I always will.

MR. TAVENNER: The Committee has information obtained in part from the *Daily Worker* indicating that, over a period of time, especially since December of 1945, you took part in numerous entertainment features. I have before me a photostatic copy of the June 20, 1947, issue of the *Daily Worker*. In a column entitled "What's On" appears this advertisement: "Tonight—Bronx, hear Peter Seeger and his guitar, at Allerton Section housewarming." May I ask you whether or not the Allerton Section was a section of the Communist Party?

MR. SEEGER: Sir, I refuse to answer that question whether it was a quote from the *New York Times* or the *Vegetarian Journal*.

MR. TAVENNER: I don't believe there is any more authoritative document in regard to the Communist Party than its official organ, the *Daily Worker*.

MR. SCHERER: He hasn't answered the question, and he merely said he wouldn't answer whether the article appeared in the *New York Times* or some other magazine. I ask you to direct the witness to answer the question.

CHAIRMAN WALTER: I direct you to answer.

MR. SEEGER: Sir, the whole line of questioning—

CHAIRMAN WALTER: You have only been asked one question, so far.

MR. SEEGER: I am not going to answer any questions as to my association, my philosophical or religious beliefs or my political beliefs, or how I voted in any election, or any of these private affairs. I think these are very improper questions for any American to be asked, especially under such compulsion as this. I would be very glad to tell you my life if you want to hear of it.

MR. TAVENNER: Has the witness declined to answer this specific question?

CHAIRMAN WALTER: He said that he is not going to answer any questions, any names or things.

MR. SCHERER: He was directed to answer the question.

MR. TAVENNER: I have before me a photostatic copy of the April 30, 1948, issue of the *Daily Worker* which carries under the same title of "What's On," an advertisement of a "May Day Rally: For Peace, Security and Democracy." The advertisement states: "Are you in a fighting mood? Then attend the May Day rally." Expert speakers are stated to be slated for the program, and then follows a statement, "Entertainment by Pete Seeger." At the bottom appears this: "Auspices Essex County Communist Party," and at the top, "Tonight, Newark, N.J." Did you lend your talent to the Essex County Communist Party on the occasion indicated by this article from the *Daily Worker*?

MR. SEEGER: Mr. Walter, I believe I have already answered this question, and the same answer.

CHAIRMAN WALTER: The same answer. In other words, you mean that you decline to answer because of the reasons stated before?

MR. SEEGER: I gave my answer, sir.

CHAIRMAN WALTER: What is your answer?

MR. SEEGER: You see, sir, I feel—

CHAIRMAN WALTER: What is your answer?

MR. SEEGER: I will tell you what my answer is.

(*Witness consulted with counsel* [Paul L. Ross].)

I feel that in my whole life I have never done anything of any conspiratorial nature and I resent very much and very deeply the implication of being called before this Committee that in some way because my opinions may be different from yours, or yours, Mr. Willis, or yours, Mr. Scherer, that I am any less of an American than anybody else. I love my country very deeply, sir.

CHAIRMAN WALTER: Why don't you make a little contribution toward preserving its institutions?

Mr. Seeger: I feel that my whole life is a contribution. That is why I would like to tell you about it.

Chairman Walter: I don't want to hear about it.

Mr. Scherer: I think that there must be a direction to answer.

Chairman Walter: I direct you to answer that question.

Mr. Seeger: I have already given you my answer, sir.

Mr. Scherer: Let me understand. You are not relying on the Fifth Amendment, are you?

Mr. Seeger: No, sir, although I do not want to in any way discredit or depreciate or depredate the witnesses that have used the Fifth Amendment, and I simply feel it is improper for this Committee to ask such questions.

Mr. Scherer: And then in answering the rest of the questions, or in refusing to answer the rest of the questions, I understand that you are not relying on the Fifth Amendment as a basis for your refusal to answer?

Mr. Seeger: No, I am not, sir.

Mr. Tavenner: I have before me a photostatic copy of the May 4, 1949, issue of the *Daily Worker,* which has an article entitled "May Day Smash Review Put on by Communist Cultural Division, On Stage," and the article was written by Bob Reed. This article emphasizes a production called *Now Is the Time,* and it says this:

> *Now Is the Time* was a hard-hitting May Day show of songs and knife-edged satire. New songs and film strips walloped the enemies of the people in what the singers called "Aesopian language."

And other persons [participated], including Peter Seeger. Lee Hays is recited to be the MC, or master of ceremonies. Did you take part in this May Day program under the auspices of the music section of the cultural division of the Communist Party?

Mr. Seeger: Mr. Chairman, the answer is the same as before.

Mr. Scherer: I think we have to have a direction.

Chairman Walter: I direct you to answer the question.

Mr. Seeger: I have given you my answer, sir.

Mr. Tavenner: The article contains another paragraph as follows:

> This performance of *Now Is the Time* was given in honor of the 12 indicted Communist Party leaders.

And then it continues with Bob Reed's account of the show:

> This reviewer has never seen a show which stirred its audience more. Add up new material, fine personal and group performances, overwhelming audience response—the result was a significant advance in the people's cultural movement. *Now Is the Time* is that rare phenomenon, a political show in which performers and audience had a lot of fun. It should be repeated for large audiences.

Mr. Lee Hays was asked, while he was on the witness stand, whether or not he wrote that play, and he refused to answer. Do you know whether he was the originator of the script?

MR. SEEGER: Do I know whether he was the originator of the script? Again my answer is the same. However, if you want to question me about any songs, I would be glad to tell you, sir.

CHAIRMAN WALTER: That is what you are being asked about now.

MR. TAVENNER: You said that you would tell us about the songs. Did you participate in a program at Wingdale Lodge in the State of New York, which is a summer camp for adults and children, on the weekend of July Fourth of this year?

(*Witness consulted with counsel.*)

MR. SEEGER: Again, I say I will be glad to tell what songs I have ever sung, because singing is my business.

MR. TAVENNER: I am going to ask you.

MR. SEEGER: But I decline to say who has ever listened to them, who has written them, or other people who have sung them.

MR. TAVENNER: Did you sing this song, to which we have referred, "Now Is the Time," at Wingdale Lodge on the weekend of July Fourth?

MR. SEEGER: I don't know any song by that name, and I know a song with a similar name. It is called "Wasn't That a Time." Is that the song?

CHAIRMAN WALTER: Did you sing that song?

MR. SEEGER: I can sing it. I don't know how well I can do it without my banjo.

CHAIRMAN WALTER: I said, Did you sing it on that occasion?

MR. SEEGER: I have sung that song. I am not going to go into where I have sung it. I have sung it many places.

CHAIRMAN WALTER: Did you sing it on this particular occasion? That is what you are being asked.

MR. SEEGER: Again my answer is the same.

CHAIRMAN WALTER: You said that you would tell us about it.

MR. SEEGER: I will tell you about the songs, but I am not going to tell you or try to explain—

CHAIRMAN WALTER: I direct you to answer the question. Did you sing this particular song on the Fourth of July at Wingdale Lodge in New York?

MR. SEEGER: I have already given you my answer to that question, and all questions such as that. I feel that is improper: to ask about my associations and opinions. I have said that I would be voluntarily glad to tell you any song, or what I have done in my life.

CHAIRMAN WALTER: I think it is my duty to inform you that we don't accept this answer and the others, and I give you an opportunity now to answer these questions, particularly the last one.

MR. SEEGER: Sir, my answer is always the same.

Chairman Walter: All right, go ahead, Mr. Tavenner.

Mr. Tavenner: Were you chosen by Mr. Elliott Sullivan to take part in the program on the weekend of July Fourth at Wingdale Lodge?

Mr. Seeger: The answer is the same, sir.

Mr. Willis: Was that the occasion of the satire on the Constitution and the Bill of Rights?

Mr. Tavenner: The same occasion, yes, sir. I have before me a photostatic copy of a page from the June 1, 1949, issue of the *Daily Worker,* and in a column entitled "Town Talk" there is found this statement:

> The first performance of a new song, "If I Had a Hammer," on the theme of the Foley Square trial of the Communist leaders, will be given at a testimonial dinner for the 12 on Friday night at St. Nicholas Arena. . . . Among those on hand for the singing will be . . . Pete Seeger, and Lee Hays—

and others whose names are mentioned. Did you take part in that performance?

Mr. Seeger: I shall be glad to answer about the song, sir, and I am not interested in carrying on the line of questioning about where I have sung any songs.

Mr. Tavenner: I ask a direction.

Chairman Walter: You may not be interested, but we are, however. I direct you to answer. You can answer that question.

Mr. Seeger: I feel these questions are improper, sir, and I feel they are immoral to ask any American this kind of question.

Mr. Tavenner: Have you finished your answer?

Mr. Seeger: Yes, sir.

Mr. Tavenner: I desire to offer the document in evidence and ask that it be marked "Seeger exhibit No. 4," for identification only, and to be made a part of the Committee files.

Mr. Seeger: I am sorry you are not interested in the song. It is a good song.

Mr. Tavenner: Were you present in the hearing room while the former witnesses testified?

Mr. Seeger: I have been here all morning, yes, sir.

Mr. Tavenner: I assume then that you heard me read the testimony of Mr. [Elia] Kazan about the purpose of the Communist Party in having its actors entertain for the benefit of Communist fronts and the Communist Party. Did you hear that testimony?

Mr. Seeger: Yes, I have heard all of the testimony today.

Mr. Tavenner: Did you hear Mr. George Hall's testimony yesterday in which he stated that, as an actor, the special contribution that he was expected to make to the Communist Party was to use his talents by entertaining at Communist Party functions? Did you hear that testimony?

MR. SEEGER: I didn't hear it, no.

MR. TAVENNER: It is a fact that he so testified. I want to know whether or not you were engaged in a similar type of service to the Communist Party in entertaining at these features.

(*Witness consulted with counsel.*)

MR. SEEGER: I have sung for Americans of every political persuasion, and I am proud that I never refuse to sing to an audience, no matter what religion or color of their skin, or situation in life. I have sung in hobo jungles, and I have sung for the Rockefellers, and I am proud that I have never refused to sing for anybody. That is the only answer I can give along that line.

CHAIRMAN WALTER: Mr. Tavenner, are you getting around to that letter? There was a letter introduced yesterday that I think was of greater importance than any bit of evidence adduced at these hearings, concerning the attempt made to influence people in this professional performers' guild and union to assist a purely Communist cause which had no relation whatsoever to the arts and the theater. Is that what you are leading up to?

MR. TAVENNER: Yes, it is. That was the letter of Peter Lawrence, which I questioned him about yesterday. That related to the trial of the Smith Act defendants here at Foley Square. I am trying to inquire now whether this witness was party to the same type of propaganda effort by the Communist Party.

MR. SCHERER: There has been no answer to your last question.

MR. TAVENNER: That is right; may I have a direction?

MR. SEEGER: Would you repeat the question? I don't even know what the last question was, and I thought I have answered all of them up to now.

MR. TAVENNER: What you stated was not in response to the question.

CHAIRMAN WALTER: Proceed with the questioning, Mr. Tavenner.

MR. TAVENNER: I believe, Mr. Chairman, with your permission, I will have the question read to him. I think it should be put in exactly the same form.

(*Whereupon the reporter read the pending question as above recorded.*)

MR. SEEGER: "These features": what do you mean? Except for the answer I have already given you, I have no answer. The answer I gave you you have, don't you? That is, that I am proud that I have sung for Americans of every political persuasion, and I have never refused to sing for anybody because I disagreed with their political opinion, and I am proud of the fact that my songs seem to cut across and find perhaps a unifying thing, basic humanity, and that is why I would love to be able to tell you about these songs, because I feel that you would agree with me more, sir. I know many beautiful songs from your home county, Carbon, and Monroe, and I hitchhiked through there and stayed in the homes of miners.

MR. TAVENNER: My question was whether or not you sang at these functions of the Communist Party. You have answered it inferentially, and if I understand your answer, you are saying you did.

MR. SEEGER: Except for that answer, I decline to answer further.

MR. TAVENNER: Did you sing at functions of the Communist Party, at Communist Party requests?

MR. SEEGER: I believe, sir, that a good twenty minutes ago, I gave my answer to this whole line of questioning.

MR. TAVENNER: Yes, but you have now beclouded your answer by your statement, and I want to make certain what you mean. Did you sing at the Communist Party functions which I have asked you about, as a Communist Party duty?

MR. SEEGER: I have already indicated that I am not interested, and I feel it is improper to say who has sung my songs or who I have sung them to, especially under such compulsion as this.

MR. TAVENNER: Have you been a member of the Communist Party since 1947?

(*Witness consulted with counsel.*)

MR. SEEGER: The same answer, sir.

CHAIRMAN WALTER: I direct you to answer that question.

MR. SEEGER: I must give the same answer as before.

MR. TAVENNER: I have a throwaway sheet entitled "Culture Fights Back, 1953," showing entertainment at the Capitol Hotel, Carnival Room, Fifty-first Street at Eighth Avenue, in 1953, sponsored by the Committee to Defend V. J. Jerome. It indicates that Pete Seeger was one of those furnishing the entertainment. Will you tell the Committee, please, whether or not you were asked to perform on that occasion, and whether or not you did, either as a Communist Party directive, or as what you considered to be a duty to the Communist Party?

MR. SEEGER: I believe I have answered this already.

MR. TAVENNER: Are you acquainted with V. J. Jerome?

MR. SEEGER: I have already told you, sir, that I believe my associations, whatever they are, are my own private affairs.

MR. TAVENNER: You did know, at that time, in 1953, that V. J. Jerome was a cultural head of the Communist Party and one of the Smith Act defendants in New York City?

MR. SEEGER: Again the same answer, sir.

MR. SCHERER: You refuse to answer that question?

MR. SEEGER: Yes, sir.

MR. TAVENNER: I hand you a photograph which was taken of the May Day parade in New York City in 1952, which shows the front rank of a group of individuals, and one is in a uniform with military cap and insignia, and carrying a placard entitled CENSORED. Will you examine it please and state whether or not that is a photograph of you?

(*A document was handed to the witness.*)

MR. SEEGER: It is like Jesus Christ when asked by Pontius Pilate, "Are you king of the Jews?"

CHAIRMAN WALTER: Stop that.

MR. SEEGER: Let someone else identify that picture.

MR. SCHERER: I ask that he be directed to answer the question.

CHAIRMAN WALTER: I direct you to answer the question.

MR. SEEGER: Do I identify this photograph?

CHAIRMAN WALTER: Yes.

MR. SEEGER: I say let someone else identify it.

MR. TAVENNER: I desire to offer the document in evidence and ask that it be marked "Seeger exhibit No. 6."

CHAIRMAN WALTER: Make it a part of the record.

(*Witness consulted with counsel.*)

MR. TAVENNER: It is noted that the individual mentioned is wearing a military uniform. That was in May of 1952, and the statute of limitations would have run by now as to any offense for the improper wearing of the uniform, and will you tell the Committee whether or not you took part in that May Day program wearing a uniform of an American soldier?

MR. SEEGER: The same answer as before, sir.

CHAIRMAN WALTER: I direct you to answer that question.

(*Witness consulted with counsel.*)

MR. SCHERER: I think the record should show that the witness remains mute, following the direction by the Chairman to answer that question.

MR. SEEGER: The same answer, sir, as before.

MR. SCHERER: Again, I understand that you are not invoking the Fifth Amendment?

MR. SEEGER: That is correct.

MR. SCHERER: We are not accepting the answers or the reasons you gave.

MR. SEEGER: That is your prerogative, sir.

MR. SCHERER: Do you understand it is the feeling of the Committee that you are in contempt as a result of the position you take?

MR. SEEGER: I can't say.

MR. SCHERER: I am telling you that that is the position of the Committee.

MR. TAVENNER: The *Daily Worker* of April 21, 1948, at page 7, contains a notice that Pete Seeger was a participant in an affair for Ferdinand Smith. Will you tell the Committee what the occasion was at which you took part?

MR. SEEGER: I hate to waste the Committee's time, but I think surely you must realize by now that my answer is the same.

MR. TAVENNER: Do you know whether Ferdinand Smith was under deportation orders at that time?

MR. SEEGER: My answer is the same as before, sir.

Mr. Tavenner: I think that he was not under deportation orders until a little later than that.

Chairman Walter: What is his name?

Mr. Tavenner: Ferdinand Smith, a Communist Party member and former vice-president of the maritime union. My purpose in asking you these questions, Mr. Seeger, is to determine whether or not, in accordance with the plan of the Communist Party as outlined by Mr. Kazan and Mr. George Hall, you were performing a valuable service to the Communist Party, and if that was the way they attempted to use you.

Mr. Seeger: Is that a question, sir?

Mr. Tavenner: That is my explanation to you, with the hope that you will give the Committee some light on that subject.

Mr. Seeger: No, my answer is the same as before.

Mr. Tavenner: Did you also perform and entertain at various functions held by front organizations, such as the American Youth for Democracy? I have here photostatic copies of the *Daily Worker* indicating such programs were conducted in Detroit in 1952, at Greenwich Village on May 10, 1947, and again at another place in March of 1948. Did you entertain at functions under the auspices of the American Youth for Democracy?

(*Witness consulted with counsel.*)

Mr. Seeger: The answer is the same, and I take it that you are not interested in *all* of the different places that I have sung. Why don't you ask me about the churches and schools and other places?

Mr. Tavenner: That is very laudable, indeed, and I wish only that your activities had been confined to those areas. If you were acting for the Communist Party at these functions, we want to know it. We want to determine just what the Communist Party plan was.

Mr. Scherer: Witness, you have indicated that you are perfectly willing to tell us about all of these innumerable functions at which you entertained, but why do you refuse to tell us about the functions that Mr. Tavenner inquires about?

Mr. Seeger: No, sir, I said that I should be glad to tell you about all of the songs that I have sung, because I feel that the songs are the clearest explanation of what I do believe in, as a musician, and as an American.

Mr. Scherer: Didn't you just say that you sang before various religious groups, school groups?

Mr. Seeger: I have said it and I will say it again, and I have sung for perhaps—

(*Witness consulted with counsel.*)

Mr. Scherer: You are willing to tell us about those groups?

Mr. Seeger: I am saying voluntarily that I have sung for almost every religious group in the country, from Jewish and Catholic, and Presbyterian and Holy Rollers and Revival Churches, and I do this voluntarily. I have sung for many, many different groups—and it is hard for perhaps one person to believe, I was looking back over the twenty years or so that I have sung around these forty-eight states, that I have sung in so many different places.

MR. SCHERER: Did you sing before the groups that Mr. Tavenner asked you about?

MR. SEEGER: I am saying that my answer is the same as before. I have told you that I sang for everybody.

CHAIRMAN WALTER: Wait a minute. You sang for everybody. Then are we to believe, or to take it, that you sang at the places Mr. Tavenner mentioned?

MR. SEEGER: My answer is the same as before.

CHAIRMAN WALTER: What is that?

MR. SEEGER: It seems to me like the third time I have said it, if not the fourth.

CHAIRMAN WALTER: Maybe it is the fifth, but say it again. I want to know what your answer is.

(*Witness consulted with counsel.*)

MR. SEEGER: I decline to discuss, under compulsion, where I have sung, and who has sung my songs, and who else has sung with me, and the people I have known. I love my country very dearly, and I greatly resent this implication that some of the places that I have sung and some of the people that I have known, and some of my opinions, whether they are religious or philosophical, or I might be a vegetarian, make me any less of an American. I will tell you about my songs, but I am not interested in telling you who wrote them, and I will tell you about my songs, and I am not interested in who listened to them.

MR. TAVENNER: According to the *Daily Worker,* there was a conference program of the Civil Rights Congress on April 2, 1949, at which you were one of the performers. On August 27, 1949, the People's Artists presented a summer musicale at Lakeland Acres picnic grounds, Peekskill, New York, for the benefit of the Harlem chapter of the Civil Rights Congress, at which you were a participant. At another meeting of the Civil Rights Congress of New York, around May 11, 1946, you were a participant. Will you tell the Committee, please, under what circumstances you performed, because you have said that you sang at all sorts of meetings. Under what circumstances were your services acquired on those occasions?

MR. SEEGER: My answer is the same as before, sir. I can only infer from your lack of interest in my songs that you are actually scared to know what these songs are like, because there is nothing wrong with my songs, sir. Do you know—

MR. SCHERER: You said you want to talk about your songs, and I will give you an opportunity. Tell us what songs you sang at Communist Party meetings?

MR. SEEGER: I will tell you about the songs that I have sung any place.

MR. SCHERER: I want to know the ones that you sang at Communist Party meetings, because those are the songs about which we can inquire. Just tell us one song that you sang at a Communist Party meeting.

MR. SEEGER: Mr. Scherer, it seems to me that you heard my testimony, and that is a ridiculous question, because you know what my answer is.

MR. TAVENNER: Mr. George Hall testified that the entertainment that he engaged in, at the instance of the Communist Party, was not songs of a political character. He did say, however, that he was expected by the Communist Party to perform in order to raise money for the Communist Party. Now, did you, as Mr. Hall did, perform in order to raise money for Communist Party causes?

(*Witness consulted with counsel.*)

MR. SEEGER: I don't care what Mr. Hall says, and my answer is the same as before, sir.

MR. TAVENNER: That you refuse to answer?

MR. SEEGER: I have given my answer.

MR. SCHERER: Was Mr. Hall telling the truth when he told the Committee about the entertainment he engaged in at the instance of the Communist Party?

MR. SEEGER: I don't feel like discussing what Mr. Hall said.

MR. TAVENNER: The American Committee for Yugoslav Relief has been designated as a front organization. According to the October 22, 1947, issue of the *Daily People's World,* in California, Pete Seeger headed the list of entertainers to appear at a picnic given by the Southern California chapter of that organization. Did you participate in that program?

MR. SEEGER: If you have a hundred more photostats there, it seems silly for me to give you the same answer a hundred more times.

MR. TAVENNER: What is your answer?

MR. SEEGER: It is the same as before, sir.

MR. TAVENNER: There are various peace groups in the country which have utilized your services, are there not?

MR. SEEGER: I have sung for pacifists and I have sung for soldiers.

MR. TAVENNER: According to the *Daily Worker* of September 6, 1940, you were scheduled as a singer at a mass meeting of the American Peace Mobilization at Turner's Arena, in Washington, D.C. What were the circumstances under which you were requested to take part in that performance?

MR. SEEGER: My answer is the same as before, sir.

MR. TAVENNER: You were a member of the American Peace Mobilization, were you not?

MR. SEEGER: My answer is the same as before.

MR. TAVENNER: Were you not a delegate to the Chicago convention of the American Peace Mobilization on September 5, 1940?

MR. SEEGER: My answer is the same as before.

CHAIRMAN WALTER: Is that organization subversive?

MR. TAVENNER: Yes.

CHAIRMAN WALTER: What is the name of it?

MR. TAVENNER: American Peace Mobilization, and it was the beginning of these peace organizations, back in 1940. Did you take part in the American Peace Crusade program in Chicago in April of 1954?

MR. SEEGER: My answer is the same as before. Of course, I would be curious to know what you think of a song like this very great Negro spiritual, "I'm Gonna Lay Down My Sword and Shield, Down by the Riverside."

MR. TAVENNER: That is not at all responsive to my question.

MR. SEEGER: I gave you my answer before I even said that.

MR. TAVENNER: If you refuse to answer, I think that you should not make a speech.

(*Witness consulted with counsel.*)

MR. TAVENNER: Did you also perform a service for the California Labor School in Los Angeles by putting on musical programs there?

MR. SEEGER: My answer is the same as before, sir.

MR. TAVENNER: Did you teach in the California Labor School?

MR. SEEGER: My answer is the same as before, sir.

MR. SCHERER: I think for the record you should state whether the California Labor School has been cited.

MR. TAVENNER: It has.

MR. SCHERER: As subversive and Communist dominated?

MR. TAVENNER: Yes, it has been.

(*Witness consulted with counsel.*)

MR. TAVENNER: Did you also teach at the Jefferson School of Social Science here in the city of New York?

MR. SEEGER: My answer is the same as before, sir.

MR. SCHERER: I ask that you direct him to answer.

CHAIRMAN WALTER: I direct you to answer. Did you teach at the Jefferson School here at New York?

MR. SEEGER: I feel very silly having to repeat the same thing over and over again, but my answer is exactly the same as before, sir.

CHAIRMAN WALTER: Has the Jefferson School of Social Science been cited?

MR. TAVENNER: Yes, and it has been required to register under the 1950 Internal Security Act.

MR. SCHERER: There are a number of people here who taught at that school, Mr. Walter.

MR. TAVENNER: I desire to offer in evidence a photostatic copy of an article from the September 21, 1946, issue of the *Daily Worker* which refers to music courses at Jefferson School, and I call attention to the last sentence in the article wherein Peter Seeger is mentioned as a leader in one of the courses. * * * According to the March 18, 1948, issue of the *Daily Worker*, it is indicated that you would entertain at a musical presented by the Jefferson Workers' Bookshop. According to the November 25, 1948, issue of the same paper you would perform also under the auspices of the Jefferson School of Social Science. Also you were a participant in a program advertised in the *Daily Worker* of June 1, 1950, put on by the Jefferson School of Social Science, and according to an issue of February 15, 1954, of the same paper, you were expected to play and lecture on songs and ballads in the Jefferson School. Will you tell the Committee, please, what were the circumstances under which you engaged in those programs, if you did?

MR. SEEGER: My answer is the same as before, sir.

MR. TAVENNER: Did you also engage in performances for the Labor Youth League in 1954?

MR. SEEGER: My answer is the same as before. Did you think that I sing propaganda songs or something?

MR. TAVENNER: In 1947, what was your connection with an organization known as People's Songs?

(*Witness consulted with counsel.*)

MR. SEEGER: I take the same answer as before regarding any organization or any association I have.

CHAIRMAN WALTER: What was People's Songs, Mr. Tavenner?

MR. TAVENNER: People's Songs was an organization which, according to its issue of February and March 1947, was composed of a number of persons on the board of directors who have been called before this Committee or identified by this Committee as members of the Communist Party, and the purpose of which, from information made available to the Committee, was to extend services to the Communist Party in its entertainment projects. Mr. Lee Hays was a member of the board of directors, was he not, along with you, in this organization?

(*Witness consulted with counsel.*)

MR. SEEGER: My answer is the same as before, sir.

MR. TAVENNER: Were you not the editor of People's Songs, and a member of the board of directors in 1947?

MR. SEEGER: My answer is the same as before.

MR. TAVENNER: You were actually the national director of this organization, were you not?

MR. SEEGER: My answer is the same as before.

MR. TAVENNER: Was the organization founded by Alan Lomax?

MR. SEEGER: My answer is the same as before.

MR. TAVENNER: Was the booking agent of People's Songs an organization known as People's Artists?

MR. SEEGER: My answer is the same.

MR. TAVENNER: Will you tell the Committee, please, whether or not during the weekend of July 4, 1955, you were a member of the Communist Party?

MR. SEEGER: My answer is the same as before, sir.

MR. TAVENNER: Were you a member of the Communist Party at any time during the various entertainment features in which you were alleged to have engaged?

MR. SEEGER: My answer is the same.

MR. TAVENNER: Are you a member of the Communist Party now?

MR. SEEGER: My answer is the same.

MR. SCHERER: I ask for a direction on that question.

CHAIRMAN WALTER: I direct you to answer.

MR. SEEGER: My answer is the same as before.

MR. TAVENNER: I have no further questions, Mr. Chairman.

CHAIRMAN WALTER: The witness is excused.

Pete Seeger was sentenced to a year in jail but appealed his case successfully—after a fight that lasted till 1962.

On August 23, 1966, Congressman William F. Ryan of New York placed in the Congressional Record the following article, reproduced here uncut, which fills in the background of Pete Seeger—"I Think I Ought to Mention I Was Blacklisted," by Millard Lampell, *The New York Times,* August 21, 1966:

In 1950, I began to keep a journal with a title borrowed from Dostoevsky: *Notes From Underground*. In it I recorded the ironic, sometimes bizarre, sometimes ludicrous experience of living in the twilight world of the blacklist. The last entry is dated 1964.

I am not by nature an injustice collector. I think martyrdom is for the saints and self-pity is a bore. So, at the Television Academy Award ceremonies, when I went up to accept an Emmy for my Hallmark drama, *Eagle in a Cage,* it was with some surprise that I heard myself saying, "I think I ought to mention that I was blacklisted for ten years."

At the press conference afterward, a reporter asked why I had said it. I had to stop and consider, and a line of the philosopher Santayana's swam into my mind, "Those who cannot remember the past are condemned to repeat it."

The Emmy broadcast brought a load of letters, including a number that asked in puzzlement, "What was this blacklist?"

Well, brothers and sisters, it was like this:

By 1950, I had been a professional writer for eight years, including the time spent as a sergeant in the Air Force that produced my first book, *The Long Way Home*. I had published poems, songs and short stories, written a novel and adapted it as a motion picture, authored a respectable number of films, radio plays and television drama, collected various awards, and seen my Lincoln cantata, "The Lonesome Train," premiered on a major network, issued as a record album, and produced in nine foreign countries.

Then, quietly, mysteriously and almost overnight, the job offers stopped coming.

Free-lance writing is a fiercely competitive arena, and when work bypasses you and goes to others, the logical conclusion is that they have more talent. At the same time, however, there was another disturbing note. I began to have increasing difficulty in getting telephone calls through to producers I had known for years.

It was about three months before my agent called me in, locked her door, and announced in a tragic whisper, "You're on the list."

It seemed that there was a list of writers, actors, directors, set designers, and even trapeze artists, choreographers and clowns who were suspected of Communist leanings and marked by all the film studios, networks and advertising agencies as unemployable. No, my agent had never actually laid eyes on this list. She had not even been officially informed that I was a pariah. It was all hints, innuendos and enigmatic murmurs. "I understand he's in a little trouble."

What made it all so cryptic was the lack of accusations or charges. Fearing legal suits, the film companies and networks flatly denied that any blacklist existed. There was no way of getting proof that I was actually on a list, no way to learn the damning details. My income simply dropped from a comfortable five figures to $2000 a year.

Finally I ran into an old friend, a producer who had downed a few too many martinis, and he leveled with me. "Pal, you're dead. I submitted your name for a show and they told me I couldn't touch you with a barge pole." He shrugged unhappily. "It's a rotten thing, I hate it, but what can I do?" and with a pat on my cheek: "Don't quote me, pal, because I'll deny I said it."

Through the next several years, bit by bit, the shadowy workings of the blacklist came into sharp focus. There were, to begin with, numerous lists. Their common chief origin was the Attorney General's unofficial and highly arbitrary index of "subversive organizations," and the published reports of the sessions of the House Committee on Un-American Activities—testimony from self-styled experts on Communism, a steamy mixture of fact, fancy and hearsay. Among those who had been named as subversives before the committee were the 16th-century playwright Christopher Marlowe* and Shirley Temple, characterized in 1938 as an unwitting Communist dupe. But also named at one session or another were hundreds of working professionals in the communications and entertainment fields. Then somebody got the profitable idea of publishing *Red Channels,* a handy, paperback compendium of the names of the suspected. Every time a name listed

* Not exactly. See page 25 above. —E.B.

in this pamphlet appeared among the critics of a film or a broadcast, it was greeted with complaints written under the letterheads of various obscure patriotic organizations. It took only a handful of these letters to stir panic in the executive corridors.

By 1951, standard equipment for every Madison Avenue and Hollywood producer's desk included, along with the onyx ash tray and pen-holder and the gold cigarette lighter, a copy of *Red Channels* in the bottom drawer.

Perhaps one has to begin by calling up the atmosphere of those days, the confusing, stalemate fighting in Korea, the flareup of belligerent patriotism, the growing government impatience with any dissent from official policy. It was a time of security checks, loyalty oaths, FBI investigations, tapped phones, secret dossiers, spy scandals, library book-burnings, and Senator Joseph McCarthy of Wisconsin waving a briefcase at the television cameras and rasping that it contained the names of a battalion of Reds in the State Department. A time of suspicion, anonymous accusation, and nameless anxiety. Friends I had known for years passed me by on the street with no sign of recognition but a furtive nod. Invitations ebbed away. I tried to be philosophical about it, but it was subtly unnerving, like being confronted on every side by advertisements insinuating dandruff, tooth decay and underarm odor, leaving me with a nagging sense of social failure.

Years later, my memories of those days were to serve me well when I sat down to write a play based on John Hersey's *The Wall,* and had to create the atmosphere of the early days of the Warsaw Ghetto.

I sold my car, moved my wife and children to a cramped apartment in a cheap neighborhood and, when my savings ran out, lived on small loans from friends and what I could earn from a thin trickle of odd, ill-paid assignments. Using a pseudonym, I wrote a few radio broadcasts for the Government of Israel, an educational film for the Government of Puerto Rico, a few scripts for benefits given by charitable organizations.

Then, in the spring of 1952, a wispy, harassed man in an ill-fitting suit appeared in my door, flipped through a bulging folder, and handed me a subpoena from the Senate Committee on Internal Security. It was in Washington, at a closed session of the committee, that for the first time I got some clues to the nature of the charges against me.

In 1940, I had come up from West Virginia and, with Pete Seeger, Woody Guthrie and Lee Hays, formed a folk-singing group called the Almanacs. Now, when every third college student seems to be toting a guitar, when used car lots advertise "Hootenanny Sale," and willowy girls drive around in Alfa-Romeos bought with the royalties from their albums of chain-gang blues and piney woods laments, it seems unbelievable that when I first came to New York the Almanacs were, to my knowledge, the only folk-singing group north of the Cumberland Gap.

Leadbelly was around, newly arrived and living in obscurity. Josh White and Burl Ives were managing to scrape out a meager living. There wasn't exactly a clamor for folk-singers, and we were grateful for any paid bookings we could get. Mostly we found ourselves performing at union meetings and left-wing benefits for Spanish refugees, striking Kentucky coal miners, and starving Alabama sharecroppers.

We were all children of the Depression, who had seen bone-aching poverty, bummed freights across country, shared gunny-sack blankets with the dispossessed and the disinherited. We had learned our songs from gaunt, unemployed Carolina cotton weavers and evicted Dust Bowl drifters. Such as they were, our politics were a crude, hand-me-down cross between Eugene Debs and the old Wobblies. A primitive, folk version of what Franklin D. Roosevelt was saying in his fireside chats. We were against hunger, war and silicosis, against bankers, landlords, politicians and Dixie deputy sheriffs. We were for the working stiff, the underdog, and the outcast, and those were the passions we poured into our songs. We were all raw off the road, and to New York's left-wing intellectuals we must have seemed the authentic voice of the working class. Singing at their benefits kept us in soup and guitar-string money.

Then came the army, and the week after I was discharged I appeared on "Town Hall of the Air" teamed with Bill Mauldin, debating two generals on the subject "What the GI Wants." It was a natural set-up for audience sympathy, enlisted men against the brass. I got almost two thousand fan letters, and overnight found myself a kind of celebrity, in demand as a public speaker. I spoke anywhere that the subject was peace or prejudice, and never thought to give a damn who the sponsoring organization was. Nobody ever tried to tell me what to say.

Years later, before the Senate Committee, I found that period haphazardly reported and presented as evidence that I had taken part in a subversive plot to bring riot and ruin to my native land. I was ordered to account for my life and to give the names of everyone I could ever remember having seen at those bygone benefits. Considering privacy of belief to be a constitutional right of all Americans, I refused.

Even though I appeared at a closed session of the committee, it didn't take very long for the news to get around. The blacklist slammed doors completely shut.

In the late summer of 1952, I gave myself a deadline of three months, resolving that if I couldn't earn a living as a writer, I would pack up my family, return to the city where I was born, and go back to work in a dye factory.

Excerpt from my journal:

This morning, nine days before the deadline, the director V. calls to offer me a job writing a documentary film about an oil boom town in North Dakota. He is aware that I am blacklisted, but is willing to take a chance. Apologizes for

> not being able to give me name credit. Disgusted by the blacklist, he will, as a protest, not ask me to use a pseudonym. The credits will not mention any writer.

If the predominant tenor of the era was fear, there was also moving evidence of courage and compassion:

> In today's mail, a letter from the prominent actor, C. Some time ago he starred in a radio play of mine, but I really do not know him very well. He is a rock-ribbed conservative, but in the envelope I find a $500 check and a brief note. "I have a feeling that life is going to get pretty rough in the days ahead. This is a gift, to use when you need to catch your breath and get back your perspective." I return the check with thanks and a dignity which I probably cannot afford.

Leafing through the journal, I come upon an entry that is pure Gogol farce:

> The television writer L. stops me on the street with a nightmare tale. A year ago, having no political activity in his past, but fearing he might become the victim of some reckless accuser, he sought out a professional investigator who does a brisk trade with the advertising agencies, checking out talent at $5 a head. L. paid to have himself investigated, asking only that, after being proved innocent, he be given a written certificate of clearance.
>
> In due time, L. was found to be free of taint, and given his document, only to discover that he was no longer able to get work. It appears that in the course of probing him, the investigator questioned a number of network executives. He assured them that it was only a routine check and L. was not under suspicion. Their reaction was skeptical. "Where there's smoke, there's fire." L. haunts the waiting room of the networks, a gaunt ghost desperately brandishing his certificate. He has not worked in eight months.

In those first years, the two major sources of work were other writers suffering from a creative block and desperate producers with deadline and budget trouble. I spent four months filling the assignments of a well-known writer who found himself unable to face his typewriter. It was a lucky and profitable arrangement that ended when he appeared one midnight and haggardly told me that his analyst had advised him that signing his name to my work was giving him an even deeper psychological problem. "He says I'm losing my identity."

By taking everything that came our way, a few dozen of us on the East Coast and in Hollywood were working sporadically and managing to survive. For every blacklisted writer who anonymously kept at his trade, ten fell by the wayside. If you could turn out a feature film in a couple of weeks or an hour television play in five days for a twenty-fifth of your former price, you had a chance.

It was a lot tougher for the directors and the actors. They couldn't work without being present in person. One brilliant clown who has since become the toast of Broadway and *Time* magazine used to go around roaring, "I'm Z., the man of a thousand faces, all of them blacklisted."

> The doorbell rings, and I find myself confronted by the well-known character actor, S. In the last decade he has appeared in more than fifty Western movies. Blacklisted now, he is peddling Christmas cards house-to-house. He displays his wares, and I regretfully explain that I can't afford to send cards this year. He settles for a cup of coffee, and reminisces about Gary Cooper and Gene Autry.

By the mid 1950's, the situation had eased a bit. A sympathetic fledgling producer, employing the talents of blacklisted writers, came up with two extremely successful network children's adventure series. And the word was getting around that such-and-such a Hollywood box-office smash, though signed by Y., was actually written by X. There even began to grow a certain mystique about the spectacular feats of the twilight writers. It was not uncommon for me to get calls from acquaintances who would chortle, "I just saw your play on television. Okay, okay, you can't say anything. But you can't kid me, I'd recognize your style anywhere." Sometimes it actually was my work, sold under another name. Sometimes it was not, my protests were of little avail, and I wasn't sure whether to feel amused or embarrassed.

> The producer T. tells me that the head of a major Hollywood studio threw the fourth draft of a script back at him, yelling, "It stinks. Do me a favor, stop wasting money, go find yourself a blacklisted writer."

It was a scramble, and I found myself writing all sorts of things I'd never tried before, industrial training films, travel shorts, doctoring Broadway plays. I wouldn't choose to go through it again, but in many ways it sharpened my skills and expanded my sense of invention.

> The actor C. invites me to lunch and proposes that I write the pilot script for a series that one of the networks has asked him and his wife to do. I explain that I am blacklisted, and while I would very much like the job, I will have to use a pseudonym. He insists that my name will be on it, brushing aside my warnings that it may cause trouble, telling me that he considers the blacklist morally repugnant.
>
> I write the pilot, and the star is delighted with it. He delivers it personally to the network's vice president in charge of production who glances at my name and hands it back. "It's lousy." C. protests that he hasn't even read it, only to be informed, "Look, even if it was Tolstoy, it would be lousy."
>
> Sobered but stubborn, C. offers me the job anyhow. I can sign my work with another name. Only it will have to be the name of an actual writer who can appear at script conferences and rehearsals. After some searching, I find a gifted young writer who is willing to collaborate, and whose name and face will represent us both.

In the end, I was writing under four different pseudonyms, including a Swedish name I used for sensitive art-house films. And there were two or three cleared writers willing to sign my work when the network or agency demanded a name with experience and a list of reputable credits.

I had read Kafka, but nothing prepared me for the emotions of living in the strange world of the nameless. A script of mine won a major award, and I remember the queer feeling of being a nonperson when another writer went up to claim it. At that, I think it was even worse for him. He tried to give me the trophy, miserably telling me that he felt like a fraud. We ended up tossing it in a trash can, and then went out and got drunk together.

Of course, there was a way to avoid all the difficulties. One could always appear before the committee and purge oneself. There were two lawyers who specialized in arranging this, one in New York and one in Hollywood. The established fee was $5000, for which one got expert advice in composing a statement of *mea culpa,* avowing that, being an artist, one was naïve about the devious ways of politics and had been the dupe of diabolical forces. One was also required to offer the names of former friends and acquaintances who were the real subversives. If one knew no such names, the lawyer would obligingly supply some, in one case arguing away the qualms of a famous choreographer who was anxious to clear himself but reluctant to become an informer with the reassuring thought, "Hell, they've all been named already, so you're not really doing them any harm. They can't be killed twice."

I find a whole section of my journal devoted to those who sought to purge themselves, pathetic case histories of the anatomy of panic:

> K. has known the playwright O. since the Thirties, a close and sentimental friendship. One of O.'s plays is currently playing in a revival, and he has insisted that K. be hired as stage manager.
>
> After being blacklisted for a number of years, O. arranged to go before the Committee and clear himself. At two in the morning, K.'s doorbell rings. It is O., looking ill and exhausted.
>
> He points at K. and says in a terrible whisper, "I named you." Then he turns and shuffles back toward the elevator. From others, I gather he spent the whole night making the rounds of the friends he turned in to the Committee.

Who can ever fully understand what fear can do to a man? There were things that happened which, even now, I find myself unable to explain:

> Opening night party at the house of the film and stage director, K. draws me into a corner and tells me that, on the road in New Haven, he was visited by an investigator from the Un-American Activities Committee. "I told him to drop dead." K. goes on for twenty minutes, describing his indignation and defiance, reviling the blacklist. The next day, I learn from his friend T. that when all this took place, K. had already appeared before the Committee and named names.

During those years, I reread the entire works of Dostoevsky, and Lord, how much better I understood them. For by then, I had had my first painful experiences with self-abasement and the need for absolution:

Walking down Broadway, someone catches my elbow from behind. It is R., whom I have known for fifteen years, and who recently appeared as a "cooperative witness" before the Committee. He asks plaintively why I passed him without saying hello, and I explain that I didn't see him. He shakes his head, "No, no, you stared right at me." He grimaces. "I don't blame you. I'm disgusting. Do you think I'm disgusting?" I am not particularly proud of the fact that I nodded yes and walked away. Who appointed me his judge? He's as much a victim as the rest of us.

In 1960, what seemed to be a wide crack appeared in the wall of the blacklist. I was offered the job of writing a film in London, working with a renowned Hollywood director who had fled a committee subpoena. It was a suspense film of, I think, considerable artistic quality, and despite the fact that our names were on it, American distribution rights were purchased by a major Hollywood company. When the first publicity came out, a few weeks before it was to open on Broadway, a Long Island post of the American Legion threatened to picket the theater. The film corporation hastily abandoned plans for the premiere. But they had half a million dollars at stake, and their lawyers met with Legion representatives to work out a deal to protect their investment. The film would have no official opening. A few months would be allowed to pass, to let things cool off. Then the picture would be quietly sneaked into the neighborhood theaters as part of a double bill with a Cary Grant comedy.

And so it went. Truce came to Korea, and McCarthy, after being outmaneuvered at one of his own hearings by Department of the Army lawyer Joseph Welch, was squashed by his colleagues in the Senate, and eventually died. Dalton Trumbo won an Oscar under the name of Robert Rich, and emerged from underground to write *Exodus* in his own name for Otto Preminger. John Henry Faulk sued several of the self-appointed patriots who had put pressure on the networks, and won a whopping award for character damage. The blacklist began to crumble and producers assured me that in their hearts they had always opposed it. Along Madison Avenue and Sunset Boulevard, people wondered exactly how it had ever happened in the first place.

Actually, blacklisting lasted longest in broadcasting. By 1961, my cantata "The Lonesome Train" was beginning to be performed again in schools and colleges. In 1962, I got my first name credit on a film for a Hollywood major studio, without picket lines or protest. But it was not until 1964 that David Susskind and Dan Melnick's Talent Associates approached me to write a script for their CBS series, "East Side West Side." I said I wouldn't consider doing it without credit, and they answered unhesitatingly, "Of course." The play I wrote was called *No Hiding Place*. It was about a Negro family moving into a white suburb. The first time my name had appeared on the home screen in more than a decade, my script won half a dozen awards, and the network scheduled a special repeat broadcast.

George Schaefer, director of Hallmark's "Hall of Fame," happened to see it, and had his assistant look up my name in the telephone book. He asked if I would accept a commission to write an original drama for the program. The result was *Eagle in a Cage,* with Trevor Howard playing Napoleon in exile on St. Helena.

Meanwhile, I had started writing for the theater. My first play opened on Broadway and my second was premiered at Washington D.C.'s Arena Stage. A long scene from that second play, *Hard Travelin',* was presented last spring at the White House Festival of the Arts, and I was invited to be there for the occasion. Then came the Emmy award, and it seemed that I had at last come in from the cold.

Or had I?

Once again we are involved in a confusing, bloody, stalemate conflict in a far-off place. Once again there is a flare-up of belligerent patriotism, signs of official impatience with dissent.

I remember arguing until dawn, some years ago, with Antek, one of the handful of surviving figures from the Warsaw Ghetto. He insisted that terror was not a matter of geography, and that the fear and savagery that exploded in Warsaw might happen anywhere. And I avowed that it could never happen here. Not in a nation with the tradition of Jefferson and Lincoln.

Assuming that we remember that heritage, and our lapses from it. Assuming that Carl Sandburg was wrong the day I heard him say, grinning crookedly in that way of his, "Man has a quick forgettery."

OCTOBER 14, 1955:

Zero Mostel

A Subcommittee of the Committee on Un-American Activities met at 10:45 a.m., in Hollywood, California, the Honorable Clyde Doyle (Chairman) presiding.

Committee members present: Representatives Clyde Doyle and Donald L. Jackson.

Staff members present: Frank S. Tavenner, Jr., Counsel; William A. Wheeler, Investigator.

MR. TAVENNER: Will you state your name, please, sir?

MR. MOSTEL: My name is Sam Mostel.

MR. TAVENNER: When and where were you born, Mr. Mostel?

MR. MOSTEL: I was born in 1915, February 28, 1915, in Brooklyn.

MR. TAVENNER: Where do you now reside, Mr. Mostel?

MR. MOSTEL: In New York City.

MR. TAVENNER: How long have you lived in New York City?

MR. MOSTEL: All my life.

MR. TAVENNER: Will you tell the Committee, please, what your formal educational training has been?

MR. MOSTEL: I went to the public schools of New York, right through college.

MR. TAVENNER: When did you complete your college work?

MR. MOSTEL: 1935.

MR. TAVENNER: Will you tell the Committee, please, briefly, what the nature of your employment or your profession has been since 1935?

MR. MOSTEL: In 1935 I was a painter, an artist, and I worked on WPA as a painter. I became an entertainer in 1942. I have been in the entertainment field since.

MR. TAVENNER: From 1935 until 1942 you followed the occupation of an artist?

MR. MOSTEL: I called myself an artist. Maybe I am the only one who did. But I also did many odd jobs so I could paint.

MR. TAVENNER: What was your first employment as an entertainer?

MR. MOSTEL: I worked in a night club in New York City.

MR. TAVENNER: What night club was that?

MR. MOSTEL: Café Society Downtown.

MR. TAVENNER: How long were you employed there?

MR. MOSTEL: About a year, I would say.

MR. TAVENNER: What was your next employment?

MR. MOSTEL: I worked in many night clubs, films, theaters, tap shows—that sort of employment—movies.

MR. TAVENNER: When did your work begin in the movies and where?

MR. MOSTEL: I did one picture for M-G-M called *Du Barry Was a Lady*. My next film was a picture called *Panic in the Streets*.

MR. TAVENNER: Were you in Hollywood or in the State of California at any time after 1942 for the purpose of carrying on your profession?

MR. MOSTEL: Oh, yes, I was. I then did films for—I did several independent films for Columbia, Warner Brothers, and I was signed to a contract with Twentieth Century–Fox. Or is it the Eighteenth Century–Fox? I don't recall.

MR. TAVENNER: What was the date of your work here in California?

MR. MOSTEL: Well, I worked sort of free lance until I got this contract, and then I stayed here for the term of my contract.

MR. TAVENNER: Did your work require you to be here from time to time?

MR. MOSTEL: Yes. Oh, I not only worked in films here. I also recently did a play here, *Lunatics and Lovers*.

MR. TAVENNER: What I am trying to find out is whether from 1942 up to the present time your work required you to be here in California from time to time.

MR. MOSTEL: From time to time.

MR. TAVENNER: Intermittently.

MR. MOSTEL: Oh, yes, of course.

MR. TAVENNER: Would you say it was as often as once a year?

MR. MOSTEL: There was quite a hiatus between the 1942 film to *Panic in the Streets,* which was done in New Orleans. And then after that—in other words, I suppose 1940, 1941, 1951 [*sic*]—that's about seven years. So I would say the next time I appeared was eight years later in a film, the greatest artistic thing that has ever come down the pike, called *The Enforcer,* with Humphrey Bogart.

MR. TAVENNER: Mr. Mostel, the records of the Committee show that you were subpoenaed on July 19, 1955, to appear in New York for hearings by this Committee on August 19, 1955. After the service of a subpoena on you, we understand, you came to the West Coast in connection with some play you were engaged in, and your counsel in New York called the Committee and represented that it would work quite a hardship on you to require you to come back for an appearance on August 19. And because of that the Committee agreed to postpone your appearance.

MR. MOSTEL: I want to thank the Committee.

MR. TAVENNER: And that is the reason for your being here now.

MR. MOSTEL: I wish to thank the Committee formally for disposing of that time. It would have worked a hardship on the cast.

MR. DOYLE: We always try to cooperate in those cases.

MR. TAVENNER: You stated your first employment in the field of entertainment was with Café Society in 1943.

MR. MOSTEL: 1942.

MR. TAVENNER: Who assisted you in obtaining that employment?

MR. [Richard] GLADSTEIN [Mostel's attorney]: If anyone.

MR. MOSTEL: Nobody assisted me. I auditioned, and quite a period elapsed before I was actually then hired for the job.

MR. TAVENNER: Who hired you?

MR. MOSTEL: Well, actually I believe it was Barney Josephson.

MR. TAVENNER: Was Barney Josephson the owner of the Café Society at that time?

MR. MOSTEL: Yes.

MR. TAVENNER: Was Ivan Black connected with Café Society at that time?

MR. MOSTEL: He was the public-relations man for it.

MR. TAVENNER: Did he play any part in your employment?

MR. MOSTEL: Well, people say all sorts of things about entertainers, but I entertain, and I don't know the part he played in my employment. I was paid by the Café Society Corporation.

MR. TAVENNER: You are also known by "Zero" as a nickname, are you not?

MR. MOSTEL: Yes, sir. After my financial standing in the community, sir.

MR. TAVENNER: Was it Ivan Black who gave you that name?

MR. MOSTEL: Well, that's also a story. I don't know who gave it to me, actually. He claims to have, I suppose. Maybe he did; I don't know.

MR. TAVENNER: Had you known Ivan Black before you became employed at Café Society?

MR. MOSTEL: No, sir.

MR. TAVENNER: Were you a member of the Young Communist League prior to being employed at Café Society?

MR. MOSTEL: That has nothing to do with my employment, obviously —your question.

MR. TAVENNER: My question was whether or not you were a member of the Young Communist League at any time before you were employed.

MR. MOSTEL: I refuse to answer that question on the grounds of the Fifth Amendment.

MR. TAVENNER: During the period of the one year when you were employed by Café Society, did you become well acquainted with Ivan Black?

MR. MOSTEL: I would say I became acquainted to the extent that it was a business relationship. As a matter of fact, personally, my attitude toward press agents is not one of the most complimentary kind, and I thought he was a necessity for a man who was in the entertainment field. He was not my great friend, although a friend.

MR. TAVENNER: While engaged in your employment at Café Society, did you acquire personal knowledge that Ivan Black was a member of the Communist Party?

MR. MOSTEL: May I confer with my attorney a moment?

(*The witness conferred with his counsel.*)

MR. MOSTEL: Do you mind if I hesitate a moment?

MR. DOYLE: Take your time.

MR. MOSTEL: It is a problem, it seems to me. That's why I am taking my time answering this question, on these private opinions, because I am not too clear on certain things, but I will be glad to answer any questions of that sort where I don't have to talk about other individuals.

MR. TAVENNER: May I ask that the witness be directed to answer?

MR. DOYLE: We are not satisfied with that answer, Witness, as being sufficient, and therefore I direct you to answer the question.

MR. MOSTEL: Well, then, I refuse to answer this question under the constitutional privileges which I have, which includes the Fifth Amendment.

MR. TAVENNER: Are you acquainted with a person by the name of Martin Berkeley?

MR. MOSTEL: Is he there again? I hesitate to answer about him, because I don't recall ever meeting him. I don't know who he is. I know about him from the newspapers, of course, but I don't know whether he knows me, and I don't know whether I met him or whether he met me. But I have to decline on the previous grounds that I have stated.

MR. TAVENNER: You mean for the same reason?

MR. MOSTEL: Yes, Fifth Amendment.

MR. TAVENNER: Mr. Berkeley testified before this Committee on January 29, 1952, relating to you as follows:

> Zero Mostel, I met him in Hollywood, I will have to say around 1938—

MR. MOSTEL: That's a—

MR. TAVENNER: All right.

MR. MOSTEL: I wasn't—

MR. TAVENNER: All right. Now, what is your reply?

MR. MOSTEL: Nothing, sir. You haven't asked me a question yet.

MR. TAVENNER: You made a statement which I understood to mean that you were not here in 1938.

MR. MOSTEL: I was not here previous to 1942.

MR. TAVENNER: Were you acquainted with Lionel Stander?

MR. MOSTEL: Yes, sir, fine actor, a very talented man.

MR. TAVENNER: Continuing with Mr. Berkeley's testimony, and repeating what I read:

> Zero Mostel, I met him in Hollywood, I will have to say around 1938, at the home of Lionel Stander. There was a meeting of the writers' fraction at which I was present, and he was among those who were there.

MR. MOSTEL: I think Mr. Berkeley is in complete error. I was never here in 1938. I did not know Mr. Stander in 1938. I was a painter.

MR. TAVENNER: When did you first become acquainted with Mr. Lionel Stander?

MR. MOSTEL: I couldn't tell you, sir. I wouldn't know that. I don't recall. It eludes my memory completely. I know I met him. I met him quite a few years ago, but not in 1938, 1939, 1940, or 1941, not in those four years.

MR. TAVENNER: But in 1942 you are not certain?

MR. MOSTEL: I am not very certain, no, sir, I might have.

MR. TAVENNER: Did you attend a meeting in the home of Mr. Stander at which Mr. Martin Berkeley was present?

MR. MOSTEL: I have never been in the home of Mr. Stander in whatever city I may have run across him.

MR. TAVENNER: Did you attend a fraction meeting of the Communist Party in the home of Lionel Stander in 1942 or any other time?

MR. MOSTEL: I have already answered that by saying I have never been at the home of Mr. Stander at any time.

MR. TAVENNER: Were you a member of the Communist Party in 1942?

MR. MOSTEL: I refuse to answer that question on the grounds previously stated, sir, constitutional liberties, which I hear are granted to every individual in this land.

MR. JACKSON: And which the Committee does not question.

MR. MOSTEL: I am sure it doesn't.

MR. TAVENNER: Mr. Mostel, during the course of our hearings in August in New York City and also during the course of other hearings the Committee has heard evidence of the assistance given by various persons to the Communist Party by entertaining at Communist Party functions, at public meetings that have been initiated by the Communist Party, and at "cause" meetings, as they have been often referred to, initiated by the Communist Party, as well as meetings held by organizations commonly known and referred to as Communist-front organizations.

MR. MOSTEL: And many other types of meetings which were held for cancer, heart, common colds, and a host of other favorites.

MR. TAVENNER: Yes, I imagine the same people who performed for the Communist Party performed for many other organizations and groups. The Committee heard evidence, for instance, by George Hall that his function in New York City was to assist the Communist Party at fund-raising campaigns by entertainment.

MR. MOSTEL: Which is a far cry from the accusation that the sole function of the Communists is to overthrow the Government.

MR. TAVENNER: I have before me a photostatic copy of the December 21, 1943, issue of *New Masses,* page 31, where there appears one-third page advertising entitled "Fund for Freedom," by the Joint Anti-Fascist Refugee Committee. It is advertised for December 26 of that year. Do you recall having engaged in that entertainment for the Joint Anti-Fascist Refugee Committee?

MR. MOSTEL: Sir, could I see it? It might refresh my memory.

MR. TAVENNER: Yes, sir.

MR. MOSTEL: Was this an organization on the Attorney General's subversive list?

MR. TAVENNER: Yes, sir.

MR. MOSTEL: Then I decline to answer that question.

MR. TAVENNER: I hand you now an advertisement of the American Youth for Democracy entitled "Support the Maritime Workers." It shows an entertainment to be given on June 14, 1946. It is called a Youth Rally. Entertainment is to be furnished by, among others, Zero Mostel, according to the advertisement. Will you examine it, please, and state whether or not you took part in that program for the American Youth of Democracy?

MR. MOSTEL: May I confer with my attorney?

MR. DOYLE: Yes, sir. You may confer with your counsel at any time. We are glad to have you do that.

(*The witness conferred with his counsel.*)

MR. MOSTEL: Sir, I don't recall about this at all. But is this organization on the Attorney General's subversive list as well?

MR. TAVENNER: Yes. I will read the citation:

> American Youth for Democracy cited as subversive and Communist by Attorney General Tom Clark December 4, 1947, and again on September 21, 1948; cited by the Special Committee on Un-American Activities March 29, 1944, as the new name under which the Young Communists League operates and which also largely absorbed the American Youth Congress.

MR. MOSTEL: Well, then, I have to decline to answer that, sir.

MR. DOYLE: May I suggest that it be understood between the witness and the Committee and the witness's counsel that wherever the witness says he declines to answer he intends to state that he relies upon his constitutional privilege of the Fifth Amendment?

MR. MOSTEL: Yes. I therefore decline to answer on my constitutional privileges. Incidentally, there are some fine names on it: [Jimmy] Durante and Milton Berle, Georgia Sothern.

MR. JACKSON: None of whom has been identified in open session as members of the Communist Party, however.

MR. MOSTEL: But, sir, the Joint Anti-Fascist Refugee Committee was on the Attorney General's list.

MR. JACKSON: There is no question but what some very worthwhile performances were given by people who were entirely sincere in their motivation and who knew nothing of the Communist Party at all. I daresay, if Mr. Durante and Mr. Berle were in your position today, they would deny that they had ever been members of the Communist Party. There is a significant difference in the nature of the testimony.

MR. MOSTEL: My point is that the organization for which they appeared apparently here—my memory isn't clear on that—was declared subversive by the Attorney General's list long after the inception of that particular organization. Also, sir, *I* wasn't accused or said to be a member of the Communist Party. You said that the testimony you have against me is that Mr. Berkeley had said I attended a fraction meeting in a certain year when I wasn't at that place.

MR. JACKSON: Certainly, Mr. Chairman, reverting back to that point, if Mr. Mostel says he was not here at that time, it seems to me that would be a misuse of the constitutional amendment, because an answer to the question would not tend to incriminate him.

MR. DOYLE: That's right.

MR. JACKSON: And in light of that, I am quite unsatisfied with the reliance on the amendment, and I ask the direction be given again on the question previously asked by counsel in that regard. If Mr. Mostel was not here at that time, if he was not in the City of Los Angeles, then a truthful answer to the question will not incriminate him.

MR. MOSTEL: I answered one question and I answered a fact, when I was asked was I a member of several organizations—I don't recall the organization at this moment—I relied on my constitutional privileges. But the fact of being present at this meeting I vehemently deny, since it was physically impossible. So, therefore, I am relying on my constitutional privilege, I feel. I am not a big legal brain.

MR. JACKSON: Were you a member of the Communist Party or of a Communist fraction of the Party in 1938 in the State of California?

MR. MOSTEL: That question I have to answer several ways. Obviously I was never in California until 1942. But on all questions about my political affiliations I wish to rely upon my constitutional privileges under the Fifth Amendment.

MR. JACKSON: I ask that direction be given inasmuch as the witness has volunteered the information that he was not in Los Angeles or in the State of California at that time.

MR. DOYLE: You understand, Witness, we are not satisfied with the answer you have given as a sufficient answer, and therefore I direct you to expressly answer the question.

MR MOSTEL: I decline to answer that question on my constitutional privilege.

MR. JACKSON: Let the record show that I am not satisfied with the answer and believe it to be an improper use of the Fifth Amendment.

MR. DOYLE: Let the record show that I believe the same.

MR. GLADSTEIN: May counsel ask a question of you gentlemen? I know it is not your rule to allow it, but under the circumstances, since you have both laid it on the record that you are not satisfied with the answer, I think the witness should be given the courtesy of having you state just why.

MR. DOYLE: Of course, we do not have time or opportunity, as counsel knows, to enter into legal arguments.

MR. GLADSTEIN: I appreciate that.

MR. DOYLE: It is not a court, and under the decisions of the Supreme Court, as you know, Counsel, it is the duty of the Committee to make it clear to the witness that we are not satisfied with an answer, and that is what I am doing.

MR. JACKSON: The witness voluntarily made a statement that he was not in the City of Los Angeles or in the State of California at the time certain events are alleged to have taken place. Which was not in response to a direct inquiry by the Committee. This was a voluntary statement on his part. Therefore, I am not satisfied with the use of the amendment in reply to a question which deals with that specific period of time. For the witness to volunteer the statement that he was not in this area at the time and then later to refuse to answer substantially the same question is to me an improper use of the amendment.

MR. MOSTEL: May I say something?

MR. DOYLE: Certainly.

MR. MOSTEL: From my limited understanding—and I appreciate your argument very much, Representative Jackson—I don't know. I understand completely your point, sir. My feeling is that when you ask me something about being physically present somewhere, then I will tell you if I were present somewhere, according to the circumstances; but if I am asked as a physical fact if I was there and it was physically impossible for me to be there, I have to tell the truth in that way.

MR. DOYLE: I think you always have to tell the truth, of course.

MR. JACKSON: If you were not in the State of California at that time, the answer to any allegation could not possibly incriminate you, in my humble opinion.

MR. TAVENNER: Mr. Mostel, the last document handed to you related to the youth rally held by American Youth for Democracy. Were you a member of American Youth for Democracy?

MR. MOSTEL: Well, I decline to answer that on my previously stated grounds, relying on the constitutional privilege.

MR. TAVENNER: Were you aware that in a report returned by this Committee in 1948 on American Youth for Democracy that it was stated there that you were an AYD member?

MR. MOSTEL: I decline to answer that question on the previously stated grounds, constitutional amendment.

MR. TAVENNER: Mr. Mostel, you mentioned the names of several people in connection with the flier put out by the Joint Anti-Fascist Refugee Committee. A little while ago you told us you would not mention the names of other people. I assume you have reconsidered your position. So I want to go back now and ask you to tell us whether or not Ivan Black was known to you to be a member of the Communist Party.

MR. MOSTEL: Well, I was merely reading that, you know, without telling you whether I know them or not. On the question of the name Ivan Black, I decline to answer on the previously stated grounds, constitutional grounds, sir. I forgot to put that in.

MR. TAVENNER: I have before me a photostatic copy of an advertisement by a Voice of Freedom Committee of a rally and show to be held at Town Hall, Thursday, May 8, 1947, New York City, together with a program of that rally. On the advertisement appears the name of Zero Mostel as one of the entertainers. Do you recall whether or not you engaged in the entertainment on that occasion?

Mr. Mostel: May I see that, sir? Is this organization on the Attorney General's subversive list?

Mr. Tavenner: Voice of Freedom was cited by the Attorney General of the United States as a Communist organization subsequent to the issuance of our guide to subversive organizations.

Mr. Mostel: I refuse to answer this question on the previously stated constitutional grounds.

Mr. Jackson: Held on May 8, 1947.

Mr. Mostel: Oh, eight-fifteen it says, p.m.

Mr. Tavenner: I have now before me a photostatic copy of a flier advertising a public meeting under the auspices of *Mainstream*. The flier is entitled "Artists Fight Back Against Un-American Thought Control." The speakers include Zero Mostel. Will you examine it and state whether or not you were a speaker on that occasion?

Mr. Mostel: I decline to answer that question on the previously stated grounds, constitutional grounds. You have more handbills about myself than I have.

Mr. Tavenner: Will you tell this Committee whether or not, on June 16, 1947, you entertained at a meeting held in the City of Washington under the auspices of the Southern Conference for Human Welfare?

Mr. Mostel: Have you got some document on that at all?

Mr. Tavenner: No, I am referring to the report that this Committee issued on that organization when it cited the organization.

Mr. Mostel: I decline to answer that on the same constitutional grounds.

Mr. Tavenner: Were you one of the sponsors of Artists' Front to Win the War program held in Carnegie Hall, October 15, 1942?

Mr. Mostel: I decline to answer that question on the same constitutional grounds.

* * *

Mr. Tavenner: I have before me a photostatic copy of a letter of October 24, 1945, on the stationery of the Spanish Refugee Appeal of the Joint Anti-Fascist Refugee Committee, from which appears a list of sponsors. Will you examine the letterhead, please, and state whether or not you see your name as one of the sponsors?

Mr. Gladstein: Doesn't the document speak for itself?

Mr. Mostel: I decline to answer this question on the same constitutional grounds.

Mr. Tavenner: I have before me a photostatic copy of a letter bearing the date of January 21, 1946, on the letterhead of the American Committee for Spanish Freedom. It is a letter written by the American Committee for Spanish Freedom to the Chairman of this Committee.

Mr. Mostel: That was foolhardy.

MR. TAVENNER: Will you examine the list of sponsors appearing on page 2—

MR. MOSTEL: Yes, I will.

MR. TAVENNER: And state whether or not your name appears there as one of the sponsors.

MR. MOSTEL: I decline to answer on the previously stated grounds, my constitutional rights.

MR. TAVENNER: I have before me a photostatic copy of part of page 12 of the April 30, 1947, edition of *PM,* showing almost a half-page advertisement by Arts, Sciences, and Professions for May Day. Will you examine the document, please, and state whether or not your name appears in the advertisement as one of the sponsors?

MR. DOYLE: I think there is a red underscoring appearing on the face of the document by the name of Zero Mostel.

MR. MOSTEL: I wish it were a blue line. I decline to answer this question on the previous grounds, my constitutional rights.

* * *

MR. TAVENNER: I have before me a photostatic copy of a letter bearing date of June 16, 1947, on the letterhead of Voice of Freedom Committee, which shows on its margin the names of the sponsors of the organization. Will you examine it, please, and state whether or not you see there the name of Zero Mostel underscored in red as one of the sponsors?

MR. DOYLE: For his convenience, I call the attention of the witness to a red line under the name of Zero Mostel on that letter.

MR. MOSTEL: I decline to answer this question on the same stated grounds, constitutional liberties.

MR. TAVENNER: In the following of your profession, Mr. Mostel, did you become a member of Actors Equity Association in New York City?

MR. MOSTEL: Well, I am a member of the Equity. Otherwise I couldn't work on the stage.

MR. TAVENNER: Did you also become a member of American Federation of Television and Radio Artists?

MR. MOSTEL: No, sir. I have been blacklisted on television.

MR. TAVENNER: During the period of your membership in 1948 were you aware of an effort made by a group of individuals within the Actors Equity to solicit the assistance of Actors Equity in behalf of the eleven Communists on trial under the Smith Act in the City of New York?

MR. MOSTEL: I decline to answer that question on the previously stated constitutional grounds.

MR. TAVENNER: Have you at any time been aware of the existence of an organized group of members of the Communist Party in the City of New York who were members—or, at least, most of whom were members—of Actors Equity?

Mr. Mostel: I have to decline to answer that question as well, on my constitutional privileges.

Mr. Tavenner: I want to ask another question or two. Have you been a member of the Communist Party at any time while you have been a member of Actors Equity Association?

Mr. Mostel: I decline to answer that question, on the same constitutional grounds.

Mr. Tavenner: Are you now a member of the Communist Party?

Mr. Mostel: I am not.

Mr. Tavenner: You are not?

Mr. Mostel: No, sir.

Mr. Tavenner: Were you a member of the Communist Party on July 7, 1955, when you were subpoenaed before this Committee?

Mr. Mostel: I decline to answer that question on the previously stated constitutional grounds.

Mr. Tavenner: Were you a member of the Communist Party at the time your counsel requested a postponement of your appearance before the Committee, which was on August 17, 1955?

Mr. Mostel: I decline to answer that question as well, on my constitutional privileges.

Mr. Tavenner: Were you a member of the Communist Party when you received your subpoena to appear here today?

Mr. Mostel: I decline to answer that question as well, on my constitutional grounds.

Mr. Tavenner: Were you a member of the Communist Party when you entered this hearing room?

Mr. Mostel: No.

Mr. Tavenner: When did you cease to be a member of the Communist Party?

Mr. Mostel: I decline to answer that question on my constitutional grounds.

Mr. Tavenner: Were you a member of the Communist Party yesterday?

Mr. Mostel: I decline to answer that question, on my same constitutional grounds.

Mr. Doyle: May I state—and I know Mr. Jackson would join me in this—that we never look forward to this sort of hearing or any hearing where any American citizen is being cross-examined. We do not look forward to it.

Mr. Mostel: I sure don't, either.

Mr. Doyle: On the other hand, we do know that there are some subversive people in our country who do advocate, when it suits their convenience, the forceful and violent overthrow of our Government. We know they exist. Do you remember Mr. Tavenner asking you if you knew George

Hall? And he stated that George Hall had testified that his job in the Communist Party was to entertain?

MR. MOSTEL: Yes, I do.

MR. DOYLE: I noticed your answer. I wrote it down. I think it is almost verbatim. Here was your interesting answer. It was voluntary, too: "It is a far cry from the claim that the sole aim of the Communist Party is to overthrow the Government by force and violence." That, to me, is quite significant, I am frank to say, Witness. Do you remember making that statement?

MR. MOSTEL: Yes.

MR. DOYLE: Why did you make that voluntary statement? That was not an issue here. We were asking you about George Hall's entertainment. We were not asking about force and violence.

MR. MOSTEL: If I remember correctly, Mr. Tavenner did not ask me a question at the time, I just volunteered.

MR. DOYLE: I know you volunteered. But why were you so anxious and prompt to volunteer the statement that this matter of entertainment was a far cry from the claim that the Communist Party advocated overthrow of the Government by force and violence?

MR. MOSTEL: Well, I volunteered because, from what I have read, this Committee believed that that is the sole aim of the Communist Party, and here suddenly came a new aim, which I was curious about, and I remarked on it, from curiosity on my part. And I'm sorry I said anything.

MR. DOYLE: Well, I assure you that it was a very interesting curiosity to me.

MR. JACKSON: Mr. Chairman, not only does this Committee have reason to believe that the Communist Party advocates the overthrow of the Government by force and violence, that finding has been made in a number of courts where Smith Act defendants were on trial.

MR. DOYLE: And of course, Mr. Jackson, my recollection is that, under the Smith Act, in all the nine or ten jury trials in our country in the last three or four years every defendant, with the exception of two, has been found guilty of violation.

MR. GLADSTEIN: Let me correct you about that, too, sir.

MR. DOYLE: I may be in error numerically, but only by a few.

MR. GLADSTEIN: Those verdicts are against the individuals on trial in those cases.

MR. DOYLE: Mr. Mostel, I cannot help but feel, Witness, that there was a time when you were a member of the Communist Party, in my own personal opinion from your testimony, because when you came into the room you were not a member of the Communist Party, according to your own testimony.

MR. MOSTEL: That is a feeling, not knowledge.

MR. DOYLE: That is a feeling. It is not a conclusion. It is not my personal knowledge.

MR. GLADSTEIN: You must be aware of Harvey Matusow, and others like him, who admitted that they falsely charged membership.

MR. DOYLE: Harvey Matusow is not before this Committee. I am making a frank statement to another American citizen.

MR. GLADSTEIN: I understand that, and every American citizen must be aware of the dangers of prosecution and persecution.

MR. JACKSON: Order, Mr. Chairman.

MR. DOYLE: Just a moment, Mr. Gladstein.

MR. GLADSTEIN: I'm sorry.

MR. MOSTEL: Don't fight, boys.

MR. DOYLE: Now, we have had so many witnesses before us who have said they were not members of the Communist Party when they appeared before the Committee, but inferentially, to me as an individual, when they answer that way they were members of the Communist Party at some time.

MR. MOSTEL: Isn't it Justice [Earl] Warren's decision—I forget the case—

MR. DOYLE: You mean in one of the three recent cases?

MR. MOSTEL: Where it says you must not infer anything of that nature. If it is a man's private affairs, he has private reasons for doing what he does do.

MR. DOYLE: That is right, and I am glad you are familiar with those three decisions, because—

MR. MOSTEL: I am not familiar, I am casually acquainted.

MR. DOYLE: Yes, casually. Well, we followed those decisions for years. That is nothing new for us, those three recent decisions. May I say this to you: Now, you are in a great field—

MR. MOSTEL: Sometimes.

MR. DOYLE: You are in a great field of entertainment of the American public. From now on, why don't you get far removed from groups that are known to be Communist dominated or Communist controlled, that sort of thing? Why don't you get so far away from them that the American public will never have any possible claim to think you ever were or ever in the future are a member of the Communist Party?

MR. MOSTEL: I have—

MR. DOYLE: Why don't you remove yourself far away from that atmosphere, sir? You can be a much better inspiration and joy to the American people if they just know that there is not a drop, not an inkpoint, not a penpoint, of a favorable attitude by you toward the Communist conspiracy?

MR. MOSTEL: My dear friend, I believe in the antiquated idea that a man works in his profession according to his ability rather than his political beliefs. When I entertain, my political beliefs are not spouted. As a matter of fact, I am casual about my political beliefs, which I wouldn't tell anybody unless you are my friend and you are in my house.

MR. DOYLE: I am not asking about—

MR. MOSTEL: And I have bad instant coffee I make, I'll tell you that.

MR. DOYLE: I am not asking about your political beliefs.

MR. MOSTEL: My dear friend, I believe in the idea that a human being should go on the stage and entertain to the best of his ability and say whatever he wants to say, because we live, I hope, in an atmosphere of freedom in this country.

MR. DOYLE: That's right, and we will fight for your right to think as you please and be as you please and do as you please, provided you do it within the four corners of the Constitution. Don't you think it is your duty, as a great entertainer, to at least find out hereafter where the money you help raise is going, whether or not it is going to some subversive cause against the constitutional form of government in our nation? Don't you think, after this sort of hearing at least, if not before, seeing the effect of these documents appearing in public, don't you think you ought—

MR. MOSTEL: Well, you see, I have such a private opinion, which, honestly, I can't speak about these documents.

MR. JACKSON: Mr. Chairman, may I say that I can think of no greater way to parade one's political beliefs than to appear under the auspices of *Mainstream,* a Communist publication, on the same program, the same platform, as it is alleged here—you have refused to state whether or not you actually did so appear—with Dalton Trumbo, Hanns Eisler, John Howard Lawson, W. E. B. Du Bois, Dorothy Parker, Howard Fast, and Zero Mostel. That program to me speaks volumes as to why you are here. Communist propaganda cannot exist without the funds that are derived from programs of this kind, and I daresay that your name on these many things for which Communist funds were being raised for Communist purposes bolstered and furthered those purposes whether or not you appeared.

MR. MOSTEL: I appreciate your opinion very much, but I do want to say that—I don't know, you know—I still stand on my grounds, and maybe it is unwise and unpolitic for me to say this. If I appeared there, what if I did an imitation of a butterfly at rest? There is no crime in making anybody laugh. I don't care if you laugh at me.

MR. JACKSON: If your interpretation of a butterfly at rest brought any money into the coffers of the Communist Party, you contributed directly to the propaganda effort of the Communist Party.

MR. MOSTEL: Suppose I had the urge to do the butterfly at rest somewhere?

MR. DOYLE: Yes, but please, when you have the urge, don't have such an urge to put the butterfly at rest by putting some money in the Communist Party coffers as a result of that urge to put the butterfly to rest. Put the bug to rest somewhere else next time.

MR. JACKSON: I suggest we put this hearing butterfly to rest.

MR. GLADSTEIN: Just to straighten out the record, may I say, Congressman Jackson, that I don't see on that anything about the Communist Party as such. It says it was under the auspices of *Mainstream*.

MR. JACKSON: The tickets, however, were on sale, significantly enough, at the Jefferson Bookshop, which I believe is a notorious Communist bookshop, and the Workers' Bookshop. They were not on sale at Macy's basement.

MR. MOSTEL: They might have been.

MR. JACKSON: Or at the public library. If they were, they did not advertise it.

MR. CHAIRMAN: I move we adjourn.

MR. GLADSTEIN: Is the witness excused, Mr. Chairman?

MR. DOYLE: The witness is excused. Thank you, Mr. Mostel. Remember what I said to you.

MR. MOSTEL: You remember what I said to you.

1956

"*Unauthorized Use of United States Passports*"

The Chairman of HUAC from 1955 to 1963 was Francis E. Walter, whose contribution to history had been, along with Pat McCarran, the Immigration Law of 1952. As the nonpartisan historian of HUAC, Walter Goodman (in *The Committee* [New York, 1968]), puts it, "The undisguised intent of the McCarran-Walter Immigration Law of 1952, based as it was on a system of national origins quotas for admitting immigrants, was to keep Eastern and Southern Europeans and Asians of all sorts out of the country."

HUAC afforded Walter the opportunity to extend his interests from immigration to emigration—or at least foreign travel. Among his targets were the churchman Willard Uphaus, the singer Paul Robeson, and the playwright Arthur Miller. Only Robeson, curiously enough, did not draw a jail sentence in these years, though Miller was acquitted on appeal, and Uphaus's crucial accuser was not HUAC but the Attorney General of New Hampshire (where Uphaus would spend his seventieth birthday behind bars in 1960). Uphaus was not actually a clergyman but, as an administrator for religious organizations, was treated as many liberal clergymen were treated in the fifties. The man who did most to round up allegedly Red clergymen for HUAC was the ex-Red J. B. Matthews, one of the most influential anti-Communists of the whole epoch, who had had much to do with the very creation of HUAC in 1938, being Martin Dies' most fertile source of "information." The McCarthy era—and to a degree Joseph McCarthy himself—brought Matthews back. The May 1953 issue of the *American Mercury* ran his article "Communism and the Colleges," and the same magazine's July issue carried an article of his, "Reds and Our Churches," which opened with this sentence: "The largest single group supporting the Communist apparatus in the United States today is composed of Protestant clergymen." Matthews named the following churchmen as top pro-Soviet propagandists: Joseph F. Fletcher, of the Episcopal Theological School, Cambridge; Kenneth Ripley Forbes, of the Episcopal League for Social Action; Jack R. McMichael, of the Methodist Federation for Social Action; Harry F. Ward, formerly of Union Theological Seminary; and—Willard Uphaus, of World Fellowship, Incorporated. Uphaus has provided a book-length account of his case in *Commitment* (New York, 1963).

MAY 23, 1956:

Willard Uphaus

The Committee on Un-American Activities convened at 10 a.m., in the caucus room of the Old House Office Building, the Honorable Francis E. Walter (Chairman) presiding.

Committee members present: Representatives Francis E. Walter, of Pennsylvania (Chairman), Morgan M. Moulder, of Missouri, Edwin E. Willis, of Louisiana, and Bernard W. Kearney, of New York.

Staff members: Richard Arens, Director, and Donald T. Appell, Investigator.

THE CHAIRMAN: The hearings which the Committee on Un-American Activities are beginning this morning deal with one of the most vital aspects of our entire security problem, the fraudulent procurement and misuse of American passports by persons in the service of the Communist conspiracy.

As a result of the investigations made by the Committee, we are now able to document in great detail the procedures by which Communists and Communist Party sympathizers obtain passports in direct violation of American law. We can document fully how, by stealth, by concealment, and by misrepresentation, members of the Communist Party and adherents to the Communist conspiracy are able to travel abroad for purposes deliberately detrimental to the United States.

The Committee has in its files hundreds of copies of fraudulent documents used by international Communist agents. These include false passport applications, false birth records, false naturalization certificates. In some cases, the purpose of the trip has been deliberately withheld; in other cases, passports have been issued to applicants who have used the identity of some other individual. Beyond this, the evidence in the possession of the Committee includes records maintained by the Communist organizations themselves, proving the real use to which these passports have been put.

Under existing law, only nationals of the United States can obtain United States passports. However, leading Soviet espionage agents have received and used American passports. Some, like the notorious Gerhart Eisler, applied for them directly. Others have received them in Moscow or in other Communist espionage centers. Some of these individuals have had as many as three passports in their possession at the same time.

* * *

MR. ARENS: Please identify yourself by name, residence, and occupation.

MR. UPHAUS: I am Willard Uphaus. I live in New Haven, Connecticut. I am executive director of World Fellowship, Incorporated.

MR. ARENS: How long have you been so employed?

MR. UPHAUS: Between three and four years.

MR. ARENS: You are appearing today in response to a subpoena which was served upon you by the House Committee on Un-American Activities?

MR. UPHAUS: That is right.

MR. ARENS: You are represented by counsel.

MR. UPHAUS: That is right.

MR. ARENS: Counsel, will you kindly identify yourself?

MR. RABINOWITZ: Victor Rabinowitz.

MR. ARENS: Your counsel a moment ago said you were submitting a statement for consideration by the Committee.

MR. UPHAUS: The statement has been submitted, and I would like to present it today.

MR. ARENS: Can you tell us to your certain knowledge whether any Communists participated in the preparation of that statement?

MR. UPHAUS: That is ridiculous. I wrote it.

MR. ARENS: Do you know whether it was edited by any Communists?

MR. UPHAUS: That is ridiculous. No Communist saw it.

MR. ARENS: Do you know whether your counsel is a Communist?

MR. UPHAUS: Certainly not. I know nothing about his political views.

MR. ARENS: Do you regard Communist Party association, affiliation, only as a question of political views?

MR. UPHAUS: No, sir.

MR. ARENS: Then why did you limit your knowledge of membership in the Communist Party to one's political views?

MR. UPHAUS: That is what you had on your mind. There are cultural and social views as well.

MR. ARENS: Do you know whether or not your counsel is a member of the Communist conspiracy?

MR. UPHAUS: That question is loaded. You ask me whether I believe in a Communist conspiracy, first.

The CHAIRMAN: He did not ask you that at all. He asked you whether you knew that your counsel was a Communist.

MR. UPHAUS: That wasn't the question. I beg to differ.

MR. ARENS: To get it straight, do you know whether your counsel is a Communist?

MR. UPHAUS: I certainly do not.

MR. ARENS: Have you made any inquiry to ascertain whether or not he is a Communist?

MR. UPHAUS: I have not.

MR. ARENS: Mr. Chairman, he has submitted this statement. I respectfully suggest the Committee may want to take it under advisement.

THE CHAIRMAN: Yes, we will take it under advisement.

MR. UPHAUS: May I present it at the present time?

THE CHAIRMAN: We have it.*

MR. ARENS: Tell us, please, whether or not in 1949 you made application for a passport to go abroad.

MR. UPHAUS: I did.

MR. ARENS: Was that passport issued to you?

MR. UPHAUS: It was.

MR. ARENS: In that passport application, where did you say were the places of destination that you wanted to go?

MR. UPHAUS: As I recall, Great Britain principally. I might have mentioned other European countries.

MR. ARENS: Did you mention in the passport application any country behind what we call the Iron Curtain?

MR. UPHAUS: As I recall, I did not.

MR. ARENS: I lay before you, Dr. Uphaus, a photostatic copy of a passport application bearing a signature and ask you whether or not that is a true and correct representation of your passport application.

MR. UPHAUS: It appears to be.

MR. ARENS: We will mark it "Uphaus exhibit No. 1," and I respectfully suggest that it be incorporated in the record and retained in the files of the Committee.

THE CHAIRMAN: It may be so incorporated.

(*Uphaus exhibit No. 1 was incorporated by reference as a part of the record.*)

MR. ARENS: Where did you go on your trip in 1949?

MR. UPHAUS: I went to Great Britain. I crossed by train, as I recall, Holland and Belgium. I visited in Germany, and I spent a short time in France.

MR. ARENS: What was the purpose of your visit?

MR. UPHAUS: I went to Great Britain as codirector of a ministers' traveling seminar to study social and religious problems in Great Britain.

MR. ARENS: Under whose auspices or sponsorship was this trip made?

MR. UPHAUS: This was an independent group of ministers.

MR. ARENS: And who paid for your expenses?

* It is printed below, right after the testimony. —E.B.

MR. UPHAUS: Each person paid for his expenses.

MR. ARENS: Did you hold these seminars?

MR. UPHAUS: I went three or four days early and set up appointments with people in all aspects of British life, conservative, labor, church, the whole broad view of church life.

MR. ARENS: How long did this trip take?

MR. UPHAUS: I stayed in Britain until the end of July.

MR. ARENS: In the aggregate, how long were you overseas?

MR. UPHAUS: I returned in early September, I think.

MR. ARENS: Then, in 1950, did you make a second trip to Europe?

MR. UPHAUS: Yes, sir.

MR. ARENS: What occasioned that trip?

MR. UPHAUS: To attend the Second World Peace Congress.

MR. ARENS: And where was that congress held?

MR. UPHAUS: It was held in Warsaw.

MR. ARENS: Did you use the same passport to go to Warsaw, Poland, that you used on your first trip to Europe?

MR. UPHAUS: This was a normal two-year passport, which was still in existence. I used it, yes, sir.

MR. ARENS: Under whose auspices did you travel to Warsaw?

MR. UPHAUS: A sponsoring committee to get delegates to the congress.

MR. ARENS: And did you attend the congress in Warsaw?

MR. UPHAUS: I attended the congress in Warsaw.

MR. ARENS: Did you make a speech to the congress at Warsaw?

MR. UPHAUS: I made a speech.

MR. ARENS: I lay before you, Doctor, a photostatic copy of a document which is a reproduction of certain speeches made at the Warsaw peace conference. I ask you whether or not you, in the course of your speech at the Warsaw peace congress, called for the admission of the People's Republic of China into the United Nations?

MR. UPHAUS: Does the document say that I did?

MR. ARENS: Yes, sir, according to this intercept.

THE CHAIRMAN: Well, did you?

MR. UPHAUS: That was five years ago, sir.

THE CHAIRMAN: Did you?

MR. UPHAUS: I do not recall. I have the complete text of the speech I made that day, if the Committee is interested.

THE CHAIRMAN: We have it, too.

MR. ARENS: We have it, too. Did you at that time call for the admission of Red China into the United Nations?

MR. UPHAUS: In all probability. I do not recall for sure.

MR. ARENS: Did you at that time attack the Federal Bureau of Investigation?

MR. UPHAUS: I criticized it.

MR. ARENS: Did you say in effect that the Federal Bureau of Investigation has been given millions of dollars to employ agents to snoop into people's lives?

MR. UPHAUS: I said that. It was the truth.

MR. ARENS: How did you know that the objective of the money which was appropriated to the Federal Bureau of Investigation was to snoop into people's lives?

MR. UPHAUS: I learned that through hard experience, sir.

MR. ARENS: What was this hard experience that you learned about the millions of dollars used by the Federal Bureau of Investigation to snoop into people's lives?

MR. UPHAUS: A friend came to my house and told me about an interview.

MR. ARENS: And who was that friend?

MR. UPHAUS: That would be contrary to my faith and belief, to bring that friend into this situation.

MR. ARENS: Mr. Chairman, I respectfully suggest that the witness be directed to answer that question.

THE CHAIRMAN: Yes, you are directed to answer that question.

MR. UPHAUS: I refuse to answer, on the following grounds: Under the First Amendment, my rights to free speech, my right to the freest exercise of religion and free assembly, are protected, and hence Congress cannot legislate on such matters. Moreover, the question includes my right to privacy. And I say to you that that was a question of private relationships.

THE CHAIRMAN: You have testified that millions of dollars were spent to snoop into private lives, and you reached that conclusion as a result of something that someone told you. Now, who was that someone?

MR. UPHAUS: I reached conclusions on the basis of my voluminous reading, sir.

THE CHAIRMAN: Well, what? What did you read that led you to that conclusion?

MR. UPHAUS: Reports.

MR. KEARNEY: What reports?

MR. UPHAUS: Well, magazine reports, documentary reports, newspaper reports.

MR. KEARNEY: Any reports from the *Daily Worker*?

MR. UPHAUS: I do not recall any reports from the *Daily Worker*.

MR. ARENS: Did you inform the State Department prior to the time that you went to the Warsaw peace conference that you were going there?

MR. UPHAUS: The State Department, I think, knew that I was going to the congress, but it was to have been held in Sheffield, sir.

MR. ARENS: Sheffield, England?

MR. UPHAUS: That is right, sir.

MR. ARENS: Did you tell the State Department that you were going to a Communist-controlled country?

MR. UPHAUS: I do not accept the presupposition in your question.

MR. ARENS: You do not accept the presupposition that Poland was controlled by the Communists, is that correct?

MR. UPHAUS: I am not prepared to testify on that.

MR. ARENS: Did you, in your own knowledge, believe that Poland was controlled by the Communist Party?

MR. UPHAUS: That was not of concern to me. I was going to a peace congress which was far, far beyond—

THE CHAIRMAN: Did you notify the United States Government that you were going to Poland?

MR. UPHAUS: No, sir.

MR. ARENS: However, you traveled on a passport which was issued to you on the basis of the representation you made to the State Department that you were going to non-Communist countries. Isn't that correct?

MR. UPHAUS: I had no relationship directly with the State Department. I had a two-year passport in hand. I did not have to apply.

THE CHAIRMAN: How do you think you got a passport, if you did not have any relationship with the State Department?

MR. UPHAUS: For that particular journey or mission, I did not make any special request.

MR. ARENS: When you made your application for a passport, you listed the countries to be visited as England, France, Germany, Holland, Switzerland, and Scotland, did you not?

MR. UPHAUS: Yes, but that was not a promise of what I was going to do for two years. That was for a specific trip.

MR. ARENS: And thereafter you used this same passport for the purpose of going to Poland, is that correct?

MR. UPHAUS: Yes.

THE CHAIRMAN: How did you get to Poland from any of the countries in which you were authorized to travel?

MR. UPHAUS: By train and by air.

THE CHAIRMAN: How did you get permission to go to Poland?

MR. UPHAUS: I presume the countries through which we passed gave us permission. We did not violate the law.

THE CHAIRMAN: What country were you in immediately before you went into Poland?

MR. UPHAUS: France.

THE CHAIRMAN: How did you get from France to Poland?

MR. UPHAUS: By way of Prague.

THE CHAIRMAN: What permission did you have when you got to the border at Prague to go into Poland?

MR. UPHAUS: It must have been the permission of the government that received us.

THE CHAIRMAN: Did you have any particular permission?

MR. UPHAUS: I didn't need permission, if the government received us.

MR. ARENS: Who was with you on this mission?

MR. UPHAUS: Which mission do you refer to?

MR. ARENS: The mission to the Warsaw peace conference.

MR. UPHAUS: Oh, there was a large American delegation of sixty-six people.

MR. ARENS: How many?

MR. UPHAUS: Sixty-six people, as I recall.

MR. ARENS: How many of them, to your knowledge, were members of the Communist Party?

MR. UPHAUS: I have no notion whatever.

MR. ARENS: When you were in Warsaw, Poland, at this Second World Peace Conference [*sic*], did you in the course of your speech make an assertion that three million noncitizens residing in the United States were being threatened with loss of their citizenship under Fascist legislation?

MR. UPHAUS: I believe something to that effect is in the address that I made.

MR. ARENS: And where did you get that information?

MR. UPHAUS: That is also ascertainable by study.

THE CHAIRMAN: You know it is not true, do you not?

MR. UPHAUS: No, I don't know it is not true.

THE CHAIRMAN: Then why did you say it if you do not know whether it is true or not?

MR. UPHAUS: Well, I would think that three million was a modest number who are intimidated by the Cold War. That was modest.

THE CHAIRMAN: What do you mean by that, "intimidated by the Cold War"?

MR. UPHAUS: Because people are afraid to open their mouths for fear they will lose their jobs.

THE CHAIRMAN: And they are going to be deported for that reason? Three million people?

MR. UPHAUS: Multitudes of people. I suppose there are that many or more who are foreign born or under surveillance due to the Walter-McCarran Act.

THE CHAIRMAN: Now, do you mean by that that an alien can be deported only because he happens to be a member of the Communist Party? Is that what you are talking about?

MR. UPHAUS: Will you please ask the question again?

THE CHAIRMAN: What did you mean about three million people being in fear of being deported?

MR. UPHAUS: Because of my acquaintanceship with the troubles and sorrows that many families have that are threatened or are deported.

THE CHAIRMAN: There are not three million aliens in the United States. And nobody is deportable under the Walter-McCarran Act unless they have committed a felony within five years after they have arrived, or are members of a proscribed organization, and then only after a trial in court. What you are objecting to is the provision in the law under which a Communist can be deported, isn't that it?

MR. UPHAUS: I don't think so, sir. I object to families being broken. I object to fathers and mothers being separated from their children. I object to older people who have given their lives here and grown up in this country being embarrassed and threatened with deportation.

MR. ARENS: You are now a member of the American Committee for Protection of Foreign Born, one of the oldest Communist fronts in the country, are you not?

MR. UPHAUS: I am not a member.

MR. ARENS: You are a sponsor and your name appears on the letterhead of the American Committee for Protection of Foreign Born, isn't that true?

MR. UPHAUS: I am a sponsor, yes.

MR. ARENS: And you have been a sponsor long since and long after the American Committee for Protection of Foreign Born has been exposed by the Committees of the Congress as an arm of the Communist conspiracy, isn't that true?

MR. UPHAUS: That has never been proved in court.

MR. ARENS: Can you tell us the names of persons who, to your knowledge, are Communists and who are identified with the American Committee for Protection of Foreign Born?

MR. UPHAUS: I positively do not know.

MR. ARENS: Do you know Abner Green, of the executive committee of the American Committee for Protection of Foreign Born?

MR. UPHAUS: Yes.

MR. ARENS: Don't you know that he is a hard-core member of the Communist conspiracy?

MR. UPHAUS: I do not know that.

MR. ARENS: Are you also a member of the National Conference to Repeal the Walter-McCarran Law and Defend Its Victims?

MR. UPHAUS: I believe that is right.

MR. ARENS: You are one of the sponsors of that organization, are you not?

MR. UPHAUS: I believe that is right.

MR. ARENS: Do you not know that that is a front in front of the American Committee for Protection of Foreign Born?

MR. UPHAUS: It has never been so declared in court.

MR. ARENS: I direct your attention to the letterhead, in which your name appears, National Conference to Repeal the Walter-McCarran Law and Defend Its Victims, with American Committee for Protection of Foreign Born right on the letterhead.

MR. UPHAUS: That is a matter of fact. But your question was something else.

MR. ARENS: The question was: Do you know that the National Conference to Repeal the Walter-McCarran Law and Defend Its Victims is a front in front of the American Committee for Protection of Foreign Born?

MR. UPHAUS: I do not accept that.

MR. ARENS: It is a creature of the American Committee for Protection of Foreign Born, is it not?

MR. UPHAUS: I do not accept that.

MR. ARENS: Explain to this Committee how the name American Committee for Protection of Foreign Born appears on the letterhead of the National Conference to Repeal the Walter-McCarran Law and Defend Its Victims.

MR. UPHAUS: I don't see the bearing of the sponsorship of the organization in its title.

MR. ARENS: To your certain knowledge, doesn't the American Committee for Protection of Foreign Born sponsor the repeal of the Walter-McCarran Law?

MR. UPHAUS: That was one of the activities, indeed.

THE CHAIRMAN: Where did you obtain your visa that enabled you to go from France to Poland?

MR. UPHAUS: In the respective countries, as I recall.

THE CHAIRMAN: You did not obtain a visa from the United States Embassy in Paris, did you?

MR. UPHAUS: No, sir.

THE CHAIRMAN: And you did not have one when you left?

MR. UPHAUS: To go to Paris?

THE CHAIRMAN: No. To go to Poland. You know what I am talking about.

MR. UPHAUS: No, sir, I didn't.

THE CHAIRMAN: Then where did you get the visa that you had when you moved from France into Poland?

MR. UPHAUS: I know of no other way I could get it than through the respective governments.

THE CHAIRMAN: The fact of the matter is you were given it by some Communists in France, were you not?

MR. UPHAUS: I could not prove that, not in two years.

THE CHAIRMAN: As a matter of fact, you do not care, isn't that it?

MR. UPHAUS: Right here is the discipline of the Methodist Church in the United States—

THE CHAIRMAN: Please, do not try to inject that. That is cowardly.

MR. UPHAUS: It is not.

THE CHAIRMAN: You just answer these questions. Do not try to hide behind religion or anything else.

MR. UPHAUS: It is part of my religion, sir.

THE CHAIRMAN: What I want to know is where you obtained the visa you had when you went into Communist Poland. That is what I want to know.

MR. UPHAUS: That would be difficult to say, except to say that it was at the hands of the governments that received us.

THE CHAIRMAN: No, the government that received you did not give you a visa. The visa had to come from somewhere else. Now, where did it come from?

MR. UPHAUS: I don't see how one can travel from country to country without some kind of official permission.

THE CHAIRMAN: Well, the official document you had that enabled you to go to Paris came from your own Government.

MR. UPHAUS: The two-year travel, that is right.

THE CHAIRMAN: And that enabled you to go to France. Now, we want to know how you were able to go behind the Iron Curtain, when no one else was permitted to travel behind the Iron Curtain. How did you get that permission?

MR. UPHAUS: Many go behind the Iron Curtain.

THE CHAIRMAN: How did you get permission to go to Poland?

MR. UPHAUS: Through the peace committee in Poland, which no doubt functioned in cooperation with the Polish government.

MR. ARENS: In this speech that you made in Warsaw, Poland, did you also attack your Government for a "trial of ideas at Foley Square setting a precedent for jailing any whose ideas can be labeled as subversive and thereby jeopardizing the freedom of thought and its expression for all Americans?"

MR. UPHAUS: I do not call it an attack. It was a criticism of the Cold War policy of that Administration.

MR. ARENS: Did you, in effect, say what I have just quoted with respect to the trial of the eleven Communist traitors at Foley Square?

MR. UPHAUS: May I see the document, please? I stand by what is in this record.

MR. ARENS: Will you give us the copy, then, of the speech that you say is the true and correct copy of your observations?

MR. UPHAUS: That is the one I used. Handle it preciously.

THE CHAIRMAN: Did you comment on the trial at Foley Square?

MR. UPHAUS: I don't recall that I did.

MR. ARENS: I lay before you a document entitled "Supplement to New Times, No. 48, November 29, 1950," in which is reproduced a speech by Dr. Willard Uphaus:

> Citizens must be careful as to their political associations in the trial of ideas at Foley Square, setting a precedent for jailing any whose ideas can be labeled as subversive, and thereby jeopardizing the freedom of thought and expression of all Americans.

Did you say that?

MR. UPHAUS: May I have the original, please? Yes, it is in there.

MR. ARENS: During the course of your speech at the Warsaw peace conference did you assert in effect that the Government of the United States was engaged in suppression and intimidation of voices for peace, and, as illustration of that, Albert Maltz and others of the Hollywood Ten are jailed, Dr. Edward K. Barsky and Mr. Howard Fast of the Anti-Fascist Refugee Committee have been serving prison sentences, and others of like ilk?

MR. UPHAUS: I really resent the use of the word "ilk."

MR. ARENS: Well, others of your—

THE CHAIRMAN: You.

MR. UPHAUS: That is in the record, yes, sir.

MR. ARENS: Did you know that these men whom you were defending as the voices of peace, the victims of suppression, were in jail because they were members of an international Communist conspiracy designed to destroy this country?

MR. UPHAUS: I did not know that.

MR. ARENS: Did you make any effort to find out before you condemned the Government of the country to which you owe allegiance?

MR. UPHAUS: Sir, I have read and thought and written on the question of the Cold War and the conspiracy, and I do not accept your basic presupposition. Right here is a document by none other than Ernest T. Weir of the National Steel Corporation, who agrees with me.

MR. ARENS: Did you, while you were at the Warsaw peace conference, receive an invitation to go a little further behind the Iron Curtain into Moscow?

MR. UPHAUS: That is right.

MR. ARENS: And who extended that invitation to you?

MR. UPHAUS: The Soviet Peace Society.

MR. ARENS: Was it an oral invitation, written, or telegraphic, or how was it?

MR. UPHAUS: The Soviet Peace Society was represented at Warsaw. Consequently, it was a face-to-face kind of invitation.

MR. ARENS: Was the person who invited you to go into Moscow—an

American citizen traveling on an American passport—known by you to be a member of the Communist Party?

MR. UPHAUS: Not at all. I didn't know.

MR. ARENS: How did you get to Moscow?

MR. UPHAUS: We flew.

MR. ARENS: Who paid your expenses?

MR. UPHAUS: I think the Soviet Peace Society paid the expenses.

MR. ARENS: How long were you in Moscow?

MR. UPHAUS: About ten days.

MR. ARENS: While you were in Moscow did you and your colleagues seek to see the then United States Ambassador to Moscow, Alan Kirk?

MR. UPHAUS: Yes. We tried to have an appointment with him.

MR. ARENS: Did the Ambassador refuse to entertain you?

MR. UPHAUS: Well, it wasn't a question of his entertaining us. He didn't receive us, no.

MR. ARENS: And what was the reason he gave for not receiving you?

MR. UPHAUS: Well, he was under the apprehension that we were there for a purpose that we weren't there for. We were there for peace solely, to understand the Soviet people. And he made a grave mistake not to see nineteen American citizens that day.

THE CHAIRMAN: Have you the list of the nineteen American citizens who were there? Will you give us the names of the citizens who accompanied you?

MR. UPHAUS: That would be in violation of my right under the First Amendment.

THE CHAIRMAN: What constitutional right have you that would be impaired or infringed upon by giving us the names of the Americans who called with you on the American Ambassador?

MR. UPHAUS: Because I have no moral ground to drag their names in.

THE CHAIRMAN: How are you dragging their names into anything?

MR. UPHAUS: I have no moral ground, no right, to bring their names in here for the newspapers.

THE CHAIRMAN: We want to know who they were.

MR. UPHAUS: I am sure the Government has the record.

THE CHAIRMAN: I direct you to answer the question.

MR. UPHAUS: I decline.

MR. ARENS: I think he wants to recite his reasons.

THE CHAIRMAN: For the reasons heretofore stated. Is that it?

MR. RABINOWITZ: Not entirely.

MR. UPHAUS: Under the Fifth Amendment, I may not be compelled to bear witness against myself. I feel that, in these circumstances, to answer about my associations with some other people is not only morally wrong but it might also subject me to unjustified prosecution under the conspiracy or other laws of the United States. The privilege is for the protection of innocent persons as well as guilty, and I claim its protection.

THE CHAIRMAN: With what crime do you think you might be charged if you give us the names of the persons who accompanied you to the American Embassy?

MR. UPHAUS: How can I tell?

THE CHAIRMAN: I direct you to answer that question.

MR. UPHAUS: I cannot anticipate actions that the Government might take.

THE CHAIRMAN: Nor can you frivolously invoke the Fifth Amendment.

MR. UPHAUS: I know it is a very serious thing, sir.

THE CHAIRMAN: I must warn you that you are in a very serious situation by refusing to answer a question which in no wise could jeopardize you in the criminal courts.

MR. UPHAUS: Suppose that, in speaking about these other eighteen persons, I would say something that would involve them wrongly. . . .

THE CHAIRMAN: But you are not going to be asked anything about them. We are merely asking who they were.

MR. UPHAUS: The Government knows who they were, sir.

THE CHAIRMAN: We do not. Now give us the names of the persons who accompanied you.

MR. UPHAUS: You can ascertain that information through the Government.

THE CHAIRMAN: I am trying to now.

MR. UPHAUS: It is accessible to you through the Government.

THE CHAIRMAN: I do not know where. And the best evidence that I know of at the moment could come from your lips. Now, who were they?

MR. UPHAUS: I cannot, sir. You have plenty of money to send an agent—

THE CHAIRMAN: I direct you to answer the question: Who accompanied you to the Embassy?

MR. UPHAUS: I refuse on the grounds already stated.

THE CHAIRMAN: All right.

MR. ARENS: Who was your host while you were in Moscow?

MR. UPHAUS: The Soviet Peace Society.

MR. ARENS: Where did you go?

MR. UPHAUS: Well, we spent the most of our time in Leningrad, Moscow, and Stalingrad.

MR. ARENS: During the course of your visit, did you make an investigation as to the great issue of freedom of religion behind the Iron Curtain and in Soviet Russia?

MR. UPHAUS: I went to church and worshiped with other people.

MR. ARENS: Did you make a comprehensive investigation of that issue?

MR. UPHAUS: One cannot do that in ten days.

MR. ARENS: After you returned from Moscow, did you join with others in issuing a report on the subject "Is There Freedom of Religion in the Soviet Union?"?

MR. UPHAUS: I believe I had nothing to do with this particular document. Is my name on that document?

MR. ARENS: I lay before you, Doctor, a photostatic copy of a document entitled "Some Answers to the Question, Is There Freedom of Religion in the Soviet Union? by British, Scottish, and American visitors to the Soviet Union in 1950," identifying a number of people who made the study, including one Dr. Willard Uphaus.

MR. UPHAUS: This simply tells that I was one person that interviewed the Metropolitan. The paragraph says nothing about what I said.

MR. ARENS: Did you participate in the preparation of this document?

MR. UPHAUS: I did not.

MR. ARENS: The report, according to its face, is issued by the National Council of American-Soviet Friendship.

MR. UPHAUS: That is not Willard Uphaus.

MR. ARENS: Were you part and parcel of the preparation of this document?

MR. UPHAUS: I was not.

MR. ARENS: Was it issued pursuant to any acquiescence of yourself?

MR. UPHAUS: I don't think I was interviewed with respect to that document. It wasn't a question of acquiescence.

MR. ARENS: Did you read the document?

MR. UPHAUS: I think I have read it.

MR. ARENS: Have you ever taken issue with this document?

MR. UPHAUS: Well, I have had discussions with people. I have never made any speeches about it, or anything like that.

MR. ARENS: Did you entertain the convictions as expressed in this document with reference to the position of the religious institutions behind the Iron Curtain, and particularly in Russia?

MR. UPHAUS: To answer that question you have to know the whole history of the Russian church and what is meant by freedom of religion to them. They have a different concept than what we have in the United States. To them, they have freedom of religion.

MR. ARENS: Here is a question. I want to ask you if you comport with this, in view of the fact that your name is identified as one of those who made this study.

> QUESTION: Do you believe the present State regime fulfills the social ideals of religion?
>
> ANSWER: The social ideals of religion—love, justice, equality, brotherhood, peace—are integral parts of the present Soviet system. Not only theoretically but realistically in this case. The Government is building for peace. All the people are equal. There is sincere brotherhood and true friendship be-

> tween the peoples of our country. The Government teaches love for labor and duty to humanity along with love, justice, equality, which help in the development of people and in living together.

Is that the essence of your conviction and your position?

MR. UPHAUS: There is a very deep distinction there. I am sure, as I talked with the churchmen in the Soviet Union, that they did teach love, brotherhood, and mercy, and all the attributes of religion.

MR. ARENS: You say here, "The Government teaches love."

MR. UPHAUS: I did *not* say that.

MR. ARENS: Do you subscribe to this conviction respecting freedom of religion in Soviet Russia, that the government teaches love, justice, equality?

MR. UPHAUS: I do not. It isn't the part of the government to teach that.

MR. ARENS: Have you ever taken issue with that?

MR. UPHAUS: Well, I am doing that today. The government of Russia doesn't do that. It is the church, the churchmen. I don't think officials officially in our country do that either.

MR. ARENS:

> QUESTION: "Do clergy have the right to criticize the Government?
>
> ANSWER: The clergy's job is not to criticize the Government but to teach and preach our sacred religion. All of his time is spent delving into religious matters and not into politics. As a citizen of the Soviet Union, however, he has the right to engage in the discussions of the problems of our country.

Is that the conviction that you had?

MR. UPHAUS: I have to distinguish between Russia and the United States in that regard, the definition of religion, its meaning, the relationship to government.

MR. ARENS: All right, sir. After your return to the United States from Soviet Russia, did you have occasion to make application for still another visit abroad?

MR. UPHAUS: I think I made application in 1952 for a passport.

MR. ARENS: And what happened to that application?

MR. UPHAUS: I was turned down.

MR. ARENS: Turned down by the State Department. Where were you going?

MR. UPHAUS: I was hoping to go to a peace conference in South America, as I recall.

MR. ARENS: Was that the American Inter-Continental Peace Conference?

MR. UPHAUS: That is right.

MR. ARENS: Thereafter did you make application for still another passport?

MR. UPHAUS: Possibly I did.

Mr. Arens: Did you propose to go to Austria in 1952?

Mr. Uphaus: Oh, yes. I think I wanted to go to Austria.

Mr. Arens: I lay before you a photostatic copy of a document entitled "Department of State Passport Application," which is dated in September 1952, bearing the signature of Willard Uphaus, and ask you whether or not that is the passport application which you made.

Mr. Uphaus: I think it is.

Mr. Arens: What was your purpose in seeking to go to Austria?

Mr. Uphaus: I wanted to meet the peoples of the different countries of Europe in the interests of peace.

Mr. Arens: Were you at that time cognizant of the fact that the Peiping peace conference was about to be held, in October of 1952, a month after you made your application to go to Austria?

Mr. Uphaus: I think I recall, yes, that that conference in China—

Mr. Arens: Did you intend to go to the Peiping peace conference?

Mr. Uphaus: I don't think I entertained any thought like that.

Mr. Arens: What was the Peiping peace conference?

Mr. Uphaus: Well, it was a conference of peoples bordering the Pacific.

Mr. Arens: Where was it being held?

Mr. Uphaus: In the capital of China.

Mr. Arens: Which China? You don't mean Formosa. You mean Red China?

Mr. Uphaus: I mean the legitimate China today.

Mr. Arens: You mean the Communist-controlled China?

Mr. Uphaus: I mean the China that is now governed by a coalition government.

Mr. Arens: Is that the government which has Communists at the head of it, atheistic, godless Communists at the head of it?

Mr. Uphaus: Can we stop long enough to discuss what materialistic philosophy of life is?

Mr. Kearney: I think he said materialistic Communism.

Mr. Uphaus: Materialistic Communists may be very devout humanists, sir, loving their fellow men and working for peace.

Mr. Arens: You honestly believe that the members of the Communist conspiracy love their fellow men and work for peace?

Mr. Uphaus: You always load the question, sir.

Mr. Arens: Tell us whether or not you do believe that the International Communists, the members of the Communist Party, are real humanists working for peace.

Mr. Uphaus: Oh, by and large, as much as people in any country or in any party.

Mr. Arens: How long have you entertained that conviction?

Mr. Uphaus: For a long time.

MR. ARENS: And you were going to go to the Peiping conference if you could, were you not?

MR. UPHAUS: Well, I had never been in the Orient, and I thought it was legitimate that I should, if I could.

MR. ARENS: Do you know a person by the name of Anita Willcox?

MR. UPHAUS: Yes, I know her.

MR. ARENS: Did you know that at the Peiping peace conference she read a greeting from you reading as follows:

> I am delighted to be able to send greetings and best wishes to your great conference through my good American friends, Mr. and Mrs. Henry Willcox. I profoundly regret that I cannot be present in person to share the spirit and deliberations that will go far to establish peace not only in Asia and Pacific regions but throughout the world.

Did you send such a message?

MR. UPHAUS: If I didn't, I should have.

MR. KEARNEY: Well, did you send such a message?

MR. UPHAUS: I think I did.

MR. KEARNEY: You think you did. Do you know whether or not you did?

MR. UPHAUS: That has been a long time, and I send many letters and telegrams in my active life.

MR. KEARNEY: You can remember what you want to remember, though.

MR. UPHAUS: That is an accusation.

MR. KEARNEY: Of course it is. You are not kidding me any by your testimony here. You know whether you sent that message or not.

MR. UPHAUS: It sounds like me, and I think possibly I did.

MR. KEARNEY: It does sound like you.

MR. UPHAUS: Indeed. It expresses my philosophy of life. I am working for peace every day of my life.

MR. ARENS: Was this a telegram, or a letter, or what was the nature of the message the Willcoxes received from you?

MR. UPHAUS: I can't say for sure whether it was a wire or an airmail letter.

MR. ARENS: Did you know the Willcoxes were going to that peace conference at Peiping before they actually departed from the United States?

MR. UPHAUS: I knew it was their hope.

MR. ARENS: Did you know whether or not they expressed that hope or belief or conviction to the Department of State prior to the time they left the United States to go to Peiping?

MR. UPHAUS: I cannot testify for them. I don't know about that.

MR. ARENS: Did you know what route they took to go to Peiping?

MR. UPHAUS: Not exactly, no.

MR. ARENS: Did you know they did not go by the most direct route to Peiping?

MR. UPHAUS: I could not possibly trace their course.

MR. ARENS: Did you actually ask the Willcoxes to attend the Peiping conference?

MR. UPHAUS: I don't think I made a categorical request. I expressed the hope that they would get there.

MR. ARENS: When did you express the hope to the Willcoxes that they would ultimately arrive at Peiping for the peace conference?

MR. UPHAUS: We were in conversation.

MR. ARENS: How long before they actually departed did this conversation take place?

MR. UPHAUS: I cannot remember that.

MR. ARENS: Where did this conversation take place?

MR. UPHAUS: I think it was in their home.

MR. ARENS: Did you receive a passport on the basis of your request to go to Austria?

MR. UPHAUS: No, sir.

MR. ARENS: Did you intend to use that passport to ultimately arrive by some devious route at the Peiping peace conference?

MR. UPHAUS: It was conceivable that I would go on, if I could find a way to go on, to that peace conference. I thought I should be there.

MR. ARENS: Did you make a representation in your application to the Passport Division of the Department of State in 1952 that you intended ultimately, if you could make it, to get on to Peiping?

MR. UPHAUS: That, I did not, no.

MR. ARENS: I lay before you a photostatic copy of your passport application of 1952, on which appears "Countries to be visited: Great Britain, France, Belgium, Germany, Switzerland, Netherlands, and Austria." Why didn't you also put on your application that you were going to go on to the Peiping conference, if possible?

MR. UPHAUS: Well, it was certainly a vague hope that I could get there, it wasn't realistic.

MR. ARENS: You knew that travel of American citizens was restricted and prohibited, isn't that correct?

MR. UPHAUS: I am not sure. Anyway, if I had known, I would have followed the United Nations Declaration of Human Rights, which says we have the right to travel into any country and return to our country.

MR. SCHERER: You follow that instead of the law of this country?

MR. UPHAUS: That is an edict that represents the majority of mankind. When I have to choose between all humanity and a particular government, a Christian has to make that choice.

MR. SCHERER: You would make the choice of following a prescribed rule or procedure or doctrine of the United Nations rather than the law of the United States?

MR. UPHAUS: It is not a prescribed rule. It is a privilege. It is historically a right inherent in society to move from one's country to another.

MR. SCHERER: You would follow that rather than the law of the United States?

MR. UPHAUS: Well, when I face that dilemma, I will decide it.

MR. SCHERER: Well, you did decide it in this particular instance, did you not?

MR. UPHAUS: I knew in my heart that I had the moral right to go to any peace congress in the world. That was according to the dictates of my church, my conscience, and my life.

MR. SCHERER: But you did know that, irrespective of what your own personal feelings might be, the law of this country prohibited you from traveling behind the Iron Curtain, did you not?

MR. UPHAUS: I did not know that.

MR. SCHERER: Well, if you did know it, which would you have followed?

MR. UPHAUS: How can one ask about what one would do?

MR. KEARNEY: You told us a minute ago that you followed the dictates of your own conscience.

MR. UPHAUS: But, when that opportunity arose, there might be new elements on which to base a decision. My conscience tomorrow may lead me to do something slightly different from today.

MR. SCHERER: I think the witness originally made his position clear and started to hedge after he had good advice from counsel.

MR. ARENS: After you made application for this passport in 1952, in what section of Austria were you to have this conference that you were to attend?

MR. UPHAUS: It was to be held in Vienna.

MR. ARENS: At the time, were you identified with the Committee for Peaceful Alternatives?

MR. UPHAUS: I think so.

MR. ARENS: Did you know that the Committee for Peaceful Alternatives has been cited as part and parcel of the Communist conspiracy?

MR. UPHAUS: Oh, yes, I knew that.

MR. ARENS: It made no difference to you anyhow, is that correct?

MR. UPHAUS: Positively not.

MR. ARENS: Now, did you send a message to this peace conference in Austria?

MR. UPHAUS: It would be my nature to do so.

MR. ARENS: Did you, in this message, include a strong plug for China assuming its rightful place among the nations of the world?

MR. UPHAUS: I probably did. That is the way I felt about it.

MR. ARENS: And your point of view at that time, and now, Doctor, is that Red China, Communist-controlled, atheistic, godless China, should be admitted into the council of the nations of the world in the United Nations?

MR. UPHAUS: I just admit that the present government of China should be admitted. I don't put all the adjectives in.

MR. ARENS: Don't you think the present government of China is controlled by the atheistic, godless international conspirators, the Communists?

MR. UPHAUS: Oh, sir, you have to define what goes on in that country before making generalizations like that.

MR. KEARNEY: Do you personally know what goes on in that country?

MR. UPHAUS: I know a great deal. My wife was a missionary seventeen years in that country, and we read a great deal about China.

MR. KEARNEY: Your wife was a missionary in old China, was she not?

MR. UPHAUS: Yes, but she knows a great deal about present China.

MR. KEARNEY: Has she been in the new China, we will say?

MR. UPHAUS: She has not.

MR. ARENS: If the Communist conspiracy would control China, and if it is an atheistic, godless conspiracy, would you still be an advocate of the admission of Red China into the council of the nations of the world?

MR. UPHAUS: That is an "iffy" question. I simply testified, sir, that I believe that the present government in China—and England and those countries are all in agreement with me—that China should be admitted to the council of nations.

MR. ARENS: What if China were controlled by the atheistic, godless conspiracy I have been talking about? Would you still be an advocate of admitting China into the nations of the world?

MR. UPHAUS: I certainly would.

MR. KEARNEY: On that question I am glad to disagree with you.

MR. UPHAUS: Well, that is why we are quoting the Declaration of Independence.

MR. KEARNEY: You have not been quoting the Declaration of Independence. You have been quoting the Declaration of the United Nations, as far as I can see.

MR. ARENS: And you are familiar with the words from the Song of David? "Blessed is the man that walketh not in the counsel of the ungodly, nor standeth in the way of sinners, nor sitteth in the seat of the scornful."

MR. UPHAUS: That was his point of view.

MR. ARENS: Whose point of view?

MR. UPHAUS: The person who wrote it.

MR. ARENS: You do not concur with David in the Book of Psalms?

MR. UPHAUS: I have a basic disagreement with a lot that I read in the Bible.

MR. ARENS: I assume you feel that David was in error when he said:

"Blessed is the man that walketh not in the counsel of the ungodly, nor standeth in the way of sinners, nor sitteth in the seat of the scornful."

MR. UPHAUS: Is this a theological seminar today?

MR. ARENS: You came with a Bible today. You have been waving it around in front of this Committee.

MR. UPHAUS: Will you give me time to discuss the theology of that verse that you quoted?

MR. ARENS: Did you participate, in New York City, in December of 1952, in a Peace on Earth Rally, which was operating in concert with the Vienna rally which you were unable to attend because you couldn't get a passport?

MR. UPHAUS: Sir, I was the director—

MR. ARENS: Can't you just answer the question? Did you participate in the rally?

MR. UPHAUS: Yes.

MR. ARENS: And in that rally did you say this: "We have a delegation of Americans there," namely at Vienna, "at least twenty, in spite of the State Department"?

MR. UPHAUS: I would have to see the text.

MR. ARENS: Let me lay before you a text as recited in a paper we call here the Communist *Daily Worker*. And I would like to read to you just a couple of paragraphs and see if this refreshes your recollection.

> "How many of us would like to be in Vienna tonight?" asked Dr. Willard Uphaus with a smile at the Peace on Earth Rally at Palm Garden Monday night. There was an answering burst of applause, and more when Dr. Uphaus, the head of the United States sponsoring committee for representation at the Congress of the Peoples for Peace, revealed that "we have a delegation of Americans there, at least twenty, in spite of the State Department."

Is that an accurate quotation of yourself at that peace rally?

MR. UPHAUS: I can't say yes or no just from a newspaper report.

MR. ARENS: Don't you have a recollection of saying in effect that you do have people at this peace conference in Vienna in spite of the State Department?

MR. UPHAUS: I honestly don't recollect just what I said.

MR. ARENS: Do you recollect that there were people at the Vienna conference?

MR. UPHAUS: Yes, I knew there were people there.

MR. ARENS: Did you know people were there from the United States?

MR. UPHAUS: I knew they were there, yes.

MR. ARENS: Did you know they were attending the conference in spite of the State Department?

MR. UPHAUS: Well, I can't answer that, because they all had passports.

MR. ARENS: Do you know how they procured those passports?

MR. UPHAUS: I cannot tell you. They made applications, I suppose, normally, the way other people do.

MR. ARENS: You know your passport application was turned down, to go to the Vienna peace conference, do you not?

MR. UPHAUS: That is right.

MR. ARENS: Do you have any recollection of saying that "they are there in spite of the State Department"?

MR. UPHAUS: I have no recollection of having said that.

MR. ARENS: Is this quotation erroneous?

MR. UPHAUS: How could I vouch for a quotation, a paper?

MR. ARENS: Did this peace rally that you had in New York City in 1952 have an international telephone hookup with Vienna so that they would be working together?

MR. UPHAUS: I think possibly there was a message sent, as I recall, to Vienna.

MR. ARENS: Who sent the message from the United States?

MR. UPHAUS: That I do not recall.

MR. ARENS: Paul Robeson did, did he not?

MR. UPHAUS: Well, I am not sure who did.

MR. ARENS: Do you remember seeing Paul Robeson there at that rally?

MR. UPHAUS: I do not remember, but it is possible that he was there.

MR. ARENS: Was Isobel Cerney there?

MR. UPHAUS: I do not remember. Oh, yes, she is from California. She was there, I think.

MR. ARENS: And she was just back from the conference at Pieping?

MR. UPHAUS: I think so.

MR. ARENS: I lay before you a document entitled "International Telephone Hookup" and ask you if that was a true representation of the program in which you participated that evening in this international hookup with Vienna.

MR. UPHAUS: I see nothing abnormal in that.

MR. ARENS: That isn't the question. Is that a true and correct representation of the program at that meeting?

MR. UPHAUS: As I recall, that represents what it was.

MR. ARENS: Did you about that time, in November of 1952, make a speech or issue a statement criticizing the State Department for undertaking to restrict travel of people to the Vienna peace conference?

MR. UPHAUS: I was very critical of the State Department for doing that. I felt that it violated the real right that we had to go to a peace meeting.

MR. ARENS: To your knowledge, did anyone attend that peace conference who did so in circumvention of the law and regulations under which the Passport Office of the Department of State was operating?

MR. UPHAUS: I cannot testify to anyone doing that.

MR. ARENS: I say, do you have knowledge of that?

MR. UPHAUS: I have no knowledge of anyone having violated the law.

MR. SCHERER: May I interrupt a minute? Do I understand that you think they had a right to go, irrespective of the law and rules and regulations of the State Department?

MR. UPHAUS: The cause of peace in the world is the primary cause and purpose which transcends the politics of the State Department.

MR. SCHERER: I did not ask you about the politics of the State Department. I asked you whether or not you felt that these people had a right to attend this peace conference irrespective of the fact that it violated the law.

MR. UPHAUS: The right of movement in the world to work for peace is a basic moral right. And restrictions in law sometimes contravene what is right and true.

MR. KEARNEY: Then, according to you, we should throw out the State Department.

MR. UPHAUS: That doesn't follow.

MR. ARENS: Incidentally, in passing, did I understand you to say you also had spent considerable time in China, or was it your wife?

MR. UPHAUS: My wife.

MR. ARENS: Did she ever tell you the old Chinese adage that "You can't carve rotten wood"?

MR. UPHAUS: I might have heard it at some time. I don't think she told me.

MR. ARENS: Don't you think that might be applicable in these peace conferences, where you sit down with traitors, materialists, atheists?

MR. UPHAUS: Listen, Mr. Arens. When the bombs fall, they are not going to ask me whether I am a Methodist or an atheist or a Communist. And I tell you now that it is the responsibility of atheists as well as Christians to work for peace and coexistence. That is the basic philosophy. And I get it right from the religion of Jesus.

MR. ARENS: Were you one of the sponsors of this Vienna peace conference, where you were going to sit down with these Communists and these atheists and these international traitors to build peace and carve out a peace for the world?

MR. UPHAUS: Didn't our President say he would go anywhere in the world for peace? President Eisenhower?

MR. SCHERER: I ask that you direct the witness to answer the question.

MR. ARENS: Weren't you the director of the sponsoring committee for this Vienna peace parley?

MR. UPHAUS: Yes.

MR. ARENS: Can you tell us who some of the other directors were of this Vienna peace parley that you set up?

MR. UPHAUS: That is a matter of record.

MR. ARENS: Well, was Dr. W. E. B. Du Bois one of them?

MR. UPHAUS: That is a matter of record.

MR. ARENS: Was he?

MR. UPHAUS: I say it is a matter of record.

MR. ARENS: Are you affirming it or denying it? Was Dr. W. E. B. Du Bois a member of this peace parley?

MR. UPHAUS: If his name is on the letterhead, then he was.

MR. ARENS: Do you have a recollection that he was?

MR. UPHAUS: I do.

MR. ARENS: Why did you not say so? You do not need to parry with us. We are just trying to seek the facts. Was Dr. John Kingsbury a member of this peace parley committee? Was he?

MR. UPHAUS: May I see the list? Then I'll know.

MR. ARENS: Do you have an independent recollection as of this moment?

MR. UPHAUS: I think he was, but I would like to see the documentation.

MR. ARENS: Do you know whether or not Louis Wheaton, chairman of the delegation to Peiping, expressed to the Department of State his intention to attend either the Peiping or Vienna conference, prior to the time he got his passport?

MR. UPHAUS: I do not know about that.

MR. ARENS: Did you make this statement:

> Dr. Willard Uphaus, Methodist churchman, declared yesterday that the recent State Department denunciation of the Congress of the Peoples for Peace, to be convened in Vienna, December 12, is more of a great deal of evidence that our top officials are opposed to any peace meeting of East and West, no matter how broadly representative, no matter how democratic the rules of procedure.

Now, what did you do toward sending that delegation to the congress, when you knew the State Department was opposed to the attendance of American citizens in that congress?

MR. UPHAUS: I think I have testified earlier that the right of assembly for peace is a prior right.

MR. ARENS: Can't you just answer the question honestly and fairly? What did you do toward sending people to that Vienna conference after you knew the State Department was trying to keep people from going to that congress?

MR. UPHAUS: Well, I looked at the purpose of the conference. I knew it was legitimate. And I encouraged everyone who could go to go.

MR. ARENS: And you did that after you knew that the State Department had issued a prohibition against American citizens attending that congress, because it was controlled by the international conspiracy of Communism, is that correct?

MR. UPHAUS: That isn't correct.

MR. ARENS: Then you state it. Did you at the time you sent these messages around know that the State Department was opposed to issuing passports to American citizens to attend that congress?

MR. UPHAUS: I knew that.

MR. SCHERER: And you did it in spite of that?

MR. UPHAUS: Indeed. Because that was our mission.

MR. SCHERER: Why did you do it?

MR. UPHAUS: Because the peace of the world transcended the Cold War for which the State Department stood.

MR. SCHERER: You set up, then, your own philosophy and followed that rather than the law of this country.

MR. UPHAUS: It is part of the Christian religion.

MR. SCHERER: I disagree with some of the Supreme Court decisions that were recently made. But I follow those decisions no matter how violently I disagree with them.

MR UPHAUS: I do not follow them when they contravene my Christian conscience.

MR. SCHERER: You mean you do not follow the decisions of the Supreme Court if they contravene your conscience?

MR. UPHAUS: I don't know of any time I have contravened a Supreme Court order. We were talking about the State Department.

MR. SCHERER: This is a new liberalism.

MR. ARENS: Is the record clear, Doctor, that despite the fact that you knew the State Department was prohibiting the issuance of passports to American citizens to attend the Vienna congress, you nevertheless were encouraging people, American citizens, to attend that congress?

MR. UPHAUS: I felt that America should be represented, that it would be wrong for her not to be represented.

MR. ARENS: Did you actually encourage people to attend the Vienna congress, notwithstanding the fact that you knew and were informed that the State Department was prohibiting people from attending that congress?

MR. UPHAUS: The answer is yes.

MR. ARENS: What did you do toward consummating this objective of yours to get American citizens to attend this congress, which was a matter of prohibition by your Government?

MR. UPHAUS: Well, I did many things. I wrote letters, I talked to people. I read the call to the congress. I agreed with it. And I tried to interest American citizens in it.

MR: ARENS: Did you actually participate in the formation of a committee?

MR. UPHAUS: I did.

MR. ARENS: A formal committee for participation in the peace conferences which we have been talking about?

MR. UPHAUS: That is right. I did.

MR. ARENS: And who worked with you in the formation of this committee to defy your Government?

MR. UPHAUS: That is a matter of record.

MR. ARENS: Well, tell us, to your recollection who were the members of that committee to defy your Government?

MR. UPHAUS: Many of them were outstanding churchmen.

THE CHAIRMAN: Well, name some of the outstanding churchmen.

MR. UPHAUS: It is a matter of record, sir.

MR. ARENS: Who participated with you in the formation of an organization whose objective it was to defy the prohibitions of your Government against attendance at Communist-controlled peace conferences?

MR. UPHAUS: I decline on the grounds of the Fifth Amendment.

MR. ARENS: Do you honestly apprehend that if you told this committee who participated with you in the formation of an organization to send people to peace conferences against the orders of the Department of State in violation of the passport regulations you would be supplying information which might be used against you in a criminal proceeding?

MR. UPHAUS: Positively, yes. I don't trust the Committee.

MR. SCHERER: Just a minute. I ask that the Chair direct him to answer the question. Because first, I think he is improperly invoking the Fifth Amendment, and second, if by chance he is properly invoking it, he certainly waived any privilege he has to invoke the Fifth Amendment, in view of his testimony on this subject.

THE CHAIRMAN: Yes. You are directed to answer the question.

MR. UPHAUS: I have to decline, your Honor.

THE CHAIRMAN: No. You do not have to. You are not under any compulsion.

MR. UPHAUS: The whole situation is compulsion around me.

THE CHAIRMAN: No, it is not. You are merely asked to answer the question. And then, when you did not, you are directed to answer.

MR. UPHAUS: I cannot in good conscience, sir.

THE CHAIRMAN: Just a minute, please. That is not a proper answer.

MR. UPHAUS: Why isn't it? I have to answer to myself, as you do, to every conduct in your life.

MR. SCHERER: I think this witness is in contempt. In order, again, to comply with a Supreme Court decision with which I do not agree, but which I recognize I must follow and will follow, I think we should say that we do not accept his answer and that in our opinion the witness, in refusing to answer, is guilty of contempt.

THE CHAIRMAN: Answer the question.

MR. UPHAUS: I cannot in good conscience, sir.

MR. ARENS: Did you encourage Mary Russak to attend the Vienna conference?

MR. UPHAUS: In all likelihood.

MR. ARENS: Did you know that Mary Russak is a hard-core member of the Communist Party?

MR. UPHAUS: No, sir.

MR. ARENS: Would it make any difference to you if you did know she was a member of the Communist Party?

MR. UPHAUS: No, sir.

MR. ARENS: What were your activities in concert with Mary Russak?

MR. UPHAUS: Well, as I recall, we met occasionally in committees to plan.

MR. ARENS: What committees did you meet with?

MR. UPHAUS: Well, they were committees of this sponsoring committee to get people to go to Vienna.

MR. ARENS: And was Mary Russak on this sponsoring committee?

MR. UPHAUS: I don't think so.

MR. ARENS: Well, what was she doing in the meetings?

MR. UPHAUS: People sometimes are invited in to take committee action who are not on the official sponsoring list. That often happens.

MR. ARENS: Mary Russak was on the Peiping sponsoring committee, was she not?

MR. UPHAUS: As far as I know, she was, yes.

MR. ARENS: Was Paul Robeson on that sponsoring committee?

MR. UPHAUS: I think he was.

MR. ARENS: And did he participate with you in encouraging these people to violate the passport regulations of this nation?

MR. UPHAUS: Well, the first half of the question is clear. He cooperated in encouraging people to go to the congress. I don't know what was in his mind as to his motive. You are writing motive into his mind.

MR. ARENS: Did he encourage people to go to the conference in violation of the State Department regulations?

MR. UPHAUS: He encouraged people to go to the congress. I don't know what his motive was.

MR. ARENS: But your motive was to send him, in spite of the State Department's regulations?

MR. UPHAUS: I thought that was my highest duty.

MR. ARENS: To your knowledge, what persons did go to the Vienna conference?

MR. UPHAUS: I honestly don't believe I can recall the names today.

MR. SCHERER: Doctor, you believe in following only such laws of this land as fit into your idea of what is right? I understand that from all of your testimony. You are only going to follow those laws and regulations which you believe to be right?

MR. UPHAUS: Do you know the history of the formation of the Christian Church? That the people were thrown to lions because of their convictions?

MR. SCHERER: I gather from all of your testimony that you are only going to follow the laws of this country that you feel are consistent with your own personal beliefs of what is basically right?

MR. UPHAUS: But look. You have drawn the wrong picture. This is one law—I suppose I am a good citizen in a thousand laws. Once in a while there is one, yes, sir.

MR. SCHERER: That you do not believe is right?

MR. UPHAUS: My conscience sometimes contravenes a statute.

MR. SCHERER: All right. And when your conscience contravenes that statute, you violate the statute, irrespective of the fact that it is the law of this land.

MR. UPHAUS: That generalization can't be made here.

MR. SCHERER: That is what all your testimony indicates. And I am shocked and surprised that a member of the Christian Church should make such a statement under oath before a Congressional Committee. It is almost unbelievable.

MR. UPHAUS: May I read something please?

MR. ARENS: If you are going to read something, read from the Psalm of David: "Blessed is the man that walketh not in the counsel of the ungodly, nor standeth in the way of sinners, nor sitteth in the seat of the scornful."

MR. UPHAUS: I want to read something from the life of Jesus.

THE CHAIRMAN: No, we have gone far enough here.

MR. UPHAUS: Jesus stood before Pilate, and He didn't answer a single question when He was asked.

THE CHAIRMAN: I hope that you won't inject this.

MR. UPHAUS: Why not this? Our nation is founded upon this book.

THE CHAIRMAN: I understand all that. But coming from this source, I just do not like it.

MR. UPHAUS: From this source, this book?

THE CHAIRMAN: No. I am talking about you.

MR. ARENS: Now would you tell us whether or not after the Peiping and Vienna conferences you participated, as head of the American Peace Crusade out in Chicago, in a meeting at which you were the recipient of gifts sent from the Vienna peace conference and from the Peiping peace conference?

MR. UPHAUS: I think we were the recipients, yes.

MR. ARENS: That is, you individually received a gift from the Vienna peace conference and a gift from the Peiping peace conference, is that correct?

MR. UPHAUS: I think I was on the platform, and I personally received a beautiful gift from the Peiping peace conference.

MR. ARENS: And who presented you with that gift?

MR. UPHAUS: Well, the lady from California that you mentioned a while ago.

MR. ARENS: And what was her name?

MR. UPHAUS: Well, I would recognize it, but I can't say now.

MR. ARENS: Was that Minnie R. Carter?

MR. UPHAUS: No.

MR. ARENS: Isobel Cerney?

MR. UPHAUS: That is right.

MR. ARENS: And she had been in attendance at the Peiping peace conference?

MR. UPHAUS: That is right.

MR. ARENS: And did you have a conversation with Isobel Cerney in Chicago?

MR. UPHAUS: It would be very likely that I did, I am sure.

MR. ARENS: And did she tell you whether or not she had gone out to the Peiping peace congress in violation of the law of this nation?

MR. UPHAUS: She did not tell me anything like that.

MR. ARENS: Did you inquire whether she had been in attendance at the Peiping peace congress in violation of the law of this nation?

MR. UPHAUS: I knew that she had been to the peace congress. I still want to read from the Bible. May I read this?

MR. ARENS: In 1950 did you make a speech in a meeting at Greenwich Village as executive secretary of the National Religion and Labor Foundation? Do you have a recollection of doing that?

MR. UPHAUS: It is possible that I did. I do not recall it.

MR. ARENS: And in that speech did you say, among other things, "Why should we, with our tradition of 1776, frustrate normal revolutions of the world with our money?"—with reference to the war in Korea?

MR. UPHAUS: Well, I think I said that. I meant that we shouldn't interfere with the people's revolution there. They had the same right that we had in 1776.

MR. ARENS: Did you not at that time impress upon your audience your conviction that the Communist aggression in Korea was just a normal revolution of patriotic people such as the revolution of 1776 in this nation, is that correct?

MR. UPHAUS: Your question presupposes some history that isn't there. I can't answer it, because the presupposition is wholly different. I still want to read about Jesus before Pilate.

THE CHAIRMAN: I certainly hope you don't put yourself in that position.

MR. UPHAUS: He didn't answer a single question, when He was—

MR. ARENS: Well, He wasn't asked whether He was hooked up with the Communist conspiracy. And He was divine. Did you in 1951 have a conference with the second secretary of the Soviet Embassy here in Washington? Do you recall? A conference with Jerome White Davis?

MR. UPHAUS: I do not recall that. I don't think I did. I don't recall a name like that. I had conferences, but not with this gentleman.

MR. ARENS: Were you also appointed to the World Peace Council?

MR. UPHAUS: Do you mean a member of the council?

MR. ARENS: Yes.

MR. UPHAUS: Yes.

MR. ARENS: Do you know that the World Peace Council and its parent organization have been cited as arms of the international Communist conspiracy?

MR. UPHAUS: Yes, I know that.

MR. ARENS: Did you in 1952 participate in a little pressure move toward the Brazilian government, which was trying to preclude a Communist-inspired peace conference to be held in Rio?

MR. UPHAUS: Well, I was interested in the conference. "Pressure" is the wrong word.

MR. ARENS: What did you do toward making representations to the Brazilian government respecting the action of that government on this proposed peace conference?

MR. UPHAUS: I don't recall any action in relation to the government. I was simply interested in the meeting that was to have been held.

MR. ARENS: Did you register a protest to the Brazilian consulate respecting the action of the government of Brazil in trying to forestall this peace conference?

MR. UPHAUS: I did.

MR. ARENS: Do you know a person by the name of William Wallace?

MR. UPHAUS: Well, he was here this morning.

MR. ARENS: Did you ever see him before?

MR. UPHAUS: Yes.

MR. ARENS: What was the occasion for your seeing him before?

MR. UPHAUS: Well, I think the only occasion I can remember is when he came to the resident board meetings of the American Peace Crusade.

MR. ARENS: He testified this morning that this American Peace Crusade, of which you were codirector, was controlled, he testified, lock, stock, and barrel by the Communist Party.

MR. UPHAUS: I disagree with his testimony.

MR. ARENS: He testified that he, at the time he was participating in it, was a member of the Communist conspiracy.

MR. UPHAUS: That may be true.

MR. ARENS: Did you know that?

MR. UPHAUS: I didn't know what his political connections were when he came to the meetings.

MR. ARENS: Did you circulate among the people you know a letter suggesting that steps be taken to preclude the United States from the use of bacteriological warfare in Korea?

MR. UPHAUS: May I see the document?

MR. ARENS: Do you have a recollection of sending such a document around?

MR. UPHAUS: There was a document that had something to do with the question, but I don't know exactly what it said.

MR. ARENS: Do you know a man by the name of Dr. James G. Endicott?

MR. UPHAUS: Yes.

MR. ARENS: And who is he?

MR. UPHAUS: He is a former missionary in China.

MR. ARENS: And what did he do that was of particular concern to you on your peace-partisan work?

MR. UPHAUS: Well, we had been friends in the peace movement for years.

MR. ARENS: He went to Korea, did he not? He went to Red China?

MR. UPHAUS: I think so.

MR. ARENS: And he came back with a propaganda statement to the effect that the United States was using bacteriological warfare, did he not?

MR. UPHAUS: You say it is propaganda. He didn't think so.

MR. ARENS: Well, did he come back with a statement to the effect that he had made a study and investigation over there in the Far East, and that the Government of the United States was engaged in bacteriological warfare?

MR. UPHAUS: After much investigation, he came to that conclusion, yes.

MR. ARENS: And did you circularize his findings and conclusions among your peace partisans?

MR. UPHAUS: I did not. We said something about that, but it had no relationship—

MR. ARENS: Didn't you say that Dr. Endicott believes there is indisputable evidence that American Armed Forces are guilty?

MR. UPHAUS: That is right.

MR. ARENS: And did you circularize that among your friends and acquaintances in this peace movement of which you were executive—whatever you were—codirector?

MR. UPHAUS: I think I signed it.

THE CHAIRMAN: You think that making a charge of that sort contributed anything toward the world peace?

MR. UPHAUS: I did not categorically charge our country.

MR. SCHERER: Let me ask a question, Counsel. Was this circulated during the time we were at war in Korea?

MR. ARENS: Yes, sir, 1952.

MR. SCHERER. Didn't you consider circulating such a thing during a time when we were at war as giving aid and comfort to the enemy?

MR. UPHAUS: Oh, not at all. Any measure for peace is far above that.

MR. SCHERER: Do you think *that* was a measure for peace?

MR. UPHAUS: When you work for world peace, you have to recognize the horrors of war regardless of who commits them.

THE CHAIRMAN: Regardless of whether it is true or false?

MR. UPHAUS: No, sir.

MR. SCHERER. Even if the description of such horrors as you say existed hurt the United States, you would still feel that you should circulate that material?

MR. UPHAUS: I don't see the relevance. It would not hurt the United States to raise the question as to whether that kind of warfare was used.

MR. SCHERER: Was that not one of the greatest weapons that the Communist conspiracy used against the United States in the councils of the world—namely, charging the United States with using germ warfare in Korea?

MR. UPHAUS: There were charges.

MR. SCHERER: And when you joined with the Communist conspiracy—

MR. UPHAUS: I did not join with the Communist conspiracy.

MR. SCHERER: When you joined with the enemies of this country—

MR. UPHAUS: I did not join with the enemies—

MR. SCHERER: When you joined with the enemies of this country, and gave vent to those charges, were you not giving aid and comfort to the enemy in time of war?

MR. UPHAUS: I deny what you said. I never joined with the enemy.

MR. SCHERER: Just a minute. Didn't you join with the enemy in making that assertion?

MR. UPHAUS: Would it be joining the enemy if I deplored the atomic bomb and the napalm bomb on innocent people?

THE CHAIRMAN: No, it would not. But you were in effect joining with the people who were making the false charges that the United States was engaged in germ warfare.

MR. UPHAUS: Can I not make that as a responsible person, irregardless—

THE CHAIRMAN: A responsible person would not make that charge, because it was not true.

MR. UPHAUS: That is still subject to research.

MR. SCHERER: Even if it had been true and you did that at a time when we were engaged in war, and that charge gave comfort and aid to the enemy in time of war, which it certainly did, is that not under our Constitution treason?

MR. UPHAUS: I don't think so. Freedom of thought and freedom of expression is never treason under our Constitution.

THE CHAIRMAN: Well, I would not go into a theater and start yelling, "Fire," if I were you, to find out something about freedom of speech.

MR. UPHAUS: That is not the proper analogy.

MR. ARENS: Did you join in 1953 in protesting to the Attorney General the proceedings which he was instituting under the Internal Security Act to cause the American Committee for Protection of Foreign Born, in a judicial proceeding pursuant to law, to be investigated, to ascertain whether or not it was a subversive organization?

MR. UPHAUS: I was under the firm conviction that it was not a subversive organization. Therefore I opposed the Attorney General's position in it.

MR. ARENS: Then how did you arrive at the conclusion that [it] was not a subversive organization?

MR. UPHAUS: By the specific things that it stood for and did, and no other things.

MR. ARENS: All right, sir. Did you at that time undertake to make an ascertainment, and did you have available for ascertainment, the Communist Party affiliation of the people who ran the American Committee for Protection of Foreign Born?

MR. UPHAUS: I did not. I was interested in what that committee was here to do to serve the American people. That was my answer, sir.

MR. ARENS: Well, did you, in the process of making that appraisal, look behind the façade of the American Committee for Protection of Foreign Born to ascertain whether or not it was living up to these glorious objectives, or whether or not it was controlled by the arm of the international Communist conspiracy?

MR. UPHAUS: I was satisfied that it was not controlled by an international arm.

MR. ARENS: How did you know that the members of the American Committee for Protection of Foreign Born who ran it were not members of the Communist conspiracy?

MR. UPHAUS: I just didn't know.

MR. ARENS: If you did not know, then how could you reach a conclusion that the American Committee for Protection of Foreign Born was not foreign controlled?

MR. UPHAUS: First of all, we have to agree on whether or not there is a conspiracy. Your whole assumption is that there is. Therefore, we can't make headway.

MR. ARENS: You do not agree that there is a Communist conspiracy?

MR. UPHAUS: Not to start an aggressive war and to overthrow this Government. I don't believe it.

MR. ARENS: How did you reach the conclusion in your own mind that the American Committee for Protection of Foreign Born should not be investigated pursuant to law?

MR. UPHAUS: Because it had done nothing that was harmful to the people.

MR. ARENS: How did you know that the members of the American Committee for Protection of Foreign Born who ran it were not Communists?

MR. UPHAUS: I didn't know. I was interested in what the committee did.

MR. ARENS: Well, if you did not know whether the American Committee for Protection of Foreign Born was controlled by Commusists, how could you then in good conscience protest to the Attorney General his investigation of it to ascertain whether or not it was controlled by the Communists?

MR. UPHAUS: That was my own judgment after thought and studying its activities. It was the general program of the Department of Justice to harangue groups with which it disagreed.

MR. ARENS: And how did you arrive at that conclusion?

MR. UPHAUS: Just by reading and studying and being intelligent, I think.

MR. ARENS: Did you know that a Committee of the Congress, after careful investigation of the American Committee for Protection of Foreign Born, after listening to the testimony of witnesses who served their country in the conspiracy to get information, found that the American Committee for Protection of Foreign Born was an arm of the international Communist conspiracy?

MR. UPHAUS: Has any court found that that is true?

MR. ARENS: Just answer that question. Did you know that the Committees of the Congress have found that the American Committee for Protection of Foreign Born was Communist controlled?

MR. UPHAUS: I think that was a pronouncement of the Congress.

MR. ARENS: Did you know that the proceeding which you protested had court review?

MR. UPHAUS: I think, probably.

MR. ARENS: Notwithstanding the fact that the proceeding which was instituted against the American Committee for Protection of Foreign Born to ascertain whether or not it was a Communist-controlled organization was a proceeding with court review, you nevertheless intervened and undertook to stop that proceeding, is that correct?

MR. UPHAUS: Well, I protested. What I did I don't know. I believed that its functions were legitimate.

MR. ARENS: In 1952, did you participate in a Civil Rights Congress dinner to pay tribute to William L. Patterson, national executive secretary of the Civil Rights Congress?

MR. UPHAUS: At the moment I don't recall.

MR. ARENS: I lay before you a photostatic copy of an article from the *Daily Worker* describing that conference and ask you if that refreshes your recollection.

MR. UPHAUS: It is a newspaper report, but I do not remember really.

MR. ARENS: Now, the Attorney General of the United States listed, after careful investigation, the American Peace Crusade as an organization that he wanted to have investigated by the Subversive Activities Control Board, to ascertain whether or not it was Communist controlled, did he not?

MR. UPHAUS: I believe that is right.

MR. ARENS: What did you do, as an American secretary of the American Peace Crusade, to undertake to avoid the law?

MR. UPHAUS: Well, I think we protested and continued to carry on our work, as I remember.

MR. ARENS: Well, now, did you call a meeting of the American Peace Crusade, or was a meeting held, for the purpose of dissolving the technical status of the American Peace Crusade as an entity?

MR. UPHAUS: There was a meeting called to dissolve the crusade. That is right.

MR. ARENS: And was it decided at that meeting in which you participated that they would dissolve the organization technically but go on actually?

MR. UPHAUS: No, sir. What do you mean? In another organization, or one by one to work for peace in other ways? What do you mean?

MR. ARENS: Just tell us if this meeting—

MR. UPHAUS: We decided to disband, and I said—and I suppose others said—Willard Uphaus will work for peace in other channels, then.

* * *

MR. ARENS: Who was present at the meeting at which it was decided to disband the American Peace Crusade, because the Attorney General had filed a petition against the organization before the Subversive Activities Control Board?

(*The witness conferred with his counsel.*)

MR. RABINOWITZ: Mr. Chairman, can we have a five-minute recess? The witness is quite tired, and so am I.

THE CHAIRMAN: Yes.

(*Short recess.*)

* * *

MR. ARENS: Where was that meeting held?

MR. UPHAUS: Well, it was held in Manhattan. I have forgotten the exact address.

MR. ARENS: And who were in attendance at that meeting?

MR. UPHAUS: Dr. France was there as I recall. I was there. Mr. Richardson was there.

MR. ARENS: Was Mary Russak there?

MR. UPHAUS: I believe she was there.

MR. ARENS: Did you know that she has been identified under oath as a member of the Communist Party?

MR. UPHAUS: No, I did not know that.

MR. ARENS: Was Betty Haufrecht there?

MR. UPHAUS: Yes.

MR. ARENS: Do you know she has been identified as a member of the Communist Party?

MR. UPHAUS: No.

MR. ARENS: Was Jessica Smith there?

MR. UPHAUS: No, I don't believe she was.

MR. ARENS: Was she a force, a moving force, in the American Peace Crusade?

MR. UPHAUS: I wouldn't say so, no. I saw very little of her.

MR. ARENS: Was Tina Ludens there?

MR. UPHAUS: I do not recall. I don't have any picture. When you say the name, I don't know whether she was there or not.

MR. ARENS: Was Eslanda Robeson there?

MR. UPHAUS: I think maybe she was.

MR. ARENS: She is the wife of Paul Robeson, is she not?

MR. UPHAUS: That is right.

MR. ARENS: Was Karen Morley there?

MR. UPHAUS: Well, I don't have a clear picture, a clear memory.

MR. ARENS: Was Mark Tarail there?

MR. UPHAUS: I don't have a clear memory about that.

MR ARENS: Was Anita or Henry Willcox there?

MR. UPHAUS: I don't believe they were.

MR. ARENS: Was a formal motion offered and carried to dissolve the organization?

MR. UPHAUS: That is right.

MR. ARENS: Did the people who were in attendance constitute a quorum of the board of directors of the American Peace Crusade?

MR. UPHAUS: Well, I should think so.

* * *

MR. ARENS: What was your livelihood or occupation at the time of the dissolution of the American Peace Crusade?

MR. UPHAUS: I was then a director of World Fellowship, Incorporated.

MR. ARENS: Are there any persons who are or were members of the American Peace Crusade who are presently directors of this World Fellowship group with which you are now identified?

MR. UPHAUS: Well, Dr. France was the attorney for the crusade, and he is one of the members of our council. That is the only one that I can think of now.

MR. ARENS: Can you tell us the principal members of the board of the World Fellowship group?

MR. UPHAUS: I am sorry. I didn't bring the letterhead.

MR. ARENS: Well, is Mary Russak on the board?

MR. UPHAUS: No.

MR. ARENS: Is Jessica Smith on the board?

MR. UPHAUS: No.

MR. ARENS: Is Karen Morley on the board?

MR. UPHAUS: No.

MR. ARENS: Is Betty Haufrecht on the board?

MR. UPHAUS: No. They are mainly clergymen or educators.

MR. ARENS: Has Mary Russak anything to do with the World Fellowship group?

MR. UPHAUS: Well, she is, I think, a friend of World Fellowship.

MR. ARENS: Does she participate in the activities of World Fellowship?

MR. UPHAUS: She came up for a vacation.

MR. ARENS: And when was that?

MR. UPHAUS: Last summer.

MR. ARENS: Did she address the World Fellowship group?

MR. UPHAUS: I think she spoke once, yes.

MR. ARENS: Did you know at that time that she was identified as a member of the Communist Party?

MR. UPHAUS: I did not

MR. ARENS: It wouldn't have made any difference if she had been, would it?

MR. UPHAUS: If she was discussing the question of peace, and not discussing politics, it would be perfectly all right.

MR. ARENS: Does William Hunton have an identfication with the World Fellowship?

MR. UPHAUS: That is right.

MR. ARENS: Has he ever come up and addressed the members of the organization?

MR. UPHAUS: Yes.

MR. ARENS: And when was he last there?

MR. UPHAUS: I think last summer.

MR. ARENS: Do you know that William Hunton has been identified as a member of the Communist Party?

MR. UPHAUS: I don't think I have ever read any official notice.

MR. ARENS: And it wouldn't make any difference to you whether he had been, would it?

MR. UPHAUS: No, sir.

THE CHAIRMAN: You know, of course, that in recent months an attempt has been made and is still being made to discredit Stalin, by the Russians and other Communists?

MR. UPHAUS: Yes.

THE CHAIRMAN: And among other things, an attempt is being made to show that these charges of germ warfare were false and were conjured up by this wicked man, Stalin. You know that?

MR. UPHAUS: I don't know, sir, where the charge started, I can't answer that at all.

THE CHAIRMAN: Would you change your position, with respect to the charges you made concerning germ warfare, if the Communist line changed in that regard?

MR. UPHAUS: I would reach my judgment, sir, on the basis of all the documentation that I could lay my hands on, regardless of its political source, whether it be Republican or Communist.

THE CHAIRMAN: Well, one certainly does not speak of the Republicans and the Communists in the same context.

MR. UPHAUS: We are all human beings, sir. We are all children of God. They are to be loved just as well as all other people.

The following is the statement submitted to HUAC by Mr. Uphaus:

MY WITNESS
by Willard Uphaus

The subpoena brought to my home on May 10 to appear at a hearing before the House Un-American Activities Committee on May 23 did not specify what the nature of subject matter of the investigation would be. The summons was not given because of any act that I had committed against any person, my state, or my country. I can only assume, from the statement made by the Committee representative who served me, that the inquiry must be concerned with my private judgments and opinions, my association with people and organizations, or my travels abroad.

Any information that I might be able to give with respect to the enactment of proposed legislation or any counsel that would be of value to my country I would gladly have given voluntarily without the embarrassment and threats that go with an enforced summons.

1. The right of movement is inherent in human society. This right is set

forth in the UN's Universal Declaration of Human Rights. "Everyone has the right to leave any country, including his own, and return to his country."

At present our government has set up unnecessary and dangerous passport restrictions as an instrument of the Cold War. It has taken away the right of travel for many as a punishment for their political and economic views. The restrictions are part of the remnants of a narrow isolationism, an educational lag, and a war against the intellect. Any country that erects barriers to prevent the free flow of friendship, ideas, culture, and trade leads the world to war and not to peace.

2. My own activities and moral judgments grow out of nurture in the Judeo-Christian faith which began in childhood. As a teacher of religion in colleges and theological schools and as a worker for brotherhood, justice, and peace, I have given special thought to the meaning, for our time, of the social and ethical teachings of the Hebrew prophets, of Jesus, and of other seers who have appeared in history. My beliefs, activities, and associations stem from my religion and not from some other ideology. Therefore, if and when I am in error in thought or behavior, not having violated any state or federal statute, it is my personal responsibility, through prayer, study, and counsel, to correct my thinking and conduct, or it is the business of my church, The Methodist Church, to instruct or discipline me; it is distinctly not the business of the government.

If the Un-American Activities Committee, through questioning or other pressure, concerns itself with my conduct in accordance with my religious views, or seeks to make moral judgments about my views, it infringes on my free exercise of religion as guaranteed by the First Amendment, and it goes contrary to the social creed of The Methodist Church.

According to the social teaching of The Methodist Church, "The American Declaration of Independence declares that life, liberty, and the pursuit of happiness are the inalienable rights of every human being. This implies that these rights are not the gifts of governments, but the gifts of God. Civil governments exist, not to confer these rights, but to guarantee them to all men alike and to protect all men in the fullest possible enjoyment of them. The right to be free implies not only the freedom of the body but the freedom of the mind."

3. I hold that, as a Christian, I have the right to choose whatever associates I desire, as long as the choices and associations are for the purpose of bringing peace and the abundant life to all people, or for the purpose of performing socially redemptive acts. I have for years worked with persons of any race, faith, nationality, or political conviction. Peace must be won through the free associations of those who have differences to resolve. It is the responsibility of individual citizens to cross barriers of the mind and of geography, as well as it is the responsibility of the official representatives of governments.

The present practice, in and out of government, of exposing people or trying to repress and frighten them is both undemocratic and un-Christian. It violates the sacredness of the individual personality and poisons social and international relations. The Methodist Church is clear in its teaching on guilt by association. It condemns the techniques of "social rejection, calling names, demands of 'loyalty oaths,' denial of employment, irresponsible accusations and assertion of 'guilt by association.' "

"In any of these cases," the teaching declares, "the results are false and inadequate information, degradation of the human mind, and shackling of the human spirit. In such an atmosphere suspicion becomes fear, fear becomes hatred, and hatred becomes war. Our role is not to suppress ideas, but to open channels of communication so that men can come to know the thoughts of their neighbors, and so that the best thoughts of all can come to be possessions of all mankind."

The Universal Declaration of Human Rights is in accord when it says that "Everyone has the right to freedom of thought, conscience and religion . . . this right includes freedom to hold opinions without interference and to seek, receive, and impart information and ideas through any media and regardless of frontiers."

No inquisitorial methods will persuade me to repudiate my associations that I have freely made whether they be with Communists in a peace movement or Democrats or Republicans in my church. I will not join in any campaign to make outcasts or pariahs out of persons because of their political opinions. The teachings of the Bible are positive on the matter of talebearing or raising false reports:

> *"Thou shalt not raise a false report; put not thine hand with the wicked to be an unrighteous witness."* Exodus 23:1

> *"Thou shalt not go up and down as a tale-bearer among thy people."* Leviticus, 19:16

> *"Be not a witness against thy neighbor without cause; and deceive not with thy lips."* Proverbs, 24:28

4. On Bill of Rights Day, December 15, President Eisenhower issued a statement in which he reminded the nation that "By our Bill of Rights our people are guaranteed the most precious of liberties: Freedom of speech, press, and religion; the right peaceably to assemble and to petition the government; freedom from unreasonable search and seizure and the right of privacy." He expressed the hope "that citizens throughout our land will renew in their hearts and minds a devotion to those freedoms and a determination to defend them against all forms of attack." And he related freedom to peace by saying in closing, "Let us also highly resolve to continue to strive for a peaceful world in which all mankind will share them [these freedoms]."

This unwarranted invasion of my freedom puts me in double jeopardy. The Committee must be aware of a prolonged attack on me by the State of New Hampshire, issuing in a contempt citation and a sentence—to me a completely unprincipled and Un-American attack—because I refused to become an informer on the people who came to World Fellowship Conference Ground to enjoy vacations and discuss present-day problems in a peaceful and democratic way. The record of my religious background and convictions, my associations and activities, and the moral and legal grounds for resisting tyrannical government in a time of fear and repression is all available to this Committee. How often must a loyal citizen and a lifelong Christian prove, under oath, that he is not going to commit violence or enter into associations that lead to violence? It seems to me that state and federal representatives might better spend their time and the taxpayers' money than by harrying innocent people to make a headline or be elected to a public office.

By any civilized criterion, Paul Robeson (born 1898) has been one of the notable Americans of his time, and Robeson the artist was generally accepted as such. It was Robeson the political activist that provided the American Establishment with the opportunity to see if it, like the Soviet authorities, could make an unperson of someone. In American history it would be hard to parallel the blackout of Robeson imposed by the Government and the press during the early and middle 1950s. It was as if the "famous actor and singer" had never existed The process began, if such things have a definite beginning, with the Peekskill riots of 1949, in which Robeson's life was threatened by vigilante and hoodlum elements. Following hard upon these incidents was the State Department's refusal of a passport (1950). In his book *Here I Stand* (1958)—which didn't even have a regular American publisher but was issued by "Othello Associates," no street address—Paul Robeson fills out the background of his passport trouble as follows:

> When my passport was revoked in 1950 (I had held one since 1922) I took the matter to court. . . . The State Department's brief . . . contained the following revealing statement: "even if the complaint had alleged, as it does not, that the passport was cancelled solely because of the applicant's recognized status as spokesman for large sections of Negro Americans, we submit that this would not amount to an abuse of discretion in view of the appellant's frank admission that he has been for years extremely active politically in behalf of independence of the colonial peoples of Africa."

On HUAC's interest in his attitude to Russia Robeson has this to say:

My views concerning the Soviet Union and my warm feelings of friendship for the peoples of that land, and the friendly sentiments which they have often expressed toward me, have been pictured as something quite sinister by Washington officials and other spokesmen for the dominant white group in our country. It has been alleged that I am part of some kind of "international conspiracy."

The truth is: *I am not and never have been involved in any international conspiracy or any other kind, and do not know anyone who is.* It should be plain to everybody—and especially to Negroes—that if the government officials had a shred of evidence to back up that charge, you can bet your last dollar that they would have tried their best to put me *under* their jail! But they have no such evidence, because that charge is a lie. By an arbitrary and, as I am insisting in the courts, *illegal* ruling they have refused me a passport. . . .

In 1946, at a legislative hearing in California [of the Tenney Committee, California's own HUAC], I testified under oath that I was not a member of the Communist Party, but since then I have refused to give testimony or to sign affidavits to that fact. There is no mystery involved in this refusal. As the witchhunt developed, it became clear that an important issue of Constitutional rights was involved in the making of such inquiries, and the film writers and directors who became known as the Hollywood Ten challenged the right of any inquisitors to violate the First Amendment's provisions of free speech and conscience. . . . I have made it a matter of principle . . . to refuse to comply with any demand of legislative committees or departmental officials that infringes upon the Constitutional rights of all Americans.

Of course, this last paragraph would only make any anti-Communist press the question if Robeson joined the Party *after* 1946, while the first paragraph fails to answer everyone's questions, not about Russia and her peoples, but about Russia and her government. This second topic, today, should interest men of the Left as well as the Right. Robeson kept being rebuked for mixing up civil rights with Marxism. But in *that* "mix-up" he today seems farsighted and not at all wrongheaded. Where there really was confusion was in identifying Marx and Stalin. But this confusion was hardly a personal eccentricity of Paul Robeson's—rather, the historic error of the world Communist movement in his time. Hence the awful irrelevance of the only recent biography, *Paul Robeson, the American Othello* by Edwin P. Hoyt (Cleveland and New York, 1967), which attempts to present these matters in terms of Robeson's personality. To be fair, the reader in search of lengthier annotation to the following testimony can find it in Hoyt's volume; unhappily, in order to hear the facts, he will also have to hear Hoyt scolding Robeson—more in sorrow than in anger, to be sure, but Hoyt is a nag, and all nags are nuisances to those they nag and bores to everyone else.

Robeson fell in love with Soviet Russia, and his love was returned. A mountain was named after him and a bust placed on the summit. He got the Stalin Prize in 1952. A biographical film was made about him. Hoyt tells all this with some emphasis but also remarks in passing that Robeson was a forerunner of the Black Power movement. This is much more important! Where Robeson the activist shows himself really significant is in siding not with Ralph Bunche but with the Communist Councilman Ben Davis. That had significance, and probably some value, but the truly significant alignment was with the future—Paul Robeson was a brother of Malcolm X, Stokely Carmichael, Rap Brown, Huey Newton, Eldridge Cleaver, before they were there to take his hand. The CP, in his mind, was a means to an end: the end was Black freedom in the United States. For believing that, Hoyt says he has a one-track mind. Perhaps. Obsession with Black freedom is, in any case, very different from obsession with Russia or Marxism.

The State Department granted Robeson a passport in 1958 with the same capriciousness with which it had refused one ever since 1950. He was then abroad, mostly in Russia, till 1963. In very ill health, he has been inactive both politically and artistically since his return.

In 1971 one can buy three albums of Robeson songs on the Vanguard label, but many recordings survive only in the collections of a few, mostly left-wing, connoisseurs.

JUNE 12, 1956:

Paul Robeson

A Subcommittee of the Committee on Un-American Activities convened at 10 a.m., in the caucus room of the Old House Office Building, the Honorable Francis E. Walter (Chairman) presiding.

Committee members present: Representatives Francis E. Walter of Pennsylvania, Clyde Doyle of California, Bernard W. Kearney of New York, and Gordon H. Scherer of Ohio.

Staff members present: Richard Arens, Director, and Donald T. Appell, Investigator.

THE CHAIRMAN: The Committee will be in order. This morning the Committee resumes its series of hearings on the vital issue of the use of American passports as travel documents in furtherance of the objectives of the Communist conspiracy. During recent hearings on this subject, it was revealed that Communists had developed a pattern procuring American passports by representing that they were going to travel for business or pleasure to certain of the countries of the free world and then, upon arriving at those countries, they used devious methods of circumventing the travel restrictions so that they could attend Communist-sponsored conferences and other propaganda efforts in the Iron Curtain countries. One of the important facts which the student of the Communist conspiracy recognizes is that Communists not only create front organizations to carry on their nefarious work, but also use people who, though not actually Communist Party members, are nevertheless witting or unwitting servants of the Communist cause. Actual technical membership in the Communist Party is not, therefore, the sole criterion to be used in undertaking to ascertain whether or not a particular individual's activities are in fact contributing to the Communist menace. Should the Government of the United States in the exercise of its sovereign power refuse to issue passports to United States citizens who propose to use those passports as tickets of admission to conferences established as propaganda efforts of the Kremlin? Should our Government require the revelation of the specific itinerary of each citizen who proposes to travel behind the Iron Curtain? Where should the balance be struck between the promotion of international travel and the security risk of couriers, propagandists, and saboteurs? These and other questions must be resolved in the light of the realisms of today. It is in this spirit of dead earnestness that the Committee is pursuing this investigation and study. Call your first witness, Mr. Arens.

MR. ARENS: Paul Robeson, will you please come forward? Please identify yourself by name, residence and occupation.

MR. ROBESON: My name is Paul Robeson. I live at 16 Jumel Terrace, New York City, and I am an actor and singer by occupation, and law on the side now and then.

MR. ARENS: Are you appearing today in response to a subpoena which was served upon you by the House Committee on Un-American Activities?

MR. ROBESON: Just a minute. Do I have the privilege of asking whom I am addressing and who is addressing me?

MR. ARENS: I am Richard Arens.

MR. ROBESON: What is your position?

MR. ARENS: I am Director of the Staff. Are you appearing today in response to a subpoena served upon you by this Committee?

MR. ROBESON: Oh, yes.

MR. ARENS: And you are represented by counsel?

MR. ROBESON: I am.

MR. ARENS: Counsel, will you kindly identify yourself?

MR. FRIEDMAN: Milton H. Friedman.

MR. ARENS: The subpoena which requires your presence here today contains a provision commanding you to produce certain documents, including all the United States passports issued to you for travel outside the continental limits of the United States. Do you have those documents?

MR. ROBESON: No. There are several in existence, but I have moved several times in the last year, and I could not put my hands on them. They probably could be produced. I lived in Connecticut and we have got a lot of stuff still packed. If they are unpacked I will be glad to send them to you.

MR. SCHERER: When was the subpoena served on you, Mr. Robeson?

MR. ROBESON: I have forgotten. It was about a couple of weeks ago.

MR. SCHERER: Did you look for the documents?

MR. ROBESON: I have looked a good deal, and Mrs. Robeson, who has charge of all of this, has looked and we have not been able to put our hands upon them. There is no reason not to produce them, certainly, if I could find them.

MR. ARENS: Did you file a passport application on July 2, 1954?

MR. ROBESON: I have filed about twenty-five in the last few months.

MR. ARENS: I lay before you a photostatic copy of a passport application bearing a signature, Paul Robeson, and ask you if that is a true and correct reproduction of the passport application which you filed on July 2, 1954.

MR. ROBESON: That is true.

MR. ARENS: I respectfully suggest, Mr. Chairman, this document be incorporated by reference in this record marked as "Robeson exhibit No. 1" and filed in the files of the Committee.

THE CHAIRMAN: It will be so incorporated.

MR. ROBESON: My counsel suggests it may not be completed.

MR. FRIEDMAN: May I make a statement, please?

THE CHAIRMAN: Counsel is permitted to accompany his client for the purpose of advising his client and not for the purpose of making statements.

MR. FRIEDMAN: I am familiar with the rules, that is why I asked your permission. May I make this statement to you, sir? I wish to make a protest against questioning Mr. Robeson with respect to his passport application, in view of the fact that there is litigation now pending concerning his passport application and Mr. Robeson's right to a passport. The litigation was tried in district court and it was the subject of a decision in the court of appeals in the circuit last week. There may be further hearings in the State Department and there may be a further appeal.

THE CHAIRMAN: Was an application made for certiorari?

MR. FRIEDMAN: No, the time has not yet elapsed for an application for certiorari but there may possibly be. I am not his counsel in that case, and I am not speaking for counsel, but there may be a hearing somewhere with respect to this matter.

THE CHAIRMAN: That is too nebulous.

MR. FRIEDMAN: The procedure now calls for it, and it is not nebulous.

MR. ARENS: Now, during the course of the process in which you were applying for this passport, in July of 1954, were you requested to submit a non-Communist affidavit?

Mr. Robeson: We had a long discussion—with my counsel, who is in the room, Mr. [Leonard B.] Boudin—with the State Department, about just such an affidavit and I was very precise not only in the application but with the State Department, headed by Mr. Henderson and Mr. McLeod, that under no conditions would I think of signing any such affidavit, that it is a complete contradiction of the rights of American citizens.

Mr. Arens: Did you comply with the requests?

Mr. Robeson: I certainly did not and I will not.

Mr. Arens: Are you now a member of the Communist Party?

Mr. Robeson: Oh please, please, please.

Mr. Scherer: Please answer, will you, Mr. Robeson?

Mr. Robeson: What is the Communist Party? What do you mean by that?

Mr. Scherer: I ask that you direct the witness to answer the question.

Mr. Robeson: What do you mean by the Communist Party? As far as I know it is a legal party like the Republican Party and the Democratic Party. Do you mean a party of people who have sacrificed for my people, and for all Americans and workers, that they can live in dignity? Do you mean that party?

Mr. Arens: Are you now a member of the Communist Party?

Mr. Robeson: Would you like to come to the ballot box when I vote and take out the ballot and see?

Mr. Arens: Mr. Chairman, I respectfully suggest that the witness be ordered and directed to answer that question.

The Chairman: You are directed to answer the question.

(*The witness consulted with his counsel.*)

Mr. Robeson: I stand upon the Fifth Amendment of the American Constitution.

Mr. Arens: Do you mean you invoke the Fifth Amendment?

Mr. Robeson: I invoke the Fifth Amendment.

Mr. Arens: Do you honestly apprehend that if you told this Committee truthfully—

Mr. Robeson: I have no desire to consider anything. I invoke the Fifth Amendment, and it is none of your business what I would like to do, and I invoke the Fifth Amendment. And forget it.

The Chairman: You are directed to answer that question.

Mr. Robeson: I invoke the Fifth Amendment, and so I am answering it, am I not?

Mr. Arens: I respectfully suggest the witness be ordered and directed to answer the question as to whether or not he honestly apprehends, that if he gave us a truthful answer to this last principal question, he would be supplying information which might be used against him in a criminal proceeding.

(*The witness consulted with his counsel.*)

THE CHAIRMAN: You are directed to answer that question, Mr. Robeson.

MR. ROBESON: Gentlemen, in the first place, wherever I have been in the world, Scandinavia, England, and many places, the first to die in the struggle against Fascism were the Communists and I laid many wreaths upon graves of Communists. It is not criminal, and the Fifth Amendment has nothing to do with criminality. The Chief Justice of the Supreme Court, Warren, has been very clear on that in many speeches, that the Fifth Amendment does not have anything to do with the inference of criminality. I invoke the Fifth Amendment.

MR. ARENS: Have you ever been known under the name of "John Thomas"?

MR. ROBESON: Oh, please, does somebody here want—are you suggesting—do you want me to be put up for perjury some place? "John Thomas"! My name is Paul Robeson, and anything I have to say, or stand for, I have said in public all over the world, and that is why I am here today.

MR. SCHERER: I ask that you direct the witness to answer the question. He is making a speech.

MR. FRIEDMAN: Excuse me, Mr. Arens, may we have the photographers take their pictures, and then desist, because it is rather nerve-racking for them to be there.

THE CHAIRMAN: They will take the pictures.

MR. ROBESON: I am used to it and I have been in moving pictures. Do you want me to pose for it good? Do you want me to smile? I cannot smile when I am talking to him.

MR. ARENS: I put it to you as a fact, and ask you to affirm or deny the fact, that your Communist Party name was "John Thomas."

MR. ROBESON: I invoke the Fifth Amendment. This is really ridiculous.

MR. ARENS: Now, tell this Committee whether or not you know Nathan Gregory Silvermaster.

[Mr. Robeson laughed. —E.B.]

MR. SCHERER: Mr. Chairman, this is not a laughing matter.

MR. ROBESON: It is a laughing matter to me, this is really complete nonsense.

MR. ARENS: Have you ever known Nathan Gregory Silvermaster?

(*The witness consulted with his counsel.*)

MR. ROBESON: I invoke the Fifth Amendment.

MR. ARENS: Do you honestly apprehend that if you told whether you know Nathan Gregory Silvermaster you would be supplying information that could be used against you in a criminal proceeding?

MR. ROBESON: I have not the slightest idea what you are talking about. I invoke the Fifth—

MR. ARENS: I suggest, Mr. Chairman, that the witness be directed to answer that question.

THE CHAIRMAN: You are directed to answer the question.

MR. ROBESON: I invoke the Fifth.

MR. SCHERER: The witness talks very loud when he makes a speech, but when he invokes the Fifth Amendment I cannot hear him.

MR. ROBESON: I invoked the Fifth Amendment very loudly. You know I am an actor, and I have medals for diction.

MR. SCHERER: Will you talk a little louder?

MR. ROBESON: I can talk plenty loud, yes. I am noted for my diction in the theater.

MR. ARENS: Do you know a woman by the name of Louise Bransten?

(*The witness consulted with his counsel.*)

MR. ROBESON: I invoke the Fifth Amendment.

MR. ARENS: I ask you to affirm or deny that on February 23, 1945, you attended a meeting in the home of Louise Bransten, at which were present Max Yergan, Frederick Thompson, David Jenkins, Nancy Pittman, Dr. Lena Halpern, and Larry Fanning?

MR. ROBESON: I invoke the Fifth Amendment.

MR. ARENS: Do you know any of those individuals?

MR. ROBESON: I invoke the Fifth Amendment.

MR. ARENS: Who are Mr. and Mrs. Vladimir P. Mikheev? Do you know them?

MR. ROBESON: I have not the slightest idea, but I invoke the Fifth Amendment.

MR. ARENS: Mr. Chairman, the witness does not have the slightest idea who they are, and I respectfully suggest he be ordered and directed to answer that question.

THE CHAIRMAN: You are directed to answer the question.

MR. ROBESON: I answer the question by invoking the Fifth Amendment.

MR. ARENS: Have you ever had contact with a man by the name of Gregory Kheifets?

MR. ROBESON: I invoke the Fifth Amendment.

MR. ARENS: Now, Gregory Kheifets is identified with the Soviet espionage operations, is he not?

MR. ROBESON: Oh, gentlemen, I thought I was here about some passports.

MR. ARENS: We will get into that in just a few moments.

MR. ROBESON: This is complete nonsense.

MR. ARENS: Tell us whether or not have have had contact and operations with Gregory Kheifets.

MR. ROBESON: I invoke the Fifth Amendment.

MR. ARENS: Who is Victor Murra—that is John Victor Murra?

MR. ROBESON: I invoke the Fifth Amendment. Your questioning leaves me completely— I invoke the Fifth Amendment.

MR. ARENS: Leon Josephson?

MR. ROBESON: I invoke the Fifth Amendment.

MR. ARENS: Do you know a Manning Johnson?

MR. ROBESON: Manning Johnson? I only have read in the papers that he said that Dr. Ralph Bunche was some kind of fellow, and he was dismissed from the FBI.* He must be a pretty low character when he could be dismissed from that.

MR. SCHERER: Whether he is a low character or not, do you know him?

MR. ROBESON: I invoke the Fifth Amendment.

MR. ARENS: I would like to read you now some testimony, under oath before this Committee, of Manning Johnson:

> QUESTION: In your vast experience in the Communist Party, did you have occasion to meet Paul Robeson?
>
> MR. JOHNSON: Yes, I have met Paul Robeson a number of times in the headquarters of the National Committee of the Communist Party, going to and coming from conferences with Earl Browder, Jack Stachel, and J. Peters. During the time I was a member of the Communist Party Paul Robeson was a member of the Communist Party. Paul Robeson, to my knowledge, has been a member of the Communist Party for many years. In the Negro Commission of the National Committee of the Communist Party, we were told under threat of expulsion never to reveal that Paul Robeson was a member of the Communist Party because Paul Robeson's assignment was highly confidential and secret. For that reason he was not permitted to attend meetings of the National Committee of the Communist Party.

MR. ROBESON: Could I protest this reading of this? If you want Mr. Manning Johnson here for cross-examination, O.K.

MR. ARENS: You tell us whether or not Manning Johnson was lying.

MR. ROBESON: I invoke the Fifth Amendment.

MR. ARENS: Have you ever been chairman of the Council on African Affairs?

(*The witness consulted with his counsel.*)

MR. ROBESON: I invoke the Fifth Amendment.

MR. ARENS: I lay before you now a document marked "Robeson exhibit No. 2" for identification purposes only in this record, entitled "For Freedom and Peace, Address by Paul Robeson, at Welcome Home Rally, in New York, June 19, 1949," with a photograph on it.

MR. ROBESON: I have a copy myself.

MR. ARENS: If you would look on the back of that pamphlet you will

* Johnson did indeed accuse Bunche of disloyalty, but the Department of Justice continued to employ him. On April 30, 1956, writes Melvin Rader, "the U.S. Supreme Court ordered the re-hearing of a case . . . because of false testimony by Manning Johnson." —E.B.

see "Paul Robeson, Chairman of the Council on African Affairs." Tell us whether or not you are the Paul Robeson alluded to in this document, a copy of which you brought with you.

MR. ROBESON: I would be the Paul Robeson.

MR. ARENS: Then you are or have been chairman of the Council on African Affairs.

MR. ROBESON: I would invoke the Fifth Amendment.

MR. ARENS: Do you know Max Yergan?

MR. ROBESON: I invoke the Fifth Amendment.

MR. ARENS: Max Yergan took an oath before this Committee and testified to tell the truth.

MR. ROBESON: Why do you not have these people here to be cross-examined? Could I ask whether this is legal?

THE CHAIRMAN: This is legal. This is not only legal but usual. By a unanimous vote, this Committee has been instructed to perform this very distasteful task.

MR. ROBESON: To whom am I talking?

THE CHAIRMAN: You are speaking to the Chairman of this Committee.

MR. ROBESON: Mr. Walter?

THE CHAIRMAN: Yes.

MR. ROBESON: The Pennsylvania Walter?

THE CHAIRMAN: That is right.

MR. ROBESON: Representative of the steelworkers?

THE CHAIRMAN: That is right.

MR. ROBESON: Of the coal-mining workers and not United States Steel, by any chance? A great patriot.

THE CHAIRMAN: That is right.

MR. ROBESON: You are the author of all of the bills that are going to keep all kinds of decent people out of the country.

THE CHAIRMAN: No, only your kind.

MR. ROBESON: Colored people like myself, from the West Indies and all kinds. And just the Teutonic Anglo-Saxon stock that you would let come in.

THE CHAIRMAN: We are trying to make it easier to get rid of your kind, too.

MR. ROBESON: You do not want any colored people to come in?

THE CHAIRMAN: Proceed.

MR. ARENS: Under date of December 17, 1948, Dr. Max Yergan testified as follows:

> [QUESTION:] Was there a group in the Council on African Affairs of Communist officials, who operated as a sort of leading caucus inside the council?
>
> DR. YERGAN: Not as such. The relation of Communists to the council was informal, and so far as I know, not organized. Toward the end of my relation to the council it became clear to me that there was a Communist core within

> the council. This was very clear to me during the last months of my relations to the council.

May I ask you now, Was there, to your knowledge, a Communist core in the Council on African Affairs?

MR. ROBESON: I will take the Fifth Amendment. Could I be allowed to read from my own statement here?

MR. ARENS: Will you just tell this Committee, while under oath, Mr. Robeson, the Communists who participated in the preparation of that statement?

MR. ROBESON: Oh, please.

MR. ARENS:

> THE CHAIRMAN: Could you identify that core clearly? Of whom did it consist?

MR. ROBESON: Could I read my statement?

MR. ARENS: As soon as you tell the Committee the Communists who participated in the preparation.

> DR. YERGAN: Dr. Doxey Wilkerson was a member of that core, and took the leading position. Paul Robeson was chairman of the council and certainly a part of that Communist-led core.

Now tell this Committee, while you are under oath, was Dr. Yergan lying?

MR. ROBESON: I invoke the Fifth Amendment. Could I say that the reason that I am here today, you know, from the mouth of the State Department itself, is: I should not be allowed to travel because I have struggled for years for the independence of the colonial peoples of Africa. For many years I have so labored and I can say modestly that my name is very much honored all over Africa, in my struggles for their independence. That is the kind of independence like Sukarno got in Indonesia. Unless we are double-talking, then these efforts in the interest of Africa would be in the same context. The other reason that I am here today, again from the State Department and from the court record of the court of appeals, is that when I am abroad I speak out against the injustices against the Negro people of this land. I sent a message to the Bandung Conference and so forth. That is why I am here. This is the basis, and I am not being tried for whether I am a Communist, I am being tried for fighting for the rights of my people, who are still second-class citizens in this United States of America. My mother was born in your state, Mr. Walter, and my mother was a Quaker, and my ancestors in the time of Washington baked bread for George Washington's troops when they crossed the Delaware, and my own father was a slave. I stand here struggling for the rights of my people to be full citizens in this country. And they are not. They are not in Mississippi. And they are not in Montgomery, Alabama. And they are not in Washington. They are nowhere, and that is why I am here today. You want to shut up every Negro who has the courage to stand up and fight for the rights of his people, for the rights of workers, and I have been on many a picket line for the steelworkers too. And that is why I am here today.

THE CHAIRMAN: Now just a minute.

MR. ROBESON: All of this is nonsense.

THE CHAIRMAN: You ought to read Jackie Robinson's testimony.

MR. ROBESON: I know Jackie Robinson, and I am sure that in his heart he would take back a lot of what he said about me. I was one of the last people, Mr. Walter, to speak to Judge [Kenesaw Mountain] Landis, to see that Jackie Robinson had a chance to play baseball. Get the pictures and get the record. I was taken by Landis by the hand, and I addressed the combined owners of the American and the National Leagues, pleading for Robinson to be able to play baseball, like I played professional football.

MR. ARENS: Would you tell us whether or not you know Thomas W. Young?

MR. ROBESON: I invoke the Fifth Amendment.

MR. ARENS: Thomas W. Young is a Negro who is president of the Guide Publishing Company, Incorporated, publishers of the *Journal and Guide* in Virginia and North Carolina. I would like to read you his testimony:

> What basis is there, if any, for believing Paul Robeson when he says that in the event of a war with Russia, the Negro would not fight for his country against the Soviets?
>
> No matter how strongly we may believe it is false, that statement coming from Robeson is not easily disposed of. His own life story is an inspiration to humble people of whom Mr. Robeson now presumes to speak. In the first place, Mr. Robeson is now so far out of touch with the Negro thinking in his everyday emotions he can no longer speak authoritatively about or for the race. Mr. Robeson does not speak for the young men who served their country so well during the recent war. He does not speak for the common people who read and believe in the Negro newspapers. He does not speak for the masses of the Negro people whom he has so shamelessly deserted. I have heard Paul Robeson declare his own personal disloyalty to the United States. He has no moral right to place in jeopardy the welfare of the American Negro simply to advance a foreign cause in which we have no real interest. It is my firm conviction that in the eyes of the Negro people this false prophet is regarded as unfaithful to their country, and they repudiate him.

Do you know the man who said that?

MR. ROBESON: I invoke the Fifth Amendment. May I now read from other Negro periodicals, [one of] which says "Paul Robeson, Negro American," and may I read from where I am a doctor of humanities from Morehouse [College, Atlanta, Georgia], and may I read from a statement by Marshall Field, when I received the Spingarn medal from the NAACP?

THE CHAIRMAN: No.

MR. ROBESON: Why not? You allowed the other statements.

THE CHAIRMAN: This was a question, Mr. Robeson.

MR. ROBESON: I have answered the question, and I take the Fifth Amendment.

THE CHAIRMAN: You have invoked the Fifth Amendment, and you have answered the question.

MR. ROBESON: Now, would you give me a chance to read my statement?

MR. KEARNEY: Would you mind reading from some of the citations you have received from Stalin?

MR. ROBESON: I have not received any citations from Stalin.

THE CHAIRMAN: From the Russian government?

MR. ROBESON: No. I received citations and medals from the Abraham Lincoln High School, and medals from the NAACP, and medals from many parts of the world, for my efforts for peace. It seems as though you gentlemen would be trying to contravene the waging of peace by your President here today. Are you for war, Mr. Walter? Would you be in the category of this former Representative who felt we should have fought on the side of Hitler? Now can I read my statement?

MR. KEARNEY: Were you in the service?

MR. ROBESON: It is a sad and bitter commentary—

THE CHAIRMAN: Just answer the question.

MR. ARENS: Did you make a trip to Europe in 1949 and to the Soviet Union?

MR. ROBESON: Yes, I made a trip. To England. And I sang.

MR. ARENS: Where did you go?

MR. ROBESON: I went first to England, where I was with the Philadelphia Orchestra, one of two American groups which was invited to England. I did a long concert tour in England and Denmark and Sweden, and I also sang for the Soviet people, one of the finest musical audiences in the world. Will you read what the *Porgy and Bess* people said? They never heard such applause in their lives. One of the most musical peoples in the world, and the great composers and great musicians, very cultured people, and Tolstoy, and—

THE CHAIRMAN: We know all of that.

MR. ROBESON: They have helped our culture and we can learn a lot.

MR. ARENS: Did you go to Paris on that trip?

MR. ROBESON: I went to Paris.

MR. ARENS: And while you were in Paris, did you tell an audience there that the American Negro would never go to war against the Soviet government?

MR. ROBESON: May I say that is slightly out of context? May I explain to you what I did say? I remember the speech very well, and the night before, in London, and do not take the newspaper, take me: I made the speech, gentlemen, Mr. So-and-So. It happened that the night before, in London, before I went to Paris . . . and will you please listen?

MR. ARENS: We are listening.

MR. ROBESON: Two thousand students from various parts of the colonial world, students who since then have become very important in their governments, in places like Indonesia and India, and in many parts of Africa, two thousand students asked me and Mr. [Dr. Y. M.] Dadoo, a leader of the Indian people in South Africa, when we addressed this conference, and remember I was speaking to a peace conference, they asked me and Mr. Dadoo to say there that they were struggling for peace, that they did not want war against anybody. Two thousand students who came from populations that would range to six or seven hundred million people.

MR. KEARNEY: Do you know anybody who wants war?

MR. ROBESON: They asked me to say in their name that they did not want war. That is what I said. No part of my speech made in Paris says fifteen million American Negroes would do anything. I said it was my feeling that the American people would struggle for peace, and that has since been underscored by the President of these United States. Now, in passing, I said—

MR. KEARNEY: Do you know of any people who want war?

MR. ROBESON: Listen to me. I said it was unthinkable to me that any people would take up arms, in the name of an Eastland, to go against anybody. Gentlemen, I still say that. This United States Government should go down to Mississippi and protect my people. That is what should happen.

THE CHAIRMAN: Did you say what was attributed to you?

MR. ROBESON: I did not say it in that context.

MR. ARENS: I lay before you a document containing an article, "I Am Looking for Full Freedom," by Paul Robeson, in a publication called the *Worker,* dated July 3, 1949.

> At the Paris Conference I said it was unthinkable that the Negro people of America or elsewhere in the world could be drawn into war with the Soviet Union.

MR. ROBESON: Is that saying the Negro people would *do* anything? I said it is unthinkable. I did not say that there [in Paris]: I said that in the *Worker*.

MR. ARENS:

> I repeat it with hundredfold emphasis: they will not.

Did you say that?

MR. ROBESON: I did not say that in Paris, I said that in America. And, gentlemen, they have not yet done so, and it is quite clear that no Americans, no people in the world probably, are going to war with the Soviet Union. So I was rather prophetic, was I not?

MR. ARENS: On that trip to Europe, did you go to Stockholm?

MR. ROBESON: I certainly did, and I understand that some people in the American Embassy tried to break up my concert. They were not successful.

MR. ARENS: While you were in Stockholm, did you make a little speech?

MR. ROBESON: I made all kinds of speeches, yes.

MR. ARENS: Let me read you a quotation.

MR. ROBESON: Let me listen.

MR. ARENS: Do so, please.

MR. ROBESON: I am a lawyer.

MR. KEARNEY: It would be a revelation if you would listen to counsel.

MR. ROBESON: In good company, I usually listen, but you know people wander around in such fancy places. Would you please let me read my statement at some point?

THE CHAIRMAN: We will consider your statement.

MR. ARENS:

> I do not hesitate one second to state clearly and unmistakably: I belong to the American resistance movement which fights against American imperialism, just as the resistance movement fought against Hitler.

MR. ROBESON: Just like Frederick Douglass and Harriet Tubman were underground railroaders, and fighting for our freedom, you bet your life.

THE CHAIRMAN: I am going to have to insist that you listen to these questions.

MR. ROBESON: I am listening.

MR. ARENS:

> If the American warmongers fancy that they could win America's millions of Negroes for a war against those countries (i.e., the Soviet Union and the peoples' democracies) then they ought to understand that this will never be the case. Why should the Negroes ever fight against the only nations of the world where racial discrimination is prohibited, and where the people can live freely? Never! I can assure you, they will never fight against either the Soviet Union or the peoples' democracies.

Did you make that statement?

MR. ROBESON: I do not remember that. But what is perfectly clear today is that nine hundred million other colored people have told you that *they* will not. Four hundred million in India, and millions everywhere, have told you, precisely, that the colored people are not going to die for anybody: they are going to die for their independence. We are dealing not with fifteen million colored people, we are dealing with hundreds of millions.

MR. KEARNEY: The witness has answered the question and he does not have to make a speech.

MR. ARENS: Did you go to Prague, Czechoslovakia?

MR. ROBESON: I sang in Prague.

MR. ARENS: And did you make a speech there?

MR. ROBESON: I do not quite remember. Let me hear it.

MR. ARENS:

> Not only as a representative of progressive America, but as a representative for the twelve Communists on trial in New York. I expect to return to New York to testify on their behalf.

MR. ROBESON: I did, and I did testify on their behalf.

MR. SCHERER: They were convicted.

MR. ROBESON: I feel that, like the Supreme Court decision against segregation, the minority opinion of Justice Black will one day rule this country.

MR. SCHERER: They were convicted.

MR. ROBESON: They were convicted certainly, and every decent American today knows that the Smith Act is a vicious document.

MR. SCHERER: That is your opinion.

MR. ROBESON: It is a vicious document, and it is not my opinion.

THE CHAIRMAN: If everyone knows that, why is it still on the statute books?

MR. ARENS: Then you did go to Moscow, on this trip?

MR. ROBESON: Oh, yes.

MR. ARENS: And while you were there, did you make a speech there?

MR. ROBESON: I spoke many times and sang.

MR. ARENS: Did you write an article that was subsequently published in the U.S.S.R. *Information Bulletin*?

MR. ROBESON: Yes.

MR. ARENS:

> Moscow is very dear to me and very close to my heart. I want to emphasize that only here, in the Soviet Union, did I feel that I was a real man with a capital "M." And now after many years I am here again in Moscow, in the country I love more than any other.

Did you say that?

MR. ROBESON: I would say— What is your name?

MR. ARENS: Arens.

MR. ROBESON: We will take this in context. I am quite willing to answer the question. When I was a singer years ago—this you have to listen to—

MR. ARENS: I am listening.

MR. ROBESON: I am a bass singer, and so for me it was Chaliapin, the great Russian bass, and not Caruso the tenor. I learned the Russian language to sing their songs—I wish you would listen now—

MR. SCHERER: I ask you to direct the witness to answer the question.

MR. ROBESON: Just be fair to me.

MR. SCHERER: I ask regular order.

MR. ROBESON: The great poet of Russia, [great] like Shakespeare of England, is of African blood.

THE CHAIRMAN: Let us not go so far afield.

MR. ROBESON: It is very important to explain this.

THE CHAIRMAN: You can make an explanation. Did you make that statement?

MR. ROBESON: When I first went to Russia in 1934—

THE CHAIRMAN: Did you make that statement?

MR. ROBESON: When I first went to Russia in 1934—

THE CHAIRMAN: Did you make that statement?

MR. SCHERER: I ask you to direct the witness to answer that question.

THE CHAIRMAN: Did you make that statement?

MR. ROBESON: In Russia I felt for the first time like a full human being. No color prejudice like in Mississippi, no color prejudice like in Washington. It was the first time I felt like a human being. Where I did not feel the pressure of color as I feel [it] in this Committee today.

MR. SCHERER: Why do you not stay in Russia?

MR. ROBESON: Because my father was a slave, and my people died to build this country, and I am going to stay here, and have a part of it just like you. And no Fascist-minded people will drive me from it. Is that clear? I am for peace with the Soviet Union, and I am for peace with China, and I am not for peace or friendship with the Fascist Franco, and I am not for peace with Fascist Nazi Germans. I am for peace with decent people.

MR. SCHERER: You are here because you are promoting the Communist cause.

MR. ROBESON: I am here because I am opposing the neo-Fascist cause which I see arising in these committees. You are like the Alien [and] Sedition Act, and Jefferson could be sitting here, and Frederick Douglass could be sitting here, and Eugene Debs could be here.

THE CHAIRMAN: Are you going to answer the questions?

MR. ROBESON: I am answering them.

THE CHAIRMAN: What is your answer to this question?

MR. ROBESON: I have answered the question.

MR. ARENS: Did you send your son to a Soviet school in New York City?

MR. ROBESON: I sent my son to a Soviet school in the Soviet Union and in England, and he was not able to go to a Soviet school in New York.

MR. ARENS: I again invite your attention to this article. Speaking of your son in a Soviet school in Soviet Russia: "Here he spent three years."

MR. ROBESON: And he suffered no prejudice like he would here in Washington.

MR. ARENS: "Then studied in a Soviet school in London."

MR. ROBESON: That is right.

MR. ARENS: "And in a Soviet school in New York."

MR. ROBESON: He was not able to.

MR. ARENS: Is that a mistake?

MR. ROBESON: That is a mistake.

MR. ARENS: That is a printer's error?

MR. ROBESON: And a wrong statement by me.

THE CHAIRMAN: Now, what prejudice are you talking about? You were graduated from Rutgers and you were graduated from the University of Pennsylvania. I remember seeing you play football at Lehigh.

MR. ROBESON: We beat Lehigh.

THE CHAIRMAN: And we had a lot of trouble with you.

MR. ROBESON: That is right. DeWysocki was playing in my team.

THE CHAIRMAN: There was no prejudice against you. Why did you not send your son to Rutgers?

MR. ROBESON: Just a moment. This is something that I challenge very deeply, and very sincerely: that the success of a few Negroes, including myself or Jackie Robinson can make up—and here is a study from Columbia University—for seven hundred dollars a year for thousands of Negro families in the South. My father was a slave, and I have cousins who are sharecroppers, and I do not see my success in terms of myself. That is the reason my own success has not meant what it should mean: I have sacrificed literally hundreds of thousands, if not millions, of dollars for what I believe in.

MR. ARENS: While you were in Moscow, did you make a speech lauding Stalin?

MR. ROBESON: I do not know.

MR. ARENS: Did you say, in effect, that Stalin was a great man, and Stalin had done much for the Russian people, for all of the nations of the world, for all working people of the earth? Did you say something to that effect about Stalin when you were in Moscow?

MR. ROBESON: I cannot remember.

MR. ARENS: Do you have a recollection of praising Stalin?

MR. ROBESON: I said a lot about Soviet people, fighting for the peoples of the earth.

MR. ARENS: Did you praise Stalin?

MR. ROBESON: I do not remember.

MR. ARENS: Have you recently changed your mind about Stalin?

MR. ROBESON: Whatever has happened to Stalin, gentlemen, is a question for the Soviet Union, and I would not argue with a representative of the people who, in building America, wasted sixty to a hundred million lives of my people, black people drawn from Africa on the plantations. You are responsible, and your forebears, for sixty million to one hundred million black people dying in the slave ships and on the plantations, and don't you ask me about anybody, please.

MR. ARENS: I am glad you called our attention to that slave problem. While you were in Soviet Russia, did you ask them there to show you the slave labor camps?

THE CHAIRMAN: You have been so greatly interested in slaves, I should think that you would want to see that.

MR. ROBESON: The slaves I see are still in a kind of semiserfdom. I am interested in the place I am, and in the country that can do something about it. As far as I know, about the slave camps, they were Fascist prisoners who had murdered millions of the Jewish people, and who would have wiped out millions of the Negro people, could they have gotten a hold of them. That is all I know about that.

MR. ARENS: Tell us whether or not you have changed your opinion in the recent past about Stalin.

MR. ROBESON: I have told you, mister, that I would not discuss anything with the people who have murdered sixty million of my people, and I will not discuss Stalin with you.

MR. ARENS: You would not, of course, discuss with us the slave labor camps in Soviet Russia.

MR. ROBESON: I will discuss Stalin when I may be among the Russian people some day, singing for them, I will discuss it there. It is their problem.

MR. ARENS: I suppose you are still going to laud Stalin like you did in 1949, or have you changed your appraisal?

MR. ROBESON: We will not discuss that here. It is very interesting, however, whether [because of] Stalin or the Soviet people, that from 1917 to 1947, in one generation, there could be a nation which equals the power of this one. Nothing could be built more on slavery than this society, I assure you.

MR. ARENS: Let me read another statement by you about the Soviet Union:

> Now, the Soviet Union is the only country I have ever been in where I have felt completely at ease. I have lived in England and America, and I have almost circled the globe, but for myself, wife, and son, the Soviet Union is our future home.

MR. ROBESON: If it were so we would be there. My wife is here and my son is here, and we have come back here.

MR. ARENS: Let me complete this paragraph and see if it helps explain why it is not your future home.

> For a while, however, I would not feel right going there to live. By singing its praises wherever I go, I think I can be of the most value to it. It is too easy to go to the Soviet Union, breathe the free air, and live happily ever afterward.

Mr. Robeson: I came back to America to fight for my people here. They are still second- and third-class citizens, gentlemen. I was born here of the Negro people and of working people, and I am back here to help them struggle.

Mr. Scherer: Did you say what he read to you?

Mr. Robeson: I do not even know what he is reading from, really, and I do not mind. It is like the statement that I was supposed to make in Paris. I thought it was healthy for Americans to consider whether or not Negroes should fight for people who kick them around, and when they took a vote up North they got very nervous because a lot of white Americans said, "I do not see why the hell they would."

Mr. Arens: Did you, while you were in Moscow, make this statement:

> Yes, the Communists march at the front of the struggle for stable peace and popular democracy. But they are not alone. With them are all of the progressive people of America, Wallace's party, and the Negroes of the South, and workers of the North.

Mr. Robeson: Now you are making it up, brother. I would have to get my own copy of the speech.

Mr. Arens: I ask you, while you are under oath, to deny that you made that statement.

Mr. Robeson: I am not denying. But do not just read anything into something. How could I say what Wallace's party would do, or what somebody else would do? That is nonsense.

Mr. Arens: While you are under oath, why do you not deny it?

Mr. Robeson: The Soviet Union and the People's Democracy in China are in the forefront of the struggle for peace, and so is our President, thank goodness, and let us hope we will have some peace, if committees like yours do not upset the applecart and destroy all of humanity. Now can I read my speech?

The Chairman: You have made it without reading it. Can you tell us what Communists participated in the preparation of that speech?

Mr. Robeson: Participated in what?

Mr. Arens: While you were in Soviet Russia, did you make statements about your academic training in Marxism? Do you recall that?

Mr. Robeson: I do not recall that, but I have read a lot of Marx.

Mr. Arens: Do you know a woman by the name of Sheila Lind?

Mr. Robeson: I do not recall.

Mr. Arens: This is the *Daily Worker*, 1949, in which she interviewed you. She is quoting: " 'When I crossed the border from Poland into the Soviet Union,' he told me, 'It was like stepping into another planet.' "

Mr. Robeson: Exactly true, no more prejudice, and no more color feeling, that is right.

Mr. Arens: " 'I felt the full dignity of being a human being for the first time.' "

Mr. Robeson: That is right, and that is still not here.

Mr. Arens: "He loved what he found there so much that, until the war, he returned to Russia for each new year."

Mr. Robeson: Every new year, and we took a little vodka.

Mr. Arens: "And he sent his son to school there. In Moscow he began to study Marxism."

Mr. Robeson: No. I started to study that in England, and all of my political education, strange to say, came in England, where I lived and worked for many years. My Marxist education is English in background, the Labour Party. I went to Republican Spain with Lord Attlee to visit the Attlee Battalion, and I knew Sir Stafford Cripps, and I knew all of the members of the Labour Party, so you cannot blame that on the Russians. You will have to blame that on the English Labour Party. They have just invited me to come to London next week to sing to a hundred and forty thousand miners up in Yorkshire. Do you think you could let me go?

The Chairman: We have nothing to do with that.

Mr. Robeson: Could you not make a suggestion to the State Department that I be allowed to go?

The Chairman: That would not do any good, because the courts have ruled that it is not in the best interests of the United States to permit you to travel.

Mr. Robeson: They have not done that. They have ruled on a very technical problem, Mr. Walter, as to whether I sign an affidavit. That is all.

Mr. Arens: In the summer of 1949 you came back to the United States, is that right?

Mr. Robeson: In the summer of 1949, yes, that is right.

Mr. Arens: And when you came back, did you make a speech in New York City, addressing a rally there? Do you recall that?

Mr. Robeson: I do not.

Mr. Arens:

> I have the greatest contempt for the democratic press, and there is something within me which keeps me from breaking your cameras over your heads.

Did you say that to the press people in New York City about the time you were addressing this rally in June of 1949?

Mr. Robeson: It is sort of out of context.

Mr. Arens: Would you want to refresh your recollection by looking at the article?

Mr. Robeson: Yes. That was not at a meeting. Why do you not say what it was? When my son married the woman of his choice, some very wild press men were there to make a sensation out of it, and this thing was at his wedding, and I did not say "democratic press," I said "a certain kind of press," and I was reaching for a camera to break it, you are quite right.

MR. ARENS: That was a misquotation?

MR. ROBESON: It was when I came out of my son's wedding, and why do you not be honest about this? There is nothing about a meeting, it was a wedding of my son.

MR. ARENS: Does not this article say, "Paul Robeson Addressing a Welcome Home Rally"?

MR. ROBESON: I do not care what it says.

MR. ARENS: That is wrong, too, is it? Now I would invite your attention, if you please, to the *Daily Worker* of June 29, 1949, with reference to a get-together with you and Ben Davis. Do you know Ben Davis?

MR. ROBESON: One of my dearest friends, one of the finest Americans you can imagine, born of a fine family, who went to Amherst [College] and was a great man.

THE CHAIRMAN: The answer is yes?

MR. ROBESON: Nothing could make me prouder than to know him.

THE CHAIRMAN: That answers the question.

MR. ARENS: Did I understand you to laud his patriotism?

MR. ROBESON: I say that he is as patriotic an American as there can be, and you gentlemen belong with the Alien and Sedition Acts, and you are the nonpatriots, and you are the un-Americans, and you ought to be ashamed of yourselves.

THE CHAIRMAN: Just a minute, the hearing is now adjourned.

MR. ROBESON: I should think it would be.

THE CHAIRMAN: I have endured all of this that I can.

MR. ROBESON: Can I read my statement?

THE CHAIRMAN: No, you cannot read it. The meeting is adjourned.

MR. ROBESON: I think it should be, and you should adjourn this forever, that is what I would say.

THE CHAIRMAN: We will convene at two o'clock this afternoon.*

MR. FRIEDMAN: Will the statement be accepted for the record without being read?

THE CHAIRMAN: No, it will not.

Some persons whom HUAC pounced on were already in process of extricating themselves from Stalinism, and the Committee's action only slowed down the process, because there was a natural unwillingness to inform on former comrades—if not also to be nice to HUAC. As Murray Kempton writes in *Part of Our Time* (New York, 1955):

* But not to hear Paul Robeson. As for his statement, see Appendix 3. —E.B.

> The Communists themselves would seem to have been much more successful than the Un-American Activities Committee in disillusioning Communists. Of the repentant Party members whose testimony before the committee was most thorough, Martin Berkeley had broken in 1943; Budd Schulberg had left in 1939; Edward Dmytryk, Frank Tuttle, Leopold Atlas, and Robert Rossen were all out by 1946. Only Richard Collins appears to have been a Communist in September 1947, when the committee began its investigation. Almost every 1947 Party member would seem to have stood fast throughout the day of the locust.* There is strong evidence that Dmytryk, Collins, Rossen and Tuttle actually postponed a public breach with the Party out of loyalty to their friends in time of trouble.

That Arthur Miller was very close to the Communist Party during the forties and early fifties reveals itself to those who look into the matter, though it was not news that at the time reached most of the audience at Miller's plays. It was the concern of such people as the members of HUAC to have it reach that audience. They also hoped to show that Miller had been an actual Party member. Such proofs were not always easy to find. Readers of the present book will recall that proof of even Hanns Eisler's membership was not forthcoming. Eisler signed an application, but it was not clear that it was accepted and that he paid dues. With Miller, the doubt was that "the application" was really an application. The point is academic, in that the Party often preferred its celebrities outside the Party—as apparently independent witnesses to its rectitude.

Miller's public political record in the fifties was somewhat as follows: In 1952 he had joined James Thurber and others in protesting against the conformist temper of the early fifties as it was affecting the theater. An article he wrote in the *New York Times* brought forth such queries as "Is Senator McCarthy Stopping Arthur Miller from Writing?" (*New Leader,* September 8, 1952). In 1953 his own *The Crucible* became Broadway's principal challenge to McCarthyism. In 1954 an even fiercer attack on McCarthyism by Miller appeared in the *Nation* (July 3) under the title "Every American Should Go to Jail: A Modest Proposal for Pacifying the Public Temper." In 1955 the City of New York threw a monkey wrench in the way of a film Miller was to make about teen-age gangs and the urban problem: "Of the eight city commissioners or their deputies who were there . . . seven voted against Miller. 'I'm not calling him a Communist,' one of the majority said afterward, 'my objection is he refuses to repent.' "

* In 1970 we learned from Dalton Trumbo's *Additional Dialogue* that "standing fast" did not have to entail Party membership. Trumbo says he was a member in 1943–1948, but not in 1948–1954. —E.B.

("How Not to Produce a Film" by Walter Goodman, *New Republic*, (December 26, 1955.) (Seldom was it so openly admitted that another of the citizenship tests of that era was repentance. And this quotation also indicates that what you repented *of* was of minor importance: just so long as you repented of it, and it was at least pink.) To add to the ironies, it would seem that Miller did begin to have doubts—perhaps one should say, more urgent doubts—about Soviet Communism in just this period. The *New York Times* of February 13, 1956, ran a story headed "Red and Anti-Red Curbs on Art Denounced by U.S. Playwright: Arthur Miller, in Message for Dostoyevsky Fete, Asks Freedom from Politics." Miller had denounced unfreedom East and West in a statement sent to the press and to the Soviet Writers' Union, the American Committee for Cultural Freedom, and the American Committee for Liberation from Bolshevism. It was just four months later that he appeared before HUAC. If the dialogue as cited here sounds rather mild on both sides, it should not be forgotten that Miller was cited for contempt. He received a thirty-day suspended sentence and a five-hundred-dollar fine. In 1958 he was exonerated by the courts, but the time, trouble, and money the process cost must be charged—with a thousand other such bills—to the House Committee on Un-American Activities. Miller made many comments, outside of his testimony, on the Committee and related topics. One is given to a character in *After the Fall* (1964):

> If everyone broke faith there would be no civilization! That is why the Committee is the face of the Philistine! And it astounds me that you can speak of truth and justice in relation to that gang of cheap publicity hounds!

The informer character in *After the Fall* bears some relation to the play's first director, Elia Kazan, whose testimony before the Committee is published above, and the informer theme had been treated by Kazan in his film *On the Waterfront,* by Miller in both *The Crucible* (1953) and *A View from the Bridge* (1955).

JUNE 21, 1956:

Arthur Miller

The Committee met at 10 a.m., in the caucus room of the House Office Building, the Honorable Francis E. Walter (Chairman of the Committee) presiding.

PRESENT: Representatives Walter, Willis, Kearney, and Scherer.

PRESENT ALSO: Richard Arens, Staff Director.

THE CHAIRMAN: Let the record show that the Chairman has appointed a Subcommittee consisting of Representatives Willis, Scherer, Kearney, and myself. I might say that the acoustics in this room are very bad and for that reason we will have to insist that there be no audible conversation.

MR. ARENS: Please identify yourself, sir, by name, residence, and occupation.

MR. MILLER: My name is Arthur Miller. I live at Roxbury, Connecticut. I am a playwright.

MR. ARENS: You are appearing today, Mr. Miller, in response to a subpoena which was served upon you by the House Committee on Un-American Activities?

MR. MILLER: That is correct.

MR. ARENS: And you are represented by counsel?

MR. MILLER: That is correct.

MR. ARENS: Counsel, will you identify yourself?

MR. RAUH: My name is Joseph L. Rauh, Jr.

MR. ARENS: Mr. Miller, please tell the Committee where and when you were born?

MR. MILLER: I was born on October 17, 1915, in New York City.

MR. ARENS: And give us a word, please, sir, about your formal education.

MR. MILLER: I went to public schools in New York City, to James Madison High School, Abraham Lincoln High School, the University of Michigan. I have a bachelor of arts degree from the University of Michigan, and an honorary doctor of humane letters.

MR. ARENS: When did you receive those degrees?

MR. MILLER: I received my bachelor's degree in June 1938 and the other degree last Saturday.

MR. ARENS: Kindly tell the Committee, Mr. Miller, the dates on which you at any time have made application for a United States passport.

MR. MILLER: I couldn't be exact about the first application, because I don't have the information with me, but to the best of my recollection it would be in 1946.

MR. ARENS: Your application was in 1946, and did you then, pursuant to the application, receive a passport?

MR. MILLER: Yes, I did.

MR. ARENS: Now tell us about any renewal of that particular passport.

MR. MILLER: That passport was renewed in Rome. I have given the passport to the State Department, in my recent applications, so I don't have all this information at my finger tips.

THE CHAIRMAN: Can you give him those dates, Mr. Arens?

MR. ARENS: I just want him to show the approximate dates. We will interrogate him at length with reference to each one.

MR. MILLER: These are all in the records.

MR. ARENS: You applied in 1946 for a passport which was issued to you in 1947?

MR. MILLER: I believe that is the case.

MR. ARENS: Then it was renewed pursuant to an application filed in Rome shortly thereafter.

MR. MILLER: Yes, a couple of years thereafter.

MR. ARENS: When was your next passport application, do you recall?

MR. MILLER: The next one was in March of 1954.

MR. ARENS: Was a passport issued to you pursuant to that application?

MR. MILLER: No, it was not.

MR. ARENS: You withdrew your passport application, did you not?

MR. MILLER: I had no further use for a passport. The passport was required because I was invited by the American-Belgian Society, which is a society in Belgium for the enhancement of relations between the United States and Belgium, and they offered to pay my transportation and my expenses from New York to Belgium for the opening of a stage theater production of one of my plays called *Crucible*. I got the cable on Monday evening. I returned the cable, saying that I would love to be there. I applied for renewal of my passport on the following day, which was Tuesday. I had to be in Brussels on the following Tuesday—that was the opening of the play—and the Belgian Airlines do not run on Monday, so I would have had to have had a passport no later than Friday. Consequently, it was a big rush. It is an abnormally short time to ask for a passport, and the week passed and I heard nothing from the State Department, so I instructed Mr. [Lloyd] Garrison, my attorney, to call and find out whether I would have it that afternoon or not. This was sometime Friday afternoon, and Mrs. [Ruth B.] Shipley, of the State Department, told Mr. Garrison that she could not issue one without further investigation. He then explained that the passport would be useless to me. I had no plans to go to Europe whatsoever, except for this free trip, which I wanted to take any time after that. That was the end of the conversation with the State Department.

MR. ARENS: Then do you have pending at the present time a passport application with the Department of State?

MR. MILLER: Yes, I do. I applied—I guess this is the fifth week now. I applied four and a half weeks ago. I wanted to go to England.

MR. ARENS: Did you, in 1955, have an employment arrangement contemplated with the Youth Board down in New York City?

MR. MILLER: I had no employment arrangement with the Youth Board. I had an employment arrangement with an independent motion-picture producing company called Combined Artists, Incorporated. My contract with Combined Artists, Incorporated was to the effect that I engage myself to write the outline and the finished screenplay of a motion picture on the subject of juvenile delinquency.

MR. ARENS: That was to be in connection with the activities or work of the Youth Board, was it not?

MR. MILLER: The Youth Board was to cooperate with me in the research which would be required for me to write this script. I ought to say that this was a kind of odd contract, but the nature of the contract was, as I understand it, that the City of New York, in return for the cooperation which it would give me, would get five per cent of the moneys of this picture.

MR. ARENS: Did you in the course of your negotiations or relationships with the Youth Board in New York City have occasion to appear before the board to express certain actions which you allegedly took in connection with a previous passport application?

MR. MILLER: Yes.

MR. ARENS: Did you make that appearance before the Youth Board in November of 1955?

MR. MILLER: It was about that time. I am not very good about dates.

MR. ARENS: Was there a controversy that arose with respect to whether or not you should be permitted to continue with your labors?

MR. MILLER: There was an attack launched upon my political fitness to write a screenplay by one newspaper. It remained with one newspaper for quite a time.

MR. ARENS: Now, did you appear before the board and, among other things, say to the board:

> Finally, some two years ago, I issued a statement which was printed in the press in reply to a State Department statement, and in this I categorically denied that I am supporting the Communist cause or contributing to it or was under its discipline or domination.
>
> Furthermore, in my application at about the same time for renewal of my passport, I had signed under the penalties of perjury that statement that I was not a member of any subversive organization. I cite these statements, which of course are still true because they are part of the public record and have been for a long time.

I ask you now, Mr. Miller, if you made the statement which I have just read to you?

MR. MILLER: I believe you read it correctly, yes, sir.

MR. ARENS: Did you, in your passport application, deny under oath that you had supported the Communist cause or contributed to it or were under its discipline or domination?

MR. MILLER: The oath that I referred to was the standard oath that I had taken some years before in my first application for a passport. My understanding of the oath was that I wouldn't have been foolish enough to have tried to mislead the New York City Youth Board by referring to an oath which everybody signs who gets a passport if I had not in this case mistakenly understood the oath years later.

MR. ARENS: Mr. Miller—I beg your pardon.

MR. MILLER: I was asked by the chairman of the Youth Board whether this was the standard oath that I was referring to or whether it was some special oath. I said no, it was the standard oath. Now, I would have to be a singularly obtuse individual to have referred the gentleman to an oath which he could have found by going across the street to the passport bureau if I had any impulse there to mislead him. I understood at that time—it was my recollection at the time, and I certainly would have signed such an oath had it been there—that that was the common oath taken. Oaths are in newspapers very often now, and that was my understanding at the time. I am sorry I made an error. It was by no means any attempt to mislead anybody. It was just my faulty memory of what I had signed some years before.

MR. ARENS: I am a little puzzled. You say you are sorry you made an error. What error?

MR. MILLER: I mistook that kind of oath for the oath that anyone takes who signs a passport application. I was referring to the oath that I had signed when I had taken out my passport application some years earlier.

MR. ARENS: Now I lay before you the photostatic copy of a passport application signed by one Arthur Miller in 1947—April 1947—and ask you if that is a true and correct reproduction of the passport application which you signed in 1947 and submitted to the Department of State in an attempt to procure a passport?

MR. MILLER: Yes, it is.

MR. ARENS: Is this the document to which you were alluding in your conversation with the Youth Board when you told the Youth Board that you categorically denied to the State Department under oath that you had been supporting the Communist cause or contributing to it or were under its discipline or domination? Is that the document to which you were alluding in your statement before the Youth Board?

MR. MILLER: I beg your pardon. There seems to be a slight misunderstanding. When my passport was denied by the State Department I issued a statement in reply to a public statement by the State Department in which I denied such affiliations. That was what I was referring to in that particular wording that you are speaking of.

MR. ARENS: Well, did you sign a statement under oath to the Department of State in the course of your attempt to procure a passport in 1947 in which you denied that you had ever been supporting the Communist cause or contributing to it or were under its discipline or domination?

MR. MILLER: The only statement I have ever signed in relation to the State Department is the oath here in this passport application.

MR. ARENS: Now, do you see, in that passport application, any oath which in essence is a denial of support of the Communist cause or contribution to it or being under its discipline or domination?

MR. MILLER: No, I do not. I have just tried to explain, sir, that that was an error on my part in referring to the oath as I did. I would have signed such an oath had it been in the passport application, and I have just stated that I made an error, and I made the error in all good faith, because I would have been a very stupid man to have referred to a passport application, thinking that no one would have the sense to look at it. I thought that is what I had said.

THE CHAIRMAN: Answer the questions, Mr. Miller.

MR. MILLER: I am sorry.

MR. ARENS: Let us get this record clear now. Would you, in 1947, have taken an oath—even though you are now mistaken as to whether or not you did take one—would you have taken an oath that you had not contributed to the Communist cause, supported it, or been under its discipline?

MR. MILLER: I would have made a statement that I had been affiliated from time to time with organizations that were cited as Communist-dominated organizations, but I would have certainly taken an oath at any time in my life that I was never under the discipline of the Communist Party or the Communist cause.

MR. ARENS: And would you have then taken an oath that you had never *contributed* to the Communist cause?

MR. MILLER: Well, that question would involve the later citation of certain organizations which I may have contributed a dollar or two to in the past which would now be called contributing to the Communist cause.

THE CHAIRMAN: What organizations are you referring to?

MR. MILLER: I have none in particular in mind.

THE CHAIRMAN: You had organizations in mind when you made that statement.

MR. MILLER: Well, let me think. I understand the Joint Anti-Fascist Committee has been cited. I believe that from time to time I would contribute to some drive of theirs during and after the Spanish Civil War.

(*Representative Doyle entered the hearing room.*)

MR. ARENS: Mr. Miller, is it a fair summary to say that in 1955, when you appeared before the Youth Board, and this controversy arose respecting what you have described as your political beliefs, that you told the Youth Board in essence that you had never contributed to the Communist cause, that you had never been under Communist discipline, and that you had made an oath to your Government to that effect when you made application for your passport?

MR. MILLER: No, I would contest that, sir.

MR. ARENS: You straighten us out as to what the position was that you took before the Youth Board when the controversy arose.

(*The witness conferred with his counsel.*)

MR. MILLER: I would like to refresh my memory with just a glance at my statement there, so I could—

MR. ARENS: The part which I read to you is here. It has been underlined so that I would be able to refer to it here in this session today.

MR. MILLER: I would just like to clear one thing up and this, perhaps —no, I guess it isn't technical. There are two statements referred to here, I think reasonably clearly, although it may seem to be a little meshed together.

> Finally, some two years ago, I issued a statement which was printed in the press in reply to a State Department statement.

That is a press statement. I believe I have a copy here which you can look at, if you don't have a copy of it, and in this I categorically denied that I was supporting the Communist cause or was contributing to it or was under its discipline or domination. That was in reply, that press statement, to a State Department statement which said, in effect, that the State Department was exercising its right to deny a passport to anyone who it was believed was then under the domination of the Communist Party, et cetera. In my statement to the press I said I was not, and that I was not supporting any Communist cause.

MR. ARENS: Did you, in essence, say to the Youth Board that you were not and had not been under Communist Party discipline and that you had not contributed to the Communist Party?

MR. MILLER: I dispute that, sir.

MR. ARENS: Did you admit to the Youth Board that you had been under Communist Party discipline and that you had been contributing to Communist causes?

MR. MILLER: I was never under Communist Party discipline, so, therefore, I would not be called upon to admit. As for contributing to causes, front groups, and so forth, I won't deny that. I am here to tell you the truth, and I wouldn't deny it there. The issue there, quite clearly, was whether I was trustworthy enough to write a screenplay on juvenile delinquency without warping the truth about this very grave problem. I tried to indicate that this would not be the case, and they already had an outline of this picture, which was not written while I was under attack at all. I was perfectly calm and quiet. It had been written some weeks or months before, and they had all their experts, and they themselves had been very enthusiastic about this outline, so there was no question about warping the material. All I was trying to get across was that I was not then supporting any group that might indicate that I would warp this material or that would make me untrustworthy.

MR. ARENS: Now, Mr. Miller, in 1947, the very year in which you made this passport application in which you stated to the Youth Board that you had sworn to the Department of State you had never been enmeshed in Communist activities, were you a sponsor of the World Youth Festival to be held in Prague?

* * *

MR. MILLER: I could not recall that, but if there is any evidence—

MR. ARENS: I should like to refresh your recollection. I lay before you now a photostatic copy of the *New York Times* of May 25, 1947, entitled "The Dance: Prague Festival."

> A movement, rather late in getting under way but vigorous, nevertheless, has been started to see that the American dance is represented at the World Youth Festival, to be held in Prague from July 20 to August 17, under the auspices of the World Federation of Democratic Youth.

Among the sponsors listed here is a person described as Arthur Miller. I lay that before you and ask you if that helps refresh your recollection?

MR. MILLER: Well, I would add, of course, that there were a good many other—

THE CHAIRMAN: Answer the question.

MR. MILLER: Mr. Walter, I have no memory of it, but I would not deny that I had done this.

MR. ARENS: Now, in 1947, did you have difficulty with the Department of State over an incident in which the Department of State refused to sponsor transportation for students and participants attending this World Youth Festival?

MR. MILLER: I don't [recall], but I would like to say now that in those times I did support a number of things which I would not do now.

THE CHAIRMAN: What things did you support that you would not support now?

MR. MILLER: I would not support now a cause or movement which was dominated by Communists.

THE CHAIRMAN: But you did at that time?

MR. MILLER: I did, yes.

MR. ARENS: Now I lay before you this photostatic copy of the *New York Times,* Wednesday, June 11, 1947, entitled "Miller Fails in Plea."

> Efforts to obtain financial assistance for the project to send Arthur Miller's play *All My Sons* to the Prague Youth Festival this summer proved disappointing at a meeting yesterday of theatrical business people and representatives of the company.

There is also in this article reference to an incident which I shall now describe by reading another excerpt:

> The gathering adopted the following resolution, recommended by Mr. Miller, to be wired to the Department of State:
>
> "Urge you seriously to reconsider refusal to sponsor availability of transportation for students and participants attending World Youth Festival in Prague this summer. To my knowledge the participants have no special political affiliations."

I lay that now before you and ask you whether that refreshes your recollection.

(*The witness conferred with his counsel.*)

MR. MILLER: This is of a slightly special nature and I would like to make one comment about it.

MR. ARENS: Please do.

MR. MILLER: It does refresh my recollection. Somebody wanted to do my play. I didn't know who they were, but I was always in favor of having my plays done. As I recall, there was no money to send them over and I wanted to do what I could to have that play sent over. This particular thing, I believe, was just in the normal course of an author's life. I would have done it if they had wanted it to go to Australia.

MR. ARENS: Did you in this year, 1947, sign a statement released by the Civil Rights Congress which, among other things, reads as follows:

> The Communist Party is a legal American political party. We see nothing in their program, record, or activities, either in war or peace, to justify the enactment of the repressive legislation now being urged upon the Congress in an atmosphere of an organized hysteria.

Did you sign the statement?

MR. MILLER: Sir, I don't— These things were coming across my desk.

MR. ARENS: I lay before you the document now. See if it refreshes your recollection. It is the Communist *Daily Worker* of Wednesday, April 16, 1947, indicating that one hundred prominent Americans had issued this statement, including a person described here as Arthur Miller.

MR. MILLER: I see my name here. I will not deny I signed it. I just don't have any recollection of it.

* * *

MR. ARENS: Now I lay before you the *Washington Post* of Tuesday, May 20, 1947: "Rob Communists of Their Rights?—Then Yours Go Out the Window, Too." It is an advertisement protesting the flagrant violation, punitive measures directed against the Communist Party, and signed by a number of persons, including one Arthur Miller, identified as a playwright. I ask you if you have a recollection of lending your name to that cause or movement?

MR. MILLER: I see my name here. I would not deny I might have signed it.

MR. ARENS: In 1947 were you cognizant of the proceedings then pending in this country against a Communist agent known as Gerhart Eisler?

MR. MILLER: I remember reading about him.

MR. ARENS: Did you sign a statement in protest of the prosecution of Gerhart Eisler?

MR. MILLER: I don't recall that, sir.

MR. ARENS: I lay before you now a press release of 1947 of the Civil Rights Congress protesting the shameful persecution of the German anti-Fascist refugee, Gerhart Eisler, signed by a number of persons, including a person identified as Arthur Miller, playwright.

MR. MILLER: I recall this. I would like to say, though, that I did sign a lot of things in those days.

THE CHAIRMAN: Wait a minute. Did you sign that or is that a press release?

MR. MILLER: Oh, no—

MR. ARENS: That is a press release, Mr. Chairman, indicating the names of people who signed it. He has now identified it, or at least admitted his signature to the press release.

MR. MILLER: I am not denying being the sponsor of many of these things.

MR. ARENS: I lay before you a passport application—

MR. MILLER: At the present time I would not be doing it, that is all.

MR. ARENS: Now I lay before you the passport application of a person where the signature appears, Samuel Liptzin, but the photograph is that of Gerhart Eisler. Did you know, at the time you signed that statement protesting the persecution of Gerhart Eisler, that he was a top-ranking agent of the Kremlin in this country, and that among other things for which he was being pursued by our Government was passport fraud?

MR. MILLER: Sir, I would have had no knowledge of that, and in those days I would not have had the mood of investigating these things at all. I tell you quite frankly this suited the mood that I was in, and I would never have gone to any trouble about investigating that kind of thing.

MR. ARENS: Did you participate in a statement issued by the Civil Rights Congress with reference to Eisler?

> The hysterical atmosphere contrived around the case indicates that this incident involving a German Communist kept here against his will is intended as the initial phase of a sweeping attack upon the entire labor and progressive movement in the United States.

MR. MILLER: I don't recall it.

MR. ARENS: Look at this exhibit here and see whether or not it helps refresh your recollection.

MR. MILLER: My point is simple.

MR. ARENS: First tell us whether or not this refreshes your recollection, whether or not you recall participating in the issuance of that statement, and then go on with your statement.

MR. MILLER: I do not recall participating in it. I do not deny I may have done it. I do not have a memory of these things. It is ten years ago. I would just make this simple point, and that is that I would have had no knowledge of the details here, and they would not have been of great interest to me at the time. I was acting not as an investigator or as a lawyer [or] as someone who would be careful to any great degree about what he was supporting providing that it met the mood of the time that I was living in.

MR. ARENS: We will get into that proposition a little later. Did you, during this period which we have been discussing—we are beginning in 1947 and coming on right up—did you during this period know a man by the name of Millard Lampell?

MR. MILLER: I did, yes.

MR. ARENS: Did Millard Lampell, to your knowledge, recollection, solicit you to participate in a movement called Veterans Against Discrimination of the Civil Rights Congress?

MR. MILLER: I would not recall that, sir. I don't remember that.

MR. ARENS: Do you recall Millard Lampell enlisting you to join in the movement to attack the House Committee on Un-American Activities?

MR. MILLER: No, sir.

MR. ARENS: Do you recall an attack on the House Committee on Un-American Activities in which you were a participant?

MR. MILLER: I would say that in all probability I had supported criticism of the Un-American Activities Committee.

MR. ARENS: Would you want to give us a little bit clearer characterization of what you mean by the word "criticism" of the House Committee on Un-American Activities?

MR. MILLER: I probably would have signed statements opposing the Committee.

MR. ARENS: Did you sign statements or lend your name, prestige, and influence toward a movement to abolish the Committee on Un-American Activities?

MR. MILLER: I have no memory of that.

MR. ARENS: I lay before you now a photostatic copy of a letter on the letterhead of the Veterans Against Discrimination of Civil Rights Congress, Millard Lampell, chairman, who, as the record reflects, has been identified as a hard-core Communist, which says, "The Un-American Committee can and must be abolished." Among others, the sponsors include the name of one Arthur Miller. I ask you whether or not that refreshes your recollection as to any of your activities?

MR. MILLER: I would say yes.

MR. ARENS: Now I lay before you a copy of an announcement of a mobilization, a rally, mobilized against the House Un-American Activities Committee, held under the auspices of the Civil Rights Congress, in which one, two, three, six people are to speak at Manhattan Center in New York City, three of whom have been publicly identified as Communist agents, including on this list of people who are to speak at this rally to destroy the House Committee on Un-American Activities one Arthur Miller. I ask you whether or not you are the Arthur Miller?

MR. MILLER: I am not clear whether I was a speaker or not.

MR. ARENS: The advertisement would so indicate, would it not?

MR. MILLER: Well, I have found that more than once there was a slight use of license, so to speak, and I found myself listed as a speaker many times, or several times at least. I recall people saying to me that I had made a speech somewhere some weeks ago and I would say, "Where?" I had been a sponsor of something but I had not made a speech. I don't recall making that speech. It is quite probable that I supported it.

MR. KEARNEY: Mr. Miller, did you ever make any protest against the use of your name?

MR. MILLER: I would occasionally, yes. I would try to find whoever was responsible, which was not always easy. It was always after the fact, of course, and there was no way for me to redress the thing. I did make remonstrances.

MR. ARENS: Did you remonstrate the use of your name appearing in the public print in connection with a public caravan to come to Washington to protest the hearings by the House Un-American Activities Committee in which they were exposing Communists in Hollywood?

MR. MILLER: No, I would not have protested that. I was supporting that.

MR. ARENS: Did you participate in the caravan?

MR. MILLER: No, I did not.

MR. ARENS: Do you recall participating in a movement to defend Howard Fast?

MR. MILLER: If I can see the material?

MR. ARENS: I lay before you now a photostatic copy of a dodger [poster?] of a protest meeting for Howard Fast "and other victims" of the House Committee on Un-American Activities, signed by approximately a dozen people, including a person listed as Arthur Miller, and ask you whether or not you are the Arthur Miller?

MR. MILLER: Yes, that was my opinion at the time. I know really very little about anything except my work and my field, and it seemed to me that the then prevalent, rather ceaseless, investigating of artists was creating a pall of apprehension and fear among all kinds of people.

THE CHAIRMAN: But did you know that those very artists were the chief source of supply for the funds that were used by the Communists in the United States? Did you know that, when you were defending these people, they were the people who contributed thousands of dollars monthly to assist in the organization of labor unions that were Communist dominated?

MR. MILLER: Mr. Walter, I will tell you—

THE CHAIRMAN: Or did you not care?

MR. MILLER: Quite frankly, the consideration in my mind was that, as far as I could see, there was a distinct pall of apprehension and fear. People were being put into a state of great apprehension and they were—

THE CHAIRMAN: Apprehension of what, Mr. Miller?

MR. MILLER: Well, in some cases, just punishment and, in some cases, unjust punishment.

THE CHAIRMAN: Do you know of any artist who was prosecuted as a result of any information obtained from these hearings who was not a member of the Communist apparatus?

MR. MILLER: Quite frankly, sir, that wouldn't have been the issue in my mind.

THE CHAIRMAN: You are talking about the issue in your mind, and, in view of the fact that you have raised this question repeatedly—about your mood, your mind—may I ask if you changed your mind since the revelations concerning Mr. Stalin have been made?

MR. MILLER: I suppose that a year has not gone by that I have not altered my opinions or beliefs or approach to life, and, long before that, I had shifted my views as to my relations or my attitude toward Marxism and toward Communism.

THE CHAIRMAN: When did you change your views about Marxism?

MR. MILLER: I was not a Saul of Tarsus walking down a road and struck by a bright light. It was a slow process that occurred over years really, through my own work and through my own efforts to understand myself and what I was trying to do in the world.

THE CHAIRMAN: This is very interesting to me, because, within the last few hours, there came to my office a very prominent lawyer, who told me of a number of performers who had invoked the Fifth Amendment, and they did it largely because they did not want to be placed in the position of being informer, but he said that there now has come to them an appreciation that the greatest informer in the world is the man who now speaks for the Communists—namely, Mr. Khrushchev. It was a very interesting thing, and he said that six of these performers now want to come before our Committee and testify, people who invoked the Fifth Amendment.

MR. ARENS: Mr. Miller, this mood that you are talking about to defend people in the arts did not strike you, apparently, in 1945, with reference to Ezra Pound, did it?

MR. MILLER: I was very troubled by Ezra's Pound's condition, and to this day I think it is a tragic fact, and I could not tell you right now in any cogent way what I think should have been done with Ezra Pound. My instinctive feeling is that he should have been let alone.

MR. ARENS: You must have changed your mind, then, since 1945, did you not?

MR. MILLER: I probably did, yes.

MR. ARENS: Let us clear the record. Who was Ezra Pound?

MR. MILLER: Who is Ezra Pound?

MR. ARENS: Who was he?

MR. MILLER: Ezra Pound is one of the great poets of this century.

MR. ARENS: And you, in effect, said in that statement which appeared in *New Masses* that he ought to be shot, did you not?

MR. MILLER: I don't recall such a statement.

MR. ARENS: Well, let me read it to you.

MR. MILLER: By the way, you didn't permit me to finish my statement. It happened one night I had bought a new radio during the war, and I had a short-wave set, and I turned on the short wave, and there was a voice which I had never heard but which spoke perfectly good American advocating the destruction of the Jewish people and justifying the cremation of Jews, and I was quite astonished because it was such a common American accent, and I waited to the end, and it was being broadcast from Italy, and it was Ezra Pound. I think I can be forgiven for feeling slightly perturbed about this man, but I will say now, despite that, it is a difficult and hard issue to settle, and I think it's a tragic one and sometimes there are no easy answers.

MR. ARENS: Ezra Pound was a poet who, during the war, was issuing statements and was writing plays and issuing poems which were anti-Communist and which were against the interests, at that time, of the United States of America. Is that not the essence of what he did? He was a propagandist, a writer, was he not?

MR. MILLER: Excuse me, sir. I had never had any knowledge of Ezra Pound's views at all, quite frankly, until I heard that broadcast and I realized that this man was a Mussolini propagandist who was broadcasting from the Rome radio.

MR. ARENS: Did you not write in *New Masses,* in effect, criticizing those who would defend Ezra Pound on the same basis that you defended the Hollywood Ten?

MR. MILLER: I would like to see the statement, if I may.

* * *

MR. ARENS: Here is Arthur Miller's statement in 1945:

> In the belief that Ezra Pound's trial for treason is of high importance to the future direction of American letters, and poetry in particular, I should like to offer my commentary on the reaction of five poets and a critic to the Pound case in the newspaper *PM* of Sunday, November 25. The majority of the reactions are alarming.
>
> All six agree that Pound's contribution to literature was of the highest order. With this no man can argue.
>
> If I may be pardoned some nonpoetical language, the boys are cutting the baloney pretty thick. [Karl] Shapiro ought to know that Pound is not accused of not "reversing his beliefs" but of aiding and abetting the enemy by broadcasting propaganda calculated to undermine the American will to fight

> fascism. And Mr. [Conrad] Aiken ought to know by now that Pound did not betray himself to "man in the abstract" but to Mussolini, whose victims are, to be sure, now buried and abstract, but who was a most real, most unpoetical type of fellow.

The article winds up:

> In conclusion, may I say that without much effort one could find a thousand poets and writers who understand not only why Pound was dangerous and treasonous, but why he will be even more so if released. In a world where humanism must conquer lest humanity be destroyed, literature must nurture the conscience of man. A greater calamity cannot befall the art than that Ezra Pound, the Mussolini mouthpiece, should be welcomed back as an arbiter of American letters, an eventuality not to be dismissed if the court adopts the sentiments of these four poets.

MR. MILLER: Mr. Arens, in the first place, this was a time of war. He [Pound] was literally and in every conceivable way a traitor and there was no question about it, I don't think, in anybody's mind. I would not now say that I share all these sentiments by any means. This is a long time ago. I don't think I would be quite as virulent about it now. I, however, can understand quite easily how I could have felt this way. I felt this man threatened me personally: I am a Jew. He was for burning Jews and you will have to pardon my excitement at the time if that was the situation.

MR. ARENS: I want this record to show that I am not undertaking by this question to defend Ezra Pound; I am only pointing out by this exhibit what would appear to be, absent any explanation, an inconsistency at least.

(*Representative Jackson entered the hearing room.*)

MR. KEARNEY: Pound was convicted as a traitor and served time?

MR. ARENS: As were the twelve Communists.

MR. JACKSON: I would like, in view of the witness's strong words of denunciation of Mr. Pound for his expressions of anti-Semitism and his understandable resentment of them, did you ever subsequently, and particularly since the denunciation in the Soviet Union of Stalin, ever make a public statement denouncing the shocking evidence of anti-Semitism in the Soviet Union?

MR. MILLER: I am sorry to say that there was none. I am sorry to say something worse: that I was not shocked. This last stuff has been no great shock to me. I have had intimate evidence from a man I know who had a brother in the Soviet Union and who was, as I remember it, the editor or writer for some literary magazine there and who, this man told me—I can't remember now, because it's possibly three years ago, four years ago—he had completely dropped out of sight and was no longer responding to any mail. They were two brothers. This fellow told me that he thought that he had been the victim of purely anti-Semitic things. Now I have ceased these kinds of statements, as I said, which were befitting the frame of mind I was in. I ceased issuing statements right and left, except when I am personally involved, because I found I was being tangled in stuff that I was really not prepared to defend a hundred per cent, and I am ashamed to say that I should have, and I did feel I was not completely ignorant of this. It isn't a matter of Khrushchev. I knew this before Khrushchev.

MR. ARENS: Did you know it in 1952 when you signed a statement in defense of the twelve Communist traitors who were convicted in Foley Square in New York City?

MR. MILLER: That I would make a differentiation about, quite frankly. This is a question which verges on—I don't know under what law this prosecution took place.

MR. ARENS: Under the Smith law: conspiring to overthrow the Government of the United States by force and violence. That is part of the International Cominform apparatus.

MR. MILLER: I am opposed to the Smith Act and I am still opposed to anyone being penalized for advocating anything. I say that because of a very simple reason. I don't believe that, in the history of letters, there are many great books or great plays that don't advocate. That doesn't mean that a man is a propagandist. It is in the nature of life, and it is in the nature of literature, that the passions of an author congeal around issues. You can go from *War and Peace* through all the great novels of time and they are all advocating something. Therefore, when I heard that the United States Government wanted to pass a law against the advocacy, without any overt action, I was alarmed. I am not here defending Communists, I am here defending the right of an author to advocate.

MR. SCHERER: Even to advocate the overthrow of this Government by force and violence?

MR. MILLER: I am now speaking, sir, of creative literature. These are risks and balances of risks.

MR. SCHERER: You understood, did you not, that the twelve Communists were prosecuted for advocating, teaching, and urging the overthrow of this Government by force and violence, through unlawful means? Now, my question is, Do you mean that you would be opposed to the prosecution of anyone today for advocating the overthrowing of this Government by force and violence? I cannot draw any other conclusion.

MR. MILLER: Mr. Scherer, there is another conclusion which I would like to speak on for just one moment. The Smith Act, as I understood it and as I understand it now, does lay penalties upon advocacy.

MR. SCHERER: Upon what?

MR. MILLER: Upon advocacy of beliefs or opinions, and so forth. What I felt strongly about then—

MR. SCHERER: Not opinions. It does not lay any upon opinions.

MR. MILLER: I am not that close to the text of it, but my understanding is that advocacy is penalized, or can be, under this law. Now, my interest, as I tell you, is possibly too selfish, but without it I can't operate, and neither can literature in this country, and I don't think anybody can question that.

MR. SCHERER: I am not asking you about advocacy generally.

MR. MILLER: But, sir, I understand your point.

MR. SCHERER: I do not understand yours.

MR. MILLER: If advocacy of itself becomes a crime or can be penalized without overt action, we are smack in the middle of literature, and I don't see how it can be avoided. That is my opinion. That is, where I can understand yours, I ask you to understand mine.

MR. SCHERER: Does your theory carry so far as for you to sit here today and say that you are opposed to prosecution of anyone who today would advocate, teach, and urge the overthrow of this Government by force and violence? Limiting it to that. Let us leave literature out of that.

MR. MILLER: If a man were outside this building and telling people to come in and storm this building and blow it up or something of that sort, I would say, "Call out the troops." There is no question in my mind about that. That is advocacy. But in the Smith Act, as I understand it, it is applicable to literature. Now, in my opinion, that cannot be equated with the freedom of literature, without which we will be back in a situation where people, as in the Soviet Union and as in Nazi Germany, have not got the right to advocate.

MR. SCHERER: Let us go into literature. Do you believe that, today, a Communist who is a poet should have the right to advocate the overthrow of this Government by force and violence? In his literature, in poetry, or in newspapers or anything else?

(*The witness confers with his counsel.*)

MR. MILLER: I tell you frankly, sir, I think, if you are talking about a poem, I would say that a man should have the right to write a poem just about anything.

MR. SCHERER: All right.

MR. JACKSON: Then I understand your position is that freedom in literature is absolute?

MR. MILLER: Well, I recognize that these things, sir, are not: the absolutes are not absolute.

MR. JACKSON: My interpretation of your position is that it is absolute that a writer must have, in order to express his heart, absolute freedom of action?

MR. MILLER: That would be the most desirable state of affairs, I say, yes.

MR. SCHERER: Even to the extent of advocating the violent overthrow of the Government of the United States at this time?

MR. MILLER: Frankly, sir, I have never read such a book.

MR. SCHERER: I did not say you have read it. I am asking you what your opinion is with reference to it.

MR. MILLER: I think that, once you start to cut away, there is a certain common sense in mankind which makes these limits automatic. There are risks which are balanced. The Constitution is full of those risks. We have rights, which, if they are violated, or rather used in an irresponsible way, can do damage. Yet they are there and the common sense of the people of the United States has kept this in sort of a balance. I would prefer any day to say, "Yes, there should be no limit upon the literary freedom," than to say, "You can go up this far and no farther," because then you are getting into an area where people are going to say, "I think that this goes over the line," and then you are in an area where there is no limit to the censorship that can take place.

MR. SCHERER: Do you consider those things that you have written in the *New Masses* as an exercise of your literary rights?

MR. MILLER: Sir, I never advocated the overthrow of the United States Government. I want that perfectly clear.

MR. SCHERER: I did not say you did. I want to get what you consider literature.

MR. MILLER: I did not advocate that. I wouldn't call it especially an exercise in freedom. It was simply an effusion of mind. It didn't require a mandate to do it. The *Masses* was widely circulated. Writers were writing for it. Some of the greatest writers today have written for the *New Masses*.

MR. SCHERER: Then you believe that we should allow the Communists in this country to start actually physical violence in the overthrow of this Government before they are prosecuted?

MR. MILLER: No, sir. You are importing.

MR. SCHERER: I cannot draw any other conclusion from what you said.

MR. MILLER: You fail to draw a line between advocacy and essence. Our law is based upon acts, not thought. How do we know? Anybody in this room might have thoughts of various kinds that could be prosecuted if they were carried into action.

MR. VELDE: Are you opposed to the Smith Act? Would you advocate its repeal?

MR. MILLER: Sir, I have not got the Smith Act in front of me. I could tell you my sentiment as it relates to the Smith Act. I am opposed to the laying down of any limits upon the freedom of literature, and I am opposed to it because I think that that way lies a kind of repression of literature which is disastrous. In the Sovet Union there has been nothing written of any value in twenty-five years.

MR. VELDE: I understand. You have a perfect right to advocate the repeal of the Smith Act if you want to.

MR. MILLER: I am just making one mitigation. I don't know the Smith

Act well enough for me to sit here under oath and say that I am opposed to every single word of it. I couldn't do that because I don't believe I have ever read the thing. All I know is that that provision, according to the widest publication of the press, is in it, and I would be opposed to that provision.

MR. VELDE: In any event, Mr. Miller, you have not had a change of heart since 1947, during the trial of the twelve Communists?

MR. MILLER: In relation to censorship, I have always had the same opinion.

MR. SCHERER: This is not censorship.

MR. MILLER: Perhaps I used the word closely [loosely?], but in relation to the limitation of the artist's right in society, I am opposed to it.

MR. SCHERER: All of us believe in freedom.

MR. KEARNEY: You are putting the artist and literature in a preferred class.

MR. MILLER: I thought we were going to get to this, and it places me in a slightly impossible position. I would be lying to you if I said that I didn't think the artist was, to a certain degree, in a special class. The reason is quite simple and maybe absurd, but, if you are asking me what I think, I will tell you. Most of us are occupied most of the day in earning a living in one way or another. The artist is a peculiar man in one respect. He has got a peculiar mandate in the history of civilization from people: he has a mandate not only in his literature but in the way he behaves and the way he lives.

MR. SCHERER: He has special rights?

MR. MILLER: I am not speaking of rights.

MR. KEARNEY: I would like to have the question I asked answered.

THE CHAIRMAN: He is trying to answer.

MR. KEARNEY: There are interruptions.

MR. MILLER: The artist is inclined to use certain rights more than other people because of the nature of his work. Most of us may have an opinion. We may have a view of life which on a rare occasion we have time to speak of. That is the artist's line of work. That is what he does all day long and, consequently, he is particularly sensitive to its limitations.

MR. KEARNEY: In other words, your thought, as I get it, is that the artist lives in a different world from anyone else.

MR. MILLER: No, he doesn't, but there is a conflict, I admit. I think there is an old conflict that goes back to Socrates between the man who is involved with ideal things and the man who has the terrible responsibility of keeping things going as they are, and protecting the state and keeping an army and getting people fed.

MR. ARENS: Did you, in 1949 in June, participate in a call for a conference on civil liberties, civil rights, to be held in the Henry Hudson Hotel in New York City?

MR. MILLER: Could I see that?

MR. ARENS: Yes, I lay before you this call to a conference which, among other things, charges the FBI with being peeping Toms and using paid informers and going into every lodge, home, church, political meeting, and labor organization; something has to be done about it, so you have a call to conference in New York City in 1949. Do you recall that? The name Arthur Miller appears there as one of those who is attacking the FBI.

MR. MILLER: I wouldn't deny having done this.

MR. ARENS: Do you recall attending the conference?

MR. MILLER: I don't believe I did, sir.

MR. ARENS: At the conference, according to the *New York Times,* there was a resolution introduced for the purpose of defending all the victims of the Smith Act about which we have been talking, but the conference decided it would not defend all the victims of the Smith Act: it would not defend the Trotskyites. According to this article, Paul Robeson, who was there, said:

> In speaking for denial of civil liberties to the Socialist Workers Party, Mr. Robeson asked the conference, "Would you give civil rights to the Ku Klux Klan?"
>
> "No," chorused the delegates.
>
> "These men are the allies of fascism who want to destroy the new democracies of the world," the singer shouted. "Let's not get confused. They are the enemies of the working class."

According to this article in the *New York Times,* July 18, 1949, this conference in which you participated—or to which you lent your name—would deny civil liberties to the Trotskyites, although they would give them to Communists. Did you protest this position?

MR. MILLER: Well, I didn't protest, but I was very put out that anyone who had been prosecuted in that sort of way should not be defended.

MR. ARENS: Were you present at the session?

MR. MILLER: I don't believe so, sir.

MR. ARENS: Did you remonstrate with the leadership of this Civil Rights Congress?

MR. MILLER: I did not know about this position at the time, because of a general lapse of interest in what was going on, but I would see the degree of responsibility that is implied in my signing that thing, and I think it was wrong. I think that the Trotskyites or anybody else who suffered the penalties should be defended.

MR. ARENS: Did you learn of the position of this Civil Rights Congress that civil rights are for everybody, including the Communists, but not for Trotskyites?

MR. MILLER: I couldn't recall that. I think I have set forth my position on that.

MR. ARENS: Did you learn of the attacks by the Civil Rights Congress on the Federal Bureau of Investigation as Fascism, American style?

MR. MILLER: I don't recall anything of that kind.

MR. ARENS: Now, did you know a man by the name of Kazan?

MR. MILLER: I did.

MR. ARENS: What was your relationship with Mr. Kazan?

MR. MILLER: He was the director of two of my plays.

MR. ARENS: And was he subsequently exposed as a Communist?

MR. MILLER: I believe so, yes.

MR. ARENS: And did he subsequently testify and admit that he had been a Communist? And identified, before an agency of his Government, people whom he had known as members of the conspiracy?

MR. MILLER: Yes.

MR. ARENS: And did you then in 1953 criticize Mr. Kazan as a renegade intellectual?

MR. MILLER: No.

MR. ARENS: As an informer?

MR. MILLER: No.

MR. ARENS: Did you protest the position of Kazan when he testified before his Government and said, in effect, he had been a Communist, and identified people as Communists?

MR. MILLER: I have never made a statement about Elia Kazan's testimony in my life.

MR. ARENS: Did you, at any time, to any person, level a criticism at Kazan because of his testimony before a Committee in which he identified people as Communists?

MR. MILLER: I didn't know what his testimony was exactly, but I have discussed him with one or two people in my life.

MR. ARENS: After Kazan had been your producer, worked with you in your plays, and came down to Washington and testified before a Congressional Committee, "Yes, I have been a Communist. Yes, I identify so-and-so and so-and-so as people who were in the conspiracy with me," did you criticize him for that position? Did you break with him?

MR. MILLER: Are you asking me whether I broke with him? Is that the question?

MR. ARENS: The question is pretty clear, I believe. What was your position with reference to Kazan after he testified before a Congressional Committee?

MR. MILLER: You are putting two things together.

MR. ARENS: Take them one by one, any way you want to.

MR. MILLER: The fact is I "broke" with him, although that word is not descriptive of my act.

MR. ARENS: We will use the word "disassociate," then.

MR. MILLER: I am not at all certain that Mr. Kazan would have directed my next play in any case. I am not one to go about in the streets proclaiming my private business, and the public or whoever is interested would not know that perhaps other elements had come into this situation which have absolutely no political interest, and I would venture to say have no interest for this Committee. The fact is that he did not direct any more of my plays. It may be in the future he will. I have said that in the *New York Post,* I believe. I hesitate to take the brunt of this kind of characterization, so to speak—not really for political reasons but because there are private reasons involved which I don't believe are of interest here.

MR. DOYLE: Mr. Chairman, may I interrupt? I do not think we should take the time of this Committee to have this witness put in a position where he tells about his private business.

THE CHAIRMAN: Well, of course not. He is volunteering this statement.

MR. DOYLE: I do not think we should let him volunteer these confidential matters of his business and profession. They are not a concern of this Committee.

THE CHAIRMAN: That is right.

MR. DOYLE: I object to that procedure. I do not think we have any business leaving this witness in that position.

THE CHAIRMAN: There is no disposition to do that.

MR. DOYLE: Let us stop it then and go to the issue.

THE CHAIRMAN: All right. Answer the question.

MR. ARENS: The question is, Did you attack Kazan because he broke with the Communist Party and testified before a Congressional Committee?

MR. MILLER: I stated earlier, sir, that I have never attacked Kazan. I will stand on that. That is it.

MR. ARENS: That is the answer, then. Did you join with others in protesting the enactment of the Internal Security Act in 1950?

MR. MILLER: I don't even remember what the act was, to tell you the truth, and I am not prepared to deny or affirm it. You will have to show it to me. If it seems familiar, I will identify it.

MR. ARENS: Were you an initiating sponsor of an emergency defense conference held in New York City in 1952 for the purpose of protesting the enforcement of the Internal Security Act?

MR. MILLER: I have no recollection of it whatever.

MR. ARENS: Now, do you recall in 1948 the proposed visit of the Red Dean of Canterbury to the United States and any participation you may have had as a part of the welcoming committee?

MR. MILLER: I don't [recall], but I probably did it.

MR. ARENS: Were you a member of the National Council of Arts, Sciences, and Professions?

MR. MILLER: Yes.

Mr. Arens: Did you know at the time of its Communist control and leadership?

Mr. Miller: Well, I suspected that the Communists were in control of it. I couldn't say that I knew it.

Mr. Arens: Excuse me. Did you protest at any time the control of the organization by the Communist Party?

Mr. Miller: In itself as such, no, but I did have actually no contact with these people excepting as I was being circulated for my name and various things and my participation in the Waldorf Peace Conference. Beyond that, I don't recall having any business with them. I would have from time to time, perhaps, taken issue on some particular thing with some person or other, but I wouldn't have lodged a formal protest.

Mr. Arens: Did you lend your name as a sponsor of the peace parleys of the World Congress for Peace held in Paris?

Mr. Miller: I don't believe that that is accurate. It is the only one that I actually believe I had nothing to do with.

Mr. Arens: I lay before you now a photostatic copy of that organization, World Congress for Peace, to be held in Paris. Among the sponsors listed, there is a person by the name of Arthur Miller. I ask you whether or not you have a recollection of that?

Mr. Miller: The reason that I doubt this: Where something was going to be carried into the international sphere I was loath, and I think there is no case that I was ready to support criticism of this country abroad. I want to just amplify that for one second. It is very important to me because it does make a difference. This is involved in this, because it is an international thing, and it is usable in Europe. After the denial of my passport by the State Department, I was literally besieged by foreign newspapermen. As far as I know, they were all from non-Communist [countries] and most of them in the country I know [a] little about, France. They were from the rightist press and from the center press. They were after me to the point where I had to go to my home in Roxbury and hide out there because they wanted me to carry on a fight in the European press against the United States. I refused to do it and I refused to do it for a good reason, and that is that, whatever I may have supported and however it looks, I do draw a line between criticism of the United States in the United States and before foreigners.

The Chairman: Do I understand that representatives of the foreign press tried to prevail upon you to attack your Government for publicity purposes in the nations they came from?

Mr. Miller: Sir?

The Chairman: Are those people still employed in this country?

Mr. Miller: I would have no way of knowing. The statement is slightly extreme, sir, as compared to the facts. I don't think it needs me to say that the passport-denial business is widely publicized in Europe, and many of these people feel disabled in the face of the Communist mockery of democratic institutions when they try to defend this, and many of them feel, I am sure, that it is an unwise policy in many cases, especially someone—not only in my case, but I think there was a question of a visa for Graham Greene once.

THE CHAIRMAN: I am talking about a particular thing because I think that those people ought not to be permitted to work in this country.

MR. MILLER: I am just telling you what I know. That is that they were eager—as a matter of fact, the brunt of their tone and of their method of talking to me on the telephone was—to aggravate this thing into an international issue of sorts, and I refused to do it because I don't believe that anybody in Europe has got anything to teach us in that regard, and it would have been a dishonest thing for me to have done. I felt very deeply about it. I felt very hurt about it, because I believe I am a good representative of this country abroad and my plays are shown everywhere where there is a theater abroad.

MR. ARENS: Do you have that position with respect to Red China?

MR. MILLER: What position?

MR. ARENS: The position that you did not want to participate in anything affecting international relations.

MR. MILLER: No. In the last few years I would not participate in anything that was a Communist front of any kind.

MR. ARENS: Did you participate in a movement to embrace Red China by this country?

MR. MILLER: I recall nothing of the kind.

MR. ARENS: I lay before you a photostatic copy of a document called "Far East Spotlight for Friendship with New China," calling for friendship cargoes to "New China," a launching dinner; and the sponsors of the dinner, or those who sent personal messages of support, included one Arthur Miller. I ask you if that refreshes your recollection.

MR. MILLER: This was, as it says here, "The China Welfare Appeal, a new relief drive to aid the Chinese people." It was headed up by Madame Sun Yat-sen, widow of the founder of the Chinese Republic. My recollection of this would be that, on the basis of its relief, which is not what I was talking about a moment ago at all, I would have supported it.

MR. VELDE: What was the date of that?

MR. ARENS: May 1949. Did you support the China Welfare Appeal in the propaganda statement which they issued over the country:

> Not only has the export of medical supplies from the United States been made subject to burdensome restrictions and procedures, but a virtual embargo has been placed on all shipments to China. The history of such restrictions shows that they did not begin with recent events in Korea

I lay before you a photostatic copy of a letter on the letterhead of the China Welfare Appeal, and ask you whether or not, although your name appears here on the letterhead, you lent yourself knowingly to that cause and movement?

MR. MILLER: You say my name does appear on the letter?

MR. ARENS: This is the reverse page. It had to be photostated on both sides. The name of Arthur Miller appears there.

MR. MILLER: It is the China Welfare Appeal. As I recall, there was a need for medicines and penicillin, et cetera, which they weren't permitted to buy, or something of that sort. I did support this.

MR. ARENS: Did you also support the Joint Anti-Fascist Refugee Committee in the Spanish Refugee Appeal, for which funds were solicited and transmitted to the Communists in Spain in 1949 and again in 1951?

MR. MILLER: This is not in mitigation of these other things. I think the Spanish case is quite different, however. I have always been, since my student days, in the thirties, a partisan of republican Spain. I am quite proud of it. I think a democracy was destroyed there. I would have carried through pretty generally my feelings of the thirties into the forties, as regards the Spanish Civil War refugees.

MR. ARENS: Now, do you recall, in view of your observations respecting your plays' being played abroad, coauthoring a play *Listen My Children*?

MR. MILLER: Coauthoring a play?

MR. ARENS: Yes, sir.

MR. MILLER: No, I don't.

MR. ARENS: Or do you recall authoring a play *Listen My Children*?

MR. MILLER: What year would this have been?

MR. ARENS: 1939.

MR. MILLER: 1939?

MR. ARENS: Yes, sir, with Norman Rosten?

MR. MILLER: Oh, yes. Yes, I do.

MR. ARENS: I lay before you now an original document in handwriting which we procured from the Library of Congress as the document there for the purpose of copyright. Could you tell us whether that is your handwriting or Rosten's?

MR. MILLER: It isn't mine.

MR. ARENS: Did you coauthor with Rosten this play?

MR. MILLER: I did. My recollection is clear now. I wrote a sketch about when I had been on relief in—well, when I got out of college.

MR. DOYLE: What year was that that you got out of college?

MR. MILLER: I graduated in June 1938. And I subsequently got on to the Federal Writers, Federal Theater Project, and I wrote a farcical sort of a play about standing and waiting in a relief office. And that was, I think, what you are referring to. It was a one-act sketch, which was later amplified. Nothing ever came of it, I am glad to say.

MR. ARENS: Did you know that Norman Rosten was a Communist when you collaborated with him in the play *Listen My Children*?

MR. MILLER: I wouldn't know anything about that.

MR. ARENS: In 1936 he was publicly identified in the *Daily Worker* as a member of the Young Communist League.

MR. MILLER: I wouldn't make a comment about that. I wouldn't know anything about it. I would be inclined strongly to say that it wasn't true.

MR. ARENS: Let me lay before you a photostatic copy of the Communist *Daily Worker* of December 10, 1936, a public proclamation.

MR. MILLER: I can't prove as to whether he was a Communist or not. It is impossible.

MR. ARENS: I asked if you knew. If you do not know, that is the answer.

MR. MILLER: By the way, I would add that that doesn't mean he was a Communist, does it?

MR. ARENS: If he was a member of the Young Communist League?

MR. MILLER: I am just asking a question.

MR. ARENS: Did *Listen My Children* pertain to Congressional investigating committees?

MR. MILLER: If it did, then it is not what I am talking about. What I am talking about is another thing. This is a long time ago.

MR. ARENS: Let me read:

> Curtain slowly opens. The committee members are engaged in activity of an extraordinary variety, amid an equally extraordinary environment. Profuse flag bunting over the walls. There are several huge clocks ticking ominously. Also a metronome which is continually being adjusted for tempo change. Secretary, at desk, pounds typewriter and, as alarm clock rings, she feeds the committeemen spoonsful of castor oil. . . . In center of room, in rocker, sits a man. He is securely tied to chair, with a gag in his mouth and a bandage tied over his mouth. Water, coming from a pipe near ceiling, trickles on his head. Nearby is a charcoal stove holding branding irons. Two bloodhounds are tied in the corner of the room.

Was that the play that you coauthored with Norman Rosten? Is that an accurate description of the play *Listen My Children*?

MR. MILLER: I would say that I find it amusing. I don't see what is so horrific about that. I think it is a farce. I don't think anybody would take it seriously.

THE CHAIRMAN: It is a little corny.

MR. MILLER: I was not, by the way, the author of that scene. I am saying this out of a kind of professional jealousy.

MR. ARENS: Was it likewise just a little farce, your play *You're Next,* by Arthur Miller, attacking the House Committee on Un-American Activities?

MR. MILLER: No, that would have been quite serious.

MR. ARENS: Did you know that the play *You're Next,* by Arthur Miller, attacking Congressional investigating committees, was reproduced by the Communist Party?

MR. MILLER: No, I have no knowledge of it.

MR. ARENS: I lay before you now a photostatic copy of the Communist *Daily Worker* of New York, Wednesday, June 18, 1947: "New York State Communist Party Building Congress—program—including *You're Next,* by Arthur Miller."

MR. MILLER: Sir, you can't tax me with that.

MR. ARENS: I ask you only whether or not you knew it, sir.

MR. MILLER: I did not know it, and I say that you can't tax me with that. My plays have gone all over the world, by all kinds of people, including the Spanish government theater, where *Death of a Salesman* has run longer than any modern play in history. I take no more responsibility for who plays my plays than General Motors can take for who rides in their Chevrolets.

MR. SCHERER: Before the Communist Party would use such a play it had to follow the Communist line?

MR. MILLER: Nothing in my life was ever written to follow a line. I will go into that, if you will.

MR. ARENS: In view of your observations respecting your plays abroad, did you donate the rights of your play *All My Sons* to the Polish League in Poland?

MR. MILLER: Polish League of what?

MR. ARENS: League of Women in Poland, in 1947, September.

MR. MILLER: I don't remember it, but you can't get any money out of Poland, and you can't get any money out of Russia, and you can't get any money out of any place on the other side of the Iron Curtain. It is quite possible—I have no recollection of it at all—that they simply took the royalties that were probably not even there and applied them to this fund. I have no communication, to my knowledge, from anybody.

MR. DOYLE: May I ask whether there is an identification of that? The Polish League of Women is a Communist organization?

MR. ARENS: Yes, sir, a branch of the Congress of American Women. I should like, if you please, sir, if it would refresh your recollection, to read you an article appearing in the *Daily Worker,* September 29, 1947.

MR. MILLER: You say the Congress of American Women. Yes, they asked me to do this on the basis of a relief drive that they were having for the Polish children.

MR. ARENS: Then you have a recollection of donating the royalties of your play?

MR. MILLER: I just said so, sir.

MR. ARENS: Are you cognizant of the fact that your play *The Crucible,* with respect to witch hunts in 1692, was the case history [*sic*] of a series of articles in the Communist press drawing parallels to the investigations of Communists and other subversives by Congressional Committees?

MR. MILLER: The comparison is inevitable, sir.

MR. ARENS: What have been your activities or associations with Howard Fast?

MR. MILLER: In what respect?

MR. ARENS: Do you know him?

MR. MILLER: I have met him.

MR. ARENS: How long do you know him?

MR. MILLER: I don't know how to describe that.

MR. ARENS: Well, have you collaborated with him?

MR. MILLER: No, sir.

MR. ARENS: Are you cognizant of the promotion of yourself by Howard Fast?

MR. MILLER: No.

MR. ARENS: I lay before you a copy of the Communist *Daily Worker* of November 8, 1955, "I Propose Arthur Miller as the American Dramatist of the Day" by Howard Fast.

MR. MILLER: The appreciation of dramatic values by people who have behind them a remorseless attachment to the political line is of no import to me. I don't believe it when they are against me, and I don't believe it when they are for me. In this case, I take no compliment out of this. It happens that *The Crucible,* which, by the way, I began thinking about in 1938, and which they now say was written about the Rosenbergs, about whom I had not heard when I started to write this play—it happened that the "line" in that play coincided at that moment. I have another example of that, which I will go into. This is not literary or dramatic criticism. This is a political article. You are taxing me with what he says. Now, the next play—as with *Death of a Salesman,* which they called "a decadent piece of trash" in the *Daily Worker*—they were against it. I am not going to guide myself by what they think or don't think. From time to time I am sure Howard Fast or similar critics of plays have praised or blamed one or another of a hundred writers, all of whom you can't tax with that criticism. It isn't fair.

MR. ARENS: Now, your present application for a passport, pending in the Department of State, is for the purpose of traveling to England, is that correct?

MR. MILLER: To England, yes.

MR. ARENS: What is the objective?

MR. MILLER: The objective is double. I have a production which is in the talking stage in England of *A View from the Bridge,* and I will be there to be with the woman who will then be my wife.* That is my aim.

MR. ARENS: Have you had difficulty in connection with your play *A View from the Bridge* in its presentation in England?

MR. MILLER: It has not got that far. I have had the censor in England giving us a little trouble, yes, but that is general. A lot of American plays have that difficulty.

MR. ARENS: Do you know a person by the name of Sue Warren?

MR. MILLER: I couldn't recall at this moment.

MR. ARENS: Do you know or have you known a person by the name of Arnaud d'Usseau?

MR. MILLER: I have met him.

MR. ARENS: What has been the nature of your activity in connection with Arnaud d'Usseau?

MR. MILLER: Just what is the point?

MR. ARENS: Have you been in any Communist Party sessions with Arnaud d'Usseau?

MR. MILLER: I was present at meetings of Communist Party writers in 1947, about five or six meetings.

MR. ARENS: Where were those meetings held?

MR. MILLER: They were held in someone's apartment. I don't know whose it was.

MR. ARENS: Were those closed Party meetings?

MR. MILLER: I wouldn't be able to tell you that.

MR. ARENS: Was anyone there who, to your knowledge, was not a Communist?

MR. MILLER: I wouldn't know that.

MR. ARENS: Have you ever made application for membership in the Communist Party?

MR. MILLER: In 1939, I believe it was, or in 1940, I went to attend a Marxist study course in the vacant store open to the street in my neighborhood in Brooklyn. I there signed some form or another.

MR. ARENS: That was an application for membership in the Communist Party, was it not?

MR. MILLER: I would not say that. I am here to tell you what I know.

MR. ARENS: Tell us what you know.

MR. MILLER: This is now sixteen years ago. That is half a lifetime away. I don't recall, and I haven't been able to recall and, if I could, I would tell you the exact nature of that application. I understood then that this was to be, as I have said, a study course. I was there for about three or four times, perhaps. It was of no interest to me and I didn't return.

MR. ARENS: Who invited you to attend?

MR. MILLER: I wouldn't remember. It was a long time ago.

* Marilyn Monroe. —E.B.

MR. ARENS: Tell us, if you please, sir, about these meetings with the Communist Party writers which you said you attended in New York City.

MR. MILLER: I was by then a well-known writer. I had written *All My Sons* and a novel, *Focus,* and a book of reportage about Ernie Pyle and my work with him in attempting to make the picture *The Story of GI Joe*. I did the research for that, so that by that time I was quite well known, and I attended these meetings in order to locate my ideas in relation to Marxism, because I had been assailed for years by all kinds of interpretations of what Communism was, what Marxism was, and I went there to discover where I stood finally and completely. And I listened and said very little, I think, the four or five times.

MR. ARENS: What occasioned your presence? Who invited you there?

MR. MILLER: I couldn't tell you. I don't know.

MR. ARENS: Can you tell us who was there when you walked into the room?

MR. MILLER: Mr. Chairman, I understand the philosophy behind this question and I want you to understand mine. When I say this, I want you to understand that I am not protecting the Communists or the Communist Party. I am trying to, and I will, protect my sense of myself. I could not use the name of another person and bring trouble on him. These were writers, poets, as far as I could see, and the life of a writer, despite what it sometimes seems, is pretty tough. I wouldn't make it any tougher for anybody. I ask you not to ask me that question.

(*The witness confers with his counsel.*)

I will tell you anything about myself, as I have.

MR. ARENS: These were Communist Party meetings, were they not?

MR. MILLER: I will be perfectly frank with you in anything relating to my activities. I take the responsibility for everything I have ever done, but I cannot take responsibility for another human being.

MR. ARENS: This record shows, does it not, Mr. Miller, that these were Communist Party meetings?

(*The witness confers with his counsel.*)

MR. ARENS: Is that correct?

MR. MILLER: I understood them to be Communist writers who were meeting regularly.

MR. ARENS: Mr. Chairman, I respectfully suggest that the witness be ordered and directed to answer the question as to who it was that he saw at these meetings.

MR. JACKSON: May I say that moral scruples, however laudable, do not constitute legal reason for refusing to answer the question. I certainly endorse the request for direction.

THE CHAIRMAN: You are directed to answer the question, Mr. Miller.

MR. MILLER: May I confer with my attorney for a moment?

(*The witness confers with his counsel.*)

MR. MILLER: Mr. Walter, could I ask you to postpone this question until the testimony is completed and you can gauge for yourself?

THE CHAIRMAN: Of course, you can do that, but I understand this *is* about the end of the hearing.

MR. ARENS: This is about the end of the hearing. We have only a few more questions. The record reflects that this witness has identified these meetings as the meetings of the Communist writers. In the jurisdiction of this Committee he has been requested to tell this Committee who were in attendance at these meetings.

MR. DOYLE: If I understand the record, the record shows that he answered that he did not know whether there were any non-Communists there, or not.

MR. MILLER: I would like to add, sir, to complete this picture, that I decided in the course of these meetings that I had finally to find out what my views really were in relation to theirs, and I decided that I would write a paper in which, for the first time in my life, I would set forth my views on art, on the relation of art to politics, on the relation of the artist to politics, which are subjects that are very important to me. And I did so, and I read this paper to the group and I discovered, as I read it and certainly by the time I had finished with it, that I had no real basis in common either philosophically or, most important to me, as a dramatist. The most important thing to me in the world is my work, and I was resolved that, if I found that I was in fact a Marxist, I would declare it, and that, if I did not, I would say that I was not, and I wrote a paper, and I would like to give you the brunt of it so that you may know me.

THE CHAIRMAN: Have you got the paper?

MR. MILLER: I think it is the best essay I ever wrote, and I have never been able to find it in the last two or three years. I wish I could. I would publish it, as I recall it, because it meant so much to me. It was this: that great art, like science, attempts to see the present remorselessly and truthfully; that, if Marxism is what it claims to be, a science of society, it must be devoted to the objective facts more than all the philosophies that it attacks as being untruthful; therefore, the first job of a Marxist writer is to tell the truth, and, if the truth is opposed to what he thinks it ought to be, he must still tell it, because that is the stretching and the straining that every science and every art that is worth its salt must go through. I found that there was a dumb silence because it seemed not only that it was non-Marxist, which it was, but that it was a perfectly idealistic position—namely, that, first of all, the artist is capable of seeing the facts, and, secondly, what are you going to do when you see the facts and they are really opposed to the line? The real Marxist writer has to turn those facts around to fit that line. I could never do that. I have not done it. I want to raise another point here: I wrote a play called *All My Sons,* which was attacked as a Communist play. This is an example of something you raised just a little while earlier about the use of my play in the Communist meeting—a different sketch that I had written. I started that play when the war was on. The Communist line during the war was that capitalists were the salt of the earth just like workers, that there would never be a strike again, that we were going to go hand in hand down the road in the future. I wrote my play *All My Sons* in the midst of this period. The story is the story of an airplane-parts manufacturer who sends out faulty parts to the Air Force. Therefore, what happened was that the war ended before I could get the play produced. The Communist line changed back to an attack on capitalists, and here I am being praised by the Communist press as having written a perfectly fine Communist play. Had the play opened when it was supposed to have opened, it would have been attacked as an anti-Communist play. The same thing happened with *Salesman*. *Death of a Salesman* in New York was condemned by the Communist press.

MR. SCHERER: There is a question before the witness—namely, to give the names of those individuals who were present at this Communist Party meeting. There is a direction on the part of the Chairman to answer that question. Now, so that the record may be clear, I think we should say to the witness, Witness, would you listen?

MR. MILLER: Yes.

MR. SCHERER: We do not accept the reasons you gave for refusing to answer the question, and it is the opinion of the Committee that, if you do not answer the question, you are placing yourself in contempt.

(*The witness confers with his counsel.*)

MR. SCHERER: That is an admonition that this Committee must give you in compliance with the decisions of the Supreme Court. Now, Mr. Chairman, I ask that you again direct the witness to answer the question.

THE CHAIRMAN: He has been directed to answer the question, and he gave us an answer that we just do not accept.

MR. ARENS: Was Arnaud d'Usseau chairman at this meeting of Communist Party writers which took place in 1947 at which you were in attendance?

MR. MILLER: All I can, sir, is that my conscience will not permit me to use the name of another person.

(*The witness confers with his counsel.*)

And that my counsel advises me that there is no relevance between this question and the question of whether I should have a passport or there should be passport legislation in 1956.

MR. ARENS: Mr. Chairman, I respectfully suggest that the witness be ordered and directed to answer the question as to whether or not Arnaud d'Usseau was chairman of the meeting of the Communist Party writers in New York City in 1947 at which you were in attendance.

THE CHAIRMAN: You are directed to answer the question.

MR. MILLER: I have given you my answer, sir.

MR. ARENS: I ask you now, sir, whether or not Sue Warren was in attendance at this meeting of the Communist Party writers held in New York City in 1947?

MR. MILLER: I have given you my answer.

MR. VELDE: Do you know Sue Warren?

MR. JACKSON: Did you decline to answer the question?

(*The witness confers with his counsel.*)

MR. MILLER: I tell you, sir, that I have given my answer.

MR. JACKSON: I am not satisfied with that. That is entirely too vague. What I want is a positive statement as to whether or not you will answer that question.

(*The witness confers with his counsel.*)

MR. MILLER: Sir, I believe I have given you the answer that I must give.

THE CHAIRMAN: Let us get that straight. As I understand, you decline to answer the question for the reason that you gave when you declined to answer the first question, or at least when you gave an answer that was not deemed acceptable, is that it?

MR. MILLER: That is correct.

MR. ARENS: Were you proposed for membership in the Stuyvesant Branch, 12th Assembly District, of the Communist Party by Sue Warren in 1943?

MR. MILLER: To my knowledge, I would not know that. I would have no knowledge of it.

MR. ARENS: Have you made application for membership in the Communist Party?

MR. MILLER: I answered that question.

MR. ARENS: I put it to you as a fact and ask you to affirm or deny the fact that you did make application for membership in the Communist Party and that the number of your application is 23345.

MR. MILLER: I would not affirm that. I have no memory of such a thing.

MR. ARENS: Do you deny it?

MR. MILLER: I would deny it.

MR. VELDE: I would just like one question. We mentioned Norman Rosten a while ago, with whom you collaborated in a play in 1938, I believe it was. Do you know where he is today?

MR. MILLER: He is in New York City.

MR. VELDE: Do you have any contacts with him at the present time?

MR. MILLER: Yes.

MR. VELDE: Are you engaged in any business with him?

MR. MILLER: No, he is a writer. I know him.

MR. DOYLE: Why do you not direct some of that magnificent ability you have to fighting against well-known Communist subversive conspiracies in our country and in the world? Why do you not direct your magnificent talents to that, in part? I mean more positively?

MR. MILLER: Yes, I think it would be a disaster and a calamity if the Communist Party ever took over this country. That is an opinion that has come to me not out of the blue sky but out of long thought. I tell you further that I have been trying for years now. I am not a fictionalist. I reflect what my heart tells me from the society around me. We are living in a time when there is great uncertainty in this country. It is not a Communist idea: you just pick up a book-review section and you will see everybody selling books on peace of mind, because there isn't any. I am trying to delve to the bottom of this, and come up with a positive answer, and I have had to go to hell to meet the devil. You can't know what the worst is until you have seen the worst, and it is not for me to make easy answers and to come forth before the American people and tell them everything is all right, when I look in their eyes and I see them troubled. I believe in democracy. I believe it is the only way for myself and for anybody that I care about; it is the only way to live; but my criticism, such as it has been, is not to be confused with a hatred. I love this country, I think, as much as any man, and it is because I see things that I think traduce certainly the values that have been in this country that I speak. I would like more than anything else in the world to make positive my plays, and I intend to do so before I finish. It has to be on the basis of reality.

THE CHAIRMAN: Mr. Miller, I trust that you will raise your important voice in what must be apparent to you now as a conspiracy. I am frank to admit that I participated in some [activities] myself: I remember making a rather sizable contribution to this Anti-Fascist Committee because they were moving Jews away from Germany, and I know that a great many other people did. But it is significant that, in all of these causes in which you participated because of the persecution of the Jewish people, you never moved toward the assistance of people who were being persecuted by the Communists. That, I think, is very unfortunate.

MR. MILLER: I think it is not only unfortunate, it was a great error. In the face of an overwhelming ideal it has been the common experience of mankind, both good people and bad people, that detail [the ideal?] goes by the board and fades into the walls. I believe now in facts. I look at life to see what is happening, and I have no line. I have no preconception. I am devoted to what is going on. The hardest thing to do is to tell what is going on. It is easy to talk about the past and future, but nobody knows what is happening now.

MR. KEARNEY: Do you consider yourself more or less of a dupe in joining these Communist organizations?

MR. MILLER: I wouldn't say so, because I was an adult, I wasn't a child. I was looking for the [a?] world that would be perfect. I think it necessary that I do that, if I were to develop myself as a writer. I am not ashamed of this. I accept my life. That is what I have done. I learned a great deal.

THE CHAIRMAN: You have learned a great deal and made a greater contribution to what we think you now stand for than you realize, because, by the errors that you committed, you are serving a very loud note of warning to a lot of other people who might fall into what you did.

1957

"Communism in the Metropolitan Music School"

Earl Robinson's name links the later and earlier parts of the present book, for, though he was not called before HUAC till 1957, he had been at least twice mentioned in 1940 in Martin Dies' *Trojan Horse in America.* Asking, "What are some of the guiding principles by which anyone may be able to recognize a Communist Trojan Horse organization when he sees one?" Dies had given eighteen numbered replies of which number eleven was:

> Does the organization use for entertainment such well-known Communists or communist-controlled groups as Earl Robinson, TAC, and Freiheit Gesangs Verein? Does it popularize camps such as Unity and Beacon?

Wherein we learn that a man can be a group. Speaking, on a later page, of a political rally, Dies reports:

> Earl Robinson's chorus was also one of the attractions. Robinson's "Ballad for Americans" is an American version of the "Internationale," the international anthem of the Communist movement. Again and again the *Daily Worker* has analyzed "Ballad for Americans" to show how Robinson skillfully set the "class struggle" to new words and music. (The "Ballad" was used to open the recent Republican National Convention in Philadelphia.)

"Ballad for Americans" provides a link not only to the 1940 Republican Convention, but also to Paul Robeson, whose recording of it around that time has been preserved for us by Vanguard Records (VSD–79193), and, further, to the Federal Theater. The song derives from the final production of Federal Theater, a musical entitled *Sing for Your Supper,* which had HUAC much exercised because it was a long time (about a year) in the making and perhaps, too, because it was of collective authorship. Here is Hallie Flanagan's account from *Arena:*

> *Sing for Your Supper* reached its climax in "Ballad of Uncle Sam," which since that time, as "Ballad for Americans," has been performed under many circumstances; it was sung over a nation-wide hook-up by Paul Robeson, and C.B.S. was buried under an avalanche of letters saying, "This is the voice of America." It was sung by the Schola Cantorum in the Lewisohn Stadium in New York to the music of the Philharmonic Symphony Orchestra, and thousands of people rose and cheered. It was chosen as the theme song of the Republican National Convention in Philadelphia in 1940—probably without knowledge of its Federal Theater origin, or of the fact that Congressman [Clifton A.] Woodrum had said, "If there is a line or passage in it [*Sing for Your Supper*] that contributes to cultural or educational benefit or uplift of America, I will eat the whole manuscript." Yet it was never sung under circumstances more momentous to human beings than on the last night of the Federal Theater by the project that originated it. As the revue of Uncle Sam surveying his world reached its climax, the stage began to fill with "engineer, musician, street-cleaner" and "all the etceteras." Over the silent house the words of the questioner and the answers of the chorus took on an urgency. Did anyone believe in liberty in those days? No one did, and yet, "out of the . . . patriotic spouting" came our "marching song," as adopted unanimously in Congress, July 4, 1776: "We hold these truths to be self-evident: that all men are created equal, that they are endowed by their Creator with certain inalienable rights, that among these are life, liberty and the pursuit of happiness."
>
> Thus Federal Theater ended as it had begun, with fearless presentation of problems touching American life. If this first government theater in our country had been less alive it might have lived longer. But I do not believe anyone who worked on it regrets that it stood from first to last against reaction, against prejudice, against racial, religious, and political intolerance. It strove for a more dramatic statement and a better understanding of the great forces of our life today; it fought for a free theater as one of the many expressions of a civilized, informed, and vigorous life.
>
> Anyone who thinks that those things do not need fighting for today is out of touch with reality.

APRIL 11, 1957:

Earl Robinson

The Subcommittee of the Committee on Un-American Activities convened at 10 a.m., in room 35, United States Court House, Foley Square, New York, New York, the Honorable Morgan M. Moulder (Chairman) presiding.

Committee members present: Representatives Morgan M. Moulder, of Missouri; Clyde Doyle, of California; James B. Frazier, Jr., of Tennessee; and Robert J. McIntosh, of Michigan.

Staff members present: Richard Arens, Director; Dolores Scotti, Investigator; Frank Bonora, Acting Clerk.

MR. ARENS: Kindly identify yourself by name, residence, and occupation.

MR. ROBINSON: My name is Earl Robinson. I am, first of all, a composer of music. I compose songs, cantatas, orchestral work. I write music for the theater, ballet, and films, for Hollywood and here. Secondly, I am a singer, something of a performer. I have sung thousands of concerts all over America, Canada, everywhere from the big concert halls to the White House. Thirdly, I am a conductor. I have conducted everything from children's choruses of six years old up through the New York Philharmonic. Fourth and fifth, down the line, I am known as something of an authority on American folk music. I give lectures on American folk music and do research in that field.

MR. ARENS: You are appearing today, Mr. Robinson, in response to a subpoena which was served upon you by the House Un-American Activities Committee?

MR. ROBINSON: Yes.

MR. ARENS: And you are represented by counsel?

MR. ROBINSON: Yes, sir.

MR. ARENS: Counsel, will you kindly identify yourself?

MR. POPPER: Martin Popper.

MR. ARENS: Are you connected with the Metropolitan Music School, Mr. Robinson?

MR. ROBINSON: Yes, sir. I teach a children's chorus there at the present time.

MR. ARENS: Are you connected with People's Songs?

MR. ROBINSON: People's Songs, as far as I know, is out of existence. I was at one time.

MR. ARENS: You were on the board of directors of People's Songs, were you not?

MR. ROBINSON: If that is the way you have it, that is right, yes.

MR. ARENS: Did you author the publication "The Quiet Man from Kansas," in honor of Earl Browder?

(*The witness conferred with his counsel.*)

MR. ROBINSON: I am sorry, I will have to decline to answer this. I have a reason, which I hope you will listen to, because it is going to relate to any further questions of this nature. As a musician, I started out very, very early in the schools of Seattle, Washington, which is my home town, learning something about our Constitution, and I had to come home from the grade school at LaFayette, occasionally, to memorize things like the preamble from the Declaration of Independence, perhaps the First Amendment. As a little boy, these were big words and they didn't mean much to me, but my father took time out to explain some of the meaning back of things like "a more perfect Union, establish justice, insure domestic tranquillity," "Congress shall make no law," and so forth, "We, the people of the United States." These became, through my father's help, very, very important words—so important that, when I started really composing, I started setting a lot of them to music. The Declaration of Independence: "We hold these truths to be self-evident, that all men are created equal, that they are endowed by their Creator with certain *inalienable* rights"—that is a tough word to set to music, but it appears in my "Ballad for Americans."

MR. ARENS: Why did you, then, join an organization that was dedicated to the overthrow of the Constitution?

MR. POPPER: Why do you not let the witness finish?

MR. MOULDER: As I understand, he refused to answer the question, and he is now giving his reasons for refusing to answer.

MR. ROBINSON: I am trying to show that the Constitution meant enough to me that I set it to music. This has been my inspiration for my work from the very, very beginning, when I first started music, when I first graduated from the university, came to New York, and so forth. I have sung the First Amendment at concerts. This piece that I spoke about, the "Ballad for Americans," has several sections of the Constitution in it, to music. So it is precious to me; it is very, very precious. It so happens that I never have set the Fifth Amendment to music, the Sixth, or the Ninth, or Tenth, all of which I recognize as interesting and good ones, but I have made very many songs, and developed a twenty-minute cantata on Abraham Lincoln, out of the Thirteenth, Fourteenth, and Fifteenth Amendments, the struggle of the Negro people to be truly free and equal. I am working on an opera on this subject right now. Anyway, when I am called before an un-American committee—pardon me, before a Committee on Un-American Activities—I not only rely on my American rights under this Constitution, but when I feel I see any of this Constitution threatened—and I believe no matter how sincere you gentlemen are, you are deeply wrong with this kind of activity, calling up people and destroying in many, many—

MR. DOYLE: Mr. Chairman, I think that this gentleman has had plenty of time to read us a lecture—and then calling this Committee "an un-American committee," which he deliberately did. Let them confine themselves to plead their constitutional privilege, if that is what they want.

MR. MCINTOSH: Would you move along, then?

MR. ROBINSON: I feel that what I am doing is the same thing as President Eisenhower when he said, "I swear to preserve, protect, and defend the Constitution of the United States." I feel this is what I am doing in refusing to answer this kind of question, which moves into fields that bring me into disrepute, try to make me look like a subversive when I am not, when I am deeply American. So I will have to decline to answer.

MR. MOULDER: You decline to answer that, claiming your privilege under the First and Fifth Amendments of the Constitution?

MR. ROBINSON: All the amendments.

MR. ARENS: Did you join an organization dedicated to the destruction of the Constitution of the United States?

(*The witness conferred with his counsel.*)

MR. ROBINSON: No, not to my knowledge, I never did.

MR. ARENS: Did you join the Communist Party?

(*The witness conferred with his counsel.*)

MR. ARENS: I respectfully suggest that counsel be admonished that his sole and exclusive prerogative is to advise the witness of his constitutional rights, because I distinctly overheard counsel now telling the witness what to say. Now, sir, kindly tell the Committee: Did you join the Communist Party?

MR. MOULDER: Counsel has the right of advising and conferring with the witness under the rules of the Committee.

MR. POPPER: Thank you, Mr. Chairman.

MR. FRAZIER: The counsel did speak out so that everybody in the courtroom heard it.

MR. ARENS: I heard the counsel give him the answer.

MR. FRAZIER: And the witness put it in verbatim, word for word.

MR. ARENS: Did you join the Communist Party?

MR. ROBINSON: I clearly am not going to answer this kind of question under the same grounds as I said before.

MR. ARENS: In the Communist *Daily Worker* of March 30, 1953, we see an article about a memorial lauding Stalin's work for peace. There was a rally, the article tells us, which was held, a memorial to Joseph Stalin, hailing him not primarily as a leader of the Russian people, but as "Our Stalin." In the course of that rally, Earl Robinson's inspiring words were quoted: "Sleep well, beloved comrade; we pledge our bodies now. The fight will go on; the fight will go on until we win." Now look at this article, if you please, Mr. Robeson—

MR. ROBINSON: Robinson is the name.

MR. ARENS: Robeson recited. I am in error. Robeson recited Earl Robinson's words, and you are Earl Robinson, are you not?

MR. ROBINSON: That is right.

MR. ARENS: Were you in attendance when Robeson recited the words of yourself: "Sleep well, beloved comrade; we pledge our bodies now. The fight will go on; the fight will go on until we win." Kindly look at that article, if you will, sir, and tell this Committee whether those are the words of you, Earl Robinson, that are quoted by Robeson?

(*Witness conferred with his counsel.*)

MR. ROBINSON: No.

MR. ARENS: Were you in attendance at that meeting?

MR. ROBINSON: I don't remember. I really don't remember. I think probably I wasn't. I usually don't write words. I write music. This is poor research.

MR. DOYLE: Isn't that a photostat of an article in the Communist paper?

MR. ARENS: Yes.

MR. DOYLE: There is not very poor research on that, Mr. Robinson. It is pretty accurate. That is a photostat of an original document.

MR. ARENS: Are you connected, or have you been connected, with the National Council of American-Soviet Friendship?

(*Witness conferred with his counsel.*)

MR. ROBINSON: I decline to answer, sir. I notice John Cashmore on there. He maybe could afford to admit it.

* * *

MR. ARENS: Do you recall affixing your signature to an appeal requesting the then President of the United States to grant amnesty to the leaders of the Communist Party who had been convicted under the Smith Act in 1952?

MR. ROBINSON: Well, the truth is that I don't remember. I am sure that I must have, since you have a nice piece of paper there. I have given my name very, very often. Maybe in some cases too often. But I am opposed to the Smith Act. I think this is another act of Congress that has come out of this whole period of hysteria that is bad for America. If I signed it, I probably meant it.

MR. ARENS Perhaps this would refresh your recollection: We will display a photostatic reproduction of the Communist *Daily Worker* of December 10, 1952, in which your name appears as one of the signers of this appeal to which I have just alluded. Would you kindly look at that and see if that refreshes your recollection?

(*The witness conferred with his counsel.*)

MR. ROBINSON: I see I am in very good company: two hundred and eighty names.

MR. ARENS: Do you recall that incident?

MR. ROBINSON: I accept that as true. I accept that.

MR. ARENS: Tell us, if you please, how do you counterattack with art, counterattack against thought control?

(*Witness conferred with his counsel.*)

MR. ROBINSON: Could you make it more specific? I don't know what you are trying to talk about.

MR. ARENS: Yes, I will be specific. I have here a Thermofax reproduction of a bulletin, "Thought Control in U.S.A.," and at the back end of it, "Earl Robinson, composer," in which Robinson, the composer, calls upon people who read this to "Join the PCA. Counterattack with our art" against what is characterized here as thought control. I want you, a prominent musician, to tell this Committee, and via this Committee the United States Congress, how art is used to counterattack against what you have characterized as thought control. Kindly look at that document and see if it refreshes your recollection.

MR. DOYLE: As long as you have stated that you were and are opposed to the Smith Act, is the Internal Security Act included in that? How would you use art to counterattack against the Internal Security Act of our Nation?

(*The witness conferred with his counsel.*)

MR. ROBINSON: America has deep fountains of strength which grew out of our struggle as a nation to free ourselves, to develop the Constitution and the Bill of Rights. I believe this is a grand and a tremendous country. When I say the word "struggle," it is because things happened that need criticism, that need fixing. The Civil War was such a fixing. We have had a continuous history of this kind of thing. In my music, as a composer with a feeling for America, I try, wherever possible, and certainly quite often, to make the music serve America in a better way. I consider that this composition of mine, "Ballad for Americans," which I teach to my kids at the Metropolitan Music School and which in 1940 was sung at the Republican National Convention, I consider that this music counterattacks, if you want to call it that, against things which would destroy the faith and the decency of the people, to make it create informers, make a guy like this* come up here this morning and name names.

MR. ARENS: Did you use your art to counterattack in the Spanish civil war?

MR. RORINSON: I wouldn't be surprised.

MR. ARENS: You mentioned Abraham Lincoln a while ago. Did you use your art to write music on the Abraham Lincoln Brigade which fought in Spain?

* Max Marlin. —E.B.

MR. ROBINSON: I think some of my music was used in Spain. I am proud to say it was.

MR. ARENS: You are helping the Committee. We are glad to find out how people who are in your status do use art in the fight to obtain their objectives.

MR. ROBINSON: I hope my music will always be used in the fight against Fascism.

MR. ARENS: Have you written any pieces to be used against Communism?

MR. ROBINSON: The Committee's chief interest, as I understand, is the subject of Communism and Communists and so forth, and getting into a political situation in which anything that I deeply believe then can be questioned and turned and used against me. So it seems to me—

MR. ARENS: You don't have any hesitancy at all in condemning Fascism and taking pride in the fact that your music is used against Fascism.

MR. ROBINSON: I said specifically in Spain.

MR. ARENS: Yes. Now tell us about anything you have done in the use of art as a weapon, and your music as a weapon, in this global struggle in which the West and the East are engaged? International Communism, godless, atheistic Communism, tell us what you have done to use your art to engage in that struggle against Communism.

MR. ROBINSON: I have gone on singing "Ballad for Americans," "The Lonesome Train," the story of Lincoln's funeral train which carried his body from Washington to Springfield. It has the lines at the end of it, "Freedom is a thing that has no ending. It needs to be cared for; it needs defending." That is what I believe in. This is what I am doing with my music all the time. I haven't stopped.

MR. ARENS: Were you inspired to write any songs condemning the Soviet invasion and massacre in Hungary?

(*The witness conferred with his counsel.*)

MR. ROBINSON: My lawyer feels that this line of questioning should be stopped. So I will decline to answer that.

MR. MOULDER: For what reasons? The same reasons?

(*The witness conferred with his counsel.*)

MR. ROBINSON: The same reasons.

MR. ARENS: Can you tell us what songs you wrote, or in what manner you used your art—to paraphrase your language in this exhibit—to assist the Abraham Lincoln Brigade forces in Spain?

MR. ROBINSON: I don't remember writing any specific songs for Spain. But I was very, very proud when I heard that two of my songs, among others, I guess, were sung over there. One was a song called "Joe Hill." Another one was called "Abe Lincoln," in which I set some of the President's first inaugural address to music. This was the brigade that went over to fight on the side of the Spanish Loyalists, so they used this song. This was based on Lincoln's words, "This country with its institutions belongs to the people who inhabit it."

MR. ARENS: Tell us, in view of your statement here about counterattacking with art: Is art a potent weapon in the ideological differences between, say, the East and the West? Is art a potent weapon?

MR. ROBINSON: I think art is a potent weapon for understanding, for making this a better world. I think it is a potent weapon to help [people] to get along with each other.

MR. ARENS: Would art be a potent weapon, say, in the hands of the Soviet Union, in undertaking to propagate its ideology?

MR. ROBINSON: Well, I suppose Shostakovich's Fifth Symphony or Seventh Symphony, which was performed over here in wartime when we were fighting together, I suppose this was propaganda for the Soviet Union. It is pretty good. I don't think that he was trying to subvert the United States with the Seventh Symphony. I think he was trying to help his own country, but that symphony was played here in Carnegie Hall, and it was played in all the major symphony orchestras in the country, and it was good.

MR. ARENS: To pursue the matter that you opened up a while ago, how can art be used as a weapon, let us say, against Fascism? Give us the techniques of it.

MR. ROBINSON: I have no idea along this line except what I told you before. Some of the men who went over to Spain to fight sang some of my songs, and I was happy about it.

MR. ARENS: Could prominent artists, say such as yourself, who bear a fine reputation in the field of music, just as a great star bears a fine reputation in the field of motion pictures and the like, could a great artist, by lending his name to a cause, serve the cause of anti-Fascism just by signing petitions and by letting his name be used on various organizations' letterheads?

(*The witness conferred with his counsel.*)

MR. ROBINSON: Well, it seems to me that my answer, of necessity, would be yes, but I do not care to go into this particular discussion of how my name or somebody's name is going to help or hurt a cause.

MR. ARENS: We want you to go into it. You have said here that art is a potent weapon to counterattack, or something like that. "We are going to counterattack with our art against thought control," and the like. I want you to tell us how. You have talked also about what you have done to serve the cause of anti-Fascism. It is very commendable to oppose Fascism. Now we want you to tell us how a prominent musician, prominent artist, can serve the cause of anti-Fascism by lending his name to various movements. Can you help us on that?

(*The witness conferred with his counsel.*)

MR. ROBINSON: I am not talking about names. I am mainly speaking about music. I do not care to go into the business of lending a name here and there, and so forth.

MR. MOULDER: May I clarify this? The question, of course, calls for an expression of an opinion on your part.

MR. ARENS: Mr. Chairman, he has commended himself as an outstanding composer. I am not in a position to either confirm or deny it. But he has also told us of his activities against Fascism. I would like him to tell us not only from the standpoint of his opinion, but from the standpoint of his own experience.

MR. MOULDER: If you know of specific instances and facts and cases where you can answer the question properly, do so.

(*The witness conferred with his counsel.*)

MR. ROBINSON: Well, in the area of opinion, I don't see what good this can do. If you want to ask me about specific songs, I will be glad to answer you. I wrote a lot of stuff during the war against Fascism.

MR. ARENS: I have an issue of *People's Songs* when you were on the board of directors. This is the issue of February–March 1947. Here is what they say in *People's Songs*: "Among the first year's most successful projects were the classes in the use of music for political action, which *People's Songs* gave at N.C.-P.A.C. schools in Washington, D.C., Chicago, Boston, New Haven, New York, and Detroit," and so forth. According to this issue of *People's Songs,* you are on the board of directors. Please tell this Committee about "the use of music for political action." There are the words taken from *People's Songs*. How do you use music for political action?

(*The witness conferred with his counsel.*)

MR. ROBINSON: Music has been used for political action all through our history.

MR. ARENS: Tell us how.

MR. ROBINSON: "John Brown's Body" is one of the most famous songs which helped to produce the Civil War and was sung by the soldiers during the war. There are dozens of examples. In the American Revolution, if you will pardon the expression, tremendous songs came out: "The Bennington Riflemen," the story of our forefathers that shot at the Redcoats from behind trees, and so forth.

MR. ARENS: Is music an effective weapon in political action?

MR. ROBINSON: I am not sure how effective it is, but it has been used a lot.

MR. ARENS: Was it used for political action in *The People's Song Book*? I have here the song "The Gol-dern Red," by Bob Claiborne. He was before the Committee yesterday. The song reads: "I went up to my boss one day to ask him for a raise. He wept and said he didn't have the dough. Well, I knew for all his crying that that plutocrat was lying. And that's just what I told the so-and-so. And what d'ya think he said? Why you're nothing but a Gol-dern Red (straight from Russia). You're nothing but a Gol-dern Red. Yes, and if the truth be told, you're receiving Moscow gold. Yes, you're nothing but a Gol-dern Red." Is that a song that you would regard as a song for political action?

MR. ROBINSON: I don't know if there is anything very political about it. It so happens I didn't write it, and I am not sure that I would have written one like that. But I sort of smiled when you read it a couple of days ago, and I smiled again today. I think it is interesting.

MR. ARENS: The purpose of that song, obviously, is to have an impact on the mind that there is false accusation of people being Communists, isn't it? That is the whole import of that song, from the standpoint of political action?

MR. ROBINSON: I suggest you interpret it.

MR. ARENS: I should like to ask you, if you please, sir, about some other activities. I have here the *Herald Tribune* of October 10, 1943. The musicians' committee of the National Council of American-Soviet Friendship will do certain things. This musicians' committee is composed of a number of people, including Earl Robinson. Kindly look at that Thermofax reproduction of that article and tell us whether or not you recall your membership on the musicians' committee of the National Council of American-Soviet Friendship.

(*The witness conferred with his counsel.*)

MR. ROBINSON: I already declined to answer this kind of question before.

MR. ARENS: Can you tell this Committee how the musicians' committee would serve the objectives of the National Council of American-Soviet Friendship?

MR. ROBINSON: The same answer.

MR. ARENS: What is a revolutionary song? Could you help us on that?

MR. ROBINSON: "The Bennington Rifles," the one I mentioned before, part of the American Revolution, that said,"Oh, the rifle, the rifle, in our hands will prove no trifle." They are talking about the Redcoats who came over here. I call that a revolutionary song.

MR. ARENS: Are there any revolutionary songs from the Soviet Union that particularly come to your mind?

MR. ROBINSON: The Soviet Union has a lot of them, I assume. You know.

MR. ARENS: You wrote about some of the revolutionary songs from the Soviet Union, did you not, in a publication called *America Sings* issued by the Workers' Bookshop?

MR. ROBINSON: I am going to decline to answer this for the same reasons.

MR. ARENS: Let me display to you, if you please, sir, a Thermofax reproduction of the bulletin, *America Sings,* issued by the Workers' Bookshop. There is a foreword to that publication by Earl Robinson, in which you talk about, among other things, revolutionary songs, and list some of the countries from which these revolutionary songs emanate, including the Soviet Union.

(*The witness conferred with his counsel.*)

MR. ROBINSON: I don't think we should waste any more time on this. This is an attempt to draw me into a political discussion, stuff that goes way, way back and so forth.

MR. ARENS: Would you kindly give a reason for declining to answer?

MR. ROBINSON: The same reason as before.

MR. ARENS: Do you honestly feel that if you told this Committee truthfully whether or not you authored this article you would be supplying information that might be used against you in a criminal proceeding?

(*The witness conferred with his counsel.*)

MR. ROBINSON: It might.

MR. DOYLE: May I see that exhibit, please, Mr. Arens?

MR. ARENS: Yes, sir. Mr. Robinson, how old are these children you teach?

MR. ROBINSON: Between six and eleven, and then a sort of teen-age group that goes up to about fourteen.

MR. ARENS: Do you teach them any revolutionary songs?

MR. ROBINSON: This is what I teach—I commend this again to you—the "Ballad for Americans," and "The Lonesome Train." Some are my compositions, some American folk songs. Sometimes we go across the border and take a foreign folk song, too. I explain to them that this is for the purpose of getting to understand other countries better. As Mr. Doyle said the other day, music is an international language.

MR. DOYLE: A universal language.

MR. ROBINSON: Pardon me. A universal language.

MR. DOYLE: I am not an authority on music, but I know that much about it.

MR. ROBINSON: O.K.

MR. ARENS: I have here a Thermofax reproduction of the Communist *Daily Worker* of January 20, 1954. I would like to ask you about this:

> The role of "The Artist and the Professional in the Age of McCarthy" is the theme of the fifth annual convention of the New York Council of the Arts, Sciences, and Professions, to be held here January 29, 30, and 31, Director Marvel Cooke announced yesterday.

According to the article, there will be four different panels on the role of artists and professions in this "age of McCarthy," including Earl Robinson as one of the speakers. Could you look at this article and tell us, first of all, whether or not you are accurately described as one of the speakers on the subject as set forth in the article?

(*Witness conferred with his counsel.*)

MR. ROBINSON: Well, I don't know how long you are going to go with this. This is clearly mine. I don't remember now all the things that I said at this particular panel, but I am sure that I was there—like I have, you know, been appearing hundreds of times, and I am not going to—

MR. ARENS: Thank you. Do you recall appearing as an artist at a concert on behalf of Morton Sobell, the young scientist in Alcatraz, who was connected with the Rosenbergs? Do you recall using your art in that respect?

MR. ROBINSON: I think that this questioning has gone on enough. I don't know how valuable the Government's time and money is, but you have gotten a picture of me. Every time you talk about any one of these organizations, you say, "connected up with the Communist conspiracy," and so forth. Because of this, I don't think I shall answer any more of these kind of things. On the basis of the Constitution.

MR. ARENS: I would like to display to you a Thermofax reproduction of the Communist *Daily Worker* of Thursday, January 22, 1954. According to this article, there will be a concert featuring a new ballad about Morton Sobell, sponsored by the Bronx Committee to Secure Justice for Morton Sobell in the Rosenberg Case. Performing artists will include Earl Robinson. Kindly look at this Thermofax reproduction of the article from the *Daily Worker* and tell us, first of all, whether or not that refreshes your recollection.

(*The witness conferred with his counsel.*)

MR. ROBINSON: I am declining on the same grounds I said before to answer this kind of question. I made my position clear, didn't I, before?

MR. ARENS: Do you honestly feel, sir, that if you told this Committee truthfully whether or not you participated in this concert you would be supplying information which might be used against you in a criminal proceeding?

MR. ROBINSON: It might. I am sure you can go on all night with this, but I think it is a waste of time from now on.

MR. ARENS: I would say, on the basis of all of these exhibits, we probably could go on quite a while. Do you instruct at the Jefferson School of Social Science?

(*The witness conferred with his counsel.*)

MR. ROBINSON: What do you mean? As far as I know, that is not even in existence.

MR. ARENS: Have you instructed, or led discussion groups, at the Jefferson School of Social Science?

MR. ROBINSON: My lawyer says I should decline. O.K., I decline to answer. The same grounds.

MR. ARENS: I want to display to you a Thermofax reproduction of the Communist *Daily Worker* of Tuesday, April 6, 1954, reading: "Earl Robinson will lead a discussion on 'Folk Music and the Contemporary Composer' this evening (Tuesday) at the Jefferson School, Sixteenth Street and Sixth Avenue, at 6:40 P.M." Kindly look at that article and see if it refreshes your recollection with reference to that panel at the Jefferson School of Social Science.

(*The witness conferred with his counsel.*)

MR. ROBINSON: Do I make my speech about the Constitution again, how much it means to me? I am not going to let you destroy either the First or Fifth Amendment with this kind of insinuation. Somehow I am made out to be subversive, and I refuse to be. I am not.

MR. MOULDER: You claim the protection of the First and Fifth Amendments in declining to answer?

MR. ROBINSON: Yes.

MR. ARENS: Do you recall in 1953 participating as an entertainer for a Freedom Festival, sponsored by the Civil Rights Congress in Philadelphia?

MR. ROBINSON: The same answer.

MR. ARENS: I have here an article (*Daily Worker,* June 11, 1953) in which your name appears as the entertainer—one of two entertainers—at a rally addressed by Elizabeth Gurley Flynn, one of the New York Smith Act defendants, and William Albertson, one of the Pittsburgh defendants, in a Freedom Festival sponsored by the Civil Rights Congress. Kindly look at this article and tell this Committee, while you are under oath, whether or not you lent your name and prestige to that enterprise.

(*The witness conferred with his counsel.*)

MR. ROBINSON: You know, I have a lot of press clippings of my own at home. I should have brought them along. I can back every one of those you have with one of mine at a university, or all kinds of places. I mean, I don't see that this is serving any purpose any more.

MR. ARENS: We are concerned at the moment with pursuing the theme that you established in your writings: that art and artists can be used as a political weapon.

* * *

MR. ROBINSON: It is a terrible shame that I cannot speak freely.

MR. ARENS: We should be very happy to have you do so.

MR. ROBINSON: It is a terrible shame that the atmosphere that this Committee has set up in this country is such that a person renders himself subject to possible prosecution and all the rest of that if he can't answer certain things. There are many, many things that I am proud of in my past.

MR. ARENS: Let's make the record clear. Do you honestly feel, sir, that if you told this Committee truthfully, while you are under oath, whether or not you lent your name and your prestige to the National Conference to Repeal the Walter-McCarran Law and to the American Committee for Protection of Foreign Born* you would be supplying information which might be used against you in a criminal proceeding?

MR. ROBINSON: Unfortunately, it might.

MR. DOYLE: You stated a few minutes ago that you lent your name to many things. It may be that you have lent your name to some of these groups that have been cited as subversive without knowing that they were subversive. I do not know. * * * I suggest to you, as a man, apparently, of great ability, that you watch your name, because there are some men about your age and a little bit younger who gave their lives in uniform so that fellows like you and I might live. They didn't do it to perpetuate the Soviet system of Communism in this country.

MR. ROBINSON: Neither did I.

MR. DOYLE: Of course, I remember that you deliberately named this Committee in your statement as an un-American committee. That is your appraisal of your Committee of Congress that is before you, an un-American committee. You did it deliberately. And you haven't denied it. I have given you three chances to say it was a mistake, and you have not.

MR. ROBINSON: I corrected myself.

MR. DOYLE: Yes, you did, deliberately. I noticed it. That is your appraisal of your Congress. Your Congress, in the very act that you say you are opposed to, declared, in the introduction to the act: "There exists a world Communist movement which in its origin, its practice, is a world-wide revolutionary movement." May I have that pamphlet, *America Sings*? I was raised, too, to recognize music as the universal language. That is why I dared say that when you were here in the room. I believe it sincerely. In noticing the introduction to the booklet *America Sings,* which has your name printed on it—but which you did not admit authoring: you pleaded the Fifth Amendment—I want to call your attention to an introduction, printed on that five-cent pamphlet. I notice it costs five cents. This, of course, helps circulation. The only reference in the introduction, apparently made by a man with your name, is to revolutionary songs from foreign countries, emphasizing the Soviet Union and Germany. There isn't a single American song called to attention in that introduction. There is not an American song called to attention. And yet they call it *America Sings*. And that is the kind of Soviet propaganda that is infiltrating our country. I have one thing more, Mr. Robinson. Can you show me in your writings—and I ask you in good faith—one single song upholding and promoting loyalty to the Stars and Stripes, to the American flag?

MR. ROBINSON: Everything I have written does this.

MR. DOYLE: Show me one in wording where you emphasize, in your lovely music and prose and poetry, where you urge the American people to uphold the Stars and Stripes. I didn't see one in that ballad.

* On which questions had just been asked. —E.B.

MR. ROBINSON: It seems to me that these lines that I quoted to you before say this.

MR. DOYLE: You urge the American people to uphold the Constitution and the Stars and Stripes?

MR. ROBINSON: Do you mean my quoting, "We hold these truths to be self-evident, that all men are created equal, that they are endowed by their Creator," I am just fooling around with that?

MR. DOYLE: That is quoting. Show me one poem where you have deliberately set to music or otherwise that the American schoolchildren, for instance, or the Americans shall support the Constitution, and so forth!

MR. ROBINSON: I have a song called, "The House I Live In, That Is America to Me." * It has sold millions and millions of copies. It has been sung by most of the big singers in the country at one time or another. This says, "What is America to me? A name, a man, the flag I see, a certain word, democracy. What is America to me? The house I live in, the plot of earth, the street, the grocer and the butcher, the people that I meet." The middle section goes on: "The words of old Abe Lincoln, of Jefferson and Paine, of Washington and Roosevelt."

MR. DOYLE: Mail me a copy and I will pay for it, gladly.

MR. ROBINSON: The biggest line in it is, "A dream that has been growing for a hundred and fifty years." This has been sung. School kids know it. You should know it.

MR. DOYLE: Why, then, do you tear down this theory by this sort of thing? Why do you tear down that magnificent conception of our country?

MR. ROBINSON: I am not tearing down. I never have torn down.

MR. DOYLE: I beg to differ with you. Mail me a copy of that, and I will pay you for it, gladly.

MR. ARENS: I want to clear the record on one thing: Are you now a Communist?

MR. ROBINSON: Do you expect me to answer that?

MR. ARENS: Yes, I would like to have you deny it while you are under oath.

MR. ROBINSON: For the same reason, that I don't feel this Committee has a right to pry into these kind of things, and also to try to make me seem subversive, when every bit of work I have done in my life has been in defense of America and helping America, I feel that you have no right to try to put me in that kind of light. I decline to answer.

* Robinson's most famous song after "Ballad for Americans." It can be heard today, as sung by Paul Robeson, on the Vanguard album *Robeson* (VSD–2015). —E.B.

1958

The New York Shakespeare Festival

JUNE 19, 1958:

Joseph Papp

The Subcommittee of the Committee on Un-American Activities met at 10 a.m., in room 129, Federal Court House, Foley Square, New York, New York, the Honorable Morgan M. Moulder, Chairman of the Subcommittee.

Committee members present: Representatives Morgan M. Moulder, of Missouri (appearance as noted); William M. Tuck, of Virginia; and Gordon H. Scherer, of Ohio.

Staff members present: Richard Arens, Staff Director, and Donald T. Appell, Investigator.

MR. ARENS: Kindly identify yourself by name, residence, and occupation.

MR. PAPIROFSKY: My name is Joseph Papirofsky. I am a producer of Shakespearean plays for Central Park.

MR. ARENS: You are appearing today, Mr. Papirofsky, in response to a subpoena which was served upon you by the House Committee on Un-American Activities?

MR. PAPIROFSKY: That is right.

MR. ARENS: You are represented by counsel?

MR. PAPIROFSKY: Yes.

MR. ARENS: Counsel, will you kindly identify yourself?

MR. LONDON: Ephraim London.

MR. ARENS: Are you also known, Mr. Papirofsky, as Mr. Papp?

MR. PAPIROFSKY: Yes, my professional name is Mr. Papp.

MR. ARENS: Where and when were you born, please, sir?

MR. PAPIROFSKY: I was born in Williamsburg, Brooklyn, June 22, 1921.

MR. ARENS: Give us a word, please, sir, about your formal education.

MR. PAPIROFSKY: High-school graduate.

MR. ARENS: And a thumbnail sketch, if you do not mind, sir, of your professional career.

MR. PAPIROFSKY: Working from the present back?

MR. ARENS: Either direction, whichever is more convenient to you.

MR. PAPIROFSKY: My present work is primarily centered around the New York Shakespeare Festival, which is an educational nonprofit organization chartered by the [New York] state education department, established for the purpose of producing plays for the general public without admission charge. The programs also include free performances of Shakespeare for high-school students.

MR. ARENS: The Shakespeare Workshop produces the Shakespeare Festival, is that correct?

MR. PAPIROFSKY: In effect, I would say that is correct.

MR. ARENS: If I am not burdening you too much here in the recitation of the facts of this particular enterprise, what is your connection with the Workshop?

MR. PAPIROFSKY: I am producer of the New York Shakespeare Festival, having the same role with the Workshop.

MR. ARENS: How long has the Workshop been in existence?

MR. PAPIROFSKY: I believe the charter was issued in September 1954.

MR. ARENS: Is it incorporated?

MR. PAPIROFSKY: It is a state-chartered organization. It is a nonprofit organization. I am the head and founder of the organization and the moving force behind the organization.

MR. ARENS: Does it enjoy tax-free status?

MR. PAPIROFSKY: Yes, it does.

MR. ARENS: Do you receive a salary from this Workshop?

MR. PAPIROFSKY: I began to receive a salary five months ago. For the first three years I received no salary.

MR. ARENS: Is this a full-time activity by yourself?

MR. PAPIROFSKY: It is a most time-consuming and full-time activity.

MR. MOULDER: How is it financed?

MR. PAPIROFSKY: It is financed through contributions from the general public, from foundations, and part of the financing, indirect finance, is the fact that we are on city property and the city, in effect, contributes facilities for making that possible.

(*The witness conferred with his counsel.*)

MR. ARENS: On that same theme, could you give us a word about the budget? What is the aggregate income and expenditure of the organization?

MR. PAPIROFSKY: It is very difficult to get an exact figure, but I can tell you what a show would cost. I mentioned the number of shows, you might add it up, because the costs have increased as we go on because we began to pay people's salaries. Prior to this point, there were no salaries paid. The production we plan to open on July 2 will cost approximately four thousand dollars a week to run and has a preproduction cost of approximately eighteen thousand dollars. This is the highest budget we have had yet.

MR. ARENS: Would the budget in the aggregate for all of the activities of the organization run in the neighborhood of a million dollars a year?

MR. PAPIROFSKY: No, I am afraid not. I would say, roughly, if we were to continue on the basis we are playing now, it would cost approximately—playing ten or eleven months a year—two hundred thousand dollars a year to operate.

MR. ARENS: Would you kindly tell us the employment you had prior to your connection with the Workshop?

(*The witness conferred with his counsel.*)

MR. PAPIROFSKY: Prior to working with the Festival, I was employed by CBS as a stage manager.

MR. ARENS: Over what period of time?

MR. PAPIROFSKY: I am still employed by CBS as a stage manager.

MR. ARENS: When did that employment begin?

MR. PAPIROFSKY: It began sometime in 1951.

MR. ARENS: What was your connection prior to CBS?

MR. PAPIROFSKY: Prior to that I was in California and I worked for the Actors' Laboratory, Incorporated.

MR. ARENS: How long did you work for the Actors' Laboratory, Incorporated?

MR. PAPIROFSKY: I came to the Actors' Laboratory as a student under the GI bill, and then I became employed there for approximately two years. I think it was from 1948 to 1950.

MR. ARENS: In what capacity?

MR. PAPIROFSKY: I worked in the office as kind of a manager.

MR. ARENS: Were there any other schools with which you were connected in California?

(*The witness conferred with his counsel.*)

MR. PAPIROFSKY: Yes, I also taught acting to working people at the California Labor School; again, this was a labor of love.

* * *

MR. ARENS: Mr. Papirofsky, are you now, or have you ever been, a member of the Communist Party?

MR. PAPIROFSKY: I am not now a member of the Communist Party.

MR. ARENS: Were you a member of the Communist Party at any time since you received your subpoena to appear before this Committee?

(*The witness conferred with his counsel.*)

MR. PAPIROFSKY: I must decline to answer that question on the grounds of self-incrimination.

MR. ARENS: Were you a member of the Communist Party during the course of the last month?

MR. PAPIROFSKY: No, sir.

MR. ARENS: Have you been a member of the Communist Party at any time since you received your subpoena on April 16, 1958?

MR. PAPIROFSKY: No, sir, I have not.

MR. ARENS: Have you been a member of the Communist Party in the course of the last year?

MR. PAPIROFSKY: No, sir.

MR. ARENS: Have you been a member of the Communist Party any time since January 1955?

MR. PAPIROFSKY: I must decline to answer that question on the grounds of self-incrimination.

MR. ARENS: Have you been a member of the Communist Party since June 1955?

MR. PAPIROFSKY: No, sir.

MR. ARENS: Have you been a member of the Communist Party any time since February 1955?

MR. PAPIROFSKY: I must decline to answer that question on the same grounds.

MR. ARENS: Are there persons presently in the entertainment industry who, to your certain knowledge, are or in the recent past have been members of the Communist Party?

(*The witness conferred with his counsel.*)

MR. PAPIROFSKY: I am afraid I do not know the answer to that question.

MR. ARENS: Have you resigned from the Communist Party?

MR. PAPIROFSKY: The assumption is that I was a member of the Communist Party, and, therefore, I must respectfully decline to answer that on the basis of the Fifth Amendment.

MR. ARENS: Are you a Communist, though not a member of the Communist Party?

MR. PAPIROFSKY: The answer to that is no.

MR. ARENS: Have you been since January 1, 1955, a Communist?

MR. PAPIROFSKY: I must decline to answer that on the same grounds.

MR. ARENS: Did I understand you to say that when you were instructing at the California Labor School there was no compensation involved, it was a labor of love?

MR. PAPIROFSKY: To the best of my knowledge, I think there was no pay.

MR. ARENS: Did you know that the California Labor School was controlled by the Communist conspiracy?

MR. PAPIROFSKY: I did not know it was so controlled.

Mr. Arens: Were you a Communist when you were teaching at the California Labor School?

Mr. Papirofsky: I must decline to answer that on the same grounds.

Mr. Arens: Were you a Communist when you were teaching at the Actors' Laboratory?

Mr. Papirofsky: I must decline to answer that on the grounds previously stated.

Mr. Arens: Are you a member of a professional trade-union?

Mr. Papirofsky: Yes, sir.

Mr. Arens: Which one?

Mr. Papirofsky: Radio and Television Directors Guild.

Mr. Arens: How long have you been connected with that organization?

Mr. Papirofsky: Approximately six years.

Mr. Arens: Have you held any post or office in that organization?

Mr. Papirofsky: I have never been an officer of the organization.

Mr. Arens: During the course of your period of instructing at the California Labor School, the People's Drama School, or the Actors' Laboratory, did you ever recruit anyone into the Communist Party?

Mr. Papirofsky: I must decline to answer that, sir, on the same grounds.

(*The witness conferred with his counsel.*)

If the intent of that question was whether I used my position to get members into the Communist Party, I must say no to that.

Mr. Arens: I have a Thermofax reproduction of an article appearing in the Communist *Daily Worker* entitled, "Theatre Groups, Noted Actors Wire Support to People's Drama." The wire of support from famous actors signed by half a dozen persons, including Joe Papirofsky, all of the executive committee of Actors' Laboratory Theater, reads in part: "Outraged at news of brutal hoodlum attack on actors. Flagrant display of direct censorship." Kindly look at that article which Mr. Appell is now displaying to you and tell this Committee whether or not it refreshes your recollection, whether or not you used your prestige in the entertainment industry in that protest.

(*The witness conferred with his counsel.*)

Mr. Papirofsky: I must say my answer is still unchanged, sir. I have always been opposed to censorship, and I would send another wire if there were censorship again, lending my support to an attack of this kind, because this was a direct attack on these people, and I felt at the time that it was absolutely wrong, and I would do it again.

Mr. Arens: Were you a Communist when you sent that wire?

Mr. Papirofsky: I must decline to answer on the same grounds.

Mr. Arens: What name did you use when you were in California?

MR. PAPIROFSKY: Joseph Papirofsky.

MR. ARENS: When did you begin the use of the name Papp?

MR. PAPIROFSKY: It was not my doing. It began at CBS. They have a very small type schedule and my name was too long, and they condensed it, they began to call me Papp, and I began to use the name.

MR. ARENS: You have expressed yourself publicly with reference to the Committee before which you are appearing today.

MR. PAPIROFSKY: Yes, I did express myself publicly, if I remember correctly, and my opinion is exactly the same today as it was then.

MR. ARENS: Is your opinion—and I am not trying to probe your opinion—still in condemnation of Larry Parks, who broke from the Communist Party and came before the Committee and identified a number of Communists? Are you still hostile to that man?

MR. PAPIROFSKY: Am I hostile to him?

MR. ARENS: Yes.

(*The witness conferred with his counsel.*)

MR. PAPIROFSKY: The feeling I would have about Mr. Parks would be the same feeling I would have about anybody who would gratuitously injure the people who work with him in the way he did.

MR. ARENS: What if Mr. Parks, instead of having been in the Communist conspiracy, had been in a narcotics ring and came before the appropriate investigating committee and identified persons active in the narcotics ring? Would you be in opposition to him then?

MR. PAPIROFSKY: I am afraid I cannot go into that question, because the one case you mentioned, with Mr. Parks, has to do with a man because of the way he functioned, hurt the employment of people, innocent people, by mentioning names, and so forth. Whereas, the narcotic situation is hurting men's bodies and not their thinking.

MR. ARENS: You acclaimed Mr. Parks publicly at one time and used your prestige and used the glamour of your position to acclaim Mr. Parks when he at first refused to cooperate with the Committee on Un-American Activities.

MR. PAPIROFSKY: I have no glamour and prestige. I think it is a misnomer to use that.

MR. ARENS: You let your name be used in acclaim of Larry Parks when he refused to cooperate with the Committee on Un-American Activities, is that correct?

MR. PAPIROFSKY: Yes, if you have a record of it there, I would have to say I did.

MR. ARENS: Do you recall doing that?

MR. PAPIROFSKY: No, sir, I do not.

MR. ARENS: Let me lay before you a Thermofax reproduction of an advertisement bearing the names of a number of persons:

The Thomas Rankin Committee Must Go!

We, the undersigned members of the acting profession, acclaim Larry Parks one of the "unfriendly nineteen." We acclaim those actors who appeared in Washington to protest the star chamber proceedings . . . those others who broadcast their indignation on the air and in the press . . . and those who remained to fight here. We are proud that they are upholding the finest traditions of our profession and our country.

This advertisement appeared just before Larry Parks decided he was going to cooperate with the Committee and it bears, among others, the name of Joseph Papirofsky. Kindly look at that and tell us whether or not you have a recollection of joining in that enterprise and letting your name be used.

MR. PAPIROFSKY: "The Thomas Rankin Committee Must Go"?

MR. ARENS: Yes, that is correct.

MR. PAPIROFSKY: That is my name here.

MR. ARENS: Did you consciously and knowingly lend your name to that enterprise?

MR. PAPIROFSKY: I think I have stated my position on the question of the Committee.

MR. ARENS: Did you do so in that instance?

MR. PAPIROFSKY: My name is there, so I certainly did.

MR. ARENS: Do you recall doing it?

MR. PAPIROFSKY: No, I do not recall.

MR. ARENS: Were you a Communist when you did it?

MR. PAPIROFSKY: I must refuse to answer on the same grounds as I mentioned before.

MR. ARENS: Have you knowingly lent your name in the course of your professional career to enterprises which to your certain knowledge were promoted by the Communist Party?

MR. PAPIROFSKY: I must decline to answer that question, sir, on the same grounds I mentioned previously.

MR. ARENS: I respectfully suggest that would conclude the staff interrogation of this witness.

MR. PAPIROFSKY: Representative Moulder, I would like to submit this. This is a magazine published by the State Department and sent to Russia—an example of American democracy at work. The work of this cover is the work of the New York Festival. Inside there is a series of pictures describing our work as descriptive of the free democratic culture. I see no mention of the Un-American Activities Committee, so I must assume what we are doing, the department feels, is a much more important function. I also submit the Voice of America tapes that I have made to various countries as an example of free democracy in this country. I feel that what I believe in can be best stated this way.

MR. SCHERER: When you were making those Voice of America tapes were you a member of the Communist Party?

MR. PAPIROFSKY: No, sir, I was not a member of the Communist Party when I was making the Voice of America tapes.

MR. SCHERER: Did you disclose to the State Department that you had been a member of the Communist Party?

MR. PAPIROFSKY: I must decline to answer that question on the same constitutional grounds as I mentioned.

* * *

MR. MOULDER: Do you have the opportunity to inject into your plays or into the acting or the entertainment supervision which you have any propaganda in any way which would influence others to be sympathetic with the Communist philosophy or the beliefs of Communism?

MR. PAPIROFSKY: Sir, the plays we do are Shakespeare's plays. Shakespeare said, "To thine own self be true," and various other lines from Shakespeare can hardly be said to be subversive or influencing minds. I cannot control the writings of Shakespeare. He wrote plays five hundred [*sic*] years ago. I am in no position to influence what the final product will be, except artistically and except in terms of my job as a producer.

MR. MOULDER: My point is, do you intentionally control the operation of the entertainment which you produce or supervise for the purpose of influencing sympathy toward Communism?

MR. PAPIROFSKY: The answer to that is obviously no. The plays speak for themselves. I began to mention the plays that we did. Maybe some of these plays might be considered propagandistic.

MR. ARENS: We are not concerned with the plays, and you know we are not, and there is no suggestion here by this chairman or anyone else that Shakespeare was a Communist. That is ludicrous and absurd. That is the Commie line. The inquiry of this Committee is solely with reference to the extent to which Communists have used their prestige in the theater to promote Communists; and for you to twist this testimony, in the presence of the public press here, to give an implication that the Chairman is trying to elicit information from you that Shakespeare was subversive, or this Committee is investigating Shakespeare, investigating that type of thing, is not only ludicrous, but it is highly unfair.

MR. PAPIROFSKY: I am sorry. I think you misunderstand me.

MR. ARENS: I did not misunderstand you.

MR. PAPIROFSKY: I am saying that, over the past years, I have been devoting all my energies to this project, in which the plays of Shakespeare are most important.

MR. ARENS: Have you been devoting some of your energy to the Communist Party?

MR. PAPIROFSKY: I think I have answered all of those questions the way you have put them forward to me.

MR. MOULDER: I was very much impressed by your straightforward and honest replies to counsel concerning your background and your work. When it comes to the question of whether you have been actively connected with the Communist Party, that is a different matter. I do not intend to interrogate you about your philosophies or beliefs unless you volunteer to submit that information.

MR. PAPIROFSKY: I voluntarily submitted that information because I think it is important in terms of how I am to be judged by anybody.

MR. MOULDER: Have you undergone any change in your beliefs, in your philosophies or social beliefs, and the form of government we should have, during the past two or three years? Have you changed your opinion in that connection?

MR. PAPIROFSKY: Changed my opinion from what?

MR. MOULDER: In your philosophy of government or form of government we should have.

MR. PAPIROFSKY: My opinions change constantly, and they have changed from time to time on many, many subjects.

MR. MOULDER: You understand, of course, the Communist philosophy is antispiritual, antireligious, and is very much in conflict with our system in the American form of government and the American way of life. Do you agree with that?

MR. PAPIROFSKY: I am not antispiritual or antireligious in any way.

MR. MOULDER: You mentioned a while ago that to give names of other people, such as Larry Parks, you considered wrong when it does injury to other people?

MR. PAPIROFSKY: Yes.

MR. MOULDER: If Communism is not subversive or a danger to our American form of government and our way of life, then what harm is done by revealing the names of people who are active in the Communist Party and the Communist movement?

MR. PAPIROFSKY: First, the question assumes I know these people.

MR. MOULDER: I am not asking you that. I am asking you, as a result of your statement, what harm is done if Communism is not subversive and is not a threat to our form of government and the American way of life, then what harm does it do to reveal the names of people who are active members of the Communist Party, if that is true?

MR. PAPIROFSKY: I understand the question, Representative Moulder. You know there is a blacklisting device in the industry, and the naming of people this way does deny these people the right to work, which I think is terribly unfair and un-American.

MR. ARENS: Who denies them the right to work?

MR. PAPIROFSKY: Because of the kinds of publicity accumulated at these hearings.

MR. ARENS: Do you think it is wrong to disassociate from public media of expression in this country people who are secret members of a conspiracy which has as its avowed objective the overthrow of this Government by force and violence?

(*The witness conferred with his counsel.*)

MR. PAPIROFSKY: I just think it is wrong to deny anybody employment because of their political beliefs.

MR. ARENS: Do you think it is wrong to employ them if they are members of a conspiratorial apparatus?

(*The witness conferred with his counsel.*)

MR. PAPIROFSKY: This question assumes that there is a conspiracy and that I know about it, and I must decline to answer it on the same grounds.

(*Witness excused.*)

1966

"Assistance to Enemies of the United States in Time of Undeclared War"

In the 1960s the country changed. While official America prepared and carried through the war against Vietnam, precisely this action brought into being a radical opposition stronger than anything of the kind that had existed since the thirties. You hear the new tone of voice as early as 1962, when Dagmar Wilson of Women Strike for Peace was asked by HUAC whether, since she was willing to have Communists in her organization she would also welcome Fascists. It was a tired old trap of a query, calculated to bring out that left-wingers tolerated Communists but not Fascists. When Mrs. Wilson showed no hesitation in saying, why, of course she would welcome Fascists because the cause of peace welcomed anybody and needed everybody, it was something new in the halls of Congress. Four years later, when a bunch of young people from the Progressive Labor [Maoist] Party—including Richard Mark Rhoads and Steven Cherkoss—were brought to HUAC's witness chair, they disconcerted Washington, and made history, by answering the sixty-four-dollar question ("Are you now or were you ever . . .") in a delighted affirmative. Sometimes, as in the first excerpt quoted below, the witness couldn't wait for the question but asked it and answered it all at once.

The new radicals considered taking the "Einstein pledge," as Dave Dellinger mentions (as cited below), but generally decided on an alternate, but equally militant, course: not to refuse to appear before the Committee but to use the Committee's facilities as a forum for their own views and attitudes. (The "attitudes" sometimes made headlines more easily, as when Jerry Rubin dressed up as a soldier in the Revolutionary War or when Abbie Hoffman wore a shirt made from the American flag.)

AUGUST 17, 1966:

Richard Mark Rhoads

The Subcommittee of the Committee on Un-American Activities met in the Caucus Room, Cannon House Office Building, Washington, D.C., the Honorable Joe R. Pool, Texas, Chairman. Members present: John M. Ashbrook, Ohio; John H. Buchanan, Jr., Alabama. Alternate member: Del Clawson, California.

Staff members present: Francis J. McNamara, Director; William Hitz, General Counsel; Alfred M. Nittle, Counsel; Donald T. Appell, Chief Investigator.

MR. NITTLE: Would Richard Mark Rhoads please come forward?

MR. POOL: Do you solemnly swear that the testimony you are about to give will be the truth, the whole truth, and nothing but the truth, so help you God?

MR. RHOADS: I came to the Committee to tell as much of the truth as I can before being interrupted by this Committee.

MR. POOL: Do you solemnly swear that the testimony you are about to give will be the truth, the whole truth, and nothing but the truth, so—

MR. RHOADS: I so affirm.

MR. POOL: Do you affirm that the testimony you are about to give will be the truth, the whole truth, and nothing but the truth?

MR. RHOADS: I affirm.

MR. NITTLE: Mr. Rhoads, would you state your full name for the purposes of the record?

MR. RHOADS: Before answering the first question, I would like to register some objections to this entire proceeding. May I do so at this time?

MR. NITTLE: You will address your request to the Chairman, please.

MR. POOL: Go ahead.

MR. RHOADS: Mr. Chairman, may I make some objections to the entire proceedings?

MR. POOL: Identify yourself.

MR. RHOADS: Will I then be allowed to object to the proceeding?

MR. POOL: Yes.

MR. RHOADS: My name is Richard M. Rhoads.

MR. NITTLE: Are you represented by counsel?

MR. RHOADS: Yes.

MR. NITTLE: Would counsel identify himself for the record?

MR. GOLLOBIN: Ira Gollobin from New York City.

MR. POOL: All right, you can state your objections now.

MR. RHOADS: Opposition in our country to the Johnson Administration war of genocide in Vietnam is enormous.

MR. NITTLE: Now, Mr. Chairman, I must object.

MR. POOL: I don't mind you making objections, but I don't want you making speeches. Just state your objections, and we will consider them.

MR. RHOADS: I am stating my objection. I will continue. In the face of militant opposition at home and revolutionary action in Vietnam, Johnson resorts to escalation—

MR. NITTLE: Now, Mr. Chairman, I must object again.

MR. POOL: You are not responding. I told you to state your objection.

MR. RHOADS: I am stating my objection.

MR. POOL: You are making a speech.

MR. RHOADS: I am stating my objection. In our country—

MR. NITTLE: These are not legal objections, Mr. Rhoads.

MR. POOL: Ask the next question, Mr. Nittle.

MR. RHOADS: I am stating my objection.

MR. NITTLE: State the time and place of your birth.

MR. RHOADS: I insist on the right to state my objection.

MR. POOL: What is the question, Mr. Nittle?

MR. NITTLE: State the time and place of your birth.

MR. RHOADS: If the Committee will not allow me to state the political basis for my objections, I will go on to the legal ones.

MR. NITTLE: State the time and place of your birth, please.

MR. RHOADS: I am continuing my objections.

MR. POOL: I direct you to answer the question.

MR. RHOADS: I am perfectly willing to answer this question, but I want to make my legal objections to this hearing.

MR. POOL: Go ahead. If you will make your objections in a short form, I will listen to them; I am not going to listen to a speech.

MR. RHOADS: I object to answering any questions of this Committee on the ground that Public Law 601, 79th Congress, 60 Statutes 812, Rule XI, authorizing the Committee on Un-American Activities "to make . . . investigations of the extent, character, and objects of un-American propaganda activities in the United States" violates the Constitution in that the statute is ambiguous and vague, the term "un-American propaganda activities" being nowhere defined and being in fact incapable of precise definition and obscuring the fact that there are not one, but two kinds of un-American activities: first, those that the vast majority of the American people deem un-American, such as undemocratic—

MR. POOL: State your objection. Go on and state your objections and answer the question.

MR. RHOADS: —and, secondly, those deemed un-American by a small minority of the wealthy privileged, who condone escalating the Vietnam war—

MR. POOL: This is argumentative also. State your objection.

MR. RHOADS: —by their political position and that of the Johnson Administration and members of this Committee. I further object to answering any questions of this Committee on the ground that the statute on its face, and as applied by the House Un-American Activities Committee during the past twenty years, and especially today its harassment of those opposing the Vietnam war—

MR. NITTLE: Mr. Chairman, this is not a legal argument, it is a diatribe.

MR. POOL: State your objections.

MR. RHOADS: If I continue, it will be very clear that it is a legal argument.

MR. POOL: Do you take the Fifth Amendment?

MR. RHOADS: I am not answering a question, I am making an objection.

MR. POOL: I am going to direct you for the last time.

MR. RHOADS: There is no question on the floor.

MR. POOL: He just asked you a question.

MR. GOLLOBIN: Mr. Chairman, you did give him permission to make a legal objection.

MR. ASHBROOK: He is not doing it.

MR. GOLLOBIN: In terms of the amendments.

MR. POOL: All right, you can make your objection.

MR. RHOADS: Its harassment of Vietnam is repugnant to freedom of speech—

MR. ASHBROOK: Mr. Chairman—

MR. POOL: If you have objections, this is the last time I am going to give you a chance to make them, and the record will show this. Now make your objection right now, and if you have a Fifth Amendment objection, state it right now, because I am going on to the next question.

MR. RHOADS: —is repugnant to the freedom of speech, assembly, association.

MR. ASHBROOK: Mr. Chairman—

MR. RHOADS: I am quoting from the Bill of Rights: This is part of my legal objection. Am I not entitled to do so?

MR. POOL: Make your objection.

MR. RHOADS: Guaranteed to the people by the Bill of Rights and—

MR. ASHBROOK: Mr. Chairman, this witness is here subject to—

MR. POOL: For the last time, I direct you to answer the question.

MR. ASHBROOK: I submit this witness is recalcitrant and we dismiss him and call him back when he wants to contain himself.

MR. POOL: I am giving an opportunity to answer the question for the last time.

MR. ASHBROOK: He is not quoting from any amendment that is applicable.

MR. RHOADS: I have further grounds for objection.

MR. POOL: It better come forth pretty quick.

MR. RHOADS: I decline to answer on the ground that this Committee is at present illegally constituted and that at least one of its members, the Congressman from Alabama—

MR. POOL: That has been ruled on before, time and again,* and it is invalid, so go on to the next objection.

MR. RHOADS: I have further objection to this Committee's entire hearing and answering any questions before this Committee. I object to the fact that the statement of purpose that this Committee handed to me yesterday morning, the fact that they handed it to me only yesterday morning. This is not a serious legislative committee, but a circus intended to harass—

MR. POOL: All right. Now, Mr. Nittle, ask the next question. I have given him plenty of chance.

MR. RHOADS: I have further grounds.

MR. NITTLE: Would you relate the extent of your formal education?

MR. RHOADS: Will you repeat the question?

MR. NITTLE: Would you relate the extent of your formal education?

MR. POOL: I want to direct to the witness's attention that failure to answer questions of this Committee could possibly, in my opinion, properly subject you to contempt.

(*Laughter.*)

MR. RHOADS: Is that a threat?

MR. POOL: No, I am just pointing it out to you.

MR. RHOADS: I see.

MR. POOL: Go ahead, Mr. Nittle, ask the question again.

MR. NITTLE: What schools did you attend and when, and what degrees have you received, if any?

MR. RHOADS: My greatest education has been provided—

MR. NITTLE: I asked you what schools you attended, I didn't ask you for a speech.

MR. RHOADS: I am going to tell you. In the last few years I have been

* On the previous day, another member of the Progressive Labor Party, Jeffrey Gordon, had had an exchange with Mr. Buchanan, Congressman from Alabama, as follows:

MR. BUCHANAN: May I suggest that you brush up on your arithmetic, since the Congress represents all the people of this country—

MR. GORDON: That is a *mis*representation—

MR. BUCHANAN: And you represent a tiny minority.

MR. GORDON: Oh, wow! That's too much: coming from Alabama and saying that.

MR. POOR: Any other questions? The witness is excused.

MR. GORDON: Get out of Vietnam!

(*Applause*)

attending what you might call a school of life known as the United States. For instance, in Times Square in New York City—

MR. NITTLE: If the Chairman pleases, I think the witness is being in contempt here.

MR. POOL: Answer the question. I direct you to answer the question.

MR. RHOADS: I am answering the question in my own way and—

MR. ASHBROOK: The question was formal education, Mr. Chairman. I believe you would know that means an institution of higher learning or a secondary school.

MR. RHOADS: I am presently a full-time student at City College in New York. At City College last June the students of the whole school were unable to—

MR. POOL: Answer the question. You are not entitled to make a speech. Just answer the questions.

MR. NITTLE: What is your present occupation?

MR. RHOADS: I am a student.

(*Laughter.*)

MR. POOL: Next question.

MR. NITTLE: Do you have any other occupation?

MR. RHOADS: I have answered that question.

MR. NITTLE: Mr. Rhoads, do you receive a source of income from any employment or source?

MR. RHOADS: Why didn't you ask that question of the fink* that testified yesterday, what was *his* source of income?

(*Applause.*)

MR. POOL: Answer the question. Officers, if there are any more demonstrations, remove the people who are demonstrating and they will not be allowed back in the room. If necessary, we will clear the whole room if we can't have orderly proceedings in this hearing.

MR. NITTLE: Mr. Rhoads, in a passport application filed by you on April 21, 1965, for travel to Nigeria, you set forth your occupation as that of editor. Do you still have that occupation either part or full time?

MR. RHOADS: May we see the document, please?

MR. NITTLE: Are you the—

MR. RHOADS: I am still conferring with my attorney.

MR. NITTLE: Mr. Chairman, I suggest that the witness has had adequate time to confer with his counsel.

MR. POOL: Is the witness ready?

MR. RHOADS: Would you repeat the question, please?

MR. NITTLE: Are you presently the editor of any publication of the Progressive Labor Party?

MR. RHOADS: No.

MR. NITTLE: Are you presently the editor of *Free Student*?

* Phillip Abbott Luce, as identified by Mr. Nittle on page 865. —E.B.

Mr. Rhoads: *Free Student* is an anti-imperialist newspaper—

Mr. Nittle: I say are you presently—

Mr. Rhoads: —of which I am on the editorial board.

Mr. Nittle: You are. Do you receive any remuneration for your services to the *Free Student*?

Mr. Rhoads: You are getting back onto this dangerous area of—

Mr. Pool: I direct you to answer the question.

Mr. Rhoads: Unlike some people who are paid agents of various Government agencies and would only do it for the fact they get paid, I am a volunteer worker for the *Free Student*.

Mr. Pool: Ask the next question.

Mr. Nittle: Mr. [Phillip Abbott] Luce testified yesterday that, during his period of membership in the Progressive Labor Movement and the May 2nd Movement, you were a member of the Progressive Labor Movement and of the national executive committee of the May 2nd Movement. Was his testimony truthful?

Mr. Rhoads: It seems to me there are several questions in that question. Could you break it down to one question at a time?

Mr. Nittle: Were you a member of the Progressive Labor Movement between the period July 1964 and January 1965?

Mr. Rhoads: I am very proud to state that, right now as I sit here before this Committee, I am a member of the Progressive Labor Party.

Mr. Pool: Next question. That is sufficient.

Mr. Nittle: Were you a member—

Mr. Pool: Mr. Nittle, what is the objective of the Progressive Labor Party? I am addressing that to the witness.

Mr. Nittle: Mr. Rhoads, the Chairman is addressing a question to you.

Mr. Rhoads: Oh, is that to me? What is the objective of the Progressive Labor Party?

Mr. Pool: That is right.

Mr. Rhoads: Let me read to you from the preamble of the constitution of the Progressive Labor Party in an attempt to answer that question from a document of our party:

> The great American dream of "life, liberty, and the pursuit of happiness" has been turned by a ruthless regime into a nightmare of death, destruction, and the pursuit of dollars. On behalf of the tens of millions of our fellow citizens who have seen their dream betrayed—

This is from our founding convention.

> In the midst of the corruption and terror of the past—and the present—we have come together to plant the flag of the future.
>
> Even as we meet, the rulers of our nation are sending off more planes, bombs, guns, and gases in a desperate effort to paralyze the progress of his-

tory, to terrorize and destroy those around the world who hold freedom more dear even than life when life means slavery. At home, these same rulers enforce a society of fear with police dogs, cattle prods and prisons.

The most hated government in the world today is the government of our country. In the remotest corner of the earth, the initials U.S.A., which once stood for hope, have replaced the crooked cross of Nazi Germany as the symbol of tyranny and death.

Yet there is another U.S.A.: the U.S.A. which once declared to the world that "whenever any form of government becomes destructive . . . it is the right of the people to alter or to abolish it, and to institute a new government laying its foundations on such principles, and organizing its powers in such forms, as to them shall seem most likely to effect their safety and happiness" (Declaration of Independence); the U.S.A. of the men and women who sweat in factories to produce goods, of the housewives who struggle to keep the homes and raise the children, of the students, artists, and honest intellectuals who want desperately to create new beauty for life and not bombs and billboards for death.

It is for this U.S.A., often fooled, sometimes silenced, but still seeking a better life, that we meet today. This U.S.A., in the ghetto streets and tenements will not go along with the gas chamber plans of this country's ruling class. This U.S.A., beaten down time and again, deceived and denied, is still ready to organize and to resist. And it is to build that organization and that resistance that we launch our Party today. . . .

With the birth of our new Party, we dedicate ourselves to end those fears and those troubles. We resolve to build a revolutionary movement with the participation and support of millions of working men and women as well as those students, artists, and intellectuals who will join with the working class to end the profit system which breeds those fears and those troubles. With such a movement, we will build a socialist U.S.A., with all power in the hands of the working people and their allies.

We recognize that the fight will be long and hard. The kings, queens, and bishops of modern finance capital and their political pawns have made it clear they will use every form of force and violence in their desperation to hold onto their stolen billions. We will be prepared to continue the struggle on whatever level and with whatever forms are necessary. Surrender is a word we will not know.

To win, we will have to work closely together, disciplined by the urgency of the goal before us; we will have to study and learn to utilize our communist principles and the science of Marxism-Leninism to evaluate honestly our own strengths and weaknesses and those of the enemy at each new stage of the campaign.

Regardless of personal sacrifice, we resolve to demonstrate through constant organized action that the struggle can be carried—and won—to defeat the present system of war and oppression; that the working class can—and will—control its own destiny.

We know full well that with this resolve we fix our fates in a future of fire.

Yet we know, too, that from the very flames of our fight—the fight of all honest working people, students, housewives, and intellectuals of our country and the world—a new society shall be built—in which our children, our children's children, and the billion, billion children to come will never be forced to hunger for food or shelter or love—a new society without exploitation of man by man, a society, a nation, a world of revolutionary socialism.

To this end, we here resolve to give our every energy, our resources, and our lives.

(*Applause.*)

MR. POOL: Then it is the objective of the Progressive Labor Party to bring a Communist government to the United States, is that correct?

MR. RHOADS: We intend to fight by every democratic means possible that the allegedly and incorrectly called democratic government of this country will allow us to fight to make this a socialist country, because that is what the people of the United States need. In a socialist United States there will be no need to pursue wars of aggression like the present genocide against the people of Vietnam and the American people.

MR. ASHBROOK: He did not respond to the question, Mr. Chairman.

MR. POOL: I know, but he did not deny the purpose of the Party was to bring a Communist government to the United States.

MR. RHOADS: The objective of the Progressive Labor Party is to fight in the best interests of the people of the United States.

MR. ASHBROOK: Mr. Chairman, in his own words he referred to "our Communist philosophy" or something of that sort. It was "our Communist." Is that what you meant to say, or are you denying it now?

MR. RHOADS: Are you trying to ask me whether I am a Communist or not?

MR. ASHBROOK: You are asking the question. Answer mine.

MR. POOL: You can answer that if you want to.

MR. RHOADS: I certainly am.

MR. POOL: I don't have to ask you the next question, then.

(*Laughter.*)

MR. POOL: Do you advocate the overthrow of the United States Government by force and violence?

MR. RHOADS: You gentlemen have some nerve to use "violence" when you are talking about what *we* advocate, because the United States Government is the prime user of violence against the people of the United States.

MR. POOL: You are not responsive to my question.

MR. RHOADS: I am completely responsive to your question.

MR. POOL: Do you advocate the overthrow of the United States Government by use of force and violence?

MR. RHOADS: We believe in the American people taking power in their own country by the use of every democratic means possible. You gentlemen, and the much more powerful gentlemen that you represent, are the ones that consistently stand in the way of that, and always have in the history of our country, that violate the Constitution every day of the week, that show your true beliefs about violence by using the most hideous genocidal violence against the people of Vietnam and by sacrificing the blood of the American people to carry that out, and by using hideous violence against Negro people in Washington, D.C., and all over the United States.

MR. ASHBROOK: Mr. Chairman, I wonder if the witness would respond to two questions without making a speech. If he is against overthrow by force and violence, what would be his position on the ruthless manner in which the Russians overcame the Hungarian rebellion? It appears that force and violence seems to—

MR. RHOADS: We are fighting to keep a society that will never again see force and violence. However, when the forces of injustice and racism and coming Fascism use force and violence against the American people and we—

MR. ASHBROOK: We are talking about Hungary.

MR. RHOADS: The North found it necessary to use force and violence against slavery.

MR. POOL: I think that the American people are sufficiently informed now as to the forces behind these movements, and your testimony is very helpful in letting the American people know how serious this movement is to our security. The witness is now excused permanently.

MR. RHOADS: Get out of Vietnam now!

(*Applause.*)

AUGUST 19, 1966:

Steven Cherkoss

The Subcommittee of the Committee on Un-American Activities met in the Caucus Room, Cannon House Office Building, Washington, D.C., the Honorable Joe R. Pool (Chairman of the Subcommittee) presiding. Subcommittee members present: Representatives Joe R. Pool, Texas; Richard H. Ichord, Missouri; and John H. Buchanan, Jr., Alabama.

Staff members present: Francis J. McNamara, Director; William Hitz, General Counsel; Alfred M. Nittle, Counsel; Donald T. Appell, Chief Investigator.

MR. NITTLE: Would Steven Cherkoss come forward? Did you take the opportunity afforded you to obtain counsel?

MR. CHERKOSS: Let us face it. This system has got to go. Now I will answer the question. I want to make a statement about not having counsel.

You have deprived me of the lawyer of my choice,* and I do not wish to be represented by any other lawyer. I could not have confidence in any lawyer who would appear at this time under the circumstances which you, as Representatives of a Government that is committing war crimes, have created in this kangaroo court. Therefore, I will proceed alone to confront this racist Committee of cowardly, yellow-bellied reactionaries, Representatives of the U.S. Government, not of the people, that is conducting a genocidal war in Vietnam that is against the best interests of the American and Vietnamese people.

MR. NITTLE: Do you desire to testify—

MR. CHERKOSS: Yes.

MR. NITTLE: —in the absence of counsel?

MR. CHERKOSS: Yes. I am not going to let you guys get off the hook.

MR. POOL: Raise your right hand. Do you solemnly swear the testimony you are about to give will be the truth, the whole truth, and nothing but the truth, so help you God?

MR. CHERKOSS: I am here to tell the truth, but I know the American people would rise up and demolish this Committee when they learn the truth about this Committee and the U.S. Government that is conducting a war and acting against their interests.

MR. POOL: Do you solemnly swear the testimony you are about to give will be the truth, the whole truth, and nothing but the truth, so help you God?

MR. CHERKOSS: I am, as I have told you, yes, but this Committee isn't interested in hearing the truth.

MR. POOL: Go ahead.

MR. CHERKOSS: I want to make a statement, state objections.

MR. NITTLE: Would you state your name for the record, please?

MR. CHERKOSS: You fellows know my name. You have been investigating me long enough.

MR. NITTLE: Is your name Steven Cherkoss and do you reside at 2732 Haste Street, Berkeley, California?

MR. CHERKOSS: I identify myself as an American Revolutionary in the tradition of others who have fought against and defeated the British imperialists in a Revolutionary War of Independence in 1776, with those who fought against slavery, with those who organized the CIO, with the working men and women who build this country, and with the millions of Americans from East to West who are fighting today for civil rights, black liberation, and to get the U.S. out of Vietnam now. Yes, I am Steve Cherkoss. I don't reside at 2732. I reside at 2929 Sixteenth Street.

MR. NITTLE: Today.

* Two days previously the lawyers of this group of unfriendly witnesses—William Kunstler, Frank J. Donner, and others—had withdrawn from the case when one of their number, Arthur Kinoy, was forcibly ejected from the room. —E.B.

MR. CHERKOSS: And I have a statement to make, state objections to this Committee's proceeding.

MR. NITTLE: Have you resided at 2732 Haste Street, Berkeley, California?

MR. CHERKOSS: I would like to make my objections.

MR. NITTLE: Before you answer that question?

MR. CHERKOSS: That's right.

MR. POOL: Let him answer the question.

MR. CHERKOSS: Opposition in America to the Johnson Administration's war of genocide in Vietnam is enormous and still growing. Johnson resorts to escalation in Vietnam. His method is kill all, burn all. In our country, it is increased political repression. The Johnson Administration has called on a discredited, racist HUAC, a circus Committee of coward yellow bellies, to launch the first official attack on the antiwar movement. HUAC, in a blaze of Red-baiting, has attempted to divide and silence militants and revolutionaries. HUAC and Johnson hope this witch hunt will frighten the massive antiwar movement into passivity or convert it into a loyal opposition. This inquisition also has been used to help ram through Congress the Joe Fool bill, the suppression of peace bill, H.R. 12047,* and to amend the Internal Security Act, title IV, section 401–3. The essence of this Fascist legislation is to stop the anti-Vietnam war activity. Millions of Americans are learning that the U.S. war of aggression in Vietnam is opposed to their interests. Because of the war and a war budget, wages and working conditions are declining. Prices of food, rent, clothes, and homes are rising. Local taxes are rising because present taxes are used for war. Federal taxes will be increased to meet the twenty-one-billion-dollar-a-year war cost in Vietnam. Ghetto conditions are worsening daily, and the only jobs for black youth today are in the Army. Black youth and young white workers are being used as cannon fodder to kill and be killed in Vietnam. Students and intellectuals recognize the university system as a market place to buy and sell minds. The universities are merely a training ground, service centers, for big business or their Government in Washington. Students and intellectuals—solid, honest intellectuals, that is—realize that their abilities are not used for social creativity, but are used to apologize, to be technicians, for this ruthless, degenerate, U.S. Government, or to produce for it. Our people also see huge profiteering from this war. Many realize that the U.S. is not in Vietnam to free the people, but that it is there to prevent the revolution from triumphing. They see the U.S. needs Vietnam for its natural resources as a political and military base to dominate Southeast Asia and to attack China. The U.S. has billions invested in Asia. It makes mil-

*The investigation of PL, in the official records, is entitled: "Hearings on H.R. 12047, H.R. 14925, H.R. 16175, H.R. 17140, and H.R. 17194—Bills to Make Punishable Assistance to Enemies of U.S. in Time of Undeclared War." —E.B.

lions in profits from these investments. If the people of Southeast Asia win their freedom, the U.S. will lose its ability to exploit them. The future of U.S. political aspirations for world domination depends on controlling Asia. The U.S. is not in Vietnam because of any accident. It is there to secure its profit and power. The U.S. ruling class and the Johnson group do not care how many die. They will murder as much as they can to hold and enlarge their base in Asia. It is the Johnson gang that is disloyal and subversive to the American people, and, by all means, this Committee. They are the enemies of the people of the world. They are the most hated force in the history of international politics. They must be defeated. They will be stopped. The American people will rise up and liberate themselves in this country, and they will stop the U.S. Government's criminal actions throughout the world. Because of deteriorating conditions, a result of the war, Americans are fighting back. Strikes increase. And this Committee knows full well about strikes, because this Committee has been used time and time again to break the back of militant strikes. Rebellion increases in ghettos. Black people organize for political power, black power. They know the fight is here and now, right here at home, not in Vietnam. Black people and Vietnam people have the same enemy—U.S. rulers. The antiwar movement snowballs in the U.S., as young Americans and Vietnamese die while profits soar. PLP [Progressive Labor Party] members have been dragged to Washington, and I am a PLP member and proud to say that, proud to say I am a Marxist-Leninist, a revolutionary Communist, because that is expressing the full aspirations of the American people. We have been dragged here to Washington in this repressive act to stifle the antiwar movement. We believe that counterrevolutionary war, like the U.S. Government is fighting in Vietnam, is a product of the system called U.S. imperialism and will only end with defeat of this imperialism. The U.S. Government today is following the pattern of Adolf Hitler. We identify with the real America. Mark Twain very ably said there are two Americas, and that one America represents the U.S. rulers and one the people of this country. We identify with the real America, the people's America, the America which has always fought for social progress at home and abroad. We believe it is necessary to have socialism in our country to achieve the flowering of real America, to end war, oppression, insecurity, and the cultural and moral decay that is choking our people. We are Communists and we are proud of it. We act in accordance with the aspirations of the overwhelming majority of the American people.

MR. POOL: Just a moment.

MR. CHERKOSS: We believe that the working people, aided by students, honest, solid intellectuals, and others, must hold political power.

MR. POOL: May I interrupt you just there?

MR. CHERKOSS: By all means.

MR. POOL: Are you a Communist?

MR. CHERKOSS: I am going to finish this statement, one more paragraph, and then I will answer the questions.

MR. POOL: All right.

MR. CHERKOSS: We seek this goal: political power by the working people of this country, created by students and solid intellectuals. HUAC, Johnson, and their ilk are opposed to the interests of most Americans. Their attack on PLP and the antiwar movement has served to unite forces of progress more than ever. Those called to the hearings, like ourselves, have fought back and will continue to fight back. We have nothing to hide. We will use this forum, and have used this forum, to expose the reactionary nature of the Administration. We have pointed out their ruthlessness, and we are using this [forum] to show that U.S. imperialism is prepared for a long fight, and we must be prepared, too, for a long and hard effort, if we want to win. Despite this attack, the antiwar movement will grow. Our people can defeat the war machine. We hail the efforts of the Vietnamese people. They are winning. We welcome their triumph. We say to U.S. rulers, "Get out of Vietnam now." I have some other objections. I am not finished.

MR. POOL: Your objection is overruled, if you made one there.

MR. CHERKOSS: That was an objection to this Committee and its hearings.

MR. POOL: All right.

MR. CHERKOSS: I associate myself with the suit against HUAC, declaring HUAC illegal, that is now pending in the Washington courts. I fully associate with that suit. I object to answering any questions of this Committee on the ground that Public Law 601, 79th Congress, 60 Statutes 812, Part 2, Rule XI, authorizing the Committee on Un-American Activities to make investigations of the extent, character, and objects of un-American propaganda activities in the U.S., violates the U.S. Constitution, in that the statute is ambiguous and vague, the term "un-American propaganda activities" being nowhere defined, being in fact incapable of one precise definition, and obscuring the fact that there is not one, but two, kinds of un-American activities: first, those that the vast majority of American people deem un-American, such as the undemocratic activities of this Committee; and, secondly, those deemed un-American by a small minority of the wealthy, privileged, the ruling class, who are now escalating the Vietnam war, and by their political spokesmen, such as members of this Committee and the U.S. power machine. I further object to answering any questions of this Committee on the grounds that the statute on its face, as applied by the House Un-American Activities Committee for more than twenty years, and especially today in its harassment of those opposing the Vietnam war, is repugnant to freedom of speech, assembly, association, and privacy guaranteed to the people by the Bill of Rights, and suppresses dissent, and thus infringes not only the rights of dissenters, but, above all, the right of the American people as a whole to be informed of the opinion of the dissenters, as a basis for the American people correctly to make decisions concerning their welfare and very survival, and results in this Committee [carrying us] further along the American road to Fascism, and further results in discarding democratic processes, openly making the Government the master over the people, and not the servant of the people, a Government not *of* the people, but *against* the people, that rules in the interest of the elite, the ruling class.

MR. POOL: Your objection is overruled.

MR. CHERKOSS: I am not finished yet. O.K., I have plenty of time here. You guys are paying the bill. You are defrauding the American people on that. I decline to answer on the grounds that this Committee is at present illegally constituted in that four or more—I am not too sure—four or more of its members, Congressman Watson of South Carolina,* and Joe Pool of Texas, and Willis of Louisiana, were elected in states which have denied the right to vote to a considerable number of Negro and poor-white citizens of the state but whose representation has not been proportionately reduced as required by section two of the Fourteenth Amendment to the Constitution of the U.S. You have subpoenaed us in an attempt to scare, intimidate, and thus split the growing American movement against the war and the U.S. Government that bears sole responsibility for that war. We have come here with clean hands, and you cannot say the same. It is you, not us, that are acting against the interests of the American people. And let us face it, gentlemen, your Government days are numbered.

MR. POOL: Are you finished?

MR. CHERKOSS: Well, just as my opener. Gentlemen, I am finished with the opener.

MR. POOL: Your objection is overruled. Would you want to answer the question whether or not you are a Communist? I think I asked you that a while ago.

MR. CHERKOSS: As I stated, the U.S. Government is acting against the needs, the real needs, and aspirations of the American people not only in Vietnam, but in the Dominican Republic, Angola, in Asia, Africa, Latin America, and in this country. Black people are systematically murdered on the streets of this country every day. And this Government that does not represent the interests of the American people and cannot be reformed—we have seen that it cannot be reformed—must be destroyed by the people, in the interest of the people. And this Committee will be demolished, like the U.S. Government, by the American people, the American working people, solid intellectuals, and solid students. And, yes, I am proud to say I am a

* Albert W. Watson of South Carolina was not yet a Committee member in 1966. The Southerners, other than Pool and Willis, were Tuck (Virginia), Weltner (Georgia), and Buchanan (Alabama). —E.B.

Communist, a Marxist-Leninist, a revolutionary, acting in accordance with the full aspirations of the American and world peoples.

MR. POOL: Does that include using violence to overthrow the Government if necessary?

MR. CHERKOSS: That sounds like a loaded question. Let us face it. The violence that was used here to get the lawyers out was all too apparent to the people in this room. The violence that the U.S. Government uses to suppress peoples throughout the world is all too apparent to all of us. Let us face it. The violence is on the hands of the ruling class, and that has been historically true. So you are the guys that are committing the violence throughout the world, who are brutally dehumanizing people throughout this country and throughout the world. You are the fellows that use violence.

MR. POOL: If necessary, would you use violence to overthrow this Government?

MR. CHERKOSS: The American working people, as I said before, along with their allied forces, are going to take power, and they'll do that any way they deem necessary at that time.

MR. POOL: Including violence, if necessary?

MR. CHERKOSS: Well, my friend, we can look at history and say no ruling class has ever surrendered power voluntarily. That is a fact in history.

MR. POOL: And that might be a fact in the future? Is that what you are saying?

MR. CHERKOSS: Well, not in the future but today, this Government brutally suppresses the peoples of the world and the people of this country. They use force and violence every single day. Black people throughout this country know all about the force and violence that the U.S. Government and their lackeys use against them.

MR. POOL: So you refuse to say that you would use violence, if necessary? Is that what you mean?

MR. CHERKOSS: Will you repeat the question? I can't understand this fellow's accent. Is there someone speaking that isn't a racist, that speaks with a more American accent?

MR. POOL: I think the American people understand what I am saying, regardless of my accent.

MR. CHERKOSS: Now, Joe—

MR. POOL: I ask you, one more time, if you want to answer. You have been very cooperative and maybe you want to answer this. Would you use violence, if necessary, to overthrow this Government, if you disagreed with it?

MR. CHERKOSS: I told you the people of this country will take power as they deem necessary at this time, and the force and violence—

MR. POOL: Is always initiated by the ruling class?

MR. CHERKOSS: That is my answer.

MR. POOL: All right. All right, Mr. Nittle, wait just a second. I haven't ruled on the— What was the previous question?

MR. NITTLE: The question, Mr. Pool, the outstanding question, is whether or not this witness has resided at 2732 Haste Street.

MR. CHERKOSS: Oh, yes, that's right. That's the question.

MR. POOL: Do you care to answer the question, or do you want me to listen to some more objections on that?

MR. CHERKOSS: State the relevancy of that question.

MR. NITTLE: Yes, I shall. Mr. Cherkoss, it is the Committee's information that you are a West Coast student organizer for the Progressive Labor Party and that you also served as a West Coast spokesman of its front organization, the May 2nd Movement—

MR. CHERKOSS: The only front I know of here is the front of the CIA for U.S. imperialism. Let us talk about fronts. Let us talk about fronts this Government has set up internationally to suppress the people throughout the world.

MR. POOL: Just a minute.

MR. NITTLE: And that pursuant to the program of the Progressive Labor Party, you caused to be formed a Medical Aid to Vietnam Committee, later established on the Stanford University campus and at the University of California in Berkeley. I have before me a copy of a postal application dated November 4, 1965, for Post Office Box 1128, for the Medical Aid to Vietnam Committee, filed under the signature of Steve Cherkoss, indicating a business address for the organization at 3382 Eighteenth Street, San Francisco, an address which was then, according to the information of the Committee—

MR. CHERKOSS: Where does the Committee get its information?

MR. NITTLE:—the headquarters of the Progressive Labor Party. In addition to the business address of the Progressive Labor Party, you gave your home address as 2732 Haste Street. I hand you a copy of that postal application as a portion of my statement of the relevancy of the question.

MR. CHERKOSS: Look, you have subpoenaed us, forced us to be subjected to harassment and public condemnation, calling us three thousand miles from Berkeley. Yes, sir, that was my address, 2732 Haste. I gave my business address at—what is it? Let us see. 3382 Eighteenth Street, San Francisco. Very good. Yes, correct.

MR. NITTLE: And that is your signature on the application?

MR. CHERKOSS: Yes, by all means.

MR. NITTLE: I offer that in evidence, Mr. Chairman.

MR. POOL: Counsel, I think we have had sufficient testimony from this witness, and at this time the witness is excused.

MR. CHERKOSS: I have a few statements to make—

MR. POOL: You are excused. Step down.

MR. CHERKOSS: —about the illegality of this Government. In the words of John Quincy Adams—

MR. POOL: The witness will step down. He has been excused. I am going to direct you to step down for the last time. You are not a witness here now. You are excused. Will you step down quietly? Will you go to the door, or sit down in the room, either one?

MR. CHERKOSS: I have just a few statements to make.

MR. POOL: You will not make any statements. You have been excused.

MR. CHERKOSS: The blood of Americans—

MR. POOL: The officer will escort him to the door.

1968

"Subversive Involvement in Disruption of 1968 Democratic Party National Convention"

The above-cited investigation of members of the Progressive Labor Party came under the heading "Hearings on . . . bills to make punishable assistance to enemies of U.S. in time of undeclared war," in other words, was part of the attempt of those who brought about and then conducted the war in Vietnam to get rid of the peace movement, and especially that part of it which was sympathetic to the enemy. That was 1966; and meanwhile the war was not going very well for the United States. "Subversive involvement in disruption of 1968 Democratic Party National Convention" (the title that covers the testimony below) seemed to offer better foothold. And it is clear enough now that the Committee's investigation of Hayden, Davis, and Dellinger in December 1968 was but a prologue to the drama acted out in Julius Hoffman's Chicago courtroom in 1969–1970. Representative Ichord's preamble, even in the excerpt reprinted here, would suggest, too, that the Committee knew what it was doing.

DECEMBER 2–3, 1968:

Tom Hayden

A Subcommittee of the Committee on Un-American Activities met, at 10:10 a.m., in room 311, Cannon House Office Building, Washington, D.C., the Honorable Richard H. Ichord (Chairman of the Subcommittee) presiding.

(Subcommittee members: Representatives Richard H. Ichord, of Missouri, Chairman; John M. Ashbrook, of Ohio; and Albert W. Watson, of South Carolina.)

Subcommittee members present: Representatives Ichord and Ashbrook [Watson attended on December 3. —E.B.].

Staff members present: Francis J. McNamara, Director; Frank Conley, Special Counsel; Chester D. Smith, General Counsel; Alfred M. Nittle, Counsel; and Herbert Romerstein, Investigator.

MR. ICHORD: The purpose of the hearing is to investigate and determine the nature and extent of Communist and subversive participation in the organization and the instigation of the disturbances that occurred during the Democratic National Convention in Chicago and the connections, if any, of certain leaders of the demonstration with foreign powers. There have been charges that the police overreacted; there have been charges that the police underreacted. Those charges are collateral to these hearings. There have also been charges that national TV did not accurately report what happened in Chicago. That is not the purpose of these hearings. The purposes are as stated. Now these are legislative hearings, a legislative investigation conducted by the House Committee on Un-American Activities, which is one of the standing Committees of Congress. These are not trial proceedings. No one is on trial here. The Committee seeks to punish no witness for conduct outside this hearing room.

MR. [Henry M.] DI SUVERO: Mr. Chairman—

MR. ICHORD: Will you come forward, sir, and identify yourself?

MR. DI SUVERO: My name is di Suvero, and I am representing Thomas Hayden. There was one matter that was left open by the Committee Chairman during the last hearings, and that was the matter under our point 11, which the Committee Chairman reserved decision on. Point 11 referred to the fact that Mr. Hayden was under pending state criminal prosecutions in the state court of Illinois. What we asked at that time was that the Committee not make inquiry, on the basis that such inquiry would violate Mr. Hayden's due-process rights, as well as violate the separation of powers, insofar as J. Campbell has ordered an inquiry by the Federal grand jury. And I would like to know what the Committee's decision has been on that ruling.

MR. ICHORD: Mr. Counsel, could you explain to the Chair the nature of the prosecution?

MR. DI SUVERO: Well, the state prosecutions are five counts. One is obstructing a police officer, two of disorderly conduct, and two of resisting arrest. The Federal prosecution, to which we have been advised Mr. Hayden is a target of that prosecution, is a prosecution under the Federal antiriot law.

MR. ICHORD: Has there been an indictment?

MR. DI SUVERO: There has not been an indictment.

MR. ICHORD: Mr. Counsel, do you propose to ask this witness any questions concerning the charges pending against him in the City of Chicago?

MR. CONLEY: Mr. Chairman, we do not contemplate any questions directed to his specific activities out of which these arrests apparently arose.

MR. ICHORD: The Chair is aware of Supreme Court decisions to the effect that, if legislative hearings are conducted for the purpose of aiding the state in the prosecution of the case, Mr. Counsel, they would not be permissible, but this is not the purpose of these hearings. The purposes are as I stated in my opening statement. Therefore, the Chair will have to specifically overrule point 11 of the motion filed by the attorneys, and the Chair would specifically instruct the counsel not to question this witness on any of the specifics contained in the charge of disorderly conduct and the other counts which the attorney has stated.

MR. DI SUVERO: And that direction, I take it, Mr. Chairman, does not extend to any subject matter which might be the inquiry of a Federal grand jury.

MR. ICHORD: Of course, the gentleman has not been indicted by the Federal grand jury. The Chair has been advised that the witness is in possession of certain facts which should be inquired into by this Committee, and I would specifically rule that the pending grand-jury proceedings would not prohibit this Committee from examining the witness. Proceed, Mr. Counsel.

MR. CONLEY: Mr. Hayden, would you give us a brief résumé of your educational background, please?

MR. HAYDEN: You mean the colleges I attended?

MR. CONLEY: High school and college, please.

MR. HAYDEN: Yes. I attended Royal Oak-Dondero High School in Royal Oak, Michigan, from 1954 to 1957. I attended the University of Michigan, 1957 to 1961. I returned to the University of Michigan 1962 through part of 1964 as a graduate student and as an instructor, and I taught political science at Rutgers University in 1967.

MR. CONLEY: Did you get a degree from the University of Michigan?

MR. HAYDEN: I did not complete my graduate studies.

MR. CONLEY: Did you get a bachelor's?

MR. HAYDEN: I got a bachelor's degree in 1961.

MR. CONLEY: Was this in English?

MR. HAYDEN: Yes.

MR. CONLEY: Now, Mr. Hayden, since your completion of your education, what particular positions have you held?

MR. HAYDEN: You mean jobs—in the sense of how I get money?

MR. CONLEY: Well, let us start with that, yes.

MR. HAYDEN: Well, I have done some teaching, as I said, at Rutgers University. I have been paid as an author and lecturer, published two books, one by New American Library–Signet, on North Vietnam, and another on the conditions in Newark at the time of the rebellion of July 1967, which was published by Random House.

MR. CONLEY: Excuse me. Was this book *Rebellion in Newark*?

MR. HAYDEN: Right. And I remain under contract, writing another book on Vietnam for the same publishing house.

MR. CONLEY: All right. Now, have you, in connection with your book-writing, also written the preface to a book called *Mission to Hanoi*?

MR. HAYDEN: You mean the book by Communist Party theoretician Herbert Aptheker.

MR. CONLEY: Yes, sir.

MR. HAYDEN: Yes, I was a fellow traveler to Hanoi with Herbert Aptheker in 1965 and I did write an introduction to his book, before I proceeded to write a book giving my own political views.

MR. CONLEY: All right. Now then, these are the jobs that you have held where you received pay, as I understand.

MR. HAYDEN: As far as I can recall.

MR. CONLEY: All right. Now, what jobs have you held in the political area, as you define it?

MR. HAYDEN: Well, I consider myself an organizer of a movement to put you and your Committee out of power, because I think you represent racist philosophy—

MR. CONLEY: Well, what group is that, sir?

MR. HAYDEN: —that has no meaning any more in the twentieth century.

MR. CONLEY: Mr. Hayden, what group do you refer to that you represent?

MR. HAYDEN: Well, I have worked for many groups. As you know, I worked very hard for several years for Students for a Democratic Society.

MR. CONLEY: Were you president of that group from June of '62 to '63?

MR. HAYDEN: I was president of SDS, yes, during the time that you designate.

MR. CONLEY: And were you the author of—

MR. HAYDEN: But before that I was an organizer of it, and afterward I remained affiliated with it for some time.

MR. CONLEY: Were you the author of the Port Huron Statement?

MR. HAYDEN: I wish that I was, but I was merely a drafter of the original document, and the author of the document was the convention itself that met in Port Huron.

MR. CONLEY: You assisted, then, in the preparation of the document which was adopted by the convention?

MR. HAYDEN: I was probably the major author of the original draft.

MR. CONLEY: All right. Was it materially changed by the convention?

MR. HAYDEN: Yes. It had a better position on American capitalism. I was not too clear about the problems of American society, and the convention straightened me out by deciding that the profit system that you represent is a fundamental thing to be moved aside so that the country can move ahead.

MR. CONLEY: All right. Now, Mr. Hayden, a minute ago, in connection with your books, you mentioned that you had written a book about Vietnam. Was this book *The Other Side*?

MR. HAYDEN: Right.

MR. CONLEY: Did you collaborate on this book with the traveler that went with you, Mr. [Staughton] Lynd?

MR. HAYDEN: Yes, I did.

MR. CONLEY: And this book came out subsequent to your preface to *Mission to Hanoi*?

MR. HAYDEN: As far as I can recall, Herbert Aptheker's book came out rather quickly after the trip, and the book that I wrote with Staughton came out some time later.

MR. CONLEY: Now, Mr. Hayden, were you the co-project director with Mr. [Rennie] Davis for the National Mobilization Committee's efforts in Chicago?

MR. HAYDEN: Yes, I was.

MR. CONLEY: When were you appointed to this position?

MR. HAYDEN: I suppose it was in the very early—in the early spring.

MR. CONLEY: Could you be specific in terms of months, sir?

MR. HAYDEN: I don't think I could, but I would guess at March or April.

MR. CONLEY. March or April. By whom were you appointed?

MR. HAYDEN: By the Mobilization, which has a structure for making such appointments, consisting of an administrative committee and a steering committee and a set of officers.

MR. CONLEY: Were you a part of the steering committee or the officers or the—

MR. HAYDEN: No.

MR. CONLEY: In other words, you were appointed by this group. How many people are represented by this group?

MR. HAYDEN. The Mobilization has representatives from nearly a hundred organizations, most of whom are active around particular subjects like the organization of the demonstration.

MR. CONLEY: Well, did a hundred people meet to decide to appoint you?

MR. HAYDEN: I can't really recall. If you will allow me one minute to go talk to Rennie Davis, who has more of an organizational mind than I do,

I am sure I could straighten it all out, but the Mobilization, through its normal process, appointed me in the spring of the year to be a project director with Rennie Davis, and I went to Chicago for that purpose.

MR. CONLEY: Did you receive this appointment in writing?

MR. HAYDEN: Oh, no, that's not the way we work.

MR. CONLEY: Do you recall who actually told you that you had been appointed?

MR. HAYDEN: No, I just knew that I had been appointed. If anyone told me that I was appointed, it was Dave Dellinger, who, as you know, is the chairman of the Mobilization.

MR. CONLEY: All right. Now, Mr. Hayden, when did you go to Chicago and begin working full time for the committee?

MR. HAYDEN: Late May or early June.

MR. CONLEY: All right. And did you work out of the 407 South Dearborn Street address?

MR. HAYDEN: Yes, I did.

MR. CONLEY: Now, at the time that you started to work for the committee were you paid any type of a salary?

MR. HAYDEN: No. I didn't take a salary. I lived from my normal income.

MR. CONLEY: Did you, during any of the time that you worked with the National Mobilization Committee, receive any salary or compensation?

MR. HAYDEN: Not that I know. I think they allocated some funds for the office staff, and those probably were in Rennie Davis's name. But I wasn't too close to that end of the organization, and my services were basically volunteer services. If Mr. Davis is here and he is listening to your questions, he can come before you with some more concrete answers.

MR. CONLEY: Then, sir, it is your testimony that you received no compensation, either by check or by cash, for your activities in Chicago?

MR. HAYDEN: As best as I can recall, I lived from my own income, but, you see, the way we live I give Rennie some money, and he might give it back to me. And in that sense, it may have gone through the Mobilization at one time or another, but basically, I always lived on my own income.

MR. CONLEY: Well, sir, I can understand with cash that this might be true, but do you have any specific recollection of having received any checks in any way that were earmarked as moneys for you as compensation for working with the National Mobilization Committee?

MR. HAYDEN: There might have been some during the summer, but if there were they were a pittance. Maybe two hundred dollars.

MR. CONLEY: All right, sir.

MR. HAYDEN: I can check that in my bank account. I just don't have the information here.

MR. CONLEY: All right, sir. You stated that you continued to live on your outside income. What was your outside income during the summer of 1968?

MR. HAYDEN: How much money did I carry around, or what?

MR. CONLEY: No, sir, what was the source of your income?

MR. HAYDEN: Source of it? Speaking—based on the notoriety that people like you and the mass media have given me.

MR. CONLEY: Your speaking appearances, then, were what you were able to derive your income from?

MR. HAYDEN: And writing.

MR. CONLEY: What particular articles were you writing at that time?

MR. HAYDEN: This summer? Well, as I said, I was at work, on the contractual basis with Random House, on a new book on Vietnam.

MR. CONLEY: All right. Now, Mr. Hayden, Mr. Davis worked with you in the Chicago office, did he not?

MR. HAYDEN: He primarily ran the office.

MR. CONLEY: Did you consider him your boss?

MR. HAYDEN: No. He was my brother.

MR. CONLEY: All right. How many other full-time employees did you have in the Chicago office?

MR. HAYDEN: I don't know, because we don't operate on that basis. As the convention approached, we had more and more people working out of the office on a multitude of problems.

MR. CONLEY: Starting in June—how many people did you have there in June?

(*Witness confers with counsel.*)

MR. HAYDEN: You see, because we have different views of the world, it sometimes may seem to you that I don't answer your questions, but that is primarily because I don't live in a world of jobs, money, and so forth.

MR. CONLEY: No, sir, you have answered my question very nicely.

MR. HAYDEN: I don't know how many people worked in the Chicago office in June. Probably ten or fifteen.

MR. CONLEY: All right, sir. And then in July—do you have any statement as to how large the staff had grown to at that time?

MR. HAYDEN: No.

MR. CONLEY: A guesstimate?

MR. HAYDEN: More. Twenty, twenty-five.

MR. CONLEY: All right, sir, and then during the first two weeks of August, what had the staff grown to?

MR. HAYDEN: I don't really know. It was larger, but, you see, it was organized not in terms of numbers. We were organizing a legal panel to handle our suit against Mayor [Richard J.] Daley, seeking to get permits for our demonstrations and rallies, and I don't know if you would consider those lawyers part of the Mobilization staff. We were organizing doctors to prepare first-aid stations, because we expected that, what with the announcement that twenty thousand troops would be brought into the city, some people were going to get hurt. And we didn't want Mayor Daley's hospitals to be the only thing we could go to if people were hit over the head. But I don't know if you would consider those doctors part of the Mobilization staff.

MR. CONLEY: You considered them part of the Mobilization staff, didn't you?

MR. HAYDEN: No, that is the doctors' group. We considered our responsibility was to make sure that sympathetic public-health students, medical students, and doctors would get themselves together and stay in touch with us about our programmatic needs, and the same with lawyers, so the question of staff involves a lot of blurred lines. That is all I am saying. Out of the central office, Room 315, 407 South Dearborn, as I say, there was always a nucleus of ten to thirty people doing the normal central office work, answering the phone and sending out mailings and protecting the doors from people who might want to come in and shoot the place up. That sort of thing occupied most of the people in the office. And as the convention approached, more and more people came to the office, at least to get some information about what was happening and where to go in the city. So it got to be a very large office situation by the time of the convention.

MR. CONLEY: You did not consider the lawyers, then, and the doctors, who were part of the over-all plan, as a part of the Mobilization Committee?

MR. HAYDEN: Well, we don't think in those terms.

MR. CONLEY: Sir, you are the one that raised question that I might think in those terms, and I am asking you what *you* thought?

MR. HAYDEN: They didn't have to accept the Mobilization structure. They were not integral parts of it, in the sense of groups that would abide by all the day-to-day decisions or general policy decisions. They were cooperating groups of doctors and lawyers.

MR. CONLEY: All right. Now, after the convention was over, Mr. Hayden, did you then leave the Chicago area and go to the West Coast?

MR. HAYDEN: Yes.

MR. CONLEY: And have you continued to remain on the West Coast, basically, since that time?

MR. HAYDEN: Basically, since that time, yes.

MR. CONLEY: All right, sir. And did you continue to receive any compensation after the convention from the National Mobilization Committee?

MR. HAYDEN: No.

MR. CONLEY: To your knowledge, you have not received any?

MR. HAYDEN: No, I haven't received it.

MR. CONLEY: Now, when you initially went to the Oakland area, did you not in fact live with Robert Scheer?

MR. HAYDEN: No.

MR. CONLEY: You did not stay at his residence?

MR. HAYDEN: I stayed at several residences, including his.

MR. CONLEY: All right, you did stay at his residence at one time, then, since the convention and prior to this time?

MR. HAYDEN: Yes.

MR. CONLEY: Now, you are now living at what was it?

MR. HAYDEN: 6000 Broadway, in Oakland.

MR. CONLEY: In Oakland. In the early months of 1968 numerous items that your National Mobilization Committee put out referred to you and Rennie Davis as co-project directors of the Chicago organization. You are familiar with the articles that I am talking about?

MR. HAYDEN: I am familiar with the titles.

MR. CONLEY: Well, your literature carried at the bottom of it you and Rennie Davis as co-project directors.

MR. HAYDEN: Right.

MR. CONLEY: Then a letter came out on August 10, 1968, on the stationery of the National Mobilization Committee and signed by Dave Dellinger, and it refers to Rennie Davis as project director and makes no mention of yourself. Were you no longer a co-project director as of August 10?

MR. HAYDEN: I don't know the letter you are referring to, but, from all that I recall, we were always the co-project directors.

MR. CONLEY: This is the letter, sir.

MR. HAYDEN: Well, this only refers to Rennie Davis as project director because Rennie would be—as I said, he was the managerial person in the office, and the section of the letter you refer to indicates that people should call the Chicago office and talk with Paul Potter, Vernon Grizzard, or Rennie Davis. And that makes sense to me, because Rennie was the one who operated the office, but that doesn't imply that I was not a co-project director, even though I can understand how you might come to that conclusion.

MR. CONLEY: Sir, I just wanted to clear it up. O.K.? Now, Mr. Hayden, did you remain in Chicago from the time you arrived there in June until the Democratic Convention in August?

MR. HAYDEN: Yes, I did, basically.

MR. CONLEY: Did you leave there on at least one occasion, though, and go overseas?

MR. HAYDEN: Yes, I went to Paris to try to do some writing about the peace talks and to have discussions with Ambassador [W. Averell] Harriman and with North Vietnamese officials.

MR. CONLEY: Now, was this trip made in July of 1968?

MR. HAYDEN: To the best of my recollection.

MR. CONLEY: And did you meet, when you were in Paris, with the North Vietnamese, Viet Cong, and U.S. representatives, including Mr. Harriman?

MR. HAYDEN: Yes, although I don't recall meeting with South Vietnamese representatives, or Viet Cong, as you call them.

MR. ASHBROOK: Mr. Counsel, he answered yes. You did meet with Mr. Harriman?

MR. HAYDEN: Yes, of course.

MR. CONLEY: Now do you recall specifically when in July these visits occurred?

MR. HAYDEN: It was the beginning of July. I remember, because I was there on the Fourth of July, and we had a Fourth of July celebration with all the Americans in Paris who wanted to come. We had a sort of a rally and a discussion with Vietnamese people and we showed films, and so on.

MR. CONLEY: Now, when you had these contacts with the North Vietnamese in Paris, did you discuss with them a meeting between U.S. and Vietnamese youth to be held in Budapest, Hungary, in September of this year?

MR. HAYDEN: No, I did not.

MR. CONLEY: You had no discussion with them at all about that meeting in September?

MR. HAYDEN: No.

* * *

MR. CONLEY: Mr. Hayden, is it your present aim to seek the destruction of the present American democratic system?

MR. HAYDEN: That is a joke.

MR. CONLEY: I am asking you, sir.

MR. HAYDEN: Well, I don't believe the present American democratic system exists. That is why we can't get together to straighten things out. You have destroyed the American democratic system by the existence of a committee of this kind.

MR. CONLEY: Well, let us use the word "system," then. Let us take the words "American" and "democratic" out of it and let us just call it the system. Is it your aim to destroy the present system?

MR. HAYDEN: What do you mean by "destroy"?

MR. CONLEY: To overturn it.

MR. HAYDEN: What do you mean by "overturn it"?

MR. CONLEY: To do away with it.

MR. HAYDEN: What do you mean by "do away with it"? By what means?

MR. CONLEY: I am asking you, sir.

MR. HAYDEN: No, you asked me whether it was my aim.

MR. CONLEY: I am asking you if that is your aim, sir.

MR. HAYDEN: The question is too ambiguous.

MR. ICHORD: We are getting into the field of political philosophy. The witness has testified at length as to his philosophy, Mr. Counsel. But it would be very difficult for the Chair to direct an answer to the question.

MR. CONLEY: Mr. Hayden, I have one final question for you. Ambrose Bierce, in his *Devil's Dictionary,* defines a conspirator as someone who finds it necessary to write down everything for his enemy to find. Mr. Hayden, you were clever enough not to be carrying any names or addresses on your person, or any slips of paper, at the time of the events in Chicago. However, in the purse of Miss Constance Brown was a complete list of names and addresses which were purportedly prepared by you. And I would ask you, sir, don't you think that the young people who follow you in these various movements should take a second look at you before they place their lives and their responsibilities in the hand of you [*sic*]?

MR. HAYDEN: ———. [Thus the Committee's records. I believe the missing word is "shit." —E.B.]

MR. ICHORD: The witness will please be seated.

MR. HAYDEN: I thought that was the final question.

MR. ICHORD: The Chair directs the witness to be seated.

MR. WATSON: Mr. Chairman, may I make this point? I know there are advocates of free speech, and the witness is one of them, but I happen to be one who will not tolerate any such language as that. We have ladies in this room, and I shall not tolerate it, and if it is necessary for me to ask the police to arrest a man for such disorderly language as that, I shall do so. I am not going to tolerate language such as that in the presence of ladies.

MR. HAYDEN: Well, will you tolerate a question of the indecent kind that was just made by your own counsel?

MR. ICHORD: Let the witness be admonished that this is a Committee of Congress, consisting of duly elected members, that this Committee is a legislative arm of Congress, and there are ways of enforcing proper order before the Committee. There is such a thing as contempt.

MR. ASHBROOK: Mr. Hayden, sometimes I get the impression that you indicate what happened in Chicago was unfortunate, a travesty, and so forth. Other times, I get the indication you believe that Chicago was valuable, in that it demonstrated certain things, brought to the surface what you consider to be unfair treatment, some of the wrongs of the political processes. There is somewhat of a dilemma here. I would like to have for the record whether you think now, looking back to the Chicago convention, what happened was good, bad, or helpful to your movement. You have talked kind of from both sides. I would like to know which is your honest point of view.

MR. HAYDEN: I have talked both sides, because we are going to win either way, Mr. Ashbrook. We would have won if it would have been safe and secure for two hundred thousand rank-and-file people, ordinary people, to come to Chicago and protest. That would have had a profoundly discrediting effect on the Democratic Party as it ratified the war in Vietnam and nominated Hubert Humphrey, and would have defeated the Democratic Party by the alienation of its grass-roots base. Since that was not allowed, because of the failure of the city to grant permits, since that was not allowed because there was too much jeopardy facing anybody with a family or job, and since they didn't come to Chicago, we won in a different way: by exposing the brute nature that underlies the supposedly democratic two-party system. I would have preferred to win the first way, but the second way was a tremendous victory of a kind for the young people in this country, people who are not voters, people who are never polled by Gallup or Harris, but people who watch on television and do not identify with the Nixon girls and David Eisenhower, but identify with the young people who are in the streets of Chicago, and watch very carefully. If you think that you have had militant people before you in these hearings, you have yet to see what the seven- and eight-year-olds are going to bring you over the next five or ten years. You have taught them to have no respect for your authority by what has happened in the City of Chicago. And that is a victory in the sense that committees like yourselves are now through. You exist only formally; you exist officially; but you have lost all authority. And when a group of people who have power lose their authority, then they have lost. You have lost, period. That is why I have been quiet. That is why these hearings aren't disrupted, that is why no one comes to these hearings to picket any more. The job has been done against HUAC, and the job has virtually been done against politicians.

MR. ICHORD: And you say you are eventually going to do the job against the whole United States?

MR. HAYDEN: Politicians like Dean Rusk, Lyndon Johnson, Richard Nixon, Hubert Humphrey, these people are in a sense already finished, because they can't exercise any authority; they have no respect from wide sections of the American people. Richard Nixon does not even believe that Beatles albums should be played. He believes that drugs are the curse of American youth.

MR. ICHORD: Of course, Mr. Hayden, you are very fortunate to have the protection of the First Amendment rights. Do you think that if you had performed the acts that you have performed and said such things that you have said in North Vietnam, in behalf of America, that you wouldn't be shot on the spot? Do you think you would be given the same amount of liberty, guarantees of First Amendment rights, which you have been given?

MR. HAYDEN: Mr. Ichord, I don't consider that I have that much freedom. Is it freedom to sit here, and under penalty of going to jail if I don't talk to you and express my opinions over and over in a committee chamber of this sort, knowing full well that the opinions are hot air, they have no effect on your ears, they will not change a thing? If that is freedom, that is a very inadequate definition of freedom.

MR. ICHORD: You have indeed a very strange philosophy, sir. You say that you don't care about electing a President. You don't care about a President at all. What kind of government do you want?

MR. HAYDEN: I want a democratic government. My views on that are spelled out in the—not so very well, perhaps, certainly not, in my opinion, but they are spelled out in exhaustive detail in all kinds of things that I have written, which I would be glad to submit to you, but I think that the question at this point would be a little bit redundant.

MR. ASHBROOK: You would have preferred to have another approach in Chicago. And from your point of view, this was pushed upon you, but, once it happened, it did pinpoint some of your criticisms of the democratic process and, as such, probably helped in the over-all situation. I gather this is what you are saying. But, from what you are saying, it comes through to me that this was not good for the democratic processes in this country, at least from your point of view, but would be good from the point of view of those who think the democratic processes are in an establishment, white majority, et cetera, and won't work. Would that be a reasonable summation of what you have said? Trying to differentiate between your point of view and our point of view. What happened in Chicago did not help the democratic process in this country?

MR. HAYDEN: From your point of view.

MR. ASHBROOK: From our point of view.

MR. HAYDEN: From my point of view, it did.

MR. ASHBROOK: Well, then, maybe that is why I have a hard time understanding your statement, which is made in the *New York Times,* on September 1, 1968, from Downers Grove, Illinois, where it quoted you directly as saying—by John Kifner, their reporter: "We're going to create little Chicagos everywhere the candidates appear." If what happened in Chicago was bad—and, of course, some of what you have said indicates that it was bad—it should be avoided; it was unfortunate; and, once happening, you had to derive some benefit for those who want change. Now you are in a position of saying that, nevertheless, you want little Chicagos, two hundred, three hundred Chicagos throughout the country. Is that a fair statement?

MR. HAYDEN: Yes, I wanted, and many of us wanted, the energy and momentum of the Chicago demonstration to be carried back to the communities where the demonstrators came from, and the criticism of the Democratic Party, criticism of the false choices in the elections, criticism of the fact that there was no way to vote for peace in the 1968 elections, to be made very clear in these local communities. And I wanted the people to go back from Chicago and interpret what happened in Chicago to students in high schools and colleges and their neighbors, and I wanted demonstrations to occur whenever candidates came to speak. And there *were* some demonstrations around the country when candidates came to speak. We wanted

Election Day demonstrations, and there *were* some Election Day demonstrations.

MR. ASHBROOK: Well, then I would be wrong in assuming, when you say you wanted to create little Chicagos in the country, you are talking from the standpoint of demonstration, where I guess I was thinking you meant that you wanted the police to be hitting people on the head, and that kind of thing.

MR. HAYDEN: Well, it takes two to do that. It takes an initiator, and I think that police learned from Chicago to temporarily pull back, in some local situations, because they wanted to get Hubert Humphrey elected President.

MR. ASHBROOK: The police wanted to?

MR. HAYDEN: No, not the police, but the people who order the police. Certainly the police *didn't* want Hubert Humphrey elected President.

MR. ASHBROOK: On one other point, I think it is very important, because we are looking at all the statements in the context of what you have said, what your meaning is to what you have said, and I think you pointed out very articulately that you do have some different meaning than what many of us might think would come from that; that is a good example there. But from your own words—and I know quite often you have been misquoted; I can understand that, everybody is misquoted—but from your own words, in the June 15, 1968, issue of *Ramparts,* page 40, where it says, "Two, Three, Many Columbias"—that is the heading—it says, "By Tom Hayden," you state the following:

> Columbia opened a new tactical stage in the resistance movement which began last fall: from the overnight occupation of buildings to permanent occupation; from mill-ins to the creation of revolutionary committees; from symbolic civil disobedience to barricaded resistance. Not only are these tactics already being duplicated on other campuses, but they are sure to be surpassed by even more militant tactics. In the future it is conceivable that students will threaten destruction of buildings as a last deterrent to police attacks. Many of the tactics learned can also be applied in smaller hit-and-run operations between strikes: raids on the offices of professors doing weapons research could win substantial support among students while making the university more blatantly repressive.

End of your direct quote. I would have to say, when I observe this and other statements you have made, most of the tenor that I get out of them is a call to more militant action. I know you have defined what you mean by "militant." Here you are talking about taking over buildings, you are talking about hit-and-run operations between strikes, raids on offices, maybe we get back to the old semantic argument of what "attack" means, of what "pinning delegates in the convention" means, what the statement "anything to stop this farce" means, of what "guerrillas" means, but it seems to me that this sets the stage for the confrontations with the police, a confrontation with the authority everywhere, which many of us feel might have happened in Chicago and might have been one of the causes. Now I hand you the whole article. I assure you I didn't take it out of context, because I have read it three or four times, and isn't it fair for any reasonable person, possibly even a Member of Congress, to feel that you are advocating more militant action, up to and including illegal action?

MR. HAYDEN: Well, we would disagree on whether it is illegal action.

MR. ASHBROOK: To take over a building?

MR. HAYDEN: I think it is unconstitutional for the Columbia board of trustees to be appointed for life.

MR. ASHBROOK: But not to prevent students from going to class?

MR. HAYDEN: I think it is illegal and unconstitutional for scientists to make weapons which are banned by Geneva agreements and other international treaties and to make them on university campuses. I think that, in the whole area of student riots and welfare, students are threatened in a way that gives them less actual legal civil rights than convicts in a penitentiary have. My views on this are extremely thoroughly written down. I don't believe that there is a democratic machinery on the campus. I don't believe the draft represents democratic machinery. And as long as there is no democratic machinery, then young people will either have to capitulate in the *status quo* or find ways to resist it. I don't really advise that people find illegal ways to resist it, because I think that the authorities are going to start putting people away. Most of my friends are on their way to jail, for one thing or another. Most of the young leaders in this country in the movements—many of them unknown to you, many of them unknown to me—are facing prison sentences already, so I beg to differ with the idea that I advocate illegal action, but I do advocate action that could bring a university to a halt, as the actions of the students and faculty at San Francisco State have brought that university to a halt, to try to straighten the university out.

MR. ASHBROOK: Mr. Hayden, maybe we would disagree on the term, but it seemed to me from what you have said that that comes very close to anarchy.

MR. HAYDEN: Well, we are living in a state of anarchy when a young man is faced by a draft board—the average age of its members is fifty-eight, one-fifth of those members are seventy-three years old—there is no mechanism for that young person to avoid intolerable choices, either of fighting in a war that he doesn't want to fight in, or copping out and letting some Puerto Rican or young black person or poor working-class person fight for him. Isn't that a state of anarchy, facing that individual, rather than a state of law? He has no recourse, he has no machinery, and that is the situation facing all young people in this country, and it is a situation that I could describe in great detail in other spheres besides the draft.

MR. WATSON: Mr. Hayden, I believe you stated, in summation, that we are going to lose, referring to the present generation, the Establishment.

MR. HAYDEN: No, I just meant HUAC has lost its authority. That is why no one pickets here any more.

MR. WATSON: I see. Of course, perhaps some of us may assign other reasons as to why they no longer picket, but—

MR. HAYDEN: I hope you don't think it is the police.

MR. WATSON: Oh, of course not. You have demonstrated that you have no fear or respect for police authority. But did I not understand—

MR. HAYDEN: Not when it is used in the way that you are using it, to protect your so-called democracy.

MR. WATSON: Did I understand you to say that the system, or whatever it is, this generation, we are going to lose?

MR. HAYDEN: I think that politicians like Dean Rusk, Lyndon Johnson, Richard Nixon, Hubert Humphrey have lost their authority with wide sections of the American people. I said that HUAC has lost its authority.

MR. WATSON: And that you—

MR. HAYDEN: And that you can't retain it by having a younger chairman, or being more reasonable, because that doesn't deal with the fundamental questions.

MR. ICHORD: Mr. Hayden, some of the newspaper columnists have stated that you and your group were very instrumental in the election of Richard Nixon. Doesn't that somewhat frustrate you, with your feeling toward Richard Nixon?

MR. HAYDEN: No. I think that the election of Richard Nixon shows that the country will continue to run down until people decide to straighten it out. It doesn't really matter to me whether Hubert Humphrey or Richard Nixon is President of the United States.

MR. WATSON: You didn't say earlier that you and those of your thinking were going to ultimately win?

MR. HAYDEN: Well, I think we will at least outlive you. (*Laughter.*) Probably much of our time will be spent in penitentiaries. I think that we are more than an existential or romantic movement, however; I think we are a calculating movement, a political movement, and we are trying to make this country a better country, and we have every reason to believe that we have some chance to be successful.

MR. WATSON: So your ultimate objective is to make this country a better country. You made that statement.

MR. HAYDEN: Well, yes, I just made that statement.

MR. WATSON: And you have, I believe, a lot of, or several comments in support of the so-called Walker Report.

MR. HAYDEN: Not quite. I don't quite agree with the Walker Report.

MR. WATSON: You don't quite. But some parts of it, you do.

MR. HAYDEN: It has a lot of evidence of what happened in Chicago between the police and demonstrators that I think is accurate evidence, solid evidence.

MR. WATSON: Well, from this report, on page 49, I would like to read a paragraph. The report says it is a typical Yippie flyer, and it reads as follows:

> Who says that rich white Americans can tell the Chinese what is best? How dare you tell the poor that their poverty is deserved? If f—— nuns—

And you know what I mean.

MR. HAYDEN: What *do* you mean, Mr. Watson?

MR. WATSON:

> —laugh at professors—

MR. HAYDEN: What do you mean, Mr. Watson?

MR. WATSON: I will give you credit for being intelligent enough to arrive at an interpretation yourself.

> —disobey your parents: burn your money: you know life is a dream and all of our institutions are man-made illusions effective because YOU take the dream for reality. . . . Break down the family, church, nation, city, economy: turn life into an art form, a theater of the soul and a theater of the future; the revolutionary is the only artist. . . . What's needed is a generation of people who are freaky, crazy, irrational, sexy, angry, irreligious, childish, and mad; people who burn draft cards, burn high school and college degrees; people who say: "To hell with your goals!"; people who lure the youth with music, pot, and acid; people who redefine the normal; people who break with the status-role-title-consumer game; people who have nothing material to lose but their flesh.

And finally:

> The white youth of America have more in common with Indians plundered than they do with their own parents. Burn their houses down, and you will be free.

End quote. That is a typical Yippie flyer. And this, in your judgment, is the way to have a better America?

MR. HAYDEN: I think that beautiful sentiments are expressed in that statement, and I wish that you could understand them, Mr. Watson.

MR. WATSON: Fine, that wraps it up real well. Thank you.

DECEMBER 3, 1968:

Rennie Davis

[Following upon the Hayden testimony.] (Subcommittee members present: Representatives Ichord and Watson.)

MR. DAVIS: My full name is Rennard Cordon Davis.

MR. CONLEY: Spell the first name.

MR. DAVIS: R-e-n-n-a-r-d. My friends call me Rennie. Police and people who are upset by what I represent call me Mr. Davis or simply Davis. I am in the process of possibly moving to Washington in response to President-elect Nixon's call to come to the inauguration and I may take up residence here in Washington, D.C., but for the time being I can receive all mail at 5 Beekman Street in New York City.

MR. CONLEY: Mr. Davis, are you appearing here today in response to a subpoena served on you by United States Deputy Marshal John Brophy on September 26, 1968, at 25 East 26th Street, New York, New York?

MR. DAVIS: I don't remember the exact time that I was subpoenaed, but that is certainly the only reason that I would appear before a committee such as this.

MR. CONLEY: Mr. Davis, where were you born, please?

MR. DAVIS: Well, I was born in Lansing, Michigan.

MR. CONLEY: The date?

MR. DAVIS: May 23, 1940.

MR. CONLEY: Would you be kind enough to give the Committee a brief résumé of your education, high school and college?

MR. DAVIS: I grew up in the Blue Ridge Mountains of Virginia. I am a Southerner. I feel that I am. I went to a small rural school just outside—about sixty-five miles southwest of Washington, called Clarke County High School. It borders right on the property of Senator Harry Byrd, who owns the largest singly owned apple orchard in the country. I attended Oberlin College in Oberlin, Ohio, and received a B.A. degree. I did graduate work—

MR. CONLEY: Was that degree in 1962?

MR. DAVIS: That is correct.

MR. CONLEY: In political science?

MR. DAVIS: Right again.

MR. CONLEY: All right. Go ahead.

MR. DAVIS: I went to graduate schools at the University of Illinois, the University of Michigan, and the University of Chicago.

MR. CONLEY: Did you attend these schools in 1964, 1965, and 1966 respectively?

MR. DAVIS: That is correct.

MR. CONLEY: Have you received any advanced degrees as a result of this graduate work?

MR. DAVIS: No, I can't seem to finish any of my degrees.

MR. CONLEY: Mr. Davis, what is your employment background since high school? What type of employment have you held?

MR. DAVIS: I have been employed by what we have been calling loosely this morning the movement since early 1960. And I think it is misleading to talk about my formal education. My education came from having a cigarette ground out in the back of my neck in the South, trying to get a hamburger with a black man. My education came with working with people from Kentucky, West Virginia, Alabama, and South Carolina who moved to Chicago thinking they could get a better deal there, only to find they were confronted with railroads who wanted to steal rents and fix up apartments in no way at all or caseworkers who live in the suburbs and made literally life-and-death decisions over their lives and they had no recourse in making those decisions. You know my background. My work has been in neighborhoods, in communities, trying to work around those kinds of grievances. That has been the basic employment of the past, and I hope for the future.

MR. CONLEY: Mr. Davis, in the years 1964–1965, were you director of SDS Economic Research and Action Project?

MR. DAVIS: Yes. Let me run through the whole list. In 1964 Students for a Democratic Society established a community-organizing program that was aimed at trying to bring people into black and poor-white communities, to develop new political centers of power that could allow individuals who are victims of police brutality or welfare bureaucracy or slum landlords or loan sharks to have an organization that they could use for their own rights and their own grievances. We established some ten organizing projects in 1964. That was the same year that some eight hundred students went to Mississippi to work against racism. Then in 1965 I moved to Chicago, Illinois, where I became a member of JOIN Community Union.

MR. CONLEY: That is J-O-I-N?

MR. DAVIS: That is correct. The purpose of JOIN was to attempt to see if the kinds of people that Mr. Watson claims to represent and that [Governor George C.] Wallace claimed to speak for could, in fact, if organized around their own grievances and their own problems, begin to understand that they have a relationship to the black community and that, in fact, it is the movement that has begun in the black community that makes the most sense as an ultimate power solution to the problems of poor whites in this country. I had the privilege to work for nearly three years with residents of Alabama, Mississippi, Tennessee, and Kentucky in this organization. In 1967, I believe it was, I became director of a research project that was aimed at supplying information, to various community groups across Chicago, that would be useful in making their challenge to an incredibly corrupt from-top-down political machine represented publicly by Mayor Daley. The name of this organization was the Center for Radical Research.

MR. ICHORD: Is that with headquarters in Chicago?

MR. DAVIS: That is right. In late 1967 I was invited to a conference in Bratislava, Czechoslovakia, along with forty other people who represented the black movement, people who represented the clergy, the lawyers, reporters, women, and others who shared at least a desire to end the slaughter in Vietnam. At that conference, invitation was extended to me to see firsthand what had been talked about at Bratislava through a trip to North Vietnam. I went at that time, October 1967, to North Vietnam, to try to document, if I could, the widespread use of antipersonnel weapons or cluster bomb units in that country. As you know, in 1967 the United States Air Force was claiming it was hitting only steel and concrete in North Vietnam. What I discovered, in cities like Nam Dinh or Son Tay or Hanoi, in the populated civilian areas, was the use of a weapon that sprays small steel pellets in every direction, splintering bodies, splintering bones, creating deep rips within the internal organs, and most people facing a death that amounts to a slow, painful bleeding to death. If such a bomb were to explode in this room, everyone here would die. But as quickly as the bodies could be removed from this room, we could have another session of Un-American Activities.

MR. ICHORD: Are you an expert on bombs, Mr. Davis?

MR. DAVIS: I have studied this particular weapon in great detail, because in 1967 one out of every two bombs dropped in North Vietnam was a cluster bomb unit. So, I attempted to go to study bomb damage and the type of experimental weapons used in Hanoi to bring that information back to the United States, since the United States military—through the press—was patently lying about what was happening in that country.

MR. ASHBROOK: Mr. Davis, on that point, have you yourself physically examined one of these bombs?

MR. DAVIS: Yes, sir. As a matter of fact, just outside of Nam Dinh, about sixty-five miles south of Saigon—it was a city that was reduced to about thirty thousand from sixty-five thousand. An early-morning raid of F-105s came across and dropped CBUs on this city. Immediately after the planes left, we immediately went into the city. There are bomblets inside the cluster bomb unit that contain the pellets, and when they hit, they then explode some three hundred steel pellets in the air—an old-fashioned hand grenade has about eighty pieces of shrapnel. One of the bomblets did not detonate, did not explode, and it was deactivated, and a peasant woman who had just lost two of her own children that morning presented me with this bomblet and asked that I take it back to America where it belongs. She was standing in front of a schoolhouse at the time, and the whole wall was just splintered with these pellets.

MR. ASHBROOK: You don't know that the bomb could have been "planted" and used for propaganda?

MR. DAVIS: If the bomb was "planted," then the North Vietnamese are spending perhaps a million man-hours a month putting little pellets in doors in Hanoi and hospitals and schools, and everywhere you go this camouflage of propaganda has been created over what I traveled, literally hundreds of miles, particularly for essentially rural areas, what amounts to the industrial or city or populated areas. So, I would judge that that was not the case, though there are Americans who believe that the Vietnamese are so vicious they would go to any extreme to create that impression. Coming back from Hanoi, I would like to talk much more about the use of experimental weapons of our military in that country and my purposes in going there, if you are interested in my connections with the Vietnamese, as I am sure you are.

MR. ICHORD: We are getting far afield from the identification.

MR. DAVIS: I was essentially a traveler and speaker about the war until the spring of 1968. At that time I became quite involved in the organization of soldiers—

MR. CONLEY: Mr. Davis, I don't mean to interrupt you or cut you off, but if we get some other information, we could get to that.

MR. DAVIS: I thought I would talk about Summer Support, which I was formerly involved in. It was the project that helped to set up antiwar coffeehouses around the country.

MR. CONLEY: We will get that. But if we can take it in a little different order—

MR. DAVIS: Fine—any way you want.

MR. CONLEY: As I understand it, you were director of SDS, Economic Research and Action Project, the director of the JOIN Community Union?

MR. DAVIS: No, I was never director of JOIN.

MR. CONLEY: Were you the director of the Center for Radical Research? Did I misunderstand you on that?

MR. DAVIS: No, that is correct.

MR. CONLEY: In connection with those three particular jobs that you held, did you receive any compensation?

MR. DAVIS: No, don't be silly. They have no money.

MR. CONLEY: In other words, you were not paid in any way for your work with SDS or with the other two organizations, JOIN or the Center for Radical Research?

MR. DAVIS: No, I never received a paycheck from any of those organizations, to the best of my knowledge.

MR. CONLEY: In connection with your work with the Center for Radical Research, did not this group undertake to investigate the Chicago Police Department for the purpose of identifying the plainclothes officers that worked within that department this past year?

MR. DAVIS: I don't remember the time that we worked on that project, but, as you know through your association with this Committee, many of the organizations that are trying to change this country are continuously infiltrated and undermined by Federal and local police agents. One of the concerns of people who are trying to build a democratic society in this country is how to operate democratically when your meetings are infiltrated and reports are written that distort your purposes and then used against you. It seemed to us that the first step in dealing with this problem was to identify who those agents might be. My recollection is that we did have some young people connected with the research center who tried to develop that information for Chicago community groups.

MR. CONLEY: Mr. Davis, moving to your involvement with the National Mobilization Committee, I would ask you if you were not in Chicago during the Democratic Convention in August of this year.

MR. DAVIS: I have a big scar on my head to demonstrate that I was in Chicago at that time.

MR. CONLEY: Did you not, in fact, serve as codirector with Tom Hayden for the Mobilization Committee's activities in Chicago?

MR. DAVIS: Yes. I wonder if I could speed it up by saying I associate myself with every statement that Mr. Hayden made in the last day and a half. I find the substance of that statement to be correct, and all questions that were put to him, I would respond to in the same way. I think that he demonstrated beautifully what he means by being a political guerrilla. I think he pinned you against the wall. I think his testimony was the best kind of example—

MR. ICHORD: What is your definition?

MR. DAVIS: I would take as an example and a definition Mr. Hayden's —Tom's—testimony because I think that it made this Committee what it is, which is: irrelevant to our movement.

MR. ICHORD: I think we could speed up, Mr. Davis, if we would let the record show that you have the same contempt for the Committee and the other institutions of Congress and our Government—

MR. DAVIS: No, let the record not show that. That would distort my position.

MR. ICHORD: Let's proceed with the questioning, then.

MR. DAVIS: What I was going to suggest, because I am very anxious to get out of here as soon as I can, as I am sure you are, [was] that Mr. Hayden's testimony stand as my testimony as well. Maybe we could now zero in on the questions which remain: how we get our money, how we organize ourselves, whatever you like.

MR. CONLEY: I do have to ask you these questions, because, as I recall Mr. Hayden's questions, he said you were in a better position to answer these next few questions than he was. The last question was, Did you serve as a co-project director? Is your answer yes to that?

Mr. Davis: Mr. Hayden said I was. That is what I was trying to get to. We could cut through the things he already said.

Mr. Conley: When were you appointed to this position, Mr. Davis?

Mr. Davis: Well, appointments don't come in some kind of mechanical way in our movement. I was interested in a demonstration at the Democratic Convention as early as October 1967 and began to go to various meetings to raise that possibility as early as December 1967. I think it was largely because of my interest in focusing on the Democratic Convention, which at the beginning, at least, appeared almost certain to renominate Lyndon Johnson for another four years of slaughter in Vietnam.

Mr. Conley: Mr. Davis, was it in January, February? Was it along in there when the letterhead first began using your name? I certainly don't intend to lead you, but I think we are getting far afield again.

Mr. Davis: I would say: in the spring of 1968 I became co-project director of the National Mobilization Committee to End the War in Vietnam.

Mr. Conley: When did you first go to Chicago to work full time in the office set up on South Dearborn?

Mr. Davis: I lived in Chicago all the time, I was always there.

Mr. Conley: Do you recall when the office was opened? I am referring to Room 315, 407 South Dearborn.

Mr. Davis: The office was opened in late January or early February.

Mr. Conley: Did you start working out of the office at that time?

Mr. Davis: Yes.

Mr. Conley: Was that office being operated at that time as a part of National Mobilization?

Mr. Davis: The Chicago office was a group of people in Chicago who were attempting to relate to a variety of organizations, not all of whom were represented by the National Mobilization coalition. It was only in May, I would guess, that the office in some sense became formally connected with the National Mobilization.

Mr. Conley: Mr. Davis, in connection with your duties as codirector or co-project director, whatever you choose to call it, did you receive any type of remuneration for your duties?

Mr. Davis: I recall that there was a period in which the Mobilization did pay me a subsistence salary that I generally gave away.

Mr. Conley: Was this by check or by cash?

Mr. Davis: It would always have been by check, if such money was given.

Mr. Conley: May I ask you, sir, who was authorized to write checks and deliver checks to you?

Mr. Davis: From the National Mobilization?

Mr. Conley: Yes.

Mr. Davis: Eric Weinberger is our treasurer.

MR. CONLEY: Do you recall on what banks these checks were drawn?

MR. DAVIS: No, I don't.

MR. CONLEY: Was it a Chicago bank or out-of-city bank?

MR. DAVIS: The Mobilization account is in New York City.

MR. CONLEY: Mr. Davis, in some of Mr. Hayden's testimony here yesterday, I believe, he indicated that you actually were the principal administrator of the Chicago office of the National Mobilization Committee, that you more or less had the over-all responsibility for the office. Is this a fair statement?

MR. DAVIS: Yes, but again it does not do justice to the way people work. People don't work in a kind of—one person gives the directions and the other people carry them out. We generally sit down and talk about what the problems are: how do we get housing for maybe five thousand people and who is best at working up a letter to explain our purposes or getting some students to go out and talk about that, and whoever is the best at that or figures they can do it they just say, "O.K., I will do that." It is not like I figure there has to be housing for this number of people and then make an assignment. People would not work with you if you worked that way. How do you explain the fact that people work for no money and live on peanut butter sandwiches?

* * *

MR. CONLEY: Mr. Davis, directing your attention to another document, and it concerns a meeting held near Chicago March 22 to March 24. You will note that it carries a National Mobilization Committee heading and a date of March 7, 1968. Have you seen this document or a document similar to it in connection with that meeting?

MR. DAVIS: This is signed by Father Daniel Berrigan, Carl Davidson, Don Duncan, Al Evanoff, Richard Flacks, Vernon Grizzard, Steve Halliwell, Clark Kissinger, Sidney Lens, Marya Levenson, Linda Morse, Sidney Peck, William Pepper, Monsignor Charles Rice, Franz Schurmann, Cora Weiss, Dagmar Wilson, Dr. Quentin Young, Leni Zeiger, and Howard Zinn. Also the temporary administrative committee: Rennie Davis, Dave Dellinger, Tom Hayden, Bob Greenblatt, and Sue Munaker. I could read my whole address book right into the record if you want it. I have about fifteen hundred names. I think we put this letter out.

MR. CONLEY: When you say "we put this out," you mean National Mobilization put this letter out?

MR. DAVIS: No.

MR. CONLEY: Who put the letter out?

MR. DAVIS: The people who signed it.

MR. CONLEY: And all of them take the responsibility for the text of the letter so far as you know?

MR. DAVIS: I would hope so. Their names are on it.

MR. CONLEY: You have not had anyone come to you and say, "I do not want my name to appear on this letter and I want you to repudiate that it is on there."

MR. DAVIS: No one has come to me about it, to the best of my recollection.

MR. CONLEY: Mr. Davis, in connection with this letter, there is a distinction made between conference sponsors and temporary administrative committee, of which it lists Davis, Dellinger, Hayden, Greenblatt, and Munaker. What is the distinction?

MR. DAVIS: One group, the conference sponsors, want to lend their name to the meeting to demonstrate the kinds of people and organizations that we hope to involve in the meeting. The second group is a group that is responsible for putting the meeting together.

MR. CONLEY: I would like, if I may, to direct our attention to a statement that appears in the *Guardian* of September 7, 1968, page 3. There are actually two paragraphs that I wish to call to your attention, if I may. The first one is a statement by Mr. Dick Gregory, which is as follows: "Gregory said it is 'your duty to overthrow this government.' " Then there is a statement attributed to Rennie Davis, which is as follows:

> Rennie Davis called for the building of an NLF in the U.S., proposed that Humphrey and Nixon not be permitted to campaign, and announced plans for a national G.I. week this fall to let the troops know "we support your right to return to civilian life."

Did you in fact call for the formation of an NLF in the United States?

MR. DAVIS: This was Thursday, after the terrible riot Wednesday night in front of the Conrad Hilton. I said something to the effect that Hubert's notorious promise to export the great society to South Vietnam was turning to its reverse: Vietnam was coming home. We saw it in the barbed wire, bayonets, the troops that had been brought into Chicago to protect the Democratic Convention from its own citizens. Hubert Humphrey had been nominated in the International Amphitheater, but outside the Conrad Hilton, standing on a garbage can, we announced our own political campaign for the people who felt that there had been a total breakdown of the democratic process when Vietnam—which had been the central issue of this campaign, and perhaps the major issue, as important as the issue of slavery, for this country—had now been buried under the slogan, "law and order." And we announced at our platform, which is appropriately a garbage can, that we intended to do all that we could to focus on the central issue facing the American people in the election in 1968. We suggested that, with a Vietnam coming in America, what was perhaps needed was a liberation movement in the United States, and that in this election what we had to do was vote and support American soldiers in their right to return to civilian life. I suggested we do it by holding love-ins at military bases around the country; that we do it by leaflets and by word [of mouth?] indicating our support for American soldiers. Those people who feel they are the real patriots in this country will stand up against the fraudulence of this country and help to bring home the American boys in 1968.

MR. CONLEY: Then do I take it you have not said what is attributed to you?

MR. DAVIS: No, I believed we needed a liberation movement in the United States. I don't know if I used "national liberation front" or not, but certainly the meaning that I intended was what I just described.

MR. CONLEY: Mr. Davis, directing your attention to something else, back in January of this year at a meeting held in New York, the Lawyers Guild, were you at that meeting?

MR. DAVIS: Is that the same meeting you talked to Tom about?

MR. CONLEY: Yes, sir.

MR. DAVIS: Yes, sir, I was at that meeting.

MR. CONLEY: Sir, apparently in connection with that meeting, you made some remarks about the manner of setting up law students. I believe your words were to the effect that Chicago operations should find subsistence for fifty law students, the guild should handle recruiting, and Chicago should handle the research in Illinois law. Right after you made this statement, Ken Cloke made the statement: "Affirmative suits should be referred to Kunstler and Kinoy. Bail problems should be referred to Detroit." Do you recall this statement having been made by Mr. Cloke?

MR. DAVIS: It does not make any sense, so I assume that he did not make it. Ken generally makes sense.

MR. CONLEY: You do not recall that statement, or one of similar import, having been made?

MR. DAVIS: No, I think whoever took the minutes for you messed up.

MR. CONLEY: These are not our minutes.

MR. DAVIS: They must be your minutes, because they are wrong from beginning to end, everything you read. You brought that up with somebody else—Bob Greenblatt—about that meeting—not a very important meeting, Mr. Conley, in the whole picture.

MR. ICHORD: What was the purpose of the meeting?

MR. DAVIS: To discuss with lawyers who had assisted the Mobilization in other national actions, particularly on permit negotiations, ways we could handle whatever legal problems might be anticipated in Chicago.

MR. WATSON: Inasmuch as we have one of the so-called coffeehouses in Columbia, my hometown, and since you acknowledge some recollection of having written a letter similar to the first two pages of the so-called secret letter sent out to those prospective workers for the coffeehouses, do you remember that letter?

MR: DAVIS: I don't remember it being so secret, Mr. Watson.

MR. WATSON: But you say you sent it out, or are familiar with it?

Mr. Davis: Yes.

Mr. Watson: What is the purpose of the coffeehouse?

Mr. Davis: The purpose is to provide a kind of an oasis for soldiers who, in many cases, feel that they are involved, or are about to be involved, in a very unjust war. Where they can come together to talk about whatever is on their mind. Where we can, hopefully, bring good entertainment, and kind of provide an antidote to the virus of the USO, with its old ladies and scaggs and very bad music.

Mr. Watson: Have you been in the service yourself?

Mr. Davis: No, I haven't been.

Mr. Watson: So, in making such a categorical statement, which has been typical of the testimony, you would not be able to say they have not had some fine young ladies in the USO across the nation of ours.

Mr. Davis: They have had some young ladies in the USO. They have also had them in whore houses and prostitution halls in the Army towns. We would like to provide something better.

Mr. Watson: Didn't you suggest your movement would suggest love-ins and—

Mr. Davis: Love is what is very much needed in the United States.

Mr. Watson: What is a love-in? You said you are against so-called prostitution, but you are going to suggest a national liberation program providing love-ins at military bases. Let's hear your explanation of a love-in.

Mr. Davis: Love is the antidote to the spirit of the bayonet.

Mr. Watson: What is a love-in?

Mr. Davis: That is where people can get together and relax and talk about whatever is on their mind and listen to good music and feel they are not going to be harassed or threatened by military officers. Love-in is a symbol of the youth culture that we are trying to create, that we hope someday will replace the sterile plastic culture that we think you represent, Mr. Watson.

Mr. Watson: Thank you. And the purpose of the coffeehouse was not to bring about desertions, AWOLs, or any outward refusal on the part of a soldier, especially the recruits, since most of these are located in or are adjacent to recruiting bases or basic-training stations?

Mr. Davis: It is the first time in two days, Mr. Watson, that you have gotten something absolutely right.

Mr. Watson: It *was* to encourage AWOLs?

Mr. Davis: You messed up again. I thought you had it, but you don't. And that is the problem with this Committee—

Mr. Watson: That is the problem in talking to a gentleman like you. I thought if we had a meaning of the word—

Mr. Davis: We strained here this morning and the day before, I think, to try to understand each other, and I think it didn't work so well. But I think that young people, as you subpoena them and bring them here, will continue to talk this way.

MR. ICHORD: Remember, Mr. Davis, you are not so young any more, you are twenty-eight.

MR. WATSON: Now I ask you the question again: Was it not a purpose of the coffeehouse to cause AWOLs, desertions, among military personnel, primarily basic trainees?

MR. DAVIS: Hell, no.

MR. WATSON: You have made it very emphatic.

MR. DAVIS: That is right.

MR. WATSON: In this two-page letter, which you agreed you had a part in its preparation, I read this sentence:

> Because of the cultural and class basis of our movement with which we are already familiar, those soldiers most likely to be turned off the Army are also those . . . most likely to welcome a coffeehouse.

What do you mean by the terminology "turned off"? Does that mean to support the Army?

MR. DAVIS: No, it is an expression that is very popular from barracks stateside to Vietnam. I would like to, at this time, quote the expression that almost every GI that I talked to, particularly those going through basic training or facing orders for Vietnam, immediately understands. That expression is "——— it." [Thus the printed record. Davis probably said, "Fuck the Army." —E.B.] That feeling is sweeping young people who are in the military and outside the military across this nation. And the reason is that Congressmen like you are forcing us to feel more and more that the military of this country is something of which we cannot be proud.

MR. WATSON: Then what is the meaning of the words "turned off"?

MR. DAVIS: Well, Mr. Watson, have you ever been turned on?

MR. WATSON: I have turned on a light and I have turned off a light.

MR. DAVIS: That is the problem.

MR. WATSON: By the common terminology or interpretation, the interpretation of the language, or the understanding of the language, would be "to cause someone to become disenchanted to the point of losing all interest in the Army, even to the point of AWOL or desertion," but that is not your meaning?

MR. DAVIS: I think a lot of young men are losing interest in the Army, and "turn off" is the opposite of "turn on."

MR. ICHORD: Is it synonymous with "cop out"?

MR. DAVIS: You are getting close to it, Mr. Ichord. Let's see if we can understand it. To feel that you do not have to give up your soul, your life, your beliefs because a sergeant yells at you to fall in or fall out, to carry a bayonet and learn the spirit which is to kill, to understand that your body may be given to Uncle Sam, but not necessarily your mind, that as an

American citizen you have certain rights, even within the military, to say that this war is immoral and unjust, that you feel you have to somehow be heard on whether or not you will be forced to commit acts of genocide against another people, and to generally let it be known, through your own deeds and through the actions of people in the military, that there are vast segments of men in the Army today who want peace, who want out of Vietnam and want an end to the kind of policies that the United States military police carries out throughout the world: to feel that and express that is not automatically to go AWOL or desert. I happen to believe young men should go into the Army and organize, in the Army, to keep thoughts going, to increase this discussion, to make it possible for more and more young to let the American public know that there are big segments of the Army that oppose this war, and to get the idea across that being against the Army is not unpatriotic, that it is one of the most patriotic and important things you can do for this country.

MR. WATSON: You have nothing but contempt for this Committee. That is fair, isn't it?

MR. DAVIS: You men are interesting. I have not found this a complete drag.

MR. WATSON: You have nothing but contempt for this Committee, for the President, Secretary Rusk, and everything else?

MR. DAVIS: No, not everything else. I don't have contempt for—

MR. WATSON: Love-ins—

MR. DAVIS: I don't have contempt for American soldiers. I don't have contempt for black people, for poor people, for welfare mothers, for university people trying to open up democratic channels. I don't have contempt for people trying to earn a living. I don't have contempt for humanity and decency. People believe in democratic processes and want to bring the democratic values and processes into this society. There are many things, Mr. Watson, for which I do not have contempt.

MR. WATSON: In other words, those things you and your organization stand for you have no contempt for. So far as what happened in Chicago, you absolutely did nothing wrong, said nothing wrong, the whole blame is to be placed at the feet of Mayor Daley and the police department?

MR. DAVIS: The whole blame is to be placed on a society or a Government that is increasingly out of touch with the young people in this country and with what the real interests of this country are. Chicago is a kind of watershed event, I think. In August of 1963, you know—Tom mentioned this—some two hundred fifty thousand people marched for jobs and justice in this city. Exactly five years later, another demonstration that was trying to mount its concern about peace in Vietnam was clubbed and brutally suppressed by police in a general military environment that had been created by officials of Chicago. During those five years we dropped more bombs in Vietnam than we did in World War II. We spent three times as much in riot control as was spent on poverty. We saw scores of cities go up in smoke out of rebellion to the conditions in those communities. We saw thousands of young people face prison rather than fight in a war they considered unjust. Chicago has to be seen in the context of a society that increasingly resorts to military and police force, rather than consensus, for insuring its policies. Well, at the same time more and more American citizens are joining in a movement to create a new basis, just basis, humane basis on which this country can operate.

MR. ICHORD: If I may interrupt, Mr. Watson, do you feel they have a democratic society in North Vietnam?

MR. DAVIS: The American people are deluded if they believe there is a small group of people at the top that terrorize. . . . The Vietnamese people are united in trying to stop the bombing, they feel that their own interest for freedom and independence is consistent with a struggle that has been going on for twenty-five years in that country, consistent with the positions of the recognized leaders of that country. But that, to me, is an irrelevant question. We have no right deciding the fate and destinies of a country twenty-five thousand miles away, and that is why American forces should be withdrawn from there.

MR. WATSON: Earlier, to establish the objectivity of Mr. Hayden, I asked him, in view of his visits to North Vietnam, how many visits he had made to South Vietnam. How many visits have you made to South Vietnam?

MR. DAVIS: I have not had the opportunity to be in South Vietnam. I would like very much to go.

MR. ASHBROOK: I have one final question. I think it ties in what you said about North Vietnam. I would like to make this a part of the record. Hanoi radio broadcast of September 14, 1968, said, and I condense it:

> The South Vietnamese people's committee for solidarity with the American people has sent a letter to the National Mobilization Committee to End the War in Vietnam thanking the progressive American people of all strata for their seething, resolute, and courageous struggle conducted last month. . . . We are daily and hourly following with great enthusiasm your persistent and valiant struggle.
>
> Your recent actions in Chicago, as well as throughout the United States, against the U.S. policy of aggression in Vietnam, have strongly stimulated our people in South Vietnam who are conducting the powerful general offensive and widespread uprisings throughout South Vietnam with the resolve to wrest back at all costs our sacred right—

Et cetera. You were somewhat critical of broadcasts emanating from Vietnam. Would a broadcast of this type be the type that you could more identify yourself [with], consistent with what you just said?

MR. DAVIS: I think it is totally within American interests to work in the way I am working for a withdrawal of troops from Vietnam. And, secondly, the forces for independence in that country are clearly lined up against American penetration.

MR. ASHBROOK: Would it be your impression that this Chicago fiasco, whoever is at fault, did help the Vietnamese?

MR. DAVIS: I think Chicago, as well as other peace demonstrations, help to convey to Vietnam, to the people around the world, that there is a significant section of the American people who would like to see us return to some of the democratic ideals for which our Revolution stood. To give hope to other nations, I think, is beautiful.

MR ASHBROOK: How can you identify with a GI, or how are you going to get through the communication barrier, when he hears broadcasts from Hanoi as to what great work, in effect, you are doing in Chicago?

MR. DAVIS: I think the way that we get through to the GI is: our essential work is to rebuild this country, to make this country something other than the people's policeman of the world.

MR. ASHBROOK: Do we do it through a peaceful process?

MR. DAVIS: It depends on you. This Committee, this Congress, and this Government generally is so unresponsive to what people are saying in this country, particularly the young, that it becomes more and more difficult for us to find any channel through which we can operate. As I said, that demonstration in August of 1963 was ignored. We petitioned the Government. We met with President Kennedy, and five years later the two Kennedys were assassinated. The spiritual leader of the civil-rights movement, Dr. King, was assassinated, and horrors both abroad and home had been reaped [wrought?] on people by the Johnson Administration. The best thing would be for you to get off of the Committee and join us in the streets of this country.

MR. ASHBROOK: Thank you for your advice.

MR. WATSON: You state the Government and the American people—the old fuddy-duddies, as I and others—are unresponsive to the young.

MR. DAVIS: There are some young people that are growing up like you.

MR. WATSON: Do you speak for all young Americans?

MR. DAVIS: No, I speak for myself.

MR. WATSON: You speak for a small fraction of them. Most young Americans are responsible citizens. They want to help bring a better America, and not help bring about an anarchy, as you and your associates wish, and the record should show you represent only a small fraction of America.

MR. DAVIS: Mr. Watson, you had better watch out.

MR. ICHORD: What are you going to do?

MR. DAVIS: If you have children—

MR. WATSON: I have three children. I assure you I will teach them responsibility and not irresponsibility.

MR. DAVIS: Keep that up, Mr. Watson, and right in your own house there will be trouble. Young people are not going to be whiplashed into an unjust society. The hope that we have is that the young people at least have the advantage of opening their eyes and seeing what this country is doing. We do not claim to speak for all young people in the United States, but we do say that there are many people who more and more understand that it is people like you that are destroying America, and that the hope of America is in the people who will stand up to people like you.

MR. CONLEY: I would request permission to introduce "Davis exhibit No. 5," which is a letter dated March 7. I would call the Committee Chairman's attention specifically to the fact that this is the letter repudiated by Dr. Quentin Young,* as to its authenticity, at an earlier hearing. Mr. Davis said he prepared this.

MR. ICHORD: Without objection from the Committee members, the document will be incorporated in the record.

MR. DAVIS: Beautiful.

DECEMBER 4, 1968:

Dave Dellinger

The Subcommittee of the Committee on Un-American Activities met at 1:40 p.m., in room 311, Cannon House Office Building, Washington, D.C., the Honorable Richard H. Ichord (Chairman of the Subcommittee) presiding.

(Subcommittee members: Representatives Richard H. Ichord, of Missouri, Chairman; John M. Ashbrook, of Ohio; and Albert W. Watson, of South Carolina.)

Subcommittee members present: Representatives Ichord, Ashbrook, and Watson.

Staff members present: Francis J. McNamara, Director; Frank Conley, Special Counsel; Chester D. Smith, General Counsel; Alfred M. Nittle, Counsel; and Herbert Romerstein, Investigator.

MR. ICHORD: Will the witness first please be sworn.

MR. DELLINGER: I am sorry. I try to tell the truth on all occasions, so I don't swear.

MR. ICHORD: Well, of course, it is the practice of the Committee that all witnesses appearing before an investigative committee such as this, Mr. Dellinger, would be sworn. Will you raise your right hand, sir? Do you solemnly—

* Who had already lit into the Committee in his testimony of October 3 and 4, 1968. That testimony was reprinted by the Medical Committee for Human Rights, to which Dr. Young belongs, as a supplement to *Health Rights News,* and then further reprinted by the National Committee to Abolish the House Committee on Un-American Activities. —E.B.

Mr. Dellinger: I am sorry. I will assure you—

Mr. Ichord: Do you wish to affirm, sir?

Mr. Dellinger: Yes, I will affirm.

Mr. Ichord: Do you solemnly affirm that the testimony you are about to give before this Committee will be the truth, the whole truth, and nothing but the truth?

Mr. Dellinger: I don't like formulas which imply that sometimes I don't tell the truth.

Mr. Ichord: It is the understanding that the witness is affirming. This is a practice before the Committee.

Mr. Dellinger: Yes, without the ritual, I affirm.

(*Off the record.*)

Mr. Ichord: Mr. Counsel, the Chair has just received a message from Mr. [Jeremiah S.] Gutman relaying a request of Mr. [Jerry] Rubin to be permitted into the hearing room. The Chair has been informed that Mr. Rubin is attired in a Santa Claus costume. It is not the purpose of the Chair to direct that Mr. Rubin attire himself in a certain manner or take other actions in regard to his body, but it is a responsibility of the Chair to maintain order in these hearings. The Chair has exercised its prerogative of excluding, and I have so instructed the police to exclude, Mr. Rubin from the hearing room, because it is the determination of the Chair that such a dress could only add to the possibilities of disorder. The Chair has been advised, Mr. Dellinger, that you have recently undergone an operation. The Chair has been advised that your doctor has informed him that you would be able to testify. I know that the operation is a very recent event. Perhaps the witness will tire. Do you feel that you are physically able to testify at this time?

Mr. Dellinger: Yes, I am anxious to talk about the incidents in Chicago. I feel a little weak, but I expect to be able to proceed without problems.

Mr. Ichord: If you do tire, will you please so advise the Chair, and we can declare a recess for you.

Mr. Dellinger: Thank you very much, sir.

Mr. Ichord: Or if you feel that you are not able to go on.

Mr. Dellinger: Thank you.

(*Off the record.*)

Mr. Ichord: Mr. Gutman, the attorney for Mr. Dellinger, has just approached the Chair and asked that the record show a renewal of the motions and the objections which were previously filed on behalf of Mr. Dellinger with regard to his appearance here. Mr. Dellinger has not been indicted?

Mr. Gutman: No, sir, but we understand from an announcement made by the Federal grand jury in Chicago that, within two weeks, indictments are expected of a group of people who have been described as "the leaders of the demonstration." Since Mr. Dellinger regards himself, and the country regards him, as one of the leaders of the demonstration on behalf of Mobilization in Chicago during the affected time, we believe it reasonable to assume that there is a substantial likelihood that he may be indicted.

MR. ICHORD: Then let the record show the Chair overrules the request.

MR. CONLEY: Mr. Dellinger, would you please state your full name and address for the record?

MR. DELLINGER: My name is David Dellinger. My office address is 5 Beekman Street, Manhattan, New York City.

MR. CONLEY: Sir, do you have a home address?

MR. DELLINGER: I have a home, but since I have received a number of death threats and attacks, including receiving grenades and bombs in the mail, which only by what the Army demolition experts called a miracle did not kill my entire family, I prefer not to give my home address publicly.

MR. CONLEY: Now, Mr. Dellinger, are you appearing here today in response to a subpoena served on you by United States [Deputy] Marshal John Brophy on September 23, 1968, at 68 Charles Street, New York City?

MR. DELLINGER: I did receive a subpoena, and I considered not coming because I think that one does not have to obey illegal and immoral orders. However, since I am anxious to tell everything that I know involving myself, the plans, the actions, and so forth, at Chicago, and since I consider the Committee largely ineffective, I am perfectly happy to be here and to discuss with you everything that I can about myself. So without necessarily recognizing the validity of the subpoena, I come in response and of my own volition.

MR. ICHORD: At that point, Mr. Dellinger, I think you have adequately expressed your contempt for the Committee, and we will let the record show that, and in order to expedite things—

MR. DELLINGER: I don't know what your word "contempt"—

MR. ICHORD: —if you want to express contempt against anybody else, go ahead.

MR. DELLINGER: I don't know where the word "contempt" is; I certainly did not use it. I consider it undemocratic for a man to represent a Congressional district in which sixty per cent of the residents are black and, by the last figures I saw, only six per cent of the black people vote. That is the type of thing that I mean.

MR. ICHORD: Of course, Mr. Dellinger, I don't want to argue with you, but you said the "immoral" acts, referring to the subpoena, and that was an act of this Committee, but if the record will show that, perhaps we can get down to the meat of the matter.

MR. CONLEY: Mr. Dellinger, in order to get some identification, where were you born, sir, and when?

MR. DELLINGER: I was born in Wakefield, Massachusetts, on August 22, 1915.

Mr. Conley: And would you be kind enough to give us your educational background, formal education?

Mr. Dellinger: Well, roughly, I graduated from high school; I graduated from Yale University in 1936; I studied for a year at New College, Oxford, on a Henry Fellowship. I returned to Yale, where, while working for the University Christian Association, known as Dwight Hall, I took some courses at Yale Divinity School. I then went to Union Theological Seminary in New York City for a year and had begun my second year when I declined my exemption from the draft and publicly refused to register and, therefore, left the seminary to go to prison, where I got the best and most thorough education of all.

Mr. Conley: When you mentioned prison, was this during the Second World War, sir?

Mr. Dellinger: It was before the Second World War. It was in 1940, when the first peacetime draft law was passed. Since I am a pacifist, but since I did not want to hide behind a clerical exemption, I publicly refused to register.

Mr. Conley: Mr. Dellinger, what have been your major employments since 1953?

Mr. Dellinger: Beginning before 1953 I worked and lived at what is sometimes called an intentional community, somewhat in the Utopian community tradition. I helped organize a producers' cooperative called the Libertarian Press, which wrote and edited and printed artwork, political material, cultural, and intellectual.

Mr. Conley: Sir, now coming forward from that venture, what was the next employment or business that you engaged in?

Mr. Dellinger: Well, in the winter of 1956 I was one of four or five people, including A. J. Muste, Bayard Rustin, and Roy Finch, and, I think, for a short period Charles Walker, who founded a magazine called *Liberation,* and in the early years we printed the magazine and did a great deal of the editing at the producer's cooperative. Later I began to work for pay, you might say, as an editor, first for two days a week, and then, perhaps about two or three years ago, I became a full-time editor.

Mr. Conley: All right, now the *Liberation* magazine to which you are making reference now is still in existence?

Mr. Dellinger: Yes, it is in its twelfth year, I believe.

* * *

Mr. Conley: Mr. Dellinger, you were in Chicago, were you not, during the period of the Democratic Party Convention of August 26 to 29?

Mr. Dellinger: Yes. I was there prior to that, also.

Mr. Conley: Were you not there in your capacity as chairman of the National Mobilization Committee?

Mr. Dellinger: Well, in part. But, you see, my approach to journalism from way back, when we started Libertarian Press, has been what is sometimes called an engaged journalism. That is, to write on many occasions about a movement or events in which the editors and the other writers, including myself, are actively involved. So when I am active in the Mobilization, I am also active as an editor of *Liberation,* which is the place where I draw my income.

MR. CONLEY: Well then, sir, would it be a fairer statement for me to then say that you were in Chicago as chairman of National Mobilization [and?] as an editor of *Liberation* magazine?

MR. DELLINGER: Yes, it would.

* * *

MR. DELLINGER: We in the United States, because we are a little smoother and more, quote, "civilized" on the surface than Nazi Germany, we must not be able to continue business as usual, making it possible for the American people to napalm people and to uproot people and commit genocide in Vietnam or in the black community at home. We must not be able to do this and [have] people think, "Well, everything is smooth and tranquil here." But, you know, it [the war] is no more real to the American people than the death camps were to the German people. So although I am, by conviction and politics and philosophy and religion, a pacifist and myself only take part in and advocate nonviolent actions, I believe that, within the nonviolent framework, and also, of course, [working with] others who in one way or another do not share all of that philosophy, it is tremendously important that we confront the American people. Not just the political figures who might be deemed by some to be responsible; I believe the responsibility goes to us all. We confront them with the reality of the situation and make it impossible for us to gorge ourselves on our high standard of living and our consumer culture and to dismiss this death of American boys and Vietnamese men, women, and children which is going on daily as long as the war continues. And it is my intention to make it impossible for the American people to sink back into apathy and acquiescence.

MR. ICHORD: Mr. Dellinger, the Chair last night read an editorial in which it was stated that we often forget the terrorist Viet Cong, who, since the beginning of 1968, have killed twelve thousand South Vietnamese civilians and abducted about twenty-five a day. Do you speak out against those kinds of atrocities, too?

MR. DELLINGER: Well, I try very hard not to fall into the trap of equating the violence of the Viet Cong or the National Liberation Front and the vast majority of the Vietnamese people, try not to equate that with the aggressive violence of the invader.

MR. ICHORD: Is terrorist activity directed against South Vietnamese civilians not aggressive?

MR. DELLINGER: Well, you see, I make a comparison between the

Vietnamese people, who feel that there is no other way to defend the independence and the sanctity of their homeland than by the use of violence, I compare them to the American patriots under George Washington who also used violence. The word "terror" is a tough one, you know, what constitutes "terror." [Our patriots] applied methods similar to those of the NLF against the British and also, by the way, against American Tories. Although I myself advocate nonviolence, I do not feel that I as an American could be self-righteous about the methods employed by the Vietnamese who are certainly fighting for the freedom and independence of the Vietnam people.

Mr. Ichord: I take it, as a pacifist, then, you do justify violence under certain circumstances?

Mr. Dellinger: Well, as a pacifist, I understand people, including the American patriots, including the Vietnamese patriots, including the Cuban patriots, including the black patriots, our internal colony, people who feel that it is necessary to resort to violence in order to throw off an oppressive force. And I do make a distinction between [them and] an imperialist country like the United States, which has its tentacles all over the world and has the highest standard of living in the world, based upon the fact that it bleeds those countries and keeps them underdeveloped and is now, as I see it, making an example of Vietnam. They can afford to lose the resources of Vietnam, but they feel that they can't afford to have the underdeveloped and underprivileged people of the world get it into their head that they can win their freedom and independence.

Mr. Ichord: Do I understand you to say that you believe such terrorist activity to be justified under the circumstances?

Mr. Dellinger: Well, as I say, I draw a distinction. I did not condemn my brother, who, during World War II, went overseas. Well, actually he was in the medical battalion, but as part of the war. Despite the fact that I had been very active in the anti-Nazi movement as a kid, I myself, partly because of the method [i.e., of violence] and partly because of the imperialist system which was backing the American war effort, did not bear arms. As I say, I went to jail rather than hide behind the clerical exemption, but I do not criticize my brother. I think these are individual decisions that people have to make when faced with a menace like Hitlerism in the thirties or like American imperialist aggression throughout the world today. I have a great deal of sympathy for people who resort to violence in order to overthrow this kind of thing, but it is not my position. When I was in Hanoi I had difficulties of a certain kind with the Vietnamese, but I pointed out to them that Norman Morrison, who was a national hero in Vietnam because he had burned himself in front of the Pentagon in order to bring home to the American people what they were doing to Vietnamese men, women, and children, that Norman Morrison was ready to give up his own life that way, but that he would not even shoot down a plane that was overhead. And I pointed out that I, Staughton Lynd, and A. J. Muste, whom the Vietnamese all knew, that none of us would engage in violent activity, but I did not feel it in my heart or in my politics to condemn them for their violence.

MR. ICHORD: I had the experience, Mr. Dellinger, the other day, of meeting a woman who had two sons, one of whom had volunteered for the Army and for Vietnam to fight for what he thought was right, and the other son, she said, was a pacifist and had stated that he was going to violate the draft laws. It is rather difficult to give a mother advice. What kind of advice could you have given her?

MR. DELLINGER: I hold strong convictions, and from a lecture platform I will always present positions as forcefully as I can, but I do not believe in indoctrinating people or giving them advice. My brother was a little younger than I, and when I came out of jail the first time he came to me a little bit in anguish because he also was suspicious of the American economic and political system which had supported Hitler earlier and had not helped the Jews, would not let them in, and now was going into this holy war. But on the other hand, he felt that it was necessary. If he came to me for advice, I wouldn't give it to him, because these are things that people wrestle with in their own conscience, and I hope to be part of what they wrestle with by what I write, but I never advise anybody to register or not to register, to go into the Army or leave the Army, to bear arms or not to bear arms.

MR. ICHORD: Go ahead with your questions, counsel.

MR. ASHBROOK: I can respect your views, but I note, in talking about Nazism and talking about what you termed American aggressive imperialism, that you did not say anything in condemnation of Communist aggressive imperialism. Was this an oversight, or do you in fact think that there is not a problem of Communist aggressive imperialism?

MR. DELLINGER: I was a little distressed that, although I made a number of public statements to the press condemning the Soviet invasion of Czechoslovakia in as strong terms as I could, normally this was not picked up. I am not saying that this was, you know, indirect censorship or anything, but it would have been helpful if at that time it could have been made clear what our attitude was. The Cold War atmosphere has been encouraged and developed by this Committee, and that's one of my deep reasons for deep opposition to this Committee.

MR. ASHBROOK: You still haven't said whether you think there is a threat or whether you have the same condemnation of Communist aggressive imperialism as that you have charged the United States with.

MR. DELLINGER: Well, I thought I indicated that I condemned the Soviet invasion of Czechoslovakia. It has not ended up in the kind of genocide that has been going on for years in Vietnam, but—

MR. ASHBROOK: Genocide? You mean the white races and others weren't suffering from genocide?

MR. DELLINGER: Well, I am indicating that I oppose aggression, including Soviet aggression, and somehow or other you seem unwilling to give up the idea that I don't.

MR. ASHBROOK: No, you have now stated, but at first I didn't think you had stated.

MR. DELLINGER: Much as I condemn the Soviet invasion of Czechoslovakia, I do not think that the Americans should wash their hands of the responsibility they play in the situation. The CIA and other Government agencies are organizing subversion and the overthrow of government and direct and indirect invasion and aggression in all of these countries. And although I do not believe that this justifies the Soviet invasion, the right wing in this country and the liberal center wing, which has been in the Administration, make it easier for the Soviet government to fool its people, because they can say, "Look, the CIA has overthrown this government and that government." I mean the bloodbath in Indonesia, as an example. And they can more easily persuade their people that the CIA and the United States and West Germany, which has never been thoroughly denazified, are about to invade Czechoslovakia. But still, my solidarity is with people like Mrs. [Yuli] Daniel and the others who protested in Moscow. One of the organizations to which I belong actually sent people to Moscow and Prague and Warsaw, where they protested against the Soviet invasion and were arrested and in some cases beaten up for it.

MR. WATSON: If apparently you do condemn the aggressive Communist activities equally with the so-called American imperialistic activities, I wonder why you do not spend at least a part of your time in articulating that condemnation? Apparently this is the first time that I have heard of it right here. I wonder why you don't give at least a little time during your lectures and your Libertarian Press, and so forth? I wonder why you wouldn't devote just a little column on one of the pages to a condemnation of that?

MR. DELLINGER: We have articles in *Liberation* magazine condemning it. I, as a member of the War Crimes Tribunal, which I believe rightly found the United States guilty of war crimes, contrary to the Nuremberg charter and contrary to humanity, I, as a member of that tribunal, was one of an overwhelming majority who signed the public statement condemning the Soviet invasion of Czechoslovakia.

MR. WATSON: I personally would find it interesting if you could supply the Committee with some of your public pronouncements condemning Soviet aggressiveness in your various publications. And one final question: Did I understand you correctly to say that it is not your business to give advice to people?

MR. DELLINGER: I give a certain type of advice all the time. I, for example, think that American soldiers should refuse to commit war crimes in Vietnam.

MR. WATSON: Oh, certainly.

MR. DELLINGER: And I will say that publicly. I think that young men should refuse to go into the Armed Forces and I will say that publicly.

MR. WATSON: And you urge them to do that?

MR. DELLINGER: I never advise anybody and say, "You drop out of the Army," or, "You refuse to register for the draft," or "You lay down your arms." But obviously that's my position, and I try to shout that from the housetops.

MR. WATSON: You advise everyone to do that, but to understand you correctly, you do not give individuals that advice?

(*Witness confers with counsel.*)

MR. DELLINGER: Excuse me, I don't mean to impute evil motives, but you seem to be obscuring what I am saying. I make very clear that I do not advise individuals. I—

MR. WATSON: But you advise everyone generally?

MR. DELLINGER: I extol the virtues of this position because I believe that if the United States does not bring a halt to its aggression, and if it does not deny the military-industrial complex the methods, the means, the manpower, money and manpower, to build a war machine and to use it in Santo Domingo and use it in Bolivia and use it in Paraguay and use it in Vietnam, why, I see a very terrible future. There is already a terrible present. But if you come to me and say, "Now I am wondering," I might be tempted to suggest you resign from the House Un-American Activities Committee. But I would rather call for its abolition. If you come to me and say, "Shall I or shall I not go into the Army?" there comes a point when I have to say, "You have to wrestle with your own conscience, you have to decide what you are prepared to do."

MR. WATSON: Of course, it wouldn't be difficult for you to suggest that I resign from this Committee, would it?

MR. DELLINGER: I say that might be a temptation.

MR. WATSON: I would agree with you, it would be a temptation.

MR. ICHORD: Let's proceed, Mr. Counsel.

MR. DELLINGER: But what I would rather do, you see, is have South Carolina turned into a democracy, which would elect people with all the citizens' votes. (*Applause.*)

MR. ICHORD: Now, ladies and gentlemen of the audience, the Chair will have to admonish you that you are guests of the Committee. The business of this Committee is the people's business and you are certainly welcome, but the Chair has the duty of maintaining order, and outbursts, applause, or any kind of disturbing activity just can't be permitted. So I would appeal to your sense of propriety and ask that you abide by the rules.

MR. WATSON: Mr. Chairman, if I might make just one statement in reference to the outburst, apparently against my state and me personally, down home we have an old saying whereby people are judged not only by their friends but by their enemies, and it is a compliment down my way to be opposed by certain individuals, so I take no personal offense to the outcry against me.

MR. CONLEY: Mr. Dellinger, I notice that you indicated that you were a pacifist during the Second World War, or, specifically, with reference to Germany. And you indicate that you still maintain a posture of being a pacifist. Is this a fair statement today?

MR. DELLINGER: I believe that the adoption of nonviolence is a necessity for the world and for the American people, and so when I, for example, went to prison during World War II, I refused to call myself a conscientious objector because that seemed to make it some special thing. I called myself a war objector. I am opposed to the use of military methods in an attempt to solve problems.

MR. CONLEY: You make no judgment in the World War II matter, other than to say you were opposed to war?

MR. DELLINGER: I did make a judgment. I was actively anti-Nazi. I picketed to try to have the United States lower its immigration barriers and allow Jews to come in. But the United States would not do that. And I always, before it was popular to do so in this country or in England, where I spent a year in 1936 to '37, condemned Hitler and Hitlerism. On the other hand, I myself was unwilling to adopt the methods which culminated in the atom bombing of Hiroshima and Nagasaki.

MR. CONLEY: What I am putting to you, sir, is that you did not, with the same fervor, make a judgment as to who was right and who was wrong in World War II, as you have in the present Vietnam situation.

MR. DELLINGER: With the same fervor, I drew a moral distinction between the Fascist forces and the popular forces, such as the resistance forces, in France and Italy and Yugoslavia and other places, who were fighting against Fascism. My endorsement of the United States Government was less enthusiastic because I felt that I could not trust a government elected and run in a largely undemocratic way, dominated by large corporations and military-industrial interests. I never condemned anybody who bore arms and I was in some ways ambivalent about it. Nonetheless, I think that my point was verified when the United States first, for example, burned half a million people alive in Tokyo with fire bombs and then unnecessarily dropped the atom bomb on Nagasaki and Hiroshima in order to improve their power position after World War II, and also prepared the climate which led to the McCarthy period and the foundation of committees like this. I believe that the self-righteous unity of the American people in World War II, even behind a good cause—namely, anti-Fascism—helped produce the assault upon the people of Korea and helped produce the war in Vietnam.

* * *

MR. CONLEY: Mr. Dellinger, are you not the author of the introduction to Mr. [Wilfred] Burchett's forthcoming book on Vietnam?

MR. DELLINGER: Yes. I was going to mention that earlier.

MR. CONLEY: Are you also not planning to address a rally tonight, the *Guardian* rally in New York City, with Mr. Burchett?

MR. DELLINGER: Not that I know of. I was earlier asked if I could come, but because of my operation I indicated that I did not expect to be able to come. I did expect to speak with Mr. Burchett at a conference in Montreal last weekend. I also had to cancel out on that. I will be happy to appear on any platform anywhere with Mr. Burchett, even though we might have differences of interpretation.

MR. CONLEY: May I suggest, on your next occasion of visiting with him, you make inquiry about the question I put to you about the Communist brainwashing campaign in Korea several years ago.

MR. DELLINGER: Yes. I think I should come to his defense a little bit on that, because I discussed with him the question of possible Vietnamese brainwashing of Americans. First of all, I became assured, insofar as it was possible, that this is not taking place. Also that the prisoners released have made this pretty clear—the first release of NLF prisoners, the men were whisked away to Okinawa and kept incommunicado for months and had not been released until they had been threatened and intimidated so that they did not speak. From these conversations with Mr. Burchett, I feel convinced that he is opposed to brainwashing and would neither support it nor take part in it, even though I have to plead ignorance of the history that has been adduced on both sides in the Korean war.

MR. CONLEY: Mr. Dellinger, moving to another area—the participation by you in the Bratislava conference—I wish to hand to you at this time a copy of a letter. It is addressed, "Dear Friend." It is dated August 22, 1967, which solicits participation in a conference then scheduled for Prague. I ask you to advise the Committee as to the identity of those people to whom this letter was sent.

MR. DELLINGER: We sent out a number of communications. Apparently this went, as near as I can tell from the way it reads in the context, it went to people who were part of the delegation. I think most of their names have appeared. Most of them wrote reports of the visit when they came back, and others were mentioned, I remember, in *Newsweek* and *Time*.

MR. CONLEY: Would you identify those that you recall.

MR. DELLINGER: I really can't. As I indicated earlier, I myself have received deadly bombs and grenades through the mail, which only by a miracle failed to kill my children, who got the mail. According to the post-office inspectors, on at least two previous occasions, bombs which were intended for me blew up in the post office when they were being handled. It is that delicate. Yet my children at that time normally picked up the mail and walked a mile with it to my country home. It was by accident I picked it up in the car, and it is a miracle when I opened it it did not explode, because I was a little suspicious and opened it cautiously. Under those circumstances, I refuse. I think it is unwise for me at this point to name people who met with the NLF and the Democratic Republic of Vietnam in Bratislava. To the best of my knowledge, they have all themselves written and talked about this. But in case there is anybody who, because of his home situation, felt that he did not want this made public because of the safety of his family, I certainly don't want to be in a position to make this public.

MR. WATSON: I notice item 5 in this letter states that there would be a limitation of forty-four pounds for luggage: "HOWEVER, please only pack thirty-nine pounds, saving five pounds for literature to take to the Vietnamese." What was the form of that literature?

MR. DELLINGER: It would vary, but naturally, I being editor of *Liberation,* what would first come to mind would be that we would send over issues of *Liberation*.

MR. WATSON: It would be anti-American literature?

MR. DELLINGER: I don't consider *Liberation* to be anti-American. I consider the House Un-American Activities [Committee] to be anti-American. There are two Americas, you know. I think I speak for the best interests of the best America.

MR. ICHORD: Let us describe the type of literature which you anticipated being taken.

MR. DELLINGER: As I said, *Liberation* is the first thing that comes to mind, but just a scattering of materials of various kinds that could be books and magazines, weekly publications. Yes, I would bring back copies of the *Vietnam Courier,* and I would take to them copies of *Liberation, Guardian,* who knows, maybe an interesting magazine section of the *New York Times*. Anything which would—

MR. WATSON: Anything which would be of encouragement to the North Vietnamese would be included in that?

MR. DELLINGER: Not necessarily, because I don't believe in encouraging contrary to the facts. For instance, on my first trip to Vietnam, I have been so brainwashed by the American press that I thought the Vietnamese were overemphasizing the value to them of the demonstrations in this country. One of the things I had in mind was to say to them, "Listen, the antiwar movement is not that strong, the demonstrators are not all that big, and we are not powerful enough to stop the war in the United States. Don't think that we are." But that was independent of whether it would encourage or discourage. That was to simply tell them the truth. When I got over there, I found out that the press had a false idea of the emphasis. Since that time, the antiwar sentiment has grown. Now it is the most unpopular war in American history.

MR. WATSON: In other words, of this reserve five pounds for literature, you would want this Committee to believe that a part was to be some proper American literature.

MR. DELLINGER: Yes, truthful literature, which I consider to be the most proper American literature, to the best interest of America, the proper American of the antiwar movement who does not want our country to be dragged into the mud and to be a war criminal and does not want his children slaughtered.

MR. WATSON: Basically, it would be that type literature which would be of encouragement or help to the North Vietnamese?

MR. DELLINGER: Well, you can put your own interpretation on it. As I say, I am sure we included *Liberation*. I am sure we included the *Guardian*. I am sure we included some things from the *New York Times* that might be of interest to them.

MR. ICHORD: Continue.

MR. DELLINGER: I believe in the free dissemination of ideas and literature everywhere, including ideas that I disagree with. Nothing would have stopped me from bringing things that I disagreed with.

MR. WATSON: At your meetings do you distribute proper American positions on Vietnam?

MR. DELLINGER: I have already indicated that I think Mobilization represents *the* proper American position on Vietnam.

MR. WATSON: Do you distribute literature of the position opposite to yours?

MR. DELLINGER: I myself take the position that, if somebody comes up and distributes anti-American literature, in other words, literature supporting the war in Vietnam, I would be perfectly happy to have them do that. I always am happy for people to hear both sides. On a number of occasions, when I was scheduled to debate with representatives of the State Department or of the Pentagon or various governmental agencies, they pulled out when they learned I was to be the opponent, because they knew I had been to Vietnam and had perhaps more facts than that particular individual felt competent to deal with. On other occasions, I have debated such people. I have always believed in fair presentation on both sides, including sides whose ideas I disagree with.

MR. WATSON: You yourself have never made any distribution, or you yourself have never articulated the position, opposite to that which you now describe as "proper American"?

MR. DELLINGER: My position is constantly developing. There is a certain core of constancy to it, but it is constantly developing.

MR. WATSON: Hardening, or developing?

MR. DELLINGER: I think it is becoming more militantly anti-imperialist through the years, but I don't think it is hardening, it is developing.

MR. WATSON: Militant is generally described as the opposite of peaceful, is it not?

MR. DELLINGER: Not in my vocabulary. I certainly do not mean it that way.

MR. WATSON: You do not?

MR. DELLINGER: No. I am a nonviolent militant.

MR. WATSON: I guess that is just like being a Catholic-Jew.

MR. GUTMAN: I can be verbally aggressive, just as I am now to you, Congressman.

MR. ICHORD: Mr. Counsel, let us abide by the rules. You have not been called to testify.

MR. CONLEY: Mr. Dellinger, I hand you now what is captioned "Purposes and Proposed Agenda of the Prague Conference," and ask you if you recognize this and whether you did, in fact, prepare it.

MR. DELLINGER: There is nothing in here that I want to repudiate, but I don't remember whether it is all mine or not.

MR. CONLEY: In this particular document, Mr. Dellinger, appears a "Possible Agenda." I read from that agenda the proposed topics:

A. The Antiwar Movement
B. The Student Movement
C. The Civil-Rights and Black-Power Movement
D. The Labor Movement
E. American Politics: 1968
F. Business and the War
G. America's Global Situation

Are these basically the topics which were the possible agenda for that meeting?

MR. DELLINGER: I can assure you that, unfortunately, we did not cover adequately all of these subjects. The time was too short.

MR. CONLEY: Are you acquainted with an individual by the name of Steven S. Schwarzschild?

MR. DELLINGER: Yes.

MR. CONLEY: Now, Mr. Schwarzschild has apparently done some writing, Mr. Dellinger, in a magazine referred to as *Dissent,* I believe, and has indicated in this magazine that he attended this particular conference. Was Steven Schwarzschild in fact at this conference held in Bratislava between September 6 and 12, 1967?

MR. DELLINGER: He was at part of it. He was in very great personal conflict, I think, over this. I myself had luncheon with him and his family, discussing the advisability of his going. He was under a lot of pressure from some members of his family about going. In addition to the usual concerns that families might have about that, if he went he might be called before the House Un-American Activities Committee or otherwise persecuted.

MR. ICHORD: Do you think you have been persecuted?

MR. DELLINGER: I think you have been very fair in the manner of this. I think a lot of the questions have no legislative purpose.

MR. ICHORD: The Chair will be the judge of those questions, if and when that question arises.

MR. DELLINGER: The history of the Committee is that it has not been honorable. In a sense, one is persecuted just by being here. It takes one away from his work and he constantly runs the danger of being cited for contempt if he makes any slight wrong step.

MR. ICHORD: The Chair will assume that you will abide by your affirmation, Mr. Dellinger.

MR. DELLINGER: Anyway, in addition, Steven Schwarzschild is a rabbi, and this was shortly after the death of an American in Czechoslovakia by the name of [Charles] Jordan, if I remember correctly, in which there were overtones of anti-Semitism. There was a great deal of emotion, both Jewish and other concerns, over this whole incident. Steven Schwarzschild was very much torn about whether he should go or not. I encouraged him to go. I thought this would give him the opportunity to express his concerns, including about Czechoslovakia and anti-Semitism, and to investigate. Anyway, as a result of the internal conflict, and perhaps due to the fact he was trying to do some of these things, I think Steven Schwarzschild attended less to the conference than anybody else. In one sense he might be said to have never quite participated; he was around the edges of it. During at least part of the conference he was in Prague instead of in Bratislava.

MR. CONLEY: You will concede with me, then, that he was at least there physically, whether he participated or not?

MR. DELLINGER: He was a delegate and he was there during part of it.

MR. CONLEY: Bearing this in mind and referring specifically to this magazine, *Dissent,* the January–February 1968 issue, I read to you, sir, the introduction to an article which he wrote, entitled "The New Left Meets the Real Thing." It goes as follows:

> During their visits to Hanoi David Dellinger (editor of *Liberation*), Tom Hayden, and Nick Egleson (recent chairman of SDS) were invited to gather a group of about 40 American radicals in order to arrange a meeting with a group of Vietnamese. The Americans were expected not only to oppose the war in Vietnam but also to favor, on balance, an NLF victory.

* * *

Sir, is this a fair statement?

MR. DELLINGER: Without meaning to reflect on Rabbi Schwarzschild's honesty, because I do believe he is an honest person, I consider this to be an inaccurate summary. First of all, Tom Hayden was not involved in meetings in Hanoi which originated the idea or made plans for this conference, and his error on this point is indicative, perhaps, of other errors. Secondly, I cannot recognize discussion at any point that the delegation would be expected, on balance, to favor an NLF victory. The very presence of Rabbi Schwarzschild—I would not consider him a radical—should indicate that fact.

* * *

MR. CONLEY: Mr. Dellinger, moving on, in this article prepared by Rabbi Schwarzschild appears the following:

> Yet out of these quasi-official reports no "hard news" whatever emerged. Even someone like myself who knows nothing about Vietnam but what he reads in the newspapers and in a few supplementary sources heard nothing that I had not known beforehand. It was, furthermore, absolutely impossible, even in private conversation, to break through the official propaganda line to which all of the Vietnamese rigorously adhered. This was especially annoying since the Americans had, after all, been selected because they supported the cause of their Vietnamese counterparts—and yet they were addressed as if they had to be indoctrinated from scratch with the crudest tools of persuasion.

Is Rabbi Schwarzschild's observation as to the way the group was treated by the Vietnamese an accurate one?

MR. DELLINGER: No. I would say Mr. Schwarzschild, who did not come to Bratislava until late and who, as I say, was somewhat on the fringes of the conference and also was, I would feel, internally torn and under great pressure from his anti-Communist associates, was probably not able to be an objective judge at that point and perhaps himself set up some of the barriers that existed between him and the Vietnamese. I have found that with all political groups that is a problem. I found that the Vietnamese, who are intensely involved in the defense of their homeland and have suffered incalculable casualties, have, on a number of occasions when I have been present, tended to start off with a rather—what should I say—a rather formal presentation of the official Vietnamese point of view, which I, on a number of occasions, have not found extremely helpful. I have discussed this with them and I try to get beyond this as soon as possible. In considering the suspicions which they are almost bound to have of Americans, considering the ability of committees like yours and the CIA and others to infiltrate all of these groups, I can see where they were perhaps a little standoffish at first. If I remember correctly, the first reports, although of value, were a little more stereotyped and a little less valuable than I had hoped. But this very quickly broke down, and we ate in the same dining room together at tables that sat four, most of them, and I think the experience of all the Americans was that these conversations were very frank and informal, and not doctrinaire and not propaganda.

MR. CONLEY: Rabbi Schwarzschild, toward the end of this article, deals with what he described as the propaganda films on guerrilla tactics exhibited to the Americans by an NLF military expert. Apparently, from reading the article, I deduce there were some motion-picture films shown of guerrilla tactics:

> The most one can say of these methods is that they possibly may be necessary, if not desirable, in defense against at least equally brutal and politically even less justified foreign invaders. One might even be prepared to go so far as to say that the Vietnamese who had to practice them might, in order to be able to live with themselves, have to get some kind of personal satisfaction out of these tactics. While some of these blood-curdling tactics were being described, I made it my business not to look at the speaker but to study the American listeners. I am sorry to have to say that, with the exception of some of the members of pacifist, especially Quaker, organizations who maintained straight faces, there was nothing but approval to be seen in any facial expressions, and there were even a few audible chuckles. So far as I know, not a word was ever said about this afterwards.

Mr. Dellinger, were you present at these events?

MR. DELLINGER: Obviously, the NLF is engaged in guerrilla warfare so, obviously, it is possible that such a session took place. But as you read this my jaw dropped, and I have been searching my memory to try to remember what it could be that he is referring to. I cannot remember any such occasion. I remember a military report, and I think this was one of the first times that the Vietnamese began to say that they were winning the war or had won the war or were about to win the war. I don't remember any such session. As I remember the Vietnamese movies, they showed bombs dropping, peasants being rounded up, peasants being tortured, kicked, hit with guns, dragged behind tanks, American tanks, this kind of thing. There are two possibilities: either that it took place when I wasn't there, or that it didn't take place, and this is a somewhat liberal interpretation of his.

* * *

MR. CONLEY: Did you have occasion, or did any of the members of the American delegation have occasion, while at this conference, to be presented with a ring which you were informed had been made from a part of an American airplane that had been shot down?

MR. DELLINGER: Well, I consider this entirely possible, because the Vietnamese make combs and rings, to the best of my knowledge, from planes that have been shot down. Mary McCarthy has written in the *New York Review of Books* about being tendered such a ring and her own reluctance to wear it. I myself, if I remember correctly, was given a comb and a ring in Vietnam, but explained that I was not interested in wearing such a ring.

MR. CONLEY: If I may, sir, I have another article, taken from *Win,* Volume III, No. 17, under October 16, 1967, captioned "Report From

Bratislava," by Eric Weinberger, which would indicate that Mr. Weinberger was also at this conference. Would you hesitate to identify him?

MR. DELLINGER: No, he was there.

MR. CONLEY: In this article Mr. Weinberger states that, prior to a year or two before his article, he had been persuaded "by A. J. Muste and Dave Dellinger, to come off it on the condemn-violence-on-both-sides-equally-bit." Do you recall the quotation?

MR. DELLINGER: I think I do now, and that is my position. The violence of the richest, most powerful nation in the world invading a little, undeveloped country of Asia should not be compared to the violence used in self-defense by that country.

MR. CONLEY: As I understand it, sir, Mr. Weinberger, up until you and Mr. Muste were able to prevail on him to come off of it, was taking the position that violence was wrong on both sides, or was equally wrong. Is it your position as a pacifist only certain violence is wrong?

MR. DELLINGER: At the beginning of the war in Vietnam, the traditional pacifist tended to say, "A plague on both your houses, we are against all violence, and there is violence being used on both sides." I believe that the violence of George Washington and of the American patriots was obviously different, morally and practically, from the violence of Adolf Hitler during World War II. I have made distinctions in violence without, however, advocating violence. I don't remember my own history in relation to the war in Vietnam, but it was not hard for me to believe that there was a distinction between the aggressive violence of the United States and the violence of the patriotic forces of Vietnam.

MR. CONLEY: In connection with this particular conference, I want to read to you a list of names, and will rather anticipate your answer, but I do have to do this, sir, for the record, if you will bear with me.

MR. DELLINGER: Could I ask you, for the record, if you might consider whether it is worth reading all of these names, in case there are people who might receive the kind of package in the mail that I have talked about? Why not show us the list?

MR. GUTMAN: Why not show us the list, and then ask us questions about them by numbers?

MR. ICHORD: Let the Chair inquire. Will you please come forward, Mr. Counsel, and let me see what you have?

MR. CONLEY: Mr. Dellinger, my question is: Were the following persons present at this conference with you: Robert L. Allen, Jr., Malcolm Boyd, Carol D. Brightman, Reverend John Pairman Brown, Bronson Pettibone Clark, Robert Merten Cook, Stoney Cooks, Rennard Cordon Davis, David Dellinger, Elizabeth P. Dellinger [Mrs. Dellinger], Thorne Webb Dreyer, Nicholas Egleson, Richard Flacks, John Ross Flanagan, Norman David Fruchter, Tom Gardner, Carol Glassman, Thomas Hayden, Steven

E. Halliwell, Christopher Jencks, Walter Russell Johnson, Carole Yvonne King, Andrew David Kopkind, Bob Kramer, Carol Cohen McEldowney, Leon Morse, Linda Morse, Raymond A. Mungo, Douglas Craig Norberg, Vivian Emma Rothstein, Steven S. Schwarzschild, Sol Stern, Dennis Sweeney, John P. Tillman, Jr., Barbara Webster, Eric Weinberger, Henry William Werner, John Augusta Wilson, Willie T. Wright, and Ron Young?

MR. GUTMAN: May I ask the legislative purpose of this question, Mr. Chairman?

MR. ICHORD: The Chair will advise the counsel that, in view of the fact that this was a meeting with the North Vietnamese and other allies, friendly nations with the North Vietnamese, in view of the purview of these hearings and that the witness was a leader in the Chicago demonstration and he has so testified, it is a pertinent question and within the subject of inquiry.

MR. GUTMAN: I fail to see the pertinency, Mr. Chairman.

MR. ICHORD: These are individuals who attended the conference with the gentleman. The counsel has advised me that they have been so identified in the newspapers. The witness was there, and the Chair will have to rule that it is a proper question.

MR. GUTMAN: Mr. Chairman, since you have just stated—

MR. ICHORD: You have the right to advise with your witness if you desire, but you haven't been called to testify, Mr. Gutman.

MR. GUTMAN: I understand. We are talking on the question of relevancy. If I advise him on the question what to say, on the legal point of relevancy, he is merely going to have to parrot what I suggest to him.

MR. ICHORD: I think we will have to abide by the rules. Go ahead. You will be given time to confer with your client.

MR. DELLINGER: If that is the way you want it.

(*Witness confers with counsel.*)

MR. DELLINGER: To the best of my knowledge, from listening carefully to the list, I would have to say that, no, that is not an accurate list of the people who attended the conference, definitely not.

MR. CONLEY: Did the people named attend that conference?

MR. DELLINGER: Some of the people named did, some did not. Some of the names appear to be inaccurate combinations.

MR. CONLEY: Are any names missing who attended the conference?

MR. DELLINGER: I have not any idea. As you read off those names, I thought, Oh, yes, I remember him, he was there. Other names, I thought, Who is he? I never heard of him.

MR. CONLEY: Mr. Dellinger, let us move on to an administrative committee meeting of the National Mobilization Committee which was held in Cambridge, Massachusetts, on October 13 of this year. Did you attend that meeting?

MR. DELLINGER: I believe I presided at that meeting.

MR. CONLEY: I will ask you, Mr. Dellinger, if those attending this meeting discussed this Committee's investigative hearings, the grand-jury investigation of the disturbances in Chicago, and the hearing of the President's Commission on the Causes and Prevention of Violence?

(*Witness confers with counsel.*)

MR. DELLINGER: Yes, I recollect that these subjects were discussed there. I would like to point out that one of the concerns expressed was whether or not some of the people present would be indicted. Since it has been reported in the newspapers that indictments are being prepared, that might influence how we proceed from here, because I don't want to say anything involving people indicted or about to be indicted.

MR. CONLEY: Again, sir, I think you are reading more into the question than what I intended.

MR. DELLINGER: I am only trying to communicate and establish some understanding here.

MR. CONLEY: Mr. Dellinger, was it decided at this meeting at Cambridge that, in view of these activities—that is, the meeting of this Committee, the grand-jury investigation, and the President's Commission on the Causes and Prevention of Violence—the persons involved in the Chicago disturbance, the demonstrators, and so forth, should be urged not to cooperate with any request received for an interview by the FBI or any other investigative agency?

MR. DELLINGER: No, this was not the decision. There were a number of different viewpoints expressed. Rennie Davis and I reported that we had already had an interview with a representative of the subcommittee of the President's Commission on Violence. Everybody was aware of the fact that some of the FBI investigation had been very partial and unfair. In fact, when the FBI approached me, I told them that I was very busy and asked them what the purpose was. They made very clear to me that the purpose of talking to me was to find out if I knew about any violations of law on the part of the demonstrators, but it was clearly demonstrated to me that they were not interested in any violations of law by anybody other than demonstrators. I reported this fact at the meeting. It was a very complicated discussion, in which there were probably four or five points of view, some advocating virtually total cooperation, because the truth was certainly in our favor and we had nothing to hide, some people advocating virtual noncooperation, because whatever we said might be twisted and distorted and used against us unfairly or used to involve other people, and there were a variety of positions in between. If my memory is correct, a subcommittee, of which I was a member, was instructed to work with the legal committee and to get out a memorandum discussing the various dangers and difficulties, but not taking a hard line as to whether people should speak or not. As I say, we are not a talk-down organization. We are heterogeneous and under no circumstances would we issue too hard a line anyway. But I think we did want people to be aware of what happened in a number of FBI interviews and also to be aware of what their rights were. They had the right to refuse to testify if they wanted to.

MR. CONLEY: Was it not also decided at this meeting in Cambridge that the minutes of all future administrative committee meetings would continue to list those in attendance, but would leave out home addresses, and while they would summarize issues and decisions, they would not attribute specific remarks to specific individuals?

(*Witness confers with counsel.*)

MR. DELLINGER: I consider this to be an example of the kind of illegal persecution that unfortunately has too often characterized the history of this Committee. This was a private meeting, protected under the First and Fourth Amendments of the Constitution. It is as if you were to get me up here and to say, "Did you vote for So-and-So in your secret ballot?"

MR. CONLEY: Nobody has put that question to you.

MR. DELLINGER: You have asked about decisions and statements of a private meeting, which is protected by the First and Fourth Amendments. I consider this a violation of privacy. Now, having registered that objection and used that as an example of the type of thing to which I object in this Committee, I will proceed to answer the question in a way that will not involve other people. I will volunteer the information, although I think you don't have the right to ask it.

MR. CONLEY: Since the meeting in Cambridge on October 13, isn't it true that the Mobilization Committee has made a mailing of a "Dear Friend" letter, bringing attention to the various investigations of your Chicago demonstration and advising that "any further cooperation"—that is, with investigating agencies—

> runs the risk of lending a legitimacy to governmental abuse of investigatory power for the purpose of harassing, intimidating, and repressing political opposition. Our experience has shown that any interview, given in the best of faith to the most liberal-minded body, can find its way into the hands of prosecuting attorneys, FBI files and HUAC smear campaigns. . . .
>
> We bring this matter to your attention as a matter of urgency. . . . Hundreds of people have already been asked for interviews by FBI agents. Since there is no obligation to grant any interviews or give any testimony unless a subpoena has been served, most people refuse these requests. We support those who select this course of noncooperation. If you are approached by any investigatory agency please keep us informed and feel free to discuss with us the manner in which you intend to respond.

Is that a fair reading of those portions of that document?

MR. ICHORD: Mr. Counsel, the Chair can't see the pertinency of that question. Let us go on to something else.

MR. CONLEY: That concludes our questions, sir.

MR. ICHORD: I thought you had one other question you wanted to ask.

MR. GUTMAN: Does the missing question begin, "Are you now, or have you ever been—"

MR. ICHORD: Counsel will be in order.

MR. DELLINGER: Mr. Chairman, while he is thinking, could I make a comment relevant to that area?

MR. ICHORD: You mean you want to answer the question when I ruled the question out of order?

MR. DELLINGER: I want to tell one thing from my own experience. When I agreed to make a lengthy tape for the subcommittee investigating the Chicago disorder—the subcommission of the President's Commission on Violence—I was told that none of that material would be turned over to the grand jury or to any other body, including HUAC. Now, I heard, on television last night, an interview with the judge presiding over the grand-jury investigation in Illinois, who said that he was anxious to see the material on which the report was based. And the impression I got from the response of Chairman [Daniel] Walker was that this material would be made available if requested. Now, I give this as an example of the kind of problem that people face.

MR. ICHORD: Mr. Dellinger, the Chair has no jurisdiction whatsoever over the Presidential Riot Commission or the grand-jury proceedings in Chicago. As I stated at the outset of the hearing, we were not interested in the grand-jury proceeding. We were interested in proceeding to search out the facts, look into the charges that have been made relative to subversives participating in the organization, in the planning, of the riots, and what connections the leaders had with foreign powers. It is the duty of the Chair to keep the hearings in these bounds.

MR. DELLINGER: I am simply trying to indicate any additional reason for my reluctance to mention the names of other people.

MR. WATSON: Mr. Dellinger, I am interested in the article that was written by Rabbi Schwarzschild, a friend of yours and a friend of your good counsel there. Obviously, the article or the author, either or both, were considered reliable enough that they would be included in the publication *Dissent,* which I assume would be one fairly recognized by the left movement. Is that not a correct statement?

MR. DELLINGER: First of all, Rabbi Schwarzschild is not an intimate friend of mine. Secondly, there are many variations within the Left, and, I think, if you want my own opinion, *Dissent* has been a little bit sick with anti-Communism. It has many valuable articles in it, but a lot of [their] people are intellectuals who, I think, have been victimized by the Cold War and perhaps, in some cases, because of the positions that they hold and the respectability that they covet—I am sorry to be imputing motivation—really have been very wrong in the things they write. At least I very much disagree with the kind of virulent anti-Communism which seeps into *Dis-*

sent magazine and always the lofty and patronizing attitude toward young people who may not be able to write as well as some of the editors of *Dissent* but who very often are closer to the struggle for social justice and human liberation.

Afterword

"The world is dividing into two camps, freedom versus Communism, Christian civilization versus paganism, righteousness and justice versus force and violence."

—Congressman George A. Dondero in the House debate on the Mundt-Nixon bill to "protect the U.S. against un-American and subversive activities," 1948

"The issue between Republicans and Democrats is clearly drawn: it has been deliberately drawn by those that have been in charge of twenty years of treason."

—Joseph R. McCarthy at the Republican Convention that nominated Dwight D. Eisenhower and Richard M. Nixon, 1952

"The simple fact is that when I took up my little sling and aimed at Communism, I also hit something else. What I hit was the forces of that great socialist revolution which, in the name of liberalism, spasmodically, incompletely, somewhat formlessly, but always in the same direction, has been inching its ice cap over the nation for two decades. This is not a charge. . . . It is a fact."

—Whittaker Chambers, in *Witness* (1952)

1

If there were a God, and we could know it for sure; if this God badly needed us to know it, needed also homage from us and much support; if, moreover, godly people were by definition free people and their freedom took concrete form in a socioeconomic system called Free Enterprise; if, conversely and consequently, the two cardinal errors for human beings were

NOT to believe in God and Free Enterprise, BUT to believe in No God, or even any other definition of God, and in Socialism, or even any other definition of freedom; then it was reasonable of the Congress to create the House Committee on Un-American Activities in 1938, and the thirty-odd years of that Committee's work may be seen as a contribution to the good, the beautiful, and the true.

To those who think this is to place too much emphasis on religion, the HUAC being by no means a religious body, I must reply that by all means there is something false and grotesquely exaggerated in the emphasis, but that the falsity and exaggeration are the Committee's own. God and Free Enterprise undoubtedly are the twin pillars of the edifice they defend. That this edifice may be a castle in the air is only to add that we are dealing here with pure opinion, indeed with ideology, the falsest of false consciousness. Such notions may have small weight in the realms of truth or logic but may nonetheless—or all the more—be deftly woven into the fabric of history. As theory, anti-Semitism was tenuous, abstract, even absurd, but the ovens of Auschwitz were of solid iron and the charred remains were of real bone. The ideologues in such cases are shrewd enough not to argue with the professors of philosophy. Their criterion is whether a given notion strikes an answering chord in classes of men whose support they and/or their masters need. Once it does, professors of philosophy will not be lacking in the ranks of those who affirm that it's a mysterious universe we live in, rationalism has lots wrong with it, and everyone knows two times two is five.

Whether or not Free Enterprise is of any use to God, He has always been of much to it. To base Free Enterprise on Him is to found it on a rock—upon the unchangeably true, upon the conveniently undebatable. And, by paradox if not magic, it is also conveniently to dissolve Free Enterprise in a mist of vagueness and undefinability. We have here the great example in modern history of having it both ways, which in logic is bad but in traditional politics—the art of manipulating human beings—is the principal end in view. You hear it said, these days, of almost everything that if it didn't exist it would have to be invented, but the great Voltairean formula was devised to describe the human need of one idea only: God. There is irony in the formula, but Voltaire was no atheist. What hurts in his irony is the strong suggestion that precisely those whose affirmation of God is prompted by their interests are irreligious: they are using God, and the God they are using is just a social force, a psychosocial factor in their political constituency: it is the members of the HUAC who are the atheists, the materialists. No wonder they protest (too much) against atheism and materialism! Conscious atheism in others is their arch enemy, first, because it challenges their own right to use the word "God," a right they most sorely need, and, second, because they are themselves atheists, if unconscious ones, and fear having this fact exposed by atheists who are out in the open. Among the various ironies, perhaps the supreme one is that, for these people, real believers in God—believers in a real God—are the ultimate atheists, for in pointing to a Being who exists outside this world, they discount the God of the Chamber of Commerce and the FBI, the God who is a concrete social fact. Not much preferable are those whose definition of God, though human, has a different social orientation, Paul Tillich, for instance, who saw "Faith" as a synonym for "ultimate concern." The lower-middle-class's concern for conformity and status is hardly ultimate. If its God is the one God, Tillich's is no God. "That guy Tillich was a Socialist from way back."

Socialists are atheists in that they propose to take charge. Under capitalism, God is in charge. The basic idea of the capitalist economy, of the whole capitalist civilization and era, was *laissez faire,* which Bernard Shaw translated: "letting things slide." That's because Shaw was an "atheist." *Laissez faire* would not be letting things slide if old Nobodaddy (the "Socialist" Blake's word for God) were everyone's Daddy and were up there arranging for the survival of the fittest through open competition, a preponderance of booms over slumps, freedom of soul through freedom of trade, and so on. To a purely rational mind this may seem a somewhat ridiculous role for God to play, but to a practical apologist for capitalism it could only seem exactly what rescued his system from absurdity by elevating luck into law, chance into destiny. Though capitalism has also had its professional economists to sell *laissez faire* to the academic establishment in the jargon of social science, that was a minor matter beside satisfying the popular need for a mythology.

> The rich man in his castle
> The poor man at his gate
> God made them high and lowly
> And ordered their estate.

In this form, the mythology goes back long before the nineteenth century: you mustn't meddle with the class structure, because it has divine sanction. The classical economics of the nineteenth century added: you mustn't meddle because, under God, the system runs itself better than men could ever run it, rich men get richer, an occasional poor man gets rich, and if the poor chiefly remain poor, or even get poorer, such is life under God.

And America was the classical country of the classical economics. Whereas Europeans in trouble always now tended to see capitalism in its death throes, and Socialism just round the corner, Americans saw capitalism as everlasting like its God, and Socialism as a totally uncalled-for idea, cranky, perverse, alien, in a word—in *the* word—*un-American.* One of those oversophisticated West European countries like France or Germany might have a Socialist government for a while, but presumably that could be taken care of. . . .

It was against this background that the news of October broke in 1917. Ten days shook the world. It was a young American that said so, and all

America realized, with a shock, that capitalism could be overthrown in a big, sprawling, underdeveloped, "new" kind of a country—a country unlike France and Germany but like, say, China . . . and America. The Chinese surprise would not come till 1949, but meanwhile radicals with their bombs had to be pounced on in the United States. What would later be called McCarthyism might well be dated from the national hysteria that attended the Red scare of 1919–1920 when Attorney General A. Mitchell Palmer played the role that was later played by Joseph R. McCarthy, and 1919 was also the year when the United States Government first investigated "efforts being made to propagate in this country the principles of any party exercising . . . authority in Russia." In 1930 came the Hamilton Fish Committee in the House of Representatives. Speaking of a resolution to investigate "all entities, groups, or individuals who are alleged to advise, teach, or advocate the overthrow by force or violence of the Government of the United States," Fish commented, "It is not the purpose of this resolution to interfere with any group except the Communists in the United States, and we propose to deport all alien Communists." In the middle thirties Representative Samuel Dickstein would fain have deflected investigative ardor toward the Nazis, but in 1938 HUAC was formed, Dickstein was not on the Committee, and its Chairman, Martin Dies of Texas, would make sure that any interests the Committee might have outside of Communism would be diversionary as to purpose and ephemeral as to duration.

The years 1929–1931 brought an even greater shock than 1917 to a middle class that had once thought itself secure. Capitalism didn't seem everlasting even in America now. The economy had broken down. *Laissez faire* had indeed meant letting things slide—into an abyss. After 1929 even ideas on how to save the capitalist system would tend to be proposals to have the Government interfere. Blasphemy and presumption! Such ideas were doubly threatening: if they worked, then classical economics had to be dropped by its own champions; if they didn't work, men would think of dropping the whole capitalist system if by that time it hadn't dropped itself.

Popular ideology generally takes the form of melodrama, and the melodrama that had come out of the Red October of 1917 might be expressed in the dictum: "Life is a battle against Soviet Russia." How many people subscribed to this notion in the twenties would be hard to say. They were just a fringe of the middle class, perhaps, the most insecure section of that class, the most vulnerable to paranoia. Certainly the image was there, and was a vivid one. In more recent lingo, it "turned people on." It was something, so to speak, to masturbate to. Alien Russia and rabid Red made a good combination; and the adjective "un-American" said it all. In the twenties, there was already this much behind the fantasy: Russia was indeed an alien and forbidding place, it did adhere to Communism, which was an alien and forbidding doctrine, it did send agents to the United States, and American Communists did fraternize with their Russian comrades and were apt to return from trips to Moscow with a headful of plans for the furtherance of the cause.

In the thirties the fantasy received a new charge of reality. Not only were Americans far more receptive, the Soviet Union was far more active. Communism does have to be world-wide if there is going to be lasting Communism at all—Stalin and Trotsky didn't really differ as to that—and the fact that one country has already had its revolution does make it a world headquarters and by that token a threat to the (prerevolutionary) world. It is understandable, then, that if a Soviet spy like Whittaker Chambers could believe he was making a sizable contribution to the overthrow of capitalism in the United States, persons of equally lurid imagination in the other camp would believe such contributions were being made. It is equally understandable that many would agree with Chambers that this is how Socialism most characteristically does spread. James Bond was not yet invented but he would be born out of the fantasies of precisely that generation. In Chambers we see the impact of art (mythology, group fantasy) on life; and we see the same thing in Chambers' enemies, who, of course, as Chambers was the first to admit, were also his friends: moving straight over from his pals in the Party to men like Luce, Nixon, and William Buckley, he never knew —never wished to know—what most of us think of as normal America, normal humanity, a ghastly irony in the life of one whose first ideological affair was with the proletariat.

It was interesting to be in America in 1939. Some groups of Americans, I recall, especially in upper-middle-class circles, were predominantly Anglophile, and spoke of little but the need of aid to Britain, possibly adding something about the threat to France. But there were others whose attention was overwhelmingly on the Soviet Union, and their attitudes tell us a lot about *them.* The Soviet Union was supposed to have betrayed them. BUT the Soviet Union had never owed them anything—on the contrary. The Soviet Union was supposed to have done the unthinkable in making a nonagression pact with Germany. BUT wasn't it equally unthinkable that anti-Communist America would ever join with the Soviet Union in a war? Yet it did so for the whole period 1941–1945. The 1939 crisis is important also in relation to the Communists themselves. No sympathizer with the CPUSA, I don't feel hurt that the Party lost members at any point, but the "moral crisis" of 1939 reveals itself as a phony in a very clear-cut fashion. The accusation against the Party was betrayal of its professed principles. Now, its professed principles are Marxist. Did those who left the Party proceed to maintain Marxism in its purity against the non-Marxism of the CPUSA? By no means. Most of them, so far as I have been able to ascertain, became regular fellows, and certainly quite a lot just switched sides in the greatest show on earth, the number-one melodrama of the twentieth century, the battle of Free Men against the Soviet Union.

One Communist sympathizer who did not make the phony switch in

1939 was J. Robert Oppenheimer, and yet, such is the irony of history, he turned out to be the greatest melodramatic protagonist of them all. If we are to believe the friend who is up to now the only source of information, Oppenheimer continued to sympathize with the Party and the Soviet Union during 1940, and it would have been strange indeed if he had switched in 1941, for in the middle of that year Russia became the ally of Britain against Hitler. In 1942, however, Oppenheimer was chosen to head the Manhattan Project and work on the atom bomb for America. It didn't take him more than a year, if that, to be converted to belief in The Great Melodrama: in 1943 he was so eager to give information to the secret police about his former comrades that one of the security officers thought he was currying favor. Later, when this period of Oppenheimer's life was reviewed by the Atomic Energy Commission, his one supporter among the three "judges" had this to say in his defense: "He hates Russia." But some people are hard to please, and the other two judges didn't feel Oppenheimer could be trusted to hate Russia uninterruptedly.

Hate Russia! Research on the bomb was started because it was feared Hitler might also come up with one. Then it was used, not indeed against Russia, but against Japan at the moment when Russia was ready to aid the Allies in the East and share the victory with them. The view of Russian historians is naturally that the two hundred thousand who died at Hiroshima did so that they might be saved from the Red Army. Better dead than Red. Whether that is whole truth, it is obviously true in some degree. It can be confirmed by all manner of evidence. To cite a small example, the American commander in the Pacific, Douglas MacArthur, was visited in 1945 by Churchill's top commander, Alanbrooke, who reported of MacArthur, "He considered the Russians a greater menace than the Nazis had ever been." That remark forces us to look back and note the consistency of Western statesmen from the time (1919) when Churchill had supported the White generals against the Red Army, through neutrality in Spain in the thirties, through a World War II in which the real betrayals were their own, to that grand design for Southeast Asia which started to go into action in 1950 and is still dragging catastrophically on in Vietnam as these words are written.

If the idea that life is a battle with Soviet Russia was fantastic in the twenties, and still fairly absurd in the thirties, the possibility of actual war between the Russian and American governments in the forties made it seem realism itself. One had many friends in 1945 who expected America and Russia to go for each other's throats the moment they were through with Germany, and we have learned since that the Nazis had entertained not unreasonable hopes of this several years earlier: they sensed the force of The Great Melodrama. If what happened was only the Cold War, that also represents the triumph of the melodrama, all the more so as the two giant powers are fighting wars with the small countries as proxies. Moscow fights Washington in Prague; Washington fights Moscow in Saigon.

The triumph of The Great Melodrama was also the triumph of the HUAC. The forties and fifties were the days of the Committee's dubious glory. After all, its only real scoop, ever, was the Hiss case (1948). This one time the HUAC grabbed the headlines and kept them and in the course of ruining Hiss made two historic reputations, that of Whittaker Chambers, and that of Richard Milhous Nixon. Whatever the gaps in Hiss's evidence, he would easily have been saved had Chambers chosen any other point in time for his "revelations." Hiss was a victim, not of justice, but of the clock: 1949 was a devastating year for the United States. Russia was found to have an atom bomb, and China went Socialist. How far hysteria went in the West may be gauged from the fact that the possibility of just up and atom-bombing Moscow was raised there by . . . Bertrand Russell! Heads had to roll, and Hiss's did. New men must present themselves, and Nixon did. Someone must help the heads to roll and the new men to make their bow, and Chambers did. On the assumption that Hiss was guilty, not only as charged, but guilty of espionage, the Committee could be said to be doing just what it had always wanted to do. It had come into its own.

Which was fun while it lasted. But it didn't last long because other committees wanted to get into the limelight, and Senator McCarthy's subcommittee succeeded. Meanwhile The Great Melodrama had reached a climax in the courtroom of Judge Irving Kaufman, who accused two alleged Communists of causing the Korean war and, in effect, got a jury to agree with him. The speech he made on April 5, 1951, when sentencing the Rosenbergs gives as pithy a description of The Great Melodrama as can be found anywhere, as well as exemplifying that melodrama in murderous action:

> They [the Rosenbergs] made a choice of devoting themselves to the Russian ideology of denial of God . . . and aggression against free men everywhere. . . . I believe your [the Rosenbergs'] conduct . . . has already caused the Communist aggression in Korea with the resultant casualties exceeding 50,000, and who knows but that millions more of innocent people may pay the price of your treason? Indeed by your betrayal you undoubtedly have altered the course of history to the disadvantage of our country. . . . I . . . assume that the basic Marxist goal of world revolution and the destruction of capitalism was well known to the defendants. . . . I must pass such sentence upon the principals in this diabolical conspiracy to destroy a Godfearing nation which will demonstrate with finality that this nation's security will remain inviolate.

I. F. Stone was one of very few Americans who maintained that the Korean war was not started by "Communist aggression" at all but by the machinations of an imperialistic United States, intent on controlling Southeast Asia; but there again it was a question of timing. Americans in large numbers did not become receptive to that kind of argument for another dozen years. Even in 1964 William Fulbright and Eugene McCarthy were unreceptive when Wayne Morse and Ernest Gruening applied the argument to Vietnam. Much blood had to flow, much cruelty and much idiocy had to be brought to their attention before even they came around, reminding one of the question in Shaw's *Saint Joan:* "Must a Christ die in every generation for the benefit of those with no imagination?"

2

Since, so far, I have been writing about the anti-Communist Establishment, it would be possible for a visitor from Mars, following my account, to assume that the Communists and their sympathizers were entirely admirable and innocent victims of "McCarthyism," that they, accused of conspiracy, were themselves the target of a conspiracy they in no way invited. At this point, one must speak specifically of the Communist Party—not of Communism, much less of radicalism generally. In the time of Stalin, the CPUSA made two decisive commitments which have nothing necessarily to do with Communism: one was to the Soviet Union, the other to a tactic of secrecy. The two commitments were all too intricately intertwined, as secrecy was a Russian tradition, and had indeed—in the times of the tsars—been a harsh necessity.

The commitment to Russia had two distinct features: it was a commitment to a foreign power and it was a promise of unquestioning obedience. Now, either of these features might have been tolerable—without the other. Taking orders from a boss who is on the premises is not unusual, nor so objectionable if you have chosen the boss and can quit at will and without reprisals. That Russia would always have had advice to offer would also have been harmless enough. What made trouble was that, whenever Moscow spoke, everyone else had to jump to attention. Not till the 1960s did the national CPs learn to talk back, if then. It is true that Moscow's modes of interference were often exaggerated by their enemies. Fewer people received direct orders from Moscow than our "Radical Right" imagined. The thing was: they didn't need to. Stalin only had to sneeze, and they all caught cold. Discipline, which is a thing our own Left today could use some of, which indeed is morally legitimate and politically necessary, became, as military discipline so often has, a mere pretext for outright domination of one man by another, and reduction of the dominated to a subhuman status. Since domination is bad for the dominant too, making them conceited, arbitrary, and cruel, we had here a trend exactly opposite to that which Communism—the philosophy of Marx and Engels—had laid down.

If the combination of unquestioning obedience with allegiance to a foreign power was damaging, the combination of both with a tactic of secrecy was fatal. A Communist was not now to be defined as a member of a political party as that term is understood in the United States. He was a "secret agent of a foreign power" and since we were at war with that power—not in fact, perhaps, but in the kind of fantasy that becomes fact—he was "guilty of treason." Spy and traitor—this is "Communist" defined after the heart's desire of militant anti-Communists. And the CPUSA handed them its confirmation of the formula on a silver platter. This is why the Hiss case was the biggest event in the history of HUAC up to that time, and it may explain, too, why Hiss was so tight-lipped about Communism and has remained so.

It is time now, I believe, to cease regarding the case as a personal duel between Hiss and Chambers. Politically, it was the Committee's attempt to nail down its thesis about Communists. It held that it succeeded; most of conservative America readily agreed; what is perhaps more interesting, a large part of liberal America was seduced into agreement. And in the long sweep of history, the personal victor was not Whittaker Chambers, who shriveled up and died, but Representative Richard M. Nixon of California, who was quoted by the Associated Press as saying:

> The hearing [on Hiss] is by far the most important the Committee on Un-American Activities has conducted because of the nature of the evidence and the importance of the people involved. It will prove to the American people once and for all that where you have a Communist you have an espionage agent.

Now the proof that Hiss was a spy was never conclusive. Chambers, as Hiss's lawyers would eventually argue, may have committed forgery by typewriter in order to frame Hiss. Suppose Hiss had got up one day and said, "Look, I was never an agent. What I was is known as *a Communist:* I was a Marxist, I believed in Socialism through revolution." He would have been falling into a semantic trap. A Communist is *by definition* an agent. (True, this definition became definitive precisely through the Hiss trial, but it was widely current earlier.) And if Hiss was indeed a Communist, this must have been why he never said so. This and the whole code and tradition of secrecy in which the CPUSA had enveloped itself. So he gambled and fought the whole battle on the question whether he had been an agent. If he had won, no one would have found out if he had done *anything*—even read the Communist Manifesto. If, on the other hand, he was found to be an agent, then obviously he was a Communist too, and would be used to prove the Nixonian axiom: "where you have a Communist you have an espionage agent."

In fact, of course, Hiss's being an agent, if he was, would NOT prove that he was a Communist, since there could be other reasons for undertaking agentry, and often are. Conversely, those who know the milieu will confirm that not only were many Communists not agents, but many wouldn't have been able even to conceive of being agents. Again, what was unfortunate to the point of the catastrophic was the over-all Stalinist commitment to secrecy and to Russia: it constantly created situations which went part way to espionage even when they didn't go the whole way, and it involved people who really could never have lived with themselves as spies, or even as nonpatriots, in actions that smacked of snooping and/or of divided allegiance.

I am not overlooking the arguments by which the CP could be defended. If you are a Socialist, and Socialism is achieved in one country, that country may reasonably enough come to mean a great deal to you, and indeed there are many Americans whose warmth of feeling toward a foreign power—Eire, Israel are examples—goes pretty far at times, as do their machinations on behalf of such powers. It can also be argued that what is in the interests of the one Socialist country must be in the interests of America too—the Socialist America we are working for—so that there is no possible conflict of loyalties. Certainly, the pro-Soviet leftists of the thirties did not see themselves as anti-American. For many of them, the then current CP slogan, "Communism is twentieth-century Americanism," was on the level. Any Russian aid in a revolution would have been regarded as analagous to French aid in 1776. The Russians would help to overthrow General Motors as the French helped to overthrow George III.

Few, of course, had projected any such thing. Had they done so, they would have run upon problems. In the American Revolution, there was small possibility of the French taking over George Washington, who in the first place professed no allegiance, public or secret, to them. Soviet Russia was simply too big a friend and did business in the wrong way—by overmuch secrecy and by outright domination. That she did so was part of a larger fact: that something had gone dreadfully wrong with Socialism in Russia, possibly through mistakes of Lenin (and Leninism) in the early days, certainly through the dictatorship of Stalin in the thirties. I state the case baldly. The CPUSA denied every word of it, and still does. This is hardly the place to have it out with them, but whatever conclusions one has reached bear directly on one's judgment of "allegiance to a foreign power" in general. The degree of allegiance an Irish American feels to Eire may be very considerable, but, first, Eire can't do much about it and, second, Eire isn't much of a threat to anything.

I had the peculiar experience not long ago of reading in the same week *Soviet Communism, a New Civilization?* (1935) by Sidney and Beatrice Webb, and *Journey into the Whirlwind* (1967) by Eugenia Semyonovna Ginzburg. Both present a picture of Russia in the thirties. The Webbs saw a beautiful new civilization there, leading the way for the rest of the world. Their only serious complaint is that discussion of fundamental principles wasn't encouraged. Eugenia Ginzburg could have got along very nicely without discussion of fundamental principles. She was a Communist in Russia and asked nothing but to be allowed to live on and work as such. She was forbidden to. And she was forbidden to on no rational grounds but on unhappily familiar irrational ones. She was confronted with human cruelty organized on the largest scale—by that very Soviet government which the Webbs admired so much. I'm afraid the Webbs wouldn't have believed such things possible even under capitalism. Under Socialism they were impossible by definition. Yet Eugenia Ginzburg can be disregarded only if (a) she is a liar or (b) her case isn't typical. I defy anyone to read the book and believe it is mendacious, and, alas, no one can look further into the record and not find it to be typical.

The revolution had been betrayed. Trotsky was right. And therefore this was a strange time indeed to decide that Communism was twentieth-century Americanism. It was a strange time for a popular front in which Communism would commonly be equated with the most idealistic forms of liberalism. At this point the tactic of secrecy reveals another dimension. *The very nature of Soviet Communism was being kept a secret from its liberal friends.* In some ways, the CP was secretive even vis-à-vis its own members: this, too, Miss Ginzburg's history illustrates. But there was no incentive in Russia to pretend to be a Jeffersonian democrat. In America there was. And in the era in which the Party to which they owed absolute obedience practiced terror that went far beyond expedient callousness into orgies of meaningless sadism, American Communists wore the sheep's clothing of idealistic liberals. If, contrariwise, a truly idealistic liberal could be suspected of Communism, the error was to be attributed not alone to the paranoia of the Right but equally to the hypocrisy of the Left.

And hypocritical Leftists were not above exploiting the situation quite grossly. In the matter of invoking the Fifth Amendment, for example. While Joe McCarthy, on his side—or, for that matter, Sidney Hook—taught a credulous public to believe that anyone who invoked this amendment was a Communist, Communists edged non-Communists toward invoking it just in order to prove McCarthy and Hook wrong and, more broadly, to blur the lines between Communism and non-Communism in their own interest. An incident I myself recall from the fifties is of such a non-Communist being actually blackmailed into invoking the Fifth Amendment by his Communist "friends," the threat being that if he didn't do it, they would report his attendance at such-and-such "Communist-front" meetings. The same horrible irony obtains in this last clause. It was the Right which decided which organizations were "fronts." An unscrupulous, over-Machiavellian Left could get certain results by accepting a definition it knew to be false. After which any discussion as to which organizations "really" were fronts could not but be Pirandellian. If they were fronts at all, they became so, in some cases at least, by being called so by the Right and by being accepted as such by the one section of the Left which was given to such shenanigans. That section was the Communist Party.

Absurd of course is all the rightist rhetoric about Communism, means, and ends. This rhetoric reiterates that the peculiar evil in Communism is the belief that the end justifies bad means. The absurdity here rests in the disregard of the fact that politics in general is committed to acceptance of bad means, otherwise politicians would never support war, let alone the system of secrecy and deceit (espionage and diplomacy) that goes with it. If Communism was worse, it was not a matter of principle but of degree. Yet even that was not the main point, which was that of Communism more was expected. Communism was supposed to be a new game, and all the Stalinists were proposing was to beat the veterans of the old game. Stalin had *more logical* concentration camps than Hitler, or so it could be claimed for a time and up to a point: in the end they were so far beyond all logic that the act of comparison becomes surrealistic, ludicrous—and inhuman. Let us suppose for the purposes of argument—or for the purpose of breaking off that particular argument—that the amount of cruelty in the Hitler and Stalin regimes was exactly equal. The Russian disaster would be many times worse than the German because it is more than a disaster, it is also a tragedy, the greatest historical tragedy of the past hundred years, because, beyond all the physical suffering, it represented the desolating disappointment of the great hope of our era: the hope of Socialist humanism, the hope, to put it modestly, of a society which, through Socialism, shall be less oppressed, less insecure, less miserable.

Just how close any part of the CPUSA was to the giant misdeeds of the Soviet government in the late thirties I do not know, but there is plenty on the record to document that, while a degree of Machiavellianism is common to all politics, the Communists delighted in maximizing that degree and have the worst record of perhaps any radical organization that ever existed for intrigue, unscrupulousness, and inhumanity. If this is even approximately true, then we cannot think of an attack upon them—however inhuman and unscrupulous *it* may be—as comparable, say, to Hitler's assault upon ordinary citizens of Jewish origin.

One of the best studies I have read in the field is *Witch Hunt* by Carey McWilliams. After twenty years, most of McWilliams' arguments stand up very well, and some are more pertinent than ever, as for example:

> Even a majority enjoys no real immunity from the modern forms of psychological warfare which governments use to coerce consent. Nowadays large majorities can be manipulated by carefully timed headlines, revelations, and a thoroughly unscrupulous exploitation of the silence and secrecy surrounding many phases of government.

Under American law, nothing save a clear-and-present physical danger could justify coming down hard on any group of citizens of any persuasion, including Communism. McWilliams' book might be regarded as a scholarly elaboration upon such views of freedom of speech as have been reiterated over the years by Justice William O. Douglas and Justice Hugo Black. He identifies a real sickness, a veritable fever, within American society, demonstrates its ravages, and suggests, for cure, adherence to the principles laid down in the Constitution and the Bill of Rights.

But it is characteristic of the liberal writing of the time (1950) that so little is said of Communism. The whole problem is seen as that of the witch-hunters themselves. On one point, however, McWilliams shows more curiosity than did the liberalism of the day: secrecy. Generally this was passed over almost as if the CPUSA was as open in its dealings as any other group. McWilliams acknowledges that it was not, and even advances a justification for secrecy, and a dignified precedent: the Abolitionists also withheld their plans from the public. But I'm afraid the CPUSA can only suffer further from any comparison with the Abolitionists. Of course, all parties involved in revolutionary, warlike, and maybe just political action will use a degree of secrecy. There is secrecy in withholding a press release till the right moment. Again, the difference from Communist practice is not one of principle but of degree; but moral differences are often differences of degree; such differences can be enormous. The Abolitionists had a deserved reputation for integrity. The opposite is true of the Communist parties of the Stalin era.

Descending from the high plateau of politics to simple personal prudence, one might defend American Communists who were secretive to avoid losing their jobs. Surely secrecy of that sort is often fully justified. If only the secrecy of the CP had stopped there! But not only was it a Machiavellian scheme of life with widely spread nets, it was a veritable mystique, respected and adhered to beyond all rational plan. It was a way of life. And therein more than a revolution was betrayed. Marxism was betrayed. The whole tradition of radicalism was betrayed. I cite the Communist Manifesto:

> The Communists disdain to conceal their views and aims. They openly declare that their ends can be attained by the forcible overthrow of all existing social conditions. Let the ruling classes tremble at a Communist revolution.

That such an "open declaration" is likely to be dangerous is obvious. That the declarer may lose his job stands to reason. Though he might forgivably do a little trembling, the emphasis of Marx and Engels is all on the trembling the other side would do.

Quite a contrast to HUAC's Hollywood hearings of 1947. The Ten went to jail and in various degrees suffered further privations later, but what were they fighting for? Materially speaking, for the maintenance of their—in some cases—absurdly high level of income. Ideologically speaking, neither for Marxism nor for Stalinism, but for the classical liberalism of Hugo Black and William Douglas, as embodied in the First Amendment. Why? What sense did that make? That wasn't the kind of people they were, obviously, whether or not they were all card-carrying members of the CPUSA. But, alas, they did *not* disdain to conceal their views. They lacked candor, and if that, humanly speaking, is quite a common lack, it is an impossible lack for real radicals. For, to radicalism, candor is no adornment, it is of the essence. It is love of candor that makes men radical thinkers: a distaste for pretense, an awareness of the prevalence of false consciousness, and a yearning for realities, an appetite for true consciousness. While in action Stalinist Communism ran to terror on a big scale, in thought it went just as far astray by creating its own false consciousness. Abandoning that strenuous and joyful quest for reality which is the spiritual life of radicalism, it addressed itself instead to the traditional task of wrapping realities in empty forms of words. So, in the HUAC hearings, the rhetoric of John Howard Lawson merely counterbalances that of the Committee. Bullshit equals bullshit.

3

It is with this in mind that Richard Rovere wrote, "The investigators and the investigated have seemed richly to deserve each other." The witticism is sharp, but what exactly is implied? If a torturer and the man he is torturing are equally terrible fellows, should one extend an equal lack of sympathy to both? Rovere does praise Walter Goodman, the principal historian of HUAC, precisely for "the evenhandedness of his contempt for the Stalinist Left and the Yahoo Right." * But aside from the question of whether contempt is a sufficient response, there is a failure to distinguish here between the mere disaster of Yahoo Rightism, and the tragedy of Communism in the Stalin era. A Yahoo is a Yahoo, but the Left was not by nature Stalinist: the Stalinization of non-Stalinoid human beings was a tragic process—how could anyone who has been on the inside, the real side, of any of this contrive to be merely contemptuous? If your brother goes wrong, you aren't contemptuous, you are devastated; and the Stalinists were our brothers, while the Yahoos were not. I speak for radicals.

Rovere and Goodman could reply that they are not radicals, and this is very true. The question remains whether their contempt for hangman and hanged alike yields any insight, let alone constitutes a tenable position. All that comes through to me is a certain delight in feeling superior to both sides: a message less about the sides than about the observer. The stance is narcissistic, and it fails to do justice not only to the investigated *but also to the investigators.*

No radical critic can bring to the investigators the kind of understanding that comes from sympathy, but a combatant does not fall, either, into the error of underestimating the enemy. Contempt entails doing just that, for in the fire of contempt, a knave dwindles into a fool, a monster into a shrimp. With this in mind, I would criticize what, over the years, I have found to be the prevailing view of HUAC among those who consider themselves agin it. It is that the HUAC hearings are an irrelevant side show beside the circus tent of American politics. As a theater man, I may be permitted to remind anyone who needs it that actual side shows were intended to lure customers into the tent: they were never irrelevant. Metaphor aside, I think it can be

* Foreword to *The Committee* by Walter Goodman. —E.B.

demonstrated that—amid so many stupid things said—HUAC itself was usually the reverse of stupid and, so far from being irrelevant or remote, was always close to the center of the political struggle. These men had their ears closer to the ground than any of your bland, clever, literate liberals.

We shall never know *how* close unless some band of revolutionaries manages to corner the FBI files, for undoubtedly the historian's key to The Whole Truth in this field lies in the connection between HUAC and the FBI. There is general agreement that it is close, which indeed can be proved from the public record, but just what it means in specific detail could only be shown from FBI files themselves. In the matter of informing, for example. The public got the impression that informers just ran to Washington and talked to HUAC while America eavesdropped. In fact, HUAC carefully dramatized the act of informing for purposes of waging political warfare: to intimidate some, to encourage others, and so on. It was theater or, if you like, ritual: a rite of purification that would also put the fear of God (HUAC's man in Heaven) into the as yet unpurified. The public confessions were as nothing to the private confessions that preceded them. One could spill all the beans to J. Edgar Hoover or one of his merry men; then HUAC would serve selected beans to the great American public via the great American press. HUAC also had its own investigators to whom beans could be privately spilled. Before we would know The Whole Truth we would need to have the records of their sessions too, as well as of "executive sessions" of the Committee, which also seem to have specialized in intimate, if not necessarily true, confessions. If the American people is not the freest ever, it is the best supervised and most listened in on. Everything from Eleanor Roosevelt's hotel-room conversation to Martin Luther King's extramarital relations is there on tape for nation-wide broadcast at the appointed time. For Big Brother isn't of 1984, he has been watching us for some decades now. Some think his name is Hoover. In which case his Little Brother's name is HUAC.

Linked in the first instance to the FBI, HUAC is linked in the second to the courts. Congressman John Rankin described it as "the grand jury of America," and in 1946 it became the only House Committee ever to have the right to subpoena witnesses. The game was then to place them in a position where the House itself would cite them for contempt of Congress. At best they would then go to jail, at worst spend some uncomfortable, expensive years keeping out of jail: such was the alternative to purification. The Committee won either way.

That HUAC has always been extremely smart is best shown in its choice of targets and therewith of headlines. One could work backward from 1970 and demonstrate this year by year. This year they are doing the Panthers. Last year they did SDS. In 1968 they were investigating the Chicago "conspiracy" even before Nixon got to the White House. In 1966 it had been

"Bills to make punishable assistance to enemies of U.S. in time of undeclared war"—i.e., the left wing of the peace movement. They had got to women's liberation as early as 1962 (Women Strike for Peace). They were on to the Oppenheimer Case as early as 1947, though for the public it didn't become a case at all till seven years later. "Alger Hiss the Spy" was a HUAC discovery or invention, as you will. They had a large share in making history of the Great Informers: first and always foremost Whittaker Chambers, but, scarcely less creative and aggressive, Elizabeth Bentley, Louis Budenz, Harvey Matusow. They shot two Eislers with one stone—a third Eisler, who got in touch with Hoover in 1946. In 1939 they wrecked the Federal Theater, that first effort at Socialist humanism in American institutions. In short, they have always been on the ball, and we needn't even ask Our Father to forgive them, for they do know what they do.

The HUAC's most notorious target of all was Hollywood, and to be sure they chose it because, in Arthur Miller's phrase, they were "cheap publicity hounds." Yet if we impute this motive alone we fall into the trap of overstressing the HUAC's frivolity and thereby underestimating its seriousness. In our America, publicity is no marginal phenomenon, and its ballyhoo, though unreal in one sense, is, in mere common sense, reality itself. At best we may hope to make it unreal later on. For now, the advertising is the most real part of television—TV exists for it, not it for TV, time is money, and TV has Father Time in a wallet on its back. The image is more important than the man, whether the name be Narcissus or Nixon, and the unreal is our quintessential reality, our *Ding an sich*. And the marriage of HUAC and Hollywood was made in Heaven, which in turn is situated between Fifth and Park. Today, if the HUAC were still in its prime, it would no doubt be wooing the TV networks, but in 1947 Hollywood was still the principal dream factory—always excepting Washington itself.

The two sets of dreamers—power wielders too, since their dreams had power, black-and-white power, not to mention Technicolor—were meant for each other and had to get together. And paranoia being what it is, and The Great Melodrama being what it is, they had to get together against the Enemy, especially the Enemy Within, the "Trojan Horse in America," the Russian agent in the White House or Disneyland. A big show? Well, naturally: the greatest show on earth, enacted by professionals of both entertainment businesses, West and East, Hollywood and Washington. And it was the only time in history that the earth seemed likely to be taken over by its greatest show.

4

How should those of us who are "unfriendly" to such a Committee behave when subpoenaed by it? I have been saying that, traditionally and essentially, radicals disdain to conceal their views. The simplest thing for them to do, then, would be to go to Washington and answer all questions.

But this would be to recognize the Committee's authority or at least existence. Should they do that? Albert Einstein thought not and, in 1953, formulated what I. F. Stone, who supported it, called the Einstein Pledge.* Einstein saw the Committee's work as a kind of Inquisition that threatened the integrity of all intellectual workers. They should therefore be conscientious objectors against it, breaking the law of the land in the name of a Higher Law, like St. Thomas More—and be prepared to suffer for this as he did.

But just as conscientious objection to military service may be applied in various degrees and at various stages along the line—one can serve in the Red Cross or one can refuse even to go to the induction center—so it has been possible to fight the Committee without taking the Einstein Pledge. Most unfriendly witnesses have responded to their subpoenas and have then confronted HUAC with some tactic calculated to help their own cause. The most famous tack has been invocation of the Fifth Amendment to the Constitution—which offers the privilege of not testifying if you judge that your testimony might prove self-incriminating. Some witnesses cited several amendments, and many invoked just the First, which guarantees freedom of speech and association.

In themselves all these choices were legitimate, even if, as Telford Taylor has shown in his book *Grand Inquest,* there was widespread misunderstanding of what the Fifth Amendment was all about. (It was never intended as a way of protecting associates; rather, and specifically, as a means of *self*-protection, whether one was innocent or guilty. When Lillian Hellman, in 1952, tried to use the Fifth to shield others while exposing herself she was performing legal gymnastics—unwittingly, of course; and in retrospect it would seem that both the ethics and the politics of her strategy were exemplary.) If there was a question, it was not really of the tactics themselves but of good faith. Was refusal to speak the honest and courageous gesture it purported to be or a disingenuous way of hiding something both from the Committee and from the world?

As I have stressed, it is the Communist Party, of all radical groups, that has made a specialty of a politics of bad faith. To match it one has to look to its archenemies in the Establishment, such as Richard Nixon, a man fascinated by Communist skulduggery. And it was the Communist Party that gave Joe McCarthy the pretext for his otherwise preposterous concept, "Fifth-Amendment Communists," and, for that matter, which gave Sidney Hook the pretext for his more sophisticated presentations of McCarthy's notion. The CPUSA, rendering suspect everything they touched, forfeited what is nowadays called "credibility," which perhaps wouldn't have mattered very much except that they thereby damaged the "credibility" of every other radical group in America. What one has to complain of, then, is less that some people's silence was in bad faith than that the good faith of what was no doubt the large majority of unfriendly witnesses before HUAC was

*** Printed above as "A Letter from Albert Einstein," pp. 667–668.**

brought into question by the bad faith of the others. Which was a double misfortune: a misfortune in ethics, since a real wrong was done by some human beings to others, and a misfortune in political warfare and "public relations" since irreparable damage was done to reputations, both of causes and of individuals.

What a pity that such a topic comes to us almost exclusively in the crude blacks and whites of journalism! For, that way, it is not just nuances of gray that are lost but the whole spectrum of colors. What I have said of the CPUSA is far from true of many members and sympathizers of that organization, for the Party was monolithic chiefly in the fertile fantasy of its enemies: it had human beings both in and around it, many of them very fine people indeed. When its most famous sympathizer, Paul Robeson, took the position before HUAC that everyone in fact knew where he stood, it was true. He may have respected certain formal taboos of CP tradition—like avoiding the mention of Communism and its Party when addressing a non-Communist audience—yet it would be ludicrous to suggest that Paul Robeson ever kept the public from knowing who he was and what he believed. When he refused, on principle, to answer the $64 question before HUAC, he had already answered it before California's "little HUAC," the Tenney Committee. But by the time he came before HUAC, he had decided to say, in effect, "I'll tell the public but I won't tell you." He was far from alone in this decision. A party may have betrayed a Revolution, but that does not make a traitor of each of its individual supporters—a traitor either to Revolution or to their country—for no man is an institution incarnate, and, despite reports to the contrary, very many Stalinists continued to be men.

Much as one may favor open declarations of faith, it would be unfair, without knowing each from the inside, to censure those individuals who did not make such declarations. Their secret was not always that they held membership in the CPUSA. There were often private reasons for silence: one person was protecting another or believing he was. Besides which, there was much sincerity, if not always as much clearheadedness, in the individual's commitment to silence. Even today many on the Left will not go along with such a condemnation of the CP as I have offered here. And yesterday—well, yesterday *Journey into the Whirlwind* had not been written and, although evidence of the nature of Stalinism had been published, it was much easier, then, to overlook it. The Webbs were a scholarly couple, yet their only comment on the murder of Trotsky (in the 1942 revision of their book) was that he fell at the hands of one of his own followers! (At the time this was a common version of what happened. The full truth had not yet been written. But one notes also a refusal to be suspicious that is highly inappropriate to the subject.)

It would in any case be a mistake both tactical and moral to go after individuals in a kind of reverse McCarthyism. Let the dead bury their dead. In the 1960s a new generation came to life. As far as HUAC is concerned, it began with Women Strike for Peace. The HUAC wanted to know if they were a Communist front. One questioned such people, didn't one, and they hedged on their answers? If they said they accepted Communists into membership of their organizations they would add that that was only because they were so broad-minded. So one pressed on and asked, Are you so broad-minded you accept Nazis? Then they said, Oh no, that was quite different and, bingo, one had them in the trap: they were, too, a front for Communism. Only Dagmar Wilson didn't hedge. She wasn't CP-trained. She wasn't CP-intimidated, -blackmailed, or even -overawed. She just answered any and all questions in her own freewheeling style, willing to talk to the HUAC, just as she would have been willing to talk to George Lincoln Rockwell or the Grand Wizard of the Klan. A woman with nothing to hide! A woman who disdained to conceal her views and openly declared them! Yes, she answered, she would accept Communists. Yes, she answered, she would accept Nazis, if she could get 'em. In the cause of peace, one needed them all, one needed everybody.

It was the fall of HUAC's Bastille. Whether or no the Committee and its unfriendly witnesses hitherto had "deserved each other," they had come to need each other as playmates in a game with by now agreed rules. It was smart to ask a question knowing that the witness would refuse to answer, and that you'd get him for contempt. How disconcerting, then, if the witness spoiled everything by answering the question and reversing the roles; playing cop to their robber, hero to their villain! Of course, silence had been heroic—in intention. And Arthur Miller had tried to apotheosize this heroic refusal to speak in dramatic literature (*The Crucible*). In real life, unhappily, such refusal was rendered suspect and ambiguous by its whole background in the life and hates of the Communist Party. Liberation from the murk of this ambiguity was to be found in ending the silence—but singing quite a different tune from the one the HUAC wanted to hear.

> . . . once the keystone of [the Fifth Amendment] privilege was removed, the entire structure of investigative exposure so carefully erected through the years came tumbling down. The witness was at liberty to dispute and challenge all of the committee's most cherished assumptions, to parry and thrust, to insist upon counterstatements. Since there is nothing in the Federal contempt statute that forces the witness to confine his answer to a narrow formula or that bars him from objecting to questions ad nauseam, the witnesses at the hearing, liberated from the Fifth Amendment and its ancillary restraints, made the committee pay an exorbitant price for the answers it received. Overnight a new kind of witness was born: the witness who boils over with talk, who pleads no privilege and fills the record with his views and objections. He is exactly the old-style friendly witness with one important exception: his testimony attacks the committee, its premises and its claimed legislative subject matter—bitingly, humorously, solemnly and fearlessly.*

* "HUAC: From Pillory to Farce" by Frank J. Donner, *The Nation,* September 5, 1966.

The hearing here described took place in August 1966. The view of Marx and Engels on concealment had finally come into its own, logically enough, by way of young members of the Marxist-Leninist Progressive Labor Party. They had prepared speeches presenting their views, and they delivered them as fully as they were allowed to, paying as much or as little attention to the questions the Committee asked, or tried to ask, as they wished. It was a matter therefore not only of open declaration but of a rather violent war of nerves—rebel sons of America against fuddy-duddy fathers. And no one could have been better cast for this father role than the Chairman of HUAC, the late Joe R. Pool of (naturally) Texas. Jerry Rubin was on hand, dressed as a soldier of the Revolutionary War. Very much, at the time, a show in its own right, the 1966 hearing seems in retrospect more of a rehearsal for Judge Julius Hoffman's courtroom (1969–1970).

But this is to forget to credit HUAC with its own rehearsal procedures. They hauled in David Dellinger, Rennie Davis, and Tom Hayden in October 1968. These three didn't run wild like the Progressive Laborites, but they did exploit the committee room as a forum for their views, and, in effect, they imposed their own rules of procedure, since there was nothing the Committee could do to stop them from talking, let alone to ensure that their vocabulary, syntax, and tone should be what Congressmen regard as proper.

The HUAC road show, after running so merrily for thirty years, stopped right there. Yes, it was to continue under another name—the House Internal Security Committee—and might well remain a menace for a long time to come. But something more than a title had ended. The 1960s killed the Committee that all of us knew and some of us didn't love, that Committee whose spirit is perhaps best caught in the utterances of its most eloquent investigator, the late Richard Arens:

> Do you remember the quotation from Lenin on that, that they will encircle the United States and it will fall in the hands of the Communists like an over-ripened fruit?
>
> Within the framework of the Communist operation, is there room for concepts of God and spiritual values as we were taught them at our mother's knee?
>
> Are you now thoroughly disgusted with the fact that you have been associated with the Communist ideology, which is atheistic, which is the very antithesis of Christian morality as we know it in this country?
>
> Are you now, or have you ever been, a member of a godless conspiracy controlled by a foreign power?

Or, finally:

> Kindly tell us, while you are under oath now, and in the aura of patriotism which you have surrounded yourself [with] in your opening statement,

> whether or not you betrayed your country by being executive secretary of this organization designed to subvert the security of this great nation?

A question which Arens reworded, when the witness objected to it, as follows:

> For the moment, may we change to say, Were you executive secretary of this innocent little organization, this patriotic organization, this organization for the uplift of humanity, the Southern California Peace Crusade?

That is unmistakably the tone of the 1950s, but the mentality is much older, as old as persecution perhaps, and certainly as old as the thirties and forties, when the lady who had falsely denounced Hallie Flanagan to HUAC as virtually a Communist was rewarded for her pains by being hired as an investigator and, after duly warning the Committee against Herman Shumlin and Woody Guthrie, reported on Helen Hayes as follows: "While Helen Hayes is one of our leading actresses, she was head of the milk fund for the North American Spanish Committee." The radicals of the sixties put the Committee—for the first time—on the defensive. Earlier, the witnesses were generally meek; now Committee members were generally meek. And in seizing the offensive, the new type of witnesses seized what was dearest to HUAC's patriotic heart: the headlines. During 1969 and 1970, the new "Committee on Internal Security" was not calling unfriendly witnesses at all. And on August 10, 1969, it was announced in the *New York Times* that, at long last, the courts had allowed a direct challenge to the Committee's constitutionality.

> The ruling, by a unanimous three-judge panel of the United States Court of Appeals for the Seventh Circuit, sitting in Chicago, will apparently have the effect of placing on trial the controversial 31-year history of the committee.

One Committee chairman was sent to jail years ago, but this was only for thievery. It is nice to think that HUAC as a whole could be found to be unconstitutional, for, in that case, what would be the difference in status between its investigators and ordinary snoopers and spies? And who would have betrayed their country, the witnesses or the Committee members? Some of both perhaps; but only the HUAC members could claim to be traitors ex officio.

Appendix 1: House Un-American Activities Committee Membership 1938–1970

(Note: the name of the Committee was changed in 1969 to House Internal Security Committee)

LISTED UNDER SELECT AND SPECIAL COMMITTEES OF THE HOUSE (1938–1944): SPECIAL COMMITTEE TO INVESTIGATE UN-AMERICAN ACTIVITIES

75th Congress 1937–1938
(1938 only)

(Democrats)
Chairman, Martin Dies, Texas
Arthur D. Healey, Massachusetts
John J. Dempsey, New Mexico
Joe Starnes, Alabama
Harold G. Mosier, Ohio

(Republicans)
Noah M. Mason, Illinois
J. Parnell Thomas, New Jersey

Secretary, Robert E. Stripling

76th Congress 1939–1940

Chairman, Martin Dies, Texas
Arthur D. Healey, Massachusetts (replaced by Joseph E. Carey, Massachusetts)
John J. Dempsey, New Mexico
Joe Starnes, Alabama
Jerry Voorhis, California
Noah M. Mason, Illinois
J. Parnell Thomas, New Jersey

Secretary, Robert E. Stripling

77th Congress 1941–1942

Chairman, Martin Dies, Texas
Joseph E. Carey, Massachusetts
Harry P. Beam, Illinois
Joe Starnes, Alabama
Jerry Voorhis, California

Noah M. Mason, Illinois
J. Parnell Thomas, New Jersey

Secretary, Robert E. Stripling

78th Congress 1943–1944

Chairman, Martin Dies, Texas
Herman P. Eberharter, Pennsylvania
Wirt Courtney, Tennessee
Joe Starnes, Alabama
John M. Costello, California

Noah M. Mason, Illinois (replaced in

2nd Session by Fred E. Busbey, Illinois)
J. Parnell Thomas, New Jersey
Karl E. Mundt, South Dakota

Secretary, Robert E. Stripling

STANDING COMMITTEE: COMMITTEE ON UN-AMERICAN ACTIVITIES

79th Congress 1945–1946

Chairman, Edward J. Hart, New Jersey (replaced as Chairman by John S. Wood, Georgia)
John E. Rankin, Mississippi
J. Hardin Peterson, Florida
J. W. Robinson, Utah
John R. Murdock, Arizona
Herbert C. Bonner, North Carolina

J. Parnell Thomas, New Jersey
Karl E. Mundt, South Dakota
Gerald W. Landis, Indiana

Secretary, Robert E. Stripling

80th Congress 1947–1948

Chairman, J. Parnell Thomas, New Jersey
Karl E. Mundt, South Dakota
John McDowell, Pennsylvania
Richard M. Nixon, California
Richard B. Vail, Illinois

John S. Wood, Georgia
John E. Rankin, Mississippi
J. Hardin Peterson, Florida
Herbert C. Bonner, North Carolina (replaced in 2nd Session by F. Edward Hébert, Louisiana)

Secretary, Robert E. Stripling

81st Congress 1949–1950

Chairman, John S. Wood, Georgia
Francis E. Walter, Pennsylvania
Burr P. Harrison, Virginia
John McSweeney, Ohio
Morgan M. Moulder, Missouri

J. Parnell Thomas, New Jersey (gone by January 3, 1950. Nixon becomes senior Republican member, with one Republican vacancy)
Richard M. Nixon, California
Francis Case, South Dakota
Harold H. Velde, Illinois

Clerk, John W. Carrington

82nd Congress 1951–1952

Chairman, John S. Wood, Georgia
Francis E. Walter, Pennsylvania
Morgan M. Moulder, Missouri
Clyde Doyle, California
James B. Frazier, Jr., Tennessee

Harold H. Velde, Illinois
Bernard W. (Pat) Kearney, New York
Donald L. Jackson, California
Charles E. Potter, Michigan

Clerk, John W. Carrington

83rd Congress 1953–1954

Chairman, Harold H. Velde, Illinois
Bernard W. (Pat) Kearney, New York
Donald L. Jackson, California
Kit Clardy, Michigan
Gordon H. Scherer, Ohio

Francis E. Walter, Pennsylvania
Morgan M. Moulder, Missouri
Clyde Doyle, California
James B. Frazier, Jr., Tennessee

Chief Clerk, Thomas W. Beale, Sr.

84th Congress 1955–1956

Chairman, Francis E. Walter, Pennsylvania
Morgan M. Moulder, Missouri
Clyde Doyle, California
James B. Frazier, Jr., Tennessee
Edwin E. Willis, Louisiana

Harold H. Velde, Illinois
Bernard W. (Pat) Kearney, New York
Donald L. Jackson, California
Gordon H. Scherer, Ohio

Chief Clerk, Thomas W. Beale, Sr.

85th Congress 1957–1958

Chairman, Francis E. Walter, Pennsylvania
Morgan M. Moulder, Missouri
Clyde Doyle, California

James B. Frazier, Jr., Tennessee
Edwin E. Willis, Louisiana

Bernard W. (Pat) Kearney, New York
Donald L. Jackson, California
Gordon H. Scherer, Ohio
Robert J. McIntosh, Michigan

Staff Director, Richard Arens

86th Congress 1959–1960

Chairman, Francis E. Walter, Pennsylvania
Morgan M. Moulder, Missouri
Clyde Doyle, California
Edwin E. Willis, Louisiana
William M. Tuck, Virginia

Donald L. Jackson, California
Gordon H. Scherer, Ohio
William E. Miller, New York
August E. Johansen, Michigan

Staff Director, Richard Arens

87th Congress 1961–1962

Chairman, Francis E. Walter, Pennsylvania
Morgan M. Moulder, Missouri
Clyde Doyle, California
Edwin E. Willis, Louisiana
William M. Tuck, Virginia

Gordon H. Scherer, Ohio
August E. Johansen, Michigan
Donald C. Bruce, Indiana
Henry C. Shadeberg, Wisconsin

Director, Frank S. Tavenner, Jr.

88th Congress 1963–1964

Chairman, Francis E. Walter, Pennsylvania (1st Session)
Clyde Doyle, California (1st Session)
Edwin E. Willis, Louisiana
William M. Tuck, Virginia
Joe R. Pool, Texas
Richard H. Ichord, Missouri (2nd Session)
George F. Senner, Jr., Arizona (2nd Session)
August E. Johansen, Michigan
Donald C. Bruce, Indiana
Henry C. Shadeberg, Wisconsin
John M. Ashbrook, Ohio

Director, Francis J. McNamara

89th Congress 1965–1966

Chairman, Edwin E. Willis, Louisiana
William M. Tuck, Virginia
Joe R. Pool, Texas
Richard H. Ichord, Missouri
George F. Senner, Jr., Arizona
Charles L. Weltner, Georgia

John M. Ashbrook, Ohio
Del Clawson, California
John H. Buchanan, Jr., Alabama

Director, Francis J. McNamara

90th Congress 1967–1968

Chairman, Edwin E. Willis, Louisiana
William M. Tuck, Virginia
Joe R. Pool, Texas
Richard H. Ichord, Missouri
John C. Culver, Iowa

John M. Ashbrook, Ohio
Del Clawson, California
Richard L. Roudebush, Indiana
Albert W. Watson, South Carolina

Director, Francis J. McNamara

91st Congress 1969–1970 (Name of Committee changed to Committee on Internal Security as of 2/18/69)

Chairman, Richard H. Ichord, Missouri
Claude Pepper, Florida
Edwin W. Edwards, Louisiana
Richardson Preyer, North Carolina
Louis Stokes, Ohio

John M. Ashbrook, Ohio
Richard L. Roudebush, Indiana
Albert W. Watson, South Carolina
William J. Scherle, Iowa

Chief Counsel, Donald G. Sanders

Appendix 2: The Measures Taken

by Bertolt Brecht and Hanns Eisler, as translated for the House Un-American Activities Committee

---

The Committee's own translation of *Die Massnahme* is reprinted here not only to clarify discussion of the play in the testimony of Hanns Eisler and of Bertolt Brecht but also as a specimen of the Committee's handiwork, here submitted to scholarly scrutiny. It is a very literal job, but not at all an accurate one. There are mistakes, beginning on page one with the title, which does not mean either "rule" or "doctrine," any more than Brecht's contribution (the words) can be designated as "drill." There are also typographical errors, which have been retained. It is clear that if you translate Brecht this way, you can attribute anything to him that you wish. And he was by no means the only foreigner to be given a Committee grilling.

For some years this was the only published translation of *Die Massnahme*. It has since appeared in two differing English versions by the present editor, corresponding to two different German versions, in, respectively: Bentley, *The Modern Theatre*, volume 6 (New York, 1960) and Brecht, *The Jewish Wife and Other Short Plays* (New York, 1967).

[Translation]

HANNS EISLER

DIE MASSNAHME
The Rule [*or Doctrine*]

Drill [libretto] by Bert Brecht

Piano score

[Published by] Universal-Edition No. 2744

Hanns Eisler
The Rule [*or Doctrine*]
Drill [libretto] by Bert Brecht
Op[us] No. 20
Piano score by Erwin Ratz

Performance right reserved
[Published by] Universal-Edition A. G.
Vienna Copyright 1931 by Universal-Edition Leipsic
Printed in Austria

CONTENTS

		Page
No. 1	Prelude (The four agitators, mixed chorus, orchestra)	3
	I. The Teachings of the Classics	
No. 2a	Recitative (The young comrade, the three agitators, orchestra)	10
No. 2b	Praise of the USSR [Hail to USSR!] (mixed chorus with orchestra)	12
	II. The Cover-up [Masking]	
No. 3a	Recitative (The director of the party headquarters, the two agitators, orchestra)	17
No. 3b	Declamation (mixed chorus with percussion [accompaniment])	22
No. 4	Praise of the illegal labor [Hail to illegal labor!] (mixed chorus with orchestra, later: The four agitators)	23
	III. The Stone	
No. 5	Song of the rice boatmen (Two coolies, the young comrade, the overseer, male chorus with orchestra)	31
No. 6	Discourse (mixed chorus a cappella)	44
No. 6b	Declamation (Lenin quotation) (mixed chorus with percussion [accompaniment])	44
No. 6c	Canon of a Lenin quotation (mixed chorus with percussion [accompaniment])	45
	IV. Justice	
No. 7a	Strike song (The young comrade, male chorus with orchestra)	46
No. 7b	Discussion	52
	V. What Actually is a Man [Human Being]?	
No. 8a	Recitative (The trader [businessman], The young comrade, orchestra)	53
No. 8b	Song of the products (The trader [businessman], The young comrade, orchestra; later: mixed chorus)	59
No. 9	Change the world—it needs it! (mixed chorus with orchestra)	68
	VI. The Treason	
No. 10	Praise of the Party [Hail to the Party!] (mixed chorus with orchestra)	75

VII. Utmost Persecution, and Analysis

No. 11 Recitative (mixed chorus with percussion [accompaniment]) 85
No. 12a Recitative (The four agitators, orchestra) 87
No. 12b We are the scum of the earth (mixed chorus with orchestra) 89

VIII. The Burial

No. 13a and b (mixed chorus a cappella) 93
No. 14 Finale (mixed chorus with orchestra) 95

LIST OF PERFORMERS

The First Agitator (to be performed by the same soloist: The director of the party headquarters; The first coolie, The trader [businessman]) .... Tenor
The Second Agitator (The second coolie) .... }
The Third Agitator (The overseer, the policeman) .... } three actors
The Fourth Agitator (The young comrade) .... }
Male chorus; mixed chorus

ORCHESTRA

Three trumpets
Two horns
Two bass horns
Piano
Percussion instruments:
Two pairs of timpanis
Big drum
Small drum
Tenor (or field) drum
Cymbals
Tomtom
Duration of performance: one hour and thirty minutes.
Performance right reserved
Droits d'exécution réservés

THE RULE [or Doctrine]

Drill [libretto] by Bert Brecht

[music by]
Hanns Eisler, op[us] No. 20

[pp. 1–9]

Above measure 23: The controlling chorus. Then, from measure 24 on: "Come forth! Your labor was successful./ In this country too marches the Revolution,/ and formed are the lines of the fighters there also./ We are in accord with you."/

After measure 65: The four agitators (calling out loudly): "Halt!/

Measure 70: The four agitators: "We have something to tell [you]! We report the death of a comrade."/

From measure 73 on: "Who killed him?"/

Above measure 83: The four agitators: "We killed him. We shot him and threw him into [a] quicklime [pit]."/

From measure 86 on: "What is it that he has done that you had to shoot him?"/

Above measure 96: The four agitators: "Often he did the right thing, sometimes the wrong [thing], but finally he became a danger to the movement. He wanted [to do] the right [thing] and did the wrong [thing]. We demand your judgment."/

From measure 99 on: "Describe how it happened, and you will hear our judgment."/

Above measure 117: The four agitators: "We shall accept your judgment."/

[p. 10–16]

I. The Teaching of the Classics

The four agitators: "We came from Moscow as agitators; we were to travel to the city of Mukden to spread propaganda and to create, in the factories, the Chinese Party. We were to report to [district] party headquarters (the one) closest to the border, and to requisition a guide. There, in the anteroom, a young comrade came toward us and spoke of the nature of our mission. We are repeating the conversation:"

(The line up; three on one side, and one on the opposite side; one of the four [agitators] represents the young comrade.)

The young comrade: "I am the secretary of the party headquarters which is the last toward the border. My heart is beating for the Revolution. The witnessing of wrong-doing drove me into the lines of the fighters [party members]. Man must help man. I am for freedom. I believe in mankind. And I am for the rules [doctrines] of the Communist Party which fights for the classless society against exploitation and ignorance."

The three agitators: "We come from Moscow."

The young comrade: "We have expected you."

The three agitators: "Why?"

The young comrade: "We do not get anywhere. There is disorder and need, little bread and much fighting. Many [people] are full of courage, but few can read. [There are] few machines, and no one understands [how to operate] them. Our locomotives are worn out [literally, "worn to pieces"—translator.]"

No. 2a Recitative

The young comrade: "Have you brought along locomotives?"

The three agitators: "No."

The young comrade: "Have you [any] tractors with you?"

The three agitators: "No."

The young comrade: "Our peasants even pull their own wooden plows. And then we have nothing to sow upon our fields. Have you brought along seed?"

The three agitators: "No."

The young comrade: "Are you at least bringing ammunition and machine guns?"

The three agitators: "No."

The young comrade: "The two of us have to defend the Revolution here. Surely you have a letter to us from the Central Committee which tells us what to do?"

The three agitators: "No."

The young comrade: "So you want to help us yourselves?"

The three agitators: "No."

The young comrade: "In our clothes we resist day and night the onslaught of hunger, ruin and counter-revolution. You, however, bring us nothing."

The three agitators: "So it is [you are right]: we bring you nothing. But across the border, to Mukden, we bring to the Chinese workers the teachings of the Classics and of the propagandists: the A B C of Communism; [we bring] to the ignorant the truth about their situation; [we bring] to the oppressed, class conscience; and [we bring] to the class-conscious, the experience[s] of the Revolution. From you we shall requisition an automobile and a guide."

The young comrade: "So I have asked badly?"

The three agitators: "No[t at all]; a good question was followed by a better answer. We [can] see that the utmost was demanded by you; but more will be demanded from you: one of you two [the two of you] must lead us to Mukden."

The young comrade: "I am leaving, therefore, my post, which was too difficult for two, for which, however, one [person] must be sufficient now. I shall go with you."

The young comrade: "Marching onward, spreading the teachings of the Communist Classics: the World Revolution."

No. 2b Praise of the USSR [*Hail to USSR!*]

(spirited)

Above measure 5: (continue spirited).

"The whole world has already discussed our misfortunes; but still shared our meager meal the hope of all oppressed which contents itself with water, and Knowledge with a clear voice taught the guest behind our collapsing door."/

Above measure 27: (spirited). From measure 27 on: "When the door [is] collapsed, we can be seen from farther afield/ [we] whom frost will not kill nor hunger—untiringly discussing the fate of the world."/

The four agitators: "So the young comrade from the border station was in accord with us as to the nature of our mission, and we—four men and a woman—proceeded toward the director of the party headquarters."

II. The Cover-up [*Masking*]

[pp. 17–30]

The four agitators: "But the work in Mukden was illegal, hence we had to 'cover up our faces'; our young comrade agreed to this. We repeat the incident . . ."

(One of the agitators represents the director of the party headquarters.)

The director of the party headquarters: "I am the director of the last party headquarters [party headquarters next to border—translator]. I am giving my approval of having the comrade from my station go along with you as a guide. There is, however, unrest in the factories of Mukden, and these days the whole world is looking toward this city [waiting to see] whether or not one of us [our comrades] is coming out of the huts of the Chinese workers, and I hear [am told] that there are gun-boats in the rivers and armored trains on the rails ready to attack us the moment one of us is seen there. I am therefore recommending to the comrades to cross the border as Chinese. (To the agitators) You must not be seen."

The two agitators: "We shall not be seen."

The director of the party headquarters: "If one [of you] is wounded he must not be found."

The two agitators: "He will not be found."

No. 3a Recitative

Above measure 1: Energetic.

Above measure 3: The director of the party headquarters.

Above measure 5: (forceful, fresh).

From measure 5 on: "Are you ready to talk as long as you can [are able to] talk,/ but to disappear before anybody is looking,/ [and] also to hide the living and [as well as] the dead?"/

Above measure 17: The two agitators (spoken [not sung]). "Yes!"

Abbreviation before measure 19: The leader of the party headquarters.

Above measure 23: (in a loud tone of voice rhythmically).

Above measure 22 in piano accompaniment: hurrying—a tempo.

From measure 20 on: "Then you will not be yourselves any more;/ you [will be] no longer Karl Schmidt of Berlin,/ you [will be] no longer Anna Kjersk of Kasan,/ and you [will be] no longer Peter Sawitsch of Moscow;/ rather, you [will] all [be] without name and [without] mother, blank pages upon which the Revolution writes its order[s]."/

Above measure 25 (again sung).

Abbreviation before measure 31: The director of the party headquarters.

Above measure 34: The two agitators (spoken [not sung]). "Yes!"

Above measure 37: (The director of the party headquarters hands them masks.) a tempo, somewhat slower.

Above measure 47: (The director of the party headquarters) (always very forceful and fresh).

From measure 47 on: "Then, from this hour on, you are no longer nobody;/ rather, from this hour on, and probably until your disappearance,/ [you will be] unknown workers, fighters, Chinese, born of Chinese mothers, yellow-skinned, speaking Chinese in [your] sleep and in [your] fever."/

Above measure 54: (spoken [not sung]).

Abbreviation before measure 58: The director of the party headquarters.

Above measure 59: The two agitators (they put on their masks).

Measure 60: "Yes!"

Above measure 70: The director of the party headquarters (calling out loudly): "In the interest of Communism,/ in sympathy with the marching on of the proletarian masses [the proletariat] of all countries,/ saying yes to [advocating] the revolutionizing of the world."/

Above measure 74: The two agitators. "Yes!"

[At the end] The two agitators: In this manner the young comrade showed his agreement with the cover-up [masking] of his face.

No. 3b Declamation

Above measure 1: (speak very distinctly) footnote: The tempo of the chorus is about 152 metronome beats, with particular stress, however, upon distinct pronunciation [of the words].

Before measure 1: Chorus.

Before measure 1 of the accompaniment: Small drum.

Above measure 23: Broad.

At the end: The four agitators: "We went as Chinese to Mukden—four men and a woman—to spread propaganda and to create the Chinese party through the teachings of the Classics and of the propagandists—the A B C of Communism; to bring truth to the ignorant about their situation; [to teach] the oppressed class conscience, and the class-conscious the experience[s] of the Revolution."

No. 4 Praise of the Illegal Labor [Hail to Illegal labor!]

Above measure 1: Hard and dry.

Before measure 1: Tenor; chorus, bass.

From measure 2 on: "How beautiful [it is] to plead the cause of class struggle,/ to call our loudly and resoundingly [to urge] the masses to the fight,/ to annihilate the oppressors, to liberate the oppressed./"

Above measure 13: flowing.

From measure 13 on: "Hard and useful is the daily toil—the persistent and secretive knotting of the great net of the Party before the rifles of the employers."/

Above measure 16: (energetic).

Above measure 22: With full force.

Before measure 22: Soprano, Contralto, Tenor, Bass.

Soprano: "To talk! To conquer! To die!

Contralto: ditto.

Tenor: ditto.

Bass: "To talk, but to secrete the talker. To conquer, but to secrete the Conqueror. To die, but to secrete the death."

Above measure 28: Somewhat hurrying.

From measure 28 on, Soprano and Contralto. "Who would not do much for fame?/ But who does it for silence?"/

From measure 29 on, Tenor and Bass: same words.

Above measure 34: In march tempo.

From measure 44 on: "But the needy eater invites honor to the table;/ out of the humble and tumbling down hut emerges inescapably greatness/, and fame asks in vain for the doers of the great deed."/

Above measure 63: (spoken [not sung]).

From measure 64 on: "Emerge for a moment, [you] unknown [with your] masked faces and receive our thanks!"

[At the end] The four agitators: "In the city of Mukden, we spread propaganda among the workers. We had no bread for the hungry, only knowledge for the ignorant; therefore we spoke of the underlying reason of the need, did not abolish the need, but spoke of the abolishing of the underlying reason."

Footnote (NB. above measure 72:) This beat must be repeated until the four agitators have finished their speech.

III. The Stone

[pp. 31–45]

The four agitators: "At first we went to the lower city. There, coolies pulled a boat from the shore on a rope. But the earth was slippery. When one [of them] slipped and the overseer kicked him, we told the young comrade: Follow them and spread propaganda among them. Tell them that in Tientsin you have seen boatmen with shoes provided with boards under the soles so that they could not slip. Try to manage that they too will demand such shoes. Don't, however, fall prey to pity! And we asked: Are you agreed, and he was agreed and hurried there and fell prey to pity. We are demonstrating:"

(Two of the agitators represent coolies, in that they tie a rope to a pole and pull the rope over their shoulders. One represents the young comrade, the other, the overseer.)

The overseer: "I am the overseer. The rice must be in the city of Mukden before nightfall."

The two coolies: "We are the coolies and drag the rice-boat up the river."

No. 5 Song of the Rice Boatmen

Above measure 4: The first coolie:

From measure 5 on: "In the city up the stream there is for us a mouthful of rice,/ but the boat is heavy which must go upstream, and the water flows downstream; we shall never get up there."/

Before measure 15: Tenor, male chorus, Bass.

From measure 18 on: "Pull faster, the mouths are waiting to be fed./ Pull evenly, do not push the man next to you!"

[Between staves, above measure 36]

The young comrade: "Ugly it is to listen to the beauty with which the men cloak the anguish of their work."

The overseer: "Pull faster!"

Above measure 38: The first coolie: "Night is falling soon; the mattress, too small for a dog's shadown, costs half a mouthful of rice./ Because the shore is too slippery, we cannot make any headway."/

Above measure 55: (but faster).

Before measure 55: Tenor, male chorus, Bass.

From measure 56 on: "Pull faster, the mouths are waiting to be fed./ Pull evenly, do not push the man next to you!"/

Above measure 73: The second coolie: (slipping) "I am stuck."

The first coolie: (while the coolies are just standing and are being whipped until the one who fell is on his feet again) "Longer than we hold the rope which cuts into the shoulder; the whip of the overseer has seen four generation, we are not the last one."/

Footnote to measure 81: If the first basses do not have the high F-major, which actually is to be executed in a yelling fashion, all basses will sing only the voice of the second basses.

From measure 82 on: "Pull faster, the mouths are waiting to be fed, to be fed./ Pull evenly, do not push the man next to you! Ohay, Ohay!"/

The young comrade: "Difficult it is to view these men without pity. (to the overseer) Don't you see that the earth is too slippery?"

The overseer: "What is the earth?"

The young comrade: "Too slippery!"

The overseer: "What? Do you claim that the shore is too slippery to pull a boat-load of rice?"

The young comrade: "Yes!"

The overseer: "So you believe that the city of Mukden does not need any rice?"

The young comrade: "When (the) people fall down they cannot pull the boat."

The overseer: "Shall I [do you want me to] put down a stone for everyone, from here to the city of Mukden?"

The young comrade: "I don't know what you should do, but I know what they should [do]. (To the coolies) Don't believe that anything that has not worked for two thousand years is never going to work. In Tientsin I have seen shoes on the [feet of the] boatmen that have boards under the soles so that they could not slip. This they have accomplished through unanimous demand. Therefore, also demand such shoes unanimously."

The coolies: "Really, we cannot pull this boat without such shoes any longer."

The overseer: "But the rice must be in the city tonight."

(He whips, they pull)

Above measure 92: The first coolie: "Our fathers pulled the boat from the mouth of the river upstream aways,/ our children will reach the spring, we are in between."/

Bass from measure 100 on: "Pull faster, the mouths are waiting to be fed, to be fed. Pull evenly, do not push the man next to you, man next to you."/

Measures 102 and 103, 106 and 107, Tenor: "Ohay! Ohay!"/

The second coolie: "Help me!"

The young comrade: "Aren't you a man [human being]? Here, I am taking a stone and putting it into the mud (to the coolie) and now step [on it]!"

The overseer: "Right. What can shoes in Tientsin do for us here? I'd rather let your pitying comrade run alongside you with a stone to put it down for anyone who slips."

Above measure 110: The first coolie: Then: "There is rice in the boat./ The peasant who harvested it got a handful of coins; we get still less; an ox would be dearer./ We are too dear."/

Above measure 125: (One of the coolies slips, the young comrade puts down the stone for him, and the coolie gets up on his feet again.)

Above measure 126: (very fast).

Tenor and Bass from measure 126 on: "Pull faster, the mouths are waiting to be fed./ Pull evenly, do not push the man next to you!"

Above measure 146: The first coolie: "When the rice arrives in the city and the children ask/ who has pulled the heavy boat, the answer will be: it has been pulled."/

Above measure 156: (One of the coolies slips, the young comrade put down the stone for him, and the coolie get up on his feet again.)

Tenor, from measure 159 on: "Ohay! Hay! Ohay! Hay! Ohay! Hay! Ohay! Hay!"

Bass, from measure 157 on: "Pull faster, the mouths are waiting to be fed, to be fed./ Pull evenly, do not push the man next to you, man next to you!"

Above measure 166: (yelling).

From measure 166 on: "The food from below comes to the eaters above. [They] who pulled it/ have not eaten./ Ohay! Hay!"/

(One of the coolies slips, the young comrade puts the stone down for him, the coolie gets up on his feet again.)

The young comrade: "I can do no more. You must demand other shoes."

The coolie: "This [He] is a fool to be laughed at."

The overseer: "No, he is one of those who agitate among the people [against] us. Halloh, grab him!"

The four agitators: And presently he was seized. And he was hunted for two days and met [up with] us, and we were chased with him through the city of Mukden for a week and could not let ourselves be seen in the lower [part of the] city.

The leader of the controlling chorus: Discussion! But it is not right to support the weak/, wherever he may be, to assist him, [to support and assist] the exploited, in his daily toil/ and oppression!/

The four agitators: He has not helped him, but he has prevented us from spreading propaganda in our section of the city./

No. 6a

Before measure 1: Soprano, Contralto.

Before measure 1: Chorus: We are in accord.

Before measure 1: Tenor, Bass.

Above measure 1: (spoken [not sung]).

The four agitators: The young comrade admitted that he had separated feeling from sense. But we consoled him and quoted to him the [following] words of Comrade Lenin:

No. 6b Lenin Quotation (Declamation [spoken chorus])

Before measure 1: Soprano, Contralto, chorus, Tenor, Bass.

"It is not he who makes no mistakes who is clever, but he who knows how to correct them quickly."/

No. 6c Canon of a Lenin Quotation

Before measure 1: Soprano, Contralto, chorus, Tenor, Bass.

Abbreviation before measure 1: Small drum.

Above measure 1: Fresh, forceful.

"It is not he who makes no mistakes who is clever, but he who knows how to correct them quickly!"

Above measure 15: (without ritardano).

IV. Justice

[pp. 46–52]

The four agitators: We founded the first cells in the factories and trained the first functionaries, established a party school and taught them the secret manufacturing of forbidden literature. But then we worked in the textile plants, and when the wages were cut down, a part of the workers went on strike. Since, however, the other part continued working the strike was endangered. We told the young comrade: Stand at the door of the factory and distribute pamphlets. We repeat the conversation [below].

The three agitators: You have failed with the rice boatmen.

The young comrade: Yes.

The three agitators: Have you learned something [from this experience]?

The young comrade: Yes.

The three agitators: Will you fare better with the strike?

The young comrade: Yes.

(Two of the agitators represent textile workers and the third, a policeman.)

The two textile workers: We are workers in the textile factory.

The policeman: I am a policeman and gain my [daily] bread through the men in power in order to fight dissatisfaction.

No. 7a Strike Song

Above measure 1: Energetic march tempo.

Before measure 7: Tenor, male chorus, bass.

From measure 10 on: "Emerge Comrade!/ Risk the penny which is a penny no more,/ the bedstead upon which it rains,/ and the place of work which you will lose tomorrow!/ Out [with you] on the street!/ Fight! It is too late for waiting!/ Help yourself in that you help us!/ Practice solidarity!/ [Repeat as refrain.]

Above measure 46: The young comrade: Give away what you have [own], comrade: you have nothing!

Before measure 47: Tenor, Bass.

From measure 47 on: "Emerge, Comrade,/ confront the rifles and insist upon your wages! When you know that you have nothing to lose,/ their policemen do not have enough rifles!/"

After measure 64: (Here follows the refrain from X to the end, measure 45.)

The two textile workers: We go home after hours, our wages are cut; we do not know, however, what to do and continue working.

The young comrade: (puts leaflet into the pocket of one of the textile workers, while the other looks idly on) Read it and pass it on. After you have read it you will know what you must do.

The first [*textile worker*]: (takes it and walks on)

The policeman: (takes the pamphlet away from the first [textile worker]) who gave you the pamphlet?

The first [*textile worker*]: I don't know, somebody gave it to me in passing by.

The policeman: (approaches the second [textile worker]) You gave him the pamphlet. We policemen are looking for such [persons] who distribute those pamphlets.

The second [*textile worker*]: I did not give a pamphlet to anybody.

The young comrade: Is it a crime, after all, to bring knowledge to the ignorant about their situation?

The policeman: (to the second [textile worker]) Your teachings have terrible consequences. When you teach in such a factory, then it does not know its owner any longer. [it belongs no longer to its owner]. This little pamphlet is more dangerous than ten canons.

The young comrade: What's in it [what is the content]?

The policeman: That I don't know. (To the second [textile worker]) What's in it [what is the content]?

The second [*textile worker*]: I don't know about the pamphlet; I did not distribute it.

The young comrade: I know that he didn't do it.

The policeman: (to the young comrade) Did you give him the pamphlet?

The young comrade: No.

The policeman: (to the second [textile worker]) Then you gave it to him.

The young comrade: (to the first [textile worker]) What will happen to him?

The first [*textile worker*]: He may be shot.

The young comrade: Why do you want to shoot him, policeman? Aren't you also a proletarian?

The policeman: (to the second [textile worker]) Come along. (hitting his head)

The young comrade: ([tries to] prevent him) He didn't do it.

The policeman: Then it was you after all.

The second [*textile worker*]: He didn't do it.

The policeman: Then it must have been both of you.

The first [*textile worker*]: Run, man, run, your pocket is full of pamphlets!

The policeman: (beats the second [textile worker] down)

The young comrade: (Points at the policeman. To the first [textile worker]) Now he beat down an innocent man; you are a witness.

The first [*textile worker*]: (attacks the policeman) You bought dog [you dirty dog]! (The policeman draws his revolver. The young comrade grabs the policeman by the neck from behind; the first coolie slowly bends his arm back. The gun goes off; the policeman is being disarmed.)

The young comrade: (yells) Help, comrades! Help! Innocent men are being killed here!

The second coolie: (Rising [from the ground], to the first [coolie]) Now we have beaten down a policeman and cannot get into the factory tomorrow morning, and (to the young comrade) it is your fault.

The young comrade: If you go to work [to the plant] you betray your comrades.

The second coolie: I have a wife and three children, and when you left and went on strike, our wages were upped. Here, I had double wages! (He shows the money).

The young comrade: (strikes the money out of the coolie's hand) Shame on you, you bought (dirty) dogs!

(The first coolie grabs him by the throat while the second picks up his money. The young comrade strikes the attacker down with the blackjack of the policeman.)

The second coolie: (yells) Help! There are agitators here!

The four agitators: And immediately the workers emerged from the plant and drove the pickets away.

Discussion

The controlling chorus: What could the young comrade have done?

The four agitators: He might have told the coolies that they could have defended themselves against the police [effectively] only if all the workers in the plant had managed to fight the police in solidarity. Then the policeman would have been in the wrong.

No. 7b

Before measure 1: The controlling chorus.

Above measure 1: (spoken [not sung]): "We are in accord!"

V. What actually is a man [*human being*]?

The four agitators: Every day we struggled with the old unions, (organizations) [with] the hopelessness and [with] the oppression; we taught the workers to change the fight for better wages into the fight for power. [We] taught them the use of weapons and the art of street-fighting. Then we heard [were told] that the businessmen had a tariff quarrel with the British who ruled the city. In order to exploit the quarrel among the ruling in favor of the ruled, we sent the young comrade with a letter to the richest businessman [in town]. In this letter was written: Arm the coolies! To the young comrade we said: Behave in such a way that you will obtain the weapons. But when the food came on the table he was not silent. We are demonstrating the incident [below]:

(One of the agitators represents the businessman)

The trader [*businessman*]: I am the trader [businessman]. I am expecting a letter from the coolie union concerning an unanimous action against the British.

The young comrade: Here is the letter from the coolie union.

The trader [*businessman*]: I am inviting you to eat with me.

The young comrade: It is an honor for me to be permitted to eat with you.

The trader [*businessman*]: While the food is being prepared I shall give you my opinion of the coolies. Please sit down here.

The young comrade: I am much interested in your opinion.

No. 8a Recitative

Above measure 1: Free is to rhythm (average tempo ca. 76 metronome beats)

Above measure 10: The trader [businessman]:

From measure 11 on: "Why do I get everything cheaper than the others/ and why does a coolie work for me for practically nothing?/"

Above measure 14: (unhurried)

Above measure 20: (spoken [not sung]).

Above measure 22: The young comrade:

Measures 22 and 23: "I don't know."

From measure 24 on: (The trader [businessman]): "Because I am a clever man./ You are also clever people because you know how to get the wages from the coolies."/

Above measure 32: The young comrade:

From measure 23 on: "We know how."/

Above measure 34: The young comrade: "By the way, are you going to arm the coolies against the British?"

Above measure 35: The trader [businessman]:

From measure 35 on: "Maybe, maybe . . . I know how to treat a coolie."

Above measure 34 in accompaniment: Free as to rythm (according to the speaker).

Abbreviation before measure 38: The trader [businessman].

From measure 39 on: You must give a coolie only rice enough to keep him alive,/ else he cannot work for you. Is that right?"

Above measure 47: The young comrade:

From measure 48 on: "Yes, that's right."

Above measure 40 (unhurried).

Abbreviation before measure 50: The trader [businessman]. "But I say: No!/ No!/ No!"

Abbreviation before measure 54: the trader [businessman].

Above measure 55: Tempo as in the same place [?].

From measure 55 on: Then, if the coolies are cheaper than the rice,/ I can take [employ or hire] a new coolie./ Is that better [literally: more correct]?"/

Above measure 63: Free as to rhythm (according to the speakers).

Above measure 63, second staff: The young comrade:

From measure 63 on: "Yes, that is better [literally: more correct]."/

Above measure 66: The young comrade: When, by the way, will you send the first [batch of] arms into the lower city?

The trader [businessman]: Soon, soon . . . .

Above measure 68: Tempo as in the same place [?]

From measure 68 on: "You should see how the coolies who load my leather eat my rice./ What do you think, do I pay much for the work?"/

Abbreviation before measure 70: The trader [businessman].

Above measure 74: Free (according to the speaker). Above that: The young comrade: No, but your rice is dear/ and the work must be good,/ but your rice is poor.

Above measure 78: The trader [businessman]:

Measures 78 and 79: You are clever [sly] people!

Above measure 79: (They are smiling at each other)

Above measure 80: The young comrade: Are you going to arm the coolies against the British?

Above measure 81: The trader [businessman]: After the meal we can [let us] view the arsenal.

From measure 83 on: "I [shall] now sing my favorite song to you."/

No. 8b Song of the Products

Above measure 1: Compact.

Above measure 2: The trader [businessman]: "There is rice downstream/ people in the upper provinces need rice/ If we leave the rice in the warehouses,/ the rice will be dearer [more expensive] for them./ Those who pull the rice-boats/ will then get less rice./ Then the rice for me will become still cheaper./

Above measure 38: The young comrade: What actually is rice?

Above measure 39: Refrain somewhat more quiet.

Abbreviation before measure 39: The trader [businessman].

From measure 39 on: "How do I know what rice is?/ I know who knows that!/ I don't know what rice is,/ I only know its price./

Above measure 68: The trader [businessman]: From then on: "Winter is coming, the coolies needs clothing,/ cotton must be bought and cotton must be held back./ When the cold arrives,/ clothing becomes more expensive./ The cotton mills pay too high wages./ There is actually too much cotton./"

Above measure 104: The young comrade: What actually is cotton?

Above measure 105: Again somewhat more quiet.

Abbreviation before measure 105: The trader [businessman].

From then on: "How do I know what cotton is,/ how do I know who knows that?/ I don't know what cotton is,/ I only know its price!"

From measure 135 on: "Such a man [human being] needs too much grub./ This makes the man dearer [more expensive]./ To provide the grub men are needed. The cooks make it cheaper, but the eaters make it dearer [more expensive]./ There are actually too few people."/

Above measure 158: The young comrade: What actually is a man [human being]?

Abbreviation before measure 159: The trader [businessman]. From then on: "How do I know what a man [human being] is,/ how do I know who knows that?/ I don't know what a man [human being] is./ I only know his price/"

Before measure 173: Soprano, Contralto, chorus, Tenor, Bass. From then on: "He does not know what a man [human being] is,/ he only knows his price."/

The trader [businessman]: (to the young comrade) And now we shall [let us] eat my good rice.

The young comrade: (gets up) I cannot eat with you.

The four agitators: This is what he said, and laughter and threat were of no avail in trying to force him to eat with him whom he loathed, and the trader [businessman] threw him out, and the coolies got no weapons.

Discussion

The controlling chorus: But isn't it right to put honor above everything else?

The four agitators: No.

No. 9 Change the world—it needs it!

Before measure 1: Soprano, Contralto, Chorus, Tenor, Bass.

From measure 2 on: "With whom wouldn't the one who is right get together in order to help the law?/ What medicine would taste too bitter for the dying [man]? What infamy haven't you committed in order to extirpate infamy?/ If you could finally change the world,/ what would you be too good for?/ Drown in the mud [literally: smut], embrace the butcher, but change the world, it needs it!/ Who are you?/"

Abave measure 49: (spoken [not sung]).

Before measure 49: Soprano, Contralto, Tenor, Bass.

From measure 49 on: "For a long time we have listened to you not only as judges but also as studients."

The four agitators: Hardly [had he arrived] at the stairs, the young comrade recognized his mistake and suggested that we send him back across the border. We clearly saw his weakness, but we still needed him, for he had a large following in the youth organizations and helped us much in those days to knot the nets of the party before the rifles of the employers.

VI. The Treason

The four agitators: During this [particular] week the persecutions increased extraordinarily. We had but a secreted room for the printing press and the pamphlets. But one [beautiful] morning strong unrest, caused by hunger, broke out in the city, and also from the country there came news concerning strong unrest. On the evening of the third day, arriving at our haven after being exposed to danger, the door was opened by our young comrade. There were sacks in front of the house in the rain. We repeat [below] the conservation.

The three agitators: What kind of sacks are those?

The young comrade: They are our propaganda pamphlets.

The three agitators: What are you going to do with them

The young comrade: I have to tell you something: the new leaders of the unemployed arrived here today and convinced me that we have to start action right away. We also want to distribute the propaganda pamphlets and to storm the barracks.

The three agitators: Then you showed them the wrong way. But tell us your reasons and try to convince us!

The young comrade: The need is becoming greater and the unrest is increasing in the city.

The three agitators: The ignorant are beginning to understand their position.

The young comrade: The unemployed have accepted our teachings.

The three agitators: The oppressed are becoming class-conscious.

The young comrade: They are going out into the street and want to demolish the [cotton] mills.

The three agitators: They are lacking the experience[s] of the Revolution. This makes our responsibility so much greater.

The young comrade: The unemployed can wait no longer and I/ can wait no longer either./ There are too many needs./

The three agitators: But there are too few fighters.

The young comrade: Their sufferings are frightful.

The three agitators: Suffering [alone] is not sufficient.

The young comrade: There are inside the house seven [persons] who have come to us at the order of the unemployed. Behind them there are seven thousand, and they know: misfortune does not grow on your chest like leprosy; poverty does not fall from the rooftops like shingles; but misfortune and poverty are man-made; want is being cooked for them, but their wailings is their food. They know everything.

The three agitators: Do you know many regiments [troops] the government has at its disposal?

The young comrade: No.

The three agitators: Then you know too little. Where are your weapons?

The young comrade: (he shows his hands) We shall fight with tooth and nail.

The three agitators: That is not sufficient. You only see the misery of the unemployed, but not the misery of the employed. You only see the city, but not the farmers. You see the soldiers only as oppressors, but not as oppressed miserables in uniform. Go, therefore, to the unemployed, recall your advice to storm the barracks, and convince them that they must participate tonight in the demonstration of the factory-workers; and we shall try to convince the dissatisfied soldiers that they should likewise demonstrate with us, in uniform.

The young comrade: I have reminded the unemployed of the many times the soldiers have shot at them. Shall I tell them now that they should demonstrate jointly with murderers?

The three agitators: Yes, for the soldiers can recognize that they were wrong to shoot at the wretched of their own class [estate]. Remember the classical advice of Comrade Lenin not to view all farmers as class enemies but to win over the village poor as co-fighters.

The young comrade: Now I ask: Is it the intention of the classics [literally: do the classics tolerate] to let misery wait?

The three agitators: They speak of methods which recognize misery in its entirety.

The young comrade: Hence the classics do not advocate equal, immediate, and primary assistance to each and every miserable?

The three agitators: No.

The young comrade: Then the classics are dirt, and I am tearing them up; for man, the living man, is roaring, and his misery breaks [tears] all the dams of their teachings. Therefore I am now taking action, now and immediately, for I am roaring and I am breaking the dams of their teachings.

(He tears up the pamphlets.)

The three agitators:

Do not tear them up! We need them/
Every one of them. Face reality!/
Your Revolution is started quickly and lasts for a day/
And tomorrow will be throttled./
But our Revolution will start tomorrow./

Will conquer and change the world./
Your revolution ends when you end [with you]./
When you have come to an end/
Our Revolution will continue [live on].

The young comrade: Listen to what I [have to] say: I [can] see with my two eyes that misery cannot wait. Therefore I oppose your resolution to wait.

The three agitators: You have not convinced us. Go, therefore, to the unemployed and convince them that they must fall into the lines of the Revolution. This is what we demand of you now in the name of the Party.

The young comrade:

Who, though, is the Party?/
Is it sitting in a house with telephones?/

Are its thoughts secret, its resolutions unknown?/
Who is it?/

The three agitators:

We are it./
You and I and all of you—all of us./
In your suit it is, comrade; in your head it thinks/;
Wherever I live there is its home; and wherever you are
attacked, there it fights./

Show us the road which we shall choose, and we/
Shall choose it as you do, but/
Do not choose the right road without us./
Without us it is/
The wrongest [road]./
Do not separate from us!/
That the short road is better than the long [road], nobody will deny,/
But if somebody knows it/ And he is unable to show us, what good is his knowledge?/
Be wise [with us]!/
Do not separate from us!/

The young comrade: Because I am right, I cannot give in. With my two eyes I [can] see that misery cannot wait.

No. 10 Praise of the Party [*Hail to the Party*]

Before measure 1: Soprano, Contralto, First Tenor, Chorus, Second Tenor, Bass.

Above measure 1: Forceful.

From measure 3 on: (Soprano part): The individual has two,/ the party has a thousand eyes./ The party sees [can see] seven states./ The party has many hours./ The party cannot be destroyed,/ for it fights with the methods of the classics which are drawn [created] from the knowledge of reality, and are destined to be changed/, in that the teachings spread through the masses./ Who, however, is the party?/ Is it sitting in a house with telephones?/ Are its thoughts secret,/ its resolutions unknown?/ Who is it?/ It is [all of] us! [We are the party!]/ You and I and all of you,—all of us!/ In your suit it is, comrade,/ and in your head it thinks,/ wherever I live there is its home,/ wherever you are attacked, there it fights./

Above measure 48: (spoken [not sung]).

Above measure 53: (again sung)

First Tenor part: The individual has two eyes./ The individual sees [can see] a city./ The individual has his hour./ The individual can be destroyed./ (continue same as Soprano part: for it fights with the methods, etc.)

The young comrade: All this is valid no longer; in view of the struggle I overthrow everything which was valid yesterday; dissolve all agreements with everybody; and am doing the only human [thing]. Here is a [plan for] action. I am going to be the leader. My heart is beating for the Revolution. Here it is!

The three agitators: Silence!

The young comrade: Here is oppression. I am for freedom!

The three agitators: Silence! You are betraying us!

The young comrade: I cannot be still, because I am right.

The three agitators: Whether you are right or wrong—if you talk we are lost! Silence!

The young comrade:
I saw too much./
Therefore I step before them./
As the one I am [as myself], and tell the truth./
(He removes his mask and yells)
We have come to help you/
We come from Moscow./
(He tears up his mask)
The four agitators:
And we looked toward him and in the twilight/
We saw his bare face,/
Human, open, and guileless. He had/
Torn the mask.
And from the houses/
Came the yelling of the exploited: Who/
Is disturbing the sleep/ of the poor?/
And a window opened and a voice yelled:/
There are strangers here! Chase the agitators!/
So they recognized us!/
And it was then that we heard that there was unrest/
In the lower city, and the ignorant waited in the/
Assembly-Halls, and the unarmed [waited] in the streets./
He, however, did not stop roaring./
And we beat him down/,
Picked him up, and left the city in a hurry./

VII. Utmost Persecution, and Analysis

No. 11 Recitative

Before measure No. 1: Soprano, Contralto, Chorus, Tenor, Bass, Small drum

Above measure 1: Temperamental, somewhat hurrying.

From measure 2 on: They left the city!/ Unrest is growing in the city, but the leadership flees across the city limits./ Your rule!/

Above measure 5: (spoken [not sung])

Above measure 12: (again sung).

The four agitators: Just wait! Easy it is to know the right [thing]/ Far ahead of the end/ If one has time—if you know months ahead./ But we had ten minutes' time and/ [Had to] think in front of the rifles!/

When during our flight we came into the neighborhood of the quicklime pits outside of the city, we saw our persecutors behind us. Our young comrade opened his eyes, heard what had happened, realized what he had done, and said: We are lost.

In the times of utmost persecution, confusion of theory,/ weighing asset [s] and possibility [liabilities]/ the fighters analyze their position./

Above measure 29: The four agitators: We repeat the analysis.

No. 12a Recitative

Above measure 1: March tempo.

Below measure 3 in accompaniment: (very short)

Above measure 4: First agitator: (spoken in exact rhythm). We must get him across the border, we said./

Measure 9: Second agitator: But the masses are in the streets./

Above measure 13: Third agitator: And we must bring them to the assemblies./

Above measure 17: First agitator: Hence we cannot get our comrade across the border./

Above measure 22: Third agitator: If we, however, hide him and he is found, what happens if he is recognized?/

Above measure 30: The first agitator: There are gun-boats ready in the rivers, and there are armored trains on the trails, to attack us if one of us is seen there. He must not be seen./

No. 12b We are the Scum of the Earth

Above measure 1: Strong march tempo (heavily stressed).

Before measure 1: Tenor, Chorus, Bass. From measure 1 on: If we are seen entering the hut[s] of the exploited,/ the canons of all exploiters will go off/ against the huts/ and against our country./ For, when the hungry repels in pain the tormentor/, we have paid him for his pain and repelling. On our foreheads it is written that we are against exploitation,/ in our handbill it is written:/ these [men] are for the oppressed! Those who help the desperate are the scum of the earth/. We are the scum of the earth./ We must not be found./

Above measure 11: (shrill)

Above measure 26: (shrill)

Above measure 40: take your time

Above measure 43: Only somewhat broader than at the beginning of the march.

VIII. The Burial

[pp. 93–100]

The four agitators: We have resolved:/ Then he must disappear, and, as a matter of fact [disappear] entirely. For we cannot take him along, and we canot leave him here/ Therefore we must shoot him and throw him into the quicklime [pit] For the quicklime will burn him./

No. 13a

Before measure 1: Soprano, Contralto, Chorus, Tenor, Bass: Was there no other way out? The four agitators: Due to the shortness of time we found no other way out./ As animal helps animal,/ We too wished to help him who/ Fought with us for our [common] cause./ Five minutes, facing the persecutors,/ We pondered a/ Better possibility/. You too are now pondering/ A better possibility./

(pause)

Thus we have resolved: Now/ [let us] sever the foot from our body. *Terrible it is to kill.* However, it is ourselves we shall kill, not only others, when necessary./ Since only force/ Can change this killing world, as/ Every living [person] knows./ However, we said,/ As yet the time has not come for us not to kill. Only with the/ Unyielding will to change the world we founded The Rule [Doctrine].

No. 13b

Before measure 1: Soprano, Contralto, Chorus, Tenor, Bass.

Above measure 1: (without expression)

From measure 1 on: "Spread [the tidings], you are assured of our sympathy,/ not easy was it to do what was right [to do the right thing]. It was not you who passed judgment on him/ but reality."

The four agitators: We [let us] repeat our last conversation.

The first agitator: We want to [let us] ask him whether he gives his consent, for he was a brave fighter. (It is true that the face which emerged from the mask was different from the face we had covered with the mask, as will the face which will be eaten by the quicklime be different from the face which at one time greeted us at the border.)

The second agitator: Even if he does not give his consent, he must disappear, and, as a matter of fact [he must disappear] entirely.

The first agitator: (to the young comrade) If you are caught, you will be shot; and since you were recognized, our work is betrayed. Therefore we must shoot you and throw you into [a] quicklime [pit], to be be eaten by quicklime. However we ask you: Do you know any other way out?

The young comrade: No.

The three agitators: So we ask you: Do you give your consent?

(pause)

The young comrade: Yes.

The three agitators: Where shall we put you?

The young comrade: Into [the] quicklime [pit].

The three agitators: Will you do it by yourself?

The young comrade: Help me!

The three agitators: Lean your head on our arm/ [and] Close your eyes!

The young comrade: (while he cannot be seen) In the interest of Communism/, In accord with the on march of the proletarian masses/ of all countries/ Saying "Yes" to the revolutionizing of the world./

The three agitators: Then we shot him and/ Threw him into [the] quicklime [pit], And when the quicklime had eaten him/ We returned to our work.

No. 14 Finale [*Final Chorus*]

Above measure 1: broad, weighty quarter-notes.

Before measure 7: Soprano, Contralto, Chorus, Tenor, Bass.

From measure 11 on: And your work was happy [successful]/, and you have spread the teachings of the Classics, the A B C of Communism: [You have brought to] the ignorant knowledge of their situation, to the oppressed class consciousness and the experience[s] of the Revolution./ And the Revolution marches there too./ And there too the lines of the fighters are orderly./ We are in accord with you./ But also, your report shows us/ how much is needed to change the world; ire and tenacity; knowledge and uprising; quick action; deep thinking; cold suffering; endless waiting: understanding of the individual and understanding of the whole [masses?]:/ Only taught by reality can we change reality./

Above measure 17: Do not hurry!

Above measure 55: With greatest force.

Before measure 62: Soprano, Contralto, Tenor, Bass, Small Drum (abbreviated).

Above measure 62: (spoken [not sung]).

(Translated by Elizabeth Hanunian, September 18, 1947)

Appendix 3: A Statement by Paul Robeson

This item should properly have followed the Robeson testimony above but did not come to hand until the present book was in page proof. It was well worth making an appendix of, however, especially as it seems never to have been printed before anywhere. It consists, of course, of the Statement that Robeson tried to make to the Committee in 1956 and was not allowed to. It was supplied to Eric Bentley, with permission to publish, by Paul Robeson, Jr., who is hereby most warmly thanked.

It is a sad and bitter commentary on the state of civil liberties in America that the very forces of reaction, typified by Representative Francis Walter and his Senate counterparts, who have denied me access to the lecture podium, the concert hall, the opera house, and the dramatic stage, now hale me before a committee of inquisition in order to hear what I have to say. It is obvious that those who are trying to gag me here and abroad will scarcely grant me the freedom to express myself fully in a hearing controlled by them.

It would be more fitting for me to question Walter, [James] Eastland and [John Foster] Dulles than for them to question me, for it is they who should be called to account for their conduct, not I. Why does Walter not investigate the truly "un-American" activities of Eastland and his gang, to whom the Constitution is a scrap of paper when invoked by the Negro people and to whom defiance of the Supreme Court is a racial duty? And how can Eastland pretend concern over the internal security of our country while he supports the most brutal assaults on fifteen million Americans by the White Citizens' Councils and the Ku Klux Klan? When will Dulles explain his reckless irresponsible "brink of war" policy by which the world might have been destroyed?

And specifically, why is Dulles afraid to let me have a passport, to let me travel abroad to sing, to act, to speak my mind? This question has been partially answered by State Department lawyers who have asserted in court that the State Department claims the right to deny me a passport because of what they called my "recognized status as a spokesman for large sections of Negro Americans" and because I have "been for years extremely active in behalf of independence of colonial peoples of Africa." The State Department has also based its denial of a passport to me on the fact that I sent a message of greeting to the Bandung Conference, convened by Nehru, Sukarno, and other great leaders of the colored peoples of the world. Principally, however, Dulles objects to speeches I have made abroad against the oppression suffered by my people in the United States.

I am proud that those statements can be made about me. It is my firm intention to continue to speak out against injustices to the Negro people, and I shall continue to do all within my power in behalf of independence of colonial peoples of Africa. It is for Dulles to explain why a Negro who opposes colonialism and supports the aspirations of Negro Americans should for those reasons be denied a passport.

My fight for a passport is a struggle for freedom—freedom to travel, freedom to earn a livelihood, freedom to speak, freedom to express myself artistically and culturally. I have been denied these freedoms because Dulles, Eastland, Walter, and their ilk oppose my views on colonial liberation, my resistance to oppression of Negro Americans, and my burning desire for peace with all nations. But these are views which I shall proclaim whenever given the opportunity, whether before this committee or any other body.

President Eisenhower has strongly urged the desirability of international cultural exchanges. I agree with him. The American people would welcome artistic performances by the great singers, actors, ballet troupes, opera companies, symphony orchestras and virtuosos of South America, Europe, Africa, and Asia, including the folk and classic art of the African peoples, the ancient culture of China, as well as the artistic works of the western world. I hope the day will come soon when Walter will consent to lowering the cruel bars which deny the American people the right to witness performances of many great foreign artists. It is certainly high time for him to drop the ridiculous "Keystone Kop" antics of fingerprinting distinguished visitors.

I find no such restrictions placed upon me abroad as Walter has had placed upon foreign artists whose performances the American people wish to see and hear. I have been invited to perform all over the world, and only the arbitrary denial of a passport has prevented realization of this particular aspect of the cultural exchange which the President favors.

I have been invited by Leslie Linder Productions to play the title role in a production of *Othello* in England. British Actors' Equity Association has unanimously approved of my appearance and performance in England.

I have been invited by Workers' Music Association Ltd. to make a concert tour of England under its auspices. The invitation was signed by all of the vice-presidents, including Benjamin Britten, and was seconded by a personal invitation of R. Vaughan Williams.

I have been invited by Adam Holender, impresario, to make a concert tour of Israel, and he has tendered to me a proposed contract for that purpose.

Mosfilm, a Soviet moving-picture producing company, has invited me to play the title role in a film version of *Othello,* assuring me "of the tremendous artistic joy which association with your wonderful talent will bring us."

The British Electrical Trades Union requested me to attend their annual policy conference, recalling my attendance at a similar conference held in 1949 at which, they wrote me, "you sang and spoke so movingly."

The British Workers' Sports Association, erroneously crediting a false report that I would be permitted to travel, wrote me, "We view the news with very great happiness." They invited me "to sing to our members in London, Glasgow, Manchester or Cardiff, or all four, under the auspices of our International Fund, and on a financial basis favourable to yourself, and to be mutually agreed." They suggested a choice of three different halls in London, seating, respectively, 3,000, 4,500, and 7,000.

The Australian Peace Council invited me to make a combined "singing and peace tour" of the dominion.

I have received an invitation from the Education Committee of the London Co-operative Society to sing at concerts in London under their auspices.

A Swedish youth organization called "Democratic Youth" has invited me to visit Sweden "to give some concerts here, to get to know our culture and our people." The letter of invitation added, "Your appearance here would be greeted with the greatest interest and pleasure, and a tour in Sweden can be arranged either by us or by our organization in cooperation with others, or by any of our cultural societies or artist's bureaus, whichever you may prefer."

I have an invitation from the South Wales Miners to sing at the Miners' Singing Festival on October 6, 1956, and in a series of concerts in the mining valley thereafter.

In Manchester, England, a group of people called the "Let Paul Robeson Sing Committee" has asked me to give a concert at the Free Trade Hall in that city either preceding or following my engagement in Wales.

I have been requested by the Artistic and Literary Director of the Agence

Littéraire et Artistique Parisienne pour les Échanges Culturels to sign a contract with the great French concert organizer, M. Marcel de Valmalette, to sing in a series of concerts at the Palais de Chaillot in Paris.

There is no doubt that the governments of those countries and many others where I would be invited to sing if I could travel abroad would have no fear of what I might sing or say while there, whether such governments be allies and friends of America or neutrals or those others whose friendship for the American people is obstructed by Dulles and Walter and like-minded reactionaries.

My travels abroad to sing and act and speak cannot possibly harm the American people. In the past I have won friends for the real America among the millions before whom I have performed—not for Walter, not for Dulles, not for Eastland, not for the racists who disgrace our country's name—but friends for the American Negro, our workers, our farmers, our artists.

By continuing the struggle at home and abroad for peace and friendship with all of the world's people, for an end to colonialism, for full citizenship for Negro Americans, for a world in which art and culture may abound, I intend to continue to win friends for the best in American life.

Index

A Note on How to Find Things

Many things that a reader might turn to an index for can, in the present book, be found by judicious use of either the table of contents or Appendix 1 or both. The table of contents lists the fifty principals in the drama and indicates where they play their big scenes. Appendix 1 lists the nine (earlier, seven) members of the Committee in each of its thirty years. These years are given again at the head of each alternate page. So it is easy to find whose name should fall where. Most of this information is given again at the head of each piece of testimony, where also committee staff members are named. *The following index does not include any of these names.* It is devoted to more than eight hundred other names in the text. Only names of persons are given, and only persons of our, and HUAC's, own time (approximately the last fifty years). But the attempt has been made to include *all* such persons with the exception of names occurring only in the long lists on pages 293, 506, 902, and 927–28, and with the further exception of names used adjectivally ("the Shakespeare play") or in subordination to a noun ("Shakespeare's play"). This would be the right place to mention that there exists a Cumulative Index to Publications of the Committee on Un-American Activities, 1938–1954, and a Supplement to this covering 1955–1968. The first runs to 1344 pages, the second to 995 pages. In various indexes (the two just mentioned being by no means all), HUAC has informed the public: "The fact that a name appears in this index is not per se an indication of a record of subversive activities." Which is just as well, since their pages contain names such as Eisenhower, Roosevelt, Wilson, and Lincoln. . . .

Abt, John, 301
Adomian, Lon, 87
Afinogenov, Alexander, 447
Aiken, Conrad, 805
Alanbrooke, 938
Albertson, Albert, 842
Alexander, Hy, 555
Allen, James, 469
Andreivsky, Alexander, 234, 235
Angoff, Charles, 473
Anisimov, A. I., 396
Antek, 708
Antokolsky, 448
Apresian, Stepan, 238
Aptheker, Herbert, 882
Aragon, Louis, 109
Ardrey, Robert, 492
Arent, Arthur, 19n
Arthur, Art, 406
Ashe, Harold J. 645, 646
Ashe, Mildred, 648
Atkinson, Brooks, 26, 27, 473, 517
Atkinson, Oriana, 127
Atlas, Leopold, 790

Attlee, Clement (Lord), 788
Auden, W. H., 3

Babel, Isaac, 446, 448
Bacall, Lauren, 365
Backus, Georgia, 343, 553, 555
Bacus, Glenn O., 639, 640
Baker, Kenny, 544
Baldwin, Roger, 247
Ball, Lucille, 495
Barmine, Alexandre, 127
Barrault, Jean-Louis, 109
Barrie, Lee, 558
Barsky, Edward K., 413, 424, 738
Baruch, Bernard, 684
Baumgardt, David, 207, 210, 211, 218, 219
Bautzer, Greg, 296
Beals, Carleton, 512, 513, 514
Behrman, S. N., 493
Bela, Nicholas, 684
Belfrage, Cedric, 647
Benchley, Robert, 115
Benson, Lieutenant, 374
Bentley, Elizabeth, xxvii, 405, 948
Bercovici, L., 390
Bergman, Ingrid, 426
Berkeley, Martin, xxvii, 194, 202, 466, 535, 536, 540, 646, 651, 652, 684, 712, 714, 790
Berle, Milton, 714
Berman, Lionel, 237, 632
Berry, Jack, 382
Bessie, Alvah, xix–xx, 110, 174n, 188, 389, 394
Biberman, Herbert, 110, 174n, 239, 240, 241, 302, 382, 390, 393, 397, 398, 452, 453, 647
Biddle, Francis, 161, 169, 474, 491
Bilbo, Theodore G., 150
Black, Hugo, 249, 783, 944, 945
Black, Ivan, 710, 711
Blake, William, 935
Blankfort, Henry, 390, 549
Bloor, Mother, 473, 474, 509
Blum, Léon, 287
Bogart, Humphrey, 302, 345, 365, 710
Bohnen, Roman ("Bohnman"), 342
Bond, Ward, 295
Bonn, John, 488
Boudin, Leonard B., 636, 646, 647, 773
Brand, Phoebe, 486, 654, 655
Bransten, Louise, 235, 237, 238, 239, 241, 242, 243, 775
Bransten, Richard (Bruce Minton), 237, 548, 549, 557, 560
Breen, 534
Brem, Georg, 213
Breuer, Bessie, 494
Brewer, Roy M., 188, 195–206, 406, 408, 409
Bricker, John W., 134
Bridges, Harry, 55, 393, 491, 564
Bridges, Lloyd, 657
Bridgman, H. A., 505
Bright, John, 450
Britten, Benjamin, 979
Bromberg, J. Edward, 341, 486, 501, 502
Brophy, John, 912
Brosman, R. J., 59
Browder, Earl, xxvi, 30, 55, 126, 226, 229, 237, 268, 389, 397, 525, 548, 565, 594, 620, 631, 776, 832
Brown, Constance, 889
Brown, Father, 130
Brown, John, xix
Brown, Rap, 770
Browne and Bioff, 638
Buchman, Sidney, 390, 496
Buchwald, Nathaniel, 474, 516, 518
Buckley, William F., Jr., xxiii, 272, 937
Budenz, Louis, xxvii, 55, 62, 405, 462, 463, 464, 475, 481, 948
Bukharin, Nikolai, 62, 72, 446, 448
Bunche, Ralph, 770, 776
Bunge, Hans, 56, 94n, 528n
Burchett, Wilfred, 920
Burman, Robert, 145
Burns, 530
Burnshaw, Stanley, 521
Butler, Hugo, 339
Byrd, Harry, 896

Cagney, James, 342
Caille, Robert, 487
Calverton, V. F., 463
Campbell, Allen, 536, 538
Campbell, J., 880
Capone, Al, 131
Carlisle, Harry, 453, 535
Carlson, Evans P., 462, 475, 476
Carmichael, Stokely, 770
Carnovsky, Morris, 341, 363, 486, 654, 655

Carroll, Madeleine, 344, 358
Carroll, Paul Vincent, 493
Carter, Minnie R., 756
Caruso, Enrico, 783
Caspary, Vera, 344
Cerf, Bennett, 473, 495
Cerney, Isobel, 749, 756
Chadwick, I. E., 406
Chaliapin, Feodor, 783
Chamberlain, John, 463
Chambers, Whittaker, xix, 21n, 272, 301, 405, 569–571, 623, 933, 937, 941, 948
Chaplin, Charles, 109, 150, 300, 307
Chase, Allan, 356, 357
Chevalier, Haakon, 225, 238, 243, 244
Chodorov, Edward, 632, 633
Chodorov, Jerome, 632, 633
Christians, Mady, xix
Churchill, Winston, 938
Claiborne, Bob, 838
Clark, Margot, 583, 584, 598
Clark, Maurice, 390
Clark, Ramsey, xxvi
Clark, Tom C., 675, 714
Clay, Lucius, 291
Cleaver, Eldridge, 770
Clements, Colin, 493
Clifford, Margaret Ellen, 21n
Cloke, Ken, 904
Clurman, Harold, 107, 489
Cobb, Mrs. Lee J., 659, 660
Cocteau, Jean, 109
Cohn, Harry, 634
Cole, Lester, 110, 240, 389, 452, 453, 645
Collins, Charles A., 419, 420
Collins, Richard, xxvii, 110, 343, 384, 395, 434, 437, 438, 439, 451, 452, 457, 563, 790
Cooke, Marvel, 840
Copland, Aaron, 93
Corelli, Alan, 414
Corey, George, 390
Corey, Jeff, 658
Cornell, Katharine, 422
Coughlin, Charles E., 597
Cowell, Henry, 93
Cowley, Malcolm, 107, 247
Crabbe, Buster, 150, 151
Crawford, Cheryl, 489
Cripps, Stafford, 788
Cromwell, John, 122
Cronyn, Hume, 125
Crosby, Bing, 176, 177
Crum, Bartley, 111, 199, 208, 220, 392, 394, 398, 404
Cukor, George, 107
Cummings, Homer, 493
Cvetic, Matthew, 308, 399

Dadoo, Y. M., 781
Dales, Jack, 406
Daley, Richard J., 885, 898, 907
Dallin, David J., 127
Damaskinos, Archbishop, 674
Daniel, Mrs. Yuli, 917
Darcy, Sam, 161
Darrow, Clarence, 261
Da Silva, Howard, 137, 300, 301, 307, 342, 364, 433
Dassin, Jules, 382
Davidson, 313
Davies, Joseph E., 121
Davies, Marian, 638
Davis, Ben J., 305, 306, 307, 416, 417, 418, 419, 432, 433, 770, 789
Davis, Jerome White, 757
Dawson, Leo A., 43
de Valmalette, Marcel, 980
De Mille, Cecil B., 132
Dennis, Eugene, 132, 161
DeSola, Ralph, 45
Devine, A., 344
Dewey, John, 463, 464
Dewey, Thomas E., 134
Dewysocki, 785
Di Suvero, Henry, 880, 881
Diamond, Milton, 398
Dickson, B. A., 357
Dickstein, Samuel, 936
Dieterle, William, 107
Dimitrov, Georgi (1), 134, 229
Dimitrov, Georgi (2), 286
Dirksen, Everett, 6
Dmytryk, Madelyn, xix
Dodd, Bella, 592
Donath, Ludwig, 658
Donlevy, Brian, 216
Dondero, George A., 933
Donner, Frank J., 869n, 951
Donovan, Colonel, 350
Dos Passos, John, 13n, 447
Douglas, Dorothy, 599
Douglas, Melvyn, 123, 453
Douglas, William O., 527, 944, 945
Dreiser, Theodore, 525

Du Bois, W. E. B., 676, 722, 751
Duclos, Jacques, 126, 397, 566
Duff, Howard, 303, 304, 306
Dugan, Stephen, 14
Duggan, Lawrence, xix
Dulles, John Foster, 977, 978, 980
Dunne, Phil, 365, 476, 477
Durante, Jimmy, 714
d'Usseau, Arnaud, 493, 683, 822
d'Usseau, Susan, 683

Eaker, Ira C., 291
Eastland, James O., 977, 978
Eastman, Max, 463
Eberlein, Hugo, 62, 72
Edwards, Don, xxiii
Edwards, Paul, 8
Egleson, Nick, 924
Eisenhower, David, 890
Eisenhower, Dwight D., 291, 564, 565, 750, 767, 933, 978
Eisler, Mrs. Ella (Tune), 64
Eisler, Rudolph, 60
Elion, Harry, 488
Eliot, T. S., 127
Ellen, Ward, 374
Ellis, Dave, 558
Eltenton, Charles, 225, 242, 243, 244
Eltenton, Dolly, 242, 243
Eluard, Paul, 109
Endicott, James G., 758
English, Richard, 400
Epp, General, 213
Ernst, Morris, 271
Evans, Alice, 488
Evans, Ward V., 669

Fadiman, Clifton, 473
Fanning, Larry, 775
Faragoh, Elizabeth, 390, 398
Faragoh, Francis E., 344, 390
Farish, Linn, 374
Farrell, James T., 447, 521, 522
Fast, Howard, 722, 738, 802, 818
Faulk, John Henry, 707
Fay, Frank, 413, 414
Fedin, Konstantin, 448
Feller, Abraham, xix
Field, Marshall, 779
Finch, Roy, 913
Fish, Hamilton, 936
Fischer, Marie Edith, 60
Fisher, J., 127
Fletcher, Joseph F., 728
Flynn, Elizabeth G., 264, 842
Folkoff, Isaac, 354, 358
Fontanne, Lynn, 422
Forbes, Kenneth Ripley, 728
Ford, Henry, 264
Forrestal, James V., 435, 674
Forsythe, Robert (Kyle Crichton), 521
Fortas, Abe, 296, 407
Foster, Joe, 83
Foster, William Z., 127, 159, 267, 268, 285, 593
France, Dr., 763
Franco, Francisco, 412
Frank, Richard, 594
Frankfeld, Phil (Frankfield?), 584, 585, 596, 597, 609
Frankfurter, Felix, 527
Frauenglass, William, 667
Freeman, Joseph, 465, 472
Freud, Sigmund, xxv, xxviii
Friedman, Milton H., 771, 772, 774, 789
Fulbright, J. William, 939
Furry, Wendell, 575, 599, 618, 623

Gandhi, 668
Gang, Martin, 369, 544
Garfield, John, xix, 248, 295, 296, 297, 298, 299, 302, 304, 305, 342, 522
Garland, Judy, 495
Garrison, Lloyd, 793
Gebert, B., 673
Geer, Will, 344
George, George [sic], 239
George, Harrison, 355
Gerlando, Jay, 521
Gershwin, Ira, 365
Gill, Eric, xxvii
Ginzburg, Eugenia S., 13n, 942, 943
Gladstein, Richard, 710, 715, 717, 721, 723
Glenn, Charles, 442, 443, 444, 556
Glenn, Elizabeth, 557, 558
Gold, Michael, 13n, 22, 227, 331, 465, 470, 471, 482, 522, 525
Golden, John, 425
Goldwater, Barry M., 272
Goldwyn, Samuel, 534, 543
Gollobin, Ira, 860, 862
Gonda, Elaine, 558

Goodman, Walter, 727, 791, 946
Goodwin, Richard, 598, 605, 607
Gordon, Hy, 583, 598
Gordon, Jeffrey, 863n
Gordon, Michael, 487
Gorky, Maxim, 94, 95, 131, 217, 446, 447, 448
Gough, Lloyd, 344, 363, 632
Gow, James, 493
Graff, Fred, 343
Grant, Cary, 430, 431
Grant, Morton, 240
Grauer, Ben, 307
Green, Abner, 735
Green, James F., xxvi
Greenblatt, Bob, 902, 903
Greene, Graham, 447
Gregory, Dick, 903
Grennman, Steve, 59
Grizzard, Vernon, 887
Grossman, Aubrey Whitney, 242
Gruening, Ernest, 939
Guthrie, Woody, 702, 953
Gutman, Jeremiah S., 911, 923, 927, 928

Hague, Frank, 232
Hall, George, 691, 695, 697, 713, 720
Halperin, Israel, 598
Halpern, Lena, 775
Hammett, Dashiell, 302, 303, 536, 538, 542, 543
Hannel, Dr., 637
Hanunian, Elizabeth, 976
Harap, Louis, 582
Harnicker, John, 374
Harriman, W. Averell, xxvi, xxvii, 887, 888
Harris, Lement, 241
Harris, Lou, 240, 535
Harris, Vera, 240
Hart, Moss, 427
Hastings, Senator, 31
Hatchard, Charles, 83, 84
Hathaway, C. A., 469, 525
Haufrecht, Betty, 763, 764
Hayes, Helen, 422, 953
Hays, Lee, 685, 689, 690, 691. 699, 702
Hazlitt, Henry, 463
Henderson, Leon, 123
Hendley, Charles, 592
Henreid, Paul, 125
Hepburn, Katharine, 191
Herbst, Josephine, 13n
Herman, John, 13n
Herriot, Édouard, 287
Hersey, John, 702
Hiss, Alger, xiii, xxvi, 13, 301, 336, 569, 570, 571, 941, 948
Hitler, Adolf, 94, 95, 115, 118, 209, 211, 221, 222, 254, 258, 259, 262, 282, 299, 412, 581, 599, 610, 871, 916, 919, 927, 944
Hobart, Rose, 657
Hoffman, Abbie, 859
Hoffman, Julius, 879
Holder, Francis, 26
Holender, Adam, 979
Holliday, Judy, 302, 304, 306
Holman, Russell, 358
Holly, Judge, 250
Holmes, Oliver Wendell, 169, 181, 253
Hood, Richard B., 171, 172, 369
Hook, Sidney, 247, 463, 464, 599, 943, 949
Hoover, J. Edgar, xxvi, 129, 142, 177, 178, 260, 262, 348, 367, 368, 369, 576, 577, 947
Hopkins, Harry, 6
Hopkins, Pauline, 548
Hopper, Hedda, 300
Horne, Lena, 304, 305, 306
Horrall, V. B., 237
Howard, Trevor, 708
Howe, Anne, 488
Hoyt, Edwin P., 769, 770
Huffman, Hazel, 5, 7, 16
Hughes, Howard, 74
Hughes, Langston, 673
Hughes, Rupert, 171, 178
Humphrey, Hubert H., 890, 892, 894, 903
Hunton, William, 764
Hurwitz, Leo, 488
Huston, John, 365, 412, 491
Hutchinson, William, 146
Huxley, Aldous, 447
Hyde, Douglas, 456

Irwin, Ben, 469
Isaacs, Edith, 17
Ivanov, Peter, 242, 243
Ivens, Joris, 84
Ives, Burl, 703

Jaffe, Sam, 342, 656
Jannings, Emil, 299
Jarrico, Paul, 235, 240, 386, 440, 451

Jasienski, Bruno, 13n
Jelagin, Juri, 449n
Jenkins, David, 775
Jerome, V. J., 92, 225, 226–233, 331, 356, 357, 366, 440, 487, 488, 516, 535, 538, 539, 596, 621, 646, 693
Joffe, Abraham, 242
John XXIII, Pope, 168
Johnson, Lyndon B., 861, 870, 872, 890, 894, 901
Johnson, Manning, 506, 507, 509, 510, 776
Johnson, Wendell, 267
Johnston, Eric, 179, 180
Jordan, Charles, 924
Josephson, Leon, 776
Jouvet, Louis, 109
Jurist, Irma, 683

Kafka, Franz, 706
Kahn, Gordon, 110, 161, 383, 453
Kalatozov, Mikhail, 234, 235
Kantorowicz, Alfred, 210
Kapitza, Peter, 243
Kaplan, Raymond, xix
Katz, Otto (André Simone), 235, 238
Kaufman, Irving, 939
Keene, William B., 300
Keller, 87
Kelly, 452
Kempner, Alexander, 406
Kempton, Murray, 789
Kennedy, John F., 909
Kenny, Robert W., 111, 219, 220, 394
Kent, Morton E., xix
Kent, Rockwell, 247, 347
Kerr, Walter and Jean, 493
Kersten, Charles J., 279–280
Kheifetz, Gregory, 56, 214, 215, 235, 239, 241, 242, 243, 775
Khrameev, 239
Khrushchev, Nikita, 803, 806
Khrushchev, Mrs. N., 199
Kifner, John, 891
Killian, Victor, Sr., 344, 658
King, Carol, 55
King, Martin Luther, 909, 947
Kingsbury, John, 751
Kinoy, Arthur, 869n, 904
Kirchwey, Freda, 107
Kirk, Alan, 739
Kline, Herbert, 522, 525
Knox, Alexander, 125, 364
Koch, Major, 374
Koch, Howard, 110, 176
Kollwitz, Käthe, 232
Koestler, Arthur, 56, 127, 405, 447, 496
Komorowski, Conrad, 506, 507, 510, 511, 513, 514
Kondratyev, Victor, 242
Kornilov, Boris, 448
Kraber, Tony, 486, 502
Kraft, Hyman, 240, 492
Kramer, Charles, 301
Krauss, Werner, 299
Kravchenko, Victor, 127, 391, 392
Kreymborg, Alfred, 233
Kunitz, Joshua, 13n
Kunstler, William, 869n, 904

Ladd, Alan, 150
La Follette, Robert, 248, 257
Laguardia, Fiorello, 416, 423
Lampell, Millard, 700–708, 801
Landis, Judge K. M., 651, 779
Lancaster, Burt, 495
Langford, Frances, 544
Langner, Lawrence, 427, 428
Laski, Harold J., 413
Lastfogel, Abe, 634
Lattimore, Owen, 296, 610
Laughton, Charles, 495
Laurence, Paula, 413
Lawrence, Marc, 342, 637, 639, 644, 645, 647, 648, 651, 653, 657
Lawrence, Peter, 692
Lawrence, Stanley, 449, 450, 451, 535
Leadbelly (Huddie Ledbetter), 702
Lee, Madeline, 632
Leech, Elizabeth, 322
Lees, Robert, 362
Lehman, Herbert H., 597
Leibowitz, Samuel, 266
Lenin, 126, 131, 213, 214, 542, 585, 599, 621, 622, 942, 952
Leonov, Leonid, 448
Lerner, Alan Jay, 494
Lerner, Tillie, 453
Leverett, Lewis, 486
Leviné, David, 213
Lind, Sheila, 787
Lipsky, 420
Littlepage, John D., 127
Loeb, Philip, xix, 344, 656

Lomax, Alan, 699
London, Ephraim, 847
Losey, Joseph, 107
Lovett, R. M., 247
Loy, Myrna, 495
Lozowick, L., 525
Luce, Henry, 937
Luce, P. A., 864n, 865
Ludens, Tina, 763
Ludwig, Emil ("Lustig"), 145
Lumpkin, K., 599
Lunt, Alfred, 422
Lurye, Moissei I. ("Lurge"), 65n
Lyman, Ellwood W., 355
Lynd, Staughton, 883, 915

MacArthur, Douglas, 938
McCarran, Pat, 303, 727
McCarthy Eugene, 939
McCarthy, Joseph R., xix, 190, 702, 707, 790, 840, 933, 936, 942, 949
McCarthy, Mary, 926
McCormick, Mrs. Larue, 161
MacDonald, Dwight, 56
McGee, Willie, 298
McKenney, Ruth, 237, 548
McLeod, 773
McMichael, Jack R., 728
McTernan, John Tripp, 242
McWilliams, Carey, 944, 945
Machado, Gerardo, 509
Mackiedo, Sergei, 373
Magil, A. B., 13n
Maisky, Ivan, 128
Malcolm X, 770
Maltz, Albert, 110, 174n, 179, 233, 385, 387, 400–405, 452, 495, 547, 558, 560, 561, 562, 628, 738
Mandel, Louis, 308, 309, 333, 338, 340, 341, 343
Mann, Thomas, 109
Manoff, Arnold, 390
Manola, Colonel, 373
Manuilsky, Dmitri, 239
Marcantonio, Vito, 247
March, Fredric, 495
Margolis, Ben, 390, 391, 392
Marlin, Max, 835n
Marshall, George C., 424
Martin, Henri ("Mate"), 132
Massing, Hede (Tune, Eisler), 65n
Matisse, Pierre, 109
Matthews, J. B., xix, 727
Matthiessen, F. O., xix, 617
Matusow, Harvey, 721, 948
Mauldin, Bill, 703
May, Alan Nunn, 127
Mayer, Louis B., 112, 116, 130, 138, 153
Mellett, Lowell, 112, 138
Merker, Paul, 69
Meyerhold, V., 448, 449
Meyers, General, 271
Mikheev, Vladimir P., 775
Milestone, Lewis, 110
Miller, Paula, 486
Minor, Robert, 268
Mockridge, Norton, 683–86
Moffitt, Jack, 171, 182
Molotov, Vyacheslav, 124, 126, 131, 134, 239, 243, 620
Montgomery, Robert, 144
Morford, Richard, 424
Moore, Sam, 390, 553
Morgan, Colonel, 639, 640
Morley, Karen, 137, 316, 322, 343, 363, 367, 376, 763, 764
Morley, Lord, 76
Morrison, Norman, 915
Morse, Wayne, 939
Munaker, Sue, 902, 903
Murphy, George, 144
Murphy, Justice, 250
Murra, Victor, 775
Murray, Ken, 544
Mussolini, Benito, 259, 437, 581
Muste, A. J., 913, 915, 927

Namkoom, David Y., 665
Nash, Ogden, 493
Nathan, Otto, 200
Nelson, Steve, 355
Newton, Huey, 770
Newton, Louie D., 675, 676
Nicolaevsky, Boris I., 127n
Nielsen, Rutgers, 429
Nizer, Louis, 296
Norman, E. Herbert, xix
North, Joseph, 235, 356, 465, 466, 469, 472, 513, 516, 525, 547, 559, 560
Novikov, Nikolai, 413
Nowell, William O'Dell, 63

Ocko, Edna, 632

O'Dwyer, William, 423
Olshevsky, 213
Olson, Senator, 51
Oppenheimer, J. Robert, 225, 244, 938
Orloff, Dr., 637
Ornitz, Samuel, 110
O'Shea, Madelyn, 42, 43, 44
Overgaard, A., 487, 503

Page, Charles A., 236, 238, 239
Page, Mary, 237
Palmer, A. Mitchell, 936
Parker, Dorothy, 536, 538, 722
Parry, William, 583
Parsons, Louella, 399
Pasternak, Boris, 446, 448
Pastoev, V. V., 235, 241
Paxton, John, 384
Peck, Gregory, 345
Pegler, Westbrook, 638
Pell, Mike, 535
Pepper, Claude, 393
Pepper, George, 390
Perelman, S. J., 493
Perlberg, William, 296
Peters, J. (Stevens, Goldberger), 240, 241, 527, 776
Petkov, Nikolai, 134
Picasso, Pablo, 108, 109
Pichel, Irving, 110
Pittman, Nancy, 775
Pius XII, Pope, 304
Platt, David, 297–299
Polonsky, Abe, 361, 366, 560
Pomerantz, Charlotte, 667
Popper, Martin, 831, 832, 833
Porter, Jean, 402
Potamkin, Harry A., 13n
Potter, Paul, 887
Pound, Ezra, 803, 804, 805
Power, Tyrone, 150, 151
Pressman, Lee, 301, 330, 393
Proctor, James, 492
Pyle, Ernie, 820

Rabinowitz, Victor, 729, 762
Radamsky, Sergei, 81, 82
Radin, Max, 455
Ratz, Erwin, 960
Rauh, Joseph L., Jr., 533, 536, 792
Ravines, Euducio, 203
Rayburn, Sam, xxviii
Reed, Bob, 656, 689
Reed, John, 20
Reinhardt, Max, 16
Reiskind, Edwin M., 296, 407, 428
Remington, William W., 436, 505
Reuther, Walter, 257n
Revere, Ann, 341, 657
Ribbentrop, Joachim, von, 124
Rice, Elmer, 14
Riesel, Victor, 293, 300, 419
Riesman, David, 600
Robbins, Herbert, 598
Roberts, Holland, 239
Robeson, Eslanda, 763
Robinson, Jackie, 779, 785
Rockwell, George Lincoln, 951
Rolfe, Edwin, xix
Roosevelt, Eleanor, 107, 108, 123, 257n, 423, 453, 947
Roosevelt, Franklin D., xx, 66, 150, 257, 261, 304, 388, 703, 844
Roosevelt, James, 123
Rose, Billy, 500
Rosenberg, Julius and Ethel, 818, 841, 939
Rosenberg, Meta Reis, 343, 395, 451
Ross, Paul L., 688
Rossen, Robert, 110, 202, 240, 343, 576, 790
Rossen, Sam, 341
Rosten, Norman, 815, 816, 823
Rothstein, Brunhilde (Hilde Eisler), 65
Rovere, Richard, 447, 946
Rubin, Jerry, 859, 911, 952
Rushmore, Howard, 55
Rusk, Dean, 890, 894, 907
Ruskin, Shimen, 657
Russak, Mary, 754, 763, 764
Russell, Bertrand, 939
Rustin, Bayard, 913
Ruthven, Madeline, 240
Ryan, William F., 700
Ryerson, Florence, 493
Ryskind, Morrie, 171

Sackin, 389
Salt, Waldo, 110, 240, 451
Sandburg, Carl, 708
Santayana, George, 700
Savoretti, Joseph, 236, 237
Schaefer, George, 708

Schary, Dore, 302, 303
Scheer, Robert, 886
Schlatter, Richard, 598, 605, 607, 618
Schlein, Charles, 657
Schlein, Gerry, 657, 658
Schneiderman, Bill, 355, 358
Schoenberg, Arnold, 75
Schneerson, G., 92
Schwarzschild, Leopold, 127
Schwarzschild, S. S., 923, 924, 925, 931
Scott, Adrian, 110, 384, 385, 386, 390, 392, 393, 396, 398, 529
Scott, Randolph, 430
Seaton, George, 296
Seaver, Edwin, 469
Seeger, Charles, 93
Selvinsky, 448
Shafer, 87
Shafran, Evan, 535
Shapiro, Karl, 804
Shapley, Harlow, 492
Shaw, Artie, 307
Shaw, Bernard, 30, 191, 935
Shepherd, Eric, 169
Sherr, Rubby, 599
Sherwood, Robert E., 238
Sherwood, William and Barbara, xx
Ship, Reuben, 556
Shipley, Ruth B., 793
Shumlin, Herman, 953
Shuster, George, 72, 73
Siegel, R. Lawrence, 628
Sillen, Samuel, 547, 559, 560, 562, 591
Silvermaster, Nathan Gregory, 774
Simonson, Lee, 233
Sirovich, William, 9
Sklar, George, 233
Sinatra, Frank, 495
Skouras, Spyros P., 495
Smelyakoff, 448
Smith, Al, 31
Smith, Art, 487, 488, 502
Smith, Ferdinand, 694, 695
Smith, Jessica, 763, 764
Smith, W. M., xix
Snow, Edgar, 229
Sobell, Morton, 841
Solodovnikov, A. V., 396
Sondergaard, Gale, 300, 301, 302, 341, 647, 657
Sorrell, Herbert K., 124, 125
Sothern, Georgia, 714
Spellman, Francis Cardinal, 168
Spender, Stephen, 447
Sproul, Gordon, 388
Stachel, Jack, 591, 592, 776
Stalin, 4, 31, 61, 66, 69, 72, 95, 115, 120, 123, 126, 131, 132, 181, 196, 203, 264, 294, 304, 305, 375, 396, 412, 446, 567, 621, 769, 780, 785, 786, 833, 937, 940, 944
Stander, Lucy, 645, 646
Stanislavski, Konstantin, 427, 472, 658, 659
Stapp, John, 365, 561
Stark, Wallace, 42, 43
Starr, Louis E., xxvi
Stassen, Harold H., 132
Steele, Walter S., xxvi, xxvii
Steiner, Ralph, 488, 489
Stern, Bernhard, 613, 616
Stever, Lettie, 631
Stewart, Donald Ogden, 247, 536, 538
Stewart, John, 547, 548, 559
Stone, I. F., 668, 939, 949
Strack, Celeste, 506, 507, 509
Strand, Paul, 488
Strasberg, Lee, 489
Sturges, Preston, 634
Sukarno, 778
Sullivan, Ed, 429
Sullivan, Elliott, 632, 658, 684, 685, 686, 691
Swanson, Pauline, 234
Swing, Raymond Gram, 107
Szulc, Tad, 272

Tabori, George, 494
Taft, Robert A., 129
Talmadge, Mrs. Julius Y., xxvi
Tarail, Mark, 763
Tarantino, Jimmie, 302–307
Tasker, Robert, 450
Taylor, John Thomas, xxvi
Taylor, Telford, 532, 949
Tenney, Jack, 171
Tito, 374
Thieman, Superintendent, 398
Thomas, Norman, 267
Thompson, Bob, 374
Thompson, Dorothy, 107, 410
Thompson, Frederick, 239, 775
Thorez, Maurice, 132
Thurber, James, 790
Tillich, Paul, 935

Tofte, Haus, 374
Tolstoy, Alexei, 448
Tompkins, Warwick M., 347, 349, 350, 353, 354, 357, 358, 366, 371, 373
Trachtenberg, Alexander, 474
Tracy, Spencer, 151, 191
Tree, Dorothy, 341, 657
Tretyakov, Sergei, 98, 213
Trivers, Paul, 384, 385
Trotsky, 937, 943, 950
Truman, Harry S., 298
Trumbo, Dalton, xxi, 110, 173, 174, 175, 188n, 303, 307, 478, 496, 707, 722, 790n
Tuttle, Frank, 339, 382, 389, 496, 576, 577, 646, 790
Tuttle, Tania, 452
Twitchell, Alice, 646, 647
Tyne, George, 658

Uerkvitz, Herta, 240
Ulbricht, Walter, 69
Utley, Freda, 127
Uris, Michael, 341, 342, 390

Vale, Rena M., 160
Vassiliyev, P., 448
Vaughan Williams, Ralph, 979
Vinson, Owen, 545, 546, 547, 550, 552, 553, 555, 557, 566
Vishinsky, Andrei, 121, 126, 131, 134
Vorhaus, Bernard, 382

Waldman, Louis, 257
Walker, Charles, 913
Walker, Daniel, 931
Wallace, George C., 897
Wallace, Henry A., xxvi, 133, 257, 269, 281, 282, 283, 375, 454, 492, 663
Wallace, William, 757
Wallis, Hal, 534
Walsh, Richard, 146, 294
Wanamaker, Sam, 307
Wanger, Walter, 291–92, 293
Ward, Harry F., 728
Warner, Jack L., 130, 153, 171, 198
Warren, Earl, 721, 774
Warren, Sue, 819, 823
Watts, Richard, Jr., 665
Waxman, Stanley, 558
Wayne, John, 291–92, 300, 430, 431
Weales, Gerald, 501n
Webb, Sidney and Beatrice, 942
Webster, Margaret, 428
Weill, Kurt, 493, 494
Weinberger, Eric, 901, 927
Weir, Ernest T., 738
Weis, P., 85
Welch, Joseph, 707
Welles, Orson, 304, 307
Welles, Sumner, xxvi, 99, 107
Wellman, Ted (Sid Benson), 487, 502, 504, 505
Wexley, John, 233, 384, 385
Wheaton, Louis, 751
White, Harry Dexter, xix, xxvi
White, Josh, 413, 703
White, Richard, 525
White, Walter, 267
White, William, 127
White, William Allen, 410
Whitney, Lynn, 558
Wilder, Thornton, 493
Wilkerson, Doxey, 778
Wilkinson, Mrs. Frank, 200
Willcox, Mr. and Mrs. Henry, 744, 745, 763
Williams, Tennessee, 494
Willkie, Wendell, 74, 392, 394, 455
Wilson, Dagmar, 859, 951
Wilson, Ruth, 240, 241
Winant, John, xix
Winiton, Paul, 127
Winsor, Kathleen, 307
Winter, Carl, 561, 562
Winter, Ella, 525
Winters, Bea, 359, 365, 371, 372
Witt, Nathan, 301
Wolfe, Thomas, 463
Wolff, Billy, 558
Woltman, Frederick, 55, 683–686
Wood, Robert, 161
Wood, Samuel G., 127, 167, 330
Woodrum, Clifton A., 830
Woodward, Ellen, 9, 10
Wortis, Joseph, 599
Wuchinich, G., 374

Yergan, Max, 239, 775, 777, 778
Young, Frances, xix
Young, Quentin, 910

Young, Thomas W., 779
Young, Stark, 517
Youngdahl, Judge, 650

Zaholotsky, 448
Zanuck, Darryl, 389
Zelinsky, Corvely, 447
Zhdanov, Andrei A., 282
Zhukovsky, Herman, 396
Ziemer, Gregor, 169
Zublin, Vassili, 238, 241
Zugsmith, Leane, 247